Middle East
on a shoestring

Andrew Humphreys   Gordon Robison
Tom Brosnahan   Diana Saad
Geert Cole   David St Vincent
Rosemary Hall   Damien Simonis
Pertti Hämäläinen   Neil Tilbury
Ann Jousiffe   Tony Wheeler
Leanne Logan

Middle East

2nd edition

Published by
Lonely Planet Publications
Head Office: PO Box 617, Hawthorn, Vic 3122, Australia
Branches: PO Box 2001A, Berkeley, CA 94702, USA
               12 Barley Mow Passage, Chiswick, London W4 4PH, UK
               71 bis rue du Cardinal Lemoine, 75005 Paris, France

Printed by
Colorcraft Ltd, Hong Kong

Photographs by
Tom Brosnahan, Eddie Gerald, Pertti Hämäläinen, Peter Jousiffe, Gordon Robison, Tony Wheeler

Front cover: Blue Valley, Sinai Desert, Egypt (Patrick Curtet, The Image Bank)
Title page: Mari Water Goddess, Mari (Tell Hariri), Syria (Margaret Jung)

First Published
April 1994

This Edition
March 1997

Although the authors and publisher have tried to make the information as
accurate as possible, they accept no responsibility for any loss, injury or
inconvenience sustained by any person using this book.

National Library of Australia Cataloguing in Publication Data

Middle East.

2nd ed.
Includes index.
ISBN 0 86442 407 8.

1. Middle East – Guidebooks. I. Humphreys, Andrew, 1965-
(Series : Lonely Planet on a shoestring).

915.60453

Andrew Humphreys

Andrew first encountered the Middle East in the form of Egypt in 1988 when a three week holiday gradually extended to a three year long stay. A part of this time he spent documenting Islamic architecture for a preservation society, later going on to work for *Egypt Today*, the country's biggest English-language periodical. In 1991, an unexpected turn of events deposited Andrew in newly independent Estonia with a ringside seat from which to observe the after-effects of the disintegration of the USSR. Initially working for a local English-language paper, Andrew moved on to co-found a new pan-Baltic newspaper, at which point a happy chance-meeting with Lonely Planet set him to work on three successive books covering post-Soviet territories. In 1995 he returned to the Middle East to work on more Lonely Planet titles, including the coordination of this second edition. He is now firmly lodged back in Cairo.

Tom Brosnahan

Tom Brosnahan was born in Pennsylvania, went to college in Boston, then set out on the road. He first went to Turkey as a US Peace Corps Volunteer, taught English, and learned to speak Turkish. He studied Ottoman Turkish history and language for eight years, but abandoned the writing of his PhD dissertation in favour of writing guidebooks.

Tom researched and wrote the Turkey chapter for both editions. He is also the author of Lonely Planet's *Turkey, İstanbul city guide, Guatemala, Belize & Yucatán: La Ruta Maya* and the *Turkish phrasebook*, as well as co-author of *Mexico, Central America on a shoestring* and other Lonely Planet guides. His e-mail address is tbros@infoexchange.com.

Geert Cole

Together with Leanne Logan, Geert updated the Egypt chapter for this edition. Born in Antwerp in Belgium, Geert swapped university and art studies in the 1970s to discover broader horizons and other cultures. Each trip resulted in an extra diary being put on the shelf and another job experience being added to life's list. In more recent times, when not running his stained-glass studio, Geert could be found sailing the Pacific, sorting Aussie sheep, and amongst other challenges, trekking through Alaska and diving tropical reefs.

Together Geert and Leanne have worked on travel guides to *France, New Caledonia, Western Europe, India, Africa* and, most recently, to *Egypt*. They also researched the first edition of Lonely Planet's *Egypt travel atlas*. Together they continue fossicking around this lovely planet.

Rosemary Hall

Rosemary was born in Sunderland, England. She graduated in fine art, but fame and fortune as an artist eluded her, so she spent a few months bumming around Europe and India. After teaching in northern England, she decided to find work somewhere more exotic, finally landing a job in Basra, Iraq. After two years she returned to London, did supply teaching and travelled in India and South-East Asia. After the Iran-Iraq War ended, she went back to research the Iraq chapter for Lonely Planet's *West Asia on a shoestring*. Rosemary has also written the Greece chapter for *Mediterranean Europe on a shoestring*, and the first edition of *Greece*.

Ann Jousiffe

Ann is a London-based writer and photographer specialising in North Africa and the Middle East. Her work has appeared in many books, magazines and newspapers in the UK and worldwide. She has also worked on several television documentaries about Libya.

Ann updated the Lebanon chapter for this edition. She is also the author of the Libya section of Lonely Planet's *North Africa* and the forthcoming *Lebanon*.

Leanne Logan

Together with Geert Cole, Leanne updated the Egypt chapter. Bitten by the travel bug before even reaching her teens, Leanne has long been lured by travel. She explored parts of her homeland as a reporter for several newspapers and Australian Associated Press after completing a journalism degree at the Queensland University of Technology. In 1987, she set off through Asia and the Middle East to London where, as deputy editor of a travel magazine, her wander lust was temporarily fed but not sated. Eventually she bought a one-way ticket to Africa and, like many others, fell in love with that amazing continent.

Leanne joined Lonely Planet in 1991 and, while conducting research into Belgium's 350-odd beers, she met a local connoisseur, Geert Cole. The pair have been a team ever since and have worked together on a variety of Lonely Planet guides.

Gordon Robison

Gordon Robison grew up in Maine and Vermont, in the north-eastern USA. He attended Westminster School in London and graduated from Pomona College in Claremont, California, with a degree in government. He later studied Arabic at Cairo's International Language Institute. After university Gordon travelled in Europe, the Middle East and Mexico and worked for a year in Saudi Arabia. From 1989 until 1994 he lived in Cairo where he worked as a freelance journalist, reporting regularly for the American ABC Radio News. His work has also been published in the *Irish Times*, the London *Sunday Times*, the *Financial Times*, the *Miami Herald* and the *Atlanta Journal-Constitution*.

For both editions, Gordon researched and wrote the Bahrain, Kuwait, Oman, Qatar, Saudi Arabia and United Arab Emirates chapters and also contributed material in the Facts about the Region chapter. He is also the author of Lonely Planet's guide to the *Arab Gulf States*. He now lives in Atlanta where he works for CNN International. He is married to Dona Stewart. They have one daughter, Halle.

David St Vincent

David, one of the few Westerners not in the arms trade to have visited both Iran and Iraq during the Iran-Iraq War, wrote the Iran chapter for the first edition of this book. He is also the author of LP's *Iran* and co-author of *Pakistan*.

Damien Simonis

Damien is a London-based journalist. He left Australia in 1989 with a degree in modern languages and several years' experience as reporter and sub-editor on such papers as the *Australian* and the *Age*. He later put in several years' hard labour on London papers like the *Guardian* and the *Independent*. He has worked and travelled widely in Europe, the Middle East and North Africa. Damien updated the Jordan and Syria chapters. He has also worked on Lonely Planet's guides for *Jordan & Syria*, *Egypt*, *Morocco*, *North Africa*, *Italy* and *Spain*.

Tony Wheeler

Tony was born in England but grew up in Pakistan, the Bahamas and the USA. He returned to England to do a degree in engineering at Warwick University, worked as an automotive design engineer, returned to university to complete an MBA in London, then dropped out on the Asian overland trail with his wife Maureen. Eventually settling down in Australia, they've been travelling, writing and publishing guidebooks ever since, having set up Lonely Planet Publications in the mid-1970s. Travel for the Wheelers is considerably enlivened by their daughter Tashi and their son Kieran.

Pertti Hämäläinen

Pertti was born in Turku, Finland, and lives in the capital of the country, Helsinki. He has an MSc in Applied Mathematics from the University of Turku and runs a consultancy company of his own, specialised in local area networks and data communications. Pertti was introduced to travelling by his first wife Tuula in the late '70s. Her great interest in Islamic architecture first led them to Southern Arabia in 1984 and many times since. In addition to researching and writing the Yemen chapter for both editions of this book, he is the author of Lonely Planet's *Yemen*. Pertti is a member of die Deutsch-Jemenitische Getsellschaft eV and the American Institute for Yemeni Studies.

Diana Saad

Diana, formerly a Lonely Planet editor, researched and wrote the Lebanon chapter for the first edition of this book.

Neil Tilbury

Neil spent a few years working in the hotel and wine trades before travelling to the USA via Europe, the Middle East, Asia and Australia. One of the countries that he visited was Israel, and he authored the first two editions of Lonely Planet's *Israel*, as well as supplying the Israel chapter for the first edition of this book.

From the Authors

Tom Brosnahan Thanks to Pat Yale, co-author of Lonely Planet's *Turkey*; Leyla Özhan of the Turkish tourism office in New York City; Mustafa Siyahhan of the Turkish tourism office in Washington DC; Cansen Bekleriz of the tourism office in İstanbul's Sirkeci station; Ersan Atsür of Orion-Tour in İstanbul; Çelik Gülersoy of the Turkish Touring and Automobile Association; Süha Ersöz of the Esbelli Evi in Ürgüp; Ann Nevens of the Hotel Empress Zoe in İstanbul; and, as always, the Turkish people (especially the cooks!) who made my research trips so enjoyable.

Pertti Hämäläinen Thanks to all the friendly Yemenis, especially those of the youngest generation, who never hesitated to offer their enthusiasm, help and advice to the visitors – you are too numerous to list here! Special thanks go to Zahra Abdrabo from Aden and Abdulaziz al-Saqqaf from San'a, who went out of their way in providing us assistance and information. And, finally, thanks to my wife Raija for her spirited support on the road.

Ann Jousiffe I would like to thank Renee and Munzer Aweida of MEA for all their kind support and help. Also many thanks to Francois and Pascale at Amchit Camping and to Bassam Lahoud for taking time out to show us many places of interest.

Leanne Logan & Geert Cole Special thanks to Richard Hoath from the American University in Cairo (AUC) and to Philip Jones of the Hurghada Environmental Protection and Conservation Association (HEPCA). Thanks to staff at the various tourist offices as well as to Nazmi Amin Farad of the Egyptian Tourist Authority in Cairo. To fellow LP author, Andrew Humphreys, and to all those in LP's Melbourne office who also worked on this book, a big *shukran*. Thank you also to Narelle & Keith Werder, Maureen & David Logan, Ray Hartley, Robin, Peter & Dylan Osborne and lastly, our best mates, Bluey & Sixy.

Gordon Robison A special thanks to my wife Dona and daughter, Halle. Thanks also to King Mallory, Ashraf Fouad, David & Mary Gore-Booth, Grainne Geraghty, Peter Smith, Khalid Alturki, Michael Georgy & Fayza Amba, Peter Dejardins & Yvonne Preston and Christine Hauser.

Damien Simonis Thanks to MEED in London for access to their library. In Damascus special thanks to the Dutch tour leaders and Jeffrey Hayes of the American Language Center. In Hama I owe a particular debt to

Bader Tonbur. In Amman, thanks go to the staff off the Bdeiwi Hotel, Hector Low of the British Council and my steadfast travel companions – Elisabeth Mead, Michelle Byrnes and Felicity Campion.

This Book
This book originally grew out of the Middle East section of Lonely Planer's *West Asia on a shoestring*. The updated information for both editions has been provided by the authors of LP's various Middle East guides.

From the Publisher
The editing and proofing of this second edition was coordinated by Michelle Glynn, with invaluable assistance from Brigitte Barta, Lindsay Brown, Helen Castle, Michelle Coxall, Liz Filleul, Lyn McGaurr, Susan Noonan, Kristin Odijk, Diana Saad and Rachel Scully.

Rachael Scott and Chris Klep coordinated the mapping; Rachael was also responsible for the design. Verity Campbell, Trudi Canavan, Sally Gerdan, Indra Kilfoyle, Michael Signal, Geoff Stringer, Paul Piaia and Margaret Jung also assisted with the mapping. Margaret designed the title page and chapter ends. Simon Bracken designed the cover with cartographic assistance from Adam McCrow.

Thanks to Dan Levin for creating the soft fonts, Paul Piaia for creating the climate charts, Anne Mulvaney for indexing, and the hard working readers' letters team. Thanks also to Peter Ward of Peter Ward Book Exports for his advice about bookshops; Dr Peter Hawden for his enthusiastic assistance with the Afghanistan and Iraq chapters, and valuable insights into travelling in Oman; Simon Goldsmith (from the LP UK office) and Brett Wells (from the LP US office) for chasing up transport information for the

introductory chapters; and Samantha Carew and Greg Herriman for their advice and support.

Finally, a special thanks to Andrew Humphreys, coordinating author, for his hard work, sense of humour and dedication.

Thanks
A special thanks to all the people who found the time and energy to write to us from all over the world with their tips, advice and travellers' tales. Their names appear at the back of this book.

Warning & Request
Things change – prices go up, schedules change, good places go bad and bad places go bankrupt – nothing stays the same. So if you find things better or worse, recently opened or long since closed, please write and tell us and help make the next edition even more accurate and useful.

We value all of the feedback we receive from travellers. Julie Young coordinates a small team who read and acknowledge every letter, postcard and email, and ensure that every morsel of information finds its way to the appropriate authors, editors and publishers.

Everyone who writes to us will find their name in the next edition of the appropriate guide and will also receive a free subscription to our quarterly newsletter, *Planet Talk*. The very best contributions will be rewarded with a free Lonely Planet guide.

Excerpts from your correspondence may appear in Updates (which we add to the end pages of books when they are reprinted), new editions of this guide, in our newsletter, *Planet Talk*, or in the Postcards section of our Web site – so please let us know if you don't want your letter published or your name acknowledged.

Contents

Map Legend

BOUNDARIES

━━━━━━━━	International Boundary
━━━━━━━━	Regional Boundary

ROUTES

	Freeway
	Highway
	Major Road
	Unsealed Road or Track
	City Road
	City Street
	Railway
	Underground Railway
	Tram
	Walking Track
	Walking Tour
	Ferry Route
	Cable Car or Chairlift

AREA FEATURES

	Parks
	Built-Up Area
	Pedestrian Mall
	Market (Souq)
+ + + + +	Cemetery
× × × × × ×	Non-Christian Cemetery
	Reef
	Beach or Desert
🌴 🌴 🌴	Oasis
	Rocks

HYDROGRAPHIC FEATURES

	Coastline
	River, Creek
	Intermittent River or Creek
	Lake, Intermittent Lake
	Canal

SYMBOLS

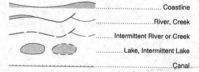

❍ CAPITAL		National Capital
◉ Capital		Regional Capital
⬭ CITY		Major City
● City		City
● Town		Town
● Village		Village
■ ▼		Place to Stay, Place to Eat
☕ 🍷		Cafe, Pub or Bar
✉ ☎		Post Office, Telephone
❶ ❸		Tourist Information, Bank
❍ ⓜ		Transport, Metro Station
🏛 ⌂		Museum, Youth Hostel
⚏ ▲		Caravan Park, Camping Ground
❒ ▬		Church, Cathedral
◖ ✺		Mosque, Synagogue
🏛 ▣		Classical Temple, Temple
✚ ★		Hospital, Police Station

❍	ⓑ	Embassy, Petrol Station
✈	✝	Airport, Airfield
▭	✿	Swimming Pool, Gardens
❖	🐘	Shopping Centre, Zoo
Ⓚ	Ⓜ	Kibbutz, Moshav
←	A25	One Way Street, Route Number
🏛	▲	Stately Home, Monument
🃁	▣	Castle, Tomb or Mausoleum
⌒	⌂	Cave, Hut or Chalet
▲	※	Mountain or Hill, Lookout
🏮	⊠	Lighthouse, Shipwreck
)(	◎	Pass, Spring
⅄	⬩	Beach, Border Crossing
∴	⊠	Ruins, Pyramid
▬▬▬▬		Ancient or City Wall / Fort
⊓⊓⊓⟶ ⟵		Cliff or Escarpment, Tunnel
┼┼┼┼▬┼┼┼		Railway Station

Note: not all symbols displayed above appear in this book

Introduction

Travellers returning from the Middle East bring back tales of unforgettable desert landscapes, spectacular archaeological sites, wonderful hospitality and an astonishing array of things to see and do. Yet turbulent politics and an often unflattering media profile have deterred others from exploring this fascinating region.

With the signing of the Israeli-PLO peace accord in late 1993, the Middle East is once again appearing on an increasing number of travel agendas. While volatile politics continue to make travel to Afghanistan or Iraq all but impossible, you can visit most of the region safely – and sometimes at a surprisingly low cost. Getting around the region is not always straightforward, but it is possible if you keep a few simple rules in mind. And the relative lack of mass tourism is an attraction in itself.

Travel in the Middle East requires patience and a willingness to have your preconceptions challenged; above all, however, it's a richly rewarding experience.

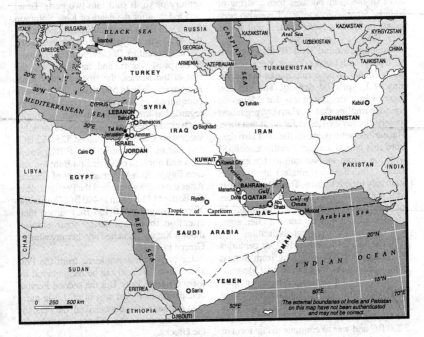

13

Facts about the Region

HISTORY
Cradle of Civilisation

If Africa is the birthplace of humanity, the Middle East can make a strong claim to be the birthplace of civilisation. Mesopotamia's Fertile Crescent and the valley of the Nile River were the sites of some of the world's earliest known organised societies.

About 5000 BC a culture known as Al-Ubaid first appeared in Mesopotamia. Little is known about it except that its influence eventually spread down what is now the coast of the Gulf but was then a string of islands. Stone Age artefacts have also been found in Israel's Negev desert and in the West Bank town of Jericho.

Sometime around 3100 BC the kingdoms of Upper and Lower Egypt were unified under Menes, whose rule marks the beginning of Egypt's 1st dynasty. The fact that there were two kingdoms for Menes to conquer implies that a relatively organised society already existed in Egypt at that time. The earliest settlements in the Gulf also date from this period and are usually associated with the Umm an-Nar culture (centred in today's United Arab Emirates), about which relatively little is known. The Levant too was well settled by this time, and local powers included the Amorites and the Canaanites. In Mesopotamia it was the era of Sumer, arguably the world's first great civilisation.

In the late 24th and early 23rd centuries BC, Sargon of Akkad, a king from Sumer, conquered much of the Levant and Mesopotamia. At its southern edge Sargon's empire contended with a powerful kingdom called Dilmun, centred on the island of Bahrain in the Gulf. Dilmun's civilisation arose around 3200 BC and was to continue in one form or another for nearly 2000 years.

The patriarch Abraham also came from Mesopotamia, having been born, according to tradition, in Ur of the Chaldees on the Euphrates River. His migration from Ur to Canaan is usually dated around 1800 BC, a

century or so before another native of Mesopotamia, the Babylonian king Hammurabi, issued his famous code of laws. Other powers in the region at that time included the Hittite and Assyrian empires and, in Greece and Asia Minor, Mycenae and Troy.

The biblical kingdom of Israel was a very minor player in this game of empires. It was established by Saul around 1023 BC, some 250 years after what is traditionally given as the date of the Israelites' exodus from Egypt. The unified Israeli kingdom lasted only a century or so. It split into two parts, Israel and Judah, after the death of King Solomon (circa 928 BC). Israel and Judah later fell to the Assyrians and Babylonians respectively.

The 7th century BC saw both the conquest of Egypt by Assyria and, far to the east, the rise of the Medes, the first of many great Persian empires. In 550 BC the Medes were conquered by Cyrus the Great, usually regarded as the first Persian shah, or king.

Over the next 60 years Cyrus and his successors Cambyses (reigned 525-522 BC) and Darius I (reigned 521-486 BC) swept west and north to conquer first Babylon and then Egypt, Asia Minor and parts of Greece. After the Greeks stemmed the Persian tide at the Battle of Marathon in 490 BC, Darius and Xerxes (reigned 486-466 BC) turned their attention to consolidating their empire, though Xerxes launched another invasion of Greece in 480 BC.

Egypt won independence from the Persians in 401 BC only to be reconquered by them 60 years later. But the second Persian occupation of Egypt was brief. Little more than a decade after they arrived, the Persians were again driven out of Egypt, this time by the Greeks.

In 336 BC Philip of Macedon, a warlord who had conquered much of mainland Greece, was murdered. His son Alexander assumed the throne and began a series of conquests that would eventually encompass most of Asia Minor, the Middle East, Persia and north-western India. The high point of Alexander's brief reign was the final crushing of Persia and the sack of its capital, Persepolis, in the winter of 331-330 BC.

The Hellenistic World

Alexander died in Babylon in 323 BC. His empire was promptly carved up by his generals, who spent the next 40 years fighting each other. Eventually three main dynasties emerged from this carnage: the Antigonids in Greece and Asia Minor; the Ptolemies in Egypt; and the Seleucids, who controlled the swath of land running from modern Israel and Lebanon through Mesopotamia to Persia.

This is not to say that peace reigned. Having finished off a host of lesser competitors, the heirs to Alexander's empire then proceeded to fight each other. Within a century huge areas of the eastern part of the Seleucid Empire (modern Iran) had broken off to become the Parthian Kingdom. Parts of Palestine and Syria eventually fell to the Nabataeans – an Arab dynasty based at Petra (in modern Jordan) – while other parts changed hands frequently among the Seleucids, Ptolemies, Nabataeans and various local dynasties. Eventually all of the western Mediterranean fell before the Romans. They conquered most of Asia Minor in 188 BC, then Syria and Palestine in 64 and 63 BC, and, finally, Egypt in 30 BC.

In the east, the Seleucids saw their territory steadily whittled away by the Parthians until it disappeared entirely at the end of the 2nd century BC. The Parthians controlled most of Mesopotamia and Persia and parts of eastern Arabia for the next several centuries before giving way to another Persian dynasty, the Sassanians.

This left the area covered by this book divided largely among two empires and their client states until the coming of Islam. Asia Minor, the Levant and Egypt were dominated by what, after 395 AD, was known as the Eastern Roman, or Byzantine, Empire. The Sassanians ruled the east, while the area in between was occupied by several small client states. Only the nomads of the desert

and the frankincense kingdoms of South Arabia remained independent of the great powers of the day.

Frankincense, arguably the ancient world's most valuable commodity, was then produced only in South Arabia and control of the trade routes by which it was sent north made the rulers of what is now Yemen some of the richest people on earth. Saba, the biblical Sheba and the greatest of the South Arabian kingdoms, was founded around 1000 BC and remained the pre-eminent power in that region until about 50 AD, when it was supplanted by another local dynasty, the Himyarites. The decline of the frankincense trade after the 3rd century AD moved Arabia to the margins of the ancient world.

The New Religion

For several hundred years prior to the coming of Islam, the Byzantines and the Sassanians were almost constantly at war, a fact which probably explains the weakened state in which the Arab armies were to find the two empires.

The prophet Mohammed was born in Mecca, in western Arabia, sometime around the year 570. In the year 610 he began to receive revelations from God, conveyed to him through the archangel Gabriel. Thus began Mohammed's ministry, which was to continue until his death, at Medina, in 632. By that time Islam had swept all other religions before it throughout most of the Arabian peninsula.

A breathtaking series of conquests followed. In the 20 years after Mohammed's death Arab armies flying the Muslim flag took Syria, Palestine, Egypt, Persia and parts of what is now Afghanistan. In 652 they crossed the Oxus River into Central Asia. Within a century of the Prophet's death the Arabs ruled an empire stretching from Spain to India and north into Uzbekistan.

The governance of this empire initially fell to the Prophet's companions. Successive leaders of the Muslim community took the title of 'caliph', an Arabic word meaning 'successor', 'lieutenant' or 'viceroy'.

Arguments over the leadership quickly

arose, and in 644 a dispute over the caliphate opened a rift in Islam that grew into today's divide between Sunni and Shiite Muslims. Those who took the side of Ali, Mohammed's cousin and son-in-law, became known as the Shiia (Shiite), or 'Partisans (of Ali)'. Ali eventually became caliph in 656, but a civil war soon broke out which ended with his assassination by followers of Mu'awiyah, the Muslim military governor of Syria, who was also a distant relative of the Prophet.

The Umayyads

Mu'awiyah moved the capital from Medina to Damascus and established the first great Muslim dynasty – the Umayyad (or Omayyad) dynasty. The name is derived from Mu'awiyah's clan, the Bani Umayyah, within the Prophet's tribe, the Quraysh.

The Umayyads were descended from a branch of the Quraysh known more for expediency than piety. Mu'awiyah's father was one of the last people in Mecca to embrace Islam and had long been Mohammed's chief opponent in the city. By moving the capital to Damascus the Umayyads were symbolically declaring that they had aspirations far beyond the rather ascetic teachings of the Qur'an (Koran).

The Umayyads gave the Islamic world some of its greatest architectural treasures, such as the Dome of the Rock in Jerusalem and the Omayyad Mosque in Damascus. History, however, has not been kind to them, remembering them largely for the high living, corruption, nepotism and tyranny which eventually proved to be their undoing.

In 750 the Umayyads were toppled in a revolt led by Abu Muslim, a freed slave who accused them of impiety and rallied the Shiites of Persia behind the Abbasid (or Abbassid) branch of the Prophet's family. The religious side of this appeal reinforced long-simmering ethnic discontent: Umayyad rule had been particularly harsh on the non-Arab peoples of Mesopotamia, Persia and Khorasan (the historical name for what is now north-eastern Iran and western Afghanistan).

The Abbasids

From the beginning the Abbasid caliphate had a distinctly Persian flavour. This was reflected in the decision of the second Abbasid caliph, Al-Mansur, to build a completely new capital close to the Abbasids' Persian power base and far from Levantine cities like Damascus, where the non-Muslim population (and, hence, Byzantine influence) remained large. Persian influence was clear in the layout of the new capital, Baghdad, and in the architecture of the caliph's palace. Even the site had significance – Baghdad is only 30 km from Ctesiphon, the Sassanian and Parthian capital. Over time the Abbasids also came to adopt a number of Sassanian practices, including concealing the ruler behind a curtain during audiences.

It should be emphasised, however, that the Abbasids were Arabs, not Persians. In fairness to the Umayyads, one ought to add that the Abbasids have not exactly gone down in history as overly high-minded or pious either. But the early centuries of their rule constitute what has been remembered ever since as the golden age of Islamic culture and society.

The most famous of the Abbasid caliphs was Harun ar-Rashid (reigned 786-809) of *The Thousand and One Nights* fame – a warrior king who led one of the most successful early Muslim invasions of Byzantium, almost reaching Constantinople. He also presided over an extraordinary burst of creativity in the arts, medicine, literature and science. Harun's son and main successor, Al-Ma'mun, founded the Beit al-Hikmah, or 'House of Wisdom', a Baghdad-based academy dedicated to translating Greek and Roman works of science and philosophy into Arabic. It was only through these translations that most of the classical literature we know today was saved for posterity.

But, as with the Umayyads before them, the Abbasids had planted the seeds of their own destruction in the first years of their rule. Though they had rallied Shiite support in their initial bid for power, the Abbasids did

PETER JOUSIFFE

TONY WHEELER

EDDIE GERALD

Top Left: Elaborate entrance to the Armenian Church of St James in Jerusalem, Israel.
Top Right: Beautifully painted door to the Queen's Hotel, Luxor, Egypt.
Bottom: Backyard of the Archaeological Museum, Eminönü, İstanbul, Turkey.

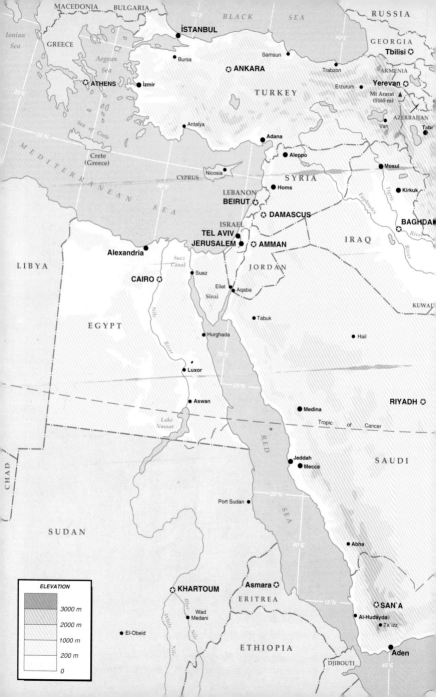

Middle East

The external boundaries of India and Pakistan on this map have not been authenticated and may not be correct.

Top: Zubara Fort, built in 1938 as a Qatari border police post.
Middle: Yacht sailing near Uğurlu off the Mediterranean coast of Turkey.
Bottom: Ramlat as-Sab'atayn desert, Yemen.

not make Shiism the official creed of the empire or otherwise address Shiite aspirations. This, along with the difficulties inherent in governing a far-flung empire, and the power struggles which seem to beset most absolute monarchies, eventually eroded their power base.

After Harun's death the empire was effectively divided between two of his sons. Predictably, civil war ensued. In 813 one son, Al-Ma'mun, emerged triumphant and reigned as caliph for the next 20 years. But Al-Ma'mun's hold on power remained insecure, and eventually he abandoned Baghdad to found a new capital at Samarra, 100 km to the north, where he surrounded himself with Turkish mercenaries.

This was a mistake. Al-Ma'mun's successors became increasingly isolated in Samarra, which was not so much a city as a giant fortified military camp. Over time the caliph's Turkish bodyguards became the real rulers of an empire which itself was rapidly shrinking.

In the first years of Abbasid rule the empire lost Spain to the lone surviving member of the Umayyad family. The tendency after that was for governors in the outer provinces to set up new dynasties whenever they felt strong enough to do so. These rulers continued to owe nominal allegiance to the caliph but in practice the empire had no control over them. North Africa slipped away in this manner at the end of the 8th century. In the early 9th century most of Central Asia and the portions of the empire in what are now India, Pakistan and Afghanistan followed.

Egypt slipped in and out of Abbasid control for a century before falling to the Fatimids – a Shiite dynasty from North Africa – in 969. The Fatimids made Cairo their capital and for the next two centuries ruled most of Syria, the Levant and western Arabia. The Fatimids' most lasting legacy was Al-Azhar, a university and mosque founded in Cairo during the early years of their rule. Al-Azhar, which is now the oldest university in the world, remains one of the Islamic world's leading centres of scholarship.

By the middle of the 10th century the Abbasid caliphs were the prisoners of their Turkish guards. Two dynasties emerged from these guards to rule the empire through figurehead caliphs: the Buyids (932-1062), who eventually moved the capital to Shīrāz, in modern Iran; and the Seljuks (1038-1194), who moved the capital back to Baghdad while extending their reach throughout Persia, Central Asia and Afghanistan.

The Crusades

In 1095 Pope Urban II called for a Christian military expedition to liberate the holy places of Jerusalem. There was a political subtext to Urban's spiritual concerns. Over the previous generation the Seljuk Turks had expanded westward to take control of Armenia, Azerbaijan and a large part of Anatolia. The resulting pressure was intense enough to cause the Byzantine emperor and the Greek Orthodox Church to swallow their pride and appeal to the Pope for help. For his part Urban was understandably eager to assert Rome's primacy in the east, particularly in the Holy Land.

After linking up with the Byzantine army in 1097, the Crusaders successfully besieged Antioch (modern Antakya, in Turkey) and then marched down the coast before turning inland, toward Jerusalem. A thousand Fatimid troops held Jerusalem for six weeks against some 15,000 Crusaders before the city fell on 15 July 1099. The victorious Crusaders massacred the local population – Muslims, Jews and Christians alike – plundered the non-Christian religious sites and turned the Dome of the Rock into a church. Four Crusader states were created in the conquered territories: the Kingdom of Jerusalem, the Principality of Antioch and the counties of Tripoli and Edessa.

These successes were short-lived. It took less than 50 years for the tide to begin to turn against the Crusaders and only 200 before they were driven out of the region once and for all.

The Muslim reconquest began in 1144 when Zengi, the founder of a short-lived Kurdish dynasty from Mosul (now in northern

Iraq), wiped out the county of Edessa. Within a few years he and his successor, Nur ad-Din, had gone on to reduce the principality of Antioch to a sliver of land along the coast.

Nur ad-Din then moved to position one of his generals in the Fatimid court in Egypt. That general, Salah ad-Din al-Ayoubi, better known in the west as Saladin, took control of Egypt in his own right in 1171 and went on to lead the Muslim army that reconquered Jerusalem in 1187. Over the next 100 years the Crusaders, who occupied a coastal strip of varying length and depth, were slowly squeezed out. Antioch and Jaffa fell in 1268, Tripoli in 1289 and, finally, Acre (modern Akko, in Israel) in 1291.

Salah ad-Din's dynasty, the Ayyubids, ruled Egypt, Syria, western Arabia and parts of Yemen until 1250, when they were unceremoniously removed by their own army. They were replaced by the strange soldier-slave kings known as the Mamluks, who were to rule Egypt, Syria, Palestine and western Arabia for nearly 300 years (1250-1517).

The Mamluks ran what would today be called a military dictatorship. But the only way to join their army was to be press-ganged into it. Non-Muslim boys were captured or bought outside the empire (often in Europe or Central Asia), converted to Islam and raised in the service of a single military commander. They were expected to give this commander total loyalty, in exchange for which their fortunes would rise (or fall) with his. The children of Mamluk soldiers were free men and women but were not allowed to join the army. Sultans were chosen from among the most senior Mamluk commanders.

After overthrowing the Ayyubids, the Mamluks ruled in their own right, paying only nominal allegiance to the Abbasid caliphs they had set up in Cairo after the Mongols sacked Baghdad in 1258.

The Mongol Invasions

As the Seljuk Empire collapsed in the second half of the 12th century, the crescent of land from Anatolia to Khorasan became a mass of warring local dynasties. A few Seljuks clung on in Anatolia to vie with the Byzantines, but throughout the rest of what had been their empire, chaos reigned for a century or so.

Enter the Mongols. In 1206 the tribes of what is now southern Siberia and Mongolia united around a single chief: Genghis Khan. He was said to have been visited in a dream by a spirit who commanded him to return humankind to its pre-civilisation 'state of nature'. By the time he died, in 1227, Genghis had done a remarkable job of fulfiling the spirit's wish.

In 1218, after more than a decade spent destroying northern China, Genghis and his armies crossed thousands of kilometres of barren steppe to invade the lands of Islam. At his death, nine years later, he had wreaked havoc throughout Central Asia, Afghanistan and Khorasan.

Genghis' grandson, Hulagu Khan, continued the family tradition. His army utterly destroyed Baghdad in 1258, killing 800,000 people in a week-long orgy of looting and pillage. Hulagu died in 1265 but the dynasty he founded, the Il-Khanids, ruled a huge Persian-Turkish empire for another 90 years, during which time the pagan Mongols were converted to Islam.

As Il-Khanid rule waned in Persia, another marauding army descended from the steppes to pillage the Middle East. Tamerlane's claim of descent from Genghis Khan was false in biological terms but 100% accurate when it came to military strategy. His army became known, among other things, for killing every living thing in the cities it conquered and then building enormous towers of skulls beside whatever ruins were left.

In a mere five years (1399-1404) he massacred his way out of Central Asia, across Persia, up to the Caucasus, across eastern Anatolia and down into Syria, then eastward across Iraq and back to Persia. Once there he turned west and went all the way to the Aegean coast before heading back across Persia yet again on his way home to Samarkand, in modern Uzbekistan.

The Rise of the Ottomans

In 1258 – the same year that Hulagu Khan sacked Baghdad – a boy named Osman was born to the chief of a pagan Turkish tribe in western Anatolia.

Osman, the first ruler of what would become the Ottoman Empire, converted to Islam in his youth. He began his military career by hiring out his tribe's army as mercenaries in the civil wars then besetting what was left of the Byzantine Empire. Payment came in the form of land.

Rather than taking on the Byzantines directly, Osman's successors patiently scooped up the bits and pieces of the empire that Constantinople could no longer control. By the end of the 14th century the Ottomans had conquered Bulgaria, Serbia, Bosnia, Hungary and all of the territory that now makes up Turkey. They had also moved their capital across the Dardanelles to Adrianople, today the Turkish city of Edirne. In 1453 Sultan Mehmet II took Constantinople, the hitherto unachievable object of innumerable Muslim wars almost since the 7th century.

The empire reached its peak, both politically and culturally, under Süleyman the Magnificent (reigned 1520-1566), who led the Ottoman armies west to the gates of Vienna, east into Persia, and south through the holy cities of Mecca and Medina and into Yemen. His control also extended throughout North Africa. He cracked down on corruption, reformed the Ottoman legal system and was the patron of the great architect Sinan, who designed the Süleymaniye Mosque in İstanbul and oversaw the reconstruction of the Grand Mosque in Mecca.

After Süleyman, however, the Ottoman Empire went into a long, slow period of decline. Only five years after his death Spain and Venice destroyed virtually the entire Ottoman navy at the Battle of Lepanto (in the Aegean Sea), a loss which eventually cost the Sublime Porte (as the Ottoman government was known) control of the western Mediterranean. North Africa soon fell under the sway of local dynasties. The Ottomans were driven out of Yemen in 1636, and conflict with the Safavids – Persia's rulers from the early 16th century to the early 18th century – was almost constant.

Enter Europe

Europe's colonial expansion into the Middle East began in 1498, when the Portuguese explorer Vasco de Gama visited Oman's northern coast, the Strait of Hormuz (then the seat of an independent kingdom) and the Sheikhdom of Julfar, near modern Ras al-Khaimah in the United Arab Emirates (UAE). In 1507 Portugal annexed the Yemeni island of Socotra and occupied Oman. Its power eventually extended as far north as Bahrain. But although Portugal retained control of Bahrain until 1602 and was not driven out of Oman until 1650, the area was important to it only as a way-station on the route to India. Little, if any, effort was made to penetrate Arabia's interior.

Portuguese influence in the Gulf gradually gave way to that of Britain's East India Company, which had trading links with the area as early as 1616. During the 17th and early 18th centuries the British concentrated on driving their French and Dutch competitors out of the region, a task they had largely accomplished by 1750.

At the beginning of the 18th century the political weaknesses of both Persia and Turkey left the way open to European powers seeking to dominate the region. The Ottoman sultans were, by then, virtual figureheads, and Persia seemed chronically unstable. After the fall of the Safavids, Persia was ruled by three different dynasties in the space of just 55 years.

Decline of the Porte

In the early 19th century the Europeans began nibbling away at the Ottoman Empire, the economy of which was not helped by the empire having to fight some half-a-dozen wars with Russia between 1768 and the end of the 19th century.

In 1798 Napoleon invaded Egypt in what he thought would be the first step towards building a French empire in the Middle East and India. The French occupation of Egypt lasted only three years but left a lasting mark:

until very recently French was the second (sometimes the first) language of choice for the Egyptian upper classes. Even today, Egypt's legal system is based on a French model.

The British forced the French out of Egypt in 1801, and several years of unrest followed. In 1805 Mohammed Ali, an Albanian soldier in the Ottoman army, emerged as the country's strongman and became the Ottoman sultan's khedive, or viceroy. Mohammed Ali, whose descendants ruled Egypt in some form or other until 1952, set about modernising the country, particularly by sending large numbers of Egyptians to study in Europe.

In 1818 Mohammed Ali obliged the sultan by sending an army, led by his son Ibrahim, to retake Arabia, much of which had been conquered by Bedouin warriors led by the ancestors of today's Saudi royal family. In the 1820s Ibrahim was dispatched to Greece to try, unsuccessfully this time, to stop the war of independence there.

As time passed, and it became increasingly obvious that the sultan was ever more dependent on him for military backing, Mohammed Ali's ambitions grew. In the 1830s he invaded and conquered Syria, and by 1839 he had effective control of most of the Ottoman Empire. İstanbul itself would probably have been his next target had not the European powers, alarmed by the idea of the Ottoman government collapsing, forced him to withdraw to Egypt. In exchange, the sultan recognised Mohammed Ali as a separate ruler owing only nominal allegiance to the Porte (which was more an acknowledgement of reality than anything else).

In 1869 Mohammed Ali's grandson, Ismail, opened the Suez Canal. But within a few years his government was so deeply in debt that in 1882 the British, who already played a large role in Egyptian affairs, occupied the country.

Throughout the early 19th century the Ottoman Empire stagnated, becoming increasingly dependent on the good will of the European powers and weakening its own position by ceding authority over its subjects

to various foreign governments. In 1860 the French sent troops to Lebanon after a massacre of local Christians by the local Druze. Before withdrawing, the French forced the Ottomans to set up a new administrative system for the area guaranteeing the appointment of Christian governors, over whom the French themselves came to have great influence.

At other times during the 19th century the Ottoman government ceded to the Russian Empire the right to 'protect' all Orthodox Christians living under Ottoman rule. Turkey became known as 'the sick man of Europe', yet powerful political forces there stymied any effort at reform. In 1856 Sultan Abdülmecit promulgated a broad programme of much-needed administrative, educational and financial reforms, but many of these were reversed under his successors. Even a coup led by reformers in 1876 did little to improve the situation.

The loss of virtually all of the empire's European provinces during the 19th century also changed the nature of the Ottoman state. For the first time in several centuries an Ottoman sultan found himself ruling an empire which was overwhelmingly eastern and Islamic. If, however, the sultan was going to stress his realm's Islamic identity (and around the end of the 19th century a conscious decision to this effect was taken in İstanbul), day-to-day control of western Arabia, and especially of the holy cities, was essential.

In 1900 Sultan Abdülhamid II (reigned 1876-1909) announced that a railway would be built from Damascus to Medina. An extension to Mecca was planned but never completed. The ostensible purpose of the project was to make it easier for pilgrims to reach the holy cities, but Abdülhamid's real motive for the project was to bring the Hejaz back under firm Ottoman control. The Hejaz Railway to Medina began operation in 1908.

Atatürk & Rezā Shāh

With the outbreak of WWI in 1914 the Ottoman Empire sided with Germany, and

Sultan Mohammed V declared a *jihad*, or holy war, calling on Muslims everywhere to rise up against Britain, France and Russia. To counter the sultan, the British negotiated an alliance with Hussein bin Ali, the Grand Sherif of Mecca. In 1916 Sherif Hussein agreed to lead an Arab revolt against the Turks (his nominal overlords) in exchange for a British promise to make him King of the Arabs after the war.

The British never had any serious intention of keeping this promise. At the same time that they were negotiating with Sherif Hussein, they were holding talks with the French on how to carve up the Ottoman Empire. Britain had also given the Zionist movement a promise, known as the Balfour Declaration after the then-British foreign secretary, that it would 'view with favour the establishment in Palestine of a national home for the Jewish people' after the war.

In the closing year of the war the British occupied Palestine and Damascus. After the war a settlement modelled on the Sykes-Picot Agreement – the secret Anglo-French accord that divided the Ottoman Empire into British and French spheres of influence – was implemented and given the formal rubber-stamp approval of the newly created League of Nations: France took control of Syria and Lebanon, while Britain retained Egypt and was given control of Palestine, Transjordan and Iraq. These territories were formally held under 'mandates' from the League of Nations, but in practice the system amounted to little more than direct colonial rule.

The war also spelled the end of the Ottoman dynasty. Stripped of its Arab provinces, the Ottoman monarchy was overthrown and a Turkish republic declared under the leadership of Mustafa Kemal, a soldier who became Turkey's first president in 1923. Atatürk, as he was known, changed the Turkish alphabet from Arabic to Latin script and launched a drive for modernisation, which he regarded as synonymous with secularism.

Under Atatürk and his successors Turkey has steadily pulled away from the Middle East and its affairs. The country is now a member of the North Atlantic Treaty Organization (NATO) and the Council of Europe and has been lobbying for membership of the European Union (EU).

In the early '50s Turkey briefly evolved into a two party democracy, albeit a rather unsteady one. This unsteadiness (violence was one feature of Ottoman political life which managed to survive Atatürk) eventually led the military to overthrow the civilian government three times between 1960 and 1980.

Atatürk's secularism found an echo in Persia where, in 1923, Rezā Khān, the commander of a Cossack brigade who had risen to become war minister, overthrew the Ghajar dynasty. To emphasise his nationalist credentials, he changed his name from Khān to the more Persian-sounding Pahlavī, which also happened to be the name of the language spoken in pre-Islamic Persia. He initially moved to set up a secular republic on the Turkish model, but after protests from the country's religious establishment he had himself crowned shah instead.

The reforms instituted by Rezā Shāh, as he was known after his coronation, were less successful than Atatürk's. His heavy-handedness probably worked against him. (One British traveller in the late '30s wrote of seeing soldiers snatching the veils from women's faces and trampling them in the mud.) In 1934 he changed the country's name to Iran.

Above all Rezā Shāh was a fierce nationalist. Before he came to power Britain and Russia had jointly dominated the country, a fact which led him to evince pro-German sympathies when WWII began. That, in turn, led the British to depose him in 1941 in favour of his son, Mohammed Rezā. Rezā Shāh died in exile in South Africa in 1944.

WWII & Beyond

The Middle East was only of marginal importance during WWII. In April 1941 a pro-German coup overthrew the government of Iraq. Iraq had gained nominal independence in 1932, though British 'advisors' remained extremely powerful there. The coup was short-lived. British and Jordanian troops marched across the desert and re-installed a pro-British government only a month later. That summer British, Jordanian and Free French forces invaded Syria and Lebanon to depose the pro-Vichy regime there.

As a battle theatre Egypt was briefly central to the war. It was at El Alamein, in the desert west of Alexandria, that the German advance across North Africa was finally turned back. The Germans, who were hampered by a lack of fuel, had planned to occupy Alexandria and Cairo before attacking Saudi Arabia in a bid to capture the oil fields around the Gulf.

The region's problems began in earnest soon after the war was over. Since taking control of Palestine in 1918, the British had been under pressure to allow unrestricted Jewish immigration to the territory. With tension rising between Palestine's Arab and Jewish residents, they had refused to do this and, in the late '30s, had placed strict limits on the number of new Jewish immigrants.

Several plans to partition Palestine were proposed during the '30s and '40s, but WWII (briefly) put an end to all such discussion. When the war ended, Britain again found itself under pressure to allow large-scale Jewish immigration, particularly in the wake of the Holocaust.

In early 1947 the British announced that they were turning the entire problem over to the newly created United Nations (UN). The UN voted to partition Palestine, but the Arab side rejected the plan and war followed.

The disastrous performance of the Arab armies in the 1948 Arab-Israeli War (known in Israel as the War of Independence) had far-reaching consequences. Recriminations over the war, and the refugee problem it created, laid the groundwork for the 1951 assassination of King Abdullah of Jordan (the grandfather of Jordan's present king, Hussein). Syria, which had gained independence from France in 1946, became the field for a seemingly endless series of military coups in which disputes over how to handle

the Palestine problem often played a large part.

It was in Egypt that the 'Disaster of 1948', as many Arabs still call it, truly made its power felt. The Egyptian army largely blamed the loss on the country's corrupt and ineffective politicians. In July 1952 a group of young officers toppled the monarchy. Initially an aged and respected army general was installed as the country's president, but it soon emerged that the real power lay with one of the coup plotters: Gamal Abdel Nasser. By 1954 he was the country's acknowledged leader.

Mossadiq & Iran

It was, however, in Iran, not Egypt, that the Middle East's first great nationalist crisis occurred. Iran was a patchwork of ethnic enclaves. The country was rich in oil but politically volatile. Rezā Shāh had held the country together with a combination of authoritarian rule and sheer force of personality. His son, Mohammed Rezā, was not cut from the same cloth.

In the late '40s relations between the Iranian government and the British-owned Anglo-Iranian Oil Company (the precursor of today's BP) became steadily more tense. The Iranian government, which already had the best deal of any of the producing countries vis-à-vis the oil companies, was demanding a larger share of oil revenues and threatening nationalisation if it did not receive satisfaction.

The always-turbulent world of Iranian politics reached a fever pitch in the spring of 1951 with the assassination of Prime Minister Ali Razmara, a general who opposed the nationalisation of Anglo-Iranian. In his place the Majles, or parliament, chose Mohammed Mossadiq, the aged chairman of the Majles oil committee and the oil company's most ardent foe. Three days later a law nationalising Anglo-Iranian went into force. The resulting crisis dragged on throughout 1952. Strikes and, later, a British-organised boycott guaranteed that no oil flowed out of Iran. The USA's attempts at mediation proved fruitless. With no solution in sight,

Mossadiq, a demagogue of the first order, resorted to governing by mob rule – manipulating and intimidating the Majles by summoning huge crowds to surround the parliament building.

Late in the year the USA and Britain began work on a secret plan, which they approved in mid-1953, to topple Mossadiq with a coup. The plan was supposed to begin with the shah dismissing Mossadiq, but things went wrong from the start, and mobs under Mossadiq's control drove the shah out of the country, first to Baghdad and, later, to Rome. Within days, however, the tide turned and by the end of August the shah was back in Tehrān.

The extent to which the USA's Central Intelligence Agency (CIA) was involved in generating the wave of public support which brought the shah back from Rome has long been the subject of fierce debate. Whatever the truth may be, most Iranians believe to this day that the USA put the shah back on the throne. That belief played no small part in the fury directed by Iran against Washington when the shah was overthrown again, this time for good, more than 25 years later.

The Suez Crisis

One outcome of the drawn-out Iranian crisis was that the British, who still ran parts of Yemen, most of the Gulf and the Suez Canal, came to feel that nationalist movements in the Middle East were best dealt with by stomping on them quickly. A pervasive British fear throughout the two year Iranian crisis had been that if Mossadiq succeeded in nationalising Anglo-Iranian, the floodgates would open throughout the region. In particular they feared that President Nasser of Egypt might try to nationalise the Suez Canal, which was still regarded as a vital lifeline of the British Empire.

With Mossadiq out of the way, the British came to see Nasser as the source of most of their problems in the region. In 1954 Britain reluctantly agreed to evacuate the Canal Zone, which it had retained control of when Egypt was granted nominal independence in 1922. Britain retained the right, however, to reoccupy the canal in the event of an attack on Turkey or any Arab League state.

Using this loophole the British almost immediately began secret talks with the French on ways to re-establish western control over the waterway. France's interest was twofold: the Suez Canal company was based in Paris, and the French believed Nasser was supporting the nationalist struggle against them in Algeria. Israel, which wanted to curb attacks from Egyptian-sponsored guerrillas operating from the Gaza Strip, was brought into the talks, and a plan emerged.

The spark for the Suez Crisis was the US decision, announced on 19 July 1956, to withdraw backing for the loan Egypt needed to finance the huge Aswan High Dam project. Washington justified its action by citing what it saw as Nasser's increasing friendliness with the Soviet Union. A week later Nasser announced that he would nationalise the canal and use its revenues to finance the dam. This prompted the British, French and Israelis to put their hitherto secret plan into action.

On 28 October 1956 Israel invaded Egypt, ostensibly to put a stop to the Gaza-based attacks. As Israeli forces entered Sinai, London and Paris, by prearrangement with Israel, issued an ultimatum demanding that both Israel and Egypt 'withdraw' from an area extending for 16 km either side of the canal. This was slightly disingenuous, as the Israelis were still far from the canal, of which the Egyptians still controlled both banks. In any case, Nasser rejected the ultimatum and Britain and France responded by bombing Egypt and landing their troops in the Canal Zone.

The crisis only ended when the USA forced Britain and France to withdraw. Though it had been a military defeat, Nasser turned the Suez Crisis into a great political victory.

From Suez to Black September

The years immediately after Suez were Nasser's heyday. The Egyptian leader emerged from the Suez Crisis as the pre-eminent figure in the Arab world and a central player in the politics of nationalism, socialism and decolonisation which gripped much of the developing world throughout the '50s and '60s.

But despite this prominence, Nasser was never able to realise his dream of a Pan-Arab state. In 1958 he merged Egypt and Syria to form the United Arab Republic. The marriage of the two countries was unhappy from the outset, and the union was dissolved three years later. A 1963 attempt to unite Egypt, Syria and Iraq never got off the ground. Soon afterwards Nasser became involved in a bloody proxy war with the Saudis in Yemen which tied down tens of thousands of Egyptian troops for years. Other Arab countries – particularly Syria and Iraq – were chronically unstable, and Israel, Arab rhetoric notwithstanding, appeared militarily unassailable.

Nasser was realistic. Privately he acknowledged that the Arabs would probably lose a war against Israel, but for public consumption he gave rabble-rousing speeches about liberating Palestine. By early 1967 the public mood engendered throughout the Arab world by these speeches was beginning to catch up with him. Nasser fell victim to accusations that he was 'hiding' behind the UN troops who had been stationed in the Sinai peninsula since the Suez Crisis.

On 16 May 1967 Nasser demanded that the UN forces be withdrawn. Somewhat to his surprise the UN Secretary-General complied immediately. The Egyptian army moved into key points in Sinai and announced a blockade of the Strait of Tiran, effectively closing the southern Israeli port of Eilat.

The Egyptian army was mobilised and the country put on a war footing. Israel responded on 5 June 1967 with a pre-emptive strike that wiped out virtually the entire Egyptian air force. The war lasted only six days, and when it was over Israel controlled all of the Sinai peninsula and the Gaza Strip. The West Bank, including Jerusalem's Old City, had been seized from Jordan and the Golan Heights from Syria. To the 'Disaster of 1948' was now added the 'Humiliation of 1967'.

As in 1948, the war's political fallout was far-reaching. In Egypt, at least, Nasser again managed to turn a military debacle into a political victory, but in the years that followed it became obvious that he had lost much of his lustre. Recriminations over the loss of the Golan Heights fuelled yet another round of coup-plotting in Syria. Even in distant Kuwait, over 1200 km from the battlefront, the government was sharply criticised for not having done enough to help the Arab cause.

It was also in the wake of the Six Day War that the Palestinians first became players in Arab politics. The Palestine Liberation Organization (PLO) had been set up by Nasser in 1964 as little more than a front for the Egyptian leader. After 1967, however, many Palestinians concluded that it was unrealistic to count on the Arab states to regain Palestine for them.

Numerous small guerrilla groups sprang up after the war. Most prominent among these was Fatah (the name is a reverse acronym in Arabic for 'Palestine Liberation Movement'), founded in Kuwait in 1958 by three young Palestinian expatriates, including a building contractor named Yasser Arafat. It was Fatah, and a host of smaller groups ranging from Marxist revolutionaries to idealist social democrats, that took over the PLO in the years after 1967. With its weak government, weighed down by hundreds of thousands of Palestinian refugees, and its long border with Israel and the West Bank, Jordan became the main base for the *fedayeen*, as the guerrilla groups were known in Arabic.

Relations between the PLO and Jordan were never particularly good. The first PLO fighter to be killed was, in fact, shot by the Jordanian army, not by the Israelis. Throughout the late '60s tension between King Hussein of Jordan and the Palestinians rose steadily as guerrilla raids from Jordanian territory prompted numerous Israeli retaliatory strikes and counter-raids.

The final showdown came in September 1970 when King Hussein moved to smash Palestinian power in his country while the Palestinians attempted to overthrow the king. The PLO assumed that Jordan's large population of Palestinian refugees would guarantee them victory. In this they badly miscalculated. Despite the defection of some predominantly Palestinian units, the Jordanian army on the whole remained loyal and moved in to wipe out Palestinian resistance. Thousands of people – mostly civilians caught in the crossfire – died in the fighting.

A hastily convened Arab summit in Cairo sent a delegation to Amman to negotiate a cease-fire. The PLO leader, Yasser Arafat, was smuggled out of Jordan dressed as a Kuwaiti official and King Hussein arrived in Egypt shortly thereafter. On 27 September 1970 it was announced that the two sides had reached an agreement to end the fighting which had, by then, been going on for almost three weeks. The agreement required most of the fedayeen to move to Lebanon (where their presence fuelled that country's slow slide toward civil war). Though it also allowed the Palestinians to maintain a presence in Jordan, this was greatly reduced in size and kept under stricter Jordanian control.

Nasser, who had been the driving force behind the agreement, spent the rest of the day seeing off the delegations at Cairo airport. He then went home, where he collapsed and died of a heart attack in the early hours of 28 September.

The October War & Its Aftermath

The year 1970 saw the ascension of new leaders in both Egypt and Syria: Anwar Sadat and Hafez al-Assad respectively. The decade also began with the last remnants of colonial rule departing from the Middle East when the British, in late 1971, pulled out of the Gulf.

Preparations were also well under way for the next Middle Eastern war. The Arab states were constantly under pressure from their citizens to reclaim the land lost in 1967. In Egypt, Sadat felt the political need to emerge

from Nasser's shadow. In Syria, Assad needed a war to counter the charge that as defence minister in 1967 he had been responsible for the loss of the Golan Heights.

The war began on 6 October 1973, when Egyptian troops crossed the Suez Canal, taking Israel almost entirely by surprise. After advancing a short distance into Sinai, however, the Egyptian army stopped, giving Israel the opportunity to concentrate its forces against the Syrians on the Golan Heights and then to turn back towards Egypt. When the war ended in late 1973 the Israelis actually occupied more land than they had when it began. Months of shuttle diplomacy by the US secretary of state, Henry Kissinger, followed. This produced a set of disengagement agreements under which Israel withdrew from some of the territory it had occupied. It also led to the reopening of the Suez Canal, which had been closed since 1967, though in exchange the Egyptians had to concede the right of Israeli ships to use the waterway.

Pressure on the USA to broker a deal was fuelled when the Gulf States embargoed oil supplies to the west 10 days after the war began. The embargo was relatively short-lived, but if the goal was to get the west's attention, it was certainly successful.

The embargo also led to a huge, and basically permanent, increase in the price of oil, which led in turn to a flood of money landing in the laps of the Gulf's sheikhs. An enormous building boom began throughout the Gulf.

In 1979 Iran's Islamic Revolution shook the Gulf States, but it also made them even richer. Not only did the price of oil soar yet again, but production was increased to fill the gap left by the absence of Iranian oil from world markets.

All of this shifted the balance of power in the Middle East. The oil states, rich but underpopulated and militarily weak, gained at the expense of poorer, more populous countries. Huge shifts of population followed the two oil booms of the '70s as millions of Egyptians, Syrians, Jordanians, Palestinians and Yemenis went off to seek their fortunes in the oil states (including Iraq where, in the late '80s, over a million Egyptians alone were working).

This further increased the Gulf's political clout. Poorer Arab governments, dependent both on hand-outs from the oil states and on the remittances sent home by their citizens working in the Gulf, found they increasingly had to defer to the Gulf rulers in general and the Saudis in particular.

Peace & Revolution

Anwar Sadat's dramatic visit to Jerusalem in 1977 opened the way for an Egyptian-Israeli peace process which culminated, in March 1979, with the signing of a peace treaty between the two countries. As Sadat and Israel's prime minister, Menachem Begin, signed the treaty in Washington, Arab leaders meeting in Baghdad voted to expel Egypt from the Arab League. All but two Arab countries (Sudan and Oman) broke off diplomatic relations with Egypt.

Meanwhile, one of the few friends Sadat had left in the region had troubles of his own. Discontent with the Shāh of Iran's autocratic rule and his personal disregard for his country's Shiite Muslim religious traditions had been simmering for years. Political violence slowly increased throughout 1978. The turning point came in September of that year, when Iranian police fired on anti-shah demonstrators in Tehrān, killing at least 300. The momentum of the protests quickly became unstoppable.

On 16 January 1979 the shah left Iran, never to return (he died in Egypt in 1980). The interim government set up after his departure was swept aside the following month when the revolution's leader, the hitherto obscure Āyatollāh Rūhollāh Khomeinī, returned to Tehrān from his exile in France.

After the Revolution

Iran's Islamic Revolution seemed to change everything in the Middle East, ushering in a period of instability which lasted until nearly the end of the '80s.

In 1979 militants seized the Grand Mosque in Mecca – Islam's holiest site – and were only ejected several weeks later after bloody gun battles inside the mosque itself. In November of that year student militants in Tehrān overran the US embassy, taking the staff there hostage. In 1980 Turkey's government was overthrown in a military coup, capping weeks of violence between left and right-wing extremists. Further east, Iraq invaded Iran, launching what would become the longest, bloodiest and, arguably, most pointless war in modern history.

Tensions escalated yet again in 1981 when President Sadat of Egypt was assassinated by Muslim militants. The following year Israel invaded Lebanon, further fuelling the cycle of chaos and destruction that had gripped that country since 1975.

Lebanon's confessional system of government, under which the president was always a Maronite Christian, the prime minister a Sunni Muslim, the speaker of parliament a Shiite Muslim and the foreign minister a Greek Orthodox Christian, was based on a census conducted by the French in the '20s and an unwritten agreement among the country's political leaders in the years immediately after WWII. It collapsed under the weight of demographic changes that made the Muslim communities more populous, and the tensions that came with playing host to a large, poor and disenfranchised community of Palestinian refugees including, after 1970, most of the Palestinian guerilla forces. The latter established a state-within-a-state in southern Lebanon and their raids into Israel prompted frequent Israeli reprisals across the border.

Over the 15 years of Lebanon's civil wars an extraordinary cast of foreign characters intervened on one side or another (in some cases switching sides as time went on): the USA, Britain, France, Iran, Iraq, Israel and Syria all got deeply involved in the Lebanese mess at one time or another. In the early and mid-80s Lebanon became a depressing metaphor for the entire region. By the end of the decade it had become so violent and so dangerous that few foreigners dared venture there. The fighting in Lebanon only limped to a close in late 1990 when Syria moved in to put an end to it with the tacit approval of the USA.

Still, there were occasional bright spots. Turkey returned to democratic rule in 1983, albeit with a new constitution barring from public office anyone who had been involved in politics prior to the 1980 coup. In 1985 the Israelis withdrew from most of Lebanon. In 1988 Iran and Iraq grudgingly agreed to a cease-fire. The following year Egypt was readmitted to the Arab League and Jordan held its first elections in more than 20 years.

The 1990s

The Gulf War On 2 August 1990, Iraq invaded Kuwait. Within days King Fahd of Saudi Arabia had asked the USA to send troops to defend his country against a possible Iraqi attack. The result was Operation Desert Shield, a US-led coalition in Saudi Arabia and the Gulf which eventually involved over 500,000 troops. On 17 January 1991 the coalition launched Operation Desert Storm to drive Iraq out of Kuwait, a goal which was accomplished after a six week bombing campaign and a four day ground offensive.

In late 1990, while attempting to solicit Arab support for the anti-Iraq coalition, US President George Bush promised to make a new effort to achieve Arab-Israeli peace once the Iraqis were out of Kuwait. After the war Bush's secretary of state, James Baker, embarked on a tortuous series of shuttles around the region in an attempt to convene a Middle East peace conference.

Israeli-PLO Peace Agreement The conference took place in Madrid at the end of October 1991. It was followed by nearly two years of relatively fruitless bilateral negotiations between the Israelis on the one hand and Jordan, the Palestinians, Lebanon and Syria on the other.

In the late summer of 1993, with the negotiations stalled and seemingly on the verge of breaking down, it was revealed that Israel and the PLO had been holding secret talks in Norway for 18 months and that they were now ready to sign the outline of a peace

agreement and to recognise each other. When the agreements were signed a few weeks later, extremists on both sides howled in protest. Egypt, feeling vindicated 14 years after signing its own peace treaty with Israel, applauded loudly. The rest of the Arab world maintained a guarded silence. Another round of Israeli-PLO talks in late 1993 and early 1994 led to an agreement under which Israel withdrew from the Gaza Strip and the West Bank town of Jericho in May 1994.

Jordan, after some initial hesitation, used the Israel-PLO agreements as an excuse to move forward in its own peace talks with the Israelis. On 26 October 1994 Jordan became the second Arab country to sign a formal peace treaty with Israel. Talks between Israel and Syria did not go as well, and continued off-and-on from 1993 through 1996.

On 4 November 1995 Israeli Prime Minister Yitzhak Rabin was assassinated as he left a peace rally in Tel Aviv. Israelis were stunned to learn that the lone gunman was not an Arab but a Jew – a law student who objected to the Rabin government's policy of handing back territory to the Palestinians. Unrepentant, the assassin said he had hoped Rabin's murder would stop the peace process in its tracks. As it was the peace process initially moved forward with renewed vigour under the leadership of Rabin's successor Shimon Peres, until in February 1996 a series of four suicide bombings by Palestinian militants left more than 60 Israelis dead.

The response from the international community showed just how much things had changed in the Middle East during the '90s: on 13 March 1996 a one day summit meeting took place in the Egyptian resort of Sharm el-Sheikh with the aim of reinvigorating the peace process. It was attended by the presidents of the USA and Russia, by most of Europe's heads of government, and by Israel's prime minister, Egypt's president and the kings of Jordan and Morocco. More significantly, the meeting was also attended by representatives of all of the Gulf States, by the president of Yemen and the foreign ministers of Algeria and Tunisia. The summit represented the first public contact between many Arab governments and Israel. However, the Israeli people remained unconvinced of the future prospects of peace and two months later voted in Binyamin Netanyahu as the new prime minister, a right-wing candidate who advocated tougher policies against the Palestinians. Since that time, relations between Netanyahu's Israel

The Arab-Israeli Conflict

There are Israelis who claim that God gave the land to the Jews and, therefore, it would be blasphemous to surrender a millimetre of it. There are Arabs who equate Israel with the Crusader states of the Middle Ages and view its destruction as a religious duty, saying it represents an infidel incursion into the sacred lands of Islam.

These are, of course, extreme examples, but they serve to illustrate the depth of the feelings and enmities born of nearly a century of conflict between Arabs and Jews over the sliver of land traditionally known as Palestine.

Zionism has its roots in 19th-century Europe (thus the Arab claim that Israel is little more than a relic of the colonial era). Though the idea of a Jewish state did not originate with him it was first put forward in a systematic way by an Austrian journalist, Theodor Herzl, who believed that Jews could never gain true acceptance in European society. Herzl's 1896 book, *Der Judenstaat* (The Jewish State), called for the establishment of a Jewish homeland, and the following year he organised the first International Zionist Congress in Basel, Switzerland. The Congress' final resolution stated that 'the goal of Zionism is the establishment for the Jewish people of a home in Palestine guaranteed by public law'.

In November 1917 the British Cabinet, in a statement known as the Balfour Declaration, gave the cause its formal backing. When British took control of Palestine near the end of WWI Zionists hoped the declaration would serve as a licence for unrestricted Jewish immigration. The arrival of Jewish settlers, however, led to tension with Palestine's Arab population and, eventually, to violence. In the late 1930s Britain clamped strict limits on Jewish immigration, a policy which was continued throughout WWII.

In February 1947 the British, despairing of ever reconciling Arabs and Jews and far more concerned with post-WWII reconstruction at home, announced that they would withdraw from Palestine the following year and turned the problem over to the United Nations.

In November 1947 the UN voted to partition Palestine into Arab and Jewish states and to turn Jerusalem into an international city. Predictably, neither side was satisfied with the plan. The Jews, however reluctantly, accepted it while the Arabs rejected it outright. War broke out when Britain withdrew in May 1948, and the formal partition lines quickly came to mean nothing. Jewish forces sought to gain control of as much of Palestine as possible while the combined armies of Egypt, Jordan and Lebanon (along with smaller contingents from Syria, Iraq and Saudi Arabia) endeavoured to wipe out the new Jewish state.

The 1949 armistice agreements which ended Israel's War of Independence effectively defined the Jewish state's borders for the next 18 years. The only portions of historical Palestine left under Arab control were the Gaza Strip, which was occupied by the Egyptian army, and the area now known as the West Bank, which was occupied, and later annexed, by the Jordanians.

By the time of the Suez Crisis in 1956 the basic elements which defined the Arab-Israeli conflict for the next 35 years were in place: Israel, its population swelled by successive waves of Jewish immigration, possessed most (after 1967, all) of historical Palestine. The Palestinians lived as refugees either in other Arab countries or under Israeli occupation. Arab governments refused to talk to Israel under any circumstances and Israel loudly proclaimed its desire for peace while working furiously to create what former Israeli Defence Minister Moshe Dayan called 'facts on the ground' – essentially geographic and demographic alterations to secure the territory under their control. These changes tended both to reinforce Israel's long-term strategic position and to convince Arabs that Israel had no intention of either giving up land or of allowing Palestinian refugees to return to what had once been their homes.

In such an explosive situation no event or gesture, however seemingly innocuous, managed to remain devoid of political content. The combination of time, physical separation and an unbroken stream of propaganda on both sides led many Arabs and Israelis to develop somewhat cartoon-like images of each other.

The 1991 Gulf War changed the strategic equation in the region by leaving both sides of the and the Arab world have remained at a stalemate.

Iran & the West Meanwhile, under Presi-

dent Hāshemī Rafsanjānī, Iran had begun to make tentative overtures to the outside world. After Āyatollāh Khomeinī's death, in June 1989, Rafsanjānī had emerged as the

Arab-Israeli conflict politically weakened and anxious to score points with the international community. Even so, it took months of US coaxing to get both sides to agree to attend a peace conference in Madrid in October of the same year. Among the major sticking points was Israel's insistence that it would not deal directly with the Palestine Liberation Organization (PLO), which it considered a terrorist group. After the ceremonial opening session in Madrid, nearly two years of inconclusive bilateral talks with Syria, Lebanon, Jordan and a group of non-PLO Palestinians followed.

Then, in August 1993, the news broke that Israel and the PLO had been holding secret talks for some 18 months in Norway. The following month Israel and the PLO formally recognised each other. Then, on 13 September, PLO Chairman Yasser Arafat and Israeli Prime Minister Yitzhak Rabin shook hands in Washington on the White House lawn after watching their deputies sign a joint Declaration of Principles. The Declaration laid out a timetable for future talks on the details of an Israeli withdrawal from the Gaza Strip and the West Bank town of Jericho, the redeployment of Israeli forces away from the West Bank's other population centres, the granting of limited autonomy to Palestinians throughout the West Bank and Gaza Strip and elections for a Palestinian Authority to run the self-rule areas.

At the Washington ceremony almost every speaker, whether Israeli, Palestinian, American or Russian, stressed the length of the road that still had to be travelled before a true and lasting peace could be achieved. Their point was driven home by the charges of betrayal with which rejectionists on both sides greeted the accords.

Between the need of Arafat and Rabin to cover their flanks politically, a series of provocations by extremists on both sides and the simple fact that neither Israel nor the PLO really had much trust in the other, the talks on a detailed agreement dragged on for months beyond the original timetable. An accord was finally signed, in Cairo, in May 1994 and Israeli troops withdrew from Gaza and Jericho. Further talks led to Palestinian elections and the withdrawal of most Israeli troops from the West Bank's main population centres at the end of 1995, a process that went forward despite the assassination of Prime Minister Rabin by a Jewish extremist opposed to the peace process on 4 November 1995.

Working with Arafat, Rabin's successor, Shimon Peres, sought to push the peace process forward. The job was complicated by an increasingly strong backlash from Hamas, a Palestinian Muslim fundamentalist group originally supported by the Israelis themselves as an alternative to the PLO, and by the doubts about the peace process that Hamas' terror bombings sowed in the Israeli public. In May 1996 these doubts brought down Peres, who narrowly lost the prime ministership to Benjamin Netanyahu in a general election. The 1996 election was also Israel's first in which the prime minister was directly elected in a separate vote from the one for seats in parliament. This gave Netanyahu much greater power within the Israeli government.

The new prime minister appointed one of the most right-wing governments in the country's history, and promised to be much tougher on security issues than his predecessor. While saying he wanted only to put the peace process on a sounder footing, he subjected Arafat to what the Palestinians, and most other Arabs, saw as a series of deliberate slights and public humiliations. Tension once again rose throughout the region. In September 1996 there were widespread clashes between Israelis and Palestinians, including the Palestinian police, that left dozens dead. Peace talks with Syria and Lebanon, slow-moving under Peres, ground to a halt with the installation of the new government.

Though Israel and Jordan have drawn increasingly close to one another on the governmental level since they signed a peace treaty in October 1994, contact between the two peoples remains more limited. As has been the case with Egypt, many Israeli tourists visit Jordan, but few Jordanians have shown any interest in holidays in Israel.

Egypt has been at peace with Israel since 1979, yet many Egyptians and Israelis continue to express bitter attitudes toward one another. That reality, and the chilly official relationship between Egypt and Israel for most of the years since 1979, underscores the fact that peace per se is neither friendship nor reconciliation. In time enemies may become friends and allies (think of Germany and France), but this is a slow process and the change in attitudes that it requires cannot be brought about overnight by a piece of paper. ■

country's political leader. In June 1993 he was elected to a second term as president – though with a much smaller margin of victory than had been expected – on a platform promising economic reform.

Though much of the fervour of the 1979 revolution has dissipated, Iran's relations with the west in the mid-90s continued to be awkward. Iranian leaders have refused to revoke Āyatollāh Khomeinī's 1989 call for the murder of the British writer Salman Rushdie, and they have been accused by the USA of trying to build an atomic bomb. Other western countries refused to join the Americans when they imposed an embargo on trade with Iran in 1995, but few have rushed to embrace the Iranians either.

Turkish Elections In April 1993 Turkey's president, Turgut Özal, who had shepherded the country's return to democracy as prime minister and, later, as president, died. Özal's long-time rival Prime Minister Süleyman Demirel became Turkey's new president. Demirel's successor as prime minister was Tansu Çiller, the first woman to head the government of a Muslim Middle Eastern country.

Çiller sought to deepen Turkey's ties with Europe and the west, pressing for a free trade agreement with the European Union. But many in Europe remained wary of Turkey because of its mixed human rights record. An offensive against Kurdish rebels in the country's south-east in the summer of 1995 tarnished Turkey's reputation in the west, while undermining Çiller's coalition government at home. Part of her problem was that while many in the west thought she had gone too far, some of her supporters at home, including some in the military, thought the drive against the rebels had not been carried nearly far enough.

Çiller's government fell in late 1995 and elections in December of that year produced no clear winner. The Islamist-oriented Welfare Party emerged from the poll with the largest share of the votes (just over 20%). After several months of negotiations Çiller's True Path Party agreed to a coalition with the Motherland Party, until then its arch-rival, designed largely to keep the Welfare Party out of government. The new coalition, led by Çiller's long-time rival Mesut Yilmaz, lasted only a few months. In the summer of 1996 the government fell, and President Demirel was left with little choice but to offer Welfare Party leader Necmettin Erebakan the prime ministership. Erebakan negotiated a coalition agreement with Çiller (something she had previously said she would never do) and Atatürk's secular republic began its first experiment with a religiously oriented government.

GEOGRAPHY

The Middle East is a somewhat vaguely defined area where the three continents of the Old World meet. The region could essentially be defined as south-west Asia, but because present international borders and age-old cultural exchanges draw Turkey and Egypt into the picture, Europe and Africa are also included. The shores of the Mediterranean, Black, Caspian, Arabian and Red seas and the Caucasus Mountains form natural boundaries. The core of the Middle East consists of the Arabian peninsula and the Levant, with Iran and, arguably, Afghanistan forming the eastern part of the region.

Topographically the area is extremely varied. Many people immediately visualise sand dunes on hearing the name of the region, but sand deserts form only a tiny percentage of the whole area. They are mainly to be found in Saudi Arabia and Egypt, and even in those countries rocky plains are much more common. Mountains and high plateaus abound in many countries: in Turkey, Iran, Afghanistan and Yemen much of the area lies above 1000m.

If the western Himalayas and the Hindu Kush of Afghanistan, with their 6000 to 7000m high peaks, are not counted, the highest mountains in the Middle East include the 5671m high Kūh-é Damāvand in Iran, the 5165m high Ararat in Turkey and the 3700m high Jebel an-Nabi Shu'ayb in Yemen.

The biggest rivers in the area include the

Nile, bringing African waters through Egypt, and the Euphrates and Tigris, flowing from the Anatolian highlands through Iraq to the Persian Gulf. Otherwise, with the exception of those in Turkey and north-western Iran, rivers flowing all year round and reaching the sea are a rarity in the region, due to the arid climate.

CLIMATE

Most of the Middle East is arid or semi-arid, including the greater part of the Arabian peninsula and Egypt, most of Jordan, Iraq and Iran, and Afghanistan. In many regions annual rainfall hardly reaches 100 mm. Most of Egypt, south-eastern Saudi Arabia and western Oman are extremely arid, with years often passing without rain. Dasht-é Kavīr, or the Great Salt Desert of Iran, is the largest area in the world with absolutely no vegetation. However, mountain ridges and two separate moist climate systems guarantee that considerable variation occurs within most of the countries.

The coast lands of Turkey, Syria and Lebanon all get an ample amount of rain from the Mediterranean climatic system. So do north-eastern Iraq and north-western Iran, where a narrow slip of this type of climate extends from the Black Sea, along the western Agros Mountains, all the way to Khūzestān and beyond, bringing cyclonic rains in winter. Annual rainfall can reach 600 mm in some areas, while in others it can even go up to 2000 mm per year. Further south there tends to be less rain, although southernmost Arabia and, occasionally, south-eastern Iran are affected by the Indian monsoon system; in the mountains of Yemen annual rainfall can exceed 2000 mm.

Temperatures vary wildly depending on the time of year and location. The low-lying coast lands of the Red Sea, Arabian Sea and Persian Gulf are hot to the extreme throughout the year, with humidity continuously exceeding 70%. Expect daytime temperatures between 40°C and 50°C during the summer, and way above 30°C in the winter, with nights not much cooler. Along the southern coasts of the Black and Caspian seas the mild climate resembles that of Central Europe.

On the other hand, temperatures drop consistently with the altitude. The rule of thumb is that for every 100m of ascent the temperature drops by 0.5°C to 0.7°C. Still, many high plateaus are quite hot during the summer days but freezing cold at night.

Mountains with snow caps are to be seen in Turkey, Iran, Afghanistan and even as far south as Lebanon and northern Israel. Winters are regularly snowy in the non-arid highlands of Turkey and Iran, and in the coldest winters it may very occasionally snow as far south as the mountains of Yemen. In the highlands of Turkey, Iran and Afghanistan you'll need extremely warm clothing in winter, which can be frosty.

ECOLOGY & ENVIRONMENT

The Middle East straddles the environmental dilemma. Until the 1960s many countries in the region had economies based completely on recyclable materials. No waste existed. Everything was usable and anything that was thrown away was immediately absorbed in a process of natural circulation. Since then, the region has wholly embraced the pre-packaged, throw-away ethos. But unfortunately, the modern synthetic waste often continues to be treated as though it were organic and is disposed of indiscriminately.

One of the worst things that could have happened to the region is plastic. It's not just the cities; even tracks in the depths of the wilderness are usually marked out by a trail of snagged polythene bags. There was a tendency a generation ago, especially in the Gulf during the region's first rush of wealth, to see the desert as a gigantic rubbish tip. On one level this made sense – for centuries the Bedouin had left their garbage behind them to be reclaimed by the desert. But that way of life presupposed a society based on communities of people who continually moved around and were in harmony with their surroundings.

Any such harmony has long since disappeared and the catalogue of environmental discord is ever increasing. Migrating birds are being killed in massive numbers while en route from Europe to Africa; waterfowl are hunted in protected wetlands breeding areas; and ivory and other illegal animal products are traded in shops. The coral reefs of the Red Sea are under enormous threat from irresponsible tourism and opportunistic development. Fresh water lakes are being poisoned by industrial and agricultural toxins. Air pollution in some cities is so thick that it is eating away at the antiquities.

The traditional excuse has been that the cash-strapped countries of the region do not have the financial resources necessary to combat pollution or to police protected

species, but many governments are waking up to the realisation that, in the long run, it makes greater economic sense to invest in environmental protection. Egyptian TV, for example, regularly screens government information programmes aimed at educating people in environmental matters, while Yemen has undertaken the development of modern waste-disposal systems. Oman's government, undeniably one of region's greenest, runs a breeding centre for endangered species, such as the Arabian oryx, Arabian leopard and houbara, at Bait al-Barakah, west of Muscat. It has also set aside an area around Ras al-Hadd as a protected breeding ground for giant sea turtles.

GOVERNMENT & POLITICS
Even leaving aside the matter of Israel and the widely unloved Iran, the countries of the Middle East are far from being a homogeneous bunch. Territorial disputes and rival claims on water rights, as well as ideological clashes, not to mention the wedges driven in by external influences, have all combined to ensure that the post-colonial notion of a powerful Pan-Arab union has rarely ever looked liked becoming a reality.

The Pan-Arab dream has its origins in 1945 with the convening of the Arab League of Nations, which brought together in a proposed political and economic union the seven independent Arab states of the time (Egypt, Lebanon, Transjordan, Syria, Iraq, Saudi Arabia and Yemen). Although the League has since swollen to 21 members, the unified front the organisation aimed to present has constantly been undermined by internal dissension to the extent that the whole idea of a political merging in the Arab world has been completely discredited.

In 1979 Egypt, home of the Arab League, was itself ostracised from the organisation after signing a peace treaty with Israel at Camp David. Respectability has since, to some extent, been restored but the downgraded Egypt now vies for the mantel of regional super-power with Jordan and Syria. Relations between the three, especially between Jordan and Syria, have traditionally

Responsible Tourism
The environmental problems of the Middle East might seem simply too insurmountable for a visitor to care about their own contribution; however, there is a lot you can do to minimise the impact of your visit.

Leave It As You Found It As long as outsiders have been searching for and stumbling over the ancient monuments of the Middle East, they have also been chipping bits off or leaving their own contributions engraved upon them. When visiting historical sites, consider how important it is for you to climb to the top of a pyramid or take home an unattached sample of carved masonry.

Don't Litter Indisputably, there is a lot of carelessly discarded rubbish strewn about the Middle East, and tidy-town awards do not feature here. Some of the refuse – plastic mineral water bottles for instance – is actually recycled in many ways, so don't be too quick to point an accusing finger at the locals. However, there is no doubt that inadequate waste disposal and little regard for environmental issues produces some ugly sights. Resist the local tendency to indifference on the subject and do as you would with rubbish at home – bin it.

Do As Requested Strange to say, but despite warnings and posted signs to the contrary, Red Sea divers and snorkellers continue to destroy coral by touching and treading. Despite instructions to the contrary, drivers in national parks still insist on heading off the beaten track, in some cases spelling disaster for the fragile environment or, in areas such as Sinai or the Golan, putting their own lives in danger from the risk of unexploded mines. ■

been, at best, lukewarm, although there has been some thawing recently in the face of Israel's Netanyahu government. (The question of Palestine affects all Middle Eastern relations to some extent; at the time of writing Turkey found itself out of favour with the Arab world because of an accord on military cooperation between itself and Israel.)

Ranks were further split by Iraq's invasion of Kuwait. During the protracted and bloody war against Iran, Iraq had enjoyed the support of most of the Middle East's Arab nations (Syria alone has good relations with the Persian mullahs), but Saddam found himself out of sympathy when he committed his act of aggression against a fellow Muslim Arab state. Only Jordan, Yemen and the Palestinians abstained from joining the US-led coalition that drove the Iraqis out of the tiny besieged Gulf state.

The 1991 Desert Storm affair also served to illustrate just how large an influence the oil-producing Gulf States had acquired in the politics of the region. Had the super-rich Saudi Arabia not itself felt threatened by Saddam and made an appeal for help, it is unlikely that the USA would have moved to directly intervene. And without coercion from the White House, it is also almost certain a country like Egypt would have remained inactive – many of the region's poorer nations still resent the Gulf States for their perceived failure to share around the dividends of their oil wealth.

ECONOMY

The Middle East is an area of great economic disparities. At one end are those citizens of the Gulf States – notably Kuwait and the UAE – who have per capita incomes comparable to those of citizens in the richest western countries. Even 'medium-income' countries are often quite well off by world standards: according to the World Bank, Israel's per capita income (US$13,760) falls immediately between Ireland's and Spain's.

At the other end of the spectrum lie Yemen – by almost any measure one of the poorest countries on earth – and Egypt, where per capita income is a tiny fraction of that enjoyed by even the 'poorer' oil states.

Amid such disparities there is obviously also great diversity. Among the oil states, for example, Saudi Arabia has a significantly lower per capita income than either Kuwait or the UAE despite having vastly larger oil reserves. The reason for this is simple: Saudi Arabia is a much larger country, with many more people. Some Gulf countries – notably Bahrain and Oman – have little oil and rely for their income on an active merchant class, services and a small but growing tourism industry.

Ultimately there are two industries – oil and tourism – that dominate the economic life of most of the countries covered by this book. This is something of an oversimplification, but while there are exceptions to the rule (agriculture, for example, remains a key sector of the economy in many countries – notably Egypt, Turkey and Yemen), oil and tourism, whether directly or indirectly, are the Middle East's main sources of income.

Oil

The Middle Eastern oil industry got its start in Persia (modern Iran), where oil was found in commercial quantities in 1908. The next major strikes were in the Kurdish region of northern Iraq in 1927 and in Bahrain in 1932. By the time WWII broke out in Europe, the Middle East in general, and the Gulf in particular, was known to contain some of the richest oil fields on earth.

Today oil is the economic mainstay of Iran, Iraq and all of the Gulf States. It is also an important source of income for Egypt, Yemen and Syria. Many of the region's countries which do not possess oil remain indirectly dependent on it in the form of remittances sent home by people working in the oil states. Jordan and the West Bank are the most obvious examples of areas dependent on such remittances, but Egypt, Lebanon and Yemen also benefit to some degree.

The oil states derive substantial income from the investment of portions of their oil and oil-related (ie refining and petrochemical industry) revenues in the western financial system. Before the 1990 Iraqi invasion, Kuwait's income from its investments actually exceeded its income from oil.

The recession of the late '80s and early '90s (and, in the case of Saudi Arabia and Kuwait, costs associated with the 1991 Gulf War) forced most of the biggest investors to reduce those holdings substantially, but that still left them with enormous cash reserves – an estimated US$51 billion in the case of Saudi Arabia, even after the bills for the Gulf War were paid.

Tourism

As the birthplace of the world's three great monotheistic religions and either the seat of, or the battleground for, many of the great empire-builders of antiquity, the Middle East is endowed with a surfeit of archaeological and religious treasures.

Though the region includes countries which either forbid tourism (Saudi Arabia) or make little effort to attract foreign tourists (Iran and Iraq), it also includes many where the government has worked hard to develop a tourist industry. Israel, with its vast wealth of religious and archaeological treasures but relative lack of natural resources, and Turkey – especially along the Aegean coast – are two obvious examples. Tourism has long been a major industry in Egypt and is growing rapidly in Jordan, Syria, Yemen, Bahrain, the UAE and Oman.

Tourism, however, is a notoriously uncertain source of income. The Gulf War destroyed the 1990-91 tourist season throughout the region, and in 1993 local political violence nearly crippled the industry in Egypt and Turkey. Until very recently the *intifada* – the Palestinian uprising against Israeli rule in the Gaza Strip and West Bank – was severely denting Israel's tourism income. The advances of the peace process initially reversed this trend. The handshake between Arafat and Rabin on the White House lawn did much to ensure a steadily increasing flow of tourist-generated foreign currency into the region throughout 1994-95, with Egypt, Jordan and Israel being particular beneficiaries. But terrorist attacks in early 1996, followed by renewed Israeli-Palestinian violence late in the year, once again made some travellers leery of the area as this book went to press. ∎

The only countries which have neither oil of their own in significant quantities nor large numbers of their citizens working in the oil states are Israel and Turkey.

Development Aid

Some poorer Middle Eastern countries also depend heavily on development aid to prop up their economies. Israel and Egypt are the two largest recipients of US foreign aid, between them accounting for over 40% of Washington's total foreign assistance budget. Egypt, Yemen and Jordan also receive fairly large sums of aid from the EU. Syria's economic crisis has been exacerbated by the loss of the generous subsidies it used to receive from the Soviet Union.

The oil states – particularly Saudi Arabia, Kuwait and Abu Dhabi (the largest of the sheikhdoms which make up the UAE) – are also large aid donors, though the substantial sums of money they used to transfer to development projects in Jordan, Yemen and Sudan have been cut off or sharply curtailed since those countries sided with Iraq after Baghdad's 1990 invasion of Kuwait. The Gulf States tend to channel their aid toward Muslim countries.

Trade & Services

The region's history as a trading centre is also reflected in today's economies. Services – particularly ports and shipping – are a major factor in many Middle Eastern economic equations, though none of the region's ports are as big as those of Singapore, Antwerp or Rotterdam.

Jebel Ali at Dubai in the UAE is the largest artificial port in the world and probably the Middle East's most active duty-free zone. In the Suez Canal the Egyptians have one of the world's key shipping channels, as well as a major source of hard currency in the form of tolls, services and the takings from sales in the Port Said duty-free area.

Agriculture & Industry

Egypt and Turkey – the two largest countries in the region by population – are also among the most economically diverse. Services (including their tourism industries) account for about half of all economic activity in both countries, and agriculture, though its share has declined in recent decades, can still claim around 20% of total output. Agriculture is also a significant element of the economy in Jordan, Israel and on the West Bank. Both also have active, if slightly creaky, industrial and manufacturing bases.

The region's other genuinely diverse economy belongs to Israel. Decades of political isolation led the Jewish state to develop a variety of industries – especially in defence and dual-use fields – found in few other small countries.

Military Spending

However, the region's overall economic health is another matter entirely. It has often been said that the Middle East is potentially one of the richest regions of the world. The problem is the way the money is used. Iraq, blessed with lots of oil, a relatively temperate climate and good agricultural land, has wasted mind-boggling sums of money on weapons and the construction of a stifling police state.

Throughout the region military spending has sucked up an enormous amount of national wealth. In some cases, such as Israel, the threats to national security are real. In others, Egypt and Syria for example, an entrenched military elite has objected to any attempt to scale back its privileges as regional tensions have eased. Some of the Gulf States, whose armed forces are dominated by members of the ruling families, have developed a fascination with high-tech weaponry that has more to do with ideas of status than with ideas of defence.

Future Challenges

Reform and modernisation of their ageing industrial bases has been a political (and financial) problem for both Egypt and Turkey. In Egypt the situation has been complicated by the lingering on of the Soviet-style economy that Nasser bequeathed to the country.

Iran and the Gulf, with their economic fortunes so closely tied to the price of oil, have also been subject to periodic economic ups and downs. All of the oil-producing countries have reaped huge profits from the UN embargo on oil sales by Iraq that was imposed in 1990. When Iraq comes back online the price of oil is likely to drop sharply, at least for a while – a prospect that worries the other producers, particularly since the price of oil was relatively low throughout the mid-90s.

The extent to which the oil producers have prepared for the day when oil runs out varies. Oman, with limited resources, has worked hard to broaden its economic base and wean itself from the foreign labour that dominates the other Gulf States. Many other Gulf countries have talked about economic diversification and the 'localisation' of their workforces, but to little obvious effect. When the oil does start to run out the effect will be felt region-wide as remittances from foreign workers and development aid from the oil states drop off.

That day, however, may be further away than some people think. Oil and gas resources in the Gulf remain extensive.

Rarer, and in some ways more precious, is water. Water resources throughout the region are stretched to their capacity and beyond. Examples of potential flashpoints abound: rights to the ground water underneath the West Bank have proven to be one of the most difficult issues for Israelis and Palestinians to negotiate; Syria and Iraq have protested to Turkey over that country's building of dams at the headwaters of the Tigris and Euphrates rivers; and Egypt has threatened military action against Sudan or any other upstream country that endangers its access to the waters of the Nile. Saudi Arabia will run out of the ground water that fuels its vast agricultural programme long before it runs out of oil. In the coming years the politics and economics of water may prove to be as interesting, and as crucial to the region, as oil has been for the last two generations.

POPULATION & PEOPLE

The most populous countries in the Middle

East are Turkey, Egypt and Iran, each with approximately 60 million inhabitants. The remaining countries have a combined population of 100 million: the smallest – Bahrain and Qatar – have only about half a million inhabitants each.

The people of the Middle East are descendants of those who built many ancient civilisations. While the Turks, Persians and Afghans are distinctive groups, with their own countries, customs and even languages, for Arabs the picture is less clear. Most of the Arab world's links with its pre-Islamic past have been broken over the centuries, and present-day Iraqis or Egyptians, for example, identify more closely with the all-embracing, but rather abstract, Arab Nation than with ancient Mesopotamia or Pharaonic Egypt.

Arabs

Exactly who are the Arabs – all people speaking Arabic, or only the residents of the Arabian peninsula?

Fourteen centuries ago, only the nomadic tribes wandering between the Euphrates River and the Central Arabian peninsula were considered Arabs, distinguished by their language. However, with the rapid expansion of Islam, the language of the Qur'an was spread to vast areas.

Although the Arabs were relatively few in number in most of the countries they conquered, their culture quickly became established through language and intermarriage. The term 'Arab' came to apply to two groups: in addition to the original nomadic Arabs, the settled inhabitants of these newly conquered provinces became known as Arabs when they adopted the language.

However, as late as in the 19th century it was often remarked that Egyptians were not 'real' Arabs. It was only in the 20th century that rising Arab nationalism legitimised the current usage.

Tribes The basic structure of Arab society has always been formed by families, extended families and tribes. Both wandering nomads and settled farmers divide into tribes and subtribes, the latter occupying a more or less strictly defined territory.

Belonging to a unit gives a member both rights and obligations. Conflicts are resolved within the smallest unit both participants belong to, and the smaller the number of people involved, the closer the opponents are to each other within the tribal structure. If a tribesman kills a member of another tribe, everybody in his tribe is responsible for compensation. In the course of recent history, tribal conflicts have increasingly been settled with money. While tribal killings are still a reality on the peninsula, their number has been on a slow but steady decline since money from oil exports has started coming into the region.

Every tribe elects a sheikh, or 'oldest one' – a respected and supposedly wise man who is to resolve the conflicts arising within the tribe according to *shari'a*, the Islamic law. In

The Bedouin

The most romanticised group of Arabs are no doubt the Bedouin (also called Bedu). While not an ethnic group, they are the archetypal Arabs – the camel-herding nomads who travel all over the deserts and semi-deserts in search of food for their cattle. From among their ranks came the warriors who spread Islam to North Africa and Persia 14 centuries ago.

Today Bedouin are found mainly in Jordan, Iraq, Saudi Arabia, Yemen and Egypt. Their numbers are unknown due to their habit of wandering in regions where no census-takers venture.

While some of them have settled down to enjoy the facilities of modern life, many maintain traditional life styles. (Well, they may bring their camels to the market on top of Toyota pick-up trucks and use plastic containers to carry drinking water, but that's just adaptation.) Their customs derive from the days of early Islam, and the hospitality towards strangers that Arabs are so famous for (and proud of) certainly takes its most genuine forms among the Bedouin.

On the other hand, some Bedouin don't want to have anything to do with strangers. As many oil explorers have found after having been forced to give up their cars, you certainly don't walk into a Bedouin camp uninvited. ■

the case of an unresolvable conflict with another tribe, it is the sheikh who is responsible for recruiting an army and organising and leading the battle against the aggressor. His power is not absolute, however; a new election may be held if he doesn't live up to expectations.

Persians

The Persians, or Fārsīs, retained their own language even though they were among the first to adopt the new religion and welcomed the Arabic script for writing Persian. Nevertheless, almost half the Iranian population is comprised of minority ethnic groups. The Turkish-speaking Āzarīs form the largest minority, with significant numbers also of Kurds, Arabs and Turkmen.

Turks

In the north, too, Byzantium was strong enough to resist Islam for several centuries, and the Turks kept their own language even after conversion to Islam. During the 400 year Ottoman Empire, when the Turks ruled most of the Middle East, they became known as the Shimaliyya, or Northerners, throughout the Arab world.

Kurds

The Kurds must be some of the most famous landless people of our time. Numbering an estimated 25 million people (most of them having scattered all over the world from their home mountains in eastern Turkey and Syria, northern Iraq and north-western Iran) these blue or green-eyed Sunni Muslims have a language of their own. Persecuted in turn by Turks, Iraqis, Syrians and Iranians over the centuries and betrayed by superpowers negotiating local solutions over their heads, they have adopted the motto 'The Kurds have no friends'. Even today it seems that they will continue to exist as the largest ethnic group in the world without a state of its own.

Data on the numbers of Kurds within Middle Eastern countries vary, but Iraq, Iran and Turkey have around three million each, while Syria has about one million. Exact numbers are difficult to get, as many members of the population seem to be constantly on the move, fleeing whichever country is currently oppressing them most.

Other Groups

There are, of course, numerous other population groups in the Middle East, including Jews, Afghans and countless ethnic minorities.

Armenians, like Kurds, form a small group badly treated by history. The Turkish massacre of Armenians is one of the great tragedies of this century. Today you can see Armenians living outside Armenia in Turkey, Syria and Iran. Their shops are distinguished by the unique Armenian script.

Another important minority is formed by the expatriate communities, mostly in oil-rich Gulf States. In the smallest countries expatriates often outnumber the original inhabitants. In addition to specialists from the west and unskilled labourers from middle and eastern Asia, there is significant labour mobility between the Middle Eastern countries themselves.

ARTS

The arts of the Middle East are largely the arts of Islam, typified in the minds of the non-Muslim by exotic curves and arabesques, and by intricate geometric patterning. Artistic tradition in the western sense of painting and sculpture has historically been largely absent, as Islam has always regarded the depiction of living beings as idolatrous. There have been exceptions. The long-standing figurative art traditions in Asia Minor, Persia and further east were never completely extinguished by Islam; the Turks and Iraqis continued to produce beautiful illuminated manuscripts, while the Persians maintained their art of miniature painting – which is still practised today in places like Esfahān in modern-day Iran.

Since the pervasive influence of Europe in the region, beginning in the 19th century, western-style painting and sculpture have come to take their place in the Middle Eastern artistic repertoire, but there are few artists that have been able to reconcile these mediums with their heritage, and all too often the results rely heavily on ill-appropriated European models.

In the areas of calligraphy, metalwork, ceramics, glass, carpets and textiles, however, Islamic art has a cultural heritage of unsurpassable richness – one that, in turn, has had great influence on the west. Middle Eastern artisans and craftspeople (Armenians, Christians and Jews as well as Muslims) have for over 1200 years applied complex and sumptuous decorations to often very practical objects to create items of extraordinary beauty. Plenty of such items are on view in the region's museums such as the Topkapı Palace in İstanbul or the Islamic Museum in Cairo, but to appreciate the achievements of Islamic art it is only necessary to visit one of the older mosques in which tiling, wood carving, inlaid panelling and calligraphy are often combined in exaltation of Allah. Islamic art is, for a Muslim, foremost an expression of faith.

Architecture

Ancient monuments aside, the most striking artistic heritage of the Middle East is its architecture, particularly that which developed after the coming of Islam. The earliest construction efforts inherited much from Byzantine models, but with the spread of the Muslim domain various styles soon developed, each influenced by local artists' tastes. The vocabulary of Islamic architecture quickly became very sophisticated and expressive, reaching its apotheosis under the Mamluks (1250 to 1517). A military dynasty of former slaves ruling out of Egypt, the Mamluks were great patrons of the arts and built many mosques, *madrassas* (theological schools), *khanqahs* (monasteries) and mausoleum complexes. Their buildings are characterised by the red and white bands of stone (a technique known as *ablaq*) and by the elaborate carvings and patterning around windows and in the recessed portals. The best examples of their patronage are found in Cairo but impressive Mamluk monuments also remain in Damascus and Jerusalem.

The Mamluks were eventually defeated by the Ottoman Turks who followed up their military gains with an equally expansive campaign of construction. Designed on the basic principle of a dome on a square, and instantly recognisable by their slim pencil-shaped minarets, Ottoman mosques can be found throughout Egypt, Israel, the Palestinian Territories, Lebanon, Syria and Iraq. The most impressive monuments of this era, however, were built at the heart of the empire – the Süleymaniye in İstanbul and the Selimiye Mosque at Edirne. Both are the work of the Turkish master architect Sinan.

Of all the non-Gulf regions of the Middle East, Persia was the one area that did not fall to the Turks. The Persian Safavid dynasty proved strong enough to hold the Ottomans at bay and thus Iran, and neighbouring Afghanistan, have a very different architectural

The Mosque

Mosques are generally built around open courtyards, off which lie one or more *iwan* (covered halls). The iwan facing Mecca is the focal point of prayer – it's indicated by a small alcove-like niche in the wall, called a *mihrab*. Beside the mihrab is often a free-standing pulpit and narrow stair, known as a *minbar*. It is from here that the imam gives the Friday *khutba* (sermon). Some of these minbars are ornately decorated.

The two most distinctive architectural components of the mosque are the dome and the minaret. In open courtyard mosques, the dome is often above the mihrab area; in Ottoman Turkish-style mosques it covers the whole prayer hall. The minaret is the tower from which, traditionally, the call to prayer is made. In the past a *muezzin* would climb the internal stair to the top of the minaret to perform the call, but these days it's more likely to be a tape recording broadcast from loudspeakers.

On the whole mosques engender a much more relaxed atmosphere than their Christian counterparts, churches. The mosque often serves as a casual community centre where often you'll find groups of children or adults receiving instruction (usually in the Qur'an). Other people wander in for respite from the heat and din outside and find a corner in which to sit and read, or even doze. Outside the Gulf States, it's usually quite OK for non-Muslims to enter most mosques. ■

tradition to anywhere else in the Middle East. Persian architecture has its roots not in Byzantium/Constantinople, but in the east with the Mongols who swept down from Central Asia. Their grand buildings are much simpler in form but made startling by the sumptuous use of cobalt blue and turquoise tiling which often covers every available surface.

See also the Arts section in the Yemen chapter for background information on that country's unique vernacular architecture.

Literature

Poetry has always been the pre-eminent literary form in the Middle East and all the best known figures of classical Arabic and Persian literature are poets – men regarded as possessing knowledge forbidden to ordinary people, supposedly acquired from demons. The favourite demon seems to have been alcohol. Abu Nuwas, faithful companion to the 8th-century Baghdad caliph Harun ar-Rashid, and a rather debauched fellow, left behind countless odes to the wonders of

wine, as did the Persian Omar Khayyām, famed 11th-century composer of the *rubaiyyat*. (The current Iranian regime now prefers to celebrate Khayyām for his work as a mathematician.)

Arab literature in the form of novels and short stories has its origins only in the 20th century. An increased exposure to European influences, combined with nascent Arab nationalism in the wake of the Ottoman Empire's putrefaction, led to the first stirrings. While, broadly speaking, it could be said that it has been the Egyptians, Lebanese and, to a lesser extent, the Palestinians who have dominated the scene, it's an unquestionable fact that the single most important Arabic fiction writer of this century is Naguib Mahfouz.

A life-long native of Cairo, Mahfouz began writing in the 1930s. Since that time he has done much to free Arabic literature from its western-copyist origins and infuse the medium with a unique regional voice, inspired heavily by the traditional Middle Eastern art of storytelling. His achievements

The Thousand and One Nights

After the Bible, *The Thousand and One Nights* (in Arabic, *Alf Layla wa Layla*), also called *Arabian Nights*, must be one of the most familiar, while at the same time unread, books in the English language. It owes its existence in the popular consciousness almost wholly to the Disneyfied tales of Aladdin, Sinbad and Ali Baba & the 40 Thieves that appear in children's books, cartoon films and Christmas pantomimes.

That the actual text itself is largely ignored is unsurprising considering that in its most famous English-language edition (that translated by the Victorian adventurer Sir Richard Burton), it runs to 16 volumes. In fact, an old Middle Eastern superstition has it that nobody can read the whole text of *The Nights* without dying.

But what constitutes the whole text is a matter of academic debate. *The Thousand and One Nights* is a portmanteau title for a mixed bag of colourful and fantastic tales, and the many historical manuscripts that carry the famed title collectively contain many thousands of stories, sharing a core of exactly 271 common tales. They all, however, employ the same framing device – that of a succession of stories related nightly by the wily Sheherazade to save her neck from the misogynistic King Shahriyar.

Sheherazade and her tales have their origins in pre-Islamic Persia, but over the ages (and in endless retellings and rewritings) they were adapted, expanded and updated, drawing on sources as far flung as Greece and India. As they're known to us now, the stories are mainly set in the semi-fabled Baghdad of Harun ar-Rashid (reigned 786 to 809 AD), and in Mamluk-era Cairo and Damascus. Regarding the last two cities in particular, *The Nights* provides a wealth of rich period detail, from shopping lists and prices of slaves, through to vivid descriptions of the types and practices of assorted conjurers, harlots, thieves and mystics. *The Thousand and One Nights* is revered as much by medieval scholars as it is by Walt's animators. ■

were recognised internationally with the award of the Nobel Prize for Literature in 1988. Much of his work is available in English-language translations – look out particularly for his *Cairo Trilogy*, the haunting *Miramar*, set in Alexandria, and *Arabian Nights & Days* which takes up where *The Thousand and One Nights* left off.

Unfortunately, mainstream publishers in the west seem content to leave Arab literature with Mahfouz, and other excellent Egyptian writers, such as Yusuf Idris and Tawfiq Hakim, are available to an English-speaking audience only through small local publishers such as the American University Press (see the Egypt chapter or email them at auc@aucacs.eun.eg). An exception is Nawal el-Saadawi, an Egyptian feminist well known in the west, with several books available in English-language editions (*Fall of the Imam* and *Death of an Ex-Minister* are two of the most widely available titles).

After Cairo, Beirut is the other literary capital of the Middle East. As well as being the focus of Lebanese literary life, it has been the refuge of Syrian writers escaping their own repressive regime and of refugee Palestinians. Of the latter category Liana Badr, who fled to Beirut after the Israelis captured her home town of Jericho, near Jerusalem, in 1967, has two books available in English (*The Eye of the Mirror* and the short story collection, *A Balcony over the Fakihani*), both of which draw heavily on her first-hand experiences of upheaval.

Of the native Lebanese writers, the best represented in translation is Hanan al-Shaykh, who writes extremely poignant but humorous novels (*Beirut Blues*, *The Story of Zahra* and *Women of Sand and Myrrh*) that resonate beyond the bounds of the Middle East.

See also Books in the Regional Facts for the Visitor chapter for Amin Maalouf and Ahdaf Soueif. For Jewish Israeli literature see the Israel & the Palestinian Territories chapter.

Music

Unlike literature which is a take it or leave it affair, in the Arab countries of the Middle East there is no getting away from music. It's impossible to take a taxi, shop, or even walk any busy street in the evening, without some imposed musical accompaniment.

The most widespread and popular style of music focuses on a star performer backed by anything from a small quartet to a full-blown orchestra. The all-time voice of classical Arabic music is unquestionably Um Kolthum, an Egyptian-born songstress – her wholesale adoration is one of the few truly unifying factors in the Arab world. She died in 1975, but backed by the Middle Eastern

Belly Dancing

For most foreigners, the only known side of Arabic musical culture is the belly dance. Beyond the Turkish Delight cliché of diaphanous veils and the hint of striptease, the Middle East does have an ancient tradition of sensual dance which, from the evidence of tomb paintings, dates back to the time of ancient Egypt. Visit any wedding in Egypt, Palestine or Syria today, and you'll see unmarried girls with their arms above their head gyrating their pelvises in a manner that attracts every male eye around. The more professional dancers, performing at clubs and hotels, also succeed in attracting very large sums of money. Those at the top of the profession who are accorded star status dance only at private functions for which they earn a small fortune – thousands of dollars for a brief appearance.

Small-time spenders can see belly dancing at many of the region's up-market hotels but the performances, laid on with the tourist in mind, tend to be lacklustre affairs. Much better is to visit some sleazy nightclub where the women make their money from tips and are prepared to expend some energy to top up the earnings. Eroticism is rarely an element of the show – pressure from Islamic groups has meant that many dancers have been obliged to cover up their bellies. ∎

Orchestra, her songs are still ubiquitous on radio and TV, and an Um Kolthum cassette remains an essential part of a taxi driver's accessory kit. Her male counterparts were Abdel Halim al-Hafez and Fareed al-Atrash, both of whom are also now dead, but continue to sell in vast quantities.

After Egypt, Lebanon is the other great centre of classical Arab music. The Lebanese torch singer Fairouz is currently *the* Arab world superstar. For anyone with unattuned ears who hears all Arabic music as wailing, then exposure to Fairouz may be the thing to bring on a change of attitude.

The kind of orchestra that backs such a singer is a curious cross-fertilisation of east and west, with such instruments as the reed pipe, oud (lute), tambourine and tabla (small hand-held drum) contributing the oriental element. There's also classical instrumental music, involving one or more of the traditional Arab instruments, especially the oud and tabla. Among the better performers is Munir Bechir, an oud player whose recordings are occasionally available in the west.

Distinct from the classical style, the Arab world also has its own particular fashion of pop music. Groups are largely unknown and, again, the vocal is the thing, delivered by a star artist over a clattering, handclapping rhythm embroidered with synthesised twirlings. There are confusingly few musical hooks, the words are numbingly repetitive (the word *habibi*, meaning 'my love' or 'my darling', seems to form the bulk of most lyrics), and the volume is usually LOUD. Even so, you had better learn to like it because once it gets inside your head there's no getting it out again.

For Jewish music see the Israel & the Palestinian Territories chapter.

RELIGION

The Middle East is the birthplace of the three big monotheistic religions of the world: Judaism, Christianity and Islam. The followers of all of these religions worship the same God, the main difference among them being their understanding of when the revelations from God ceased to flow unto earth. While Judaism adheres to the Old Testament, Christianity in addition follows the teachings of the New Testament, and the Muslims' holiest book is the Qur'an which, according to their belief, contains the final revelation of God, covering the points not made clear by earlier prophets.

Islam

Islam was founded in the early 7th century by the Prophet Mohammed, born around 570 AD in Mecca. Mohammed got his first revelation at about the age of 40, in the form of a voice commanding him to 'Recite'. The voice, according to Mohammed, belonged to the archangel Gabriel, who revealed to him the words of God.

The revelations continued for the rest of Mohammed's life, and the oral recitations were, during and after his lifetime, written down in the Qur'an (the name meaning literally 'recitation'), the book which came to establish the form of written Arabic for centuries. To this day not one dot has been changed in the holy Qur'an – the speech of God – and foreign translations are never definitive, merely introductory.

Mohammed's teachings were not an immediate success. He started preaching in 613, three years after the first revelation, but could only attract a few dozen followers. Having attacked the ways of Meccan life – especially the worship of a wealth of idols – he also made many enemies. In 622 he and his followers retreated to Medina, an oasis town some 360 km from Mecca. It is this *hijra*, or migration, that marks the start of the Muslim calendar.

In Medina Mohammed quickly became a successful religious, political and military leader. After several clashes with the Meccans he finally gathered 10,000 troops and conquered his home town, demolishing the idols worshipped by the population and establishing the one God. In Mohammed's time, Islam was a revolutionary concept that countered existing social inequalities by stating that all Muslims, both men and women, were equal in their submission to God.

Mohammed died in 632, but the new religion continued its rapid spread, reaching all of Arabia by 634, Egypt, Syria and what is now Iraq and western Iran by 642, and most of Iran and Afghanistan by 656. The Jews and Christians in those regions were often discontented with their rulers and welcomed Arab armies as liberators. From the Middle East, the Islamic Empire continued to spread in all directions during subsequent centuries.

The area of present-day Turkey, however, was a tough challenge. Even though the Arabs were at the gates of Constantinople by 674, the Christian Byzantines resisted successfully, and it was only in the 10th and 11th centuries that the Turkish Seljuk tribes converted most of Asia Minor to Islam. Constantinople was not taken until 1453.

Following this period of rapid expansion, the Islamic Empire started a long decline in 1000 AD, splitting under various states and foreign occupiers. Even then the religion itself continued its spread, being ousted only from relatively limited areas, mainly in Europe. The Christian Crusaders in the early centuries of this millennium hardly made a dent in Islam's prevalence in the Middle East.

Sects All big religions have a host of different factions, and Islam is no exception. The major division within Islam stems from a dispute about who should succeed Mohammed, who died with no sons. Competing for power were Abu Bakr, the father of Mohammed's second wife Aisha; and Ali, Mohammed's cousin and the husband of his daughter Fatima. Initially, the power was transferred to Abu Bakr, who became the first caliph, or successor, with Ali reluctantly agreeing.

Ali's sect, the Shiite, got its second chance in 656, when the third caliph, Uthman from the Umayyad family, was murdered. In the ensuing power struggle Ali was victorious, moving his capital to Kufa (later Najaf, in Iraq), only to be assassinated himself in 661. The Umayyad dynasty, after defeating Ali's successor, Hussein, in 680 at Kerbala, rose to rule the vast majority of the Muslim world,

marking the start of the Sunni sect. The division between the two sects is evident even today. Sunnis comprise some 90% of the world's more than 800 million Muslims, but Shiites are close to being a majority of the population in Iraq and constitute a clear majority in Bahrain and Iran. There are also Shiite minorities in almost all Arab countries.

Furthermore, there are numerous subsects within both the Sunni and Shiite sects. The main Sunni schools developed within the first 200 years of Islam: the Hanafi, Maliki, Shafai and Hanbali schools are all still active. Saudi Wahhabis are from the Hanbali school, while the rest of Arabian, Egyptian and Iranian Sunnis follow the Shafai teachings. The Hanafi school is active in Turkey, Iran and Afghanistan, while the Maliki school is confined to Egypt and other North African countries.

Many Shiite subsects have, at some point in history, stuck to the teachings of a certain caliph or imam, not recognising his follower. A well-known Shiite subsect is the 'Seveners', or Ismailis, named in the 9th century after Ali's seventh descendant, Ismail. The Ismailis later split into Egyptian, Persian and Syrian wings, of which the latter two have survived to this day, with millions of followers in the Middle East, Asia and East Africa. The leaders of these two lines are the Aga Khans. In Iran the 'Twelvers' are a prominent subsect.

Among other Shiite subsects are the Zaydis of Yemen, stemming from Zayd ibn Ali, a direct descendant of Ali. They recognise only the first four imams,. The Alawites of Syria are another well-known Shiite subsect, with the Syrian president, Hafez al-Assad, a prominent member. The mysterious Druzes of Syria, Lebanon and Israel are sometimes regarded as a Shiite subsect, sometimes as a non-Muslim group.

The Belief Islam is based on the belief of total submission to God, and this principle is very visibly present in the daily life of every Muslim. In fact, the very word Islam literally means 'submitting', while 'Muslim' means 'submitter' to God. The faith is expressed by observance of the five so-called pillars of Islam: the creed, performance of prayer, giving of alms, observance of fasting and performance of pilgrimage.

There is almost a sixth pillar, jihad – or striving in the way of God – which has been much disputed and misunderstood by Muslims and non-Muslims alike. It is often translated as 'holy war', and indeed it may mean a holy war against the godless, the unbelievers, as well as an internal struggle against humankind's basic unholy instincts. But while the latter interpretation is much preferred at present, there are always plenty of people who use the word for propagandist purposes of war and disorder. It is for this reason that Islam has gained a reputation as a dangerous religion of fanatics in the eyes of many westerners. However, in its essence Islam is as peaceful a religion as any.

The Creed The core of Islamic belief is expressed in beautiful calligraphy on the flag of Saudi Arabia: 'There is no God but God and Mohammed is the Prophet of God'. Anybody who utters this phrase in the presence of two reliable witnesses may be regarded as a Muslim.

Muslims also believe in the angels who brought God's messages to humans, in the prophets who received these messages, in the books in which the prophets expressed these revelations, and in the last day of judgement. The Qur'an mentions 28 prophets, of whom Mohammed was last, the one who received the final revelation from God: there will be no more prophets. The Qur'an is thus the last of the books towards which the revelations of earlier prophets progress. The day of judgement will be announced by the archangel Asrafil blowing a trumpet, and all people will be summoned to either paradise or hell, according to whether they have struggled along God's path or abandoned it.

Islam shares many holy men and scriptures with Judaism and Christianity. Twenty-one of the prophets are also mentioned in the Bible, and Adam, Noah, Abraham, David, Jacob, Joseph, Job, Moses and Jesus are given particular honour, although the divinity of Jesus is strictly denied. The Qur'an also recognises the Scriptures of Abraham, the Torah of Moses, the Psalms of David and the Gospels of Jesus as God's revelation.

Prayer The ritual of prayer is an essential part of the daily life of a believer. Every Muslim should pray at least five times a day: at sunrise, noon, late afternoon, sunset and night. Five times a day the muezzin calls male believers to the mosque for prayer. It is perfectly permissible to pray at home or elsewhere – only the noon prayer on Friday should be conducted in the mosque. It is preferred that women pray at home, although some mosques have a separate screened-off area for female worshippers.

The act of praying consists of a series of predefined movements of the body and recitals of prayers and passages of the Qur'an, all designed to express the believer's absolute humility and God's sovereignty. First the believer washes himself to show his will to purify himself – there are fountains or ablution pools in mosques for this purpose. Then he goes to the place of prayer, orientates himself towards Mecca – the proper orientation is indicated by the alignment of the mosque – and performs one or more *rakats*, or cycles of prayer, during which he reads certain passages of the Qur'an, prays, bows and prostrates himself in a different series for each of the day's five prayer times.

Alms A Muslim should pay one-fortieth of his yearly revenue to the poor as *zakat*, or alms; this institution is as essential as prayer. This practice reflects as much the need to 'purify' earthly wealth as the individual's willingness to demonstrate social responsibility.

Previously the giving of alms may have been an act of a more individual nature than it is today, when the institution has developed along lines significantly similar to those used by western welfare states in taking care of their poor. In many Arabic countries, a special ministry of waqfs and religious guidance controls the dispensation of religious charitable endowments.

Fasting The ninth month of the lunar year, Ramadan, is the month of fasting. During this month, Muslims abstain from eating, drinking, smoking and sexual intercourse from sunrise to sunset. Extra prayers and recitations of the Qur'an are encouraged, since the purpose of fasting is to bring people closer to God.

The considerable effort needed to adhere to this rule greatly contributes to each individual's sense of belonging to the Muslim community, since everybody shares this experience at the same time. Fasting has a great influence on the daily routines of any Muslim country too, since during the fast all daily activities are of necessity kept at the lowest possible level. Ramadan is not a detested month, though. In fact, Muslims love it, since fasting during the daylight hours gives them a reason for feasting in the dark. Nights are lively and joyous occasions, many people staying awake all night and sleeping in the afternoon.

Pilgrimage Every Muslim capable of affording it should perform the *haj*, or pilgrimage, to the holiest of cities, Mecca, at least once in his or her lifetime. The pilgrimage takes place every year during Zuul-Hijja, the last month of the Muslim calendar. The reward is considerable: the forgiving of all past sins. It is possible to make the pilgrimage at other times of the year, but the benefits of such an *umra*, or small pilgrimage, are fewer.

Nearly two million Muslims make the haj each year. The number of pilgrims is restricted by a quota system run by the Saudis, who issue one haj visa to every 1000 Muslims in any country.

Calendar The Muslim calendar is used side by side with the western Gregorian calendar in most Middle Eastern countries. All religious feasts are celebrated within the framework of the Muslim calendar, while secular activities are planned according to the Christian system, except in Saudi Arabia,

where the Muslim calendar is the principal one used, and in Iran, where the Iranian solar calendar is used.

The Muslim year is based on the lunar cycle and is divided into 12 lunar months, each with 29 or 30 days. Consequently, the Muslim year is 10 or 11 days shorter than the Christian solar year, and the Muslim festivals gradually move around our year, completing the cycle in roughly 33 years.

The religious festivals are attended to with different devotion in different countries: in more secular countries they don't affect you so much, while in more traditional ones you should take them into account when planning your schedule. Immediately after Ramadan, the first four days of the Shawwal month make up the Eid al-Fitr, or Festival of Breaking the Fast. Another major holiday, when the celebrations may take up to six days, is Eid al-Adha, or Feast of Sacrifice, beginning on the 10th of Zuul-Hijja, the month of pilgrimage. Other important festivals include the Hijra, or New Year, and Mawlid an-Nabi, the Prophet's Birthday. For dates see the table of holidays near Public Holidays & Special Events in the Regional Facts for the Visitor chapter.

Judaism
The foundation of the Jewish religion is the Torah, or the first five books of the Old Testament. The Torah contains the revelation from God via Moses more than 3000 years ago, including, most importantly, God's commandments (of which there are 613 in all). The Torah is supplemented by the rest of the books of the Old Testament, of which the most important are the prophetic books, giving much of the substance to the religion.

These books are complemented by the Talmud, a collection of another 63 books, written in the early centuries AD and containing most of what separates Judaism from other religions. Included are plenty of Rabbinical interpretations of the earlier scriptures, with a wealth of instructions and rulings for the daily life of a Jew.

The Talmud was written when the Jewish Diaspora began: after the Romans crushed the Jewish state and destroyed the Temple in Jerusalem in 70 AD, many Jews were either exiled or sold into slavery abroad. The Jewish religion was kept intact, however, within families, who passed the teachings from generation to generation. Unlike Christians or Muslims, Jews have never actively sought converts from the followers of other religions.

Up to the first half of the 20th century there existed sizeable Jewish minorities in all countries in the Middle East. However, in the late '40s and early '50s the newly founded State of Israel began to seek the repatriation of Jews from all over the world, after 19 centuries of Diaspora, to fulfil the prophet Isaiah's prediction. Mass emigrations were facilitated from country to country, more or less with the cooperation of local authorities. Today most Middle Eastern countries have only a few hundred Jews left, many of them still planning to emigrate to the Promised Land.

Christianity

Jesus preached in what is today Israel, but Christians form only minority groups in all Middle Eastern countries. Their numbers range from zero in Saudi Arabia (only Muslims can have Saudi nationality) to about 13% of the population of Egypt and Syria.

By far the biggest Christian sect in the region is formed by the Copts of Egypt, who make up most of that country's Christian population. Originally it was the apostle Mark who established Christianity in Egypt, and by the 4th century it had become the state religion. The Coptic Church split from the Byzantine Orthodox Church in the 5th century after a dispute about the human nature of Jesus, with Dioscurus, the patriarch of Alexandria, declaring Jesus to be totally divine. Internationally, the most famous Egyptian Copt today is the UN secretary-general, Boutros Boutros-Ghali.

The Christians of Syria belong to many churches in all main branches of the religion – Orthodox, Catholic and Protestant. This richness reflects the country's location on major routes along which the religion spread to Europe and Asia, and by which people and ideas have flowed into the area for centuries.

Lebanon and Jordan have sizeable Christian populations too, and the former's one million Maronites also have followers all over the world.

And of course, while Christians form only 2.4% of the population of Israel, almost all factions of the religion are represented there, keeping watch over Christianity's holy sites.

LANGUAGE

Arabic is the official language of all Middle Eastern countries except Afghanistan, Iran, Israel and Turkey. (For information about languages spoken there, see the respective country chapters.) English is widely spoken in the area, as, to a lesser extent, is French (spoken mainly in Lebanon and Syria), but any effort to communicate with the locals in their own language will be well rewarded. No matter how far off the mark your pronunciation or grammar might be, you'll often get the response (usually with a big smile), 'Ah, you speak Arabic very well!'.

Learning the basics for day-to-day travelling doesn't take long at all, but to master the complexities of Arabic would take years of constant study.

It is worth noting here that transliteration from the Arabic script into English – or any other language for that matter – is at best an approximate science.

The presence of sounds unknown in European languages and the fact that the script is 'defective' (most vowels are not written) combine to make it nearly impossible to settle on one method of transliteration. A wide variety of spellings is therefore possible for words when they appear in Latin script – and that goes for place names and people's names as well.

The matter is further complicated by the wide variety of dialects and the imaginative ideas Arabs themselves often have on appropriate spelling in, say, English: words spelt one way in a Gulf country may look very different in Syria, heavily influenced by French (not even the most venerable of western Arabists have been able to come up with a satisfactory solution).

There are four vowel sounds in Arabic not represented in the alphabet:

'	glottal stop, like the nonvoice before *Oh, Lord!*
a	as in *hat*, or as in *hut* (with emphatics)
i	as in *hit*
u	as in *put*

The alphabet itself consists of 28 consonants:

Arabic	Name of Letter	Transliteration Exact	Informal	Pronunciation
ا	'alif	a:	aa	as in *man* but longer
ب	ba:'	b	b	as in *big*
ت	ta:'	t	t	as in *tongue*
ث	tha:'	th	th	as in *thin*
ج	ji:m	j	j	as in *jam*; or in some countries like *g* in *go*
ح	Ha:'	H	h	strong *h* from back of throat, like blowing on spectacles to clean them
خ	kha:'	kh	kh	like *ch* in Scottish *loch* or German *achtung*
د	da:l	d	d	as in *dim*
ذ	dha:l	dh	dh	like *th* in *this*
ر	ra:	r	r	prolonged *r* with quick taps of tongue against upper gum; as in Spanish *caro*
ز	za:	z	z	as in *zip*
س	si:n	s	s	as in *sock*
ش	shi:n	sh	sh	as in *shoe*
ص	**s**a:d	**s**	s	emphatic *s*; a bit like in *sum*
ض	**d**a:d	**d**	d	emphatic *d*; a bit like in *dumb*
ط	ta:'	**t**	t	emphatic *t*; a bit like in *tar*
ظ	za:'	**z**	dh	emphatic *dh*; a bit like *z* in *czar*
ع	'ayn	'	'	nothing like this in English; gag muscles at back of throat for voice like when puking; often *a* as in *but* is close
غ	ghayn	gh	gh	Parisian *r*
ف	fa:'	f	f	as in *fat*
ق	qa:f	q	q	like *k* but darker, further back in throat; or *g* as in *go* (common in Yemen)
ك	ka:f	k	k	as in *king*
ل	la:m	l	l	as in *lamb*
م	mi:m	m	m	as in *man*
ن	nu:n	n	n	as in *name*
ه	ha:'	h	h	as in *ham*
و	wa:w	w	w	as in *wet*; or
		u:	u	long *u* as in *mood*; or
		aw	aw	diphthong as in *how*
ى	ya:'	y	y	as in *yes*; or
		i:	i	long *i* as in *meet*; or
		ay	ay	diphthong as in *why* or in *way*

Place Name Spellings

While we have tried to standardise all spellings in this book there are some instances in which flexibility seemed to be more appropriate than consistency. For example, while we use the more accepted 'beit' (meaning house) and 'sheikh' throughout the book, in the Gulf State chapters we decided to go with 'bait' and 'shaikh' as these are the spellings any visitor to those countries will find on local maps and road signs.

Differences in spelling also arise through the same word appearing modified in the different languages of the region – 'square' in Arabic is traditionally transliterated as 'midan', but in Turkish it's written 'maydan' and in Persian 'meidun' (or 'meidun-é'; 'the square of'). Here lies great potential for confusion, as in the case of 'hamam' which is Turkish for the famed 'bathhouse', but Arabic for 'pigeon'; if you're looking for a good steam-cleaning in Arabic you ask for 'hammam', with two distinctly sounded syllables.

We have also been forced to modify some spellings because of regional differences in Arabic pronunciation. The most obvious example of this is the hard Egyptian sounding of the letter *ji:m*, like the 'g' in 'gate', whereas elsewhere in the Arab world it's a softer 'j' as in 'jam' – hence we have used both 'gadid' and 'jadid' (new), and 'gebel' and 'jebel' (mountain). ∎

In this book, don't be surprised if you come across several versions of the same thing! TE Lawrence, when asked by his publishers to clarify 'inconsistencies in the spelling of proper names' in *Seven Pillars of Wisdom* – his account of the Arab Revolt in WWI – wrote back:

Arabic names won't go into English...There are some 'scientific systems' of transliteration, helpful to people who know enough Arabic not to need helping, but a washout for the world. I spell my names anyhow, to show what rot the systems are.

Pronunciation

Much of the vocabulary that follows would be universally understood throughout the Arab world, although some of it, especially where more than one option is given, reflects the region's dialects. Arabic pronunciation is not easy, and to reflect sounds unknown in English, certain combinations of letters are used in transliteration.

Greetings & Civilities

Arabs place great importance on civility, and it's rare to see any interaction between people that doesn't begin with profuse greetings, enquiries into the other's health and other niceties.

Arabic greetings are more formal than greetings in English, and there is a reciprocal response to each. These sometimes vary slightly, depending on whether you're addressing a man or a woman. A simple encounter can become a drawn-out affair, with neither side wanting to be the one to put a halt to the stream of greetings and well-wishing. As an *ajnabi* (foreigner), you're not expected to know all the ins and outs, but if you come up with the right expression at the appropriate moment, they'll love it.

The most common greeting is *salaam alaykum* ('peace be upon you'), to which the correct reply is *wa alaykum as-salaam* ('and upon you be peace'). If you get invited to a birthday celebration or are around for any of the big holidays, the common greeting is *kul sana wa intum bi-kheer* ('I wish you well for the coming year').

After having a bath or a haircut, you will often hear people say to you *na'iman*, which roughly means 'heavenly' and boils down to an observation along the lines of 'nice and clean now, huh'.

Arrival in one piece is always something to be grateful for. Passengers will often be greeted with *al-hamdu lillah 'al as-salaama*, meaning 'Thank God for your safe arrival'.

Hi.	*marhaba*
Hello. (literally 'welcome')	*ahlan wa sahlan/ ahlan*
Hello. (response)	*ahlan beek*
Goodbye.	*ma'a salaama/ Allah ma'ak*
Good morning.	*sabah al-khayr*
Good morning. (response)	*sabah an-noor*

Good evening.	*masa al-khayr*
Good evening. (response)	*masa an-noor*
Good night.	*tisbah 'ala khayr*
Good night. (response)	*wa inta min ahalu*
Please. (request)	*min fadlak* (m)
	min fadlik (f)
Please. (formal, eg in restaurants)	*law samaht* (m)
	law samahti (f)
Please. (come in/ go ahead)	*tafadal* (m)
	tafadali (f)
	tafadalu (pl)
Thank you.	*shukran*
Thanks a lot.	*shukran jazeelan*
You are welcome.	*'afwan or ahlan*
How are you?	*kayf haalak?* (m)
	kayf haalik? (f)
Fine. (literally 'thanks be to God')	*al-hamdu lillah*
Pleased to meet you. (departing)	*fursa sa'ida*
Pardon/Excuse me.	*'afwan*
Sorry!	*'assif*
Congratulations!	*mabrouk*

Small Talk

What is your name?	*shu-ismak?* (m)
	shu-ismik? (f)
My name is ...	*ismi ...*
Where are you from?	*min wayn inta?*
Do you speak ...?	*btah-ki/hal tatakallam ...?*
I speak ...	*ana bah-ki/ana atakallam ...*
English	*ingleezi*
French	*faransi*
German	*almaani*
I understand.	*ana af-ham*
I don't understand.	*ma bif-ham/la af-ham*
What does this mean?	*yaanee ay?*
I want an interpreter.	*ureed mutarjem*
I (don't) like ...	*ana (ma) bahib /ana (la) uhib ...*
Yes.	*aiwa/na'am*
No.	*la*
No problem.	*mish mushkila*
Never mind.	*ma'lesh*

I am sick.	*ana mareed* (m)
	ana mareeda (f)

Questions like 'Is the bus coming?' or 'Will the bank be open later?' generally elicit the inevitable response *in sha' Allah* – God willing – an expression you'll hear over and over again. Another less common one is *ma sha'Allah* – God's will be done – sometimes a useful answer to probing questions about why you're not married yet!

Getting Around

How many km?	*kam kilometre?*
bus station	*mahattat al-baas*
railway station	*mahattat al-qitaar*
airport	*al-mataar*
car	*as-sayaara*
1st class	*daraja awla*
2nd class	*daraja thani*
here/there	*hena/henak*
left	*yasaar*
right	*shimal/yameen*
straight ahead	*'ala tuul*

Around Town

Where is (the) ...?	*wayn ...?*
bank	*al-masraf/al-bank*
hotel	*al-funduq*
market	*as-souq*
Mohammed St	*sharia Mohammed*
mosque	*al-jaame'/al-masjid*
museum	*al-mat'haf*
passport & immigration office	*maktab al-jawazaat wa al-hijra*
pharmacy	*as-saydaliyya*
police	*ash-shurta*
post office	*maktab al-bareed*
restaurant	*al-mat'am*
tourist office	*maktab as-siyaha*

Accommodation

Do you have ...?	*fi 'andakum ...?*
a room	*ghurfa*
a single room	*ghurfa mufrada*
a double room	*ghurfa bi sareerayn*
a shower	*doosh*
hot water	*mai harr*

a toilet	twalet/mirhad/
	hammam
soap	saboon
air-con	kondishon/takyeef
electricity	kahraba

Shopping

How much?	qaddaysh/bikam
How many?	kam wahid?
How much money?	kam fuloos?
money	fuloos/masaari

big	kabeer
small	sagheer
bad	mish kwayyis/mu
	kwayyis
good	kwayyis
cheap/expensive	rakhees/ghaali
cheaper	arkhas
closed	maghlooq/musakkar
open	maftooh

Time

When?	mata/emta?
yesterday	imbaarih/'ams
today	al-yom
tomorrow	bukra/ghadan
minute	daqiqa
hour	sa'a
day	yom
week	usbu'
month	shaher
year	sana

| What is the time? | as-sa'a kam? |
| It's 5 o'clock. | as-sa'a khamsa |

Days of the Week

Monday	al-itneen
Tuesday	at-talata
Wednesday	al-arbi'a
Thursday	al-khamees
Friday	al-jum'a
Saturday	as-sabt
Sunday	al-ahad

Months

The Islamic year has 12 lunar months and is 11 days shorter than the western (Gregorian) calendar, so important Muslim dates will fall 11 days earlier each (western) year.

There are two Gregorian calendars in use in the Arab world. In Egypt and the Gulf States, the months have virtually the same names as in English (January is *yanaayir*, October *octobir* and so on), but in Lebanon, Jordan and Syria, the names are quite different. Talking about, say, June as 'month six' is the easiest solution, but for the sake of completeness, the months from January are:

January	kanoon ath-thani
February	shubaat
March	azaar
April	nisaan
May	ayyaar
June	huzayran
July	tammooz
August	'aab
September	aylool
October	tishreen al-awal
November	tishreen ath-thani
December	kanoon al-awal

The Hijra months, too, have their own names:

1st	Moharram
2nd	Safar
3rd	Rabi' al-Awal
4th	Rabi' ath-Thani
5th	Jumada al-Awall
6th	Jumada al-Akhira
7th	Rajab
8th	Shaaban
9th	Ramadan
10th	Shawwal
11th	Zuul-Qe'da
12th	Zuul-Hijja

Numbers

Arabic numerals, unlike the written language, run from left to right.

0	•	sifr
1	١	waahid
2	٢	itneen
3	٣	talaata
4	٤	arba'a
5	٥	khamsa

6	٦	*sitta*	19	١٩	*tisata'shar*	
7	٧	*sab'a*	20	٢٠	*'ishreen*	
8	٨	*tamanya*	21	٢١	*wahid wa 'ishreen*	
9	٩	*tis'a*	30	٣٠	*talateen*	
10	١٠	*'ashra*	40	٤٠	*arba'een*	
11	١١	*hida'shar*	50	٥٠	*khamseen*	
12	١٢	*itna'shar*	60	٦٠	*sitteen*	
13	١٣	*talat-ashar*	70	٧٠	*sab'een*	
14	١٤	*arba'at-ashar*	80	٨٠	*tamaneen*	
15	١٥	*khamas-ta'shar*	90	٩٠	*tis'een*	
16	١٦	*sitta'shar*	100	١٠٠	*miyya*	
17	١٧	*sabata'shar*	1000	١٠٠٠	*alf*	
18	١٨	*tamanta'shar*				

Body Language

Arabs gesticulate a lot in conversation, and some things can be said without uttering a word. Certain expressions also go together with particular gestures.

Many often say 'no' merely by raising the eyebrows and lifting the head up and back. This is often accompanied by a 'tsk tsk' noise and it can all be a little off-putting if you're not used to it – don't take it as a snub.

Shaking the head from side to side (as westerners would to say 'no') means 'I don't understand'. Stretching out the hand as if to open a door and giving it a quick flick of the wrist is equivalent to 'what do you want?', 'where are you going?' or 'what's your problem?'

If an official holds out a hand and draws a line across the palm with the index finger of the other hand, he or she is not indicating a long life-line but asking to see your passport, bus ticket or any other document that may seem relevant at the time.

Guys asking directions should not be surprised to be taken by the arm or hand and led along. It is quite natural for men to hold each other by the hand and, despite what you may think, rarely means anything untoward is happening. Women should obviously be more careful about such helpfulness.

A right hand over your heart means 'no, thanks' when you are offered something. When you've had enough tea, Turkish coffee or anything else to drink, you put your hand over the cup. The polite thing to say is *dayman* ('always', more or less meaning 'may it ever be thus'). Arabic coffee has its own rituals – see the Drinks section in the Regional Facts for the Visitor chapter.

As the left hand is associated with toilet duties, it is considered unclean, so you should always use the right hand when giving or receiving something. ■

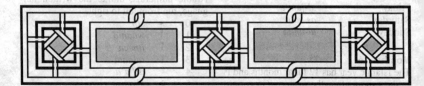

Regional Facts for the Visitor

PLANNING

When to Go

When planning a trip to the Middle East, two things to keep in mind are the weather and the religious holidays and festivals.

The Weather Factor Most of the Middle East is best visited from autumn to spring (October to May), though water-sport lovers and sun-worshippers may want to visit the Mediterranean countries in summer (June to September). The latter months, however, are definitely to be avoided in the Arabian peninsula and Egypt.

Afghanistan, Iran, Iraq, Israel, Jordan, Lebanon, Syria, Turkey and Yemen have their best weather in autumn and spring. The Gulf States and Egypt are best in winter (November to March).

There are a number of local variations, however. For example, the most agreeable time to visit the southern coast of Iran is from December to February, and the north-west and north-east are at their best between late

---

The Middle East in Brief

Afghanistan Definitely off limits until real peace is restored, and there's little chance of that happening any time in the near future.

Bahrain Bahrain is the easiest of the Gulf States to visit and a good bet for travellers on a budget. But periodic political violence is something to be aware of, and keep an eye on, when planning a trip.

Egypt Sporadic attacks continue in Middle Egypt and visitors should completely avoid travelling in this region, but there should be no fears around the tourist magnets of Aswan, Luxor, Sinai and Cairo.

Iran The Iranians are the region's most welcoming and hospitable people and their vast country is home to some spectacular scenery and sites – the only problem lies in obtaining a visa.

Iraq At the time of writing Iraq is not issuing visas to travellers, although a handful of determined souls have managed to find their way in.

Israel & the Palestinian Territories Despite the occasional scary headlines, Israel and the Palestinian Territories are a safe destination, offering a great deal of cultural and scenic variety with minimum hassles.

Jordan Still one of the safest and most friendly countries in the region, and after the Pyramids, Petra is the Middle East's most unmissable site.

Kuwait While not entirely recovered from Saddam's invasion, Kuwait is nevertheless open to visitors.

Lebanon Now the fighting is over Lebanon is starting to regain the interest of the adventurous traveller. Keep away from the south and it is fairly safe to travel.

Oman One of the least developed and most charming of the Gulf States, Oman probably has the greatest potential for the traveller.

Qatar Though Qatar opened its doors to tourists in 1989 its remoteness has kept it off the agendas of even the most intrepid travellers – not that there's much there to see.

Saudi Arabia Saudi Arabia actively discourages tourism, and visas are hard to come by. Once in, the country is surprisingly fascinating.

Syria Despite its bad political reputation Syria is an extremely safe and straightforward country to visit.

Turkey The tourist boom continues. Western Turkey is admirably safe, but east of Amasya, Kayseri and Gaziantep, exercise caution: travel on major routes to major cities and tourist sites in daylight only. Avoid completely the border areas with Syria and Iraq.

United Arab Emirates A union of seven very different sovereign sheikhdoms that are rapidly becoming a major up-market tourist destination. The best place in the Gulf for the independent traveller.

Yemen A country with a unique and long-isolated cultural heritage that is more accessible today than ever before. A lack of resources and recurrent political crises have hampered the development of the tourism industry but this is amply compensated by the natural hospitality of the ever-optimistic Yemenis.

Highlights of the Middle East

Country	Highlight	Features
Bahrain	Manama	Capital city; National Museum; Heritage Centre; Bait al-Qur'an; souq
	Near Manama	Ad-Diraz and Barbar temples; Suq al-Khamis Mosque; burial mounds
Egypt	Cairo	Pyramids; Egyptian Museum; Islamic Cairo, the greatest assembly of medieval architecture in the Muslim world
	Luxor	Grand pharoanic temples of Luxor and Karnak; the Valley of the Kings
	Aswan	Abu Simbel, one of the most impressive pharoanic monuments
	Sinai	Explore the fascinating coral gardens of the Red Sea
Iran	Esfahān	Mosques, gardens and town planning from the golden age of Persia
	Persepolis	Extensive hillside remains of the palace of Darius
Israel	Jerusalem	Semi-fabled historical Old City steeped with history and significance
	Dead Sea	Rejuvinating waters and mud baths; mountain-top fortress of Masada
Jordan	Petra	Ancient 'rose-red city' of the Nabataeans
	Aqaba	Diving and snorkelling on the beautiful coral reefs in the Gulf of Aqaba
	Wadi Rum	Lawrence of Arabia's stamping ground; desert treks; climbing; camel rides
Kuwait	Kuwait City	Parliament; Sadu House; ruined National Museum; Tareq Rajab Museum
	Al-Jahra	Red Fort – site of the famous 1920 siege
Lebanon	Baalbek	Spectacular ruined temples
	Byblos	Classical ruins and medieval city around a picturesque harbour
	Kadisha Gorge	Dramatic mountain landscape; early convents carved into the rock; nearby Biblical cedars of Lebanon
	Tripoli	Medieval Arab town and Crusader castle
	Beiteddine	Lavish Arab palace
Oman	Muscat	Capital city; famous port; Mutrah souq; forts; museums
	Nizwa	Can be centrepiece of longer trip around north of country; fort; souq
	Salalah	Archaeological sites; nearby Taqa Fort; Job's Tomb; beaches
	Musandem Peninsula	Spectacular scenery; old forts in Khasab and Bukha
Qatar	Doha	National Museum; Ethnographic Museum; National Theatre
	Zubara	Well-preserved four-bastioned desert fort
Saudi Arabia	Riyadh	Modern architecture; Masmak Fortress; National Museum; Dir'aiyah
	Jeddah	Well-preserved old city with houses built from coral; souq; museum
	Madain Salah	Ancient Nabatean city
	Najran	Fort; dam; museum; traditional architecture
	Hofuf	Huge oasis; ruins; Qasr Ibrahim Fortress
Syria	Crac des Chevaliers	One of the best preserved Crusader castles in the world
	Palmyra	Spectacular archaeological remains of famous Roman-era oasis city
	Aleppo	Fabulous covered souqs; museum; mosques; citadel
Turkey	İstanbul	Great mosques; museums; meals; views; shopping
	Cappadocia	Moonlike volcanic landscape; ancient cave-churches and dwellings
	Ephesus	Well-preserved Roman city, beaches nearby
United Arab Emirates	Abu Dhabi	Capital city; beaches (including a women-only beach); restored fortress
	Dubai	Creek and waterfront; museum; best gold souk in Middle East; nightlife
	Al-Ain/Buraimi	Oasis shared by UAE and Oman; museum; souq; restored forts; Jebel Hafit
	Fujairah	Base for exploring the archaeological sites/scenic areas of the east coast
Yemen	Old San'a	Unique architecture; lively town
	Wadi Hadhramawt	Spectacular valley with historic towns

Suggested time required to see the highlight
(unless specified, doesn't include travel to and from the highlight)

Days*	Getting There & Around	Accommodation
3	Bus, taxi, foot	All price ranges; quality usually good at low end
1	Bus, taxi, rental car	Day-trip from Manama
3-5	Taxi, minibus	All prices; good variety at the bottom end
2	Ferry over the Nile and then bicycle	All types and prices
1-2	Bus to Abu Simbel and a felucca to Edfu	All types and prices
2-3	Bus there and service taxis to get around	Inexpensive beach huts
2-3	Overnight train from Tehrān	US$4 (hostel) to US$95 (the grandest hotel)
1	Best visited from Shīrāz	Plenty on offer in Shīrāz
3-7	Local buses	Wide variety for all budgets
1	Bus	Expensive hostels
2-3	Bus, minibus, service taxi	All types and prices
3	Air, minibus, service taxi, taxi	Camping to top-end hotels
2-4	Minibus from Petra and Aqaba or 4WD	Camping or basic resthouse
3	Bus, taxi	Expensive even at bottom end
1	Intercity bus	Day-trip from Kuwait City
1-2	Service taxi	Cheap hotels, famous old Palmyra Hotel (expensive)
1-2	Service taxi, bus	Expensive hotels but cheap camping nearby
2	Service taxi	Some mid-range hotels
1-2	Bus, service taxi	Cheap hotels
1	Service taxi	No accomodation except luxury hotel
3-5	Bus, microbus, service taxi, rental car	High standard; moderate to very expensive
1	Intercity bus, microbus, service taxi, rental car	Two hotels: one expensive, one *very* expensive
2-4	Intercity bus, microbus, rental car	Moderately priced guesthouses, expensive hotels
2-4	Air, service taxi	Only one hotel in Khasab (expensive)
2	Taxi, rental car	Good; moderate to very expensive
1	Taxi, rental car	Day-trip from Doha
2-4	Taxi, local bus, rental car	All prices; quality usually very good
2-4	Air, sea, taxi, intercity bus, minibus	All prices; range of quality
2-3	Rental car or tour	Camping (tours), hotels in nearby Al-Ula
2-3	Air, intercity bus, service taxi, rental car	All prices; quality very high
1-2	Air, intercity bus, service taxi	Youth hostel and two moderately priced hotels
1	Microbus from Homs or bus from Tartus	Plenty in Hama, Homs and Tartus
2-3	Several buses to/from Damasus per day	From camping to five-star
3-7	Air, bus service taxi, train	All prices
3-5	Local buses, taxis, dolmuş (jitney)	All types and prices
2-4	Bus, dolmuş, moped, hiking	All types and prices
1-3	Bus, dolmuş, hiking	All types and prices
1-2	Intercity bus, minibus taxi	Medium to expensive
2-4	Minibus, taxi, rental car	All prices; excellent youth hostel
2-3	Bus (from Abu Dhabi only), service taxi	Four hotels: one medium priced, others expensive
2-3	Service taxi, rental car	All prices; quality generally good
2	Bus, taxi (all cheap)	Cheap; traditional Yemeni; expensive luxury
3-7	Air, bus, taxi, extensive tours with rented 4WD	Cheap to medium priced hotels in towns

spring and early summer and between late summer and early autumn.

The monsoon season in southern Oman is June to September – a good time to avoid this part of the country.

In Egypt, temperatures increase as you travel south from Alexandria, but the Sinai peninsula has unique weather. The desert is typically hot during the day and cold at night, but the mountains can be freezing, even during the day.

Israel's and Lebanon's climates are not so extreme that there is a specific time to avoid, though the coast can be extremely hot and humid in August. The winter months have the heaviest rainfall and there is very cold weather in many areas then, although Eilat is popular at that time.

Winter can be downright unpleasant in Syria and Jordan, especially in the mountains, when temperatures drop. If you find Amman too cool in winter, you can head down to Aqaba on the Red Sea; it enjoys fine weather and is something of a winter resort.

As a general rule, you should not venture into the east of Turkey before mid-May or after mid-October unless you're prepared, as there will still be lots of snow around, perhaps even enough to close roads and mountain passes.

In Yemen, climatic conditions vary greatly between regions. If you are planning to visit Aden and Hadhramawt, summer is certainly the season to avoid. In contrast, the highlands can get quite cold in winter.

Religious Holidays & Festivals One time of year not to visit staunchly Islamic nations is during the month-long fast of Ramadan (see the table of holidays near Public Holidays & Special Events later in this chapter). For that entire month no Muslim may eat, smoke or drink from sunrise to sunset. During Ramadan, Muslims rise early to breakfast before dawn, fast all day then feast again after sunset. Technically, non-Muslims are not bound by the fast of Ramadan but it certainly affects travel in the region. For a start most restaurants will be closed (five-star hotels in the big cities are a discreet exception) and in the stricter Islamic nations you are strongly advised not to be seen eating or drinking during daylight hours. Going all day without food or drink doesn't put people in a good mood either and you'll find people less helpful and more argumentative at this time. All in all, Ramadan is not the ideal time to visit the region.

You may also want to stay away during the Muslim festivals marking the end of Ramadan and the annual pilgrimage to Mecca (the haj).

In Iran, Moharram, the month of mourning, can also be a difficult time to travel. For the second half of March, transport and accommodation become very difficult as Iranians return to their home towns and villages for the Persian New Year celebrations (Nō Rūz, usually 21 to 24 March). It is better to avoid travelling around Iran at all during this period.

At haj time, it is a good idea to avoid Saudi Arabia.

In Israel, religious holidays cause the country to fill up with pilgrims, prices to double and public transport to grind to a halt. Although spring is the nicest time to visit, avoid Passover and Easter. There are several Jewish holidays in autumn that make it almost as tricky to get around then as during Passover.

Note that many sites of interest are closed for days at a time during these holiday periods.

What to Bring

As little as possible is the basic message, but not so little that you become a burden on other people. The super-light travellers generally seem to get along by continuously scrounging things. At the other extreme, starting off with an overload of useless junk is a continual hassle and becomes impossible as soon as you start accumulating more baggage along the way.

Backpacks are still the most popular luggage as they are commodious and the only way to go if you have to do any walking. On the debit side they are awkward to load on and off buses and trains, they don't offer too much protection for your valuables and some airlines may refuse to be responsible if they are broken into or damaged.

The combination backpack and shoulder bags are recommended. Their straps can be zipped away when not needed so they combine the carrying ease of a pack with the added strength of a bag. Another alternative is a large, soft zip-bag with a wide shoulder strap so it can be carried with relative ease if necessary. You can also get some tabs sewn on to this type of bag so you can partially thief-proof it with small padlocks.

Inside? The secret of successful packing is plastic bags or 'stuff bags'; they not only keep things separate and clean but also dry. You will no doubt be buying local clothes on the way so start light. A good list would be:

- underwear, socks and swimming gear
- one pair of jeans and one pair of shorts
- a few shirts and T-shirts
- a sweater for cold nights
- one pair of sneakers or a strong pair of shoes
- a pair of sandals or thongs (flip-flops)
- a lightweight wind and waterproof jacket
- a set of clothes for more formal occasions

Modesty rates highly in most Middle Eastern countries, especially for women. Wearing short skirts or shorts is asking for trouble in Muslim countries – long, loose clothing is always the best idea. In Iran, it is essential for women to cover all parts of the body except the hands, feet and face (from hairline to neckline), and to ensure that the outer layer of clothing gives no hint of the shape of the body. In Israel, most religious sites are not open to anyone dressed immodestly. (For more details see the Women Travellers' section in this chapter.)

It's always advisable to have one set of completely conventional 'dress up' clothes to wear when you arrive at embassies or consulates for visas, at the border to enter a country, or at docks or airports. You'll find life much simpler if you look neat and affluent; particularly disliked are thongs (flip-flops), shorts, jeans (especially with patches on them), local attire, T-shirts, etc.

On the nonclothing side, the following items may be useful:

- washing detergent and a universal plug
- pegs
- a length of cord for a makeshift washing line
- a Swiss army knife
- a money belt
- a tennis ball cut in half to use as a universal sink plug
- medical and sewing kit
- a pair of sunglasses
- a hat
- a torch (flashlight)

- a padlock
- a towel
- a sleeping bag
- a canteen
- a short-wave radio

A sleeping bag not only serves to sleep in but can double as a coat on cold days, a cushion on hard train seats, a seat for long waits on railway platforms and a bed top-cover, since hotels rarely give you one. A padlock will lock your bag to the luggage rack or to the seat in trains and will fortify your hotel-room doors – they very rarely lock with a latch. Although soap, toothpaste and other toiletries are readily obtainable, in the more backward areas toilet paper is unknown. So unless you can adapt to the Middle Eastern watering can and left-hand method, bring along some loo rolls. Tampons are not always easy to find outside big cities so bring along a supply. Toiletries, when available, can be expensive, so you may as well bring your own supply.

VISAS & DOCUMENTS
Passport
Make sure your passport is valid for a reasonably long period of time and has plenty of space; it could be embarrassing if you run out of blank pages and you are too far away from your embassy to be issued a new one.

Visas
Visas are an annoying, expensive and time-consuming piece of red tape. Effectively they are permits to enter certain countries and are stamped in your passport. You can either get them before you go or along the way. The advantage of predeparture collection is that it doesn't waste travelling time, the post office can do the leg work, and 'difficult' embassies are sometimes less difficult when you are in your own country. The two major drawbacks are that some countries may not be represented in your own country and often visas have a limited 'tenability' – it is no good getting a visa which will expire in three months if you are not going to arrive in that country for four months. You can

usually get a visa at an embassy or consulate in a neighbouring or nearby country, and often visas are available at the border or, even more likely, at the airport of arrival.

Some visas are free but most require a stack of forms, a gallery of photos and a pocketful of money. Sometimes, other requirements can pop up. You may have to have a certain amount of money or travellers' cheques, your hair length (if you are male) or appearance may have to meet certain standards and you may have to provide the dreaded 'ticket out'. That means before you can obtain a visa to enter the country you must have a ticket to leave it. This can often be a real nuisance if you want to leave by some obscure method and obtain tickets within the country. The answer in this situation is to get the simplest and cheapest airline ticket available from a reputable international airline – so that refunding it later, if you don't use it, is easy. A miscellaneous charges order (MCO) is a not quite so acceptable an alternative to a real airline ticket. An MCO is rather like a gift certificate redeemable as an airline ticket, and shows suspicious Immigration officials that you have the ability to get a ticket when necessary.

Visa headaches often seem to wax and wane; countries go through a period of making visas easier, then about-turn and make them more difficult. Egypt, Israel and Turkey issue visas on arrival to most nationals. Saudi Arabia refuses entry to people of the Jewish faith and most Middle Eastern countries deny entry to anyone whose passport betrays evidence of a visit to Israel (see the visa section in the Israel & the Palestinian Territories chapter).

How ready the Iranians are to let you into their country depends very much on the state of their relations with your government at the time. Citizens of small inoffensive countries like Ireland, New Zealand and San Marino are the greatest beneficiaries of this policy; Americans and Israelis are the greatest losers. Whoever you are, the situation is bound to change within the life of this book, and the best source of information is still going to be other travellers or your embassy.

If you hit a sticky visa problem, shop around. In some other city or country the situation may be better. Full details follow in the individual country chapters in this book, but remember the most important rule: treat embassies, consulates and borders as formal occasions – dress up for them.

Photocopies

Get a photocopy or two of your student card; this is required by some airlines before they give you your student-discounted tickets and photocopy machines are few and far between in some places in the Middle East. It's also worth taking photocopies of other relevant documents too, such as your passport data pages and your airline tickets, just in case you lose them.

Travel Insurance

However you're travelling, it's worth taking out travel insurance. Work out what you need. You may not want to insure that grotty old army surplus backpack but everyone should be covered for the worst possible case: an accident, for example, that will require hospital treatment and a flight home. It's a good idea to make a copy of your policy, in case the original is lost. If you are planning to travel for a long time, the insurance may seem very expensive but if you can't afford it, you may not be able to afford to deal with a medical emergency in the Middle East. For more on health and travel insurance see the Health Appendix.

Student Cards

An International Student Identity Card (ISIC), a green and white card with your photograph on it, usually supplied in laminated plastic, can come in surprisingly useful in the Middle East. As well as student discounts on flights and rail travel there are often reduced admissions at museums, archaeological sites and monuments for student card holders. Bear in mind that a student card issued by your own university or college may not be recognised elsewhere, it really should be ISIC.

Photographs

Raid the piggy bank, rush around to your favourite photo booth and get dozens of mug shots. Three dozen wouldn't be too many; every visa seems to require two or three, plus photos are needed for ID papers, passports, driving licences and student cards. Take plenty as they will be cheaper and easier to get in your own country.

Other Documents

An International Health Certificate is usually available from a doctor – see the Health section later in this chapter for more details. If you plan to drive, get an International Driving Permit from your local automobile association. They are valid for one year only. If you plan to take your own car you will need a *carnet de passage* and third-party insurance or a Green Card (see Car & Motorcycle in the Getting Around the Region chapter for more information).

EMBASSIES

Embassies – that is your own embassies abroad – are really not much use; they won't bail you out of trouble and generally won't hold mail for you, and even their newspapers tend to be well out of date. Of course there are some honourable exceptions; some embassies have excellent libraries with up-to-date newspapers and magazines, and brazen travellers recommend the 'government-employees-only' cafeterias for food from back home. Some embassies also post useful warning notices about local dangers or potential problems. The US embassies are particularly good for providing this information and it's worth scanning their notice boards for warnings about health problems, epidemics, dangers to lone travellers, etc.

For the addresses and contact details of embassies and consulates, see the individual country chapters.

MONEY

Bring as much as you can of this desirable commodity. Everybody will have their own idea of how much is enough although the main expense is likely to be your air tickets at one end or the other. On top of those basic transportation costs are your living costs. In parts of the Middle East, if you're just lazing around on the beach, that can still cost a dollar (or two) a day, and in other places it is much higher. This aspect completely depends on your personal comfort needs and where you decide to spend your time.

Costs
Leaving aside big expenditures (eg a plane ticket), most travellers will average from US$12 to US$20 a day for food, accommodation and day-to-day travelling in most of the Middle Eastern countries except the Arab Gulf States and perhaps Israel, where travellers can expect to spend US$40 a day. The real shoestringers might get down to less than US$10 while people who like a little more luxury will spend more. Remember that visa costs can mount rapidly if you travel back and forth a lot, and that buying things would put an extra hole in your budget. And when you have finished travelling you will want money to get back home. But remember you are not on some sort of travelling economy run – being too tight with your money can mean you miss out on the whole purpose of being there.

Carrying Money
The safest place to carry your money is next to your skin. A money belt or pouch, or an extra pocket inside your jeans, will help to keep things with their rightful owner. You can pick up nice leather money belts or pouches in a number of countries. Remember that if you lose cash you have lost it for ever, so don't go overboard on the convenience of cash versus the safety of cheques. A useful idea is to put aside a totally separate little emergency stash, say US$50, for use if everything else disappears. If there are two of you the money carrying duties can be split to minimise the risk of a total loss.

Cash & Travellers' Cheques
You should carry your money partly in travellers' cheques and partly in cash. US dollars and all major currencies are widely

recognised and easily converted in Middle Eastern countries. American Express (Amex) and other major travellers' cheques are available in a variety of currencies apart from the US dollar. Amex and Thomas Cook are probably the best known travellers' cheques. If you're travelling to more remote areas it's wise not to take all your cheques from the same company. It's not unknown to arrive in some small town to find that none of the three banks will accept cheques from a particular bank.

Easy replacement if they are stolen is the key to travellers' cheques, which is why you shouldn't bother with lesser known brands. To get stolen cheques replaced, you need to have serial numbers and proof of initial purchase to hand in to the relevant company before they even talk to you.

Carry some cheques in small denominations for last-minute conversions but don't have them all in small amounts – sometimes you get charged a per cheque service fee and, in any case, changing money is often a time-consuming activity.

ATMs
Most of the larger banks in the region – with the exception of those in Egypt, Iran, Lebanon, Syria and Yemen – now have Automatic Teller Machines (ATMs) linked up to one of the international networks (eg Cirrus or Plus systems). Look for the sticker on the machine showing the logo of their operating system. Major credit and credit/debit cards, especially Visa and MasterCard, are readily accepted and many machines will also take bank-issued cash cards (which you use at home to withdraw money directly from your bank account). Make sure you remember your PIN (personal identification number), and it is also a good idea to check out what sort of transaction fees you are likely to incur from both your own bank and the banks whose machines you will be using while you travel. See the individual country chapters for more details.

Credit Cards
These days credit cards are fairly widely

accepted in the Middle East although often only at the more expensive establishments. Visa, MasterCard and Amex are the most popular.

International Transfers

If you run out of money it is usually a fairly simple matter to have funds transferred from a bank account in your home country. Insist that the money is telexed or cabled and allow plenty of time.

Ask your bank to send the money to a specific bank in the city you nominate or to inform you which bank the money is being transferred to. It is better to arrange this before you go. Waiting for money is a well-known, wasteful occupation which is best avoided by taking enough to begin with. Money transferred to you will be converted into local currency. You can then reconvert it into hard currency and buy travellers' cheques with it if you wish.

Currency Exchange

Check around when looking to exchange your cash as rates do vary. Also be on the lookout for hidden extras like commission. Official moneychangers rather than banks often offer the best deals. Throughout the Middle East avoid accepting torn or particularly tatty notes as you may have difficulty disposing of them except to a bank.

Black Market

There is still some black-market activity in some Middle Eastern countries. If you do play the black market don't do it on the street – a dealer with a front, a travel agent or tailor shop, for example, is safest. Big notes are worth much more than small ones – 100 US$1 bills are worth less than one US$100 bill. Sometimes it's the same story with quite legal moneychangers. In some countries you may be asked to declare your cash and cheques on entry and exit and account for the difference in bank receipts, but this is often more for appearance's sake than for real. All you have to do is declare less than you actually have and make sure they don't see it. Requiring to see bank receipts for major

purchases like airline tickets (or requiring payment in foreign currency) is more rigorously enforced.

Tipping & Bargaining

Tipping is expected in all Middle Eastern countries except Yemen, where this practice simply does not exist. Called *baksheesh* in the Middle East, it is usually more than just a reward for having performed a service properly. Salaries and wages in these countries are much lower than in western countries, so baksheesh is regarded as a means of supplementing income – an often essential means.

For western travellers not used to almost continual tipping, demands for baksheesh for doing anything can be quite irritating. But it is the accepted way of getting things done in many Middle Eastern countries. Carry lots of small change with you but keep it separate from bigger bills, so that baksheesh demands don't increase when they see that you could supposedly afford more.

Almost all prices are negotiable in the Middle East, especially in the souqs (markets) and bazaars, where bargaining is expected. Prices of souvenirs are always inflated to allow for it. Many travellers find bargaining a hassle, but if you keep your cool and look at it as part of your travel experience, it can be quite enjoyable, especially if you manage to obtain the price you planned to pay in the first place.

There are different strategies for bargaining. A good rule is not to show too much interest in the item you want to buy. Start the bargaining with a much lower price than you really want to pay and then barter up to that point. When you state your first price the shopkeeper will inevitably huff about how absurd that is and then tell you the 'lowest' price. If it is still not low enough, then be insistent and keep smiling. Tea or coffee might be served as part of the bargaining ritual; accepting it doesn't place you under any obligation to buy. If you still can't get your price, then just walk away. There are hundreds of shops in the bazaars.

It is essential that you have a good idea of

the item's value both locally and overseas and not to be intimidated.

BOOKS

Most books are published in different editions by different publishers in different countries. As a result, a book might be a hardcover rarity in one country while it's readily available in paperback in another. Fortunately, bookshops and libraries search by title or author, so your local bookshop or library is best placed to advise you on the availability of the following recommendations.

The books listed here contain general information about the Middle East. Other books relevant to individual countries are listed in each chapter.

Lonely Planet

In addition to this book, Lonely Planet has several detailed guides to various countries in the Middle East, including travel survival kits for the following: *Arab Gulf States, Egypt, Iran, Israel & the Palestinian Territories, Jordan & Syria, Turkey* and *Yemen*. There are also city guides for Jerusalem and İstanbul, travel atlases for Egypt, Israel & the Palestinian Territories, and Jordan, Lebanon & Syria, and an Arabic phrasebook.

Lonely Planet's new travel literature series, *Journeys*, includes *The Gates of Damascus* by Lieve Joris and *Kingdom of the Film Stars: Travels in Jordan* by Anne Caulfield.

Travel

Byron, Robert, *The Road to Oxiana*. A classic of the travel writing genre. Recorded in Byron's admirably terse style, it is a vividly observed and often hilarious diary of a slow passage from England to the Oxus (now Amu-Darya) River in northwest Afghanistan, with lengthy wanderings in Iran en route.

Danziger, Nick, *Danziger's Travels*. An incredible modern-day overland odyssey through Turkey, Iran, Afghanistan, Pakistan, China and Tibet – without regard for visas, immigration posts, civil wars and the like. Although Danziger suffers from an inflated sense of self-importance and a propensity for melodrama, his trip is loaded with enough adventures to make all but the most seasoned traveller feel like a package tourist.

Horwitz, Tony, *Baghdad Without a Map*. Should really be subtitled, 'the trials and misadventures of a freelance journalist awash in the Middle East'. Amongst other places, Cairo-based Horwitz trips up in Baghdad, Beirut, Tehrān and Yemen. Sober reading for anyone who thought they might make some easy cash by flogging their travel diary on getting back home.

Lawrence, TE, *Seven Pillars of Wisdom*. Not exactly a travelogue, this is more a classic of modern literature, as well as an extraordinarily self-serving account of the Arab revolt in Hejaz and Transjordan during WWI.

Paine, Sheila, *Afghan Amulet*. In search of an embroidered amulet, Paine had herself smuggled into Afghanistan in 1993, from where the trail led to Iraq and eventually Turkish Kurdistan.

Raban, Jonathan, *Arabia Through the Looking Glass*. One of the most readable of English travel writers, in this early book Raban visits the Arab Gulf countries during the oil boom. His observations on expatriate life in the region are as valid today as they were when he visited in early 1979. The same journey also resulted in rather more dated chapters on Cairo and Amman.

Stark, Freya, *East is West, Valleys of the Assassins, Beyond the Euphrates*. Probably the most famous of a number of distinguished women travellers in the Middle East, Stark wrote more than 20 books recounting her travels throughout the region. The ones listed above are just a few of her better known titles.

Theroux, Paul, *Pillars of Hercules*. The normally acerbic and grumpy Theroux lightens up a little as his exploratory jaunt around the fringes of the Mediterranean takes in seaside Turkey, Syria, Israel and Egypt. You still wouldn't want him as your travelling companion but he's great in book form.

Theroux, Peter, *Sandstorms*. A memoir of Theroux's seven years stationed as a journalist in Riyadh.

Thesiger, Wilfred, *Arabian Sands, The Marsh Arabs*. These two classic books describe Thesiger's visits to Iraq, and Arabia in the late 1940s and 50s.

Thubron, Colin, *The Hills of Adonis, Mirror to Damascus, Jerusalem*. The most feted British travel writer of the moment, Thubron has written books on Lebanon, Syria and Jerusalem – see Books in the Israel and Lebanon country chapters.

History & Politics

Cooley, John K, *Payback: America's Long War in the Middle East*. Cooley chronicles, in depressing detail, the degree to which Washington created many of its own, and the west's, problems in the region through the 1980s.

Friedman, Thomas, *From Beirut to Jerusalem*. The recent history of the Middle Eastern conflicts as witnessed by a Pulitzer prize-winning journalist. The book is an excellent read for anyone seeking a fuller understanding of the causes and effects of the constant strife that afflicts the region.

Fromkin, David, *A Peace to End All Peace: Creating the Modern Middle East, 1914-1922*. For some background on how the Middle East came to be the mess that it is, this book is absolutely essential. Fromkin defines the region broadly, even taking in Central Asia, as he details the western machinations during and immediately after WWI that laid the groundwork for the Middle Eastern politics we know today.

Glass, Charles, *Money For Old Rope, Tribes With Flags*. Two collections of articles and essays on Levantine politickings by veteran journalist Glass. Both include accounts of his kidnapping and subsequent escape from pro-Iranian guerrillas in Beirut.

Halliday, Fred, *Arabia Without Sultans*. This book gives a detailed and quite accurate account of the development of the Arab Gulf countries in recent decades, with some 180 pages devoted to Yemen.

Hourani, Albert, *A History of the Arab Peoples*. While not exactly holiday reading, this is possibly the single best book on the development and sociology of the modern-day Arab world.

Lewis, Bernard, *The Middle East*. A very recent and very erudite overview of Middle Eastern history from the rise of Christianity to the present day.

Mansfield, Peter, *The Arabs*. In addition to an overview of the history of the Middle East, Mansfield comments on the individual countries in the region.

People & Society

Brooks, Geraldine, *Nine Parts of Desire*. An investigation into the life of women under Islam. As befits a *Wall Street Journal* correspondent, the book succeeds in maintaining a degree of objectivity, and interview sources range from village girls to Queen Noor of Jordan and the daughter of President Rafsanjānī of Iran.

El-Saadawi, Nawal, *The Hidden Face of Eve: Women in the Arab World*. Considers the role of women in world history, Arab history and literature, and contemporary Egypt. El-Saadawi is a psychiatrist, feminist, novelist and writer of nonfiction and all her books, many of which have been translated into several languages, are well worth reading for the insight they provide into the lives of women in the Arab world.

Goodwin, Jan, *Price of Honour*. The blurb on the back of this book includes the terms 'horrific', 'abused', 'oppressed' and 'restrictions', and that's all within a single sentence. Goodwin has clocked up the miles and the hours in her quest to expose the Muslim world's mistreatment of women, but you can't help but suspect she already had her script written long before she set about her research.

Mansfield, Peter, *The New Arabians*. An introduction to both the history and society of the Gulf, though the focus is mostly on Saudi Arabia and the general tone of the book is fairly uncontroversial.

Islam

Ahmed, Akbar, *Living Islam*. Highly recommended as a sensitive introduction to Islam by a Pakistani scholar who has dedicated himself to bridging the mutual ignorance and misunderstanding between the Muslim and non-Muslim worlds, based in part on a BBC TV series.

Guillaume, Alfred, *Islam*. Dry as dust but dense with information on history, doctrine and practice.

Literature

The Thousand and One Nights. About as much to do with the modern Middle East as the tales of Hans Christian Anderson have to do with NATO, but nevertheless a great read. Dawood or Haddawy are reckoned to have produced the best English-language translations, while the Mardrus/Mathers or Burton versions have added farting and lusting.

Reference Books

A useful general reference on both artistic and architectural forms throughout the Islamic world is David Talbot Rice's *Islamic Art*. Another book carrying the same title has been written by Barbara Brend.

If you are serious about looking for quality rugs, kilims and the like it could definitely pay to first consult *Oriental Rugs & A Buyer's Guide* by Essie Sakhi. As well as colour photographs, the book includes useful information on the history of Persian carpets, how they are made, and even more importantly, what to look for when buying one. Also recommended (and with the same title) is *Oriental Rugs & A Buyer's Guide* by Lee Allane.

For those with a shoppers eye on the region's souqs and markets, Heather Colyer Ross' *The Art of Bedouin Jewellery* would be a very useful asset.

There are also several good books dealing with the intricate and complex art form of Arabic calligraphy; one such study is *Calligraphy and Islamic Culture* by Annemarie Schimmel. ■

Maalouf, Amin, *Leo the African, Samarkand, Tanios the Rock*. Lebanese-born Maalouf is a beguiling storyteller who writes oriental-flavoured epics that inject Middle Eastern history with the pace and wonder of a Spielberg movie.

Soueif, Ahdaf, *Aisha, Eye of the Sun, Sandpiper*. An Anglo-Egyptian authoress whose Tolstoyian novel and two short story collections share England and Cairo as backdrops to some well-wrought emotional vignettes.

For literature by Middle Eastern writers see the Arts section in the Facts about the Region chapter.

ONLINE SERVICES

For those lugging laptops around, the Middle East is joining the communications revolution, but as yet hooking up is still difficult in most of the region's countries – with the notable exception of Israel and perhaps Turkey. Compuserve has nodes in both of these countries and, in each case, there are several other competing servers. The only

Middle Eastern internet cafe that we're aware of is Strudel (email strudel@inter.net.il) in Jerusalem (see the Israel chapter) but check the international cyber cafe listing on http://www.easynet.co.uk/pages/cafe/ccafe.htm for the latest information.

Elsewhere you will have great trouble getting online. The best places to start making enquiries are computer dealers or universities – the American University in Cairo, for instance, is sufficiently net savvy to have its own web site.

PHOTOGRAPHY & VIDEO
Film & Equipment

Most types of film are available in the Middle East though they may not be easily found in remote villages. Colour-print processing is usually quite adequate, while B&W and slide processing is not that good.

Film prices are usually similar, if not more expensive, to prices in western countries, so

---

Web Sites

Type in somewhere as seemingly obscure as Afghanistan into a Web search engine and you'll be amazed at the number of matches it throws out. Point and click surfers can dig up heaps of practical information on the Net that may be of use to anyone planning a visit to the Middle East or even living there. The following are just a few suggestions of places to start:

http://www.lonelyplanet.com
This is the award-winning Lonely Planet site homepage, containing destination updates, recent travellers letters and a useful travellers' bulletin board.
http://www.city.net/countries/israel
Lots of links specifically geared to the visitor, including categories such as travel & tourism, maps, museums & galleries and lodgings. The site may also now include Middle Eastern countries other than Israel.
http://www.arab.net
This site has information on the history, geography, business, culture, government and tourism of 16 Arab countries. It also includes some more general information on matters close to the Arab heart – food and camels.
http://gauss.technion.ac.il/nyh/israel/cities.html
Bills itself as the Complete Guide (almost) to the World Wide Web in Israel and boasts over 950 links broken down into categories such as arts, reference etc.
http://www.jpost.co.il
The Internet version of the English-language daily *The Jerusalem Post*, it includes daily news, columns, features and reviews – and there's no subscription fee.
http://www1.huji.ac.il/jeru/jerusalem.html
A virtual tour through the Old City of Jerusalem with links to information on other parts of the country.
http://163.121.10.41/tourism
The homepage of the Egypt Tourism Authority with pictures and information on all the major sites.

you may want to bring your own supply. In some countries, film may have been stored for ages in less than ideal conditions, so always check the 'use by' date.

Cameras and lenses collect dust quickly in desert areas. Lens paper and cleaner can be difficult to find in some countries, so bring your own. A dust brush is also useful.

Photography

In most Middle Eastern countries, early morning and late afternoon are the best times to take photographs. During the rest of the day, sunlight can be too bright and the sky too hazy, causing your photos to look washed out. There are a few remedies for this: a polarisation filter will cut glare and reflection off sand and water; a lens hood will cut some of the glare; Kodachrome film, with an ASA of 64 or 25, and Fujichrome 50 and 100 are good slide films to use when the sun is bright.

Many religious sites and other buildings are not lit inside and you'll need long exposures (several seconds), a powerful flash or faster film. A portable tripod can be very useful.

For good people pictures, a powerful lens is helpful.

Video

Properly used, a video camera can give a fascinating record of your holiday. As well as videoing the obvious things – sunsets, spectacular views – remember to record some of the ordinary everyday details of life in the country. Often the most interesting things occur when you're actually intent on filming something else. Remember too that, unlike still photography, video 'flows' – so, for example, you can shoot scenes of countryside rolling past the train window, to give an overall impression that isn't possible with ordinary photos.

Video cameras these days have amazingly sensitive microphones, and you might be surprised how much sound will be picked up. This can also be a problem if there is a lot of ambient noise – filming by the side of a busy road might seem OK when you do it, but viewing it back home might simply give you a deafening cacophony of traffic noise. One good rule to follow for beginners is to try to film in long takes, and don't move the camera around too much. Otherwise, your video could well make your viewers seasick! If your camera has a stabiliser, you can use it to obtain good footage while travelling on various means of transport, even on bumpy roads. And remember, you're on holiday – don't let the video take over your life and turn your trip into a Cecil B de Mille production.

Make sure you keep the batteries charged and have the necessary charger, plugs and transformer for the country you are visiting. In most countries, it is possible to obtain video cartridges easily in large towns and cities, but make sure you buy the correct format. It is usually worth buying at least a few cartridges duty free to start off your trip.

Finally, remember to follow the same rules regarding people's sensitivities as for still photography – having a video camera shoved in their face is probably even more annoying and offensive than a still camera. Always ask permission first.

Restrictions

In most Middle Eastern countries, it is forbidden to photograph anything even vaguely military in nature (bridges, railway stations, airports and other public works). The definition of what is 'strategic' differs from one country to another, and signs are not always posted, so be careful – otherwise you may get your film and camera confiscated. (In some countries people have been arrested but this is very unlikely to happen.)

Photography is usually allowed inside religious and archaeological sites, unless there are signs indicating otherwise. As a rule, however, do not photograph inside mosques during a service.

Also, be aware that certain countries, like Iran, are very suspicious of video cameras and may not allow you to take one into the country. See individual country chapters for further details.

Photographing People

As a matter of courtesy, do not photograph people without asking their permission first. Children will almost always say yes, but their parents or other adults might say no. In the more conservative Muslim countries you should not photograph women. In countries where you can photograph women, show them the camera and make it clear that you want to take a picture of them. Some may object, and if they don't, their male companions may instead. Make sure you've got the OK before shooting if you don't want to risk having your camera smashed or stones thrown at you. In Israel, Orthodox Jews do not like you to point the camera at them.

Many Middle Easterners are sensitive about the negative aspects of their country, so exercise discretion when taking photos in poorer areas.

Airport Security

Some but not all airports have X-ray machines for checking luggage. Despite assurances that they are safe for camera film, it's better to keep any unexposed film somewhere where it can easily be removed for examination.

TIME

Egypt, Israel, Jordan, Lebanon, Syria and Turkey are two hours ahead of GMT/UTC. Bahrain, Iraq, Kuwait, Qatar, Saudi Arabia and Yemen are three hours ahead; Iran is 3½ hours ahead and Afghanistan is 4½ hours ahead. See the comparative times table below to find out what the time is in your city when it's noon in the Middle Eastern capitals and which countries have daylight saving.

Time is something that Middle Eastern people always seem to have plenty of – something that should take five minutes will invariably take an hour. Trying to speed things up will only lead to frustration. It is better to take it philosophically than try to fight it.

ELECTRICITY

The electric current in most Middle Eastern countries is 220V AC, 50 Hz, though in some both 220V and 110V are in use in different areas. Most of the plugs are of the British or European variety. You'd be well advised to bring along an adaptor and transformer if necessary.

As some Middle Eastern countries suffer from power shortages, it is a good idea to

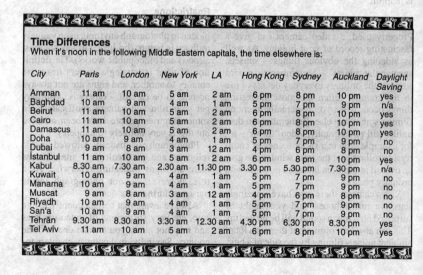

Time Differences

When it's noon in the following Middle Eastern capitals, the time elsewhere is:

City	Paris	London	New York	LA	Hong Kong	Sydney	Auckland	Daylight Saving
Amman	11 am	10 am	5 am	2 am	6 pm	8 pm	10 pm	yes
Baghdad	10 am	9 am	4 am	1 am	5 pm	7 pm	9 pm	n/a
Beirut	11 am	10 am	5 am	2 am	6 pm	8 pm	10 pm	yes
Cairo	11 am	10 am	5 am	2 am	6 pm	8 pm	10 pm	yes
Damascus	11 am	10 am	5 am	2 am	6 pm	8 pm	10 pm	yes
Doha	10 am	9 am	4 am	1 am	5 pm	7 pm	9 pm	no
Dubai	9 am	8 am	3 am	12 am	4 pm	6 pm	8 pm	no
İstanbul	11 am	10 am	5 am	2 am	6 pm	8 pm	10 pm	yes
Kabul	8.30 am	7.30 am	2.30 am	11.30 pm	3.30 pm	5.30 pm	7.30 pm	n/a
Kuwait	10 am	9 am	4 am	1 am	5 pm	7 pm	9 pm	no
Manama	10 am	9 am	4 am	1 am	5 pm	7 pm	9 pm	no
Muscat	9 am	8 am	3 am	12 am	4 pm	6 pm	8 pm	no
Riyadh	10 am	9 am	4 am	1 am	5 pm	7 pm	9 pm	no
San'a	10 am	9 am	4 am	1 am	5 pm	7 pm	9 pm	no
Tehrān	9.30 am	8.30 am	3.30 am	12.30 am	4.30 pm	6.30 pm	8.30 pm	yes
Tel Aviv	11 am	10 am	5 am	2 am	6 pm	8 pm	10 pm	yes

Electrical Conversions

Country	Voltage	Plug
Afghanistan	n/a	n/a
Bahrain	230	3-pin UK-style
Egypt	220 & 110	round 2-pin
Iran	220	round 2-pin
Iraq	n/a	n/a
Israel	220	round 2-pin
Jordan	220	round 2-pin
Kuwait	220 & 240	2 & 3-pin UK-style
Lebanon	220 & 110	round & flat 2-pin
Oman	220 & 240	3-pin UK-style
Qatar	230	3-pin UK-style
SA	220 & 110*	n/a
Syria	220	round 2-pin
Turkey	220	round 2-pin**
UAE	240 & 220#	3-pin UK-style
Yemen	220	3-pin UK-style

* Both 220 and 110 are found at various places in the kingdom, but the latter is more widespread.
** There are two sizes in use in Turkey. Most common is the small-diameter prong; the other is the large-diameter, grounded plug used in Germany and Austria.
# The current is 240V in Abu Dhabi and 220V in the rest of the Emirates.

keep a torch (flashlight) or a few candles in a handy place in your backpack.

WEIGHTS & MEASURES

All the countries in this book use the metric system. There is a standard conversion table at the back of this book.

In Iran, you may still come across the *sīr* (about 75g) and the *chārak* (10 sīr) in some remoter places. Gold and other precious metals are still measured by the *mesghāl*, equal to 4.7g. The *farsang* (sometimes known in English as the parasang) is an old Persian measure of distance which always used to differ from place to place but is quoted in one recent reference book as measuring exactly 6.24 km. You may still hear the farsang used.

Feet and nautical miles continue to be used in aeronautical and naval circles.

In the souqs of Oman, silver jewellery is often sold according to weight measured in tolas. Tolas are sometimes called 'thallers'

after the Maria Theresia dollar, an 18th century Austrian coin which became the model for Arabia's common currency of the 19th and early 20th centuries. One tola is equal to 11.75g.

HEALTH

Travel health depends on your predeparture preparations, your day-to-day health care while travelling and how you handle any medical problem or emergency that does develop. While the list of potential dangers can seem quite frightening, with a little luck, some basic precautions and adequate information few travellers experience more than upset stomachs. For more information, see the Health Appendix and the individual country chapters.

WOMEN TRAVELLERS

Middle Easterners are generally conservative, especially about matters concerning sex and women; Muslim countries simply aren't the place to make a feminist statement. Islam, and in particular the more conservative interpretation of Islam, does impose a number of strict constraints on women, and a western woman is better off not visiting conservative Muslim countries unless prepared to fit in with the social code.

On the other hand, unaccompanied women on occasion are treated with extra courtesy and indulgence because of their perceived vulnerability.

Attitudes to Women

Attitudes towards women can range from the fairly liberal (the Mediterranean coast), where women can wear anything they like, to the very conservative (Afghanistan, Iran and Saudi Arabia), where women must cover almost all parts of their body. Conversely, treatment of foreign women tends to be at its best in strictly Islamic societies such as Iran (providing of course you adhere to the prevailing social mores), and at its worst in Egypt and Israel where sexual harassment can be a real holiday-souring nuisance.

Local Women According to both men and

women, the role of a woman is as mother and matron of the household, and it is this which the men seek to protect. They don't want their wives to have to work, as it is a man's role to provide for the family. Most Middle Eastern women are still raised to want or expect nothing else. Consequently, very few have broken away from the house and family. The traditional role is still taken very seriously by the women themselves as well as by the men. Premarital sex is considered a violation of this role – for women that is.

Western Women Unfortunately, many Middle Eastern men have a slightly twisted view of western women. Muslims are very conservative when it comes to sex and women, and men have little or no contact with either before marriage. Western movies and TV give them the impression that all western women are promiscuous and will jump into bed at the drop of a hat. It doesn't actually take much on your part to perpetuate this belief – bare shoulders or shorts on a woman are 'proof' enough. Unfortunately, this doesn't necessarily mean that western women travellers are guaranteed to be free of harassment if they dress modestly.

Unaccompanied women will routinely be stared at and will often have lewd comments directed at them. They will often be misunderstood and, in turn, misunderstand. They may be followed and may find strange and unwanted visitors turning up outside their hotel rooms. In shops, you may be served only after the men, including those who enter after you.

Some hotels and restaurants do not serve lone women at all, and staying in the budget hotels can be problematic. You'll often have to take a room for yourself, and it's not a bad idea to look around for holes in the wall in interesting places. Some women swear they feel better with some tissue stuffed into key holes and the like.

Most of the incidents recounted by women travellers in the area are nonthreatening nuisances; physical harassment and rape are not significant threats in the Middle East.

Safety Precautions

You can travel independently if you follow a few tips: avoid direct eye contact with a man unless you know him; try not to respond to an obnoxious comment from a man – act as if you didn't hear it; be careful in crowds where you are crammed between people, as it is not unusual for crude things to happen behind you; never hitchhike alone or with only female companions and, most of all, do not flirt with strange men.

Try to stay in better hotels (possibly a moot point in the Gulf countries where many bottom-end hotels will not rent rooms to single women), dress conservatively and do not ride in the front seat of taxi cabs.

Generally, Middle Eastern men seem to have more respect for a married woman. A wedding ring will immediately add to your respectability, but a photo of your children and even husband can clinch it – if you don't have any, borrow a picture of your nephew or niece.

Normally, it is best to totally ignore the predictable and constant come-ons. If a person or a situation becomes troublesome head for a busy place, preferably where a lot of other foreigners and a few policemen are gathered (a shopping mall or the lobby of a big hotel, for example).

If you need more information and tips, refer to an article by Ludmilla Tüting titled 'The Woman Traveller', which has appeared in both *The Globetrotters Handbook* and *The Traveller's Handbook*. Another good source of information and tips is a British book called *The Guidebook for Women Travellers*. Its section on travel in Middle Eastern countries is particularly useful.

What to Wear

This differs from country to country, though on the whole a certain amount of modesty is advisable. In Egypt, Iraq, Israel, Jordan, Lebanon, Syria and Turkey, attitudes towards women are more relaxed than in Iran, the Gulf countries and Afghanistan. Women can generally wear what they like at beach resorts and in big cities. Outside these areas, however, it is better not to wear tight-fitting or revealing garments, and to ensure that legs, arms, shoulders and neckline are covered. Wearing a bra will avoid countless unwelcome confrontations, and a hat or headscarf is also a good idea.

In the more conservative states of Bahrain, Kuwait, Oman, Qatar, the UAE and Yemen, it is again better not to wear very tight or revealing clothing.

In the very traditional societies of Afghanistan, Iran and Saudi Arabia, although it is not necessary for foreign women to wear the *chador* (the one-piece cloak associated with Muslim countries), it is essential for them to cover all parts of the body except the hands, feet and face (from hairline to neckline), and to ensure that the outer layer of clothing gives no hint of the shape of the body.

Standard dress for western women in these countries tends to be a full-length skirt, or a long-sleeved shirt and trousers (jeans are OK), worn underneath a loose-fitting, below-the-knees black or dark blue coat. A large, plain headscarf should cover the hair and neck (a hat will not do) and thick socks should cover any visible parts of the legs.

GAY & LESBIAN TRAVELLERS

With the exception of Egypt, Turkey and Israel, homosexuality is illegal in all Middle Eastern countries. Penalties include fines and/or imprisonment, and in Iran, Saudi Arabia and Yemen the death penalty may be invoked. Even in Israel, Egypt and Turkey, where homosexuality is not prohibited by law, it remains fairly low key. However, in general, as a westerner, you are unlikely to encounter prejudice or harassment as long as you remain discreet, although this may not be the case if you become involved with a local. For more information on gay-friendly bars and hotels see the *Spartacus International Gay Guide* and the individual Egypt, Turkey and Israel chapters.

DISABLED TRAVELLERS

Generally speaking, scant regard is paid to the needs of disabled travellers in the Middle East. Steps, high kerbs and other assorted obstacles are everywhere, streets are often badly rutted and uneven, roads are made virtually uncrossable by heavy traffic, while many doorways are low and narrow. Ramps and specially equipped lodgings and toilets are an extreme rarity. You will have to plan your trip carefully and probably be obliged to restrict yourself to luxury-level hotels and private, hired transport. The happy exception is Israel – see the Disabled Travellers section in that chapter. Visitors to Egypt can also contact ETAMS (☎ (02) 575 4721; fax 575 4191) at 13 Sharia Qasr al-Nil in central Cairo. This tour company specialises in custom-made tours, accommodation and sightseeing in specially equipped buses. It also has information on hotels claiming to have facilities catering to the disabled.

Otherwise, before setting off for the Middle East disabled travellers could get in touch with their national support organisation (preferably with the travel officer, if there is one) – in the UK contact RADAR (☎ (0171) 250 3222) of 250 City Rd, London EC1V 8AS.

TRAVEL WITH CHILDREN

Taking the kids can add another dimension to a trip to the Middle East, although there are a few provisos that should be born in mind. Firstly, it's a good idea to avoid travel in the summer as the extreme heat can be quite uncomfortable and energy sapping. With infants, another problem may be cleanliness. It is impractical to carry more than about a half dozen washable nappies around with you, but disposable ones are not always that easy to come by – although in Egypt, Israel, Lebanon and Turkey there should be no problem. Powdered milk is widely available, as is bottled water. As for hotels, you are going to want something with a private bathroom and hot water, which will normally preclude most budget accommodation. The good news is that children are made a big fuss of in the Middle East. They'll help break the ice and open doors to closer contact with local people.

For more comprehensive advice on the dos and don'ts of taking the kids in your luggage, see Lonely Planet's *Travel with Children* by Maureen Wheeler.

DANGERS & ANNOYANCES

The Middle East has a reputation for being a dangerous area because of political turmoil, the Arab-Israeli conflict and the emergence of Islamic fundamentalism in many countries. Don't let this deter you from travelling. The trouble spots are usually well defined, and as long as you keep track of political developments, you are unlikely to come to any harm; in fact, the Middle East is a remarkably safe area.

At the time of writing, Iraq was off limits to tourists and fighting had re-erupted between Afghanistan's rival factions. In Israel, certain areas of the West Bank and Gaza Strip can be dangerous to visit at certain times, depending on the political climate.

The situation in Lebanon had regained a semblance of normality until the Israeli assault of April 1996; even so, except for Israeli-occupied southern Lebanon, it is quite safe to visit.

Tourists have been attacked in Egypt but the incidents remain isolated ones and the Egyptian authorities are at great pains to reassure the world that Egypt is safe.

For further details, check the Middle East in Brief box on page 51 and also the individual country chapters.

Security Checks

In Iran, Israel and Lebanon, there are security checks at several public buildings where your baggage may be inspected. There are also checkpoints along major routes around the country where you may be asked for identification. Foreigners are expected to carry their passports with them at all times.

Theft & Violence

In general theft is not much of a problem in Middle Eastern countries and robbery (mugging) even less of one, but don't let the relative safety lull you. Take the standard precautions.

Always keep valuables with you or locked in a safe – never leave them in your room or in a car or bus. Use a money belt, a pouch under your clothes, a leather wallet attached to your belt, or extra internal pockets in your clothing. Keep a record of your passport, credit card and travellers' cheque numbers separately; it won't cure problems, but it will make them easier to bear.

However, beware of your fellow travellers; there are more than a few backpackers who make their money go further by helping themselves to other people's.

Sexual Harassment

Men should be prepared for a certain amount of sexual harassment from other men in some Middle Eastern countries, especially the Gulf States. It is not unusual to be propositioned in a restaurant or on the street. Women should see the Women Travellers section earlier in this chapter.

Power & Water Cuts

Electricity blackouts are still a more or less daily occurrence throughout Iran, Lebanon and Syria. Take a torch (flashlight) with you at all times, or leave it where you can easily find it in the dark.

Water cuts are much less frequent, and there's not much you can do about them, except perhaps filling all available receptacles every night just in case.

BUSINESS HOURS

The end-of-week holiday throughout the Middle East is Friday except in Israel, Lebanon and Turkey. In Israel it's Saturday (Shabbat) while in Lebanon and Turkey it's Sunday. In countries where Friday is the holiday, most embassies and government offices are also closed on Thursday, though private businesses and shops are open on Thursday mornings and many stores will reopen in the evening on Friday.

In many countries, shops have different hours at different times of the year, depending on the seasons (they tend to work shorter hours in summer) and on Ramadan, the month-long fasting month for Muslims, when almost everything shuts down in the afternoon in many countries.

PUBLIC HOLIDAYS & SPECIAL EVENTS

All Middle Eastern countries observe the main Islamic holidays of Eid al-Fitr, which marks the end of Ramadan, and Eid al-Adha, which marks the pilgrimage to Mecca. Countries with a major Shiite population also observe Ashura, the anniversary of the martyrdom of Hussein, the third imam of the Shiites. Most observe both the Gregorian and the Islamic new year holidays, but they also have other religious and public holidays (for details refer to the individual country chapters). Following is a list of the dates for Muslim holidays up to the year 2001. These dates may vary by several days in either direction as the Islamic calendar is based on the cycles, and the sighting, of the moon. See the Religion and Language sections in the Facts about the Region chapter for information about the Islamic calendar and the names of the 12 lunar months of the Islamic calendar respectively.

Ramadan

Ramadan (Ramazan in Iran and Turkey) is the ninth month of the Muslim calendar, when Muslims fast during daylight hours to fulfil the fourth pillar of Islam. There are no public holidays but it is difficult to deal with officialdom then because of unusual opening hours.

During this fasting month, pious Muslims will not allow *anything* to pass their lips in daylight hours.

Although many do not follow the injunctions to the letter, most conform to some extent. Foreigners are not expected to follow suit, but it is generally impolite to smoke,

drink or eat in public during Ramadan. In the bigger cities it is less of a problem, but it remains sensible to avoid flaunting your kebabs.

Business hours tend to become more erratic and usually shorter, and in out-of-the-way places you may find it hard to find a restaurant that opens before sunset.

The evening meal during Ramadan, called *iftar* (breaking the fast), is always a bit of a celebration. Go to the bigger restaurants and wait with fasting crowds for sundown, the moment when food is served – it's quite a lively experience. For more information see Religion in the Facts about the Region chapter.

ACTIVITIES

From deserts to beaches to snowcapped mountains, the variety of terrain in the Middle East can offer the visitor a few special-interest activities. Following is a general breakdown of some of these activities; for more details (and other activities) see the individual country chapters.

Water Sports

The Red and Mediterranean seas, the Sea of Galilee and the Persian Gulf provide ample opportunities for swimming, windsurfing, sailing, yachting, rowing, water-skiing, snorkelling and scuba diving almost year-round. You can enjoy some or all of these activities in Egypt, Israel, Jordan and Turkey.

Climbing, Trekking & Walking

There's a wealth of superb hiking opportunities, both leisurely and more strenuous, in

Table of Holidays

Hijra Year	New Year	Prophet's Birthday	Ramadan Begins	Eid al-Fitr	Eid al-Adha
1417	20.05.96	28.07.96	10.01.97	09.02.97	18.04.97
1418	09.05.97	17.07.97	31.12.97	29.01.98	08.04.98
1419	28.04.98	06.07.98	19.12.98	18.01.99	28.03.99
1420	17.04.99	26.06.99	09.12.99	08.01.00	16.03.00
1421	06.04.00	14.06.00	27.11.00	27.12.00	06.03.01

Israel, Jordan and Turkey. In Iran, the Alborz Mountains are a popular destination for walking.

Skiing

It's possible to ski in Iran, Israel, Lebanon and Turkey. The season starts around the middle of January and lasts until late March or April.

Desert Safaris & Drives

There are lots of deserts in the Middle East and, in many countries, driving around the desert in a 4WD is a popular activity. There are also organised desert safaris and trips in Israel, Oman and the UAE.

Language Courses

Egypt, Jordan, Syria and Saudi Arabia offer short intensive courses in Arabic. It's also possible to take up Hebrew and biblical studies in Israel.

Archaeological Digs

With its wealth of ancient history, the Middle East offers unparalleled opportunities for visiting archaeological sites. In Israel, it is also possible to work on archaeological digs. The busy archaeological season is May to September.

Turkish Baths

There are Turkish baths in Syria and Turkey where you can be steam-cleaned, have a massage, relax and sip tea at an affordable price.

ACCOMMODATION

Accommodation in the Middle East ranges from the cheap to the very expensive, and in many countries, such as Jordan and the Arab Gulf States, it can be difficult to find really cheap accommodation at all.

Between the two price ranges there's something to suit almost everyone. There are hotels, pensions, youth hostels and, in some countries, camping grounds.

In many countries it can be hard for women to find cheap accommodation because these are often male-only dorms that usually cater to local workers. In addition, unmarried couples travelling together will be given separate rooms in the more conservative Muslim countries.

Most hotels in Syria that are officially two-stars and above charge foreigners in US dollars, and often they want the payment in cash. In Israel, paying in US dollars will save you paying the 15% VAT.

Camping

Camping is possible in several places around the Middle East, but it is better to stick to officially sanctioned camping sites because many areas are military or restricted zones and are not always marked. There are camping grounds in Egypt, Iran, Israel, Lebanon and Saudi Arabia. It is also possible to camp out in some of the other countries. If you do camp out, always ask the locals before pitching your tent as you may be on somebody's land.

Hostels

There are youth hostels in Bahrain, Egypt, Israel, Qatar, Saudi Arabia and the UAE. Many may require the hostel cards and HI members often get discounts.

Hotels

At the bottom end of the market, conditions can be very primitive with prices starting at US$4 per bed in a small town up to US$20 or US$25 for a double room in a large city.

Often you might be sharing the room with a few other men, or you may get a mattress with no sheets but plenty of filthy blankets. The toilets are often the hole-in-the-ground type and there may be a washbasin, with cold water only, either in the room or near the toilet.

At the five-star end of the price range are hotels representing most of the world's major chains: Hilton, Sheraton, Holiday Inn etc, with prices starting at about US$90 and going up to US$250 or more for a double, depending on the country.

For details and other types of accommodation see the individual country chapters.

FOOD

The food is essentially the same in all the countries of the Middle East. If you're familiar with Lebanese and Turkish food then the region will hold no surprises for you. It's also pretty much the same in Israel and closely related in Iran. Although the food is generally quite healthy and tasty, if you're travelling on a shoestring you will also find it quite monotonous. High cuisine in the Middle Eastern countries comes with an equally high price tag.

Fuul, *felafel* and *houmos* are the three staples of the region and you'll find them at breakfast, lunch and dinner time. *Fuul* is a paste made from fava beans, garlic and lemon, usually served swimming in oil. *Felafel* is even more widespread. It's deep-fried balls of chickpea paste with spices and is served in a piece of Arabic flat bread *(khobz)* with pickled vegetables or tomato. Felafel is one of the cheapest foods to eat and you'll be thoroughly sick of it by the time you leave. *Houmos* is cooked chickpeas ground into a paste and mixed with garlic and lemon. It is available in virtually every restaurant and is usually excellent.

Arabic bread is eaten with absolutely everything and is also called *aish*, meaning 'life'. It is round and flat and makes a good filler if you are preparing your own food.

Baba ghanouj is another dip which is eaten with bread. It's made from mashed eggplant and *tahina* – sesame-seed paste. *Shwarma* is the meat (lamb or chicken) equivalent of the felafel and since it's cheap and convenient you'll also get your fair share of it. Shwarma stalls have their vertical spits set up along the footpath and when you order one the guy will slice off the meat and pack it into a piece of flat bread with tomato or pickled vegetables. On the same stall you will usually find *kibbih*, which are deep fried balls made of meat and cracked wheat and stuffed with more meat fried in onions.

Main dishes are usually chicken, kebabs, or meat and vegetable stews. Chicken *(farooj)* is usually roasted on spits in large ovens out the front of the restaurant. The usual serving is half a chicken *(nus farooj)* and it will come with bread and a side dish of raw onion, chillies and sometimes olives. With the optional extras of salad *(salata)* and houmos, you have a good meal.

Kebabs are another common favourite and are usually sold by weight. The spicy minced lamb is pressed onto skewers, grilled over charcoal and served with bread and a side dish. Stews are usually meat or vegetable or both and although not available everywhere, make a pleasant change from chicken and kebabs. *Fasooliya* is bean stew, *baseela* is peas and *batatas*, potato. They are usually served on rice *(ruz)* or macaroni *(makarone)*, which are extra.

Mezze is actually a selection of appetisers but makes a meal in itself. Served on a tray with tea, you get houmos, baba ghanouj, sardines, cucumbers, tomato, liver and kidneys, fried eggs, spice and oil.

Arab desserts are usually overpoweringly sweet – buy the pastries in small quantities.

Soup

soups	*shurba*
lentil soup	*shurbat 'aads*

Vegetables

vegetables	*khudrawat*
potatoes	*batatas*
green beans	*fasooliya*
lentils	*'aads*
peas	*baseela*
cauliflower	*arnabeet*
cabbage	*kharoum, malfouf*
carrot	*jazar*
turnip	*lift*
okra	*baamiyya*
eggplant	*batinjan*

Salad

salad	*salata*
lettuce	*khass*
tomato	*tamatin, banadoura*
onion	*bassal*
garlic	*tuum*
cucumber	*khiyaar*

Meat

meat	*lahm*

lamb	*lahm danee*
camel	*lahm gamal*
chicken	*farooj*
liver	*kibda*
kidney	*kelawwi*

Desserts

mahalabiyya	*a milk pudding*
mahalabiyya wa festa	*same but with pistachio nuts*
baklawah	*multilayered flaky pastry with nuts drenched in honey*
kinaafa	*shredded wheat over goat cheese baked in syrup*
zalabiyya	*pastries dipped in rose-water*
booza	*ice cream*

Fruit

fruit	*fawaka*
apricot	*meesh-meesh*
apple	*tooffah*
orange	*burtuaan*
lime	*limuun*
banana	*mohz*
date	*tamr*
grape	*einab*
fig	*tiin*
pomegranate	*rumman*
watermelon	*batteekh*

Miscellaneous

salt	*milh*
pepper	*filfil*
bread	*khobz* or *eish*
eggs	*bayd*
cheese	*gibna*
sugar	*sukkar*
yoghurt	*laban*
butter	*zibda*

DRINK

Nonalcoholic Drinks

Tea & Coffee In the Middle East tea *(shay)* and coffee *(qahwa)* are drunk in copious quantities and are served strong.

Tea is served in small glasses, often with *na'ana* (mint), and is incredibly sweet unless you ask for only a little sugar *(shwayya sukkar)* or medium *(wassat)*. If you want no sugar at all, ask for it *bidoon sukkar* (without sugar), but it tastes bitter and has a strong tannin aftertaste.

Coffee is usually Turkish coffee in small cups and is also sweet. If you want less sugar ask for it *mazboota*; without sugar ask for *sada* (plain). It is very thick and muddy so let it settle a bit before drinking. Don't try and drink the last mouthful (which in cups this size is only about the second mouthful) because it's like drinking silt.

The traditional Arabic or Bedouin coffee is heavily laced with cardamom and drunk in cups without handles which hold only a mouthful. Served without sugar, it is poured from a silver or brass pot and your cup will be refilled until you make the proper gesture that you have had enough – hold the cup out and cover it with your hand. It is good etiquette to have at least three cups although you are unlikely to offend if you have less. Coffee is then followed by tea ad infinitum.

Western-style instant coffee is usually called Nescafé. It comes in a small packet with a cup of hot water and a jug of milk.

The Coffeehouse

The coffeehouse (in Arabic *qahwa*, the same word as for coffee; in Persian they're *chāykhūné*, or teahouse) is the great social institution of the Middle East. Or rather it is for around half the population – with very few exceptions, no Arabic woman would enter a qahwa. There's no reason, however, why a western women shouldn't, especially in the less staunchly Muslim countries like Egypt, Jordan, Lebanon and Syria.

Typically just a collection of battered chairs and tables in a sawdust-strewn room open to the street, the qahwa is a relaxed and unfussy place to meet locals who are often curious to question any *khwagas* (foreigners) who come and sit among them. Conversation is inevitably accompanied by the incessant clacking of slammed domino and backgammon pieces and the bubbling sound of smokers drawing hard on their nargilehs (the cumbersome water pipe, also known as a shisha). ■

Other Nonalcoholic Drinks Juice stalls selling delicious freshly squeezed fruit juices (*'aseer*) are quite common. Popular juices include lemon, orange, carrot, banana, pomegranate and rockmelon, and you can have combinations of any or all of these. Steer clear of the stalls which add milk to their drinks.

Other traditional drinks include *'ayran* (yoghurt and water mixed), which is tangy, refreshing and healthy. Another favourite, served hot in the winter, cold in the summer, is *sahlab* (*sahlep* or *salep* in Turkey). It is made up of sahlab powder (like tapioca), milk, coconut, sugar, raisins, chopped nuts, rose-water and a glacé cherry garnish (most cheap places will have simpler versions).

Soft drinks are popular and you'll find a few of the major brands, including Coca-Cola, Sport Cola, 7-Up, Fanta, Schweppes and Pepsi, in several countries in the Middle East.

Water Tap water may not be always safe to drink, but bottled mineral water, local and imported, is widely available.

Alcohol
Many Middle Eastern countries have several locally brewed alcoholic beverages, including beer (and nonalcoholic beer), wine (red, white and rosé) and *arak*, the indigenous firewater. It is similar to Turkish *raki* and, yes, the effect is the same. It is usually mixed with water and ice and drunk with food. The best arak is said to come from Lebanon.

In most larger cities and tourist resorts, you can find spirits and beer imported from all over the world.

Forget about alcohol in the more staunchly Muslim countries of the Gulf. Where it is available (in restaurants and bars attached to top-end hotels), it has been imported from the west and is sold at top-end prices. In dry countries such as Iran and Saudi Arabia, the punishment for possessing or drinking alcohol remains severe.

THINGS TO BUY
One of the highlights of the Middle East is the covered souqs and bazaars where anything can be found if you look long and hard enough. Nothing beats the excitement of the expedition up and down the back alleyways of the bazaars, past pungent barrels of basil and cloves from the spice stalls through to medieval caravanserais. Take your sense of humour and curiosity with you, and if you want to buy something, be prepared to bargain for it; it is expected.

The list of things to buy varies from country to country (see the individual country chapters), but it includes handicrafts; *kilims* (rugs) and carpets; pearls, silver and gold; cotton clothing including *kaffiyeh* (headscarves), *galabiyya* (long, loose robes worn by men), caftans and embroidered dresses; Bedouin woven bags; decorative daggers and swords; copperware and brassware; olive and cedar woodcarvings; bottles of coloured sand; kohl; silk scarves; inlaid backgammon boards and jewellery boxes; water pipes and meerschaum pipes; embroidered tablecloths and cushion covers; leather and suede material; frankincense and incense.

In addition there's a plethora of tacky souvenirs and kitsch, from Khomeini watches to hieroglyphic drawings.

At the other extreme are the duty-free shops of the UAE airports, reputed to be among the largest and cheapest in the world, where you'll find the latest in electronic goods and hi-tech gadgets.

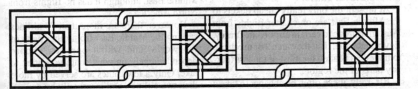

Getting There & Away

AIR

The Middle East has many hubs of global air travel that have for decades been transit points on many intercontinental routes. There is a huge number of flights with many different airlines from most major airports in Asia, Europe and Africa, a smaller number from North America and one from Australasia.

However, most of the Middle East is still seen primarily as a business destination and that fact is reflected in the relative expense of flying there. The situation may improve if the region picks up more tourists, but as yet the demand isn't there.

At present the only really cheap tickets to the Middle East are on charter flights from Western Europe to certain airports in Turkey, Egypt and Israel. But they aren't of much use to travellers headed for most of the less touristy parts of the region.

Bizarrely, it can often be cheaper to take a transcontinental flight involving a change of planes or a transit stop in the Middle East than to buy a ticket just to that place: this can be true even for tickets sold through the same travel agency and with the same airline. For example a London-Karachi ticket via Dubai may cost less than the cheapest available London-Dubai ticket. The catch is that the first ticket may not allow a stopover in Dubai, may restrict it to the return leg or may only allow it for an extra charge. There are many similar anomalies to puzzle you.

Airports & Airlines

Dubai is the Middle East's gateway airport *par excellence*. Not only does it handle more flights to/from the region than any other Middle Eastern airport, but it has the best connections within the region. Furthermore, it's the base of the Middle East's best airline, Emirates, and has a duty-free shop deservedly famous the world over. Some airlines have been known to advertise the fact that their flights make a transit stop there.

Other airports with a relatively large number of flights to/from the region include Bahrain, Riyadh, Jeddah, İstanbul and Cairo, but these aren't generally as good as Dubai for onward connections in the Middle East. Tel Aviv has many international connections, but is next to useless as a gateway to the rest of the Middle East. Even a ticket to/from Israel is enough to have you refused entry to many Muslim countries. However, this situation may change.

The airline with by far the most flights to and within the Middle East is Gulf Air; it's the only carrier flying from Australia to the Middle East, although it has no flights from North America.

However, there are more than 70 airlines serving the Middle East from other parts of the world, and which one you choose depends largely on what route you want to take. Only a few routes are served by more than two airlines, and many only by one.

Buying Tickets

The air ticket will probably be the single most expensive item in your budget, and buying it can be an intimidating business. There's likely to be a multitude of airlines and travel agents hoping to separate you from your money, and it's always worth putting aside a few hours to shop around. Start early: some of the cheapest tickets have to be bought months in advance, and some popular flights sell out early. Talk to other recent travellers: they may be able to stop you making some of the old mistakes. Look at the ads in newspapers and magazines (not forgetting the press of the ethnic group whose country you plan to visit), consult reference books and watch for special offers. The *OAG World Airways Guide* (formerly the *ABC World Airways Guide*) lists virtually all flights in the world and is invaluable for working out routes and which airlines serve them, directly or indirectly. It's kept at air travel agencies worldwide and some public libraries.

With this information you're at a great advantage if you want to find the cheapest available ticket to a given destination. Just telephone each airline serving your route and ask for the name of its consolidator (the travel agent which sells its discounted tickets through other travel agents or direct to the public). This will almost certainly quote you the cheapest fare available for that airline. If the airline doesn't have a consolidator, then it probably doesn't discount tickets at all.

You may decide to pay more than the rock-bottom fare by opting for the safety of a better known travel agent. Firms such as STA, which has offices worldwide, Council Travel in the USA or Travel CUTS in Canada aren't going to disappear overnight and offer good prices to most destinations.

If you're travelling from the UK or the USA, you may find that the cheapest flights are being advertised by obscure bucket shops whose names haven't yet reached the telephone directory. Many such firms are honest and solvent, but there are a few rogues who will take your money and disappear. If you feel suspicious about a firm, don't hand over all the money at once: leave a deposit of 20% or so and pay the balance when you get the ticket. If it insists on cash in advance, go somewhere else. Once you have the ticket, ring the airline to confirm that you're actually booked on the flight.

Find out the fare, the route, the duration of the journey and any restrictions on the ticket (see the Air Travel Glossary, later). Then sit back and decide which is best for you.

Airlines can supply information on routes and timetables. However, except at times of interairline war, they almost never supply the cheapest tickets. The cheapest official excursion fare is just a useful starting point. One rare exception is the Syrian Arab Airlines office in London, which even undercuts its own consolidator on some fares.

You may discover that those impossibly cheap flights are 'fully booked, but we have another one that costs a bit more', or the flight is on an airline notorious for its poor safety standards and leaves you in the world's least favourite airport in mid-journey for 14 hours. Or that the agency claims to have the last two seats available for the whole of July, which it will hold for you for a maximum of two hours. Don't panic: keep ringing around.

All this homework is likely to be wasted, however, if you're buying a ticket in a country with strict regulations on what airlines are allowed to charge. The market is slowly opening up around the world, but there are still plenty of countries where the fare the airline office quotes is the only one available. You can often get around this problem by buying your tickets all in one go at a bucket shop somewhere else in the world, but sometimes it's just impossible to get a discount on some routes wherever you buy the ticket.

Use the fares quoted in this book as a guide only. They are approximate and based on those advertised by travel agents at the time of writing. Quoted airfares don't necessarily constitute a recommendation for the carrier.

Once you have your ticket, write its number down, together with the flight number and other details, and keep the information somewhere separate. If the ticket is lost or stolen, this will help you get a replacement.

It's sensible to buy travel insurance as early as possible. If you buy it the week before you fly, you may find, for example, that you're not covered for delays to your flight caused by industrial action.

Round-the-World Tickets

Round-the-World (RTW) tickets have become very popular in the past few years.

The airline RTW tickets are often bargains, and can work out no more expensive or even cheaper than ordinary round-trip tickets.

The official airline RTW tickets are usually put together by a combination of two airlines, and permit you to fly anywhere you want on their route systems so long as you do not backtrack. Other restrictions are that you usually must book the first sector in advance and cancellation penalties then apply. There may be restrictions on how

Air Travel Glossary

Apex Tickets Apex, or 'advance purchase excursion' is a discounted ticket that must be paid for in advance. There are penalties if you wish to change it.

Baggage Allowance This will be written on your ticket; usually one 20 kg item to go in the hold, plus one item of hand luggage.

Bucket Shops An unbonded travel agency specialising in discounted airline tickets.

Bumped Just because you have a confirmed seat doesn't mean you're going to get on the plane – see Overbooking.

Cancellation Penalties If you have to cancel or change an Apex or other discount ticket, there may be heavy penalties involved; insurance can sometimes be taken out against these penalties. Some airlines impose penalties on regular tickets as well, particularly against 'no show' passengers.

Check In Airlines ask you to check in a certain time ahead of the flight departure (usually two hours on international flights). If you fail to check in on time and the flight is overbooked, the airline can cancel your booking and give your seat to somebody else.

Confirmation Having a ticket written out with the flight and date on it doesn't mean you have a seat until the agent has confirmed with the airline that your status is 'OK'. Prior to this confirmation, your status is 'on request'.

Courier Fares Businesses often need to send their urgent documents or freight securely and quickly. They do it through courier companies. These companies hire people to accompany the package through customs and, in return, offer a discount ticket which is sometimes a phenomenal bargain. In effect, what the courier companies do is ship their freight as your luggage on the regular commercial flights. This is a legitimate operation – all freight is completely legal. There are two shortcomings, however: the short turnaround time of the ticket, usually not longer than a month; and the limitation on your luggage allowance. You may be required to surrender all your baggage allowance for the use of the courier company, and be only allowed to take carry-on luggage.

Discounted Tickets There are two types of discounted fares – officially discounted (such as Apex – see Promotional Fares) and unofficially discounted (see Bucket Shops). The latter can save you more than money – you may be able to pay Apex prices without the associated Apex advance booking and other requirements. The lowest prices often impose drawbacks, such as flying with unpopular airlines, inconvenient schedules, or unpleasant routes and connections.

Economy Class Tickets Economy-class tickets are usually not the cheapest way to go, though they do give you maximum flexibility and they are valid for 12 months. If you don't use them, most are fully refundable, as are unused sectors of a multiple ticket.

Full Fare Airlines traditionally offer first class (coded F), business class (coded J) and economy class (coded Y) tickets. These days there are so many promotional and discounted fares available that few passengers pay full fare.

Lost Tickets If you lose your airline ticket, an airline will usually treat it like a travellers' cheque and, after inquiries, issue you with a replacement. Legally, however, an airline is entitled to treat it like cash, so if you lose a ticket, it could be forever. Take good care of your tickets.

MCO An MCO (Miscellaneous Charges Order) is a voucher for a value of a given amount, which resembles an airline ticket and can be used to pay for a specific flight with any IATA (International Air Transport Association) airline. MCOs, which are more flexible than a regular ticket, may satisfy the many stops you are permitted and usually the tickets are valid from 90 days up to a year.

One official RTW ticket that includes the Middle East is with Gulf Air between London and Melbourne or Sydney with one stopover in either Bahrain or Muscat and two stopovers in Asia. The only condition is that you have to exit Asia by Singapore to get to Australia. From the UK the ticket costs from UK£659 to UK£1045, with the lowest fare being for departures between April and June, the highest for departures around Christmas.

An alternative type of RTW ticket is put together by a travel agent using a combination of discounted tickets. This can be cheaper than an airline RTW ticket but there may be less choice of routes. As it's difficult to find discounts on flights within the Middle East, an RTW ticket of this kind with a few stopovers in the region will probably be a lot more expensive than a ticket with one

irritating onward ticket requirement, but some countries are now reluctant to accept them. MCOs are fully refundable if unused.

No Shows No shows are passengers who fail to show up for their flight for whatever reason. Full-fare no shows are sometimes entitled to travel on a later flight. The rest of us are penalised (see Cancellation Penalties).

Open Jaw Tickets These are return tickets which allow you to fly to one place but return from another, and travel between the two 'jaws' by any means of transport at your own expense. If available, this can save you backtracking to your arrival point.

Overbooking Airlines hate to fly with empty seats, and since every flight has some passengers who fail to show up (see No Shows), they often book more passengers than they have seats available. Usually the excess passengers balance those who fail to show up, but occasionally somebody gets bumped. If this happens, guess who it is most likely to be? The passengers who check in late.

Promotional Fares These are officially discounted fares, such as Apex fares, which are available from travel agents or direct from the airline.

Reconfirmation You must contact the airline at least 72 hours prior to departure to 'reconfirm' that you intend to be on the flight. If you don't do this, the airline can delete your name from the passenger list and you could lose your seat.

Restrictions Discounted tickets often have various restrictions on them, such as necessity of advance purchase, limitations on the minimum and maximum period you must be away, restrictions on breaking the journey or changing the booking or route etc.

Standby This is a discounted ticket where you only fly if there is a seat free at the last moment. Standby fares are usually only available directly at the airport, but sometimes may also be handled by an airline's city office. To give yourself the best possible chance of getting on the flight you want, get there early and have your name placed on the waiting list. It's first come, first served.

Student Discounts Some airlines offer student-card holders 15% to 25% discounts on their tickets. The same often applies to anyone under the age of 26. These discounts are generally only available on ordinary economy-class fares. You wouldn't get one, for instance, on an Apex or a RTW ticket, since these are already discounted.

Tickets Out An entry requirement for many countries is that you have an onward or return ticket, in other words, a ticket out of the country. If you're not sure what you intend to do next, the easiest solution is to buy the cheapest onward ticket to a neighbouring country or a ticket from a reliable airline which can later be refunded if you do not use it.

Transferred Tickets Airline tickets cannot be transferred from one person to another. Travellers sometimes try to sell the return half of their ticket, but officials can ask you to prove that you are the person named on the ticket. This may not be checked on domestic flights, but on international flights, tickets are usually compared with passports.

Travel Periods Some officially discounted fares, Apex fares in particular, vary with the time of year. There is often a low (off-peak) season and a high (peak) season. Sometimes there's an intermediate or shoulder season as well. At peak times, when everyone wants to fly, both officially and unofficially discounted fares will be higher, or there may simply be no discounted tickets available. Usually the fare depends on your outward flight – if you depart in the high season and return in the low season, you pay the high-season fare.

stopover. But one stopover will probably allow you plenty of time to visit other parts of the region by land or sea. A customised RTW ticket may also be the only affordable option if you want to include Africa or South America in your plans.

Travellers with Special Needs

If you have special needs of any sort – you've broken a leg, you're vegetarian, eat only kosher or halal food, travelling in a wheel-chair, taking the baby, terrified of flying – you should let the airline know as soon as possible so that they can make arrangements accordingly. You should remind them when you reconfirm your booking (at least 72 hours before departure) and again when you check in at the airport. It may also be worth ringing round the airlines before you make your booking to find out how they can handle your particular needs.

Airports and airlines can be surprisingly helpful, but they do need warning. Most international airports will provide escorts from check-in desk to plane where needed, and there should be ramps, lifts, accessible toilets and reachable phones. Aircraft toilets, on the other hand, are likely to present a problem; travellers should discuss this with the airline at an early stage and, if necessary, with their doctor.

Guide dogs for the blind will often have to travel in a specially pressurised baggage compartment with other animals, away from their owner, though smaller guide dogs may be admitted to the cabin. All guide dogs will be subject to the same quarantine laws (six months in isolation, etc) as any other animal when entering or returning to countries currently free of rabies, such as Britain or Australia.

Deaf travellers can ask for airport and in-flight announcements to be written down for them.

Children under two travel for 10% of the standard fare (or free, on some airlines), as long as they don't occupy a seat. They don't get a baggage allowance either. 'Skycots' should be provided by the airline if requested in advance; these will take a child weighing up to about 10 kg. Children between two and 12 can usually occupy a seat for half to two-thirds of the full fare, and do get a baggage allowance. Push chairs can often be taken as hand luggage.

North America

From Montreal and Toronto Air Canada and Royal Jordanian fly twice weekly to Amman, and El Al flies three times a week to Tel Aviv. There are more flights from the USA, but still not that many. Royal Jordanian flies New York-Amman five times a week and Chicago-Amman twice weekly. EgyptAir flies between New York and Cairo four times a week and Los Angeles and Cairo once a week. Other New York-Cairo flights are run by Trans World. To/from Israel, you can choose from El Al's Tel Aviv links with New York and Los Angeles and Trans World's New York-Tel Aviv flights. PIA flies New York-Damascus once a week. Saudia services operate to/from Jeddah and Riyadh, linking with both New York and Washington. Kuwait Airways flies between New York and Kuwait City three times per week.

As well as these direct flights there are connections with changes for other Middle Eastern airports from various cities in North America. The cheapest way to get from North America to the Middle East by air might be to fly to London and buy a ticket from a bucket shop there, but this would depend on the fare to London and the time spent in London waiting for a flight out.

The *New York Times*, the *Los Angeles Times*, the *Chicago Tribune* and the *San Francisco Examiner* all produce weekly travel sections filled with travel agents' ads. Council Travel and STA Travel have offices in main US cities.

The magazine *Travel Unlimited* (PO Box 1058, Allston, MA 02134) publishes details of the cheapest air fares and courier possibilities for destinations all over the world from the USA.

Travel CUTS has offices in main Canadian cities. The *Toronto Globe & Mail* and the *Vancouver Sun* carry travel agents' ads. The magazine *Great Expeditions* (PO Box

8000-411, Abbotsford, BC V2S 6H1) is also useful.

Australasia

There are no longer tight constraints on ticket discounting in Australia, but for Australians and New Zealanders there are very few route options to the Middle East. Gulf Air flies four times per week from Melbourne and Sydney to Bahrain, and Middle East Airline (MEA) flies between Sydney and Beirut once a week. The Sydney-Bahrain flight takes about 17 hours. Gulf Air's RTW fare could be good value if you also want to visit London and stop over in Asia.

Alternatively you could fly to Hong Kong, Bombay or Karachi and proceed by land from there. There are also plenty of connections with changes for Abu Dhabi, Amman, Beirut, Cairo, Damascus, Dhahran, Doha, Dubai, İstanbul, Jeddah, Kuwait, Muscat and Riyadh with various combinations of the following airlines: Alitalia, British Airways, Royal Brunei Airlines, Cathay Pacific, Emirates, Garuda, Gulf Air, Kuwait Airways, Malaysian Airlines, EgyptAir, Olympic Airways, PIA, Philippine Airlines, Qantas, Syrian Arab Airlines, Royal Jordanian, Singapore Airlines, Aeroflot, Saudia, Thai Airways International, Turkish Airlines and Air Lanka.

Possibilities for discounts are with Aeroflot on its Sydney-Moscow-Beirut and Sydney-Moscow-İstanbul connections (all involving changes). Another possibility is with Philippine Airlines from Sydney or Brisbane to Riyadh via Manila. Emirates is planning to start flights from Sydney to Dubai.

From New Zealand the only regular connections with changes for the Middle East are from Auckland to Cairo via Bangkok with Air New Zealand and EgyptAir, to Dubai with Cathay Pacific via Hong Kong and to İstanbul via Bangkok or Singapore with Air New Zealand and Turkish Airlines.

In both Australia and New Zealand, STA and Flight Centres International are big dealers in cheap air fares. Check the travel agents' ads in the Yellow Pages and ring around. Fares start at A$1650 in the low season.

Europe

You can get to the Middle East on direct flights from almost any European city of any size. London has the greatest number of flights there, closely followed by Frankfurt.

Fares from London are often cheaper than from other European cities. Following is a sample of some of the cheapest high and low season single/round-trip fares to the Middle East. Low-season (generally October to June) prices are mostly around 12% lower than the high-season rates.

Unique Tours (☎ (0171) 495 4848):
    San'a £225/390 (high season)
    Sharjah £225/385 (high season)
    Tehrān £240/390 (high season)
Syrian Arab Airlines (☎ (0171) 493 2851):
    Aleppo £208/301 (high season; 2 month return)
Nouvelles Frontières (☎ (0171) 629 7772):
    Amman £210/240 (low season)
    Bahrain £242/341 (low season)
    Cairo £210/240 (low season)
    Damascus £210/240 (low season)
    Dubai £252/348 (low season)
    İstanbul £204/216 (low season)
    Tel Aviv £210/240 (low season)
Bright Sun Travel (☎ (0171) 287 4949):
    Damascus £240/330
Green Island Holidays (☎ (0171) 637 7338):
    İzmir £129/207 (low season)
Eastman Travel (☎ (0171) 433 3177):
    Muscat £225/435 (high season)

London and Amsterdam have countless bucket shops selling tickets to almost any conceivable part of the world. However, shops specialising in fares to the Middle East are pretty thin on the ground and even these often don't advertise their services or prices. In the UK the Air Travel Advisory Bureau (☎ (0171) 636 5000) will give the names of agencies offering cheap tickets to virtually any destination. One reputable budget agency is Trailfinders (☎ (0171) 938 3366), 42-50 Earls Court Rd, London W8 6FT. It's particularly recommended for tailor-made RTW tickets or any other complicated routings. The useful travel newspaper *Trailfinder* is available through its office. One reliable bucket shop specialising in flights to and via the Middle East is Skylord Travel (☎ (0171) 439 3521), 2 Denmark St, London W1V 7RH.

Most British travel agents are registered with the Association of British Travel Agents (ABTA). If you have bought a ticket from an ABTA-registered agent who then goes out of business, ABTA will guarantee a refund or an alternative. Unregistered bucket shops are riskier but sometimes cheaper.

The cheapest fares from Western Europe to the Middle East are often with Aeroflot or Tarom for flights connecting in Moscow or Bucharest, although they don't serve every Middle Eastern country. Some other Eastern European airlines also offer generous discounts on tickets to the Middle East sold through agents.

From Germany and the UK there are also many charter flights to resort towns in Turkey, Egypt and Israel. Usually these cater for package tour groups, but often spare seats will be sold off at short notice to the public. In summer, especially, you may be able to find some very good deals if you're fairly flexible about your travel plans. Look out for last-minute ads posted outside travel agencies. For cheap tickets on both charter and scheduled flights also check the travel pages in local and national newspapers, but don't treat the fares quoted as gospel.

The Belgian newsletter for 'passionate travellers', *Farang* (☎ (019) 699823), La Rue 8, 4261 Braives, Belgium, deals with remote destinations. So does the French club, Aventure du Bout du Monde (☎ 01 43 35 08 95), 7 Rue Gasande, 75014 Paris.

Some of the best deals from Amsterdam or Brussels are offered by the student travel agency NBBS Reiswinkels (☎ (020) 624 09 89), Roskin 38, Amsterdam; and Acotra (☎ 5127078), Rue de la Madeline 51, 1000 Brussels. Their fares to Cairo and some other Middle Eastern destinations are comparable with those from London bucket shops.

Athens is another place with thriving bucket shops. Agencies around the Plaka and Syntagma Square offer the best available fares. If you're headed for Egypt a bus trip to Athens and a cheap flight from there to Cairo will work out quite a lot cheaper than a flight from elsewhere in Europe. Agencies in Athens recommended by travellers include Fantasy Travel at 10 Xenofontas St (near Syntagma Square), Speedy Ways Travel Agency; and Lin Travel (☎ 322 1237), at 39 Nikis St, Syntagma.

Across Western Europe many travel agencies have ties with STA, where you can buy cheap tickets and alter STA tickets free of charge (once only). Outlets in main transport hubs include CTS Voyages (☎ 01 25 00 76), 20 Rue des Carmes, Paris; SRID Reisen (☎ (069) 430 191), Berger Str 118, Frankfurt; and ISYTS (☎ 322 1267), 2nd floor, 11 Odos Nikis, Syntagma, Athens.

Bucket shops have yet to spread to Eastern Europe, although strangely tickets from Western Europe to the Middle East routed via Eastern Europe are often the cheapest available. Some of these do, however, allow you to stop over at little or no extra cost.

Africa
You can fly directly to the Middle East from 29 airports in 24 African countries (excluding Egypt), but the budget possibilities are somewhat slender. Unfortunately it's difficult to avoid flying at least once if you're going from Africa to the Middle East.

By far the greatest number of flights are from Khartoum. Although you're unlikely to find any discounted tickets in Khartoum itself, Sudan Airways is known for cheap fares on flights via Khartoum: you can look for discounts from other African countries served by it. Aeroflot may offer special deals to the Middle East via Moscow from some places in Africa. There are now flights from Johannesburg to Abu Dhabi, Cairo and Tel Aviv, but there isn't much discounting on these.

Nairobi is reputed to be the best place in Africa for discounted air fares, although most of these are to Europe; you may have to search hard to find much on offer to the Middle East. Bucket shops in Nairobi sell one-way Emirates and Gulf Air tickets to

Dubai (US$440), Doha (US$440), Jeddah (US$370), San'a (US$270) and Aden (US$270).These shops may also have special deals via Cairo to other places in the Middle East You can also probably get a good deal on PIA flights from Nairobi to Karachi via Dubai, or just to Dubai.

Now that Ethiopia has reopened to tourism, one reasonably inexpensive land and air combination would be to travel through the country to Djibouti and fly from there to Ta'izz or Aden.

India & Pakistan

Apart from Western Europe, the Indian subcontinent has the greatest concentration of flights to the Middle East. Although there are more flights to the Middle East from Bombay and Karachi, Delhi is the best place on the subcontinent to buy cheap tickets. You're unlikely to find much of a discount on tickets to Turkey or Iran, however. Probably the best bargain is with Aeroflot from Delhi to Cairo via Moscow, but you may also be able to find cheap tickets to Dubai, Jeddah and some other places. Tickets to Africa or Europe via the Middle East are another possibility, although you'll probably find that a stopover costs extra.

If you're headed for the Arab Gulf States, the cheapest flight is with Pakistan International Airways (PIA) from Gwadar to Muscat, at US$103/195 for single/round trip. This, together with a domestic ticket from Karachi to Gwadar costing about US$50 is much cheaper than a direct Karachi-Muscat flight (US$283/412). However, a major detraction of the cheaper fare is that these two flights do not connect, and accommodation in Gwadar is scarce.

Asia

Hong Kong, Bangkok and Singapore are Asia's main centres for bucket shops and they also have direct flights and transfer connections to the Middle East, although Hong Kong has rather fewer than the others. Manila and Kuala Lumpur also have a fair number of flights but are not as good for buying cheap tickets. Tokyo has very few

and is in any case a hopeless place to find discounts.

In Singapore you may find the best direct deals are to/from Dubai with Aeroflot. From Bangkok try Emirates, Thai Airways International or Royal Brunei. From Hong Kong the only direct flights are to Dubai with Emirates and Cathay Pacific, and to Abu Dhabi, Bahrain and Muscat with Gulf Air. To/from Dubai you may find cheaper flights on transfer connections via Colombo with Air Lanka or via Bombay with Air India.

Bucket shops in Asia are at least as unreliable as those elsewhere: ask the advice of other travellers before buying a ticket. A reliable Hong Kong agency for budget travel is Hong Kong Student Travel Bureau, at Room 1021 Star House, Tsimshatsui, Kowloon (☎ 2730 3269), or Wing On Central Bldg Room 901 , 26 Des Voeux Rd, Central (☎ 2810 7272), plus half a dozen other branches in the colony.

STA has branches in Bangkok (☎ 233 2582), Singapore (☎ 734 5681), Kuala Lumpur (☎ 2305720) and Tokyo (☎ 5391 2922).

Transcaucasia & Central Asia

There are a small but rapidly growing number of flights from Transcaucasia and Central Asia to Tehrān, İstanbul and some other Middle Eastern airports. At present there are flights to the Middle East from Almaty, Ashghabad, Baku, Sochi, Tashkent, Tbilisi, Urumqi and Yerevan. These can be a lot more straightforward than going by land on the same routes.

There are regular flights between İstanbul and Almaty (Turkish Airlines; three times a week), Bishkek (Kyrgyzstan Airlines; twice weekly), Baku (Turkish Airlines; three times a week) and Tashkent (Uzbekistan Airways; twice weekly). There are also daily İstanbul-Ashghabad flights on Turkmenistan Airlines for US$600 return.

Other Middle Eastern flights out of Ashghabad with Turkmenistan Airlines are to Abu Dhabi (three times a week), and Damascus (once a weekend). There is a flight once a week to Mashhad, Iran, for

US$70 one way. There is also an Iran Air flight between Tehrān-Ashghabad each Tuesday (US$305 return).

Uzbekistan Airways flies from Tashkent to Tel Aviv once or twice a week, Bahrain and Sharjah two or three times a week, and Jeddah weekly.

There are irregular charter connections from Dushanbe, Tajikstan, to Aleppo and Abu Dhabi, mainly for small-time importers and smugglers. They fly out of Dushanbe half empty but return overloaded with cargo; generally there is space only on flights *out* of Tajikstan; contact Intourist at the Hotel Tajikistan (☎ (3772) 21 68 92; fax 21 52 36).

Leaving the Middle East

Buying cheap tickets from the Middle East isn't easy. Usually the best deal you can get is an airline's official excursion fare, and no discount on single tickets unless you qualify for a youth or student fare. Some travel agencies in the Middle East will knock the price down by up to 10% if you're persistent, but may then tie you into fixed dates or flying with a less popular airline. Or, if you pay the full fare, there may be a perk like free connecting domestic flights. If you're paying the full fare, you might as well choose the airline you prefer and go straight to its booking office.

The nearest thing you'll find to a discount ticket market in the Middle East is offered by some travel agencies in Israel, particularly in Tel Aviv, and in İstanbul, especially around Taksim Square and in Sultanahmet. However, in both cases they only usually offer much of a discount on tickets to Western Europe and North America, not to other parts of the world. You'll do much better in Athens.

Of course it's best to leave the Middle East on a return ticket or as a stopover destination from some other part of the world where you can buy discounted tickets.

LAND

Regardless of your budget, you will probably appreciate being in the Middle East more if you go there by land and have a chance to take in the cultures of neighbouring countries.

There are still plenty of possibilities – more than might first meet the eye – and several new ones have opened up in recent years, especially since the collapse of the USSR. At the same time a few have become somewhat more difficult.

For some years the most usual overland routes to the Middle East have been through the Balkans into İstanbul or, coming from the east, through Pakistan entering Iran at the border post near Zāhedān. Both offer a choice between going by rail, taking a bus or driving one's own vehicle. The two are frequently combined.

If you travel the route through Turkey, you must take into account the longstanding conflict between the Turkish armed forces and the PKK Kurdish guerillas. Fighting breaks out in different locations in the east and south-east of the country. It's impossible to predict exactly where it may occur, but it is usually in villages and towns off the main highway.

Overall, it is not a significant threat to travellers who follow a few simple rules: travel during daylight hours, stay on main roads (or railways), and keep to major destinations (ie, don't go exploring in the villages and mountains of the south-east). It looks like safety will gradually improve as time goes on; that has been the trend recently.

Routes through Turkey to Syria are normal, with no special danger; to Iran via Doğubeyazıt the danger is minimal, though the road via Hakkari and Esendere should be avoided. The road to Iraq via Cizre, Silopi, Habur and Zakhu must be avoided, however, as this area is very sensitive due to operations supporting the 'Kurdish safe haven' in northern Iraq.

Until the Soviet invasion of Afghanistan in 1979, the most popular route with westbound travellers was through the Khyber Pass from Peshawar to Jalalabad, west to Kabul and on through Herat into Mashhad in Iran. However, because of the continuing turmoil, at present Afghanistan is issuing visas only to aid workers and journalists.

Entering from almost any part of Africa is difficult, dangerous or both, depending on the route, but it's still possible to get all the way from southern Africa to Egypt without taking a single flight. Most people give up or don't even try, however.

It's important to seek consular advice before attempting any of the following routes.

Transcaucasia

Georgia To travel to Georgia, you must first obtain a visa from the Georgian consulate in Trabzon. A bus to Batumi departs Trabzon's Russian bazaar at 7 pm daily, but it arrives in Batumi in the middle of the night. You may prefer to take a morning minibus to Rize or Hopa and pick up another one heading for the border at Sarp (US$5 in all). On the other side of the border taxis will be waiting for you to Batumi (US$10). Ask to be dropped near the railway station.

Armenia Two trains daily run out to the Armenian border at Doğu Kapı. See the Turkey chapter for more details.

No safe land route exists between Armenia and Iran. Check with Yerevan's Iranian embassy or Tehrān's Russian embassy before making this trip.

Azerbaijan Two border posts between Azerbaijan and Iran are open. The road crossing point is at Astara on the Caspian coast, 220 km south-south-west of Baku and 68 km north-east of Ardabīl. Supposedly one train a day links Baku and Astara. From Astara savaris and minibuses run to Ardabīl and Rasht (190 km). This route can be used by independent motorists. Only people from the immediate region may cross between Julfa and Jolfā by road. Everyone else must go by train.

Check with Baku's Iranian embassy or Tehrān's Russian embassy before making this trip. It may be safer to fly or take the ferry.

Central Asia

Turkmenistan Although there is a regular bus service between Mashhad in north-eastern Iran and the Turkmen capital, Ashghabat, it is not allowed for independent travellers to cross the land border between Iran and Turkmenistan. In 1996 a link from Mashhad to the Turkmen railway network was opened but, at least initially, there are no passenger services operating on this line.

The Turkmenistan-Afghanistan border post of Kushka can be reached by train from Ashghabat (one train a day) but it's in a military exclusion zone, and even those in possession of an Afghan visa will also require special travel permission from the Turkmen Foreign Ministry.

Uzbekistan For anyone able to get a visa, it's possible to enter Afghanistan by road from the Uzbek railhead of Termez, linked daily with Tashkent (US$18) and also a brief halt for the daily Moscow-Dushanbe service (US$76 to Moscow). All three of these trains also stop in Samarkand (US$13).

Tajikistan The whole length of Tajikistan's Afghanistan border is a Russian-patrolled military exclusion zone and no civilian crossing is permitted.

China

No legal way exists of crossing the Chinese-Afghan border.

Pakistan

There is a weekly express service between Quetta and Zāhedān, leaving Quetta early on Saturday afternoon, and Zāhedān on Monday morning. It takes about 28 hours, including formalities at the Pakistani border post of Taftan (Kuh-i-Taftan) and the Iranian one of Mīrjāvé. A second (regular) service goes only to/from the border, leaving Quetta early on Tuesday morning or Taftan on Wednesday afternoon, taking about 22 hours. The fare is Rs 403/112 in 1st/2nd class between Quetta and Taftan, 590 rials in 1st class between Mīrjāvé and Zāhedān.

The express train has 1st-class sleeper accommodation only, and in either direction you have to buy a fresh ticket in local currency at the border. There's also a Rs 10 fare between Taftan and Mīrjāvé. Eastbound passengers can reserve a sleeper out of Zāhedān on ☎ (0541) 26024.

Alternatively, you can take a long, dusty and unpleasant bus trip between Quetta and Taftan for around Rs 85, with several departures daily. Westbound buses leave from the New Quetta bus station, Sariab Rd. Frequent buses also link Mīrjāvé and Zāhedān, a two hour trip costing foreigners an outrageous 3000 rials plus baggage charges.

Check current timetables before you head for the border. Expect to spend at least four hours in Taftan, a depressing fly-blown smugglers' den that is as hot as an oven in summer. Don't even think about spending the night here.

Take food and drink however you go. Those driving their own vehicles through the interior of Pakistani Baluchistan should go in a convoy for safety. Roadside facilities are scant; people travelling between India and Europe in their own transport often describe this as the worst leg of their journey. It's advisable to check present conditions with Zāhedān's Pakistani consulate or Quetta's Iranian consulate before setting out. If in doubt follow the railway line. See Lonely Planet's *Iran* and *Pakistan* for important details.

North Africa

Although it's fairly straightforward to get to Egypt from its African neighbours – Libya and Sudan – the problem is in getting to either of these countries in the first place. As war-torn south and west Sudan are off limits to foreigners, few overland travellers even try to enter it from any other country but Egypt. It may be safe and relatively easy to cross from Ethiopia, depending on the situation locally: you should take consular advice before making any plans. For more details see Lonely Planet's *Africa on a shoestring*.

Libya There are direct buses running daily between Cairo and Benghazi (20 hours) and twice weekly between Cairo and Tripoli (Tarabulus; 36 hours). You can also get buses

to the same destinations from Alexandria, and fares from here tend to be slightly cheaper. A more laborious but even cheaper alternative would be to get local transport to Sallum and a service taxi to the border. From there you can get Libyan transport heading west. Information about buses and service taxis from the border can be found in the Sallum section of the Egypt chapter.

Sudan It's theoretically possible to travel overland between Sudan and Egypt, but not very practical unless you have your own 4WD, or fancy joining a camel caravan, as no public transport by land exists between the two countries. However, it's extremely unwise to attempt any of these at the present in view of the deteriorating relationship between Egypt and Sudan.

The Balkans

Greece Relations between Greece and Turkey have never been good and crossing from one to the other can be a harrowing experience. However, a relatively large proportion of overlanders do still enter or leave the Middle East through their mutual frontier.

Bus Buses to İstanbul via Thessaloniki depart from Athens' Peloponese railway station several times daily. The journey takes about 22 hours from Athens – slightly less than the train and a somewhat more pleasant prospect. Try to book your seat a day ahead. Varan Turizm (☎ (01) 513 5768) runs services daily as does Ulusoy (☎ (01) 524 0519; fax 524 3290). Check with Magic Bus (☎ 323 7471), Fileninon 20, Athens, for student discounts.

Train This is a must for masochists. Greece's sole rail link with Turkey is the daily Thessaloniki-İstanbul service. Although it's an overnight international journey, only 2nd class seats are available. The train leaves İstanbul late in the evening, arriving in Thessaloniki late in the afternoon the next day, and Athens very late in the evening. From Athens the train leaves at breakfast time, arrives in Thessaloniki after lunch and gets to İstanbul at breakfast time the next morning. Although the 1400 km trip is supposed to take 24 hours, delays of more than five or six hours at the border are common, especially on the eastbound leg, and the train can get uncomfortably crowded. If you're coming from or heading for Athens, you'll have to change at Thessaloniki.

Car & Motorcycle The two Greek road border posts with Turkey are at Kastanies and Kipi. If you're lucky you may get through in an hour or two.

Hitching Although many travellers hitch-hike, it is not a totally safe way of getting around. Just because we explain how hitching works doesn't mean we recommend it.

From Greece, the main road goes to Kastanies and Pazarkule (Turkey), seven km south-west of Edirne on the Meriç River, two km past the Turkish village of Kraağaç to a border post originally meant to serve the railway line. You'll probably have to take a Greek taxi (US$6; two minutes) to the actual border, which is halfway across the one-km-wide neutral territory separating the two border posts. On the Turkish side, you can walk to or from Pazarkule. From Pazarkule, or from the nearby railway station, you'll probably have to take a Turkish taxi (US$5; 15 minutes) into town as there's little traffic and hitching isn't too easy, though you may be lucky.

If you're crossing from Turkey, do so as soon after 9 am as possible in order to catch one of the few buses or fewer trains from Kastanies heading south to Alexandroupolis.

Bulgaria Relations aren't good between Bulgaria and Turkey, but with Greece now somewhat out on a limb as far as land communications are concerned, many more travellers are entering Turkey from Bulgaria.

Bus There are direct buses to İstanbul from Sofia and, at least in summer, from some other places in Bulgaria.

Train The İstanbul Express, from Munich, and the Balkan Express, from Budapest, both link Sofia and İstanbul via Plovdiv, taking around 15 hours. Westbound, it may be cheaper to buy a ticket only as far as the Turkish border town Kapıkule and then pay the additional fare into Bulgaria on the train itself. In Bulgaria, tickets can be bought at any Rila railway ticket office.

Car & Motorcycle Bulgaria's main road crossing point with Turkey, open 24 hours a day, is at Kapitan-Andreevo on the E5 road from Svilengrad; over the fence lies the Turkish border post of Kapıkule, 18 km west of Edirne. The second is at Malko Tarnova, 92 km south of Burgas. Motorists in transit through Bulgaria may only be allowed to cross at Kapitan-Andreevo, depending on the current regulations.

Hitching A cheaper option is to catch a domestic train to Svilengrad and take a bus or taxi or hitch the 14 km from here to Kapitan-Andreevo. You may not be allowed to walk to the border on the Bulgarian side; you may be required to hitch a lift or hire a taxi. After the formalities, you enter the Turkish town of Kapıkule by crossing the river Tunca at the Gazi Mihal Bridge and passing some fragments of Byzantine city walls. City bus No 1 runs from Kapıkule to the centre of Edirne; there are dolmuşes on this route as well, but both are infrequent in early morning and late at night. It's also easy to enter Bulgaria this way, although the Bulgarian taxi drivers will probably want hard currency.

The Rest of Europe

All direct bus and train services from Europe to the Middle East terminate at İstanbul. It's still fairly easy to get to İstanbul by train or bus, at least indirectly, from most parts of Europe without a great deal of planning or difficulty. Many parts of the former Yugoslavia are still safe for foreigners, but it's advisable to find out from consular sources which these are before going there. Alternatively one can avoid it altogether by following a less direct route through Hungary, Romania and Bulgaria. For more details on the following routes see Lonely Planet's shoestring guides to Eastern Europe and Mediterranean Europe.

Bus As yet no scheduled bus services from Europe serve any Middle Eastern destination other than İstanbul.

Turkish scams on buses to Europe have been part of travellers' lore for many years. Two favourite tricks are selling tickets for fictitious connecting services and running buses which don't have the correct documentation to enter a particular country. If you ask for a ticket to Timbuktu or Ulan Bator, you'll no doubt find some unscrupulous operator only too happy to sell you a ticket on its nonexistent service there. By the time you find out that the company isn't going to take you to the place you've paid for, it's too late to do anything. However, such scams are only likely to be an issue with buses run by Turkish carriers from İstanbul, not with those to İstanbul from other parts of Europe or for buses run by foreign companies from İstanbul.

Buses to İstanbul run from many European cities. One of the main operators from Western Europe is Eurolines, which sells tickets through various agencies. Two of the best Turkish companies – Ulusoy and Varan – operate big Mercedes buses on European routes and are also reliable. For details get in touch with the bookings office of any international bus station or any travel agency dealing in bus tickets.

During the summer there are regular bus services to İstanbul from the following cities: Bucharest, Tirana, Rome and Turin, Bregenz, Graz, Innsbruck, Salzburg, Vienna and Wiener Neustadt in Austria, several German cities, Paris and Strasbourg in France, Basel and Zurich in Switzerland, Amsterdam, Brussels and London (other towns are also linked). Sample one-way fares to İstanbul are US$175 from Frankfurt, US$155 from Munich and US$110 from Vienna. Round-trip fares are discounted about 20%. Ask about student, youth or child

discounts. Addresses of some of the companies running these services follow.

Austria
    Varan Turizm, Kaiserschutzen Str 12, 5020 Salzburg (☎ & fax (662) 87 50 68)
    Varan Turizm, Adamgasse 9A, 8020 Innsbruck (☎ & fax (512) 57 53 78)
Germany
    Ulusoy Turizm, Deutsche Touring GmbH, Römerhof 17, 60486 Frankfurt (☎ (069) 79 03 50; fax 70 47 14)
    Ulusoy Turizm, Deutsche Touring Stadtbüro, Starnberger Bahnhof, Arnulfstrasse 3 (☎ (089) 59 18 24; fax 59 61 33)
İstanbul
    Ulusoy Turizm, İnönü Caddesi 59, Taksim (☎ (212) 244 1271, 244 2823)
    Varan Turizm, İnönü Caddesi 29/B, Taksim (☎ (212) 243 1903, 244 8457)
Switzerland
    Varan Turizm, Josefstrasse 45, 8005 Zurich (☎ (01) 272 04 77; fax 241 80 19)

Train The *Thomas Cook European Timetable*, updated several times yearly, covers all international and many domestic train services within Europe. But for details of those in other continents, or between Europe and Asia, you'll need the *Thomas Cook Overseas Timetable*. Both also list many bus and ferry services. They can be bought from Thomas Cook offices worldwide and are also kept at many travel agencies and some reference libraries. Copies can be ordered from Thomas Cook Publishing (☎ (1733) 268 943; fax 267052), PO Box 227, Thorpe Wood, Peterborough PE3 8BQ, UK.

Tehrān Although the Moscow-Tehrān train no longer exists, in theory it is still possible to make this journey. You would have to catch a train from Moscow to Baku (once or twice a week), and another from Baku to Julfa on the Azerbaijani side of the Azerbaijan/Iran border. Here there would be a change of trains to take you across the iron bridge to Jolfā on the Iranian side, from where another train would have to be caught to Tabrīz in north-western Iran. From Tabrīz there are two trains a day to Tehrān or several daily buses.

İstanbul All trains from Europe to the Middle East terminate at İstanbul's Sirkeci station. While trains also run from Asian İstanbul to Syria and Iran, through tickets are difficult or impossible to obtain: you may have to spend a few days in İstanbul waiting for the first available seat.

When it is running, the daily *İstanbul Express* from Munich departs each evening at dinner time, reaches Belgrade at breakfast time, Sofia at dinner time and İstanbul at breakfast time on the third day, taking about 35 hours (if it's on time).

The train hauls sleeping and couchette coaches, a restaurant car and (three days weekly) auto-train carriages so you can take your car with you. The auto-train service runs Tuesday, Friday and Saturday from Munich; Wednesday, Thursday and Sunday from İstanbul. The fare for a car and driver from Munich to İstanbul (one way) is from US$660 to US$900; round-trip fares are discounted about 12%.

A second train, the *Skopje-İstanbul Express* departs from Munich later each evening, reaching Sofia in about 25½ hours. At Sofia it is met by the *Sofia Express* from Moscow and Bucharest before continuing to İstanbul overnight, arriving around lunch time, 38 hours after having left Munich, 37 hours after having left Moscow.

A nightly train from Vienna connects with the *İstanbul Express* at Zagreb, departing from Vienna after dinner, arriving in Zagreb several hours after midnight. You reach İstanbul in the morning after two nights on the train.

With a change of trains it's possible to get to İstanbul from more European cities. Through tickets can be bought at almost any international railway booking office in Europe, but it's advisable to make enquiries some weeks ahead, especially in summer when demand is greatest. See also Lonely Planet's *Mediterranean Europe on a shoestring* and *Turkey*. If you're arriving from Western Europe (although perhaps not Eastern or Central Europe), you may find that flying or taking a bus to İstanbul is slightly cheaper than going by rail. However, the trains are more civilised, offer the opportunity to break your journey more or less when you like – and as a travel experience in their own right they are hard to beat. Paul Theroux managed to write a bestseller about just such a trip.

If you're planning to get from Western Europe to İstanbul and back within a month, an Inter-Rail or Eurail card could save you money: this is valid for free travel on most of Europe's and all of Turkey's railways, but not those of the former USSR or any Middle Eastern country except Turkey. But both cards wouldn't allow you very much time inside the region and are unlikely to cost less than a single ticket. If you're under 26 you can take advantage of the Wasteels BIGE Youth Train, with special low fares.

Car & Motorcycle The E5 highway makes its way through the Balkans to Edirne and İstanbul, then onward to Ankara, Adana and the Syrian frontier. Though the road is good in most of the countries it passes through, you will encounter heavy traffic and lots of heavy vehicles along the route, as this is a very important freight route between Europe and the Middle East. It deteriorates very badly east of Ankara. Your automobile association may be able to help you plan a route across Europe. See also Lonely Planet's *Mediterranean Europe on a shoestring*.

Car ferries can shorten driving times considerably, but are unlikely to save you any money.

SEA & RIVER
Sailing is still a feasible and affordable method of reaching or leaving the Middle East. On most routes it's quite a lot cheaper than flying, more interesting and it can often bypass tedious or difficult land journeys. On the other hand, except on some of the Mediterranean services, it's not likely to be especially comfortable, particularly in midsummer. It can also call for a degree of patience and flexibility.

The Mediterranean routes have been popular with western travellers for many years and are fairly well publicised. However, it's not always easy to find out information about many of the other services, as the usual travel trade publications tend to ignore their existence. Your best bet is to get in touch with the carrier or its nearest agent some time in advance, and not to take too seriously what other sources tell you. This advice is particularly important if your itinerary depends on catching a particular ferry, or if you intend to ship your vehicle on one.

You're unlikely to regret taking an adequate supply of food and drink with you on any of these ships; even if it is available on board you're pretty stuck if it doesn't agree with you or your budget. Many people may find deck class on some of the longer sailings, such as the eight-day Karachi-Jeddah run, a little too much to bear.

As well as the services listed below, some cruise liners call at Middle Eastern ports such as Aden, Suez, Alexandria or Muscat, but these are somewhat outside the scope of this book. A good travel agent should be able to tell you what's available this season.

Unless stated otherwise, all services run in both directions and all fares quoted below are single. A slight discount may apply on round-trip tickets as well as student, youth or child fares on some lines. Schedules tend to change at least annually according to demand; fares, too, often fluctuate according to season, especially on the Mediterranean routes.

Although vehicles can be shipped on most of the following routes, bookings for them may have to be made some time in advance. The charge usually depends on the length or volume of the vehicle and should be checked with the carrier. As a rule motorcycles cost almost nothing to ship and bicycles go free.

Strand Cruise & Travel in the UK claims it can book tickets on most of the services in this and the following chapter, given enough time, but may levy a handling fee.

Mediterranean Sea

Of all the scheduled services listed in this chapter, those in the Mediterranean offer the nearest thing to most people's idea of a cruise. Some of the ships even have discos,

duty-free shops, casinos and swimming pools. However, travelling in deck class on the Piraeus-Haifa run is unlikely to damage your shoestring credentials.

Thomas Cook's *Greek Island Hopping* covers most domestic and international services in the east Mediterranean, not just those between the Greek islands. It includes summaries of sights and budget accommodation in most ports.

Greece Salamis Lines and (from early in April to late in October) Vergina, Stability, Afroessa and Poseidon lines operate weekly ferries between Piraeus, the port of Athens, and Haifa (see the Israel chapter). All stop at Rhodes and Limassol (Cyprus), some also at Iraklion. The run takes about 58 hours and the cheapest accommodation is in deck class.

In summer the MS *Dahab* links Alexandria with Limassol and Rhodes. See the Alexandria section in the Egypt chapter.

Between Italy, Greece & Turkey Several shipping lines operate car and passenger ferries from Italy and Greece to Turkey in summer, and small ferries shuttle between the Greek islands and the Turkish mainland. A hydrofoil service operates in high summer between Rhodes and Fethiye. Timetables and fares are notoriously fickle and the few dependable services generally vary according to demand and are most frequent in summer; some stop running or only operate irregular services at other times. Various petty restrictions apply; it's easier to get a ticket with a Turkish ship from Turkey, a Greek ship from Greece, unless you already hold a return ticket. Turkish Maritime Lines (Venice to Çeşme, İzmir, and Antalya), European Seaways (Brindisi/Bari-Mykonos-Çeşme), Med Link Lines (Brindisi-Igoumenitsa-Patras-Çeşme) and Stern Ferrylines (Brindisi/Bari-Çeşme) have all been recommended. For more information see the Getting There & Away section of the Turkey chapter.

Cyprus Turkish Maritime Lines sails three times weekly from Famagusta (Magosa) on north Cyprus to Mersin. Catamarans run daily between Larnaca and Beirut; hydrofoil and ferry services run daily from Kyrenia (Girne) to Taşucu, and three times a week in summer between Limassol and Haifa (see the Israel chapter).

Black Sea

Georgia Crowded hydrofoils run between Batumi and Trabzon, however, irregular timetables and avoiding ticket swindlers makes travelling via this route very frustrating.

Russia Karden Line ferries run between Trabzon and Sochi in Russia, departing Trabzon on Monday and Thursday at 6 pm and return from Sochi on Tuesday and Friday at 6 pm. Cabin tickets (US$60) are available in Trabzon from Navi Tour, İskele Caddesi Belediye Duükkanları (☎ (462) 326 4484). At the time of writing most people would have to have obtained a visa from a Russian consulate in their home country in order to use this service, but that may change.

Red Sea & Gulf of Aden

Sudan Ferries bound from Port Sudan leave from Suez; the voyage, via Jeddah in Saudi Arabia, takes about four days. Information and tickets are available from Yara Tours & Shipping (☎ 393 8861) at Sharia Mohammed Sabri Abu Alam in central Cairo. Fayez Trading, Construction and Shipping (☎ (02) 647 4208) is one of the main companies in Jeddah. See the Egypt and Saudi Arabia chapters for more information.

Djibouti It's possible to sail cheaply on a cargo ship between Djibouti and Al-Makha. Fares, schedules and ticket conditions are available locally.

Arabian Sea & Indian Ocean

The Pan-Islamic Steamship Company sails about once a month between Karachi and Jeddah. In the haj season only pilgrims are carried. The sailing to Jeddah takes seven or eight days. For information and tickets contact their office in Karachi (see Shipping-

Line Addresses, following). There are also offices in Yemen and the other Gulf States.

Caspian Sea

Azerbaijan You can sail to Baku from Bandar-é Anzalī in Iran on Sunday or back on Thursday (both depart at 7 pm, arriving next morning at 9 am), year-round. The oneway fares are US$100 for third class (like airline economy seating) and US$130/160/200 for a 2nd/1st/super class cabin. Tickets should be bought at least three days ahead. Outside the two countries, tickets and information can be obtained through IRISL (Iran's national shipping line) in London on ☎ (0171) 378 7121.

Nile River

Sudan The twice-weekly steamer service linking the railheads of Wadi Halfa in Sudan and Aswan in Egypt was suspended in 1994 because of deteriorating relations between the two countries, and it's anyone's guess when it will resume.

Shipping-Line Addresses

The head office of each shipping line is listed first under each heading, followed by a selection of any offices or agents outside the Middle East.

Adriatica Line
    Zattere 1411, PO Box 705, Venice 30123, Italy (☎ (041) 781611; fax 781894)
    Crete Travel Bureau, 20-22 Odos Epimenidou, PO Box 1069, Iraklion, Greece (☎ (081) 227 002; fax 223749)
    Charilaos Cacouris Company, Odos Othonos Amalias 8, PO Box 1012, Patras, Greece (☎ (061) 421995)
    Serena Holidays, 40-42 Kenway Rd, London SW5 0RA, UK (☎ (0171) 373 6548)
Afroessa Lines
    1 Odos Harilaou Tricoupi, 18536, Piraeus, Greece (☎ (01) 418 3777; fax 418 1121)
Arkadia Lines
    215 Kifissias Ave, Maroussi, 15124, Athens, Greece (☎ (01) 612 3402; fax 612 6206)
    42, Akti Posidonos & Loudovikou Strs, 18531, Piraeus, Greece (☎ (01) 422 2127; fax 422 3640)
Black Sea Steamship Company
    Potyomkintsev ploshcha 1, 270026 Odessa, Ukraine (☎ (0482) 25 35 39)

Fayaz Trading, Construction & Shipping Company
Al Mina'a St, Jeddah, Saudi Arabia
(☎ (02) 647 4208)
Khazar Shipping Company
IRISL, TR House, 134-8 Borough High St,
London SE1 1LB, UK (☎ (0171) 378 7121)
Minoan Lines
64B Odos Kifissias, 15125 Maroussi, Athens,
Greece (☎ (01) 689 8340; fax 689 8344)
17, Odos 25 Avgustou, Iraklion, Crete
(☎ (081) 330301; fax 330308)
Euroferries Ancona Ltd, Stazione Marittima
Porto, Ancona, Italy (☎ (071) 207 1068;
207 0874)
Misr Edco Shipping Co SAE
1 El Central St, El Manshia, Alexandria, Egypt
(☎ (03) 483 2397; fax 483 8898)
Yusuf bin Ahmed Kanoo, PO Box 812, Kilo 4,
Mekka Road, Jeddah, Saudi Arabia (☎ (02) 682
3759, 647 5251)
Telstar Travel & Tourism, Jebel Amman, 3rd
Circle, Riyadh Centre, El Riyadh building, PO
Box 194, Amman, Jordan (☎ (06) 40213/4;
fax 40168)
Pan-Islamic Steamship Company
Writers' Chambers, Mumtz Hasan Road, PO Box
4855, Karachi, Pakistan (☎ (021) 241 2110;
fax 241 2276)
Poseidon Line
Akti Miaouli 35-39, Piraeus, Greece 18536
(☎ (01) 429 2046; fax 429 2041)
Shipping Corporation of India
Shipping House, 245 Madame Cama Rd,
Bombay, India 400021 (☎ (022) 202 6666;
fax 202 2949)
Stability Line
11 Odos Sachtouri, Piraeus, Greece, 18536
(☎ (01) 413 2392)

Kouros Travel, Rhodes Town, Greece
Olymbion 3B, Honey Court 7, Limassol, Cyprus
(☎ (05) 43978)
Strand Cruise & Travel Centre
Charing Cross Shopping Concourse, Strand,
London WC2N 4HZ, UK (☎ (0171) 836 6363;
fax 497 0078)
Turkish Maritime Lines
BassaniSpA, Via XXII Marzo 2414, 30124
Venice Italy (☎ (41) 520 8819; fax 520 4009)
Kıbrıs Türk Denizcilik Ltd Şti, Bülent Ecevit
Bulvarı 3, Gazimagosa (Famagusta), Turkish
Republic of Northern Cypres (☎ (392) 366 5786;
fax 366 7840)
Meclisi Mebusan Caddesi 18, Salipazari,
İstanbul 80040 (☎ (212) 252 1700; fax 251 5767)
Sunquest Holidays Ltd, 23 Princes St, London
W1R 7RG, UK (☎ (0171) 499 9992;
fax 499 9995)
TDİ Denizyolları Acentesi, Rıhtım Caddesi,
Karaköy, İstanbul, Turkey (☎ (212) 249 9222 for
reservations, 244 2502 for information;
fax 251 9025)

LEAVING THE MIDDLE EAST

Many countries, including several Middle
Eastern ones, impose a departure tax on air
or sea passengers, some even for people
leaving by land. Usually this is payable only
in local currency and there may be a different
rate for foreigners and local people, or
depending on the country of destination.
Check what, if any, departure tax applies
when you buy your tickets out of a country.
See also the individual country chapters.

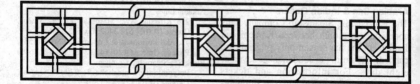

Getting Around the Region

AIR

Flying is certainly the most user-friendly method of transport in the Middle East. Because of the distances and the physical and political obstacles, the region has invested more of its oil wealth in air communications than in any other form of transport. For many Middle Easterners flying is the preferred means of travel for any but the shortest of journeys. For some it is the only conceivable means.

Except for in Israel, Afghanistan and Iraq, even if you have to change aircraft once, you're unlikely to have to wait long for a connection. Tickets are more flexible than for buses or trains, schedules more rigidly adhered to and refunds easier to get, and obtaining information is rarely a problem.

In the Middle East conditions and attitudes conspire against overlanders in a way they do in few other parts of the world. Several countries make it difficult for foreigners who require visas to enter by any means but air, if at all, while many borders are closed altogether. In other parts of the world, if one country won't let you in or is too dangerous to visit, it's usually possible to go through another country instead. This is often not an option in the Middle East.

Many Middle Eastern people also find it hard to comprehend why any westerner would actually prefer to travel by land or sea when it's possible to fly instead.

Flying isn't an option for getting to or from Iraq, thanks to a UN air embargo. Nor is flying possible between Israel and most other Middle Eastern countries, except for Egypt and Turkey.

Flying within the Middle East, except sometimes on domestic flights, is expensive. If the alternative is hiring a car or taxi for the same journey, it might possibly represent a saving, but otherwise it almost certainly won't. You don't always have even this choice.

There are no regional air passes.

BUS

Bus transport is variable in the Middle East – while there are some countries where buses are a perfectly feasible means of getting around most of the time, other states in the region virtually have no public bus services at all. On an extensive tour of the whole region it would be almost impossible to avoid more expensive forms of transport entirely.

Buses are the most popular form of long-distance public transport in Iran, Turkey, Egypt, Israel and, to a lesser extent, Syria and Iraq. In these countries buses will take you to almost anywhere of any size; on many routes there may be no other form of public transport. However, bus services are generally geared towards the needs of local people; so a place which has great touristic appeal but few inhabitants may be impossible to reach by bus. In Jordan and Lebanon, shared taxis are common means of transport between towns.

Car ownership levels in the Gulf States are so high that little demand for public bus services exists on most routes. It's not too difficult to get between the main towns in Saudi Arabia and Oman by bus, but Bahrain, Kuwait, the UAE and Qatar have few, if any, domestic services.

Most Middle Eastern countries can be reached by direct international bus from other parts of the region. Even in those countries without any international bus services it's usually possible to get to at least one neighbouring country by changing buses at the border, or by a combination of buses and taxis. The city that has by far the most buses to other countries in the region is İstanbul, with Riyadh, Jeddah, Ankara and Damascus competing for second place.

It's possible to cover quite considerable distances in the Middle East on single bus journeys. For example you could get from İstanbul to Riyadh in one marathon bus trip, although if you did you probably wouldn't feel like travelling again for a while. One problem with international bus services in the region is that you have to wait for both the vehicle and everyone else on it to clear customs at each border you cross. At many frontiers this can mean delays of 12 hours or more. While a direct international bus will be more convenient and probably more comfortable, using domestic services (where they exist) to get to and from borders can often work out to be quicker. They are sometimes quite a lot cheaper, too.

In general it's advisable to book bus seats in advance at the bus station; usually there's no other ticket outlet or reliable source of information about current services; international tickets often have to be booked a few days ahead. Even at stations, trying to find information can be frustrating, especially if you don't speak the language.

Return or through tickets are often not issued, and no regional bus passes exist. Tickets usually correspond to a particular seat number: depending on the make of vehicle, some seats are much more highly rated than others.

The cost and comfort of bus travel vary enormously throughout the region, and details are given in the individual country chapters. The video coach has reached the Middle East but the no-smoking bus hasn't, at least not on long-distance routes. Loud music on buses is a potential annoyance in many Middle Eastern countries, but at least it helps keep the driver awake.

TRAIN

No Middle Eastern country has an extensive railway network and there are few international services. Most railway lines in the region were built primarily for strategic or economic reasons, and many are either no longer in use or only carry freight. However, where there is a choice the trains are usually more comfortable than the buses and compare favourably in price. On the other hand they are less frequent and usually slower, while many stations are some distance out of the town centres they serve. In general, tickets are only sold at the station and reservations are either compulsory or recommended.

Most trains in Turkey are very slow and decrepit but in Iran, Iraq, Syria, Saudi Arabia, Jordan, Israel and Egypt they are a pleasant way to travel, and a better way of meeting people than taking most other forms of public transport.

At present the only functioning international passenger services within the region run between İstanbul and Tehrān, İstanbul and Aleppo and Amman and Damascus, with through services between Tehrān and Damascus planned for the near future.

TAXI

In the west taxis are usually an avoidable luxury. In the Middle East they are often neither. Many cities, especially in the Gulf States, have no other form of urban public transport, while there are also many rural routes that are only feasible in a taxi or private vehicle.

The ways in which taxis operate vary widely from country to country, and often even from place to place within a country. So does the expense of using them. Different types of taxi are painted or marked in different ways, or known by different names, but often local people talking to foreigners in English will just use the blanket term 'taxi'. If you want to make the best use of them for your money, it's important to know which is which. Details of local peculiarities are given in the country chapters.

Regular Taxi

The regular taxi (also known as agency taxi, telephone taxi, private taxi or, in Israel, special taxi) are found in almost every Middle Eastern town, sometimes even in quite tiny settlements.

In some places there's no other public transport, but in most, regular taxis exist alongside less expensive means of getting around (although these usually shut down overnight). They are primarily of use for transport within towns or on short rural trips, but in some countries hiring them for excursions of several hours is still cheap. They are also often the only way of reaching airports or seaports.

For details see the individual country chapters.

Shared Taxi

A compromise between the convenience of a regular taxi and the economy of a bus, the shared taxi picks up and drops off passengers at points along its route and runs to no particular schedule (although in most places to a fixed route). It's known by different names – collect, collective or service taxi in English, *servees* in Arabic, *sherut* in Hebrew, *dolmuş* in Turkish, and just *tāksī* in Persian. Most shared taxis take up to four or five passengers, but some seat up to about 12 and are indistinguishable for most purposes from minibuses.

Shared taxis are much cheaper than private taxis and, once you get the hang of them, can be just as convenient. They are dearer than buses, but more frequent and usually faster, because they don't stop so often or for so long. They also tend to operate longer hours than buses. They can be used for urban, intercity or rural transport, but not necessarily all three in a particular place.

Fixed-route taxis wait at the point of departure until full or nearly full. Usually they pick up or drop off passengers anywhere en route, but in some places they have fixed halts or stations. Sometimes each service is allocated a number, which may be indicated on the vehicle. Generally a flat fare applies for each route, but sometimes it's possible to pay a partial fare.

Shared taxis without routes are supreme examples of market forces at work. If the price is right you'll quickly find a taxi willing to take you almost anywhere, but if you're prepared to wait a while, or to do your journey in stages, you can get around for almost nothing. Fares depend largely on time and distance but can also vary slightly according to demand.

Beware of boarding an empty one, as the driver may assume you want to hire the vehicle for your exclusive use and charge you accordingly. It's advisable to watch what other passengers pay and to hand over your fare in front of them. Passengers are expected to know where they are getting off. 'Thank you' in the local language is the usual cue for the driver to stop. Make it clear to the driver or other passengers if you want to be told when you reach your destination.

CAR & MOTORCYCLE

The advantages of having your own vehicle are obvious. You aren't tied to schedules, you can choose your own company, set your own pace, take the scenic route, declare your vehicle a smoking or no-smoking zone, and won't be at the mercy of dishonest taxi drivers or have to fight for a place on a bus. And you can avoid all the hassles that go with carrying your world on your back.

Many Middle Eastern countries and cities are very much car-oriented and chastise those without their own wheels. In the Gulf States, in particular, a car can make a great difference to the success of your travels. It also makes getting between each country by land much easier than for people relying on public transport. Your chances of obtaining a Saudi road transit visa increase immeasurably if you're attached to a private vehicle.

Almost throughout the region, as you might expect, petrol is both cheap and readily available. Desert roads are the exception, where petrol stations can be few and far between.

But for the vast majority of short-term visitors to the Middle East the advantages of being attached to one vehicle are far outweighed by the disadvantages. The main problem isn't the expense of obtaining a *carnet de passage* (see following). It's not the often hair-raising driving found on Middle Eastern roads. Nor is it the variable quality of the roads themselves or the sheer distance between places of interest. Nor is it even the millstone-around-the-neck worry of serious accident, breakdown or theft.

The one overwhelming obstacle that puts all these difficulties into the shade is simply establishing a feasible route through the Middle East. This can be hard enough if you're relying on public transport, but at least there's nearly always the alternative of flying if a particular overland route proves too difficult or dangerous. This is hardly an option if you have a car with you, and air freighting even a motorcycle isn't cheap. Selling or dumping a temporarily imported vehicle in the Middle East is more or less ruled out by customs regulations. It's at least theoretically possible to have it put under customs seal in one country and to return for it later, but this is a hassle to arrange, requires backtracking and somewhat negates the point of bringing a vehicle in the first place. Car ferries can get around some of these problems but shipping a car isn't cheap, often requires an advance booking and won't help you out in every eventuality.

Overland access from Europe being restricted, it's hard to think of a route through the Middle East that would justify the expense and hassle of bringing a car and getting it out again. Even in the Gulf States, it would make more sense for short-term visitors to rent a car locally. For long-term residents it would probably be cheaper and more straightforward to buy one there and sell it before leaving.

Motorcycles can be shipped or, often, loaded as luggage onto trains, but they are a rare form of long-distance transport in the Middle East and other road users have scant consideration for them.

Even if you do work out a feasible route that justifies taking your own vehicle, you'll face mountains of paperwork and red tape before you leave home. The documents usually take a month or more to obtain, and just finding out the current regulations can be difficult. It's best to get in touch with your automobile association (eg the AA or RAC in the UK) at least three months in advance. Note that the rules and conventions following may not apply if you stay more than three months in any one country, or if you're going for any purpose but tourism.

Carnets

A *carnet de passage* is a booklet that is stamped on arrival in and departure from a country to ensure that you export the vehicle again after you've imported it. It can be issued by a motoring organisation in the country where the vehicle is registered. The situation on carnets alters frequently, but many Middle Eastern countries currently require them.

The sting in the tail with a carnet is that you have to lodge a deposit to secure it. If you default on the carnet – that is, you don't have an export stamp to match the import one – then the country in question can claim your deposit, and that can be up to 300% of the new value of the vehicle. You can get around this problem with bank guarantees or carnet insurance but you still have to fork out in the end if you default.

Should the worst occur and your vehicle is irretrievably damaged in an accident or catastrophic breakdown, you'll have to argue it out with customs officials. Having a vehicle stolen can be even worse, as you may be suspected of having sold it.

Other Documents

An International Driving Permit (IDP) is compulsory for foreign drivers and motorcyclists in Afghanistan, Bahrain, Egypt, Iran, Iraq, Saudi Arabia, Syria and Yemen. Most foreign licences are acceptable in the other Gulf States, Israel, Lebanon and Turkey, and for foreign-registered vehicles in Jordan, but even in these places an IDP is recommended.

For the vehicle you'll need the registration documents. Check with your insurer whether you're covered for the countries you intend to visit and whether third party cover is included. You'll also need a green card, issued by insurers. Insurance for some countries is only obtainable at the border.

Breakdowns & Spare Parts

Mechanical failure can be a problem as spare parts – or at least official ones – are often unobtainable. Fear not: ingenuity often compensates for factory parts.

Generally Land Rovers, Volkswagens, Range Rovers, Mercedes and Chevrolets are the cars for which spare parts are most likely to be available, although in recent years

Japan has been a particularly vigorous exporter of vehicles to the Middle East. In more anti-western countries, such as Iran, Syria and Iraq, spare parts for US vehicles may be very hard to find. One tip is to ask your vehicle manufacturer for a list of any authorised service centres it has in the countries you plan to visit. The length of this is likely to be a pretty good reflection of how easy it is to get spare parts on your travels.

Although a virtual necessity in Afghanistan, a 4WD is not essential in most of the rest of the region except for driving in the desert and other off-road activities. These require planning and experience; even seasoned local motorists tend to go in a convoy for their own safety. One good introduction to the subject is *Staying Alive in the Desert* by KEM Melville.

Road Rules & Conditions

Whatever memories you lose of the Middle East, you're unlikely to forget the driving standards. With the partial exception of Oman, these are appalling by western norms. Fatalism rules supreme. Many regulations are, in practice, purely cautionary. Car horns, used at the slightest provocation, take the place of caution and courtesy. At least theoretically, driving throughout the region is on the right, although many motorcyclists consider themselves exempt from this convention. You're unlikely even to know what the speed limit is on a particular road, let alone to be forced to keep to it.

As a rule only non-Middle Easterners wear motorcycle helmets or car safety belts in most countries of the region.

The main roads are good or at least reasonable in most parts of the Middle East: Afghanistan and Lebanon are exceptions. But there are plenty of unsurfaced roads, and the international roads are generally narrow and crowded.

Remember that an accident in the more remote parts of the region isn't always handled by your friendly insurance company. 'An eye for an eye' is likely to be the thought in the mind of the other party and his or her relatives, whether you're in the wrong or not. Don't hang around to ask questions or gawp. Of course we're not saying that you shouldn't report an accident, but it may be more prudent to head for the nearest police station than to wait at the scene. Except in well-lit urban areas, try to avoid driving at night, as you may find your vehicle is the only thing on the road with lights.

A warning triangle is required for vehicles (except motorcycles) in most Middle Eastern countries; in Turkey two triangles and a first-aid kit are compulsory.

One book worth a place in your glove compartment is *Overland and Beyond* by Jonathan & Theresa Hewatt.

Petrol

Usually two grades are available; if in doubt get the more expensive one. Petrol stations are few and far between on many desert roads. Away from the main towns, it's advisable to fill up whenever you get the chance. Locally produced maps often indicate the locations of petrol stations. Diesel isn't easily available in every Middle Eastern country, nor is lead-free petrol.

Motorcycle

Motorcycles are rare sights in most of the Arabian peninsula; elsewhere in the region they are fairly popular as a means of racing around in urban areas, but little used as long-distance transport. They are particularly popular in Afghanistan, where two wheels are better than four at swerving around potholes, and few people can afford cars anyway. Women motorcyclists are a very rare breed throughout the region.

If you do decide to motorcycle through the Middle East, try to take one of the more popular Japanese models if you want to stand any chance of finding spare parts. Even then, make sure it's in very good shape before setting out.

Rental

In most large Middle Eastern cities it's fairly easy, if rarely cheap, to rent a vehicle. Some agencies can arrange vans, minibuses and buses for groups, but most deal only in cars;

extremely few rent out motorcycles or bicycles. Before hiring a self-drive vehicle, ask yourself seriously how well you think you can cope with the local driving conditions and whether you know your way around well enough to make good use of one. Also compare the cost with that of hiring a taxi for the same period.

BICYCLE

While there are a few places and occasions in the Middle East where a bicycle would be useful, there are many more where it would be a distinct liability. Many long-distance routes in the Middle East are arduous even for motorists, and for a cyclist they would be both difficult and dangerous. The distances, the climate, the terrain and the politics all make cycling a most improbable method of long-distance transport. As a rule bicycles are the preserve of children and their natural environment is, at best, the pavement. Drivers rarely have much consideration for other motorised road users, let alone those relying on pedal power, and in most parts of the region bicycles on the open road are a very rare sight.

There are some towns and rural areas where the distances and traffic are manageable enough to make cycling feasible, but many more where it would be a somewhat hazardous pursuit. Even in the places where a bike would come in handy, the problem would be getting it there in the first place. The compromise of renting one locally is only possible in a few places, mostly in Egypt and Israel. It's not much of a problem to load one as luggage on trains, planes and ships, but on most other forms of public transport in the region it would have to be very sturdy to put up with a lot of rough handling. It would be wise to assume that any spare part is unavailable locally, although motorcycle repair shops may come up with an ingenious substitute.

If you want to try, bear in mind that the usual dress restrictions are not waived for cyclists. Ones who wear shorts, for example, are liable to have stones thrown at them in many of the more conservative regions.

HITCHING

Although many travellers hitchhike, it is not a totally safe way of getting around. There is no part of the Middle East where hitching can be recommended for unaccompanied women. Just because we explain how hitching works doesn't mean we recommend it.

Hitching as commonly understood in the west hardly exists in the Middle East (except Israel). Although in most countries you'll often see people standing by the road hoping for a lift, they will nearly always expect (and be expected) to offer to pay. Hitching in the Middle Eastern sense is not so much an alternative to the public transport system as an extension of it. The going rate is usually roughly the equivalent of the bus or shared taxi fare, but may be more if a driver takes you to an address or place off his or her route. You may well be offered free lifts from time to time, but you won't get very far if you set out deliberately to avoid paying for transport.

Hitching is not illegal in any Middle Eastern country and in many places it is extremely common. However, while it's quite normal for Middle Easterners, Asians and Africans, it isn't everywhere something which westerners are expected to do. In many Middle Eastern countries, westerners who try to set a precedent of any kind often attract considerable attention. While this can work to your advantage, it can also lead to suspicion from the local police.

Throughout the Middle East a raised thumb is a vaguely obscene gesture. A common way of signalling that you want a lift is to extend your right hand, palm down.

WALKING

This is probably the most neglected means of transport in the whole Middle East. Middle Easterners tend to regard foreigners who walk more than short distances as slightly mad, and they have a point.

While it's true that your legs can take you to places that no other form of transport can, in the Middle East the distances are too great and the terrain and climate too harsh for walking to be a very attractive option most of the time. Both urban and rural roads are designed with scant regard for pedestrians, while in remote areas off the main roads life-sustaining facilities are often few and far between. However, trekking in mountainous areas can be rewarding and relatively accessible, although it's very much a do-it-yourself pursuit.

BOAT

The Middle East is one of the few regions of the world where passenger shipping is still a growth market. The number of services in the Persian Gulf in particular has risen rapidly in the last few years.

The ferries meet an obvious need, as they're the only way, apart from flying, of avoiding long detours by land through such trouble spots as Israel or eastern Turkey – or through or around Iraq. Moreover, most are cheaper than any other form of public transport on the same route.

Practicality is, however, the essence of these services, not luxury. Even in 1st class you shouldn't expect your voyage to be a pleasure cruise, while deck class often means just that. In summer, conditions may be a little too hot for many people. While food and drink of some sort may be available on board, many passengers prefer to take their own. Vehicles can be shipped on all the following services, but advance arrangements may have to be made.

For the latest information, get in touch with the head office or local agent of the respective company some time in advance.

See the Shipping-Line Addresses list in the Sea & River section of the Regional Getting There & Away chapter for more information.

Red Sea

The Amman-based Arab Bridge Maritime Company sails at least once daily between Nuweiba in Sinai and Aqaba. The journey takes three hours or so. There is also a speedboat plying the same route which does the journey in one hour. See the Egypt and Jordan chapters for more details.

The Alexandria-based Misr Edco Shipping Company and four Saudi companies sail between Jeddah and Suez. The journey takes about 36 hours direct, about 72 via Aqaba. Buy tickets and check timetables and routes directly from the shipping company or its agent rather than through a travel agency if you don't want to be given misleading information (see the Shipping-Line Addresses list in the Sea & River section of the Regional Getting There & Away chapter). Misr Edco sails about twice weekly between Port Safaga (Egypt) and Jeddah.

Persian Gulf & Sea of Oman

If you want to visit the Gulf States but don't want to fly and can't get into Saudi Arabia, don't neglect the possibility of sailing. The shortest sailing, across the Strait of Hormuz between Bandar-é Abbās and Sharjah takes about 12 hours. Fares start at around US$50 in 3rd (deck) class. Other, less frequent, services link Būshehr and Bahrain, Būshehr and Kuwait, Bandar-é Abbās and Muscat, Bandar-é Abbās and Doha and Chābāhār and Muscat. These only have 1st-class (cabin) accommodation but all are considerably cheaper than the equivalent airfare. Most are overnight journeys. All these ships are operated by Valfajre-8 Shipping Company, owned by Islamic Republic of Iran Shipping Lines (see the Getting Around section of the Iran chapter). Outside the region information and tickets can be obtained through IRISL in London.

ORGANISED TOURS

A tour is unlikely to be the cheapest or only way of reaching your destination in the Middle East, or of getting around once you arrive there. No Middle Eastern state requires tourists to enter in a group, while the less accessible countries simply don't feature on any tour. There are occasions when a place on an organised tour can be a short cut to obtaining a difficult visa, but usually one pays handsomely for the privilege.

Packages on offer cater for a wide range of tastes and budgets, ranging from sun, sand and sea holidays on Turkey's Mediterranean coast, to tours of desert monasteries in Syria escorted by a lecturer from the British Museum. The most popular package-tour destinations by far are Turkey, Egypt and Israel, with Syria and Jordan some way behind, but the popularity of each one of these often wavers dramatically depending on political developments.

The following operators offer some of the more interesting tours in the Middle Eastern region (all are UK based):

British Museum Traveller, 46 Bloomsbury St, London WC1 3QQ (☎ (0171) 323 8895; fax 580 8677). Archaeological-oriented tours led by leading academics; the 1997 programme includes a week spent excavating in the Jordan Valley, Byzantine and Seljuk Turkey and Early Travellers in Egypt. There are also more general tours of Jordan, Syria and Yemen.

Classic Tours, 148 Curtain Rd, London EC2A 3AR (☎ (0171) 613 4441; fax 613 4024). Itineraries include Syria, Lebanon, Ancient Turkey, the Persian Empire as well as a combined biking and hiking tour from Jerusalem to Eilat for around UK£700 (flights and bike rental included).

Dragoman, 96 Camp Green, Kenton Rd, Debenham, Suffolk IP14 6LA (☎ (01728) 861 133; fax 861 127). A long-established overland specialist, whose programme includes a five week expedition taking in Turkey, Syria, Jordan and Egypt, for a starting price of around UK£600, flights not included.

Encounter Overland, 267 Old Brompton Rd, London SW5 9JA (☎ (0171) 370 6951; fax 244 9737). Encounter's Middle Eastern itineraries include

21 days exploring Egypt (UK£550), or alternatively trucking it from London to Cairo in seven weeks via Turkey, Syria and Jordan (UK£1500). Their classic overland trip from London to Kathmandu (11 weeks; UK£1700) includes Turkey and Iran.

Exodus Expeditions, 9 Weir Rd, London SW12 0LT (☎ (0181) 673 0859; fax 673 0779). A highly respected company with several (pricey) Middle Eastern trips on their books, including highlights of Turkey (16 days), Yemen & the Hadhramawt (20 days), and Petra & Palmyra (18 days).

Explore Worldwide, 1 Fredrick St, Aldershot, Hampshire GU11 1LQ (☎ (01252) 319 448; fax 343 170). Its 1997 brochure has numerous Middle East tours, including seven focused on Egypt, a Lawrence's Arabia package centred on Jordan, a 15 day expedition of Yemen, and 11 days touring Oman.

Hinterland Travel, 2 Ivy Mill Lane, Godstone, Surrey RH9 8NH (☎ (01883) 743 584; fax 743 912). Anyone with time on their hands could join an 88 day overland journey which begins in İstanbul before moving on to Syria, Lebanon, Jordan, Egypt, Saudi Arabia, UAE, Oman, Iran and winding up in Pakistan; the cost is UK£2450, flights not included. The company also runs a 19 day Syria, Jordan and Lebanon trip (UK£299, flights not included), and a 16 day exploration of Iran (UK£600, flights not included).

Jasmin Tours, High St, Cookham, Maidenhead, Berks SL6 9SQ (☎ (01628) 850 788; fax 529 4444). The company has numerous packages involving Egypt, Jordan, Lebanon and Syria, as well as a 13 day escorted tour of Yemen (from UK£1500), 12 days in Oman (from UK£1600), and an 8 day fly-drive deal in the UAE (from UK£970).

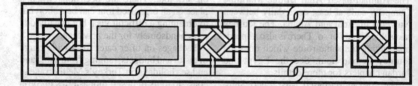

Afghanistan

At the time of writing the sound of gunfire and shelling still reverberates over Kabul as it has done with depressing regularity since the late 1970s. Hopes are high that the latest faction to win control over the war-torn capital, the Islamic Taliban fighters, may eventually succeed in bringing peace and order but for the time being Afghanistan remains unsafe to visit. This is tragic for the country and unfortunate for travellers, as Afghanistan is vastly appealing, with endless empty deserts, soaring barren mountains, old historic towns and ruins and, best of all, the proud, independent and detached Afghans.

Facts about the Country

HISTORY

Afghanistan's history as a country spans little more than two centuries, although in the past it has been part, or even the centre, of great empires. As with many eastern countries the rise and fall of political power was inextricably tied to the rise and fall of religions.

It was in Afghanistan that the ancient religion of Zoroastrianism started in the 6th century BC. Later, Buddhism spread west from India to the Bamiyan Valley where it remained strong until the 10th century AD. The eastward sweep of Islam had reached Afghanistan in the 7th century and the whole country to this day remains Muslim.

During these centuries Afghanistan had been ruled by local kings or invaders from abroad, such as Alexander the Great, but Mahmud of Ghazni established the first great Afghan power centre in the south of the country in the 11th century. He repeatedly descended to the rich plains of India to carry off anything that could be moved. Altogether he made no less than 17 raids under the pretext of taking Islam to the Hindus. It was

Democratic Republic of Afghanistan

Area: 650,000 sq km
Population: 20.6 million
Population Growth Rate: 6.7%
Capital: Kabul (pop: 1,036,407)
Head of State: Unclear at present
Official Language: Pashto and Fārsī
Currency: Afghani
Exchange Rate: 4750 afghanis = US$1
Per Capita GNP: US$23,240
Inflation: 56.7%
Time: GMT/UTC +4½

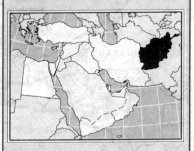

Travel Warning
Both the British Foreign Office and US State Department strongly advise against travel to Afghanistan. The situation remains extremely volatile and there are recurrent outbreaks of fighting throughout the country. At the time of research Afghan embassies and consulates were only issuing visas to accredited journalists and aid workers. For these reasons it was not possible to visit Afghanistan for the update of this edition. However, the Afghan border is notably porous and occasionally travellers have managed to enter the country. Those who propose to attempt this are strongly urged to check the situation before setting out. The British High Commission in Islamabad, Pakistan (☎ (51) 822 131/5), can supply limited advice, but visitors should be aware that there is no British or US mission in Afghanistan to provide consular help. ■

a profitable business but Ghazni soon fell to a neighbouring king. Afghanistan's worst foreign invasion then occurred.

Between 1220 and 1223 Genghis Khan tore through the country destroying all before him. Balkh, Herat, Ghazni and Bamiyan were all reduced to rubble and the damage done to the irrigation system was never repaired. Genghis specialised in pleasant little acts of psychological showmanship like building towers of skulls outside the citadel walls of cities he was besieging. No future conqueror could match the rapacity of

Genghis, and his name is still spoken with awe.

Tamerlane later swept through in the early 1380s but he had nothing on the mighty Genghis. His real name was Timur the Turk but after being wounded in battle in Afghanistan he was named Timur-leng, 'Timur-the-lame', which became Tamerlane. The rise of the Great Mogul Empire again lifted Afghanistan to heights of power. Babur had his capital in Kabul in 1512, but as the Moguls extended their power into India, Afghanistan's status declined as it went from

Afghanistan

The external boundaries of India and Pakistan on this map have not been authenticated and may not be correct.

being the centre of the empire to being simply a peripheral part of it.

In 1774, with European strength threatening the declining Moguls on the Indian subcontinent, the Kingdom of Afghanistan was founded. The 19th century was a period of often comic-book confrontation with the British, who were afraid of the effects of unruly neighbours such as Afghanistan and Burma on their great Indian colony. Additionally the spectre of Russian influence resulted in a series of remarkably unsuccessful preventative wars being fought on flimsy pretexts. To a large extent they came about because the Afghan kingdom was now too weak to stand up by itself and needed help from outside. An approach was made to the British, who stalled on it initially but sent in the troops as soon as a similar approach was made to the Russians.

The first war took place between 1839 and 1842. Dost Mohammed, ruler of Kabul, had made just such approaches to the British and Russians in turn. In 1841 the British garrison in Kabul, finding things a little uncomfortable, attempted to retreat to India and were almost totally wiped out in the Khyber Pass – only one man survived. Despite re-occupying Kabul and doing a little razing and burning to show who was boss, the British ended up with Dost Mohammed back in power, just as he had been before the war.

Round two, from 1878 to 1880, was almost the same: Afghanistan agreed to become more or less a protectorate of the British, happily accepted an annual payment to keep things in shape and agreed to a British resident in Kabul. No sooner had this diplomatic mission been installed in Kabul than all its members were murdered. This time the British decided to keep control over the external affairs, but to leave the internal matters strictly up to the Afghans themselves. A treaty with Russia further improved things – since nobody felt safe putting a foot in the country the Russians and British decided to make a little Afghan no-man's-land between themselves. That is the reason for the strange little strip of Afghanistan, the Wakhan Corridor, poking out of the top

north-eastern corner. In 1893 the British also drew Afghanistan's eastern boundaries and neatly partitioned a large number of the Pathan tribes into India in what today is Pakistan. That has been a cause of Afghan-Pakistani strife for many years and is the reason the Afghans refer to the western part of Pakistan as Pashtunistan.

Finally in 1919 the British, who by this time had totally lost interest in the place, got involved in one last tangle. And lost again. After that Afghanistan managed to go its own way right up to the late 1970s. It was the USA which replaced Britain in worrying about Russian influence, but in the post-WWII period it was nice, new roads that the superpowers used to influence Afghanistan – not troops marching over the Khyber. Nevertheless the USA tacitly recognised that Afghanistan was firmly in the Soviet sphere of influence and the Soviet presence was strongly felt. Afghanistan's trade was tilted heavily towards the USSR and Soviet foreign aid to Afghanistan far outweighed western assistance. Only in tourism did the western powers have a major influence on the country.

Internally Afghanistan remained precariously unstable, despite its relatively untroubled external relations, and it was this internal instability that eventually led to the sad situation in Afghanistan today. Attempts to encourage Turkish-style progress in the country failed dismally between WWI and WWII. The post-war kingdom ended in 1973 when the king, a Pathan like most of those in power, was neatly overthrown while away in Europe. His 'progressive' successors were hardly any more progressive than he had been, but the situation under them was far better than that which was to follow.

After the bloody pro-Moscow revolution that took place in 1978 Afghanistan rapidly fell into complete turmoil and confusion. Its pro-communist, anti-religious government was far out of step with the strongly Islamic situations that prevailed in neighbouring Iran and Pakistan, and soon the ever-volatile Afghan tribes had the countryside up in arms. A second revolution brought in a government leaning even more heavily on Soviet support and the country took another step towards complete anarchy.

Finally in late 1979, the Soviet regime decided that enough was enough. Another 'popular' revolution took place and a Soviet puppet government was installed in Kabul, with what looked like half the Soviet army lined up behind it to keep things in order. Despite an ineffectual storm of western protests it soon became clear that the Soviets were there to stay but the Soviet army soon found Afghanistan just as unpleasant as the Americans had found Vietnam. They had the advantage of short supply lines, no organised protests from home and a divided enemy but, divided or not, the Afghan mujahedeen were every bit as determined as the Viet Cong.

The war ground on through the '80s with huge numbers of Afghans seeking refuge in neighbouring countries, particularly Pakistan. The Afghan tribal warriors remained disorganised and badly trained but to their determination and undoubted bravery they also began to add modern weaponry, and soon the Soviet regime only held the cities. Even supplying the cities became increasingly difficult as road convoys were ambushed and aircraft brought down with surface-to-air missiles. Then Gorbachev's new pragmatic approach arrived in the Kremlin and suddenly they wanted out.

The Soviet withdrawal in 1989 weakened the Russian-backed government of President Najibullah. In an attempt to end the civil war, Najibullah proposed a government of national unity but the mujahedeen refused to participate in any government which included him or his Watan (Homeland) Party. In April 1992 Najibullah was ousted and a week later fighting erupted between rival mujahedeen factions that took over parts of Kabul. An interim president was installed and replaced two months later by Burhanuddin Rabbani, a founder of the country's Islamic political movement.

The accession of Rabbani did nothing to stop the fighting. Constant warfare between the presidential forces and the armies of Gulbuddin Hekmatyar, a rival mujahedeen warlord, devastated the country, doing more damage than the Soviet occupation. The two bitter rivals were, however, forced into an alliance in May 1996 by the spectacular military successes of a group of Islamic fighters called the Taliban who were sweeping through the Afghan provinces with the announced intentions of vanquishing Afghanistan's warring factions. In September 1996 they entered Kabul unopposed – Rabbani and Hekmatyar's forces had already fled north. The former communist president Najibullah was not so foresighted, and one of the first acts of the new rulers of Kabul was to drag him from the UN compound where he had been sheltering for the last 4½ years, execute him and string up the body for public viewing. Medieval acts such as this and the Taliban's unprecedentedly severe interpretation of Islamic shari'a law – forbidding women to work, closing girls' schools, making beards compulsory for men – have caused great unease in the capital.

At the time of writing, the group controls four-fifths of Afghanistan's territory; reports from within the country indicate that if the Taliban can enforce peace and unity throughout the land then imposed Islamic law would be a small price to pay. However, for the traveller, one of the most interesting countries in Asia looks likely to remain off limits for some time to come.

GEOGRAPHY

Afghanistan is totally landlocked and has an extremely rugged topography. Total area is 650,000 sq km. The mighty Hindu Kush

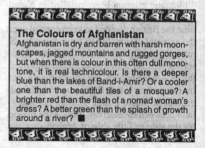

The Colours of Afghanistan
Afghanistan is dry and barren with harsh moonscapes, jagged mountains and rugged gorges, but when there is colour in this often dull monotone, it is real technicolour. Is there a deeper blue than the lakes of Band-i-Amir? Or a cooler one than the beautiful tiles of a mosque? A brighter red than the flash of a nomad woman's dress? A better green than the splash of growth around a river? ■

mountain range, the western extremity of the Himalayas, runs across the country from east to west. The average elevation of this mountainous interior is a lofty 2700m and the highest mountains reach 7500m. South is the dry, dusty Dasht-i-Margo, where the climate can be uncomfortably cold on the northern plateau in winter.

CLIMATE

The weather in Afghanistan is distinctly on the harsh side – very cold in the winters, very hot in the summers. If you are in the country between December and March make sure you have plenty of warm clothing. Spring is pleasant although the winter thaw can make the ground very muddy.

Summer (from June to August) is blisteringly hot, dry and dusty – not pleasant, particularly in the south. The best time of year is autumn (September and October). Kabul is very high up, at over 2000m, which tempers the summer heat but makes the winter cold even more severe.

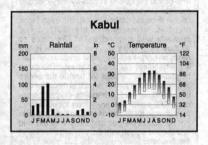

GOVERNMENT & POLITICS

According to Afghanistan's 1987 constitution the Loya Jirga, a traditional gathering of tribal leaders, elects an executive president for a seven year term. The president then appoints a Council of Ministers which must be approved by the bicameral National Assembly.

At present the country is without elected leaders – President Burhanuddin Rabbani and Prime Minister Gulbuddin Hekmatyar have fled Kabul. Power rests in the hands of

the Taliban who are led by Maulana Mohammed Omar, a former mujahedeen. On taking the capital the Taliban announced that Afghanistan would be ruled by an interim six-member council led by Omar's deputy, Mullah Mohammed Rabbani (no relation to the fleeing president).

ECONOMY

A country primarily of agricultural and nomadic shepherding people, Afghanistan trades chiefly with the former republics of the Soviet Union and the Eastern European countries. The only natural resource which has been exploited is natural gas, most of which is piped into the former USSR republics which border Afghanistan in the north.

It is a country where nothing goes to waste – old car and truck tyres become sandals or buckets, food tins become containers or cooking utensils. If it can't be made out of something else then they will make it from scratch whether it is a car part for a broken down vehicle or those amazing old rifles,

Irrigation Ingenuity

The *karez* is a peculiarly Afghan means of irrigation and of great interest to outsiders. Like many dry, arid countries Afghanistan has great underground reservoirs of water which can transform otherwise barren stretches of land – if you can get the water up. This subterranean water is often so far underground that drilling or digging for it, with primitive equipment, is virtually impossible.

Long ago the Afghans devised a better way. They dig a well, known as the 'head well', on higher ground where the distance to the water is much less. A long tunnel is then dug to conduct this water down to the village farmland. A whole series of wells are dug along the path of this tunnel during its construction. These are later used as entry points to maintain the tunnel and when not in use are covered with dirt which makes them look like gigantic ant hills. Digging a karez is skilled and dangerous work and the *karez-kans* are respected and highly paid workers. The cost of making a karez and later maintaining it is usually split between a whole village and the karez is communally owned. ■

perfect imitations of out-of-date British army weaponry.

POPULATION & PEOPLE

The population of Afghanistan is about 20.6 million although exact figures are hard to come by due to the nomadic habits of many of the people. There are millions of Afghan refugees in neighbouring countries, the overwhelming majority in Pakistan. Approximately 60% of the population is Afghan, the balance a mixture of minority groups. Kabul is the capital and largest city; other cities are Herat, Kandahar, and Mazar-i-Sharif.

Afghanistan was somehow totally unlike any other country along the (Asia) overland trail. The people were as poor as you would see, yet beggars were few. Pride is a big thing with the Afghans and 'fierce' is the only adjective to describe their spirit of independence. They are most definitely not a subject people. Compared to the countries on either side – Iran to the west, Pakistan and India to the east – it was a totally relaxed country. The hassles seemed to disappear.

SOCIETY & CONDUCT

Afghanistan's geographical position – surrounded by Iran, Turkmenistan, Uzbekistan, Tajikistan, Pakistan and China – and its varied geological terrain have both contributed to the great diversity of languages and traditions that form Afghanistan's cultural heritage. However, the turmoil produced by the civil war and the enormous number of people fleeing the country have placed all this under great pressure.

The seclusion and veiling of women has not been enforced since 1959, but with the Taliban's accession to power, at the time of writing Afghan women were being flogged or otherwise punished for being on the street at all, and especially for showing any part of leg, arms and neck uncovered. If the extreme orthodox Islamic regime persists great care will be needed to exercise respect for prevailing customs. Women should not enter mosques.

RELIGION

Afghanistan is an intensely Muslim country but although the Blue Mosque in Mazar-i-

Sharif is a most important Shiite Muslim shrine, the country is 80% Sunni. There are very small percentages of Hindus, Sikhs and Jews.

LANGUAGE

Afghanistan has two main languages. One is a Persian dialect very similar to the Fārsī spoken in Iran – see the Iran chapter for some words in that language.

The other is Pashto, which is also spoken in the Pathan (Pashtun) regions of Pakistan. Persian is the language of the government and officials and is the one to generally use. In the south and to some extent in the east, Pashto is more generally spoken. The following words are in Pashto.

The conventional greetings are delightfully descriptive. Remember that most important word, the one for foreigner –

Bloody Games

In a nation populated in part by fiery-blooded mountain tribesmen, no one would expect cricket to be the national sport. But even those prepared for excitement are likely to find *buzkashi* wild beyond belief. As close to warfare as a sport can get, buzkashi is like rugby on horseback – a game in which the 'ball' is the headless carcass of a sheep. The game begins with the carcass (or *boz*) in the centre of a circle at one end of a field; at the other end is a bunch of wild, adrenaline-crazed horsemen. At a signal, it's every man for himself as they charge for the carcass. The aim is to gain possession of the boz and carry it up the field and around a post, with the winning rider being the one who finally drops the boz back in the circle. All the while there's a frenzied tug-of-war on horseback as each competitor tries to steal the boz. While knives are not allowed, whips are. Smashed noses, wrenched shoulders and shattered thigh bones are all part of the fun. Unsurprisingly, the game is said to date from the days of Genghis Khan when, tradition has it, human carcasses were used rather than those of sheep.

In more peaceful times Friday was the big day for buzkashi and the main towns to see it in were Mazar-i-Sharif and Kunduz in the north, although there were also big games in Kabul each year. ■

farangi. And spend 10 minutes learning your Arabic numerals or the possibility of getting ripped off will become a certainty.

Basics

How are you?	*sa hal deh?*
Where are you going?	*charta zi?*
Goodbye.	*da khudai paman*
Thank you.	*tashakur/shukria*
Yes/No.	*ah/na*
expensive/cheap	*gran/arazan*
good/very good	*kha/der kha*
beautiful	*khesta*

Food

bread	*nan*
tea	*chai*
water	*ubuh*
boiled water	*ishedeli ubuh*
room	*khuma*
vegetables	*sabzi*

Time

tomorrow/yesterday (according to context)	*balauroz*
today	*nun/nunroz*
day after tomorrow/ before yesterday	*dremoroz*
now	*oos*

Numbers

1	١	*yow or yo*
2	٢	*dva*
3	٣	*dreh*
4	٤	*salor*
5	٥	*pinzo*
6	٦	*shpaag*
7	٧	*uwa or wo*
8	٨	*atta or atto*
9	٩	*naha*
10	١٠	*laas or loos*
100	١٠٠	*saal*

Facts for the Visitor

VISAS & DOCUMENTS

Few visitors, apart from journalists, try to enter Afghanistan today. However, it is possible to obtain visas to Afghanistan for accredited journalists and aid workers.

EMBASSIES

Some Afghan embassies and consulates overseas include:

France
  32 Ave Raphael, Paris 75016 (☎ 01 45 25 05 29)
India
  5/50-F Shantipath, Chanakyapuri, New Delhi (☎ (60) 3331)
Pakistan
  House No 8, St No 09, G-6/3, Islamabad (☎ (051) 822566)
  17CB-1 Gul Mohar St, Peshawar University Town, Peshawar (☎ (0521) 40503)
Russia
  Sverchkov pereulok 3/2 (☎ (095) 923 5515)
UK
  31 Princes Gate, London SW7 (☎ (0171) 589 8891)
USA
  2341 Wyoming Ave NW, Washington DC 20008 (☎ (202) 234 3770)

MONEY

Afghanistan was always a place where changing money on the street was much easier and faster than changing it in the banks and at present the economy is, no doubt, all based on foreign currencies.

The local currency, the afghani, is divided into 100 puls.

BOOKS

One of the modern classics of travel writing is Eric Newby's *A Short Walk in the Hindu Kush*. It describes the adventures of two Englishmen who trekked through the Hindu Kush to Nuristan, north of Kabul, in the 1950s. Two more latter-day travelogues are *Under a Sickle Moon* by Peregrine Hodson and *Adventures in Afghanistan* by Louis Palmer, both of which describe the authors' experiences with the mujahedeen, and recount meetings with some extraordinary characters. Few characters in the travel literature genre, however, are as memorable as the show-stealing Afghan consul to Iran as portrayed by Robert Byron in his *Road to Oxiana*, still, more than 60 years after it was written, the best book on Persia and Afghanistan.

For a general flavour of Afghanistan, James Michener's *Caravans* is a rather ridiculous and overly romantic novel, but it provides gripping reading and it does tell you how to pronounce Kabul!

See also *Afghan Amulet* by Sheila Paine and *Danziger's Travels* by Nick Danziger, in the Books section of the Regional Facts for the Visitor chapter.

ACCOMMODATION

Kabul had a great number of cheap hotels, but even before the Soviet invasion the government was closing many of them down.

FOOD & DRINKS

Food in Afghanistan is basic. Very basic. Kabul had a selection of those 'international traveller's menu' places, but elsewhere there are a lot of kebabs and omelettes, with little else available. Pilau and kebabs are the two main Afghan dishes. Kebabs – mutton or, less frequently, chicken – are served with rice or with the delicious Afghan bread known as nan.

Pilau are the rice-meat-vegetable dishes you find all across Asia. *Zarda* or *norang pilau* is made with chicken and flavoured with strips of orange peel. More common is *gaubili pilau* which uses mutton. Nuts, raisins and spices are all standard additions to a pilau. *Chelow*, like the Iranian Chelo, is made by cooking the rice separately. *Qurma*, or korma, is like a pilau with a heavy sauce.

The hygiene of Afghan bakeries was not all one could ask for, but nan being made was a performance not to be missed. If you arrived early you could buy the nan hot from the pit. The bakery would have about half a dozen men all working on their appointed tasks. The oven was reached through a circular hole in the ground, narrower at the neck than the base. The bread, like a half-metre-long oval pancake, was stuck against the side. When ready it was peeled off with a long shovel and stacked straight on to the road. At least while it was hot the flies seemed to keep off – unusual for food in Afghanistan.

Afghan fruit was usually very good, particularly in Kabul, where pomegranates, citrus fruit, grapes and melons were all excellent. Great care had to be taken with fruit. It had to be washed and carefully peeled if you wanted to avoid stomach problems. *Chai* (tea), of course, is the number one Afghan drink. There are *chai khanas* (teahouses) almost everywhere in Afghanistan. Small and dark, they're very much a male meeting place where endless cups of the delicious Afghan tea are consumed. You could often find simple food in chai khanas, and in remote places they also offered accommodation to travellers.

Supposedly Coca-Cola is still on sale in Afghanistan. Wine and beer are more difficult to find and prohibitively expensive.

THINGS TO BUY

Due to the much smaller number of visitors to Afghanistan today it's very much a buyers' market and you can pick up real bargains in handicrafts in Kabul. Afghan carpets are justly renowned and many carpet aficionados prefer them to the more formal Persian carpets.

Clothes were always an interesting and colourful buy although quality was not always too high. When buying *posteens* – the colourful embroidered Afghan coats – it was necessary to check carefully how well they had been cured. Many coats began to smell very badly after they left Afghanistan.

Kandahar was famed for its embroidery and you could buy mirrored panels to be made up into skirts or dresses elsewhere. Afghan coats were said to be particularly good in Ghazni. Leatherwork of all kinds could be found in Herat – hats, belts, bags and strong, cheap sandals. Recycling things is an Afghan speciality so sandals usually had old car tyres for their soles – better cornering power with Goodyear or Michelin?

Afghan rugs were also good buys – handmade and in a variety of tribal designs. If you were into jewellery Afghanistan was noted for lapis lazuli. There were also a lot of antiques (new and old) around, particularly venerable-looking guns. And, of course, there was Afghanistan's famous dope.

Getting There & Away

If you can enter Afghanistan at all at present Kabul is probably the gateway. Ariana Afghan Airlines, the national flag carrier, used to make regular connections with Pakistan and India.

There were three main road entry points into Afghanistan. One crossed from Mashhad in Iran to Herat, the second from Quetta in Pakistan to Kandahar and the third from Peshawar in Pakistan over the Khyber Pass to Kabul.

Getting Around

Flying is probably the only means of travel within Afghanistan today. Afghanistan has one good road loop, built with Russian and US aid, from Herat through Kandahar to Kabul. Good roads continue north from Herat into Turkmenistan and north from Kabul to Mazar-i-Sharif and Tajikistan. A poor road completes the loop from Mazar-i-Sharif to Herat. Another rough route runs through the centre of the country from Herat to Kabul via Band-i-Amir and Bamiyan – shorter in distance but longer in time. Once there were frequent bus services between Herat and Kandahar, Kandahar and Kabul, and Kabul and Mazar-i-Sharif.

The surfaced roads were only built in the 1960s and travel through Afghanistan, previously hard going, became a breeze. The road made its great southern loop from Kabul to Herat via Kandahar in order to skirt the southern extremities of the Hindu Kush. The road north to Mazar-i-Sharif passed through the long Salang Tunnel. Traffic was always light and apart from occasional brown hills the only things to see were nomads and their camels. The nomad cos-

tumes are brilliant and the women are quite unlike the traditional Afghan women who are usually shrouded from head to toe.

Kabul

The capital of Afghanistan was never a terribly attractive or interesting city and that has certainly not been improved by the almost constant fighting that has gone on since the Soviets pulled out in 1989. They left a reasonably intact city, but since then Kabul has been virtually destroyed by bombardments and street battles with an estimated loss of some 30,000 lives. The Kabul Museum, which used to have one of the finest collections of antiquities in Asia, has had nearly three-quarters of its finest collections looted by the various factions that have controlled the building during the ebb and flow of fighting.

City Wall & Citadel
It was not possible to visit the old citadel, Bala Hissar, even prior to the invasion, as it was still used by the military, but it was possible to walk the entire length of the often crumbling walls. They run from the southern side of Koh-i-Asamai, the hill close to Shah-i-Nan, down to the river then up and over Koh-i-Sher Darwaza on the other side of the river, finally terminating at the citadel. It took about five hours to walk the full length of the walls.

Other Sights
The pleasant **Gardens of Babur** were a cool retreat near the city walls. The noon gun (which was fired every noon, believe it or not!) was here too. It was once used for rather messy executions. It was not possible to go inside the **Pol-i-Khisti**, the most important mosque in Kabul. The **bazaar** – twisting, turning streets of shops – flanks Jodi Maiwand Ave to the south of the river. There is a **camel market** just outside Kabul on the Jalalabad road.

Places to Stay & Eat

Kabul had a lot of places to stay and you had no trouble finding something to suit. Today the choice is probably limited to the *Kabul Inter-Continental*. The bazaar hotels, south of the river around Jodi Maiwand Ave, were cheap and grotty. Most people stayed in the newer diplomatic quarter known as Shah-i-Nao. Here you once found 'Chicken St', the freak centre of Kabul and one of those great Asian 'bottlenecks' through which every overland traveller seemed to pass. It was packed with restaurants, souvenir and craft shops, cheap hotels and crowds of travellers.

Amongst the popular eating places, now no doubt all shut down, were *Sigi's Restaurant* on Chicken St and the *government restaurant* in central Pashtunistan Square – famous all across Asia for its apple pies.

Getting Around

Buses in Kabul were absurdly cheap and none too reliable. They tended to depart only when full and were inclined to stop for prayers and other calls! Taxis were un-metered but had a flat charge within the city limits.

Around the Country

NURISTAN

The region north-east of Kabul, known as Nuristan, the 'land of light', is interestingly described in *A Short Walk in the Hindu Kush*. Once known as Kafiristan, it had been a non-Muslim thorn in the side of the central government until Islam was forcibly taken to the people around the turn of the century – 'do you believe in Mohammed or would you like your head chopped off?'. It's still remote, little visited and of great ethnological interest.

BAMIYAN

There were two ways of getting to the great Buddhas of Bamiyan from Kabul. The longer, easier route heads north then turns west and is about 250 km. The shorter, more difficult route heads directly west from Kabul then turns north through the Unai and Hajigak passes – only 180 km but much more severe dirt roads. You could also approach Bamiyan, during the dry season, from Herat on the central route.

When the intrepid Chinese priest Hsuan-tsang visited Bamiyan in 632 AD there were 'more than 10 monasteries and more than 1000 priests'. This was one of the great Buddhist centres, but the arrival of Islam spelt disaster. The Muslims abhorred representations of the human form and on several occasions they mutilated or damaged the huge buddha statues that dominate the valley. The Russians didn't help the situation either. The latest traveller reports indicated that the Buddhas of Bamiyan are now within a military base and access to them may be barred. Try checking in Kabul before setting out.

Giant Buddhas

The smaller of the two buddhas stands a towering 35m high. This buddha is thought to have been carved out in the 2nd or 3rd century AD and has elements of the Graeco-Buddhist style. It is much more badly disfigured than the later, better and larger buddha which stands 53m high. This buddha is estimated to be two or three centuries younger and is in a later, more sophisticated style. The buddhas were carved roughly out of their niches then the final design applied with mud and straw covered them in a type of cement. Cords draped down the body were built up to form the folds of the figures' robes. The holes that make exposed parts of the figures look like a cheese were used to peg and stabilise this outer 'skin'.

Around the buddhas is an absolute honeycomb of caves which were once covered in painted frescoes – the buddhas too were at one time brightly painted. Most of the frescoes have long since deteriorated, partly due to the actions of the local inhabitants who have used the caves as dwellings. The best remaining paintings can be seen around the smaller buddha.

Other Sights

The **Red City**, the remains of an ancient citadel which guarded Bamiyan, is about 17 km before Bamiyan itself. It took a couple of hours to scramble around it. **Shar-i-Gholgola** is the ruined city in the valley – the name means 'city of sighs', the sighs being those of the inhabitants after Genghis had dropped in for a spot of massacring. There are many more caves and other attractions in the area. A climb to the top of the cliff on the other side of the valley to look across at the buddhas was a popular activity.

Places to Stay & Eat

A lot of places had sprung up at Bamiyan to cater for travellers but the basic places were very basic.

BAND-I-AMIR

It's not really possible to describe the lakes of Band-i-Amir. To appreciate them you had to go there. The lakes – clear, cold blue surrounded by towering cliffs – are 75 km beyond Bamiyan. It was worth suffering the pre-dawn chill to see the sunrise over them. Most accommodation at Band-i-Amir operated in summer only; it was far too cold to hang around for long in the winter.

THE NORTH

North of the Hindu Kush is a quite different Afghanistan – if the south is related to the Iranian plateau, the north is akin to the Russian steppes and indeed, prior to modern attitudes about borders, the Afghan nomads were quite at home on both the Russian and Afghan sides of the border. Until the Salang Pass tunnel was completed in the mid-1960s this was also a totally isolated part of the country. To get there before that time you either had to climb up and over the highest part of the Hindu Kush, north of Kabul, or cross the lower western extremity near Herat and make a long desert crossing.

Archaeologists found remains of Greek cities and buildings from Alexander the Great's day near Mazar-i-Sharif but there was nothing much for the visitor to view. The road westwards to Herat gets progressively worse after Balkh, and after Shibarghan it is just a sandy wasteland.

Mazar-i-Sharif

The main town of the northern region is actually quite new, particularly in comparison with neighbouring Balkh. Its main attraction considerably predates the rest of the town, however. The **Blue Mosque**, or Tomb of Ali, marks the centre of the town and is the holiest spot in Afghanistan. Of course whether or not Ali really does rest within is open to question. After his assassination, Ali, adopted son and then son-in-law of the Prophet, was said to have been buried in Iraq. Quite why his skeleton should then turn up near Balkh we are not sure. Nevertheless in the 12th century a small shrine was built for him, but later hidden with earth during Genghis Khan's little visit. The current shrine dates from 1481 but has been considerably modified since; only the two main domes are original.

Balkh

A Chinese visitor in 663 AD said Balkh had three of the most beautiful buildings in the world and it was known to the Arabs as the 'mother of cities'. Today all that is left are a few timeworn buildings and the crumbling remains of the city walls. Balkh was once the capital of Zoroaster and a principal centre for his religion. Later, under the Arabs, it became an important Muslim centre with a huge mosque and a reputation for culture and trade. Then, in 1220, Genghis Khan massacred the inhabitants and toppled the walls in the most terrible slaughter Afghanistan was to suffer at his hands.

When Marco Polo passed through in 1275 he found only ruins. Later Tamerlane rebuilt the walls but efforts to re-establish Balkh were unsuccessful and it has been a ghost town for centuries. The 15th century **Green Mosque** (Mosque of Abu Nasr Parsā) and piles of rubble are pretty much all there is to see.

GHAZNI

Like Balkh in the north the modern town of

Ghazni is just a pale shadow of its former glory although there was much more to see here than in the northern centre. Ghazni is only 150 km south-west of Kabul on the road to Kandahar so it was easy to get to, but it is slightly off the main road, making it just as easy to drive straight by.

A thousand years ago, at its peak, the Ghazni kingdom stretched to India in the east and Persia in the west. Mahmud, who ruled from 990 to 1030, specialised in swooping down on the plains of India and carting off treasure by the camel load. All these easily acquired riches turned Ghazni into a great and beautiful city, but in 1151 it was burnt out by a local king – who was so pleased with his arsonist abilities that he named himself the 'world burner'. Only 70 years later, in 1221, Genghis dropped by and knocked over whatever was left. Although it was later partially restored, Ghazni today is known mainly for its fine **bazaar**.

The **tomb of Mahmud** is not one of Ghazni's greatest buildings although he was undoubtedly the most important ruler of the kingdom. The carefully restored **tomb of Abdul Razzak** and the museum within are of greater interest. There are also some very fine minarets, the excavations of the **Palace of Masud** and, most surprisingly, a recently discovered **Buddhist stupa** which has survived from long before the Arab invasion that preceded even Mahmud.

KANDAHAR

Situated in the far south of Afghanistan, about midway between Kabul and Herat, Kandahar is the point on the main highway where it stops going south and starts going north. It is also the place where the road branches off south to Quetta in Pakistan. In fact it is today pretty much what it has always been – an important crossroads and little else. In the summer, when Kandahar becomes excessively dry, hot and dusty, it is not a place to hang around for very long.

Mosque of the Sacred Cloak

Kandahar's great treasure, a cloak which once belonged to the Prophet, is safely

locked away from infidel eyes in this mosque. Next door is the uninspiring tomb of Ahmed Shah, father of modern Afghanistan and the man who brought the cloak back to Kandahar. Apart from the mosque itself there is little to see in Kandahar, although a few km out of town there are a couple of attractions.

Chihil Zina

The 'Forty Steps' are only a few km from the centre towards Herat. They lead up to a niche carved in the rock by Babur, founder of the Mogul Empire, guarded by two stone lions. Here, overlooking his capital city (nice views), he carved a record of his many victories. Akbar, his grandson, appended his list too.

Tomb of Mir Waiss

The tomb is pleasantly situated by a cool green garden on the banks of the Arghandah River, just a little further out from the centre of Kandahar.

Places to Stay

The cheap hotels were mainly clustered around the central bus terminal or along the Herat road.

HELMAND VALLEY

The Helmand Valley was once the centre of a sophisticated karez underground irrigation system. Unfortunately Genghis, on one of his rape-pillage-destroy visits, did it no good at all and the area has pretty much reverted to desert. The Helmand River Project was intended to re-irrigate this area.

Bost

If you head towards Herat for about 100 km then turn south at Girishk, another 50 km on a good dirt road brings you to the site of Bost. Way back when Ghazni was the centre of power in this part of Asia, this was the second city. Today it is a jumble of ruins and remains – shattered remnants of a once mighty city. The superb arch, **Qalai Bost**, was the high point of a visit to this old centre.

Kajaki

If you head back to the main road from Bost, then cross it and continue 90 km (again on a good dirt road) north you'll find yourself at this pleasant place on the banks of the Helmand River.

HERAT

Herat is a small, provincial, relatively green, laze-about place which everyone seemed to like. Part of its attraction was the contrast to everything around it. It was an easy-going oasis after a lot of hassle and dry desert. It was also a place with a quite amazingly violent history even in recent years. At one time in 1979, before the conclusive Russian takeover, every Russian in Herat was massacred by angry Afghans.

Friday Mosque

The Friday Mosque, or Masjid-i-Jami, is Herat's number one attraction and one of the finest Islamic buildings in the world, certainly the finest in Afghanistan. Although there have been religious buildings on this site for well over 1000 years everybody and their brother has had a go at knocking them down, including Genghis Khan, who destroyed an earlier mosque. The current one was built in 1498 and since 1943 has been gradually restored to its former magnificence. It has some extremely fine tilework to complement its graceful architecture and you could visit the small workshop where tiles were still being made for the restoration project. The mosque is also unusual, in Afghanistan, for permitting non-Muslim and women visitors.

Citadel

Herat's ancient citadel was still used as an army post so you could not get in for a look around although you could walk right round its outer wall. Only in this past century has the citadel been allowed to deteriorate badly but it makes a sad, though impressive, contrast with the great mosque.

Covered Bazaar

The covered bazaar in Char souq is a complex of all sorts of shops and artisans' workshops. It is in the south-western corner of the old walled city. At various points around the bazaar area and elsewhere in Herat you could see the old covered wells for which Herat is known.

Gazar Gah

This monastery complex, dating from 1425, is about five km east of Herat. The tomb of Abdullah Ansar, a famous Sufi mystic and poet who died in Herat in 1088, is the main attraction. Qivam ad-Din, the architect who later remodelled the shrine, is buried in the small tomb, which is fashioned in the form of a crouching dog, in front of the shrine. There is also a unique black-marble tombstone in the complex. On the road back to Herat there is a small **park** offering a fine view over the town.

Other Sights

A short walk from the centre on the road that runs north and intersects the road to the Iran border are a number of interesting sights. First there is a small **park** with a beehive-shaped tomb then, further on, four immense, broken **minarets**. They are all that remains of an old madrassa or theological school, which was built by the Empress Gaur-Shad, who also built the mosque at Mashhad. She was a remarkable woman who followed Tamerlane and kept his empire intact for many years after his death.

Unhappily the destruction of the minarets was due to a visiting British adventurer in 1838. Finding the Persians about to invade the town, he decided to lend a hand to the locals and had parts of the religious school blown up to give the artillery a clearer line of fire. Further up the road are some interesting old **windmills**, examples of which could also be seen between Herat and Islam Qala, the border point to Iran.

Places to Stay & Eat

The cheap hotels were mainly clustered along the main street in the old city.

Bahrain

Since the dawn of history Bahrain has been a trading centre. Occupying a strategic position on the great trade routes of antiquity, with good harbours and abundant fresh water, the Bahrainis are natural merchants. The islands' prosperity today is built not on oil but on banking, tourism and other service industries. It is the easiest of the Gulf countries to visit, and one of the best values for those on a budget.

Bear in mind, however, that while Bahrain is one of the most liberal countries in the Gulf it is still, by western standards, a very conservative place. In comparison to other Arab countries it is less open than Egypt or Jordan, and it certainly does not share those countries' long experience with tourism. Political tensions in recent years have made discretion on the part of visitors even more important.

Facts about the Country

HISTORY

Bahrain's history goes back to the roots of human civilisation. From the 3rd millennium BC it was the seat of Dilmun, one of the great trading empires of the ancient world. Dilmun was founded during the Bronze Age, probably sometime around 3200 BC, and continued in some form or other for more than 2000 years. It evolved here because of the islands' strategic position along the trade routes linking Mesopotamia with the Indus Valley.

From 2200 to 1600 BC Dilmun controlled a large section of the western shore of the Gulf. At times its power probably extended as far north as modern Kuwait and as far inland as the Al-Hasa Oasis in eastern Saudi Arabia. Between 1600 and 1000 BC, however, Dilmun fell into decline and by about 600 BC it had been fully absorbed by Babylon.

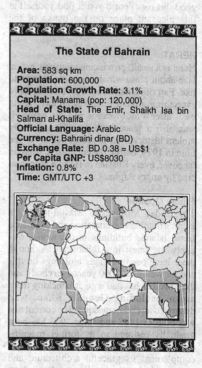

The State of Bahrain

Area: 583 sq km
Population: 600,000
Population Growth Rate: 3.1%
Capital: Manama (pop: 120,000)
Head of State: The Emir, Shaikh Isa bin Salman al-Khalifa
Official Language: Arabic
Currency: Bahraini dinar (BD)
Exchange Rate: BD 0.38 = US$1
Per Capita GNP: US$8030
Inflation: 0.8%
Time: GMT/UTC +3

From the 9th to the 11th century Bahrain was part of the Umayyad (Omayyad) and, later, Abbasid empires. It was under Abbasid rule that its reputation as a stronghold of Shiite Islam was established. Although during this period Bahrain had neither the wealth nor the importance it had enjoyed some 2000 years earlier, it appears to have been reasonably prosperous. It was once again on the trade routes between Mesopotamia and the Indian subcontinent, and as one of the Gulf's main pearling ports Bahrain clearly had economic value.

It was not until the mid-18th century that the Al-Khalifa, the family which now rules Bahrain, first arrived in the area. They initially settled in Zubara, on the north-western edge of the Qatar peninsula, and involved themselves in the region's lucrative pearling trade. They drove the Persians out of Bahrain in 1782 or 1783. Three years later, however, the Al-Khalifa were driven out by an Omani invasion and they did not return until 1820.

Shortly thereafter a treaty was signed with the British in which the Bahrainis agreed to abstain from what the British defined as piracy. The treaty was updated in 1835 and 1861, becoming the first of the so-called Exclusive Agreements, under which the ruler of Bahrain (and other Gulf rulers who later signed similar documents) ceded control of foreign affairs to Britain in exchange for military protection. Britain's main concern was to keep other western powers out of the area and safeguard its supply routes to India – with a few notable exceptions, the British largely stayed out of local politics during the 19th century.

Bahrain was the first place on the Arabian side of the Gulf where oil was discovered. The first oil concession was granted in 1925 and oil in commercial quantities was found in June 1932. Exports began soon afterwards. The discovery of oil could not have come at a better time for Bahrain, as it roughly coincided with the collapse of the world pearl market. Until that time pearling had been the mainstay of Bahrain's economy.

Equally important was the fact that oil was discovered in Bahrain before it was discovered elsewhere in the Gulf. The Bahrainis were the first to enjoy the benefits that came from the oil revenues – notably a dramatic improvement in the quality of education and health care. This led to the island assuming a larger role in Britain's operations in the Gulf. The main British naval base in the region was moved to Bahrain in 1935. In 1946 the Political Residency, the office of the senior British official in the region, was also moved to Bahrain.

Bahrain's modernisation began under Shaikh (Sheikh) Hamad bin Ali and accelerated under his son, Shaikh Salman, who came to power when Shaikh Hamad died in 1942. Salman's 19 years on the throne saw a vast increase in the country's standard of living as oil production boomed in Saudi Arabia, Kuwait and Qatar. At that time none of these other areas could match Bahrain's level of development, health care or education. As a result, Bahrain became the Gulf's main entrepôt.

Shaikh Salman died in 1961 and was succeeded by his son, the present emir, Shaikh Isa bin Salman al-Khalifa.

Bahrain became independent on 14 August 1971 and a Constituent Assembly charged with drafting a constitution was elected at the end of 1972. The emir issued the constitution in May 1973 and an elected national assembly convened that December. The Assembly, however, was dissolved only 20 months later when the emir decided that radical assembly members were making it impossible for the executive branch to function.

During the '70s and '80s Bahrain experienced a huge degree of growth, partly from the skyrocketing price of oil but also because in the mid to late '70s it was still well ahead of much of the rest of the Gulf in terms of infrastructure. In recent years its status as an entrepôt has declined somewhat, but its economy has also become more diversified and less oil-dependent.

While the '90s have seen a vast improvement in relations with Iran, Bahrain's relations with Iraq have gone sharply downhill. Bahrainis will not soon forget that Iraq's Saddam Hussein ordered a missile attack on their country during the Gulf War (the missile landed harmlessly in the sea). A dispute with Qatar over ownership of the Hawar Islands, over which Bahrain has de jure control, has dragged on for years and remains a diplomatic sore spot between the two countries.

In recent years, however, the quiet world of Bahraini life has been rocked by sporadic waves of unrest. The trouble began in late 1994 when the emir refused to accept a petition, reputedly signed by some 25,000 Bahrainis, calling for greater democracy. Anger at this incident boiled over into rioting that November, with protests centred in the

BAHRAIN

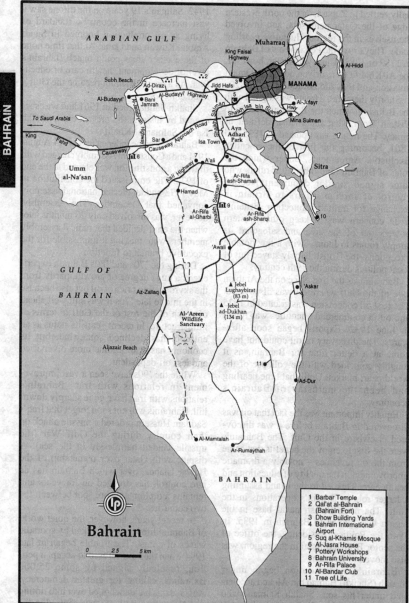

ARABIAN GULF

Muharraq

King Faisal
Highway

Al-Hidd

Subh Beach

Ad-Diraz

Jidd Hafs

MANAMA

Al-Budayyi' Highway

Al-Budayyi'

Bani
Jamrah

Al-Jufayr

Shaikh Isa bin Sulman Hwy

To Saudi Arabia

King
Fahd

Causeway

Sar

Causeway Approach Road

Isa Town

Ayn
Adhari
Park

Mina Sulman

Umm
al-Na'san

A'ali

Nali Highway

Isa bin Sulman Hwy

Ar-Rifa
ash-Shamali

Sitra

Hamad

Ar-Rifa
al-Gharbi

Ar-Rifa
ash-Sharqi

GULF OF
BAHRAIN

'Awali

Az-Zallaq

Al-'Areen
Wildlife
Sanctuary

▲ Jebel
Lughaybirat
(83 m)

'Askar

▲ Jebel
ad-Dukhan
(134 m)

Aljazair Beach

Ad-Dur

Al-Mamtalah

Ar-Rumaythah

BAHRAIN

Bahrain

0   2.5   5 km

1	Barbar Temple
2	Qal'at al-Bahrain (Bahrain Fort)
3	Dhow Building Yards
4	Bahrain International Airport
5	Suq al-Khamis Mosque
6	Al-Jasra House
7	Pottery Workshops
8	Bahrain University
9	Ar-Rifa Palace
10	Al-Bandar Club
11	Tree of Life

BAHRAIN

Suggested Itineraries

Almost everything worth seeing in Bahrain can be covered in four or five days – a week at the most. There are no hotels outside the capital, **Manama**, but the country is so small that this hardly matters.

In Manama itself be sure to see the **National Museum**, **Beit al-Qur'an** and the **dhow building yard**. Also leave some time free for exploring the **souq**.

Outside the capital, the burial mounds and pottery workshops at **A'ali**, the ruined **Ad-Diraz** and **Barbar temples** and the ancient **Suq al-Khamis Mosque** should be at the top of your itinerary. On **Muharraq**, Bahrain's second-largest island, be sure to see **Bait Shaikh Isa bin Ali**, a restored house that gives you an idea of how the country's elite lived in the days before oil. ■

predominantly Shiite villages west of the capital. There was more unrest in April 1995 and again in the spring of 1996, when bombs exploded at both the Diplomat and Meridien hotels. The government, through the state-controlled media, accused Iran of inciting the violence.

GEOGRAPHY

The country is a low-lying archipelago of about 33 islands (including the disputed Hawar group) of which Bahrain Island (about 50 km by 16 km) is the largest. Muharraq, Sitra and Umm al-Na'san are the only other islands in the group of any significant size. The total area of the country is 583 sq km. The highest point in Bahrain, Jabal ad-Dukhan, is only 134m above sea level.

CLIMATE

This is one area in which Bahrain duplicates all of its neighbours. It can get extremely hot and humid from June to September, with temperatures averaging 36°C during the day. November to March tends to be quite pleasant with warm days and cool (though not really cold) nights. Temperatures vary between a minimum of 14°C to a maximum of 24°C.

FLORA & FAUNA

Bahrain has long been famous for its greenery in the midst of the region's deserts. Recently, however, this has been changing. Though parts of the island are still thickly covered in date palms, the island is a lot less green than it used to be. Some of the trees have been cut down and others have died as increasing demands are made on the underground springs which water them.

As for fauna, aside from domesticated donkeys you won't see many animals. Even that old Arabian standby, the camel, is a relatively rare sight in Bahrain.

GOVERNMENT & POLITICS

Bahrain is an absolute monarchy, though the emir, Shaikh Isa bin Salman al-Khalifa, consults often with government ministers and is readily available to citizens. The prime minister is the emir's brother, Shaikh Khalifa bin Salman al-Khalifa. The crown prince, Shaikh Hamad bin Isa al-Khalifa, is also the head of the Bahrain defence forces. Bahrain is the only Gulf state to have adopted a strict rule of primogeniture within the royal family.

ECONOMY

With relatively limited oil reserves Bahrain has developed a more diversified economy than many other Gulf states. The island is home to the largest aluminium smelter in the Middle East, a large shipbuilding and repair yard and one of the region's busiest airports. It is also a centre for offshore banking and other investment-related activity.

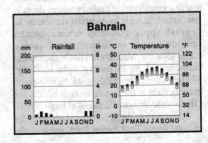

POPULATION & PEOPLE

About 600,000 people live in Bahrain, of whom some 150,000 are foreign workers. There are many North American and British people working in the islands' oil and financial industries. Services are dominated by Filipinos. That said, Manama is probably the most cosmopolitan city in the Gulf.

The Bahrainis themselves are Arabs, though many are at least partially of Persian ancestry.

ARTS

Traditional craftwork continues in several places around Bahrain: dhow building on the outskirts of Manama and on Muharraq; cloth weaving at Bani Jamrah; and pottery making at A'ali. The tourist office in Manama has a selection of all of these (except the dhows!) on sale, and you can also drive out to the villages and bargain with the craftspeople yourself.

SOCIETY & CONDUCT
Traditional Culture

As flashy and modern as central Manama may be, the basic rhythms of life in the islands' many villages, and in parts of Manama itself, remain remarkably traditional. Starting from Bab al-Bahrain in Manama, the further you go back into the souq the more conservative life gets. The same can be said for much of the rest of the country. It is a side of Bahrain that visitors all too often miss.

Dos & Don'ts

Bahrain is relatively liberal as Gulf countries go, but the Gulf itself remains one of the most conservative places on earth. Bahrain is still a conservative country where dress is concerned, at least by western standards. In general apply common sense: women shouldn't wear miniskirts, short shorts, bikini tops etc. Men should not walk around bare-chested or in overly tight clothing. Women should probably stick to one-piece bathing suits at the beach, though bikinis are OK to wear around the pools at large hotels.

Conservative dress is particularly in order in rural areas. That means long, loose clothing. Short sleeves are usually OK, even for women, but sleeveless clothes (especially on women) may cause offence in more traditional areas.

RELIGION

Bahrain's population is 85% Muslim, with indigenous Christian, Jewish, Hindu and Parsee minorities (according to the Ministry of Information). Islam is the state religion. The majority of Muslims, probably upwards of 70%, are Shiites.

LANGUAGE

Arabic is the official language but English is very widely spoken. Farsi is also widely spoken, though it is most often used at home rather than in public.

Facts for the Visitor

PLANNING
When to Go

For information see the Regional Facts for the Visitor chapter. Note also that Bahrain's cheaper hotels can be extremely crowded over New Year's Eve.

Maps

The *Bahrain Map* (BD 1 at the tourist office) is very comprehensive and includes good inset maps of Manama and Muharraq. It is also very out of date but still your best bet for getting around the capital. The glossy tourist map (BD 1.500 at the tourist office) is a lot more up to date but a lot less detailed, particularly in the central area. This map should be your first choice for trying to find the tourist sites outside the capital.

What to Bring

For information see the Regional Facts for the Visitor chapter at the beginning of the book.

VISAS & DOCUMENTS
Visas

British citizens do not need a visa to enter Bahrain for periods of up to one month.

People of most other western nationalities can obtain a 72 hour transit visa or a seven day tourist visa on arrival at Bahrain airport or at the Bahraini customs post on the Saudi Arabia-Bahrain causeway. The three day visa costs BD 10 and the seven day visa BD 15. Fees can be paid in Bahraini dinars or Saudi riyals. Possession of an onward or return plane or bus ticket is not formally required but travellers are often asked to produce these.

If your passport has an Israeli stamp you will be denied entry (and customs do check).

Women travelling alone and holders of non-western passports – particularly people from South-East Asia or the Indian subcontinent – should obtain visas in advance through a hotel. To have a hotel arrange a visa for you, send them a fax about three weeks prior to arrival with all your passport data as well as arrival and departure dates and the purpose of your visit ('tourism' is fine). You'll also need to specify the exact flight on which you plan to arrive (airline, flight number, day and time) and include a telephone or fax number where you can be reached. It might be a good idea to double-check everything by telephone. The hotel will act as your sponsor and make all of the visa arrangements for a small fee (usually BD 2 to BD 4), which will be added to your bill. You can then pick up the visa at the airport, port or on the causeway.

Visa Extensions Hotels that can issue visas can also get your visa extended once you are in the country. If you are staying in a cheap hotel and want to extend your stay, your only practical option is to move up-market and stay there. Extending your visa through a hotel is painless and requires nothing from you except a few extra dinars (usually BD 10 for a one week extension plus a hotel charge of BD 2 to BD 4). It usually takes about two days so don't wait until the morning your visa runs out to organise this!

Other Documents
Health certificates are not required to enter Bahrain unless you are coming from an area

of endemic yellow fever etc (eg Sub-Saharan Africa).

If you plan to rent a car in Bahrain, you will need to obtain an International Driving Permit from your local automobile association.

EMBASSIES
Bahraini Embassies Abroad
Bahraini embassies overseas are of little use to the traveller. They usually handle only residence and work visas, which are only issued after approval has been received from Manama.

Foreign Embassies in Bahrain
Embassies are in the capital, Manama. Most are open Saturday to Wednesday from 7.30 or 8 am until noon or 1 pm.

Australia
    Australian interests are looked after by the UK embassy
Canada
    Canadian interests are looked after by the UK embassy
France
    Diplomatic Area, Al-Fatih Highway, near the National Museum; entered from Exhibition Ave (☎ 291 734)
Germany
    Al-Hassaa building, 1st floor, near Beit al-Qur'an (☎ 530210)
Jordan
    Diplomatic Area, Al-Fatih Highway, near the National Museum (☎ 291 109)
Kuwait
    King Faisal Highway, opposite the Holiday Inn (☎ 534 040)
New Zealand (consular agency)
    Yateem Centre, Level 2 (☎ 223 600)
Oman
    Diplomatic Area, Al-Fatih Highway, near the National Museum. The building is entered from the side facing Exhibition Ave (☎ 293 663).
Saudi Arabia
    King Faisal Highway, opposite the Holiday Inn and near the Kuwaiti embassy (☎ 537 722)
UK
    Government Ave, opposite the Bahrain Commercial Complex (☎ 534 404)
USA
    Just off the Shaikh Isa bin Sulman Highway, in the Al-Zinj district, next to the Ahli Sporting Club (☎ 273 300)

BAHRAIN

BAHRAIN

CUSTOMS

Non-Muslims are allowed to import two litres of alcoholic beverages. All passengers are allowed to bring in 400 cigarettes or 50 cigars and 250g of loose tobacco. You may be asked whether you are carrying a video camera and, if so, this fact is likely to be recorded in your passport to guarantee that you take it out again.

MONEY
Costs

If you stay in the souq, walk a lot and have no huge appetite for either food or booze, it is quite possible to get by on BD 10 per day.

Currency

The Bahraini dinar (BD) is divided into 1000 fils. Coins are 5, 10, 25, 50 and 100 fils. Notes come in denominations of BD ½, one, five, 10 and 20. For small transactions most businesses will accept Qatari or Saudi riyals at a flat rate of BD 1 = QR/SR 10. The Bahraini dinar is a convertible currency and there are no restrictions on its import or export.

Currency Exchange

Australia	A$1	=	BD 0.300
France	FF1	=	BD 0.074
Germany	DM1	=	BD 0.250
UK	UK£1	=	BD 0.620
USA	US$1	=	BD 0.380

Changing Money

Banking hours are Saturday to Wednesday from 7.30 am to noon. Most banks close at 11 am on Thursday. Some moneychangers keep slightly longer hours and may open for a while later in the afternoon. Moneychangers usually have better rates than banks. Be sure to shop around. Credit cards are widely accepted in Bahrain, and most of the major banks are linked to one or more of the international ATM networks.

Tipping & Bargaining

A service charge is added to almost every bill but it generally goes to the shop, not the staff. While tips are not expected, especially in cheap places, waiting staff are often paid appalling wages and a tip, even a small one, will be much appreciated.

In many small shops you will probably be offered an immediate discount on the marked price, and you might be able to talk the price of souvenirs on sale in the souq down by an additional 10% or so (but not the ones in the Bab al-Bahrain government tourist shop as the prices there are fixed). Hotel rates are almost always negotiable, though, again, to what extent depends mostly on how business has been over the last few days.

Prices of meals, books and organised tours are generally not negotiable.

POST & COMMUNICATIONS
Post

Mail to and from Europe and North America takes about a week. Allow 10 days to Australia. The main post office is in Manama on Government Ave across from Bab Al-Bahrain.

International postal rates are measured in 10g increments. Postage per 10g is 200 fils to Europe and the Indian subcontinent, and 250 fils to Australia, Africa or North America. Postage for aerogrammes is 150 fils to anywhere in the world. Postcard rates are 150 fils to Europe and 200 fils to Australia, Africa or North America.

The GPO on Government Ave has poste restante facilities. Letters should be addressed c/o Poste Restante, Manama Post Office (Counter Section), Manama, Bahrain.

Telephone

Bahrain's country code is 973, followed by the local six digit number. There are no area or city codes. Payphones usually take telephone cards, which are widely available throughout the country. For coin phones you need to insert a minimum of 100 fils.

Bahrain also has an extensive set of Home Country Direct services. By dialling a special number these connect you directly to an operator in the question. You may then make a collect (reverse charges) call or bill the call to a phone company credit card issued in that country. Home Country Direct services available from any phone in Bahrain include:

Australia	800-061
Canada	800-100
Ireland	800-353
UK	800-044
USA	800-001 (ATT)
USA	800-002 (MCI)
USA	800-777 (Sprint)

Fax, Telex & Telegraph

Fax, telex, and telegraph services are available from the telecommunications office in the Yateem Centre on Al-Khalifa Ave in Manama. See the Manama section later in this chapter for more details.

BOOKS

Possibly the best book on Bahrain is *Looking for Dilmun* by Geoffrey Bibby, an Anglo-Danish archaeologist who supervised the early professional archaeological work on the island. It is an account of Bibby's digs in Bahrain, but it also provides a fascinating picture of life on the island and the rest of the Gulf in the '50s and '60s. Archaeology buffs might also want to pick up *Bahrain Through the Ages – The Archaeology* by Shaikha Haya Ali al-Khalifa & Michael Rice. Hotel bookshops in Bahrain are the easiest places to find this one, which is only available in hardback.

The best all-round guide to the country's architecture, archaeology and curiosities is *Bahrain: A Heritage Explored* by Angela Clark. It can be found at all hotel bookshops and costs about BD 5. The book, an updated version of Clark's 1981 book, *The Islands of Bahrain*, includes the best general descriptions of the country's archaeological sites (outside of the Al-Khalifa/Rice book which is a bit bulky to haul around). For more general book information, see the Books section in the Regional Facts for the Visitor.

NEWSPAPERS & MAGAZINES

The *Gulf Daily News* is Bahrain's English-language newspaper. It's a bit disappointing in terms of news but hugely useful as a source of 'what's on' information. There is no Friday edition. All of the larger hotels stock the usual array of international publications.

RADIO & TV

Radio Bahrain broadcasts 24 hours a day on 98.5 FM. The fare consists, broadly, of pop music in the mornings, feature programmes in the afternoons and light music at night.

Channel 55 is Bahrain TV's English programme service. It carries a mix of British and US programmes every day from 5 or 6 pm until around midnight. Bahrain TV also broadcasts BBC World Service TV 24 hours a day on a local UHF frequency.

PHOTOGRAPHY & VIDEO

Bahrain is fairly relaxed about both tourists and cameras, and as long as you don't try to take a picture of something obviously military or taboo (eg women, especially in rural areas) you should have no problems.

Film is easily available anywhere in Manama, as is processing for colour prints.

HEALTH

The quality of medical care in Bahrain is very high. Hygiene standards for food preparation are also quite high, except in a few of the darker corners of the souq. Cases of travellers' diarrhoea almost always originate in the cheaper parts of the souq and if you exercise a little common sense you will probably be alright. The tap water is not suitable for drinking. For more detailed health information please refer to the Health Appendix.

WOMEN TRAVELLERS

Bahrain is without a doubt one of the easiest countries in the Gulf for women to travel in. The country's long trading history and traditional openness account for its relatively progressive attitude toward women.

Outside of mosques it is never necessary for female visitors to Bahrain to cover their heads, though extra caution should be taken in village areas. Modest shorts or above-knee skirts, which would be perfectly acceptable

BAHRAIN

in Manama, will not go down well in the villages.

DANGERS & ANNOYANCES
Bahrain is a very safe place. Violent crime is quite rare and you can walk around central Manama late at night without fear. That said, young unaccompanied males (that's right, males) should steel themselves for a certain amount of petty harassment. It seems that foreign women encounter far less trouble than they would in, say, Cairo or Athens, but we cannot guarantee this. Be firm, maintain your composure and everything will probably be OK.

BUSINESS HOURS
Shops and offices are generally open from around 8 am until 1 pm. Many shops, particularly in the Manama souq, reopen later in the afternoon from 4 or 5 until 7 pm. Friday is the weekly holiday and many businesses also close early on Thursday.

PUBLIC HOLIDAYS & SPECIAL EVENTS
The Islamic holidays of Eid al-Fitr (the end of Ramadan), Eid al-Adha (Pilgrimage) and the Islamic New Year are all observed. Bahrain's large Shiite community also marks Ashura, though this is not an official government holiday. See the table of holidays near Public Holidays & Special Events in the Regional Facts for the Visitor chapter.

Bahrain also celebrates New Year's Day (1 January) and National Day (16 December).

ACTIVITIES
Most activities on the island are centred around clubs, societies and sports organisations. The *Gulf Daily News* and Radio Bahrain are good sources of information for events and gatherings around the island. Otherwise, social life on the island consists mainly of eating and/or drinking out.

WORK
Throughout the Gulf regulations controlling work visas are quite strict. Working in the country requires that you have a Bahraini sponsor, and casual travellers should not expect to pick up short-term work, either legally or illegally.

ACCOMMODATION
Bahrain's youth hostel is in the suburb of Al-Jufayr, south-east of Manama's centre. If you are not a Hostelling International (HI) member, membership cards are available to foreigners for BD 7. See Places to Stay in the Manama section later in this chapter for more details.

Hotel rooms bottom out at about BD 7/10 for singles/doubles with bath. Rooms without private baths are a dinar or so less. Bahrain's five-star hotels sometimes offer unusually good weekend (ie Wednesday and Thursday nights) packages which are worth looking into, though they usually have to be booked in advance.

FOOD
While a bit thin on Arabic food Bahrain offers a bonanza of Asian specialities. From Indian and Pakistani to Thai and Filipino you can find almost any sort of cuisine in the area around Al-Khalifa Rd. Good meals are usually about BD 3, but if you stick to simple things like *shwarma* (beef or chicken carved from a large spit and rolled in pita bread with some or all of the following: lettuce, tomatoes, houmos and hot sauce) you can easily eat for under BD 1.

DRINKS
Nonalcoholic drinks consist of Pepsi or Coke, 7-Up, orange soda or fruit juice (not usually fresh unless you buy from a large hotel). Alcohol is draught beer and Bahrain has the same selection of harder stuff that you would find in any bar. Booze is not cheap. Expect to pay at least BD 1 for a can of beer and BD 1.500 for an English pint.

ENTERTAINMENT
Bahrain has one of the most lively entertainment scenes in the Gulf. See the Manama section later in this chapter for the complete lowdown on Bahrain's nightlife.

THINGS TO BUY
Good handicrafts are on sale at the tourist office at Bab al-Bahrain, which has displays showing where various items come from on the island. Locally produced items include pottery from A'ali, and hand-woven cloth from Bani Jamrah. See Things to Buy in the Manama section for details.

Getting There & Away

AIR
Bahrain is the base of operations for Gulf Air, and is one of the Gulf region's main transport centres. The best service into Bahrain from outside the region is from major hubs like London (Gulf Air has several flights daily) and Bangkok, and from large cities on the Indian subcontinent, such as Karachi, New Delhi and Bombay. Gulf Air also has regular flights from Bahrain to New York and Melbourne. Special offers to any given city will be advertised at most of the travel agents in the souq in Manama. London, New Delhi, Cairo and Singapore are probably your best bets for discounts.

Don't look for bargains on flights around the Gulf, though special 'weekend' fares to the United Arab Emirates (UAE) and Oman are often available. These allow travel only on Wednesday, Thursday and Friday, and are a bit cheaper than the lowest regular return fares. Return fares to Dhahran (flying time of nine minutes) start at BD 33 (US$88). The cheapest return ticket to Kuwait costs BD 59 (US$157), Dubai BD 60 (US$160) and Muscat BD 92 (US$245).

LAND
Land travel to/from Bahrain is via the causeway to Saudi Arabia. The Saudi-Bahraini Transport company runs five buses daily to and from Dammam via Alkhobar. The trip takes about three hours. For more details see the Manama section later in this chapter.

SEA
There are passenger services between Iran and Bahrain. See the Manama section for more details.

LEAVING BAHRAIN
If you depart by air there is an Airport Usage Fee of BD 3. There is a BD 2 toll for leaving the country via the causeway to Saudi Arabia, and a BD 3 port tax if you leave by boat.

Getting Around
Bahrain has a fairly comprehensive bus system linking most of the major towns to terminals in Manama and Muharraq. The fare is a flat rate of 50 fils per trip.

Car rental rates start at around BD 15 per day. To rent a car you will need an International Driving Permit. This must be obtained before you arrive in Bahrain. For more details on car rental see Getting Around in the Manama section later in this chapter.

There are also taxis in Manama, which are metered.

ORGANISED TOURS
Bahrain's tourist industry is still largely aimed at stopover and transit passengers and weekend visitors from Saudi Arabia. A number of airlines offer short-stay stopover packages in Bahrain aimed at people travelling between Europe and Asia. These generally include a one or two night stay, some meals and one or more half-day tours. Some of these cost less than US$100, including accommodation, and are pretty good deals. See under Organised Tours in the Manama section for a listing of local tour companies.

Manama

Manama is the very new capital of a very old place – many of the hotels and official buildings along Government Ave sit on reclaimed land. But don't be fooled – only a few blocks inland from the shiny new hotels are sections of the city which have changed little in the last 50 years.

Orientation

Manama's main street is Government Ave, which runs roughly east-west through the city. The central section of this street is the stretch from the Delmon Hotel to the large roundabout by the Hilton and Sheraton hotels. Al-Khalifa Ave runs more or less parallel to, and one block south of, Government Ave. Here you will find many of Manama's cheaper hotels and numerous small restaurants. The hub of all activity is Bab al-Bahrain and the small roundabout in front of it. The area south of Government Ave is the souq. The western limit of the centre is the Pearl Monument roundabout, while the National Museum and the causeway to Muharraq mark the centre's eastern boundary.

Exhibition Ave, running south from the Shaikh Hamad Causeway Rd to Shaikh Daij Ave and roughly paralleling the Al-Fatih Highway, is the other road you should know. Along it are a number of smaller hotels notable mostly for containing a few of Bahrain's better known nightspots. A few airline and car rental offices and fast-food joints can also be found in the same neighbourhood.

Information

Tourist Office The tourist office (☎ 231 375) and a government-run souvenir shop are both in Bab al-Bahrain and are entered from the Al-Khalifa Ave side. They are open daily from 8 am to 1 pm and 4 to 8.30 pm. Organised tours run by government-owned Gulf Tours can be booked through the tourist office. The shop sells the best available maps of the country (see the earlier Facts for the Visitor section for more information on available maps).

Money Several banks are on the side street which runs from Bab al-Bahrain to the Regency Inter-Continental Hotel. There are also a number of banks and moneychangers

on Government Ave between Bab al-Bahrain and the Delmon Hotel. You are likely to get better rates from moneychangers so it's worth taking a few minutes to shop around.

American Express (Amex) is represented in Bahrain by Kanoo Travel (☎ 249 346). The office, on Al-Khalifa Ave just behind Bab al-Bahrain, is open Saturday to Wednesday from 8 am to 12.30 pm and 3 to 6 pm, and on Thursday from 8 am to noon. It is closed on Friday. It will cash personal cheques for Amex card holders but does not provide mail service. The big Amex office in the Bahrain Commercial Centre is Amex's Middle East regional administrative headquarters; you won't need to go there unless you have a bill to pay.

Post The GPO is opposite Bab al-Bahrain on Government Ave. It is open daily except Friday from 7 am to 7.30 pm, and poste restante facilities are available.

Telephone The main Telecommunications Centre is on the ground floor of the Yateem Centre shopping complex on Al-Khalifa Ave. It is open every day from 6.30 am to 11.30 pm. Services include local and international telephone calls, telex, fax and telegraph facilities. International calls can be direct-dialled on either coin or card phones, or booked through the operator. You should be aware that booking a call is much more expensive than calling direct on the card phones.

Travel Agencies More travel agents than one would think the market could possibly support have offices on both Government and Al-Khalifa Aves. Prices are government controlled and do not vary enough from agent to agent to be worth mentioning. However, since agents offer different fares, it is worth checking out at least three or four places to find the cheapest price.

Bookshops The Family Bookshop, between the American Mission Hospital and the UK embassy, is the best in Bahrain with an excellent (if pricey) selection of the latest

BAHRAIN

Manama

ARABIAN GULF

To Muharraq &
Bahrain International
Airport

Al-Fatih Highway

To Gulf Hotel,
Al-Julayr &
Youth Hostel

Diplomatic Area
Office Buildings

Vacant
Lot

Ras
Rumman

Awadiya

Exhibition Avenue

Palace Avenue

Al-Hura

Dhuwawdah

Zubara Avenue

Al-Qudaybiyah Avenue

Shaikh Daij Avenue

Al-Qudaybiyah

Tafta Bin Al-Abd

Avenue

Kuwait Road

Shaikh Hamad Causeway

King Faisal Highway

Bani Otbah Avenue

Palace Avenue

Andalus
Garden

Old Palace

Al-Adliya

Fadhel

Kanoo

Hammam

Shaikh Isa Avenue

Isa al-Kabeer Avenue

Cemetery

Al-Sulmaniya
Garden

Al-Sulmaniya Avenue

Al-Sulmaniya

Busitra

Souq

Commercial
Area

Mukharqah

Khalaf al-Asroor Ave.

Al-Mutanabi Avenue

Kuwait
Avenue

See Central Manama
Hotel District Map

Zararie

Mohammed Avenue

Shaikh Hamad Avenue

Lulu Avenue

An Naim

Kuwait
Avenue

Al-Budayi

Qasari
Garden

Qatal Al-Bahrain &
Saudi Arabia

Shuwaifiyah Avenue

King Faisal Highway

Shaikh Salman Highway

Al-Qutool

Delmon
Roundabout

0   250   500 m

PLACES TO STAY
4   Tylos Hotel
8   (Joyce's Bar)
9   Sheraton Bahrain
11 Bahrain Hilton
12 Holiday Inn
22 Baisan International
    Hotel (The Warbler
    & Bacchus Bars)
25 Omar Khayam Hotel
26 Ramada Hotel

OTHER
1   Pearl Monument
2   Manama Central Market
3   Buses to Saudi Arabia
5   American Mission
    Hospital
6   UK Embassy
7   Bahrain Commercial
    Complex
10 Kuwaiti Embassy
13 German Embassy
14 Beit al-Qur'an
15 Sail Monument
16 National Museum
17 Omani Embassy
18 Jordanian Embassy
19 French Embassy
20 South Korean Embassy
21 Abu Bakr al-Sadiq
    Mosque
23 Al-Sulmaniya Medical
    Centre
24 Old Palace
27 Al-Qudaybiyah Palace
28 Al-Fatih Mosque

best-sellers. Also try the Al-Hilal Bookshop on Tujjaar Ave with its rather eclectic selection of English books, ranging from romance novels to technical books to the occasional out-of-print account of some 18th or 19th century explorer's voyages.

Cultural Centres The main western cultural centres in Bahrain are:

Alliance Française, Isa Town, behind Bahrain University's Polytechnic College, off the 16th December Highway (☎ 683 295)
British Council, Ahmed Mansour al-Ali building (opposite the BMW showroom) on the Shaikh Salman (or Sulman) Highway. The library, which is on the ground floor, is open Saturday to Wednesday from 9 am to noon and 3 to 6 pm (☎ 261 555).
USIS has a library (open to all) at the US embassy with US newspapers and magazines. It is open Saturday to Wednesday from 8 am to 4 pm (☎ 273 300).

Medical Services The American Mission Hospital (☎ 253 447) on Isa al-Kabeer Ave offers walk-in consultations for BD 7 (BD 9.500 if you have to see a specialist) plus the cost of any medicine or X-rays required. Similar services are available at the Awali Hospital (☎ 753 434) and the International Hospital (☎ 591 666).

Emergency For fire, police or ambulance services dial ☎ 999 from any telephone.

National Museum

This is the large white building at the northern end of the Al-Fatih Highway, near the Bahrain Island end of the Muharraq causeway. Its collection is exceptionally well displayed, and most exhibits are marked in both English and Arabic. The museum is open Saturday to Wednesday from 8 am to 2 pm, Thursday from 10 am to 5 pm and is closed on Friday. Admission is 500 fils. Photography is permitted except in the Document Hall and the Dilmun Gallery.

Heritage Centre

The centre occupies a villa on Government Ave across from the Bahrain Commercial Centre. The villa was built in 1937 to house the law courts.

The Heritage Centre's exhibits aim to give the visitor some idea of traditional Bahraini culture through a combination of dioramas, traditional costumes and old photograph displays. There are also exhibits on pearl diving, sea hunting, folk music instruments, the various uses of the date palm and a reconstruction of the high court, whose sessions used to be held in the building.

The centre is open Saturday to Wednesday from 8 am to 2 pm and Thursday from 10 am to 5 pm, but it's closed Friday. Admission is free, and photography is prohibited.

Wind Towers

Bahrain's pre-electricity form of air-conditioning can be seen in several places in the older parts of town. The towers are designed to catch even slight breezes and funnel the air down into the houses.

The easiest one to find is 10 to 15 minutes walk from the Hilton/Sheraton roundabout. With your back to the two hotels follow Palace Ave. Turn right on Rd 609 (on the corner with signs for Creative Ads and the Al-Baraka Car Centre). Follow this street for about 200m; it is on the left. The same house also has a well-preserved covered balcony. (If driving, note that Palace Ave is a limited access road and you cannot turn onto Rd 609 from either lane.)

Friday Mosque

This mosque, built with the islands' first oil revenues in 1938, is easily identifiable by its colourful mosaic minaret. The mosque is at the intersection of Al-Khalifa Ave and Shaikh Isa Ave.

Bab al-Bahrain

Built by the British in 1945 to house government offices and serve as a formal entryway to the city, the Bab, as it is known locally, now houses the tourist office. Its gateway was designed by Sir Charles Belgrave, the long-time British adviser to the rulers of Bahrain. The small square in front of the Bab was once the terminus of the customs' pier (which gives some idea of the extent of land reclamation in the area).

The Bab serves as the main entrance to the **souq**, which covers roughly the area between Al-Khalifa Ave and Shaikh Abdulla Ave, from Municipality Ave to Bab al-Bahrain Ave.

Beit al-Qur'an

A striking bit of architecture at the eastern end of Government Ave, Beit al-Qur'an (Koran House) was opened in 1990 as a museum and research centre. The museum's centrepiece is a large, and quite striking, collection of Islamic art, including Qur'ans, manuscripts, wood carvings etc. The museum is open Saturday to Wednesday from 9 am to noon and 4 to 6 pm, and until noon on Thursday. It is closed Friday. Admission is free, but a donation is requested.

Dhow Builders

Manama's dhow building yard is in the non-descript-looking sheds just west of the Pearl Monument roundabout. In the same area you can also see fish traps being woven from wire. No admission fee is charged but ask before taking photographs or climbing on the half-built dhows, the latter being a matter of safety as well as courtesy.

Al-Fatih Mosque

Also known as the Great Mosque, the Al-Fatih Mosque dominates the Al-Fatih Highway on the coast south of central Manama. It's the largest building in the country and is said to be capable of holding up to 7000 worshippers. Non-Muslims are welcome to visit the mosque Saturday to Wednesday from 8 am to 2 pm, except during prayer time.

Beach Clubs

Several of Bahrain's beach clubs are open to visitors upon payment of a dinar or two for a day ticket. Clubs worth trying include the Bahrain Yacht Club, at the southern tip of Sitra Island, and the Al-Bandar Club next door. To get into either club on a Friday you will probably need to be accompanied by a member. You can also usually get access to the pools at any of the larger hotels upon payment of a small fee, approximately BD 2.

Organised Tours

Gulf Tours (☎ 213 460), a division of the government-run Tourism Projects Company, offers a number of itineraries around Manama and the main archaeological/historical sites. These cost BD 7 or BD 8 (BD 5 for children aged three to 10 on all trips – no charge for children under three), and most last three hours. Check the tourist office for an exact schedule.

Other companies offering tours include Bahrain Explored (☎ 211 477) and Sunshine Tours (☎ 223 601).

Places to Stay – bottom end

The *Youth Hostel* (☎ 727 170) is at No 1105 Rd 4225 in Al-Jufayr, south-east of the city centre. It is opposite the Bahrain School and just beyond the United Nations Development Programme (UNDP) and UNICEF offices. If you are coming from the airport the route is well signposted. Beds are BD 2 per night, most of them in twin-bed rooms. There is also a family section and kitchen facilities are available. The management's attitude toward unaccompanied women can best be described as problematic.

All of the following hotels have air-conditioning. Service charges, where applicable, are included in the rates quoted here. Also note that the rates listed are initial quotes and are definitely negotiable, at least during the week. Most of Bahrain's cheap hotels raise their rates over the weekend, which usually means on Wednesday and Thursday nights. If you check in before the weekend and stay through it, you should only be charged the weekday rate, but check first with the management to avoid any misunderstandings.

After a bad patch a few years ago the *Al-Burge Hotel* (formerly the Abu Nawas Hotel) (☎ 213 163; fax 213 512) on Municipality Ave has undergone a modest face-lift and is once again the best cheapie in town. The rooms are spartan but clean, and the staff are friendly. Rooms cost BD 8/10 with bath, BD 6/8 without.

The *Central Hotel* (☎ 233 553) used to be one of Bahrain's better values but has fallen on hard times recently. It is a bit out of the way, on an alleyway off the east side of Municipality Square, and it's not really worth going out of your way for. The rates are BD 8/12 for singles/doubles, some of which have attached baths.

At the southern end of Municipality Square, the *Al-Dewania Hotel* (☎ 263 300; fax 259 709) is a so-so deal at BD 12.360/15.450 a single/double.

The *Al-Kuwait Guest House* (☎ 210 781) has small, spartan, uncarpeted rooms for BD 7/12, some with Turkish toilets (the hole-in-the-floor variety). Some rooms have attached baths. The clientele seems to be mostly low-income Saudis. Unaccompanied women might want to look somewhere else.

On Al-Khalifa Ave, near the Al-Jazira Hotel, the *Awal Hotel* (☎ 211 321; fax 211 391) is overpriced at BD 15/19.550. The rooms are large but rather musty, and for that sort of money one expects much cleaner bathrooms. Nearby, the *Ambassador Hotel* (☎ 277 991) costs BD 15/20 a single/double.

The *Seef Hotel* (☎ 244 557; fax 593 363) is just off the north side of Government Ave behind the Standard & Chartered Bank building. Singles/doubles cost BD 8/12, all with bath, TV and fridge. The rooms are OK but nothing to write home about. The toilets are all Turkish-style.

On Tujjaar Ave in the souq, the *Capital Hotel* (☎ 255 955; fax 211 675) is quite good value at BD 10/14 a single/double, including breakfast. The somewhat pricier *Oriental Palace Hotel* (☎ 233 331; fax 214 141), with rooms at BD 16.100/20.700, is just around the corner.

It is somehow comforting to know that a few things in any city never change. In Manama one of those things is the *Al-Gindoul Hotel* (☎ 210 353), on Municipality Ave, which remains the worst hotel in Bahrain. Beds are between BD 6 and BD 10, some with bath and some without, depending on what the manager thinks you might be able to afford.

Further afield, the recently spiffed-up *Bahrain Hotel* (☎ 227 478; fax 213 509) is good value at BD 9/16 a single/double for simple but very clean rooms, all with private bath, telephone and TV. The hotel is in two old houses which have been reconstructed. It's on Al-Khalifa Ave, two blocks east of the Tylos Hotel.

Places to Stay – middle

Bahrain's mid-priced hotels are a varied lot. A 15% service charge (included, where applicable, in the prices quoted here) can be assumed at this level, as can amenities such as a fridge, TV and telephone. During slow periods you may be able to bargain a dinar or two off the rates quoted here, but don't count on it. Most hotels in this category do not raise their rates on weekends.

If you want or need to have your entry visa sponsored by a hotel the cheapest place providing this service is the *Oasis Hotel* (☎ 229 979; fax 224 421) on Government Ave opposite the Delmon Hotel. At BD 14/18 the rooms are excellent value and we recommend it for unaccompanied women.

If you are looking for a place to stay centrally, it is hard to beat the *Bab al-Bahrain Hotel* (☎ 211 622; fax 213 661) on Government Ave right next to the Bab itself. It is an extremely clean place, with good, medium-sized rooms at BD 20.700/28.750. A few doors down the street, the *Gulf Pearl Hotel* (☎ 213 877; fax 213943) is a bit more expensive for singles at BD 23, but its doubles cost BD 28.750.

Once you reach the *Al-Jazira Hotel* (☎ 211 810; fax 210 726) on Al-Khalifa Ave in the souq you'll know you have reached the cheap hotel district. Rooms are BD 21.240/28.320 for singles/doubles, which is a bit pricey all things considered. None of these hotels sponsor visas.

The *Sahara Hotel* (☎ 225 580; fax 210 580) on Municipality Square also has a good spot. Singles/doubles are BD 20.700/28.750. The clientele is mostly Gulf Arabs in town for short visits. Across the square, the *Adhari Hotel* (☎ 224 343; fax 214 707) charges BD 17.250/23 but will readily discount its prices.

BAHRAIN

PLACES TO EAT
2 Kwality Restaurant
5 Al-Aswar Sandwiches
5 Al-Osra Restaurant
19 East Restaurant & Coffee
25 Ahmed Abdul Rahim's
   Coffee House
28 Money Restaurant
35 Wendy's Corner
   (Restaurant)
38 Cafe Hanan
39 Charcoal Grill Restaurant

PLACES TO STAY
16 Regency Inter-
   Continental
18 Seef Hotel
21 Delmon Hotel
23 Gulf Gate Hotel
26 Oasis Hotel
29 Al-Burge Hotel
30 Bahrain International
   Hotel
32 Awal Hotel
33 Al-Kuwait Guest
   House
34 Al-Jazira Hotel
37 Gulf Pearl Hotel
41 Bab al-Bahrain Hotel
45 Oriental Palace Hotel
46 Capital Hotel
49 Aradous Hotel
52 Bahrain Hotel
53 Adhari Hotel
54 Sentral Hotel
55 Sahara Hotel
56 Al-Dewania Hotel

OTHER
1 Government House
4 Friday Mosque
6 Gulf Air
7 Manama Centre
8 Kuwait Airways
9 British Bank of the
   Middle East (ATM)
10 Heritage Centre
11 Saudia Airlines
12 ABN-AMRO Bank (Amex
   Express Cash Machine)
13 Dutch Consulate
   (2nd Floor)
14 GPO
15 Banks
17 Standard &
   Chartered Bank
20 Municipality Building
22 Avis Rent-a-Car
24 Manama Bus Station
27 Ebrahim Abu Ahmed
   Antiques
31 Bradran Persian Store
36 Bank of Bahrain &
   Kuwait (ATM)
40 Tourist Office
42 Kanoo Travel (Amex)
43 British Airways
44 Yateem Centre
   (Telecommunications
   Office)
47 Souvenir Shops
48 Al-Hilal Bookshop
50 National Bank of
   Bahrain
51 Al-Awal Exchange
   (Money Exchange)

Central Manama
Hotel District

0   100   200 m

Its bar, the Hunter's Lounge, is popular with US sailors on shore leave.

The *Aradous Hotel* (☎ 241 011), on Wali al-Ahed Ave, is under the same management as the Adhari and has roughly the same prices.

Further west, along Government Ave moving away from the town centre, is the *Tylos Hotel* (☎ 252 600; fax 252 611), with rooms at BD 23/32.200 a single/double. It also arranges visas.

The *Gulf Gate Hotel* (☎ 210 210; fax 213 315) is a relatively new three to four-star hotel with a quiet but central location just behind the Delmon Hotel. Singles/doubles cost BD 20.600/30.900.

Places to Eat

There are lots of cheap places to eat in the city centre, especially on Government and Al-Khalifa Aves around Bab al-Bahrain. If your taste does not run to burgers and fries, try the *Charcoal Grill* restaurant next to Bab al-Bahrain. It features a wide selection of Indian, Chinese and Filipino food. Try the mixed fried rice at BD 1.700. Those on tight budgets can get sandwiches for 500 fils to BD 1. We recommended this place.

Nearby, also on Government Ave, *Cafe Hanan* offers a mix of burgers and sandwiches at 300 to 700 fils and Filipino food for BD 1 to BD 1.200.

The *Honey Restaurant* on Municipality Ave, next to the Al-Burge Hotel, is slightly more expensive. The menu is heavy on Filipino noodle dishes. A change of name since the last edition of this book has been accompanied by an unfortunate slide in the quality of the food.

One block north of Government Ave, the *East Restaurant & Coffee*, next to the Seef Hotel, has Thai food but not much of a selection. Meals cost BD 3 to BD 4.

Further east, immediately across from the entrance to Government House on Government Ave, the *Al-Osra Restaurant* has the usual blend of 'Arabic, Indian, Chinese and Continental Foods' (to quote its sign). Entrees cost 300 to 500 fils and main dishes cost anywhere from 500 fils to BD 3, includ-

ing an extensive list of curries, most for between 500 fils and BD 1. The Indian food is the cheapest, while steaks are the most expensive.

The *Kwality Restaurant*, further along Government Ave in the direction of the Hilton/Sheraton roundabout, has a similar menu and nicer decor, but the food isn't as good.

For a quick snack it is hard to beat *Al-Aswar Sandwiches*, a tiny restaurant on a side street off Al-Khalifa Ave near the Friday Mosque. Large servings of fresh juice cost 250 to 400 fils and burgers can be had for 200 to 500 fils. This place is recommended.

One of the best value eateries in Bahrain is *La Taverna*, the Italian restaurant on the 2nd floor of the Oasis Hotel at the other end of Government Ave. Main dishes cost BD 3 to BD 5 and pasta main courses around BD 2.500. It serves what is arguably the best Italian food in the country. Try the pasta with clams. Across the hall from La Taverna is *Tarbouche*, a Lebanese restaurant that is also one of the best in town. Meals here similarly cost BD 3 to BD 5.

There are very few traditional coffee houses left in central Manama. A good one, however, is *Ahmed Abdul Rahim's Coffee House* on Government Ave, west of the Oasis Hotel. The sign is only in Arabic but you'll find it hard to miss with all those old men sitting on blue benches sipping tea from tiny glasses. You may join them for 50 fils per cup.

Entertainment

There are a couple of small cinemas in town which show mostly Indian films. Check the *Gulf Daily News* for listings.

Conventional hotel bars range from comfortable-but-generic (the *Clipper Bar* at the Regency Inter-Continental) to the bizarrely thematic (the *Sherlock Holmes Bar* at the Gulf Hotel and the 1st floor *bar* at the Al-Jazira Hotel, featuring Tudor decor), to the carefully targeted (the *Hunter's Lounge* at the Adhari Hotel). *The Warbler* at the Baisan International Hotel, off the west side of Exhibition Ave on Avenue 2005, is popular with younger western expats. Another popular watering hole is *Joyce's* at the Tylos Hotel. *Spats*, a wine bar on the 2nd floor of the Oasis Hotel, and *Henry's*, the bar on the 1st floor of the Mansouri Mansions Hotel, both draw a much more mixed (ie expat and Arab) crowd than most other bars in Bahrain.

The island's longest-established disco is *Layali* at the Sheraton Hotel.

Western rock stars occasionally drop in for one-off performances and the five-star hotels regularly bring theatre companies out from the UK (and occasionally France) for three or four night runs. Arab singing stars feature occasionally. The best source for information on these events is Radio Bahrain or the monthly 'What's On' brochure published by the government-run Tourism Projects Company.

Things to Buy

A wide selection of local crafts are on sale at the tourist office shop in Bab al-Bahrain. The shop also stocks some quite striking wood and brasswork, though most of it is not locally made. Prices in the tourist office shop are fixed.

For interesting antiques and regional (though rarely Bahraini) crafts, try the Bradran Persian Store (☎ 228 655) on Rd 467 (an alley off Government Ave near the Bahrain Islamic Bank). It has a selection of Iranian, Indian and Chinese goods. The shop's speciality, however, is printed table-cloths from Isfahan in Iran. After a bit of bargaining these sell for BD 3 to BD 15, depending on size.

Another good place to look for souvenirs is Ebrahim Abu Ahmed Antiques (☎ 270 872). Its main shop is just off Municipality Ave in the city centre near the Oasis Hotel. It stocks a wide variety of goods, including coffee pots, wooden inlay boxes from Iran, brass and copperwork and some jewellery.

Getting There & Away

Air Bahrain international airport (☎ 325 555 for flight information) is one of the busiest in the Gulf. Check-in time for most flights is officially one hour before a flight but it can

be a good idea to turn up a bit earlier than that. Most of Manama's airline offices are in the city centre on or around Government Ave, and are open Saturday to Wednesday from 8 or 8.30 am to 12.30 pm and 3 to 5 or 5.30 pm (morning hours only on Thursday). The booking office for Gulf Air (☎ 335 777) is in the Manama Centre on Government Ave.

Bus The Saudi-Bahraini Transport Company (☎ 263 244) runs five buses daily to and from Dammam via Alkhobar. The fare is BD 4 one way, BD 7 return. Buses leave Bahrain for Saudi Arabia at 8.30 am, noon, and at 3, 6 and 8.30 pm. Buses leave Dammam for Bahrain at 8 and 11 am, and at 2, 5 and 8.30 pm. The buses come and go from a stop near the central market buildings, on Lulu Ave, between the King Faisal Highway and Government Ave. The ticket office is in the small brown trailer. The trip between Bahrain and Alkhobar takes about two hours, with the bus arriving in Dammam about 45 minutes later.

The office also sells other international bus tickets that involve a change of bus in Dammam. Destinations include Abu Dhabi/Dubai (18 hours; BD 30), Amman (approx 36 hours; BD 40), Damascus (approx 48 hours; BD 40) and Kuwait (nine hours; BD 21).

Car Rates for compact cars start at around BD 13 per day or BD 70 to BD 80 for a week, including insurance and unlimited mileage. To rent a car in Bahrain you need an International Driving Permit. This cannot be obtained in Bahrain if you do not already have one. Foreigners resident in another GCC country can rent a car using a licence from that country.

Some of the well-established international agencies include Thrifty Rent-a-Car (☎ 801 100) on Zubarah Ave near the intersection with Exhibition Ave, Avis (☎ 211 770), with an office on Government Ave next door to the Delmon Hotel, and Budget (☎ 534 100) in the Bahrain Commercial Centre on Government Ave.

Boat There are passenger services between

Iran and Bahrain. The boats leave from Mina Sulman on the outskirts of Manama, and there is only one class of service. The trip takes 16 hours and costs BD 36 one way, BD 63 return, plus a BD 3 port tax. Contact International Travel (☎ 250 883) on Al-Khalifa Ave for tickets and details.

Getting Around

The Airport Bahrain international airport is on Muharraq Island, six km from the city centre. Bus No 1 runs between the airport and the central bus station in Manama every 35 minutes from around 6 am until 8.45 pm. The fare is 50 fils and the trip takes about 20 minutes.

A taxi from central Manama to the airport should cost BD 2 or less depending on where exactly you pick it up. For trips into town from the airport there is a BD 1 surcharge, so these tend to run BD 2 to BD 3.

Bus Bahrain's bus system links routes around Greater Manama with the outlying towns. Fares are a flat 50 fils per trip. Manama's main bus station is on Government Ave between the Delmon and Tylos hotels. Some of the main Manama-based bus routes are:

Route 1 – Al-Hidd, Bahrain airport, Muharraq bus station, Ras Rummaan, Municipality, Manama central market, Manama bus station and vice-versa

Route 2 – Isa Town, Al-Sehlah, Al-Khamis, Al-Sulmaniya, Manama bus station, Manama Municipality, Ras Rummaan, Muharraq

Route 3 – Manama bus station, Manama Municipality, UK embassy, American Mission Hospital, Kuwaiti building (Shaikh Isa Ave), Radio Station, Al-Jufayr, Mina Sulman

Route 5 – Al-Budayyi', Ad-Diraz, Abu Saybi, Jidd Hafs, Al-Budayyi' Highway, Manama bus station, Manama Municipality, Ras Rummaan, Old Palace Ave, Al-Sulmaniya Ave and vice-versa

Taxi Taxis have meters and are a fairly inexpensive way to get around because the fares tick over pretty slowly.

Around Bahrain Island

QAL'AT AL-BAHRAIN

Bahrain's main archaeological site, also known as Bahrain Fort or the Portuguese Fort, is a complex containing four separate excavations. At the time of writing, the site was undergoing extensive renovation, apparently with the goal of restoring the ruined Portuguese fortress to its original form. Despite the construction work, the site remains open every day during daylight hours. Admission is free.

The site appears to have been occupied from about 2800 BC, the time when Dilmun was coming into its own as a commercial power. The settlement here was then fairly small. The oldest excavated part of the site is the portion of a defensive wall from the City II period (circa 2000 BC). The largest visible section of the wall lies just east of the Portuguese ruins.

The excavated remains of Cities III and IV are referred to as the Kassite and Assyrian buildings. These date from 1500 to 500 BC and lie just south of the Portuguese fortress. At the time of writing, a team of French archaeologists was digging in this part of the site and the excavated area had almost doubled in size. The ongoing dig, however, may mean limited access to this part of the site.

The site is about five km west of Manama and is easy to reach by car: keep driving along King Faisal Highway past the Pearl Monument roundabout. Take the Al-Budayyi' Highway and turn off it to the right at the roundabout just beyond the exhibition centre (which will be on your left). This turn puts you on Ave 40 at a sign for the Al-Seef district (there is another turn for Al-Seef before you reach the roundabout. Ignore this as it is the access road for the Meridien Hotel). After another 100m take the first left off Ave 40. Follow the asphalted street which directs you through a village until you come to a five-way junction. Look for a dirt track going to your right over a low hill. This takes you to the fort.

BARBAR TEMPLE

Barbar is a complex of three 2nd and 3rd millennium BC temples. These were probably dedicated to Enki, the God of Wisdom and The Sweet Waters Under the Earth. In a country as blessed with natural springs as Bahrain this god of fresh waters was, understandably, an important one to the people who lived here.

To reach the temple take the Al-Budayyi' Highway west from Manama and turn right off the highway at a green sign for Barbar. Follow this road just over half a km and the temple will be on your right, about 50m off the road. The site is open during daylight hours and there is often an attendant there with a guest book, which you will be expected to sign. Admission is free.

The closest bus stop to the Barbar Temple is near the Ad-Diraz temple, a 20 to 30 minute walk away.

AD-DIRAZ TEMPLE

Ad-Diraz is the other Dilmun-era temple to the west of Qal'at al-Bahrain. Less is known about it than some of the other contemporary Dilmun temples. It dates from the 2nd millennium BC, and is several centuries younger than the Barbar Temple, from which it differs significantly.

Unlike Barbar, the Ad-Diraz Temple is quite close to the Al-Budayyi' Highway. The turn for the temple is clearly signposted as you come from Manama (but not if you are driving in the other direction). It is open during daylight hours and admission is free. Bus No 5 stops very close to the Ad-Diraz Temple.

BANI JAMRAH

This village, just south of the Al-Budayyi' Highway, near the road's western end, is known for its cloth weavers. The looms themselves are very complex. The weaver sits in a small hollowed-out concrete area inside a shack drawing the yarn into the loom from a skein placed in a bag secured to a wooden post eight to 10m away. Taking pictures is no problem, though visitors are not usually welcome in the village itself.

SUQ AL-KHAMIS MOSQUE

Approximately 2.5 km south of Manama on the Shaikh Salman Highway, this is the oldest mosque in Bahrain. The original mosque is believed to have been built in the late 7th century by Omar, one of the first caliphs. As for what you see today, an inscription puts the construction in the second half of the 11th century. It is possible, however, that some fragments of the original mosque remain.

The site is open Saturday to Wednesday from 7 am to 2 pm, and Thursday and Friday from 8 am to noon. Admission is free.

To reach the mosque, leave Manama via the Shaikh Salman Highway. Once in the village of Al-Khamis you'll see the mosque on the right side of the road as you come from Manama.

A'ALI BURIAL MOUNDS

There are about 85,000 burial mounds in Bahrain. They are, literally, all over the island, though many are concentrated in about half a dozen major mound fields. The most impressive group of mounds are the so-called 'Royal Tombs' in the village of A'ali, south-west of Manama. The mounds were originally pronounced 'royal' simply because of their size. The largest are 12 to 15m high and up to 45m in diameter.

A'ali is also the site of Bahrain's best known pottery workshop. A'ali pottery is on sale in the tourist office shop and at several stalls around the village.

To reach A'ali from Manama, take the Shaikh Salman Highway south past Isa Town, then turn west on A'ali Highway. Continue past the first turn for A'ali and turn off the highway at a small green sign pointing to the left. Once you reach the village turn right on Ave 42 (there's a small blue street sign) to reach both the mounds and the pottery workshop.

AL-JASRA HOUSE

This historic house, the birthplace of the present emir, Shaikh Isa bin Salman al-Khalifa, is a traditional building of coral and gypsum. The house was built in 1907. It is open Saturday to Wednesday from 8 am to 2 pm, Thursday from 10 am to 5 pm and Friday from 3 to 6 pm. Admission is free.

To reach the house take the Causeway Approach Rd out of Manama and exit at the turn for Al-Jasra. If you are coming from Qal'at al-Bahrain and the other sites along the north coast of Bahrain continue west on the Al-Budayyi' Highway past Bani Jamrah and turn south on the Al-Janabiyah Highway – look for signs pointing to Saudi Arabia. The Al-Jasrah exit is part of the same interchange where the Al-Janabiyah Highway links up with the Causeway Approach Rd.

When you exit the Causeway Approach Rd get onto the Mazare'a Highway. Follow this through a residential area and two roundabouts then turn left at a sign for the Al-Jasra House.

AL-'AREEN WILDLIFE SANCTUARY

This 10 sq km preserve in the south-west of Bahrain Island is a conservation area for species indigenous to Arabia, such as the Arabian oryx, although other animals not native to Arabia (eg zebras) have been introduced as well. The tour is conducted from a special 'tour' bus. The tour takes about 40 minutes. Admission is BD 1 for adults, 500 fils for children under 13 and free for children under four. The sanctuary is open from 7 am to 4.30 pm. Call the sanctuary office at ☎ 836 116 for more information, including specific tour times.

To reach the sanctuary take the Causeway Approach Rd out of Manama to the Al-Jasra exit, then turn south on the Zaid bin Omera Highway.

THE TREE OF LIFE

This lone tree, apparently fed by an underground spring, has been the subject of much speculation. It is the centrepiece of the 'Bahrain-was-the-Garden-of-Eden' theory advanced by some archaeologists, scholars and, most enthusiastically, by the tourist office. It's very hard to find and your best bet is either a resident with a car, a map and a lot of patience, or an organised tour.

Muharraq Island

There is no place to stay on Bahrain's second most important island, but there is a lot to see. Most of it is within walking distance of Muharraq's bus station. The bus station is near the end of the causeway to Manama and there are several tea stalls and restaurants in the neighbourhood, as well as a post office. To reach the bus station as you come off the causeway turn right at the first roundabout. The station will be on your right after about 100m.

Bait Shaikh Isa bin Ali & Bait Seyadi

These two traditional houses are well worth visiting for a look at pre-oil life in Bahrain. To reach them go straight through the roundabout as you come off the causeway from Manama. Follow the road as it swings around to the left, then turn right on Shaikh Abdulla bin Isa Ave (you should see two small blue-and-white signs pointing the way to the houses). Further up Shaikh Abdulla bin Isa Ave you will see two small signs pointing to the left, the upper one to 'Sh. Isa bin Ali House' and the lower one to 'Seydai House'.

To reach Bait Seyadi from Bait Shaikh Isa bin Ali, go straight and a bit to the right as you come out the door of the house, and cross a patch of waste ground keeping the mosque to your right and the electrical transformer to your left. This will take you into a narrow alley for about 50m. When you emerge from the alley the minaret of the mosque attached to Bait Seyadi will be right in front of you. The entrance to the house itself is on the far side of the building.

Both houses are open Saturday to Wednesday from 8 am to 2 pm and Thursday from 9.30 am to 5 pm. They are closed Friday. Admission is free.

Walking to either house from the Muharraq bus station should not take more than 10 or 15 minutes.

Qal'at Abu Mahir (Abu Mahir Fort)

This small fort dates as far back as the 16th

century, though it has been rebuilt several times since then. It was originally on an island, but land reclamation work has made it part of Muharraq's shoreline. It is within the grounds of the Muharraq coast guard station so access is sometimes limited. Generally, however, if you present yourself at the gate on a weekday (Saturday to Wednesday) between 7 am and 2 pm and ask nicely they will let you in. You will be escorted to the fort. Be especially careful to ask permission before taking pictures here – it is, after all, a military base.

Muharraq Dhow Building Yard

Muharraq's small dhow yard is on the coast between Qal'at Abu Mahir and the turn-off for the airport. There is no admission charge, but you should remember to ask permission before taking pictures.

Qal'at Arad (Arad Fort)

The foundations of this fort date from the 16th century when the site was fortified by the Portuguese, though much of what is visible today was built during the brief Omani occupation of Bahrain at the beginning

BAHRAIN

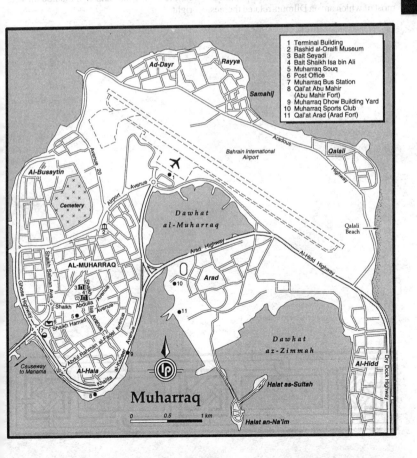

1 Terminal Building
2 Rashid al-Oraifi Museum
3 Bait Seyadi
4 Bait Shaikh Isa bin Ali
5 Muharraq Souq
6 Post Office
7 Muharraq Bus Station
8 Qal'at Abu Mahir
  (Abu Mahir Fort)
9 Muharraq Dhow Building Yard
10 Muharraq Sports Club
11 Qal'at Arad (Arad Fort)

Ad-Dayr

Rayya

Samahij

Aradous

Bahrain International Airport

Qalali

Qalali Beach

Al-Busaytin

Avenue 20

Airport Avenue

Avenue

Cemetery

Dawhat al-Muharraq

Arad Highway

Al-Hidda Highway

AL-MUHARRAQ

Ghose Highway

Shaikh Salman Ave

Shaikh Isa Avenue

Shaikh Abdulla

Shaikh Hamad

Abdul Rahman al-Fadel Avenue

al-Kabeer Avenue

Arad

10

11

Dawhat az-Zimmah

Causeway to Manama

Al-Hala

Khalifa

9

8

Dry Dock Highway

Al-Hidd

Halat as-Sultah

Muharraq

Halat an-Na'im

0   0.5   1 km

of the 19th century. It is open Saturday to Wednesday from 7.30 am to 2 pm, Wednesday afternoon from 3.30 to 5.30 pm, Thursday from 10 am to 5 pm, and Friday from 9 to 11 am and 3.30 to 5 pm. The relatively new 'tower' by the entrance gate has a small display on the fort's history. Admission is free.

Rashid al-Oraifi Museum

Bahrain's newest museum (it opened in 1994) is really a private art gallery dedicated to the work of its artist-owner. It is built around a collection of Al-Oraifi's paintings, most of which are on Dilmun-related themes.

The museum is open Saturday to Thursday from 8 am to noon and 4 to 8 pm, and Friday until noon. Admission is BD 1.

To reach the museum from Manama, take the Muharraq causeway road to the first roundabout. Continue straight through the roundabout and turn left at Shaikh Salman Ave. Follow Shaikh Salman Ave until you reach Airport Ave (at the second traffic signal past the roundabout). Turn right here and follow it to Ave 1. Turn right onto Ave 1 and go straight, into a small alley, for a few hundred metres. When you reach a stop sign turn left – the museum will then be on your right.

Egypt

Birthplace of one of the greatest civilisations the world has known, modern Egypt still retains the glory of the Pharaohs in the extraordinary monuments they left behind, in their pyramids and the splendours of their temples.

The centuries following the long era of Pharaonic rule brought Greeks, Romans, Arabs, Turks and Europeans – to mention only the main players – to the seat of power, and all have left their mark. Islamic Cairo has some of the most remarkable medieval Islamic architecture in the world, while a city like Alexandria still has a Mediterranean grace despite the neglect of decades.

Through it all, the Nile, Egypt's eternal lifeblood, has flowed on, nourishing the lives of the fellahin (peasants) who have worked the land, and of those who have lived from their toil. In a sense, nothing has changed. Without the mighty river and its army of farmers, modern Egypt, a cacophonous mixture of ancient and modern, a crossroads between east and west, Asia and Africa, could not exist. On either side of the Nile lie harsh deserts, occasionally softened by pockets of life in the oases. South-east of the famous Suez Canal stretches Sinai, a region of awesome beauty and a place of refuge and conflict for thousands of years. An unparalleled paradise off the Red Sea coast combines with the natural and architectural marvels on land to make this a fascinating destination.

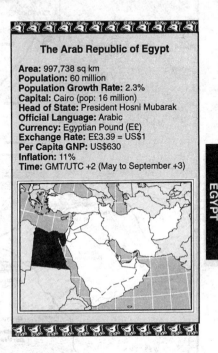

The Arab Republic of Egypt

Area: 997,738 sq km
Population: 60 million
Population Growth Rate: 2.3%
Capital: Cairo (pop: 16 million)
Head of State: President Hosni Mubarak
Official Language: Arabic
Currency: Egyptian Pound (E£)
Exchange Rate: E£3.39 = US$1
Per Capita GNP: US$630
Inflation: 11%
Time: GMT/UTC +2 (May to September +3)

EGYPT

Facts about the Country

HISTORY

About 5000 years ago an Egyptian king named Menes unified Upper and Lower Egypt for the first time. For centuries beforehand, communities had been developing along the Nile. The small kingdoms eventually developed into two important states, one covering the valley as far as the Delta, the other consisting of the Delta itself. The unification of these two states, by Menes in about 3000 BC, set the scene for the greatest era of ancient Egyptian civilisation. More than 30 dynasties, 50 rulers and 2700 years of indigenous – and occasionally foreign – rule passed before Alexander the Great ushered in a long, unbroken period of foreign domination.

Pharaonic Times (3000-341 BC)

Little is known of the immediate successors of Menes except that, attributed with divine ancestry, they promoted the development of a highly stratified society, patronised the arts and built many temples and public works.

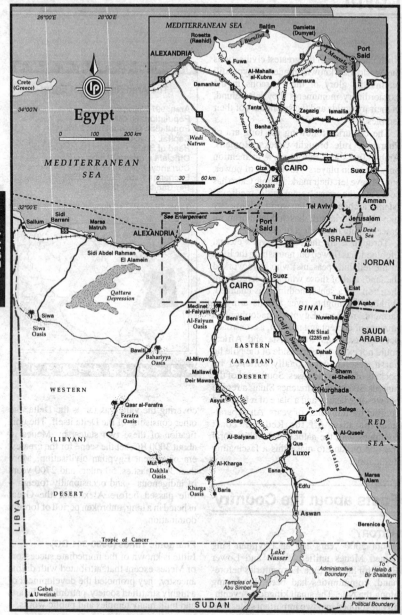

Suggested Itineraries

You can see many of Egypt's most famous sights in a week-long whirlwind tour. You'll need two days in **Cairo** to cover the **pyramids** and the **Egyptian Museum**, after which you could take the overnight train to **Luxor** and spend two days visiting the ancient necropolis of **Thebes** and Luxor itself. Jump on a morning bus to **Aswan** (five hours) and you'll be able to spend the afternoon sailing on a **felucca** on the Nile. Real travel buffs could fit in a trip to **Abu Simbel** the next day, before hightailing it by train or bus back to Cairo.

A fortnight will give you enough time to explore parts, but not all, of Egypt. If ancient monuments are your thing, just stick to combing the Nile Valley. Those who like a cocktail of sights could consider three days in and around Cairo, two days in Luxor and another two days in Aswan, taking in Abu Simbel and the **Temple of Philae** too, before moving into relaxation mode with two nights on a felucca from Aswan to Edfu followed by a couple of days snorkelling around **Hurghada** on the Red Sea.

If you prefer to concentrate less on temples and tombs, head straight to Luxor after Cairo and then backtrack across the Eastern Desert to Hurghada. From there you can get a ferry across the Red Sea to southern **Sinai**, where you can delight in the underwater world before climbing to the peak of **Gebel Katherina (Mt St Catherine).** ■

In the 27th century BC Egypt's pyramids began to appear. King Zoser and his chief architect, Imhotep, built what may have been the first, the Step Pyramid at Saqqara. Zoser ruled from the nearby capital of Memphis.

For the next three dynasties and 500 years – a period called the Old Kingdom – the power of Egypt's Pharaohs and the size and scale of their pyramids and temples greatly increased. The size of such buildings symbolised the Pharaoh's importance and power over his people. The pyramid also gave the Pharaoh steps to the heavens, and the ceremonial wooden barques buried with him provided him with symbolic vehicles to the next life. The last three Pharaohs of the 4th dynasty, Cheops, Chephren and Mycerinus, built the three Great Pyramids of Giza.

By the beginning of the 5th dynasty (about 2490-2330 BC) it is clear the Pharaohs had ceded some of their power to a rising class of nobles. In the following centuries Egypt broke down into several squabbling principalities. The rise of Thebes (Luxor) saw an end to the turmoil and Egypt was reunited under Mentuhotep II, marking the beginning of the Middle Kingdom. For 250 years all went well, but more internal fighting and 100 years of occupation by the Hyksos, invaders from the north-east, cast a shadow over the country.

The New Kingdom, its capital at Thebes and later Memphis, represented a blossoming of culture and empire in Pharaonic Egypt. For almost 400 years, from the 18th to the 20th dynasties (1550-1150 BC), Egypt was a great power in north-east Africa and the eastern Mediterranean. Renowned kings and queens ruled an expanding empire from Memphis, and built monuments which even today are unique in their immensity and beauty. The most startling of them is perhaps the Temple of Amun at Karnak, just north of Luxor. But by the time Ramses III came to power (1198 BC) as the second king of the 20th dynasty, disunity had again set in. The empire continued to shrink, and Egypt was attacked by outsiders. This was the state of affairs when Alexander the Great arrived in the 4th century BC.

From Alexander to Islam (332 BC to 638 AD)

Egypt was chaotic when Alexander arrived in 332 BC. Over the previous several centuries Libyans, Ethiopians, Persians and Assyrians had invaded the country at different times. Alexander, who was in the process of conquering all of the Middle East and beyond (see History in the earlier Facts about the Region chapter), established a new capital, Alexandria, which he named after

The Preparation for Eternal Life

Prior to dynastic times the dead in Egypt were simply buried in shallow graves on the edge of the desert and covered with sand. Because of the dry atmosphere and hot sand this practice often caused the bodies to dehydrate before the tissues decomposed and this natural method of preservation did not go unnoticed.

As the ancient Egyptians changed their burial rituals and introduced coffins, the technique of mummification was developed to artificially preserve the dead bodies of those who could afford the process, as well as to preserve an incredible number of sacred birds, reptiles and other animals. In the case of the Pharaohs, this preservation process was essential, as the survival of the Pharaoh's *ka* – the life force which emanated from the gods – depended on the continued existence of the body.

For humans the mummification process took about 70 days. The most important aspect was the removal of the vital organs (which were subsequently stored in containers known as Canopic jars) and the drying of the body using a dehydrating agent called natron (a mineral of hydrated sodium carbonate). The actual wrapping of the body in bandages played no role in the preservation of the corpse. ■

himself. After his death, Egypt was ruled for 300 years by the Ptolemies, a family descended from one of his generals.

The expanding Roman Empire took an increasing interest in Egypt and, after a long and complicated story of murder and intrigue involving Cleopatra, Julius Caesar, Marc Antony and a disgruntled Roman Senate, Egypt became a province of Rome in 30 BC.

When the Roman Empire split into two in the 4th century AD, Egypt came under the control of Byzantium, the eastern half of the empire ruled from Constantinople (modern İstanbul). During this time a separate Christian church, which came to be known as the Coptic Church, developed and thrived; it still exists today.

Apart from the odd invasion by Persians, Egypt remained well off centre stage until the arrival of the Muslim Arab invaders in 638-639 AD.

Muslim Dynasties & Ottoman Suzerainty (639-1798)

Amr ibn al-As brought Islam to Egypt, and by 642 he had established a new capital at Fustat – the precursor of Cairo. Egypt was to become one of the many players in an ever changing game of musical chairs within the Islamic world. Ruled at first by the Damascus-based Umayyads and then from Baghdad by the Abbasids, Egypt became an increasingly independent power. With the arrival of the Shiite Fatimids from the west, Cairo was established in 969. After the coming of the Crusaders to the Middle East in the 11th century, Egypt fell under the control of Saladin (or more properly, Salah ad-Din, 'Righteousness of the Faith'), a warrior leader of Turkish descent. His line was followed by the topsy-turvy dynasty of freed Turkish slave-mercenaries – the Mamluks – who stayed in control until Egypt was absorbed into the mighty Turkish Ottoman Empire. See the History section of the Facts about the Region chapter for more details of this period.

European Intervention (1798-1952)

Although the Ottoman Empire remained nominally in control of Egypt until WWI, the reality was different. Napoleon embarked on what was to prove one of the first of many military adventures when still a servant of the Republic in 1798, landing a force in Egypt – supposedly in support of the Ottomans, whose capacity to control Egypt was by now severely limited. Napoleon had his own schemes, including gaining control of trade routes to India (which were important to Britain) and 'civilising' Egypt. His success was limited, and after Nelson sank his fleet off Abu Qir near Alexandria he was finally forced to withdraw in 1801.

A headstrong local ruler, Mohammed Ali, an Albanian in the service of Constantinople, became a thorn in everyone's side by pursuing a truly independent policy from 1805 to 1849. He even took Syria from the Ottomans, and was compelled to abandon it only by European intervention aimed at maintaining the imperial status quo.

He and his successors also hoped to make Egypt economically independent. A large-scale cotton industry was nurtured – particularly in the 1860s, as civil war crippled the US producers – and various monumental public works projects were undertaken, the greatest of them being the Suez Canal. Mismanagement sent the country bankrupt, however, and by 1882 British and French comptrollers were in charge of its finances. Of the two, Britain clearly exercised the greater political control; when war broke out in 1914 Egypt was made a British protectorate. In 1922 Egypt was granted nominal independence and elections were held for a constitutional monarchy under King Fuad, but the British remained pulling the strings behind the scenes.

Egypt was left in chaos following WWII and then defeat in Israel's 1948 War of Independence. By 1952 only a group of dissident military officers had the wherewithal to take over the government.

Post-Revolution Egypt

The Free Officers, led by Colonel Gamal Abdel Nasser, overthrew King Farouk, Fuad's son, in a bloodless coup that was quickly dubbed the Revolution of 1952. The first independent Arab Republic of Egypt was formed and Nasser, who after some manoeuvring became head of state, wasted no time in getting embroiled in international politics.

He became one of the architects of the Nonaligned Movement, and distanced himself from the west. In a gesture of defiance he nationalised the Suez Canal Company, prompting a short-lived Israeli-British-French attack in November. Eleven years later, fearing an imminent Arab attack, Israel launched a pre-emptive war against her neighbour. In six days she had destroyed the Egyptian airforce and occupied all of the Sinai peninsula. Nasser remained in power until his death in 1970, when he was succeeded by Anwar Sadat, who in 1973 attempted to retake Sinai. He failed, but four years later was in Jerusalem and on the road to peace. The Camp David Accord was signed in 1979, and by 1982 most of Sinai was back in Egyptian hands. Sadat paid with his life, assassinated in 1981 by people presumed to be Muslim fundamentalists.

To the Present

Hosni Mubarak, Sadat's deputy, took over and remains in power to this day. He has steered a middle course in most fields – maintaining peace with Israel but also returning to the Arab fold after some years of excommunication. He has slowly rolled back Nasser's socialism, dropping subsidies and privatising some areas of the economy, but there remains much to do. He has loosened the reins politically but himself admits democracy is limited – he says that Egypt is not yet ready for it. Astutely, he sided with the Allies in the 1991 Gulf War with Iraq, and won a US$14 billion cut in debt. His biggest headache remains how to deal with rising Islamic fundamentalist violence – hundreds of people were killed between 1992-95 in sectarian violence and fighting between government forces and members of the Gama'a al-Islamiyya (Islamic Association). A number of those killed were tourists, for the Gama'a has declared tourism, and hence tourists, a legitimate target in its fight with the government over the introduction of *shari'a* (Islamic law) – a fight that hides the more pressing issue of a young population increasingly frustrated by economic woes.

The government has hit back hard. Under special laws introduced in 1992 a total of 66 alleged terrorists had been sentenced to death by late 1995, and 48 of the sentences carried out. The government has taken great pains to assure the world that the militants at home have been all but wiped out. However, the unsuccessful attempt in mid-1995 to assassinate Mubarak while on a visit to Addis Ababa, Ethiopia, followed five months later by the bombing of the Egyptian embassy in Islamabad and the 1996 massacre of 16 Greek tourists in Cairo, put paid to official claims that the militants were being defeated.

GEOGRAPHY

Egypt is almost square in shape. The distance from north to south is 1030 km; from east to

EGYPT

west it's 965 km in the north and 1240 km in the south. For most Egyptians the Nile Valley is Egypt. To the east of the valley is the Eastern (Arabian) Desert – a barren plateau bounded on its eastern edge by a high ridge of mountains. To the west is the Western (Libyan) Desert – a plateau punctuated by huge clumps of bizarre geological formations and luxuriant oases.

Terrain in Sinai slopes from the high mountain ridges, which include Mt Sinai (Gebel Musa) and Mt St Catherine (Gebel Katherina; the highest in Egypt at 2642m), in the south to desert coastal plains and lagoons in the north.

CLIMATE

Egypt's climate is easy to summarise. Most of the year, except for the winter months of December, January and February, it is hot and dry. Temperatures increase as you travel south from Alexandria. Alexandria receives the most rain – approximately 190 mm a year – while far south in Aswan any rain at all is rare.

Summer temperatures range from 31°C (87°F) on the Mediterranean coast to a scorching 50°C (122°F) in Aswan. At night in winter the temperatures sometimes plummet to as low as 8°C, even in the south.

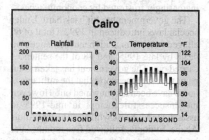

ECOLOGY & ENVIRONMENT

Despite being a signatory to various international conventions aimed at protecting vulnerable or endangered species and important natural habitats, Egypt has a long way to go where environmental awareness

and protection is concerned. Irresponsible tourism, pollution and poaching are all still major problems. However, the government has started to set aside protected zones, such as the Zaranik area on Lake Bardawil, the Elba region on the Red Sea coast, and the Naqb, Ras Abu Gallum and Dahab regions in Sinai. Unfortunately, with the exception of Ras Mohammed National Park in Sinai where full-time rangers are employed to patrol the park, there is little active enforcement of protection laws within these zones. See also the Ecology & Environment section in the Facts about the Region chapter.

FLORA & FAUNA

The lotus that symbolises ancient Egypt can be found in the Delta area, but the papyrus reed is now only found in botanical gardens. More than a hundred kinds of grasses thrive in areas where there is water, and the date palm is seen in every cultivable area.

Egypt's deserts used to be sanctuaries for an amazing variety of larger mammals, such as leopards, cheetahs, oryx, aardwolves, striped hyenas and caracals. Unfortunately, all of these are on the brink of extinction due to persecution by hunters. These days you'll be lucky to see any mammals other than camels, donkeys, domesticated horses and buffalo. There is also a variety of small desert rodents and similar animals.

Bird life is rich, with about 430 species having been sighted in Egypt. Marine life is equally as impressive – the Red Sea is teeming with an amazing spectacle of colour and form, from dolphins and turtles to colourful corals, sponges and sea cucumbers.

GOVERNMENT & POLITICS

The bulk of power is concentrated in the hands of the president, who is nominated by the People's Assembly and elected by popular referendum for six years. The president appoints vice presidents and ministers, as well as 10 members of the 454 member assembly and 70 of the 210 member Majlis ash-Shura (Advisory Council). Elections are supervised by the Ministry of the Interior. President Mubarak's National Democratic

Party won a resounding victory in the election of 1995, though opposition parties claimed that there was electoral fraud.

The republic is divided into 25 governorates, known as *muhafazat*, for administrative purposes.

ECONOMY

Egypt exports 1½ times as much cotton as the USA sells overseas. Other important crops include wheat and various fruits, especially citrus.

Raw materials mined include iron ore, manganese, phosphates, chromium and small amounts of coal. Some uranium has also been found in Sinai, and Egypt remains a net exporter of oil. Textiles and cement are produced on a large scale.

However, the Suez Canal is Egypt's largest single foreign currency earner. Dues from commercial users now amount to more than US$2 billion per year.

A rapidly expanding sector is tourism. In 1991 it produced US$1 billion in revenue but the Gulf War and attacks by extremist Islamists on tourists between 1992-94 sparked a fall in business of anything up to 75%, depending on which source you believe. The government reported a 19% growth in tourist numbers in the first half of 1995 compared with the previous year and the days of empty Nile cruisers lining the river, semi-deserted temples and despondent bazaar workers appeared to be over. However, the shooting of 18 tourists in April 1996 could once again put the brakes on the tourist sector.

POPULATION & PEOPLE

Egypt's population has, in a sense, become its greatest problem. Estimated at 60 million in 1995, it is predicted to reach 65 million by the year 2000.

Anthropologists divide the Egyptian people very roughly into three racial groups, of which the biggest is descended from the Hamito-Semitic race that has peopled the Nile for millennia. These are the 'real Egyptians'. The truly Arab element is made up of the Bedouin Arab nomads who migrated from Arabia and live in desert areas, particularly Sinai. Their numbers are estimated at about 500,000. The third group are the Nubians, from the Aswan area.

EDUCATION

Although nine years of primary school education are supposedly compulsory in Egypt, and about 97% of children from six to 15 years attend school, the adult illiteracy rate was estimated by UNESCO to be 50% in 1992. To westerners that may seem startlingly high, but 16 years earlier the level was 61.8%! Two-thirds of Egypt's illiterates are women.

ARTS

For a general discussion about Islamic music, architecture and literature see Arts in the Facts about the Region chapter.

Painting

Painting was first incorporated into Egyptian tomb art in the 24th century BC in the Pyramid of Unas at Saqqara. However, it was the Pharaohs of the New Kingdom (1550-1150 BC) who really brought this art to the fore, adorning their tombs with spectacular images of the netherworld and resurrection. You'll find no better example of this than the reliefs in the tomb of Nefertari in the Valley of the Queens near Luxor.

SOCIETY & CONDUCT

Although mostly easy-going, Egyptians are often genuinely offended by the behaviour of western visitors to their country. Men and women should dress modestly. This means long skirts or pants (nothing too figure hugging), and arms covered down to the elbows for women and generally long trousers for men. This is especially true when visiting mosques and churches. In the Sinai resorts you can relax a bit. Public displays of affection – anything from holding hands – are generally frowned upon.

RELIGION

The official state religion is Islam, and the majority of Egyptians are Muslims. Although the figures are much disputed, it is

EGYPT

thought about 13% of the population are Coptic Christians. A brief outline of the basic elements and evolution of Islam appears in the Facts about the Region chapter.

For three centuries prior to the arrival of Islam in Egypt, Christianity was the official religion of the country, by then under control of the eastern half of the crumbling Roman Empire, later to become known as Byzantium.

The Coptic (the word is derived from the Greek for Egyptian) Church broke away from the main body of the eastern church over the question of Christ's humanity. The Egyptians would not accept the official line that He was human as well as divine, considering such an assertion blasphemous. The Copts have had a mixed run with their Muslim co-nationals. Violence between Copts and extremist Muslims ebbs and flows, and through the 1980s and '90s it has been a constant feature of Egyptian political life.

Pharaonic Religion

Ancient Egypt produced a wealth of gods and goddesses, animal deities and magical practices that have both captured modern imagination and defied attempts to create for them neat and tidy categories. Ancient Egyptian deities could be local or universal or both; they could assume the characteristics of one another; and they could be at once destructive and beneficial, evil and good. The deities, on whom the preservation of cosmic order depended, required constant attention, which meant for mortals strict adherence to rite and ritual. Detailed descriptions of how particular rituals were to be carried out are today the major source of information we have on religion in Pharaonic times, the thinking behind them having been largely lost.

It is no surprise that a sun-god became one of Egypt's most important deities. The sun-god was usually known as Ra; Aten was the name of the visible disc of the sun. Ra was the creator and ruler of other deified elements of nature. There was Nut, the sky-goddess, Shu, the god of air, and Geb, the earth-god.

If you wish to learn more about religion in ancient Egypt, refer to Books in the following Facts for the Visitor section.

LANGUAGE

Egyptian colloquial Arabic differs from the Arabic of neighbouring countries in various ways. The most striking changes in pronunciation are the use of a hard 'g' for 'j' in northern Egypt, and the 'q', which becomes a glottal stop (qala'a, meaning citadel, is pronounced 'ala'a).

Facts for the Visitor

PLANNING

When to Go

Winter is the best time to be in Upper Egypt (the south) – even then it gets pretty hot during the day. Elsewhere, spring and autumn are generally the most pleasant times of year, although the Mediterranean coast can be a bit nippy well into April.

Maps

Lonely Planet's *Egypt Travel Atlas* breaks the country down into about 40 pages of detailed maps (scales 1:900,000 and 1:1,800,000) and so gives unrivalled coverage. It's fully indexed and the book format means it is easy to refer to, especially on buses and trains.

There are many other maps of Egypt available, including one published by Kümmerly & Frey, a Swiss company. It covers all of Egypt and Sinai, on a scale of 1:950,000, and sells for about US$9.

There is an expanding plethora of maps of Cairo or Cairo suburbs available in the better bookshops in the city. Some are OK, others pathetic, and most of little interest to the traveller passing through.

What to Bring

Egypt is generally a hot country but a sweater, and even a jacket in winter, may come in very handy.

Most toiletries are available, although you

may want to bring your own contact lens solution. Some women's products, such as sanitary pads, liners and tampons, though available, can be hard to find or low quality.

VISAS & DOCUMENTS
Visas
All foreigners entering Egypt, except nationals of Malta and Arab countries, must obtain visas from Egyptian consulates overseas or at the airport or port upon arrival. In the UK, a single-entry tourist visa costs most western applicants the equivalent of UK£15 (about US$22). As a general rule, it is cheaper to get a visa on arrival at Cairo airport (see later in this section), but this depends on your nationality and where you apply for the visa.

The single-entry visa is valid for presentation for three months and entitles the holder to stay in Egypt for one month. Multiple-entry visas (for three visits) are also available.

Visas can be obtained in most neighbouring countries with little fuss. In Jordan, you can get them at the embassy in Amman or the consulate in Aqaba on the same day. Most people pay JD12, although UK citizens pay a whopping JD40. In Israel, visas can be obtained at the embassy in Tel Aviv or the consulate in Eilat for 40 NIS, but 60 NIS (US$20) for Israelis. Egypt also has an embassy in Benghazi, Libya, and in Damascus, Syria.

You can get a visa upon arrival in Egypt at various points. At Cairo airport's new terminal the process is simple, and visas cost US$19 or UK£12 – get them from the Bank Misr desk just before immigration. While you can't get a visa at the border with Israel, it is possible to visit Sinai between Sharm el-Sheikh and Taba (on the Israeli border) without a visa. You are also permitted to visit St Catherine's Monastery. On arrival, you are issued with an entry stamp free of charge allowing you up to 14 days in the area. If you are coming from Israel, you can have the stamp put on a separate piece of paper.

You can get a visa, with much fuss, on the boat from Jordan.

Registration You must register with the police within one week of your arrival in Egypt. Most hotels will take care of this, some for a small fee, but you can do it yourself in the Mogamma building in Cairo or passport offices in the bigger cities.

Visa Extensions & Re-Entry Visas Extensions of your visa beyond the first month can be obtained for either six or 12 months and cost E£12.10/38.10 respectively. You need one photograph and a modicum of patience.

If you do not have a multiple-entry visa, it is also possible to get a re-entry visa, valid to the expiry date of your visa and any extensions, at most passport offices, including the Mogamma in Cairo. A single/multiple re-entry visa costs E£10.10/13.10.

Note that there is a two week grace period beyond the expiry date of your visa.

Other Documents
Vaccination Certificate A vaccination certificate proving that you have been vaccinated for yellow fever and/or cholera is only necessary if you are coming from an infected area (such as most of sub-Saharan Africa and South America). If you are staying over 30 days, evidence of an AIDS test is required.

Student Cards Legitimate International Student Identification Cards (ISIC) are available in Cairo from two places – the Medical Scientific Centre (MSC; ☎ 363 8815), 103 Sharia al-Manial on Roda Island, and Cairo University's Faculty of Engineering on Sharia Gamat al-Qahira in Giza. Cards are issued in a matter of minutes and cost E£20 from the MSC, or E£30 from the Faculty of Engineering. No proof is needed but you'll require a passport photo. A student card entitles you to half-price entry to most monuments and up to half-price on train tickets.

EMBASSIES
Egyptian Embassies Abroad
Following are the addresses and telephone

numbers of Egyptian embassies and consulates in major cities around the world:

Australia
1 Darwin Ave, Yarralumla, Canberra, ACT 2600 (☎ (06) 273 4437/8)
Consulate: 9th floor, 124 Exhibition St, Melbourne, Vic 3000 (☎ (03) 9654 8869/8634); 335 New South Head Rd, Double Bay, Sydney, NSW 2028 (☎ (02) 9362 3483)

Canada
454 Laurier Ave East, Ottawa, Ontario K1N 6R3 (☎ (613) 234 4931/35/58)
Consulate: 1 Place Sainte Marie, 2617 Montreal, Quebec H3B 4S3 (☎ (514) 866 8455)

Denmark
Kristianiagade 19, 2100 Copenhagen (☎ 35 43 70 70, 35 43 71 52)

France
56 Ave d'Iena, 75116 Paris (☎ 01 47 23 06 43, 01 53 67 88 30)
Consulate: 58 Ave Foch, 75116 Paris (☎ 01 45 00 49 52, 01 45 00 77 10); 166 Ave d'Hambourg, 13008 Marseilles (☎ 04 91 25 04 04)

Germany
Kronprinzenstrasse 2, Bad Godesberg, 53173 Bonn (☎ (228) 9 56 83 11/12/13)
Embassy branch: Waldstrasse 15, 13156 Berlin (☎ (30) 4 77 10 48)
Consulate: Eysseneckstrasse 34, 60322 Frankfurt/Main (☎ (69) 59 05 57/8)

Ireland
12 Clyde Rd, Dublin 4 (☎ (1) 660 6566, 660 6718)

Israel
54 Basel St, Tel Aviv (☎ (03) 546 4151/2)
Consulate: 68 Afraty St, Bna Betkha, Eilat (☎ (07) 597 6115)

Jordan
4th floor, Karbata Ben el-Dawar St, Amman or PO Box 35178 (☎ (6) 605202)
Consulate: Al-Wahdat al-Jarbiyya, al-Istiqlal St, Aqaba (☎ (3) 316171/81)

Libya
5th floor, Omar Khayam Hotel, Benghazi (☎ (61) 92488)

Netherlands
Badhuisweg 92, 2587 CL, The Hague (☎ (070) 354 20 00)

UK
26 South St, Mayfair, London W1Y 6DD (☎ (0171) 499 2401)
Consulate: 2 Lowndes St, London SW1 (☎ (0171) 235 9777)

USA
3521 International CT NW, Washington DC 20008 (☎ (202) 224 4319, 224 5131)
Consulate: 1110 2nd Ave, New York, NY 10022

(☎ (212) 759 7120/1/2); 3001 Pacific Ave, San Francisco, CA 94115 (☎ (415) 346 9700/2); suite 2180, 1990 Post Oak Blvd, Houston, TX 77056 (☎ (713) 961 4915/6); suite 1900, 500 N Michigan Ave, Chicago, IL 60611 (☎ (312) 828 9162/64/67)

Foreign Embassies in Egypt

The addresses of some of the foreign embassies and consulates in Egypt are:

Australia
11th floor, World Trade Centre, 1191 Corniche el-Nil, Cairo (☎ 575 0444); hours are from 8 am to 3 pm, Sunday to Thursday

Belgium
20 Sharia Kamel ash-Shennawi, Garden City, Cairo (☎ 354 7494)

Canada
3rd floor, 4 Sharia Kobra, Garden City, Cairo (☎ 354 3110); hours are from 8.30 am to 4.30 pm, Sunday to Thursday

Denmark
12 Sharia Hassan Sabri, Zamalek, Cairo (☎ 340 2503)

France
29 Sharia al-Giza, Giza (☎ 728649, 728346)
Consulate: 2 Midan Orabi, Mansheya, Alexandria (☎ 482 7950)

Germany
8 Sharia Hassan Sabri, Zamalek, Cairo (☎ 341 0015)
Consulate: 5 Sharia Mena, Rushdy, Alexandria (☎ 545 7025)

Ireland
7th floor, 3 Sharia Abu al-Feda, Zamalek, Cairo (☎ 340 8264)
Consulate: Honorary Consul, Hisham Helmy, 36 Sharia Kafr Abdu, Rushdy, Alexandria (☎ 546 4686)

Israel
18th floor, 6 Sharia Ibn al-Malek, Giza (☎ 361 0528); hours are from 10 am to 12.30 pm, Sunday to Thursday
Consulate: 207 Sharia Abdel Salem Aref, Alexandria (☎ 586 0492)

Jordan
6 Sharia Gohainy, Doqqi, Cairo (☎ 348 5566)
Hours are from 9 am to 3 pm, Saturday to Thursday. The embassy is two blocks west of the Sheraton Hotel. Visas cost from nothing for Australians to E£63 for UK citizens, E£77 for US citizens and E£91 for Canadians. You apply in the morning and come back to collect the visa at 2 pm. You'll need one photo. It is generally quite easy, and cheaper, to get a Jordanian visa upon arrival in the country (JD10 for UK and US citizens; free for Australians). At Aqaba, there is

a police and immigration station at the passenger ferry terminal, where visas are issued on the spot, although you may have to wait a bit.

Netherlands
18 Sharia Hassan Sabri, Zamalek, Cairo (☎ 340 1936)
Consulate: 3rd floor, 18 Tariq al-Hurriya, Alexandria (☎ 482 9044, 483 4210)

New Zealand
New Zealand's affairs are handled by the UK embassy

South Africa
21-23 Sharia al-Giza, Giza, Cairo (☎ 571 5897)

Syria
18 Sharia Abdel Rahim Sabri, Doqqi, Cairo (☎ 377 7020)

UK
7 Sharia Ahmed Ragheb, Garden City, Cairo (☎ 354 0850); hours are from 7.30 am to 2 pm, Sunday to Thursday
Consulate: 3 Sharia Mena, Rushdy, Alexandria (☎ 546 7001/2); hours are from 8 am to 1 pm, Sunday to Thursday

USA
5 Sharia Latin America, Garden City, Cairo (☎ 355 7371); hours are from 8 am to 4.30 pm, Sunday to Thursday.
Consulate: Unit 64904, 110 Tariq al-Hurriya, Alexandria (☎ 482 1911); hours are from 8.30 am to 4.30 pm, Sunday to Thursday

Yemen
28 Sharia Amin ar-Rafi'i, Doqqi, Cairo (☎ 361 4224)

For a visa you will need two photographs and a letter of recommendation from your embassy. The visa costs from E£140 for US, Canadians and French citizens to E£186 for UK citizens. Visas are usually issued within two days of applying, but before going ahead with the application you should check how long the visa is valid. Upon arrival you will be granted a one month stay. The embassy is open from 9 am to 3 pm, Sunday to Thursday.

CUSTOMS

A grand total of E£1000 can be imported into or exported out of the country, although you'd be unlucky to be searched thoroughly enough to be caught with more. You can import one bottle of liquor and 200 cigarettes. You will be asked to declare video cameras. You can purchase a variety of items from duty-free shops at ports of entry and in the large cities up to 30 days after arrival – liquor is a good buy.

MONEY

Costs

Despite high inflation and a steady currency, Egypt is still a cheap place to travel. You can get by on US$10 a day or even less if you're willing to stick to the cheapest end of the food and accommodation range and take 3rd class trains.

To give some indication of daily costs, the staple snacks – fuul and ta'amiyya (felafel) sandwiches – cost about 35 pt. A cup of tea/coffee costs 30/50 pt, a beer retails for E£5 to E£5 and a bottle of mineral water is E£1.50. Entry to the bulk of monuments and museums costs from E£6 to E£10. Baksheesh (tips) is expected everywhere – 25 to 50 pt is enough for small services such as taking luggage to your room.

In Sinai, everything from bus fares to soft drinks costs more than elsewhere.

Currency

The official currency of Egypt is called the pound (E£). In Arabic it is called a *guinay*. One pound = 100 piastres (pt – sometimes indicated by ـﭙ), or 1000 millims. The Arabic word for piastre is *irsh* or *girsh*. Coins in circulation are in denominations of 1, 5, 10, 20 and 25 pt. There are notes in denominations of 25 and 50 pt, and E£1, 5, 10, 20, 50 and 100.

Currency Exchange

The E£ was partly floated in 1987 and has been fairly steady since late 1990. At the time of publication, exchange rates for a range of foreign currencies were as follows:

Australia	A$1	=	E£2.96
Canada	C$1	=	E£2.53
France	FF10	=	E£6.70
Germany	DM1	=	E£2.25
Israel	NIS	=	E£1.05
Japan	¥100	=	E£3.05
Jordan	JD1	=	E£4.78
UK	UK£1	=	E£5.66
USA	US$1	=	E£3.39

Changing Money

Most foreign hard currencies, cash or

travellers' cheques, can be readily changed in Egypt. Money can be officially changed at American Express (Amex) and Thomas Cook offices, commercial banks, foreign exchange (forex) bureaus and some hotels.

Amex, Visa, MasterCard, JCB cards and Eurocard are good for purchases in a wide range of shops displaying the appropriate signs.

Visa and MasterCard are good for cash advances from many branches of Banque Misr and the National Bank of Egypt, as well as Thomas Cook. Outside the big cities and tourist hubs, cash advances are more problematic. Excess E£ can be exchanged into hard currency at the end of your stay, or during if you wish, at some banks, forex bureaus and Thomas Cook and Amex offices.

Eurocheques can be cashed at various banks, but watch the charges. You need your Eurocheque card and passport.

The black market for hard currency is negligible and few travellers can be bothered hunting it out for the fraction of the difference it makes.

Tipping & Bargaining

Tipping in Egypt is called baksheesh, although it is more than just a reward for having done a service properly. Salaries and wages in Egypt are much lower than in western countries, so baksheesh is regarded as a means of supplementing income – an often essential means. Services such as opening a door or carrying your bags warrant 25 to 50 pt. A guard who shows you something off the beaten track at an ancient site should receive about E£1. Baksheesh is not necessary when asking for directions.

In hotels and restaurants, a 12% service charge is included at the bottom of the bill, but the money goes into the till rather than into the pocket of the staff. If you want to tip someone, you'll have to do so directly.

Bargaining is part of everyday life in Egypt. Almost everything is open to haggling – from hotel rooms to the fruit juice you buy at a local stand. When buying souvenirs in bazaars, don't start bargaining until you have an idea of the true price, and never quote a price you're not prepared to pay.

POST & COMMUNICATIONS
Post

The Egyptian postal system is slow but eventually most mail gets to its destination. Receiving and sending packages through customs can cause tremendous headaches, though there is generally little problem with letters and postcards. They can take anywhere from four to 10 days to get to the UK and one to three weeks to reach the USA or Australia. Postcards and letters up to 10g cost 80 pt. There is also an Express Mail Service (EMS).

Mail can be received at Amex offices or via poste restante in most Egyptian cities. Amex offices are the better option.

Telephone

Local telephone calls cost 10 pt from payphones – if you can find one that works. Many kiosks and small shops have telephones for public use at 50 pt per local call. Major hotels usually charge E£1.

Card phones are on the increase. You'll find these bright orange phones mainly in telephone offices, where you can buy phonecards (135 units for E£15). Use them to call direct anywhere in Egypt or abroad (dial 00 and the country code). Otherwise you'll have to book a call at the exchange, with a three minute minimum. Cheap rates are available from 8 pm to 7.59 am.

The country code for Egypt is 20.

Fax & Telegraph

Fax machines are available for sending and receiving documents at the main telephone and telegraph offices in the big cities, at EMS offices, at most three to five-star hotels and at some of the smaller hotels. Telexes and telegrams can also be sent from telephone offices.

BOOKS

The following is a short list of books that can further introduce you to Egypt and the Egyptians. Most can be found in Egypt. For more general information, see the Books section in the Regional Facts for the Visitor chapter

For information on Egyptian authors and their works, see Arts in the Facts about the Region section.

Travel

Gerard de Nerval's *Journey to the Orient* was first published in the 19th century. This book will prime you for exploration of the mysteries of Egypt.

Beyond the Pyramids, by Douglas Kennedy, is one of the few travelogues written about Egypt in recent years and is an entertaining, often humorous read.

Mike Asher's book *In Search of the 40 Days Road* recounts his search for the trail which Sudanese camel traders follow when taking their camels north to Egypt.

History

The Penguin Guide to Ancient Egypt, by William J Murnane, is one of the best overall books on the life and monuments of ancient Egypt. There are plenty of illustrations and descriptions of almost every major monument in the country.

The British Museum Book of Ancient Egypt, edited by Stephen Quirke and Jeffrey Spencer, gives an authoritative overview of ancient Egypt, but is surprisingly short on plans and diagrams of monuments.

The Ancient Egyptians: Religious Beliefs & Practices, by Rosalie David, is one of the first books to trace the evolution of religious beliefs and practices in ancient Egypt. It is a very thorough and comprehensive treatment of a complex subject.

People & Society

Amitav Ghosh's *In an Antique Land* is a superb account of life in a Nile Delta village. *Shahhat: An Egyptian*, by Richard Critchfield, is an in-depth portrait of a young man named Shahhat and his life in an Egyptian village. Critchfield lived and worked for an extended period in a west bank village near Luxor to write this.

Khul-Khaal: Five Egyptian Women Tell their Stories, edited by Nayra Atiya, reveals the life stories of five contemporary Egyptian women from a variety of backgrounds. Fascinating information for anyone interested in Egyptian life.

NEWSPAPERS & MAGAZINES

By Middle Eastern standards, Egypt's press suffers a moderate level of censorship. There is a range of local publications, and most major foreign newspapers and news magazines can be obtained in Cairo, Alexandria and some of the main tourist centres, usually a day late. Among the local press, the Egypt edition of the *Middle East Times*, a weekly digest, is the best in English. The *Egyptian Gazette* is Egypt's daily English-language newspaper. *Cairo Today* is an interesting monthly magazine with quite a lot of useful listings information.

RADIO & TV

Local English news can be heard on FM95, 557 kHz. The station also broadcasts news in French, German, Italian and Greek. In the evenings, the BBC and VOA can be heard on medium wave. TV news is usually shown at 9 pm in English and at 7 pm in French.

PHOTOGRAPHY & VIDEO

Film costs are similar to western prices, if not more, so you might choose to bring some with you. There are quite a few places to have film processed in Cairo and the other main cities. As usual in the Middle East, it pays to watch where you point your camera. Public utilities, bridges, dams, airfields, and anything military are out.

Outrageous fees for shooting videos have been introduced at many ancient sites. In most cases it costs around E£25, but fees of E£100 are becoming increasingly common. The Manial Palace Museum in Cairo charges E£150.

LAUNDRY

There are a few self-service laundries around Cairo but virtually none elsewhere. Another option is to take your clothes to one of Egypt's many 'hole-in-the-wall' laundries, where they wash and iron your clothes by hand. Some hotels in Luxor and Aswan have so-called washing machines, but they are laborious contraptions.

HEALTH

There are hospitals throughout Egypt, but facilities are often dubious. If you need an operation, don't have it here. London or other European cities are only a few hours away by plane. If you need a doctor, your embassy should be able to help find one. Vaccinations for cholera and yellow fever only are done at the International Vaccination Centre in the former Hotel Continental on Sharia al-Gomhurriya facing the Ezbekiya Gardens. Bring your own sterilised syringe. See the Health Appendix for more detailed health information, especially the section on Schistosomiasis (bilharzia).

TOILETS

Public toilets are bad news: fly infested, dirty and stinky. Some toilets are still of the squat-over-a-hole-in-a-little-room variety. Only in mid-range and top-end hotels will toilet paper be provided; most toilets simply come equipped with a water squirter. If you do use toilet paper, put it in the bucket.

WOMEN TRAVELLERS

Egyptians are conservative, especially about matters concerning sex and women; Egyptian women that is, not foreign women. An entire book could be written from the comments and stories of women travellers about their adventures and misadventures in Egypt. At the very least, pinching bottoms, brushing breasts or making lewd suggestions seem to be considered a perfectly natural means of communication with the unknown foreign woman by some Egyptian men. Flashing and masturbating in public occasionally occurs, however, serious physical harassment and rape are not significant threats in Egypt.

GAY & LESBIAN TRAVELLERS

While lesbian relationships are uncommon in Egypt, male homosexuality is not. It is, however, clandestine. No man will attest to being gay as Egyptians in general perceive gay men to be weak and feminine.

No national support group exists, and only in Cairo will you find gay bars. The Taverne du Champs de Mars and Jackie's Disco, both in the Nile Hilton Hotel in Cairo, are popular gay hang-outs.

DANGERS & ANNOYANCES

Egypt is generally a safe place, although you should be on your guard for pickpockets and the like in the main tourist centres, especially on crowded public transport.

Terrorism

What began as one or two isolated incidents in 1992 took on all the signs of a concerted campaign against tourism by Islamist extremists in 1993-94. The authorities have embarked on campaigns to reassure the world of Egypt's safety, but the danger of being caught in the crossfire, however statistically slight, should at least be borne in mind. (See under History in the earlier Facts about the Country section for background information.)

Drugs

Marijuana and hashish are quite freely available in places around Egypt where travellers gather – most notably Aswan and Dahab. Harder drugs are also in circulation at Dahab. Penalties for smuggling and dealing include 25 years in jail or death by hanging.

Mines

A leftover from the Israeli-Egyptian wars and WWII, land mines are still littered along the Red Sea and Mediterranean coasts and throughout Sinai. If you're a sun worshipper in search of the perfect beach or simply an off the road adventurer, seek local advice before wandering off the beaten track.

Marine Creatures

Don't be completely fooled by the beauty of the Red Sea's blue-green waters and coral reefs – they do have their share of hazards. Avoid bumping into sea urchins and coral, especially fire coral, as it is extremely sharp and can cause a painful, burning sensation where it breaks your skin. The best policy for your own protection and that of the reef is simply not to touch the reef.

Before diving or snorkelling, you should learn to recognise potentially dangerous creatures such as stonefish, lionfish, scorpionfish, barracuda and Moray eels. There are sharks in the Red Sea.

BUSINESS HOURS

Banking hours are from 8 or 8.30 am to 2 pm Sunday to Thursday. Many banks in Cairo and other cities open again from 5 or 6 pm for two or three hours, largely for foreign exchange. During Ramadan, banks are open between 10 am and 1.30 pm. Foreign exchange offices tend to be open longer hours.

Most government offices operate from about 8 am to 2 pm Sunday to Thursday.

There are no hard and fast rules for shop trading hours. Most open at about 9 am and close for a few hours in the afternoon (especially in summer) before reopening in the evening.

PUBLIC HOLIDAYS & SPECIAL EVENTS

In addition to Islamic holidays (see the table of holidays in Public Holidays & Special Events in the Regional Facts for the Visitor chapter), the following Coptic Christian and national holidays are observed.

New Year's Day
    1 January
Christmas
    7 January
Epiphany
    19 January; celebrating the baptism of Jesus
Annunciation
    23 March
Easter
    This is the most important date on the Coptic calender. It's preceded by 55 days of fasting, and is celebrated on different dates each year.
Sham an-Nessim (Sniffing the Breeze)
    A special Coptic holiday with Pharaonic origins, it literally means 'the smell of a fresh wind'. It falls on the first Monday after Easter and is celebrated by all Egyptians, with family picnics and outings.

Sinai Liberation Day
    25 April
May Day
    1 May
Revolution Day
    23 July
National Day
    6 October (a day of military parades and air displays)

ACTIVITIES

Diving

Many people simply jet into Sinai or Hurghada from Europe for a week or two of diving. The waters of the Red Sea are teeming with a dazzling array of colourful coral and fish life, so it's little surprise really. There's a plethora of dive operators in Sinai (at Na'ama Bay, Sharm el-Sheikh, Dahab and Nuweiba) and on the Red Sea coast (Hurghada, Port Safaga and Al-Quseir); Na'ama Bay and Hurghada have the greatest concentration of operators.

Most of the clubs offer every possible kind of dive course. The average open-water certification course for beginners, either with CMAS, PADI or NAUI, takes about five days and usually includes several dives. The total cost varies between US$280 to US$400 depending on the operator and location.

A day's diving (two dives), including equipment and air fills, costs US$50 to US$95. An introductory dive is around US$60. Full equipment can be hired for about US$20 per day.

Camel Treks

For some, the eerie silence and star-studded night sky of the desert are a dream, and in Sinai it's quite possible to arrange with the Bedouin to enjoy this and more for a few hours or a few weeks on the back of a camel.

COURSES

The American University in Cairo (AUC) is one of the premier universities in the Middle East. The AUC offers degree, non-degree and summer-school programmes, but it's not cheap. More information can be obtained from the AUC, PO Box 2511, Cairo (☎ 354 2964, ext 5011/12/13; fax 355 7565).

EGYPT

It is also possible to study at Egyptian universities such as Al-Azhar, Alexandria, 'Ain Shams and Cairo.

The AUC, the bigger language schools (see the following Work section) and some of the cultural centres offer Arabic-language courses. Quality and intensiveness vary greatly.

WORK

The most common source of work is teaching English as a foreign language in Cairo and, to a lesser extent, in Alexandria. If you have TEFL qualifications, try the British Council (☎ 345 3281) at 192 Sharia el-Nil, Cairo, the AUC's Center for Adult and Continuing Education (☎ 354 2964), or either of the International Language Institute's (ILI) two offices: 3 Sharia Mahmoud Azmy, Sahafayeen, Cairo (☎ 346 3087); and 2 Sharia Mohammed Bayoumi, Heliopolis, Cairo (☎ 291 9295; fax 418 7275). Also, check the monthly magazine *Cairo Today* for schools requiring fewer or no qualifications.

Diving instructors can often find work on the resorts along the Red Sea and Sinai coasts, and film and TV extras are sometimes needed in Cairo.

ACCOMMODATION

Places to stay in Egypt range from cheap to expensive and rough to luxurious. There are resorts, hotels, flotels (Nile cruisers), pensions, youth hostels and a few camping grounds.

Camping

There is only a handful of official camping grounds and few of them are much good.

Hostels

There are 15 hostels recognised by Hostelling International (HI) but, frankly, some of them are awful. They range in price from E£3 to E£16. The Egyptian Hostelling International office (☎ 575 8099) at 7 Sharia Dr Abdel Hamid Said, Cairo, can give you the latest information.

Cheap Hotels

The two, one and zero-star hotels form the budget group. Often the ratings mean nothing at all, as a hotel without a star can be as good as a two-star hotel, only cheaper. You can spend as little as E£10 per night for a clean single room with hot water or E£40 plus for a dirty double room without a shower.

Other Hotels

Most of the world's major chains are represented. The four-star hotels start at about E£100 and head upwards. Generally the standards are fairly high. Some of the three-star places, which charge around E£50 to E£100, are also quite OK.

Note Residents in Egypt are often entitled to something closer to the local rate for rooms in the bigger hotels.

FOOD

Egyptian food is basically a variation on the Middle Eastern theme. *Fuul* and *ta'amiyya* (known as *felafel* elsewhere) are the unofficial national staples of Egypt. Fuul is fava beans, with a variety of ingredients such as oil, lemon, salt, eggs and onions to spice it up.

Egypt shares with its neighbours dishes like *houmos*, *baba ghanouj*, *tahina*, *shwarma*, *kebab* and *kibbih*. Some of these will be accompanied by *torshi*, pickled vegetables. See Food in the Regional Facts for the Visitor chapter for more details of Middle Eastern cuisine.

Molokhiyya is also very popular and is one of the few truly Egyptian dishes. It's a green, slimy, delicious soup made by stewing a strange leafy vegetable, rice and garlic in chicken or beef broth.

Other popular dishes are *kushari*, a combination of noodles, rice, black lentils, fried onions and tomato sauce, and *fiteer*, which is a cross between pizza and pastry, and can be either sweet or savoury. Both are served at a place called a *fatatri*.

DRINK

Shay and *awha* (tea and coffee) are the two liquid mainstays in Egypt and the rest of the Middle East. Another favourite is fruit juice, from plain orange to weird and wonderful cocktails. An Egyptian staple is *asab* (sugar cane juice). Soft drinks are very popular.

Stella, the local beer, is widely available. It costs about E£5 to E£9 in most bars. The smaller bottles of Stella Export cost up to E£15. Neither are great but better than nothing at all. There are also several locally produced wines – the Omar Khayyam red is not too bad. Spirits, too, are made locally. There are some brandies and Egypt's version of ouzo, raqi and arak – *zibiba*.

ENTERTAINMENT
Cinemas
It is quite possible to catch a good recent mainstream movie in both Cairo and Alexandria. Check the *Egyptian Gazette* for details.

Discos, Nightclubs & Bars
Most western-style discos are in the middle to top-end hotels, but they're often not so hot. Belly dancing can be seen in the big hotels, expensive nightclubs or rather tacky but atmospheric joints for locals in central Cairo. Many hotels have bars and, in Cairo especially, you'll find a lot of low-key bars, known as 'cafeterias', catering to the locals.

THINGS TO BUY
Egypt is a budget souvenir and kitsch shopper's paradise. Hieroglyphic drawings of Pharaohs, queens, gods and goddesses embellish and blemish everything from ashtrays to engraved brass tables. Gold, silver, jewellery, leather, woodwork, basketry, copperware and brassware, ceramics and alabaster and, of course, the ubiquitous papyrus are just some of the possibilities. The Khan al-Khalili and surrounding markets in Cairo have the greatest range.

Gold and silver jewellery can be made to specification for not much more than the cost of the metal. A cartouche with the name of a friend or relative spelled in hieroglyphs makes a great gift.

Although gold shops are concentrated in the centre of Khan al-Khalili, gold can be bought all over Islamic Cairo. It's generally sold by weight. Caution should be exercised when buying any jewellery – examine closely what you're getting.

Papyrus is a popular buy. Avoid machine printed stuff and remember that better quality papyrus should not be damaged when rolled up.

Egyptian cotton is renowned. You can have *galabiyyas* (full-length robes worn by men) made up, or tailor-made suits prepared. T-shirts abound, and some of the appliqué and hand-sewn cushion covers and wall-hangings are truly unique. They can cost anything from E£20 to E£1000 depending on workmanship.

For carpets it may be worth visiting the tapestry schools on the Saqqara road near the pyramids – the Wissa Wassef Art Centre is particularly interesting.

Leather goods of all descriptions can be bought – but watch the workmanship.

Plates, coffee pots and a variety of other objects in brass and copper are often fairly cheap, going for as little as a few pounds for something small and basic. Engraved trays and plates start at around E£15.

Along with papyrus, inlaid backgammon boards and jewellery boxes are a popular buy. As long as you're not fooled by claims they are made with mother-of-pearl, they make an attractive and typically Egyptian souvenir.

Avoid the ivory products – elephants have been decimated for their ivory tusks, despite numerous edicts supposedly protecting them. Stuffed birds and desert creatures are illegally sold at Kerdassa, a village near the pyramids in Cairo, and stuffed crocodiles in the bazaar in Aswan. Please don't buy them.

Getting There & Away

AIR
Egypt's main international gateway is Cairo airport, which has two terminals. The new terminal, known as Terminal II, services most international airlines. The old Terminal I is mainly used by EgyptAir (domestic and international flights). Lufthansa and Olympic

Airways have flights to Alexandria, and charter airlines are the main international customers at Luxor, Aswan, Hurghada and Sharm el-Sheikh airports.

The USA

EgyptAir flies from New York and Los Angeles to Cairo. The advance purchase fares from New York and Los Angeles are US$1280/2176 one way/return and US$ 1630/3358 one way/return respectively. EgyptAir has no connections to Canada.

Lufthansa has connections to Cairo via Frankfurt from 12 cities in the USA. Advance purchase and youth fares are available. From Los Angeles, the cheapest return fare is US$2032, and entails a minimum stay of seven days and a maximum of two months. The cheapest one-way ticket from Los Angeles is US$1718. From New York, the same two tickets are US$1606 and US$1088 respectively.

Australia & New Zealand

Some of the best fares from Australia to Cairo are offered by STA Travel. Fares start at A$1220/1830 one way/return from Melbourne or Sydney. Round-The-World (RTW) fares with a stopover in Cairo start from A$2080 but vary according to season. EgyptAir commenced flying between Egypt and Australia in late 1995.

The UK

London is one of the best centres in the world for discounted air tickets. If you are planning to travel onto Africa, it is worth checking out tickets from Europe with stopovers in Cairo, as air travel within Africa is expensive. The Africa Travel Shop (☎ (0171) 387 1211) at 4 Medway Court, Leigh St, London WC1, has one-way tickets to Nairobi with a stop in Cairo for UK£295 – much better than anything you'll find in Cairo.

Middle East

Arab Gulf States There are regular flights between Egypt and all the Gulf states.

Israel Air Sinai and El Al regularly fly between Cairo and Tel Aviv for about E£637 one way or E£907 return.

Jordan There are regular flights with Royal Jordanian and EgyptAir between Cairo and Amman. Amman-Cairo costs JD84 (about US$120) one way and double return. Going the other way, the fare is E£571 one way and E£1010 return. There are no student reductions.

Turkey The Sultanahmet area in İstanbul is the closest the city comes to the bucket shop scene. Occasionally there are some OK deals from here travelling with EgyptAir and Turkish Airlines, and travellers planning to skip Syria and Jordan going either way have reported getting reasonable fares.

Africa

Sudan Sudan Airways and EgyptAir both have two flights a week between Cairo and Khartoum. The 2½ hour flight costs E£1326 one way or E£1444 return (valid for one month). Sudan Airways also has a youth fare (for those under 25 years) which costs E£849 one way or E£1565 return (open for one year).

Tunisia Tunis Air and EgyptAir offer student discounts on flights between Cairo and Tunis, but that doesn't make it cheap. The one-way fare is E£840. If you're over 31, it costs E£1550.

Other African Countries There is nothing cheap about travelling by air between African capitals. About the best you can do to Nairobi is E£2129 one way with Kenyan Airways (or E£1678 for a student fare). The flight to Addis Ababa in Ethiopia costs E£1820 one way, or E£2545 return with Ethiopian Airlines.

LAND

Israel & the Palestinian Territories

There are two crossing points into Israel, one at Taba on the Gulf of Aqaba and the other at Rafah on the north Sinai coast.

There are daily buses direct from Cairo to

Tel Aviv every day, except Saturday, departing at 5.30 am from in front of the Cairo Sheraton. A one-way fare is about E£100 or E£120 (return E£150) and tickets can be bought from various agencies, including Misr Travel at the Sheraton.

Local transport is a cheaper option. Take a bus from Abbassiya Sinai terminal (E£25) or a service taxi from Midan Ramses (E£15) to Rafah, where you can connect with an Israeli bus for Tel Aviv (which costs the shekel equivalent of US$10) at the border – beware, however, there's only one bus a day, departing at 3 pm. Alternatively, take a bus for Taba (E£65) from Abbassiya Sinai terminal, walk over the border and catch a local bus for Eilat (US$1) from where there are frequent services to Tel Aviv and Jerusalem. There's an E£17 departure tax to be paid at Rafah. From Taba the fee is E£2.

Libya
There are direct buses running between Cairo (or Alexandria) and Benghazi and Tripoli. Refer to the Sallum section later in this chapter for information about getting to/from the border itself.

SEA
Europe
Menatours acts as the agent for the limited passenger-ship services that operate between Port Said or Alexandria and various Mediterranean destinations (for details see the Port Said and Alexandria Getting There & Away sections later in this chapter).

Jordan
There are car ferries, regular ferries and a speedboat service between Nuweiba, in Sinai, and Aqaba, Jordan's only port. You can reach the Nuweiba port directly by bus from Cairo's Abbassiya Sinai terminal. The trip takes about eight hours and costs US$23. Some buses for Cairo, Ismailia and the Delta, in Nuweiba, wait for the arrival of the boat. In Aqaba, the ferry terminal is seven km south of the town centre. A taxi from the terminal to the centre costs JD1.500, but they'll try for more.

There are two ferry sailings a day each way and they take three hours. From Nuweiba, they are supposed to leave at 11 am and 6 pm; the fare is US$32. The speedboat takes one hour and costs US$42.

Saudi Arabia
Direct ferries take about three days between Suez and Jeddah. Frequency varies, but getting a berth during the *haj*, the pilgrimage to Mecca, is virtually impossible. The price of berths ranges from E£145 for deck class to E£300 for 1st class. You can get information at Menatours or Misr Travel agencies, or buy a ticket directly in the latter's office in Port Tawfiq, Suez.

There are also passenger boats from Port Safaga to Duba and Jeddah.

RIVER
Sudan
The most common way of travelling between Sudan and Egypt used to be by steamer from Wadi Halfa along Lake Nasser to Aswan; however, this service has been indefinitely cancelled. For more details refer to the Aswan section later in this chapter.

LEAVING EGYPT
Departure fees seem to vary. There is a E£2 departure fee when leaving from Taba, or leaving Nuweiba for the Aqaba boat or crossing the Libyan border. An Egyptian departure tax of E£17 is charged from Egypt to Israel via Rafah, but there is no Israeli entry fee.

A E£21 embarkation fee is payable when you leave Alexandria by ship, but the E£21 airport departure tax is incorporated into the price of air tickets.

Getting Around

AIR
In Egypt, air fares are about average by international standards. It costs E£497 one way from Cairo to Aswan, E£361 to Luxor,

E£412 to Sharm el-Sheikh and E£214 to Alexandria.

If you do have to travel by plane, EgyptAir flies from Cairo to Abu Simbel, Al-Arish, Al-Kharga, Alexandria, Aswan, Hurghada, Luxor, Marsa Matruh and Sharm el-Sheikh, as well as from Luxor to Aswan and Hurghada, and from Aswan to Abu Simbel.

Air Sinai (to all intents and purposes EgyptAir by another name) has flights from Cairo to Sharm el-Sheikh and Taba (Ras an-Naqb; in winter only).

BUS

Buses service just about every city, town and village in Egypt. Inter-city buses, especially on shorter runs and in Upper Egypt, tend to become quite crowded and you'll be lucky to get a seat.

There are four main companies: Superjet (luxury buses only); West Delta Bus Co; East Delta Bus Co; and Upper Egypt Bus Co.

Deluxe buses travel between some of the main towns, especially Cairo and Alexandria. They are fast and comfortable, with air-con (it doesn't always work), toilet and, unfortunately, nonstop noisy video.

A direct bus between Cairo and Aswan will cost about E£50, and E£15 to E£28 between Cairo and Alexandria. The direct buses from Cairo to Sinai destinations tend to be expensive.

TRAIN

Trains travel along more than 5000 km of track to almost every major city and town in Egypt. A timetable for the main destinations, in shoddy English, is updated every year (valid to 30 June) and is available for E£1.

A train with wagon-lit sleepers runs daily between Cairo, Luxor and Aswan. Tickets must be reserved, often a couple of days in advance. The one-way trip from Cairo to Aswan costs E£451/293 in 1st/2nd class, which is the plush way to travel. Less classy sleepers are not available to foreigners.

Other trains range from the sleek Turbos connecting Alexandria with Cairo four times a day on a nonstop, two hour run to rattling old 3rd class museums, packed to the hilt

with passengers, chickens and just about every imaginable kind of baggage and household items. Student discounts of up to 50% are available for ISIC card holders. You can travel from Cairo to Aswan for less than E£10 in 3rd class with a student card – it's painful but cheap.

TAXI

Travelling by 'ser-vees' taxi (you'll occasionally hear them referred to rather quaintly as *bijous*) is the fastest way to go from city to city. They travel on set routes, and in most places congregate near bus and railway stations. Each driver waits with his Peugeot 504 taxi (or increasingly Toyota microbus) until it's full. Fares tend to be a little higher than on the buses.

MICROBUS

A slightly bigger version of the service taxi is a van that would normally take about 12 people. More often than not they cram on as many as 22. These run on fewer routes than the service taxis, though generally cost the same.

PICK-UPS

Toyota and Chevrolet pick-up trucks cover a lot of the routes off the main roads between smaller towns and villages. The general rule is to get 12 passengers inside the covered rear of the truck, with a few more hanging off the back.

CAR & MOTORCYCLE

Driving in Cairo is a crazy affair, but in other parts of the country, at least in daylight, it isn't so bad. Driving is on the right-hand side in Egypt. For more information on road rules, suggested routes and other advice, it might be worth picking up a copy of *On the Road in Egypt – A Motorist's Guide* by Mary Dungan Megalli.

Petrol is readily available. *Benzin aadi*, or normal, costs 90 pt a litre. *Mumtaz*, or super, is more expensive at E£1 a litre. Unleaded petrol was introduced in 1995 but it's not a big seller yet.

Several car-rental agencies have offices in

Cairo and Alexandria and the major tourist centres. They include Avis, Hertz and Budget. Their rates are on a par with international charges.

BICYCLE

Cycling is a practical way of getting around a town and its surrounding sites. In most places you can rent bicycles quite cheaply; prices start at around E£5 per day.

HITCHING

It is easy to hitch in Egypt; however, drivers are used to being paid for giving you a ride so you probably won't save very much money.

CAMEL

While the more intrepid travellers will probably want to buy their own 'ship of the desert', there are easier and less costly alternatives. It's easiest to hire a camel for a couple of hours and take a tour around the Pyramids of Giza, the temple complex at Saqqara or to the Monastery of St Simeon in Aswan. A guide usually accompanies you. It is also easy to arrange a camel safari in Sinai or from Siwa Oasis.

BOAT
Felucca

The ancient sailboats of the Nile are still the most common means of transport up and down the river. Sunset is one of the best times to take a felucca ride, but you can arrange a few hours of peaceful sailing at any time from just about anywhere on the Nile. The best trip is the journey between Aswan and Esna, Edfu or Kom Ombo; this takes from one to three days.

Yacht

It is possible to take a yacht into Egyptian waters and ports. There are 12 designated ports of entry, including Alexandria, Dahab, Ismailia, Nuweiba, Port Said, Suez and Sharm el-Sheikh. A security permit is required to enter the Nile River, and transit fees of US$10 per person and US$20 for the yacht need to be paid to negotiate the Suez

Canal. These and other fees are liable to change. It may be possible to pick up work on passing yachts in Suez.

LOCAL TRANSPORT
Bus

Cairo and Alexandria are the only cities in Egypt with their own bus systems. It's a cheap way to get around, but they can get ridiculously crowded at times.

Metro

Cairo is the only city in Egypt (indeed in Africa) with a metro system. It's a single line of 33 stations that stretches for 43 km from the southern suburb of Helwan to Al-Marg near Heliopolis. The metro is fast, inexpensive (30 pt from Midan Tahrir to Ramses railway station) and usually not crowded.

Tram

Cairo and Alexandria are also the only two cities with tram systems. Alexandria's trams are relatively efficient and go all over the city but they also get quite crowded. Cairo's trams (actually known to Cairenes as the 'metro' – confused?) are similar but only a few lines remain.

Taxi

There are taxis in most cities in Egypt. A short run in Cairo costs E£2, while a journey across town, say from Zamalek to Khan al-Khalili would be E£3.50. If you bargain you will inevitably pay two or three times more than you ought to – the only way to pay the proper fare is to know it before you get into the cab and not to raise the subject of money at all, just hand the driver the proper sum at your destination.

Multiple hire is the rule rather than the exception.

Microbus

Privately owned and usually unmarked microbuses (in the form of a minibus) shuttle around all the larger cities. For the average traveller, they can be difficult to use, as it is quite unclear where most of them go. The exception is the route from Midan Tahrir in

Cairo to the pyramids. Most of the smaller cities and towns have similar microbuses doing set routes around town.

Hantour & Careta

Hantours, also known as *caleches*, are horse-drawn carriages which are popular tourist vehicles in Luxor and Aswan.

Caretas are donkey-drawn carts with plastic awnings and wooden seats, and are used as local taxis in some towns on the Mediterranean Coast. They're also common in Siwa Oasis.

ORGANISED TOURS

It is possible to organise day tours, Nile cruises and longer trips in Egypt, but as a rule they are not very cheap and won't suit the budget traveller's pocket.

However, those wanting to splash out may like to consider the new five-star MS *Eugénie*, which sails between Aswan High Dam and Abu Simbel once a week, visiting a few ancient sites along the way. The three day trip up (or alternatively down) Lake Nasser on this turn-of-the-century style boat costs US$100/120 per person per day in a single/double cabin, including meals. Information and reservations can be made through 17 Sharia Tunis, New Ma'adi, Cairo (☎ (02) 352 4775; fax 353 6114).

Cairo

To the 16 million or more people who live here, Cairo is the Mother of the World. In this city, east and west clash in a raucous mix of old and new. Dubbed Al-Qahira, which means 'the victorious', by her new Fatimid rulers in 969 AD (hence Cairo), the city had already won its place as one of the key capitals in the Muslim world.

Its precursor, the Christian city of Babylon under Byzantine tutelage, has long since been swallowed up by the rapidly expanding metropolis, and is now known as Old Cairo.

In 1171 Saladin (Salah ad-Din) restored

Sunni rule in Cairo after the Shiite Fatimid dynasty had petered out.

His dynasty met its end in 1250, when the Mamluks took the reins of power. They are owed a great many of the monuments remaining in what today is called Islamic Cairo. The city's days as an imperial centre came to an end with the arrival of the Ottoman Turks in 1517.

In 1992 the city was rocked by an earthquake that left hundreds dead, thousands homeless and many of its great monuments badly shaken.

Orientation

Most travellers wind up in Midan Tahrir at the beginning of their visit to this surprisingly compact city. From Midan Tahrir, north-east to Midan Talaat Harb and Ezbekiya Gardens, you will find most of Cairo's western-style shops and many of the budget hotels.

Further east are some of Cairo's poorer districts, the market and medieval neighbourhoods of Al-Muski, Darb al-Ahmar and the City of the Dead. South of Darb al-Ahmar is the ancient Citadel. Continuing farther east towards the airport you will enter Heliopolis, also called Misr al-Gadida (New Cairo).

North of Midan Tahrir along the metro line is the main railway station on Midan Ramses.

West of Midan Tahrir is Gezira, a large island in the Nile, the northern end of which is the posh central Cairo district of Zamalek.

Beyond are the newer districts of Agouza, Doqqi, Mohandiseen and Giza. Where Giza meets the desert lie the Great Pyramids and the Desert Highway to Alexandria.

South of Midan Tahrir is Garden City, a British-designed diplomatic district. Further south again is Old Cairo.

Information

Registration You must register your arrival in Egypt within seven days. The Mogamma offices are open (for registration only) Saturday to Thursday from 8 am to 2 pm. Outside these hours you can register at the little booth marked 'Registration' on the 1st floor at the top of the stairs. This booth is open daily from 2 to 4 pm, and 7 to 9 pm (winter) and 8 to 10 pm (summer).

Visa extensions and re-entry visas are also issued at the Mogamma.

Tourist Office The head office of the Egyptian Tourist Authority (☎ 391 3454), 5 Sharia Adly, is about half a block west of Midan Opera. It's open every day, usually from 8.30 am to 8 pm.

Money The Banque Misr exchange offices at the Nile Hilton and inside Shepherd's Hotel are open 24 hours a day. The money-changing booths at the airport are open 24 hours also. A growing number of exchange bureaus are springing up around Cairo.

Amex has several offices in Cairo. Its central office (☎ 574 7991), at 15 Sharia Qasr el-Nil, is open Saturday to Thursday from 8.30 am to 4.30 pm, Friday from 9 am to 3 pm. Thomas Cook also has a handful of offices in Cairo; in central Cairo its office (☎ 574 3955) is at 7 Sharia Mohammed Bassiuni, and is open daily from 8 am to 5 pm.

Post & Communications Cairo's GPO, in Midan Ataba, is open from 7 am to 7 pm, supposedly seven days a week (be wary on Friday and public holidays). Poste restante is through the last door down the side street to the right of the main entrance, opposite the EMS fast mail office, and is open from 8 am to 6 pm (Friday and holidays from 10 am until noon). To send a package abroad you must go to the Post Traffic Centre at Midan Ramses. It is open daily, except Friday, from 8.30 am to 3 pm.

There are several telephone offices around Cairo, and most have a few card phones. There are offices on the north side of Midan Tahrir, near the tourist information office on Sharia Adly, on Sharia Alfi Bey, on Sharia Mohammed Mahmud in the Telecommunications building and on Sharia 26th of July, Zamalek, near the Zamalek Bridge.

The telephone code for Cairo is 02.

Travel Agencies The area around Midan Tahrir is teeming with travel agents. Fairly efficient is De Castro Tours (☎ 574 3144) at 12 Sharia Talaat Harb. Just down the road at No 10 is Norma Tours (☎ 760007), which touts itself as being a cheap air-fare specialist.

Bookshops Among the better bookshops for guides, maps and general literature in English are the Anglo-Egyptian Bookshop at 165 Sharia Mohammed Farid; the AUC Bookstore inside the university entrance on Sharia Mohammed Mahmud; Lehnert & Landrock at 44 Sharia Sherif; and Shorouk, on Midan Talaat Harb.

If it's books in French you're after, head straight for the Livres de France on Sharia Qasr el-Nil.

Libraries The best public library is the new and very grand Great Cairo Library (☎ 341 2280) at 15 Sharia Mohammed Mazhar, Zamalek. It's open daily, except Monday, from 9 am to 7 pm.

Cultural Centres Most cultural centres run libraries, show films and stage various lectures, exhibitions and performances. The American Cultural Center (☎ 354 9601) is at 5 Sharia Latin America in Garden City, while the British Council (☎ 345 3281) is in a villa near the circus grounds at 192 Sharia el-Nil in Agouza.

Canada, France, Germany, India, Italy, Japan and the Netherlands also have cultural centres in Cairo.

Emergency Some important numbers in Cairo are:

Ambulance
    Cairo Ambulance Service (☎ 123, 770123/230); possibly slow
    Giza (☎ 720385)
    Heliopolis (☎ 244 4327)
    Ma'adi (☎ 350 2873)
Police
    Central (☎ 13)
    Emergency (☎ 122, 900112)
    Tourist Police (☎ 126)

EGYPT

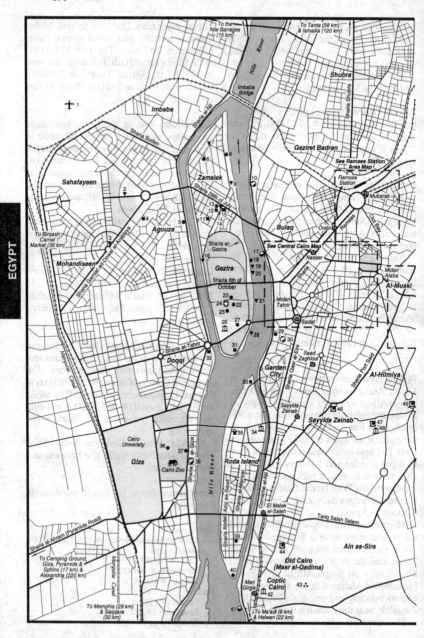

EGYPT

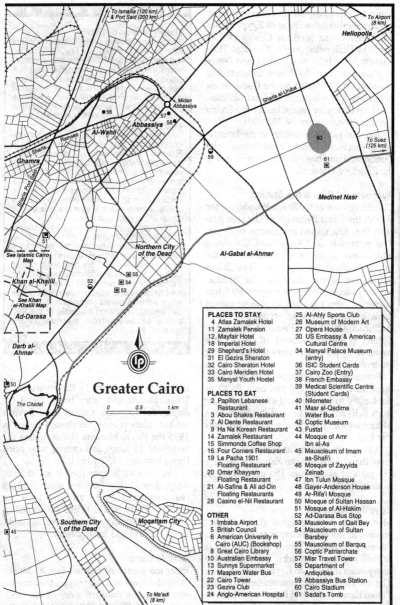

Greater Cairo

0   0.5   1 km

PLACES TO STAY
4   Atlas Zamalek Hotel
11 Zamalek Pension
12 Mayfair Hotel
18 Imperial Hotel
29 Shepherd's Hotel
31 El Gezira Sheraton
32 Cairo Sheraton Hotel
33 Cairo Meridien Hotel
35 Manyal Youth Hostel

PLACES TO EAT
2   Papillon Lebanese
    Restaurant
3   Abou Shakra Restaurant
7   Al Dente Restaurant
9   Ha Na Korean Restaurant
14 Zamalek Restaurant
15 Simmonds Coffee Shop
16 Four Corners Restaurant
19 Le Pacha 1901
    Floating Restaurant
20 Omar Khayyam
    Floating Restaurant
21 Al-Safina & Ali ad-Din
    Floating Restaurants
28 Casino el-Nil Restaurant

OTHER
1   Imbaba Airport
5   British Council
6   American University in
    Cairo (AUC) (Bookshop)
8   Great Cairo Library
10 Australian Embassy
13 Sunnys Supermarket
17 Maspero Water Bus
22 Cairo Tower
23 Gezira Club
24 Anglo-American Hospital

25 Al-Ahly Sports Club
26 Museum of Modern Art
27 Opera House
30 US Embassy & American
    Cultural Centre
34 Manyal Palace Museum
    (entry)
36 ISIC Student Cards
37 Cairo Zoo (Entry)
38 French Embassy
39 Medical Scientific Centre
    (Student Cards)
40 Nilometer
41 Masr al-Qadima
    Water Bus
42 Coptic Museum
43 Fustat
44 Mosque of Amr
    Ibn al-As
45 Mausoleum of Imam
    as-Shafi'i
46 Mosque of Zayyida
    Zeinab
47 Ibn Tulun Mosque
48 Gayer-Anderson House
49 Ar-Rifa'i Mosque
50 Mosque of Sultan Hassan
51 Mosque of Al-Hakim
52 Ad-Darasa Bus Stop
53 Mausoleum of Qait Bey
54 Mausoleum of Sultan
    Barsbey
55 Mausoleum of Barquq
56 Coptic Patriarchate
57 Misr Travel Tower
58 Department of
    Antiquities
59 Abbassiya Bus Station
60 Cairo Stadium
61 Sadat's Tomb

There are three hospitals in Cairo with more modern facilities than most of Egypt's other hospitals: Cairo Medical Centre (☎ 258 0566) in Heliopolis; Anglo-American Hospital (☎ 340 6162), next to the Cairo Tower in Zamalek; and As-Salam International Hospital (☎ 363 8050) on the Corniche el-Nil in Ma'adi, which has 24 hour facilities. It has another more central branch at 3 Sharia Syria in Mohandiseen (☎ 302 9091).

You can get vaccinations at the International Vaccination Centre in the former Hotel Continental on Sharia al-Gomhurriya facing the Ezbekiya Gardens.

Pyramids of Giza & the Sphinx

Considered one of the Seven Wonders of the World, the Great Pyramids of Giza are possibly the most visited monuments of Egypt. The pyramids of Cheops and Chephren, which have stood for 46 centuries, are the largest, while that of Mycerinus is much less impressive. Before them lies the Sphinx. Mystery surrounds the meaning of this feline character, 50m long and 22m high, carved from a single block of stone. Known in Arabic as Abu al-Hol (Father of Terror), the Sphinx is the centrepiece of the nightly sound & light performances (E£30, half for students).

Entrance to the grounds of the pyramids, open from 7 am to 7.30 pm, costs E£20, as does entry to the Pyramid of Cheops (open from 8.30 am to 4 pm) and the Solar Boat Museum (open from 9 am to 4 pm). Students pay E£5.

A taxi from Midan Tahrir should not cost more than E£10. You can also get minibuses (35 pt) and microbuses (50 pt) directly in front of the Nile Hilton.

Egyptian Museum

Much of the archaeological glory of Egypt resides, in somewhat chaotic fashion, in this museum on Midan Tahrir. The museum is full of statuary, artworks, sarcophagi and many other relics from Egypt's ancient past. The star attractions are the treasures found in Tutankhamun's tomb in Luxor – particularly the gold mask of the boy king. Mummies are

The Pyramids of Giza

It was not an obsession with death, or a fear of it, on the part of the ancient Egyptians that led to the construction of these incredible mausoleums; it was their belief in eternal life and their desire to be at one with the cosmos. A Pharaoh was the son of a god, and the sole receiver of the *ka*, or life force, that emanated from the god. The Pharaoh, in turn, conducted this vital force to his people, so in life and death he was worshipped as a god.

A pyramid was thus not only an indestructible sanctum for the preservation of a Pharaoh's *ka*, nor simply an incredible, geometric pile of stones raised over the mummified remains of a Pharaoh and his treasures to ensure his immortality. It was the apex of a much larger funerary complex that provided a place of worship for his subjects, as well as a visible reminder of the absolute and eternal power of the gods and their universe.

The mortuary complexes of Cheops, Chephren and Mycerinus, who were father, son and grandson, included the following: a pyramid, which was the Pharaoh's tomb as well as a repository for all his household goods, clothes and treasure; a funerary temple on the east side of the pyramid; pits for the storage of the Pharaoh's solar boats (known as barques), which were his means of transport in the afterlife; a valley temple on the banks of the Nile; and a causeway from the river to the pyramid. ■

second in popularity to the treasures of Tutankhamun and, after being taken off display for 15 years, a selection of Egypt's ancient rulers is again on show. Opened in 1995 the Royal Mummy Room houses the bodies of 11 kings and queens who ruled Egypt between 1552-1069 BC.

The museum is open from 9 am to 5 pm daily; closed Friday between noon and 2 pm (summer) and 11.30 am and 1.30 pm (winter). Entry is E£10 (E£5 for students). The Royal Mummy Room costs an additional E£60 (E£35 for students).

Islamic Cairo

Enter the warren of districts like Al-Muski, Darb al-Ahmar and Baatiniyya, between the two remaining northern gates of the medieval city of Cairo and the Citadel to the south, and you submerge yourself in a world that, but for cars and radios, has hardly changed in hundreds of years.

Saladin (Salah ad-Din) began building the **Citadel** in 1176. Over the centuries, various edifices have been added within its imposing crenellated walls. The most impressive of them is the **Mosque of Mohammed Ali**, built by the 19th century ruler of the same name. The Turkish-style mosque dominates the whole of Islamic Cairo, an unmistakable landmark in the sea of minarets. The Citadel is open from 8 am to 5 pm (winter) and 6 pm (summer); entry is E£20.

Just north of the Citadel rise the **Mosque of Sultan Hassan** and the **Ar-Rifa'i Mosque**, where the Shah of Iran is interred. Entry to the former costs E£12; baksheesh is needed to see the Shah's tomb.

To the south-west is one of the largest mosques in the world – the **Ibn Tulun Mosque**. Although not in great condition, it is an impressive monument to the 9th century Abbasid commander sent to rule in the name of Baghdad, but who established his own dynasty instead. Entry is E£6. You may want to visit the **Gayer-Anderson Museum** next door.

EGYPT

Islamic Cairo

1	Beit as-Suhaymi
2	Sabil-Kuttab of Abdul Katkhuda
3	Qasr Beshtak
4	Mosque of Barquq
5	Mausoleum of an-Nasir Mohammed
6	House of Uthman Katkhuda
7	Musafirkhanah
8	House of Gamal ad-Din
9	Upper Egypt Bus Co Station
10	Museum of Islamic Art
11	Abdel Harraz Spice & Herb Shop
12	Mosque of Sultan Mu'ayyad Sheikh
13	Said Delta Papyrus Centre
14	Turkish Hammam
15	Bab Zuweila
16	Mosque of Salih Talai
17	Mosque of Qijmas al-Ishaqi

Heading north from the Citadel, you pass through a labyrinth of ancient mosques and twisting lanes to **Bab Zuweila**, the only surviving southern gate and once a place of execution. The **Mosque of Sultan Mu'ayyad Sheikh** by the gate was finished in 1420 by the Mamluk Mu'ayyad Sheikh, a freed Circassian slave who came to rule Egypt. There are some great views from the minarets. Entry is E£6.

Walk up the market street, Sharia al-Muizz li-Din Allah, and you emerge at a grand square. **Al-Ghouri**, the mausoleum and madrassa complex here, is the site of

twice-weekly Sufi dancing performances. See Entertainment later in this section.

Off to the right is the mosque and university of **Al-Azhar**, built in 970 and the oldest university in the world. Admission is E£12. Cross Midan al-Azhar and you find yourself in the maze of the **Khan al-Khalili**, a souvenir shopper's paradise – bargain hard.

Continue heading north along Sharia al-Muizz li-Din Allah, and you will pass a series of impressive mausoleums and mosques dating to Mamluk times, including the **Mausoleum of Qalaun** and, a little further up, the **Mosque of Barquq**. The street leads on

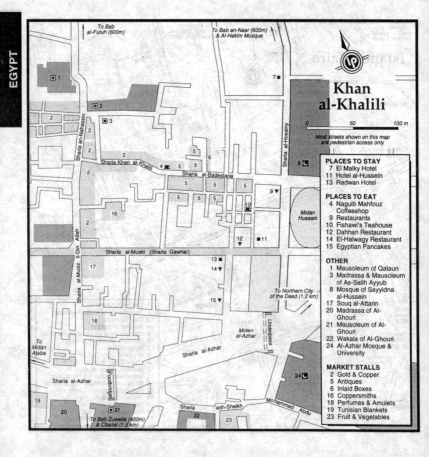

Khan al-Khalili

0   50   100 m

Most streets shown on this map are pedestrian access only

PLACES TO STAY
7 El Malky Hotel
11 Hotel al-Hussein
13 Radwan Hotel

PLACES TO EAT
4 Naguib Mahfouz Coffeeshop
9 Restaurants
10 Fishawi's Teahouse
12 Dahhan Restaurant
14 El-Halwagy Restaurant
15 Egyptian Pancakes

OTHER
1 Mausoleum of Qalaun
3 Madrassa & Mausoleum of As-Salih Ayyub
8 Mosque of Sayyidna al-Hussein
17 Souq al-Attarin
20 Madrassa of Al-Ghouri
21 Mausoleum of Al-Ghouri
22 Wakala of Al-Ghouri
24 Al-Azhar Mosque & University

MARKET STALLS
2 Gold & Copper
5 Antiques
6 Inlaid Boxes
16 Coppersmiths
18 Perfumes & Amulets
19 Tunisian Blankets
23 Fruit & Vegetables

EGYPT

to **Bab al-Futuh** and **Bab an-Nasr**, the two remaining northern gates of the old city. Beyond the gates and to the east lies the **City of the Dead**, which contains some equally impressive mausoleums and mosques.

Museum of Islamic Art

Established in 1881, this comparatively little-visited museum on Midan Ahmed Mahir houses an extensive collection of Islamic decorative art, and is well worth a look. You can see outstanding *mashrabiyyah* (ornately carved wooden panel or screen) woodwork, tapestries, glassware, manuscripts and weaponry. It is open from 9 am to 4 pm (closed Friday); admission costs E£8.

Old Cairo

Once known as Babylon, this remains the seat of the Coptic Christian community. There is a **museum** with mosaics, manuscripts, tapestries and other Christian artwork. Al-Muallaqa, or the **Hanging Church**, is the centre of Coptic worship. Among the other churches and monasteries here, **St Sergius** is supposed to mark one of the resting places of the Holy Family on its flight from King Herod. The easiest way to get here from Midan Tahrir is by metro (30 pt). Get out at the Mari Girgis station.

Felucca Rides

You can hire a felucca for about E£10 an hour from points such as Garden City, opposite the Cairo Meridien; along the south-east end of Gezira, between 6th of October and Tahrir bridges; and in Ma'adi.

Special Events

Held in late November/early December every year, the 14 day Cairo International Film Festival is a veritable feast of modern (although not always the latest) cinema, and most of it is uncensored. The *Egyptian Gazette* usually carries details.

Held at the Opera House in early November, the annual Arab Music Festival brings together some of the best musicians from 14 Arab countries. Programmes are usually in Arabic only but the tourist office should have details.

Places to Stay

Camping The *Motel Salma* (☎ 384 9152) is about the only camping possibility. It's next to the Wissa Wassef Art Centre at Harrania, south of Giza. Camping costs E£7 per person with your own tent or campervan, or you can stay in overpriced, claustrophobic cabins.

Hostels The *Manial Youth Hostel* (☎ 364 0729) at 135 Sharia Abdel Aziz as-Saud is near the Manial Palace on Roda Island. It's in reasonable nick with clean toilets, although the beds are nothing great; it costs E£8.60 with a Hostelling International card, E£12.10 without.

Hotels – Central Cairo The area of central Cairo from Midan Tahrir to Sharia 26th of July is full of budget possibilities. About the cheapest are three places all in a building in the market lane around the corner from the Casablanca Restaurant. On the 1st floor is the friendly and popular *Sultan Hotel* (☎ 772258), while the 5th floor is home to the *Tawfikia* (☎ 755514) and *Safary* hotels. They are all basic and offer beds in simple dorms for about E£7.

The *Pensione de Famille* (☎ 574 5630) on Sharia Abdel Khaliq Sarwat, just off Sharia Talaat Harb, is in a building that should have been condemned years ago. The beds are a little lumpy, but at E£8/11 for a single/double room (excluding breakfast), you can't go too wrong. There's a grotty kitchen if you're desperate to cook something.

Two of Cairo's most popular backpackers' haunts are down by Midan Tahrir. One is the new *Sun Hotel* (☎ 578 1786) at 2 Sharia Talaat Harb (9th floor), which has decently sized singles/doubles with big comfortable beds for E£25/40, or E£15 per person in a four bed room. The communal bathrooms are clean. It arranges a tour to the Birqash camel market every Friday (for details see the Around Cairo section). The other is the 8th floor *Ismailia House Hotel* (☎ 356 3122), right on Midan Tahrir (No 1). It is

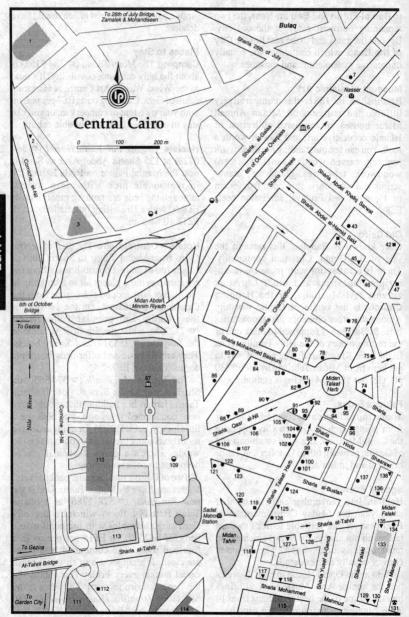

To 26th of July Bridge,
Zamalek & Mohandiseen

Bulaq

Sharia 26th of July

Central Cairo

Nasser

0   100   200 m

Sharia al-Galaa

6th of October Overpass

Sharia Ramses

Sharia Abdel Khaliq Sarwat

Sharia Abdel al-Hamid Said

Comiche el-Nil

Sharia Champollion

6th of October
Bridge

To Gezira

Midan Abdel
Minnim Riyadh

Sharia Mohammed Bassiuni

Nile River

Comiche el-Nil

To Gezira

Sharia Qasr el-Nil

Midan Talaat
Harb

Sharia

Sharia

Hoda

Shaarawi

Sharia al-Bustan

Midan
Falaki

Sharia Talaat Harb

Sharia Yusef al-Gendi

Sharia Falaki

Sharia Mansur

Sadat Metro
Station

Midan
Tahrir

Sharia at-Tahrir

At-Tahrir Bridge

To Gezira

To
Garden City

Sharia at-Tahrir

Sharia Mohammed

Mahmud

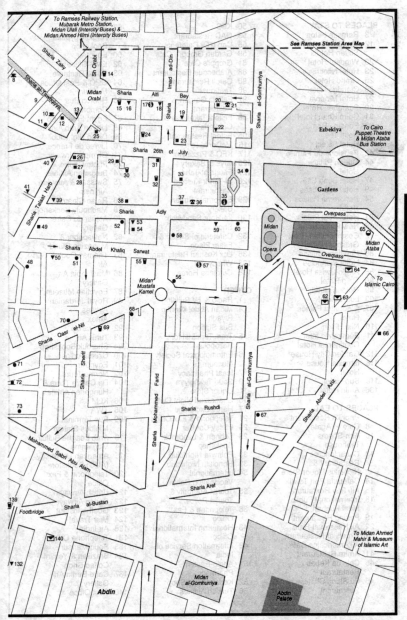

To Ramses Railway Station,
Mubarak Metro Station,
Midan Ulali (Intercity Buses) &
Midan Ahmed Hilmi (Intercity Buses)

See Ramses Station Area Map

Sharia Zaky

Sh Orabi

Sharia al-Tawfikiyya

Midan
Orabi

Sharia

Alfi

Imad ad-Din

Bey

Sharia al-Gomhurriya

Ezbekiya

To Cairo
Puppet Theatre
& Midan Ataba
Bus Station

Sharia 26th of July

Sharia Talaat Harb

Gardens

Sharia Adly

Overpass

Midan
Opera

Midan
Ataba

Sharia Abdel Khaliq Sarwat

Sharia Mustafa Kamel

Overpass

To
Islamic Cairo

Midan
Mustafa
Kamel

Sharia Qasr el-Nil

Sharia Sherif

Sharia Mohammed Farid

Sharia Rushdi

Sharia al-Gomhurriya

Sharia Abdel Aziz

To Midan Ahmed
Mahir & Museum
of Islamic Art

Mohammed Sabri Abu Alam

Sharia al-Bustan

Footbridge

Sharia Aref

Abdin

Midan
al-Gomhurriya

To Midan Ahmed
Mahir & Museum
of Islamic Art

Abdin
Palace

EGYPT

PLACES TO STAY
3 Ramses Hilton
12 Tawfikia, Safary & Sultan Hotels
20 Windsor Hotel
23 Hotel Nitocrisse
25 Grand Hotel
26 Claridge Hotel
27 Hotel Minerva
29 Scarabee Hotel
31 Cairo Khan Hotel
33 Pension Roma
37 Hotel Tee
38 Hotel Select
42 Pensione de Famille
44 Odeon Palace Hotel
47 Hotel Beau Site
49 Hotel des Roses
54 Panorama Palace Hotel
61 Hotel Petit Palais
66 New Riche Hotel
72 Cosmopolitan Hotel
77 Gresham Hotel
80 Pensione Suisse
84 Hotel Viennoise
85 Anglo-Swiss Hotel
95 Tulip Hotel
99 Golden Hotel
103 Lotus Hotel
107 Cleopatra Palace Hotel
110 Nile Hilton
111 Semiramis Inter Continental Hotel
112 Garden City House
118 Ismailia House Hotel
119 Sun Hotel
136 Amin Hotel

PLACES TO EAT
2 Paprika Restaurant
8 Cafe el-Agatey
10 Ash-Shams Teahouse
13 Casablanca Restaurant & Nicolakis Liquor Store
14 Cafeteria Port Tewfik
16 Alfi Bey Restaurant
18 International Public Meal Kushari
19 Peking Restaurant
22 Ali Hassan al-Hatti
39 Excelsior Restaurant
40 À l'Américaine Café
41 Amira Restaurant
45 Coin de Kebab Restaurant
46 Fu Shing Chinese Restaurant

50 KFC
53 GAD Restaurant
55 Cap d'Or Cafeteria
59 Garden Groppi's Cafe
81 Groppi's Cafe
88 Arabesque Restaurant
90 Caroll Restaurant
96 Teahouse
97 Felfela Garden Restaurant
98 Felfela Takeaway & Cafeteria
105 Estoril Restaurant
116 McDonald's
117 KFC & Pizza Hut
125 Crystal Bakery
127 Fatatri at-Tahrir
128 El-Tahrir Kushari Restaurant
129 El-Fornaia Etman Bakery
130 24-Hour Sandwich Shop
132 Cafeteria el-Shaab & Fiteer Place
135 Lux Kushari Restaurant
138 Wimpy Bar
139 Cafeteria Horea

OTHER
1 Radio & TV Building
4 Midan Abdel Minnim Riyadh Bus Station
5 Tram Terminal for Heliopolis
6 Entomological Society Museum
7 Isaaf Pharmacy
9 Souq Tawfiqiyya
11 Liquor Store
15 Shahrazad Night Club
17 Horus Exchange
21 Telephone & Fax Office
24 Pussy Cat Bar
28 Lehnert & Landrock Bookshop
30 Palmyra Nightclub
32 Honolulu Nightclub
34 International Vaccination Centre
35 Tourist Authority & Tourist Police
36 Telephone & Fax Office
43 Hostelling International Office
48 Information Service of India
51 Anglo-Eastern Pharmacy
52 Kodak Photo Shop
56 Turkish Airlines

57 Banque Misr
58 Anglo-Egyptian Bookshop
60 EgyptAir
62 EMS Office
63 Poste Restante
64 GPO & Post Office Museum
65 Hebton Bus Company
67 Egypt Free Shop
68 Libyan Arab Airlines
69 Disco Nightclub
70 Livres de France
71 Olympic Airways
73 Photo Centre
74 Bulgarian Airlines
75 Swissair & Austrian Airlines
76 Radio Cinema
78 Madbouly Bookshop
79 Atelier du Caire Gallery
82 Newspaper & Magazine Stand
83 Thomas Cook & Gulf Air
86 Mashrabia Art Gallery
87 Egyptian Museum
89 Royal Jordanian Airlines
91 Amex
92 Air France
93 Tunis Air
94 Shorouk Bookshop
100 Czech Airlines
101 EgyptAir
102 Norma Tours
104 De Castro Tours & Hungarian Airlines
106 KLM
108 TWA
109 Bus Terminal & Minibus Station
113 Arab League Building
114 Mogamma
115 American University (AUC) Bookstore
120 Telephone & Fax Office
121 British Airways
122 Sudan Airways
123 Goethe Institut
124 Misr Travel
126 Air India
131 Telephone Office
133 Souq Mansur
134 Brazilian & Yemini Coffee Shop
137 Cairo-Berlin Art Gallery
140 Post Office

clean and bright, and the showers are piping hot. Singles, a few of which are pretty dingy, cost E£20. Doubles come at E£40 and are the best value. A bed in a shared room (a double with two extra rickety beds crammed in), costs E£12 to E£15.

Also owned by the Ismailia is the *Hotel Petit Palais* (☎ 391 1863) at 45 Sharia Abdel Khaliq Sarwat. The bathrooms are spotless, and unlike at the Ismailia, each room has hot water; prices are comparable.

The *Gresham Hotel* (☎ 575 9043), on the 3rd floor at 20 Sharia Talaat Harb, hasn't changed its room rates in years and is now pretty good value. Single rooms cost E£25, or E£35 with private bath and air-con. Doubles without/with bath go for E£40/45 and are all air-con.

The *Pension Roma* (☎ 391 1088) at 169 Sharia Mohammed Farid, near the junction with Sharia Adly, is tucked away in a side alley. All the rooms have shiny hardwood floors and antique furniture. Single/double/triple rooms without a bath are E£20/38/50. A room with four beds costs E£66.

The *Happyton Hotel* (☎ 928671) at 10 Sharia Aly el-Kassar, in a quiet backstreet off Sharia Imad ad-Din, is one of the best value-for-money mid-range options, and it's handy to both central Cairo and Ramses station. A relaxed place with a small, open-air rooftop bar and a restaurant, it has singles/doubles with air-con and private bathroom for E£40/52. There are triples also. Some of the rooms are a tad small.

The *Lotus Hotel* (☎ 575 0966) at 12 Sharia Talaat Harb (opposite Felfela Cafeteria) is another good mid-priced hotel. You'll pay E£35/65 for a single without/with a bath; doubles are E£65/85. There are also some triples.

The *Cosmopolitan Hotel* (☎ 392 3663) on Sharia Ibn Taalab, just off Sharia Qasr el-Nil, has beautifully plush old rooms with dark lacquered furniture, central air-con and tiled bathrooms with tubs. Some rooms have balconies and there's a wonderful old open elevator. Singles/doubles cost US$40/50.

Hotels – Elsewhere There are two places worth investigating in Zamalek, away from the hubbub of central Cairo. The *Mayfair Hotel* (☎ 340 7315) at 9 Sharia Aziz Osman has singles/doubles without bath for E£20/22, or air-con doubles with bath for E£37.

Two blocks down and to the right along Sharia Salah ad-Din is the *Zamalek Pension* (☎ 340 9318). It has clean, comfortable singles/doubles for E£35/70. It is not bad for what you get.

In Islamic Cairo, the *Hotel al-Hussein* (☎ 591 8089), on Midan Hussein, is right by the Khan al-Khalili bazaar. Clean rooms with bath and views over the midan cost E£50/60. Smaller rooms without bath or view are E£30/40.

The *Hotel Mena House Oberoi* (☎ 383 3444) is the closest hotel to the Great Pyramids of Giza. It's a grand old hotel with an abundance of elegance and opulent oriental decor. Prices are about US$112/140 for single/double rooms, plus taxes.

Places to Eat

Cairo is full of cafes and snack bars where you can eat staple snacks such as shwarma, kushari, fuul and ta'amiyya for no more than E£1. For those with a more timid palate there are also plenty of western fast-food places around.

A great place to introduce yourself to Egyptian shopping strategies is *Souq Mansur*, which occupies a converted warehouse off Sharia Mansur in central Cairo. This market does not cater at all for tourists, and is a real sensory experience. Another colourful central market, this time for fruit and vegetables only, is the *Souq Tawfiqiyya* along Sharia al-Tawfiqiyya just west of Midan Orabi.

If it's a supermarket you're in need of, head to *Sunnys* on Sharia Aziz Osman in Zamalek.

Central Cairo One of the best places for a cheap meal in Cairo is *El-Tabie El-Domiati* at 31 Sharia Orabi, not far from Orabi metro station. The portions are large, the service fast and friendly, the setting clean and the food is excellent. It's predominantly vegetarian and

EGYPT

has a great salad bar and delicious ta'amiyya. A filling meal for two costs as little as E£6 to E£8.

The *International Public Meal Kushari*, on the corner of Sharias Imad ad-Din and Alfi Bey, is a popular kushari joint. The woodchip floor, eager waiters and large servings (E£1.25) all add to the flavour of this authentic little place.

The *Casablanca*, opposite the Grand Hotel on Sharia Talaat Harb, serves an excellent meat or cheese fiteer (pizza) for E£6. The latter is a good vegetarian dish if you eat eggs.

Ali Hassan al-Hatti, just north of Sharia 26th July, is a real gem – a kebab and kofta place with chandeliers. Try its speciality called 'moza', which is roast lamb on rice, for E£15.

Excelsior, on the corner of Sharias Talaat Harb and Adly, is popular with the cinema crowds. Again, the main dishes are around the E£15 mark, but many of the meat dishes are overcooked. It serves great ice creams for E£3.50 to E£5.

Directly across the road from the Excelsior is the *Amira*, a 24 hour eatery where film extras are sometimes recruited. You can get a delicious lentil soup for E£1.50, or a number of other small dishes for a couple of pounds.

The *Felfela Garden* at 15 Sharia Hoda Shaarawi, just off Sharia Talaat Harb, is one of the better all-round restaurants in Cairo, although its enormous popularity with locals and foreigners alike means there are quite a few dishes you could get elsewhere for less.

Felfela Cafeteria, just around the corner from the main restaurant, has excellent ta'amiyya, shwarma, kofta and fuul sandwiches, from 40 pt to E£1.25.

At 166 Sharia at-Tahrir is the 24 hour *Fatatri at-Tahrir*, an excellent place for a sweet or savoury fiteer – E£6 for small ones, E£8 for medium and E£10 for large. For more sweets and pastries, try *Groppi's* on Midan Talaat Harb.

The *Caroll Restaurant* at 12 Sharia Qasr el-Nil is a popular place for European and Egyptian food. It serves a wide range of meat and fish dishes for E£25 plus. Some of the pastas are very good and considerably cheaper.

The *Peking* at 14 Sharia al-Ezbekiya serves Cantonese meals for about E£30.

Islamic Cairo The 24 hour *El-Halwagy* on a side street off Sharia al-Muski is an excellent ta'amiyya, fuul and salad place (E£10 for a meal for two), which has been around for nearly a century. Next door is *Egyptian Pancakes*.

Zamalek The closest thing you'll find to a real Italian cafe this side of the Mediterranean is the little *Simonds Coffee Shop* on Sharia 26th of July, where the owner, Mohammed Eid, has been serving pastries and cappuccinos (E£1.70) to an eclectic clientele for more than 40 years.

The *Al Dente Restaurant* at 26 Sharia Bahgat Ali Isa is a tiny new Italian place frequented by students from the nearby AUC and young expats. Pasta meals cost between E£6 to E£10; there's no alcohol.

The *Zamalek Restaurant* is a cheap little kebab house on Sharia 26th of July.

The *Four Corners* at 4 Sharia Hassan Sabri, is four restaurants – French, Italian, Chinese and American – in one. None are really cheap.

The *Ha Na* Korean restaurant on Sharia Mohammed Mazhar serves high-quality food in generous helpings. For E£20 a head you'll get an authentic meal that would cost four times as much in a city like London.

Mohandiseen *Papillon* is a popular Lebanese restaurant on Sharia 26th of July. It has a wide range of oriental dishes, some of them a pleasing variation on Egyptian cuisine.

Abou Shakra, 17 Sharia Gamiat ad-Dowal al-Arabiyya, is owned by Abou Shakra, also known as the 'King of Kebab'. He has several other restaurants of the same name around town; his original establishment is in Garden City.

Giza *Andrea's Chicken & Fish Restaurant* and *La Rose* are both about one km from

Pyramids Rd on the left bank (when heading towards Kerdassa) of Maryutia Canal. Andrea's is usually a bit overrun by tour groups, making La Rose the quieter, more preferable option.

Felfela Village (☎ 383 0574) is down the road and across the canal from Andrea's. It puts on a show with the food – call for details.

Just on the turn-off for the Desert Highway from Pyramids Rd is an overpriced fish restaurant called *Christo*. It has set menus ranging from E£25 to E£42.

Entertainment

On Wednesday and Saturday nights from 9 pm (9.30 pm in winter) you can treat yourself to a display of *raqs ash-sharqi*, or Sufi dancing, in the Madrassa of Al-Ghouri in Islamic Cairo. (Sufis are adherents of a Muslim mystical order which emphasises dancing as a direct personal experience of God.) Admission is free and it's advisable to come early (we suggest 45 minutes to an hour), especially in winter, as the small auditorium can get quite crowded.

There are a few cinemas that occasionally show decent movies. Check the *Egyptian Gazette* or *Al-Ahram* newspapers. Quite often there are interesting performances at the Opera House. Pick up a programme – you can see international troupes for much less than it would cost in the west.

Some of the big hotels have discos. One of the better ones is at the *Atlas Zamalek Hotel* near Midan Sphinx in Mohandiseen.

You can see fairly contrived belly-dancing at some of the big hotels and in expensive nightclubs along Pyramids Rd. Otherwise, you can try the local product. It's a bit tacky, but interesting. The *Palmyra*, run by Madame Monocle, is a good example of the genre. The Odeon Palace Hotel has a 24 hour *bar*, or you could try the Windsor Hotel's atmospheric *Barrel Lounge*.

There are several spit-and-sawdust bars, known as 'cafeterias' around town – one of the better ones is *Cafeteria Horea* on Midan Falaki. It's a huge airy place with enormous windows and is great for having a cold Stella with your game of backgammon.

Cairo is dotted with thousands of coffee and teahouses where waiters hustle back and forth carrying water pipes and trays of glasses, while in the background there's a constant clatter of domino tiles and backgammon pieces. One of the oldest is the famous *Fishawi's*, a few steps off Midan Hussein in Khan al-Khalili. Another authentic place is the colourful *Ash-Shams*, hidden from the crowds in a side lane between Sharias 26th of July and al-Tawfiqiyya at the northern end of Sharia Talaat Harb. Although most of these places are predominantly menonly establishments, western women should have no qualms about having a drink here.

Getting There & Away

Air Cairo is the main point of entry into Egypt. The bulk of the travel agents are around Midan Tahrir and along Sharia Talaat Harb. EgyptAir flies all over the country, and Air Sinai has limited runs.

Bus There are several bus stations scattered throughout Cairo. From Midan Abdel Minnim Riyadh, just around the corner from the Ramses Hilton along Sharia al-Galaa, there are frequent services to Alexandria ranging in price from E£8 to E£28. There is at least one bus a day to Marsa Matruh (E£35; five hours) with more frequent services in summer. Nine Superjet buses go to Port Said (E£10 to E£16; three hours) and there's also a Superjet bus to Sharm el-Sheikh (E£50) at 11 pm. There are buses to destinations throughout the Delta, and the Upper Egypt Bus Co has daily buses to Aswan (E£50; 12 hours), Hurghada (E£25 to E£30; six hours) and Luxor (E£40; 10-11 hours).

The same company has cheaper buses to those destinations and to most towns along the Nile leaving from Midan Ahmed Hilmi, behind Ramses railway station. From Midan Ulali, also near Ramses station, the East Delta Bus Co has buses to the Suez Canal towns. To Suez costs E£5. Buses to Libya also leave from here.

Nearly all the East Delta Bus Co buses to Sinai leave from the Sinai Terminal at Midan

Abbassiya, on the way to the airport. The exception is the 5 pm bus to Sharm el-Sheikh which leaves from Midan Ulali. These bus trips are expensive: to Sharm el-Sheikh costs from E£30 to E£50; to St Catherine's is E£40; and to Nuweiba costs E£40 to E£55.

Buses to the Western Oases leave from a small lot at 45 Sharia al-Azhar, off the main road to Khan al-Khalili.

Train Trains to all destinations leave from Ramses station at Midan Ramses. The daily wagon-lit train to Luxor and Aswan leaves

at 7.45 pm, arriving in Luxor at 5 am and in Aswan at 11 am. For either destination it costs E£451 one way in a 1st class sleeper compartment, or E£293 in 2nd class (E£540 return), including all meals. There is no student reduction.

Tickets for 1st and 2nd class seats on the overnight air-con express trains to Luxor (E£48/28) and Aswan (E£60/34) must be bought in advance at a window on platform 11. Ordinary 2nd and 3rd class tickets must be bought at separate windows.

First class tickets to Alexandria must be

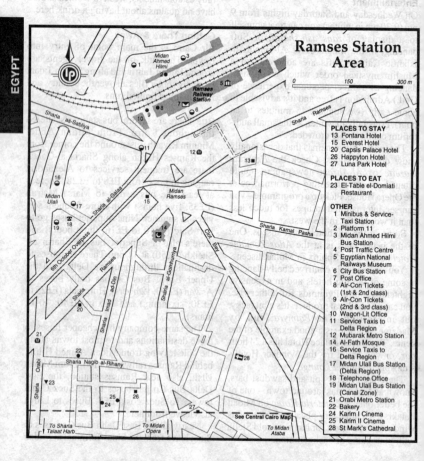

Ramses Station Area

0   150   300 m

PLACES TO STAY
13 Fontana Hotel
15 Everest Hotel
20 Capsis Palace Hotel
26 Happyton Hotel
27 Luna Park Hotel

PLACES TO EAT
23 El-Table el-Domiati Restaurant

OTHER
1 Minibus & Service-Taxi Station
2 Platform 11
3 Midan Ahmed Hilmi Bus Station
4 Post Traffic Centre
5 Egyptian National Railways Museum
6 City Bus Station
7 Post Office
8 Air-Con Tickets (1st & 2nd class)
9 Air-Con Tickets (2nd & 3rd class)
10 Wagon-Lit Office
11 Service Taxis to Delta Region
12 Mubarak Metro Station
14 Al-Fath Mosque
16 Service Taxis to Delta Region
17 Midan Ulali Bus Station (Delta Region)
18 Telephone Office
19 Midan Ulali Bus Station (Canal Zone)
21 Orabi Metro Station
22 Bakery
24 Karim I Cinema
25 Karim II Cinema
28 St Mark's Cathedral

See Central Cairo Map

bought at windows in the main building. The Turbo is the best train (E£22; two hours). Second class with air-con (E£17) is quite comfortable.

Service Taxi Cairo's service taxis depart from various places around the city. By Ramses station, they stretch around from the Midan Ulali bus station up to the railway station. They depart for Al-Arish (E£12; five hours), Alexandria (E£8 to E£10), Damietta (Ras al-Bar), Ismailia (E£5), Mansura, Port Said (E£8), Qantara, Rafah (E£15; six hours) and Suez (E£5).

Service taxis for Alexandria (E£9 to E£11) also leave from in front of Ramses station and the Nile Hilton. Taxis for destinations in and around Al-Faiyum leave from the Faiyum bus stop at Midan Giza (E£4). Note that sometimes 'service taxis' are in fact microbuses.

Getting Around
The Airport Bus No 422 runs hourly between 6 am and midnight to the new Terminal II from Midan Tahrir for 25 pt. Several buses operate from various points in the city to the old terminal I – some shuttle to the new terminal too. Bus No 400 goes from Midan Tahrir, as does minibus No 27 (50 pt). Taxis should not cost more than E£20.

Bus & Minibus The Greater Cairo General Transport Authority operates a dense bus and minibus network, but it never seems to be enough. The main station is in front of the Nile Hilton at Midan Tahrir. Fares for buses are usually 25 pt. Minibus fares range from 25 to 50 pt.

Bus No 815 goes from Midan Tahrir to Al-Azhar and the Khan al-Khalili. Minibus No 83 goes from Midan Tahrir to the Great Pyramids of Giza and Minibus No 54 goes to the Citadel. The numbers are sometimes in Arabic numerals only, so it pays to learn them.

Metro The 33 station metro system is a surprisingly modern, clean and efficient mass transit service. It costs 30 pt to ride up to nine

stops, and E£1.20 to ride the length of the line.

Tram The bulk of Cairo's trams (known to Cairenes, confusingly for outsiders, as 'metros') have been phased out. Three lines run in the north-east of town, merging at Midan Roxy just south of Heliopolis, and coming from Nozha, Merghany and Abdel Aziz Fahmy. The trams are as cheap, and often as crowded, as the buses.

Taxi Catching a taxi is the easiest way around Cairo, but be prepared to fight over fares. Short hops around the city centre are worth E£3. Longer drives, say from Midan Tahrir to Al-Azhar, should be around E£4.

Waterbus Opposite the Radio & Television building, waterbuses head south along the Nile as far as Old Cairo and north to the Nile barrages at Qanater, a popular day trip with Cairenes. The fare costs only 10 to 25 pt.

Around Cairo

MEMPHIS & SAQQARA
There is not much left of the former Pharaonic capital of Memphis, 24 km south of Cairo, but the museum contains a fairly impressive statue of Ramses II. A few km away is Saqqara, a vast site strewn with pyramids, temples and tombs. The star attraction here is the **Step Pyramid** of Zoser, the first decent attempt at a pyramid. Entrance for the whole of the North Saqqara area is E£20. It's open from 7.30 am to 4 pm (5 pm in summer).

It is possible to hire a horse or camel at the Pyramids of Giza to head down to Saqqara but you'll spend much of the day in the saddle. You really need to set a whole day aside to get even a superficial view of the area, and transport to get around the Saqqara site is essential.

Getting There & Away
A taxi from central Cairo will cost about

E£60 to E£70 shared among a maximum of seven people. This is the best way for those on a tight budget to get to and around Saqqara. Stipulate the sights you want to see and how long you want to be out, and bargain hard.

Alternatively, you could join one of the inexpensive tours run by Salah Mohammed Abdel Hafiez (☎ 768537) in Cairo; you'll need to book a day in advance.

BIRQASH CAMEL MARKET

Until 1995 Egypt's largest camel market, or Souq al-Gamaal, was located among run-down tenements in Imbaba, one of Cairo's western suburbs. The city's burgeoning population forced its relocation to Birqash, 35 km north-west of Cairo, on the edge of the Western Desert.

The market is an easy half-day trip from Cairo but, like all of Egypt's animal markets, it's not for animal lovers or the faint-hearted. Hundreds of camels are sold here everyday, most having been brought up the 40 Days Road from western Sudan. The market is most lively on Friday and Monday mornings from about 6 to 9 am; admission is E£2.

Getting There & Away

The cheapest way to get to the market is to take a taxi (E£4) to the site of the old camel market at Imbaba, from where microbuses (E£1) shuttle back and forth to Birqash.

Alternatively, on Friday only, the Sun Hotel (☎ 578 1786) at 2 Sharia Talaat Harb organises a minibus tour (E£20 per person; minimum five), which departs from the hotel at 7 am.

A taxi there and back will cost around E£60; make sure to negotiate waiting time.

The Nile Valley

The ancient Greek traveller and writer Herodotus described Egypt as 'the gift of the Nile'. The ancient Egyptians likened their land to a lotus – the Delta being the flower, the oasis of Al-Faiyum the bud and the river and its valley the stem. With very little rain

throughout the year, the Nile is the lifeblood of the country.

Travelling south from Cairo you pass through a world where ancient and medieval monuments almost seem to be part of the present. The daily labour and recreation of the fellahin in the 20th century seems to differ little from the images depicted in the wall paintings of the ancient monuments. For most travellers, however, it is not the green fields but the temples of Luxor, the Valley of the Kings (where many of the Pharaohs, including Tutankhamun, had their final resting place), the towering statued facade of Abu Simbel and a string of other imposing temples dotted like milestones along the Nile that draw them ever further south. A few flee the monuments for an excursion of another type altogether, to the islands of green formed by the Western Oases in the Western (Libyan) Desert.

AL-FAIYUM

About 100 km south-west of Cairo, Al-Faiyum is a huge irrigated oasis, about 60 km long and 70 km wide. There's not an awful lot to see in the main town, Medinet al-Faiyum, but you can explore such features of the oasis as the salty lake of **Birket Qarun** and the Ptolemaic temple known as **Qasr Qarun**, the springs of '**Ain as-Siliin**, the Hawara, Lahun and Meidum **pyramids**, or the **Museum of Kom Aushim** at Karanis on the road to Cairo.

Places to Stay & Eat

It is possible to camp in the grounds of the Museum of Kom Aushim for E£4, or at the lake; get a permit from the tourist police.

The *Youth Hostel* (☎ (084) 323682), down by the Cairo bus station, almost two km from the centre of Medinet al-Faiyum, costs E£3 for members (E£5 for non-members) for a bed in a room of six.

The *Palace Hotel* (☎ (084) 321222), in the town centre near the canal, has good, clean singles/ doubles (including breakfast) without bath for E£20/35; with bath E£30/45.

Apart from the usual stalls, about the only

restaurant in town is the overpriced *Cafeteria al-Medina*, right by the waterwheels and tourist office in the centre of town.

Getting There & Away

There are regular buses to Cairo (E£3; two hours). The bus station is east of the town centre. Buses for Beni Suef (E£1; one hour) leave from another station west of the town centre. Service taxis also run to both these destinations.

AL-MINYA

The 'Bride of Upper Egypt' (*Arous as-*Sa'id*), Al-Minya marks the divide between Upper and Lower Egypt. A semi-industrial provincial capital 247 km south of Cairo, it does not offer much to see, but it's not a bad base for day trips to the Pharaonic tombs and temples of Beni Hasan, Tuna al-Gebel and Hermopolis.

Information

There's a tourist information office (☎ (086) 320150) in the Governorate building and another branch in the railway station (☎ (086) 342044). There are a couple of banks, and the main Banque Misr does cash

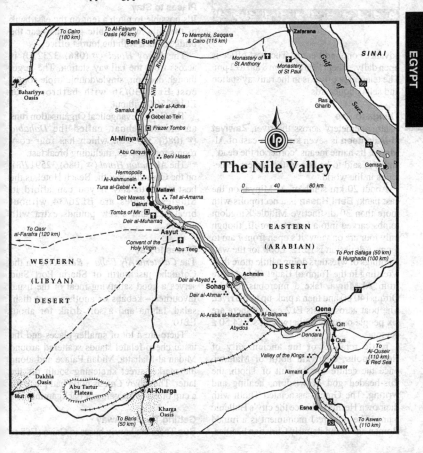

EGYPT

EGYPT

Troubles in the Nile Valley

Al-Minya has a large Christian population and is part of the belt of towns, including Mallawi, Dairut, Asyut and Sohag, where clashes between Christians and Muslims (usually said to be fundamentalists) have taken place since the early 1990s – although feuding of the sort has long been a part of the territory. If you haven't already felt the tension caused by this sectarian violence and the occasional pot shots taken at tourists in the area, you may start to here. It's likely the local police will insist on providing you with an armed escort to many of the ancient sites along this stretch of the Nile. ■

---

advances on credit cards. The post office is open daily, except Friday, from 8 am to 2 pm. The telephone office is in the railway station and sells phonecards.

Things to See

A large cemetery across the river, **Zawiyet al-Mayyiteen** is seven km south-east of Al-Minya. Its name means 'corner of the dead', and it is said to be one of the largest cemeteries in the world.

About 20 km south of Al-Minya, on the east bank, **Beni Hasan** is a necropolis with more than 30 distinctive Middle Kingdom tombs carved into a limestone cliff, though only four are on view; it's open from 7 am to 5 pm. Admission is E£12. Look for the wall paintings of wrestlers doing a little more than wrestling in the Tomb of Baqet. To get there from Al-Minya, take a microbus to Abu Qirqus (40 pt) and then a pick-up to the river. The boat across costs E£2 each if there are six people or more. Otherwise it's E£4.50 a person.

Little remains of the ancient city of **Hermopolis**, eight km north of Mallawi, once the centre for the cult of Thoth, the ibis-headed god of wisdom, healing and writing. The Greeks associated Thoth with their own Hermes – hence the city's Hellenic name. The only real monument is a ruined Roman agora and its early Christian basilica,

the largest of its type in Egypt. At the time of writing, Hermopolis was closed – the tourist office in either Asyut or Al-Minya should know if it has reopened.

Seven km south-west of Hermopolis is the necropolis of **Tuna al-Gebel**. The most interesting things to see here are the dark catacomb galleries, once filled with thousands of mummified baboons, and the mummy of Isadora, a woman who drowned in the Nile about 150 AD. The site is open from 7 am to 5 pm, and admission costs E£12.

Places to Stay

It's possible to pitch a tent on the east bank of the Nile in the public gardens near the bridge; check with the tourist office.

The *Savoy Hotel* (☎ (086) 323270) is across from the railway station. The large, though decrepit, single/double/triple rooms cost E£20/30/36 with bathroom, or E£15/25/30 without.

The Coptic Evangelical Organisation runs an old houseboat, called the *Dahabia* (☎ (086) 325596), which has four cosy rooms for E£30/55, including breakfast.

The *Akhnaton Hotel* (☎ (086) 325917/8), on the Corniche near the Beach Hotel, is the best place to stay if you can afford it. Singles/doubles are E£26/34 without breakfast, and a few pounds extra with air-con.

Places to Eat

The *Cafeteria Aly Baba – Patisserie* on the Corniche just north of Sharia Port Said serves a good satisfying meal of the usual favourites – kebabs or another meat dish, salad, tahina and a soft drink for about E£10.

There are a lot of smaller places and the usual cheap felafel stands scattered around Midan al-Mahatta, Midan Palace and along the market street stretching south off the latter. The *Savoy Cafe* is not a bad place for a cup of tea and a game of backgammon.

Getting There & Away

Bus There are hourly buses to Cairo (E£8 to

E£11; four hours) from 5 am to 4 pm. Buses to Asyut (E£3.50; two to three hours) leave every half hour from 6 am to 5 pm, and on Sunday, Monday and Wednesday mornings there's a bus to Hurghada (E£24).

Train The trip from Cairo (four hours) costs E£14/6.50 in 2nd class with/without air-con.

Trains heading south depart fairly frequently, with the fastest trains leaving Al-Minya between about 11 pm and 1 am. Fares (2nd class with air-con/2nd class without) from Al-Minya are: Aswan E£27/13.20; Asyut E£8/3.40; Luxor E£21/10; Qena E£19/9; and Sohag E£13/5.80.

Service Taxi From Cairo the three to four hour trip to Al-Minya costs E£8. Service taxis to Asyut cost E£4.50 for the two hour trip.

TELL AL-AMARNA

The scant remains of this once-glorious city, 12 km south of Mallawi, may be a little disappointing when compared to its fascinating, albeit brief, moment in history. This is where Akhenaten and his wife Nefertiti built their new city dedicated to the worship of a single god, the sun disc Aten. The faith did not outlast their deaths and nor did the city. There are two sets of **tombs** spread out over a wide area. The site is open from 7 am to 4 pm in winter; 5 pm in summer. Admission is E£7. The bus tour to the northern tombs costs about E£4 per person; to the south it's more expensive. Take a service taxi to Deir Mawas from Mallawi or Asyut and a boat across the river for 25 to 50 pt.

ASYUT

The biggest town in Upper Egypt, for several centuries Asyut was an important trading centre at the end of the 40 Days Road caravan route out of Sudan. It has more recently become known as a centre of violence between Copts and Muslim extremists. There is not much to see here, although it could be a base for visiting Tel al-Amarna. It is also a gateway to the oases.

Places to Stay & Eat

The *Youth Hostel* (☎ (088) 324846) is at Lux Houses, 503 Sharia al-Walidiyya, and costs E£4 for a bed in a crowded dorm of eight.

The *YMCA* (☎ (088) 323218), about 500m down Sharia Salah ad-Din al-Ayoubi, deservedly gets rave reviews from many travellers. A bed in the old dorm section costs E£6. The new building has singles/doubles with air-con, TV, minifridge and private bath for E£25/35.

Moving up the scale, the *Akhnaton Hotel* (☎ (088) 337723) has pretty reasonable rooms with clean linen, TV, hot water and soap in the bathrooms for E£28/35 for singles/doubles.

There's not much in the line of restaurants, although the *Cafeteria Majestic* in front of the railway station is lively and serves decent food. The popular restaurant at *Akhnaton Hotel* serves an escalope for E£10.50 – with real chips – as well as good pizzas (E£6.50) and soup.

Getting There & Away

Bus From Asyut buses depart for Cairo (E£10 to E£15; six to seven hours) at 12.30, 7, 8, 10 and 11 am, noon and 2, 3, 5, 7, 10, 11 pm and midnight. Buses leave for Al-Minya (E£3.50; two to three hours) every two hours from 6 am to 5 pm. There are buses to Luxor and Hurghada also.

If you are heading out to the oases, there are buses to Kharga (E£6 to E£7; four hours) at 7 and 8 am, and 1, 3, 5 and 10 pm.

Train There are about 20 trains throughout the day to Cairo and Al-Minya, and about half that number to Luxor.

EGYPT

Service Taxi Service taxis to Al-Minya, Cairo and Kharga cost E£4.50, E£15 and E£8 per head respectively.

SOHAG

Apart from a couple of nearby **monasteries** and the **statue of Queen Meret Amun** in neighbouring Achmin, there is little to make you want to stop in this governorate capital, 115 km south of Asyut, although you could use it as a base for visiting the temples of Abydos. There are a few cheap hotels near the railway station.

ABYDOS

According to mythology, the head of the god Osiris was buried here after his brother Seth killed him, and so Abydos became the most important site of his worship. The first building complex you see is one of the most complete temples in Egypt. The **Cenotaph Temple of Seti I** honours seven gods, including Osiris and the deified Pharaoh himself. To the north-west lies what's left of the **Temple of Ramses II**, built by Seti's son. The site is open from 7 am to 5 pm, and admission is E£12.

Places to Stay

Right in front of Abydos is the *Osiris Park Restaurant & Camp* (☎ 812200), where a bed in a tent costs E£5. You can pitch your own tent for E£3 per person.

The only other option is the *Abydos Hotel* (☎ 812102), 200m before the Osiris. It has simple, overpriced rooms for E£30/50.

Getting There & Away

Trains from Asyut, Sohag, Qena and further afield sometimes stop at the township of Al-Balyana. Buses drop you at Al-Balyana, from where service taxis (75 pt) and microbuses (30 pt) go to the temple complex.

QENA & DENDARA

Qena has little going for it other than its proximity to the **Temple of Hathor**, Dendara. The temple is dedicated to the goddess Hathor, and, although built by the Ptolemies, retains the Egyptian style and serves their beliefs. Hathor, the goddess of pleasure and love, is figured on the 24 columns of the Outer Hypostyle Hall, and on the walls are scenes of Roman emperors as Pharaohs. The views from the roof are magnificent. It's open from 7 am to 6 pm, and admission is E£12.

Places to Stay & Eat

You can stay by the temple. A bed in the hotel that calls itself a 'camp' is E£25. In Qena, about four km away on the east bank of the Nile, is the *New Palace Hotel* (☎ (096) 322509), with singles/doubles for E£12/20. There are a few small restaurants selling the standard fare.

Getting There & Away

Eleven buses go to Aswan (E£8.50) from 6.30 am to 7.45 pm, and most stop in Luxor (E£1.50 to E£2). You can also get buses heading to Hurghada (E£8; 3 hours) and on to Suez (E£22 to E£38; nine to 10 hours). There are also buses to Cairo and Port Safaga.

LUXOR

The sheer grandeur of Luxor's monumental architecture, and its excellent state of preservation, have made this village-city one of Egypt's greatest tourist attractions. Built on and around the 4000 year old site of ancient Thebes, Luxor is an extraordinary mixture of exotic history and modern commercialism.

Its attraction for tourists is by no means a recent phenomenon. Travellers have been visiting Thebes for centuries, marvelling at the splendid temples of Luxor, Karnak, Ramses II and Hatshepsut. As far back as Graeco-Roman times visitors would wait in the desert to hear the mysterious voice of Memnon emanating from the colossal statues of Amenophis III (the result of a flaw later repaired by the Romans), and in the past 100 years or so curious travellers have been following the footsteps of the excavators into the tombs of the Valley of the Kings.

What most visitors today know as Luxor is actually three separate areas: the city of Luxor itself, the village of Karnak a couple of km to the north-east, and the monuments and necropolis of ancient Thebes on the west bank of the Nile.

History
Following the collapse of centralised power at the end of the Old Kingdom period, the small village of Thebes, under the 11th and 12th dynasty Pharaohs, emerged as the main power in Upper Egypt. Rising against the northern capital of Heracleopolis, Thebes reunited the country under its political, religious and administrative control, and ushered in the Middle Kingdom period. The strength of its government also enabled it to re-establish control after a second period of decline and bring in the New Kingdom dynasties.

At the height of its glory and opulence, from 1570 BC to 1090 BC, the New Kingdom Pharaohs made Thebes their permanent residence; the city had a population of nearly one million and the architectural activity was astounding.

Orientation
There are only three main thoroughfares in Luxor: Sharia al-Mahatta runs between the railway station and the gardens of Luxor Temple; the Corniche runs along the river; and Sharia al-Karnak runs parallel to it and out towards the Karnak temples. The bulk of the cheap hotels are clustered around Sharia Television.

Information
Passport Office Opposite the Isis Hotel, south of the town centre, the passport office is open from 8 am to 2 pm daily, except Friday.

Tourist Office The main tourist office (☎ 373294) is next to the New Winter Palace hotel. It's open daily from 8 am to 8 pm, and staff let you leave messages for other travellers.

Money The main banks have branches on or near the Corniche. There is an exchange booth open long hours on the Corniche in front of the tourist office. Amex (☎ 372862) and Thomas Cook (☎ 372196) have offices at the Old Winter Palace Hotel.

Post & Communications The GPO is on Sharia al-Mahatta, and there's a branch office in the Tourist Bazaar next to the New Winter Palace Hotel.

The central telephone office is on Sharia al-Karnak and is open 24 hours; there's another, open from 8 am to 10 pm, below the resplendent entrance of the Old Winter Palace Hotel.

The telephone code for Luxor is 095.

The East Bank
Luxor Museum This museum has a small but well-chosen collection of relics from the Theban temples and necropolis. The displays include pottery, jewellery, furniture and stelae. A new section has recently been opened containing 16 statues, some of them sublime pieces of art, found in Luxor Temple.

The museum is open daily from 9 am to 1 pm and 4 to 9 pm (winter) or 5 to 10 pm (summer). Entry costs E£15.

Luxor Temple Built by the New Kingdom Pharaoh Amenophis III, on the site of an older sanctuary dedicated to the Theban triad, Luxor Temple is a strikingly graceful piece of architecture on the banks of the Nile. It was added to over the centuries by Tutankhamun, Ramses II, Nectanebo, Alexander the Great and various Romans. At one point the Arabs built a mosque in one of the interior courts.

The temple is open daily from 6 am to 9 pm (winter) and 10 pm (summer), and admission is E£20.

Temples of Karnak This site is possibly one of the most overwhelming monuments of the Pharaonic legacy; work was carried out on the temples of Karnak for over 1500 years. Most was done in the New Kingdom period, although the original sanctuary of the main enclosure, the Great Temple of Amun, was

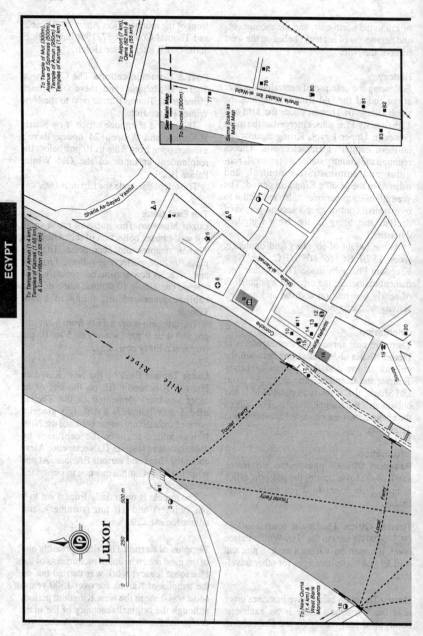

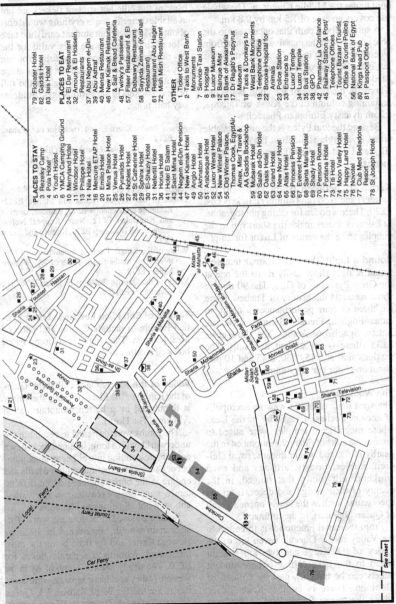

PLACES TO STAY
3 Rezeiky Camp
4 Pola Hotel
5 Youth Hostel
6 YMCA Camping Ground
10 Merryland Hotel
11 Windsor Hotel
13 Philippe Hotel
14 Nile Hotel
16 Mercure ETAP Hotel
20 Emilio Hotel
21 Mina Palace Hotel
25 Venus Hotel
26 Pyramids Hotel
27 Nobles Hotel
28 St Catherine Hotel
29 Sphinx Hotel
30 El-Shazly Hotel
31 Nefertiti Hotel
36 Horus Hotel
41 Hotel El Salam
43 Saint Mina Hotel
44 New Karnak Hotel
47 New Karnak Hotel
49 Anglo Hotel
50 Akhnaton Hotel
51 Arabesque Hotel
52 Luxor Wena Hotel
54 New Winter Palace,
   New Winter Palace
55 Old Winter Palace,
   Thomas Cook, EgyptAir,
   Amex, Misr Travel &
   AA Gaddis Bookshop
59 Mubarak Hotel
60 Salah ad-Din Hotel
62 Oasis Hotel
63 Grand Hotel
64 New Nour Hotel
65 Atlas Hotel
66 Everest Pension
67 Santa Maria Hotel
68 Shady Hotel
69 Pension Roma
70 Fontana Hotel
73 Titi Hotel
75 Moon Valley Hotel
76 Novotel
77 Club Med Belladona
   Resort
78 St Joseph Hotel
79 Flobater Hotel
82 Gaddis Hotel
83 Isis Hotel

PLACES TO EAT
24 El Dar Restaurant
32 Amoun & El Hossein
   Restaurants
37 Abu Negem el-Din
39 Abu Ashraf
40 Mensa Restaurant
46 New Karnak Restaurant
   & Salt & Bread Cafeteria
48 Twinky's Patisserie
57 Fiteer Restaurant & El
   Dabaawy Restaurant
58 Sayyida Zeinab (Kushari
   Restaurant)
61 Restaurant Abu Hager
72 Mish Mish Restaurant

OTHER
1 Ticket Office
2 Taxis to West Bank
   Monuments
7 Service-Taxi Station
8 Hospital
9 Luxor Museum
12 Banque Misr
15 Bank of Alexandria
17 Dr Ragab's Papyrus
   Museum
18 Taxis & Donkeys to
   West Bank Monuments
19 Telephone Office
23 Brooke Hospital for
   Animals
33 Police Station
   Entrance to
34 Luxor Temple
35 Bus Station
38 GPO
42 Pharmacy La Confiance
45 Railway Station & Post/
   Telephone Offices
53 Tourist Bazaar (Tourist
   Office & Tourist Police)
56 National Bank of Egypt
80 Kings Head Pub
81 Passport Office

EGYPT

built under the Middle Kingdom. The whole site covers an area of 1.5 km by 0.8 km.

A sphinx-lined path that once went to the Nile takes you to the massive 1st Pylon, from where you end up in the Great Court. To the left is the Temple of Seti II, dedicated to the triad of Theban gods – Amun, Mut and Khons. In the centre of the court is the one remaining column of the Kiosk of Taharqa, a 25th dynasty Ethiopian Pharaoh.

Beyond the 2nd Pylon is the unforgettable Great Hypostyle Hall. Built by Amenophis III, Seti I and Ramses II, it covers 6000 sq metres.

General admission to the temples of Karnak is between 6 am and 5.30 pm (winter) and 6.30 pm (summer); tickets cost E£20. There's no fee for taking photographs. Local microbuses make the short run to the temples from the centre of Luxor for 25 pt.

Sound & Light Show The Karnak temples' sound & light show easily rivals the one at the Great Pyramids of Giza. The 90 minute show recounts the history of Thebes. There are three or four performances a night, in either English, French, German, Japanese, Italian, Spanish or Arabic. The show costs E£33 (there is no student discount). The sessions start at 6.15, 7.30, 8.45 and 10 pm; about one hour later in summer.

The West Bank

The west bank of Luxor was the necropolis of ancient Thebes, a vast City of the Dead where magnificent temples were raised to honour the cults of Pharaohs entombed in the nearby cliffs, and where queens, royal children, nobles, priests, artisans and even workers built tombs that ranged, in the quality of their design and decor, from the spectacular, such as the newly opened Tomb of Queen Nefertari, to the ordinary.

From the canal junction it is three km to the Valley of the Queens, seven km to the Valley of the Kings and two km straight ahead to the ticket office (where student tickets can be bought), past the Colossi of Memnon. There is another ticket office where the tourist ferries land on the west

bank of the Nile but student tickets are not available there. To see everything would cost about US$65 (without student card) and take a lot of time. Tickets are only valid for the day of purchase, so choose carefully. You can buy tickets for the Valley of the Kings at the site itself. The following list gives the full prices of tickets to the various sites. Students pay half price.

Assasif Tombs: Kheru-Ef and Anch-Hor E£6; Pabasa E£12
Deir al-Bahri (Temple of Hatshepsut) E£12
Deir al-Medina E£6; Tomb of Peshedu E£12
Medinat Habu (Temple of Ramses III) E£12
Ramesseum E£12
Temple of Seti I E£12
Tombs of the Nobles: Nakht and Menna E£12; Rekhmire and Sennofer E£12; Ramose, Userhet and Khaemhet E£12; Nefer-Ronpet, Nefer-Sekheru and Dhutmosi E£20; Khonsu and Benia E£12
Valley of the Kings: Tomb of Tutankhamun E£20; three other tombs E£10; Tomb of Ay (Western Valley) E£12
Valley of the Queens: Tomb of Nefertari E£200(!); other tombs E£12

Temple of Seti I Seti I expanded the Egyptian Empire to include Cyprus and parts of Mesopotamia. The temple is seldom visited but well worth a look.

Valley of the Kings Once called the Gates of the Kings, or the Place of Truth, the valley is dominated by a barren mountain called Al-Qurn (The Horn).

The tombs were designed to resemble the underworld, with a long, inclined rock-hewn corridor descending into either an antechamber or a series of sometimes pillared halls and ending in the burial chamber. More than 60 tombs have been excavated in the valley, although not all belong to Pharaohs.

Some are closed for restoration work. Tutankhamun's tomb, discovered in 1922 by Howard Carter and far from being the most interesting, requires a separate ticket for E£20. The newly opened Tomb of Ay in the Western Valley also has a separate admission. Better are the tombs of Ramses VI, Queen Tawsert/Sethnakt, Tuthmosis III and Saptah.

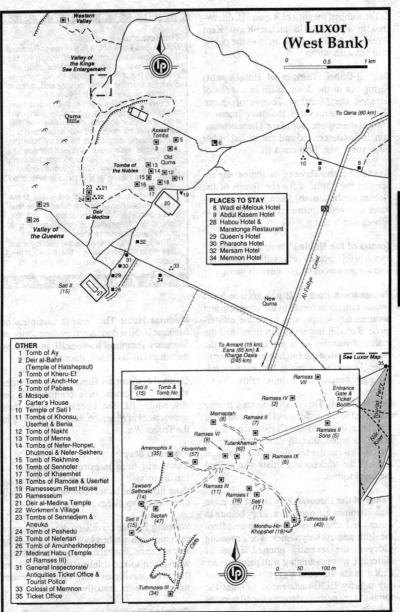

Luxor
(West Bank)

0   0.5   1 km

To Qena (60 km)

Western Valley

Valley of the Kings
See Enlargement

Qurna Hills

Assasif Tombs

Old Qurna

Tombs of the Nobles

Deir al-Medina

Valley of the Queens

Seti II (15)

New Qurna

Al-Fadliya Canal

To Amant (15 km),
Esna (65 km) &
Kharga Oasis
(245 km)

PLACES TO STAY
8 Wadi el-Melouk Hotel
9 Abdul Kasem Hotel
28 Habou Hotel &
   Maratonga Restaurant
29 Queen's Hotel
30 Pharaohs Hotel
32 Mersam Hotel
34 Memnon Hotel

OTHER
1 Tomb of Ay
2 Deir al-Bahri
   (Temple of Hatshepsut)
3 Tomb of Kheru-Ef
4 Tomb of Anch-Hor
5 Tomb of Pabasa
6 Mosque
7 Carter's House
10 Temple of Seti I
11 Tombs of Khonsu,
   Userhet & Benia
12 Tomb of Nakht
13 Tomb of Menna
14 Tombs of Nefer-Ronpet,
   Dhutmosi & Nefer-Sekheru
15 Tomb of Rekhmire
16 Tomb of Sennofer
17 Tomb of Khaemhet
18 Tombs of Ramose & Userhet
19 Ramesseum Rest House
20 Ramesseum
21 Deir al-Medina Temple
22 Workmen's Village
23 Tombs of Sennedjem &
   Aneuka
24 Tomb of Peshedu
25 Tomb of Nefertari
26 Tomb of Amunherkhepshep
27 Medinet Habu (Temple
   of Ramses III)
31 General Inspectorate/
   Antiquities Ticket Office &
   Tourist Police
33 Colossi of Memnon
35 Ticket Office

EGYPT

See Luxor Map

Seti II (15) — Tomb & Tomb No

Ramses VII

Ramses IV (2)

Memeptah (8)

Ramses II (7)

Ramses VI

Amenophis II (35)

Horemheb (57)

Tutankhamun (62)

Ramses II Sons (5)

Ramses IX (6)

Tawsert/Sethnakt (14)

Ramses III (11)

Ramses I (16)

Seti I (17)

Seti II (15)

Saptah (47)

Tuthmosis IV (43)

Monthu-Hir-Khopshef (19)

Cliffs

Tuthmosis III (34)

Entrance Gate & Ticket Booth

Nile Tourist Ferry

Nile River

0   50   100 m

The tomb of the sons of Ramses II, discovered in 1995 by US archaeologist Kent Weeks, is expected to be open to the public in about a decade.

Deir al-Bahri (Temple of Hatshepsut)
Rising out of the desert plain in a series of terraces, the Mortuary Temple of Queen Hatshepsut merges with the sheer limestone cliffs of the eastern face of the Theban mountain. It was desecrated and vandalised by her bitter successor, Tuthmosis III.

Assasif Tombs Three of the tombs here are open to the public. Like the Tombs of the Nobles further south, the artwork concentrates on events from everyday life such as fishing and hunting.

Tombs of the Nobles There are at least 12 tombs in this group worth visiting; tickets are sold for groups of two or three of them.

Ramesseum Ramses II was keen to leave behind him monuments to his greatness and his mortuary temple was to be the masterpiece. Sadly, it lies mostly in ruins, and the shattered remains of a giant statue of the Pharaoh inspired the English poet Shelley to write 'Ozymandias' in the 19th century, ridiculing his aspiration to immortality.

Deir al-Medina This small Ptolemaic temple dedicated to the goddesses Hathor and Maat was later occupied by Christian monks – hence its name, literally 'the monastery of the city'. Near the temple are the tombs of some of the workers and artists who created the royal tombs.

Valley of the Queens Only five of the more than 70 tombs are open here. They belong to queens and other royal family members from the 19th and 20th dynasties. The crowning glory is the recently opened Tomb of Nefertari, whose stunning wall paintings are hailed as the finest in Egypt. Visitors must pay a hefty E£200 admission to enter the tomb and are permitted to stay for 10 minutes only.

The Tomb of Nefertari
Nefertari was one of the five wives of Ramses II, the New Kingdom Pharaoh known for his colossal monuments of self-celebration. However, the tomb he created for his favourite queen is a shrine to her beauty and, without doubt, an exquisite labour of love.

Every inch of the walls in the tomb's three chambers and connecting corridors is adorned with colourful scenes of Nefertari in the company of the gods and with associated text from the *Book of the Dead*. Invariably, Nefertari is depicted wearing a divinely transparent white gown and a golden headdress featuring two long feathers extending from the back of a vulture. The ceiling of the tomb is festooned with golden stars.

Like most of the tombs in the Valley of the Kings, this one had been plundered by the time it was discovered by archaeologists in 1904. Only a few fragments of the queen's pink granite sarcophagus remained.

The tomb was opened to the public for the first time in 1995 following a US$6 million restoration project that lasted for five years. ∎

Medinat Habu The temple complex of Medinat Habu is dominated by the enormous Mortuary Temple of Ramses III, inspired by the temple of his father, Ramses II.

Colossi of Memnon These 18m high statues are all that remain of a temple built by Amenophis III. The Greeks believed they were statues of Memnon, slain by Achilles in the Trojan War.

Places to Stay
The tourist trade is extremely seasonal in Luxor, so visitors in winter will often pay more than in the hotter months. Luxor is full of pretty cheap places to stay.

Warning Female travellers should exercise extreme caution when looking for a place to stay in Luxor. Several have reported that they were given spiked drinks at the hotel where they were staying and then taken to a room where they were sexually assaulted.

Camping The *YMCA* campground on Sharia

al-Karnak costs E£3 per night. It's very basic. The *Rezeiky Camp* (☎ 381334), just up the road, charges E£10 per person, which allows you access to the dinky swimming pool and showers. A bed in a small mud bungalow costs an exorbitant E£15.

Hostels The *Youth Hostel* (☎ 372139) is in a street just off Sharia al-Karnak. Rooms are clean and have at least three beds. It costs E£6.10 with a membership card, or E£7.10 without. Breakfast is E£2 extra. It is a little out of the hustle and bustle but close to the service-taxi station.

East Bank – south of Sharia al-Mahatta
Close to the railway station is the *Anglo Hotel* (E£10/15 for a single/double room with breakfast and shared bathroom). It's clean and the management is friendly.

Sharia Abd al-Moneim al-Adasi leads away from the railway station to Sharia Mohammed Farid and then on to what everyone seems to know as Sharia Television or Television St, which is about a 10 minute walk from the railway station. Around these two streets teems a growing family of little budget pensions and hotels. The *Oasis Hotel* (☎ 381699) is off to the left. The double rooms are considerably better than the more pokey singles and have their own bath. All rooms have fans and comfortable beds. The bathrooms are new and clean, and there's plenty of hot water. Singles/doubles cost E£6.50/13, or E£8/16 with air-con.

Two streets past the Oasis, then down a dead-end alley off to the right, is the *Grand Hotel* (☎ 374186). Newly renovated and, for the time being, very clean, it has a small rooftop terrace with great views, and decent shared bathrooms with hot water. Doubles with fans and a bit of furniture go for E£5. There's a washing machine, and bikes are for hire for E£4 per day.

If you walk up Sharia Ahmed Orabi and turn right into the second dusty laneway on your right, you'll find the *Atlas Hotel* (☎ 373514). At E£6 a person (plus E£2 if you want breakfast), this is not a bad place. Continue down this lane, turn right and take the

next two lefts, and you'll find the *Fontana Hotel* (☎ 380663), which is popular with backpackers, although at E£10/15 for a room with shared facilities, or E£20 for a double with air-con and private bathroom, the rooms are a tad overpriced.

In a lane off Sharia Television (it's blocked off) is the *Everest Hotel* (☎ 370017). The rooms come with air-con or fan and attached bathrooms (even toilet paper is provided!), and cost E£15/20.

The 2nd-floor *Pension Roma*, in a lane opposite the old garage on Sharia Television, is run by a friendly Egyptian guy and his English wife. It's small, homey and OK value at E£5 for a poky double with shared facilities, though some of the beds are saggy.

A few streets away is the *Happy Land* (☎ 371828) run by Mr Ibrahim. The cheapest rooms are E£5 a person, including breakfast which is served on the unfinished 3rd floor. A good single with private bath costs E£10.

Down on Sharia Television, there are two mid-range places offering comfortable rooms with all the necessary mod-cons. Both are prepared to discuss discounts when business is slow. The *Shady Hotel* (☎ 381262) charges E£100/128 for rooms on the street side, E£10 extra for the quieter pool side. Taxes are extra. Doubles drop to about E£84 in winter. Across the street, the much cheaper *Santa Maria Hotel* (☎ 380430) offers singles/doubles for E£50/70.

East Bank – north of Sharia al-Mahatta
The *Hotel El Salam* (☎ 372517), in a lane just off Sharia al-Mahatta, is deservedly a popular haunt for the impecunious. At E£5/10 the prices are reasonable and include use of a washing machine. The rooms have fans. A double with bath costs E£15.

The *Saint Mina Hotel* (☎ 386568) is a very good deal if you've got a little extra to pay. The 20 room hotel is relatively new, and, although the rooms are small, they are modern and clean with air-con or fans. A single with bath is E£30, but singles/doubles without bath go for E£20/35.

The *Sphinx Hotel* (☎ 372830) on Sharia Houssef Hassan has singles/doubles for

E£10/20, which may or may not include breakfast depending on how well you can haggle. The rooms have clean, private baths, and the staff are friendly.

Across the road, the *Venus* (☎ 382625) has 25 reasonable rooms with bath. Singles/doubles cost E£10/20, and the hotel has a restaurant and bar.

On Sharia al-Karnak, about a block north of Sharia al-Mahatta, you'll see the *Horus Hotel* (☎ 372165). Rooms cost E£35/45 and are clean and comfortable, with air-con and relatively new bathrooms.

The *Mina Palace Hotel* (☎ 372074) is on the Corniche north of Luxor Temple. It is popular with German groups and has singles/doubles with air-con and private bathrooms for E£65/88.

The *Windsor Hotel* (☎ 375547) is on a small alley just off Sharia Nefertiti. It's a good 120 room hotel, although some of the rooms are a little shoddy. It's popular with European tour groups and singles/doubles cost E£60/80.

Across from this is the *Merryland Hotel* (☎ 371746). Its 32 rooms are more modest than those of the Windsor, but with the same facilities: TV, phone, air-con, bath and balcony. The price of E£40/60 is very reasonable.

West Bank Opposite the Medinat Habu temple complex is the *Habou Hotel* (sometimes spelt 'Habu'). It has dark, dingy, overpriced singles/doubles for E£10/20.

The rooms at the nearby *Queen's Hotel* (☎ 384835) are slightly better than those at the Habou Hotel, but the view is not the best. The roof restaurant has a good panorama.

The *Mersam Hotel* (☎ 382403), also known as the *Ali Abd el-Rasul Hotel* or the *Sheik Ali Hotel*, is opposite the Antiquities Office. Rooms in the main building are somewhat better than the primitive mud-wall rooms in an adjacent building. Singles/doubles cost E£25/30 in summer, though prices double in winter.

The *Abdul Kasem Hotel* (☎ 310319) is near the Temple of Seti I on Sharia Wadi

al-Melouk. It has rooms for E£20/30 and is one of the best lower-budget places on the west bank. It rents bicycles for E£5 a day.

Pharaohs Hotel (☎ 310702) is the only mid-range place to stay on the west bank. It's near the Antiquities Office and has 14 rooms, most with air-con or strong overhead fans, wallpaper and tiled floors. Single/double rooms with fan cost E£30/40, or E£60/70 with air-con. There's a small restaurant which is renowned for its sun-baked bread.

Places to Eat

The *New Karnak Restaurant* and the *Salt & Bread Cafeteria* next-door serve cheap meals for about E£4. The latter offers many entrees, including kebab, pigeon and chicken; the former has rather small portions of chicken or other meat dishes.

The *Mensa Restaurant* on Sharia al-Mahatta has basic food that's slightly overpriced. Dishes include chicken, pigeon stuffed with rice, sandwiches, and chicken with French fries and mixed vegetables. You can have almost a full meal for about E£8.50.

There are a few juice stands at the Luxor Temple end of Sharia al-Mahatta. This street also has a number of good sandwich stands and other cheap-eats possibilities.

A little more expensive is *El-Hossein* on Sharia al-Karnak. Most main dishes cost E£7 to E£10 before service is added to the price. It serves tasty fish in a tomato and basil sauce, and acceptable, if smallish, pizzas for E£7. The soups are sometimes good, sometimes watery. The *Amoun Restaurant* next door serves oriental kebab, chicken, fish, and various rice and vegetable dishes for similar prices.

Up the road from the El-Hossein is the small and busy local hang-out, the *Abu Negem el-Din*, where half a chicken will cost you E£5, and a plate of makarone E£2. Try the tagen, a kind of stew, with or without meat, in a clay casserole pot.

There is a huddle of small eateries and cafes in the lanes around Sharia al-Mahatta between the Amoun Restaurant and the police station, where the food is cheap and the atmosphere busy. One of them, the tiny

El-Dar Restaurant, is on the 1st floor of a building on a laneway off Sharia al-Karnak. The portions tend to be a bit small, but you can get a beer here for E£6.

At the northern end of Sharia Television is another cluster of small diners, a juice stand and a very good, no-name, open-air *fiteer restaurant*. It's sandwiched between a teahouse and the El-Dabaawy Restaurant – just look for the flashing 'Pizza' sign.

A little further along Sharia Television is *Sayyida Zeinab*, one of Luxor's best kushari joints. The prices are written in English, so there's no attempt to rip off tourists, and the portions are large.

Further up Sharia Television, near the Titi Hotel, is the *Mish Mish* restaurant. Try its Mish Mish salad – a kind of mixed salad with houmos and cold meats, enough to constitute a light meal for E£6. It serves a version of pizza too.

The *Marhaba Restaurant* is an oriental-style dining room on the roof of the Tourist Bazaar building on Sharia al-Karnak, near Luxor Temple. This place commands great views of the river, but the food is rather expensive (main courses average E£20).

The air-conditioned *Restaurant Abu Hager* on Sharia Abdel al-Moneim al-Adasi serves shish kebab and kofta for E£6.50 and soups for E£1.50.

A new and very trendy travellers' hangout is the 24 hour *Kings Head Pub* on Sharia Khaled ibn el-Walid near the passport office. This place is England through and through – from the dart board and billiard table to the western music and counter meals. The food is very good though the prices are inflated.

Most of the mid-range hotels have their own restaurants, generally rooftop jobs of varying quality.

The Mercure ETAP Hotel has the *Champollion* snack bar, where you can get pizza, cakes and beer. The old *Winter Palace* serves reasonable buffet meals throughout the day should you feel like splashing out. Breakfast goes for E£35, lunch costs E£52 and dinner is E£60, not including taxes.

If you're hunting around for sweets or ice cream after all this, you could pop into *Twinky's*, around the corner from the New Karnak Hotel.

Getting There & Away

Air EgyptAir flies daily between Cairo, Luxor and Aswan. A one-way ticket to Luxor from Cairo costs E£361. There are frequent daily departures. There are also daily flights from Luxor to Aswan (E£163) and two flights per week to Sharm el-Sheikh (E£412). In the high season, there are flights to Abu Simbel via Aswan and to Hurghada.

Bus The bus station is behind Luxor Temple on Sharia al-Karnak (the garage on Sharia Television is not a pick-up point).

From Luxor, there are two departures to Cairo: at 4.30 pm (E£34); and 7 pm (E£40). The trip takes 10 to 11 hours. Buses leave for Aswan (E£5.50 to E£6.50; four to five hours) about every hour from 6 am to 3.30 pm. The same buses go to Esna (E£2) and Edfu (E£4). Buses to Hurghada (E£8 to E£16; five hours) leave at 6.30 am, 2.30, 4 and 7 pm – the 7 pm bus is the deluxe service costing E£31.

Train The wagon-lit train for Cairo leaves at about 8.30 pm. See Getting There & Away in the earlier Cairo section for more details.

First and 2nd class sitting fares to Cairo are E£48/28 for the 11.30 am train, and E£51/31 for the slightly faster 11.30 pm service.

First and 2nd class tickets to Aswan (four hours) cost E£20/12 on the 6.30 am train, and E£22/14 on the 4.30 pm service. Fares to Al-Minya are E£34/21 on the 11.30 am train, and E£3 more for the 11.30 pm train.

Service Taxi The service taxi station is on a street off Sharia al-Karnak, a couple of blocks inland from the Luxor Museum. Regular destinations include Aswan (E£7.50; 3½ hours), Edfu (E£5; two hours), Esna (E£2; 45 minutes), Kom Ombo (E£6.50; 2½ hours), Qena (E£2) and Qus (E£1.25).

Getting Around
The Airport Luxor airport is seven km east

of town and the official fare for a taxi is E£10.

Bicycle Luxor is bursting with bicycle rental shops. Prices range from E£4 to E£10 a day.

Hantour For about E£4 per hour you can get around town by horse and carriage. Bargain hard.

Ferry Five ferries cross the Nile – two tourist and three local, at least one of which also carries vehicles. Foreigners pay E£2.50 on all of them.

The tourist boats drop you off at the tourist landing, where you can buy full-price tickets to the sights, about one km north of the town landing.

ESNA

The hypostyle hall, with its 24 columns still supporting a roof, is all that remains of the **Temple of Khnum** constructed by Egypt's Ptolemaic rulers. The temple is open from 6 am to 5.30 pm (6.30 pm in summer), and admission costs E£8.

Getting There & Away

Buses from Luxor cost E£2 but service taxis are often more convenient and cost the same.

EDFU

The attraction in this town 53 km south of Esna is the Greek-built **Temple of Horus**, the falcon-headed son of Osiris. It took about 200 years to complete and its completeness has helped fill in a lot of gaps in knowledge about the Pharaonic architecture it imitates. It is open from 7 am to 4 pm in winter and 6 am to 6 pm in summer. Admission is E£20.

There are two cheap hotels in Edfu, near the temple, and a couple of small places to eat off the square.

Getting There & Away

There are frequent connections to Edfu from Luxor and Aswan. Service taxis are the best bet. They cost E£5 from Luxor and E£3.50 from Aswan. The buses are E£4 and E£2.50

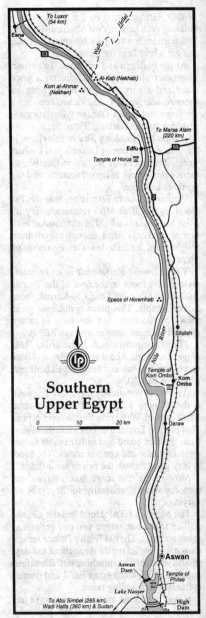

Southern
Upper Egypt

0   10   20 Km

respectively. There is a morning bus to Marsa Alam (E£7) and Bir Shalatayn (E£12) on the Red Sea coast.

KOM OMBO

The dual **Temple of Sobek & Haroeris** (the local crocodile-god and the falcon-headed sky-god, respectively) stands on a promontory at a bend in the Nile near the village of Kom Ombo, where in ancient times sacred crocodiles basked in the sun on the river bank. The temple is open from 8 am to 4 pm, and admission costs E£4.

Getting There & Away

Kom Ombo is an easy day trip from Aswan. Service taxis cost E£1.25 and can drop you at the turn-off from where it's a two km walk or hitch to the temple. Otherwise, from the Cleopatra Hotel in Kom Ombo, take a covered pick-up (25 pt) to the boat landing on the Nile about 800m north of the temple, then walk the remainder.

ASWAN

Over the centuries Aswan, Egypt's southernmost city, has been a garrison town, the gateway to Africa and the now inundated land of Nubia, a prosperous marketplace at the crossroads of the ancient caravan routes and, more recently, a popular winter resort.

In ancient times the area was known as Sunt and the Copts called the place Souan, which means 'trade', from which the Arabic 'Aswan' is derived. In and around Aswan you can see a variety of Pharaonic monuments, a Coptic Christian monastery, the High Dam and Lake Nasser, the huge artificial lake that backs up behind the dam into Sudan. It is the most attractive of the Nile towns – a drink on the terrace of the Old Cataract Hotel overlooking the river, Elephantine Island and the flocks of felucca sails on the Nile will convince the most sceptical.

Orientation

There are only three main avenues and most of the city is along the Nile or parallel to it. The railway station is at the northern end of town, three blocks east of the river and its boulevard, the Corniche el-Nil, along which you'll find most of the public utilities and better hotels and restaurants.

Information

Tourist Office There are two tourist offices: one (☎ 312811) is next to the railway station; and the other (☎ 323297) on a side street, one block in from the Corniche. Both offices are open Saturday to Thursday from 8.30 am to 2 pm and 6 to 8 pm; Friday from 10 am to 2 pm and 6 to 8 pm.

Money The main banks have their branches on the Corniche. Banque Misr and the Banque du Caire will issue cash advances on Visa and MasterCard. The Bank of Alexandria accepts Eurocheques. The Amex office (☎ 322909) is in the Old Cataract Hotel. Thomas Cook (☎ 304011) is on the Corniche.

Post & Communications The GPO is also on the Corniche, next to the municipal swimming pool. However, poste restante must be collected from the smaller post office on the corner of Sharia Abtal at-Tahrir and Sharia Salah ad-Din (go around to the back opposite the Victoria Hotel). Both are open daily, except Friday, from 8 am and 2 pm.

International telephone calls can be made from the telephone office, which is on the Corniche towards the southern end of town, just past the EgyptAir office.

The telephone code for Aswan is 097.

Sharia as-Souq

This busy street is humming with the activity of one of the most colourful markets you'll find in Egypt.

Elephantine Island

Once the core of what is now Aswan, the island is characterised by its huge grey boulders. Excavations have revealed a small town, temples, fortifications and a Nilometer at the southern end of the island. There is a small museum.

Kitchener's Island

Lord Kitchener turned this island into a flourishing garden, which it remains. Entry is E£5 and you have to hire a boat to get there.

Mausoleum of Aga Khan

The elaborate resting place of the Aga Khan is modelled on Fatimid tombs in Cairo. It's open from Tuesday to Sunday.

Monastery of St Simeon

This well-preserved 6th century Coptic Christian monastery is a half-hour hike or short camel ride from the felucca dock near the Mausoleum of Aga Khan.

Tombs of the Nobles

A few of these Old and Middle Kingdom tombs of local dignitaries are worth exploring. Admission to the tombs is E£6. Hours are from 8 am to 4 pm (winter) and 5 pm (summer).

Nubian Museum

This museum is under construction on the road to the Aswan Dam and is planned to be

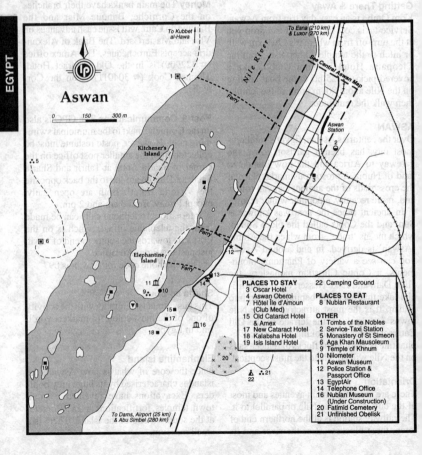

Aswan

To Kubbet al-Hawa

To Esna (210 km) & Luxor (270 km)

Nile River

Ferry

See Central Aswan Map

Aswan Station

Kitchener's Island

Ferry

Ferry

Elephantine Island

PLACES TO STAY	22 Camping Ground
3 Oscar Hotel	**PLACES TO EAT**
4 Aswan Oberoi	8 Nubian Restaurant
7 Hôtel Île d'Amoun (Club Med)	**OTHER**
15 Old Cataract Hotel & Amex	1 Tombs of the Nobles
17 New Cataract Hotel	2 Service-Taxi Station
18 Kalabsha Hotel	5 Monastery of St Simeon
19 Isis Island Hotel	6 Aga Khan Mausoleum
	9 Temple of Khnum
	10 Nilometer
	11 Aswan Museum
	12 Police Station & Passport Office
	13 EgyptAir
	14 Telephone Office
	16 Nubian Museum (Under Construction)
	20 Fatimid Cemetery
	21 Unfinished Obelisk

To Dams, Airport (25 km) & Abu Simbel (280 km)

a showcase of Nubian art and architecture. Ask the tourist office if it has opened.

Fatimid Cemetery & Unfinished Obelisk

The Fatimid Cemetery, opposite the Nubian Museum, is a collection of low stone buildings with domed roofs topped by crescents. It's a 15 minute walk from the EgyptAir office.

Across the road from the cemetery (a five to 10 minute walk away if you follow the road) is the Unfinished Obelisk, a huge discarded obelisk on the edge of the northern granite quarries. Entry to the site costs E£5.

Places to Stay

Camping There's a camping ground next to the Unfinished Obelisk. Facilities are basic (cold showers only), but there are grassy spaces and a few trees to provide shade. It costs E£3 per person plus E£5/2 for a car/motorcycle.

Hostels The *Youth Hostel* (☎ 322235) is on Sharia Abtal at-Tahrir, not far from the railway station. At E£8 for a bed in a shared double or triple, it's not a bad deal (though breakfast is not included). The rooms have fans, the showers and toilets are clean and the place is generally empty.

Hotels – north of the railway station The 27 room *Rosewan Hotel* (☎ 324497) has clean, simple, rather small singles/doubles with shower/toilet combinations for E£16/26, or E£14/25 without shower. All rooms have fans and tiled floors, and, according to some disgruntled travellers, bugs.

The *Hotel El-Saffa* (☎ 322173) next door is starting to show its age but is still OK at E£5/10 for rooms with sinks and balconies. A few rooms also have showers with hot water.

A few blocks north is the *Mena Hotel* (☎ 324388). The cool, carpeted rooms each have a TV, phone, shower, toilet and small balcony. Singles are E£15, doubles (with the choice of one large bed or two singles) cost E£25.

Hotels – south of the railway station Across the street from the youth hostel is the *Marwa Hotel*, which at E£4 is about as cheap as you'll find. Another cheapie is the *Bob Marley Hotel*, one block east of the Medina restaurant. For E£5 per person you get a reasonable double room with fan and balcony. The newer air-con rooms cost a bit more.

The relatively new *Nubian Oasis Hotel* (☎ 312126/123), just off Sharia as-Souq, is one of Aswan's most popular travellers' haunts. It has good clean rooms for E£8 per person with private bath, or E£6 without. There's a large lounge area and a roof garden where Stellas cost E£5.

On a quiet side street towards the southern end of the souq is the relatively new *Hotel Al-Oraby* (☎ 317578). Its central location is an advantage for exploring the souq and the Corniche, the staff are friendly and the communal bathrooms are clean (though prone to flooding). It charges E£7 per person in a room with fan; air-con is a few E£ more. It's a 15 to 20 minute walk from the railway station.

Further away from the Nile is the *Oscar Hotel* (☎ 323851), which has become something of a travellers' favourite. Rooms cost E£25/35. There's a rooftop terrace where beers (E£5) are available.

The *Abu Simbel Hotel* (☎ 322888) on the Corniche used to be a mid-range place but the hotel is so decrepit that it is now a definite bottom ender. Double rooms with shower cost E£28 for one or two people. The views from here are superb.

Continuing south along the Corniche, the new 34 room *Memnon Hotel* (☎ 322650) is above the National Bank of Egypt (but can only be entered through the back alley). Air-con doubles with private bath, comfortable beds and views over the alley/Nile cost E£25/35; singles are E£5 cheaper. It's good value.

The *Ramses Hotel* (☎ 324000) on Sharia Abtal at-Tahrir is a good deal and, according to some travellers, the best value-for-money hotel in Aswan. Singles/doubles with shower, toilet, air-con, colour TV, minirefrigerator and Nile views cost about E£35/55.

EGYPT

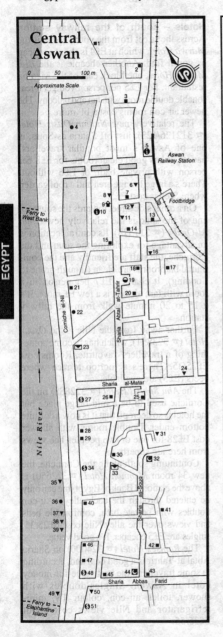

Central Aswan

Approximate Scale
0   50   100 m

Aswan
Railway Station

Footbridge

Ferry to
West Bank

Comiche el-Nil

Sharia Abtal al-Tahrir

Nile River

Sharia al-Matar

Sharia as-Souq

Sharia Abbas Farid

Ferry to
Elephantine
Island

PLACES TO STAY
1   New Abu Simbel Hotel
2   Mena Hotel
3   Rosewan & El-Saffa
     Hotels
7   Marwa Hotel
9   Youth Hostel
13 Noorhan Hotel
14 El-Amin Hotel
15 Ramses Hotel
17 Bob Marley Hotel
18 Cleopatra Hotel
20 Nubian Oasis Hotel
21 Abu Simbel Hotel
25 Aswan Palace Hotel
26 Happi Hotel
28 El-Salam Hotel
29 Hathor Hotel
30 Victoria Hotel
40 Horus Hotel
41 Molla Hotel
42 Hotel al-Oraby
43 Abou Shelib Hotel
45 El Amir Hotel
46 Memnon Hotel
47 Philae Hotel

PLACES TO EAT
6   Restaurant Derwash
8   El Dar Restaurant
11 Esraa (Kofta Place)
12 El Nasr Pizza Place
16 Medina Restaurant
24 El Masry Restaurant
31 Al-Sayed Nafesa
     Restaurant
35 Saladin Restaurant
37 Aswan Moon Restaurant
38 Emy Restaurant
39 Monalisa Restaurant
49 Panorama & El-Shati
     Restaurants
50 Restaurant el-Nil

OTHER
4   Governorate Building
5   Tourist Office
10 Tourist Office & Nile
     Valley Navigation
     Office
19 Bus Station
22 Cultural Centre
23 GPO
27 Banque Misr
32 Mosque
33 Post Office (Poste
     Restante)
34 Bank of Alexandria
36 Dr Ragab Papyrus
     Museum
44 Mosque
48 Banque du Caire
51 Thomas Cook

The *Old Cataract Hotel* (☎ 316002) is an impressive Moorish-style building surrounded by gardens on a rise above the river, with splendid views of the Nile. Doubles start at US$110/120 for a standard room with a garden/Nile view.

Places to Eat

Along Sharia as-Souq is a veritable smorgasbord of small restaurants and cafes in the midst of the lively souq atmosphere. There are also plenty of cafes by the railway station.

The *Restaurant Derwash* on the south side of the Aswan railway station square has been recommended by some travellers. A block from the railway station is *Samah*, a little ta'amiyya stall. Down a side street, a bit further, is *El-Nasr*, which has pizza (or 'betza' as they prefer to spell it), as well as fried fish and chicken.

Next to the youth hostel is an OK place called the *El-Dar*, which serves a nice, if smallish, vegetable soup. Alternatively you could try *Esraa*, a tiny kofta place just down the road.

The *Medina Restaurant* on Sharia as-Souq, across from the Cleopatra Hotel, is recommended for its kofta and kebab deals. It also serves a vegetarian meal for E£4.50 which includes a cola.

The *Al-Sayed Nafesa*, tucked away in a side alley in the heart of the souq, is a good-value, little place, serving kofta for E£5, soup for E£1, and a meal of rice, salad, vegetables and bread for E£2.50.

There are three places on the Corniche where you can sit out on a barge in the river and get decent food and beers. Of the trio, the *Aswan Moon Restaurant* remains the most popular among foreigners and Egyptians. Main courses go for about E£12 and a beer is E£6. It serves generous soups and pizzas (E£10), but the salads tend to be small. Another of the trio, the *Emy Restaurant*, does especially nice fruit cocktail drinks. The view from its top deck at sunset is bliss, and the beers are the cheapest in town.

The tiny *Restaurant el-Nil* is on the Corniche a few doors along from Thomas Cook.

A full meal of fish (carp from Lake Nasser), chicken or meat with rice, vegetables, salad, tahina and bread should cost about E£9.

Those intending to splurge at the restaurant at the Old Cataract should note that, while the decor is delightful, the French cuisine is average and the Egyptian woman crooning away on old Frank Sinatra classics is decidedly off-putting. The Nubian musicians and dancers who come on later, however, liven things up.

Getting There & Away

Air EgyptAir flies daily from Cairo to Aswan (E£497 one way; 1½ hours). The one-way hop to Luxor is E£163; to Hurghada via Luxor it's E£323.

The return flight from Aswan to Abu Simbel costs E£439 and includes bus transfers between the airport and the temple site.

Bus The bus station is in the middle of town. There are two daily buses to Abu Simbel (E£26 return) but neither of them are air-conditioned. One leaves at 8 am and arrives back at about 5.30 pm; the other is a night service departing at 5 pm. You should book in advance.

There are hourly buses to Edfu (E£2; 1½ hours), Esna (E£2.50; two hours), Kom Ombo (E£1.25; one hour) and Luxor (E£5.50 to E£6.50; four to five hours). A direct bus for Cairo (12 hours) leaves at 3.30 pm and costs E£50. The bus leaving an hour later costs E£10 less.

There are buses to Hurghada at 8 am (E£16) and 3.30 pm (E£30). The bus to Marsa Alam (E£10.50; five hours), also on the Red Sea coast, departs at 6.15 am and continues all the way south to Bir Shalatayn (E£18).

Train There's a handful of trains running daily between Cairo and Aswan, although only three of them can be used by foreigners. The most expensive is the wagon-lit train (No 85) which costs E£293 one way in 2nd class to Cairo (which is the same fare as from Luxor) and departs at 3 pm. See the Cairo

Getting There & Away section earlier in this chapter for more details on this train.

Express trains No 981 and 997 to Cairo leave at 5.45 am and 6.30 pm. The 1st/2nd class fare is E£60/34. The trip to Cairo is scheduled to take about 15 hours but can take more than 20.

Tickets for the train to Luxor (four hours) cost E£20/12 in 1st/2nd class on the afternoon service, and a couple of pounds more on the morning train.

To get to the High Dam, 13 km south of Aswan, take one of the six daily trains to Sadd al-Ali railway station (65 pt) at the end of the Cairo-Aswan line.

Service Taxi The service-taxi station is across the railway tracks on the east side of town. Service taxis (which are sometimes actually microbuses) depart regularly for Daraw (E£1.50; 30 minutes), Edfu (E£3.50; 1½ hours), Kom Ombo (E£1.50; one hour) and Luxor (E£7.50; 3½ hours).

Felucca A trip down the Nile would not be complete without at least a short felucca ride, but the most popular trip is downstream from Aswan to Edfu which takes about two or three days – most captains won't go further. There's no shortage of captains or touts along the Corniche trying to sell rides. Get a group of people to go together (a comfortable number is six; more than eight is a tight squeeze). Officially, feluccas can carry a minimum of six passengers and a maximum of eight for the following prices: E£25 to Kom Ombo, E£45 to Edfu and E£50 to Esna. On top of this you must add E£5 for police registration and the cost of food supplies. Check the boat for adequate space, blankets, cushions etc, and if the deal includes food it is an idea to accompany the captain when shopping. Don't forget water or you'll be drinking and cooking with Nile water.

Boat Boat services along Lake Nasser to Wadi Halfa in Sudan were stopped in late 1994 and it's anyone's guess when they will resume. The Nile Valley Navigation Office (☎ 322348) is the best place to direct enquiries. It is next to the tourist office, one street in from the Corniche. This used to be the place to buy tickets; the office is open from 9 am to 1.30 pm.

Getting Around
The Airport The airport is 25 km south-west of town and the taxi fare is about E£20.

Taxi A taxi tour that includes the Temple of Philae, the High Dam and the Unfinished Obelisk near the Fatimid Cemetery costs around E£25 for five to six people.

Bicycle There are a few places at the railway station end of Sharia as-Souq where you can hire bicycles for about E£4 a day. Try around the Marwa and Ramses hotels.

Boat A ferry shuttles across the Nile to just below the Tombs of the Nobles on the west bank. It departs either from near the tourist office or opposite the Abu Simbel Hotel. The fare is 50 pt each way.

Ferries to Elephantine Island costs 25 pt each way and leave from landings in front of the telephone office and opposite Thomas Cook.

AROUND ASWAN
Temple of Philae
South of Aswan and relocated to another island to escape flooding in the 1960s, the Temple of Philae was dedicated to Isis, who found the heart of her slain brother, Osiris, on Philae Island (now submerged). Most of the temple was built by the Ptolemies and Romans, and early Christians turned the hypostyle hall into a chapel. It is possible to organise taxi trips to the boat landing at Shellal south of the Old Dam, or you can walk if you can get a lift to the dam.

The temple complex is open from 8 am to 4 pm (winter) and 7 am to 5 pm (summer); admission is E£20. Tickets are purchased from the small office before the boat landing at Shellal. The boat costs about E£14 (maximum eight people) for the round trip. A sound & light show is held here – there are usually three performances a night.

The High Dam

In 1956 after the USA, the UK and the World Bank suddenly refused the financial backing they had offered for building the High Dam, Nasser ordered the nationalisation of the Suez Canal as a means of raising the capital. The Soviet Union then offered the necessary funding and expertise, and work began on the High Dam in 1960 and was completed in 1971.

As a result of the dam, the area of Egypt's cultivable land was increased by 30%; the High Dam's hydroelectric station has doubled the country's power supply and a rise in the Sahara's water table has been recorded as far away as Algeria.

On the other hand, artificial fertilisers now have to be used because the dam hinders the flow of silt that was critical to the Nile Valley's fertility. In turn, the authorities are faced with the problem that the silt will eventually fill the lake. The dam also spelt the end of the Nubian people's homeland. The greatest fear is that should the dam ever break or be sabotaged, most of Egypt would be swept into the Mediterranean.

Another consequence of the dam's construction was the fact that a great many valuable and irreplaceable ancient monuments were doomed to be drowned by the waters of Lake Nasser. In response, teams of local and foreign archaeologists descended on Nubia to set in motion UNESCO-organised projects aimed at rescuing as many of the threatened treasures as possible. While some temples disappeared beneath the lake, 14 were salvaged and moved to safety. Ten of them, including the temple complexes of Philae, Kalabsha and Abu Simbel, were dismantled stone by stone and rebuilt on higher ground. ∎

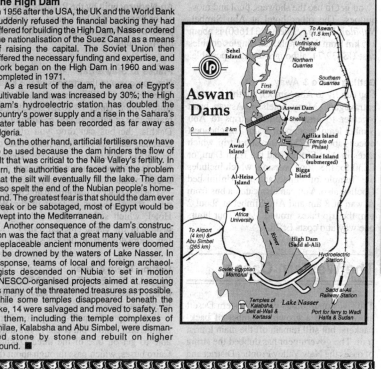

Aswan Dams

EGYPT

High Dam

This colossal structure controls the unpredictable annual flooding of the Nile and is a source of hydroelectric power. It's 3600m long and 111m deep. Trips to Abu Simbel (see the following section) usually include a stop at the dam.

ABU SIMBEL

Thanks to a US$40 million UNESCO effort, Ramses II's **Great Temple of Abu Simbel** was moved out of the way of the rising waters of Lake Nasser in the 1960s.

The temple was dedicated to the gods Ra-Harakhty, Amun, Ptah and the deified Pharaoh himself. Guarding the entrance, the four famous colossal statues of Ramses II sit majestically, each more than 20m tall, with smaller statues of the king's mother, Queen Tuya, his wife Nefertari and some of their children.

The other temple at the Abu Simbel complex is the rock cut **Temple of Hathor**.

The admission fee for both temples is E£21 (E£12 for students).

Places to Stay

There are two hotels at Abu Simbel. The *Nefertari Hotel* (☎ 316402) is about 400m from the temples. It has singles/doubles/

triples for US$60/75/90, including breakfast and taxes. You can also camp for about E£20 – you get to use the showers, pool and mosquitoes. The other hotel at Abu Simbel, *Nabalah Ramses Hotel* (☎ 311660) is about 1½ km from the temple site. Singles/doubles cost US$39/74, although deals are possible.

Getting There & Away
You can fly to Abu Simbel, but this is a little extravagant. Many hotels in Aswan band together to arrange minibus trips to Abu Simbel leaving at about 5 am. The cheapest price is about E£25 for the 'short' trip, which takes in Abu Simbel and the High Dam, or E£30 for the 'long' version, which includes the Temple of Philae and the Unfinished Obelisk also. You can also catch a bus from Aswan at 8 am and Abu Simbel at about 2 pm; the trip takes around 3½ to four hours one way and costs E£26.

The Western Oases

The fives main oases of the Western Desert are attracting a growing number of backpackers, but still remain off the main tourist trail. The government has dubbed the string of oases the New Valley Frontier District and hopes to develop the area, and so create new possibilities for an exploding population. Asphalt roads link all the oases now, four of them in a long loop from Asyut round to Cairo. Siwa, out near the Libyan frontier, is now linked by road to Bahariyya, but no public transport uses this route as yet. There is limited accommodation in all of the oases, and infrequent buses link all but Siwa.

KHARGA OASIS
About 235 km south of Asyut is the largest of the oases, Kharga. The town, Al-Kharga, is the administrative centre of the New Valley governorate, which also includes Dakhla and Farafra oases. The town is of little interest, but to the north you'll find the **Temple of Hibis**, built to the god Amun by

the Persian Emperor Darius I. To the east are the crumbling remains of the **Temple of An-Nadura**, built by the Romans. Just north of the Temple of Hibis is the Coptic **Necropolis of Al-Bagawat**, dating as far back as the 4th century.

Places to Stay & Eat
You can *camp* in the grounds of the Kharga Oasis Hotel for E£7 per person. The four storey *Waha Hotel* (☎ (092) 900393) is a reasonable cheapie. If you're coming from Dakhla, the bus can drop you off at the entrance. Singles/doubles without bath cost E£5.50/11, or E£12/17 with bath. There are also several government resthouses and a couple of mid-range hotels in Al-Kharga.

The best places to eat are the hotels. Otherwise, try *Al-Ahram*, in front of the Waha Hotel, which sells chicken and vegetable dishes, or the cheap chicken (only) place a few doors down from the bus station.

Getting There & Away
EgyptAir flies from Cairo to Al-Kharga and return on Sunday and Wednesday; the fare is E£399 one way.

Buses depart from Al-Kharga for Cairo at 6 am (E£21) and 7 pm (E£32). You may be able to get on one of the three Dakhla to Cairo buses, which pass through about three hours after leaving Dakhla. There are buses from Al-Kharga to Asyut (E£6 to E£7; four hours) at 6, 7, 11 am and 2 pm. Two other buses pass through from Dakhla to Asyut. Buses to Dakhla (E£5 to E£7; three hours) leave at 7 am and 1 pm.

A service taxi from Asyut (three to four hours) costs E£8 per person. To Dakhla (three hours) costs E£7.

DAKHLA OASIS
Located 190 km west of Kharga is the oasis of Dakhla, containing two small towns, Mut and Al-Qasr. The former is the bigger and has most of the hotels and public utilities. There are government-run hot **springs** three km to its north. Another 30 km brings you to the remarkable medieval mud-brick town of **Al-**

Qasr. Watch out for the 12th century minaret.

Places to Stay & Eat

It's possible to *camp* near the dunes west of Mut or in Al-Qasr, or at the Mut Talata springs for E£4 per person.

The only option in Al-Qasr is the friendly *Al-Qasr Hotel* (☎ (092) 940750) on the main road near the entry to the old town. It has four, big rooms for E£7 per person. On the ground floor is a teahouse and restaurant which serves good basic fare such as chicken, rice, fuul and salad.

The best deal in Mut is the *Gardens Hotel* (☎ (092) 941577), where singles/doubles without bath or fan cost E£10/12; with bath E£12/16 (triples E£21). It also has a restaurant and it rents bikes for E£5.

Getting There & Away

Bus services to Kharga Oasis (E£7) and on to Asyut (E£15) and Cairo leave every day at 6 am and 5 pm and, sometimes, 7 pm. The respective fares to Cairo (12 to 14 hours) are E£26/35/37. Other buses to Asyut (E£12) via Kharga (E£5) leave every day at 8.30 am and 4 pm. There's a bus to Kharga only at 2.30 pm.

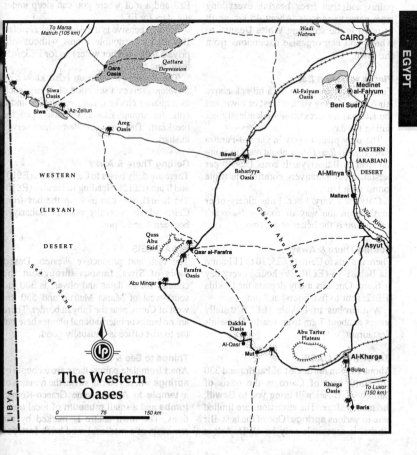

The Western Oases

0   75   150 km

EGYPT

LIBYA

There is one bus a day to and from Farafra Oasis (E£12; four to five hours). There are no buses direct to Bahariyya Oasis.

Service taxis leave from the bus station, and cost E£7 to Kharga and E£15 to either Farafra or Asyut.

There are also microbuses to Farafra for E£12.

FARAFRA OASIS

Approximately 300 km north-west of Dakhla, Farafra is the smallest and most untouched of the oases. There is really nothing much to see here, except for the palms and fruit trees bearing everything from dates to apricots. About 45 km north of town is the stunning **White Desert**, to which you can organise excursions from the town.

Places to Stay & Eat

There is a *camping site* on a hillock above Bir 6, a hot spring six km west of town, but the site has no trees so it's relentlessly hot during the day.

The only place to stay in Qasr al-Farafra is the *Tourist Rest House* about one km along the road to Bahariyya. It costs E£9.40 per person in comparatively comfortable triple rooms with fans.

Only two very basic little diners offer anything in the way of food – *Hussein's Restaurant* is the better of the two.

Getting There & Away

There is a bus to Cairo (E£25; 10 to 11 hours) via Bahariyya (E£10; 2½ hours) every day at 6 am. One bus a day departs for Dakhla (E£12; four to five hours) at 2 pm.

A microbus to Dakhla (E£12) usually leaves at about 7 am from nearby Hussein's Restaurant.

BAHARIYYA OASIS

About 185 km north-east of Farafra and 330 km south-east of Cairo is the oasis of Bahariyya. Buses will bring you to **Bawiti**, the main village. The attractions are limited here to various **springs**. One of the best, Bir Ghaba, is accessible only by 4WD. Ask at

the Alpenblick Hotel in Bawati, which has a camp site there. You can also walk to **Black Mountain**.

Places to Stay & Eat

The *Paradise Hotel* is a pretty dingy place in the centre of Bawiti which charges E£3.50 a bed.

Ahmed's Safari Camp, about four km out of Bawiti, has become a bit of a favourite among travellers and trans-Africa groups. It has cool, pleasant, domed double rooms with private bathroom for E£10, rooms with shared facilities for E£5, basic reed huts for E£3 and a roof where you can sleep under the stars for E£2.

More expensive is the *Alpenblick Hotel* in Bawiti. Large double rooms without/with private bath (and hot water) go for E£35/45, including breakfast.

The *Popular Restaurant* (also known as *Bayoumi*) serves a selection of dishes, such as a quarter chicken, rice, vegetables and a cola, for around E£8 and is also open for breakfast. The *Paradise Restaurant* serves kushari.

Getting There & Away

There are daily buses to Cairo at 7 am (E£10) and 9 am (E£12). Heading to Farafra (E£10; 2½ hours), you can pick up the bus from Cairo which generally reaches Bahariyya between 1 and 2 pm.

SIWA OASIS

The lush and productive Western Desert oasis of Siwa, famous throughout the country for its dates and olives, is 300 km south-west of Marsa Matruh and 550 km west of Cairo, near the Libyan border. There are no banks or international phones here but the tourist office is unusually good.

Things to See & Do

Apart from date palms, there are a couple of **springs** where you can swim, the remains of a **temple** to Amun, some Graeco-Roman **tombs** and a small **museum** of local traditions. The town centre is marked by the remnants of a medieval mud brick **fortress** and **minaret** – the only one in the country where the muezzin still climbs to the top and doesn't use a loudspeaker. Several shops around town sell local crafts such as basketware and jewellery.

Places to Stay & Eat
There are about half a dozen places to stay in Siwa. The *Yousef Hotel* is an OK deal at E£5 a night in a shared room. The *Palm Trees Hotel*, just off the main square, is more tranquil and has clean rooms with fans, screened windows and small balconies for E£5 per person.

The town's top hotel is the 20 room *Arous el-Waha* (☎ (03 934026) 6100). Recently renovated, all the rooms have bathrooms with constant hot water and fans. Singles/doubles cost E£36/59.

In the centre of town, you can eat at a handful of restaurants. The longest-standing is the ever popular *Abdu Restaurant*, across the road from the Yousef Hotel. Equally as popular these days is the nearby *Alexander Restaurant*, where you can get excellent lentil soup (E£1), vegetarian shakshooka (E£2.50) (baked vegetable dish with an egg on top) and couscous (E£2.50).

Getting There & Away
The West Delta Bus Co station is on the main square in Siwa. There's a daily bus at 6.30 am to Alexandria (E£13.50; 10 hours), stopping at Marsa Matruh (E£7; five hours) on the way. On Sunday, Tuesday and Thursday, there's a second bus to Alexandria, once again via Marsa Matruh. It departs at 10 am, is air-conditioned and costs E£20 to Alexandria and E£10 to Marsa Matruh. You should book ahead for these services. An additional daily service to Marsa Matruh leaves at 1 pm and costs E£7; no bookings are taken.

There is a 425 km road to Bahariyya Oasis, but no public transport.

Alexandria & the Mediterranean Coast

On the north coast of Egypt, west of where the Rosetta branch of the Nile leaves the Delta and where the barren desert meets the sparkling waters of the Mediterranean, is the charming, although somewhat jaded, city of Alexandria – once the shining gem of the Hellenistic world. Nearby is the famous

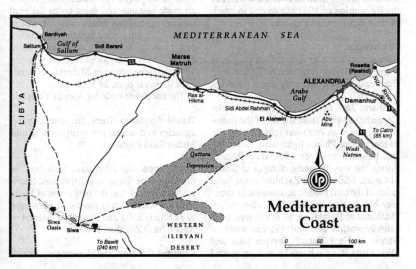

Mediterranean Coast

MEDITERRANEAN SEA

LIBYA

Bardiyah
Sallum
Gulf of Sallum
Sidi Barani
Marsa Matruh
Ras al-Hikma
Sidi Abdel Rahman
El Alamein
Arabs Gulf
ALEXANDRIA
Rosetta (Rashid)
Damanhur
Nile River
Abu Mina
To Cairo (85 km)
Wadi Natrun

Qattara Depression

Siwa Oasis
Siwa
To Bawiti (240 km)

WESTERN (LIBYAN) DESERT

0   50   100 km

EGYPT

town of El Alamein, where the tide of the African campaign during WWII was changed in favour of the Allies and, further west, the Mediterranean resort of Marsa Matruh.

ALEXANDRIA

Born the capital and jewel of Ptolemaic Egypt, Alexandria was eclipsed and reduced to a backwater in the 7th century when the conquering Muslims made their capital in what was to become Cairo. Napoleon's arrival 11 centuries later changed all this, and the modern metropolis still retains something of the cosmopolitan port city.

History

Established in 332 BC by Alexander the Great, the city became a major trade centre and focal point of learning for the whole Mediterranean world. Its ancient library held 500,000 volumes and the Pharos lighthouse was one of the Seven Wonders of the World. Alexandria continued as the capital of Egypt under the Romans and their eastern offshoot, the Byzantine Empire. From the 4th century onwards the city declined into insignificance. Napoleon's arrival and Alexandria's subsequent redevelopment as a major port attracted people from all over the world, but the Revolution of 1952 put an end to much of the city's pluralistic charm.

Orientation

Alexandria, home to five million people, is a true waterfront city, nearly 20 km long from east to west and only about three km wide.

Sharia 26th of July (also known as the Corniche) sweeps from the tip of the promontory, where an Arab fort stands on the site of the ancient Pharos lighthouse, east along the beaches towards Montazah Palace. Along the way its name changes to Sharia al-Geish. Midan Saad Zaghloul is the focal point of the city. Hotels, restaurants, an intercity bus station and the main tram station (Mahattat ar-Ramla) are all in this area. Misr railway station is about 1½ km south of Sharia an-Nabi Daniel. Service taxis and West Delta Bus Co buses leave from around

the square in front of Misr railway station. The port is on the Western Harbour, near Ras at-Tin Palace.

Information

Registration You can register or get a visa extension at the passport office at 28 Sharia Talaat Harb.

Tourist Office The main tourist office (☎ 807 9885), on the south-west corner of Midan Saad Zaghloul, is quite helpful with local information. It's open from 8 am to 6 pm.

Money Many of the main banks have branches along Sharia Talaat Harb, in the centre of town. To exchange travellers' cheques you'll need to head to the Bank of Alexandria's branch at 2 Sharia Saad Zaghloul, or to Banque Misr's branch in the Cecil Hotel. Amex (☎ 851708) is somewhat inconveniently located at 34 Sharia el-Moaskar el-Romani in Rushdy to the east of the city centre. Thomas Cook (☎ 483 5118) is at 15 Midan Saad Zaghloul.

Post & Communications The GPO is a small office just east of Midan Orabi. To pick up poste restante you must go to the mail sorting centre one block west of Midan Orabi. It's a little stone building (opposite a new 15 storey high-rise), and is open daily, except Friday, from about 6.30 am to 6 pm. The telephone office at Mahattat ar-Ramla tram station is open 24 hours a day.

The telephone code for Alexandria is 03.

Travel Agencies There are several travel agencies and airline representatives around Midan Saad Zaghloul.

Bookshops The Al-Ahram bookshop, on the corner of Tariq al-Hurriya and Sharia an-Nabi Daniel, has the best range of books in town. Alternatively there's Al-Mustaqbal at 32 Sharia Safia Zaghloul or Al-Maaref on Midan Saad Zaghloul.

Cultural Centres The Americans, British,

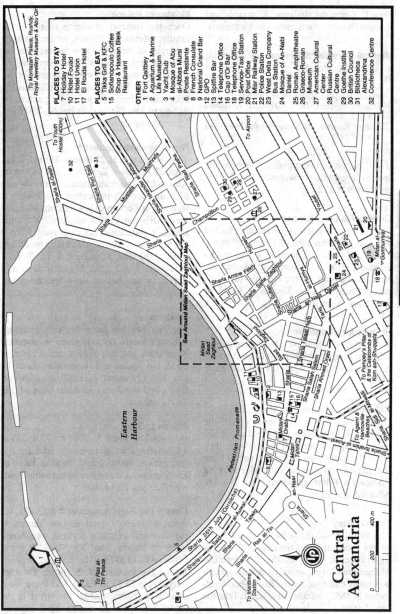

PLACES TO STAY
7 Holiday Hotel
10 Hotel Fouad
11 Hotel Union
17 El Rouda Hotel

PLACES TO EAT
5 Tikka Grill & KFC
15 Sofianopoulo Coffee
Shop & Hassan Bleik
Restaurant

OTHER
1 Fort Qaitbey
2 Aquarium & Marine
Life Museum
3 Yacht Club
4 Mosque of Abu
al-Abbas Mursi
6 French Consulate
9 Poste Restante
12 National Grand Bar
13 GPO
14 Spitfire Bar
16 Telephone Office
18 Cap d'Or Bar
19 Telephone Office
20 Service-Taxi Station
21 Post Office
22 Misr Railway Station
23 Police Station
24 West Delta Company
Bus Station
25 Mosque of An-Nabi
Daniel
26 Roman Amphitheatre
27 Graeco-Roman
Museum
28 American Cultural
Center
29 Russian Cultural
Centre
30 Goethe Institut
31 British Council
32 Bibliotheca
Alexandrina
Conference Centre

Central
Alexandria

French, Germans, Italians, Spaniards and Russians have cultural centres in Alexandria.

Medical Services & Emergency
Hospitals in Alexandria include:

University Hospital, Shatby (☎ 482 2929)
Al-Moassa Hospital, Tariq al-Hurriya, Al-Hadara (☎ 421 2885)
El Seginy Hospital, 10 Sharia Bilous, Ibrahimiya (☎ 597 0671)

If you have a real emergency, telephone the special 'urgent help' number ☎ 123. For the police call ☎ 122.

Graeco-Roman Museum
There's very little left of the ancient city, but you can get some idea of the splendours it must have once contained in a visit to this museum. It's at 5 Sharia al-Mathaf ar-Romani and is open from 9 am to 4 pm daily, except Friday, when it closes at 11.30 am for two hours. Admission is E£8.

Roman Amphitheatre
This is the only example of a Roman theatre found in Egypt and it is in quite good condition. It's open from 9 am to 4 pm, and entry is E£6.

Catacombs of Kom ash-Shuqqafa
Dating back to the 2nd century AD, the tombs of Kom ash-Shuqqafa held about 300 corpses. Open from 8.30 am to 4 pm, they are in the south-west of the city, not far from the famed, misnamed and disappointing **Pompey's Pillar** and tram line No 16. Admission is E£6.

Fort Qaitbey
The Mamluk sultan Qaitbey built a fortress on the foundations of the destroyed Pharos lighthouse in 1480. In the 19th century Mohammed Ali expanded its defences, but it was badly damaged during British bombardments in 1882. Admission is E£12. Take the No 15 tram.

Montazah Palace
Once the summer residence of the royal family, Montazah Palace, at the eastern extremity of the city, is now reserved for the president and his VIPs but the gardens are still a pleasant place to wander around for the day. Entry to the grounds costs E£2. Bus No 260 from Midan Orabi passes the gardens on its way to Abu Qir, as does bus No 250 from Misr railway station.

Royal Jewellery Museum
This museum is at 27 Sharia Ahmed Yehia Pacha, Zizinia (or Zezeniya), and is one of Alexandria's prize attractions. Formerly one of King Farouk's palaces, it now houses a stunning collection of jewels from Mohammed Ali's early 19th century rule until Farouk's abdication. It's open daily from 9 am to 4 pm (closed for two hours on Friday from 11.30 am). Admission is E£10. Take blue tram No 2 from Mahattat ar-Ramla station or any bus on the Corniche going towards Montazah.

Beaches
The city beaches are not overly enticing, although locals flock to them in summer. Maamoura, just east of Montazah Palace, is good, but Agami and Hannoville, about 17 km west of central Alexandria, are better. Buses and minibuses go there from Midan Saad Zaghloul.

Places to Stay
Hostels The *Youth Hostel* (☎ 597 4559) at 13 Sharia Port Said costs E£6.10 for members in dorms (eight beds) or E£10 to E£15 in one of the new double rooms. Non-members pay E£4 extra.

Hotels The *Hotel Acropole* (☎ 805980), 4th floor, 1 Sharia Gamal ad-Din Yassin, is pleasant and centrally located, one block west of Sharia Saad Zaghloul. It costs between E£15 to E£20 for a single, depending on the location of the room. Doubles range from E£25 to E£30, and there are a couple of triples. Across the street is the *Hotel Triomphe*. Its rooms have sagging

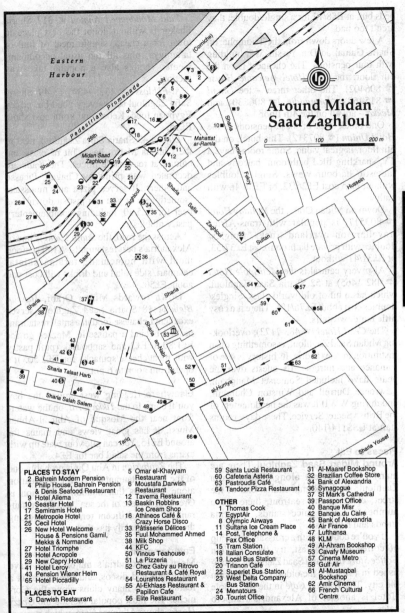

Around Midan Saad Zaghloul

Eastern Harbour

0   100   200 m

EGYPT

PLACES TO STAY
2 Bahrein Modern Pension
4 Philip House, Bahrein Pension & Denis Seafood Restaurant
9 Hotel Allema
10 Seastar Hotel
17 Semiramis Hotel
21 Metropole Hotel
26 Cecil Hotel
26 New Hotel Welcome House & Pensions Gamil, Mekka & Normandie
27 Hotel Triomphe
28 Hotel Acropole
29 New Capry Hotel
41 Hotel Leroy
43 Pension Wiener Heim
65 Hotel Piccadilly

PLACES TO EAT
3 Darwish Restaurant

5 Omar el-Khayyam Restaurant
6 Moustafa Darwish Restaurant
12 Taverna Restaurant
13 Baskin Robbins Ice Cream Shop
16 Athineos Café & Crazy Horse Disco
33 Pâtisserie Délices
35 Fuul Mohammed Ahmed
38 Milk Shop
44 KFC
50 Vinous Teahouse
51 La Pizzeria
52 Chez Gaby au Ritrovo Restaurant & Café Royal
54 Lourantos Restaurant
55 Al-Ekhlass Restaurant & Papillon Cafe
56 Elite Restaurant

59 Santa Lucia Restaurant
60 Cafeteria Asteria
63 Pastroudis Café
64 Tandoor Pizza Restaurant

OTHER
1 Thomas Cook
7 EgyptAir
8 Olympic Airways
11 Sultana Ice Cream Place
14 Post, Telephone & Fax Office
15 Tram Station
18 Italian Consulate
19 Local Bus Station
20 Trianon Café
22 Superjet Bus Station
23 West Delta Company Bus Station
24 Menatours
30 Tourist Office

31 Al-Maaref Bookshop
32 Brazilian Coffee Store
34 Bank of Alexandria
36 Synagogue
37 St Mark's Cathedral
39 Passport Office
40 Banque Misr
42 Banque du Caire
45 Bank of Alexandria
46 Air France
47 Lufthansa
48 KLM
49 Al-Ahram Bookshop
57 Cavafy Museum
57 Cinema Metro
61 Gulf Air
61 Al-Mustaqbal Bookshop
62 Amir Cinema
66 French Cultural Centre

beds but, at E£8/12 for a single/double, they aren't too bad.

A few doors down from the Triomphe, on Sharia Gamal ad-Din Yassin, is a building with four pensions. The cheapest is on the 5th floor: the *New Hotel Welcome House* (☎ 806402). The other three – the *Gamil* (☎ 815458), *Normandie* (☎ 806830) and *Mekka* – are all on the 4th floor.

One block west of these pensions is the *Hotel Union* (☎ 807312). This hotel, on the 5th floor, is great value. Some rooms have a TV, sparkling tiled bathroom, balcony and fantastic harbour views. Singles/doubles without bath cost E£26/32, or E£36/46 with bath.

Down on Midan Orabi, the *Holiday Hotel* (☎ 803517) is popular with trans-Africa travellers on overland trucks. Singles/doubles with private bathroom cost E£37/53, or E£31/41 without.

Also very central is the *Metropole Hotel* (☎ 482 1465) at 52 Sharia Saad Zaghloul, which has a bit of old world class. Singles/doubles cost about E£76/106. There is a cosy little bar downstairs.

The *Cecil Hotel* (☎ 483 7173), overlooking Midan Saad Zaghloul, is something of an institution in Alexandria. Its history is one of romance and intrigue. Its guests over the years have included Somerset Maugham, Lawrence Durrell and Winston Churchill, and during WWII it was the headquarters of the British Secret Service. These days, rooms start at US$114/140.

Places to Eat

Around Midan Saad Zaghloul There are many places to eat along Sharia Safia Zaghloul. At the Ramla station end of the street, close to the seafront, there are a number of cafes, juice stands, shwarma stands and bakeries.

If you're content with a croissant and a cup of coffee for breakfast, try the *Brazilian Coffee Store* on Sharia Saad Zaghloul. Established in 1929, it's the oldest coffee shop in the city. The *Trianon Café* in the Metropole Hotel is another of Alexandria's superb cafes.

Fuul Mohammed Ahmed at 317 Sharia Shakor is without doubt the best place in town for a cheap, simple meal of fuul or ta'amiyya, plus all the usual accompaniments. There's also a popular takeaway section.

Al-Ekhlass (☎ 482 4434) at 49 Sharia Safia Zaghloul serves very good but pricey Egyptian food. Kebab and kofta cost about E£15.

Elite at 43 Sharia Safia Zaghloul, next to the Cinema Metro, has a bit of class and culture at reasonable prices. The walls are decorated with prints by Chagall, Picasso and others. It serves pizza and moussaka (sometimes), or you can just sit down for a beer for E£5.30, including complimentary pastry nibbles.

Across the road, the *Santa Lucia* is one of Alexandria's best restaurants. A full seafood meal with homemade tarama salata, calamari, side salad and drinks will cost you about E£50.

Down towards Midan Orabi, *Hassan Bleik* at 18 Sharia Saad Zaghloul serves excellent Lebanese food in a small restaurant nestled behind a patisserie. Mezzes go for E£1.80 to E£3 and sanbousak (puff pastry with meat/cheese/spinach) for E£2.50. It's open from noon to 6 pm.

Elsewhere Heading west around the bay you'll come to the *Tikka Grill*, on the waterfront near the Mosque of Abu al-Abbas Mursi. It has great views and mains for around E£15. You can pile your plate up with extras from the salad bar for E£4.

The *Zephyrion* in Abu Qir is probably one of the best restaurants in Egypt. Its location alone warrants that honour. Zephyrion is Greek for 'breeze of the sea', and this restaurant, on a magnificent terrace overlooking the ocean, certainly has that.

Entertainment

Most of Alexandria's major hotels have nightclubs and discos, and live music is a feature of the many clubs along the Corniche. The most popular include the *Crazy Horse*, above Athineos Café, which starts at

11 pm, features a belly dancer and costs E£50, including a meal.

There are several cinemas that show English-language films – try the *Amir* on Tariq al-Hurriya and the *Metro* on Sharia Safia Zaghloul.

If you want a drink in a tucked away bar with low lights and decent pub music, head straight for the tiny *Spitfire Bar* just back from the GPO. It closes at midnight. The quaint *Cap d'Or Bar*, 4 Sharia Adib, just around the corner from the Hassan Bleik restaurant, is open until 3 am.

Getting There & Away

Air There are direct international flights from Alexandria to Athens (Olympic Airways) and Frankfurt (Lufthansa), and to Saudi Arabia and Dubai (EgyptAir).

The one-way fare for the 40 minute flight from Cairo to Alexandria is E£214.

Bus The West Delta Bus Co runs buses from Midan Saad Zaghloul, Sidi Gaber railway station and from in front of Misr railway station *(mahattat Misr)*. Superjet runs its luxury buses from Midan Saad Zaghloul only.

Superjet buses leave for Cairo (E£19 to E£21) and Cairo airport (E£24 to E£30) every half hour from 5.30 am to 9.30 pm. There's a daily service to Marsa Matruh (summer only) for E£22 at 7.15 am and 4 and 8 pm; Port Said (E£28) at 7.45 am; Hurghada (E£60) at 8 pm; and Sharm el-Sheikh (E£71) at 6.30 pm.

Next door is the West Delta Bus Co stand. You can buy tickets for same-day travel to Cairo and Marsa Matruh here, but if you want to book a seat for later on, or for services leaving from other stations, go to the office around the corner from the New Imperial restaurant.

West Delta's comfy buses to Cairo (E£15) and Cairo airport (E£20) run every hour from 5.30 am to 10 pm from Midan Saad Zaghloul. In summer, three buses leave here for Marsa Matruh (E£17; four hours) at 7 and 9 am and 3 pm.

West Delta and Superjet both run buses to Benghazi and Tripoli in Libya from Midan Saad Zaghloul.

In front of Misr railway station, the blue and white no-frills buses of the West Delta Bus Co depart for a variety of destinations. Buses to Cairo leave hourly from 7 am to 6 pm, and cost E£8 to E£10. There are also services to Sallum (the Libyan border), and to Siwa (E£13.50; nine hours) via Marsa Matruh at 10 am. On Saturday, Monday and Wednesday there's a second bus to Siwa for E£20. It has air-con and departs at noon, arriving in Siwa by 9 pm.

Train Cairo-bound trains leave Alexandria at least every hour. The longest trip can take five hours; the shortest about two hours. The direct trains to Cairo, some of which are Turbos, leave at 7 and 8 am and 2, 3, 6, 7 and 10.10 pm. They cost E£22/17. The 10.10 pm train (No 934) goes on to Luxor.

Two trains a day leave Alexandria for Marsa Matruh and take about eight hours. This is the painful way to go.

Service Taxi The service-taxi station is a sprawling mess opposite Misr railway station. The fares are E£8 to E£10 to Cairo or Marsa Matruh.

Boat There's one passenger boat linking Alexandria with Beirut (Lebanon), Lattakia (Syria) and Antalya (Turkey). Menatours (☎ 808407) on Midan Saad Zaghloul can provide you with more information and up-to-date schedules.

Getting Around

The Airport The airport is south-west of the city centre. To get there, you can take bus No 203 from Ramla station or No 703 from Midan Orabi. A taxi should cost about E£10.

Bus & Minibus Most of Alexandria's local buses leave from Midan Saad Zaghloul or adjacent Mahattat ar-Ramla, but some leave from Midan Orabi, Ras at-Tin and Misr railway station. Services operate from 5.30 am to 1 am the next morning. Single trips around Alexandria cost 10 to 25 pt, and 50 pt to the beaches of Agami and Hannoville.

Train The slow 3rd class train from Misr railway station to Abu Qir stops, among other places, at Sidi Gaber, Montazah and Maamoura. The fare is 40 pt.

Tram You can get to most places around central Alexandria by tram. Ramla station is the main tram station. Lime-yellow coloured trams go west from Ramla station: No 14 goes to Misr railway station and Moharram Bey; No 15 goes to the Mosque of Abu al-Abbas Mursi and Fort Qait Bey; and No 16 goes past Pompey's Pillar to Karmous station. Blue trams go east from Ramla: No 2 goes about two-thirds of the way to Montazah via Zizinia, Nos 3 and 7 to Sidi Gaber North; Nos 4 and 6 to Sidi Gaber South; and Nos 5 and 8 to San Stefano. Tram No 6 goes from Ras at-Tin to Moharram Bey.

Taxi A short trip, say from Midan Saad Zaghloul to Misr railway station, will cost E£1, and E£3 to E£4 is reasonable for a trip to the eastern beaches.

ROSETTA (RASHID)

The ancient city of Rosetta, also known by its newer name of Rashid, is 65 km east of Alexandria, where the western (Rosetta) branch of the Nile empties into the Mediterranean. Founded in the 9th century Rosetta is most famous for the Rosetta stone, an inscribed stone that was unearthed by Napoleon's soldiers in 1799. The basalt slab, which dates from about 196 BC, was inscribed in Egyptian hieroglyphs, demotic Egyptian and Greek. The combination of written languages enabled a Frenchman Jean-François Champollion to finally decipher the ancient Pharaonic language.

EL ALAMEIN

The beginning of General Montgomery's offensive on 23 October 1942 ruined Field Marshall Rommel's hopes of pushing his Afrika Korps through to the Suez Canal forever. Within two weeks he was on the run,

and El Alamein went down as the first great turning point of WWII. Today, a **war museum** and the Commonwealth, German and Italian **war cemeteries** mark the scene of one of the biggest tank battles in history.

Places to Stay & Eat

The *Al-Amana Hotel*, almost opposite the museum, has simple double rooms that are a damn sight better than the rooms in the resthouse down the road. For E£15 you'll get a double without bath, or E£20 with (though running water can be problematic). It can generally scratch up something to eat.

Getting There & Away

Bus West Delta Bus Co buses on route between Marsa Matruh and Alexandria usually stop at El Alamein (E£4). Note that the summer-time luxury bus services to Marsa Matruh generally do *not* stop at El Alamein. The trip from Alexandria is about 1½ hours; from Matruh 2½ hours.

Service Taxi Service taxis leave from the lot in front of Misr railway station, Alexandria, and cost about E£6. It's pretty easy to pick up one of these from El Alamein to get back to Alexandria.

MARSA MATRUH

The large waterfront town of Marsa Matruh, built around a charming bay of clear Mediterranean waters and clean white sandy beaches, is a popular summer destination for Egyptians.

Orientation

There are really only two streets in Marsa Matruh that you need to know: the Corniche, which runs right around the waterfront, and Sharia Iskendariyya (Alexandria), which runs perpendicular to the Corniche.

The more expensive hotels are along the Corniche. Others are dotted around the town, mostly not too far from Sharia Iskendariyya. The bulk of the restaurants and shops are on or around Sharia Iskendariyya.

Information

Passport Office The passport office is just off Sharia Iskendariyya, a couple of blocks in from the railway station.

Tourist Office Marsa Matruh's tourist office (☎ 931841) is on the ground floor of the Governorate building one block west of Sharia Iskendariyya, on the corner of the Corniche. It is open daily from 8.30 am to 6 pm (until 9 pm in summer).

Money You can change cash and cheques at the National Bank of Egypt, a few blocks west of Sharia Iskendariyya and in from the Corniche. You *might* be able to convince the Banque Misr branch on Sharia al-Gala'a to accept Visa or MasterCard for a cash advance.

Post & Communications The GPO is on Sharia ash-Shataa, one block south of the Corniche and two blocks east of Sharia Iskendariyya. The 24 hour telephone office is across the street from the GPO. The telephone code for Marsa Matruh is 03.

Rommel Museum

Set in the caves Rommel used as his head-quarters during part of the El Alamein campaign, this pretty poor excuse for a museum contains a few photos, a bust of the Desert Fox and what is purported to be Rommel's great coat. It's closed in winter. Nearby is **Rommel's Beach**, where he used to take a break from warring.

Folklore Museum

This one room museum is just round the corner from the tourist office (where you must ask for the key). On display is a Bedouin tent and bridal costumes from Siwa. Entry is free.

Beaches

The best of the beaches are outside the grotty town. The pick is **Agiba**, 24 km west of Marsa Matruh. A pick-up goes out there. You could also try **Cleopatra's Bath**, 14 km to the west.

Places to Stay

Camping It's best to inform the folks at the tourist office if you plan to camp along the coast or at Rommel's Beach.

Hostels The *Youth Hostel* (☎ 932331), a couple of blocks south of the Awam Mosque, is OK. Members pay E£5.10 for a comfortable enough bunk bed in a cramped room of six or eight.

Hotels A popular backpackers' stop is the *Ghazala Hotel* (☎ 933519) just off Sharia Iskendariyya; the entrance is sandwiched between some shops and is easily over-looked. It charges E£7.50 a head for a basic but clean bed.

Queen Mary is a four storey pension (there's no sign or telephone) one block back from the water next to the Awam Mosque. In winter, it has doubles with private bathrooms for E£15 (prices are five times higher in summer).

The *Dareen Hotel* (☎ 935607), near the road to Sallum and Siwa, has reasonably comfortable rooms with private bath and breakfast for E£26/40 (E£10 more in summer).

On Sharia Iskendariyya is the *Riviera Palace* (☎ 933045). In winter, rooms cost E£36/55 without breakfast; in summer you must also pay half-board, which comes to E£75/132.

There's a string of places on the waterfront heading west of Sharia Iskendariyya. The first two, the *Royal Palace Hotel* (☎ 934295) and the *Arous al-Bahr* (☎ 934419) are both quite reasonable with singles/doubles for about E£35/60.

Places to Eat

The *Panayotis Greek Restaurant* is on Sharia Iskendariyya. It serves a decent plate of fish for E£18 and calamari for E£15. You can also get a Stella beer here, or take it away. Across the road is the *Alex Tourist Restaurant*, where you can also down a Stella. It serves kebabs, kofta and the like. Next door is a small pizza place with a shwarma takeaway stand. The pizzas are OK, and cost E£10 with the lot. Next to this is an unassuming little fuul place. A filling meal of fuul, ta'amiyya, tahina, salad and bread costs all of E£1.70.

For excellent pizza (summer only), head down to the Corniche. Just after the Negresco Hotel you'll find *Pizza Gaby*, where most of the pizzas cost around E£10.

Getting There & Away
Air There are three flights a week to Cairo for about E£350.

Bus Marsa Matruh has two bus stations: one near the tourist office; and the other, the main station, up near the railway line. Superjet buses to Alexandria (E£22, summer only) leave at 8 am, noon, 3 and 5 pm. Also during summer only, Superjet has three buses to Cairo (E£35) at 8 and 11 am and 3.30 pm. All of these buses depart from the bus station near the tourist office.

West Delta Bus Co has buses to Alexandria (E£17; four hours) at 9 am and 3 pm, and to Cairo (E£30 to E£35; five hours) leaving at 2.30 pm throughout the year; as well as at 8.30 am and 3.30 and 5 pm in summer only. These all leave from the bus station near the tourist office.

From the main bus station, there is a daily bus (without air-con) to Cairo (E£18) at 7.30 am, and at least nine buses make the run to Alexandria (E£9 to E£11).

Buses for Siwa (E£7 to E£10; five hours) leave at 7.30 am and 3.30 pm, and on Saturday, Monday and Wednesday at 5.30 pm. Buses for Sallum (E£7 to E£8; 3½ hours) leave at 7 am, 3.30 and 5 pm.

Train Two trains a day leave for Alexandria at 4 and 9.20 pm. Second class air-con costs E£17, and ordinary 2nd/3rd class tickets are E£6.40/2.80. The trip takes anywhere from six to seven hours.

Service Taxi The service-taxi lot is across from the main bus station. The fare to Sallum is E£10. Service taxis run to Alexandria (E£8) and sometimes Siwa (E£10).

Getting Around
Caretas, or donkey carts, are the most common form of transport around the streets of Marsa Matruh. A ride across town should cost no more than E£1. From the town centre to Rommel's Museum is E£1.50.

In summer there are supposedly regular buses to Cleopatra's Bath and Agiba beach. Failing this, you can get a pick-up to Agiba from in front of the Ramses Hotel for E£2 a person.

SALLUM
Some 214 km west of Marsa Matruh, Sallum is the last town before the Libyan border. There's not much to it, but you can visit a Commonwealth **war cemetery** or go for a swim at one of the outlying **beaches**. There are a couple of small hotels and cafes.

Getting There & Away
Buses for Marsa Matruh (E£7 to E£8; 3½ hours) depart three times a day; some of these go on to Alexandria (E£16). A service taxi to Marsa Matruh will cost about E£10. The train from Marsa Matruh is apparently reserved for military purposes alone.

Libya The border crossing point of Amsaad, just north of the Halfaya Pass, is 12 km on from Sallum. Service taxis run up the mountain between the town and the Egyptian side of the crossing for E£2 to E£3. Once through passport control and customs on both sides (you walk through), you can get a taxi to Al-Burdi. From there you can get buses to Tobruk and Benghazi.

The Suez Canal

The Suez Canal, one of the greatest feats of modern engineering, links the Mediterranean with the northern end of the Red Sea. Opened in 1869 the canal severed Asia from Africa, and is now an important source of revenue for Egypt in the form of fees charged for its use by the world's tankers.

The three principal cities along the canal

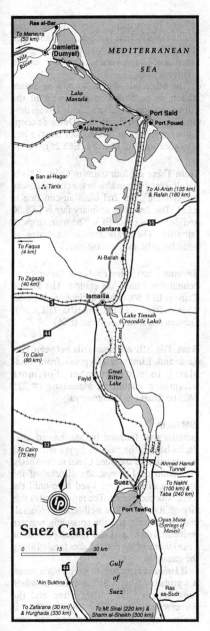

are not top of the list of tourist attractions, but the sight of tankers negotiating the canal is well worth the effort of getting to Port Said or Suez. Port Said and, to a lesser extent Ismailia, are full of some of the best examples of late 19th and early 20th century colonial-style architecture, but Suez, victim of the wars with Israel, has little attraction. Because it is an important transport hub, however, many people end up there, if only to change buses.

PORT SAID

A city of 400,000 people, Port Said, founded in 1859, is a duty-free zone. It is effectively built on an island, connected to the mainland by a bridge to the south and a causeway to the west. Ferries cross the canal to Port Fouad, a civil servants' town built in the 1920s.

Information

The tourist office, telephone exchange and various banks are on Sharia Palestine, which runs north-south along the canal. Other banks, Thomas Cook and the GPO are on or around Sharia al-Gomhurriya, which runs parallel to Sharia Palestine, a couple of blocks in.

Customs Because Port Said is a duty-free zone, there are customs controls on the way in and out of Port Said, and at the railway and bus stations. If you are shopping, check before you buy whether the items will be subject to duties.

Things to See

You can't miss **Suez Canal House**, the Moorish-style building right on the canal. Unfortunately, you can't go inside. Many canal-side streets are lined with four storey buildings with wooden balconies and verandas. The **National Museum** has a good collection of artefacts from all stages of Egyptian history. It merits more visitors than it gets. Admission is E£6. The **Military Museum** is west of the City Council buildings. To cool off, you can use one of the public beaches on the Mediterranean coast.

EGYPT

Places to Stay & Eat

The *Youth Hostel* (☎ (066) 228702), near the stadium, costs E£3.25 with membership card and E£1 more without. It has basic bunks in rooms of about 20 beds.

The area around the canal is crawling with little dives. The very basic *Pension Rivoli*, on a lane off Sharia al-Gomhurriya, charges E£5 a night for a bed. A much better deal is the *Akri Hotel* (☎ (066) 221013) at 24 Sharia al-Gomhurriya. It has clean singles and doubles without bath for about E£15/21. The rooms have a bit of charm and are nicely furnished. The *El-Ghazal Hotel* at 42 Sharia 23rd of July has doubles for E£16.50, but tends to fill up in summer.

The *Hotel de la Poste* (☎ (066) 224048), on Sharia al-Gomhurriya, has a fading but renovated elegance. Singles/doubles on the street with bath and balconies cost E£33/40. Rooms off the street cost E£22/27.

A notable fish restaurant is *Galal*, on the corner of Sharia al-Gomhurriya and Sharia Gaberti, one block from the Hotel de la Poste.

Around the corner from Hotel Akri is the very cheap and very good *Restaurant Soufer*, where arguably the best houmos in Egypt is prepared.

Across the road from Hotel Akri is *Reana*, a Chinese-Korean restaurant, and *Cecil*, a spit-and-sawdust bar, which is open until quite late.

On a street about three blocks north of Sharia al-Gomhurriya there's a lively fruit and vegetable market, as well as the popular *New Rex* bakery.

Getting There & Away

Bus There are three bus stations. The Superjet buses to Cairo (E£15; three hours) leave 11 times a day from in front of the railway station. It also has a bus to Alexandria (E£28; four hours) at 3.30 pm. Book ahead.

The East Delta Bus Co runs buses to destinations outside the Delta (and Tanta in the Delta for some reason) from its terminal near the Farial Gardens. Buses to Cairo (E£10 to E£16) leave hourly from 6 am to 6 pm. There are four buses to Alexandria (E£15 to E£20),

at 7 and 10 am, and 1.30 and 4.30 pm. Other destinations include Ismailia (E£5) and Suez (E£9). For Al-Arish, you must first go to Ismailia or Qantara and take a bus or service taxi from there.

The other bus station, known as Salam station, is on Sharia an-Nasr, west of the railway station. It predominantly covers destinations throughout the Delta (except Tanta). Every hour (on the half hour) a bus also goes south to Qantara (E£2.25).

Train There are four trains to Cairo. This is the slowest, but can also be the cheapest, way to get there. The 2nd class air-con fare is E£14. The 2nd class ordinary fare is E£5.50 and 3rd class costs E£3. The train stops in Ismailia. There are five other trains to Ismailia only. Tickets cost E£2.30/1.

Service Taxi Service taxis leave from behind the Salam bus station. The fare to Cairo is E£7.50. Other destinations include: Alexandria (E£11); Ismailia (E£3.50); Qantara (E£2.50); and Suez (E£6).

Boat The MS *Atalante* sails between Port Said and Limassol (Cyprus) from mid-March to mid-November. For more information enquire at Menatours (☎ 225 742) on Sharia al-Gomhurriya.

ISMAILIA

Ismailia was founded by and named after Pasha Ismail, the ruler of Egypt during the construction of the Suez Canal in the 1860s. Ferdinand de Lesseps, the director of the Suez Canal Company, lived here until the canal was completed. The railway splits this city of 300,000 into a well-tended colonial-era eastern side and the sprawling western residential districts. Lake Timsah (Crocodile Lake) is one of the Bitter Lakes located along the canal.

If Ismailia can claim to have a main street, it's probably Sharia Sultan Hussein, which runs between the railway line and the Sweetwater Canal. The tourist office is useless here. Banks, telephone and post office can all be found near the railway station.

Things to See & Do

The small **Ismailia Museum** has an interesting collection of ancient artefacts. The house where Ferdinand de Lesseps lived is not open to the public, but is one of many buildings built here by Europeans that are worth a look. You might want to spend time on some of the **beaches** of Lake Timsah.

Places to Stay & Eat

The relatively new *Youth Hostel* (☎ (064) 322850), on a beach around Lake Timsah, has rooms with two/four/six beds for E£18/15/8 per person, including breakfast.

The *Hotel des Voyageurs*, on Sharia Ahmed Orabi, a short way in from the railway station, offers basic but quite acceptable lodgings for E£10/16. The *Isis Hotel* (☎ (064) 227821) on Midan Orabi, opposite the railway station, has clean and comfortable rooms with bath for E£18/25.

The *Crocodile Inn* (☎ (064) 331555), on the corner of Sharia Saad Zaghloul and Sharia Sultan Hussein, offers somewhat musty singles/doubles for E£45/61.

Around the corner from the Hotel des Voyageurs is an excellent little ta'amiyya place; you can dine in or take away. There are some cheap eateries in the mall off Sharia Sultan Hussein. *George's* and the *Nefertiti*, both on Sharia Sultan Hussein, serve fish and meat dishes for about E£10 to E£15.

Getting There & Away

Bus You can get buses to Cairo from two bus stations. On Midan Orabi, the West Delta Bus Co has frequent departures for E£5. Buses leave for Alexandria (E£12) at 7 am and 2.30 pm.

Buses for Cairo also leave from the main bus station (East Delta Bus Co) on the other side of the railway line, with the same frequency and at the same price. Other destinations serviced from here include: Al-Arish (E£7); Port Said (E£5); Suez (E£3); and Sharm el-Sheikh (E£15).

Train There are about 10 trains from Ismailia to Cairo (three hours); tickets cost E£8/4.20/1.80 for 2nd class air-con, 2nd class ordinary and 3rd class. To Port Said (1½ hours) it costs E£6/2.30/1.

There are at least nine 2nd/3rd class trains to Suez for E£2/1.

Service Taxi Service taxis depart from the lot across the road from the East Delta Bus Co station. Destinations include: Al-Arish (E£6); Cairo (E£5); Port Said (E£3.50); and Suez (E£3).

SUEZ

Suez, which sprawls around from the entrance of the canal at Port Tawfiq down along the west side of the gulf, suffered badly in the 1967 and 1973 wars, and is above all a transit point for tankers, pilgrims to Mecca and people travelling between Sinai and the rest of the country. It's a good place to watch the passing tankers.

Information

The tourist office is in Port Tawfiq, the GPO on Sharia Hoda Shaarawi and the telephone exchange on Sharia Saad Zaghloul. Most banks have branches around town.

Places to Stay & Eat

The *Youth Hostel* (☎ (062) 221945) is on the main road heading west out of Suez. It's cheap (E£5 with membership card or E£6 without), grungy and a long way from anything.

In the centre of town, there's a handful of budget hotels clustered around Sharias at-Tahrir and Talaat Harb. One of the cheapest is the *Haramein Hotel* (☎ (062) 320051) near the end of Sharia at-Tahrir. Dingy rooms cost E£5/6. Marginally better is the *Hotel Al-Madena* (☎ (062) 224056), which charges E£7/12 for singles/doubles.

The *Star Hotel* (☎ (062) 228737) on Sharia Banque Misr has quite decent rooms with fans for E£9/12 without bath. Just up the street at No 21 is the *Sina Hotel* (☎ (062) 220394), which has singles/doubles/triples for E£12.30/20.50/30.

The *White House Hotel* (☎ (062) 227599) at 322 Sharia as-Salaam is a clean, respectable and popular place, although a bit worn around the edges. Singles/doubles with showers and breakfast are E£35/45.

On the eating front, there are cheap ta'amiyya and shwarma stands in the area bounded by Sharias Talaat Harb, Abdul as-Sarawat, Khidr and Banque Misr. The spotlessly clean *Fresh Food Suez* snack bar on Sharia Abdul as-Sarawat sells hamburgers for E£1.

The restaurant in the *White House Hotel* offers a wide range of meat and fish dishes for about E£11, and soups and salad for E£1.50 to E£3. Beers cost E£6.

The *Fish Restaurant*, near the White House Hotel, serves large meals for E£20. Almost next door is the cheaper *Riviera*.

Getting There & Away

Bus All buses leave from Arbaeen bus station on Sharia al-Faarz, near the centre of town. Most tickets should be booked well ahead. Buses to Cairo (E£5) and Ismailia (E£4.50) leave frequently. There are three buses directly to Port Said (E£9) at 7 and 9 am and 3.30 pm. There are six services a day to Hurghada (E£17; five hours). Most of these buses go on to Qena (E£22 to E£38) via Port Safaga. At 10.30 am there is a bus to Aswan (E£26; 15 hours) via Luxor (E£24; 10 hours). There is another bus to Luxor at 6 pm (E£31).

The bus to Nuweiba (E£25) via Taba (E£30) leaves at 3 pm. Buses to Sharm el-Sheikh (E£20; 5½ hours) depart at 11 am and 3 pm, and go on to Dahab (E£22; 6½ hours) and Nuweiba (E£20). There's a bus for St Catherine's (E£17; five hours) via Wadi Feran at 11 am.

Train The railway station is a good couple of km west of the Arbaeen bus station. Six Cairo-bound trains that only make it as far as 'Ain Shams depart here. Second class is E£2.60 and 3rd class E£1.05. There are also trains to Ismailia and Port Said.

Service Taxi Service taxis go to many of the destinations serviced by buses and trains. The fares to Cairo, Hurghada, Ismailia and Port Said are E£5, E£20, E£3 and E£6 respectively.

Boat It is possible to travel by boat between Suez, Jeddah and Port Sudan. The Suez-Jeddah leg of the trip takes about three days; the Jeddah-Port Sudan section is another 24 hours. If you have a transit visa for Saudi Arabia, you will not be allowed off the ship during that time.

For more information, enquire at Misr Travel (☎ (062) 223949) or at the Wadi Al-Nil Company (☎ (062) 228849) at 2 Sharia el-Gasha, both in Port Tawfiq.

The Red Sea Coast

Egypt's Red Sea coast stretches for more than 800 km from Suez to the village of Bir Shalatayn near the disputed border with Sudan. Famed for its brilliant turquoise waters, splendid coral and exotic creatures of the deep, the Red Sea coast attracts more than 200,000 tourists annually. It is Egypt's most rapidly developing region. Unfortunately, much of the development has gone unchecked, resulting in damage to the coral reefs around the region's premier resort town, Hurghada.

Warning Although some of the coast is said to be mined, most beaches seem to be OK. If you have any doubts, ask the local authorities.

MONASTERIES OF ST ANTHONY & ST PAUL

The Coptic Christian monasteries of St Anthony and St Paul, about 150 km south of Suez, are open for day trips between 9 am and 5 pm. It's possible to stay overnight at either, but if you plan to stay at St Paul's you'll need prior permission from its residence (☎ 590 0218) in Cairo.

The two monasteries are 82 km apart by road, or 35 km as the crow flies. Both were

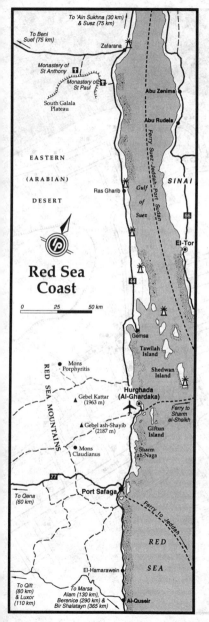

To 'Ain Sukhna (30 km)
& Suez (75 km)

To Beni
Suef (75 km)

Zafarana

Monastery of
St Anthony

Monastery of
St Paul

South Galala
Plateau

Abu Zenima

Abu Rudeis

EASTERN

(ARABIAN)

DESERT

Ras Gharib

SINAI

Gulf
of
Suez

66

El-Tor

**Red Sea
Coast**

0   25   50 km

Gemsa

Tawilah
Island

Shedwan
Island

RED SEA MOUNTAINS

Mons
Porphyritis

Gebel Kattar
(1963 m)

Hurghada
(Al-Ghardaka)

Gebel ash-Shayib
(2187 m)

Giftun
Island

Mons
Claudianus

Sharm
an-Naga

Ferry to Sharm
el-Sheikh

77

Port Safaga

To Qena
(60 km)

RED

SEA

El-Hamarawein

To Qift
(80 km)
& Luxor
(110 km)

To Marsa
Alam (130 km),
Berenice (290 km) &
Bir Shalatayn (365 km)

Al-Quseir

Ferry Suez-Jeddah-Port Sudan

Ferry to Jeddah

EGYPT

built in the 4th century AD and consist of
chapels, churches, bakeries and the like. St
Paul's, 15 km east of the Hurghada to Suez
road and 25 km south of Zafarana, is the
more interesting of the two. St Anthony's is
south of the Zafarana to Beni Suef road.
There are occasional tours from Hurghada.
Otherwise you'll have to use public transport
between Hurghada and Suez, and then
attempt to hitch (which may not be an easy
task).

HURGHADA (AL-GHARDAKA)

The only attraction of this one-time fishing
village is the water, or rather what's in it. The
town and the coast for 20 km south resemble
a kind of permanent building site – every sq
cm of beach will soon be backed by some
hotel resort – and the disease is spreading
down the coast.

The main town area, Ad-Dahar, where
virtually all the budget accommodation is
located, is at the northern end. South is the
port area of Sigala and then the resort strip.
The Suez-Port Safaga road is called Sharia
an-Nasr as it passes through Ad-Dahar.

Despite being a popular resort, Hurghada
is still a traditional town and local sensibilities must be considered when you move
away from the beach area. Don't wander
around the market quarter in Ad-Dahar in
shorts and skimpy tops.

Information

The passport and registration office is near
the northern exit of Ad-Dahar. The tourist
office (☎ (065) 546513), just off Sharia an-
Nasr beside the Ritz Hotel, is open daily,
except Friday, from 8.30 am to 3 pm.

Banque Misr, the National Bank of Egypt
and the Bank of Alexandria all have branches
along Sharia an-Nasr in Ad-Dahar. Thomas
Cook has a new office on Sheraton Rd in
Sigala.

The GPO is on Sharia an-Nasr, towards
the southern end of Ad-Dahar. The telephone
office is a 20 minute walk north along the
same road.

The new Aboudi Bookshop, opposite
Market Place in Ad-Dahar, has foreign and

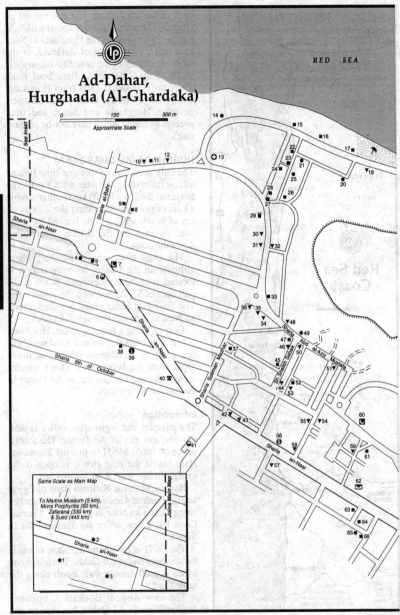

RED SEA

Ad-Dahar,
Hurghada (Al-Ghardaka)

0   150   300 m

Approximate Scale

See Inset

Sharia al-Bahr

Sharia an-Nasr

Sharia an-Nasr

Sharia 6th of October

Sharia an-Nasr

Sharia Suliman Mazhar

Sharia Sheikh Sabak

Abd al-Aziz Mustafa

Same Scale as Main Map

To Marine Museum (5 km),
Mons Porphyritis (60 km),
Zafarana (330 km)
& Suez (445 km)

Sharia an-Nasr

Joins Main Map

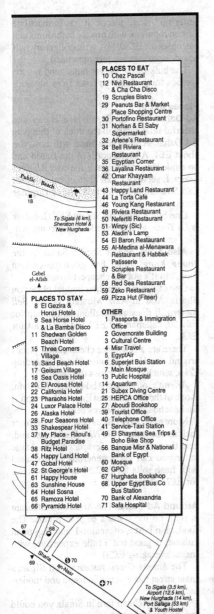

PLACES TO EAT
10 Chez Pascal
12 Nivi Restaurant
   & Cha Cha Disco
19 Scruples Bistro
29 Peanuts Bar & Market
   Place Shopping Centre
30 Portofino Restaurant
31 Norhan & El Saby
   Supermarket
32 Arlene's Restaurant
34 Bell Riviera
   Restaurant
35 Egyptian Corner
36 Layalina Restaurant
42 Omar Khayyam
   Restaurant
43 Happy Land Restaurant
44 La Torta Cafe
46 Young Kang Restaurant
48 Riviera Restaurant
50 Nefertiti Restaurant
51 Winpy (Sic)
53 Aladin's Lamp
54 El Baron Restaurant
55 Al-Medina al-Menawara
   Restaurant & Habbak
   Patisserie
57 Scruples Restaurant
   & Bar
58 Red Sea Restaurant
59 Zeko Restaurant
69 Pizza Hut (Fiteer)

PLACES TO STAY
8 El Gezira &
   Horus Hotels
9 Sea Horse Hotel
   & La Bamba Disco
11 Shedwan Golden
   Beach Hotel
15 Three Corners
   Village
16 Sand Beach Hotel
17 Geisum Village
18 Sea Oasis Hotel
20 El Arousa Hotel
22 California Hotel
23 Pharaohs Hotel
24 Luxor Palace Hotel
26 Alaska Hotel
28 Four Seasons Hotel
37 My Place - Raoul's
   Budget Paradise
38 Ritz Hotel
45 Happy Land Hotel
47 Gobal Hotel
52 St George's Hotel
61 Happy House
63 Sunshine House
64 Hotel Sosna
65 Ramoza Hotel
66 Pyramids Hotel

OTHER
1 Passports & Immigration
   Office
2 Governorate Building
3 Cultural Centre
4 Misr Travel
5 EgyptAir
6 Superjet Bus Station
7 Main Mosque
13 Public Hospital
14 Aquarium
21 Subex Diving Centre
25 HEPCA Office
27 Aboudi Bookshop
39 Tourist Office
40 Telephone Office
41 Service-Taxi Station
49 El Shaymaa Sea Trips &
   Boho Bike Shop
56 Banque Misr & National
   Bank of Egypt
60 Mosque
62 GPO
67 Hurghada Bookshop
68 Upper Egypt Bus Co
   Bus Station
70 Bank of Alexandria
71 Safa Hospital

Public Beach
18

To Sigala (6 km),
Sheraton Hotel &
New Hurghada

Gebel
el-Afish

67
68

Sharia
an-Nasr

69
70
71

To Sigala (3.5 km),
Airport (12.5 km),
New Hurghada (14 km),
Port Safaga (53 km)
& Youth Hostel

Egyptian literature, maps, guidebooks and foreign newspapers.

There are two hospitals in Ad-Dahar: the private Safa hospital is near the Upper Egypt Bus Co station while the public hospital (☎ (065) 546740) is near Shedwan Golden Beach Hotel. Emergency telephone numbers include: ambulance (☎ 546490), police (☎ (065) 546723) and tourist police (☎ (065) 546765).

Water Sports

Hurghada is crawling with dive clubs and agents for snorkelling trips.

One of the popular snorkelling day trips is to Giftun Island, which costs between E£25 to E£40. Some of the reputable dive clubs take snorkellers out to better sites and, by going with one of them, you're almost assured of reef protection practices being put into action.

Diving trips of one day or more are possible. Subex (☎ (065) 547593) in Ad-Dahar is highly recommended for shorter trips, and Rudi Kneip (☎ (065) 442960) in Sigala has years of experience taking diving safaris.

When diving or snorkelling, take care not to touch or stand on coral or fish, and to be aware of potentially dangerous fish.

To get a rough idea of prices, see Diving in the Activities section of Facts for the Visitor earlier in this chapter.

EGYPT

Choosing a Dive Club

Many of the dive companies that have sprung up in Hurghada in recent years are simply out to make a fast buck, and care little about reef conservation or safety measures for divers. Some of these outfits don't even have the minimum of safety equipment – such as a dive boat fitted with a VHF radio and oxygen for handling decompression accidents – and they employ dive instructors with very little experience. The Hurghada Environmental Protection and Conservation Association (HEPCA), located just behind the Subex dive club in Ad-Dahar, can provide you with a list of recommended clubs. ■

Organised Tours

Travel agents around town organise day trips to Cairo (E£174), Luxor (E£250), the Monasteries of St Anthony and St Paul (E£150), and the sites of two Roman settlements, Mons Claudianus and Mons Porphyritis (E£120).

Places to Stay

Hostels Hurghada's old *Youth Hostel* (☎ (065) 442432) is on the resort strip, opposite the Sonesta Beach Resort. It costs E£8 a night (E£9 for non-members). By the time you read this guide, a large new hostel should be operating about five km north of Ad-Dahar.

Hotels Hurghada is full of places to bed down. Captain Mohammed's *Happy House*, on the main square by the mosque in the centre of Ad-Dahar, is a clean basic place to stay for E£7 per person. Near the main Coptic church is the homey *My Place – Raoul's Budget Paradise*. It's not a bad deal at E£5 a head.

The *Hotel Sosna* (☎ (065) 446647) is a bit over the top, with clean rooms for E£20/30 without bath, or E£25/35 with. Better value is the *Shakespear Hotel* (☎ (065) 446256) at the top end of Sharia Abd al-Aziz Mustafa. Its very spacious, comfortable doubles with communal baths cost E£22.

On the slope behind the Aboudi Bookshop in Ad-Dahar is the comfortable *Alaska* (☎ (065) 548413), which charges E£8.50 per person plus E£2 for breakfast. Close by is the small *Luxor Palace Hotel* (☎ (065) 549260), with singles/doubles for E£10/20, breakfast included.

The *Sea Horse Hotel* (☎ (065) 54804), north of the main mosque, is an old but quite OK three-star place. In winter, rooms costs E£98/110 with breakfast, but come down about E£25 in summer. The nearby *El Gezira Hotel* (☎ (065) 547785) is quite a good deal, if you don't mind taking half board (obligatory), with single/double/triple rooms for E£68/88/114.

The *El Arousa Hotel* (☎ (065) 548434) near the waterfront in Ad-Dahar is one of the better mid-range places. It has immaculate air-con rooms all with private bathrooms and balconies for E£80/140, with obligatory half board. Bookings are recommended.

The bulk of the bigger hotels and resorts spreads south along the coast from Sigala.

Places to Eat

Ad-Dahar The *El Baron* is a cheap and cheerful little eatery in the thick of things in Ad-Dahar. A satisfying meal will cost you about E£4. A block north of the Baron and on a side lane to the right is the cosy *Aladin's Lamp*. It serves a small plate of calamari for E£5.50 and chicken for E£8, and can arrange beers.

One block north on Sharia Sheikh Sabak is *La Torta*, a pristine little cafe serving pastries and cakes.

Also along Sharia Sheikh Sabak is the *Young Kang* which has good far-eastern food, but it's not the cheapest around.

One of the most popular budget places on Sharia Abd al-Aziz Mustafa is the *Bell Riviera*. It does an excellent lentil soup for E£1.50, calamari for E£9 and breakfast for E£3.

There are a few other cheap eating places around the Happy House Hotel, including *Zeko*, which is just across the square.

Arlene's, on Sharia Abd al-Aziz Mustafa, is one of the few places in Egypt where you'll find nachos. It also serves beer.

More expensive places near the waterfront include the rather chic *Nivi Restaurant* and, near the public beach, *Scruples Bistro*. At the latter you can get a generous tahina salad with fresh rolls for E£2.50 and sandwiches for E£7; a beer is E£5.

Around Ad-Dahar The *Al-Sakia* restaurant is right on the water's edge at Sigala. The food, a mixture of seafood and Egyptian cuisine, is good but a little expensive, with mains averaging E£20.

The *Samos* Greek restaurant on Sigala's main street has a versatile menu and moderate prices.

For really cheap fare in Sigala you could try the kushari and ta'amiyya places just up from Samos or, better still, *Baracoda* (sic) near Thomas Cook. This tiny place serves passable pizzas for E£4.

A couple of km along the road, past the Moon Valley Village, is the best located *Felfela* restaurant in the country. Sitting on a rise and gentle bend on the coastline, it is a splendid place for a modestly priced meal.

Entertainment

The *Cha Cha Disco* next to the Nivi Restaurant in Ad-Dahar usually has a happy hour from 10 pm. The *La Bamba Disco*, at the Sea Horse Hotel, is one of the *in* places and has a E£35 minimum charge.

If it's just a beer you're after, try the new *Peanuts Bar* opposite the Aboudi Bookshop in Ad-Dahar. It's open 24 hours and offers unlimited unshelled peanuts and pricey German and local beers.

Getting There & Away

Air From Hurghada, EgyptAir has daily flights to Cairo (E£391) plus two flights per week to Aswan (E£323, via Luxor), Luxor (E£163) and Sharm el-Sheikh (E£286).

Bus Superjet's bus terminal is near the main mosque in Ad-Dahar. It has buses to Cairo (E£40 to E£45; six hours) at noon, 2.30 and 5 pm, and a daily bus to Alexandria (seven hours; E£60) at 2.30 pm.

The Upper Egypt Bus Co operates from the main bus station at the southern end of Ad-Dahar. It runs buses almost hourly to Cairo (E£25 to E£40; six hours) from 6 am to midnight; some of them stop in Suez. There are other buses bound only for Suez (E£17; five hours) leaving at 7, 9.30, 10 and 10.30 am, and 1 and 3 pm. About 10 buses a day go to Qena (E£8; three hours). Buses leave also to Luxor (E£8; five hours) at 6 am, noon and 4 pm; to Aswan (E£27; seven hours) at 3.30 pm; to Bir Shalatayn via Al-Quseir (E£7) and Marsa Alam at 7 am; and to Beni Suef, Al-Minya (E£24), Sohag and Asyut (E£16).

Service Taxi The service-taxi station is near the telephone office. Taxis go to Al-Quseir

(E£10); Cairo (E£30, six hours); Port Safaga (E£5); Qena (E£10); and Suez (E£20; 3½ to four hours).

Boat One vessel plies the waters from Hurghada to Sharm el-Sheikh, departing Sunday, Tuesday and Thursday from Hurghada. It's wise to book ahead. You can do this at El Shaymaa Sea Trips (☎ (065) 546901) on Sharia Abd al-Aziz Mustafa, Ad-Dahar. The trip costs E£100 one way and the boat departs from the port in Sigala sometime between 9 and 10 am. The voyage takes seven hours and it can be rough. At the time of writing, there were rumours that a second boat would be operating, in which case there would be almost daily voyages.

Getting Around

The Airport A taxi fare from the airport, which is close to the resort strip, to Ad-Dahar is E£10.

Bus In the morning, microbuses full of day labourers go south to the resorts for about E£1. Throughout the day, microbuses regularly run to New Hurghada, as far south as the InterContinental for E£1.

Taxi Taxis will take you as far south as the Sheraton for about E£10 (or more if there are plenty of tourists around). Taxi drivers in this area are, appropriately enough, a school of sharks.

Bicycle Bicycles can be rented in town for E£1/10 per hour/day.

PORT SAFAGA

Port Safaga, 53 km south of Hurghada, is first and foremost a port for the export of phosphates, but the hotel plague is here too. The main waterfront road, Sharia al-Gomhurriya, has most of the services you might need, including bus station and service-taxi lot, banks, GPO and telephone exchange.

There's only one cheap place to stay here, the *Maka Hotel*, at the northern end of town. A string of posh resorts is a few km north of town.

Getting There & Away

Bus Five buses a day go to Cairo (E£25 to E£40), stopping en route in Suez (E£35). There are seven buses to Hurghada (E£2.50 to E£5) and two to Al-Quseir (E£8; at 5 am and 2 pm). To Marsa Alam and Bir Shalatayn, there are buses on Tuesday, Thursday and Sunday at about noon. There are more or less regular services to Aswan (E£30), Luxor (E£17) and Qena (E£10).

Service Taxi The taxis run to Al-Quseir (E£3.50, try early in the morning), Hurghada (E£5; 40 minutes) and Qena E£8.

Boat Ferries sail daily to Duba (E£100 deck class; seven hours) and twice a week to Jeddah (E£200; 30 hours), both in Saudi Arabia.

AL-QUSEIR

A medieval port town of 4000 inhabitants, Al-Quseir is 85 km south of Port Safaga. Until the 10th century it was one of the most important exit points for pilgrims travelling to Mecca. There's not much to do but explore some of the **beaches** out of town on a hire bicycle.

Places to Stay & Eat

The obvious choice for those on a tight budget is the *Sea Princess Hotel* (☎ (088) 430044), just south of the bus station. Small cabin-like singles/doubles with fan cost E£12/20.

There are a few ta'amiyya and fish joints nearby and around the bus station.

Getting There & Away

Bus There is a bus to Cairo (E£42; 11 hours) via Port Safaga, Hurghada and Suez which leaves at 5 am. The bus to Marsa Alam (E£5) and beyond leaves Tuesday, Thursday and Sunday at 1.30 pm. There are two connections to Qena (E£6.50; four hours) at 7 am and 12.30 pm.

Service Taxi The officially prescribed fares are: Cairo E£30; Hurghada E£10; Luxor E£10; Port Safaga E£3.50; Qena E£8; Qift E£7; and Suez E£25.

MARSA ALAM

Marsa Alam is a fishing village 132 km south of Al-Quseir. A road also connects the village with Edfu, 230 km across the desert to the west. There are some quiet beaches around and, if you have the equipment, some reasonable diving.

Places to Stay & Eat

You can ask for a room at a mining exploration company's resthouse (*istiraha*) on the northern edge of town. The only alternative, apart from simply pitching a tent somewhere on the beach, is the *Beach Safari Camp* (☎ 364 7970) draped around two azure bays about seven km north of town. It has large tents for E£35 per person per night with breakfast, or E£65 with half board.

At the junction, there are a couple of cafes where you may be able to get ta'amiyya, as well as a pair of grocery shops with scant supplies. The only other option is the *Kavaterya* (read 'cafeteria'), next to the service station, which serves stale sandwiches, packet soups and frozen hamburgers. There's a bakery next door.

Getting There & Away

The bus to Aswan (E£10.50) via Edfu (E£7) leaves from the cafes at the junction at about 7 am. There's a bus to Al-Quseir (E£5) at 8 am on Monday, Wednesday and Saturday.

BERENICE

The military centre and small port of Berenice, 150 km south of Marsa Alam, was founded in 275 BC by Ptolemy II Euergetes I and was an important trading post until the 5th century AD. Near the town, the ruins of the **Temple of Seramis** can be seen.

BIR SHALATAYN

This tiny village 90 km south of Berenice marks the administrative boundary between Egypt and Sudan, although Egypt at least considers the political boundary to be another 175 km south, beyond the town of

Halaib, once an important Red Sea port but long fallen into obscurity.

Sinai

It was in Sinai, on Mt Sinai, that Moses received the Ten Commandments, but over the centuries the sixth has been broken here with monotonous regularity. Armies have crossed backwards and forwards, most recently from Israel, which occupied the peninsula from 1967 until 1982, when, under the Camp David Agreement, it agreed to pull out. Wedged between Africa and Asia, its northern coast is bordered by the Mediterranean Sea, and its southern peninsula by the Red Sea gulfs of Aqaba and Suez.

The area is populated mainly by Bedouin, although Egyptians are settling here, mostly to take advantage of the tourist trade.

The splendours of the underwater world of the Red Sea and the grandeur of the desert mountains are Sinai's main attractions.

Information

Visas If you're entering Egypt from Israel, or by air or sea, and intend only to visit the coastal resorts of eastern Sinai from Taba down to Sharm el-Sheikh, you can get a 14 day pass on arrival. See the earlier Facts for the Visitor and Getting There & Away sections in this chapter for more information on crossing from Israel into Egypt.

Warning Despite what local tour operators may tell you, some areas of Sinai still contain land mines leftover from the wars with Israel. Be very wary about going off the beaten track.

Diving & Snorkelling

Before leaping into the water, it is an idea to become familiar with dangerous creatures like lionfish, stonefish, barracuda and Moray eels. Remember not to touch or stand on the coral – it can be painful and certainly does the coral no good.

Daily rental costs at Sinai dive centres for

a mask, snorkel or fins will be around E£6 to E£10.

For general information about diving, see the Activities section in the Facts for the Visitor section of this chapter.

OYUN MUSA

Oyun Musa (Springs of Moses) is said to be the place where Moses, on discovering that the water there was too bitter to drink, took the advice of God and threw a special tree into the springs, miraculously sweetening the water.

Oyun Musa is about 25 km south of the Ahmed Hamdi Tunnel, which goes under the Suez Canal north of Suez.

EL-TOR

El-Tor, the administrative capital of southern Sinai, is something of a boom town, 265 km south of the Ahmed Hamdi Tunnel. There are a couple of hotels in town and some impressive coral and sea life to observe. This is the nearest place for visa extensions to the resorts of Sharm el-Sheikh and beyond – go to the town's Mogamma, the main administrative building.

Getting There & Away

Sinai buses between Cairo, Suez and Sharm el-Sheikh stop at El-Tor.

RAS MOHAMMED NATIONAL PARK

Declared a national marine park in 1988, the headland of Ras Mohammed is about 30 km short of Sharm el-Sheikh, on the road from El-Tor. Camping permits (E£5 per person per night) are available from the visitors' centre inside the park but camping is allowed only in designated areas. Vehicles are permitted to enter (US$5 per person), but access is restricted to certain regions and, for conservation reasons, it's forbidden to drive off the official tracks. Take your passport with you, and remember that it is not possible to go to Ras Mohammed if you only have a Sinai permit in your passport.

SHARM EL-SHEIKH & NA'AMA BAY

The south coast of the Gulf of Aqaba,

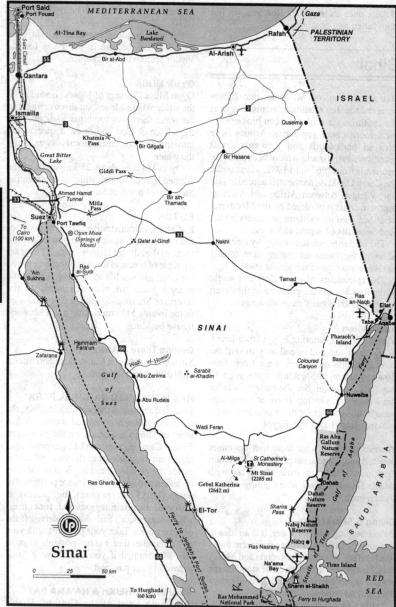

EGYPT

Sinai

0   25   50 km

MEDITERRANEAN SEA

Port Said
Port Fouad
At-Tina Bay
Lake Bardawil
Bir al-Abd
55
Qantara
Ismailia
3
Khatmia Pass
Bir Gifgafa
Great Bitter Lake
Giddi Pass
Ahmed Hamdi Tunnel
Mitla Pass
33
Suez
Port Tawfiq
To Cairo (100 km)
Oyun Musa (Springs of Moses)
Qalat al-Gindi
'Ain Sukhna
Ras al-Sudr
Hammam Fara'un
Zafarana
Gulf of Suez
Wadi el-Humur
Abu Zenima
Sarabit al-Khadim
Abu Rudeis
Ras Gharib
Wadi Feran
Al-Milga
St Catherine's Monastery
Mt Sinai (2285 m)
Gebel Katherina (2642 m)
El-Tor
Sharira Pass
Ras Nasrany
Ras Mohammed National Park
Na'ama Bay
Sharm el-Sheikh
Ferry to Hurghada
To Hurghada (60 km)

Al-Arish
Rafah
Gaza
PALESTINIAN TERRITORY
ISRAEL
Quseima
3
Bir Hasana
Bir ath-Thamada
Nakhl
33
Tamad
Ras an-Naqb
Eilat
Taba
Aqaba
Pharaoh's Island
Coloured Canyon
Basata
Nuweiba
66
Ras Abu Gallum Nature Reserve
Dahab
Dahab Nature Reserve
Nabq Nature Reserve
Nabq
Tiran Island
Straits of Tiran
RED SEA
SAUDI ARABIA
Gulf of Aqaba
Ferry to Jeddah & Port Sudan
44

SINAI

between Tiran Island in the strait and Ras Mohammed, features some of the world's most amazing underwater scenery.

Na'ama Bay is a resort that has grown from virtually nothing since the early 1980s, while Sharm el-Sheikh, initially developed by the Israelis, is a long-standing settlement. They are six km apart.

Information

Registration You can register at the passport office to the left of the port at Sharm el-Sheikh, but visa extensions can only be obtained in El-Tor.

Money The main banks have branches in both towns. Banque Misr handles Master-Card and the Bank of Alexandria Visa card. Amex operates through the Egyptian American Bank (EAB) in the shopping bazaar just off the mall at Na'ama Bay. Thomas Cook has an office on the main road in Na'ama Bay.

Post & Communications The post office is on the hill in Sharm. The nearby telephone office is open 24 hours a day. The telephone code for Sharm el-Sheikh & Na'ama Bay is 062.

Diving & Snorkelling

Na'ama itself has no reefs, but the stunning Near and Middle gardens and the even more incredible Far Garden can be reached on foot from the bay. Some of the most spectacular diving is off Ras Mohammed and in the Strait of Tiran. There is also good snorkelling at most of the popular coastal dive sights, including Ras um Sid near the lighthouse at Sharm. The deep drop-offs and strong cross currents at Ras Mohammed are not ideal for snorkelling. There are several wrecks, including the prized *Thistlegorm*. Any of the dive clubs and schools can give you a full rundown of the possibilities. Among the better and more established are Aquamarine Diving Centre (☎ 600276); Aquanaute (☎ 600187); Camel Dive Club (☎ 600700); Red Sea Diving Club (☎ 600342); and Red Sea Diving College (☎ 600313). There's a

modern decompression chamber just outside Sharm el-Sheikh.

Other Activities The big hotels at Na'ama Bay offer the whole range of watersport possibilities, from windsurfing to water-skiing. Camel and jeep treks in the desert are also on offer, and there are a couple of stables from where you can go horse-riding. There are also organised tours to other parts of Sinai, notably St Catherine's.

Places to Stay

Sharm el-Sheikh The *Youth Hostel* (☎ 600317), on the hill in Sharm el-Sheikh near the Clifftop Hotel, costs E£14 with breakfast. It's open from 7 to 9 am and 2 to 11 pm.

Safety Land (☎ 600359), almost opposite the bus station, has dorm beds in a large tent for E£22 or hot cement bungalows with fans at E£39/60 for singles/doubles.

The *Clifftop Hotel* (☎ 600251) has quite pleasant singles/doubles/triples with TV, air-con, fridge, phone and bathroom for US$43/56/67, including breakfast.

Na'ama Bay *Pigeon House* (☎ 600996), on the northern edge of town, has comfortable huts with fans and breakfast for E£38/56.

At the charming *Sanafir* (☎ 600197) you'll be looking at US$45/56/63 for a 'superior' air-con single/double/triple room in the low season, and US$64/82/93 in the high season. Breakfast is included.

The remaining hotels are more expensive still. The best deals for divers are available by booking packages for a week or more with discounted accommodation included.

Places to Eat

Sharm el-Sheikh There are a couple of small restaurants/cafes in the shopping bazaar behind the bus station. The *Sinai Star* serves some excellent fish meals for about E£12 a person. The nearby *Brilliant Restaurant* does a range of traditional Egyptian food at moderate prices. *Safety Land* can arrange meals (fish or calamari for E£24) and snacks (omelettes and salad), and you can dine within metres of the water. Beers are a reasonable E£6.

Self-caterers will find a well-stocked supermarket in the bazaar.

Na'ama Bay The *Tam Tam Oriental Cafe* is one of the cheapest restaurants in Na'ama and is deservedly popular. Jutting out onto the beach, it's a laid-back place where you can delve into a range of Egyptian fare.

Viva on the promenade is popular with divers and instructors. Two Chinese-Korean restaurants include the *Shin Seoul* in the mall and another in the Sanafir Hotel.

Getting There & Away

Air EgyptAir has daily flights to Cairo (E£412) and twice a week to Hurghada (E£286) and Luxor (E£412). Air Sinai flies to Cairo in winter only.

Bus The main bus station is in Sharm el-Sheikh; buses occasionally stop on the highway in Na'ama Bay but don't count on it. Superjet has a bus to Cairo (E£50) leaving at 11 pm. The East Delta Bus Co's direct services to Cairo (seven hours) cost from E£26 to E£50. They depart at 7, 8 and 10 am and 1, 4, 11.30 pm and midnight.

Buses to Suez (E£20; 5½ hours) depart at 7.30, 9 and 10.30 am.

Buses go to Dahab (E£7 to E£8; 1½ hours) at 7.30, 9 and 10.30 and 3, 5 and 11.30 pm. The same 9 am and 5 pm buses go on to Nuweiba (E£10); the 9 am bus continues to Taba (E£15); the 7.30 am bus goes on to St Catherine's Monastery (E£15).

Boat There's a ferry to Hurghada on Monday, Wednesday and Saturday, leaving Sharm el-Sheikh at 9 or 10 am. Tickets (E£100) can be booked through most hotels or at Thomas Cook in Na'ama Bay.

Getting Around

The Airport The airport is eight km north of Na'ama Bay. A taxi between Na'ama Bay and the airport will cost about E£15.

Bus An open sided public bus, known as a

tof-tof, runs every 40 minutes or so until about 11 pm between Sharm el-Sheikh and Na'ama Bay for E£1. Pick-ups do the same run for the same price.

SHARK BAY

Also known as Beit al-Irsh, this low-key resort camp is about five km from Na'ama Bay (about two km down a track off the main road). At the *Shark's Bay Camp* (☎ 600941) you can stay in clean and comfortable huts for E£40/55 for singles/doubles, or pitch a tent on the beach for E£15. Meals are available for E£21.

DAHAB

The village beach resort of Dahab (literally, 'gold') is 85 km north of Sharm el-Sheikh on the Gulf of Aqaba. There are two parts to Dahab: in the new part, referred to by the locals as Dahab City, are the more expensive hotels, bus station, post and phone offices and bank. The other part of Dahab, named Assalah, was a Bedouin village, about 2½ km north of town. It now has more low-budget travellers and Egyptian entrepreneurs than Bedouin in residence. Most travellers come here simply to laze around.

Tap water in Dahab is not drinkable (plenty of shops sell bottled water). Also, please respect local sensitivities and refrain from sunbathing topless. There's a lot of dope around, but be discreet.

Activities

There are seven dive clubs – among the better are Inmo (☎ 640370), Nesima (☎ (062) 640320) and Fantasea (☎ (062) 640043). They offer the full range of diving services, as well as combined camel/diving safaris.

Snorkellers tend to head for Eel Garden, just north of town. You can hire snorkelling gear from places along the waterfront.

In the morning, camel drivers and their charges congregate along the waterfront to organise camel trips to the interior of Sinai. Prices for a one day trip including food start at E£50.

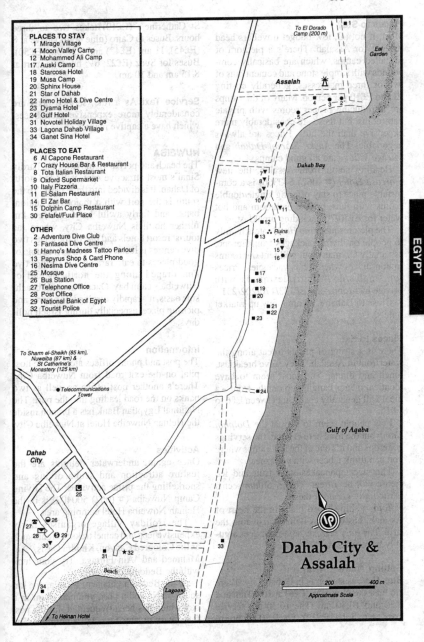

PLACES TO STAY
1 Mirage Village
4 Moon Valley Camp
12 Mohammed Ali Camp
17 Auski Camp
18 Starcosa Hotel
19 Musa Camp
20 Sphinx House
21 Star of Dahab
22 Inmo Hotel & Dive Centre
23 Dyama Hotel
24 Gulf Hotel
31 Novotel Holiday Village
33 Lagona Dahab Village
34 Ganet Sina Hotel

PLACES TO EAT
6 Al Capone Restaurant
7 Crazy House Bar & Restaurant
8 Tota Italian Restaurant
9 Oxford Supermarket
10 Italy Pizzeria
11 El-Salam Restaurant
14 El Zar Bar
15 Dolphin Camp Restaurant
30 Felafel/Fuul Place

OTHER
2 Adventure Dive Club
3 Fantasea Dive Centre
5 Hanno's Madness Tattoo Parlour
13 Papyrus Shop & Card Phone
16 Nesima Dive Centre
25 Mosque
26 Bus Station
27 Telephone Office
28 Post Office
29 National Bank of Egypt
32 Tourist Police

To El Dorado
Camp (200 m)

Eel
Garden

Assalah

Dahab Bay

Ruins

To Sharm el-Sheikh (85 km),
Nuweiba (87 km) &
St Catherine's
Monastery (125 km)

Telecommunications
Tower

Dahab
City

Beach

Gulf of Aqaba

Dahab City &
Assalah

0   200   400 m
Approximate Scale

Lagoon

To Helnan Hotel

EGYPT

Places to Stay

Most, if not all, low-budget travellers head straight for Assalah. There's a plethora of so-called camps, which are basically compounds with simple stone and cement huts of two or three mattresses, generally costing E£5 to E£10 per person. Many of the camps are introducing proper rooms with private bathrooms, but these are considerably more expensive than the huts. Prices are always negotiable. The *Auski*, *Star of Dahab* and *Mirage Village* are all good camps.

Heading south from Assalah, the new *Starcosa Hotel* (☎ (062) 640366) is a comfortable place to stay offering single/double rooms with fans, private bathroom and hot water for E£50/70, including breakfast.

The picturesque *Inmo Hotel* caters mainly to people on diving packages from Europe, especially Germany, but will rent out rooms to non-divers when it has vacancies. Prices for singles/doubles/triples/quads with private bathrooms are E£133/170/202/231.

Close to Dahab City are a few up-market hotels.

Places to Eat

There is a string of places to eat along the waterfront in Assalah. They serve breakfast, lunch and dinner, and most seem to have identical menus hanging up out the front – a meal will generally cost you between E£6 to E£15.

Few people seem to stay at the *Dolphin Camp* but the food here is good, the servings generous and it's one of the few camps where you can drink a beer with your meal.

The sweet pancakes with fruit and ice cream will be a treat. The *El Salam* seems particularly good for these.

Tota, a ship-shaped place in the heart of Assalah, has the best Italian cuisine on the strip. The *Italy Pizzeria* next-door does arguably better pizzas.

Getting There & Away

Bus The bus station is in Dahab City. There are buses to Nuweiba (E£6) at 10.30 am and 6.30 and 10.30 pm. The 10.30 am service goes on to Taba (E£10). The 9.30 am bus to

St Catherine's (E£10) takes two to three hours. Buses to Cairo (nine hours) leave at 8 (E£45), 11 am (E£42) and 9.30 pm (E£50). Buses for Suez (E£22; 6½ hours) depart at 8.15 am and 10 am.

Service Taxi As a rule, service taxis are considerably more expensive than buses, which have a captive market.

NUWEIBA

The beach and port town of Nuweiba, hardly Sinai's most attractive spot, is 87 km north of Dahab. It is divided into three parts. To the south is the port with a major bus station, banks and fairly awful hotels. A few km further north is Nuweiba City, where the tourist resort hotels and one of the area's two dive centres is located, as well as a couple of good places to eat. Tarabin is a further two km, draped along the northern end of Nuweiba's calm bay. Once a tranquil beachside oasis, it's rapidly turning into a party and pick-up place, especially during Israeli holidays.

Information

The post and phone offices are near the hospital on the exit road from Nuweiba City. There's another post office as well as two banks on the road leading into the port. The National Egyptian Bank has a branch inside the Helnan Nuweiba Hotel at Nuweiba City.

Activities

Once again, underwater delights are the feature attraction and scuba diving and snorkelling the prime activities. The Diving Camp Nuweiba (☎ (062) 500402) is in the Helnan Nuweiba Hotel camping area.

The Holiday Village organises fairly expensive jeep and camel treks to sights such as the Coloured Canyon, Khudra Oasis, 'Ain Mahmed and 'Ain Furtaga. Try your luck with the Bedouin of Tarabin.

At the Bedouin village of Mizela, one km south of Nuweiba port, you can swim in a bay which has been frequented, for the past few years at any rate, by a dolphin. The village elders charge visitors E£6 to swim and E£5 for a mask and snorkel.

Places to Stay

Nuweiba Port There are three fairly unimpressive hotels you can stay in by the port. The new *Motel Marina* is the best of the trio. Small doubles with shower and air-con are E£30; larger quads cost E£70. There's also a new *Hilton* just north of the port.

Nuweiba City With your own tent, you can camp at the *Morgana Restaurant* for E£3, but there's precious little shade. The *Helnan Nuweiba Hotel* (E£10) and *City Beach Village* (E£5) also take campers.

There are a couple of simple camps with a few huts along the beach south of the Al-Waha Tourism Village, including the overpriced *Sinai Star* and the relaxing *Duna*.

The *Helnan Nuweiba Hotel* has cabins for E£40/50/60 a single/double/triple.

The nearby *Al-Waha Tourism Village* (☎ (062) 500420/1) has large tents at E£15/18/24 for one/two/three people, or stuffy bungalows (no fan) for E£25/35/45.

The *City Beach Village*, halfway between Nuweiba City and Tarabin, is one of the best options. You can camp out in one of its reed huts for E£10 per person, or go for a clean, comfortable room for E£35/50 for singles/doubles.

Tarabin You can get a mattress in a bamboo or concrete hut at one of the camps for E£5. Arguably the nicest camp is *Petra*, which has double huts for E£15. *Elsebaey Village* (☎ (062) 500373), a new hotel in the heart of Tarabin, has double rooms with communal bathroom facilities for E£40.

Places to Eat

Besides the hotels and camps, there's not much to speak of at the port or in Tarabin. In Nuweiba City, *Dr Shishkebab* and *Sendbad* are both excellent budget diners.

Getting There & Away

Bus Buses going to or from Taba stop at the Helnan Nuweiba Hotel and Dr Shishkebab

in Nuweiba City. They usually also call in at the port but do not stop at Tarabin.

Buses generally meet incoming ferries. The bus from Taba to Cairo (E£40) via St Catherine's (E£10) stops at the Helnan Nuweiba Hotel around 11 am (sometimes earlier). There's another bus to Cairo (E£55) at 3 pm. Buses to Sharm el-Sheikh (E£10) via Dahab (E£6) leave at 6.30 am and 4 pm; to Taba (E£6 to E£8) at 6 am and noon; and to Suez at 6 am (E£20; six hours via Nakhl).

Service Taxi There is a big service-taxi station by the port. The fare to Suez is E£30 and E£35 to Cairo.

Boat For information about ferries and speedboats to Aqaba in Jordan, refer to Sea in the Getting There and Away section earlier in this chapter.

NUWEIBA TO TABA

Beaches

Despite ongoing development in the region, there are still some desolate beaches backed by stunning blue waters and pockets of fringing reefs along this stretch of road. At **Maagana**, there's a row of huts in honeycomb formation stretched out along a lovely bay.

Another seven km on is **Barracuda Village**, which has a series of waterfront stone huts.

At **Basata** (☎ (062) 500481), 23 km north of Nuweiba, is another simple, clean and carefree travellers' settlement. Its bamboo huts cost E£18 per person. A set dinner costs between E£12 to E£18 depending on whether it's vegetarian or with fish. It's advisable to book ahead if you want to stay here.

The Fjord

This small protected bay is a popular sunbathing spot only about 15 km south of Taba. Up on the rise to the north is the small *Salima Cafeteria*, with six basic rooms for E£35/50. Meals are available.

Pharaoh's Island

Only seven km south of Taba, Pharaoh's Island (Geziret Fara'un) lies about 250m off the Egyptian coast. The islet is dominated by the much restored **Castle of Saladin**, a fortress actually built by the Crusaders in 1115, but captured and expanded by Salah ad-Din in 1170. It's open from 9 am to 5 pm. Entry costs E£8 but the boat ride there and back is an outlandish E£10.50.

TABA

This busy crossing point into Israel is open 24 hours daily.

There is a small post and telephone office in the 'town', along with a hospital, bakery and an EgyptAir office (often closed). You can change money at booths of Banque du Caire (unreliable opening hours) and Banque Misr (open 24 hours) booths, both 100m before the border, or at the Taba Hilton Hotel.

Getting There & Away

Air Air Sinai runs flights twice weekly (winter only) from Cairo to Ras an-Naqb airport (38 km away from Taba) for E£430.

Bus East Delta Bus Co runs several buses from Taba. The 10 am bus goes to Nuweiba (E£8), St Catherine's Monastery (E£20) and on to Cairo (E£50). Another bus to Cairo (E£65) leaves at 2 pm but goes via Nakhl. Also via Nakhl there's a bus to Suez (E£30; five hours) at 7 am. Other buses leave at 9 am and 3 pm for Sharm el-Sheikh (E£15), stopping at Nuweiba (E£6) and Dahab (E£10). To Nuweiba only there's another bus at 2 pm.

Service Taxi A taxi (up to seven people) to Nuweiba costs E£175 and E£300 to Sharm el-Sheikh. You may also find a minibus or two which will take you to Dahab for about E£15 per person. Your bargaining power increases if the bus is not too far off.

ST CATHERINE'S MONASTERY

Twenty-two Greek Orthodox monks live in this ancient monastery at the foot of Mt Sinai. The monastic order was founded in the 4th century AD by the Byzantine empress Helena, who had a small chapel built beside what was believed to be the burning bush from which God spoke to Moses. The chapel is dedicated to St Catherine, the legendary martyr of Alexandria, who was tortured on a spiked wheel and then beheaded for her Christianity.

In the 6th century, Emperor Justinian ordered the building of a fortress, with a basilica and a monastery, as well as the original chapel, to serve as a secure home for the monks of St Catherine's and as a refuge for the Christians of southern Sinai. St Catherine's is open to visitors from 9 am to noon daily except on Friday, Sunday and holidays, when the monastery is closed.

Information

In the village of Al-Milga, about 3½ km from the monastery, there's a post office, a phone exchange, a bank and a few small eateries.

Things to See

At a height of 2285m, **Mt Sinai** (Gebel Musa is the local name) towers over St Catherine's Monastery. It is revered as the place Moses received the Ten Commandments from God. It is easy to climb – you can take the gentle camel trail or the **3000 Steps of Repentance**, carved out by a monk. It takes two to three hours, and most people either stay overnight or climb up in time for sunrise – bring a torch (flashlight). It gets freezing cold in winter.

Places to Stay & Eat

St Catherine's Monastery runs a *hostel* which offers a bed in a single-sex dormitory (seven beds) for E£35, and rooms with three beds and private bathroom for E£40 a head. The facilities are basic but clean.

Right by the roundabout, two km west of the monastery, is the expensive *St Catherine's Tourist Village*, where single/double rooms cost US$114/135, including breakfast and dinner. Next door is the somewhat grubby *Al-Fairoz Hotel*, where a dormitory bed costs E£15 and a mattress in a big tent or in the open air is E£8.

On the hill opposite Al-Fairoz is the new three-star *Daniela Village* (☎ 470279). It has a collection of stone bungalows with comfortable rooms for US$45/60/70; there's a restaurant and bar.

In Al-Milga there's a bakery opposite the mosque and a couple of well-stocked supermarkets in the shopping arcade. Just behind the bakery are a few small restaurants, the most reasonable of which is *Look Here*.

The new *Panorama Restaurant*, on the main road near the post office, has pizzas for E£5 to E£18 and sandwiches, pancakes, burgers and soups.

Getting There & Away

Bus Buses leave from the square in Al-Milga to Cairo (E£40 – from Taba via Nuweiba) at 10 am; Suez (E£17) at 6 am; Sharm el-Sheikh (E£15) via Dahab (E£10) between noon and 1 pm; and Taba (E£20) via Nuweiba (E£10) at 3.30 pm.

Service Taxi Service-taxis travel in and out of the village irregularly and infrequently, and you'll have to bargain hard – they have the upper hand.

WADI FERAN

The Bedouin oasis of Wadi Feran is between the west coast of Sinai and St Catherine's Monastery. There is a **convent** on the western edge of the oasis but you need permission from St Catherine's Monastery to visit it.

AL-ARISH

Much of the north coast of Sinai, from Port Fouad most of the way to Al-Arish, is dominated by the swampy lagoon of **Lake Bardawil**, separated from the Mediterranean by a limestone ridge. Al-Arish, beyond Lake Bardawil, is the capital of the North Sinai governorate and has a population of about 40,000. The palm-fringed beaches and comparatively unspoiled nature of the place make it a pleasant place for a swim.

Orientation & Information

The main coastal road, Sharia Fouad Zekry, forms a T-junction with Sharia 23rd of July, which runs a couple of km south (changing its name to Sharia Tahrir on the way) to the bus and service taxi stations. There is a GPO, telephone office and a few banks between the bus station and the beach.

Things to See & Do

The **Sinai Heritage Museum**, on the outskirts of town along the coastal road to Rafah, informs people about traditional life in Sinai. The main attraction is the **beach**. The parade of palms, fine white sand and clean water makes this one of the nicer Mediterranean spots in Egypt.

Places to Stay

The *Golden Beach Hotel* has rooms with up to three beds for E£15. Just up the road is the *Moon Light Hotel*, which has singles/doubles at E£10/20. Both places are on the beach but facilities are ultra basic.

Better is the *El Salam Hotel* (☎ (068) 331219) on Midan al-Baladiyya near the bus station. Rooms with two or three beds cost E£12.50.

Surely one of the better deals is the *Green Land Beach Hotel* (☎ (068) 340601), virtually on the beach near the junction of Sharias Fouad Zekry and 23rd of July. Clean and comfortable triple rooms with bathroom cost just E£15, however many occupants there are.

The nearby *Mecca Hotel* (☎ (068) 344909), just off Sharia 23rd of July, is a friendly, clean place that has singles/doubles with fan for E£30/40.

Further west are Al-Arish's two luxury establishments: the *Semiramis* and *Egoth Oberoi*.

Places to Eat

There's not a huge range of places to get a meal in Al-Arish. About as good as you'll find in the budget range is the *Aziz Restaurant* on Midan al-Baladiyya. It has decent meals of fuul and ta'amiyya, as well as grilled chicken, kofta, rice and spaghetti, and it is also open for breakfast.

Sabri, opposite Aziz in the back corner of a little square, makes the best felafel in town.

At the junction of Sharias Fouad Zekry and 23rd of July is the *Fairuz Restaurant*. It serves reasonably generous proportions.

Right on the beach nearby is the classier *Maxim*, which specialises in fish dishes costing about E£20 to E£35. It's open in summer only.

Getting There & Away
Air EgyptAir has two flights a week between Cairo and Al-Arish for E£328.

Bus Buses for Cairo (E£25 to E£35; five hours) leave at 7 am and 4 pm. There's a bus via Qantara (E£5) to Ismailia (E£7; three hours) every hour until 3 pm. For Suez, you have to go to Ismailia and take another bus from there.

At 7.15 and 10.30 am there's a bus to Rafah (E£1), which can drop you about a km short of the border at the T-junction where the bus turns left to Rafah.

Service Taxi Service taxis to Cairo cost about E£12. To Qantara they're E£5, Ismailia E£6, and to the border (or vice versa) you'll be charged anything from E£5 to E£7.

RAFAH
This coastal town, 48 km north of Al-Arish, is actually split in two by the Egypt-Israel border and its northern half lies within the Gaza Strip.

Getting There & Away
There is a service-taxi stand at the border. The trip to Cairo should be E£20, while to Al-Arish the fare is E£5.

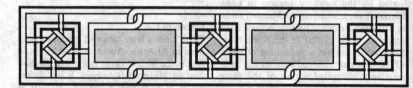

Iran

Iran is a strange sort of country. The Iranian authorities make little effort to attract foreign tourists, and for the most part holidaymakers respond with equal scorn to the idea of spending even a day in the Islamic Republic. Yet the country has managed to attract a steady stream of international visitors, and many of them have returned with stories of almost overwhelming hospitality from private Iranians, and of a magnificent cultural legacy entirely unspoilt by tourism.

Iran will appeal to the genuine traveller who is prepared to respect the local people and their traditions, be open-minded and adapt to unfamiliar circumstances. For such people, Iran is one of the most exciting, interesting, welcoming and rewarding countries yet to be discovered by tourists.

Facts about the Country

HISTORY
The Achaemenian Empire
In the 6th century BC Cyrus the Great emerged as the first notable Persian ruler. The Achaemenian Empire he founded lasted from 558 to 330 BC and his successors, Darius I and Xerxes, expanded their rule all the way to India in the east and the Aegean Sea in the west. Even Egypt came under Persian rule and the magnificent complex of Persepolis became the hub of the empire.

Xerxes' defeat by the Greeks at Marathon marked the end of the great Achaemenian period of Persian history. It was Europe's turn to conquer and, in the 4th century BC, Alexander invaded Persia and 'accidentally' burned down Persepolis. After his death the Greek influence rapidly waned, starting with the breakaway region of north-east Persia which was ruled by the Parthians.

Islam & the Seljuk Era
The Sassanians controlled Persia from 224

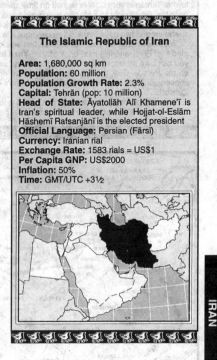

The Islamic Republic of Iran

Area: 1,680,000 sq km
Population: 60 million
Population Growth Rate: 2.3%
Capital: Tehrān (pop: 10 million)
Head of State: Āyatollāh Alī Khamene'ī is Iran's spiritual leader, while Hojjat-ol-Eslām Hāshemī Rafsanjānī is the elected president
Official Language: Persian (Fārsī)
Currency: Iranian rial
Exchange Rate: 1583 rials = US$1
Per Capita GNP: US$2000
Inflation: 50%
Time: GMT/UTC +3½

to 638 AD, but through these years Persian history was of continuing conflict with the Roman and, later, the Byzantine empires. Weakened by this scrapping, the Zoroastrian Persians fell easy prey to the spread of Islam and the Arabs. Between 637 and 642 nearly all of Persia was taken by the Arabs and the Zoroastrian religion was superseded by Islam. Arab control over Persia continued for nearly 600 years but towards the end of that period they were gradually supplanted by the Turkish Seljuk dynasty. The Seljuks heralded a new era of Persian art, literature and science, marked by such people as the mathematician-poet Omar Khayyām. Then in 1220 the Seljuk era abruptly collapsed when

Suggested Itineraries

If you only have a week to spend in Iran it's probably best to restrict yourself to two or three main towns. Tehrān is very slow to pay off on time spent there and it's best to pass through as quickly as possible. Go straight to **Esfahān** which deserves at least a couple of days and then on to **Shīrāz**, with the nearby remains of **Persepolis** and rock-face tombs of **Naghsh-é Rostam**. Again aim to spend around two days there. If you can squeeze it in, **Kermān** is well worth at least a day.

With more time on your hands, say two weeks, use Kermān as a base to visit **Bam**, with its medieval European-like mud-brick citadel. **Yazd** also repays time spent exploring. If you book early you can take advantage of Iran Air's incredibly low domestic fares to make quick trips to **Būshehr** on the Persian Gulf, the holy city of **Mashhad** or to Ahvāz, an uninspiring city itself but the most convenient place from which to visit one of Iran's most memorable sights, the ziggurat at **Choghā Zambīl**.

In spring, summer or autumn, try to spend a few days touring along the Caspian littoral, where there are some very attractive small coastal towns, such as **Rāmsar** and **Sārī**. ■

the Mongol Genghis Khan swept in and commenced a cold-blooded devastation that was to last for two centuries.

The Safavid Era

Another invasion by Tamerlane in 1380 didn't help matters, but in 1502 the Safavid era commenced and heralded a Persian renaissance. Under Shāh Abbās I (1587-1629) foreign influences were again purged from the country, and the architectural miracles he later performed in Esfahān have left a permanent reminder of this period.

The decline of the Safavids following Shāh Abbās I's death was hastened by an invasion from Afghanistan, but in 1736, Nāder Shāh, a tribal leader from the northeast, overthrew the impotent Safavids and proceeded to chuck out Afghans, Russians and Turks in all directions. He then rushed off to do a little conquering himself, returning from India loaded with goodies, but virtually exhausted Persia with his warring. It was a relief to all, both within Persia and without, when he was assassinated in 1747.

The Pahlavī Era

The following Zand and Ghajar periods were not notable except for a brief reign of glory under Karīm Khān-é Zand at Shīrāz. In 1926 Rezā Khān Pahlavī, a Cossack officer in the imperial army, founded the Pahlavī dynasty. Foreign influence – and oil – then became an important element in Iran's story. In WWII Iran was officially neutral, but Rezā Shāh was exiled to South Africa because he was thought to be too friendly with the Axis powers. His 22 year old son, Mohammad Rezā, succeeded him. After the war, the invading Russian forces were persuaded to depart (with difficulty and US conniving), the shāh assumed near-absolute power and Iran firmly aligned itself with the west.

The government of Mohammad Rezā was repressive, but forward-looking, and Iran was rapidly modernised – at least in some ways and in some places. Illiteracy was reduced, women were emancipated, land holdings redistributed, health services improved and a major industrialisation programme was embarked upon. The 1974 oil price revolution became the shāh's undoing. He allowed American arms' merchants to persuade him to squander Iran's vast new wealth on huge arsenals of useless weapons. Fortunes were wasted on inappropriate development schemes, and sycophants and courtiers grew rich beyond their wildest dreams. The flood of petrodollars ended up lining the pockets of a select few, while galloping inflation made the majority worse off than before.

Since the early days of the Pahlavī era there had been a smouldering resistance that occasionally flared into violence. Students wanted faster reform, devout Muslims wanted reforms rolled back, and everybody attacked the Pahlavīs' conspicuous consumption. As the economy went from bad to worse under the shāh's post-oil-boom mismanagement, the growing opposition made its presence felt with sabotage and massive street demonstrations. The shāh responded with all the power and brutality available to the absolute ruler of an oil-rich country who enjoyed unquestioned backing from the major western powers. His security force, Savak, earned a horrific reputation.

Āyatollāh Khomeinī

His Holiness Grand Āyatollāh Hajj Sayyed Rūhollāh Mūsavī Khomeinī was increasingly acknowledged as the leader of the shāh's opponents – a ramshackle group covering every political shade from fundamentalist Muslims to Soviet-backed leftists. Many saw him as a figurehead who, once the shāh was ousted, would retire to a position akin to that of a constitutional monarch. They were wrong.

Khomeinī first came to public attention in 1962, when he opposed the shāh's plans to reduce the clergy's property rights and emancipate women. In 1964 he was exiled to Turkey, then pushed on to Iraq. The shāh put pressure on the Iraqis to withdraw their hospitality from Khomeinī, with the result that in 1978 he was expelled from the Middle East region altogether and wound up in

France. In a development unforseen by the shāh, the Āyatollāh was placed in the arena of the international press corps, amplifying his message a thousand fold.

In the late '70s, in the face of the shāh's increasingly desperate and brutal attempts to save his regime, US support began to falter. In November 1978 he imposed martial law and hundreds of demonstrators were killed in street battles in Tehrān. He finally fled the country on 16 January 1979. In exile he was harried from country to country and died in Egypt in 1980.

The Islamic Republic

Āyatollāh Khomeinī returned to Iran on 1 February 1979 to be greeted by adoring millions. His fiery brew of nationalism and Muslim fundamentalism had been at the forefront of the revolt, but at this stage few realised how much deep-rooted support he had and how strongly he reflected the beliefs and ideals of millions of his people.

Once in control Khomeinī was soon to prove the truth in the adage that 'after the revolution comes the revolution'. His intention was to set up a clergy-dominated Islamic republic – the first true Islamic state in modern times – and he went about achieving this with brutal efficiency.

Much of the credit for undermining the shāh lay with groups like the Peoples' Fedā'īyīn and the Islamic Peoples' Mojāhedīn, but once the shāh was gone they were swept bloodily aside. People disappeared, executions took place after brief and meaningless trials and minor officials took the law into their own hands. It looked as if the country might topple into civil war.

Almost from its inception, the Islamic Republic of Iran found itself at loggerheads with the rest of the world. Under the banner 'Neither East nor West – Islamic Republic!', a set of policies was implemented that were confrontationist and unashamedly designed to promote similar Islamic revolutions elsewhere.

The main opponent in this primordial battle between Islamic right and ungodly evil was (and to a great extent continues to be)

the 'Great Satan', the name by which Iranian polemicists refer to the USA. Aside from its godless culture (in Iranian eyes), the USA provided key support to the Pahlavīs and, later, to Iraq during its seven year war with Iran. The US navy was responsible in 1988 for the accidental downing of an unarmed Iranian airliner over the Persian Gulf with a loss of more than 200 lives. Furthermore, the USA has always been viewed as the main backer of the hated Jewish State of Israel and has always shown remarkable selectivity in its support for UN resolutions in the Muslim world.

As a consequence post-revolutionary Iran has been *the* major thorn in the side of US foreign operations. The first and worst nightmare for the USA was the hostage crisis that began in October 1979 when so-called students seized the US embassy in Tehrān along with 52 hostages. The hostages (spies according to the Iranians) were held for 444 days and the crisis effectively destroyed US President Carter. Since then various Iranian-backed groups, most notably Hezbollah, have been responsible for holding hostages in Lebanon, killing 241 US marines in a truck-bombing in Beirut and numerous other actions.

The Iran-Iraq War

All this pales into insignificance, however, compared with the ghastly Iran-Iraq War that consumed hundreds of thousands of lives. In 1980 Saddam Hussein made an opportunistic land grab in south-west Iran, taking advantage of Iran's domestic chaos, on the doubtful pretext that the oil-rich province of Khūzestān was historically part of Iraq. (It's easy to see the connection with the invasion of Kuwait a decade later, even though the international reaction couldn't have been more different.) It was a tragic miscalculation. Saddam Hussein presented the shaky Islamic Republic with an outside enemy and an opportunity to spread the revolution by force of arms. Although Iraq was better equipped, Iran drew on a larger population and an often suicidal fanaticism fanned by the rhetoric of the mullahs (Muslim teachers). For the first time since WWI the world witnessed the hideous spectre of trench warfare and poison gas. A cease-fire was finally negotiated in mid-1988, with neither side having achieved its objectives.

The 1990s

On 4 June 1989 Khomeinī died leaving an uncertain legacy to the country he had dominated for a decade. It's difficult to unravel the complicated power structures within Iran, where the mullahs and Revolutionary Guards have established their own, sometimes competing, spheres of influence and bureaucracies, and the parliament is faction-ridden. While Khomeinī, with his divine authority, was alive the factions had no choice but to follow his dictates. Āyatollāh Alī Khamene'ī was appointed his successor as Iran's spiritual leader but inherited little of his popular appeal or political power. In August 1989 the speaker of the parliament, Hojjat-ol-Eslām Hāshemī Rafsanjānī, was elected president. In true Gorbachev style, he soon changed the presidency from a largely ceremonial to an executive post and made economic reform a priority over the more extreme revolutionary dogma.

Iran's problem now is the open rift between the reforming Rafsanjānī and the deeply conservative Khamene'ī, with both parties constantly jockeying for position. However, the Iranian constitution permits a maximum of two terms in office and Rafsanjānī's time is up in 1997. The elections held then will decide whether the liberalising element prevails and Iran begins to open up to the outside world, or the hardline elements come out on top and slam the door even more tightly shut.

GEOGRAPHY

Iran covers some 1,680,000 sq km, most of it a great dry plateau between 1000 and 1500m in altitude. In the north it's bordered by the Alborz Mountains where Kūh-é Damāvand, west Asia's highest peak and Iran's only volcano, towers to over 5000m only a short distance north of Tehrān. Beyond the Alborz is the desert republic of

Turkmenistan, formerly of the USSR. In the west, towards Iraq and Turkey, and in the south, towards the Persian Gulf, the plateau is bordered by the Zāgros Mountains. A number of smaller ranges rise towards the Afghan border in the east.

Much of the eastern part of the plateau is practically uninhabited desert – Dasht-é Kavīr (Great Salt Desert) to the north and Dasht-é Lūt (Great Sand Desert) to the south. Apart from the fertile northern slopes of the Alborz Mountains running down to the Caspian Sea, most of Iran is a parched, arid country – dependent since ancient times on ingenious artificial underground water channels known as *ghanāt*s.

CLIMATE

With a few exceptions, Iran is hot and dry in summer and cold and dry in winter. North of the Alborz Mountains, especially along the Caspian coast, rainfall is heavy, but the rest of Iran sees little precipitation. The summer can get pretty mean down south. In the desert and along the Persian Gulf coast, summer temperatures way over 40°C are common and usually come in tandem with debilitating humidity. Temperatures over 40°C aren't uncommon in Tehrān but the humidity is nowhere near as bad. Away from the coast most of the main cities are at a fairly high altitude, which tends to moderate the heat; on the other hand it makes the winters that much colder. In January, Tehrān and Mashhad are usually icy, while Āzarbāyjān and the west are extremely cold: high mountain passes may be snowbound.

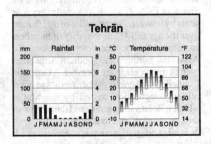

GOVERNMENT & POLITICS

It's difficult to begin to grasp how Iran's political system works without a grounding in Shiite Islam, and even then it's still something of a mystery.

The Islamic Republic of Iran was voted into existence by national referendum on 1 April 1979. Its constitution was approved by a second ballot on 3 December 1979.

The Ja'fari Twelver school of Shiite Islam, the majority creed, maintains that there were 12 hereditary imams (emāms in Persian), or leaders of the Muslims, but that the 12th (Mahdī) went into occultation and will return one day to earth. In his temporary absence, the constitution allows for the assumption of supreme spiritual and temporal leadership of the Islamic state by an appropriately qualified cleric who emerges as valī-yé faghīh (guardian jurisprudent), by general consent of a decisive majority of the people. As such he is the earthly deputy of the 12th emām and has the duty of 'supervising and correlating government policies with divine decrees', and has more or less the same powers as an absolute monarch, so long as he acts within Islamic law. An elected Assembly of Experts (Majles-é Khebregān), comprising about 70 leading Islamic jurists and scholars, has the power to appoint the leader on behalf of the people, or dismiss him if he is deemed to have broken Islamic laws and regulations. If no suitably qualified candidate should emerge as leader by popular consent the Majles is empowered to elect one itself, as was the case with Āyatollāh Alī Khamene'ī, the present (spiritual) leader.

There's also a legislative parliament, the Islamic Consultative Assembly (Majles-é Shūrā-yé Eslāmī) which is elected every four years by universal secret ballot of all Iranians over the age of 14. The majority of members are Shiite clerics. The Jews, Zoroastrians, Assyrians, northern and southern Armenians each currently elect one member. A Guardian Council (Shūrā-yé Negāhbān) exists to overrule any legislation passed by the Majles which it deems to contravene Islamic law or the constitution, and to administer the presidential and parliamentary elections. It comprises six jurisprudents nominated by the leader and six jurists elected by the Majles after nomination by the Supreme Judicial Council, an independent elected body responsible for the administration of justice.

After the spiritual leader, the highest official is the president, who is elected for a four year term by universal suffrage and can serve no more than two terms. He (or theoretically at least, she) is responsible for appointing and dismissing members of the Cabinet, subject to the vote of the Majles.

For the purposes of administration, Iran is divided into 24 provinces (ostāns), each administered by a provincial governor (ostāndār).

ECONOMY

Iran's economy has looked decidedly shaky since the 1979 revolution, and oil production has only recently approached pre-1979 levels. Significant quantities of oil were first discovered in Iran in 1908 but its known reserves are more modest than those of some other Gulf states. Current production levels are estimated at about three million barrels a day. In 1978 Iran's oil exports – 4.4 million barrels a day – accounted for 14% of the world total, but fell in 1981 to 0.7 million barrels a day, just 2.8% of the world total. Even so, petroleum is still far and away the mainstay of the economy. Were it not for Iran's oil wealth the path towards ultimate collapse would have been steep and slippery.

Other important exports include caviar, carpets, pistachios, dried fruits, spices, ores and cotton, but they're a trifle compared with oil, which alone nets about 80% of government revenue and 95% of foreign currency earnings. Iran has large numbers of goats and sheep (the latter providing wool for the carpets), while agriculture is extensively practised in the Caspian region and the other smaller fertile areas.

POPULATION & PEOPLE

Iran's population is around 60 million. Around 66% can be classified as Persians, descendants of the Aryans who first settled in the central plateau in ancient times and gave Iran its name. Other inhabitants of Iran include the Lors (Lurs), thought to be part Persian, part Arab, a semi-nomadic people who inhabit the western mountains south of Kermānshāh. They form about 1% of the country's total population. A closely related group, the Bakhteyārīs inhabit the Zāgros Mountains west of Esfahān. Both speak Lorī, a Persian dialect. The Baluchis (Balūch) are semi-nomadic and inhabit Balūchestān, a formerly semi-autonomous territory now divided between Iran and Pakistan. They speak Baluchi, a language related to Persian, and are probably of Persian origin.

People speaking Turkic languages form Iran's second main group, accounting for about a quarter of the population. Mostly they are Āzarīs (Azeris), natives of Āzarbāyjān, the north-westernmost region of Iran. There is some debate over whether the Āzarīs are actually of Turkic or Persian origin. The two undisputed Turkic groups are the Turkomans, a fierce nomadic race of

horse people and warriors inhabiting Iran's far north-east, and the Ghashghā'īs of the south-west, traditionally wandering herds-people.

About 5% of the population are Kurds, mostly inhabiting the western mountains between Orūmīyé and Kermānshāh. Iran's treatment of the Kurds compares favourably with that of certain neighbouring countries. Roughly 4% of the population are Arabs, mostly living on the south coast and islands and in Khūzestān. There are also some people who are at least partly of Negro origin, especially around and east of the Strait of Hormuz (Hormoz to the Iranians).

SOCIETY & CONDUCT

Iranian culture is essentially a development of survival in a desert society, where hospitality to strangers is a simple matter of life and death. One of the most appealing things about Iran is how strongly the tradition of hospitality is preserved – even in circumstances where the question of survival is no

IRAN

Dress Code

From the moment you enter Iran you are legally obliged to observe its rigid dress code. You will be reprimanded for any lapses, although as a foreigner you are unlikely to get into serious trouble providing you quickly make amends. The dress code is particularly strictly enforced in Ramadan (Ramazān in Persian), when Iranians avoid wearing red and other loud colours. Colours are also subdued in the month of Moharram.

Women Females older than about seven must wear the *hejāb* (modest dress) whenever in the actual or potential sight of any man who isn't a close relative. This requires that all parts of the body, except the hands, feet and face above the neckline and below the hairline, be covered and the shape of the body be disguised. The outfit commonly associated with Iranian women is the *chādor*, a tent-like black (occasionally grey) cloak, draped loosely over the head, legs and arms; however, it is not necessary to go this far. Standard dress for many Iranian women is a full-length skirt, or trousers (jeans will do), worn beneath a loose-fitting, below-the-knees black or dark blue coat, known as a *roupush*. Hair is hidden beneath a large, plain headscarf.

As a foreign woman visiting Iran you could get away with a long, generously cut, ankle-length skirt and over it a big, baggy shirt or loose-fitting jacket which comes down at least to your mid-thighs. You will also have to wear socks and a headscarf. Once in Iran you may find it more comfortable to buy yourself a roupush (they cost the equivalent of around US$20). Not only will you then attract far less attention but the roupush allows you the freedom of wearing just a light vest or bra only underneath – you'll be much cooler this way. Apart from plain rings, jewellery and make-up should be discreet to the point of invisibility.

Men Men must wear full trousers, not shorts, and keep their arms covered. In some places, one can get away with shirts rolled up below the elbow (except in Ramadan), but it's better to have them done up at the wrist. ■

longer an issue. Everywhere you go in Iran you are *mehmūn*, or guest. On our visits to Iran we've had taxi drivers refuse to accept payment, fellow queuers at bus offices insisting on paying for our tickets, and countless offers of meals and beds for the night. Frequently, facilities are made available to foreigners that would be virtually unobtainable for Iranians in the same situation.

The rules of etiquette are complex and Iranians are usually very forgiving of innocent gaffes by foreigners. The obligations aren't that different from those in the Arabian peninsula, except that in some matters they're more strongly enforced. Flirting in public with the opposite sex or wearing a ripped T-shirt and shorts, for example, is just as offensive to many Muslims in the Arab world as in Iran. The difference is that in Iran you're more likely to be arrested for it. On the other hand, Iran looks positively liberal compared with Saudi Arabia, especially as regards women. For more information for women travelling in Iran, see Women Travellers in the Facts for the Visitor section later in this chapter.

RELIGION

Most Iranians belong to the Shiite branch of Islam and the Twelver Ja'fari school is the state creed. Less than 8% of the population (specifically most Kurds, Baluchis and Turkomans and about half the Arabs) are Sunni. According to the 1986 census, 99.38% of Iranians are Muslim, 0.30% Christian, 0.05% Jewish and 0.02% Zoroastrian.

Most Iranian Christians are Armenians, predominantly members of the Gregorian Church. The rest are mainly Assyrians, divided between Nestorians and Uniate Catholics (Chaldeans). A legacy of European missionary activity, there are also a few Protestants, including Adventists, Anglicans and Lutherans, and Latin-rite Catholics. Tehrān has a Greek Orthodox cathedral, Orūmīyé a Russian Orthodox church. Jews first settled in Iran following the Babylonian captivity of 597 BC at the invitation of Xerxes I, whose wife, Esther, was Jewish. Some 30 synagogues are said to operate in Iran today.

Zoroastrians are found mainly in Yazd, Tehrān and Kermān. There are also a few Hindus and Sikhs, spread throughout Iran but most numerous in Tehrān.

LANGUAGE

Although the vast majority of Iranians can speak Persian (Fārsī), the national language, it's the parent tongue of only about 60%. The most important minority languages are Āzarī, Kurdish, Arabic, Baluchi and Lorī.

Pronunciation

A macron indicates a long vowel.

ā	between *a* in *hurrah* and *a* in *what*
ī	as *i* in *machine*
ō	as *o* in *bone*
ū	as *u* in *ruse*
a	like *a* in *map*
e	like *e* in *beg*
é	like *é* in French *café*
o	between *o* in *god* and *oo* in *good*
ei	like *ei* in *rein*

The letters **b, d, f, j, k, l, m, n, p, s, sh, t, v** and **z** are pronounced as in English.

ch	as in *chip*
g	as in *gas*
y	as in *yak*
zh	as in *Zhivago*
r	slightly trilled as in Italian
h	always pronounced wherever it falls in a word and, as **r**, doesn't lengthen the preceding vowel
kh	like *ch* in Scots *loch*
gh	a soft guttural sound like the noise made when gargling
'	a weak glottal stop, like double *t* in the Cockney pronunciation of *bottle*

Doubled consonants are always pronounced distinctly. The last syllable of a word is usually stressed, although *é* never is.

Greetings & Civilities

Hello.	*salām*
Peace be upon you.	*salām aleikom*

Goodbye.	khodāfez or more formally khodā hāfez
Good morning.	sobh bekheir
Good night/Good evening.	shab bekheir
Please. (request, literally 'kindly')	lotfan
Please. (offering something)	befarmed/befarmā'īd
Thank you.	mersī/tashakkor/motashakkeram
Don't mention it.	ghābel nabūd
Excuse me/I'm sorry.	bebakhshīd
Yes.	balé
No.	nakheir/na (less polite but not rude)
OK.	dorost

Small Talk

Where do you come from?	shomā ahl-é kojā hastīd?
Do you know ...?	shomā ... baladīd?
English	engelīsī
French	ferānsé
German	ālmānī
I'm sorry, I don't speak Persian.	bebakhshīd, fārsī balad nīstam

Getting Around

Where is the ... to Tabrīz?	... betabrīz kojāst?
bus	otōbūs
train	ghetār
boat	ghāyegh
ship/ferry	kashtī
taxi (any kind)	tāksī
car (or taxi)	māshīn
minibus	mīnībūs
airport	forūdgāh
jetty/dock/harbour	eskelé
bus/railway station	termīnāl/īstgāh
ticket	belīt
ticket office	daftar-é belīt forūshī
open/closed	bāz/ta'tīl
left	dast-é chap
right	dast-é rāst

far (from)	dūr (az ...)
near (to ...)	nazdīk (-é ...)
straight ahead	mostaghīm

Around Town

Excuse me, where is the ...?	bebakhshīd, ... kojāst?
town centre	markaz-é shahr
embassy	safārat
consulate	konsūlgarī
post office	postkhūné
mosque	masjed
church	kelīsā
restaurant	restōrān/chelō kabābī /sālon-é ghezā
toilet	dast shū'ī
street/avenue	kheyābūn

Shopping

How many?	chand tā?
How much is it?	chand é?
cheap/expensive	arzūn/gerūn

Accommodation

hotel	hotel/mehmūnkhūné
cheap hotel/guesthouse	mosāferkhūné
Do you have a ... for tonight?	emshab ... dārīd?
room	otāgh
single room	otāgh-é ye nafarī
double room	otāgh-é do nafarī
cheaper room	otāgh-é arzūntar
better room	otāgh-é behtar
How much is a room for one night?	otāgh shabī chand é?

Time & Dates

When?	kei?
At what time?	chī vaght?
(at) ... o'clock	sā'at-é...
today	emrūz
tonight	emshab
tomorrow	fardā
(in the) morning	sobh
(at) night, evening	shab

IRAN

Saturday (1st day of Muslim week)	shambé
Sunday	yekshambé
Monday	doshambé
Tuesday	seshambé
Wednesday	chahārshambé
Thursday	panjshambé
Friday	jom'é

Numbers

1	yek
2	do
3	sé
4	chahār
5	panj
6	shesh
7	haft
8	hasht
9	noh
10	dah
11	yāzdah
12	davāzdah

Facts for the Visitor

PLANNING

When to Go

Although spring and autumn are the best times to tour Iran, some part of the country will be ideal for visiting anytime of year. The climate in most areas is mild and pleasant from late March to early June and late September to early November. However, winter is the most agreeable time to visit the south coast and islands, while Āzarbāyjān, the west and the north-east are at their best from late spring to early summer and late summer to early autumn. Many people prefer not to visit during Ramadan, which is rigidly enforced in Iran. For the second half of March, transport and accommodation can become very scarce as Iranians return to their home towns and villages for the Nō Rūz celebrations (usually 21 to 24 March). It's better to avoid travelling around Iran at this time, unless your transport and accommodation have been prearranged. Rooms are also hard to find in Tehrān during the International Trade Fair held in spring.

Maps

There is an excellent 1:2,000,000 country map published by GeoCenter of Germany retailing internationally for about the equivalent of US$10. Otherwise, fairly decent home-produced maps are readily available in Iran. The best city, country and regional maps, not all in English, are published by Gītā Shenāsī and can be bought at its Tehrān office (Kheyābūn-é Enghelāb, Chahārrāh-é Valī-yé Asr, 15 Kheyābūn-é Arfa') or at some bookshops. A useful free tourist map of Iran, marking all main roads, petrol stations etc, is available from Iranian tourist offices or diplomatic missions.

What to Bring

The backpack has bad connotations in Iran and is likely to be associated with the hippy ethos which does not fit in very well with the Islamic Revolutionary ideal. To avoid the disdain of hotel receptionists, if at all possible bring a shoulder bag or hold-all of some description instead. For clothing see under Society & Conduct and Climate in the Facts about the Country section earlier in this chapter, and for other miscellaneous suggestions, the What to Bring section in the Regional Facts for the Visitor chapter.

TOURIST OFFICES

The Ministry of Culture & Islamic Guidance has a tourist office (daftar-é sīr va seyāhat) in each provincial capital, as well as Ghom and Ghazvīn, but none overseas. Most tourist offices are listed in the relevant city entries later in this chapter. While the staff do often try to be helpful, giving tourist information to foreigners is only a tiny part of their job: don't expect lots of glossy hand-outs or even necessarily anything in English. In most places they'll be genuinely surprised if you manage to track them down. Most offices have free maps of the relevant city or province; Tehrān is a notable exception.

VISAS & DOCUMENTS
Visas

Everyone must have a visa to visit Iran, except Turkish and Japanese passport holders. How ready the Iranians are to issue you a visa depends very much on the state of their relations with your country at the time. As we write, Iranian officialdom is not very keen on the British, and Americans without a very cogent reason for visiting or a place on an organised tour are still unlikely to get in. Any evidence in a passport of a previous or intended visit to Israel (but not Iraq or South Africa) is a definite bar to entry.

There are two general types of travellers' visa; transit and tourist. Transit visas are valid for at most two weeks, tourist visas for a month, but this is entirely dependent on how much the Iranians like you. As a rule they do not like independent travellers and will not issue them with tourist visas, only transit. Apply in person at an Iranian mission (which involves filling in two forms and supplying two photographs) and wait. The amount of time that you must wait and your chances of success vary with each individual embassy and consulate. At the UK consulate all applications are sent for consideration to the Ministry of Foreign Affairs (MFA) in Tehrān and it can take four weeks or more before a reply, without any guarantee of success. On the other hand, we have met travellers who applied for their transit visas at the Iranian embassy in İstanbul and got them within 24 hours.

If relatives or business contacts invite you to Iran, they can arrange a visa on your behalf through the MFA. Applicants stand a much better chance of success if they have a sponsor.

It's impossible to predict which applications will be successful but it is important to give as good an impression as possible. Obviously it makes sense to apply at least a month or two before you plan to travel. Women should wear a veil or scarf for the photos they submit with their application, and when visiting the mission.

Fees are supposed to be reciprocal, which means UK£33 for UK passport holders while the cost is nil for Australian passport holders.

Once you succeed in securing a visa, check it carefully and ask for an explanation of any entries you don't understand. Any amendments should be officially stamped and signed, or you may later be suspected of having made them yourself.

Some specialist tour agencies may be prepared to help travellers get visas without necessarily having to buy into a tour package. See Organised Tours in the Getting Around section later in this chapter.

Visa Extensions Once in Iran you can generally get two extensions of up to two weeks each for both transit and tourist visas – sometimes more, again depending on the officials considering your request and how good an impression you make on them. To apply for an extension, simply present yourself at one of the visa offices found in any provincial capital a few days before the visa is due to expire. These are usually located inside the police headquarters, or *shahrbānī* – the addresses are given in the Information section of each city entry in this chapter. The Tehrān office is the least friendly and waits of several days are common there; the Tabrīz and Shīrāz offices are reportedly the most accommodating. You need two photographs and there is a fee of between 1000 and 5000 rials.

Other Documents

It's important that you have photocopies of the information pages of your passport. You will quite often have to leave your passport with the hotel reception or at a visa office and in this instance the photocopies will be a good substitute ID for any curious officials in the meantime. Also, bring extra passport photos; you need a couple every time you extend your visa. Iranians also like to swap mugshots with 'new friends'. A student card is of limited use but will get you reductions on admission fees at Persepolis and the Arg-é Bam, amongst other places.

EMBASSIES
Iranian Embassies Abroad

Following are the addresses and telephone

numbers of Iranian embassies and consulates in major cities around the world:

Australia
14 Torres St, Red Hill, Manuka, Canberra
(☎ (06) 290 2421)
Azerbaijan
4 ulitsa Bouniat Sardarov, Baku
(☎ (8922) 926177)
Canada
411 Roosevelt Ave, Ottawa K2A 3X9
(☎ (613) 729 0902)
Egypt
12 Sharia Rifah, Doqqi, Cairo (☎ (02) 486400)
France
4 Ave d'Iena, Paris 75116 (☎ 01 47 23 61 22)
Consulate: 16 Rue Fresnel, Paris 75116
(☎ 01 47 20 30 80)
Germany
Godesberger Allee 133-7, 5300 Bonn 2
(☎ (0228) 8 10 05 21)
Consulate: Peter Lenne Strasse 26, Berlin
(☎ (030) 8 32 40 61); Abtei Strasse 25, Hamburg
(☎ (040) 41 03 75); Mauerkircherstrasse 59,
Munich (☎ (089) 98 43 22)
Pakistan
House 222-238 St 2, G-5/1, Islamabad
(☎ 822694)
Consulate: 81 Iran Rd Clifton, Karachi
(☎ 532037)
Russia
7 bulvar Pokrovskiy, Moscow
(☎ (095) 297 8440)
UK
27 Prince's Gate, London SW7 1PX
(☎ (0171) 584 8101)
Consulate: 50 Kensington Court, London W8
5DB (☎ (0171) 937 5225)
USA
Interests Section: 2209 Wisconsin Ave NW,
Washington DC 20007 (☎ (202) 965 4990)

Foreign Embassies in Iran

All of the following embassies are in Tehrān (telephone code 021) unless stated otherwise. Most embassies and consulates tend to be open from 9 am to 2 or 3 pm, and are closed on Friday and Saturday. (Street names mostly appear in full on maps; Kh represents Kheyābūn-é, K represents Kūché-yé, B represents Bozorgrāh.)

Afghanistan
Kh Beheshtī, Kh Pākestān corner of
K Chahārrom (☎ & fax 873 5600)
Consulate: Kh Bāhonar, K Konsūlgarī,
Mashhad (☎ (051) 97551)

Australia
Kh Eslāmbōlī, 13 K Nōzdahom (☎ 872 4456;
fax 872 0484)
Azerbaijan
Kh Dr Sharī'atī, 10 K Malek (☎ 750 2404;
fax 750 2724)
Bahrain
Kh Eslāmbōlī, 16 K Sī o Yekom (☎ 226 2079;
fax 226 9112)
Canada
Kh Motahharī, 57 Kh Sarāfrāz (☎ 873 2623;
fax 873 3202)
Egypt
Interests Section: B Afrīghā, 70 K Esfandyar
(☎ 222 1163)
France
85 Kh Nōfl Lōshātō (Neauphle-le-Château)
(☎ 676001; fax 676544)
Germany
324 Kh Ferdōsī (☎ 311 4111)
Iraq
494 Kh Valī-yé Asr (50m south of Meidūn-é
Valī-yé Asr) (☎ 278386)
Ireland
Bolvār-é Mīr Dāmād, 8 Kh Rāzān-é Shomālī
(☎ 222 7672; fax 222 2731)
Jordan
Kh Mahmoudieh, Kh Shadavār (☎ 204 1432;
fax 205 2515)
Kuwait
B Afrīghā, 15 K Mayhar (☎ 204 0990;
fax 204 9967)
Lebanon
Kh Nejātollāhī, 31 Kh Kalāntarī (☎ 898451;
fax 897345)
New Zealand
Kh Beheshtī, Kh Mīrzā-yé Shīrāzī, 29 K Mīrzā
Hasanī (☎ 871 5061; fax 886 1715)
Oman
B Afrīghā, 12 Kh Tandis (☎ 228 8277;
fax 228 5423)
Pakistan
Kh Fātemī, 1 Kh E'temād Zādé (☎ 934332;
fax 935154)
Consulates: Kh Emām Khomeinī, Mashhad
(☎ (051) 29845); Kh Shahīd
Razmjū Moghaddam, Zāhedān
(☎ (0541) 23389)
Visas are free, require two photos and are issued
in one week. You may need to show inward and
outward tickets.
Qatar
B Afrīghā, 4 Kh Gol Āzīn (☎ 222 1256)
Saudi Arabia
B Afrīghā, 10 Kh Saba (☎ 222 0081;
fax 222 0083)
Syria
B Afrīghā, 22 Kh Arash (☎ 222 9031;
fax 808 9409)

Turkey
  314 Kh Ferdōsī (☎ 311 5299)
  Consulates: 30 Kh Shahīd Beheshtī, Orūmīyé (☎ (0441) 28970); 516 Kh Sharī'atī-yé Shomālī, Tabrīz (☎ (041) 52417)
Turkmenistan
  Kh Pāsdārān, 39 K Golestan (☎ 254 2178; fax 258 0432)
UAE
  Kh Valī-yé Asr, Kh Dastgerdī (☎ 222 1333)
UK
  143 Kh Ferdōsī (☎ 675011; fax 678021)
  Also for other Commonwealth countries not directly represented.
USA
  Interests Section: Swiss embassy, Kh Eslāmbōlī, 5 K Hefdahom (☎ 871 5223)
  Open from 8 to 11 am only.

CUSTOMS

Customs checks on arriving passengers are much laxer than they once were. For instance, in theory visitors are not allowed to bring in more than five rolls of photographic film, or two cassettes for a video camera, but in practice this ruling is frequently waived. However, a ban on all alcohol, 'vulgar' films, 'unpleasant' records and cassettes, and books and magazines with 'indecent' pictures is strictly enforced. Cassettes are often listened to before being given the OK and magazines will be carefully examined. Something that may seem perfectly innocent to you may well be considered indecent or offensive in the eyes of a customs officer. Fashion and style magazines are an absolute no-no, although you will probably manage to hold on to your copy of *Time* or *Newsweek*.

Currency Declaration

In the past all foreign visitors to Iran were obliged to fill out a currency declaration form on arrival. On our last visit we were told that this was only necessary for anyone carrying more than US$1000. It does seem that currency checks are being phased out, but, nonetheless, we advise that you ask what the existing regulations are when you arrive.

MONEY

Costs

Iran is extremely inexpensive by interna-

tional standards, especially when it comes to getting around; a 1st class sleeper on a 12 hour train journey costs roughly the equivalent of US$3, while you can fly from one end of the country to the other for less than US$30. There are fairly decent hotels for around US$20 for a single, although it's also possible to pay as little as US$2 or US$3 (bear in mind, you don't get what you don't pay for). Dining out will rarely set you back more than a couple of dollars either. If you are not too fussy about where you sleep, a daily budget of US$15 is ample; as little as US$30 a day will ensure a very comfortable stay.

Currency

Iran's currency is the rial (*reyāl*). In conversation, although rarely in writing, Iranians usually talk in terms of *tōmāns*: one tōmān equals 10 rials. When you are quoted a price for anything, make sure that you aren't thinking rials while they're talking tōmāns. There are coins for 2, 5, 10, 20 and 50 rials, marked only with Persian numerals, and notes in denominations of 100, 200, 500, 1000, 5000 and 10,000, printed in English and Persian.

Currency Exchange

At the time of our last visit the official rate was US$1 equals 1583 rials.

Changing Money

Plenty of banks in Tehrān and several in Esfahān and Shīrāz have exchange desks, always indicated by a sign in the window. Elsewhere, cash can be changed at Bank Melli Iran's head office in any provincial capital, but foreign-currency travellers' cheques can be a major hassle to off-load. Bank Melli offices at international border-posts and airports change both cash and travellers' cheques. Exchange commission charges for cash and travellers' cheques are nominal; all banks offer the same rate.

Some private exchange offices exist in the big cities, usually around the town square. They keep longer hours than the banks and offer a faster service, but don't normally list their exchange rates; you may have to negotiate to get a good deal.

Almost any major hard currency is acceptable at banks. Major travellers' cheques can be cashed, but it's difficult to find anywhere willing to touch American Express. Credit cards (but again not American Express) are accepted by some foreign airline offices but are otherwise useless.

Black Market

There is a very active and high profile black market for currency exchange. At the time of our last visit it was possible to get as much as 4000 rials to the dollar. Considering how laborious it can be to change money in a state bank (on one occasion it took visits to four separate desks, three different cashiers' signatures and two of mine, and a grand total of 25 minutes to exchange one US$50 note), the favourable exchange rate is not the only benefit to be gained from making use of the black market. The easiest way to go about it is to ask any hotel reception if they know of somewhere you can change money; in most cases they themselves will oblige. How legal this is we don't know and we certainly advise discretion.

Tipping

Tipping is not obligatory, but it is worth remembering that many Iranians working in a service capacity do make a special effort to help foreigners and probably deserve some small token of appreciation.

POST & COMMUNICATIONS
Post

The mail service is reliable and inexpensive, though fairly slow, to all parts of the world except Israel. Poste restante is available at the head post office *(edāré-yé koll-é post)* in any provincial capital. Post offices open from at least 8 am to noon, except Friday. Outside Tehrān it's best to go to a head post office to mail parcels, or anything registered or express, overseas. Parcels have to be wrapped by postal staff.

Telephone & Telegraph

Local calls can be made from public telephone boxes, which take any combination of 10 or 20 rial coins, depending on the age of the cashbox. You may find one that works. A rapid bleeping tone is the signal to insert more coins. You can make trunk calls from some telephone boxes; they have English instructions. All towns have at least one telephone office *(telefonkhūné)*, which can place trunk calls within about 30 minutes.

For international calls your best bet is to try from a hotel. Otherwise, go to a head telephone office *(edāré-yé koll-é telefon)*, which will double as the head telegraph office *(edāré-yé koll-é mokhābarāt)* in some places. If possible save overseas calls for Tehrān, where connections are usually made quite quickly; elsewhere they may have to be booked hours ahead. Reverse-charge (collect) calls can't be made to or from Iran.

BOOKS

See also the Books section in the Regional Facts for the Visitor chapter for other titles that cover Iran.

By far the best single background read is *Lifting the Veil* (originally published as *Behind Iranian Lines*) by John Simpson & Tira Shubart. Simpson, foreign affairs editor for the BBC, shared Khomeinī's fateful flight from Paris to Tehrān in 1979. Since then, he and Shubart have returned numerous times, travelling extensively and interviewing hundreds of Iranians. The result is a supremely well informed and engrossing portrait of contemporary Iran.

Death Plus Ten Years is the story of the 5¼ years author Roger Cooper spent in a Tehrān jail after his arrest on charges of spying. The title comes from the sentence the Iranian court passed on him – to which his immediate reply was, 'Which comes first?'. *Out of Iran* by Sousan Azadi is a considerably more bitter autobiography, penned by a member of the westernised Iranian elite who stayed on after 1979, resolutely refusing to give up the pleasures of life outlawed by the newly empowered Islamic regime.

The intrepid dame Freya Stark has written

several books on her various uncompromising forays into Persia; *Beyond Euphrates* recounts her lone exploration of the Luristan region, undertaken in the 1950s, while *Valley of the Assassins* recounts her travels in the mountainous Caspian region in the 1930s.

NEWSPAPERS & MAGAZINES

There are three English-language newspapers available in Iran. The 16 page daily (except Friday) *Tehran Times* is the most widely available – it's fairly interesting and surprisingly balanced. The *Iran News* and *Kayhan International* (English edition) are much thinner and considerably harder to find outside of Tehrān. All three carry a limited amount of international news picked up from western news agencies as well as a lot of locally focused commentary.

RADIO & TV

The BBC World Service can be picked up in most parts of the country and is regularly listened to by millions of Iranians, rightfully distrustful of the state media network. Even Āyatollāh Khomeinī was reportedly an avid follower, if not supporter, of the BBC Persian Service. Frequencies to try for the BBC English-language programming include 9410, 12095 and 15050 kHz. There are three national TV channels, on all of which religious programming is still very much a priority. There is a short English-language news bulletin each evening at 10.45 pm on Channel 3.

PHOTOGRAPHY & VIDEO

Some restrictions on photography apply. You can get into deep water for even pointing your lens in the same general direction as any of the following forbidden subjects: airports; security installations; prisons; post, telephone and telegraph offices; railway stations; bridges; all other government buildings; and anything within several km of any land border or marked 'No Photography' or with the sign of a crossed out camera. If in doubt ask first. Cameras are best carried inside a bag. Video cameras require a permit.

HEALTH

There are no compulsory vaccinations needed before visiting Iran; for other health information, see the Health Appendix.

WOMEN TRAVELLERS

Women in Iran are not as 'downtrodden' or 'discriminated against' as some misguided journalists would report. In contrast to much of the Islamic world where women are forbidden to travel without male accompaniment, it's not uncommon to meet pairs or groups of young women travelling about on Iran's trains or buses, off somewhere on a sightseeing trip, maybe even staying overnight. Unlike Saudi Arabia, women are allowed to drive cars, and this they do – and they are no slouches either when it comes to hitting the horn or hurling abuse at fellow road users.

That said, the Iranian interpretation of Islam does impose a number of strict constraints on women, most notably in terms of dress – see the boxed story near the Society & Conduct entry in the Facts about the Country section earlier in this chapter. Foreign women travelling in Iran should be prepared to fit in with the social code if they wish to avoid some unpleasant experiences.

If you do become harassed, tell the person firmly but politely to go away. If the problem persists, say the word, 'Komīté' (the word for the Islamic Revolutionary Guards Corps), which should have the intended effect (but if you do want to make an official complaint, go to the police first). There have been a few reports of problems in eastern Iran, in conservative places like Zāhedān and Zābol.

DANGERS & ANNOYANCES

Crime against foreigners is pretty rare and violent crime almost unheard of; however, it pays to take the usual precautions. The police have a better reputation for probity and efficiency in Iran than in many other countries in the region. If for any reason they try to arrest you or take you away for questioning, demand identification, insist on your right to telephone your consul before going anywhere and, unless you speak fluent Persian, refuse to answer any questions until an interpreter has been found. It's a good idea to register with your consulate in Tehrān upon arrival and to memorise its telephone number.

Be prepared for body frisks, identity checks and baggage inspections when entering public buildings or undertaking long-distance travel. If you must leave your passport somewhere (eg at a hotel or visa office) ask for a receipt. You can carry on travelling inside Iran without a passport but you'll need some other proof of your identity (preferably with your photo on it) and a contact number for the person who has your passport.

Marg Bar Amrika

Open hostility towards foreigners, whatever their nationality, is actually very rare. The lobbies of Tehrān's top-end hotels may be hung with banners proclaiming 'Down with America', but city buses still carry slogans exhorting the populace to 'Drink Coca Cola'. The anti-western rhetoric is these days largely a sham, and, if it is encountered at all, it's as an expression of hatred of western governments, not their private citizens. In *Lifting the Veil*, journalist John Simpson writes of meeting three young Iranians who, on ascertaining he was English, countered with, 'Marg bar Thatcher' ('Death to Thatcher'). As Simpson tells it, they were completely taken aback that he should be offended.

Most visitors are constantly surprised by the kindness and generosity shown towards them by Iranians, regardless of their own country's position in the official demonology. Providing that you observe the restrictions on dress, it's unlikely that you'll be met with anything but courtesy. ■

BUSINESS HOURS

In general, government and private offices open from 8 am to 2 pm (noon on Thursday) and close on Friday and public holidays; some also close on Thursday. As a rule it's best to complete all official business before noon between Saturday and Wednesday.

On the south coast, places close at noon, usually reopening for a couple of hours in the early evening, year-round. Shops generally stay open until about 8 pm; bazaars usually operate according to daylight hours. Transport terminals, most bakeries, museums and some food shops stay open on Friday. Non-Muslims should avoid visiting mosques during services or on Friday unless specifically invited. Most museums open daily (except Monday) at least from 10 am to 4 pm, sometimes with a lunch break. In Ramadan many places open before sunrise and close well before noon.

PUBLIC HOLIDAYS & SPECIAL EVENTS

In addition to the traditional Muslim holidays of Ramadan (Ramazān in Iran), Eid al-Fitr and Eid al-Adha (see the table of holidays near Public Holidays & Special Events in the Regional Facts for the Visitor chapter), the Iranian calendar is marked by several other festivals.

The main one is Nō Rūz, the Persian New Year, which falls around 21 March each year. This is not an Islamic holiday, but a celebration of spring which dates back to Achaemenian times. As such, the Khomeneī regime tried to discourage people from bothering too much with the event, but without much success, and Iran still closes down for two or three days at this time as everybody travels to their home villages and towns to celebrate with family and friends.

The other big disruptive holiday, when everything closes for a couple of days, is Ashura, which marks the death of Hussein, the third emām of the Shiites. The event is traditionally celebrated with religious passion plays and sombre parades of devout black-shirted men scourging themselves with flails whilst chanting 'Ya Hussein! Ya Hussein!' ('Oh Hussein! Oh Hussein!'). Resist the temptation to take photographs. Ashura follows the lunar calendar; in 1997 it falls around 16 May, in 1998 around 5 May and in 1999 around 24 April. Similar displays of grief also take place annually on 4 June to mark the 'Heart-Rending Departure of the Great Leader of the Islamic Republic of Iran', in other words, the anniversary of the death of Āyatollāh Khomeinī.

ACCOMMODATION

The usual word for hotel is *hotel*, but *mehmānkhūné* is also used. A cheap lodging-house, usually offering both dormitory accommodation and some private rooms, is a *mosāferkhūné*. Many mosāferkhūnés offer few opportunities for personal hygiene, but there'll nearly always be a *hammūm* (public bathhouse) nearby with some private showers. Hammūms have separate sections or opening times for men and women.

In places where better accommodation is available many mosāferkhūnés won't accept foreigners. A *mehmūnpazīr* is one step up from a mosāferkhūné. A *mehmūnsarā* is a resthouse owned by a governmental or semi-governmental organisation; it'll usually take members of the public if it has any vacancies. A *mehmūnsarā-yé jahāngardī* is a resthouse specifically designed for tourists. Iran has no youth hostels. Camping is fairly popular along the Caspian coast; elsewhere ask first. Shīrāz has an official camp site.

Although most mid-range and upper-end hotels display their room prices in US dollars, you should, in theory, be able to pay in rials (calculated at the official exchange rate of US$1 to 1583 rials).

FOOD

At its best, Iran's cuisine is very good indeed. With its emphasis on the freshest ingredients, especially vegetables and fruit, and its relatively low levels of red meat and fat, it's also remarkably healthy. Meals are heavily based on rice, bread, fresh vegetables, herbs and fruit. Meat, usually minced or diced, is used to add flavour but is rarely the dominant ingredient. The standard meat is mutton or lamb, although beef and veal also turn up from time to time. Chicken, cheap and widely available, is often spit-roasted and served whole or by the half. Game is sometimes available, especially in the Caspian region. Nuts and fresh or dried fruit are commonly included in meat and poultry dishes to create a peculiarly Iranian blend of sweet and savoury.

Rice *(berenj)* is served in vast helpings with almost every main dish. Prepared in several stages over 24 or more hours, boiled and steamed and often tinted with saffron, it's always fluffy and tender, never sticky and soggy. It's often steamed with yoghurt, butter or egg yolk to make a crunchy golden crust at the base of the pan, which is broken up and served on top of the rest of the rice. *Chelō...* is a dish served with rice cooked separately from the other ingredients, while *...polō* is one in which rice has been cooked with them. Yoghurt and butter are frequently stirred into rice at the table. Often a raw onion – said to clear the stomach – and a salad are served before the main course.

Iranian bread *(nūn* or *nān)* is arguably Asia's best. It's made in flat rounds, oval or square in shape. It accompanies almost every meal, sometimes replacing rice or cutlery. Four main varieties exist. *Lavāsh* is a flat and very thin version folded twice into a square. *Sangak* is a thicker bread, oval-shaped and pulpy, baked on a bed of sterilised stones to give it a dimpled look; make sure these are removed before taking a bite. *Taftūn* is crisp, about a cm thick and oval-shaped, with a characteristic ribbed surface. *Barbarī* is the elite of Iranian breads – crisp and salty with a glazed and finely latticed crust.

Lumpy and unsweetened, yoghurt *(māst)* is another great staple. It's sometimes served on its own with bread, sometimes sits as a side dish and sometimes acts as a cooking ingredient. It is often stirred with diced vegetables, fresh herbs, spices or – in the Caspian region – garlic.

Iranian soup *(sūp)* is thick and filling. Even thicker is *āsh*, more of a pottage or broth, and thicker still is *ābgūsht* or *dīzī*. A brew of potato chunks, meat and lentils, it's mashed in a bowl and scooped up with sangak. There's an art to eating it properly. It's the only meal on offer at many teahouses and workers' restaurants. The dividing lines between sūp, āsh and ābgūsht can be hazy. *Khōresh (khōresht)* is a blanket term for any thick meaty stew with vegetables and chopped nuts.

The staple dish, served up everywhere, is *chelō kabāb*, a long strip of lean lamb, marinated overnight in seasoned yoghurt, grilled

IRAN

at a high temperature for a few minutes and served with a mound of rice. *Somāgh*, a reddish sour-tasting seasoning made from dried berries of the sumac tree, is sprinkled over it. Chelō kabāb is Iran's national dish and comes in several varieties. When made with lamb fillet it's known as *fillé kabāb* and is invariably delicious. *Chelō kabāb-é makhsūs* is a larger strip of meat than average and is also made of good-quality lamb. *Chelō kabāb-é barg* is thinner and varies in quality but is usually quite good. A vastly inferior version known as *chelō kabāb-é kūbīdé* is made of ground meat of some description; a good one is rarely found.

Jūjé kabāb is a dish of diced chicken prepared and served in the same way as chelō kabāb. *Shīshlīk* is similar to Turkish şiş kebap. Sturgeon kabābs, available on the Caspian coast, are recommended, as are prawn and shrimp kabābs (*chelō meigū*) on the south.

Kūkū is a very thick omelette cut into wedges. *Dolmé* is a vegetable, fruit or vine leaf stuffed with vegetables, meat or both. *Ghormé-yé sabzī* is a lamb, spinach and dried lime stew. Meatballs are *kofté*. One of Iran's culinary triumphs is *fesenjūn*, a stew of duck, goose, chicken or quail in a rich sauce of pomegranate juice and chopped walnuts.

DRINK

In almost any social, business or official context, tea *(chāy)* precedes any sort of serious conversation. Served scalding hot, black and strong in small glass cups, it's perfect for anyone with a tannin deficiency but hard to enjoy without sugar. A sugar lump, clenched in the teeth, is *ghand*; granulated sugar, stirred with a teaspoon, is *shekar*. The teahouse *(chāykhūné)* is a great (all-male) Iranian institution. Most bazaars have at least one. Many teahouses provide hubble-bubbles (tobacco pipes); some serve ābgūsht.

Fruit juice is readily available from street stalls. Restaurants and snack bars sell Iranian-made orangeade, lemonade and cola (the local stuff is known as Zam Zam) at around 200 rials a bottle. It's possible to buy beer – Islamic beer. Known as *mā'-osh-sha'īr*, it's quite drinkable, although it does of course lack one vital ingredient. *Dūgh* is a yoghurt and mineral water drink which is widely available and very popular, particularly in summer when it's a superb thirst quencher. A speciality of Shīrāz, *pālūdé (fālūdé)* is a rose-flavoured iced drink with fresh lemon juice. Iranian coffee *(ghahvé)* is Turkish coffee, unless it's Nescafé.

THINGS TO BUY

Perhaps largely due to its dearth of tourists, Iran is a buyers' market for souvenirs. Mass production is rare, quality fairly high even at the bottom end of the market and prices are astoundingly low. Some good buys among many are hand-beaten bronzeware and copperware, inlaid boxes and furniture, tea sets, block-printed cottonware, calligraphy, rugs, cashmere, jewellery, religious items, Khomeinī mementos, coffee sets and, of course, Persian miniatures, Persian slippers and Persian carpets. Esfahān is undoubtedly the best place for souvenir hunters.

Most main bazaars have a selection of local handicrafts ranging from the largely functional to the purely decorative. There are also many handicrafts shops in Tehrān (especially on Ferdōsī, Karīm Khān-é Zand and upper Valī-yé Asr), some in Esfahān and Shīrāz and a few elsewhere. The Iranian Handicrafts Organization (IHO) has three well-stocked shops in Tehrān (on Nejātollāhī, on Valī-yé Asr facing Pārk-é Mellat and in Hotel-é Bozorg-é Āzādī) and one in Kermān. Except in IHO shops, where prices are fixed, bargaining is the order of the day even at the flashiest places. Unless you speak fluent Persian and know the market, you'll probably end up paying more than an Iranian would. If in doubt about your own negotiating skills, or the quality of the goods, try to take an Iranian companion with you.

Caviar, once extremely cheap and fairly easily obtainable, is now only sold openly to departing international passengers at Tehrān airport's duty-free shop. Pistachios and saffron, however, are still widely available and sold at prices well below their international market value.

Getting There & Away

AIR

Iran Air operates flights to many countries in the region and to Beijing, Bombay, Singapore, Sydney, Tokyo, several destinations in the USA and Western Europe, but tickets, at full IATA rates, are too expensive for most budget travellers to consider.

In the UK, the cheapest tickets to Tehrān are with Syrian Arab Airlines (☎ (0171) 493 2851), who offer return flights with a maximum two month stay for UK£341 (plus UK£25 taxes). Other carriers flying to Tehrān include Aeroflot, Air France, Austrian Airlines, British Airways, Emirates, Lufthansa and PIA, and you may be able to get discount fares with one of these airlines through a bucket shop – see the introductory Getting There & Away chapter.

Outside the UK, there is little around in the way of cheap fares. In the USA, Explorer Travel Consultants (☎ (212) 239 1012) in New York and Travelure (☎ (818) 247 6960; fax 244 3882) in California both specialise in air travel to Iran and may be able to offer low rates. Otherwise, Aeroflot is worth a try. Another possibility is to get a cheap ticket to Dubai, then hop across the Persian Gulf to Bandar-é Abbās with Iran Air or, less expensively, by ferry from Sharjah.

Most international and all intercontinental services operate out of Tehrān's Mehrābād airport. There are also flights from several Gulf ports to Bandar-é Abbās, Esfahān, Mashhad and Shīrāz, and from Mashhad to Quetta, in Pakistan, and Ashghabat in Turkmenistan. Middle Eastern airports served from Tehrān are Damascus, Dubai, İstanbul, Kabul, Kuwait and Sharjah.

LAND
Iraq

Iran's border post with Iraq is at Khosravī, 187 km west of Kermānshāh by road. No organised public transport links the two, but you can take a bus from Kermānshāh to Ghasr-é Shīrīn and a taxi from there for the final 20 km to Khosravī. For the latest information ask at Tehrān's Iraqi embassy or the Kermānshāh tourist office.

Turkey

Several direct bus services run between Tehrān's west bus station and İstanbul weekly. Single fare from Tehrān is approximately 600,000 rials (US$200). The best buses on this route are run by Cooperative Bus Company No 1. A few direct Tehrān-Ankara, Tehrān-Erzurum and Esfahān-İstanbul services also exist.

Many travellers prefer, however, to change transport at the border to avoid a potential wait of several hours for the bus and its passengers to clear customs. Coming from Turkey, you can work your way through to dismal Doğubeyazıt, then take a minibus to Ağri Ili border post (30 minutes), open from 7 am to 2 pm. The Iranian border post (Bāzargān) is a huge compound with a large truck-parking area, replete with a mosque. The border itself runs along a ridge and it's a 20 minute walk from the official buildings on the ridge to the gate of the compound; taxis run back and forth from one end to another. From the gate, shared taxis run to Mākū, the nearest town. Mākū is a fairly pleasant overnight stop with several hotels. Many people prefer to keep moving to Tabrīz, which has more accommodation options.

If you're heading west out of Iran make sure you leave Tabrīz very early on the first bus. The best option is to get a shared taxi from Mākū to take you right through the compound to the border. If this doesn't work out, you should be able to get a taxi inside the compound at the point where the road forks right towards the mosque (and various other buildings) and left up the hill to the border.

At Bāzargān, if you're coming from Mākū, from left to right there's a bank, customs, then adjoining customs, the police. The first step is to go to the police for an exit stamp. Next you negotiate customs. Whether you're entering or leaving, expect a thorough baggage search.

IRAN

Relations here are tense, and the customs officers at Ağri Ili have a reputation for discourtesy; a few travellers entering Turkey have reported having had bribes extorted from them. One consolation for westbound passengers is Ağri Ili's duty-free shop.

A much quieter border post is at Serō, 50 km north-west of Orūmīyé by road, but no organised public transport serves this route. See the Orūmīyé section later in this chapter for more information.

The CIS

See the introductory Getting There & Away chapter.

Afghanistan

While to all intents Afghanistan is a closed country to westerners, buses go from Mashhad to Tāybād, 224 km south-east by road, and shared taxis and minibuses continue on to the Iranian border post at Eslām Ghal'é, 11 km away. From the Afghan side, buses run to Herat.

Pakistan

Buses and trains link Zāhedān with Quetta. See the introductory Getting There & Away chapter for details.

Syria

Buses run at least weekly between Tehrān's west bus station and Damascus.

SEA

See the Getting Around the Region chapter for details of ferries between Bandar-é Anzalī and Baku. There are no passenger ferries between Iran and Iraq across Arvand Rūd (Shatt al-Arab). The state-run Valfajre-8 Shipping Company (see the following Getting Around section for the addresses of it's offices) operates passenger services in the Persian Gulf and Sea of Oman from Bandar-é Abbās to Muscat and Sharjah, from Būshehr to Kuwait, and from Chābahār to Muscat. All are overnight sailings with afternoon or early evening departures. Tickets bought in Iran are payable in US dollars.

LEAVING IRAN

If leaving Iran by air you must reconfirm your flight. There is a departure tax of 70,000 rials – with some airlines this is included in the ticket (eg Air France) but with others it isn't (eg Lufthansa). This tax must be prepaid and cannot be paid at the airport.

Getting Around

AIR

Because Iran Air's domestic fares are so incredibly low, flying is the preferred means of travel. As a result, the most popular flights are booked up weeks ahead, and it's often impossible to buy a ticket in advance to fit in with your travel plans. One possible solution is to go to the airport two or three hours before you want to fly and ask to be put on the waiting list. Alternatively, if you have a planned itinerary you could book your domestic flights in advance through the Iran Air office in your own country. While foreigners pay in rials for flights in Iran, from overseas you'll have to pay in dollars at an unfavourable exchange rate.

For fares see the Getting There & Away entries in the individual city sections later in this chapter.

BUS

Nearly 20 cooperative bus companies link the country and the business is highly competitive. The bus companies are referred to simply as Cooperative No X (Sherkat-é Ta'āvonī Shomāré-yé X). The best and most popular is Cooperative No 1 (Iran Peyma), followed by No 15 (TBT) and No 5.

Although some companies have city booking offices, it's generally easiest to get a ticket at the bus station itself. Iranian bus stations are like chaotic bazaars – each bus company has a stand loudly hawking tickets. Each company serves a variety of routes and there's much overlapping. There is never a central enquiry point where you can find out who goes where and when – it's a matter of asking at desk after desk for available seats on the bus that best suits you. To confuse matters, a few cities have more than one bus station, each serving different destinations. If in doubt it's best to ask locally which is the right station for buses to a particular place. Tickets are numbered and correspond to particular seats. It's not usually a problem for couples to sit together.

On long hauls, buses are never overloaded and getting a seat at short notice is not usually a problem, except on Friday and in the run-up to public holidays . The buses are usually clean with comfortable, reclining seats. Fares are absurdly cheap, for example, Zāhedān to Mashhad, a 16 hour journey, costs just 12,000 rials. You can pay a bit more and travel 'super' with some companies. This gets you more leg room. Cooperative No 1 has 'super' buses with only three seats across, as opposed to four in normal buses.

Buses drive through the night and stop for meals at roadside cafes. Even in spring and autumn it can get very cold at night, so make sure you have warm clothes. Try to get a seat near the front, as the heater's usually only powerful enough to keep the driver and the first couple of rows of passengers happy.

TRAIN

Iranian trains are reasonably fast and comfortable, and tickets are extremely cheap. The one drawback is the limited extent of the rail network.

Two classes of accommodation exist, but not all trains have both. The main difference between the two is that 2nd class seats six people, while 1st class admits only four. Seats can be converted into beds at night but in 2nd class the sleeping arrangements are incredibly cramped. The guard will come around and take orders for tea and meals – fairly good and inexpensive – to be served in your compartment.

It's difficult to find a train timetable in Iran. Ring Tehrān ☎ 556114 for the latest information. Although foreigners may be found seats at short notice, it's a wise precaution to book as early as possible. Esfahān has a city booking office but elsewhere tickets are only sold at the railway station.

CAR & MOTORCYCLE

Iran has some of the best roads on the Asian overland route, although it also has some pretty terrible desert tracks. Fuel is still extremely cheap. You'll notice that only foreigners normally wear motorcycle helmets or car safety belts in Iran. Iranian driving habits can be hair-raising.

HITCHING

If you are seen trying to hitch a lift it will probably be assumed that you think the car is a taxi and, if you do get a lift, you'll be charged accordingly.

Iranians are hospitable people and you may well be offered occasional free lifts, but you won't get very far if you deliberately set out to avoid paying. If you're hellbent on hitching across Iran, try holding a placard with the name of your destination written in Persian and make it obvious that you're a foreigner.

A raised thumb is a vaguely obscene gesture in Iran. Remember hitching is not a particularly safe way of travelling.

BOAT

Valfajre-8 operates several passenger ferries weekly between Kīsh and Bandar-é Kong for 120,000 rials. It has offices in:

Ahvāz – ☎ (061) 34081
Bandar-é Abbās – Iran Air building, Kheyābūn-é Emām Khomeinī (☎ (0761) 29095)
Bandar-é Kong – ☎ 3632
Bandar-é Lengé – Kheyābūn-é Pāsdārān (☎ 3448)
Būshehr – Kheyābūn-é Solhābād (☎ (0771) 2314)
Chābahār – Kheyābūn-é Mōlavī (☎ (05423) 3012)
Kīsh – ☎ (07653) 27973
Shīrāz – ☎ (071) 25103
Tehrān – Kheyābūn-é Karīm Khān, Kūché-yé Ābyār (☎ (021) 899288)

There are small motor boats from Bandar-é Abbās to Hormoz and Gheshm. No passenger services operate along Iran's Caspian coast nor along Rūd-é Kārūn, Iran's only navigable river. If you want to hire a boat in Bandar-é Abbās the tourist office there can advise you.

IRAN

LOCAL TRANSPORT
Bus
Local bus services exist in most Iranian cities. Tickets must be bought at special roadside booths. Bus numbers and destinations are written only in Persian, so unless you can read Persian or know exactly where you're going and which bus to take they're difficult to use. There are also some very crowded minibuses where you pay the driver a few tōmān in cash.

Taxi
Shared taxis, painted orange and white or blue and white according to city, supplement or even replace local bus services. They take up to five passengers in whatever direction the driver thinks it's worthwhile to go at the time. The custom is to stand by the pavement, preferably on a main road, and shout out your destination to every passing taxi. Once you've learnt how to use them, shared taxis are an excellent and very inexpensive way of getting around. Often you'll have to take a number of them to get from one part of town to another, and a map is very helpful. Fares vary from place to place. The best advice is to watch what other passengers pay, pay in front of them and avoid being a solo passenger if possible.

There are also private or 'telephone' taxis, which can be ordered by telephone or at an agency office. It's essential to fix the fare before boarding, either at a flat rate or by the hour. Hotel and mosāferkhūné receptionists can order private taxis and help negotiate fares.

On arrival at a bus or railway station or airport, don't accept a lift from the first taxi driver who approaches you; you're almost bound to be overcharged. If possible, arrange to share a taxi with some Iranians going in the same direction, get them to fix the fare and confirm it with the driver when boarding. It's almost a point of honour among Iranian private taxi drivers to overcharge foreigners, given the chance. Even the poorest Iranians will usually take a taxi from the station or airport: there's rarely any practical alternative. At some places, for example Tehrān airport and Shīrāz bus station, you can buy tickets in advance to pay for your fare. Ask locally whether any buses serve your destination.

Car
Outside some bus and railway stations and on city access roads you can find drivers offering intercity transport by private car (savārī), which may be worth considering if you can't get a seat for any other means of transport. In some parts of Iran, for example the Caspian region, savārīs are the main or only form of long-distance public transport. They're no more comfortable and much dearer than buses, but faster and more convenient.

ORGANISED TOURS
Australia, Canada, the UK and the USA offer tours to Iran. See also the Organised Tours section in the Getting Around the Region chapter.

Australia
Top Deck Adventure Holidays (☎ (02) 9299 8844) in Sydney do an overland tour from Kathmandu to London which passes through Iran.

Canada
Voyage Afrolympic (☎ (514) 274 0000; fax 270 5457) in Montreal specialises in travel to Iran.

UK
Exodus Expeditions (☎ (0181) 673 0859; fax 673 0779) at 9 Weir Rd, London SW12 0LT, has a 19 day 'Journey to Persia' taking in all the highlights for about UK£1700, including flights and accommodation. Explore Worldwide (☎ (01252) 319448; fax 343170), 1 Fredrick St, Aldershot, Hampshire GU11 1LQ, runs a tour very similar to Exodus, though for 16 days only, costing UK£1395 including flights. Hinterland Travel (☎ (01883) 743584; fax 743912), 2 Ivy Mill Lane, Godstone, Surrey RH9 8NH, offers an extensive 16 day truck-tour of Iran

for UK£650, not including accommodation or flights.

Jasmin Tours (☎ (01628) 850788; fax 529 4444), High St, Cookham, Maidenhead, Berks SL6 9SQ, has a reasonable eight day 'Iran Express' package taking in Tehrān, Shīrāz and Esfahān for around UK£800, including flights and three-star accommodation.

Magic Carpet Travel (☎ (0171) 385 9975; fax 381 2304) is the UK's premier Iran specialist. It caters to small groups, offering tailor-made tours which can be anything from two weeks exploring the Valleys of the Assassins to skiing in the Alborz Mountains. It also offers a visa-only service for independent travellers. Steppes East (☎ (01285) 810267; fax 810693; email sales@steppeseast.co.uk), Castle Eaton, Cricklade, Wiltshire SN6 6JU, a Central Asia specialist, also has a couple of different Iran trips, one taking in the major Persian cities while the other heads off the beaten track.

USA

A New York-based company, Citad (☎ (800) 876 2704; fax (212) 768 3898), run by a former Iranian diplomat, organises seven-day package tours taking in Tehrān, Esfahān and Shīrāz. The deal includes visa, air fare and all meals, and costs US$2000.

Tehrān

Iran isn't blessed with one of the world's loveliest capitals. Pollution, chronic overcrowding and a lack of any responsible planning have all helped to make Tehrān a city which even a travel agent would have difficulty praising. And yet, take a gas mask or a blindfold if you will, it does deserve a day or two of anyone's time. For a start, Tehrān is the country's largest city by far and a leader in almost every field of Iranian life. In addition, it was the centre of Iran's Islamic Revolution, the world's first of its kind and, in many ways, is still a revolutionary city nearly 20 years later. Tehrān also has some

fine museums and Iran's best restaurants, shops and hotels.

Like so many Iranian cities, Tehrān started life as a small village in the foothills of a mountain, in this case Kūh-é Damāvand (5628m). Human settlement of the region dates from Neolithic times. The neighbouring city of Rei overshadowed Tehrān until it was destroyed by the Mongols in 1197. Tehrān then developed in its place as a small, moderately prosperous trading centre, which is how it would have remained had it not been chosen somewhat inexplicably as the capital by Āgha Mohammad of the Ghajar dynasty. When he made his choice in 1783, Tehrān was a dusty town of around 15,000 souls.

Despite its lengthy history, precious little evidence remains to remind you of it. In fact anything over 50 years old more or less qualifies as a historic relic, and most of what you see may make you think that Tehrān was prefabricated en masse in some grim East European factory during the Cold War era. Although sightseers may roam the streets in vain, sociologists will find it fascinating for its rapid population growth – from under three million in 1966 to a peak of around 12 million in barely 25 years. Go to the teeming slums in the south of Tehrān and see for yourself. Things are getting better, however; many internal refugees returned home from Tehrān after the end of the Iran-Iraq War and the population is now back to around 10 million.

At an altitude of 1191m, Tehrān can get pretty cold in winter, and snow isn't unusual.

Orientation

Tehrān is so vast and devoid of landmarks that getting hopelessly lost on a regular basis is a near certainty. The city proper has an area of roughly 600 sq km and a north-south diameter of over 25 km. Walking is futile unless you know exactly where you're going. The best advice is to buy a good map as soon as you arrive and to take a taxi everywhere. Orientation is at least easy as the Alborz Mountains are almost always

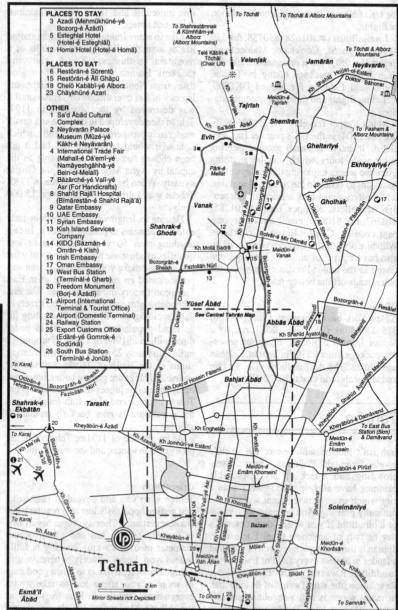

PLACES TO STAY
3 Azadi (Mehmūkhūné-yé Bozorg-é Āzādī)
5 Esteghlal Hotel (Hotel-é Esteghlāl)
12 Homa Hotel (Hotel-é Homā)

PLACES TO EAT
6 Restōrān-é Sörentö
15 Restōrān-é Ālī Ghāpū
18 Chelō Kabābī-yé Alborz
23 Chāykhūné Azari

OTHER
1 Sa'd Ābād Cultural Complex
2 Neyāvarān Palace Museum (Mūzé-yé Kākh-é Neyāvarān)
4 International Trade Fair (Mahall-é Dā'emī-yé Namāyeshgāhhā-yé Bein-ol-Melalī)
7 Bāzārché-yé Valī-yé Asr (For Handicrafts)
8 Shahīd Rajā'ī Hospital (Bīmārestān-é Shahīd Rajā'ā)
9 Qatar Embassy
10 UAE Embassy
11 Syrian Embassy
13 Kish Island Services Company
14 KIDO (Sāzmān-é Omrān-é Kish)
16 Irish Embassy
17 Oman Embassy
19 West Bus Station (Termīnāl-é Gharb)
20 Freedom Monument (Borj-é Āzādī)
21 Airport (International Terminal & Tourist Office)
22 Airport (Domestic Terminal)
24 Railway Station
25 Export Customs Office (Edāré-yé Gomrok-é Sodūrkā)
26 South Bus Station (Termīnāl-é Jonūb)

visible to the north through the clouds of smog.

Tehrān is bisected by Valī-yé Asr (claimed to be the world's longest street), which runs north from the railway station right up into the hills, and Enghelāb, which runs east from Meidūn-é Āzādī. Officially, Meidūn-é Emām Khomeinī (see the Central Tehrān map), a square so shabby as to dishonour the great leader's name, is Tehrān's centre, but the main commercial and hotel district has shifted north in recent years. A central landmark is the head telegraph office's satellite tower just south of Meidūn-é Emām Khomeinī.

Information

Tourist Offices There's a not particularly useful tourist office (☎ 892212) at 11 Kheyābūn-é Demeshgh, off Valī-yé Asr. There's also an information booth at the airport's international station where you might find someone who speaks English.

Visa Extensions For visa extensions go to the aliens' bureau (marked 'Police Department of Foreign Affairs') on Motahharī near the Mofatteh intersection.

Money Head for Kheyābūn-é Ferdōsī where there are two official moneychanging offices opposite the main gate to the British embassy compound. A little over 100m south, the central Bank Melli Iran also has an exchange counter (counter No 12) and it will cash travellers' cheques. Otherwise, try at the larger hotels.

Post & Communications The main post office is on the north side of Kheyābūn-é Emām Khomeinī, 150m west of Meidūn-é Emām Khomeinī – you can recognise it by the postboxes outside. The main telegraph office (for telephones, telegrams and faxes), the tall grey tower block with the satellite dishes on top, is on the south side of Meidūn-é Emām Khomeinī. It's open 24 hours a day.

The telephone code for Tehrān is 021.

Travel Agency Golriz on Kheyābūn-é Nosrat next to the Emām Khomeinī hospital has a very friendly and helpful staff, some of whom speak fluent English. It also accepts Visa cards.

Bookshops The two best bookshops are on Kheyābūn-é Karīm Khān-é. The Zand, 100m west of Meidūn-é Haft-é Tir, has a small, faded selection of English fiction and academic books, and you may be able to pick up *Time* magazine there. A further 100m west is an excellent bookshop for glossy, locally produced, English-language gift books.

Emergency In any case of emergency seek help from your embassy.

Museums

The **Archaeological Museum of Iran** (Mūzé-yé Īrān-é Bāstān; ☎ 672061) is perhaps Iran's finest museum. The ground floor houses items from prehistoric to Sassanian times, mostly the fruits of recent foreign excavations in Iran. Apart from the usual pots, vases and necklaces, half the contents of Persepolis have been moved here. The 1st floor has items from the Islamic era, including glassware, ceramics, inscriptions and carpets, among many other things. There's so much to see that it's best not to try and fit everything into one visit. The museum (also known as the National Museum) is on Kheyābūn-é Shahīd Yārjānī, one block north of Kheyābūn-é Emām Khomeinī (see the Central Tehrān map). Opening hours are Wednesday to Monday from 9 am to noon and 1 to 4 pm.

Hidden beneath Bank Melli Iran's head office on Ferdōsī is the stunning collection of the **Crown Jewels Museum** (Mūzé-yé Javāherāt; ☎ 311 0101). The most famous piece of the original collection, the Kūh-é Nūr (Koh-i-Noor) diamond, was pilfered by the British, and you'll have to go to the Tower of London to see that. Enough remains, however – including the Daryā-yé-Nūr diamond weighing 182 carats, the throne of Nāder Shāh encrusted with 26,000 gems, and enough crowns for all the crowned heads of Europe – to make this one of the

IRAN

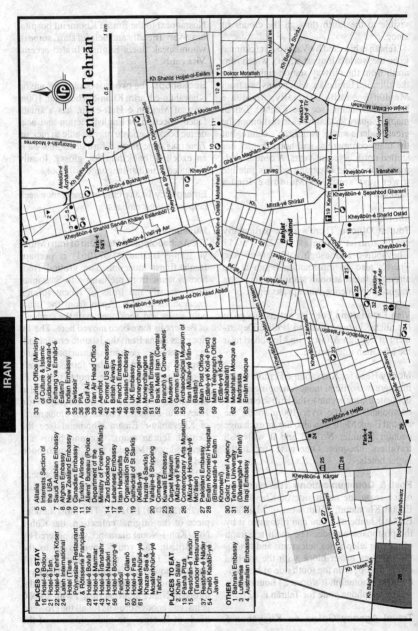

Central Tehrān

PLACES TO STAY
16 Hotel-é Bolour
21 Hotel-é Iran
22 Hotel-é Tehrān Kōser
24 Laleh International Hotel (Tiare Polynesian Restaurant & Rôtisserie Française)
29 Hotel-é Bolour
41 Hotel-é Marmar
43 Hotel-é Irānshahr
47 Hotel-é Naderi
56 Hotel-é Bozorg-é Ferdosi
57 Hotel-é Gilanō
60 Hotel-é Fars
61 Mosaferkhūne-yé Khazar Sea & Mosaferkhūne-yé Tabriz

PLACES TO EAT
2 Khan Sālār
13 Pasha Pitzā
15 Restōrān-é Tandūr (Tandoor Restaurant)
37 Restōrān-é Nader
54 Cheló Kabābi-yé Javān

OTHER
1 Bahrain Embassy
3 Lufthansa
4 Australian Embassy

5 Alitalia
6 Interests Section of the USA
7 Saudi Arabian Embassy
8 Afghan Embassy
9 New Zealand Embassy
10 Canadian Embassy
11 Pakistani Embassy
12 Aliens' Bureau (Police Department of the Ministry of Foreign Affairs)
14 Zand Bookshop
17 Lebanese Embassy
18 Iran Handicrafts Organisation Shop
19 Cathedral of St Sarkis (Kelisā-yé Hazrat-é Sarkis)
20 Vollāyie-B Shipping
23 Kuwaiti Embassy
25 Carpet Museum (Mūzé-yé Farsh)
26 Contemporary Arts Museum of Iran (Mūzé-yé Honamā-yé Mo'āser)
28 Emām Khomeini Hospital (Bimārestān-é Emām Khomeini)
31 Goîrtz Travel Agency
32 Iraqi Embassy

33 Tourist Office (Ministry of Culture & Islamic Guidance; Vezārat-é Farhang va Ershād-é Eslāmi)
34 Indian Embassy
35 Aeroflot
36 PIA
38 Gulf Air
39 Iran Air Head Office
40 Aeroflot
42 Former US Embassy
44 British Airways
45 French Embassy
46 Russian Embassy
48 UK Embassy
49 Moneychangers
50 Moneychangers
51 Turkish Embassy
52 Bank Melli Iran (Central Branch & Crown Jewels Museum
53 German Embassy
55 Archaeological Museum of Iran (Mūzé-yé Irān-é Bāstān)
58 Main Post Office (Edāré-yé Koll-é Post)
59 Main Telegraph Office (Edāré-yé Koll-é Mokhābarāt)
62 Motahhari Mosque & Madrassa
63 Emām Mosque

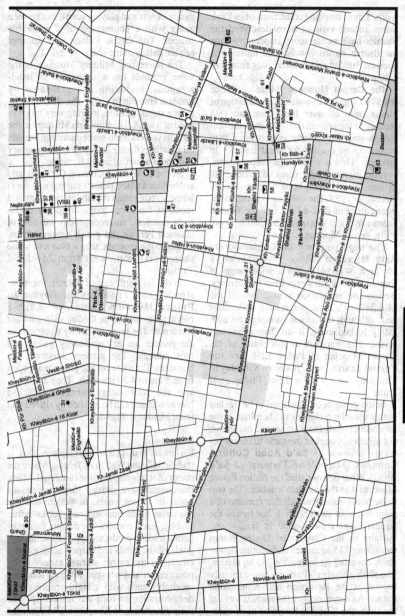

world's most stunning collections of its kind. Some recent visitors have described the baubles here as far more impressive than the British crown jewels. The museum is open on Sunday and Tuesday only from 2 to 4.30 pm.

The **Carpet Museum** (Mūzé-yé Farsh; ☎ 657707) has an eye-watering exhibition of pieces from all over Iran, from the 18th century to the present day. Although the collection isn't particularly vast, it more than makes up in quality for what it lacks in quantity. This is a must for carpet lovers. Foreign dignitaries are often taken here: ask to see the visitors' book's entry for 19 December 1989. The museum is at the north-west corner of Park-é Lālé (see the Central Tehrān map). It's open from 9 am to 5 pm daily, except Monday.

The large purpose-built **Contemporary Arts Museum** (Mūzé-yé Honarhā-yé Mo'āser; ☎ 655411) has a wide range of foreign and Iranian works from this century. Before the revolution it had one of the Middle East's most progressive collections and, although the raciest paintings are now safely locked away, it still has a few surprises. The museum is just south of the Carpet Museum in Park-é Lālé (see the Central Tehrān map). It's open Saturday to Thursday from 9 am to 7 pm, Friday until 2 pm.

In the grounds of what used to be the last shāh's summer residence in Shemīrān, in the far north of town, there are several museums, not all always open at the same time, collectively known as **Sa'd Ābād Cultural Complex** (Majmū'é-yé Farhangī-yé Sa'd Ābād). What is now called the Nation Palace Museum was the last shāh's palace. The two stone boots outside are all that remains of a giant statue of Rezā Shāh. It has two of the largest carpets ever made in Iran – one upstairs in the Ceremonial Dining Room measuring 145 sq metres and another downstairs covering an incredible 243 sq metres. The Shāh's Mother's Palace is now curiously known as the Reversion and Admonition Palace. As a comment on the wicked ways of the shāh, the 'Gamble Room', full of back-

gammon sets and playing cards, can be seen along with a photograph of a miserable pauper. The Green Palace was another private palace of the shāh.

The interesting Military Museum in the same grounds has a collection of hand-weapons, including one presented by Saddam Hussein in 1979. The shāh's Rolls-Royce stands outside, looking very much in need of a wash. The Fine Arts Museum to the right as you enter has some charming Persian oil paintings dating back to the 18th century and some beautiful inlaid furniture.

At the Sa'd Ābād Cultural Complex and at Neyāvarān (see below) the palaces seem homely rather than royally extravagant and much of the decor looks decidedly dated, even tasteless, an incongruous mixture of classical Persian and garish western styles. To get to the grounds, take a blue and white shared taxi north-west from Meidūn-é Tajrīsh.

In the far north-east of Tehrān, the monstrosity now known as the **Neyāvarān Palace Museum** (Mūzé-yé Kākh-é Neyāvarān) used to be the last shāh's winter residence. The imperial family's portraits in the parlour are extraordinarily gaudy and most unregal. The gardens, however, are beautiful. The museum and grounds are open from 8 am to 4.30 pm daily. They are opposite the south-west corner of Pārk-é Neyāvarān and can be reached by shared taxi from Meidūn-é Tajrīsh.

Bazaar

Far more than just a marketplace, this is traditionally the Wall St of Tehrān, where the prices of staple commodities are fixed. Many merchants have moved their businesses north in recent years, however, and the bazaar is in decline and now looks rather shabby. Each corridor specialises in a particular trade or product: copper, shoemaking, gold, plastic goods and carpets among many others. In the carpet section expect to be pounced on and whisked off on a tour that inevitably ends with a highly professional demonstration of hard-sell marketing. The main entrance is on Kheyābūn-é 15 Khordād and just to the south is the busy **Emām Mosque** (Masjed-é Emām).

Motahhari Mosque & Madrassa

More correctly known as the Masjed-é Sepahsālār, this is Tehrān's largest and most important mosque. It was built (1878-90) long after the golden age of Persian architecture had passed and is very ungainly and gaudy, but the massing of eight minarets is quite impressive and it has a marble-pillared room with an amazing echo.

Former US Embassy

Not exactly open to the public, this vast complex is currently used as a computer training centre for Revolutionary Guards. Nowadays it's predictably called the 'US Den of Espionage'. A booth outside sells copies of secret incriminating documents pieced together from the shredder after the fall of the embassy. Don't photograph or linger here.

Freedom Monument

Built in 1971 to commemorate the Persian Empire's 2500th anniversary, the extraordinary inverted-Y-shaped Borj-é Āzādī is close to the airport and the west bus station. Upstairs there's a historical museum of Iran and you can take a lift to the top for a lofty view, smog permitting.

Mausoleum of Emām Khomeinī

Despite the implied grandeur of the golden dome and minarets, once inside, the Ārāmgāh-é Hazrat-é Emām Khomeinī resembles not so much a holy shrine or mosque but a sports stadium. Around the green cage that contains the body of Khomeinī, children skid on the polished floor and play tag while their parents picnic and chat in family groups. Around the mausoleum, a laundry, supermarket and hotel/ restaurant complex are under construction. It's a curiously egalitarian place.

Appropriately, the site is midway between Tehrān, the city that launched the Islamic Revolution, and Ghom, the city where the great man underwent his theological train-

ing. Not far from Tehrān's south edge, it can be reached by bus No 434 from Meidūn-é Emām Khomeinī.

Behesht-é Zahrā

Stretching as far as the eye can see, this is the cemetery for those who died in the Iran-Iraq War. It is probably the world's largest graveyard, and also holds a supermarket and a computer centre for locating individual graves. There's even a metro station planned for the cemetery but until that is completed the best way to get here is to take a taxi from the Mausoleum of Emām Khomeinī just a few km north.

Places to Stay – bottom end

Tehrān has a serious accommodation shortage. Unless you arrive early in the morning or make a reservation you can't afford to be too choosy, at least not on your first night. As with most things in Tehrān, the accommodation improves in quality and rises in price the further north you go.

Tehrān's cheapies cluster around Meidūn-é Emām Khomeinī within a radius of about two km, the cheapest and grottiest of all being just north of the bazaar. Many Tehrānīs consider this a no-go area at night. Most of these places are only used to taking Iranians on zero expense accounts and you may have a long search to find one that isn't 'full' to westerners.

The mosāferkhūnés most likely to take westerners are on or just off Amīr Kabīr, the street leading east from Meidūn-é Emām Khomeinī. Try *Mosāferkhūné-yé Khazar Sea*, which charges 8000 rials for a double; coming from Meidūn-é Khomeinī it's down the fourth alley on the left. *Mosāferkhūné-yé Tabrīz*, which is next door to the Khazar Sea, has also been recommended by travellers; singles/doubles here are 10,000/12,000 rials.

Considerably better quality than the mosāferkhūnés but still in the budget bracket, *Hotel-é Gilanō* (☎ 311 8264) charges just 24,000 rials for clean doubles. It's on Kheyābūn-é Ferdōsī about 200m north of Meidūn-é Khomeinī.

There are also a few cheap but decent

IRAN

places on the southern extension of Kheyābūn-é Sa'dī, such as the *Hotel-é Fars* (☎ 305011; fax 311 1976), which charges the rial equivalent of US$20 for a double. (South Sa'dī is the main road that's first on the right when walking down Amīr Kabīr, away from Meidūn-é Khomeinī.)

Places to Stay – middle

The mid-range hotels are about 10 times as comfortable as the places on Amīr Kabīr. One place that is particularly good, with clean air-con rooms and a convenient central location, is the *Hotel-é Īrānshahr* (☎ & fax 883 4976, 882 0518) on Kheyābūn-é Īrānshahr. Doubles cost US$35. One block west, *Hotel-é Marmar* (☎ 830083; fax 882 0521) on Kheyābūn-é Sepahbod Gharanī charges US$52 for a double, while on the same street, just south of the junction with Kheyābūn-é Karīm Khān-é Zand, *Hotel-é Bolour* (☎ 884 8585) has singles/doubles for US$20/25.

Readers have also recommended the Armenian-run *Hotel-é Naderi* (☎ 678610), where decent air-con singles/doubles with a private bathroom go for just US$12/25. It's at 485 Kheyābūn-é Jomhūrī-yé Eslāmī.

Set back off a little side alley just northeast of Meidūn-é Valī-yé Asr, the *Hotel-é Tehrān Kōser* (☎ 898 1215; fax 889 1615) is a good three-star option which charges US$47 for a double. Another attractive but fairly pricey option is the *Hotel-é Bozorg-é Ferdōsī* (☎ 645 9991; fax 645 1449), very well situated on Kheyābūn-é Ferdōsī, but rates are US$35/52.

Tehrān's luxury hotels all charge around US$75/110 and include the *Laleh International* (Hotel-é Lālé-yé Bein-ol-Melalī; ☎ 656021), the *Hotel-é Esteghlāl* (ex-Hilton; ☎ 204 0011; fax 204 7041), the *Hotel-é Homā* (ex-Sheraton; ☎ 226 3021) and the *Āzadī* (ex-Hyatt; ☎ 207 3021; fax 207 3038). Of these, only the Laleh is remotely central; the other three are in north Tehrān. Each has pleasant coffee lounges where foreigners go to meet each other and Iranians go to watch them, discreetly.

Places to Eat

Chelō kabāb is definitely standard rations at most of Iran's cheaper restaurants, and Tehrān is no exception. If you're staying in the city centre, you won't have to look very far, as even richer Tehrānīs often head south when they're hungering for a good feed. At almost any restaurant in this area you can fill up for around 8000 rials and at the snack bars for under half that. Avoid sausages at all costs, however. A slightly better class of chelō kabāb is found along Ferdōsī. The absolute best kebāb in town is said to be served at *Chelō Kabābī-yé Alborz* on upper Sohrevardī, but also very popular is *Chelō Kabābī-yé Javān* on Saf off Jomhūrī-yé Eslāmī.

The best place for pizzas (around 4000 rials) is the busy *Pāshā Pīzzā* on Jahāntāb, near the Motahharī and Mofatteh crossroads.

One inexpensive place popular with thrifty Iranians looking for a good meal out is *Restōrān-é Nāder*, halfway up Nejātollāhī. On the same street, *Ray's Pitza* serves reasonable Mexican food and has an agreeably conspiratorial air. The genuinely Indian-owned *Restōrān-é Tandūr*, on Kūché-yé Ardalān off Mofatteh, is Tehrān's best Indian restaurant. It's not particularly expensive and one reader recommended its vegetarian dishes.

The following are recommended for steaks and the like: *Restōrān-é Sōrentō* on Valī-yé Asr, facing Pārk-é Mellat; and *Restōrān-é Ālī Ghāpū*, on Gāndhī near Meidūn-é Vanak. You can fill up at these places for around 12,000 rials.

If your budget can stretch then we recommend a visit to the *Khān Sālār*. The food, while not exceptional, is good, but the traditionally inspired surroundings are really something special. Main courses are around 15,000 rials and you can expect a bill for two to come to 40,000 rials minimum. It's on Kūché-yé Alvānd, off Meidūn-é Ārzhāntīn.

Also worth splashing out on is a visit to the *Chāykhūné Azari* (☎ 537 3665), a large, traditional-style teahouse in south Tehrān, complete with tiling and fountains, and Persian classical music recitations. It's extremely popular with rich north Tehrānīs and reservations are recommended. The Azari is just north of the railway station at the very bottom end of Kheyābūn-é Valī-yé Asr.

Getting There & Away

Air Iran Air has city centre offices on Meidūn-é Ferdōsī (☎ 882 6532) and Kheyābūn-é Nejātollāhī (☎ 882 9080). Most of the foreign airlines and Iranian travel agents are either on Nejātollāhī or along Kheyābūn-é Enghelāb. They're generally open Saturday to Thursday from 9 am to 4 pm.

Bus Tehrān has three intercity bus stations. The busiest, the west bus station (termīnāl-é gharb; ☎ 607 1044), is close to the airport, just north-west of the Freedom Monument, and has buses travelling to Armenia, Azerbaijan, Syria, Tabrīz, Turkey and all other places west of Tehrān, plus Chālūs and Rāmsar. The south bus station (termīnāl-é jonūb; ☎ 550047), near the railway station, has buses to Esfahān, Ghom, Kermān, Shīrāz, Yazd, Zāhedān and other places to the south or south-east. The east bus station (termīnāl-é shargh; ☎ 781040) at the far east of Kheyābūn-é Damāvand, the extension of Enghelāb, caters for buses to north-east Iran, for example, Mashhad, and the Caspian region except Rāmsar and Chālūs. The bus stations, especially the west one, can be bedlam even for Iranians; allow plenty of time to book your ticket or catch your bus.

Train Tehrān's railway station is in the south of the city on Meidūn-é Rāh Āhan. Tickets are bought from a separate building (unmarked in English – it's a single storey whitewashed concrete structure) on Kheyābūn-é Shush, about 200m east of the station and square. They should be purchased at least 24 hours in advance. All departures are in the afternoon or early evening. Trains to Kermān leave on Monday, Wednesday and Friday to Esfahān (10 hours; 10,000 rials 1st class) and Sīrjān on Saturday, Monday and Wednesday at 9.30 pm; to Gorgān on Monday, Wednesday and Saturday; and to Yazd daily except Saturday.

Other domestic services are at least daily. For timetable information call ☎ 556114.

Getting Around

The Airport From the airport it's best to pre-pay your taxi fare at the taxi desk outside the terminal, straight ahead over the road, otherwise you'll find it very hard to bargain for a reasonable fare. Official airport taxis are marked in English. A taxi to Meidūn-é Ferdōsī should cost about 6000 rials per person.

Bus Extensive bus services cover most parts of town, but for a foreigner they're difficult to use, crowded and painfully slow. There's rarely any need to subject yourself to them, since shared taxis are so plentiful and cheap. Meidūn-é Emām Khomeinī has a large city bus station where you might find someone to guide you onto the right bus.

Underground Tehrān's underground system has been nearing completion for something like 10 years now. Consequently, we do not expect it to start operating during the lifetime of this book.

Taxi Although the orange and white shared taxis take some getting used to, they are the best way of getting around the maze of Tehrān. Fares are roughly 500 rials a km but depend partly on demand, time of day and traffic conditions. If you want to go to the airport or to cover a long distance quickly, it's best to book a telephone taxi at one of the many agencies all over town or by calling ☎ 840011-20.

Central Iran

Although geographically vast and boasting several largish cities, this part of Iran is mostly desert; almost every centre of population here grew up around an oasis. The place that most visitors most want to see is Esfahān, one of the architectural highlights of the Islamic world, but there are plenty of other interesting places for culture vultures. Long-distance travel by land can be an ordeal, especially in summer.

GHOM

Ghom, 125 km south of Tehrān en route to Esfahān by bus or train, is sacred to Shiites as the place where Emām Rezā's sister, Fātemé, died in 816. Shiites revere her as the embodiment of feminine virtue, and Ghom is one of their seven holy cities. Her extensive shrine complex, **Āstāné**, was started by Shāh Abbās I, its magnificent golden cupola later added by Fath Alī Shāh. If you're not a Muslim, however, your presence is not wanted inside (English signs to that effect are displayed at all entrances) and you'll have to content yourself with a tantalising peek from the threshold. Photography is forbidden.

Places to Stay

The cheapies around the holy shrine cater principally to pilgrims and probably won't take non-Muslims. One fairly comfortable place that will is *Hotel-é Gol* on Meidūn-é Emām Khomeinī, the first main square inside Ghom on the Tehrān road, with rooms at US$15/20 for a single/double.

ESFAHĀN

The half-rhyme *Esfahān nesf-é jehān* (Esfahān is half the world) was coined in the 16th century to express the city's grandeur, and you may well agree that it has a ring of truth even today.

Esfahān had long been an important trading centre, strategically situated in the south of modern Iran, but it came to its peak during the reign of Shāh Abbās I. Iran had been in a period of decline until, in the early 16th century, the first Safavid rulers chucked the Mongols out of the country. Shāh Abbās came to power in 1587, extended his influence over rivals within the country, then pushed out the Ottomans, who had occupied a large part of Persia. With his country once more united and free of foreign influence, he set out to make Esfahān a great and beautiful city. Its period of glory lasted for little over 100 years. An invasion from Afghanistan

hastened the decline following Shāh Abbās' death and the capital was subsequently transferred to Shīrāz and then to Tehrān.

The power and breadth of Shāh Abbās' vision are still very much in evidence, although what remains is just a small taste of the city at its height. Not only is its architecture superb and its climate pleasant, but it has a more relaxed atmosphere than many other Iranian cities. It's a place for walking, getting lost in the bazaar, dozing in beautiful gardens and meeting people. The more time you have in Esfahān the better, because here it's easy to appreciate many of the best aspects of Persian culture.

Orientation

The main street, Chahār Bāgh (Four Gardens), runs north-south right through the city. If you use it to orient yourself, you can't go far wrong. Most of the main sights and the hotels are within easy walking distance – Meidūn-é Emām Khomeinī, the centrepiece of Esfahān is 500m east of Chahār Bāgh.

Information

Tourist Office The fairly helpful tourist office (☎ 21555) is on the ground floor of the Ālī Ghāpū palace on the west side of Meidūn-é Emām Khomeinī.

Visa Extensions Visas can be extended at the provincial police headquarters (shahrbānī) on Khōrshīd, a small street off Meidūn-é Emām Khomeinī just south of the Ālī Ghāpū palace.

Money Probably the most efficient places to change money are the offices on the west side of Meidūn-é Emām Khomeinī, or the Bank Melli Iran on Kheyābūn-é Sepāh.

Post & Communications The main post office is on Kheyābūn-é Neshāt, south-east of Meidūn-é Emām. The central telephone and telegraph office is on the west side of Kheyābūn-é Dastgheib. As elsewhere in the provinces, international and even trunk calls are difficult to make and it's worth paying a little more and trying from the Abbāsī hotel.

The telephone code for Esfahān is 031.

Meidūn-é Emām Khomeinī

Previously Meidūn-é Shāh, this huge open square laid out in 1612 is a majestic example of town planning. Many of Esfahān's most interesting sights are clustered around it and it's one place to which you'll keep coming back. With an area of over 8.1 hectares (20 acres), *The Guinness Book of Records* lists it as second only to Tiananmen Square in terms of size.

Shops line the square. Many specialise in brasswork, others in miniatures, and there's some interesting stuff among the gimcrack souvenirs and postcards. Times are hard and tourists are scarce, but you'll still need all your bargaining skills: Esfahān's merchants are notorious throughout Iran for their wiliness. 'An Esfahānī buys a cucumber, paints it yellow and sells it as a banana' is one of many popular gibes.

Emām Mosque Previously Masjed-é Shāh, the magnificent Masjed-é Emām anchors the south side of the square. It is completely

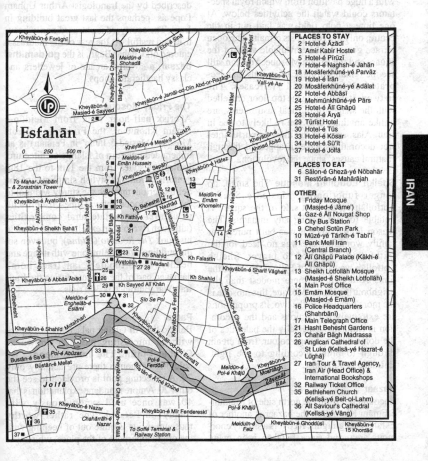

PLACES TO STAY
2 Hotel-é Āzādī
3 Amir Kabir Hostel
5 Hotel-é Pīrūzī
7 Hotel-é Naghsh-é Jahān
18 Mosāferkhūné-yé Parvāz
19 Hotel-é Īrān
20 Mosāferkhūné-yé Adālat
22 Hotel-é Abbāsī
24 Mehmūnkhūné-yé Pārs
25 Hotel-é Ālī Ghāpū
28 Hotel-é Āryā
29 Tūrist Hotel
30 Hotel-é Tūs
33 Hotel-é Kōsar
34 Hotel-é Sū'īt
37 Hotel-é Jolfā

PLACES TO EAT
6 Sālon-é Ghezā-yé Nōbahār
31 Restōrān-é Mahārājah

OTHER
1 Friday Mosque (Masjed-é Jāme')
4 Gaz-é Ālī Nougat Shop
8 City Bus Station
9 Chehel Sotūn Park
10 Mūzé-yé Tārīkh-é Tabī'ī
11 Bank Melli Iran (Central Branch)
12 Ālī Ghāpū Palace (Kākh-é Ālī Ghāpū)
13 Sheikh Lotfollāh Mosque (Masjed-é Sheikh Lotfollāh)
14 Main Post Office
15 Emām Mosque (Masjed-é Emām)
16 Police Headquarters (Shahrbānī)
17 Main Telegraph Office
21 Hasht Behesht Gardens
23 Chahār Bāgh Madrassa
26 Anglican Cathedral of St Luke (Kelīsā-yé Hazrat-é Lūghā)
27 Iran Tour & Travel Agency, Iran Air (Head Office) & International Bookshops
32 Railway Ticket Office
35 Bethlehem Church (Kelīsā-yé Beit-ol-Lahm)
36 All Saviour's Cathedral (Kelīsā-yé Vāng)

IRAN

covered, inside and out, with the pale blue tiles that became an Esfahān trademark, and is a particularly inspiring sight at night when they glow with a soft sheen.

Although the entrance, with its twin minarets, faces squarely onto the courtyard, the mosque itself is at an angle facing towards Mecca. It was built in 26 years by an increasingly impatient Shāh Abbās I and completed in 1638. Entrance is 300 rials.

Ālī Ghāpū Palace On the west side of the square, this is a seven storey palace (*kākh-é*) with a huge pavilion from which royal spectators could watch the activities below. At one time a polo field was laid out in the centre; only the goal-posts remain. The open terrace gives the best available view of the square and the Emām Mosque. You can still see the remains of intricate murals that decorated the rooms and staircases. The fretwork stalactites on the top floor, chiselled with the shapes of musical instruments, are unlike anything else you're likely to see in Iran. Alas, some of the most colourful interior decorations have disappeared through 'natural causes' since the revolution.

Sheikh Lotfollāh Mosque The small, no longer functioning, Masjed-é Sheikh Lotfollāh on the east side of the square is notable for not having any minarets. The reason is that since it was built purely for family worship there was no need for the faithful to be called to prayer. Sheikh Lotfollāh was a sort of Billy Graham of the time. Although far more modest than the neighbouring Emām Mosque, this mosque is the more beautiful of the two; its proportions are extremely harmonious and the decoration is exquisite, especially the pale tiles of the dome which change colour, from cream through to pink, according to the light. Entrance is 300 rials.

Bazaar
Encountered from the north side of Meidūn-é Emām Khomeinī, the bazaar is another of Esfahān's highlights. It covers a simply enormous area, and since Esfahān is in many

ways Iran's artistic and craft centre, it's one of the country's best shopping venues. As there are something like five km of paths to stroll through, allow plenty of time. Aside from shops and stalls selling almost every imaginable item, you will also encounter mosques, teahouses and even gardens.

Chahār Bāgh Madrassa
On Chahār Bāgh, this theological college was built by Shāh Sultan (Sóltān in Persian) Hosein, the last Safavid ruler, between 1706 and 1714, in his mother's honour. It was described by the Iranologist Arthur Upham Pope as 'perhaps the last great building in Iran'. The courtyard is extraordinarily beautiful and restful. At the rear of the madrassa, entered off Chahār Bāgh, is the **goldsmiths' bazaar**, a covered arcade of jewellers and classy handicrafts shops.

The Friday Mosque
A brisk half-hour walk from Meidūn-é Emām Khomeinī, the Friday (or Great) Mosque (Masjed-é Jāme' in Persian) is an unheralded museum of Islamic architecture. It displays styles from the 11th to the 18th centuries, from the stylish simplicity of the Seljuk period, through the sturdy Mongol to the more baroque Safavid times. It's difficult to unravel the architectural complexities (although Byron is an excellent guide here in his book *The Road to Oxiana*), but even so, the building overwhelms one with its age and beauty. Unfortunately, an Iraqi bomb damaged part of the mosque during the Iran-Iraq War. Entrance is 300 rials.

Parks
Behind the Ālī Ghāpū palace there's a park with an interesting pavilion known as **Chehel Sotūn**. The name means '40 columns', although there are actually only 20. A reflecting pool is provided to see the other 20. A more mundane explanation is that 40 was once used synonymously with 'many' in Persian. The rather worthy museum inside is quite out of keeping with the original purpose of the place, which was

built by Shāh Abbās I as a reception hall for some notoriously wild parties.

Hasht Behesht, or the Eight Paradises, is a Safavid garden palace east of Chahār Bāgh, approached from Kheyābūn-é Fathīyé. It has some charming mosaics and stalactite mouldings, and is slowly being restored to its former glory. Only the ground floor is open.

Bridges

A number of historic bridges cross Zayāndé Rūd, the river that runs east-west through Esfahān. **Sīo Sé Pol**, or 33 Bridge, so-called for its number of arches, lies at the southern end of Chahār Bāgh and dates from 1602. Downstream 1.5 km is the slightly smaller and even more attractive **Pol-é Khājū** (pronounced 'KA-jew'). Built to double as a dam in about 1650, it has two levels of terraces and has always been a popular meeting place. It also serves as a teahouse. Three km further on, the stone and brick **Pol-é Shahrestān** is Esfahān's oldest surviving bridge. Its foundations are Sassanian but most of the present structure is believed to date from the 12th century.

Jolfā

Just south of the river by Sīo Sé Pol is Jolfā, the Armenian quarter. During his wars with the Turks, Shāh Abbās I gained a large number of Armenian subjects. While the skills of these industrious Christians were coveted, it was preferred that they be kept in one area and away from the main Islamic centres. So in 1606 the shāh founded this quarter just outside the city of Esfahān, granted land to the Armenians whom he resettled and encouraged them to carry on their religion and commerce here. Jolfā is still almost exclusively Christian and has for many years been the seat of the Armenian Archbishop of Iran and India.

The most important building is the **All Saviour's Cathedral** (Kelīsā-yé Vang), built between 1655 and 1664. The influence of Islam on architecture has been so strong since the Arab conquest that even Christian buildings incorporate many Islamic features, and this one, with its onion dome, pointed arches and even a minaret-like spire, is no exception. A museum stands in the grounds, as well as a memorial to the estimated 1.5 million Armenians massacred in Turkey in 1915. Jolfā has 12 churches, all dating from the 17th century; the most interesting one is **Bethlehem Church** (Kelīsā-yé Beit-ol-Lahm), founded in 1628.

Manar Jombān

The Shaking Minarets are so known because if you climb to the top of one of them and lean hard against the wall it will start to sway and so will its twin. These perpendicular pinnacles probably date from Safavid times, although the mausoleum beneath them was built in the 14th century. About seven km west of the city centre, they are best reached by taxi. Entrance is 300 rials.

Zoroastrian Tower

On your right about a km further along the road, past many adobe houses with *bādgīr* (wind towers), is a Zoroastrian tower of silence (Āteshgāh), now disused. From it you get a good view of the city and it becomes very clear that Esfahān is a green oasis town.

Places to Stay

There are several cheapies on Kheyābūn-é Masjed-é Sayyed (for example, the *Hotel-é Sepīd* and *Hotel-é Persepōlīs*) and on Chahār Bāgh (*Tūrīst Hotel* and *Hotel-é Tūs*); none of these places are particularly clean, although the doubles at the Tūs (☎ 260068) do at least have fresh sheets and private showers and toilets. They go for 25,000 rials.

The best of the lower end accommodation is probably the *Amir Kabir Hostel* (☎ 236813), run by an enthusiastic English-speaking management. It offers clean three or four-bed dormitories with separate toilets/showers, and the hostel's garden courtyard is a good place to meet other independent travellers. Beds are 16,000 rials. It's on Chahār Bāgh just south of the junction with Kheyābūn-é Masjed-é Sayyed. Another very decent budget option is *Hotel-é Īrān*

(☎ 262010), which charges 30,000 rials for clean doubles with bathroom. It's down a little alley just off the west side of Chahār Bāgh.

Moving up-market, the *Hotel-é Āzādī* (☎ 239011; fax 233713) is excellent value; a three-star hotel with immaculate air-con rooms, it charges just 60,000/90,000 rials for singles/doubles. It's on Kheyābūn-é Masjed-é Sayyed immediately west of the junction with Chahār Bāgh.

There are a couple of other mid-range options on Chahār Bāgh, such as the *Hotel-é Pīrūzī* (☎ 261043) and the *Hotel-é Ālī Ghāpū* (☎ 231282; fax 239519), both of which are nice enough hotels but a little overpriced at US$45/65.

Immediately south of Sīo Sé Pol, the riverside *Hotel-é Sū'īt* (☎ 246071) offers better value at US$20/30, while the nearby *Hotel-é Kōsar* (☎ 240230), reputably one of the town's best, charges US$45/65.

Esfahān's most luxurious and famous accommodation is the *Hotel-é Abbāsī* (☎ 226009; fax 226008), a conversion of a grand Safavid-era caravanserai. Rooms cost US$65/95 – if you can't afford to stay here at least come for breakfast to admire the lavish decoration. The Abbāsī is on Kheyābūn-é Shahīd Āyatollāh Madanī, next door to the Chahār Bāgh Madrassa.

Places to Eat

There are several typical chelō kabābīs on Chahār Bāgh. One of the best value is *Sālon-é Ghezā-yé Nōbahār*, where main dishes are around 6000 rials. It's open from 11 am to 3 pm and 7 to 10 pm, and is just north of Meidūn-é Emām Hussein. *Restōrān-é Mahārājāh* at the southern end of Chahār Bāgh isn't bad either. Despite the name it has a standard kabāb menu, with India represented by just four unimaginative dishes. The food is reasonably good and the price range is 6000 to 10,000 rials.

At the restaurant in *Hotel-é Abbāsī* it seems you're paying dearly for the elegant setting rather than the food, which is mediocre. The food at *Hotel-é Ālī Ghāpū*'s restaurant outstrips that of the Abbāsī's in all

but price, making this the town's best value top-end eatery.

There is an atmospheric *teahouse* under the arches of Pol-é Khājū, where you can sip tea or smoke the hubble-bubble surrounded by slumbering Esfahānīs. Benefiting from the river breezes, this is often also one of the coolest places in town.

One famous Esfahānī speciality is 'gaz' (nougat made with chopped nuts, usually pistachios). It's sold at confectionery shops, of which perhaps the best is *Gaz-é Ālī*, across the road and 50m north of the Amir Kabir Hostel.

Getting There & Away

Air The most central of the town's Iran Air offices (☎ 221045) is in the new shopping complex opposite Hotel-é Abbāsī. From Esfahān there are two flights daily to Tehrān (one hour; 35,000 rials one way), four flights a week to Mashhad (95 minutes) and two a week to Zāhedān (90 minutes). For airport information call ☎ 251017.

Bus The new bus station, called Soffé Terminal, is about five or six km south of the city centre. It's well organised and possibly the least chaotic station in all of Iran. From here, it's about seven hours by bus to Tehrān (6000 rials), eight hours to Shīrāz (6000 rials), five hours to Yazd and 21 hours to Zāhedān.

Train Three trains a week run overnight to Tehrān (10 hours; 10,000 rials 1st class) via Kāshān and Ghom; at the time of writing departures were on Sunday, Tuesday and Thursday at 8.30 pm. The railway station is about eight km south of the city, beyond the bus station (about 3000 rials in a taxi). Tickets can also be booked at the office on Meidūn-é Enghelāb-é Eslāmī.

Getting Around

Although Esfahān's shared taxis are cheap and fairly easy to use, their drivers have a particularly bad reputation for cheating visitors. Try to avoid being a solo passenger.

KĀSHĀN

Some 3½ hours by bus from Esfahān, Kāshān is an attractive oasis town which has for many centuries been famous for its tiles, carpets and silk. Shāh Abbās I liked this place so much that he chose to be buried here, in the mausoleum of a 13th century ancestor. His tomb is in the crypt of **Zeyārat-é Habīb ebn-é Mūsā**, near the railway station. Kāshān has many other interesting monuments, the most notable being the 12th century **Masjed-é Jāme'** and **Manār-é Zein-od-Dīn**, an 11th century Seljuk minaret. **Bāgh-é Tārīkhī-yé Fīn** at Fīn, eight km south-west of the centre, is a historic garden containing the remains of several Safavid royal buildings.

The simple *Hotel-é Sayyāh* (☎ (02521) 4535) is 1.5 km west of the railway station. The large, modern *Hotel-é Amīr Kabīr* (☎ (02521) 30091) is next to the gardens at Fīn.

YAZD

Midway between Esfahān and Kermān, Yazd is particularly interesting for its relationship with the desert. It stands on the border between the north Great Salt Desert, Dasht-é Kavīr, and the south Great Sand Desert, Dasht-é Lūt, and has some of the region's best adobe architecture. Look out for the tall bādgīrs designed to catch even the lightest breezes and direct them down to the subterranean living rooms. In a city where summer temperatures hit 42°C, they are very necessary. Yazd's water reservoir has six such towers. Average annual rainfall here is only about 60 mm.

Yazd has 12 busy bazaars, a number of fine mosques and several other interesting buildings. For over 1000 years it has been famous for its silks and other textiles, and you can still see some traditional weaving factories here. Yazd was also an important religious centre in pre-Islamic times and still has a substantial population of Zoroastrians today – probably around 12,000, the largest single population in Iran.

Orientation & Information

Most of the main sights are within a short walking distance of the town square, Meidūn-é Beheshtī. Yazd is not a good place to have to change dollars so make sure that you have enough rials to see you through; at a push you could try the Bank Melli Iran on the west side of Kheyābūn-é Emām Khomeinī about one km north of Meidūn-é Beheshtī. The main post office is a few doors on beyond the bank. The dismally unhelpful tourist office (☎ 38046) is on Kheyābūn-é Āyatollāh Kāshānī, attached to the Ghasr-é Ā'īné Museum (Mūzé-yé Ghasr-é Ā'īné), which is a muddled museum housing a miscellany of knick-knacks assembled since the revolution.

The telephone code for Yazd is 0351.

Alexander's Prison

Zendān-é Eskandar, beneath a modern theological college on Kūché-yé Kūshk off Sayyed Gol-é Sorkh, is a medieval dungeon which must have been a pretty nasty place to end up by any standards. Its history is murky, but it certainly has nothing to do with Alexander the Great. Ask its caretaker for the key to the 11th century **Tomb of the 12 Emāms** (Maghbaré-yé Davāzdah Emām), diagonally opposite, so named because it has a Seljuk inscription bearing the names of each of the early Shiite religious leaders. It has a brick dome and some interesting plaster mouldings.

Friday Mosque

The well-preserved 14th century Friday (or Great) Mosque (in Persian Masjed-é Jāme') has a wonderfully impressive towering entrance portal flanked by twin minarets. Inside, it is also graced by some exquisite mosaic tiling and a beautiful faience mihrab (niche in the wall indicating the direction of Mecca). The Masjed-é Jāme' is on the left off Kheyābūn-é Emām Khomeinī about a km north of Meidūn-é Beheshtī. Don't confuse it with the **Takieh-yé Amir Chakhmāgh**, which is to the right off Kheyābūn-é Emām Khomeinī about 500m north of Meidūn-é Beheshtī. This is another high, twin-minareted entrance portal, in this case dating from the 19th century. This particularly imposing facade does not belong to a mosque; it was built to serve as a grandstand for the traditional passion plays performed during the mourning month of Moharram.

Āteshkadé

The Āteshkadé is a modern Zoroastrian fire-temple housing a sacred flame said to have been burning since about 470 AD. You can see it through a window inside the museum, which also has a few religious paintings and other artefacts. The temple is a km south-east of Meidūn-é Beheshtī on Kheyābūn-é Āyatollāh Kāshānī. It's open to the public Saturday to Thursday from 8 to 11 am and 2.30 to 4.30 pm.

Towers of Silence

About 15 km south-west of Yazd and best reached by shared taxi, Dakhmé-yé Zartoshtīyān is a tower of silence which fell out of use some 50 years ago. At the base of the hill you can see the remains of a well, two small bādgīrs, a kitchen and a lavatory – all for the convenience of the relatives of the dead, who would camp out for two or three

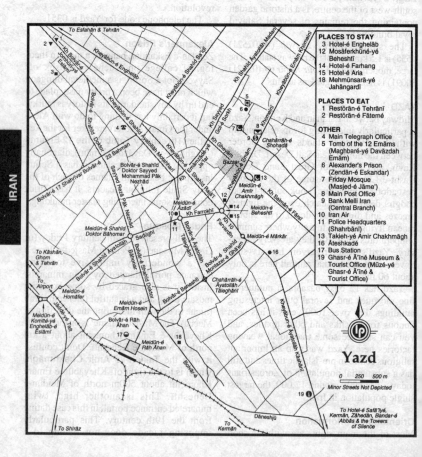

PLACES TO STAY
3 Hotel-é Enghelāb
12 Mosāferkhūné-yé Beheshtī
14 Hotel-é Farhang
15 Hotel-é Aria
18 Mehmūnsarā-yé Jahāngardī

PLACES TO EAT
1 Restōrān-é Tehrānī
2 Restōrān-é Fātemé

OTHER
4 Main Telegraph Office
5 Tomb of the 12 Emāms (Maghbaré-é Davāzdah Emām)
6 Alexander's Prison (Zendān-é Eskandar)
7 Friday Mosque (Masjed-é Jāme')
8 Main Post Office
9 Bank Melli Iran (Central Branch)
10 Iran Air
11 Police Headquarters (Shahrbānī)
13 Takieh-yé Amir Chakhmāgh
16 Āteshkadé
17 Bus Station
19 Ghasr-é Ā'īné Museum & Tourist Office (Mūzé-yé Ghasr-é Ā'īné & Tourist Office)

Yazd

0   250   500 m

Minor Streets Not Depicted

IRAN

days waiting for the vultures to do their work. Bones still litter the hill.

Places to Stay & Eat

The prospects here aren't good for budget travellers. While there are some cheap mosâferkhūnés, mostly on Kheyâbūn-é Āyatollāh Kāshānī south of Meidūn-é Beheshtī, they're terribly basic, unhygienic, and mostly showerless. We stayed at the *Mosâferkhūné-yé Beheshtī* (5000 rials per person) just north of the square, and were driven out at 4 am by a combined assault of bedbugs and mosquitoes. According to readers' letters, a far better option is the *Hotel-é Aria* (☎ 60411), which charges 5500 rials per person, and has an extremely friendly management.

We advise that you spend a little more and check into the *Hotel-é Farhang* (☎ 35011), 80m north of Meidūn-é Beheshtī, which is reasonably clean and friendly, and charges US$15/20 for a single/double with bathroom.

All of the mid-range places are some way out of the city centre and include *Hotel-é Safā'īyé* (☎ 49813) on Kheyâbūn-é Shahīd Tīmsar Fallāhī in the far south of Yazd, *Hotel-é Jomhūrī-yé Eslāmī* north-west of the city centre, and the comfortable and popular *Mehmūnsarā-yé Jahāngardī* (☎ 47222), a km east of the railway station on Bolvār-é Dāneshjū, all at US$30/45.

The two best places to eat are up near the Hotel-é Enghelāb on Kheyâbūn-é Bolvār-é Jomhūrī-yé Eslāmī; they are the *Restōrān-é Tehrānī*, which serves excellent chelo kabâb as well as fish, chicken and khōresh, and the *Restōrān-é Fātemé*.

Getting There & Away

Air There are flights connecting Yazd to Tehran (70 minutes), daily except Monday and Tuesday, and to Mashhad (85 minutes) every Monday. The Iran Air office (☎ 28030) is on Kheyâbūn-é Shahīd Āyatollāh Motaharī, 50m north of Meidūn-é Āzādī.

Bus The bus station is south of the city centre at Meidūn-é Rāh Ahān. There are bus company offices here and also, rather more conveniently, along Kheyâbūn-é Emām Khomeinī north of Meidūn-é Beheshtī. From Yazd, it's five hours to Esfahān by bus, six hours to Kermān (4000 rials), seven to Shīrāz (4500 rials), 10 to Tehrān and 14 to Zāhedān.

Train There are three trains weekly to Tehrān (12 hours) via Kāshān and, in the opposite direction, to Kermān (five hours).

SEMNĀN

Probably dating from Sassanian times, dusty Semnān lies on the north edge of Dasht-é Kavīr and owes its origins and mixed fortunes to its place on the historic trading route between Tehrān and Mashhad. Despite the many invasions of Semnān, the old part of town around the bazaar is well preserved and has a number of interesting buildings.

Dating from 1424, the **Friday (or Great) Mosque** (Masjed-é Jāme') has an impressive entrance portal and some interesting stucco around its mihrab. A free-standing Seljuk minaret nearby, probably built in the 11th century, has a charming octagonal balcony. Founded under Fath Alī Shāh in the 1820s, the large **Mosque of Emām Khomeinī** (Masjed-é Emām Khomeinī) is one of the best surviving examples of its period and shows a particularly fine use of colour. Almost nothing of architectural worth was built in Iran after this.

There are some cheap hotels on Ghods. The comfortable *Mehmūnsarā-yé Semnān*, on Jāddé-yé Mehdīshahr in the town's north-west outskirts, charges US$20/30 for a single/double.

Semnān is best reached by rail, from Tehrān or Mashhad.

AROUND SEMNĀN
Dāmghān

Dāmghān's **Mosque of Tārīkhūné** (Masjed-é Tārīkhūné) is probably Iran's oldest surviving mosque. Dating from about 760 AD, it's almost entirely pre-Islamic Sassanian in appearance, although its layout is

Arabian. It has four barrel-vaulted chambers, or *iwans*, opening onto an almost square inner courtyard. Its minaret was added in the early 11th century and the building has been restored many times, but the original very simple design has been faithfully preserved. There are also a number of very early minarets and tomb towers in the same area.

The mid-range *Mehmūnsarā-yé Dāmghān* is in a garden off Bolvār-é Āzādī. Dāmghān is about four hours by train from Semnān on the Mashhad line.

East & South-East Iran

This is the most sparsely populated and least developed part of Iran. Away from Mashhad, don't expect travelling to be either very easy or very comfortable, although it can be rewarding. If you've just arrived from Pakistan, east and south-east Iran will be a gentle introduction to Iranian culture, but if all your travelling has been in the rest of Iran prepare yourself for something rather different. The highlights are Mashhad's Shrine of Emām Rezā, the medieval citadel at Bam and the city of Kermān.

MASHHAD

This major city in the far north-east of Iran used to be known for three things: religion, commerce and tourism. While there was war and revolution in Iran and chaos in Afghanistan, transit trade all but dried up, tourism collapsed, and the only thing remaining was religion. Iran being Iran, this one commodity was more than enough to keep the city going.

Mashhad (literally, Place of Martyrdom) is sacred to Shiites as the site where their eighth emām, Rezā, died in 817 after eating some grapes. The story spread that he had been poisoned, and his tomb became a major

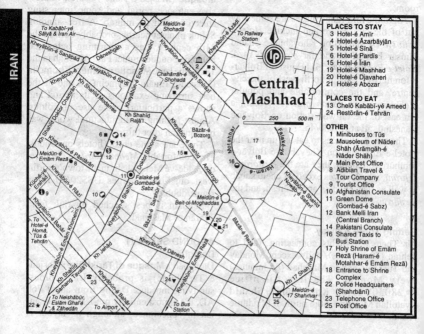

Central Mashhad

0   250   500 m

PLACES TO STAY
3 Hotel-é Amīr
4 Hotel-é Āzarbāyjān
5 Hotel-é Sīnā
6 Hotel-é Pardīs
15 Hotel-é Īrān
19 Hotel-é Mashhad
20 Hotel-é Djavaheri
21 Hotel-é Abozar

PLACES TO EAT
13 Chelō Kabābī-yé Ameed
24 Restōrān-é Tehrān

OTHER
1 Minibuses to Tūs
2 Mausoleum of Nāder Shāh (Ārāmgāh-é Nāder Shāh)
7 Main Post Office
8 Adibian Travel & Tour Company
9 Tourist Office
10 Afghanistan Consulate
11 Green Dome (Gombad-é Sabz)
12 Bank Melli Iran (Central Branch)
14 Pakistani Consulate
16 Shared Taxis to Bus Station
17 Holy Shrine of Emām Rezā (Haram-é Motahhar-é Emām Rezā)
18 Entrance to Shrine Complex
22 Police Headquarters (Shahrbānī)
23 Telephone Office
25 Post Office

pilgrimage site. What had been a small village grew into a large city and, in time, the capital of Khorāsān, Iran's largest province. In the busy pilgrimage season (Nō Rūz and late June to mid-July) you're likely to feel very small.

Orientation & Information

Mashhad is a big and relatively featureless city. As you might expect, all roads in Mashhad lead to the Holy Shrine of Emām Rezā, which is delineated by a roundabout, Falaké-yé Haram-é Motahhar. Despite Mashhad's size, most points of interest, except the airport and bus station, are a short walk from the shrine.

The helpful tourist office (☎ 48288) hides on the 2nd floor of the Ministry of Culture and Islamic Guidance building (not marked in English) on Kūché-yé Ershād off Kheyābūn-é Bahār. Visa extensions are dealt with at the police headquarters (shahrbānī), which is also on Kheyābūn-é Emām Khomeinī but some two km south of the bank and post office. The central branch of Bank Melli Iran is on Kheyābūn-é Emām Khomeinī, with the main post office opposite.

The telephone code for Mashhad is 051.

Holy Shrine of Emām Rezā

The Haram-é Motahhar-é Emām Rezā and the surrounding buildings of the *haram-é motahhar* (holy precincts) together comprise one of the marvels of the Islamic world. To visit Iran and not to come here is a bit like going to Italy and missing the Vatican. Little else in Mashhad need detain you long, but there's so much to see here in such a confined area that it's impossible to take everything in during one visit. Unfortunately, not all of the precincts are open to non-Muslims.

The walled island of the shrine complex is a city within a city, containing two mosques, 12 lofty iwans (two coated entirely with gold), six theological colleges, two main and two lesser courtyards, several libraries and even a post office, among many other buildings.

Emām Rezā's original tomb was built by Caliph Hārūn ar-Rashīd in the early 9th

century but was later destroyed, restored and destroyed again, and the present mausoleum in the centre of the complex was built under Shāh Abbās I at the turn of the 17th century.

Perhaps even more impressive than the mausoleum itself, with its shimmering gilded cupola, is the **Grand Mosque of Gōhar Shād**, (Masjed-é Azīm-é Gōhar Shād), with its 50m high blue faience dome and cavernous golden doorway. Queen of a mighty empire, wife of Tamerlane's eldest son, Shāhrokh, patron of the arts and a powerful personality in her own right, Gōhar Shād was one of the most remarkable women of Islamic history. While she also founded many great buildings in her capital, Herat, this mosque, constructed between 1405 and 1418, is the best preserved testament to her genius.

There are also two interesting **museums**, both displaying a lavish collection of precious articles donated by pilgrims almost since Emām Rezā's time. In Mūzé-yé Moghaddas, inside the precincts, look out for the 16th century gold bas-relief door once belonging to the mausoleum and, a recent addition, the *Carpet of the Seven Beloved Cities* (ie Mecca, Medina, Jerusalem, Najaf, Karbala, Mashhad and Ghom). It's said to have taken 10,000 weavers 14 years to make, and to have 30 million knots. The Mūzé-yé Ghods-é Razavī, approached from the roundabout, has what's claimed to be Iran's largest public display of Qur'ans, as well as some priceless carpets.

Although non-Muslims aren't allowed into the shrine itself, they can enter the precincts under certain constraints. It's essential to dress extremely conservatively and to behave with due reverence. A single incident could lead to a ban on non-Muslim visitors. Discreet photography is tolerated. A guided tour is highly recommended: individual and group tours in English can be arranged through Adibian Travel & Tour Company (☎ 98151) at 56 Kheyābūn-é Pāsdārān, next to the Hotel-é Jam.

Bazaars

Around the holy precincts there are three bazaars, none of any great interest. The biggest, Bāzār-é Rezā, has the usual tacky merchandise and a few shops selling turquoises mined near Mashhad.

Green Dome

Gombad-é Sabz, on Kheyābūn-é Shahīd Doktor Bāhonar, is probably Mashhad's most interesting building outside the holy precincts. This mausoleum is used by adherents of the mystical Naghshbandī Sufi school and was built in the Safavid era.

Mausoleum of Nāder Shāh

The Ārāmgāh-é Nāder Shāh is a modern Italian-designed concrete monstrosity covering the tomb of the warmongering Nāder Shāh and a small museum of various militaria, mostly from his time (18th century). The museum is open from 7.30 am to 12.30 pm and 2 to 4.30 pm, and it's on Kheyābūn-é Azādi.

Places to Stay

There are many mosāferkhūnés around the holy shrine to cater for pilgrims, but they're unlikely to accept non-Muslim foreigners. One exception is the Hotel-é Abozar (☎ 94223); it's extremely grotty (to be expected at only 7000 rials per person) but it does at least have showers. It's down a narrow alley just north of the Hotel-é Djavaheri on Kheyābūn-é Emām Rezā. The Hotel-é Djavaheri (☎ 91519) itself is not a bad budget option, charging 40,000 rials for a double with bathroom.

Mashhad has a lot of mid-range hotels. Some of the cheaper ones are the Hotel-é Amir (☎ 21300), with a friendly English-speaking manager, the Hotel-é Āzarbāyjān (☎ 54001) and Hotel-é Sīnā (☎ 28543), all on Kheyābūn-é Azādi and charging US$15/20.

More expensive places include the Hotel-é Mashhad (☎ 22701; fax 26767) on Kheyābūn-é Emām Rezā, and the excellent Hotel-é Īrān (☎ 28010; fax 28583) on Shahīd Andarzgū, both of which charge US$30/45. Another slightly more expensive option is the Hotel-é Pardīs (☎ 55715; fax 23914), a very new, swish place on Kheyābūn-é Emām Khomeinī. Doubles cost US$52.

Mashhad's top-end place is the over-rated Hotel-é Homā (☎ 832001), two km west of the city centre on Kheyābūn-é Feizīyé; rooms here start at US$65/95.

Places to Eat

Ābgūsht is popular and especially cheap here. One good place for it is Restōrān-é Tehrān on Emām Rezā. Around the holy shrine there are some cheap kabābīs and ābgusht places which may appeal to the more adventurous. Kabābī-yé Sālyā on Ebn-é Sīnā, 250m south-east of its intersection with Kheyābūn-é Sanābād, serves excellent fillé kabāb but, in our opinion, the best is served at Chelō Kabābī-yé Ameed, an immaculately clean, plate glass-fronted restaurant opposite the Pardis hotel on Kheyābūn-é Emām Khomeinī.

Getting There & Away

If you are heading for Afghanistan or Turkmenistan, see the Getting There & Away section earlier in this chapter.

Air Iran Air has its main Mashhad office (☎ 80003) on Kheyābūn-é Sanābād, two or three km west of the city centre. There's also a smaller office at the Hotel-é Homā. From Mashhad there are flights twice a week to Bandar-é Abbās (two hours), four times a week to Esfahān (1⅓ housr), five times a week to Shīrāz (one hour 50 minutes; 64,000 rials), once a week to Tabrīz (2¼ hours), three or four times daily to Tehrān (1⅔ hours), 40 minutes; 55,000 rials) and once a week to Zāhedān. The airport is five km south of town and is linked by shared taxi.

Bus All long-distance buses leave from the bus station on Bozorgrāh-é Kalāntarī, south of the city centre, around 200 rials by shared taxi from the main square. Buses run to most major cities, although if you're going any further than Tehrān you may wish you'd flown or taken a train by the time you arrive. Neishābūr is 2½ hours away by bus, Tehrān 14 hours, Zāhedān 16 hours (12,000 rials),

Yazd 21 hours, and Esfahān and Tabrīz 22 hours.

If you want to hire a taxi for the return trip to Neishābūr and Ghadamgāh, the Hotel-é Homā has a reasonably priced service. Minibuses to Tūs leave from Chahārrāh-é Shohadā hourly.

Train Two or three rains run daily to Tehrān (12 hours; 7200 rials, 2nd class) from the railway station two km north of the shrine.

AROUND MASHHAD
Tūs

This town is 23 km from Mashhad on a turning east off the Gorgān road. Sacked in 1389 and abandoned soon afterwards, Tūs was the regional capital before Mashhad. It's revered by Iranians as the home town of the epic poet Ferdōsī. His mausoleum was built in 1933 in preparation for the 1000th anniversary of his death the following year, but rebuilt in 1934 because the first version was thought too plain. A small museum is attached to it. The original city of Tūs' only remaining structure, **Bogh'é-yé Hārūnīyé**, is a large crumbling building whose history and purpose are cause for speculation.

Neishābūr

A major centre of learning in the early Islamic era, Neishābūr (Nishapur) is the place where modern Persian, newly adapted to the Arabic script, first became a literary medium. It was the home town of Omar Khayyām, poet, mathematician and astronomer, whose quatrains were made famous in the west in the 19th century by the translator Edward Fitzgerald.

Khayyām's monument lies about a km south of the modern town. His very simple tombstone sits in uneasy contrast with the modernist structure, formed of several interconnected concrete lozenges, towering over it.

A historic garden nearby, **Bāgh-é Mahrūgh**, encloses an attractive 16th century mausoleum. Almost nothing older remains. Set in a water-garden 26 km from Neishābūr on the Mashhad road, **Bogh'é-yé Ghadamgāh** is a delightful, tiny 17th century shrine built around what are said to be Emām Rezā's (very large) footprints.

ZĀHEDĀN

Despite a colourful mixture of Afghans, Baluchis, Persians and Sikhs on the street, Zāhedān is quite possibly Iran's least appealing and least friendly town. Zāhedān's only claim to fame for travellers is that it's the nearest town to the border post at Mīrjāvé, which lies across the barbed wire from Taftan on the Pakistani side. Anyone who has come from Quetta will be prepared for Zāhedān's slight air of tension. The Komīté are particularly active here, and gun law is in force around Zāhedān. Avoid travelling near the Afghan border without the advice of the police or the provincial government.

Zāhedān is an almost inevitable overnight stop on the overland trail between Turkey and Pakistan. If you're entering Iran from Pakistan don't be put off by it, for most of the rest of the country is a different place entirely.

A lot of smuggled goods are sold here fairly openly, including very cheap cigarettes in the bazaar in the Gārāzh area.

Orientation & Information

Zāhedān is a flat and largely featureless town. The main bazaar (Bāzār-é Rūz) is at the intersection of the main east-west street, Emām Khomeinī, and the north-south artery, Nīkbakht.

All overnight visitors must register their passports at the Visitors' Registration Bureau (Edāré-yé Amāken-é Komīté), next to the police headquarters on Tāleghānī, after finding a room. The office is open from early in the morning to late in the evening.

The telephone code for Zāhedān is 0541.

Places to Stay & Eat

Many travellers have had difficulty finding a place to stay here. As all available beds can fill up very quickly, try to get into town as early as possible and not look too scruffy. Either may be difficult to achieve if you're coming straight from Pakistan, as there seems to be a conspiracy to keep you at the

IRAN

dusty border as long as possible. Make sure you take the first available minibus.

Don't come here looking for luxury. The *Hotel-é Abūzar* is the least objectionable of the several undistinguished places in the noisy Gārāzh area, costing 6000 rials per person. However, if you're not in a tearing hurry to catch the first bus out, it's more pleasant to stay in the city centre. The *Hotel-é Khāvar* (☎ 28880) is supposedly Zāhedān's best hotel (it's certainly the priciest at US$60 for a double) but it's almost permanently full. We preferred the look of the *Hotel-é Salé* (☎ 3197; fax 2630), which also has much friendlier staff and charges US$20/30.

There are a limited number of places to eat. The *Restōrān-é Vanak* on Kheyābūn-é Āzādī is good value and has a slightly adventurous menu, and, despite surly staff, the restaurant at the *Hotel-é Khāvar* is acceptable. In the Gārāzh area try the cheap and cheerful *Restōrān-é Abūzar*, next to the hotel of the same name.

Getting There & Away

For entry into Pakistan, see the introductory Getting There & Away chapter.

Air The Iran Air office (☎ 20812) is in a small arcade on the east side of Kheyābūn-é Azādī. There are flights from Zāhedān twice weekly to Esfahān and Tehrān, and once a week to Mashhad.

Bus The bus company offices, with their own stations, are in the Gārāzh area in the north-west of town. Although Kermān is only seven hours away, many travellers go straight through to Shīrāz. This is a long journey – 17 hours – but it puts an awful lot of desert behind you. Other destinations include Yazd (14 hours), Mashhad (16 hours; 12,000 rials), Esfahān (21 hours), Tehrān (22 hours) and Gorgān (26 hours), but not Tabrīz.

CHĀBAHĀR

This small fishing town is the main coastal settlement of the Iranian Makrān, a region known for its harsh climate and poor communications. Although there isn't a great deal to see or do in Chābahār, its relaxed pace of life and the friendliness of its Baluchi inhabitants may well persuade you to spend some time here happily without bothering much with sights or activities. It's so sleepy that you may have to wake up stallholders to

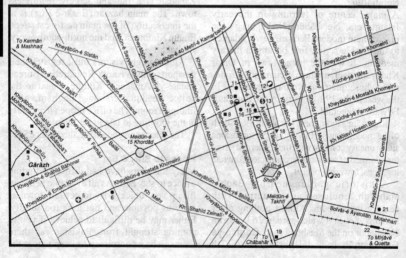

get served in the bazaar. The climate is very pleasant in winter but not at other times. The village of **Tīs**, nine km north, has an attractive arboretum and a ruined Portuguese castle.

Places to Stay & Eat

Despite erratic plumbing, the beachside *Mehmūnsarā-yé Jahāngardī* at $20/30 for singles/doubles is the town's only remotely comfortable place to stay. It has an inexpensive restaurant. The mosāferkhūnés on the main street, Kheyābūn-e Ghods, have dorm accommodation only.

Getting There & Away

Chābahār is connected by a once weekly flight to Mashhad, Tehrān and Zāhedān. The airport is actually at Konārak, 61 km west of Chābahār by road, linked by shared taxi. Buses take 12 hours to reach Chābahār from Zāhedān on a poor road.

KERMĀN

Kermān has a long and turbulent history. Believed to have been established in the 3rd century BC by Ardashīr I, founder of the Sassanian dynasty, it was in turn occupied by the Arabs, Buyids, Seljuks, Turkomans, Mongols and various local dynasties. It was restored to central government in the 19th century, but its relative remoteness and lack of natural resources have denied it any great prosperity in recent times. Until the Safavid dynasty it was principally a staging-post on the Asian trade routes, but since then, the local economy has largely depended on the production of carpets. The local dialect is so distinctive that you may have problems making yourself understood even in Persian. Some Kermānīs actually look more Indian than Persian.

Thanks to the altitude (1749m) Kermān isn't too hot in summer.

Orientation & Information

Most places of interest lie between the two main squares, Meidūn-é Āzādī and Meidūn-é Shohadā, which are about 3.5 km apart at either end of Kheyābūn-é Doktor Beheshtī/ Kheyābūn-é Sharī'atī.

The very helpful tourist office (☎ 25098) hides on Kūché-yé Ershād off Kheyabūn-é Ferdōsī. The office is unmarked in English, but it is beyond the gate at the end of the lane. Visas can be extended at the police headquarters in Kheyābūn-é Adālat, near the eastern entrance to the bazaar. For moneychanging purposes, Bank Melli Iran has a central branch on Meidūn-é Valī-yé Asr, which is midway between Āzādī and Shohadā . The post and telegraph offices are on Kheyābūn-é Adālat, south of Meidūn-é Valī-yé Asr.

The telephone code for Kermān is 0341.

Things to See

One of Iran's oldest surviving covered bazaars is Kermān's **Vakil Bazaar** (Bāzār-é Vakīl). Much of its present structure dates from Safavid times. It has some interesting handicrafts stalls, including metalwork shops selling brass trays and the like, noisily hammered into shape on site. Also within the bazaar is the **Ganj'ali Khān Bath Museum** (Mūzé-yé Mardom Shenāsī-yé Ganj'alī Khān), a historic bathhouse with waxworks performing various ablutionary functions. **Hammūm-é Ebrāhīm Khān** nearby is

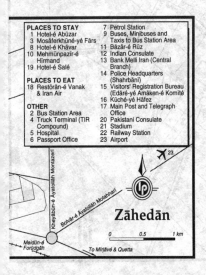

PLACES TO STAY	7 Petrol Station
1 Hotel-é Abūzar	9 Buses, Minibuses and
3 Mosāferkhūné-yé Fārs	Taxis to Bus Station Area
8 Hotel-é Khāvar	11 Bāzār-é Rūz
10 Mehmūnpazīr-é	12 Indian Consulate
Hirmand	13 Bank Melli Iran (Central
19 Hotel-é Salé	Branch)
	14 Police Headquarters
PLACES TO EAT	(Shahrbānī)
18 Restōrān-é Vanak	15 Visitors' Registration Bureau
& Iran Air	(Edāré-yé Amāken-é Komité
	16 Kūché-yé Hāfez
OTHER	17 Main Post and Telegraph
2 Bus Station Area	Office
4 Truck Terminal (TIR	20 Pakistani Consulate
Compound)	21 Stadium
5 Hospital	22 Railway Station
6 Passport Office	23 Airport

Zāhedān

0   0.5   1 km

To Mīrjāvé & Quetta

IRAN

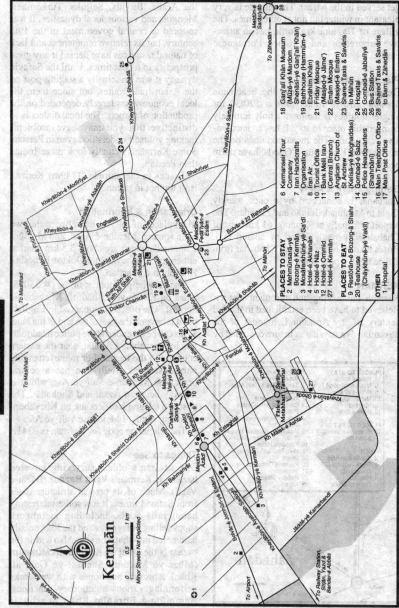

Kermān

0   0.5   1 km

Minor Streets Not Depicted

Meidān-é Sardesháb

To Zāhedān

PLACES TO STAY
2   Mehmūnsarā-yé Bozorg-é Kermān
3   Mosāferkhūné-yé Sa'di
4   Hotel-é Akhanān
5   Hotel-é Náz
12 Hotel-é Ommid
27 Hotel-é Kermān

PLACES TO EAT
9   Restōrān-é Bozorg-é Shahr
20 Teahouse (Cháykhūné-yé Vakil)

OTHER
1   Hospital
6   Kermanseir Tour Company
7   Iran Handicrafts Organisation
8   Iran Air
10 Tourist Office
11 Bank Mélli Iran (Central Branch)
13 Anglican Church of St Andrew (Kelisā-yé Moghaddas)
14 Gombad-é Sabz
15 Police Headquarters (Shahrbáni)
16 Main Telephone Office
17 Main Post Office
18 Ganj'ali Khān Museum (Mūzé-yé Mardom Shenási-yé Ganj'ali Khān)
19 Bathhouse (Hammám-é Ebrāhim Khán)
21 Friday Mosque (Masjed-é Jāme')
22 Emām Mosque (Masjed-é Emām)
23 Shared Taxis & Savāris to Máhān
24 Hospital
25 Gombad-é Jabalíyé
26 Bus Station
28 Shared Taxis & Savāris to Bam & Zāhedan

To Māshhad

To Māshhad

Kheyābūn-é Firúz Abádi

Kheyābūn-é Shohadá

Kheyābūn-é Modiníyat

Kheyābūn-é Shohadá

Kheyābūn-é Shahid Báhonar

Kheyābūn-é Fath Ali Sháhi

Kheyābūn-é Shohadá-yé Atashán

Shohadá-yé Áindáh

Kheyābūn-é

Engheláb

Meidān-é Shohadá

Shahrivar

17

Meidān-é Fedá'iyán-é Eslám

Bolvār-é 22 Bahman

Bazār-é Vakil

Kh Doktor Chamrán

Falastin

Kh Keltár

Kheyābūn-é

Kheyābūn-é Shahid Ghárani

Kh Shahid Rajei

Kheyābūn-é Shahidi Doktor Motahari

Kheyābūn-é Shahid Doktor Motahari

Meidān-é Vali-yé Asr

Chahrráh-é Somíyé

Kh Hafez

Kh Doktor

Kh Beheshti

Kh Dádcoi

Kheyābūn-é Shahab

Kheyābūn-é Adálat

Ferdosi

Kheyābūn-é Eman

Kheyābūn-é Shahab

To Máhān

Sarbáz

Kh Adálat

Kh Málek-é Ashtar

Kh Esteghlál

Park-é Moáhhari

Serdy-é Terminal

Kheyābūn-é Ghods

Meidān-é Azádi

Kh Bahmaníyé

Kh Khálú-yé Kermáni

Bolvār-é Jomhúri-yé Eslámi

Bolvār-é Áyatolá Sadúqi

Jádéd-é yé Kamarbandi

Jádéd-é yé Kamarbandi

To Railway Station, Sirján, Yazd & Bandar-é Abods

To Airport

IRAN

another traditional bathhouse, still in use, but for men only.

The **Masjed-é Jāme'** is a large mosque dating from the 14th century, with many Safavid additions. Its clock tower is unique. Founded in the 11th century the **Masjed-é Emām** is notable for its original Seljuk mihrab and (partly destroyed) minaret.

Just east of town on Shohadā, **Gombad-é Jabalīyé** is a curious double-domed structure of unknown history or purpose, although it appears to predate the AD era and may have been used by Zoroastrians. It's remarkable for being of stone (the name means 'stone dome') rather than the much more usual brick.

Places to Stay & Eat

Hotel-é Kermān (☎ 224070), at the bus station, can only be recommended if you're in a desperate rush to leave Kermān, which would be a shame. It charges 30,000 rials for a double. If you're looking for something cheaper, one reader recommended the *Hotel-é Ommid* (☎ 220571) on Kheyābūn-é Shahīd Gharanī in the city centre (no sign in English); the rates are half those of the Kermān.

The family-managed *Hotel-é Akhavān* (☎ 41411; fax 49113) is popular with overland tour groups and well attuned to the needs of independently minded foreign travellers. Air-con singles/doubles with private bathrooms are US$20/30. Across the road from the Akhavān is the slightly cheaper but adequate *Hotel-é Nāz* (☎ 46786).

The town's best hotel, the *Grand Kermān* (Mehmūnsarā-yé Bozorg-é Kermān; ☎ 45203), is comfortable if not luxurious, and charges US$30/45. It has a good but expensive restaurant.

One of the most enchanting places to eat in all of Iran is the tiled *teahouse* inside the Vakīl bazaar. It serves lunch from noon to 2 pm and tea from 10 am to 7 pm, except Friday and public holidays. About halfway along the main vaulted street of the bazaar, it is recognisable by its ornately tiled entrance. The *Restōrān-é Bozorg-é Shahr* (Big Restaurant of City), on the south side of

Kheyābūn-é Doktor Beheshtī, is good and inexpensive, with friendly service.

Getting There & Away

Air The Iran Air office (☎ 235153) is on Kheyābūn-é Doktor Beheshtī, half a km east of Meidūn-é Azādī. There are flights from Kermān daily to Tehrān (95 minutes) and twice weekly to Esfahān, Mashhad and Zāhedān.

Bus The bus station is three km south of the town centre – all the bus company offices are here. By bus it's three hours to Bam, six hours to Yazd, eight hours to Shīrāz, nine hours to Zāhedān, 12 hours to Esfahān and 15 hours to Mashhad.

Shared taxis and savārīs to Māhūn (40 minutes) go from Meidūn-é Fedāīyān-é Eslām, while those for Bam and Zāhedān go from Meidūn-é Sarāsīyāb.

Train The railway station is some way east of the town centre. Three trains a week run to Tehrān.

AROUND KERMĀN
Māhūn

This small town is 35 km from Kermān on the Bam road. A restful pleasant place, it has a fine 15th century mausoleum, **Ārāmgāh-é Shāh Ne'matollāh Valī**, inside a complex of buildings from the Safavid era, and an attractive Ghajar garden, **Bāgh-é Tārīkhī**.

Bam

This pleasant fertile town is famous for its dates, said to be the best in Iran and possibly in the Middle East. Almost every spare patch of cultivable land is profitably devoted to palm trees.

Its main interest, however, is as the site of a remarkably well-preserved medieval citadel, **Arg-é Bam**, which sits on a hillock at the northern edge of town. The Arg was probably founded in Sassanian times but most of the present site dates from the Safavid era. It's quite similar to a large medieval European castle except that the material isn't stone but mud-brick. It was built with a

IRAN

large outer citadel at the base of the hill, comprising a bazaar, a mosque, a caravanserai and residential quarters for the majority of the population. It also had a smaller inner citadel at the top of the hill, comprising an artillery yard, stables and a palace for the elite and the military. The inner and outer citadel walls are intact and you can walk to the top of them for a breathtaking view. To get to the Arg, head east from the bus office (Co-op No 7), turning north (left) at the second roundabout; in all it's about a three km walk. It's open from 8 am to noon and 2 to 5 pm daily, and admission is 10,000 rials.

Places to Stay There is only one place to stay in town but it's a good one; the privately run *Tourist Guesthouse* has basic dorms and twin-bed rooms at 10,000 rials per person, or you can beat the heat and sleep in a cool carpeted cellar for 8000 rials. The toilet/bathroom facilities aren't too great but there's a kitchen, a common room and a large walled courtyard where women can bask in the sun unveiled. To get there, if you've arrived by bus from Kermān, turn right out of the bus yard (belonging to Co-op No 7) and walk 300m to take the first street on your left; the guesthouse is 100m ahead on your right. If you've arrived from Zāhedān, then you'll get off at the offices of Co-op No 8; turn left (west) and walk for about a km.

A second, poor option is the *Bam Tourist Inn* (☎ (03447) 3323) out near the airport, a shabby modern hotel which is well overpriced at US$40/65 for singles/doubles.

South Iran & the Persian Gulf Islands

The southern coastal region is hot and humid year-round, except from November to March when its climate is the most pleasant in Iran. The town of Būshehr and Kīsh Island are then very agreeable places to stay. The landlocked province of Fārs is more congenial and is rarely excessively hot or cold.

The indigenous people of the coast and islands are often loosely called Bandarīs, from the Persian word for 'port'. Of Arab, Negro or mixed stock they retain their own Arabic dialect, culture and dress, and many are Sunni. Most of the inhabitants of Fārs (Fārsīs) are, as you'd expect, Persian, although there are also some migratory tribes whom even Genghis Khan and Tamerlane never tried to pacify.

Fārs is where the Persians first settled and the mighty Achaemenian and Sassanian empires were once centred. Persepolis was the greatest city of the region and is the principal attraction today, but it's far from the only reminder of Persia at its peak. Shīrāz, the provincial centre since the 7th century, claims its own glory as a capital of several Islamic dynasties and, perhaps more importantly, an artistic centre. Outside Fārs, various imperial dynasties have left evidence of their splendour at Choghā Zambīl, Susa and Hormoz among other places.

BANDAR-É ABBĀS

Strategically overlooking the Strait of Hormuz, this is Iran's busiest port. In summer it gets sizzling hot, but in winter it's pleasant enough to visit when it's snowing in Tehrān.

It was founded by Shāh Abbās I in 1622 to replace Hormoz as the entrepôt of the region, but nowadays about the only thing you'll find to remind you of Bandar-é Abbās' origins is its name. There isn't a whole heap of reasons to hang around here, but Bandar-é Abbās is a stepping-off point for some interesting islands. A walk along the promenade, Bolvār-é Tāleghānī, is rewarding. Bandar-é Abbās has Iran's most animated beach, with a surprising number of activities you'd expect at any seaside resort elsewhere in the world. A few brave souls paddle here, but swimming isn't a good idea because of the sharks and jellyfish.

There's a lively early-morning fish market (Bāzār-é Māhī) at the west end of the promenade, and to the north there's a bustling bazaar. Many goods re-exported from the UAE find their way here, and prices are competitive on a wide range of consumer items.

Orientation & Information

The town stretches out for many km along a narrow coastal strip. The main west-east thoroughfare changes its name from Bolvār-é Pāsdārān to Emām Khomeinī and then to Beheshtī (the main road out in all directions). Bolvār-é Tāleghānī runs parallel to, and about a km south of, Emām Khomeinī. The main square, Meidūn-é Valī-é Asr, is on Emām Khomeinī. The main passenger harbour (Eskelé-yé Shahīd Bāhonar) is eight km west of this, the bus station seven km south-east and the airport nine km east.

The tourist office hides in an alley behind the provincial police headquarters on the town square. The UAE consulate (☎ 23063) is on Bolvār-é Pāsdārān, half a km west of the fish market.

The telephone code for Bandar-é Abbās is 0761.

Places to Stay & Eat

The town has a severe accommodation short-age. In winter, when everyone else wants to visit, it's inadvisable to arrive here without a reservation.

There are some mosāferkhūnés in the bazaar area. These may be unbearably stuffy outside winter. One of the very best is *Mosāferkhūné-yé Hormozān* (☎ 24856) on Bolvār-é Asadābādī.

Hotel-é Ghods (☎ 28788), on Emām Khomeinī, is tolerable and charges US$15/20 a single/double. Other places in the same category are *Hotel-é Hamzé* (☎ 23771), on Sharī'atī, *Hotel-é Sa'dī* (☎ 22637), opposite Pārk-é Shahr on Emām Khomeinī, and *Hotel-é Āzādī*, on Bolvār-é Pāsdārān, which has a good view over the Persian Gulf. If you can't get into any of these, try *Hotel-é Naghsh-é Jahān* (☎ 28369), about a km west of Shahīd Bāhonar docks or 10 km west of the town centre. This truckers' dive has clean rooms with fans and private showers, and an adequate restaurant.

The top hotel is *Hotel-é Homā* (☎ 53080), Bolvār-é Pāsdārān, with singles/doubles at US$45/65, but it isn't up to the chain's usual high standards and conspicuously doesn't need your custom.

Despite its abundance of fresh fish and seafood the town doesn't have any very inspiring restaurants. One good inexpensive dish widely available is chelō meigū (battered shrimps or prawns with boiled rice). Two fairly good if unspectacular restaurants are *Chelō Kabābī-yé Shahrzād*, by the cinema on the town square, and *Restōrān-é Sajjād*, three km east. *Lādan Bastanī Forūshī*, on the town square, is a pleasant ice-cream parlour. *Hotel-é Homā* has a safe but unexciting restaurant. At night, kabāb stalls pop up around the main square.

Getting There & Away

The best way of getting to or from most points is by air. Iran Air's main office (☎ 39595) is on Emām Khomeinī. There are flights daily to Tehrān (two hours) and twice weekly to Mashhad (two hours).

Bandar-é Abbās is rather cut off by land; the best road is to Kermān, eight hours away by bus.

See the Getting There & Away section earlier in this chapter for details of ferries to Muscat in Oman. An almost constant stream of boats leaves Bandar-é Abbās beach for Gheshm (45 minutes) and Hormoz (30 minutes) more or less within daylight hours. Valfajre-8 Shipping Company has an office in the Iran Air building on Emām Khomeinī.

BANDAR-É LENGÉ

This small, sleepy town is an overnight stop for people sailing to/from Kīsh Island. It's a pleasantly laid-back place and the lethargy is infectious. Although it has no hotels, the central *Mosāferkhūné-yé Amīd* has doubles at 4000 rials and communal hot showers. The other mosāferkhūnés don't even have showers. Buses to Bandar-é Abbās (four hours) go from outside the teahouse facing the docks. Bandar-é Kong, the port for ferries to Kīsh, is five km east by shared taxi. Valfajre-8 has an office in Lengé on Pasdāran.

SHĪRĀZ

Shīrāz was one of the leading cities in the medieval Islamic world and Persia's capital for a short spell during the Zand dynasty from 1753 to 1794. Many of its most beautiful buildings were built or restored in that era.

Two of the most famous Persian poets were born and lived in Shīrāz – Hāfez (about 1324-89) and Sa'dī (about 1207-91). Both have their mausoleums here. Through them, Shīrāz has been synonymous with learning, nightingales, poetry, roses and, at one time, wine. Omar Khayyām, though probably the best known Persian poet in the west, is esteemed by Iranians more for his abilities as a mathematician.

To many, Shīrāz is simply the most pleasant of the large Iranian cities. It's a place that captivates many visitors, although its charm is less immediately perceptible than that of Esfahān – more poetic and less visual. Shīrāz also has one of the most agreeable climates in Iran and is rarely very cold or hot; it's especially pleasant between February and May and between October and November.

Even if you only have a short time here, try not to miss the ruins of Persepolis, 57 km away on the Esfahān road. Shīrāz also has plenty to see, and is a big university town with lots of students eager to practise their English. The medical faculty here is particularly prestigious and the only one in Iran where English is the medium of instruction. In many ways, Shīrāz continues to justify its historic epithet of Dar-ol-Elm, or Seat of Learning.

Orientation

The main street, wide tree-lined Bolvār-é Karīm Khān-é Zand (Zand for short), stretches as far west and east as you would want to go without leaving Shīrāz. Since most things to see and nearly all the hotels are along or within easy walking distance of Zand, this is a boulevard you'll keep coming back to. The best landmark for the city centre is the Arg, a large brick citadel on the north side of Zand, immediately east of the main square, Meidūn-é Shohadā. A small city bus terminus stands in front of it.

Information

Tourist Office The helpful tourist office (☎ 38032) is just south of Zand. To get there head north-east from Meidūn-é Enghelāb, take the first left turning onto Asad Ābādī and walk straight ahead for about 100m, past the first left turning but before the second. It's a ground-floor office with maps on the wall, visible through a glass facade.

Visa Extensions The visa office is on the 1st floor of the police headquarters to the north-west of Meidūn-é Shohadā. Travellers' reports claim that this is a particularly good place to apply for extensions.

Money Bank Melli Iran has a big central branch on Zand, just east of the Arg. There are also private exchange offices on the north side of Zand, west of Meidūn-é Shohadā.

Post & Communications The main post and telegraph office is on an alley behind the central Bank Melli. The telephone office is to the north; however, the best place to make an international call would be from the Hotel-é Homā.

The telephone code for Shīrāz is 071.

Arg-é Karīm Khānī

This imposing fortress was built by Karīm Khān as part of a royal courtyard which he intended to rival that of Esfahān's, although it's no longer recognisable as such. The Arg is now occupied by the police and is inaccessible to visitors.

Opposite the fortress is the **Pars Museum** (Mūzé-yé Pārs), housed in an attractive pavilion that Karīm Khān originally had built as a reception hall. It became his tomb for a short while until the vengeful Āgha Mohammad, the first Ghajar ruler, moved the corpse to his new capital of Tehrān out of spite for the Zand dynasty he overthrew.

Vakil Bazaar

Bāzār-é Vakīl, the town's chief bazaar, was

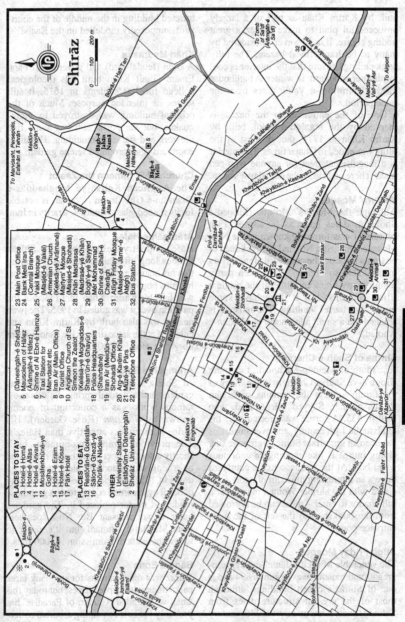

Shīrāz

0   100   200 m

PLACES TO STAY
3   Hotel-é Homā
4   Hotel-é Atlas
11   Hotel-é Anvari
12   Mosāferkhūné-yé Golhā
14   Hotel-é Eram
15   Hotel-é Kosar
17   Pārk Hotel

PLACES TO EAT
13   Restorān-é Golestān
16   Sālon-é Ghezā-yé Khōrāk-é Nāderé

OTHER
1   University Stadium (Estādyúm-é Dāneshgāh)
2   Shēraz University (Dāneshgāh-é Shērāz)
5   Mausoleum of Hāfez (Āramgāh-é Hāfez)
6   Shrine of Alī-é Hamzé
7   Taxi Station for Marvdasht etc
8   Iran Air (Main Office)
9   Tourist Office
10   Anglican Church of St Simeon the Zealot (Kelésā-yé Moghaddas-é Sham'ún-é Ghayúr)
18   Boghé-yé Sayyed Mér Mohammad
19   Shāh-é Cherāgh (Shāhchérāgh)
20   Arg-é Karém Khāni
21   Mūzé-yé Pārs
22   Telephone Office
23   Main Post Office
24   Bank Melli Iran (Central Branch)
25   Vakil Mosque (Masjed-é Vakil)
26   Armenian Church (Kelésā-yé Arāmané)
27   Martyrs Mosque (Masjed-é Shohadā)
28   Khān Madrassa (Madrasé-yé Khān)
29   Police Headquarters (Shahrbāni)
30   Shrine of Shāh-é Ātegh
31   Atigh Friday Mosque (Masjed-é Jāme'-é Atigh)
32   Bus Station

28   Vakil Bazaar

built by Karīm Khān as part of a largely unsuccessful plan to make Shīrāz a great trading centre. It is, however, considered by many to be Iran's finest bazaar. The lofty brick ceilings ensure that the interior is cool in summer and warm in winter. A bathhouse inside, **Hammūm-é Vakīl**, dates from the same period.

One of the entrances to the bazaar is marked by the **Masjed-é Vakīl**, built by Karīm Khān in 1773, though most of the tiling was added in Ghajar times. The interior is a magnificent treat for anyone who can make it here on Friday, the only day it's open.

Martyrs' Mosque

Although the Martyrs' Mosque (Masjed-é Shohadā) dates back as far as the 13th century, it was formerly known as the New Mosque (Masjed-é Nō) and it is reckoned to be Iran's largest. The courtyard alone covers over 11,000 sq metres. It has been partly rebuilt many times and little of the original tiling remains, but it does have some impressive barrel vaulting. The mosque is reached via a small alley north of Meidūn-é Ahmadī.

Shrine of Shāh-é Cherāgh

Just south of Meidūn-é Ahmadī, this tomb (Bogh'é-yé Shāh-é Cherāgh) of the 'King of the Lamp' covers the remains of Emām Rezā's brother, Sayyed Mīr Ahmad, who died in 835. A shrine was erected over his tomb in the 14th century, and ever since, this has been an important Shiite pilgrimage site. Going into it is like entering an enormous jewel box. At the entrance to the courtyard there's an interesting museum of items associated with the shrine. Women must wear a full chador to enter – these can be borrowed from the bookshop to the left of the main entrance portal.

Atīgh Friday Mosque

The venerable Masjed-é Jāme'-é Atīgh congregational mosque was begun in 894 and is one of Shīrāz's oldest buildings, although most of the present structure dates from Safavid times. It has an unusual 14th century

turreted building in the middle of the courtyard, supposedly modelled on the Kaaba.

Khān Madrassa

A *khān* (feudal lord) and governor of Fārs, Emām Gholī Khān built this theological college for 100 students in 1615. It still serves its intended purpose. Much of the original building was destroyed by earthquakes, but the portal still has some fine tilework and stalactite moulding. The inner courtyard is set around a serene garden.

Church of St Simeon the Zealot

The Anglican Kelīsā-yé Moghaddas-é Sham'ūn-é Ghayūr, on Nōbahār, is notable for its stained-glass windows, a rarity in Iran.

Ārāmgāh-é Hāfez

Hāfez's poetry helped to make Shīrāz famous long after his death and it's fitting that his mausoleum, with its restful gardens, remains popular today. The tombstone itself was laid by Karīm Khān in 1773, but the pavilion over it was added in 1935. The iwan nearby was also built by Karīm Khān and enlarged at the same time as the canopy went up. Admission is 1000 rials.

Ārāmgāh-é Sa'dī

At Shīrāz's eastern edge, this tomb has gardens and a natural spring. Sa'dī's most famous work was a collection of poems known as *Golestān* (Rose Garden). His shrine is much less attractive than Hāfez's. The previous simpler monument, built shortly after the poet's death and renovated by a long succession of rulers, was ripped down in 1952 after being deemed unworthy of Sa'dī by a learned committee. A grandiose modernist horror replaced it. The gardens, however, are pleasant. Bus No 7 goes here from Meidūn-é Ahmadī, but it's easier to take a shared taxi. Admission is 1000 rials.

Bāgh-é Eram

Shīrāz was once famous for its many large parks thick with cypress trees, but today this small well-tended 'Garden of Paradise' has probably the best remaining arboreal collection. A 19th century **Royal Palace** (Kākh-é Eram) stands in the grounds. The Ghajar architectural style which it represents is widely regarded today as tasteless and flimsy but a few examples such as this one do show a certain informal charm.

Other gardens worth a stroll include the ancient **Bāgh-é Afīf Ābād** and **Bāgh-é Delgoshā**, as well as the newer **Bāgh-é Khalīlī**.

Places to Stay

There are plenty of mosāferkhūnés around Kheyābūn-é Lotf Alī Khān-é Zand and on or off the south side of Zand (especially on Anvarī and Tōhīd). They are all pretty much alike but a couple that have been recommended by readers are the *Hotel-é Anvarī* on Kheyābūn-é Anvarī, which has doubles at 20,000 rials, and the *Mosāferkhūné Golha*, on Zand midway between Anvarī and Nōbahār, which charges 12,000 rials for a double.

In the mid-range there are two good hotels on Zand; the *Hotel-é Kōsar* (☎ 335724; fax 333117) and the *Hotel-é Eram* (☎ 337201), both three-star standard charging US$20/30. The *Hotel-é Atlas* (☎ 47748) isn't bad either but it's inconveniently located, north of the river and some 1.5 km from the centre of the city. Singles/doubles are US$25/35.

The *Pārk Hotel* (☎ 21426), just off Zand, while supposedly one of the city's top hotels, is gloomy and has unwelcoming staff. Rates are US$45/65. By its official classification, the *Hotel-é Homā* (☎ 28001) is Iran's best hotel. Nothing's too much trouble for the staff here and almost every luxury Iran has to offer is at your fingertips. Rooms are US$65/95.

Places to Eat

Two good inexpensive chelō kabābīs are *Sālon-é Ghezā-yé Khōrak-é Nāderī*, on the corner of Zand and Kheyābūn-é Rūdakī, and *Restōrān-é Golestān* almost opposite Hotel-é Eram. The restaurant at the *Eram* isn't bad either, and it's often open when most other places are closed. The restaurant at the *Hotel-*

é Homā serves Iran's best European food outside Tehrān.

Shīrāz has two wonderfully atmospheric *teahouses*, one at each of the tombs of the city's two famed poets. At the Mausoleum of Hāfez the teahouse is in a walled garden with cushioned niches in the wall for seats. It also serves soup, cakes and a thirst-quenching local speciality called pālūdé (this is what you get if you ask for ice cream), a kind of vermicelli sorbet flavoured with rose water. At the Mausoleum of Sa'dī the teahouse is in an underground chamber with a fish pool at its centre. Both teahouses are open daily from around 9 am to 6 pm.

Getting There & Away

Air Iran Air has an office on Zand just west of Meidūn-é Shohadā, but the main office (☎ 330041) is on the same street 150m west of Meidūn-é Enghelāb. There is also a third office at the Hotel-é Homā. Flights to/from Shīrāz include Bandar-é Abbās (55 minutes) daily, Esfahān (45 minutes) daily, Mashhad (90 minutes) five times a week and Tehrān (75 minutes; 50,000 rials) twice daily.

Bus The main bus station is north of the river on Bolvār-é Salmān-é Fārsī, about two km east of central Meidūn-é Shohadā (about 500 rials each in a shared taxi). Although there are some bus company offices on Zand, west of Shohāda, the majority of them are here at the station. From Shīrāz there are frequent services to Esfahān (eight hours; 6000 rials) and Tehrān (16 hours; 11,500 rials), and two buses a day to Kermān (eight hours; 6000 rials) and Yazd (seven hours; 4500 rials), among other places.

Buses and minibuses to Marvdasht and Pasargadae go from the forecourt in front of the bus station.

PERSEPOLIS

The earlier Achaemenian capital was at Pasargadae, further north, but in about 512 BC Darius I (the Great) started construction of this massive and magnificent palace complex (Takht-é Jamshīd in Persian). It sits on a plateau on the slopes of Kūh-é Rahmat

IRAN

and at one time was surrounded by a wall 18m high.

In 323 BC Alexander burnt it to the ground in an uncharacteristic act of wanton destruction, fortunately after having the enormous library translated into Greek. The ruins you see today are just a shadow of Persepolis' former glory but this is still one of the Middle East's most exciting archaeological sites.

The only entrance to the palace is by the four flights of steps of the **Grand Stairway**. At the top they lead to **Xerxes' Gateway**, with three entrances flanked east and west by two seven metre high stone bulls.

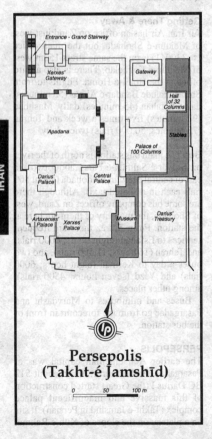

Persepolis (Takht-é Jamshīd)

0   50   100 m

The south door leads to the immense **Apadana**, where the kings once held audiences and received visitors. The roof was supported by 36 stone columns each 20m high, but the main interest today is in the superb reliefs that decorate the stairways. Altogether they are over 300m long and when, as in Persepolis' heyday, they were brightly coloured they must have been a dazzling spectacle. The quality of the work is still astounding. The *Parade of Nations* shows people and animals bringing tributes to the Persian king, who was always symbolically depicted as taller and higher than any other mortal. Other reliefs depict the 'Immortals', the 10,000-strong palace guard – so-called because as soon as one fell he was immediately replaced by another from the reserve. The famous travel writer Herodotus, known as both the father of history and the father of lies, is an entertaining, if not always entirely reliable, source of information on the Graeco-Persian Wars.

Behind the Apadana are the smaller **Palace of Darius** and **Palace of Xerxes**, as well as a small **museum** (separate entry fee). The eastern door from Xerxes' Gateway leads to the **Hall of 32 Columns**, behind which is the now totally demolished **Treasury of Darius**. Below Persepolis are the remnants of a tent city which was assembled for the Persian Empire's 2500th anniversary in 1971, a swansong by the last shāh.

Persepolis is well worth the effort to visit; the lack of visitors is very pleasant and refreshing as, except on Friday and public holidays, you have the site practically to yourself. In summer it's wise to visit in the early morning or late afternoon, avoiding the intense midday heat. Admission is 10,000 rials (half for students). There are sometimes guides here. There's a fairly good restaurant a short walk right as you leave the site.

Naghsh-é Rostam

Hewn out of a cliff three km north of Persepolis, the four lofty tombs of Naghsh-é Rostam are believed to be those of Darius I, Xerxes, Artaxerxes and Darius II, but only that of Darius I (second from right) has been positively identified. There are also reliefs cut into the stone from the far later Sassanian era and a probable fire-temple from Achaemenian times. From Persepolis to Naghsh-é Rostam entails a walk of at least an hour or more and you might prefer to pick up a taxi; from Persepolis to Naghsh-é Rostam and back to Marvdasht should cost about 5000 rials.

Pasargadae (Pāsārgād)

Cyrus the Great's capital is 130 km from Shīrāz and further off the main road. Visually it's nowhere near as interesting as Persepolis and what remains is fairly widely scattered. Begun under Cyrus the Great in about 546 BC, it was succeeded soon after his death by Darius I's magnificent palace and some historians suggest that Persepolis' construction may actually have started under Cyrus. The first structure you'll come to is **Cyrus' stone cenotaph**, known locally (incorrectly) as Ghabr-é Mādar-é Soleimān (Solomon's Mother's Tomb). Its custodian can point you in the direction of the other less impressive remains, which include three ruined Achaemenian palaces and several stone plinths and platforms.

Getting There & Away

Allow at least a whole day for the return trip from Shīrāz to these three sites. The cheapest way to make it is to catch a minibus to Marvdasht (one hour; 600 rials) from Shīrāz's bus station, then take a taxi on to Persepolis (ask for Takht-é Jamshīd), which should cost about 3000 rials. If you want to visit Pasargadae on the same trip, return to Marvdasht, take a shared taxi to Sā'adatshahr and another one from there. Some direct buses link Shīrāz and Pasargadae within daylight hours.

You'll save time if not money by chartering a taxi in Shīrāz. Persepolis is only 57 km away but you'll probably want to spend at least two or three hours wandering around and soaking up the atmosphere. If you're also going to Naghsh-é Rostam and Pasargadae the whole return trip will probably take eight hours or so. It's better to hire

a taxi by the hour (aim for about 5000 rials an hour) rather than at a flat fare, so that the driver doesn't rush you in the shortest possible time.

BŪSHEHR

Jutting out like a shark's fin into the Persian Gulf, Būshehr (Bushire) is a naval, commercial and passenger port of growing importance. It has historically been Shīrāz's main outlet to the sea, as Bandar-é Abbās has been for Kermān. Būshehr was heavily bombed in the Iran-Iraq War but is fast regaining its regional status. At one time it was the seat of the British Political Residency in the Persian Gulf (later moved to Bahrain) and the town has been occupied by the British more than once, with several monuments to their presence still around. The atmosphere here is more relaxed than in Bandar-é Abbās, and this is with little doubt the most pleasant of the larger towns along Iran's south coast. Kheyābūn-é Khalīj-é Fārs (Persian Gulf St) is one of Iran's best promenades.

Unlike many other of Iran's Persian Gulf ports, Būshehr is a manageable size for exploring. Most points of interest are north of the town square, Meidūn-é Ghods (2.5 km south of Kheyābūn-é Leyān), except the tourist office, which is 200m south, and the airport, which is four km south-west.

The telephone code for Būshehr is 0771.

Things to See

The **Old City** (Shahr-é Ghadīm) at Būshehr's narrowest northern end, enclosed to the south by Leyān and on the coast by Kheyābūn-é Khalīj-é Fārs, has some fine examples of Bandarī architecture. This is characterised by mud-brick buildings covered with a thin layer of sand-coloured plaster, with tall facades, latticed glassless windows, arched balconies, sturdy wooden doors with metal studs and carved jambs, protruding joists and overhanging balconies on flat roofs where people sleep in the hotter months. One of the best examples is the **shahrdārī** (municipal headquarters) building on the west seafront.

IRAN

The docks *(eskelé)* are east of the old city: look out for traditional ship-building activities at **Kārgāh-é Lenjsāzī**. A small historic water-reservoir *(ābambār)* stands near Hotel-é Khalīj-é Fārs. A small beach, **Pelāzh-é Shahrdārī**, lies two km south-west of Meidūn-é Ghods.

Now used by Armenians, the small stone **Kelīsā-yé Arāmané**, on Enghelāb, was founded by Anglicans in 1819 when the British were gaining a foothold over the Persian Gulf. It's well worth a visit.

Places to Stay & Eat

There are some squalid dives around Leyān and Enghelāb, such as the prison-like *Mosāferkhūné-yé Ghasr-é Telā'ī*, on Leyān, and the slightly better *Mosāferkhūné-é Tōhīd* (doubles for 6000 rials), a minute's walk south-east. The basic *Hotel-é Sa'dī* (☎ 22605) on Hāfez charges US$15/20 a single/double. The old colonial *Mehmūnsarā-yé Khalīj-é Fārs* (☎ 22228), on Valī-yé Asr, also charging US$15/20, has a fine seafront setting but is rather dilapidated.

A recommended mid-range place is *Hotel-é Rezā* (☎ 27171) on Emām Khomeinī, just south of Meidūn-é Ghods, with rooms for US$20/30. The seafront *Mehmūnsarā-yé Jahangardī* on the corner of Kheyābūn-é Khalīj-é Fārs and Īlām has a similar standard but better views.

Restōrān-é Āzādī on the corner of Shohadā and Mo'allem is inexpensive and excellent.

Getting There & Away

Buses leave from outside the bus company offices off Chahārrāh-é Shohadā. Shīrāz is five hours away by bus, Bandar-é Abbās 16 hours. The mountainous Shīrāz road is particularly scenic. See the Getting There & Away section earlier in this chapter for details of ferries to Kuwait and Bahrain.

AHVĀZ

This sprawling industrial city spanning both banks of Rūdkhūné-yé Kārūn owes its prosperity to the discovery of oil at nearby Masjed-é Soleimān in 1908. Ahvāz isn't in any way beautiful and was mercilessly bombed in the Iran-Iraq War, but it is the best base to explore Susa and Choghā Zambīl. All over town there's evidence of the oil trade. At its northern edge, huge beacons burning off excess gases from the refining process ensure that Ahvāz never gets dark. Perhaps as a result, it stays up much later than many other Iranian cities. At night it's pleasant to walk along the river bank, where there are several parks with floodlit fountains.

Orientation & Information

Ahvāz is so vast and featureless and its transport terminals, hotels and other points of interest are so spread out that you're probably best off hiring telephone taxis to get around. Ahvāz is bisected by Rūd-é Kārūn, which flows from its north-east to south-west edge. This and the four modern bridges spanning it are about the only things to orient you. The main square, Meidūn-é Shohadā, is just east of the suspension bridge, Pol-é Sefīd or Pol-é Mo'allagh. Beneath this bridge there's a small harbour where you can join a brief river cruise.

The very helpful tourist office (☎ 32725) is on Enghelāb, a km south-west of the railway station, which is 800m west of Pol-é Sefīd.

The telephone code for Ahvāz is 061.

Places to Stay & Eat

The mid-range *Hotel-é Oksīn* (☎ 442133) opposite the airport is highly recommended, if a long way from the city centre. Singles/doubles cost US$20/30. *Hotel Grand Fajr* (Hotel-é Bozorg-é Fajr; ☎ 20091), just north of the main square, with rooms at US$45/65, is central and comfortable, but the service is a little grudging. Both have fairly good restaurants.

Restōrān-é Khayyām at Pol-é Sefīd's east end is a good river-fish restaurant. *Restōrān-é Rūdkenār* on the west bank, 300m north of Pol-é Sefīd, is a popular meeting place with locals and expats.

Getting There & Away

The bus companies for long-distance trips

are mostly on Enghelāb, three km north-east of the railway station. Buses to Shīrāz take 10 hours. Minibuses to Susa (90 minutes) go from Termīnāl-é Shūsh further out on the same road. Minibuses and shared taxis to Ābādān, two to 2½ hours away, go from Chahārrāh-é Ābādān in the south-east of town.

SUSA

Although Susa (Shūsh) was one of the great ancient cities of Iran, there's no longer very much to see compared with the much better-preserved site of Persepolis. Susa was an important regional centre from at least the 4th millennium BC but it reached its first peak as the administrative capital of the Elamite ruler and founder of Choghā Zambīl, Untash Gal, in the 13th century BC. It was burnt around 640 BC by Ashurbanipal at the same time he destroyed Choghā Zambīl, but came back to prominence in 521 BC when Darius I set it up as his winter capital, Ecbatana being his summer quarters. He fortified the town and built several palaces here and, at one time, Susa must have been of similar grandeur to Persepolis. In 331 BC Susa with all its riches fell to Alexander. Although it was restored as the capital in the Sassanian era, it lost its importance once more after the Arab conquest and faded away completely after the 12th century. It was first surveyed in 1852 by the British archaeologist WK Loftus. From 1884 the French Archaeological Service carried on his work more or less continuously until the revolution.

The site is built on four small mounds. English signposts explain the remains. As you enter from the road you can't fail to notice the so-called **château** on top of the tallest mound, the **Acropolis**. This remarkable fortress was built at the end of the 19th century as the camp for the French Archaeological Service, as a defence against the unpacified Arab tribes of the region. At present its sole incumbent is a caretaker paid by the French embassy, and visitors aren't allowed inside. In contrast, almost nothing remains of the mound's earlier buildings.

The **museum** at the site's entrance was closed at last report.

The largest mound, west of the Acropolis, is the **Royal Town**, once the court officials' quarter, which has revealed remains of many buildings from Elamite to early Islamic times. North-west of this is the most impressive mound, the **Apadana**, where Darius built his residence and two other palaces. The remains of 72 columns and bulls' head capitals here show how similar this site must have been to Persepolis, constructed soon afterwards. Two famous foundation tablets that Darius laid here are now in Tehrān's archaeological museum. The **Artisans' Town** mound further west dates from Parthian times. Traces of an Arab mosque were found here but little else of substance remains.

A short walk west of the site, **Ārāmgāh-é Dānyāl**, with its characteristic white sugar-loaf tower, covers what are claimed to be the prophet Daniel's bones. It has, however, been rebuilt many times.

Choghā Zambīl

This is the world's best-preserved remaining example of a *ziggurat*, and one of Iran's most memorable sights. A ziggurat is a pyramidal temple with a series of tiers on a square or rectangular plan. The Elamites (like the Zoroastrians) revered the mountains as holy places. They made their own imitations where, as here, there were no mountains, thus creating this distinctive style of building. There are also some ziggurats in Iraq, including one just outside Baghdad and another at Nineveh.

The ziggurat was the focal point of the town of Dur Untash founded by the Elamite king, Untash Gal, in the 13th century BC as his realm's chief pilgrimage centre. It was later sacked by the Assyrian king Ashurbanipal, around 640 BC, and was lost to the world until it was accidentally rediscovered in 1935. The ziggurat was dedicated to the Elamites' chief god, Inshushinak, and originally a temple to him sat on its summit, accessible only to the elite of society. Each side of the pyramid measures 105m and its original height is believed to have exceeded 50m. There were once five tiers but only three remain intact. At one time there was a complex of chambers, tombs, tunnels and water channels in the lowest storey, as well as 13 temples and three palaces away from the ziggurat, but little of these now remains.

Getting There & Away You'll have to hire a taxi in Susa for the return trip, which takes about four hours. The ziggurat is in a restricted military area and you have to pass several checkpoints to reach it. At the penultimate one, you hand over your passport and any cameras, and collect an armed escort. All visitors need a routinely issued permit from Susa's archaeological office (Daftar-é Mīrās-é Farhangī) just west of the archaeological site. It opens from 7 am to about 2.30 pm (noon on Thursday) except Friday and public holidays. You must show your passport and give the registration number of the vehicle taking you here. The road is heavily rutted and may be impassable after rains. For the latest information ask at the Ahvāz tourist office (see the previous Ahvāz section for details).

ĀBĀDĀN

The Iran-Iraq War made this frontline city within rifle range of Iraq out of bounds to all foreigners not belonging to the press corps. Nowadays it's accessible once more, by air or bus, although the city was virtually destroyed in the war and it'll be some years before its reconstruction is complete.

Ābādān doesn't rank very highly in the history and culture stakes, but it would deserve a long entry in any book about the oil multinationals. It was and is becoming once again a major centre for the refining industry. Pre-revolutionary Ābādān was one of Iran's most important places for foreign influences as thousands upon thousands of foreigners came to exploit its oil wealth.

THE PERSIAN GULF ISLANDS

Iran possesses 16 of these islands; three (Abū Mūsā and the Tomb islands) are also claimed by the UAE. Eleven islands are inhabited. Although all have something to offer the adventurous traveller, probably the most interesting are Hormoz, Gheshm, Khārk and Kīsh. Try to go in winter, as the Persian Gulf is too hot and humid for anyone's comfort for the rest of the year.

Iran Air flies to Kīsh and Khārk from the mainland, and ferries sail to Kīsh from Bandar-é Kong. However, seats to Kīsh on all forms of transport, particularly planes, are often very hard to obtain at short notice in winter and spring. Since accommodation on Kīsh is also in short supply, your best bet is probably to go on an inclusive tour. Hormoz and Gheshm are easily reached by boat from Bandar-é Abbās.

The other islands are more difficult to get to; NIOC (National Iranian Oil Company) or Bandar-é Abbās' tourist office can give more information. To visit Khārk, the site of Iran's main oil export terminal, you need permission at least 48 hours in advance from NIOC or Būshehr's provincial governorate (ostāndārī). Gheshm has some mosāferkhūnés and a mehmūnsarā (☎ (07625) 2001), and Khārk has an NIOC guesthouse.

Hormoz Island

Jazīré-yé Hormoz has the most historical interest of all the Iranian islands, and an excursion here is very worthwhile. The main attraction is its **Portuguese Castle** (Ghal'é-yé Portoghālīhā) – probably the last thing you'd expect to find in this part of the world.

Hormoz had been an important trading centre from about 1300 AD under its own emir, although it produced virtually nothing but salt. Contemporary visitors described it as heavily fortified, bustling and opulent. At the turn of the 16th century, Portugal was a thrusting imperial power determined to establish its presence in Asia. The talented Portuguese admiral Affonso d'Albuquerque, aware of Hormoz's potential, besieged and conquered the island in 1507. The castle, which he started in the same year, was finished in 1515. In the meantime he went on to do a bit more empire building in Goa and Malacca.

The Portuguese kept on the emirs and quickly controlled all shipping in the Persian Gulf. Virtually all European trade with India, Asia, Muscat and the Persian Gulf ports was funnelled through Hormoz. At its peak, the island supported a population of over 50,000. However, when Shāh Abbās I started to rid his country of foreign influences, he couldn't fail to resent Portugal's presence on Hormoz. So with the help of the English, in 1622, he sent an expeditionary force to recapture it.

Soon supplanted by Bandar-é Abbās, Hormoz fell into a decline from which it never recovered. Only about 4000 people live here today, all in the small town of Hormoz at the island's north tip, overlooked by the castle's still impressive remains. Make sure you don't miss the last boat back as there is nowhere to stay in Hormoz.

Gheshm Island

More than twice as big as Bahrain, the mountainous Jazīré-yé Gheshm is the largest in the Persian Gulf. The largest of its mainly coastal settlements is Gheshm at the eastern tip, followed by Dargahān, 22 km west on the north shore. Some vans carry passengers along the coast road, and you may be able to hire one for a tour. The island has many interesting historic water reservoirs, as well as a ruined Portuguese castle in Gheshm, but perhaps its main appeal is to trekkers and naturalists, or people who just like getting way off the beaten track. The largely unexplored interior has deer, scorpions and snakes, while the mud flats off the north-west shore host pelicans and other birds.

Iran has grandiose development plans for the island. It's going to be a 'free area' attracting foreign and Iranian companies to exploit the vast offshore reserves of natural gas and crude oil, with a super port on the south coast and a causeway connecting the island with the mainland, as well as an international airport. To date, however, the island is astoundingly undeveloped. Now's a good time to explore it before it gets spoiled.

Kīsh Island

Jazīré-yé Kīsh is Iran's first and only free port. Before the revolution it was virtually a private retreat for the last shāh and his guests. He built a palace here, Iran's only casino and an international airport equipped for Concorde, as well as a luxury hotel. After the revolution, a Kish Island Development Organization (KIDO) was established to make these facilities available to a slightly wider public, albeit an affluent one, and to generate some income into the bargain. The plans have been so successful that KIDO – currently under direct presidential control – has more money than it knows what to do with. The pace of development is phenomenal by post-revolutionary Iranian standards.

It's possible for anyone to visit Kīsh, purchase a duty-exemption permit from KIDO, and buy imported electronic and luxury goods at one of the island's more than 100 shops. The goods can then be resold on the mainland and a tidy profit can still be made after covering all air transport and accommodation expenses, and with a pleasant short holiday thrown in. However, since half the population of Iran knows about this legalised smuggling racket, it's not easy to buy tickets here at short notice. There are also annual limits on how much one can buy duty free. For more information consult KIDO (☎ 681491), Bozorgrāh-é Afrīghā, Chahārrāh-é Haghghānī, 3 Kheyābūn-é Kīsh, in Tehrān, or whoever arranges your tickets to Kīsh.

Even if buying and selling doesn't interest you, Kīsh is worth a visit in its own right. It has several buildings associated with the last shāh, as well as a couple of Arab villages, an aquarium, some pleasant beaches and several parks.

Hotel-é Kīsh (☎ (07653) 2771), the only hotel, has luxurious doubles at US$65. Alternatively, you can rent a small *villa*, accommodating several people, from Daftar-é Vīllāhā-yé Seyāhatī-yé Morvarīd (☎ (07653) 2743, or 646 7398 in Tehrān). Try to book one before arriving. The best place to eat is *Restōrān-é Mīr Mohammad*,

IRAN

but Hotel-é Kīsh and the former casino also have some good restaurants and cafes.

Khārk Island

Jazīré-yé Khārk was an important trading centre in pre-Islamic times and hosted a Palmyrene Christian community from about the 3rd century till the Arab conquest. There's a temple to Poseidon in the centre of Khārk, of which a staircase remains. A fire temple was constructed in Sassanian times over this, followed later by a mosque. Some Christian tombs lie hereabouts, as well as a sugarloaf tomb tower of unknown date. A ruined Nestorian church and monastery on the west coast probably date from around the 5th century.

West Iran

Most of west Iran's population isn't Persian; Kurds, Lors and Āzarīs are the dominant races. Evidence exists of settlement here as early as the 6th millennium BC, and some of Iran's earliest empires and kingdoms had their capitals here. Standing at the frontier with Mesopotamia, the region has been vulnerable to incursions from the west since ancient times. It came out of the Iran-Iraq War none too well: it was bombed, partly occupied by Iraqi forces and generally thrown into turmoil. As one extreme example, the town of Ghasr-é Shīrīn's population fell from 102,000 in 1976 to just 107 in 1986. To make matters worse, during the Gulf War and Saddam Hussein's attacks on the Kurds, large numbers of refugees from Iraq ran here to escape persecution.

The situation for more fortunate visitors is that demand outstrips supply for accommodation and many other facilities in the region, and that some time will pass before it's fully equipped for tourists. Communications are poor: only one town in the west is on Iran Air's schedule and the railways won't get you far.

The main attractions are Bīsotūn, Tāgh-é Bostān, Hamadān and Ghazvīn.

KERMĀNSHĀH

Probably dating from the 4th century, Kermānshāh (also Bākhtarān) is west Iran's largest city by far. Although nothing of historical interest remains here, it is a pleasant enough base for exploring other sites in the region. It's also a good place for meeting Kurds, who form the majority population. At an altitude of 1322m, Kermānshāh has a beautiful setting framed by permanently snow-clad mountains. It gets very cold in winter but the climate is mild most of the rest of the year.

The tourist office (☎ 55472) is on Bolvār-é Beheshtī about 1.5 km north-east of the town square, Meidūn-é Āzādī.

The telephone code is 0431.

Tāgh-é Bostān

At the town's north edge, just north of the Bīsotūn road, the bas-reliefs and carved alcoves at Tāgh-é Bostān overlook a large pool and a garden. The first one you come to depicts the investiture of the Sassanian king Ardeshīr II (379-83). The next is a small arched recess showing Shāpūr II (309-79) and his grandson, the future Shāpūr III (383-88). The third is a larger grotto with an armed figure on horseback, believed to represent Khosrō II (591-628). A coloured tableau of three royal princes on the inner wall was added in Fath Alī Shāh's reign (1797-1834). Originally decorated in bright colours, the figures at Tāgh-é Bostān are somewhat more formal and stylised than those on Bīsotūn's Darius relief. Lighting conditions are best in mid-afternoon.

Bīsotūn

The bas-reliefs of Bīsotūn (Behīstūn) are hewn out of a cliff 33 km from Kermānshāh on the Hamadān road. The location was deliberate for this has, since ancient times, overlooked the main highway between Mesopotamia and Persia. Their significance can't have been lost on Alexander when he passed this way in 324 BC. The carvings were made at various times and each one was designed to portray the glory of the ruler who commissioned it. Some incorporate Zoroastrian symbols, which alone were allowed to overshadow the figure of the king.

The site has probably been continuously inhabited since Neolithic times. The present village is overlooked by a **tablet of Darius I** depicting his hard-won victory over rebel princes. Against this is a trilingual inscription in Old Persian, Akkadian and Elamite. Sir Henry Rawlinson, then a British army officer, studied this inscription between 1833 and 1834 to unlock the key to the then lost Akkadian language. A staircase below leads to a 2nd century BC **sculpture of Heracles** reclining contentedly on a lion. Above and about 50m right of this are a couple of worn **Parthian bas-reliefs**. About 40m left of the Darius tablet is a vast smooth **stone panel**, probably from the 7th century BC, whose intended purpose is unknown. Bīsotūn has plenty of other remains from various periods, but most visitors are happy merely to see the famous bas-reliefs. Lighting conditions are best in the early morning.

Places to Stay & Eat
There are some mosāferkhūnés on Modarres, immediately south of the town square. *Hotel-é Āzādī* (☎ 33347) and *Hotel-é Tōhīd* (☎ 22713) on this square have doubles at US$20. The top hotel is the undistinguished *Hotel-é Resālat* (☎ 24056) on Meidūn-é Ferdōsī in the far south of town; it has rooms at US$20/30 for singles/doubles and a fairly good restaurant. Rice cakes are a local speciality sold at confectioneries. Bīsotūn and Tāgh-é Bostān have some pleasant cafes and restaurants.

Getting There & Away
The bus station is north of the river on Bolvār-é Keshvarī, the airport some 10 km further out on the same road. Shared taxis to Tāgh-é Bostān, Bīsotūn and the bus station run from the town square. See the Getting There & Away section earlier in this chapter for details of travel to Iraq.

HAMADĀN
Once known as Ecbatana, this was the Achaemenians' summer capital when Susa was their winter capital, and it's claimed to be one of the world's longest continually inhabited towns. Like Kermānshāh, it owes its importance to its place on the ancient royal road between Persia and Baghdad. As legend has it, the town was founded by the mythical King Jamshīd, and it certainly has been settled since at least the 2nd millennium BC. It became the capital under Cyrus the Great in the 6th century BC; contemporary sources describe Ecbatana in its heyday as the most opulent of cities, with splendid palaces, buildings plated with precious metals and seven layers of city walls, the inner two coated in gold and silver. Some valuable finds from the upper levels have been unearthed this century but excavating the lower layers would mean demolishing much of the rather drab modern city.

Later occupiers include the Seleucids, Parthians, Alexander and the Sassanians. It became briefly the Seljuk capital in the 12th century but was devastated by the Mongols in 1220 and again by Tamerlane in 1386. Yet it soon returned to prosperity as a trading centre, which is how it remains today. It's also an important centre for Judaism. Jews first settled here in the 5th century BC following the Babylonian captivity, later spreading east to Shīrāz, Tehrān, Esfahān and elsewhere. In the '70s, Hamadān's Jews numbered 4000, and there are still a few left.

Hamadān sits on a high plain below Kūh-é Alvand at an altitude of 1747m. It's a popular retreat with Iranians in summer when its climate is mild and pleasant. Winters, however, are long and severe and Hamadān is sometimes snowbound.

Orientation & Information
Six straight roads radiate from the town square, Meidūn-é Emām Khomeinī, just south of the bazaar. The other main square, Meidūn-é Bū Alī Sīnā, lies 750m south, connected by Kheyābūn-é Bū Alī Sīnā. The tourist office (☎ 25065) is 200m west of this square.

The telephone code is 081.

Things to See

The only distinct monument of ancient Ecbatana is the 4th century **Stone Lion** (Sang-é Shīr) in south-east Hamadān. It originally guarded a city gate and may have been built on Alexander's orders. The **Mound of Ecbatana** (Tappé-yé Hekmatāné), north of the bazaar, is only rubble.

The **Ārāmgāh-é Ester va Mōrdekhāy**, 200m west of the town square, is Iran's foremost Jewish pilgrimage site. The mausoleum is popularly believed to contain the tombs of Esther, Xerxes I's Jewish wife – credited with organising the first Jewish emigration to Persia – and her uncle, Mordecai. In fact, the remains are much more likely those of a much later Jewish queen, Shūshān, and an unknown companion. (Shūshān is said to have persuaded her husband, Yazdgerd I, to allow a Jewish colony here in the 5th century.)

Gombad-é Alavīyān is on Kūché-yé Sa'ādatī, 750m north-west of the town square. This mausoleum of the Alavī family probably dates from the 12th century and is Hamadān's finest monument. It's notable for the outstanding quality of its stucco ornamentation.

Borj-é Ghorbān is an interesting 13th century tomb tower 600m east of Meidūn-é Bū Alī Sīnā. On this square is the distasteful-looking **Mausoleum of Avicenna** (Ārāmgāh-é Bū Alī Sīnā), the tomb of the author of a famous medical treatise who died in 1307. The museum inside fractionally makes up for the monument.

Another modernist atrocity, the **Ārāmgāh-é Bābā Tāher**, 1.3 km north-west of the town square, houses the tomb of Omar Khayyām's grandson, Bābā Tāher, a mystic poet. Resembling a giant petrified spider, this building is to the Persian architectural tradition what Emām Khomeinī is to cancan dancing.

Ganjnāmé, 35 km south-west by road, is the site of a pair of Achaemenian rock carvings of Darius I (left) and his son Xerxes I. Inscribed in Old Persian, Akkadian and Elamite, these tablets list the kings' titles and hence the extent of their empires at the time.

Shared taxis here run from Meidūn-é Abbās Ābād at Hamadān's south-west edge.

Places to Stay & Eat

Mosāferkhūnés on Ekbātān include the grotty *Rāsfī*, the grim *Ordībehesht* and the dismal *Ekbātān*. The slightly better *Hotel-é Yās* (☎ 23464), on the town square, has doubles at US$20. The top hotel is the unspectacular *Hotel-é Bū Alī* (☎ 33071), 200m south of Meidūn-é Bū Alī, which has doubles at US$30. Its restaurant has a safe if minimalist menu. There are some chelō kabābīs nearby and around the bazaar. Ganjnāmé has some outdoor cafes.

Getting There & Away

The bus companies are around the town square. Kermānshāh is three hours away by bus.

SANANDAJ

Although Sanandaj, the rather ramshackle capital of Kordestān (Kurdistan) Province, dates back at least to the Middle Ages, it's not of any great architectural or historical interest. Its main appeal is that it's the chief market town of Iran's Kurds, who have given it a very distinctive character. Unless you have plenty of time it's not easy to visit the interior of Kordestān, but the Kurds are renowned for their hospitality and you're unlikely to be short of invitations. It's notable that Iran has a province called Kordestān at all; in Turkey and Iraq, Kurds don't even officially exist.

The main street, Ferdōsī, runs south from Meidūn-é Āzādī to Meidūn-é Enghelāb.

The tourist office is on Kheyābūn-é Hammūm, which leads east from the first square. The **city museum** (Mūzé-yé Sanandaj) is 400m north-west of the second square. The **Masjed-é Jāme'**, opposite, dates from 1813 and has some attractive tilework.

Places to Stay & Eat

Hotel-é Ābīdar (☎ 23810) and *Hotel-é Hedāyat* (☎ 24117) on Ferdōsī charge US$15/20 for singles/doubles. The best place, *Mehmūnsarā-yé Sanandaj*, with rooms for US$20/30, is some distance southeast of the town centre on Bolvār-é Pāsdārān, the airport road. It also has a restaurant.

Getting There & Away

Buses to Kermānshāh (two hours) go from the bus station on the airport road, almost a km south-east of Meidūn-é Āzādī. Buses elsewhere (eg Hamadān, three hours) leave from the main station on the Tehrān road. Iran Asseman may fly here from Tehrān.

GHAZVĪN

Ghazvīn was founded in the 3rd century BC and later became prosperous under the Seljuks. It again rose to prominence briefly under the Safavid Shāh Tahmāsb I (1524-76), who transferred the capital here from Tabrīz, then considered too exposed to Ottoman invasion. He embarked on an ambitious architectural plan for Ghazvīn, but the fine buildings founded here were only a dress rehearsal for Esfahān, where his indirect successor, Shāh Abbās I, set up court in 1598. Earthquakes have taken a heavy toll on Ghazvīn but a few Safavid and Seljuk structures remain.

The local tourist office (☎ 33879) is on Kheyābūn-é Azadi. The telephone code for Ghazvīn is 0281.

Things to See

The **Masjed-é Jāme'** in part dates back to the early Islamic era. Some even claim it was founded by Hārūn ar-Rashīd in the late 8th century. The dome dates from the 12th century, as does the exquisitely decorated main prayer hall. The two minarets and the south iwan were added in Safavid times.

Some 600m east is the **Ālī Ghāpū pavilion**, which dates from Tahmāsb's time and is notable for its fine south facade. It once formed the entrance to a Safavid palace, now entirely destroyed, and may well have been the inspiration for its namesake in Esfahān.

The **Heidarīyé Madrassa** (Madrasé-yé Heidarīyé), 250m south-east of Ālī Ghāpū, was built around a 12th century Seljuk mosque, but most of this seminary dates

from the Ghajar era. The plaster mihrab, however, is original, as are the ornamentations in the dome-chamber.

Soltānīyé

The Mongols had an infamous reputation, but occasionally they were capable of the highest forms of cultural expression. Nowhere was this more evident than at Soltānīyé's **Gombad-é Soltān Oljeitū Khodābandé**.

Now nothing more than a small village, Soltānīyé was a Mongol capital in the 14th century. Its ruler, Sultan Oljeitū Khodābandé, converted to Shiism after visiting Najaf, burial place of the prophet Mohammed's son-in-law, Alī. So keen was he to show his new-found religious zeal that he built a colossal octagonal mausoleum here in Emām Alī's honour. Over 50m high and nearly 25m in diameter, it had eight minarets, several vast portals and an enormous egg-shaped cupola, which is said to be the largest supported dome in the history of Islamic architecture. Even today the building is visible from far across the surrounding plain. The whole surface was adorned with the most exquisite inscriptions, tilework and mouldings. Everything was in place for it to become one of the foremost Shiite pilgrimage sites, but for one essential detail – namely Emām Alī's mortal remains. However, the people of Najaf were understandably loath to hand over the holy bones which had brought prominence to their town, and Oljeitū was left with a vast mausoleum and no one to fill it. So after toning down some of the decorations which were only appropriate for the shrine of a great religious figure, he pragmatically converted it into his own resting place, which it became around 1317. Although some of the original structure has collapsed, what remains still warrants a long detour; the dome chamber's decorations are particularly stunning.

Soltānīyé is 146 km west of Ghazvīn on the road to Zanjān and can be reached by bus from either place.

Places to Stay

Two acceptable places in Ghazvīn's centre

are *Hotel-é Alborz* (☎ 22631) and *Hotel-é Ghods* (☎ 27437), both with singles/doubles for US$15/20.

Getting There & Away

Ghazvīn is 2½ hours by bus from Tehrān, four from Hamadān.

Āzarbāyjān

Āzarbāyjān is the north-west pocket of Iran squeezed between Turkey to the west and Armenia and Azerbaijan to the north. It's a mountainous region, with extremely cold winters and mild summers, and much of the scenery is breathtaking. All that many travellers see of it is Tabrīz and whatever else can be glimpsed through a train or bus window, but it does have a number of interesting sights. At least try to cross it in daylight. One distinguishing feature of the region is that its people are predominantly Āzarīs rather than Persians.

ORŪMĪYÉ

This small city (formerly Rezā'īyé) west of the lake of the same name is rather cut off from the rest of Iran, although it is linked to Turkey by road. It may date back to the mid-2nd millennium BC and is one of many claimants to be Zoroaster's birthplace. After the Arab conquest it was conquered in turn by the Seljuks and Mongols but its history has been less eventful and more peaceful than that of Tabrīz, and it has a more relaxed and friendly air. It's also of interest as the site of one of Iran's largest and longest established Christian communities. The main groups are Chaldeans, Nestorians and Armenians, whose denominations predate even the Church of Rome, but several others are also represented, including Eastern Orthodoxits, remnants of a White Russian influx in the 1920s. Orūmīyé's Christians only narrowly averted massacre by invading Turkish troops in 1918.

The main street, Kheyābūn-é Emām, runs south-west from Meidūn-é Velāyat-é Faghīh, the main square, to Meidūn-é Enghelāb.

The tourist office (☎ 20241) is on Kheyābūn-é Ghods-é Jonūbī. The telephone code for Orūmīyé is 0441.

Things to See

The bazaar's Seljuk **Masjed-é Jāme'** dates in part from the 13th century and is notable for its enormous dome and the very fine plaster mouldings of its mihrab. **Sé Gombad**, 1.25 km south, is a 12th century tomb-tower with interesting stucco and stalactite decorations. Several ancient and modern churches lie around the city centre – the most noteworthy is **St Mary's Church** (Kelīsā-yé Maryam-é Moghaddas) facing the tourist office.

The **Church of St Thaddaeus**, known also as the Black Church (Ghara Kelīsā), is probably Iran's most interesting and remarkable Christian monument. While not easy to reach, it warrants a detour. One of the 12 disciples, Thaddaeus (also Jude), was martyred while spreading the Gospel to this part of Iran in the 1st century. He's revered as an apostle of the Armenian Church. As legend has it, a church dedicated to him was first built on the present site in 68 AD. Nothing appears to remain of this original church, which was extensively rebuilt in the 13th century, but some parts around the altar may date from the 10th century. Most of the present structure dates from the 17th century and is of carved sandstone. The earliest parts are of black and white stone.

The church is protected within a thick wall, which also forms the outer ramparts of some abandoned monastery buildings. It only has one service a year, around 1 July (check the date at the Orūmīyé tourist office), attended by Armenian pilgrims from all over Iran. Ask for the key (*kelīd-é kelīsā*) in the Kurdish hamlet below the church. There are quite a few other more or less abandoned Armenian churches in the surrounding hills.

No public transport runs to the Church of St Thaddaeus. To reach it you'll have to hire a taxi for the day from Orūmīyé or Mākū.

leaving early in the morning. Although Mākū is only 23 km away, no direct road goes from it. As your driver probably won't know how to get here, make sure he follows the signs to Ghara Zeyā'-ed-Dīn, then takes the main road to Seyah Cheshmé 65 km west, turning right nine km before Seyah Cheshmé at the T-junction marked 'Ghareh Kelisa'. The church is about 10 km on by a dirt track.

Places to Stay & Eat

The clean and comfortable *Hotel-é Tak Setāré* (☎ 36861) on Kheyābūn-é Emām charges US$15/20 for a single/double. *Hotel-é Be'sat* (☎ 336128) on Be'sat is friendly and reasonable value at US$15/20. *Hotel-é Rezā* (☎ 26580), 100m north-west of the Be'sat, is the best hotel in the city centre and has doubles at US$30. The ugly *Mehmūnsarā-yé Orūmīyé* (☎ 23080), with rooms for US$20/30, is better still but tends to be booked up heavily; it's on Kheyābūn-é Kashani, 1.5 km south of Meidūn-é Enghelāb.

Don't expect gourmet food here. The flashest restaurants are in Hotel-é Rezā and the mehmūnsarā. Some cheaper chelō kababīs and sandwich bars lie along Kheyābūn-é Emām, and there are one or two ābgūsht places in the lanes running off it.

Getting There & Away

Buses leave from Termīnāl-é Bozorg on the town's north-east edge. Getting to Tabrīz by bus involves a long and bumpy, if scenic, detour around Lake Orūmīyé and takes five hours or so. Cars can cut the journey time in 2½ hours by taking the twice weekly ferry between Bandar-é Golmānkhūné, the port for Orūmīyé, and Sharafkhūné, the port for Tabrīz.

The border post of Serō is 50 km north-west by road. No bus runs there, but shared taxis from the bus station charge around 10,000 rials. Count on at least five hours to get through both border posts. If you leave Orūmīyé early in the morning you should be able to reach Van the same day. Take a day's supply of food and water. For the latest information ask at the Turkish consulate (see Embassies in the Facts for the Visitor section earlier in this chapter) or the tourist office.

MĀKŪ

Straggling along either side of a gorge at an altitude of 1634m, this little town is a pleasant if not particularly exciting stop on the Tabrīz to Bāzargān road. The mountainous backdrop at least is rather inspiring. This is where westbound travellers bid farewell to civilisation until at least as far as Erzurum, 342 km away.

Some small but adequate hotels line the main road, Kheyābūn-é Emām, probably the best being *Hotel-é Alvāné* (☎ (04634) 3491) and *Mehmūnsarā-yé Mākū* (☎ (06434) 31385).

Several buses link Mākū with Tabrīz daily, and there are regular minibuses and shared taxis to Bāzargān. Many people entering Iran at Bāzargān rush straight onto Tabrīz, as often as not arriving there exhausted at dead of night. Unless you're in a tearing rush, it's worth considering an overnight stop here, giving you the chance to reach Tabrīz at a more civilised hour. If you're heading west, bear in mind the considerable journey time between Tabrīz and Erzurum, not to mention the inevitable hassles and delays at the border.

TABRĪZ

This large industrial and commercial centre had a short period as the Persian capital during the Safavid era. It's no longer a particularly attractive city, but it does have a very fine 15th century covered bazaar. The Arg, a huge and crumbling brick citadel, is a notable landmark built on the site of a massive mosque which collapsed over 500 years ago. The **Blue Mosque** (Masjed-é Kabūd) dates from 1465 and, although much damaged by earthquakes, is still notable for its tilework. Tabrīz also boasts a number of Armenian churches, including one mentioned by Marco Polo in his travels.

Tabrīz was particularly strife-torn after the revolution and was heavily bombed in the Iran-Iraq War. The Tabrīzīs have a popular

IRAN

reputation for surly inhospitality, and most people will only spend as long as necessary here, on their way to or from the Turkish, Armenian or Azeri border.

Orientation & Information

Surrounded by mountains, Tabrīz itself is flat and featureless. Kheyābūn-é Emām Khomeinī, the main east-west street, is the entry point by bus from Tehrān and it ends at the railway station. Virtually everything important lies south of the river and north of Emām Khomeinī, and most things are within easy walking distance. The exceptions are

the railway station, five km west of the city centre and the new bus station, which is a couple of km to the south.

The tourist office (☎ 46041) is on Dāneshsarā, just east of Meidūn-é Shohadā. The telephone code for Tabrīz is 041.

Places to Stay & Eat

There are lots of hotels and mosāferkhūnés from the railway station to the city's east edge, stretched along Kheyābū-é 22 Bahman and Emām Khomeinī. The dirt-cheap places, most of which probably won't let you in, are around the park. Two cheapies which may let

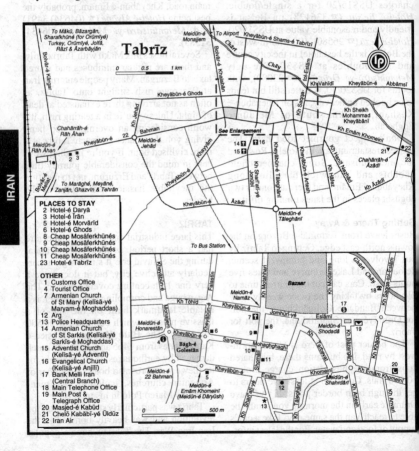

PLACES TO STAY
- 2 Hotel-é Daryā
- 3 Hotel-é Irān
- 5 Hotel-é Morvārīd
- 6 Hotel-é Ghods
- 8 Cheap Mosāferkhūnés
- 9 Cheap Mosāferkhūnés
- 10 Cheap Mosāferkhūnés
- 11 Cheap Mosāferkhūnés
- 23 Hotel-é Tabrīz

OTHER
- 1 Customs Office
- 4 Tourist Office
- 7 Armenian Church of St Mary (Kelīsā-yé Maryam-é Moghaddas)
- 12 Arg
- 13 Police Headquarters
- 14 Armenian Church of St Sarkis (Kelīsā-yé Sarkīs-é Moghaddas)
- 15 Adventist Church (Kelīsā-yé Ādventīt)
- 16 Evangelical Church (Kelīsā-yé Anjīlī)
- 17 Bank Melli Iran (Central Branch)
- 18 Main Telephone Office
- 19 Main Post & Telegraph Office
- 20 Masjed-é Kabūd
- 21 Chelō Kabābī-yé Ūldūz
- 22 Iran Air

Tabrīz

you in are *Mosāferkhūné-yé Darya* and *Mosāferkhūné-yé Karon*, both just north of Kheyābūn-é Sargord Mohaghghaghī, west of the park; expect to pay about 8000 rials. The much better *Hotel-é Daryā* (☎ 459501) and *Hotel-é Īrān* (☎ 459515), just 600m east of the railway station charge around US$10/20 for a single/double.

On Meidūn-é Emām Khomeinī, *Hotel-é Morvārīd* (☎ 56398) is reasonable if a bit grotty; doubles are 18,000 rials. One of the best deals in Tabrīz is the *Hotel-é Ghods* (☎ 68098), on Kheyābūn-é Sargord Mohaghghaghī at the north-east corner of the park. Recently renovated, the Ghods has immaculate rooms with clean sheets supplied daily. The management are friendly and rates are just 50,000 rials for a double.

Hotel-é Tabrīz (also known as the International; ☎ 459501) is the city's best hotel. It's modern and comfortable, if not luxurious, but a long walk from the city centre. Singles/doubles are US$45/65.

Tabrīz is the spiritual home of ābgūsht, a filling stew of fatty meat, lentils and potatoes served in a pipkin and poured out slowly into a dish before being ground to a pulp with a pestle and scooped up with bread. Watch someone else doing it before taking the plunge. Ābgūsht elsewhere in Iran is rarely as good. There are many places to try it around the bazaar, some more wholesome than others.

Getting There & Away
Air The Iran Air office (☎ 343515) is in its own building on Chahārrāh-é Āzādī. There are daily flights to Tehrān (one hour), and twice a week to Mashhad (1¾ hours).

Bus The new bus station, one of the more orderly in Iran, is a couple of km south of the city centre; you'll need to take a taxi – ask for 'Terminal Tabrīz'. All the bus company offices are here. Buses depart for most destinations and you don't necessarily have to change in Tehrān (nine hours). One exception is Zāhedān, to which there are no direct buses; head for Shīrāz (24 hours) and change there.

If you're aiming to enter Turkey the same day, make sure you leave on the first bus to Mākū (four hours), which is around 6 am.

Train Two trains run daily to Tehrān (14,000 rials 1st class), taking about 12 hours. For details of the Azerbaijan and Turkey services, see the introductory Getting There & Away chapter.

ARDABĪL
Approximately 218 km east of Tabrīz and only 70 km from the Caspian Sea, this small town is renowned for the **Shrine of Sheikh Safī** (Bogh'é-yé Sheikh Safī-od-Dīn). Foreparent of the Safavid dynasty, Sheikh Safī (1252-1334) was one of the foremost Sufi leaders of his time and it's indirectly due to him that Shiism later became Iran's state creed. The shrine, or *bogh'é*, is in the northwest of town.

Hotel-é Sheikh Safī (☎ (0451) 24111) charges US$15/20 for a single/double. By bus it's four hours to Tabrīz, 11 to Sārī. Frequent savārīs and minibuses run to Āstārā (1½ hours) on the border with Āzarbāyjān.

MARĀGHÉ
Marāghé, east of the lake, has a number of interesting tomb-towers from the 12th to 14th centuries, the oldest and most interesting being **Gombad-é Sorkh**. You can see some old pigeon towers around **Bonāb**, 17 km west. Marāghé is 2½ hours by bus from Tabrīz, four hours from Orūmīyé.

The Caspian Region

The Caspian Sea isn't actually a sea at all; it's the world's largest lake and particularly famous for its sturgeon from which comes that gourmet's delight – caviar. You may be able to see it being processed at Bandar-é Anzalī or Bābolsar. Until recently it was also possible to buy caviar fairly easily at absurdly low prices but nowadays virtually all of it is exported.

To Iranians the Caspian region, or *shomāl*

(the North), is a popular holiday resort, frequently compared to Switzerland. The coastal strip north of the Alborz Mountains is a green and lush countryside in total contrast to the arid plateau to the south. Rainfall is heavy, especially between September and November, and is enough to support Iran's small tea, cotton and rice industries. In summer, the tourist season, humidity can soar to 98%. The summer water temperatures hover around the mid-20°Cs – very pleasant for swimming. Of course, women have to wear the hejāb, except on segregated beaches safe from prying male eyes. Tourism here is pretty much a do-it-yourself affair. How much you enjoy it depends on whether you view its relative lack of development as a holiday destination as an advantage or a disadvantage. It's a great place to go if you like being a novelty.

Good roads run all along the coast and you can easily stop off here between Mashhad and Tehrān, or make a longer trip between Tehrān and Tabrīz by way of the coast. Not much public transport exists within the region, but on any main road it's easy enough to catch a savārī heading at least as far as the next town, motel or mosāferkhūné. There are four main road routes from Tehrān to the coast as well as the scenic railway line terminating at Gorgān, a good stretch of the way between Tehrān and Mashhad. The main resort towns are Rāmsar, Chālūs, Nōshahr, Bandar-é Anzalī and Bābolsar.

For details of transport options between the Caspian region and Āzarbāyjān and Turkmenistan, see the introductory Getting There & Away chapter.

RASHT

Some 324 km north-west of Tehrān on a good motorway, sprawling Rasht is the main city of the south Caspian region and the centre for the local rice and silk industries. With an average annual rainfall exceeding 1300 mm, it's also one of Iran's wettest towns. A popular staging-post between Tehrān and the Caspian coast, Rasht isn't, however, of much interest in its own right. It became a town around the 14th century, and

since then the Russians have occupied it several times, most recently in 1920 when the Bolsheviks torched the bazaar and drove many of the townspeople into temporary exile.

Orientation & Information

Most of the hotels and other places of interest lie within easy walking distance of the vast main square, Meidūn-é Shohadā. It hosts the police headquarters, a telephone office and the post office. Sharī'atī leads off northeastwards, Emām Khomeinī (the Tehrān road) south-eastwards, A'lam-ol-Hodā south-westwards and Sa'dī (the Bandar-é Anzalī road) northwards.

The tourist office (☎ 22026) is next to Bank Tejarat on Sa'dī, five minutes walk north of the town square.

The telephone code for Rasht is 0231.

Things to See

The **Mūzé-yé Rasht** on Kheyābūn-é Tāleghānī, less than a km south-west of the town square, has a small collection of archaeological exhibits.

Fifty-six km south-west by road, **Māsūlé** is one of the most beautiful villages in the Caspian region. Approached from Fūman by a dramatic mountain pass and completely surrounded by forest, it clings to a hillside at an altitude of 1050m. Because of the steepness of the hill, there are no lanes as such; instead the slate roof of each terrace, at a slight gradient, forms a pathway for the level above, connecting with the next one and so on. Māsūlé makes a pleasant outing by private taxi from Rasht, but beware of snowdrifts in winter.

Places to Stay & Eat

There are some mosāferkhūnés in the bazaar south of Sharī'atī. *Mehmūnpazīr-é Kārvān* (☎ 22967), 50m south-east of the town square, is friendly and charges US$24 for a clean triple with shared bathroom. Most foreigners end up at the *Hotel-é Ordībehesht* (☎ 22210), a concrete eyesore immediately west of the main square. Although draughty, it's fairly comfortable and very convenient.

Doubles are US$30. A slightly cheaper and less ugly place is *Hotel-é Pardīs* (☎ 31177) on the corner of Bolvār-é Emām Khomeinī and Bolvār-é Āzādī. The comfortable *Mehmūnsarā-yé Bozorg-é Gīlān* on Bolvār-é Āzādī charges US$20/30 for singles/ doubles.

There are quite a few good restaurants and fast food places on or a short walk south of Sabzé Meidūn, the large green square 300m south-west of Meidūn-é Shohadā, and in the bazaar area.

Getting There & Away

There are several bus company offices around Meidūn-é Shohadā. By bus it's nine hours to Gorgān or Tabrīz. Savārīs to Bandar-é Anzalī (one hour; 2000 rials each) and Rāmsar (2¾ hours) leave from outside the post office; those to Tehrān (five hours) leave from a rank over the road.

BANDAR-É ANZALĪ

This is the main port of the south Caspian, with ships from Baku regularly in harbour. It looks like a provincial outpost of the Russian Empire gone to seed at the turn of the century, which in a sense it is, for imperial Russia virtually controlled trade in the lake until WWI. Anzalī has a long windswept promenade around its central harbour and several good eating places. It's a very laid-back place, good for spending a couple of relaxing days. The nearby lagoon is a fascinating site for birdwatchers; its outlet to the lake bisects Anzalī.

Places to Stay

The comfortable *Hotel-é Īrān* (☎ (0181) 32524) on Dādgostarī commands a fine view of the harbour; doubles are US$30.

Getting There & Away

The bus companies are on Meidūn-é Emām Khomeinī, the town square, although the bus station is actually around five km south of town. Savārīs to Rasht (one hour; 2000 rials) also go from the square. See the introductory Getting There & Away chapter for details of ferries to Baku.

SĀRĪ

Some 267 km north-east of Tehrān by road, Sārī is smaller, better preserved and much more attractive than Rasht. Sārī's origins are lost in antiquity, but it's known to have been a regional capital in Sassanian times and into the 8th or 9th century.

Orientation & Information

The town square has that most unusual of Iranian landmarks, a public clock tower, hence its name Meidūn-é Sā'at (Time Square). The old part of town and most points of interest are within walking distance. The bazaar lies immediately south-west, the railway station 1.5 km south. The tourist office (☎ 2008) is on Khayyām, about half a km north of Sā'at.

The telephone code for Sārī is 02431.

Things to See

The **Emāmzādé-yé Yahyā** in the bazaar is a 15th century mausoleum notable for its fine wooden doors and tomb box. You can enter on Thursday afternoons and Friday. A few metres west, **Borj-é Soltān Zein-ol-Ābedīn**, another tomb-tower, also dates from the 15th century. The tomb inside is said to bear an exquisitely carved inscription, but the door's usually locked. Off Bolvār-é Dāneshjū east of the river, the **Emāmzādé-yé Abbās** is a large complex housing three 15th century tombs.

Places to Stay & Eat

The basic *Hotel-é Sārī* and *Hotel-é Nāder* just off Sā'at have doubles at US$20, but the best place is *Hotel-é Bādelé* (☎ 3128), 10 km east on the Gorgān road, with singles/ doubles for US$30/45. It has comfortable rooms, friendly service and a good restaurant, but is some way out if you don't have your own transport. It also tends to fill very quickly.

Getting There & Away

Minibuses to Bābol (45 minutes) leave from a small station just west of Pol-é Tajan, the river bridge for the Gorgān road. Long-distance buses go from the bus station on

IRAN

Jāddé-yé Kamarbandī, two km north-east of Sā'at. Rasht is seven hours away by bus.

RĀMSAR

This is with little doubt the most attractive of Iran's Caspian resorts. Since the thickly wooded Alborz Mountains stop only a few hundred metres short of the lake here, the backdrop is magnificent and the scope for urban development limited. The last shāh built a **palace** in the hill overlooking Rāmsar, and who could blame him? The palace opens to visitors in summer. Rāmsar is principally a place for relaxing, although avid trekkers and naturalists can find much to occupy themselves in the **forest** (jangal). There's also a small **beach**. Look out for the colourful **fish market** at Rāmsar's west edge, on the Rasht road. Outside the tourist season, Rāmsar is remarkably quiet.

Places to Stay & Eat

There's a tiny mosāferkhūné on the main street, Motahharī. The 1st class Hotel-é Rāmsar (☎ (01942) 3593) overlooking Rāmsar has as splendid a setting as any hotel in Iran. For the views alone some may think it worth splashing out upwards of US$45/65 a single/double. In summer it's advisable to book.

The large unpretentious Chelō Kabābī-yé Gol-é Sorkh is excellent for fish and other dishes. Sturgeon and salmon-trout may sometimes be available. Hotel-é Rāmsar's restaurant has a more sophisticated menu, higher prices and finer views.

Getting There & Away

Savārīs and minibuses to Rasht (2¾ hours) depart from diagonally opposite the fish market.

NŌSHAHR & CHĀLŪS

Nōshahr is Iran's second Caspian port, but you can still walk from one end to the other in 10 minutes. The resort town of Chālūs seven km west is now virtually a suburb of its larger neighbour; frequent public transport links the two until late at night. There isn't actually that much to do in either town,

but they're very popular with domestic holidaymakers and great places for seeing Iranians enjoying themselves. Nōshahr is also a good place for fishing, though, unfortunately, its beach has been eaten up by the commercial harbour.

Places to Stay & Eat

Some grotty mosāferkhūnés fester at the western approach to Chālūs. Nōshahr's Hotel-é Shālīzār (☎ (0191) 32090) has doubles at US$20 and is recommended. Chālūs' Hotel-é Malek and Hotel-é Jamshīd (☎ (0191) 22939) charge the same price.

The mid-range Restōrān-é Māzandarān and Restōrān-é Gīlān-é Fard are recommended for fish and game.

Getting There & Away

The bus company offices are in the Gārāzh at the western approach to Chālūs. Savārīs to Tehrān (3½ hours) leave from Nōshahr: book tickets at the office just west of the Friday Mosque (Masjed-é Jāme'). Savārīs also run from Nōshahr to Rāmsar and other coastal points, and from Chālūs' main square to various places inland.

BĀBOLSAR

Before the revolution, this port was a fashionable seaside hotel complex owned by the shāh. Nowadays, however, the harbour is idle, the hotel complex closed and Bābolsar is no longer a very inspiring place, although it does have a sandy beach some four km north of the main square.

The beachside Hotel-é Mīchkā (☎ (01291) 24656), built like a Mediterranean villa, is a very pleasant place to stay, with rooms at US$20/30. It has a good restaurant, but there's a cheaper one on the corner.

Frequent minibuses to Bābolsar (30 minutes) leave from the main square. Bābolsar has savārīs to Chālūs (two hours), Rasht and Tehrān.

GORGĀN

For many centuries this small town on the

north edge of the Alborz Mountains and the south of the north-eastern steppe marked the final secure outpost of civilisation within Persia for traders and travellers heading for Central Asia. This was the place to enjoy a short spell of tranquillity and make sure your horse or camel was in good shape. So fierce were the Turkomans to the north and east that no one even attempted to pacify them. This century, however, they started to give up their nomadic and pillaging ways, many settling in Gorgān. It retains something of a frontier air today and despite being a railhead is still little more than a provincial market town. There are many examples of traditional Caspian buildings, with tiled sloping roofs and charming wooden balconies, in the bazaar area west of the main square.

Things to See

In an alley just west of the main square, the **Masjed-é Jāme'**) has a very unusual Seljuk minaret, still in use. Squat, sturdy and top-heavy, it clearly shows the original, purely functional, purpose of the minaret – an elevated structure with a loft from which to call the faithful to prayer. It's quite unlike the more familiar graceful needles of later Islamic architecture. About 200m west is the **Emāmzādé-yé Nūr**, a 14th or 15th century tomb-tower. It has a good early example of stalactite moulding.

The nearby Caspian port of **Bandar-é Torkaman** has a lively Monday morning market for horses, leatherware and handicrafts.

Place to Stay

The clean and adequate *Hotel-é Khayyām* has doubles for US$20.

Getting There & Away

Minibuses to Sārī (two hours) go from Gārāzh-é Sāhel, about a km west of the town centre. Minibuses and buses elsewhere leave from Termīnāl-é Jorjān on the Mashhad road. The railway station is at Gorgān's north edge.

Gombad-é Kāvūs (Gombad)

This small Turkoman town on the Mashhad to Gorgān road is famous for a spectacular tomb-tower, Gombad-é Kāvūs, built by a local prince, Ghābus ebn-é Vashmgīr, in 1006. Its vital statistics alone are astounding. Built on a mound with foundations over 12m deep, this fluted colossus is a full 55m tall, including a conical dome 18m high, and can be seen on a clear day as far as 30 km away. Looking more like a rocket than anything else, it's so perfectly preserved that it's hard to believe it was constructed nearly a millennium ago. Originally, Ghābus' glass coffin hung from the dome but it vanished long ago and there's no longer anything to see inside.

Gombad is 1½ hours by minibus from Gorgān, eight by bus from Mashhad.

IRAN

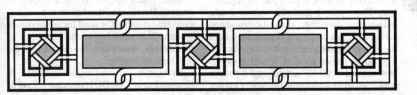

Iraq

Long ago in the fertile valleys between the Tigris and Euphrates rivers, a great civilisation was born, which was to leave an indelible mark on the whole future of the world. This land was known as Mesopotamia from the Greek meaning 'between two rivers' and is now part of modern Iraq. It was here where human beings first began to cultivate their land and where writing was invented.

Recent history has dealt less kindly with Iraq; few countries have experienced such political turbulence and so many changes of regimes. In the mid-1970s, as the country became a little more stable politically, it also began to reap the benefits of its considerable oil reserves and planned to plough some of this money into tourism.

But things took a dramatic turn for the worse in 1980 when Iraq, led by Saddam Hussein, went to war against Iran. The war lasted eight years, at the end of which Iraq's economy was pretty well battered. Before the country had a chance to rebuild it was plunged once again into crisis when Iraq invaded Kuwait. The invasion led to the Gulf War, which liberated Kuwait and destroyed Iraq's military capabilities, and to the imposition of UN economic sanctions against Iraq that are still in force.

Facts about the Country

HISTORY

Sometime around 10,000 years ago during the last ice age in northern Europe, nomads were living in what is now part of northern Iraq. These people gradually moved south, built simple dwellings, domesticated sheep and goats, grew crops and eventually settled the valleys between the Tigris and Euphrates. The Sumerian civilisation which grew up here around 4000 BC established a pattern which led to Mesopotamia becoming known

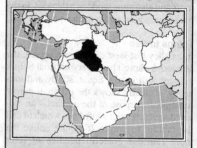

The Republic of Iraq

Area: 434,924 sq km
Population: 20.7 million
Population Growth Rate: 3.5%
Capital: Baghdad (pop: 5 million)
Head of State: President Saddam Hussein
Official Language: Arabic
Currency: Iraqi dinar
Exchange Rate: 2500 Iraqi dinars = US$1
Per Capita GNP: US$1950
Time: GMT/UTC +3

Travel Warning

Since the Iraqi invasion of Kuwait in August 1990 and the subsequent Gulf War, Iraq has been virtually closed to visitors. Baghdad's airport remains shut and, at the time of writing, no Iraqi visas were being issued to foreigners. It was therefore not possible to do a first-hand update of Iraq for this edition. ■

as the Cradle of Civilisation. Ur of the Chaldees was one great city which dates from this time.

Trade routes opened up and transport of crops and textiles to other countries by camel caravans produced the need for an inventory system. This need led to the invention of pictographs, which later developed into the first form of writing.

Eventually the civilisation collapsed in disunity but in 1700 BC Hammurabi, king of the then small town of Babylon, reunited the people and the country now called Babylonia flourished once again. King Hammurabi is most renowned for his Code of Law, forerunner of today's laws. After his death Babylonia fell into obscurity and suffered 200 years of domination by neighbouring Assyria. Under Nebuchadnezzar II Babylon's most glorious age followed. It became the most splendid city of the ancient world, renowned for its Hanging Gardens, but after Nebuchadnezzar's death it once again fell into obscurity.

In the following centuries it was conquered by different invaders until the 2nd century AD when it became part of the Persian Sassanian Empire.

In 637 AD the country was captured by Arab Muslims. In 750 the Abbasids, descendants of the uncle of Mohammed, moved the capital from Damascus to Baghdad. The city soon became a leading medieval cultural and commercial centre. In 1258 Mongol invaders murdered the last Abbasid caliph and destroyed Baghdad. In the 16th century the country was conquered by the

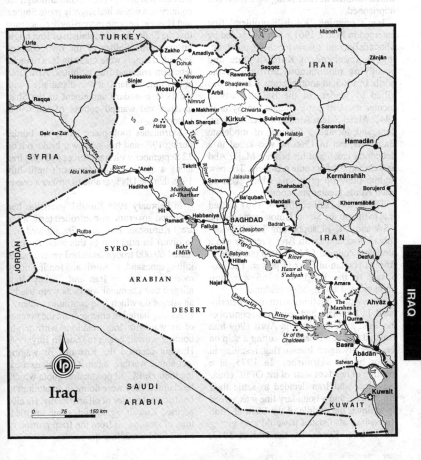

Iraq

Turks and became part of the Ottoman Empire, and until the 20th century little development took place.

During WWI the Ottoman Empire collapsed, Iraq became a British Mandate and Emir Faisal became king. Efforts were made to improve living conditions, and full independence was achieved in 1932. On 14 July 1958, King Faisal was killed in a military coup and Iraq became a republic. Conflict soon developed between the coup's two protagonists, Abdel Karim Kassem the prime minister and Abdel Salem Aref his deputy, which resulted in Aref being dismissed and imprisoned.

Iraq's ongoing 'Kurdish problem' first emerged in March 1961 when Kurds, led by Mustafa Barzani, rose in rebellion, proclaiming an independent Kurdish state and occupying mountainous territory in the north. In 1963, in another coup, Kassem was killed by leaders of the Ba'ath Party, a secular socialist party founded in Syria in 1942. Abdel Salem Aref now became president and formed a Cabinet of moderate Ba'athists, but in 1966 he was killed in a helicopter crash and his brother Major Abd ar-Rahman Aref became president. The new regime drew up proposals which were to grant Kurds greater autonomy.

The Arab-Israeli conflict of 1967 caused Iraq to turn to the Soviet Union, accusing the USA and UK of supporting Israel. Widespread discontent with Aref's regime and a bloodless coup on 17 July 1968 put General Ahmad Hassan al-Bakr in power. The proposals to the Kurds in 1966 were not implemented and fighting resumed.

Meanwhile relations with Iran deteriorated. In 1937 Iraq had been given control of the Shatt al-Arab River. In April 1969 Iran violated this agreement by sailing a ship on the river, flying an Iranian flag, resulting in minor border skirmishes. In 1975, at a meeting of heads of state of the OPEC countries, Iraq and Iran decided to settle their differences, and a boundary line was agreed upon down the middle of the Shatt al-Arab River. Iran also stated it would stop giving aid to Iraqi Kurds. By the end of 1977,

Kurdish had become an official language and greater autonomy had been granted. These factors resulted in Iraq becoming a more stable country, and the growing oil revenues brought about an unprecedented improvement in the economy.

In 1979 Saddam Hussein replaced Al-Bakr as president, the revolution in Iran took place and relations between the two countries quickly sank to an all time low. Arabs living in Iran in an area called Khuzestan demanded autonomy, a demand which Iran accused Iraq of encouraging. The Iraqi government had always been Sunni although the country as a whole had slightly more Shiites, and Hussein became increasingly concerned that the Shiite fundamentalism of Iran might influence the Shiites of his own country. Indeed, attempts were made by Iran to incite rebellion amongst Iraq's Shiites. Also, Iraq at this time declared it was dissatisfied with the 1975 boundary agreement of the Shatt al-Arab and wanted control of the whole waterway.

Skirmishes took place along the border during 1980 and full-scale war broke out on 22 September with Iraqi forces entering Iran along a 500 km front. It wasn't until July 1988 that the UN was able to broker a cease-fire.

In February 1988 Kurdish guerrillas had occupied government-controlled territory in Iraqi Kurdistan. The cease-fire allowed Iraq to divert its attention to this area. An estimated 60,000 troops launched an offensive, killing thousands of Kurds and forcing many more to escape to Iran and Turkey. It is alleged that chemical weapons were used – an allegation which Iraq continues to deny.

As Iraq started to emerge from the ravages of its war with Iran, relations with neighbouring Kuwait began to sour. In July 1990 Hussein accused the Kuwaitis of waging 'economic warfare' against Iraq by exceeding their OPEC oil production quota which, he claimed, they were doing in an attempt to hold down the price of oil artificially. He also accused Kuwait, again with some justification, of stealing oil from the Iraqi portion of an oil field straddling the border.

Arab attempts to mediate a peaceful end to the dispute failed and on 2 August 1990 Iraq sent its troops and tanks into Kuwait.

The UN quickly passed a series of resolutions calling on Iraq to withdraw from Kuwait. Instead, on 8 August, Iraq annexed the emirate.

An emergency summit of the Arab League was held in Cairo on 10 August but Saddam refused to attend. The Iraqis contended that Saudi Arabia's decision a few days earlier asking the USA for troops to defend the kingdom was at least as significant a threat to the region's security as Iraq's annexation of Kuwait, and a number of the League's members agreed. The League passed a resolution condemning the invasion but was deeply split.

Western countries, led by the USA, began to enforce a UN embargo on trade with Iraq by stopping and searching ships bound for Iraq and Jordan. In the months that followed US and other forces flooded into Saudi Arabia as the diplomatic stand-off over Kuwait deepened.

The anti-Iraq coalition's forces eventually numbered 425,000 US troops and 265,000 troops from 27 other countries. They were backed up by an increasingly long list of UN Security Council resolutions calling on Iraq to withdraw from Kuwait. At the end of November, the USA and the UK secured a UN resolution authorising the use of force to drive Iraq out of Kuwait if Baghdad did not pull out voluntarily before 15 January 1991.

With less than a week to go before the expiration of the 15 January deadline the US secretary of state, James Baker, met with the Iraqi foreign minister, Tariq Aziz, in Geneva. The talks lasted for nearly six hours but came to nothing. In the final hours before the deadline a number of national leaders, including President Mubarak of Egypt and the French president, François Mitterrand, televised appeals to Saddam to withdraw from Kuwait before it was too late. Yasser Arafat of the PLO rushed to Baghdad to try to broker a deal.

The deadline passed, the Iraqis did not budge, and within hours a barrage of Tomahawk cruise missiles were launched against strategic targets in Baghdad and other places. Then waves of Allied (mostly US) aircraft began a five week bombing campaign over Iraq and Kuwait.

The ground offensive, when it finally came, lasted only 100 hours and was something of an anti-climax. Iraq's army, which had been touted in the west for the previous six months as one of the most fearsome military machines on earth, simply disintegrated. While there were relatively few casualties on the Allied side, controversy has persisted over the number of civilian and military deaths in Iraq and Kuwait: estimates range from 10,000 to 100,000 or more.

A cease-fire was announced by the US on 28 February and Iraq agreed to comply fully with all UN Security Council resolutions. The Security Council imposed strict conditions on Iraq, demanding full disclosure, inspection and destruction of the country's biological, chemical, ballistic and nuclear weapons stockpiles and development programmes. Iraq was also ordered to pay reparations to Kuwait to compensate the victims of its invasion.

Meanwhile inside Iraq, Iraqi forces attempted to crush Kurdish and Shiite rebellions against the regime in the north and south. The fighting forced some two million Kurds to flee to mountainous regions on the Turkish and Iranian borders. In the south of the country, Shiites continued to be attacked by Iraqi government forces. This led the Allied forces to impose two 'no-fly' zones, in the north and south, to protect Kurds and Shiites from Iraqi air raids, and to a UN resolution requiring Iraq to stop oppressing the Shiites and Kurds.

Despite attempts by Iraq to have UN sanctions eased, the Security Council decided on 29 March 1993 to maintain the economic embargo because it concluded that Iraq had not fully complied with its obligations, especially those concerning the Kurds and Shiites. Also Iraq had failed to produce evidence of destroying its biological, chemical and nuclear weapons stockpiles and programmes, and there were fears that if sanctions were lifted, full production would resume.

Food and medicine were always excluded from the sanctions, but the ban on oil sales meant that there was no hard currency to pay for imported goods. As malnutrition increased and medical care became inadequate, Iraq negotiated a deal that allowed it to sell oil and buy food and medicine. In mid-1996, two French oil companies set up provisional agreements to allow Iraq to export 700,000 barrels of oil a day over a period of six months. The deal was close to agreement when on 31 August Iraq sent troops to Arbil to help the Kurdistan Democratic Party (KDP) displace the Patriotic Union of Kurdistan (PUK). The consequence of the army's incursion into an area forbidden to it by international rules was the destruction of Iraqi air defences in southern Iraq by the US and an amassing of US troops in Kuwait. The food for oil deal was placed on hold, at least until the country was considered safe for UN monitors to supervise it.

GEOGRAPHY

Iraq has a total land area of 434,924 sq km, consisting of four distinct regions. The first, the upper plain, stretches from Hit and Samarra to the Turkish border between the Euphrates and Tigris rivers and is the most fertile region, although high soil salinity reduces the cultivable potential to 12% of the arable land. The second, the lower plain, stretches from Hit and Samarra to the Arabian Gulf and contains the marshes – an area of swamps, lakes and narrow waterways, flanked by high reeds. The third, the mountainous region, is in the north-east. The fourth, the desert region, lies to the west of the Euphrates, stretching to the borders of Syria, Jordan and Saudi Arabia.

The Tigris and Euphrates rivers converge near Baghdad, then diverge again, before meeting at Qurna to form the wide Shatt al-Arab River which flows through Basra into the Gulf. Above Baghdad the rivers have strong retaining banks, further south they often flood in spring.

CLIMATE

Iraq is hot in summer; the average summer temperature in Baghdad is 34°C and in Basra 37°C; the north is slightly cooler. In the south there is high humidity and in the central plains there are dust storms. Contact-lens wearers beware – these storms can be agonising. The summer is between May and September.

Winter can be cold and the mountains become covered with snow. The average winter temperature in Baghdad is 11°C and in Basra it is 14°C. Rain falls between October and March and is pretty scanty, except in the north-east.

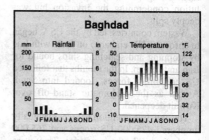

GOVERNMENT & POLITICS

Iraq is officially a republic, but because of the revolutionary nature of Iraqi politics, all legislative and executive powers are exercised by the Revolutionary Command Council (RCC). The RCC elects the president from its own members. The president, who is also commander of the armed forces, has executive power and appoints the Council of Ministers. There's also a 250 member National Assembly, elected every four years under a system of proportional representation.

ECONOMY

At the end of WWI, Iraq was a backward, poverty-stricken country, an almost forgotten outpost of the Ottoman Empire. The discovery of oil should have eased modernisation of independent Iraq (Iraq holds the world's second largest oil reserves), but political instability, and the financial drains and disruptions of the Kurdish problem and the Iran-Iraq War have been obstacles to Iraq realising its full economic potential. Dates are another important source of revenue – Iraq grows 80% of the world's dates and was the world's major date exporter.

Since the Gulf War and the imposition of UN economic sanctions, Iraq's economy has been in tatters. Unemployment is estimated at 50% and inflation reached an unprecedented annual rate of 1000% in early 1993.

In 1996, a new right allowed citizens to own trade and open bank accounts in a foreign currency as part of new economic guidelines to prop up the value of the local currency and curb the spiralling inflation.

POPULATION & PEOPLE

The population of Iraq was estimated to be 20.7 million in 1993. Baghdad has a population of about five million, Basra nearly two million and Mosul 1.5 million.

Mountains, swamps and desert have meant that communications until quite recently were poor, resulting in communities developing in isolation from one another with much cultural diversity.

Arabs make up 80% of the population and Kurds 15%. Other minority groups are the Marsh Arabs, Yezidis, Turkomans, Sabaeans, the nomadic tribes who live in the western desert and the Jazirah Bedouin who live in the highlands of the north.

EDUCATION

Education is compulsory between the ages of six and 12 and free between the ages of six and 18. There is an official estimated literacy of 80%.

RELIGION

The official religion is Islam. Muslims make up 95% of the population, with slightly more Shiites than Sunni. The Shiites tend to live in the south of the country, the Sunni in the north.

The largest group of non-Muslims are Christians who belong to various sects, including Christian Chaldeans, Syrian and Roman Catholics, Orthodox Armenians and Jacobites. Other religious minorities are the Yezidis, often erroneously called devil worshippers, and the Sabaeans who are followers of John the Baptist.

LANGUAGE

Arabic, the official language, is spoken by 80% of the population. The Kurds speak Kurdish, an Indo-European language. The Turkomans, who live in villages along the Baghdad to Mosul highway, speak a Turkish dialect. Persian is spoken by minorities near the Iranian border. English is spoken only by a small minority.

Facts for the Visitor

VISAS & DOCUMENTS

At the time of writing, Iraqi embassies overseas were not issuing visas to visitors.

EMBASSIES

Some of Iraq's embassies overseas include:

Australia
  48 Culgoa Circuit, O'Malley, ACT
  (☎ (06) 286 1333)
France
  53 rue de la Faisanderie, Paris 75016
  (☎ 01 45 01 51 00)
Jordan
  1st Circle, Jebel Amman, Amman (☎ 621 375)
UK
  22 Queen's Gate, London SW7
  (☎ (0171) 584 7141)
USA
  Iraqi Interests Section, c/o Embassy of Algeria, 1801 P St NW, Washington DC 20036
  (☎ (202) 483 7500)

MONEY

There are 1000 fils to the Iraqi dinar.

BOOKS

If you are interested in archaeology, there are many books available about Iraq's ancient sites. *Nineveh & its Remains* by Austen Henry Layard is particularly interesting; Layard was the pioneer as far as excavations

IRAQ

in the Middle East are concerned. This book also gives an insight into the lives of ordinary people in Iraq in the 19th century.

Essential reading for anyone hoping to catch a glimpse of the marshes is the excellent *The Marsh Arabs* by Wilfred Thesiger. Thesiger felt a great affinity with the Marsh Arabs and lived with them for five years in the 1950s.

Gavin Young visited the marshes in the '50s at the instigation of Thesiger. He returned again in the '70s to see how much, if at all, the Marsh Arabs had changed. *Return to the Marshes* is an account of this visit. Large colour photographs by Nik Wheeler accompany the text. Another collaboration by these two is *Iraq, Land of Two Rivers* which has interesting descriptions and photographs of the landscape and people. *The Longest War* by Dilip Hiro (Grafton, London, 1989) is a detailed, objective account of the Iran-Iraq War from start to finish. For more general information on Iraq see the Books section in the Regional Facts for the Visitor chapter.

BUSINESS HOURS

All businesses are closed on Friday. Government offices are open from 7.30 am to 2.30 pm Saturday to Wednesday, banks from 8.00 am to 12.00 pm Saturday to Thursday and shops from 8.00 am to 1.00 pm and 4.00 pm to 8 pm Saturday to Thursday.

ACCOMMODATION

Finding budget accommodation used to be the biggest problem in Iraq. It was difficult enough for men, even more so for women. There was no lack of budget hotels, but many seemed reluctant to take foreigners.

The very cheapest hotels were pretty basic and often dirty, but for just a little more money it was possible to find clean and pleasant hotels. In places without hotels, such as the marshes or Kurdish villages in the north, tourists were sometimes invited to stay with families.

Hotels above three star must be paid for in US dollars.

FOOD & DRINK

Food here is similar to that of other Middle Eastern countries. The tastiest food used to be found on street stalls and in snack bars.

Tea, drunk sweet without milk, is the most popular hot drink, followed by thick black coffee. Other drinks include fruit juices, soft drinks and alcohol, including locally made arak.

THINGS TO BUY

Iraq is known for Bedouin and Kurdish rugs, copperware and jewellery.

Getting There & Away

AIR

Although there are international airports at Baghdad and Basra, Iraqi Airways, Iraq's flag carrier, has been grounded since the Gulf War.

LAND & SEA

At the time of writing, the only overland routes to Iraq were from Jordan and Iran.

There used to be a train from İstanbul to Baghdad, but this service has been suspended since the Iran-Iraq War. There have been no passenger ships operating to or from Iraq since the start of the Iran-Iraq War.

Getting Around

AIR

It used to be possible to fly between Baghdad, Basra and Mosul.

BUS

Iraq has a good road network and there are buses between towns and cities.

TRAIN

There's a rail line connecting Baghdad to Mosul and Basra.

TAXI

Shared taxis are used between towns and cities in the north of Iraq. Both ordinary and shared taxis are orange and cream.

Baghdad

For most people the name of this ancient city conjures up vivid images, perhaps of star-spangled skies, golden domes and minarets, or women shrouded in black gliding through narrow streets with old houses leaning precariously towards one another; or perhaps of shafts of sunlight filtering through gloomy bazaars, their open shop fronts overflowing with exotic merchandise. Compared with these images, one's first impression of Baghdad can be disappointing, for it is not a city which makes an immediate impact. The old Baghdad has almost disappeared and the Iran and Gulf wars destroyed much of the modern city.

Baghdad was founded by Al-Mansur, the second caliph of the Abbasid dynasty, in 762 AD. The city he built was on the west bank of the Tigris, enclosed within a circular wall and called Medinat as-Salam, which meant City of Peace, and it became known as the Round City. The caliph's palace and the grand mosque were in the centre with four roads radiating from them. The city expanded beyond the wall and was eventually joined by a bridge of boats to the east bank, where a district called Rusafah grew up. By 946 this district had grown sufficiently big to rival the Round City.

Baghdad reached the height of its prosperity and intellectual life in the 8th and 9th centuries under the caliphs Mahdi and Harun ar-Rashid. It was the richest city in the world, the crossroads of important trade routes to the east and west. Arabic numbers, the decimal system and algebra all came into being at this time. Advances were also made in medicine and magnificent buildings were constructed with beautiful gardens.

From the mid-9th century onwards, the Abbasid caliphate became weakened by internal conflict, and civil war between Ar-Rashid's two sons resulted in partial destruction of the Round City. Total destruction came about when the Mongols sacked Baghdad, killed the caliph and many of the residents, and destroyed the irrigation system. In 1534 it became part of the Ottoman Empire and hundreds of years of neglect followed.

Efforts were made to improve the city in the early years of the 20th century. The administration was reformed, hospitals and schools were built and a postal service developed, but these improvements were belated and inadequate. Baghdad's greatest developments took place when large oil revenues started to flow in after 1973. However, all developments were curtailed by Iraq's two wars.

Orientation

The city extends along both sides of the Tigris. The east side is known as Rusafah and the west as Karkh, and they are connected by 11 bridges. The core of the city is about 3.5 by two km in Rusafah, extending from Muadham Square in the north to Tahrir Square in the south. Rashid St is the main street of this area and contains the city's financial district, the copper, textile and gold bazaars and lots of cheap hotels and restaurants.

Running parallel to Rashid St is Al-Jamouri St which has some historical mosques, government offices and more cheap hotels. South of Rashid St is Sadoun St, a newer commercial area with expensive hotels, cinemas, airline offices and travel agencies. Parallel to here along the riverbank is Abu Newas St with many outdoor cafés.

Damascus St in Karkh stretches from the Iraqi Museum to the international airport road. The Central railway station, Alawi al-Hilla bus/taxi garage, Al-Muthana airport and Zawra Park are along here. Haifa St, parallel to the river, is another important street in Karkh.

Since the 1950s the city has expanded enormously, and planned middle-class neighbourhoods have sprung up between the

IRAQ

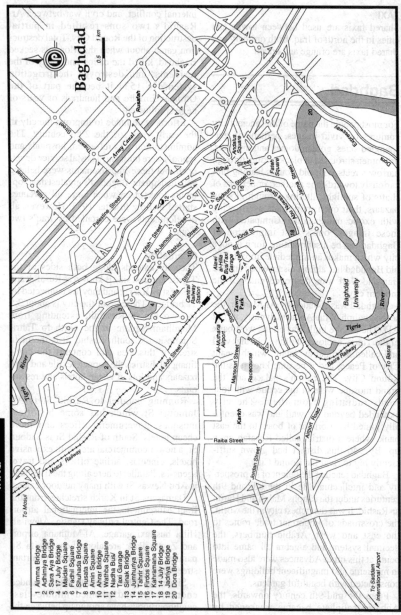

Baghdad

1. Aimma Bridge
2. Adhimiya Bridge
3. Sara Aya Bridge
4. 17 July Bridge
5. Maidan Square
6. Fadhil Square
7. Shuhada Bridge
8. Rusafa Square
9. Amin Square
10. Ahrar Bridge
11. Wathba Square
12. Nadha Bus/
    Taxi Garage
13. Sinak Bridge
14. Jumhuriya Bridge
15. Tahrir Square
16. Firdos Square
17. Kahramana Square
18. 14 July Bridge
19. Jadriya Bridge
20. Dora Bridge

To Mosul

Tigris River

Mosul Railway

To Mosul

Rusafah

Army Canal

Quaba Street

Palestine Street

Al Hilla Street

Andalus Square

Nidhal Street

Sadoun Street

Fateh Square

Abu Nawas Street

Kindi St

Krah Street

Al Jamouri Street

Rashid Street

Haifa Street

Central Railway Station

Al-Muthana Airport

Sawra Park

Alawi al-Hilla Bus/Taxi Garage

Baghdad University

Tigris River

Karkh

Racecourse

Damascus Street

Mansour Street

Basra Railway

To Basra

Raiba Street

Jordan Street

Airport Road

To Saddam International Airport

Dora Expressway

Baghdad

0 0.5 1 km

city centre and the Army Canal. On the west bank there are a number of residential areas including affluent Mansour which is surrounded by a race track and has trendy boutiques and fast-food restaurants. A number of embassies are in Mansour.

Information

The main telegraph & telex office is on the east side of Rashid St, near the Sinak bridge. The central post office is a small shabby building opposite the entrance to the Iraqi Museum. There are some banks on Rashid St. Most travel agencies, airline offices and car-hire companies are on Sadoun St.

Museums

Baghdad has numerous museums and interesting mosques. All of the museums are excellent. Many are free, others have only a nominal fee, and most are closed on Friday. In Karkh, near the Alawi al-Hilla bus/taxi garage, is the large, well-organised **Iraqi Museum** which has a carefully labelled collection (in English and Arabic) from prehistoric, Sumerian, Babylonian, Assyrian and Abbasid times. The **Baghdad Museum**, between Rusafa Square and the Shuhada bridge, houses an interesting collection of life-size models in tableaux depicting traditional Baghdadi life.

The **Museum of Pioneer Arts**, on the road opposite the telegraph & telex office on Rashid St, is worth a visit just for the wonderful old Baghdadi house in which the art collection is hung. The rooms are built around a central courtyard with a fountain in the middle. It's a peaceful retreat where you can sit and relax after the hustle and bustle of Rashid St. Some of the rooms are traditionally furnished, and the guest rooms upstairs are the nicest of all.

Housed also in a large traditional Baghdad house, the **Museum of Popular Heritage**, on the west side of Haifa St near the Ahrar bridge, has some fine examples of traditional Iraqi crafts, including woodwork, metalwork, basketwork and carpets, all tastefully displayed.

The **Saddam Art Centre**, on the west side

of Haifa St (turn left over Shuhada bridge) is a beautiful building with high ceilings, white walls and chandeliers. It was opened only in 1986 and the works in the permanent collection are mainly from the '70s and '80s. The **Museum of Modern Art** on Nafura Square, near Tahrir bus garage, is a bit of a letdown after the Saddam Art Centre, but it has some interesting temporary exhibitions.

Mosques

Never go into a mosque in Iraq unless you are invited. If you want to go inside one, stand at the entrance and someone will soon appear and indicate whether or not you are welcome inside. You must of course be dressed modestly and women must cover their heads.

The **Kadhimain Mosque** is the most important in Iraq after those at Kerbala and Najaf. Inside are the shrines of the two imans Musa al-Kadhim and Muhammad al-Jawad. The very large and elaborate mosque has gold-coated domes and minarets and was built in 1515.

The **Caliph's Mosque** is on the east side of Al-Jamouri St, between Wathba and Amin squares. It's a new mosque with an ancient minaret which dates from 1289. Built 40 years ago, the **14th Ramadan Mosque** on Firdos Square, Sadoun St, has lovely arabesques and glazed wall tiles. Another attractive mosque is the **Ibn Bunnieh Mosque** in front of Alawi al-Hilla bus garage. Yet another is the **Um Attuboul Mosque** on the road to the international airport. It has an unusual architectural style, very ornate and delicate, and gives one the impression of being modelled in icing sugar.

The **Marjan Mosque**, on the east side of Rashid St, was built in 1357, and in its early days served as a school (Murjaniya School). Early this century most of it was pulled down and rebuilt as a mosque. A little way down the road opposite is the Murjin Khan, where the scholars used to live. It has been converted into a restaurant.

Mustansiriyah School

Opposite the Baghdad Museum turn left at

the mosque to get to the school entrance. The school was built in the reign of the 37th Abbasid caliph, Mustansir Billah, and was the most highly esteemed university of that time. It was completed in 1232 and is an outstanding example of Abbasid architecture.

Abbasid Palace

From Rashid St, turn left at Maidan Square and take the road to the right of the mosque. The palace is at the bottom of the road on the right, overlooking the Tigris. Because of its resemblance in style and structure to the Mustansiriyah school, some scholars believe it is the Sharabiya school mentioned by old Arab historians.

Zawra Park

This vast park on Damascus St, opposite Al-Muthana airport, is a little parched-looking compared with European parks, but parts of it, like the Islamic garden where fountains play, are attractive. There's a good view of the city from the 54m high Baghdad Tower in the park.

There is also a zoo, a swimming pool and a planetarium in the park.

Other Attractions

When it's not too hot Baghdad is a fascinating city to explore on foot. If and when it gets onto the tourist map the bazaars of Rashid St will be where visitors go to see the 'real' Baghdad.

A far more interesting area, and one which gives a greater insight into the city, is the area behind the Saddam Art Centre on Haifa St. Here, you will see men in *galabiyyas* (long loose shirts), sitting in teahouses smoking waterpipes or sitting cross-legged on the pavement selling their wares; little shops selling fresh herbs, others selling spices and fruit and vegetables; men covered in oil mending old cars; narrow streets of old crumbling houses with overhanging balconies; barefoot children playing in the streets. Fascinating though this area is, it is also a sad testimony to Iraq's enormous social and economic problems.

Places to Stay & Eat

There used to be lots of *budget hotels* in Rashid St but most were basic, dirty and refused to let women stay. There were also cheap hotels on Al-Jamouri St between Amin and Wathba squares.

There used to be many cheap *snack bars* on Rashid St, around Wathba Square and just past Tahrir Square bus garage.

Getting Around

For local transport there are municipal double-decker buses, minibuses and taxis.

Around Baghdad

BABYLON, KERBALA & NAJAF

Ancient Babylon and the important Muslim shrines of Kerbala and Najaf all lie south of Baghdad, and it's quite possible to visit them all in a day trip from Baghdad.

Babylon

Babylon lies 90 km south of Baghdad and 10 km north of Hilla, and is perhaps the most famous of all Iraq's ancient sites. The ancient city reached its height during the reign of Nebuchadnezzar II (605-563 BC). With its high walls and magnificent palaces and temples it was regarded as one of the most beautiful cities in the world. It was most renowned for its Hanging Gardens, one of the Seven Wonders of the World and reputed to have been built for the king's wife Amytas, who was a Mede, so that she would not miss her mountain home.

All that remains of the ruins of Babylon is a huge and magnificent lion, eroded by time and the weather.

Kerbala

Kerbala is 108 km south-west of Baghdad and is of great religious significance to Muslims because of the battle of Kerbala in 680 AD between the Sunni and Shiite sects of Islam. Hussein ibn Ali, leader of the Shiite sect, and his brother Abbas, grandsons of the prophet Mohammed, were killed in the battle, and their shrines are contained in the two mosques here, making Kerbala one of the greatest pilgrimage centres in the Islamic world. Non-Muslims are not allowed to enter the shrines but, with the permission of an attendant, may be able to walk around the courtyards surrounding them.

Najaf

Najaf is 160 km south of Baghdad, just west of the Euphrates. It was founded by the caliph Harun ar-Rashid in 791 AD. In the city centre is the mosque containing the tomb of Ali ibn Abi Talib (600-661), cousin and son-in-law of Mohammed and founder of the Shiite Muslim sect, making this mosque one of the sect's greatest shrines. It is regarded by many Shiites as even more sacred than the shrines of Kerbala.

It is a great honour for Muslims to be buried in graveyards in either Kerbala or Najaf. The latter especially seems to have graveyards all over the place and it's quite fascinating, if a little macabre, to wander around them. Many of the graves are actually small shrines.

Places to Stay & Eat

There used to be a number of *budget hotels* and cheap *eating places* on the road leading up from the minibus station to the shrine in Najaf.

THE ARCH OF CTESIPHON

Little is left of the city of Ctesiphon, apart from the arch. It is 30 km south-east of Baghdad, east of the Tigris. The city was built in the 2nd century BC by the Parthian Persians. The arch was part of a great banqueting hall and, according to experts, is the widest single-span vault in the world. It survived the disastrous flooding of the Tigris in 1887 which destroyed much of the rest of the building.

HABBANIYA TOURIST VILLAGE

This tourist village is 85 km from Baghdad. Before the Iran-Iraq War, Iraq had embarked upon a major development programme to establish a vast system of tourist facilities that would cover its cities, historical sites and resort areas. The aim of this project was to meet the needs of wealthy Iraqi business people and tourists from Europe and the USA with pockets stuffed with dollars.

The project, like many others in Iraq, was curtailed by the war, but nevertheless, some facilities were completed. One of these is Habbaniya tourist village, definitely not a place for budget travellers to spend the night, although if you fancy a break from the ancient sites and mosques while you're in the Baghdad area, then it's a convenient distance for a one day visit. You can almost imagine you're at the seaside – there is a large lake in which you can swim, as well as a swimming pool.

Basra

Basra was founded by Caliph Omar in 637 AD, originally as a military base, but it rapidly grew into a major Islamic city. It became the focal point of Arab sea trade during the 16th century, when ships left its port for distant lands in the east. During this time and frequently since, because of its strategic position, it was the scene of many battles, sometimes between the Marsh Arabs and the Turks (for Iraq at this time was part of the Ottoman Empire) and sometimes between invading Persians and Turks.

In 1624 Ali Pasha repulsed a Persian attack and, in the period of peace that followed, Basra became a mecca for poets, scientists and artists. The peace was short-lived; Ali Pasha's son imposed a buffalo tax upon the Marsh Arabs and the fighting and instability resumed.

Basra is Iraq's main seaport and second-largest city, 550 km south-east of Baghdad and 130 km from the Gulf. There are extensive palm groves on the outskirts of the city and most of Iraq's dates are grown in and around Basra.

Orientation & Information

The city comprises three main areas – Ashar,

IRAQ

Margil and Basra proper. Ashar is the old commercial area and includes the Corniche which runs alongside the Shatt al-Arab River; Al-Kuwait St, where the cheap hotels and restaurants are; and Al-Thawra St, where the banks, the main Iraqi Airlines office and more restaurants are found. Basra's bazaars are also here and behind them is the Ashar bus garage. The central post office is on the road to the west of the bus garage.

The Basra railway station is in Margil, which also includes the port and a modern residential area to the north-west of Ashar.

Basra proper is the old residential area to the west of Ashar. Here you can see the lovely 19th century houses called *shenashils* by the canal which flows into the Shatt al-Arab. One of these is the Basra Museum. Further along this road is the Baghdad bus garage where intercity buses leave from.

Basra Museum

The contents of the museum are nothing special – just a few objects from Sumerian, Babylonian and Islamic times – but it's worth coming here to see the beautiful shenashil houses with high pointed windows and ornate, wooden overhanging balconies.

If you turn left after coming out of the museum and walk past five bridges, you'll come to a shop with a red canopy. Turn left here and take the first turning left and you'll see a derelict church with a notice in English announcing that it is Saint Thomas Chaldean Church.

Floating Navy Museum

This museum is in Ashar at the north corner of the Corniche. Its exhibits include guns from both sides in the Iran-Iraq War, models of ships and parts from wrecked Iranian aircraft and ships.

Museum for the Martyrs of the Persian Aggression

This white building has some war-wrecked vehicles in the grounds, while inside there are heart-rending displays of the sufferings of the ordinary people of Basra during the war with Iran. The museum is on the north-eastern corner of Istikal St.

Basra Bazaar

Basra's bazaar in Ashar is one of the most atmospheric in Iraq. In parts you can see old houses with wooden facades and balconies tilting at such precarious angles that it's amazing they manage to stand at all. There used to be a particularly good gold bazaar with some very fine pieces of jewellery.

Sinbad Island

Sinbad is supposed to have started his voyages from here. It used to be an attractive island, with outdoor restaurants and gardens, but it suffered extensive bombing, so now it's a bit of a dreary place. The landing stage for motor boats to the island is near the River View Hotel.

Places to Stay & Eat

Most of Basra's *budget hotels* were on Al-Kuwait St. There used to be cheap *eating places* on Al-Kuwait St and near the bazaar.

Getting Around

Basra has a collection of privately owned single-decker buses and minibuses operating from the Ashar garage. There are also taxis.

The railway station is seven km from Ashar, in Margil.

Nasiriya

Nasiriya is 375 km south-east of Baghdad, on the north bank of the Euphrates. Most people used to stay here only to visit Ur of the Chaldees, but it's a pleasant, relaxed place to spend a day or two. The centre of Nasiriya is Haboby Square.

Nasiriya Museum

The museum has an interesting collection from Sumerian, Assyrian, Babylonian and Abbasid times. It's on the south side of the river, a pleasant 20 minute walk along the river bank. Walk south along Neel St and turn right into the road which runs by the river, walk along here and cross over the second bridge; take the first turning right and the museum is along here on the right.

Places to Stay & Eat

There used to be a couple of cheap but cramped and dirty *hotels* on Jamharlya St. There were many *cheap restaurants* along Neel St which runs from Haboby Square to the river. Coming from the square, Jamharlya St is second on the left along Neel St. There were more *cheap restaurants* here.

AROUND NASIRIYA
Ur of the Chaldees

Ur is one of the most impressive ancient sites in Iraq. It was mentioned in the Bible as being the birth place of Abraham, and its earliest buildings date from 4000 BC. For three successive dynasties it was the capital of Sumeria although it reached its height during the third and last dynasty (2113-2095 BC). The ziggurat is impressive and the royal tombs well preserved.

The Marshes

The marshes originally covered an area of approximately 10,000 sq km between the Tigris and the Euphrates, stretching from Basra in the south, Nasiriya in the west and Kut in the north. Some parts were permanent, and other parts were temporary marshland, changing with the seasons.

The marshes were a unique world of vast expanses of water and shallow lagoons. Here it is sometimes possible to see the Marsh Arab dwellings known as *sarifas* with their ornate lattice-work entrances. The people row long slender canoes known as *mashufs* through the high reeds. There is archaeological evidence that life has continued here, almost unchanged, for 6000 years and the marshes are also home to many species of water birds. Sadly most of the marshes were drained in the late 1980s and most Marsh Arabs have moved to refugee camps, mainly in Iran.

Mosul

Mosul, 396 km north of Baghdad, is Iraq's third-largest city. It's also the most ethnically mixed with Arabs, Kurds, Assyrians and Turkomans.

In Abbasid times, Mosul achieved commercial importance because of its position on the caravan route from India and Persia to the Mediterranean. Its most important export was cotton. The word 'muslin' is derived from Mosul, and cotton is still produced here today. Mosul was devastated by the Mongols in the 13th century but began to revive under the Ottomans.

The main street and commercial area is Nineveh St. There were fashionable boutiques here, as well as old houses which are fine examples of 19th century Mosul architecture. The old part of the city is a maze of narrow streets off both sides of Nineveh St, west of the bazaar.

The city centre is Babatub Square, a huge open area with a fountain in the middle. The bazaar is between here and Nineveh St. Duwasa St, with many cheap hotels and restaurants, runs south from Babatub Square. Behind the east side of the square is the Babatub bus garage. The central post office is on the east side of the garage.

Mosul Museum

This museum has a large collection of finds from the successive civilisations of Iraq, from prehistoric to Islamic times, with emphasis on finds from Nineveh to Nimrud. It's on the west side of the river, opposite the Hurriya bridge.

Mosul House

This beautiful old house, built around a central courtyard, has a facade of Mosul marble. It houses life-size models depicting traditional Mosul life, similar to the Baghdad Museum. Admission is free but the museum is difficult to find and doesn't have a sign in English. Walking west along Nineveh St, turn left at the crossroads before the Clock &

IRAQ

Latin Church, take the second turning left along here, go under the arches and the house is on the right. It has a large wooden entrance.

Mosques

Believed to be the burial place of Jonah, the **Mosque of Nebi Yunus** is built on a mound beneath which are buried some ruins of Nineveh, but because of the sanctity of the site excavation is impossible. A little community of mud-brick houses and narrow winding streets has grown up around the mosque which is on the east side of the Tigris. Take a bus from Babatub garage towards Al-Shamal garage and look out for the mosque on the right, about three km from Hurriya bridge.

The **Great Nur ad-Din Mosque** was built in 1172 by Nur ad-Din Zanqi and is famed for its remarkably bent minaret which stands 52m high and has elaborate brickwork. To get there, walk west along Nineveh St and turn right at the crossroads before the Clock & Latin Church, and the mosque is on the right.

Churches

Mosul has a higher proportion of Christians than any other Iraqi city. The **Clock & Latin Church** is a good place to start because it's easy to find and also sells a booklet called *The Churches of Mosul*. It has a numbered list in Arabic and English of the major churches in Mosul, and a map of sorts which will help you find them, or at least enable you to get assistance from someone. The church is on the south side of Nineveh St. Inside it has lots of blue Mosul marble, lovely brickwork in blue, brown and cream, and stained-glass windows of abstract patterns.

Many of the churches are near this one, but hidden away in the labyrinth of old Mosul's fascinating back streets.

Other Attractions

The imposing ruins of **Bash Tapia castle**, rising high above the Tigris on its western bank, are now the only part of Mosul's city wall still in existence. Just a few minutes away, a little further south on the river bank, are the remnants of the 13th century palace of the sultan Badr ad-Din called **The Black Palace** (Qara Serai).

Between the two ruins is the **Chaldean Catholic Church of Al-Tahira**, or the Church of the Upper Monastery. The oldest part was built in 300 AD as a monastery, and in 1600 it was added to and became a church. In the street running parallel to this one is the Syrian Orthodox Al-Tahira Church which dates from 1210.

Places to Stay & Eat

There used to be *budget hotels* on and around Babatub Square.

The west side of Babatub bus garage used to be one of the liveliest places in Mosul in the evening, with lots of *outdoor cafés* producing good food at low prices as well as stalls with puddings and watermelon.

On the east side of the river opposite the university there were *snack bars* selling ice cream, pizzas and kebabs.

Getting Around

There are buses of all shapes and sizes, with destinations in Arabic on the front but no numbers, operating from Babatub garage. Mosul is also served by taxis.

AROUND MOSUL
Nineveh

The ancient city of Nineveh was the third capital of Assyria. Up until King Hammurabi's death it was a province of Babylonia, but after this time it developed as an independent kingdom. By 1400 BC it had become one of the most powerful countries in the Middle East, but by 500 BC it had been destroyed by the Medes of Northern Persia. For 200 years prior to this, however, Nineveh was the centre of the civilised world.

Nineveh is on the outskirts of Mosul on the east bank of the Tigris. Its walls measured 12 km in circumference and there were 15 gates, each called after an Assyrian god. Several have been reconstructed. The Shamash gate is just beyond the Al-Shamal bus garage. Nergal gate is about two km from the university and has a small museum with some Assyrian reliefs and a model of the city of Khorsabad, the fourth capital of Assyria. To get there, walk south from the university and turn left just before the reconstructed walls on both sides of the road. The gate is along here on the right.

Nimrud

Nimrud, the second capital of Assyria, is 37 km south-east of Mosul and one of the best preserved of Iraq's ancient sites. The city wall has an eight km circumference containing several buildings, the most impressive being King Assunasirpal II's palace. On either side of the entrance are two huge sculptures of human-headed lions with hawk wings. Inside are some beautiful bas-relief slabs.

Hatra

Hatra is 110 km to the south-east of Mosul. Once an important city, it dates from the 1st century AD. In architecture, sculpture, metalwork and military expertise, Hatra was no less advanced than Rome. The ruins contain many fine pieces of sculpture.

North-East Mountains

Scenically this area contrasts starkly with the rest of the country, consisting of high mountains and fertile valleys. Much of it is in the Kurdish Autonomous Region. The Kurds are descendants of the Medes and have inhabited 'Kurdistan' since Parthian times (see History in the Facts about the Region chapter).

ARBIL

Arbil, 84 km from Mosul, is one of the oldest continuously inhabited cities in the world, and headquarters of the Kurdish Autonomous Region. Its beginnings are buried in the mists of antiquity, but there is archaeological evidence that Neolithic peoples roamed the area 10,000 years ago.

Fortress

The modern town occupies the top of a mound formed by successive building over a long period of time. It is dominated by a fortress, behind which are three large 19th century Kurdish houses which, along with the fortress, have been turned into museums. The houses have ceilings decorated with floral patterns and coloured glass windows. One has a room with an interesting collection of everyday Kurdish objects and handicrafts, another an art gallery showing works by contemporary Iraqi artists. Nearby is a large bathhouse, also part of the house.

Arbil Museum

The museum was opened in 1989 and has a comprehensive collection from Sumerian to Abbasid times. From Nishteman Square, walk away from the fortress, along the main road, cross over Media Square and the museum is on the left.

SHAQLAWA & GULLY ALI BEG

The road from Arbil winds steeply upwards to Salah ad-Din at 1090m above sea level, and then on to Shaqlawa, 50 km from Arbil. This is an idyllic town surrounded by mountains and orchards where pears, apples, grapes, pomegranates, almonds and walnuts grow in profusion. There are a few *budget hotels* on the main street.

Gully Ali Beg is 60 km from Shaqlawa. From Shaqlawa the mountain ranges begin to close in and the scenery becomes more rugged and dramatic. The gully is a narrow 10 km long pass and a lovely 80m high waterfall tumbles into it.

DOHUK

Dohuk is a small Kurdish town, 73 km north of Mosul. It's a pleasant place, with an interesting market, but serves mainly as a base from which to explore the surrounding mountains. There are cheap *snack bars* on the main road.

AMADIYA

Amadiya is 90 km from Dohuk. The road makes its way through scenery which, as the

IRAQ

road unfolds, becomes more and more spectacular. It winds its way through several villages – firstly Zawila, then Suara Tuga, which has a wonderful view of the plain of Sarsang, then through Anshki to Sulaf, a village with waterfalls and lots of cafes where you can sit and enjoy the views. The road finally ends at Amadiya, an extremely picturesque village on a high plateau, 1985m above sea level, surrounded by magnificent mountains and endless green valleys.

ZAKHO

Zakho, near the Turkish border, is Iraq's most northerly town and is famous for its old stone bridge, well preserved and still in constant use. Its age is unknown but it's reputed to have been built by a local Abbasid ruler and is at the far side of town. The approach to Zakho is spectacular, crossing over many

high mountain ridges. There are lots of cheap *snack bars* and *restaurants* on the main road.

SINJAR

The town of Sinjar is 160 km west of Mosul on the slopes of the Jenel Sinjar mountain in the desert, near the Syrian border. It is most renowned for being the town of the Yezidis, the so-called Devil worshippers who are of Kurdish stock.

What they actually believe is that the Devil is a fallen angel, bringing evil to the world, and must be appeased in order that he will once again take up his rightful place amongst the angels. They will never say his name *Shaitan* or any similar sounding word.

Their religion contains elements of nature worship, Islam and Christianity. In October they hold a festival at the shrine of Sheikh Adi, the sect's founder. Like the Kurds, they are friendly and hospitable.

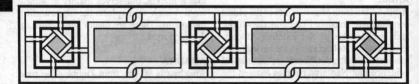

Israel & the Palestinian Territories

One of the golden rules for successful travelling is to avoid discussing religion and politics. In Israel, however, they collide inseparably, both with each other and with virtually everything else. This is the Holy Land; this is Palestine.

A land of incredible contrasts, Israel offers a wealth of changing landscapes, different climates, culture, history and, of course, religion. Its tiny size makes this all the more remarkable. Slightly smaller than New Jersey or Belgium and about half the size of Tasmania, Israel contains almost every type of geographical terrain: mountains, subtropical valleys, fertile farms, and deserts.

Jewish, Muslim and Christian pilgrims are drawn here by the conviction that 'this is where it happened'. Such beliefs, combined with Israel's strategic location, have made this probably the most hotly disputed area in the world.

Facts about the Country

HISTORY

The strategic position of Israel, or Palestine as it was once known, long made it a much fought over prize. A Jewish kingdom existed here over 2500 years ago under a succession of rulers that included David and Solomon, but after conquest by the Assyrians, the Babylonians and the Greeks, it finally fell prey to the Romans in 63 BC. The Jews revolted but were defeated. As a punishment Jerusalem was destroyed and the Jews were sent into an exile that could be said only to have come to an end after WWII with the establishment of the independent Jewish state of Israel.

Small communities of Jews always remained in the region despite the action of the Romans but the re-creation of the Jewish homeland (Zionism) was an idea born of the

The State of Israel

Area: 28,000 sq km (including the Gaza Strip and the West Bank)
Population: 5.57 million (including the Gaza Strip and the West Bank)
Population Growth Rate: 2.2%
Capital: Israel claims Jerusalem (pop: 567,100) – this is disputed by Palestinians and unrecognised by the international community
Head of State: Prime Minister Binyamin Netanyahu, with a president, Ezer Weizmann, having a largely symbolic role
Official Languages: Hebrew & Arabic
Currency: new Israeli shekel (NIS)
Exchange Rate: 3.23 NIS = US$1
Per Capita GNP: US$13,760
Inflation: 14.5%
Time: GMT/UTC +2

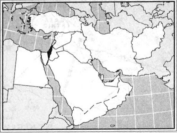

Warning

Travellers should make themselves aware of the current political situation and its possible consequences for travel in the country. At the time of writing, there are still many potentially explosive obstacles in the way of the peace process and periodic flare-ups can be expected. Generally speaking most of Israel is safe, but check on the state of play before travelling in the Golan and Upper Galilee, the West Bank and Gaza. ■

Suggested Itineraries

Allow as much time as you can for **Jerusalem**, a place that needs to be absorbed not 'done'; two days here is the absolute minimum but give it a week if you've got it. Jerusalem is also the best base for visiting the **Dead Sea** and **Masada**, two sites which come high on most visitors' itineraries.

From the Holy City, head up to **Tiberias** on the shores of Galilee and aim to spend a full day there, perhaps cycling around the lake. Next morning head for **Safed** and plan to spend the night in the Crusader city of **Akko**.

Depending on how much time you have left, you might want to visit **Caesarea**, one of the country's most satisfying archaeological sites; from here you can loop back to Jerusalem or head instead for **Tel Aviv**, in our opinion a greatly underrated Mediterranean resort. All of this can be done in eight to 10 days. If you have more time available then consider using Tiberias as a base for visiting **Banias** in the Golan and extend your stay in Jerusalem in order to make a day trip to one of the Palestinian West Bank towns such as **Nablus**. ■

19th century and the nationalist sentiments prevalent throughout Europe. Inspired by activists and visionaries, Jews from Eastern Europe began heading back for the ancient lands of Judea and Samaria. Then Ottoman backwaters, these territories came under the mandatory authority of the British on the collapse of the Turkish Empire. The Zionists managed to extract from the British the promise of a 'Jewish national homeland' in a 1917 declaration by Foreign Secretary Lord Balfour.

The immigration intensified in the 1930s as Hitler's rise to power sent hundreds of thousands of Jews fleeing from Europe to swell the numbers in the 'Promised Land'. The indigenous Arabs of Palestine saw no reason why they should suffer for the misfortunes of war-torn Europe and responded with riots against the unwelcome and ever-increasing number of newcomers. In 1948 Britain washed its hands of the whole mess and cleared out. Immediately the Jews declared the land as their own independent state, called Israel, and began to fight it out with the Arabs.

Israel emerged victorious from that first Arab-Israeli bout, as it did again during the 1956 Suez Conflict. An even more decisive victory over the combined forces of Egypt, Jordan and Syria achieved in just six days in 1967 established Israel as the Middle East's pre-eminent military superpower. However, early defeats in the following 1973 war left Israel considerably less sure of its security. Negotiations began which resulted in the signing of the Israel-Egypt Peace Treaty of 1979 (the Camp David Accord), a peace which although a little frosty has so far been maintained.

Peace with Egypt failed to address the issue of the Palestinian Arabs, great numbers of whom had been made refugees in 1948 and 1967, while those remaining in Gaza and the West Bank lived under Israeli occupation. During the 1970s and '80s, under the spearhead of Yasser Arafat's PLO, a campaign of international terrorism was waged to bring the Palestinian plight to international attention. The world response was repulsion. This began to change in 1987 with the *intifada*, a spontaneous popular uprising to which the Israelis were seen to respond with a brutal heavy-handedness. Worldwide TV screenings of Israeli soldiers firing on unarmed Arab youths did much to rehabilitate the Palestinians and demonise the Jewish state.

In 1991 Israeli officials sat down to talk with a Palestinian delegation for the first time. This ultimately led to the White House lawn where Arafat and Israeli Prime Minister Rabin signalled their intentions of peace and made their Nobel Peace Prize-winning handshake.

Since then the Gaza Strip and several towns in the West Bank have been handed over to Palestinian autonomous rule and

ISRAEL

elections have confirmed Arafat as undisputed leader of his people. However, a comprehensive settlement with the Palestinians is still some distance in the future with the really sticky issues such as the status of Jerusalem and the future of the two million Palestinian refugees in Egypt, Jordan and Lebanon still to be discussed. Add to that Syria's demands for the return of the Israeli annexed Golan Heights and the continued confrontation with Hezbollah in southern Lebanon and Israel is still some way off sleeping easy at nights. For more information about Israel's relations with its Arab neighbours, see the Arab-Israeli Conflict box on page 28 in the Facts about the Region chapter.

GEOGRAPHY

Israel (including the Gaza Strip and the West Bank) has a total area of 28,000 sq km.

The country's physical geography is dominated by the Rift Valley, part of the great Syrian-African Rift and the longest valley in the world stretching from East Africa to southern Turkey. This great trough runs the entire length of the eastern side of Israel, starting off in the south as the arid Arava Valley, then filling with the Dead Sea before becoming the Jordan Valley, swelling to contain the Sea of Galilee and furrowing between the mountains of the Golan Heights and the Galilee as the Hula Valley.

Between the mountain-fringed 'Valley' and the Mediterranean is the narrow sandy coastal plain which forms the heartland of Israel. The population centres are denser toward the more mountainous and better-watered north – to the south is the Negev, an arid desert plain.

CLIMATE

Climatic conditions vary considerably from region to region. In general, Israel's climate is temperate with two seasons: winter, at which time it's cold and rainy, and summer, which is hot and dry. Rainfall is concentrated between November and March, and can vary from over 1000 mm a year on Mt Hermon in

the Golan to less than 100 mm in Eilat on the Red Sea.

Temperature-wise, Israeli winters can be surprisingly severe, often catching travellers with inadequate clothing. Even in the summer months a warm sweater is needed in many places, as the evening temperatures drop considerably from the daytime high.

The regional climatic variations are part of what makes Israel so fascinating. For example, in Jerusalem during the winter months it is generally cold and wet and you may even experience snow, but hop on a bus down to the Dead Sea, little more than an hour's ride away, and you can change into shorts and T-shirts and bask in 23°C of sunshine.

FLORA & FAUNA

Due to its position at the junction of three natural zones, Israel enjoys an incredible and diverse wealth of plant and animal life. It serves as the northern limit for many southern plant and animal species, and the southern limit for many northern ones.

Israel's skies are also teeming with an enormous variety of birds. Some, such as storks and swallows, rest en route to other climes; coots and ducks spend the winter; African species, such as the turtle dove, prefer the summer. It's the world's second largest flyway (after South America) for migratory birds.

As far as plants and animals are concerned the richness and abundance of species is not entirely down to nature. The Israelis have devoted a lot of energy to reviving the land after centuries of neglect and abuse. Nearly 300

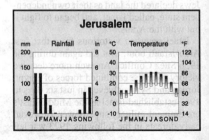

ISRAEL

Society for the Protection of Nature in Israel (SPNI)

The aims of the SPNI are the conservation and protection of antiquities, plant and animal life and the environment. For the traveller, the SPNI provides an excellent source of information on all of these areas. The main offices are in Tel Aviv and Jerusalem, both with large and extremely well stocked shops with the best range of books and pamphlets on nature and wildlife that you're going to find in Israel.

The SPNI also operates around 20 to 30 field schools throughout the country. Staffed by enthusiastic specialists these are great places to visit for information on local hikes, places of beauty and indigenous wildlife. Some of the schools also offer accommodation. Contact one of the two main offices for a complete list of addresses:

Tel Aviv – 4 Hashfela St, Tel Aviv 66183, near the central bus station (☎ (03) 537 4425; fax 383940)
Jerusalem (office and bookshop) – 13 Heleni HaMalka St, PO Box 930, Jerusalem 91008 (☎ (02) 222357, 244605)

GOVERNMENT & POLITICS

Israel is a secular, parliamentary and democratic republic, figureheaded by a largely symbolic president – a post held presently by Ezer Weizmann.

The government, headed by the prime minister, is the main policy-making body. The Knesset is Israel's parliament, a single-chambered house of 120 members (MKs). The Israeli political scene is dominated by the Israel Labour Party and Likud. Labour is generally characterised as being left of centre and it was led by Yitzhak Rabin until his assassination in November 1995 at which point Shimon Peres stepped in. Peres was ousted from office little more than six months later when he lost in elections to the Likud candidate and current incumbent, Binyamin Netanyahu. Likud is resolutely right-wing and advocates tougher policies where the Palestinians are concerned.

ECONOMY

In the past two decades Israel has switched directly from an agricultural to a post-industrial economy concentrating on the production of chemicals, plastics, electronic equipment, military technology (get the T-shirt: 'Uzis Do It Better') and computers. The country is now a world leader in various fields, such as computerised printing techniques and the genetic crossbreeding of plants and livestock and it's also a world-class centre for diamond cutting.

A crippling 60% of the national budget is still eaten up by defence spending and foreign debt but as long as the peace process stays on course prospects are good. A lasting peace with the Palestinians may lead to a lifting of the Arab boycott on all foreign companies that do business with Israel and result in increased investment from abroad. Peace also means increased revenues from tourism, one of the country's major sources of income.

POPULATION & PEOPLE

Israel, including the Gaza Strip and the West Bank, has a population of 5.57 million. Of this number 4.51 million (81%) are Jews, 805,000 (14.4%) are Muslims, 160,000 (2.9%) are Christians and 95,000 are Druze (1.7%).

The Jews

'Two Jews equals three opinions' is more than just an amusing aphorism – despite the international image of the Jews of Israel as a homogenous people the truth is that they are a deeply divided nation, riven by a bewildering array of schisms. Divisions exist along the lines of secular vs non-secular, hawks vs doves, oriental vs European, those who use coffee creamer vs those who don't – everything is an issue here to be debated and argued in cafes and newspaper columns, on TV talk shows and over the dining room table.

The most basic ethnic divide is into the Ashkenazi Jews from Eastern Europe, and

ISRAEL

the Sephardic Jews, originally from Spain but more recently from the Arab and Muslim countries (also called oriental Jews).

The Palestinian Arabs

The Arab population is concentrated mainly in Gaza and the West Bank. Over 80% are Sunni Muslims, the remainder are Christians.

Considerable controversy exists over the origins of the Palestinians and this subject is at the very heart of the Palestine 'problem'. The Israelis commonly contend that they are descended from the Arabs who invaded Palestine in the 7th century or even that most of them are descendants of immigrants from neighbouring countries who came to Palestine at the turn of the 19th century. Palestinians, on the other hand, claim that their ancestry goes back beyond that and that their ancestors appeared along the south-east Mediterranean coast more than five millennia ago and settled down to a life of fishing, farming and herding. Nearly 10% of the Arabs are Bedouin, mainly concentrated in the Negev where they continue to live in tents, breeding sheep, goats and camels.

The Druze

Nearly 10% of the non-Jewish population belong to this mysterious religious sect. The Druze have no homeland or language of their own and their nation, such as it is, is defined by their religion, an off-shoot of Islam. Like Muslims, the Druze believe in Allah and his prophets but they believe that Mohammed was succeeded by a further divine messenger. The Druze also hold the non-Islamic belief of reincarnation.

Most of the Druze nation lives in Lebanon and Syria; in Israel they inhabit a few villages in Galilee, on Mt Carmel, and also in the Golan.

ARTS
Music

Israel has long been associated with excellence in classical music. This really started in the 1930s when Jewish musicians, including some of the best of Europe's composers, performers and teachers, fled to Palestine to escape Nazism. The Israel Philharmonic Orchestra remains world-renowned and the country still produces top class musicians, most notably in the person of violinist Yitzhak Perlman.

Klezmer More elementally Jewish in nature, klezmer is traditional Yiddish dance music born in the communities of Eastern and Central Europe – think *Fiddler on the Roof*. Centred on violins, the sound can range from weeping melancholy through to wild thigh-slapping, high-kicking exuberance. In the last 20 years it's a musical form that has experienced something of a revival and Perlman recently dug around in his Jewish roots to record a klezmer album which was extremely well received.

Literature

Israeli The Israeli author SY Agnon was honoured with the Nobel Peace Prize for Literature in the 1960s but these days the most well represented Israeli writer in translation is Amos Oz, whose books appear in no less than 22 languages. Although much of the charm and colour in his novels is drawn from the Jewish characters and settings, the themes are universal and rise above national self-absorbency. Almost anything he's written is worth reading. Almost rivalling Oz in his collection of international accolades, David Grossman's novel *See Under Love* has drawn comparisons with Gunter Grass and Garcia Marquez. Belonging to a generation older than the above two, AB Yehoshua, a native of Haifa, is still producing highly regarded work. His most recent work in English translation is *Mr Mani*, a sweeping six generational epic of a wandering Jewish family.

SOCIETY & CONDUCT
Israeli Society

If the USA with its rich mix of peoples and creeds can be described as a melting pot, Israeli society is more of a chaotic and far from cohesive mosaic, as visualised by Jackson Pollock.

The nation-founding, pioneering spirit is

still very much in evidence, and Israel remains an outdoor society with a strong emphasis on healthy living and hard work – it sometimes feels like the country is one big scout jamboree. However, the pre-eminence of the kibbutz ethos is on the wane – only about 3% of the population actually live on a kibbutz. Instead, the last 20 years have seen the emergence of an Israeli *nouveaux riches* with a serious addiction to consumerism. While hedonism may be a slight exaggeration, the prevailing credo is 'live now pay later'. As it was put to us by one resident of Tel Aviv with little faith in the peace process, 'Why worry about bills when you may never get to pay them?'.

Even though these people regard them-

Sorry For What?

Two recent immigrants, one from Russia and one from the USA, together with a native Israeli are at the supermarket where they come across a sign reading 'We're sorry but due to shortages we have no meat'. The Russian turns to the other two and says, 'What is meat?' The American shrugs, 'What do they mean by shortages?'. The Israeli shakes his head and looks perplexed, 'What do they mean by this sorry?'.

The Israelis tell this joke about themselves, and any visitor who's been in the country more than five minutes will nod despairingly at the punchline. The Israelis, as they'll readily agree, are not hot on the niceties of social intercourse. No official or sales assistant will acknowledge your presence until addressed directly. Dining out, the waitress will frisbee a menu at the table, then indicate she's ready to take the order with a disinterested, 'Yeah?'. Likely looking places to ask for directions or timetables ward off all potential enquiries with prominently displayed 'No Information' notices.

For those who perceive the difference, it's not, explains writer Stephen Brook, that the Israelis are bad mannered but rather that they have no manners at all. Faced with a waiter who shrugs aside your complaints of cold food with 'People don't like it if it's too hot', anyone might feel that such subtleties are irrelevant but one thing to remember is never lose your temper and don't start shouting because there's nothing Israelis love more than a good row. ■

selves as secular they still maintain such traditions as circumcision and bar mitzvah – the spiritual roots of the country lie firmly in Judaism. Because of this, the country's outspoken religious minority, the Ultraorthodox Jews, wields a disproportionate influence in the life of all Israeli Jews. The religious courts have exclusive jurisdiction of several areas including marriage and education. There is a real attempt by the *haredim* (the general term for the Ultraorthodox) to force their strict ideology on the less observant majority of society. In recent years haredim have burnt down bus stops for carrying lewd advertising, invaded football pitches hosting Shabbat fixtures and, in Jerusalems Mea Shearim neighbourhood, have taken to assaulting improperly dressed women. This cross-cultural collision seems likely to intensify with the empowerment brought about by Ultraorthodox gains in the 1996 elections.

Palestinian Society

The traditional Palestinian lifestyle revolves strongly around the extended family. Despite the adversities of the past 50 years, outside the big cities and towns the Palestinians are extremely friendly and helpful to strangers and have no qualms about opening up their homes. Weddings are the big events and tend to involve whole villages.

In general, the Palestinians are quite accepting of foreigners' ways, but when visiting the Gaza Strip or the West Bank towns it is essential that you dress modestly – both men and women should cover their legs, and women should not expose their shoulders or upper arms.

RELIGION
Judaism

Judaism is the official state religion. According to high Jewish doctrine, Jews are in the world to be witnesses to the claim that there is one God with whom humans can have contact: God has chosen them to act as messengers, whose task it is to pass on these details to the rest of the world. What God has said is written in the Torah, the first five books of the Old Testament.

Judaism is a complex faith, and the Torah is only the foundation of Jewish sacred literature. There are also the prophetic, historical and poetical books that constitute the rest of the Old Testament. Another major written part of the Jewish faith is the Talmud, which contains rabbinical interpretations of the scriptures and commentaries.

Islam

Israel's Muslims are Sunni, followers of the succession of the caliph (see the Facts about the Region chapter).

LANGUAGE

Israel's national language is Hebrew, followed by Arabic. English is widely spoken; there will nearly always be someone nearby who understands it. Most of the important road signs are in all three languages. With Jews arriving in Israel from around the world, many other languages are commonly understood. French, German and Yiddish are the main ones, but also Spanish and Russian. Most Arabs are fluent in Hebrew and English as well as Arabic. Many also speak other European languages very well, especially in the tourist centres.

The Palestinian Arabs' common language is a Syrian dialect of Arabic (see the Facts about the Region chapter).

Facts for the Visitor

PLANNING

When to Go

Read the general notes given in the Regional Facts for the Visitor chapter. If you can, avoid visiting Israel during the Jewish holidays of Pesah (Passover), which coincides with the Christian Easter, and Rosh Hashanah, Yom Kippur and Sukkot, which fall around October (the dates vary each year). At these times shops and all businesses including cafes and restaurants close, public transport is non-existent and accommodation prices double.

Maps

Lonely Planet has a highly detailed, slimline 1:250,000 *Israel travel atlas*, designed specifically to complement their *Israel & the Palestinian Territories* guide. Otherwise, the best of the internationally available sheet maps is Hallwag's 1:500,000 *Israel Road Map*, which clearly marks the hierarchy of roads, denotes the territory of the West Bank (many maps don't), includes within its bounds Beirut, Damascus and Amman, and also has inset street plans of the major Israeli cities. Hildebrand's 1:360,000 *Travel Map of Israel* isn't bad either, although despite the larger scale it's not as clear as Hallwag.

For a wider choice or something more specialised, wait until you reach Israel where you'll be able to pick up high quality locally produced city maps, street atlases, topographical surveys – in fact more or less anything you could imaginably want.

What to Bring

For information see the Regional Facts for the Visitor chapter. Also, beware Israel can be very cold during the winter; anyone visiting from October through to March and not intending to spend all their time in Eilat should bring a sweater.

VISAS & DOCUMENTS
Visas

With all but a few exceptions, a tourist visa is not required to visit Israel – just a passport, valid for at least six months from your date of entry. Those exceptions include holders of passports from most African and Central American countries, India, Singapore and some of the ex-Soviet republics.

As a tourist you are normally allowed a three month visit, although visitors entering through the land borders with Egypt and Jordan are often initially only granted a month's stay.

If you look 'undesirable', or are suspected of looking for illegal employment, on arrival immigration officials may question the purpose of your visit and ask to see evidence of a return flight/ferry ticket and financial support. Travellers singled out and then found to have insufficient money to cover their proposed stay have, in the past, been prevented from entering the country and put on the next flight home. More commonly, if unimpressed, immigration may only allow you a shorter stay, say one month.

Visa Extensions If after your initial three month stay you want more time, you need to apply for a visa. You do this at offices of the Ministry of the Interior, which are located in most major towns and cities. You have to be able to convince the civil servants that you can support yourself without needing to work illegally. The process costs 90 NIS and one passport-sized photo is required.

The Israeli Stamp Stigma

Israel is, of course, the venue for that popular Middle Eastern game, the Passport Shuffle which involves getting in and out of the country but avoiding being stamped with any incriminating evidence to tell that you were ever there. This game was devised because those countries which refuse to recognise Israel (Iran and all Arab countries other than Egypt and Jordan) refuse to allow anyone across their borders whose passport is marred by evidence of a visit to the Jewish state. Israeli immigration officials will, if asked, stamp only your entry permit and not your passport. This is fine if you are flying both into and out of Israel but if crossing by land into either Egypt or Jordan, the Arab immigration officers are generally not so obliging and their entry stamps will be a dead giveaway – although some wily travellers have reported getting away with stamps on a separate piece of paper, especially at the Allenby Bridge border crossing into Jordan.

Other Documents

The only officially required document for travellers in Israel is a valid passport but, if you have them, bring along your Hostelling International (HI) card and International Student Identity Card (ISIC), which entitles the holder to a 10% discount on Egged bus fares over 10 NIS, 20% off fares on Israel State Railways and substantial discounts at most museums and archaeological sites. Student cards issued by your individual university or college are often not recognised.

EMBASSIES
Israeli Embassies Abroad
Australia
> 6 Turrana Ave, Yarralumla, Canberra, ACT 2600 (☎ (06) 273 1309)
> Consulate: 37 York St, Sydney, NSW 2000 (☎ (02) 9264 7933)

Canada
> 50 O'Conner St, Suite 1005, Ottawa, Ontario KIP 6L2 (☎ (613) 567 6450)
> Consulate: 115 Blvd Rene Levesque Ouest, Suite 2620, Montreal, Quebec H3B 4S5 (☎ (514) 393 9372)

Ireland
> Berkeley Court Hotel, Suite 630, Landsdowne Rd, Ballsbridge, Dublin 4 (☎ (1) 668 0303)

New Zealand
> DB Tower, The Terrace 111, PO Box 2171, Wellington (☎ (4) 472 2362)

UK
> 2 Palace Green, London W8 4QB (☎ (0171) 957 9547)

USA
> 3514 International Drive NW, Washington DC 20008 (☎ (202) 364 5500)
> Consulate: 800 Second Ave, New York NY10017 (☎ (212) 499 5300)
> There are a total of nine Israeli consulates in the USA; phone one of the above two for contact details of the rest.

Foreign Embassies in Israel

Although the Israelis lay claim to Jerusalem as the capital of the Jewish state this is not recognised by most of the international community. Instead, most foreign embassies are in Tel Aviv. Some countries also maintain consulates in Jerusalem and a few in Haifa too.

Australia
> 37 HaMelekh Shaul Ave, Tel Aviv (☎ (03) 695 0451)

Canada
> 220 HaYarkon St, Tel Aviv (☎ (03) 527 2929)

Egypt
> 54 Basel St, off Ibn Gvirol St, Tel Aviv (☎ (03) 546 4151)
> Consulate: 68 Ha'Efroni St, Eilat (☎ (07) 367 882)
> Visas are processed the same day (hand in applications Sunday to Thursday from 9 to 11 am, then

pick up that afternoon). At the time of writing single-entry tourist visas, valid for one month, cost 60 NIS (US$20), plus you need one photo.

Ireland

Consulate: Hotel Dan Accadia, Herzlia
(☎ (09) 950 9055)

Jordan

14 Abba Hillel Silver St, Ramat Gan, Tel Aviv
(☎ (03) 751 7722)

Visas are issued Sunday to Thursday 9 am to 1 pm or they can also be obtained at the Arava and Jordan River crossing points (not at the Allenby/Hussein Bridge). The cost of the visa varies by nationality; for UK citizens it's JD22, for US citizens JD15, for Australians and New Zealanders JD16, for Canadians JD30, down to just JD4 for French, Belgians and the Irish. (JD1 = US$1.41 = UK£0.85, approximately).

South Africa

16th floor, 50 Dizengoff St, Tel Aviv
(☎ (03) 525 2566)

UK

192 HaYarkon St, Tel Aviv (☎ (03) 544 0250)

USA

71 HaYarkon St, Tel Aviv (☎ (03) 517 4338)

MONEY

Most Israelis talk in terms of US dollars, not shekels, and up-market hotels, HI hostels, most car hire companies and many airlines all accept payment in US dollars – this is worth doing as it saves you the 17% Value Added Tax (VAT). After the dollar one foreign currency is as good as any other and moneychangers and banks will take whatever you've got, though exchange rates on the Egyptian pound are very poor.

Credit cards are accepted almost everywhere and many bank foyers are equipped with cash dispensing ATMs which accept, among others, American Express (Amex), Diners, EuroCard and Visa. Holders of travellers' cheques will have no trouble getting them cashed – Eurocheques can even be exchanged at branches of the post office. Beware though, commission charges can be as high as 20 NIS *per cheque* regardless of the amount, so shop around. The best bet is to go to one of the no-commission currency exchange bureaus or to one of the Amex or Thomas Cook offices or agents – see the individual city sections for addresses.

For anyone unfortunate enough to run out

of money, the Israeli Post Office operates a Western Union international money transfer service.

Costs

There are no two ways about it: compared to other countries in the region like Egypt, Jordan or Turkey, Israel is expensive. Compare prices with Australia, New Zealand, the UK or USA, however, and there's little to complain about.

Accommodation can be quite cheap – many private hostels offer clean sheets, hot showers and possibly air-con for somewhere between 20 to 30 NIS per night (US$7 to US$10). Dining could well be the area that busts your budget apart. While it is possible to survive on three felafel sandwiches a day at a cost of around 6 NIS, a more realistic figure would be 30 to 50 NIS (US$10 to US$16) per day, which allows for a little indulgence bolstered with a lot of street food.

Museum and gallery admissions are pricey, often in the region of 20 NIS (US$7) but this is offset by the relatively cheap cost of transport; the hour long bus ride between Tel Aviv and Jerusalem, for instance, is less than 14 NIS (approximately US$4.50).

On an individual budget of 80 to 100 NIS per day (approximately US$25 to US$30) it should be possible to get decent accommodation, eat well and travel around.

Currency

The national currency is the new Israeli shekel (NIS). The Hebraically correct plural is *shekelim* but even Israelis when speaking English tend to Anglicise and use 'shekels'. The new shekel is divided into 100 agorot. There are coins of 10 and 50 agorot, one and five NIS and notes of five, 10, 20, 50, 100 and 200 NIS.

Currency Exchange

Australia	A$1	=	2.55 NIS
Canada	C$1	=	2.41 NIS
Egypt	E£1	=	0.95 NIS
France	FF1	=	0.63 NIS
Germany	DM1	=	2.14 NIS
Jordan	JD1	=	4.56 NIS

UK	UK£1	=	5.38 NIS
USA	US$1	=	3.23 NIS

Changing Money

Generally speaking there is little variation in the rates of exchange on offer but you ought to check on the commission charged by the banks because sometimes this can be extremely voracious. The best deals are offered by the Arab moneychangers in Jerusalem and the specialist exchange bureaus in Jerusalem and Tel Aviv, none of which take any commission at all.

Although banking hours vary, generally they are Sunday to Tuesday and Thursday from 8.30 am to 12.30 pm and 4 to 5.30 pm, and Wednesday, Friday and eves of holy days from 8.30 am to noon.

Some bank branches also have currency exchange ATMs which accept several of the major international currencies and offer the convenience of 24 hour accessibility, seven days a week; the drawback is a whopping transaction charge.

Tipping & Bargaining

Not so long ago, apparently, no one tipped in Israel. Now your bill arrives appended with a large handwritten 'Service is not included' and delivered by a waiter or waitress with a steely smile that reads, '15%. No less'.

Note that taxi drivers in Israel do not expect to be tipped; they're usually content just to overcharge.

Taxes & Refunds

Israel slaps VAT (Value Added Tax) on a wide range of goods but tourists in Israel are entitled to a refund on most items purchased with foreign currency in shops that are registered with the Ministry of Tourism (there'll be a sign in the window or at the till). The purchases need to be wrapped in a sealed plastic bag, of which at least one side must be transparent with the original invoice displayed inside the bag so that it can be read without opening the bag. The bag needs to remain sealed for the duration of your time in Israel. Claim your refund from the Bank

Leumi counter in the departure lounge at Ben-Gurion airport.

POST & COMMUNICATIONS
Post

Letters posted in Israel take from seven to 10 days to reach North America and Australia, and a little less to Europe. Incoming mail is fairly quick, taking about three or four days from Europe and around a week from places further afield. Poste restante seems to work quite well; for poste restante addresses see the individual city sections. Remember that Amex offices (found in Israel in Jerusalem and Tel Aviv) will receive mail for card holders.

Telephone

Israel has a state-of-the-art card-operated public telephone system. International calls can be made from any street call box with telecards bought from lottery kiosks, newssellers or bookshops.

For the purposes of charging, standard rate operates between 8 am and 10 pm; from 10 pm to 1 am and all day Saturday and Sunday calls are 25% cheaper, while all week between 1 am and 8 am calls are 50% cheaper. A 10 unit phonecard will get you just a couple of minutes, if that, phoning to the USA at peak rates.

You can also make discount international calls from the offices of Solan Telecom, located in most towns and cities throughout Israel and open 24 hours, although in practice the savings are nothing substantial.

The international country code for Israel is 972.

Fax, Telegraph & Email

To send a fax or telex, call by a post office. Faxes are charged at 17 NIS for the first sheet and 9 NIS for subsequent sheets. Faxes can also be sent from Solan offices at a cost of 12 NIS per sheet, irrespective of the destination and they'll receive faxes for you for a small fee.

In main post offices a 24 hour telegram service is provided, although you might have to wake up the person on duty. Alternatively

ISRAEL

Solan Telecom (see above) will send telegrams at a cost of 25 NIS for the first seven words, address included, and 1.70 NIS for each word thereafter.

Electronic mail can be sent and received at Strudel (☎ (02) 623 2101; fax 622 1445; email strudel@inter.net.il) at 11 Mounbaz St in the Russian Compound in Jerusalem's New City.

BOOKS
The Israeli propensity for navel-gazing means that most of the titles mentioned here are also available in bookshops in Tel Aviv and Jerusalem too. Try the stores belonging to the Steimatzky chain.

Travel
Winner Takes All by Stephen Brook, despite being a little dated (it was written in 1990), is nevertheless still the best available primer for a visit to Israel. Not ageing quite so well is the slightly pompous *Jerusalem* by Colin Thubron, one of the earliest and least successful books by the now fêted travel writer. Far more illuminating and entertaining is *Jerusalem: City of Mirrors* by Amos Elon, an internationally respected Israeli writer who has spent most of his life in the city of which he writes.

Not to forget *The Innocents Abroad* by Mark Twain, written in 1871 and still one of the best books dealing with the tourist experience in the Holy Land.

History & Politics
For the uninitiated a good place to start is with Amos Oz who, although primarily a novelist, has had three collections of essays (*In the Land of Israel, The Slopes of Lebanon* and *Israel, Palestine and Peace*) published on the state of Israel and the prospects of peace. *From Beirut to Jerusalem* by Pulitzer Prize-winning journalist Thomas Friedman is the recent history of the Middle Eastern conflicts as witnessed by an outsider. It's excellent for anyone seeking a fuller understanding of the causes and effects of the constant strife that afflicts the region.

Of the authors writing from a Palestinian perspective, the most eloquent is Edward Said whose views are expounded in *The Palestinian Question*. Far more emotive and gritty is *Gaza: Legacy of Occupation* by Dick Doughty and Mohammed El-Aydi, which focuses on the tragedies of Palestinian life in the Strip.

General
To be enjoyed rather than believed at face value *O Jerusalem* by Dominique Lapierre & Larry Collins is a novelisation of the events of the 1948 War and the birth of Israel, while *The Source* by James A Michener and *Exodus* by Leon Uris are two of the all-time most popular novels with an Israeli theme. For other general information on Israel, see the Books section in the Regional Facts for the Visitor chapter.

NEWSPAPERS & MAGAZINES
Unless you read Hebrew or Arabic, your appreciation of Israel's extensive press will be limited. The *Jerusalem Post* is the country's only English-language daily (but no Saturday edition). Though indispensable for its coverage of Israeli life, its pronounced right-wing leanings are a turn-off to many. Buy it on Friday, however, for the extensive 'what's on' supplement. In East Jerusalem only, you can pick up the weekly pro-Palestinian adi Jerusalem Times. Also, look out in the hostels and bars for the freebie *Traveller*, an occasional features-based newspaper aimed squarely at the backpacking fraternity. It carries some useful pieces like a round-up of the Jerusalem and Tel Aviv bar scenes and hints on budget eating.

Western newspapers and magazines are easily found and they're usually only a day old – the best selection is carried by the Steimatzky bookshops.

RADIO & TV
National Radio 1 (576 AM in Tel Aviv and the central region, 1458 AM in Jerusalem and Eilat) has English-language news bulletins at 7 am and 1 and 8 pm, as well as a current affairs magazine at 5 pm daily. The BBC World Service can be picked up on 639

and 1323 kHz and 227 MW, while Voice of America is on 1260 kHz.

Israel has two state TV stations, both of which carry masses of English-language programming (English news on Channel 1 is at 6.15 pm during the week, 4.30 pm Friday and 5 pm Saturday). These are supplemented by Arabic language Jordan TV and Middle East TV, a Christian station administered by North Americans. The majority of the Israeli population also has cable which gives access to an additional 32 channels including CNN, Sky, BBC World, Discovery and MTV.

For TV and radio listings pick up the *Jerusalem Post.*

PHOTOGRAPHY & VIDEO

Whatever you run out of or whatever needs replacing, you'll be able to find it in Israel but there's little doubt that it would have been way cheaper back home.

Other than military installations there's little that can't be photographed – even the Israeli Defence Force (IDF) soldiers are happy to preen and pose for a visitor's camera. The exceptions are the Orthodox Jews who extremely dislike having their photograph taken.

LAUNDRY

Many of the better hostels have a laundry room, otherwise coin-operated laundrettes are common. One machine load costs about 8 NIS and dryers are about 4 NIS for a 10 minute cycle.

WOMEN TRAVELLERS

Unfortunately a lot of what we say in the Regional Facts for the Visitor chapter also applies in Israel. Although Israeli men are not known for their gentlemanly conduct towards women most of the problems will occur in Arab areas, particularly those that are most heavily visited by tourists. We recommend women take special care in the Old City of Jerusalem and on the Mount of Olives where attacks have frequently occurred, and in the towns of Nazareth and Akko.

GAY & LESBIAN TRAVELLERS

Homosexuality is not illegal in Israel but it's anathema to the country's large religious population and as a result the gay and lesbian community is obliged to keep a low profile. Not surprisingly, the biggest scene is in largely secular, free-wheeling (though little cruising) Tel Aviv, but don't expect too much. The most popular gay spot is the *Cafe Nordau* at 145 Ben Yehuda St, where homosexuality is one of the causes they champion along with animal rights and ecology. In Jerusalem, as far as we could discern the choices were the *Q Bar* or go straight. The *Tmol Shilshom* cafe/bookshop in the central Nahalat Shiv'a quarter is gay-run but other than a shelf of second-hand gay fiction that doesn't amount to much.

There must be more and we suggest that you call the gay switchboard (☎ (03) 629 2797) Sunday, Tuesday and Thursday from 7.30 to 11.30 pm. The Society for the Protection of Personal Rights (SPPR: ☎ (03) 620 4327; fax 525 2341) at PO Box 37604, Tel Aviv 61375 also operates a gay hotline (☎ (03) 629 3681) and publishes an English-language newsletter *Israel Update* – send a self-addressed envelope.

DISABLED TRAVELLERS

Many hotels and most public institutions in Israel provide ramps, specially equipped toilets and other conveniences for the disabled. In particular, several of the HI-affiliated hostels, including the one in Tel Aviv and the Beit Shmeul in Jerusalem, have rooms specially adapted for wheelchair access. Anyone with any particular concerns might try contacting in advance Milbat – The Advisory Centre for the Disabled (☎ (03) 530 3739) – at the Sheba Medical Centre in Tel Aviv for information and advice.

The Yad Sarah Organisation (☎ (02) 624 4242) at 43 HaNevi'im St in Jerusalem also provides wheelchairs, crutches and other aids on free of charge loan (though a deposit is required). It's open to visitors Sunday to Thursday from 9 am to 7 pm and Friday from 9 am to noon.

ISRAEL

BUSINESS HOURS

The most important thing to know is that on Shabbat, the Jewish sabbath, most Israeli shops, offices and places of entertainment close down. Shabbat starts at sundown Friday and ends sundown Saturday. During this time you'll find it tough to get anything to eat, you can't easily change money and your movements are restricted because most buses aren't running. You need to plan for Shabbat in advance and work out where you'll be and what you can do to avoid being overtaken by the countrywide inactivity. The country kicks back into action on Saturday evening, when the cafes, bars and restaurants always experience a great post-Shabbat rush.

Predominantly Muslim areas like East Jerusalem, the Gaza Strip and the West Bank towns remain open on Saturday but are closed all day Friday. And, of course, Christian-owned businesses (concentrated in Jerusalem's Old City and in Nazareth) close on Sunday.

Standard Israeli shopping hours are Monday to Thursday from 8 am to 1 pm and 4 to 7 pm or later, and Friday from 8 am to 2 pm, with some places opening after sundown on Saturday, too.

PUBLIC HOLIDAYS
Jewish

Be well prepared for any Jewish religious holidays that are celebrated during your visit. The Jewish holidays are effectively like long bouts of Shabbat and if you're caught off-guard you can be rendered immobile for a couple of days at a time. The main ones to beware of are Rosh HaShanah, Yom Kippur, Sukkot and Pesah.

Rosh HaShanah The 'head of the year', or Rosh HaShanah, is Jewish new year. As with all Jewish holidays, prayer services begin on the eve of the holiday, in this case continuing for two days.

Yom Kippur Known as the Day of Atonement, Yom Kippur ends the 10 days of penitence which begin on New Year's Day. For the observant, Yom Kippur means 25

hours of complete abstinence from food, drink, sex, cosmetics (including soap and toothpaste) and animal products. The time is spent in prayer and contemplation and all sins are confessed. Yom Kippur is the quietest day of the year in most of Israel.

Sukkot & Simhat Torah On the Festival of Sukkot most Jews, religious or not, erect home-made *sukkot* (shelters) in commemoration of the 40 years which the ancient Israelites spent in the wilderness after the exodus. The sukkot, hammered together from plyboard but with a roof only of loose branches through which the sky can be seen, sit out on the balconies of apartments, in gardens and even in hotels and restaurants.

Hanukah Also known as the Festival of Lights, Hanukah celebrates the triumphant Maccabaean revolt. Its symbol is the menorah, and one of its candles is lit each night for a week. A special Hanukah lamp should also be displayed by each house, usually hung in the window – in Mea She'arim these are often hung outside the building making it an enchanting district to wander through during the time of the festival.

Purim Purim, the Feast of Lots, is a remembrance of the hatred born of the Jews' refusal to assimilate and their unwillingness to compromise religious principle by bowing before the secular authority. Despite such a serious, if highly relevant, theme, the holiday has a carnival atmosphere with fancy dress as the order of the day. The streets are filled with proud parents and their Batmen, Madonnas and Power Rangers. In the evening it's the turn of the dames, fairies and gangsters.

A nation of non-drinkers, Purim is an annual opportunity for the Israelis to atone: according to tradition they are supposed to get so drunk that they can't distinguish between the words 'bless Mordechai' and 'curse Haman'. The most popular Purim food is Haman's Ears (Oznei Haman) – fried, three-cornered pastries filled with apricots or other fruits and covered in poppy seeds.

ISRAEL

Pesah Pesah, the Feast of Passover, celebrates the exodus of the Jews from Egypt led by Moses. The festival lasts a full week during which time most Jewish shops (including food shops and markets) are closed (or, if not, then open for limited hours). The production of everyday bread is substituted for *matza*, a flat tasteless variety which is made in discs of up to a metre in diameter. There's no public transport on either the first or last day of the festival.

Holocaust Day (Yom HaSho'ah) Periodically throughout the day sirens wail to signal two minutes of silence in remembrance of the six million victims of the Holocaust – it's an incredibly moving and eerie experience as everyone on the streets stops and puts their bags down, and all traffic comes to a halt, engines are extinguished and nothing moves.

Independence Day (Yom Ha'Atzmaut) On 14 May 1948 Israel became an independent state and since then the day has been celebrated by Jews worldwide (note, the date changes with the lunar calendar). In Israel expect parades, aerial flypasts, concerts, picnics and fireworks all over the country.

Muslim
The Muslim holidays have been described in the Regional Facts for the Visitor chapter. For the dates, see the table of holidays near Public Holidays & Special Events in the Regional Facts for the Visitor chapter.

Christian
Many visitors with a Christian background will find the festivals celebrated very differently from the way they are used to. This is largely due to the domination of the Orthodox Church, and also to the fact that Christianity is very much in third place in the religious stakes here. Christmas Day, for example, is just another day for most people.

ACTIVITIES
Hiking
With its changing landscapes, Israel offers a wealth of superb hiking opportunities, both leisurely and more strenuous. In particular look at exploring the Maktesh Ramon (see Mitzpe Ramon in the Negev section), the world's largest crater, and Ein Avdat (also in the Negev) which involves some canyon climbing to reach an ice cold spring. Other excellent hikes include the route through Wadi Qelt (see Around Jericho in the West Bank section) and various trails up in the Golan region – see the introduction to that particular section.

We really can't stress enough that anyone interested in hiking should visit the SPNI in Jerusalem and Tel Aviv (see Flora & Fauna earlier in this chapter).

Cycling
See the entry in the Getting Around chapter. Tours can be arranged with the Israel Cyclists' Touring Club, an affiliate of the International Bicycle Touring Society. Each tour is accompanied by a certified guide and an escort there to handle any technical problems. You might also contact the Jerusalem Cycle Club (☎ (02) 016 062, 561 9416).

Horse Riding
Widely available in the Galilee and Golan regions and at numerous places along the coast north of Tel Aviv, including:

Kibbutz Nahsholim (☎ (06) 639 9533; fax (06) 639 7614) at Dor Bay on the coast north of Netanya
The Farm (☎ (09) 866 3525) at HaVatzelet HaSharon, near Netanya
Cactus Ranch (☎ (09) 865 1239), in Netanya
Herod's Stables (☎ (06) 636 1181) at Caesarea
Mekhora Stables (☎ (04) 984 2735) at Kerem Maharal, five km north of Zichron Ya'acov
Riders' Ranch (☎ (04) 830 7242) at Beit Oren, 10 km south of Haifa.

Elsewhere try Moshav Neve Ilan (☎ (02) 534 8111) 15 km from Jerusalem, the Municipal Farm (☎ (07) 672 6608) at Migdal in Ashkelon and at the Texas Ranch in Eilat (see the Negev section).

Water Sports
While Eilat is over-rated, the beaches at Bat Yam, a suburb of Tel Aviv, Tel Aviv itself,

Netanya and Dor are all excellent. As you start getting up towards Haifa the water becomes polluted and jellyfish start to be a problem. With the Red and Mediterranean seas and the Sea of Galilee, there are ample opportunities to enjoy the pleasures of swimming, windsurfing and sailing. Eilat is the water sports capital offering everything from parascending to waterskiing. It's also a major scuba diving centre – although the sites along the Sinai coast are far superior. An interesting option is to dive at Caesarea where you can explore the underwater ruins of Herod's city. Contact the Diving Club at Caesarea (☎ (06) 636 1787).

Skiing

Israel has just the one ski centre, at Mt Hermon in the extreme north of the country. The season begins late December/January and lasts through until mid-April. There are long and short-distance chair lifts, a ski school and equipment for hire. It's not cheap, however. See the Mt Hermon Ski Centre in the Upper Galilee & the Golan section.

Birdwatching

Israel is the world's second largest bird migratory flyway, after South America. Eilat's International Birdwatching Centre (☎ (07) 374 276; fax 370 098; PO Box 774, 88106 Eilat), on HaTemarim Blvd across from the central bus station, is the best place for information.

WORK

Many people automatically associate a visit to Israel with a spell as a kibbutz or moshav volunteer and every year thousands of young people from the world over descend on the Holy Land for the experience. Many volunteers are actually very disappointed with what they find. The hostels of Tel Aviv are full of ex-kibbutzers who couldn't wait to get out. Before committing yourself to a volunteer programme you should study carefully what it actually involves.

Kibbutz Volunteers

There are basically three ways to go about becoming a volunteer. The first two involve contacting a kibbutz representative office in your own country and either joining a group of about 15 people or travelling as an individual. The kibbutz representatives charge a basic registration fee (about US$50) and arrange your flight – which generally costs more than you'd pay if you shopped around yourself. If you choose to join a group you have no option but to fly with them, but as an individual you can register and then make your own travel arrangements. To find out more, contact your nearest kibbutz representative's office:

Australia
  Darlinghurst: Kibbutz Program Centre, 104 Darlinghurst Rd, NSW 2010 (☎ (02) 9360 6300)
  Melbourne: Kibbutz Program Desk, 584 St Kilda Rd, Victoria 3004 (☎ (03) 9272 5331; fax 9272 5640)
Canada
  Ontario: Kibbutz Aliyah Desk, 1000 Finch Ave West, Downsview, M3J 2E7
  Montreal: Kibbutz Aliyah Desk, 5800 Cavendish Blvd, Cote St Luc, PQ H4W 2TS
New Zealand
  Wellington: Kibbutz Program Desk, Jewish Community Centre Building, Kensington St, PO Box 27-156, Wellington (☎ (4) 844 229)
UK
  London: Kibbutz Representatives, 1A Accommodation Rd, NW11 (☎ (0181) 458 9235) Project 67, 10 Hatton Garden, EC1 (☎ (0171) 831 7626; fax (0171) 404 5588)
USA
  New York: Kibbutz Aliyah Desk, 110 East 59th St, New York (☎ (212) 318 6130)
  San Francisco: Kibbutz Aliyah Desk, 870 Market St (1083), San Francisco, California 94102
  Florida: Israel Aliyah Centre (Kibbutz), 4200 Biscayne Blvd, Miami, Florida 33137
  Chicago: Kibbutz Aliyah Desk, 2320 W Peterson, Suite 503, Chicago, Illinois 60659

Alternatively, would-be volunteers can make their own way to the kibbutz offices in Tel Aviv to apply there in person for a place. Your success at being accepted is dependent not only on there being a suitable vacancy, but on your being able to convince the kibbutz officials that you are not a drug-crazed, beer-guzzling, youngster-perverting layabout – the British have a particularly hard task here.

There are three main offices in Tel Aviv to apply to:

Meira's
73 Ben Yehuda St, entrance behind the restaurant (☎ (03) 523 7369; fax 524 3811). Open Sunday to Thursday from 9.30 am to 3 pm.

Project 67
94 Ben Yehuda St (☎ (03) 523 0140; fax 524 7474). Open Monday to Thursday from 9 am to 5 pm and Friday from 9 am to noon.

Kibbutz Volunteer Centre
18 Frishman St, corner of Ben Yehuda (☎ (03) 527 8874). Open Sunday to Thursday from 8 am to 2 pm.

Moshav Volunteers

The major differences between being a volunteer on a moshav as opposed to a kibbutz are that the work is generally much harder, though often more varied and occasionally more interesting, and the money is slightly better.

Although there are moshav representatives in some countries, prospective volunteers can save themselves around US$100 by making their own way to Tel Aviv. The official moshav main office (☎ (03) 258 473) is downstairs at 19 Leonardo de Vinci St. From Tel Aviv central bus station take bus No 70. It's open Sunday to Thursday from 9 am to noon. You can also try Project 67 or Meira's (see above for addresses).

Each volunteer has to take out a health insurance policy which includes coverage for hospitalisation. Volunteers are often in short supply, so as long as you present yourself as hard-working, punctual and well behaved, you should have no problems and will probably find work in a day or two.

ACCOMMODATION
Camping

While there are numerous countrywide camping areas, usually equipped with all

---

Black (& Blue) Labour

It's not difficult to find work in Israel, it's just difficult to make it pay. In many cases employers are just out to exploit a plentiful supply of cheap, sometimes desperate, foreign labour. Working conditions are often poor, wages are low and you're not even assured of always being paid. We spoke to far too many people who had worked for up to a month only to realise that their employer had no intention of paying them – Eilat, in particular, is badly shark-infested and we're not talking the type with fins. Unfortunately, as you're working illegally you have very little come-back. We can only recommend that you check out the reputation of any potential employer with fellow travellers. Also don't allow a backlog of unpaid wages to build up – get paid weekly.

As anywhere else, the catering industry soaks up the largest number of illegal workers. It's unlikely, however, that you'll be waiting on tables and benefiting from the heavy tipping; instead you'll be washing dishes or cleaning. There's a lot of labouring work going, particularly in construction – an area that South African travellers seem to have monopolised. Most of the hostels also employ people to work at reception or the bar – the pay is nothing great but you get your bed for free and maybe enough money to cover food and beer. Down in Eilat the work can be a little more interesting or at least a little less like work; travellers we met were paid to hire out deck chairs on the beach, hose down the Dolphinarium daily, even to paint people's names on grains of rice.

In terms of pay you can expect something in the region of 10 to 15 NIS (US$3 to US$5) per hour. The best paid 'work' we came across was also the least savoury – a request at a travellers' bar for women to take part in an amateur strip night at 200 NIS (US$70) a performance. Women might find more appeal in au pair work. There are a couple of reputable agencies in Tel Aviv who match applicants with families on a short-term basis and pay US$500 to US$700 a month with accommodation and meals on top. The *Traveller* newspaper carries ads for the au pair agencies.

For other work check out the notice boards and ask around at hostels (Central, Seaside, Momo's, Gordon and the Dizengoff in Tel Aviv; Palm, Al-Arab and Tabasco in Jerusalem) and at bars. In Eilat hang out in the Peace Cafe from about 5 am, when foremen arrive looking for casual workers, and in Tel Aviv be outside the Sea & Sun Hostel on Nes Ziona St at 6 am. ■

ISRAEL

necessary amenities, they aren't always the expected cheap alternative and it's often better value to check into a hostel. Pitching your tent for free seems to be tolerated on most public beaches, though notable exceptions include the Dead Sea shore, the Mediterranean coast north of Nahariya and in the Gaza Strip. Be careful, theft is very common on beaches, especially in Eilat, Tel Aviv and Haifa.

Hostels

Israel had, at last count, 32 HI-affiliated hostels. In the Dead Sea region and Mitzpe Ramon they are the sole budget accommodation choice but elsewhere privately owned hostels usually offer better value and service. For a list of HI hostels and further information contact the Israel Youth Hostels Association (☎ (02) 625 2706; fax 625 0676) at 3 Dorot Rishonim St, Jerusalem 91009.

Kibbutz Guesthouses

The kibbutzim have had to search for alternatives to agriculture for income, and in recent years they have been developing the guesthouse concept. They mainly fit into the middle price range and have good facilities such as swimming pools or beaches, renowned restaurants and special activities for guests. The Kibbutz Hotels Reservations Office (☎ (03) 524 6161; fax 527 8088), 90 Ben Yehuda St, PO Box 3194, Tel Aviv 61031, publishes a booklet listing all their hotels, restaurants and camp sites with prices, amenities and a map (also available at government tourist offices).

B&Bs

In many popular tourist areas you will find accommodation in private homes. In some places they form the bulk of moderately priced rooms. They can be found by enquiring at the local tourist office, looking for signs posted in the street or in some places by simply hanging out at the bus station with your bags.

Hotels

In comparison to the number of lower and mid-price beds available, Israel has a disproportionately high percentage of luxury accommodation. Prices at these hotels compare favourably with those in other parts of the world and attuned as they are to a predominantly North American clientele, the facilities and level of service are top class.

FOOD

Despite constant claims that Israel has an incredible variety of international cuisine due to its worldwide immigration, you'll find much of the food expensive and disappointing.

Budget travellers can shop in the street markets, grocery shops and supermarkets, choose from the good range of quality vegetables and fruit and cook for themselves in their hostel's communal kitchen.

Much of what's on offer is little different from standard Middle Eastern fare with the exception of the traditional Eastern European dishes such as schnitzel, goulash and gefilte fish.

Kashrut & Kosher

Kashrut is the noun derived from the adjective 'kosher' which, roughly translated, means 'ritually acceptable'. Jewish law dictates which foods can be eaten and how they should be prepared and served. For example, all fruit and vegetables can be eaten, but certain meats and fish cannot: eg pork and shellfish. It is forbidden to eat meat and dairy products together or prepare them with the same utensils. Foods which are neither milk nor meat are *parve* or *pareve*. Prepared, they may be used with milk or meat.

Kosher restaurants serve either meat or dairy products, and they will not serve cheeseburgers, a cream sauce with chicken, or tea with milk in a meat restaurant.

DRINKS

Although alcohol is absolutely permissible Israelis do not drink very much. Usually, wine is only drunk on holy days such as Shabbat and during Passover. Spirits are hardly touched at all. However, vines and wines have existed in Israel since 3000 BC, making it one of the world's oldest wine-producing areas. Notable wine producers here are Christian monks.

Israel also has a national brewery and its product, bottled under the labels Maccabee and Gold Star, isn't bad.

ENTERTAINMENT

Israel has a much more liberal society than its Middle East neighbours. You can find an increasing number of bars in most towns, along with different versions of discos and live music venues. For more traditional nightlife, Jerusalem, Tel Aviv and Beersheba, in particular, feature venues where Israeli folk dancing and traditional live music from the Diaspora are regularly performed. Classical music concerts are frequently staged throughout the country.

For sports fans, Israel's small population and political isolation reduces the choice of spectator sports to soccer, basketball, the occasional tennis tournament and the Maccabeeah Games (a Jewish Olympics).

Arab entertainment sources are limited to music from the neighbouring Arab nations, most notably Egypt, and a small theatre in East Jerusalem (see Jerusalem).

THINGS TO BUY

Israel is full of shops stocked with tacky souvenirs more expensive than in neighbouring countries. To find bargains and quality items you will need time to shop around and patience to haggle. It is hard to think of much in Israel that will appeal to budget travellers that cannot be found for less elsewhere in the Middle East. Exceptions are items of religious interest and Armenian ceramics.

Getting There & Away

AIR

Airfares to Israel vary considerably, depending on the season. July to September and Jewish holidays in particular mean much higher prices. It is often difficult to get a flight out of Israel in a hurry, so think carefully before getting there on a one-way ticket. There is a choice of carriers from the USA, Canada, the UK and Europe. Many, especially Jews and Americans, prefer to fly El Al for security reasons. In all locations, consult the advertisements in Sunday newspapers and do not rely on your local travel agent for the lowest price. Eastern European carriers offer the cheapest tickets, although their bad reputations are deserved. Charter flights are the most popular budget option from the UK and Europe.

There are no direct flights between Australia/New Zealand and Israel. One option is to buy RTW tickets with, say Qantas or British Airways (about A$2700), with a side trip to Israel. If you are flexible, you can be better off flying to London or Athens and then looking for a cheap ticket. When checking out fares also look into flights to Ovda, a small airport just outside Eilat which is commonly used by cheap charters.

There are El Al and Air Sinai flights available between Israel and Egypt, which avoid an Egypt-Israel border stamp in your passport; about US$130 one way.

Cheap Tickets in Israel

Despite the long queues, the Israel Student Travel Association (ISSTA) offices do not always offer very competitive fares. See the Travel Agencies listings under Information in the individual city entries. It's worth checking around the hostels and travellers' bars as many of these advertise cut-price flights. In Tel Aviv, for example, ask at the No 1, Greenhouse or Gordon hostels and look at the noticeboard in The Leprechaun bar; in Jerusalem ask at the Al-Arab, Palm or Tabasco hostels; and in Eilat try at Max & Merran's. The average cheapest prices that we saw were US$180 single to London and US$280 to New York.

LAND

Egypt and Jordan have open land borders with Israel; Lebanon and Syria do not. If you are planning to visit either of these last two then do so before going to Israel, as evidence of a visit to the Jewish state will without exception bar you from entry (see the Israeli Stamp Stigma in the Visas & Documents section earlier this chapter).

Private cars may cross the borders but not taxis or hire cars. Drivers and riders of motorcycles will need the vehicle's registration papers and liability insurance, although for Israel an international drivers' permit is not necessary – a domestic licence will do.

Egypt

There are two border crossing points, Rafah and Taba, and which one you use depends on where you are in Israel and whether it's Sinai you're heading for or Cairo.

Note, if your visit to Egypt is confined to just Sinai (crossing at Taba only) then no Egyptian visa is necessary – you'll be issued a 14 day pass at the border.

Tel Aviv & Jerusalem Tour operators provide coach services from Tel Aviv and Jerusalem nonstop to Cairo via the border at Rafah in the Gaza Strip (where there is a change of bus). The journey takes roughly 10 hours and a ticket from Tel Aviv or Jerusalem is about US$30 one way or US$45 return. To that has to be added an Israeli departure tax of 90 NIS (US$30) (payable usually to the bus company) and an Egyptian entry tax of E£7 (US$2.50). You can change money at the border.

There are two main operators:

Egged Tours
  Tel Aviv: 59 Ben Yehuda St (☎ (03) 371 101). Daily departures at 8.30 am.
  Jerusalem: 224 Jaffa Rd, by the bus station (☎ (02) 304 883). Buses depart Thursday and Sunday at 6.30 am.
Mazada Tours
  Tel Aviv: 141 Ibn Gvirol St (☎ (03) 544 4454). Daily buses departing at 9 am, arriving Cairo 7 pm. Also Tuesday, Thursday and Sunday overnight buses departing 8.30 pm arriving 7 am next morning.
  Jerusalem: 9 Koresh St (☎ (02) 623 5777). Buses depart Monday to Friday at 7.30 am. There are also overnight services on Tuesday and Thursday, departing 7 pm.

Alternatively, you can do it yourself from Tel Aviv. An Egged bus departs for Rafah (also spelt Rafiah) at 9 am each day from the central bus station. The journey takes about two hours and costs 27 NIS. After passing through Israeli immigration catch the shuttle bus (approx US$2) over to the Egyptian hall. Once through procedures there you can catch a local Egyptian bus or service taxi for Cairo, some five hours distant.

Eilat This is the most convenient place to cross if you are planning a visit to Sinai. The border is open 24 hours but this is subject to occasional change and you will want to time your crossing to be able to find transport on the other side. Unlike Rafah, where you can be held up for three or four hours, it's normally possible to stroll through the formalities at Taba in around 30 minutes. There is a 50 NIS (US$16) Israeli departure tax to be paid at Taba as well as a E£24 (US$8) Egyptian entry tax. Visitors to Taba only are exempt from these payments.

Once on the Egyptian side change money at the Taba Hilton and then it's a further one km walk to the small tourist village and the bus stop.

Jordan

The Allenby/Hussein Bridge which until very recently served as the only meeting point of the two neighbours has been supplemented by two other crossings.

Allenby/King Hussein Bridge This crossing is only 30 km from Jerusalem on one side and 40 km from Amman on the other. You can get here easily by taking a 30 NIS service taxi from opposite Damascus Gate in Jerusalem – ask for 'Al-Malek al-Hussein' not Allenby Bridge, which is the Israeli name and may not be understood. The journey takes about 45 minutes. Remember, anyone turning up here without a valid visa will be sent back. However, the flip side is that the Jordanian officials here can be asked not to stamp visa holders' passports – this is the only crossing at which travellers looking to move on to Syria or Lebanon can avoid incriminating evidence of a trip to Israel.

ISRAEL

Crossing can take anything up to three hours depending on the traffic – try to avoid being there between 11 am and 3 pm which is the busiest time. The Israeli exit tax is 83.50 NIS (and rising all the time).

The bridge is open Sunday to Thursday from 8 am to 10.30 pm, and Friday and Saturday from 8 am to 1 pm, although these times are subject to frequent change and it's advisable to check with the tourist office in Jerusalem.

From Tel Aviv there are two buses a day (7 am and 2 pm), Saturdays excepted, departing the central bus station for the King Hussein Bridge (23 NIS) which are met on the Jordanian side by an onward bus to Amman.

Jordan River The least used of the three border crossings is six km east of Beit She'an up in the Galilee region and not particularly convenient for anywhere. However, if you don't already have your Jordanian visa they are issued here and it is considerably closer to Jerusalem than the Arava crossing at Eilat – take a Tiberias bus and change at Beit She'an for a bus for the border (8.40 NIS). Once across the border, however, you're in the middle of nowhere. The options are to take a minibus to Irbid (JD0.30) or take a taxi to the main road some three km distant from where you can try and hitch on to somewhere more life-supporting.

The border is open Sunday to Thursday from 8 am to 8 pm, and Friday and Saturday from 8 am to 5 pm. The Israeli exit tax here is 50 NIS.

The Jordanians refer to this crossing as Jisr Sheikh Hussein (Sheikh Hussein Bridge) and you may see it marked on some maps as such.

Arava Opened in August 1994 this crossing (known as Wadi Araba to the Jordanians) is just two km north-east of central Eilat. The huge volume of coach traffic at this crossing often means lengthy delays of up to three hours. The border is open for business Sunday to Thursday from 6.30 am to 10 pm, and Friday and Saturday from 8 am to 8 pm.

There's an Israeli exit tax of 48.70 NIS and anyone without a Jordanian visa can get one here. Both sides have money changing facilities but the Jordanians offer far more favourable rates.

A direct bus service between Eilat and Aqaba was due to start in late 1996 – enquire at Eilat central bus station or new tourist office for the latest information.

SEA

Israel is connected via Haifa to mainland Europe with a regular ferry service from Piraeus, near Athens in Greece. The Piraeus-Haifa run usually involves a stopover in Rhodes, or sometimes in Crete instead, with all ferries stopping additionally at Limassol in Cyprus. Departures at the time of writing were every Thursday and Saturday with an additional Friday sailing for Cyprus only.

The cheapest tickets to Piraeus are US$77 for deck, US$85 for a pullman seat and from US$100 per person in a four-berth cabin. Students and under-26s get a discount of about 20%. These prices are for one-way voyages in the low season; in the high season (July to the end of September) prices go up by about 15%. For return voyages, 20% reductions are made (although not from the student and under-26 prices).

Buying Your Ticket

There are two major ferry companies, the Stability Line (☎ (01) 413 2392; 11 Sachtouri St, Piraeus) whose Israeli agent is Jacob Caspi, and Afroessa Lines (☎ (01) 418 3777; 1 Harilaou Tricoupi St, Piraeus) whose Israeli agent is Mano Passenger Lines:

Caspi
    Tel Aviv: 1 Ben Yehuda St, Migdalor Building (☎ (03) 517 5749)
    Haifa: 76 Ha' Atzmaut St (☎ (04) 867 4449)
Mano Passenger Lines
    Tel Aviv: 97 Ben Yehuda St (☎ (03) 522 4611)
    Haifa: 39/41 HaMeginim Ave (☎ (04) 835 1631)

In Jerusalem try Allalouf & Co Shipping (☎ (02) 625 2344; fax 624 9805) at 3 Yanei St, off HaMelekh David St. It may also be worth enquiring at the Al-Arab hostel

ISRAEL

(☎ (02) 628 3527) on Souk Khan as-Zeit St in the Old City – they claim to be able to get the cheapest ferry tickets to Cyprus and Greece.

When you buy your ticket make a point of asking what time you need to show up at the port; the Friday departure for Cyprus is at 7 pm but the port closes up at 1 pm and anyone arriving later won't be able to get in.

Getting Around

AIR
Arkia, Israel's domestic airline (which also flies overseas) operates flights variously between Jerusalem, Tel Aviv, Haifa, Rosh Pina and Eilat. With Israel's short driving distances, such flights are not viable for most travellers.

BUS
Israel's small size and excellent road system have combined to make bus travel the choice of public transport to be developed. Israel's bus network is dominated by Egged, the second largest bus company in the world, after Greyhound. For information on schedules and prices call ☎ 1770-225 555 (no area code).

In Nazareth, East Jerusalem and the West Bank around 30 small Arab companies provide buses. While the Jewish buses tend to be modern, air-conditioned, cleaner and faster, Arab services are antiquated and slow.

Fares are generally very cheap and ISIC holders are entitled to a discount of about 10% on inter-urban fares.

Jewish bus schedules are affected by public holidays and these buses usually don't run at all on Shabbat. Arab buses operate every day as normal.

TRAIN
The small passenger network of the Israel State Railways (IRS) is even cheaper than the buses but, due to the location of most of the stations away from city and town centres, it is less convenient. ISIC holders get a 20%

discount. The main line is from Tel Aviv Central (North) to Haifa, with some trains continuing to Nahariya. There is a daily train running in each direction between Haifa and Jerusalem.

TAXI
Sherut/Service Taxi
Like its neighbours, Israel is the land of the shared taxi. Most commonly called the *sherut*, the Arabs call it the service taxi, or taxi service. On Shabbat, sheruts provide the only transport on certain major intercity routes. In the West Bank, where Egged is limited to Jewish settlements, the service taxis save hours of travelling time compared to the local Arab buses.

Special Taxis
Drivers of 'special' (ie non-shared) taxis have a lousy reputation for overcharging, unhelpfulness and being impolite. Be sure that the meter is used; tourist offices can advise how much to pay. Taxi drivers are not normally tipped.

CAR & MOTORCYCLE
Good roads, beautiful scenery and short distances make Israel a great place to hire a car. Also, in places like the Golan and the Negev, the buses do not cover so much ground and having your own vehicle can help you to really see the area. If you are on a tight budget, a few people sharing a car can still be the most economical way to see specific areas, if not the whole country. Eldan and Reliable are cheaper local firms.

With overland entry to Israel so limited, bringing your own vehicle makes little sense.

BICYCLE
If planning a bicycle tour, bear in mind the hot climate, frequent rainfall in certain areas, innumerable steep hills, and the fact that most drivers fail to recognise your status as a road user. Despite these factors, there are a few cyclists to be seen pedalling around.

HITCHING
This was once a common way for locals and

travellers to get around Israel. Hitching is still possible but not as easy as it used to be. Women should not hitchhike without male company. Israelis are actively encouraged to give lifts to male soldiers, so bear in mind that if you are hitchhiking you will be last in line for a lift if there are any soldiers to be seen. Female soldiers are now forbidden to hitchhike because of potential dangers.

Sticking out your thumb is not the locally accepted way to advertise to drivers that you are hitchhiking. The local signal is to point to the road with your index finger.

Jerusalem

Jerusalem, highly disputed capital of Israel, is perhaps the most fascinating city in the world, as well as one of the most beautiful. It is, surely, the holiest city of all.

History

Originally a small Jebusite settlement on the slopes of Mt Moriah, Jerusalem was captured in 997 BC by the Israelite King David, who made it his capital. Mt Moriah was the plateau on which Abraham, patriarch of the Jews, is said to have offered his son as a sacrifice to God, and so on this site David's son and successor, Solomon, built the great First Temple which though long gone still remains central to the Jewish faith. The temple was destroyed during the conquest of Nebuchadnezzar, King of Babylon, in 586 BC and the Jews suffered their first period of exile.

The Babylonians gave way to the Persians under whose benevolent rule the Jews were allowed to return and reconstruct the temple (the 'Second Temple'). The Persians went, swept aside by Alexander the Great who died shortly after to be succeeded by the Seleucid dynasty which in turn collapsed before the Romans around 63 BC. Herod the Great was installed to rule what the Romans called the Kingdom of Judea. Later, the city was administered through a series of procurators;

Pontius Pilate, who ordered the crucifixion of Jesus, was the fifth.

Jesus had very little impact on the course of history while he was alive and it wasn't until some 300 or more years after his death with the conversion of Constantine that the ministry of the Nazarene began to make any historical impact. He was one of many orators critical of the materialism and decadence of the wealthy Jerusalemites, and contemptuous of Roman authority. The swell of discontent flooded into open revolt in 66 AD (the First Revolt) resulting in the Romans destruction of the Second Temple. A Second Revolt occurring in 132 AD took the Romans four years to put down and in its aftermath they banished the Jews from Jerusalem and all Palestine. The Jews were scattered north to Babylon and Europe and west across northern Africa to Spain creating a Diaspora which, in popular myth, remained in exile until the creation of the State of Israel in 1948. The Romans also razed Jewish Jerusalem and rebuilt the city as Aelia Capitolina, the basis of today's Old City.

The conversion of the Eastern Roman Emperor Constantine to Christianity in 331 AD and the religion's subsequent legalisation triggered a wave of biblically inspired building in the 'Holy City', with churches and monasteries being erected over many of the sites associated with the life of Jesus.

After weathering a short-lived invasion by the Persians, the Byzantines buckled under the sudden onslaught of Islam. Jerusalem fell in 638 AD and was designated a Holy City of Islam because of the Muslim belief that their Prophet Mohammed had ascended to heaven from within its walls. For a time Christians, Muslims and Jews were all permitted access to the city but persecution of non-Muslims in the 10th century led to the Crusades. The Christian knights held the city from 1099 but lost it to Salah ad-Din (known to the west as Saladin) in 1187 who did, however, once again open the city to all faiths.

In 1517 the Ottoman Turks absorbed Jerusalem into their expanding empire and the city remained under rule from Istanbul for

ISRAEL

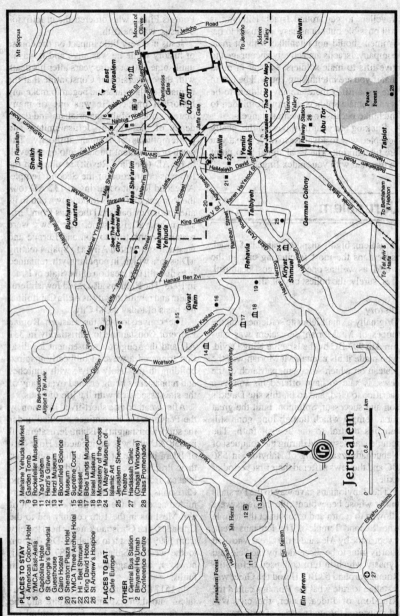

Jerusalem

PLACES TO STAY
4 American Colony Hotel
5 YMCA East-Aelia
   Capitolina Hotel
6 St George's Cathedral
   Guesthouse
8 Cairo Hostel
20 Sheraton Plaza Hotel
21 YMCA Three Arches Hotel
22 HI - Beit Shmuel
23 King David Hotel
26 St Andrew's Hospice

PLACES TO EAT
7 Cafe Europe

OTHER
1 Central Bus Station
2 Binyanei Ha'Uma
   Conference Centre

3 Mahane Yehuda Market
9 Garden Tomb
10 Rockefeller Museum
11 Yad Vashem
12 Herzl's Grave
13 Herzl Museum
14 Bloomfield Science
   Museum
15 Supreme Court
16 Knesset
17 Bible Lands Museum
18 Israel Museum
19 Monastery of the Cross
24 L.A. Mayer Museum of
   Islamic Art
25 Jerusalem Sherover
   Theatre
27 Hadassah Clinic
   (Chagall Windows)
28 Haas Promenade

400 years. However, Turkish interest in the region was minimal and a vacuum existed in which petty landlords fought for authority. It was into this vacuum that large numbers of Jewish immigrants began arriving from the mid-19th century on.

Jerusalem became a hotbed of Arab-Jewish nationalistic struggles which intensified during the 1930s. A proposal put forward by the British, successors in Jerusalem to the Ottomans, to make the city an international enclave were rejected. The city was fought over in 1948 with the end result that the Arabs got the Old City and East Jerusalem while the Jews held the western, newer parts of the city.

The Six Day War in 1967 saw the city re-unified under Israeli rule. The city continues to play a key role in the Palestine problem. According to opponents of Israel, the Jewish state has no right to declare Jerusalem its capital. There is a sincere resentment among Arabs of what Israel has done and continues to do, regardless of the many cosmetic changes made. The Israelis, meanwhile, are determined to maintain Jerusalem as capital regardless of opposition.

Orientation

Jerusalem can be divided into three parts: the walled Old City; predominantly Arab East Jerusalem; and the rapidly expanding Jewish New City (also referred to as West Jerusalem).

Information

Tourist Offices The main city tourist office (☎ 625 8844) is at 17 Jaffa Rd, just northwest of the Old City walls. It's open Sunday to Thursday from 8.30 am to 4.30 pm, and Friday from 8.30 am to noon; closed on Saturday. There is also a tourist office just inside Jaffa Gate in the Old City.

The Christian Information Centre (☎ 627 2692; fax 286 417) on Omar ibn al-Khattab Square, opposite the entrance to the Citadel, is very good on everything pertaining to the city's Christian sites. Practising Catholics apply here for tickets for the Christmas Eve Midnight Mass in Bethlehem. The centre is open Monday to Saturday from 8.30 am to 1 pm; closed Sunday. The Jewish Student Information Centre (☎ 628 2643; fax 628 8338; email jseidel@jer1.co.il) is at 5 Beit El St in the Jewish Quarter of the Old City (adjacent to the Hurva Synagogue).

Money If you want the best deal when changing money, go to the legal moneychangers in the Old City and East Jerusalem. The two just inside Damascus Gate seem to give a better price than anywhere else. The moneychanger just inside the Petra Hostel near Jaffa Gate seems to be open when the others are closed. In the New City go to Change Point at 33 Jaffa Rd or 2 Ben Yehuda St, neither of which charge commission. Both close early on Friday and are closed all day Saturday.

The American Express Travel office (☎ 623 1710; fax 623 1520) is at 40 Jaffa Rd in the New City; the local agent for Thomas Cook is Awadieh Tours (☎ 628 2365; fax 628 2366) at 23 Salah ad-Din St in East Jerusalem.

Post & Communications The main post office (☎ 624 4745) and poste restante is at 23 Jaffa Rd. The main section is open Sunday to Thursday from 7 am to 7 pm, and Friday 7 am to noon; closed Saturday.

For discount international telephone calls go to Solan Telecom which is at 2 Luntz, a small pedestrianised street running between Jaffa Rd and Ben Yehuda St. It's open 24 hours a day, seven days a week. The telephone code for Jerusalem is 02.

Travel Agencies The student travel agency ISSTA (☎ 625 7257) is at 31 HaNevi'im St, open Sunday to Tuesday and Thursday from 9 am to 6 pm, and Wednesday and Friday from 9 am to 1 pm; closed Saturday. Egged Tours (☎ 625 3454) is at 44A and 224 Jaffa Rd, while Mazada Tours (☎ 623 5777), which operates a bus service to Cairo, is at 9 Koresh St, almost behind the Jaffa Rd tourist information office.

Bookshops Steimatzky has three branches in Jerusalem's New City all within a couple

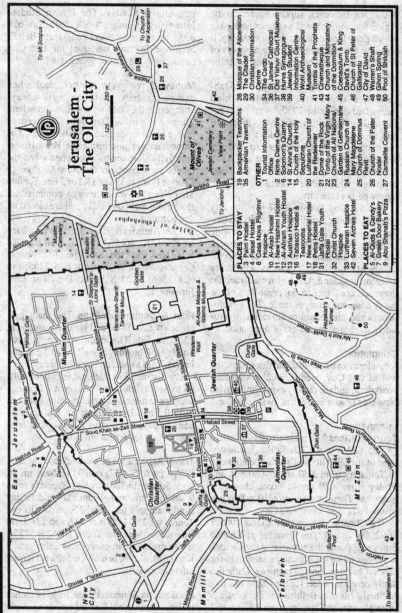

Jerusalem – The Old City

0   125   250 m

of hundred metres of each other; they're at 39 Jaffa Rd, just east of Zion Square, at 7 Ben Yehuda St and at 9 King George V St. Probably Jerusalem's best bookshop, however, is Sefer VeSefel, a creaky little place with floor to ceiling new and second-hand titles, fiction and nonfiction. It's upstairs at 2 Ya'Avetz St, which is a little alley linking Jaffa Rd with Hillel St. It's open Sunday to Thursday from 8 am to 8 pm, Friday 8 am to 2.30 pm and Saturdays from the end of Shabbat to 11.30 pm.

Laundry With only two machines but plenty of charm, coffee and good home cooking while you wait, Tzipor Hanefesh (☎ 624 9890) is a friendly three storey cafe/laundrette. One machine load costs 7 NIS and a 45 minute drying cycle costs the same. It's at 10 Rivlin St, in the trendy central area of Nahalat Shiv'a.

Medical Services
In case of medical emergencies call ☎ 101 or contact the Magen David Adom (☎ 523 133). In the Old City, the Orthodox Society (☎ 627 1958), on Greek Orthodox Patriarchate Rd in the Christian Quarter, operates a low-cost clinic that, we're told, welcomes travellers. It also does dental surgery. The clinic is open Monday to Saturday from 8 am to 3 pm; closed Sunday.

Emergency The central police station (in emergencies dial ☎ 100) is in the Russian Compound in the New City. The city's lost & found office is also here. The city's rape crisis centre can be contacted on ☎ 514 4550.

The Old City
Tightly bound by muscular stone walls, the Old City is divided into four quarters (Armenian, Christian, Jewish and Muslim) and focused on three centres of gravity: the Haram ash-Sharif (Temple Mount) site of the Dome of the Rock; the Jewish Western Wall; and the Church of the Holy Sepulchre, built over the site of the Crucifixion.

Walls, Gates & the Citadel The Old City

walls are the legacy of Süleyman the Magnificent and were built between 1537 and 1542, but have been extensively renovated since. One of the best ways to see the Old City and its surroundings is to stroll around the ramparts. It isn't possible to make a complete circuit of the wall because the Haram ash-Sharif stretch is sealed off for security reasons. Instead the walk is in two sections: Jaffa Gate north to St Stephen's Gate (via New, Damascus and Herod's Gates) and Jaffa Gate south to Dung Gate (via Zion Gate). While you can descend at any of the gates, getting up onto the walls is only possible at Jaffa and Damascus. Women should not do this walk alone because of the danger of assault or sexual harassment.

There are seven open gates. The recently restored **Jaffa Gate**, so named because it was the start of the old road to Jaffa, is now the main way of entry to the Old City from the New City. It's dominated by the minaret and towers of the **Citadel (Tower of David)** – one of the country's most impressive restoration projects, and a major museum complex which is definitely worth a visit.

Moving clockwise **New Gate**, which also gives access to the New City, is the most recent gate and dates from 1887. Down the hill, **Damascus Gate**, which gives access to/from East Jerusalem, is both the most attractive and the most crowded of all the city gates. **Herod's Gate** also faces Arab East Jerusalem; it was close to here that the Crusaders first breached Jerusalem's walls in 1099.

St Stephen's Gate, facing the Mount of Olives, is named for the first Christian martyr, who was stoned nearby. The curious name of **Dung Gate** may be due to its location nearby what was the local rubbish dump. Its official name is Gate of the Moors because North African immigrants lived nearby in the 16th century. **Zion Gate** became known as the Gate of the Jewish Quarter in late medieval times and the many bullet marks are signs of the fierce fighting that took place here during the 1948 War.

Haram ash-Sharif & Dome of the Rock
The Haram ash-Sharif (Temple Mount to the

ISRAEL

Jews) is the biblical Mt Moriah on which Abraham was instructed by God to sacrifice his son in a test of his faith. Today it's a tranquil flat paved area the size of a couple of adjacent football pitches, fringed with some attractive Mamluk buildings and with the distinctive **Dome of the Rock** mosque positioned roughly in the centre. The Dome was built between 688 and 691 by the Caliph Omar over the sacred sacrificial rock, also the spot from which the Prophet Mohammed ascended to heaven.

To the south of the Dome is the 10th century **Al-Aqsa Mosque** and beside it an uninspiring **Islamic Museum**.

There are nine gates connecting the enclosure to the surrounding narrow streets but although you can leave the compound by any of them, non-Muslims are only allowed to enter through two (the gate at the end of Bab as-Silsila St and another gate approached from the Western Wall piazza).

Entrance to the Haram itself is free, but to visit the two mosques (highly recommended) and the museum, a ticket must be purchased. Visiting hours are slightly confusing as they are based around Muslim prayer schedules which follow the lunar calendar. Basically, the Haram is open Saturday to Thursday from 8 am to 3 pm. During prayers (approximately 11.30 am to 12.30 pm winter and 12.30 to 1.30 pm summer) the museum shuts and entry to the mosques is for Muslims only. Note also that during the month of Ramadan the Haram is only open from 7.30 to 10 am and it is completely closed on Muslim holidays such as the Eid. Visitors must be suitably dressed.

Western Wall The Western Wall is part of the retaining wall built by Herod in 20 BC to support the Temple's esplanade. As such it is the only remaining physical evidence of what was the Jew's most holy ancient shrine. The area immediately in front of the Wall now operates as a great open-air synagogue.

The Wall is accessible 24 hours daily, no admission. We very much recommend that you make several visits here at different times of the day especially at sundown on Friday.

The Jewish Quarter Flattened during the fighting in 1948, the Jewish Quarter has been almost entirely reconstructed since its recapture by the Israelis in 1967. There are few historic monuments above ground level but the digging that went on during construction unearthed a number of interesting archaeological finds, the most significant of which is **The Cardo** the main (north-south) street of Roman and Byzantine Jerusalem. A part of it has been restored to something like its original appearance while the rest has been reconstructed as an arcade of expensive gift stores and galleries of Judaica.

West of the Cardo is the **Old Yishuv Court Museum** at 6 Or HaChaim St, set up as a house with each room showing an aspect of Jewish life in the Quarter before the destruction of 1948; east of the Cardo is Hurva Square identifiable by its graceful landmark of a lone single-brick arch, almost all that remains of the **Hurva Synagogue**. Down a narrow alleyway off the east side of the square is the **Wohl Archaeological Museum**, perhaps the Jewish Quarter's most impressive complex, featuring renovated examples of the houses of wealthy Jews in Herod's Upper City.

The Muslim Quarter This is the most bustling and densely populated area of the Old City and depending on your tastes it's either claustrophobic and a hassle or completely exhilarating. Clustered around the Haram ash-Sharif in narrow medieval alleys are some fine examples of **Mamluk architecture** while down by St Stephen's Gate is **St Anne's Church**, the finest example of Crusader architecture in Jerusalem. The road leading from St Stephen's Gate down into the heart of the Old City is the **Via Dolorosa**, the route traditionally believed to have been followed by Jesus as he carried his cross to Calvary. Though the biblical connection is of dubious authenticity, the Franciscan Fathers lead a procession along the Via Dolorosa every Friday at 3 pm.

The Christian Quarter The Christian Quarter is centred around the **Church of the Holy Sepulchre** which occupies the site generally agreed to be where Jesus was crucified, buried and resurrected. The church is a messy collision of styles, originally Byzantine, extensively rebuilt by the Crusaders and interfered with since and tarted up on numerous occasions since – the interior has best been described as looking like 'a cross between a building site and a used furniture depot'. The church is open daily to anyone suitably dressed. It's worth visiting the neighbouring **Lutheran Church of the Redeemer** for the excellent views over the Old City from the tower.

The Armenian Quarter & Mt Zion This small and secluded quarter is not much visited but the Armenian **St James' (Jacques') Cathedral** has a sensuous aura of ritual and mystery lacking from every other Christian site in this most holy of cities. Unfortunately the church is only open for services, held Monday to Friday from 6.30 to 7.15 am and 2.45 to 3.30 pm, and Saturday and Sunday from 2.30 to 3 pm.

The Armenian Quarter's Zion Gate leads out to Mt Zion, site of the **Coenaculum** (also known as the Cenacle), traditionally held to be where the Last Supper took place. On the other side of the same building is **David's Tomb**, claimed resting place of the legendary Jewish king, while around the corner is the **Church & Monastery of the Dormition** where the Virgin Mary fell into 'eternal sleep'.

Mount of Olives East of the Old City, reached through St Stephen's Gate, the Mount of Olives is where Jesus was arrested and later ascended to heaven. There are several interesting churches here as well as the biblical **Garden of Gethsemane** and the attractive **Tomb of the Virgin Mary**. However, the biggest draw is the **panorama** of the Old City from the top of the mount – visit early in the morning for the best light. Sadly, Lonely Planet has received a number of letters from women readers who suffered unpleasant experiences whilst walking around here and so we have to advise females not to visit alone.

East Jerusalem
The modern, blaring, fume-hazed Palestinian part of Jerusalem, this is a district of small businesses, shops and aged hotels. On Sultan Suleyman St, just outside the Old City walls, the **Rockefeller Museum** has some impressive archaeological and architectural exhibits although the presentation is off-puttingly dour and musty compared to other more modern Israeli museums. Opposite the Sultan Suleyman St bus station **Solomon's Quarry** is a vast cave beneath the north wall of the Old City – while there's little to see it does offer cool refuge on a hot day. On Nablus Rd the **Garden Tomb** is a pretty spot, believed by some to be the site of Jesus' death and resurrection.

The New City
The New City is roughly centred on the triangle of Jaffa Rd, King George V St and pedestrianised Ben Yehuda St but the most colourful and bustling district is **Mahane Yehuda**, the Jewish food market. Possibly one of the world's most reluctant tourist attractions the Ultraorthodox Jewish district of **Mea She'arim** is the only remaining example of a *shtetl* (ghetto) as existed in pre-Holocaust Eastern Europe. Dress conservatively and photograph with discretion. The Holocaust itself is remembered at **Yad Vashem**, a moving memorial and museum complex on the outskirts of town at the edge of the Jerusalem Forest.

The country's major museum complex is the **Israel Museum**, just west of the New City. An assemblage of several major collections it has an excellent art section and includes the Shrine of the Book, which houses some of the Dead Sea Scrolls.

Organised Tours
Coach A good introduction to the city is Egged Tours' **Route 99**, Circular Line. This service takes you on a comfortable coach to 36 of the major sites, with basic commentary

ISRAEL

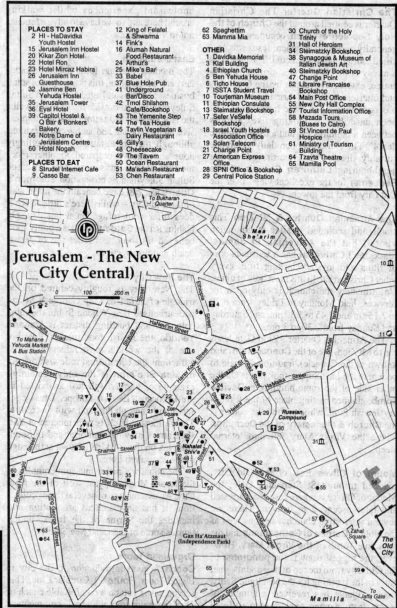

PLACES TO STAY
2 HI - HaDavidka Youth Hostel
15 Jerusalem Inn Hostel
20 Kikar Zion Hotel
22 Hotel Ron
23 Hotel Mircaz Habira
26 Jerusalem Inn Guesthouse
32 Jasmine Ben Yehuda Hostel
35 Jerusalem Tower
36 Eyal Hotel
39 Capitol Hostel & Q Bar & Bonkers Bakery
56 Notre Dame of Jerusalem Centre
60 Hotel Nogah

PLACES TO EAT
8 Strudel Internet Cafe
9 Casso Bar
12 King of Felafel & Shwarma
16 Alumah Natural Food Restaurant
24 Arthur's
33 Babel
37 Blue Hole Pub
41 Underground Bar/Disco
42 Tmol Shilshom Cafe/Bookshop
43 The Yemenite Step
44 The Tea House
45 Tavlin Vegetarian & Dairy Restaurant
46 Gilly's
48 Cheesecake
49 The Tavern
50 Ocean Restaurant
51 Ma'adan Restaurant
53 Chen Restaurant

14 Fink's
62 Spaghettim
63 Mamma Mia

OTHER
1 Davidka Memorial
3 Klal Building
4 Ethiopian Church
5 Ben Yehuda House
6 Ticho House
7 ISSTA Student Travel
10 Tourjeman Museum
11 Ethiopian Consulate
13 Steimatzky Bookshop
17 Sefer VeSefel Bookshop
18 Israel Youth Hostels Association Office
19 Solan Telecom
21 Change Point
27 American Express Office
28 SPNI Office & Bookshop
29 Central Police Station

30 Church of the Holy Trinity
31 Hall of Heroism
34 Steimatzky Bookshop
38 Synagogue & Museum of Italian Jewish Art
40 Steimatzky Bookshop
47 Change Point
52 Libraire Francaise Bookshop
54 Main Post Office
55 New City Hall Complex
57 Tourist Information Office
58 Mazada Tours (Buses to Cairo)
59 St Vincent de Paul Hospice
61 Ministry of Tourism Building
64 Tzavta Theatre
65 Mamilla Pool

Jerusalem - The New City (Central)

0   100   200 m

in English (sort of) provided by the driver. The bus leaves from Ha'Emek St by Jaffa Gate but you can board at any of the stops and it's a continuous circular route (taking 1½ hours), ending up where it started.

Zion Walking Tours The three hour 'Four Quarters' tour of the Old City departing Sunday to Friday at 9 and 11 am and 2 pm, costing 24 NIS (students 18 NIS) per person, is particularly good value. Other tours include the Pre-Temple Period route, the Underground City of Jerusalem and Mea She'arim. Zion (☎ 628 7866; fax 629 0774) has its office on Omar ibn al-Khattab Square, opposite the entrance to the Citadel.

Free Walking Tours The municipal tourist office organises a free Saturday morning walking tour around a different part of the city each week. Meet at 10 am by the entrance to the Russian Compound at 32 Jaffa Rd.

The Jewish Student Information Centre (see Information earlier in this section) which is committed to giving young Jews a fresh awareness of being Jewish organises free walking tours of Jewish sites in the Old City's Jewish and Muslim quarters.

Places to Stay – hostels
The best location to stay really depends on your requirements. The Old City and East Jerusalem tend to have the cheapest places, the best atmosphere and, of course, they're the most convenient for the major sites nearby. However, some hostels and hospices have strict curfews, and being at least a good 20 minute walk from the New City centre nightlife, they aren't so great for those who want to stay out late (the Old City and East Jerusalem almost completely close down at dusk). On the other hand, with only one or two unappealing exceptions, accommodation in the New City tends to be considerably more expensive. If you plan to stay a week or more ask about reduced rates.

The Old City In the vicinity of Damascus Gate *Al-Arab* (☎ 628 3537) on Souq Khan

as-Zeit St has large airy dorms (beds 14 NIS), mattresses on the roof (12 NIS) and a couple of private double rooms at 40 NIS. Showers and toilet facilities are inadequate but there's a kitchen with free tea, a table tennis room and each night videos are shown in the cushion-strewn common room. The other main contender in the popularity stakes is the *Tabasco* (☎ 628 3461) just off Souq Khan as-Zeit (look for the sign overhead). This place is noisy, cramped and incredibly dirty but it has a lively atmosphere, a busy notice board, no curfew and downstairs is the Old City's most partyin' venue – dorm beds are 12 NIS, a mattress on the roof is 10 NIS and private rooms are 35 NIS.

Cleaner and quieter, dorms at the *New Hashimi Hostel* (☎ 628 4410; fax 628 4667), just two doors along from Al-Arab on Souq Khan as-Zeit, have only eight beds (15 NIS) and each room has its own shower and toilet, as do the very attractive private doubles at 90 NIS. There's a large common area with plenty of tables and chairs and a well-equipped kitchen. Reception is open 24 hours. Next to the mosque on Al-Wad Rd is the *Al-Ahram Youth Hostel* (☎ 628 0926), another fairly quiet and reasonably clean place that seems to attract an older crowd. Dorm beds are 15 NIS, less for a comfortable mattress up on the roof terrace. There is an enforced midnight curfew.

Across from the Al-Ahram, on the corner with the Via Dolorosa, is the almost monastic *Austrian Hospice* (☎ 627 1466), redeemed for many by the wonderful garden terraces which overlook the streets below. Dormitory beds are 30 NIS and doubles start at 120 NIS (for married couples only). There's a 10 pm curfew but a deposit gets you the keys to the door.

In the Jaffa Gate area, the *Jaffa Gate Youth Hostel* (☎ 627 6402) is a popular, occasionally crowded place with a kitchen and cosy TV lounge. Dorm beds are 25 NIS, doubles 90 NIS, and there's a midnight curfew. It's located behind the Christian Information Centre. The *Petra Hostel* (☎ 628 2356) has a superb location on Omar ibn al-Khattab Square and if you can get in a room with a

ISRAEL

balcony overlooking the action that's great but otherwise give it a miss.

Try for the *Lutheran Hospice* (☎ 628 2120, 628 5105; fax 628 5107), the closest thing we've ever seen to a 'five-star' hostel. There are shady cloisters, a huge spotless kitchen and a palm garden with a fountain and views of the Dome of the Rock. The dorms are single sex and beds are 22 NIS. The hospice is on St Mark's Rd, one block south of the David St bazaar, and is closed from 9 am to noon and has a strict 10.45 pm curfew, though you may stay out later if you inform the front desk of the time you'll be back.

East Jerusalem 'Hostel Row' is the stretch of HaNevi'im St across from Damascus Gate, beside the service taxi rank. There are four possibilities here but we only recommend two. The *Faisal Hostel* (☎ 627 2492) is the closest to the city walls and it has a nice terrace and a kitchen with free tea and coffee. Dorm beds (a bit cramped) are 12 or 15 NIS depending on the room and there are a few doubles at 50 NIS. There's a flexible 1 am curfew. The *Palm Hostel* (☎ 627 3189), next door to the Faisal, has a great common room with plants and a glass roof. There's also a kitchen with a fridge stocked with cold beers, and videos are shown most nights. There's no curfew. Beds in large spacious dorms are 16 NIS and there are a few private rooms at 60 NIS.

One street east and just north of the bus park is the *Cairo Hostel* (☎ 627 7216) at 21 Nablus St. It's a bit soulless and not particularly friendly but there's a large lounge with satellite TV and free coffee and tea in the kitchen. Dorm beds are 15 NIS or there are also some private rooms for 60 NIS that take three, maybe four people.

The New City The *Jerusalem Inn* (☎ 625 1294) at 6 HaHistradrut St, just off pedestrianised Ben Yehuda St, is kept immaculately clean and there's a no smoking policy. There's no kitchen but at the reception/bar area you can get breakfast, snacks, tea, coffee and beer. The place has a midnight curfew but a deposit will get you a front door key. Dorm beds are 42 NIS, singles are 96 NIS while doubles are from 120 NIS up.

Another good one is the *Jasmine Ben Yehuda Hostel* (☎ 624 8021; fax 625 3032) up on the 3rd floor at 23 Ben Yehuda St. Again, this place is clean and well run – there's no kitchen, but there's tea and coffee and breakfast if you want it. There's no curfew. Dorm beds are 30 NIS.

It is possible to get cheap beds at the *Capitol* (☎ 623 4582) – dorm beds are only 20 NIS – but the hostel is right above one of the city's loudest discos and as well as the noise you've got to deal with sinks clogged with vomit and cigarette butts.

There are several HI-affiliated hostels in the New City, the best of which is *HI-Beit Shmuel* (☎ 620 3466) at 6 Shama St, next to the Hebrew Union College near the junction of HaMelekh David and Agron Sts. Highly recommended, this place is more like a hotel than a hostel and it's only a few minutes walk from both the Old City and the central area of the New City. Dorm beds are around 50 NIS and there are usually also private singles/doubles for around 90/120 NIS, breakfast included.

Places to Stay – hotels & hospices
The Old City The *Christ Church Hospice* (☎ 627 7727; fax 627 7730) at Omar ibn al-Khattab Square, opposite the Citadel entrance, has pleasant staff and is very clean, quiet and comfortable, with a pretty courtyard and nice public rooms. Singles cost from US$35 to US$42, and doubles from US$64 to US$72. As well as its cheap dorm beds, the very popular *Lutheran Hospice* (see Hostels) has an attached guesthouse in which singles/doubles go for US$40/60, with breakfast provided.

The *Casa Nova Pilgrims' Hospice* (☎ 628 2791) run by the Franciscans has singles/doubles at US$35/60. It's at 10 Casa Nova St; from Jaffa Gate take the second left, Greek Catholic Patriarchate Rd, and follow it until it eventually becomes Casa Nova St. The *Greek Catholic Patriarchate Hospice* (☎ 628 2023) is a bit unfriendly but the basic singles/doubles (US$32/48) are comfortable and breakfast is included. It's on St Dimitri's Rd, also an extension of Greek Catholic Patriarchate Rd, and the hospice is on the right on the bend.

Although owned by the Greek Orthodox Church, the *New Imperial Hotel* (☎ 628 2261), on your left as you enter Jaffa Gate, has few religious trappings. It was built in the late 19th century and retains an air of dusty, faded grandeur although the rooms have all been cleaned up and are very comfortable. Singles/doubles are a bit of a bargain starting at US$20/35.

East Jerusalem One of the best accommodation deals in the city, *St George's Cathedral Guesthouse* (☎ 628 3302; fax 628 2253) is at 20 Nablus Rd, part of the St George's Cathedral compound, just 10 minutes walk from the Old City. It's a delightful cloistered building with an attractive garden. The atmosphere is very relaxed and friendly, with no curfew. The comfortable rooms, most with private bathroom, cost US$40/60 for singles/doubles, with breakfast.

On the same street but a little closer to Damascus Gate is the *YMCA East-Aelia Capitolina Hotel* (☎ 589 4271) at 29 Nablus Rd, next door to the US Consulate. The decor is dowdy but there are good facilities, including squash and tennis courts, and a swimming pool; singles/doubles are US$55/75.

The New City Facing New Gate (and just 10 minutes walk from the city centre) the guesthouse at the *Notre Dame of Jerusalem Centre* (☎ 627 9111; fax 627 1995) is one of the city's most attractive mid-range accommodation options. The rooms have three-star-style facilities while the majestic surroundings and views are unquantifiably excellent. Singles cost US$65 and doubles US$85, breakfast included. Similarly enchanting is the *YMCA Three Arches Hotel* (☎ 625 7111; fax 625 3438), probably the best-looking YMCA in the world. Guests also have free use of the pool, gym and the

squash and tennis courts. It's on HaMelekh David St and singles are US$90, doubles US$110.

Another place of great character is *St Andrew's Hospice* (☎ 673 2401; fax 673 1711). Belonging to the church of the same name, it has a friendly Scottish country house atmosphere – very comfortable and peaceful. Singles/doubles are US$55/75, with breakfast included. However, despite its appealing location near Bloomfield Park, overlooking Mt Zion and the Old City, the hospice is a little far away from the action. It's 15 to 20 minutes steep walking to Jaffa Gate and more than that to the New City centre.

In the New City centre the *Jerusalem Inn Guesthouse* (☎ 252 757; fax 251 297) has an almost Scandinavian looking interior with masses of open space and a large lounge and bar/restaurant. Prices are US$52/58. It's at 7 Horkenos St; from Zion Square head north up Eliashar St (look for MacDavid's on the corner), up the steps at the end and it's on the left. At 44 Jaffa Rd the *Hotel Ron* (☎ 253 471; fax 250 707) has large and reasonably pleasant rooms although those facing the front may be a little noisy; singles/doubles are US$49/59.

Places to Eat

The *Mahane Yehuda Market* is Jerusalem's cheapest source of food; cheaper even than the Old City. To save even more, go along just as the market closes (about 7.30 to 8.30 pm Sunday to Thursday, and 3 to 4 pm Friday) when prices are at their lowest. It's closed on Saturday.

The Old City There are surprisingly few felafel places in the Old City and none of them are particularly good. The most convenient is a stall at the bottom of the slope as you enter from Damascus Gate, in the narrow frontage between the two forking roads. As you face the felafel stall, 90° to your left is Aqabat ash-Sheikh Rihan St along which is the *Green Door Bakery*, where Mohammed Ali tends a furnace-like oven and bakes for the local neighbourhood.

ISRAEL

For travellers, he rustles up crude cheese, egg and tomato pizzas (4 NIS) while you wait.

Abu Shanab's at 35 Latin Patriarchate Rd (the first left as you enter Jaffa Gate) also specialises in pizza, made on the premises, which comes in three sizes: filling (10 NIS), very filling (15 NIS) and 'do you want half of this?' (25 NIS). Abu Shanab also does hot sandwiches, salads, lasagne and spaghetti, all in the 10 to 15 NIS range. It's open daily from 10 am to after midnight. The other travellers' favourite is the *Tabasco Tearooms* underneath the Tabasco hostel. The place is like a college common room, dimly lit, smoky and shaken by stereo but the food is extremely cheap (mainly fry-ups).

In the Jaffa Gate area is the *Armenian Tavern*, at 79 Armenian Orthodoxy Patriarchate Rd, which has a beautiful tiled interior with a fountain gently splashing in one corner. The strongly flavoured meat dishes (25 to 35 NIS) are without exception excellent and we recommend trying the khaghoghi derev, a spiced mince meat mixture bundled in vine leaves.

East Jerusalem Sultan Suleyman St running alongside the Old City walls is the premier place in Jerusalem for oriental-style fast foods – it's also the rumoured location of that fabulous Jerusalem legend, 'the two shekel felafel'. Down towards the junction with Salah ad-Din St, *Al-Quds* and neighbouring *Candy's* both do superb shwarma (8 NIS) and shashlik (10 NIS) and the takeaway price for a whole roasted chicken hot off the skewer is only 16 NIS.

Cafe Europe at 9 As-Zahra St, east of Salah ad-Din, offers some of the best value quality eating in the whole of the city, East, West and Old. The platters are particularly recommended; a huge plate of ham, egg, chips and vegetable garnishes with bread, for example, is 18 NIS. The ice cream cocktails are excellent too although a little pricey. It's open daily from 10 am to 10.30 pm.

The New City Most New City felafel is sold on King George V St between Jaffa Rd and Ben Yehuda St – just follow the trail of tehina, salad and squashed felafel balls on the pavement. Many of the places selling felafel also have shwarma. Non-vegetarians should not miss trying the city's speciality meorav Yerushalmi, literally 'Jerusalem meats'. This is a mix of chopped livers, kidneys, hearts and beef with onions and spices sizzled on a great hot plate and scooped into pockets of bread. The best place to try it is on Agrippas St, in the vicinity of the Mahane Yehuda market where there are dozens of restaurants frying from early evening through until early morning.

The *Ticho House Cafe* is a fine place to take coffee and browse the newspapers or read a book – the ground floor of a museum and gallery, it's off the top end of Harav Kook St, open Sunday to Thursday from 10 am to midnight, Friday from 10 am to 3 pm, and Saturday from sundown to midnight. *Tmol Shilshom* is a furniture-crowded cafe with ambitions to be a bookshop. The place gets packed at lunch times but it's quieter early on and there's a good breakfast spread including waffles with homemade jam. It's in Nahalat Shiv'a at 5 Yoel Salomon St, round the back.

Jerusalem has an enormous *McDonald's* on Shamai St one block south of Ben Yehuda but anyone wanting a good burger would do better to head for *Babel*, 50m shy of the golden arches, at 19 Hillel St. It's more expensive (25 NIS and up) but Babel burgers actually taste like meat and they come accompanied by fries and salad. The meal-sized sandwiches are great too. It's open Monday to Wednesday from 7.30 am to 1 am, and nonstop from 7.30 am Thursday until 1 am Sunday morning.

There are several good pasta places in the central area, the best of which we consider to be *Spaghettim* at 8 Rabbi Akiva St, off Hillel St. The menu is spaghetti-only but served up in over 50 different ways from the predictable bolognaise through to ostrich in hunter sauce. Prices are 20 to 30 NIS and it's open from noon to 1 am.

Entertainment

East Jerusalem and the Old City close up

completely at sundown with just *Abu Shanab's*, the *Tabasco Tearooms* and *The Backpacker Tearooms* providing any alternative to beer and a book back at the hostel. The New City, on the other hand, is buzzing, especially the Nahalat Shiv'a quarter and the area immediately west of the Russian Compound. Yoel Salomon and Rivlin, the two parallel main streets in Nahalat Shiv'a, are lined with enough late night bars and cafes to defeat even the most alcohol-absorbent of pub-crawlers. *Arizona* is the favoured travellers' haunt, a bar/disco with low beer prices and nightly happy hours – it's between Zion Square and the Steimatzky bookshop on Jaffa Rd. For live music – rock, folk and blues – squeeze in at *Mike's* a tiny place on Horkenos St off Heleni HaMalka in the Russian Compound area. For jazz, try the *Pargod Theatre* (☎ 623 1765) at 94 Bezalel St. Friday afternoons used to be jam sessions from 1.30 to 5.30 pm – maybe they still are, call and find out.

The *Jerusalem Sherover Theatre* (☎ 561 7167) at 20 David Marcus St in Talbiyeh has simultaneous English-language translation headsets available for certain performances. The Sherover is also home to the Jerusalem Symphony Orchestra while the *Binyanei Ha'Umah Conference Centre* (☎ 622 2481), opposite the central bus station, is the national residence of the Israel Philharmonic Orchestra. Free classical performances are held on occasion at a number of venues including the *YMCA Auditorium* on Ha-Melekh David St, the *Music Centre of Mishkenot Sha'ananim* (alternate Fridays) and *Beit Shmuel*, part of Hebrew Union College on King George V St (Saturday morning). Immigrant musicians also give performances at *Ticho House* every Friday morning.

Al-Masrah Centre for Palestine Culture & Art and *Al-Kasaba Theatre* (☎ 628 0957), on Abu Obeida St off Salah ah-Din St, perform plays, musicals, operettas and folk dancing in Arabic, often with an English synopsis.

Pick up the *Jerusalem Post*, in particular the Friday edition, for an up-to-date and comprehensive list of events and also stop by the tourist offices for their current 'Events in Jerusalem' brochure.

Getting There & Away

Air Arkia flights depart from the airport at Atarot, north of the city. These connect directly with Eilat and Rosh Pina, with further connections to Haifa and Tel Aviv. There are no flights on Saturday.

Bus The Egged central bus station on Jaffa Rd is where most people first arrive. Buses connect to all the major areas in the country. Although the inter-urban buses usually fill up, you only need to make advance reservations for the Eilat bus. Buses for the Dead Sea are always busy and depart erratically so try to make as early a start as possible.

Tel Aviv costs 13.70 NIS, takes 50 minutes and buses depart every 10 minutes; Eilat is 43 NIS, takes 4½ hours and four buses depart each day. There's an express bus for the 40 minute trip to Ben-Gurion airport near Tel Aviv at least every hour for US$3.

For travel in the West Bank and to Gaza use the service taxis.

Train Jerusalem's railway station (☎ 673 3764) is in David Remez Square, at the southern end of HaMelekh David St. This is the end of the little used line running from Haifa via Tel Aviv. There are only two trains a day, departing at 8.30 am and 3 pm (3 pm only during the winter) and the fare to Tel Aviv is 12 NIS and to Haifa 18 NIS. The journey to Tel Aviv takes over two hours but the scenery is said to be beautiful.

Service Taxis Service taxis make an affordable alternative to the buses and on Shabbat they are the only way of getting around. Service taxis for Tel Aviv depart from the corner of Harav Kook St and Jaffa Rd and cost 11 NIS per person (20 NIS on Friday and Saturday).

In East Jerusalem the service taxi rank is across from Damascus Gate. All West Bank destinations as well as Gaza depart from here. The taxis are much faster than the buses, depart more frequently and cost only a few shekels more.

Getting Around

The Airport United Tours bus No 111 departs hourly from the central bus station for Ben-Gurion airport (45 minutes; 20 NIS). Alternatively, take a Nesher sherut from 21 King George V St, on the corner of Ben Yehuda St, for 30 NIS. For no extra charge Nesher (☎ 623 1231, 625 7227) will also pick up from your hostel/hotel, seven days a week, 24 hours a day, but reserve one day ahead.

Bus Currently, these are some of the major bus routes:

Bus No 1 goes from platform D of the central bus station to Mea She'arim, Jaffa gate, Mt Zion and then to the Old City's Jewish Quarter.

Bus No 7 goes from the bus station down Keren HaYesod, through Talpiot and out to Ramat Rachel.

Bus No 9 goes from Jaffa Rd to the Knesset, the Israel Museum and the Givat Ram campus of the Hebrew University and then into Rehavia via Ramban St and down Keren HaYesod.

Bus No 13 goes from Kiryat HaYovel via Jaffa Rd to Jaffa Gate.

Bus No 17 goes to Ein Kerem.

Bus No 18 runs the length of Jaffa Rd connecting the New City centre with the bus station.

Bus No 20 goes from Yad Vashem via Jaffa Rd to Jaffa Gate.

Bus No 23 goes from Yad Vashem via Jaffa Rd to Damascus Gate.

Bus No 27 goes from Hadassah Medical Centre to Mt Herzl and Yad Vashem, along Jaffa Rd past the central bus station, left along HaNevi'im and via Strauss and Yezehekel Sts to the Nablus Rd bus station near Damascus Gate.

Bus 28 goes from Jaffa Rd to Mt Scopus and French Hill.

Mediterranean Coast

TEL AVIV

Tel Aviv is a greatly underrated Mediterranean city, barely a century old, that thumbs its nose at the 3000 year history of Jerusalem. Forsaking synagogues for stock exchanges and tradition for fadism, the concerns of secular Tel Aviv are finance, business and fun. The city possesses an absorbing array of distinctive neighbourhoods, a result of the diverse backgrounds of its inhabitants, all of whom have arrived with the last few generations with piles of cultural baggage intact. A short walk can encompass the spicy orientalism of the Yemenite Quarter, the seedy vodka cafes of Russified lower Allenby St and the Miami chic of pastel pink and blue glass beachfront condominiums.

Orientation

Tel Aviv is a large conglomeration of connecting suburbs sprawling across a coastal plain. Most of your time will be spent in the city's well-defined central district which occupies about six km of seafront estate and is focused on four main streets running north-south, more or less parallel to the beachline. Closest to the sand is the Herbert Samuel Esplanade while a block inland is hotel-lined HaYarkon St. Further back is backpacker-central Ben Yehuda St, while the trendy shopping zone, Dizengoff, more or less marks the easternmost limit of Tel Aviv for the visitor. These four streets all run virtually the entire length of the central city area, from the northern tip bordered by the Yarkon River, down as far as Allenby St and the Yemenite Quarter, the original 1930s centre of town.

Allenby St, almost a continuation of Ben Yehuda, is a fifth major street which runs south from the city centre towards the vicinity of the central bus station.

Information

Tourist Office The city tourist information office (☎ 639 5660; fax 639 5659) is on the 6th floor of the central bus station, opposite stand 630. It's open Sunday to Thursday from 9 am to 6 pm, and Friday from 9 am to 1.30 pm; closed Saturday.

Money The best currency exchange deals are given at the private bureaus around town, places that also don't charge commission. Try Sinai Exchange at 68 Ben Yehuda St,

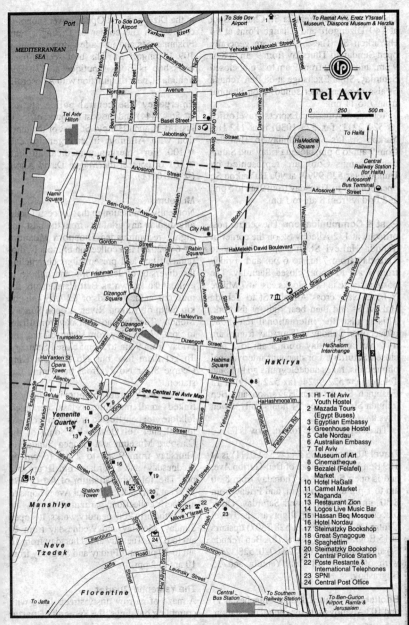

Port

To Sde Dov Airport

Yarkon River

To Sde Dov Airport

To Ramat Aviv, Eretz Y'Israel Museum, Diaspora Museum & Herzlia

MEDITERRANEAN SEA

Yirmiyahu

Yehuda HaMaccabi Street

Yeshayahu

Nordau

Avenue

Pinkas

Basel Street

Jabotinsky

Tel Aviv

0   250   500 m

To Haifa

Tel Aviv Hilton

HaMedina Square

Central Railway Station (for Haifa)

Namir Square

Arlosoroff Street

Arlosoroff Bus Terminal

Arlosoroff Street

Ben-Gurion   Avenue

HaMelekh

City Hall

Gordon   Street

Bloch

Rabin Square

HaMelekh David Boulevard

Frishman

Dizengoff Square

Dizengoff Centre

HaMelekh Shaul Avenue

HaNevl'im Street

Trumpeldor

Dizengoff Street

Kaplan Street

HaShalom Interchange

HaYarden St Opera Tower

Habima Square

Marmorek

HaKirya

Allenby

Esplanade

Ge'ula   Street

See Central Tel Aviv Map

HaHashmona'im

Yemenite Quarter

Sheinkin   Street

Shalom Tower

Manshiye

Neve Tzedek

Jaffa

Road

Shomron

To Jaffa

Lilienblum

Levinsky Street

Florentine

Central Bus Station

To Southern Railway Station

To Ben-Gurion Airport, Ramla & Jerusalem

1   HI - Tel Aviv
    Youth Hostel
2   Mazada Tours
    (Egypt Buses)
3   Egyptian Embassy
4   Greenhouse Hostel
5   Cafe Nordau
6   Australian Embassy
7   Tel Aviv
    Museum of Art
8   Cinematheque
9   Bezalel (Felafel)
    Market
10 Hotel HaGalil
11 Carmel Market
12 Maganda
13 Restaurant Zion
14 Logos Live Music Bar
15 Hassan Beq Mosque
16 Hotel Nordau
17 Steimatzky Bookshop
18 Great Synagogue
19 Spaghettim
20 Steimatzky Bookshop
21 Central Police Station
22 Poste Restante &
    International Telephones
23 SPNI
24 Central Post Office

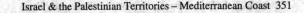

Change at 37 Ben Yehuda St, Change Spot at 140 Dizengoff and Change Point at 94 HaYarkon St. These offices are generally open Sunday to Thursday from 9 am to 8 or 9 pm, and Friday from 9 am to 2 pm; closed Saturday. Sinai Exchange at 68 Ben Yehuda St also re-opens after sundown on Shabbat from 7 to 11 pm.

Tel Aviv's American Express Travel office (☎ 524 2211; fax 523 1030) is at 112 HaYarkon St. It's open Sunday to Thursday from 9 am to 5 pm, closed Friday and Saturday. Thomas Cook are represented by Unitours (☎ 520 9999) at 90a HaYarkon St, open Sunday to Thursday from 9 am to 5 pm, and Friday from 8 am to 1 pm.

Post & Communications The central post office is at 132 Allenby St, on the corner of Yehuda HaLevi St. It's open Sunday to Thursday from 7 am to 6 pm and Friday from 7 am to noon; closed Saturday. The poste restante is two blocks east at 7 Mikve Y'Israel St – cross Allenby St to Yehuda HaLevi St and then bear right at the fork. This is also the international telephone office, open Sunday to Thursday from 8 am to 6 pm, and Friday from 8 am to 2 pm; closed Saturday. For discount international phone calls, faxes and telegrams go to Solan Telecom (☎ 522 9424; fax 522 9449) at 13 Frishman St, between HaYarkon and Ben Yehuda Sts. It's open 24 hours daily, seven days a week.

The telephone code for Tel Aviv is 03.

Travel Agencies ISSTA (☎ 517 0111) is at 109 Ben Yehuda, corner of Ben-Gurion Ave, and is open Sunday to Thursday from 8.30 am to 1 pm and 3 to 6 pm, and Friday from 8.30 am to 1 pm; closed Saturday. Other places to look for cheap flights are the Travel Centre (☎ 528 0955; fax 528 7307) upstairs at 15 Bograshov St (also at 18A Ben Yehuda St) and Mona Tours (☎ 523 0920, 528 3248) with offices at 48 Ben Yehuda and 25 Bograshov.

Bookshops Steimatzky has branches at 71 and 103 Allenby St, in the central bus station,

in the Dizengoff and Opera Tower shopping centres, on the corner of Dizengoff and Frishman Sts and just a few doors along at 109 Dizengoff St. The best second-hand bookshop is Book Boutique at 170 Ben Yehuda St, near the junction with Arlosoroff.

Emergency The central police station (☎ 564 4444) and the lost & found office is just off Yehuda HaLevi St, east of the junction with Allenby; in emergencies call ☎ 100. For emergency medical aid call ☎ 101 or contact the Magen David Adom (☎ 546 0111).

Museums
Not really a museum, in that it doesn't actually display any artefacts from the past, the highly recommended **Diaspora Museum** (☎ 646 2020) is a collection of models, dioramas, films and presentations chronicling the diversity of Jewish life and culture in exile. Also known as Beit Hatefutsoth, the museum, in the grounds of Tel Aviv Uni one km north of Yarkon River, is open Sunday, Monday, Tuesday and Thursday from 10 am to 5 pm, Wednesday from 10 am to 7 pm, and Friday from 9 am to 2 pm; closed Saturday. To get there take bus No 25 from King George St or No 27 from the central bus station.

The **Eretz Y'Israel Museum** is actually 11 linked small museums (glass, ceramics, folklore etc) constructed around an archaeological site, Tel Qasile. It's south of the Diaspora Museum and is open Sunday to Thursday from 9 am to 2 pm (6 pm on Wednesday) and Saturday from 10 am to 2 pm. The **Tel Aviv Museum of Art** (☎ 696 1297) at 27 HaMelekh Shaul Ave is home to a superb collection, particularly strong on late 19th/early 20th century works. It's open Sunday, Monday and Wednesday from 10 am to 6 pm, Tuesday and Thursday from 10 am to 10 pm, and Friday and Saturday from 10 am to 2 pm.

The Yemenite Quarter
A maze of narrow dusty streets lined with crumbling buildings, the **Yemenite Quarter**

is imbued with an oriental flavour at odds with the clean cut modernism of the rest of the city. It's one of the few places in the city that reminds the visitor of Tel Aviv's Middle Eastern location, especially loud and crowded **Carmel Market**. Push your way past the first few metres of clothing and footwear to reach the more aromatic and enticing stalls of fresh fruits and vegetables, hot breads and spices. Nearby **Nahalat Binyamin St** is a busy pedestrianised precinct full of fashionable cafes and arty shops. On Tuesday afternoon and Friday the street is also host to a craft market and filled with buskers, mime artists and dancers.

One block west of Nahalat Binyamin is the imposing bulk of Tel Aviv's major landmark, the **Shalom Tower**; the lower floors are a shopping mall while the top (30th) floor is an observation deck with great views over the city and beyond.

Beaches

Possibly the major attraction in Tel Aviv is the lengthy stretch of fine white sand fringing the city centre. When the sun is out (and it usually is) the beaches are a strutting ground for the local poseurs and a vast sandy court for pairs playing *matkot*, Israeli beach tennis. On summer nights the beaches remain crowded as they serve as impromptu sites for concerts and discos.

Bear in mind that drownings are a tragically regular occurrence – a combination of the strong undertow and reckless swimmers overestimating their capabilities. It's wise to take heed of the warning flags posted along the beaches: a black flag means that swimming is forbidden; red means that swimming is dangerous and you certainly shouldn't swim by yourself; white means that the area is safe.

Places to Stay – hostels

Virtually all of Tel Aviv's hostels and hotels are found on or around Ben Yehuda and HaYarkon Sts, all with locations just minutes from the beaches, popular eating and shopping places and nightspots. The flip side is that a lot of these places, especially in the

lower price bracket, tend to be quite noisy, especially if you are in a room facing the street. If serenity is your bag then consider staying in neighbouring Jaffa to the south.

The charge per night for a dorm bed in a Tel Aviv hostel is generally 25 to 30 NIS – exceptions noted below. For slightly less, many places will also let you sleep on the roof. There's no curfew unless noted.

The *Saskia Hostel* (☎ 528 0955) at 18A Ben Yehuda St is in a fairly pristine state, particularly the women-only dorms. There are also a couple of private rooms with their own toilet, shower and fan for 100 NIS. Cheaper rates are available for longer term stays and there's a bar and kitchen for guests' use. Round the corner, on Trumpeldor St, the *Seaside Hostel* (☎ 620 0513) has air-con and cheaper non-air-con dorms, each eight-bed room with its own shower and toilet. There are no cooking facilities but there's a bright and cheerful common room with bar, TV and fridge for guests' use.

Although some 10 to 15 minutes walk from the beach the *Dizengoff Hostel* (☎ 522 5184; fax 522 5181) compensates with a great location on bustling Dizengoff Square, close to plenty of cheap eating places. There's a kitchen and a roof terrace bar overlooking the square. The hostel also has private rooms at 90 NIS per night. Another good one is the *No 1 Hostel* (☎ 523 7807) up on the 4th floor at 84 Ben Yehuda, just south of the intersection with Gordon St. There's a kitchen and a lovely conservatory-like common room overlooking the city rooftops. The single-sex dorms have their own bathrooms and there are reductions for longer stays. There are also two private rooms (90 NIS). The same company behind the No 1, Sleep in Israel (fax 523 7419), also runs the *Gordon Hostel* (☎ 522 9870), on the seafront at 2 Gordon St. There's a kitchen, a video room, a rooftop bar and a 24 hour bar on the ground floor below.

Just east of Ben Yehuda St, the *Josef Hostel* (☎ 525 7070) at 15 Bograshov St isn't bad either, with a large air-con bar open 24 hours, TV lounge, kitchen and even a travel agency on the premises. Dorms have only four beds and, depending on whether there's an attached bathroom or not, they go for as little as 23 NIS. A couple of the dorms are also women-only. There's one private room at 95 NIS.

Recommended by many readers, the *Greenhouse Hostel* (☎ 523 5994) at 201 Dizengoff St, between Arlosoroff and Jabotinsky Sts, is quiet, ultra-clean and nicely furnished. There's a TV lounge, kitchen and a pleasant rooftop bar open until midnight in the summer. Beds in the spacious dorms are 33 NIS (only four or five beds per

room) and there are also some private doubles for 72 NIS.

Places to Stay – hotels
Unless otherwise stated, prices include breakfast and private bathrooms. Note rates can vary dramatically according to the season.

The *Gordon Inn Guest House* (☎ 523 8239; fax 523 7419) at 17 Gordon St is a hybrid hostel-hotel, beautifully kept and good value with singles from US$33 to US$39 and doubles from US$47 to US$54.

Central Tel Aviv

Benefiting greatly from a beachfront setting the *Ambassador* (☎ 517 7301; fax 517 6308) at 2 Allenby St has singles/doubles at US$60/85.

Also recommended is the *Adiv* (☎ 522 9141; fax 522 9144) at 5 Mendele St between Ben Yehuda and HaYarkon Sts, which has an excellent self-service restaurant worth visiting for breakfast even if you're not staying here. Singles/doubles are US$62/85.

The hotels belonging to the Atlas chain are all modern, three-star-style establishments with high standards of service. Atlas hotels in the city centre include the *City Hotel* (☎ 524 6253; fax 524 6250) at 9 Mapu St, between Ben Yehuda and HaYarkon Sts; the *Top Hotel* (☎ 517 0941; fax 517 1322) at 35 Ben Yehuda St; and the *Center Hotel* (☎ 629 6181; fax 629 6751) at 2 Zamenhoff St, just off Dizengoff Square. In all cases single rooms cost somewhere between US$74 to US$96 and doubles from US$98 to US$125.

For character, look to the faded elegance of the Yemenite Quarter. The *Hotel Nordau* (☎ 560 6612) at 27 Nahalat Binyamin St is housed in a creaking 1920s townhouse, recently renovated by enthusiastic management. Large double rooms with balconies, bathroom and fan are US$30. At the *Hotel HaGalil* (☎ 517 5036, 510 1782) at 23 Beit Josef Ave it's years since anybody dusted let alone renovated but that all adds to the antiquated charm of the place. Singles are US$25, doubles are US$40, toilets and showers are shared.

Places to Eat

For fresh fruit head for Carmel Market. For one-stop shopping there's a convenient *Supersol supermarket*, at 79 Ben Yehuda St, between Gordon and Mapu Sts. It's open

PLACES TO STAY			
3	Carlton Hotel	61	Miami Hotel
6	Radisson-Moriah	62	Hotel Bell
	Plaza	64	Dizengoff Hostel
7	Holiday Inn	65	Center Hotel
8	Ramada Continental		
10	Gordon Inn	**PLACES TO EAT**	
	Guest House	15	Kassit Cafe
13	Gordon Hostel	17	Akapulko
19	No 1 Hostel	18	Supersol Supermarket
22	City Hotel	21	Chicken 'n' Chips
23	Tel Aviv Sheraton	26	Mulligan's
27	Astor Hotel	35	Espresso Mersand
31	Dan Tel Aviv	37	Eternity Cafe
33	Adiv	44	Osteria da Fiorella
38	The Travellers' Hostel	57	The Leprechaun
40	Yamit Towers	63	The Beer Bar
42	Aviv Hotel	67	Davka Po
43	Top Hotel	68	Chinn Chinn Chinese
45	Josef Hostel & The		Takeaway, Cameri
	Travel Centre		Theatre & Steimatzky
47	Momo's Hostel		Bookshop
48	Hotel Metropolitan	73	The White Gallery
49	Hotel Imperial		
51	Seaside Hostel	**OTHER**	
52	Saskia Hostel	1	No 181 HaYarkon St
53	Sea & Sun Hostel	2	Book Boutique
54	Hotel Eilat & The	4	Ben-Gurion's House
	Church Bar	5	ISSTA Student Travel
55	Moss Hotel	9	British Council
56	Hotel Nes Ziona	11	Change Spot (Currency
59	Ambassador		Exchange, Phones &
60	Tayelet Hotel		Fax)
		12	Project 67
		14	Kibbutz Hotels
			Reservation Office
		16	Steimatzky Bookshop
		20	Meira's Kibbutz &
			Moshav Office
		24	Unitours (Thomas
			Cook Agents)
		25	French Embassy
		28	American Express
		29	Solan Telecom
		30	Arkia (Domestic
			Filghts) Booking
			Office
		32	Branch Post Office
		34	Egged Tours
		36	Laundrette
		39	Mona Tours
		41	US Embassy
		46	Mona Tours
		50	Branch Post Office
		58	Travel Centre
		66	Branch Post Office
		69	Gan Ha'Ir Shopping
			Centre
		70	Rabin Memorial
		71	City Hall
		72	Jabotinsky Institute
		74	Habima Theatre
		75	Helena Rubenstein
			Pavilion

ISRAEL

Sunday to Thursday from 7 am to midnight, Wednesday and Thursday for 24 hours, and Friday from 7 am to 3 pm; closed Saturday.

Felafel in Tel Aviv isn't always the best but one guaranteed good place is *Bezalel Market*, near Allenby St and the Yemenite Quarter. The 'felafel market', as it's also known, is no more than two stalls side by side but each has a fantastic array of salads and for 6 NIS you are free to stuff your own pitta bread with as much felafel and greenery as you can fit in. Otherwise the heaviest concentration of Middle Eastern fast food staples are on the southern stretches of Ben Yehuda and Dizengoff Sts.

Tel Aviv's many cafes exist as centres of gossip and to provide ringside seating for the ongoing pavement carnival. Good or cheap food is not always a priority and the locals tend to fuel themselves on black coffee, croissants and cheesecake. *Espresso Mersand* on the corner of Ben Yehuda and Frishman Sts is typical of the city's cafes – come in a morning to observe its unique collection of regulars, comprising journalists and actors and elderly German Jews. At the *Cafe Nordau*, at 145 Ben Yehuda St, the place mats are printed on recycled paper, the cafe serves as a collection point for used batteries, dogs have their own menu and upstairs is a gay club. The food here is actually very good, ranging from light lunches such as soups and baked potatoes (actually, not so light) to full blown meals. The place gets packed in the evenings so come early if you want to eat.

If you take your tea without frills then the *Shakespeare* is a pleasant unpretentious place, with air-con and large picture windows onto the beach. It's part of the British Council on HaYarkon St, just north of Gordon St.

The unique tofu-cuisine at the Black Hebrew restaurant *Eternity*, at 60 Ben Yehuda St, is well worth a try. Even avid meat lovers should at least sample the vegetable shwarma, cheaper and perhaps more enjoyable than the real thing.

Felafel aside, easily the cheapest eating in Tel Aviv is at the travellers' bars. *The Beer Bar*, *The Leprechaun* and *Mulligan's* (see Entertainment following) all have constantly changing menus, typically featuring English breakfasts, stir fries and spaghetti. In all cases the cooks are resident travellers (and you don't find many cordon bleu chefs hiding under a backpack) but if the quality is variable, the quantity gives little cause for complaint.

On Frishman St, near the corner with Dizengoff, is *Chinn Chinn*, a cheapie Chinese place with vegetable dishes at 13.50 NIS and chicken/pork/beef dishes at around the 20 NIS mark. Open from noon to midnight, they also offer takeaway. Across the road, the cafe/restaurant *Akapulko* does great Zeppelin-sized mushroom blintzes (22 NIS), after which you won't need to eat for another week.

Looking like a refugee from South Beach Miami, the puce-painted *Chicago Pizza Pie Factory* (☎ 517 7505) at 63 HaYarkon St (on the corner of Trumpeldor St) serves two-person deep pan pizzas from 27 to 50 NIS, as well as chilli (19 NIS) and lasagne (22 NIS). It also has draft beer and American sports on TV. For more State-side vibes there's a *Hard Rock Cafe* (☎ 525 1336) on Dizengoff St, part of the Dizengoff Centre.

In the Yemenite Quarter the atmospheric *Restaurant Zion* (☎ 510 7414), at 28 Peduyim St, serves oriental Jewish specialities like grilled meats and offal including such lovelies as ox testicles (35 NIS) and veal brains (32 NIS), and a variety of stuffed vegetable dishes at 8 NIS. The nearby *Maganda* (☎ 517 9990) at 26 Rabbi Meir St does more of the same but in a livelier and louder setting.

Pasta fans should head for *Spaghettim* (☎ 566 4467) at 18 Yavne St, one block north of Allenby. It's spaghetti only but there's a choice of more than 50 sauces – we tried about eight and they were all good. It's open from noon to 1 am.

Entertainment

There's a collection of travellers' bars around the southern end of HaYarkon and Ben Yehuda Sts. At the time of writing, the big favourite is *The Leprechaun*, a small bar with loud music and an even louder crowd. It's on HaYarden St, at the back of the Opera Tower. Right around the corner is *The Church Bar*, underneath the Hotel Eilat at 58 HaYarkon St, while north on the same street, just beyond the junction with Frishman St, is *Mulligan's*, another really popular place with a terrace out the back overlooking the seafront, a couple of pool tables and satellite TV for desperate football fans.

For live music visit *Logos*, which has local blues, R&B and rock bands playing every night at about 10 pm. It's at 8 HaShomer, a side street running off Nahalat Binyamin St to HaCarmel St.

Anyone seriously interested in good cinema should drop by the *Cinematheque* (☎ 691 7181), part of a membership chain which shows a variety of classics, avant-garde, new wave, and off-beat movies – it's at 1 Ha' Arba'a St; follow Dizengoff St south to the junction with Ibn Gvirol St. Continue south on Ibn Gvirol, forking left onto Carlibach St and the Cinematheque will be visible to your left across a triangular piazza. During the summer months, check to see if free films are being screened at night on the beach, near Allenby St.

Performances at the *Cameri Theatre* at 101 Dizengoff St (entrance on Frishman St) are simultaneously translated into English on Tuesday. At the *Habima Theatre* (on Habima Square, between Rothschild Ave and Dizengoff St), home of Israel's national theatre group, performances on Thursday have simultaneous English-language translation.

Getting There & Away

Air Arkia flights depart from the Sde Dov airport, north of the Yarkon River. These connect directly with Eilat (several flights daily; US$80 one way) and Rosh Pina in Upper Galilee, with further connections to Haifa and Jerusalem. There are no flights on Saturday. Arkia's city offices (☎ 699 2222) are at 11 Frishman St.

Bus Doubling as a multistorey shopping centre, Tel Aviv's central bus station is a mammoth complex in which, if unlucky, you could easily spend the first few days of your visit trying to find the way out. Outgoing intercity buses depart from the 6th floor, where there's also an efficient if sullenly staffed information point. Suburban and city buses depart from the 4th floor but these are not so well signposted and you'll need to ask to find the correct bay.

There are buses to Jerusalem (one hour; 13.70 NIS) departing every 10 minutes; to Haifa (1½ hours; 17.50 NIS) every 15 to 20 minutes; and to Eilat (five hours; 46 NIS) hourly between 6.30 am and 5 pm, plus an overnight service departing at 12.30 am.

There is also a second bus station in Tel Aviv, the Arlosoroff terminal, which is up by the central railway station in the north-east part of town. One or two services from Jerusalem and Haifa finish up here rather than the central bus station. To get into town walk over to the bus stands on the main road and catch a No 61 which runs down Arlosoroff St and then south along Dizengoff and King George Sts to Allenby St.

Train Tel Aviv has two railway stations. The central railway station (☎ 693 7515) serves Haifa (14.50 NIS) with trains leaving virtually every hour between 6 am and 8 pm. It's at the junction of Haifa Rd, Arlosoroff St and Petah Tikva Rd – take bus Nos 61 or 62 north up Dizengoff St.

A second railway station south of the central bus station serves Jerusalem (12 NIS). There are only two trains a day (just one in the winter). It's on Kibbutz Galuyot Rd – take bus No 41 from Levinsky St near the central bus station, or take a taxi.

Service Taxis Service taxis operate from outside the central bus station (where bus Nos 4 and 5 alight) to the suburbs, Jerusalem (10 NIS) and Haifa (16 NIS). On Saturday they leave from HaHashmal St, east of the bottom of Allenby St and cost about an extra 20%.

Getting Around

The Airport Bus No 222 runs up HaYarkon

St to the airport, with departures at 45 minute intervals between 4 am and midnight (last bus Friday 6.45 pm; first bus Saturday at noon). There are timetables posted at the stops. The city-airport fare is 13.90 NIS and the journey takes from 45 minutes to an hour.

Bus Bus No 4 goes from the central bus station via Allenby, Ben Yehuda and north Dizengoff Sts to the Reading terminal, north of the Yarkon River, passing most of the city centre hostels along the way; bus No 5 goes from the central bus station, along Allenby St, up Rothschild Ave, along Dizengoff St, Nordau Ave, Ibn Gvirol, Pinkas, Weizmann and Yehuda HaMaccabi Sts and then back – useful for the HI hostel, the Egyptian embassy, Habima Square and the Dizengoff St hostels.

JAFFA

Founded, according to the Old Testament, by Japheth, in the wake of the famed flood that shot his father Noah to fame, Jaffa came to prominence as a port during the time of Solomon. Now swallowed up by Tel Aviv, the Jaffa (in Hebrew, Yafo) of today exists largely as a quaint harbour-side setting for an expensive seafood meal.

Every Wednesday, a free three hour guided walking tour of Old Jaffa departs from the clock tower at 9 am.

Things to See & Do

The central attraction is **Old Jaffa**, a prettified area of narrow twisting alleys, home to galleries, artists' studios and a variety of unnecessary shops. The **Museum of Antiquities** at 10 Mifraz Shlomo St was originally a Turkish administrative and detention centre but is now home to a display of local archaeological discoveries. It's open Sunday to Thursday from 9 am to 2 pm (until 6 pm on Wednesday), and Saturday from 10 am to 2 pm; closed Friday. The grassy knoll behind the museum, known as the **HaPisga Gardens**, has a small amphitheatre with a panorama of the Tel Aviv seafront as its backdrop.

A footbridge connects the gardens to

Kedumim Square (Kikar Kedumim), Old Jaffa's reconstructed centre, ringed by restaurants, clubs and galleries but dominated by the bulk of orange-painted **St Peter's Monastery**. In a chamber underneath the square is the well-designed **Visitors' Centre** where you can view partially excavated remains from the Hellenistic and Roman era and watch a six minute film on Jaffa. You can also pick up an informative free map down here. It's open daily from 9 am to 10 pm (2 pm on Friday).

Close to the **Ottoman clock tower**, east

PLACES TO STAY
7 Old Jaffa Hostel

PLACES TO EAT
5 Dr Shakshouka
6 Said Abu Elafia & Sons Bakery
10 Greek Plate Smashing Restaurant
12 Michel's Aladdin Restaurant
20 Little Spain Restaurant

OTHER
1 Police
2 Clock Tower
3 Tel Aviv Bus Stop
4 Mahmudiya Mosque
8 Museum of Antiquities
9 Amphitheatre
11 Sea Mosque
13 Sculpture & Viewpoint
14 Armenian Church
15 St Michael's Greek Orthodox Church
16 St Peter's Monastery
17 Visitors' Centre
18 Simon the Tanner's House
19 Ilana Gur Museum
21 The Israel Experience
22 St George's Church

Jaffa

of Yefet St, is the **flea market**, which has a decent reputation for antiques and interesting oriental bits and pieces.

Places to Stay

A pleasant Israeli couple have converted a beautiful old Turkish house into the lovely *Old Jaffa Hostel* (☎ 682 2370/16). There's a large bar/common room and airy dorms complete with armchairs and tables. A dorm bed is 25 NIS while private doubles are 80 NIS. There's also the option of taking a mattress on the roof for 19 NIS. The hostel is in the flea market area at 8 Olei Zion St although the entrance is a little difficult to find – there's no sign at eye level, it's under your feet set in stone at the foot of an unmarked door.

Places to Eat

Almost reason alone to visit Jaffa, *Said Abu Elafia & Sons*, a bakery at 7 Yefet St, has become near legendary in Israel. The main attraction is their version of pizza, prepared in the traditional Arab manner of cracking a couple of eggs on top of pitta bread, stirring in tomato, cheese and olives and baking it in the oven. Other items include 24 varieties of bread, such as pitta coated in sesame seeds or spices (ask for za'atar; thyme) and sambusa, triangular shaped pastries with various fillings; try sambusa mayorav, which contains mushrooms, potato, egg and cheese, and costs 6 NIS.

For Israelis, the main culinary attraction in Jaffa is fish and both Mifraz Shlomo St and the port area have numerous outdoor restaurants, some of which also serve meat grilled on the fire. Although extremely popular with Israelis, we weren't greatly impressed by the food, service or prices. We do though recommend *Michel's Aladdin* at 5 Mifraz Shlomo St, if only for the views from its terrace. The restaurant is housed in an 800 year old building that was originally a Turkish bath. Most of the menu is priced up in the 30 to 60 NIS range but there are things like blintzes at 25 NIS.

Getting There & Away

From the centre of Tel Aviv it's a pleasant 2.5 km stroll along the seafront to Old Jaffa. If you don't fancy walking then catch bus No 10 from Ben Yehuda St, bus No 18 from Dizengoff St, or bus Nos 18 or 25 from Allenby St. In the reverse direction, bus No 10 for Ben Yehuda St departs from beside the clock tower.

HERZLIA

North of Tel Aviv this town is popular for its beaches. Most of them charge admission but Sidna Ali Beach, a short walk north of the central hotel district, is free and often less crowded – it also has the attraction of the Sidna Ali caveman and his post-apocalyptic home. Herzlia is just a 40 minute ride from Tel Aviv's central bus station.

RAMLA

Established by the Arabs in 716 AD Ramla was the country's capital prior to the Crusades. Now, by-passed by the major roads, of no interest to modern-day pilgrims and unknown to tourists, Ramla minds its own business with just one or two worn Islamic monuments standing as testaments to former glories. However, the mix of an old Arab quarter of crumbling stone buildings with lots of green parkland and eucalyptus tree-lined avenues makes for a very attractive small town, definitely worth a visit, especially on Wednesday, market day. There are buses every 20 minutes from Tel Aviv's central bus station (45 minutes; 6.80 NIS).

ASHKELON

Situated 56 km south of Tel Aviv, Ashkelon is a small town ambitiously marketing itself as the new resort capital of Israel. Its attractions include a seafront **national park** strewn with archaeological excavations dating from the Bronze Age to the Crusader period, a 5th to 6th century **mosaic floor** in the Byzantine church ruins near the central district of Afridar, and an old Arab quarter, **Migdal**, now depressingly Russified. All in all it's a fairly dull place although we're sure the local tourist office (☎ (07) 673 2412)

ISRAEL

would beg to differ – they're at Zefania Square in central Afridar, open Sunday and Tuesday from 8.30 am to 1.30 pm, and Monday, Wednesday and Thursday from 8.30 am to 12.30 pm; closed Friday and Saturday.

There are buses every 20 minutes from Tel Aviv (1¼ hours; 15 NIS) and hourly services from Jerusalem (19 NIS).

NETANYA

As a sun and sand resort we would recommend francophile Netanya over more popular Eilat. It has an 11 km stretch of **free beaches**, which are some of the best in the country (beware of the undertow) and a lively pedestrianised main street lined with patisseries. The local tourist information office (☎ (09) 882 7286) is housed in a small kiosk-like building on the south-western corner of Ha'Atzmaut Square, open Sunday to Thursday from 8.30 am to 6 pm, and Friday from 9 am to noon; closed Saturday.

Places to Stay

Unfortunately budget accommodation is severely limited to the *Atzmaut Hostel* (☎ (09) 862 1315), occupying a prime position right on the south side of seafront Ha'Atzmaut Square. The rooms are air-con, clean and comfortable but a little on the expensive side at 40 NIS per person. The similarly pricey alternative is the *Hotel Orit* (☎ (09) 861 6818), at 21 Chen St, a guesthouse run by friendly Swedish Christians. Doubles are 69 NIS per person, breakfast included. It's often full with parties of Scandinavians so try booking ahead.

Getting There & Away

There are buses about every 15 minutes to and from Tel Aviv (30 minutes; 7.50 NIS) and services to Haifa (one hour; 15 NIS) and Jerusalem about every 30 minutes. To reach Caesarea, Megiddo, Nazareth or Tiberias, take a bus from Netanya to Hadera and change there.

HAIFA

While Jerusalem is swathed in historical mystique and Tel Aviv buzzes with unbounded credit card hedonism, Haifa, Israel's third largest city, contents itself with being the solid cornerstone of the country's technological industry. However, clinging to the wooded slopes of Mt Carmel, Haifa is not an unattractive place and the upper sections of the city include some pleasant residential areas and promenades with superb panoramic views north along the coastline. There are quite a few destinations nearby that are worth a brief visit and as the regional transport hub, Haifa makes a convenient base for some good day trips.

The Haifa Tourism Development Association organises a free guided walking tour every Saturday at 10 am. Meet at the signposted observation point on the corner of Sha'ar HaLevenon and Ye'fe Nof Sts up in Carmel Central.

Orientation

Haifa is divided into three tiers ascending the slope of Mt Carmel. Whether you arrive by bus, train or boat, the first place you will see is the port area, also known as Downtown. Uphill is Hadar; most shops, businesses, eating places and hotels are here. The Carmel district occupies the higher slopes of the city, where exclusive residences benefit from cool breezes and magnificent views. Carmel Central, focused on HaNassi Ave, is a small commercial district with a cluster of bars and eating places all charging fittingly high-altitude prices.

Information

Tourist Offices Haifa's main tourist information office (☎ 866 6521/2) is at 18 Herzl St in Hadar. It's open Sunday to Thursday from 8.30 am to 5 pm, and Friday from 8.30 am to 2 pm; closed Saturday. There are also tourist offices at the central bus station, in the City Hall at 14 Hassan Shukri St, and in Carmel Central at 106 HaNassi Ave. There's also a pre-recorded, English-language 'What's On' line – call ☎ 837 4253.

Money Banks are easily found on Ha'Atzmaut St in the port area and in Hadar on and around

HaNevi'im St. All banks are closed on Saturday and Monday, and on Wednesday and Friday afternoons. If you're caught short of shekels out of banking hours then Haifa's port area is a popular haunt for black marketeers. While they offer a better rate than the banks they take cash only and there's a definite risk of being ripped off.

Post & Communications The main post office, poste restante and international telephones are at 19 HaPalyam Ave in the port area. It's open Sunday to Thursday from 8 am to 8 pm, and Friday from 8 am to 2 pm; closed Saturday.

The telephone code for Haifa is 04.

Emergency The central police station is at 28 Jaffa Rd in the port area (emergency ☎ 100). First aid is available at the Haifa Medical Centre (☎ 830 5222) at 15 Horev St in Carmel Central or through the Magen

David Adom (☎ 851 2233). In an emergency call ☎ 911.

Baha'i Shrine & Gardens

Sited amid the beautifully manicured and dizzily sloped Persian Gardens, Haifa's most impressive attraction is the golden-domed **Shrine of the Bab**. This is one of the two main spiritual centres of the Baha'i faith. Completed in 1953, the shrine combines the style and proportions of European architecture with designs inspired by the orient. To get to the shrine take bus No 22 from the central bus station; Nos 23, 25 and 26 from HaNevi'im or Herzl Sts (in Hadar) also stop outside. The shrine is open daily from 9 am to noon. Admission is free. Remove your shoes before entering and don't wear shorts or bare your shoulders. The gardens remain open until 5 pm.

Higher up the hill, 200m beyond the Baha'i shrine, is the **Sculpture Garden**

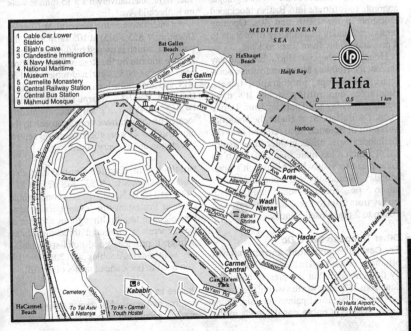

1 Cable Car Lower Station
2 Elijah's Cave
3 Clandestine Immigration & Navy Museum
4 National Maritime Museum
5 Carmelite Monastery
6 Central Railway Station
7 Central Bus Station
8 Mahmud Mosque

(Gan HaPesalim), a small park peopled with bronze sculptures.

Museums

The **Haifa Museum** at 26 Shabtai Levi St is ostensibly three museums in one – ancient art, modern art, and music and ethnology – however the combined displays would hardly fill a telephone kiosk and there's more bare wall here than in China. It's open Tuesday, Thursday and Saturday from 10 am to 1 pm and 6 to 9 pm, and Sunday, Monday, and Wednesday from 10 am to 1 pm only; closed Friday. The same ticket admits you to the **National Maritime Museum** at 198 Allenby Rd, west of the bus station, which presents a rather dry history of shipping in the Mediterranean area. It's open Sunday to Thursday from 10 am to 4 pm, and Saturday from 10 am to 1 pm.

Much more interesting is the neighbouring **Clandestine Immigration & Navy Museum** (☎ 853 6249) which deals with the successes and failures of the Zionists' illegal attempts to infiltrate into British blockaded Palestine in the 1930s and 40s. Opening hours are Sunday to Thursday from 9 am to 4 pm, and Friday from 9 am to 1 pm.

Housed in the old Haifa East railway station, the **Railway Museum** features a collection of stamps, photographs, tickets, timetables and rolling stock; it's open Sunday, Tuesday and Thursday from 9 am to noon. On Balfour St in Hadar the **National Museum of Science** (also referred to as the Technodea) specialises in interactive exhibits, of which it has more than 200, and it's a great place to visit with children. It's open Monday, Wednesday and Thursday from 9 am to 5 pm, Tuesday from 9 am to 7 pm, Friday from 9 am to 1 pm, and Saturday from 10 am to 2 pm; closed Sunday.

Other Things to See & Do

The **Carmelite monastery and church** was originally established in the late 12th century by the Crusaders but the present buildings date from 1836. It's worth visiting the church to view the beautiful painted ceiling. From the monastery a **cable car** descends to the Bat Galim Promenade below, beside the maritime museum and a small grotto known as **Elijah's Cave**. This is where the prophet Elijah is believed to have hidden from King Ahab and Queen Jezebel after he slew the 450 priests of Ba'al (I Kings:17-19). Holy to all three of the major monotheistic faiths the cave is usually crammed full of praying Jews while outside the garden is a favourite picnic spot for local Christian Arabs.

Places to Stay

Hostels There's not much to choose from and most travellers end up at the pleasant and friendly *Bethel Hostel* (☎ 852 1110) at 40 HaGefen St. There are no private rooms (separate male and female dorms; 30 NIS per night) nor a kitchen, but there is a lounge with tea and coffee-making facilities, a snack bar open for breakfast and a free evening meal on Friday. To get to the hostel from the central bus station take bus No 22, get off at the first stop on HaGefen St, walk back past Ben-Gurion Ave and it's on your right; alternatively it's a 15 minute walk up Rothschild Ave.

An alternative is the peaceful *St Charles Hospice* (☎ 855 3705) at 105 Jaffa Rd in the port area, which is owned by the Latin Patriarchate and run by the Rosary Sisters. Dorm beds are 50 NIS, singles/doubles 60/120 NIS, and all include breakfast. A third option exists in the *HI – Carmel Youth Hostel* (☎ 853 1944) but it's very inconveniently located on the south-western approach to the city. Bus No 43 goes there from the central bus station about every hour.

Hotels Up in Carmel Central the *Beit Shalom Guesthouse* (☎ 837 7481/2; fax 837 2443) at 110 HaNassi Ave is a comfortable German Protestant-run 'evangelical guesthouse', open to all (although, in summer at least, there's a minimum three night stay policy). It provides good hotel-style facilities with singles/doubles at 120/180 NIS. You need to book ahead as it's often full.

Places to Eat

For fruit and vegetables, shop at the great little market occupying a couple of alleyways

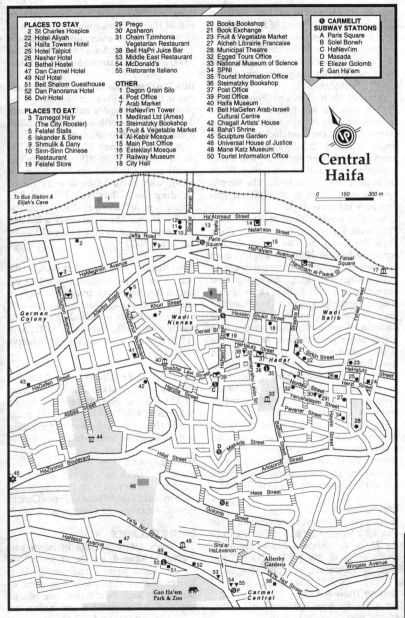

PLACES TO STAY
2 St Charles Hospice
22 Hotel Aliyah
24 Haifa Towers Hotel
25 Hotel Talpiot
26 Nesher Hotel
43 Bethel Hostel
47 Dan Carmel Hotel
49 Nof Hotel
51 Beit Shalom Guesthouse
52 Dan Panorama Hotel
56 Dvir Hotel

PLACES TO EAT
3 Tarnegol Ha'Ir
(The City Rooster)
5 Felafel Stalls
6 Iskander & Sons
9 Shmulik & Dany
10 Sinn-Sinn Chinese
Restaurant
19 Felafel Store

29 Prego
30 Apsheron
31 Chaim Tzimhonia
Vegetarian Restaurant
38 Beit HaPri Juice Bar
53 Middle East Restaurant
54 McDonald's
55 Ristorante Italiano

OTHER
1 Dagon Grain Silo
4 Post Office
7 Arab Market
8 HaNevi'im Tower
11 Meditrad Ltd (Amex)
12 Steimatzky Bookshop
13 Fruit & Vegetable Market
14 Al-Kebir Mosque
15 Main Post Office
16 Esteklayl Mosque
17 Railway Museum
18 City Hall

20 Books Bookshop
21 Book Exchange
23 Fruit & Vegetable Market
27 Alcheh Librairie Francaise
28 Municipal Theatre
32 Egged Tours Office
33 National Museum of Science
34 SPNI
35 Tourist Information Office
36 Steimatzky Bookshop
37 Post Office
39 Post Office
40 Haifa Museum
41 Beit HaGefen Arab-Israeli
Cultural Centre
42 Chagall Artists' House
44 Baha'i Shrine
45 Sculpture Garden
46 Universal House of Justice
48 Mane Katz Museum
50 Tourist Information Office

**Ⓢ CARMELIT
SUBWAY STATIONS**
A Paris Square
B Solel Boneh
C HaNevi'im
D Masada
E Eliezer Golomb
F Gan Ha'em

**Central
Haifa**

0   150   300 m

between Ha'Atzmaut St and Jaffa Rd down in the port area. For some of the country's best felafel and shwarma head for the HaNevi'im end of HeHalutz St in Hadar. This is also the place for bakeries producing sweet pastries, ring doughnuts, sticky buns and other delights.

Tarnegol Ha'Ir (The City Rooster – no English sign but just look for a frontage adorned with big red chickens) at 17 Ben-Gurion Ave is an excellent chicken restaurant (roast, schnitzel, kebab, shashlik, wings, livers etc) with some interesting side dishes available from a self-service trolley. Prices are in the 20 to 25 NIS range. The place is open from 11.30 am to midnight and gets very busy in the evenings.

In Hadar, head for 30 Herzl St and *Chaim Tzimhonia Vegetarian Restaurant – Dairy Farm Food*, only the latter part of which is written in English. Here you will find plain but tasty vegetarian dishes served in a fairly busy, though unexciting, atmosphere. You can eat for as little as 12 NIS. The restaurant is open Sunday to Thursday from 9 am to 8 pm, and Friday from 9 am to 1 pm; closed Saturday. There's plenty of cheap eating places along pedestrianised Nordau St in Hadar – try *Apsheron* at 18 Nordau, which has a fairly extensive menu of meat dishes, pizzas and pasta priced quite reasonably at between 15 and 25 NIS. Next door at No 20, *Prego* is considerably more classy and its pastas weigh in at 30 NIS or more.

A self-service cafeteria on the 1st floor of the *Dan Panorama Centre*, part of the hotel of the same name on HaNassi Ave, provides some of the cheapest eating in Carmel with an odd selection ranging from burgers (6 NIS and up) to Chinese stir-fry (15 to 20 NIS).

Entertainment

Haifa is not renowned for entertainment but pick up a copy of the free leaflet *Events in the Haifa & Northern Region* from the tourist office or dial ☎ 837 4253 and you might find something of appeal going on.

Getting There & Away

Air Arkia, the Israeli domestic airline, flies in and out of the airport in the industrial zone east of Haifa. Flights connect directly with Eilat, with further connections to Tel Aviv and Jerusalem. The Arkia city office (☎ 864 3371) is at 80 Ha'Atzmaut St in the port area.

Bus The central bus station, on HaHaganah Ave in the Bat Galim neighbourhood of the port area, has intercity buses arriving and departing on the north side, and local buses operating from the south side.

Buses depart every 20 minutes for Tel Aviv (1½ hours; 17.50 NIS) while there's an hourly service to Jerusalem (two hours; 24 NIS), with extra buses at peak times. Heading north, bus Nos 271 and 272 (express) go to Nahariya (45 to 70 minutes; 10.50 NIS) via Akko, and bus Nos 251 and 252 (express) go to Akko only (30 to 50 minutes; 8 NIS).

Train Haifa has three railway stations but the one to use is Bat Galim, adjacent to the central bus station and reached through an underground passage next to bus platform 34. Timetables are given in English for the hourly trains south, via Netanya, to Tel Aviv (14.50 NIS) and north, via Akko, to Nahariya (8.50 NIS).

Ferry For sailings to Athens, Crete and Cyprus contact Mano Passenger Lines (☎ 853 1631) at 39/41 HaMeginim Ave or SOL Lines (☎ 867 4444) at 76 Ha'Atzmaut. See the Getting There & Away section earlier in this chapter for further details.

Getting Around

Haifa has Israel's only subway system, the Carmelit, which runs from Paris Square in the port area through Hadar and up to Carmel Central – it saves a lot of legwork.

DRUZE VILLAGES

The dusty Druze villages of **Isfiya** and **Daliyat al-Karmel**, on the slopes of Mt Carmel, are a popular attraction for both foreign visitors and Israelis who come to shop at the high-street bazaar (the mix of imported Indian clothing and trinkets on offer is unlikely to hold much appeal for the well-travelled). There isn't much to see here, however, a visit does provide an opportunity to observe and possibly meet the Druze, a people that have a reputation for being extremely friendly and hospitable.

It is possible to stay in Isfiya, the nearer of the two villages to Haifa. The *Stella Carmel Hospice* (☎ (04) 839 1692), in an idyllic setting on the outskirts of the village, was originally built as an Arab hotel and provides clean and comfortable accommodation in a quiet atmosphere. Dorm beds are 30 NIS (with breakfast), 45 NIS (half board), and 60 NIS (full board). Single rooms cost from 54 to 105 NIS, doubles from 108 to 144 NIS.

The Druze villages are a half-day trip from Haifa. Bus No 192 runs from Haifa's central bus station, via Herzl St, Sunday to Friday, *but* there are only two or three departures a day – all are in the afternoon. It's much better to take a service taxi; they leave continually all day till about 5 pm from Eliyahu St, between Paris Square and Ha'Atzmaut St in the port area. They take about half the time of the bus and at 7.50 NIS are no more expensive.

DOR

On the coast road, about 29 km south of Haifa, Dor is a modern settlement mainly populated by Greek Jews. It is next to the site of an ancient town and near one of the country's loveliest and most peaceful stretches of sand, **Tantura beach**. The area is ideal for camping and there are many appealing places to pitch a tent. There is a nearby site run by the Dor Moshav (☎ (06) 639 9121) with bungalows as well as tents for hire. To get there take any of the buses going along the Haifa-Hadera highway and ask the driver to drop you off at Dor.

CAESAREA

One of the country's premier archaeological sites, Caesarea is also a fast developing coastal resort with commercialisation continuing apace with the excavations. It was originally a port founded by Herod the Great and the impressive remains are spread along

a three km stretch of the Mediterranean coast. The central attraction is a walled **Crusader city** with citadel and harbour. North, beyond the walls, littered across the beach are the skeletons of the **Roman aqueducts**, while to the south is a **Roman amphitheatre**, reconstructed as a modern-day venue for concert performances.

There is a free beach south of the amphitheatre but take heed of any 'No Bathing' signs – they indicate waters dangerously polluted by the factory of the nearby kibbutz.

Places to Stay

Most people visit Caesarea as a day trip from either Tel Aviv or Haifa as accommodation here is expensive – the neighbouring *Kibbutz Sdot Yam* (☎ (06) 636 4444) charges US$52/56 for its air-con singles/doubles. Free camping on the beach is possible but beware, theft is common.

Getting There & Away

From Haifa or Tel Aviv and Netanya take any bus going along the coastal road to Hadera. You then have two choices: you can get off at Hadera bus station and hope for a reasonable connection with the No 76 bus which goes to Caesarea; alternatively, you can jump off the bus at the Caesarea intersection and make the 3.5 km hike to the excavations.

BEIT SHE'ARIM

About 19 km south-east of Haifa, the archaeological site of Beit She'arim features a network of burial caves and a few ruins from the 2nd century. Get there on bus No 338 from Haifa to Kiryat Tivon.

AKKO

Surpassing even Jerusalem, there is no city in Israel more timeless than Akko, a sturdy stone fortress-city by the sea. The town has had an exceptionally long and varied history under Alexander the Great, the Egyptians and the Romans but it came to prominence as the Crusader city of Acre. It was a hotbed of Arab hostility towards Jewish immigration in the 1930s but in the end the Jews more or less left Old Akko to the Arabs, preferring

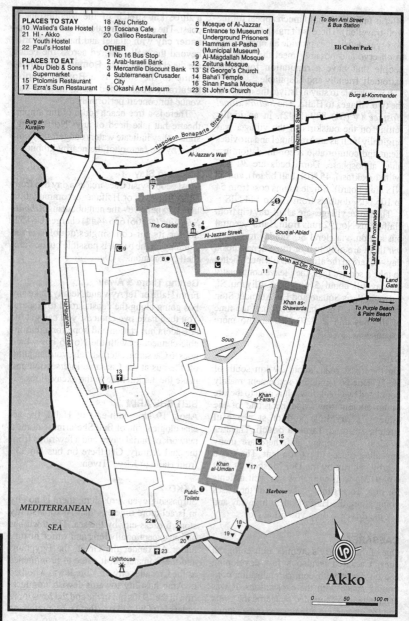

PLACES TO STAY
10 Walied's Gate Hostel
21 HI - Akko
      Youth Hostel
22 Paul's Hostel

PLACES TO EAT
11 Abu Dieb & Sons
      Supermarket
15 Ptolomis Restaurant
17 Ezra's Sun Restaurant

18 Abu Christo
19 Toscana Cafe
20 Galileo Restaurant

OTHER
1 No 16 Bus Stop
2 Arab-Israeli Bank
3 Mercantile Discount Bank
4 Subterranean Crusader
     City
5 Okashi Art Museum

6 Mosque of Al-Jazzar
7 Entrance to Museum of
     Underground Prisoners
8 Hammam al-Pasha
     (Municipal Museum)
9 Al-Magdallah Mosque
12 Zeituna Mosque
13 St George's Church
14 Baha'i Temple
16 Sinan Pasha Mosque
23 St John's Church

To Ben Ami Street
& Bus Station

Eli Cohen Park

Burg al-Kommander

Burg al-Kuraijim

To Purple Beach
& Palm Beach
Hotel

Napoleon Bonaparte Street

Al-Jazzar's Wall

Weizmann Street

Land Wall Promenade

The Citadel

Al-Jazzar Street

Souq al-Abiad

Salah ad-Din Street

Land Gate

Hahaganah Street

Khan as-Shawarda

Souq

Khan al-Faranj

Khan al-Umdan

Public Toilets

MEDITERRANEAN SEA

Harbour

Lighthouse

Akko

0   50   100 m

ISRAEL

to develop their own new town outside the city walls. A fortuitous result as Akko has been passed over for development and investment and while every other place in Israel is busy packaging up its heritage for the tourist buck, Akko soldiers on oblivious, with families not artists in its houses, household goods not souvenirs in the souq and the fish on the quayside in nets and buckets not white wine sauce.

Orientation & Information

From the bus station it's a short walk south to Old Akko; turn left as you leave the station, walk one block to the traffic lights and turn right onto Ben Ami St. After walking through the pedestrianised shopping precinct, turn left onto Weizmann St and you'll see the city walls ahead.

The ticket office at the subterranean Crusader city doubles as an information bureau, which is open Sunday to Thursday from 9 am to 6 pm, Friday from 8.30 am to 2.30 pm, and Saturday from 9 am to 6 pm.

Old Akko

Enter through walls built by Ahmed Pasha al-Jazzar in 1799 which today serve as a very physical division between the predominantly Arab Old Akko and the sprawl of the modern Jewish town to the north. The sea walls date from the 12th century but were refaced by Al-Jazzar. The north-west corner of Old Akko is secured by a fortress built, also by the ubiquitous Al-Jazzar, on 13th century Crusader foundations. The fortress is now home to the **Museum of Underground Prisoners**, dedicated to the Jewish resistance during the British Mandate. The **Mosque of Al-Jazzar**, with its distinctly Turkish green dome and pencil minaret, provides the dominant element on the Akko skyline.

Across the street from the mosque is the entrance to the **subterranean Crusader city**, a haunting series of echoing vaulted halls that lie eight metres below the street level of present-day Akko and were at one time the quarters of the crusading Knights Hospitallers. It's accessible Sunday to Thursday from 8.30 am to 6.30 pm, Friday from 8.30 am to 2.30 pm and Saturday from 9 am to 6 pm. The admission cost also includes entry to the **Hammam al-Pasha** (also called the Municipal Museum), the bathhouse of Al-Jazzar built in 1780 and in use until the 1940s.

As you exit the bathhouse, following the alleyway south will bring you into the **souq** and another slice of unadulterated orient. Beyond the souq down by the harbour is the **Khan al-Umdan**, once a grand caravanserai (or khan) that served the camel caravans bringing in grain from the hinterland, and is now Akko's unofficial soccer stadium. Atop the khan is an ugly Ottoman **clock tower** which you can sometimes ascend for a great view of the **harbour** below. The harbour is still very much in service and if you are around early enough you can watch the fishing boats chug in and off-load the day's catch. Throughout the day and until well after sundown, the *Akko Princess* departs regularly from the end of the breakwater and makes a 20 minute **cruise** around the walls.

Places to Stay

Paul's Hostel (☎ (04) 991 2857) is a small family-run concern in a converted Arab house near the harbour. There are two mixed dormitories (beds are 20 NIS) and a couple of nice private rooms at 70 NIS. To find the place go to the souvenir stall with the dark blue Kodak-emblazoned awning by the lighthouse and ask for Jerry, the manager. The nearby *HI – Akko Youth Hostel* (☎ (04) 991 1982) is housed in a grand old building which was at one time the residence of the Turkish Governor. Beds are 28 NIS (24 NIS for card holders) in large single sex dorms or 45 NIS (41 NIS) with breakfast included. To get to the hostel follow HaHaganah St down to the lighthouse and then continue round to the left.

There is a third hostel in Akko, *Walied's Gate Hostel*, but we really do not recommend this place.

Places to Eat

For cheap eating there are several felafel and

shwarma places around the junction of Salah ad-Din and Al-Jazzar Sts.

The romance of a waterfront moonlit meal means that the restaurants around the lighthouse and the harbour are easily the most popular venues for dining. *Ezra's Sun Restaurant* and the adjacent *Ptolomis* on the harbour front both serve a standard meat menu of kebabs, entrecôtes, schnitzels etc at prices ranging between 20 and 30 NIS. The location is better than the food, which is just average. The food at the *Galileo* and *Abu Christo* restaurants, on the other hand, is excellent, but it's pricey – 30 NIS minimum. They're both to be found east of the lighthouse in the vicinity of the HI youth hostel.

If you've got the use of a kitchen then supplies can be bought at *Elias Dieb & Sons* (no English sign) a great little cave-like supermarket on Salah ad-Din, opposite the Souq al-Abiad.

Getting There & Away

Departing frequently, bus Nos 252 and 272 connect Akko with Haifa (30 to 50 minutes; 8 NIS), as do bus Nos 251 and 271, but these are slower services. Bus Nos 270, 271 and 272 (express) run north to Nahariya (15 to 25 minutes; 5 NIS). There are also buses about every 30 minutes to and from Safed.

NAHARIYA

One of Israel's quietest seaside resorts, Nahariya, the definitive one-street town, seems to exist in a perpetual state of Shabbat. The town's appeal – if it can be said to have any – lies solely in its beaches, although there is also an uninteresting Canaanite temple and a dull museum. The local tourist office is on the ground floor of the municipality building, just west of the bus station on HaGa'aton Blvd – maybe they can whip up some enthusiasm for the place.

Bus Nos 270, 271 and 272 (express) run to Akko (15 to 25 minutes; 5 NIS), with the 271 and 272 services continuing to Haifa (45 to 70 minutes; 10.50 NIS). Departures are every 20 minutes until 10.30 pm.

AROUND NAHARIYA
Rosh HaNikra

On the sensitive Israel-Lebanon border (photography could be risky), carved by the sea into the base of tall white cliffs, this series of caves was enlarged by the British for a railway and by the Israelis to improve access for visitors. The road up from Nahariya (10 km to the south) halts at an observation point/tourist centre (☎ (04) 985 7109) from where the only practical way to reach the caves is by cable car. The cars operate Sunday to Thursday from 8.30 am to 6 pm, and Friday from 8.30 am to 4 pm.

Bus Nos 20 and 22 from Nahariya go direct to Rosh HaNikra (15 minutes; 5 NIS) but there are only three services a day. Other more frequent services pass the Rosh HaNikra junction but from there it's a three km walk to the site.

Peqi'in & Beit Jan

A predominantly Druze village, Peqi'in has a Jewish community which, according to tradition, has never been exiled from the Holy Land. The town has a pitta bread speciality served up in the *Jewish Community Restaurant* (actually owned by Arabs) and a Druze *cafe* across the road by the bus station. Bus No 44 runs about every hour from Nahariya; get off at the old village Peqi'in Atika, the modern settlement of Peqi'in Hadasha one stop before. Nearby Beit Jan, another Druze settlement, is the highest village in Israel.

Montfort Castle

Montfort is not the most impressive of Israel's Crusader castles but it is interesting and a visit involves a pleasant hike. Get there from Nahariya by bus to Goren from where it's then a 1½ hour walk.

The Galilee

With its rich combination of beautiful scenery and religious heritage Galilee is probably the most popular area of the country, both with Israelis and foreign visitors alike. This is Israel's lushest region, with green valleys, verdant forests, lots of fertile farmland and, of course, the Sea of Galilee itself. Serious Bible territory, Galilee is where Jesus did most of his preaching as well as a spot of water walking and some fish multiplying.

NAZARETH

Generally believed to be the home of Mary and Joseph and the infant Jesus, Nazareth usually fails to match the high expectations of pilgrims and tourists. The several important churches are unfortunately overshadowed by the unattractive and rapidly expanding modern town. Beyond the holy sites there's little here, and with few places to eat and limited accommodation options most visitors will be content to make just a half day visit of Nazareth.

Orientation & Information

The main places of interest are concentrated in the centre of the old Arab town on and around Paul VI St. The other important street is the short Casa Nova St which intersects Paul VI St and continues up to the market – the local tourist information office (☎ 657 3003; fax 657 5279) is here, just downhill from the Basilica; it's open Monday to Friday from 8.30 am to 5 pm, and Saturday from 8.30 am to 2 pm; closed Sunday.

The telephone code for Nazareth is 06.

The Holy Sites

One of the Christian world's most holy shrines, the **Basilica of the Annunciation** is held by believers to stand on the site where the Angel Gabriel appeared to Mary to inform her that she was pregnant with the son of God. It's commemorated by a ponderous modern (1969) structure which is at least partially redeemed by an inventive interior.

Just up Casa Nova St from the Basilica is **St Joseph's Church**, built in 1914 and occupying the traditional site of Joseph's carpentry shop. This belief probably originated in the 17th century and today's church was built over the remains of an existing

medieval church. Down in the crypt you can see an underground cave used for grain storage in pre-Byzantine times. Up the side street across from the Basilica (the one with the Casa Nova Hospice on the corner), the **Sisters of Nazareth Convent** boasts one of the best examples of an ancient tomb sealed by a rolling stone; it lies under the present courtyard and can only be viewed by appointment.

At the top of Casa Nova St is the **Arab market** occupying a maze of steep and narrow, winding streets, in the midst of which is the **Greek Catholic Church** located on the site of the synagogue traditionally believed to be where Jesus regularly prayed and later taught. There's also a very attractive Greek Orthodox church, **St Gabriel's**, about a 10 minute walk north of the Basilica, two blocks west of where Paul VI St ends. Close by St Gabriel's is **Mary's Well**, also known as the Virgin's Fountain, now an unimpressive

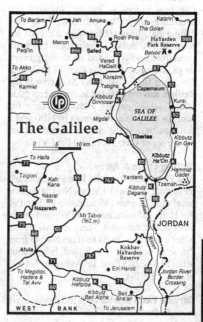

The Galilee

faucet but claimed by some as an alternative site for the appearance of the Angel Gabriel before Mary.

Places to Stay
The *Sisters of Nazareth Convent* (☎ 655 4304) provides by far the best accommodation in town. Dorm beds cost 18 NIS and there are also singles/doubles for 42/72 NIS. At Easter, especially, and through the summer, the place is busy with pilgrim groups from Europe so you'd be well advised to make a reservation if possible. To get there, go up Casa Nova St, turn left opposite the Basilica and it's up the street on the right. The *Casa Nova Hospice* (☎ 657 1367), across from the basilica on Casa Nova St, is also very popular and usually filled by Italian pilgrim groups. The rooms are pleasant and the food served is good. Singles/doubles are 90/126 NIS, breakfast is included.

Places to Eat
The best places to eat in Nazareth are undoubtedly in the Christian hospices. Failing that, the next best thing is to cook for yourself. The market is the place to buy fresh vegetables and fruit, and there are grocery shops and bakeries along Paul VI St in both directions from Casa Nova St. Between the Basilica and the bus station are several good felafel stalls, whilst a decent place for houmos (10 NIS) and shwarma (10 NIS) and a bottle of beer is the *Astoria Restaurant* on the corner of Casa Nova and Paul VI Sts.

Getting There & Away
Bus From outside of the Hamishbir department store on Paul VI St bus No 431 departs hourly for Tiberias (45 minutes; 12.30 NIS). For Haifa (45 minutes; 13 NIS) stand on the other side of the street. There are also several buses a day direct to Akko (take No 343 from the stop opposite the Egged information office; 13.40 NIS) and Tel Aviv (bus No 823 or 824; 22 NIS).

Service Taxis Service taxis to Tiberias leave from in front of the Hamishbir department store. For Haifa and Tel Aviv go to the street by the side of the Paz petrol station.

MEGIDDO
Otherwise known as Armageddon (from the Hebrew *Har Megiddo*, meaning Mt of Megiddo), the site synonymous with the last great battle on earth is today an uninspirational mound of baked earth maintained by the National Parks Authority. Excavations have unearthed the remains of 20 distinct historical periods from 4000 to 400 BC, but it takes some stretch of the imagination to see any traces of former grandeur in the modern-day site. Help, however, is given in the form of some excellent models in the visitors' centre museum and by informative signs planted around the site. It's open Saturday to Thursday from 8 am to 5 pm, and Friday from 8 am to 4 pm.

The archaeological site is two km north of Megiddo Junction, a well-signposted intersection of the main Haifa road with the Afula-Hadera highway. There are several Haifa-Afula buses passing by daily as well as half-hourly Tiberias to Tel Aviv services – ask the driver to let you off at Megiddo Junction and then walk or hitch a lift up the slight hill.

BEIT SHE'AN
The attraction here is one of the country's most extensive archaeological sites, including its best-preserved Roman amphitheatre. Excavations and restoration work are ongoing but among the other structures so far revealed are a temple, a basilica, a nymphaeum, a wide colonnaded Roman street leading down to the great theatre, and extensive Byzantine baths covering over half a hectare.

The site is open to visitors Saturday to Thursday from 8 am to 5 pm and Friday from 8 am to 4 pm (closing one hour earlier in the winter). Beit She'an is a stop-off point for the Tiberias-Jerusalem bus and there are also regular services between here and Afula, making it accessible from Nazareth.

BELVOIR

Belvoir is a ruined 12th century Crusader castle with great views over the Jezreel Valley, Jordan's Gilead Mountains and, on a clear day, even the Sea of Galilee. It's one of those places which perhaps isn't worth making a great detour for but if you happen to be passing then it's definitely worth stopping by.

The castle is part of the **Kokhav Ha-Yarden Reserve** (open Saturday to Thursday from 8 am to 5 pm, and Friday from 8 am to 4 pm), 30 km south of the Tzemah junction at the southern tip of Lake Galilee. Buses running between Tiberias and Beit She'an will drop you off at the signposted intersection with the road that leads up to the castle. From here it is a steep six km walk or hitchhike.

TIBERIAS

As the only town on the shores of the Sea of Galilee, Tiberias is the obvious base from which to enjoy the surrounding lakeside beauty spots. With its mix of natural spas and tombs of venerated sages, the town is a popular holiday centre where observant Jews can combine treatment of the body with purification of the soul, while the not so observant flock here too for lakeside wine and fish dining and the lively nightlife.

Although there isn't much to be seen of the town's rich history, there is a free two hour guided tour that goes a little way to pointing out the evidence; it departs from outside the tourist information office (in the Archaeological Park beside the Jordan River Hotel) on Sunday, Monday and Thursday at 6 pm, and Wednesday at 9 am.

The telephone code for Tiberias is 06.

The Old Town

As out of place as a pin-stripe suited gent at a teenage rave, the dignified little **Al-Omri Mosque** is one of the few structures of any age (mid-18th century) in Tiberias' not-so-old Old Town. A second mosque, the waterfront Jamaa al-Bahr (1880), now serves as the **Antiquities Museum** with displays of archaeological artefacts, maps and prints.

Part of a modern waterfront development across from the museum, the **Galilee Experience** is a 37 minute summation of the history, geography and spiritual significance of the region presented in the form of a state-of-the-art slide show.

St Peter's Church, on the restaurant-lined waterfront promenade, was originally built in the 12th century by the Crusaders but the present structure dates from 1870. The boat-shaped nave is a nod to St Peter's profession as a fisherman.

A few minutes walk along Ben Zakkai St from the centre of town, the **Tomb of Rabbi Moshe Ben Maimon** is worth visiting to observe some of the rituals of Jewish sacred life. Maimonides, as Ben Maimon is better known, was one of the 12th century's most highly regarded sages and personal physician to Saladin. Modest dress is essential.

Hammat Tiberias

Tiberias owes its existence to the hot springs two km south of the modern town, which were the focus of the original Roman settlement of Hammat Tiberias. The ancient site has been packaged up as the **Hammat Tiberias National Park**, which comprises the Ernest Lehman Museum, housed in what was originally part of a Turkish bathhouse; the ruins of a 6th century bathhouse; and the partially excavated remains of the 4th century Severus Synagogue, which has a beautiful zodiac **mosaic floor**. The park is open Sunday to Thursday from 8 am to 5 pm, and Friday from 8 am to 4 pm. To get there you can either walk along the lake shore road south from the town centre, which will take about 20 to 25 minutes, or you can try waiting for the infrequent bus No 2 or 5.

The traditions of Hammat Tiberias are maintained by the **Tiberias Hot Springs complex**, which consists of a Health Springs Centre for people with serious skin problems and a modern lakeside Relaxation Springs Centre open to the general public to enjoy a good soak or massage. It's very pricey.

Up the hill from the national park and

ISRAEL

springs is one of Judaism's holiest sites, the **tomb of Meir Ba'al Hanes**, the 2nd century rabbi who helped to compile the Mishnah, which is part of the Talmud.

Places to Stay

Hostels Beds in Tiberias generally cost a little more than in other parts of Israel; dorm beds (unless otherwise stated) are from 25 to 30 NIS while private rooms start at a minimum of 70 NIS. Add about 25% on top of that during the Jewish holidays.

One of the most popular places in town is the *Aviv Hostel* (☎ 672 0007, 672 3510), a large whitewashed building on HaGalil St on the southern edge of town. The windowless dorms are a little claustrophobic but they are at least air-conditioned. Private doubles are available at 120 to 150 NIS. The Aviv is the main place in town for bike rentals, charging 40 NIS per day (or 30 NIS for ungeared bikes). The management also run full-day tours around Upper Galilee and the Golan for 90 NIS per person.

A good alternative is the *Maman Hostel* (☎ 679 2986) on Ha'Atzmaut St, well

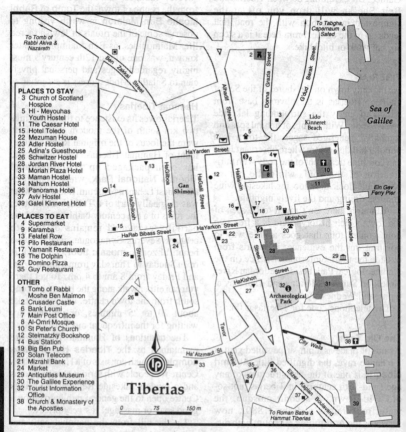

PLACES TO STAY
3 Church of Scotland Hospice
5 HI - Meyouhas Youth Hostel
11 The Caesar Hotel
15 Hotel Toledo
22 Mezuman House
23 Adler Hostel
25 Adina's Guesthouse
26 Schwitzer Hostel
28 Jordan River Hotel
31 Moriah Plaza Hotel
33 Maman Hostel
34 Nahum Hostel
36 Panorama Hotel
37 Aviv Hostel
39 Galei Kinneret Hotel

PLACES TO EAT
4 Supermarket
9 Karamba
13 Felafel Row
16 Pilo Restaurant
17 Yamanit Restaurant
18 The Dolphin
27 Domino Pizza
35 Guy Restaurant

OTHER
1 Tomb of Rabbi Moshe Ben Maimon
2 Crusader Castle
6 Bank Leumi
7 Main Post Office
8 Al-Omri Mosque
10 St Peter's Church
12 Steimatzky Bookshop
14 Bus Station
19 Big Ben Pub
20 Solan Telecom
21 Mizrahi Bank
24 Market
29 Antiquities Museum
30 The Galilee Experience
32 Tourist Information Office
38 Church & Monastery of the Apostles

To Tomb of Rabbi Akiva & Nazareth

To Tabgha, Capernaum & Safed

Sea of Galilee

Lido Kinneret Beach

Ein Gev Ferry Pier

The Promenade

HaYarden Street
HaYarkon Street
HaKishon Street
Midrahov
HaRab Bibass Street

Ben Zakkai Street
Alhadif Street
Donna Grazia Street
G'dud Barak Street
HaGalil Street
HaGiboa
HaShiloah
HaBanim Street
Tavor Street

Gan Shimon

Archaeological Park

City Walls

Elizer Kaplan Boulevard

Tiberias

0   75   150 m

To Roman Baths & Hammat Tiberias

ISRAEL

looked after with large airy dorms and spotless showers, and there's a garden and terrace round the back. The *Nahum Hostel* (☎ 672 1505), two minutes away from the Maman on Tavor St, is another backpackers' standby. It has a bar, a kitchen and there are bicycles for hire (30 NIS per day). They have some very attractive air-con double rooms at 140 NIS, with their own shower/toilet, and kitchen area.

The *HI – Meyouhas Youth Hostel* (☎ 672 1775; fax 672 0372), formerly the prestigious Hotel Tiberias (built 1862), is now one of the country's nicest HI hostels. Accommodation is in two to four-bed dorms at 42 NIS per night to non-members, breakfast included. There are also single/double rooms at 90/126 NIS.

Hotels Just past the Meyouhas Youth Hostel, towards the lake, is the comfortable *Church of Scotland Hospice* (☎ 672 3769; fax 679 0145) with excellent facilities including a garden and private beach. B&B is 90 to 120 NIS per person in larger than average singles/doubles.

Places to Eat

With a lengthy parade of felafel stands on HaYarden St, just west of the junction with HaGalil St, Tiberias is a great place for fans of the deep-fried chickpea. The cheapest shashlik and shwarma is at the shops on the west side of HaGalil; try *Al-Farsi*, the grubby kiosk (no English sign) on the corner of HaGalil and HaYarkon Sts for shashlik and salad in pitta for 10 NIS.

The cheapest sit-down dining is at the restaurants and cafes along HaBanim St, at the top end of the *midrahov* (pedestrian mall). *The Dolphin*, on the corner, does inexpensive standards like kebab or schnitzel with salad and chips for 20 NIS, while the *Yamanit Restaurant* next door serves up malawach, large flaky-pastry pancakes, filled with either meat, mushrooms, egg or honey, for 14 to 16 NIS each.

Across the road from the above two is the *Pilo* (no sign in English), easily identified by the crowds at the tables outside, all devour-

ing what is easily Tiberias' best dining deal: grilled St Peter's fish with chips and salad for 25 NIS.

For picnicking supplies there's a small *market* with some fruit and vegetable stalls, just south of Gan Shimon (Shimon Park), off HaYarkon St. It's open Sunday to Friday. There's also a very convenient *supermarket* behind the Al-Omri Mosque, open Sunday to Thursday from 7 am to 6.45 pm, Friday from 7 am to 3.30 pm, and Saturday 8 to 10 pm.

Most of the town's liveliest restaurants are to be found on the midrahov, along the promenade and on HaKishon St. The majority serve a very similar menu with little variation in price from one place to the next. The staple speciality is St Peter's fish but despite its obvious popularity it is not likely to be a gastronomic highlight of your trip to Israel. For a break from grilled fish and meat, try the *Karamba*, a vegetarian restaurant serving up soups or crepes (12 to 15 NIS), baked potatoes (18 to 22 NIS), vegetables au gratin (24 NIS), salads (22 NIS upwards) and various desserts. Karamba is at the north end of the promenade and it's open daily from about noon until the early hours.

Entertainment

The cafes and bars on and around the midrahov are where the crowds form in the evening, bunching at *La Pirat* and *Big Ben*, both of which are loud and raucous until well after midnight. There are a couple of other popular places at the northern end of the promenade, too. All these bars, however, are geared to the Israeli tourist which means 12 NIS or more a beer and awful music to boot. Budget travellers might prefer the rooftop bar at the *Nahum Hostel* which serves bottled beer at 7 NIS and shows videos most nights.

Through the summer there are discos on the Lido Beach and, for the suitably inebriated, departing from the same place each evening at 8 pm there's a disco cruise ship (15 NIS per person).

Also, check the tourist information office for special events. For example, every Passover there's the Ein Gev Music Festival and there's also an annual summer Sea of Galilee Festival which attracts a lot of attention.

Getting There & Away

Bus There's a direct bus to Tel Aviv (2½ hours; 24 NIS) departing at least every hour and services to Jerusalem (2½ hours; 28 NIS) are even more frequent. There are also regular services to Haifa (75 minutes; 16 NIS), Nazareth (45 minutes; 13.20 NIS), Safed (60 minutes; 14 NIS) and to Beit She'an.

Service Taxis Outside the bus station and across the grass is where a few service taxis leave in the morning for Nazareth and occasionally Haifa.

SEA OF GALILEE

Not just a natural beauty spot, the Sea of Galilee is also Israel's major water supply. A freshwater lake fed by the Jordan River, the 21 km long Sea of Galilee lies 212m below sea level and, in a good summer, the lake can be as warm as 33°C.

The best way to explore the Sea of Galilee is to use Tiberias as a base and spend a day or two on a bicycle. It's 55 km all the way round the Sea of Galilee and if you're in shape it's perfectly possible to cycle the whole way round in a day, taking time out at one or two of the sites. But perhaps a better way of tackling it is to take the lake in two halves, each day finishing up at Kibbutz Ein Gev, opposite Tiberias, from where there's a regular ferry crossing back.

Six km north of Tiberias the lakeside road passes ancient **Migdal**, birthplace of Mary Magdalene; a tiny, white-domed shrine marks the site.

Within the grounds of Kibbutz Ginossar is the **Yigol Allon Centre** (☎ (06) 672 1495), a museum devoted to the theme 'man in the Galilee'. Its most celebrated exhibit is what shrewd tour operators have dubbed **'the Jesus boat'**, the skeletal remains of a fishing vessel, discovered only in 1986, that scientists have dated to the time of Christ's ministry.

Generally considered to be the most beautiful and serene of the Christian holy places **Tabgha** is associated with three of the New Testament's most significant episodes: the Sermon on the Mount, the Multiplication of the Loaves & Fishes, and Jesus' post-Resurrection appearance where he conferred the leadership of the church on Peter. Each one of these events is celebrated with a church, all located within a short distance of each other.

Capernaum also has various New Testament connections – it was the home base of Jesus when he started his ministry. The ruins of a 4th century church built on the supposed site of Jesus' lodgings are now one of the major attractions of a well-labelled **archaeological museum**.

Although its marketing department would have you believe otherwise there is little of interest at **Kibbutz Ein Gev** except the landing stage for the ferry over to Tiberias. Kibbutz Ha'On has an **ostrich farm** but that's easily topped at **Hammat Gader** where an alligator farm is just one of many attractions – others include some impressive Roman ruins and hot springs. Hammat Gader (☎ (06) 675 1039; fax 675 2745) is open Monday to Thursday from 7 am to 9.30 pm, Friday from 7 am to 11.30 pm, and Saturday and Sunday from 7 am to 6.30 pm. Admission is 27 NIS (students 23 NIS), which gives access to all the amenities, although some health and beauty facilities are charged extra. The site is eight km southeast of the Sea of Galilee (21 km from Tiberias). From Tiberias bus No 24 departs Sunday to Thursday at 8.45 and 10.30 am, and Friday at 8.30 and 9.30 am. Departures from Hammat Gader are Sunday to Thursday at noon and 3 pm, and Friday at noon and 1 pm. No buses run on Saturday.

Places to Stay

Camping If you thought camping was an alternative to paying high prices, think again. Camp sites on the shores of the Sea of Galilee, mostly run by kibbutzim, are quite expensive. However, if you have your own tent then there are 20 or so spots around the lake where you can pitch for free. The SPNI

Field School and the tourist information centre at Tzemah, at the southern tip of the lake, can give you details.

Hostels An attractive alternative to Tiberias for many visitors is to stay outside the town for at least some of their time in the region. In Tabgha the modern and extremely elegant *HI – Karei Deshe-Yoram Youth Hostel* (☎ (06) 672 0601; fax 672 4818) is set in attractive grounds with eucalyptus trees, a rocky beach and a few peacocks. Dorm beds are 18 NIS for members, and non-members pay 24 NIS.

Hotels The four-star-styled *Nof Ginnosar Guesthouse* (☎ (06) 679 2161; fax 679 2170), run by Kibbutz Ginnosar, provides comfortable accommodation beside the lake. It offers gardens, a private beach and watersports facilities in a very quiet and unhurried atmosphere. Singles cost from around US$73 to US$83 and doubles from US$83 to US$99. Just south of Tabgha, the kibbutz is off the main road from Tiberias, and is clearly signposted.

Getting Around
Bicycle The most popular way of getting around the lake is by bicycle. The lake shore road is relatively hill-free and with so many sites so close together then as long as you can deal with the heat, a bike is the ideal means of transport. You can rent bicycles from several of the hostels in Tiberias, including the Aviv (☎ (06) 672 3510), Nahum (☎ (06) 672 1505) and Adler (☎ (06) 672 0031). It isn't necessary to be a guest at these places. Expect to pay 30 or 40 NIS for the day.

Ferries Three times a day a ferry belonging to the kibbutz departs Ein Gev for Tiberias and then shuttles back. In summer 1995 the sailing times from Tiberias were 11.30 am, 1.30 and 4 pm. A one-way crossing takes 45 minutes and costs 15 NIS (25 NIS return). Bicycles are carried for free.

SAFED
Alternatively spelt Zefad, Tzfat or Tsfat, this is an attractive hilltop town with a rich heritage of Jewish mysticism, a heavy quota of new immigrants and an industrious artists' colony. The town is also blessed with a beautiful high-altitude setting and a temperate climate. The shortage of good budget accommodation and lack of evening entertainment weigh against an overnight stay but it's definitely worth a day visit (best made from Tiberias). Avoid Safed on the Shabbat when even the birds stay grounded.

Orientation & Information
Safed is spread over one perfectly rounded hill, with the bus station on the east side and the old town centre 180° away, directly opposite on the west side – Yerushalayim (Jerusalem) St makes a complete loop connecting the two.

Safed's local tourist information office (☎ 692 0961) is in the lobby of City Hall at 50 Yerushalayim St and is open Sunday to Thursday from 8 am to 4 pm; closed Friday and Saturday. Every Monday to Thursday at 9.45 am, and Friday at 10 am, Aviva Minoff (☎ (06) 692 0901) leads a walking tour of Safed from the tourist information office.

Although the main post and telephone office is on HaPalmach St (look for the radar dish next door, visible from the corner of Aliyah Bet St) some way from the centre, there is a convenient branch office at 37 Yerushalayim St. Bank branches are all on Yerushalayim St west of the Citadel. Opening hours are generally Sunday, Tuesday and Thursday from 8.30 am to 12.30 pm and 4 to 6 pm, Monday and Wednesday from 8.30 am to 12.30 pm, and Friday from 8.30 am to noon; closed Saturday. An exception is the First International Bank at 34 Yerushalayim St, which is closed Sunday, Tuesday and Thursday afternoons but open from 4 to 7 pm on Monday and Wednesday.

The telephone code for Safed is 06.

Things to See & Do
At the top of the hill, the pleasant breeze-cooled park and viewpoint **Gan HaMetsuda** was once the site of a Crusader citadel. Its

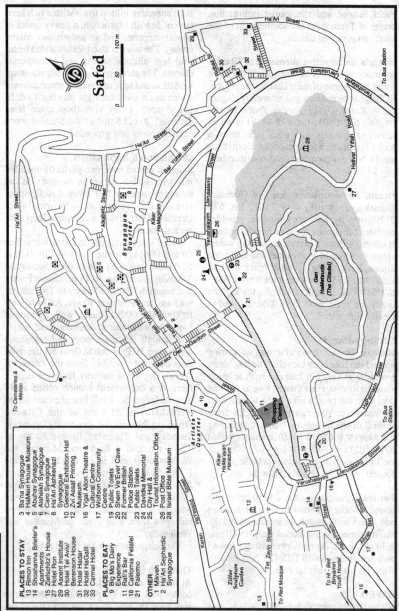

Safed

PLACES TO STAY
13 Rimon Inn
14 Shoshanna Briefer's Apartments
15 Zelfschitz's House
27 Hotel Ron
29 Ascent Institute
30 Hotel Tel Aviv
31 Berenson House
32 Hotel HaGalil
33 Carmel Hotel

PLACES TO EAT
9 Big Mo's Dairy
11 California Felafel
21 Palermo

OTHER
1 Mikveh
2 Ha'Ari Sephardic Synagogue
3 Ba'na Synagogue
4 HaMeiri House Museum
5 Abuhav Synagogue
6 Alsheikh Synagogue
7 Caro Synagogue
8 Ha'Ari Ashkenazi Synagogue
10 General Exhibition Hall
12 Assaf Printing Museum
16 Yigal Allon Theatre & Cultural Centre
17 Wolfson Community Centre
19 Public Toilets
20 Shem Ve'Ever Cave
22 Former British Police Station
23 Public Toilets
24 Davidka Memorial
25 Post Office
26 Tourist Information Office
28 Israel Bible Museum

outer walls once followed the line now marked by Yerushalayim St but you can only see remains of one of the inner walls on Hativat Yiftah Rd, near the inappropriately named **Israel Bible Museum**, actually a collection of biblical themed sculpture, painting and lithography by an American-Jewish artist.

The old quarters that are the heart of central Safed tumble down from Yerushalayim St in a snakes and ladders compendium of ankle-straining stairways and slithering alleys. They are divided uncompromisingly in two by **Ma'alot Olei HaGardom**, a broad, stiff stairway running down from Yerushalayim St. It was built by the British after the riots of 1929 to divide the town and keep the Arab and Jewish communities apart. The area to the north of the stairway is known as the **Synagogue Quarter**, the town's old traditional Jewish neighbourhood, centred on **Kikar HaMaginim** (Defenders' Square), reached by descending the steps just north of City Hall.

Of the many synagogues in this quarter there are two that should be visited; just down from the Kikar is the **Ha'Ari Ashkenazi Synagogue** while a little south is the **Caro Synagogue**. They are usually open throughout the day to visitors, and admission is free although donations are requested. Suitable clothing must be worn (no shorts, no bare shoulders) and cardboard yarmulkes are provided to cover men's heads. Photography is permitted except on the Shabbat (sundown Friday to sundown Saturday).

The part of the old town south of the Ma'alot Olei HaGardom St stairway used to be the Arab quarter but since their defeat and subsequent withdrawal in 1948 the place has been developed by the Jews as an **artists' colony**. The best place to start any walk is at the **General Exhibition Hall**, housed in a white-domed Ottoman-era mosque just a little to the south of the stairway. The opening hours of the exhibition hall vary but it's usually open for at least a part of every day, Saturday included. Many of the individual artists' studios are also open on Saturday, which makes art appreciation one of the few possibilities for a Shabbat in Safed.

Places to Stay

Shoshanna Briefer's Apartments (☎ 697 3939) are run by Shoshanna Briefer, a Rumanian lady with distinct grey-black hair who rents out beds (25 NIS) in a couple of centrally located but dingy apartments. Look for her at the central bus station where she often waits to greet potential guests. If you don't see her or, even less likely, she doesn't see you, phone her and arrange to meet at the apartments (she lives elsewhere); from the bus station climb the stairs up to Yerushalayim St, turn left and follow the road to the bridge, climb the stairs up to the bridge and cross, heading south away from the hill. Take the first alley to your right, running diagonally in the same general direction as HaPalmach St. The apartments are towards the end – one is on the right, with a grey door, about two-thirds of the way along and the other is at the end, on the left, behind a large green metal door.

On the same alley, just before Shoshanna's apartments, is *Ziefschitz's House*. The Orthodox family of the same name offer accommodation from 20 NIS per night. The rooms, off a central courtyard, have from two to four beds and are quite attractive in a spartan sort of way.

Easily mistaken for a modern high school, the *HI – Beit Binyamin Youth Hostel* (☎ 692 1086; fax 697 3514) at 1 Lohamei HaGeta'ot St in South Safed suffers badly from being a steeply gradiented 20 to 25 minute walk from the town centre. It also has a very off-putting institutional air about it. A dorm bed is 42 NIS and there are also single (90 NIS) and double (126 NIS) rooms available.

Places to Eat

Safed is not the place to plan on breaking your diet of felafel and shwarma – away from street food our experiences of dining here were invariably disappointing.

Most cafes and restaurants are on the pedestrianised part of Yerushalayim St

ISRAEL

although there are several good felafel places on the stretch between the bus station and HaPalmach, one of the best of which is *California Felafel*, right beside the bridge. Another good snacking place is the *Palermo*, which serves up reasonably priced pizza by the slice; it's on Yerushalayim St right by the top of the Ma'alot Olei HaGardom stairway.

In the Synagogue Quarter, *Big Mo's Dairy Experience* offers kosher fast food, including pizza, bagels, blintzes and sandwiches. Run by Orthodox Jews from the USA, current US sports news is provided for patrons. It's on Tarpat St, just north of Ma'alot Olei HaGardom.

Although the food is neither cheap nor particularly good at *Rafi's Bar* (☎ 697 4032), we mention it here as the only place open for eating on a Friday night (from 9 pm to 2 or 3 am). It's on the 3rd floor of the shopping centre – entering from Yerushalayim St go down two floors.

Getting There & Away

There are services to Haifa (two hours; 21 NIS) every half hour until 9 pm (5.45 pm on Friday) and hourly to Tiberias (one hour; 14 NIS) until 7 pm (4 pm on Friday). Three buses a day go to Tel Aviv (otherwise change at Haifa) and one a day to Jerusalem (otherwise change at Rosh Pina).

The Upper Galilee & the Golan

The Upper Galilee is an area of lush greenery watered by the run-off from the surrounding mountains. These streams come together in the Hula Valley to form the Jordan River, provider of most of Israel's fresh water. The chain of high peaks known as the Golan (or the Golan Heights) rises to form a barrier between the fertile Jordan Valley and the arid Syrian lands to the east. The Golan also acts as a political wedge between the two neighbouring countries, with Syria asserting

that there will never be peace while the Israelis occupy the Heights.

A relative lack of frequent public transport makes the Upper Galilee and Golan considerably more difficult to explore than most other parts of Israel. Those who have limited time and money might decide to participate in one of the tours mentioned below and visit the area for a day with a guide to point out the major places of interest. If you're following your own schedule then we recommend planning for a couple of days in the area, staying for one or possibly two nights. The only budget accommodation to be found is in the far north at Tel Hai, near Kiryat Shmona, or in the south at Katzrin.

Information

There's a local tourism authority information station (☎ (06) 693 5016) at the Mahanayim Junction, three km north of Rosh Pina. They'll be able to help with current details of accommodation and local sites. They're open daily from 8 am to 4.30 pm.

For updated hiking and day-trip information, the best bet is to call in at one of the three SPNI field schools in the region:

Golan – Katzrin (☎ (06) 696 1234; fax 696 1233).
Keshet Yehonatan – Moshav Keshet, 12 km east of Katzrin, just off road No 98 (☎ (06) 696 2506; fax 696 1702)
Hermon – south off road No 99, near Kibbutz Snir, midway between the Tel Dan and Banias Nature Reserves (☎ (06) 694 1091; fax 695 1480)

Organised Tours

From Akko, Walied's Gate Hostel (☎ (04) 991 0410, 991 4700) runs a bus trip two or three times a week depending on the demand. Departing at 8.30 am, the tour takes in Safed, the Good Fence, Banias and Majdal Shams, returning to Akko about 6 pm. The cost is 100 NIS per person. From Tiberias, the Aviv Hostel (☎ (06) 672 0007, 672 3510) organises something similar charging 90 NIS per person.

Also operating from Tiberias on Tuesday, Thursday and Saturday (April to October only) Egged Tours (☎ (06) 672 0474) takes an air-con bus on a circuit of Capernaum,

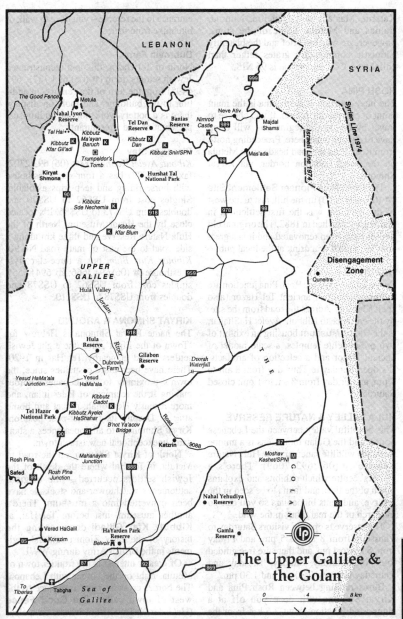

LEBANON

SYRIA

999

The Good Fence

Metula

Neve Ativ

Nahal Iyon
Reserve

Tel Dan
Reserve

Banias
Reserve

Nimrod
Castle

989

Majdal
Shams

Tel Hai

Kibbutz
Ma'ayan
Baruch

K

Kibbutz
Dan

K

Kibbutz
Kfar Gil'adi

Trumpeldor's
Tomb

99

Kibbutz Snir/SPNI

Mas'ada

99

Kiryat
Shmona

Hurshat Tal
National Park

90

Kibbutz
Sde Nechemia

K

918

978

98

Kibbutz
Kfar Blum

K

UPPER
GALILEE

959

Disengagement
Zone

Hula Valley

Quneitra

918

Hula
Reserve

Dubrovin
Farm

Gilabon
Reserve

Dvorah
Waterfall

Yesud HaMa'ala
Junction

Yesud
HaMa'ala

Kibbutz
Gadot

K

Tel Hazor
National Park

Kibbutz Ayelet
HaShahar

K

B'not Ya'acov
Bridge

91

Katzrin

9088

87

Moshav
Keshet/SPNI

M

Rosh Pina

Mahanayim
Junction

888

Safed

89

Rosh Pina
Junction

Nahal Yehudiya
Reserve

808

98

Vered HaGalil

Korazim

85

HaYarden Park
Reserve

Belvoir

Gamla
Reserve

869

Tabgha

87

92

To
Tiberias

Sea of
Galilee

**The Upper Galilee &
the Golan**

0   4   8 km

ISRAEL

Katzrin, Mas'ada and Quneitra, Nimrod, Banias and Metula. Some of the stops, however, are way too brief and the blatantly Zionistic commentary grates rather than enlightens. Cost per person is 96 NIS.

ROSH PINA

The busy junction at Rosh Pina is the main point of entry to the region. If you choose to travel by bus in the region you will often have to change buses here. Proceeding north from Rosh Pina the road heads up to Metula on the Israel-Lebanon border, via Kiryat Shmona.

The **Rosh Pina Pioneer Settlement Site** (☎ (06) 693 6603) up the hill, just to the west of the junction, was the first settlement in Galilee, established in 1882. The original old houses have been renovated and it is a great spot for a meal or a drink at the local pub.

HAZOR

Seven km north of the Rosh Pina junction are the excavations of ancient Tel Hazor (also spelt Khatsor). Across the road from the site, by the entrance to Kibbutz Ayelet HaShahar, is the **Hazor Museum** housing an exhibit of two pre-Israelite temples, a scale model of ancient Hazor and a selection of artefacts. It's open Sunday to Thursday from 8 am to 4 pm, and Friday from 8 am to 1 pm; closed Saturday.

HULA VALLEY & NATURE RESERVE

This beautiful valley between the Lebanese border and the Golan mountains is a unique wetlands wildlife sanctuary, the Hula Nature Reserve (☎ (06) 693 7069). There's a visitors' centre which exhibits and explains much of the flora and fauna to be seen in the reserve, and rents binoculars so you can go in search of the real thing in the wild.

The reserve is open to visitors Saturday to Thursday from 8 am to 5 pm, and Friday from 8 am to 4 pm, and there are free guided tours on Saturday, Sunday, Tuesday and Thursday between 9.30 am and 1.30 pm.

Buses running between Rosh Pina and Kiryat Shmona will drop you off at a signposted junction about 2.5 km from the entrance to the reserve – you have to walk or hitchhike from there.

Dubrovin Farm

North of Tel Hazor, this is a reconstructed Jewish settlers' farm (☎ (06) 693 7371, 693 4495) from the turn of the century. In addition to the buildings and tools on display, there is a pottery workshop, an audiovisual presentation and a restaurant.

Places to Stay

Kibbutz Ayelet HaShahar (☎ (06) 693 2302; fax 693 4777) has a four-star guesthouse with horse riding and jeep trips available. Singles cost from US$62 to US$70 and doubles from US$73 to US$86. It's located close by the Hazor Museum. North of the Hula Nature Reserve and three km along a side road to the east of main road No 90, *Kibbutz Kfar Blum* has a three-star style guesthouse (☎ (06) 694 3666; fax 694 8555); singles cost from US$62 to US$78 and doubles from US$78 to US$110.

KIRYAT SHMONA & AROUND

The name Kiryat Shmona is Hebrew for 'Town of the Eight', after the eight Jewish settlers killed at nearby Tel Hai in 1920. There have been more casualties since, the town's proximity to the Lebanese border making it the recipient of Palestinian, and more recently Hezbollah, rocket and bomb attacks. Despite its frontier-post position, Kiryat Shmona is to all appearances a standard, unexceptional new Israeli town.

North of Kiryat Shmona, on the road to Metula, is **Tel Hai** where the death of the Jewish settlers occurred – the original settlement's watchtower and stockade have been converted into a **museum**. There's another museum, just before Tel Hai, at **Kibbutz Kfar Gil'adi** documenting the history of the early Zionist settlers' regiments in the British Army during WWI.

Of greater interest is the frontier town of Metula, right on the border with Lebanon. The border crossing point is a place to the west of town called **The Good Fence** (HaGader HaTova) from where, on a clear day, you can see across the border to several Lebanese Christian villages and Beaufort Castle to the north-west.

East of the Kiryat Shmona-Metula road is the **Nahal Iyon Nature Reserve**, which encompasses the valley of the Iyon River and its several waterfalls, the most impressive of which is the 18 metre high **Tanur Fall**.

Places to Stay & Eat

In Kiryat Shmona there's only the *Hotel North* (also called *HaTzafon*; ☎ (06) 694 4703), across the street from the bus station; singles/doubles are US$50/65. The *HI – Tel Hai Youth Hostel* (☎ (06) 694 8043; fax 694 1743) is a cheaper alternative offering dorm beds for 48 NIS. Breakfast is included and other meals are available. At the *Kfar Gil'adi Kibbutz Guesthouse* (☎ (06) 694 1414; fax 695 1248) singles cost from US$62 to US$78, and doubles from US$78 to US$110.

Getting There & Away

Kiryat Shmona is the major junction of the Upper Golan with connecting services to Tel Hai, Metula and the Israel-Lebanon border to the north, and Tel Dan, Banias, Nimrod Castle, Mt Hermon and Katzrin to the east. It's connected to the rest of Israel via bus Nos 541, 841 and 963, which run down to Tiberias (14 NIS) via the Hula Valley and Rosh Pina.

THE GOLAN

Main road No 99 heads east from Kiryat Shmona, across the Iyon River and then the Snir River, one of the principal sources of the Jordan River, to reach **Hurshat Tal National Park** after some five km. A popular and often crowded picnic spot, this forested area is famous for its ancient oaks. Bus Nos 25, 26 and 36 from Kiryat Shmona will drop you off here.

Further along road No 99 is Kibbutz Dan and the **Beit Ussishkin Museum** featuring audiovisuals, dioramas and other exhibits covering the flora and fauna, geology, topography and history of the region. There is also a birdwatching centre here.

The **Banias Nature Reserve** is probably the most spectacularly beautiful and popular spot in the whole Upper Galilee/Golan region. The heart of the reserve is a cave sanctuary while about one km distant is the **Banias waterfall**, the largest in the region. Less than two km east of Banias, **Nimrod Castle** is the most impressive and best preserved of Israel's Crusader castles. Bus No 55 from Kiryat Shmona passes by Banias twice a day; alternatively, walk the five km west to Kibbutz Dan where bus Nos 25, 26 and 36 run a bit more often.

Up in the north-east corner of the Golan region is the **Mt Hermon Ski Centre**. At 2224m Mt Hermon is Israel's highest peak (though only 7% of Hermon is actually in Israeli territory). There are surprisingly decent, albeit limited, skiing facilities here, based around the settlement of **Neve Ativ**, where there's a ski information centre (☎ (06) 698 1337). The snow season is usually late December to early April. Prices are as bad as you probably expect them to be.

Majdal Shams and **Mas'ada** are the two largest of four Druze villages in the area. Unlike the communities on Mt Carmel, these Druze are fiercely anti-Israeli and they have protested against the occupation and subsequent annexation of this area from Syria. About 15 km south from Mas'ada, the road reaches a high mound with an observation point. From here you can look across the UN-patrolled border to the Syrian ghost-town of **Quneitra**, abandoned as a result of the fighting in 1967. Damascus is a mere 30 km north-east of here.

Places to Stay

There's a *Camping Ground* (☎ (06) 694 2360) at the Hurshat Tal National Park where tent space costs 20 NIS per person, and three-bed bungalows are 110 NIS. The *SPNI Hermon Field Study Centre* (☎ (06) 694 1091; fax 6951 480) has guest cottages set among oak tree-shaded lawns. The price per night is approximately 60 NIS per person but call in advance because this place is often booked up. The Field Study Centre is near Kibbutz Snir, which is south of road No 99 about three km west of Banias.

KATZRIN & AROUND

The new 'capital' of the Golan, **Katzrin** is not an attractive town but it's as near to an ideal base from which to explore the area as you can get, especially for those on a tight budget. Around town there's the **Golan Archaeological Museum** and the **Ancient Katzrin Park**, with the remains of a 3rd century synagogue and two reconstructed houses. There is also an excellent SPNI Field Study Centre on Daliyat St on the southern edge of Katzrin.

There are some terrific hiking opportunities in the area – ask at the field school for details about the attractive **Dvorah Waterfall** and other waterfalls, water pools and hiking in the **Gilabon Nature Reserve**.

South of Katzrin is **Gamla**, a spectacular site overlooking the Sea of Galilee, believed to be the ruins of an ancient Jewish stronghold where, as at Masada on the Dead Sea, a Roman siege ended with mass suicide.

Places to Stay

The SPNI's *Golan Field Study Centre* (☎ (06) 696 1234; fax 696 1233) in Katzrin has a modern, clean and comfortable guesthouse in which beds in air-con dorms are 60 NIS per person. To the south it has a camp site with tent sites for 16 NIS.

Getting There & Away

Bus Nos 55, 56 and 57 connect Katzrin with Rosh Pina (30 minutes; 7.50 NIS), just a couple of km east of Safed, and bus Nos 15, 16 and 19 go to Tiberias (45 minutes; 11.50 NIS).

Bus No 55 goes twice a day from Katzrin to Kiryat Shmona via Mas'ada.

The Dead Sea

It's the ultimate Israel cliche, the picture of the swimsuited bather lying in – almost on – the water, feet up and newspaper open, like a Sunday morning in bed. But unlike a camel ride at the pyramids or wrapping a *kaffiyeh* round your neck, this is one Middle Eastern

cliche well worth indulging in. With a shoreline of some 90 km there is no one bathing spot but you are advised to take your dip somewhere with shower facilities – the Dead Sea has a slightly slimy quality. After the obligatory float, the next popular thing to do is to visit Masada, a place which readers' letters consistently rate as Israel's number one attraction. Not as well known or as well frequented by travellers, the Ein Gedi Nature Reserve also rates some exploration.

Be aware that bus services in the Dead Sea region are very infrequent and to avoid hanging around, wilting under the sun, you

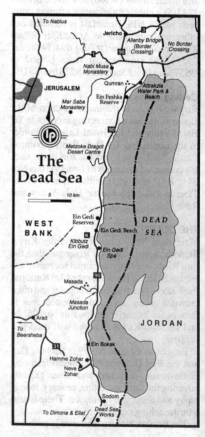

The Dead Sea

0   5   10 km

need to plan your itinerary in advance. You also, incidentally, need to carry plenty of water as dehydration can be a very real problem.

Organised Tours

By far the cheapest way of sampling the Dead Sea region is to sign up for the 12 hour tour you'll see advertised in almost all the hostels in Jerusalem. It departs the Old City at 3 am each morning, getting you down to Masada in time to watch the sunrise over the desert. There's a visit to the Ein Gedi reserves and a float in the Dead Sea before photostops at Qumran and Jericho's Mount of Temptation. Despite the stopwatch-timed schedule most travellers find that they get to see all they want. SPNI Tours operates a very similar programme but it's about three times more expensive.

Dead Healthy?

Compared to regular sea water, the water of the Dead Sea contains 20 times as much bromine, 15 times as much magnesium and 10 times as much iodine – it is, in effect, a 33% solid substance. Bromine, a component of many sedatives, relaxes the nerves; magnesium counteracts skin allergies and clears the bronchial passages; iodine has a beneficial effect on certain glandular functions – or so it's claimed, especially by local health spa owners and the various Dead Sea cosmetic companies.

Due to the low altitude, there is 10% more oxygen in the air than at sea level, and the lack of urban development has kept it free of pollution. All of this increases the body's metabolic rate and has a bracing effect.

Healthy or not, soaking in the water of the Dead Sea can also be extremely painful. Wade in with any exposed cuts or grazes and you will gain instant enlightenment as to the meaning behind the phrase to 'rub salt in ones' wounds'. We guarantee that you are going to discover scratches and sores that you never knew you had. The magnesium chloride in the water gives it a revolting bitter taste and swallowing any can induce retching. Don't get the water in your eyes either as it will sting and inflame – if this happens then rinse them immediately with fresh water. ■

Metzoke Dragot (☎ (02) 964 501/4; fax 964 505) offers various tours and activities in the Judean Desert, either with or without accommodation. They are highly recommended by those who have experienced them.

Getting There & Away

The entire west coast of the Dead Sea, about 90 km in length, is served by a single main road (No 90) which comes off the Jerusalem-Jericho highway in the north and follows the shoreline southwards to Sodom, continuing to Eilat. The most comprehensive bus service is from Jerusalem's central bus station. Buses from there to Eilat and Beersheba go by Qumran (60 minutes; 14 NIS), Ein Gedi (90 minutes; 18 NIS) and Masada, and there should be something departing at least every hour or so.

QUMRAN

Described as 'the most important discovery in the history of the Jewish people', the **Dead Sea Scrolls**, now on display in Jerusalem, were found here in 1947. The site includes the settlement and caves of the Essenes, a Jewish sect who wrote the scrolls between 150 BC and 68 AD when the Romans dispersed them. The bus stops on the main road; follow the turn-off up the hill. There is a self-service *cafeteria* at the site. It's a hot climb up to the caves, so bring drinking water.

EIN GEDI

One of the country's most attractive oases, Ein Gedi is a lush area of freshwater springs, waterfalls, pools and tropical vegetation nestled in the arid desert landscape of the lowest place on earth. It's a haven for desert wildlife, which hangs in there despite the terrifyingly raucous coach loads of kids that rampage through the reserves on an almost daily basis. The beach is, undeservedly, one of the most popular on the Dead Sea.

Ein Gedi sprawls over four km – the nature reserves, field school and youth hostel are to the north, on the west side of the road.

ISRAEL

The field school has a small museum of local flora and fauna.

One km further south are the bathing beach, restaurant and camp site. Another 2.5 km to the south is the turn-off for Kibbutz Ein Gedi, with the Ein Gedi Spa (Hamme Mazor) sulphur baths 2.5 km beyond. Avoid weekends and holidays when Ein Gedi is noisy and crowded.

Places to Stay & Eat
You can sleep for free by the beach, but watch your gear as theft is not uncommon.

The *HI – Beit Sara Hostel* (☎ (07) 658 4165) charges 54 NIS for a place in an air-con eight bed dorm; a double room is 138 NIS (non-members pay a few shekels more). In both cases breakfast is included. Dinner is also available in the evenings. Check-in is from 4 pm onwards and check-out is 9 am. The hostel is about 250m north-west from the Ein Gedi Reserve bus stop.

One km to the south by the beach, *Ein Gedi Camping Village* (☎ (07) 658 4444; fax (07) 658 4455) has tent space for 24 NIS per person and air-con cabins for US$64 for a double, plus US$10 for each extra person. There is a self-service restaurant, a mini-market for supplies and a clubhouse with a snack bar, TV and video lounge.

Surrounded by tree-filled gardens beside the Dead Sea, with a swimming pool and hot spa all included in the price, the guesthouse at *Kibbutz Ein Gedi* (☎ (07) 659 4222; fax 658 4328) is one of the most popular in the country. Terms are half board only; singles cost from US$76 to US$109 and doubles from US$113 to US$153. Booking in advance is recommended.

MASADA
A free-standing, sheer-sided plateau high above the Dead Sea, Masada was fortified by Herod the Great. In 66 AD the Jews rose up against the Romans in what's known as the First Revolt, and a group of them called the Zealots captured the lightly guarded Masada. After suppressing the uprising in the rest of the country the Romans turned their attention finally to the mountain-top strong-hold. When defeat was inevitable the 967 men, women and children atop Masada committed mass suicide leaving only a couple of survivors left to tell the tale. The event figures large in the Israeli national psyche and the melodramatic utterance 'Masada shall not fall again' is a favoured pearl of political rhetoric.

The site and views are superb, and you can reach the top by cable car or on foot.

Places to Stay & Eat
The *HI – Isaac H Taylor Hostel* (☎ (07) 658 4349), by the Masada bus stop, provides air-con dorms at 46 NIS per person, with breakfast included. Sleeping out on top of Masada is no longer permitted but the hostel does have tent-pitching space.

Getting There & Away
There are about eight buses a day to Jerusalem (105 minutes; 21 NIS), four a day to Eilat and several to Beersheba.

The Negev

Stretching south-west from the Dead Sea, the Negev Desert accounts for almost half of Israel's land area. Most of the Negev remains largely uninhabited and there are only a handful of towns together with kibbutzim, moshavim and an estimated 75,000 Bedouin who live a nomadic lifestyle. Many visitors only see the Negev through a bus window en route to Eilat but there are places worth a visit, not far from the main roads.

Hiking
There are some excellent hikes in the Negev region taking in a surprising variety of landscapes. Particularly recommended are those around Sde Boker, Ein Avdat and Mitzpe Ramon (see individual entries in this section). The SPNI have field schools at Sde Boker, Mitzpe Ramon and Eilat, and at Hatzeva, 50 km south of the Dead Sea on road No 90 – these are the places to visit for

detailed maps and information, and recommendations on routes and desert sights.

ARAD

The relatively new town of Arad has commanding views of the desert and, in the distance, the Dead Sea but other than that for most people it's just a place to change buses. Nearby Tel Arad, the country's best example of an Early Bronze Age city, may be of interest to keen archaeologists.

BEERSHEBA

Unattractive, with little to see and little to do,

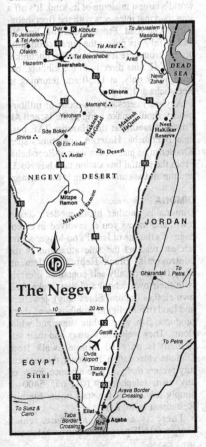

The Negev

Beersheba is unlikely to impress many visitors. It's the kind of town that gives most satisfaction when seen from the rear window of your departing bus. For the visitor, probably the greatest point of interest is the weekly Bedouin market held every Thursday morning. The museum is also pleasant but it won't take much time and as accommodation is so pricey there's little reason to stay overnight.

Information

The local tourist office (☎ (07) 623 6001/2) is on Nordau St, across from the entrance to the central bus station. You have to look hard to find it as it's marked by just a small sign in the window – look instead for Avis; the tourist office is next door. It's open Sunday to Thursday from 8 am to 4 pm; closed Friday and Saturday.

The main post office is just north of the central bus station on the corner of HaNessi'im and Nordau Sts while there are plenty of banks in the modern Kanion shopping centre beside the bus station.

The telephone code for Beersheba is 07.

Things to See

The much vaunted Thursday **Bedouin market** is rather disappointing; the only traces of authenticity are found very early in the morning. The exhibits at the **Negev Museum**, which occupies an old Turkish mosque in a park on Ha'Atzmaut St in the Old Town, include a history of the town itself as well as a series of archaeological artefacts from the whole Negev region. There is also a section on Bedouin culture, a collection of medieval maps of the Holy Land, and a 6th century mosaic floor depicting animals in its geometric design. The museum was closed for structural renovations at the time of our last visit but it's hoped that it will re-open early in 1997. The elegant building across from the museum is what used to be the Governor's Residence and was for a spell the city hall before becoming a small contemporary **art gallery**.

The site of an ancient incarnation of the town, **Tel Beersheba** is some five km north-east of modern Beersheba on the Jerusalem road. Here you can see remains of city walls and houses – it's a good idea to visit the Negev Museum first (if open) to have a better idea of what it's all about. Next to the ruins is a Visitors' Centre with a cafeteria, a restaurant and a small museum dealing with the Bedouin. To reach Tel Beersheba, take the thrice-daily bus for nearby Tel as-Sab, a new Bedouin village that is part of the Israeli programme of nomad settlement, and get off at the signs for the archaeological site.

Places to Stay

The *HI – Beit Yatziv Youth Hostel* (☎ 627 7444) isn't quite the cheapest place in town (there's a squalid hotel in the centre of town that's a few shekels cheaper) but overpriced as it is, it still offers the best value for money. It's a clean, modern complex with a swimming pool, pleasant gardens and no curfew. Comfortable dorm beds, in a room for six with toilet and shower, are 65 NIS. An adjoining guesthouse has singles/doubles for 126/186 NIS. To get there from the bus station cross the main Eilat Rd and head for the three large radio antennae visible above the buildings in front and slightly to your right. The road that runs in front of the antennae compound is Ha'Atzmaut; follow it past the mosque and the hostel is on the left-hand side, a further 400m on.

Places to Eat

The best place to eat is the Kanion shopping mall, which has the whole lower ground floor given over to felafel, shwarma and various fast-food franchises. The other place for inexpensive food is on and around Keren Kayemet Le-Y'Israel St, which is lined with cafes that serve the standard versions of grilled meats and salads, along with ice-cream parlours and fast-food outlets. If you fancy sitting down to dine try *Yitzhak's Bulgarian Restaurant* at 112 Keren Kayemet Le-Y'Israel St, which does kebabs, schnitzels, liver etc for around 20 NIS.

Getting There & Away

Bus Nos 370 and 380 run every 20 minutes

to Tel Aviv (80 minutes; 17.50 NIS), headed for the central bus station and Arlosoroff terminal respectively. Bus Nos 470 and 446 head for Jerusalem (90 minutes; 23.50 NIS), with one or the other departing every 30 minutes or so between. For Eilat (three hours; 35 NIS), there's the hourly No 394 via Mitzpe Ramon (80 minutes; 17.50 NIS) and a slow stopping service, No 397, which departs twice a day.

AROUND BEERSHEBA

Kibbutz Lahav has the Joe Alon Centre with its **Museum of Bedouin Culture**, the world's largest museum of its kind. It's off a side road that intersects with the Beersheba-Kiryat Gat road. From Beersheba, bus No 369 to Tel Aviv passes the intersection quite often – from here it's an eight km hitchhike; bus No 42 runs directly to the kibbutz, but once a day only, at 11.50 am, returning to Beersheba at 1.20 pm.

Anyone interested in aircraft or military history should make a trip to the **Israeli Air Force Museum** at the Hazerim IAF base near Beersheba. Hazerim (sometimes spelt Khatserim) is just six km west of Beersheba. From the central bus station take bus No 31 and the air base and museum is the last stop.

DIMONA

Dimona is another bleak modern desert town, and unless you're involved in espionage (it's the site of Israel's no-longer-secret nuclear reactor) the sole attraction is the controversial Black Hebrew settlement. They live a virtually self-contained lifestyle with their own school and they make their own clothes (natural fibres only), jewellery and food (their religion prohibits meat, dairy products, fish, eggs, white sugar and white flour). They welcome visitors and their settlement is only 10 minutes walk from Dimona's bus station. However, the community prefers that you give advance notice of any visit; telephone ☎ (07) 655 5400 or simply ask any of the staff in the Eternity Restaurant in Tel Aviv.

There is a small *guesthouse*, which charges 60 NIS per person with breakfast and dinner included. Alternatively, you can stay at the *Drachim Youth Hostel* (☎ (07) 655 6811) at 1 HaNassi St (the bus will pass the hostel as it comes into town) where dorm beds are 44 NIS.

With frequent buses from Beersheba (40 minutes) Dimona is not difficult to reach. There are also occasional buses from Arad and Mitzpe Ramon.

KIBBUTZ SDE BOKER & EIN AVDAT

A pioneering desert kibbutz, this was also where Israel's most celebrated prime minister David Ben-Gurion chose to live when he retired. His home is now a museum. South of the kibbutz, and overlooking the spectacular Wilderness of Zin, is the Sde Boker campus of the Ben-Gurion University. The graves of Ben-Gurion and his wife are nearby.

Ein Avdat is one of those freaks of nature – a pool of icy water in the hot expanse of desert, fed by waters that flow through an intricate network of channels. Dominated by a steep, winding canyon, reaching it involves an easy hike through the incredible scenery. The best way to reach Ein Avdat is by the Wilderness of Zin trail beginning near the Ben-Gurion University campus.

There is a SPNI field school (☎ (07) 656 5016; fax 558 352) on the campus of the Ben-Gurion University, where you should enquire about other hikes in the surrounding desert.

AVDAT

Not to be confused with Ein Avdat, this is a well-preserved Nabatean, Roman and Byzantine city perched on a nearby hill that dominates the desert skyline. Its impressive ruins and incredible vistas makes the steep climb well worth the effort.

MITZPE RAMON

Mitzpe is Hebrew for lookout and this small, struggling desert town is so named for its location overlooking the massive **Maktesh Ramon**, or Ramon Crater, one of Israel's geological highlights. While difficult to describe without going overboard, the crater

is said to remind visitors a little of the Grand Canyon and a lot of the moon. Its vital statistics are: 300m deep, eight km wide and 40 km long. A few nature trails have been marked out which lead through some of the most attractive and interesting sections.

Perched right on the edge of the Maktesh Ramon is an attractive aspirin-shaped **Visitors' Centre** which aims to explain everything you might want to know about the massive and intriguing crater. The roof of the building serves as an excellent viewing platform. The neighbouring **Bio-Ramon** complex is home to a collection of desert creatures.

The **SPNI** have a field school (☎ (07) 658 8615/6; fax 658 8615) on the edge of the crater which is possibly worth visiting for anybody planning any serious hiking. It's open Sunday to Thursday from 8 am to 5 pm, and Friday from 8 am to 1 pm; closed Saturday. The school is about a two km walk from the southern end of Ben-Gurion Blvd.

One of the new wave of desert tour centres that are springing up in the Negev, **Desert Shade** (☎ (07) 658 6229; fax 658 6208) offers desert tours on camel (30 NIS per hour) or in a 4WD (80 NIS per person for two hours), rents mountain bikes (45 NIS for a full day) and organises activities like rappelling. While the camel tours are little more than a trot down the road and back, the 4WD tour is a real off-the-road trip, accompanied by a well-informed and interesting commentary. Desert Shade is located a few hundred metres north of the petrol station, back towards Beersheba, east of the main road at the end of a dirt road.

Places to Stay & Eat

Beautifully located near the edge of the Maktesh Ramon, the modern *HI – Mitzpe Ramon Youth Hostel* (☎ (07) 658 8443; fax 658 8074) is also just a short walk from the Visitors' Centre. Dorm beds cost 58 NIS and singles/doubles are 117/166 NIS, all with breakfast.

Desert Shade (see above) can put up guests in long wooden huts which are divided into two person cubicles. Showers/toilets are

ISRAEL

shared by the whole block. The location is great, right on the edge of the maktesh, and the food, served in a large Bedouin-style tent, is excellent. Call for prices.

Getting There & Away

Bus No 932 stops here en route between Beersheba and Eilat (27 NIS), via Dimona, but there are only about four buses a day, three of them before noon – check at the youth hostel or Visitors' Centre for the current timetables. Catch bus No 932, in both directions, at the petrol station.

Bus No 060 shuttles between Beersheba (17.50 NIS) and Mitzpe Ramon, via Sde Boker and Ein Avdat, with departures about every hour between 6 am and 6 pm. Again check the youth hostel and Visitors' Centre for timetables. Catch it from Ben-Gurion Blvd, near the commercial concourse.

EILAT

Distanced from the Israel of international headlines by a 200 km sea of empty desert, Eilat exists almost as an 'offshore', sybaritic, mini city-state in which the major concerns are a good spot on the beach and an even tan. It's a wannabe beachfront Las Vegas with glitzy ziggurat-like hotels surrounding a turquoise blue artificial lagoon from which Walt Disney-styled glass-bottomed boats set out on cruises around the bay. However, the town's sun, sand and sea image isn't all it's cracked up to be: while there's plenty of sun, decent beaches are limited to a cluttered strip in the hotel area and views across the bay tend to be blotted by great tankers docking at the port. Eilat remains a popular travellers' stopover only by dint of its proximity to border crossing points with Egypt and Jordan.

Orientation & Information

Eilat has three parts: the town centre, the hotel area and a trailing five km coastal strip running down to the border with Egypt at Taba. Eilat's excellent new tourist information centre is just south of the town centre on Ha'Arava Rd above the Burger King; it's open Sunday to Thursday from 8 am to 9 pm,

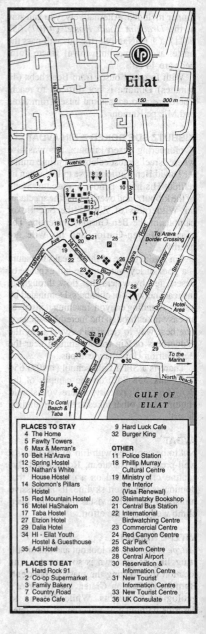

Eilat

0   150   300 m

PLACES TO STAY
4 The Home
5 Fawlty Towers
6 Max & Merran's
10 Beit Ha'Arava
12 Spring Hostel
13 Nathan's White House Hostel
14 Solomon's Pillars Hostel
15 Red Mountain Hostel
16 Motel HaShalom
17 Taba Hostel
27 Etzion Hotel
29 Dalia Hotel
34 HI - Eilat Youth Hostel & Guesthouse
35 Adi Hotel

PLACES TO EAT
1 Hard Rock 91
2 Co-op Supermarket
3 Family Bakery
7 Country Road
8 Peace Cafe
9 Hard Luck Cafe
32 Burger King

OTHER
11 Police Station
18 Phillip Murray Cultural Centre
19 Ministry of the Interior (Visa Renewal)
20 Steimatzky Bookshop
21 Central Bus Station
22 International Birdwatching Centre
23 Commercial Centre
24 Red Canyon Centre
25 Car Park
26 Shalom Centre
28 Central Airport
30 Reservation & Information Centre
31 New Tourist Information Centre
33 New Tourist Centre
36 UK Consulate

To Arava Border Crossing

Hotel Area

To the Marina

North Beach

GULF OF EILAT

To Coral Beach & Taba

ISRAEL

Friday from 8 am to 2 pm, and Saturday from 10 am to 2 pm. The best place to change money is at one of the no-commission exchange bureaus in the old Commercial Centre off HaTemarim Blvd in the town centre. Alternatively, the post office in the Red Canyon Centre also changes money and there are a couple of banks in the vicinity of the central bus station.

The police station (☎ 332 444, or in an emergency call ☎ 100) is on Avdat St, at the eastern end of Hativat HaNegev Ave. They're very used to travellers turning up here to report stolen bags and packs.

For medical aid call the Magen David Adom (☎ 372 333) or in emergencies dial ☎ 101.

The telephone code for Eilat is 07.

Things to See & Do
At **Dolphin Reef** visitors can observe training demonstrations, help out at feeding time or even swim or dive with the dolphins; it's south of the port on the road down to Taba. Further south is the **Coral World Underwater Observatory**, a glass-walled viewing chamber sunk 4.25m below the water's surface. In case the fish outside fail to put in an appearance there are plenty of captive specimens in the accompanying **aquarium**. For a deeper look at the underwater world, visitors can dive down to 60m in the observatory's **Yellow Submarine**, a viewing craft that takes passengers on a 50 minute cruise along the seabed and the sheer-sided coral cliff wall. None of the above is cheap.

The Red Sea marine life can also be observed on a **glass-bottomed boat cruise**; the Stingray-like *Jules Verne Explorer* sets off from the North Beach marina four times a day for a two hour cruise around in the tight little area hemmed in by the Egyptian and Jordanian borders. Cost per person is 55 NIS (children 40 NIS).

Originally built as a movie set, **Texas Ranch** is an unimpressive mock Wild West town inspired by the resemblance of the local terrain to that of American cowboy country. The complex also offers horse riding and half-day camel treks. Located 800m up the

dirt track beside the Texas Ranch, an **ostrich farm** has around 30 of the big birds, and other animals such as goats, ponies and peacocks.

Other than the glass-bottom boats, all the above attractions are off Mizrayim Rd, south of the HI – Eilat Youth Hostel; take bus No 15 from HaTemarim Blvd.

Beaches
Eilat's beaches are less than impressive. The most convenient is the North Beach strip fringing the hotel area but the sands are incredibly crowded and cluttered – the best chance of avoiding the rush-hour commuter feeling is to head east toward the Jordanian border. Of the five km of coastline stretching down to the Egyptian border, much of it resembles a building site of stones and gravel and muddy furrows, while one stretch is cordoned off and posted with unexploded mine notices. The only decent options seem to be the crowded, admission-charging Coral Beach Nature Reserve, south of the port, or the free HaDekel Beach, just north of the port.

Activities
Despite the enthusiastic PR, Eilat's waters do not offer world-class diving – serious divers should head to nearby Sinai. The best place, however, to check out the local options is around Coral Beach where you'll find the Red Sea Sports Club (☎ 379 685; fax 373 702) and Aqua Sport (☎ 334 404; fax 333 771) facing off across the street. Both charge about US$40 for an introductory dive, or US$250 for a six day diving course leading to PADI open-water certification – this includes all equipment except mask, snorkel and fins, which can be hired for about US$8 per day.

For snorkelling head to the Coral Beach Reserve – where as well as finding equipment for hire you can find lockers and showers, and there are a number of special trails to follow, marked out by buoys.

Both Aqua Sport at Coral Beach and the North Beach branch of Red Sea Sports Club rent out windsurfers; expect to pay about 30

ISRAEL

to 40 NIS per hour. Red Sea also offers water skiing (approx 60 NIS) and parasailing (about 100 NIS), while Aqua Sport have underwater scooters for hire.

Places to Stay

Camping Camping is illegal on most of Eilat's beaches and it's a law that is enforced. Exceptions are the areas toward the Jordanian border and south of the Red Rock Hotel/north of the port. Remember that there is a high theft rate on Eilat's beaches and if you sleep near the beach-front hotels you will also share your sleeping space with the rats who are attracted by the refuse areas.

Those who wish to pay for a rodent-free, amenity-served camp site should head for the Coral Beach area. *Caroline Camping* (☎ 375 063) offers pitching sites for 15 NIS or two-person bungalows for 80 NIS. It has clean bathrooms and showers, and a basic cafeteria. Just a couple of hundred metres south *Mt Zefahot Camping* (☎ 374 411; fax 375 206), next to the SPNI field school, charges 14 NIS for a pitching site, which gets you access to hot showers, toilets and an electricity supply if wanted.

Hostels The *Red Mountain Hostel* (☎ 374 936; ☎ & fax 374 263) is the best of four accommodation options lined up along Hativat HaNegev Ave, immediately north of the bus station. The Red Mountain is clean, and each of the six-bed air-con dorms has its own toilet and shower. The place also has a fine hotel-style lobby and a patio bar. Not quite as well maintained, the *Solomon's Pillars Hostel* (☎ 376 280) next door isn't a bad alternative but the other two in the row, the *Motel HaShalom* (☎ 376 544) and the *Taba Hostel* (☎ 375 982) are very basic and cramped. Dorm beds at all four are 20 NIS.

Walk past Solomon's Pillars and scramble up over the grassy area to reach Agmonim St and *Nathan's White House Hostel* (☎ 376 572) with dorm beds (four to eight per room) again at 20 NIS, and beyond it the very good *Spring Hostel* (☎ 374 660), a large place that may lack the homely touch of neighbouring Nathan's but it is clean and each air-con, six

to eight-bed dorm has its own modern toilet/shower. There's a kitchen and patio bar, and reception is open 24 hours. Beds are 25 NIS.

One place recommended by readers is *Beit Ha'Arava* (☎ 374 687), which is clean with comfortable air-con dorms (25 NIS per bed) and a wonderful view from the patio. There's a kitchen and people can camp in the garden for 15 NIS. To get there from the bus station, turn right onto Hativat HaNegev Ave, walk down to the end and turn left up Hativat HaGolani Ave.

There are several places favoured by Eilat's long-termers which feel more like boarding houses, the best of which is *Max & Merran's* (☎ 373 817) on Agmonim St; beds (22 NIS) are squeezed in about 10 to a room and the place could do with another bathroom to reduce the queues, but otherwise it's an easy-going and friendly place; it has a lounge with TV and VCR and free tea and coffee in the kitchen.

The *HI – Eilat Youth Hostel & Guesthouse* (☎ 370 088; fax 375 835) is immaculate and beautiful, and something of a bargain at the price. There are good views out over the Gulf from some of the balconies too. Dorm beds are 54 NIS, singles and doubles are 90/126 NIS. It's on Mizrayim Rd, south of the New Tourist shopping centre.

Hotels The single and double rooms at the *HI – Eilat Youth Hostel & Guesthouse* (see above) are equal in standard to much of the accommodation on offer in the mid-price range.

Next to the Commercial Centre at the bottom of HaTemarim Blvd is the *Etzion Hotel* (☎ 374 131; fax 370 002). It has a sauna, pool and nightclub, with singles from US$60 to US$70, and doubles from US$74 to US$87.

Up the hill and behind the New Tourist shopping centre off Yotam Rd, the *Adi Hotel* (☎ 376 151/3; fax 376 154) is fairly well hidden; look for the red and white 'ADI' sign on its wall. Singles cost from US$42 and doubles from US$55.

In the expensive hotel area by the lagoon,

there are some more moderately priced beds available. Near to the Galei Eilat Hotel, the *Dalia Hotel* (☎ 334 004; fax 334 072) has singles from US$53 to US$79, and doubles from US$68 to US$112. The *Americana Eilat* (☎ 333 777; fax 334 174) has a pool, nightclub and tennis courts with singles from US$55 to US$75, and doubles from US$65 to US$99.

A reader has also recommended Villa Kibel (☎ 376 911 or (050) 345 366; fax 376 911), an apartment with 12 air-con rooms which are US$40 each but are suitable for sharing between three or four people. The owner, Russel Kibel, also has several other properties on his books. The villa is at 18 Peres St; head north up Yotam Rd, left at the junction with Elot Ave, and Peres St is the second on the left.

Places to Eat

The one saving grace of dining in Eilat is that the thermometer-busting heat means appetites tend to be smaller. If you can be satisfied with just a sandwich then there's a *Co-op supermarket* on Elot St, on the corner of HaTemarim Blvd, and another in the Shalom Centre.

Eilat's bakers win the prize for baking Israel's smallest pitta, and getting both felafel and salad into the same piece of bread is an acquired art. Most of the felafel and shwarma places are on HaTemarim Blvd near the bus station – there's a particularly good one next to the International Bird-watching Centre. On the same boulevard, mainly between Hativat HaNegev Ave and Almogin St, are a couple of good bakeries; the *Family Bakery* where Ofarim Ave meets HaTemarim Blvd, is worth noting as it stays open 24 hours and has a seated patio and a jukebox.

For something more substantial, the *Underground* pub in the New Tourist shopping centre serves up heaped plates of spaghetti, stir-fry or chips, eggs and bacon for around 10 NIS. Nothing to do with its near-namesake, *Hard Rock 91* is a dim little cellar bar but it does serve decent burgers with fries, and a few other dishes besides.

Prices are around 10 to 15 NIS. It's at 179 Elot Ave, just east of HaTemarim Blvd. The local branch of *Nargila*, next to the bus station, provides passable Yemenite-inspired food.

None of the shopping malls has a truly recommendable eating place and you may find yourself having to resort to the *Burger Ranch* in the Red Canyon Centre or the *Burger King* at the junction of Yotam and Ha'Arava Rds.

For fish, try the *Fisherman's House*, across from Coral Beach. It offers a self-service meal of fish (seven kinds), various salads and baked potato – it's average quality at best, but you can eat as much as you like for little more than 20 NIS.

Entertainment

The nightlife in Eilat is firmly bar-based, however, pick up the free *What's On in Eilat* leaflet from the tourist office to find out what else is happening.

The most popular place with travellers at the time of our last visit was the *Underground*, in the New Tourist shopping centre, where cheap beer and food fuel a loud and lively crowd. Over in the hostel area the *Peace Cafe*, *Hard Luck Cafe* and *Country Road* are three seedy bars which serve as hang-outs for beached travellers. Come here early in the morning to try for a job on a building site. They're all virtually next to each other around the junction of Almogin and Agmonim Sts.

A little more pricey perhaps but the bars over on North Beach among the hotels are at least a lot more cheerful. The best of them is *Yatush-BaRosh*, which translates as 'Mosquito in the Head', located by the marina bridge. Not far away is *The Yacht Pub*, part of the King Solomon's Palace Hotel complex on the marina, which features live music of varying quality.

Getting There & Away

Air Arkia flights depart several times daily from the central airport for Jerusalem (US$80) and Tel Aviv (US$80) and less frequently for Haifa (US$94). The Arkia

ISRAEL

booking office (☎ 376 102) is in the Red Canyon centre, above the post office.

Bus Bus No 394 departs for Tel Aviv (five hours; 46 NIS) every 1½ hours between 8 am and 5 pm, with an additional overnight service leaving at 12.30 am. Last bus on a Friday is at 3 pm; the first bus on Shabbat is at 1 pm. Bus No 444 departs for Jerusalem (4½ hours; 42 NIS) at 7 and 10 am, and 2 and 5 pm daily. On Friday there is no 5 pm bus, while on Shabbat there is only one bus, departing at 4 pm. There is also a Haifa service (6½ hours; 51 NIS), bus No 991, departing Sunday to Thursday at 8.30 am and 11 pm, and Saturday at 11 pm only. For all of these services it's advisable to book at least a day beforehand. If there are no Jerusalem or Tel Aviv buses available, go to Beersheba and change there.

Egypt If you are heading to or from Sinai, local bus No 15 runs between Eilat's central bus station and Taba (4 NIS). The service runs every 15 to 20 minutes between 7 am and 9.30 pm (last bus Friday at 5 pm; first bus on Shabbat at 9 am). You can also catch the less frequent bus No 16 which goes Arava-central bus station-Taba but check in which direction it's heading first.

See the Getting There & Away section earlier in this chapter for complete border crossing details.

Jordan Bus No 16 runs from Eilat's central bus station to the border at Arava every 20 minutes Monday to Thursday from 7 am to 4 pm.

See the Getting There & Away section for complete border crossing details.

Getting Around
Bus Local bus No 15 is the most used service, running every day between the bus station and Taba via the Hotel Area and Coral Beach. Distances within the town are not so great and most people walk everywhere.

Bicycles & Scooters The heat may prove to be too much of a deterrent, but you can hire

a bicycle for 45 NIS a day from ETI (☎ 370 380; fax 370 434), whose office is in the new tourist information centre at the bottom of Yotam Rd. Alternatively, beat the heat and let the wind whip your hair by slapping down 100 NIS for 24 hours rental of a scooter; also from ETI.

AROUND EILAT
Places that should be seen if you have a car or decide to take a tour include **Ein Netafim**, a small spring at the foot of a 30m waterfall, which attracts many animals who come to drink; the **Red Canyon**, one of the area's most beautiful sights, 600m long, one to three metres wide at its narrowest and some 10m at it deepest; and **Moon Valley**, which is Egyptian territory but can be seen from the Red Canyon.

Some 25 km north of Eilat and accessible by public bus, **Timna Park** is the site of some stunning desert landscapes enlivened with multicoloured rock formations. Any bus heading to or from Eilat passes the turn-off for the park but from the main road it is a 2.5 km walk to the park's entrance.

Hai-Bar Arava Biblical Wildlife Reserve was created to establish breeding groups of wild animals threatened by extinction. Within the reserve is also the **Yotvata Visitors' Centre** (☎ 376 018) which features an audio-visual presentation that describes the region's natural attractions, and an exhibition of maps, diagrams and photographs on the zoology, botany, geology, archaeology and history of settlement in the area. The reserve is some 40 km north of Eilat and all buses to and from town pass by.

The Gaza Strip & the West Bank

Formerly known as the Occupied Territories, the Gaza Strip and the West Bank are predominantly Palestinian territories captured by Israel during the Six Day War. They have remained in political limbo ever since,

Warning

For the most part the Gaza Strip and the West Bank are absolutely safe to visit. There are no problems with independent travellers just turning up in Bethlehem, Jericho, Nablus or Ramallah. Anyone intending to travel to Gaza city or Hebron should make enquiries about the current situation before setting out (contact your embassy if necessary). Remember, this is a part of the world in which things can change dramatically from day to day.

Take Arab rather than Egged buses or, best of all, Arab service taxis. Note that cars with yellow Israeli registration plates, even rental cars, are not allowed into the Gaza Strip and have in the past been a target for stone-throwers in the West Bank.

This is a place to emphasise that you are a tourist. Speaking Hebrew or voicing pro-Israeli opinions is not a smart idea. ■

neither annexed outright by Israel (as were East Jerusalem and the Golan Heights), nor granted outright autonomy – although this may eventually be the result of the ongoing peace process.

Although the extents of the Gaza Strip are well defined by razor wire and watchtowers, the pre-1967 border between Israel and the West Bank (known as the 'green line') is not marked by any signs, let alone border posts, and most Israelis would be hard pressed to point out exactly where one region ends and the other begins. At the present time this has yet to become an issue as the handing back of all West Bank territories to the Palestinians is still some way down the line.

Since 1994 the Palestinians have existed under limited self-rule in the Gaza Strip and Jericho. In late 1995, the IDF also withdrew from several West Bank towns, including Jenin, Nablus, Bethlehem and Ramallah, releasing them to the direct control of the Palestinian National Authority.

GAZA

Gaza was at one time one of the most strategically important towns in the Levant, a staging post on several well-trafficked trade routes linking Central Asia and Persia with Arabia, Egypt and Africa. It is said that Gaza has been taken and destroyed in war more than any town in the world.

Since the establishment of limited self-rule in 1994, Gaza is experiencing a post-intifada pick-up, although normal service is still some way off being resumed.

Orientation & Information

There is one long street, Omar al-Mukhtar St, which runs about four km from Al-Shajaria Square to the seafront. Most of the city's shops, businesses and other facilities are either on Omar al-Mukhtar or just off it. The centre of activity is Palestine Square (Midan Filisteen) which is 500m west of Al-Shajaria Square on Omar al-Mukhtar. All Gaza's hotels and most of the restaurants are on the seafront at the extreme west end of Omar al-Mukhtar. This coastal district is known as Rimal ('Sand') and it's the posh area, full of cool villas and Mediterranean apartment blocks, home to wealthy ex-émigré Palestinians, expat aid workers and Yasser Arafat and family.

Money is best changed at the official moneychangers around Palestine Square, which is also where most of the town's banks are located. There's an international telephone office, El-Baz (☎ 682 1910; fax 686 4120) just east of Gaza's only traffic lights on Omar al-Mukhtar. The police station (☎ 100) is on the north side of Al-Shajaria Square, while around the corner is the post office – open Saturday to Thursday from 8 am to 6 pm; closed Friday.

The telephone code for Gaza is 07.

The Old Town

The area surrounding Palestine Square is the oldest part of town and contains most of the city's sites of historical interest. Although mostly obscured by the surrounding buildings, the **Jamaa al-Akbar (Great Mosque)**, a conversion of a Crusader-era church, is the town's most distinguished structure. Non-Muslims are usually allowed to enter the mosque in between the daily prayers. Along the southern side of the mosque runs the short, vaulted **Goldsmiths' Alley**, all that remains of what, during the Mamluk-era, was a much larger covered market, similar to that in Jerusalem's Old City.

During his Egyptian campaign, Napoleon Bonaparte camped in Gaza in 1799 and commandeered an attractive Mamluk-era building as his headquarters. Known as **Napoleon's Citadel** it's now a girls' school. It stands on Al-Wahida St, north of the Great Mosque. Head west (toward the sea) from the citadel and take the second right for the **Mosque of Said Hashim**, erected on the grave of the Prophet Mohammed's great-grandfather.

Places to Stay

The cheapest place in town is the *Al-Amal Hotel* (☎ & fax 682 1798) on Omar al-Mukhtar St, 300m east of the seafront.

Refugee Camp Visits

There are eight refugee camps in the Gaza Strip, all administered by UNRWA (United Nations Relief & Works Agency), who first began providing emergency aid to the refugees in 1950.

UNRWA's headquarters (signposted by a large blue UN flag) is in Gaza City, opposite the Islamic University on Al-Azhar St, just south of Talatin St – follow the veiled women. If contacted in advance, the public information department (☎ 686 7044) may, workload permitting, be able to arrange a visit to one of the refugee camps in the Strip. Try to avoid your visit coinciding with any Muslim holidays, including Ramadan, when almost everything grinds to a halt.

If UNRWA are otherwise occupied then it's possible to visit at least one of the camps on your own. Beach Camp is right on the fringes of Gaza City and a 15 minute walk north from where Omar al-Mukhtar meets the seafront road. The camp is home to just over 63,000 refugees housed in rank upon rank of single storey huts.

Generally speaking the Palestinians are delighted to welcome visitors and appreciate any outside interest in their living conditions. However, visitors must dress modestly: upper arms and shoulders covered and absolutely no shorts for either men or women. UNRWA also advise that you avoid any olive-drab or military style clothing. ■

Though the plumbing is a little old, it's a well-run place, immaculately clean and not too badly priced at US$35 for a single. For those with a fatter wallet, the other good option is *Marna House* (☎ & fax 682 3322, 682 2624) a comfortable private villa, in a quiet residential street. Singles/doubles are US$60/70, with breakfast. Marna House is two blocks north of Omar al-Mukhtar St, just west of An-Nasser St.

Places to Eat

Felafel is easily found in the Palestine Square area and some of the best shwarma is here at a shop on the short street that connects the east end of the square to Wahida St; a huge piece of lafah bread stuffed with meat and salad is only 5 NIS. For cheap grilled meat dishes go to the *Palm Beach* on Omar al-Mukhtar, a couple of hundred metres up from the seafront. They do kebabs and steaks, liver and hearts, all served with chips and salad and costing 10 to 15 NIS.

Getting There & Away

The only entry/exit point at the time of writing is Erez, in the north of the Strip. To get there, the most convenient way is to take a service taxi from opposite Damascus Gate in Jerusalem. They depart every day but you may have to wait a considerable time for the car to fill up (on our last trip we waited almost three hours for the required seven people). The cost is 20 NIS per person and the ride takes about an hour. Alternatively, if it's time you're short of not money, you can opt for a 'special' and pay for the whole taxi yourself, in which case the cost is 140 NIS.

The other possible way to get to Erez is via the Israeli coastal town of Ashkelon, which is served by regular buses from Tel Aviv. From Ashkelon take a southbound bus and ask to be let off at the Yad Mordechai junction. This is only about five km from Erez and there are usually taxis at Yad Mordechai that will ferry you to the border.

Once at Erez, for non-Israeli or non-Arab passport holders crossing into the Strip is painless and takes minutes. The only headache is the swarm of taxi drivers beyond the

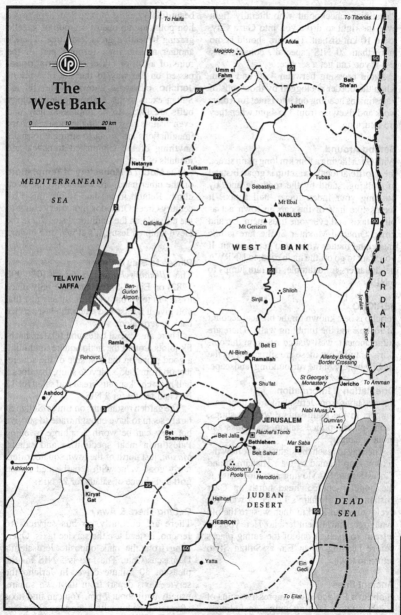

Palestinian checkpoint who literally fight over the right to drive you into Gaza City, some 10 km distant. The fare should be no more than 20 NIS 'special', considerably less if you can get a service.

Avoid crossing between 4.30 and 6 am when the border is clogged by thousands of Palestinians heading out into Israel for a days work and likewise from 3 to 4 pm when they are returning.

Getting Around
With Gaza having a four km long main street, the unofficial local taxi setup is great. Instead of walking, stand by the roadside and, by pointing your index finger, hail a taxi. It seems like half of the cars in town act as pirate taxis and everyone uses them. Up and down Omar al-Mukhtar St the fare is one shekel, no matter where you get in or out. If you want to go off the main road, to UNRWA headquarters for example, the fare jumps to 5 NIS.

JERICHO
Jericho is best known for the biblical account of Joshua and the tumbling walls. There are some ancient, well-visited ruins on the out-skirts of town but these are surpassed by the shabby beauty of the surrounding landscape.

Orientation & Information
Service taxis from Jerusalem drop their pas-sengers in the main square with its shops, eating places, police station, taxi ranks and moneychanger.

The way to reach the sights is to follow the six km loop formed by Qasr Hisham St and Ein as-Sultan St. Moving anti-clockwise is the popular choice: head north up Qasr Hisham St to Hisham's Palace, a walk (or cycle) of about 2.5 km, then west to the old synagogue and ancient Jericho. Here you can refresh yourself at one of the eating places before heading down Ein as-Sultan St to return to town.

Ancient Sites
Hisham's Palace is the impressive ruins of a 7th century hunting lodge, including a

beautiful Byzantine mosaic floor depicting a lion pouncing on one of a group of gazelle grazing beneath a great leafy tree. There's another mosaic floor forming part of the ruins of a 5th or 6th century **synagogue**, passed on the way to the site of **ancient Jericho**, otherwise known as the Tel as-Sultan excavations. Only true archaeology buffs are likely to be impressed here and even visitors blessed with the most visionary imaginations are going to struggle to make anything of the signposted trenches and mounds of dirt.

The **Mount & Monastery of Temptation**, on the other hand, are well worth the steep climb. Rebuilt in the late 1800s, this 12th century Greek Orthodox monastery clings to the cliffside on the traditional site where the Devil tempted Jesus. It's closed on Sunday.

Places to Stay & Eat
The *Hisham's Palace Hotel* (☎ (02) 992 7282) on Ein as-Sultan St is the only place to stay in town but we strongly suggest that you give it a miss and catch the last service back to Jerusalem.

There are several cafes and felafel/shash-lik joints around the main square, including a good place on the east side of the square, just up from Zaki's bicycle shop, that does a half roast chicken plus bread and salad for 12 NIS and felafel for 2 NIS.

The garden restaurants on Ein as-Sultan St rarely seem to have enough trade to survive but they can be worth a splurge to enjoy Palestinian meat specialities and salads. *Maxim*, just north of the town square, offers fairly good value with a barbecued mixed grill and choice of salads for 24 NIS.

Getting There & Away
There are currently no bus services to Jericho, instead use the service taxis. Oper-ating from the rank opposite Jerusalem's Damascus Gate. The fare is 5 NIS for the pleasant 30 minute drive. In Jericho the service taxis depart from the town square, usually until about 7 pm. You can find taxis after this time but with a shortage of passen-

gers you may have to fork out for a higher fare.

It is possible to get a service taxi from Jericho to other West Bank towns such as Bethlehem, Nablus and Ramallah; ask at the rank on the southern side of the square.

Getting Around

With the distance involved between the town and the sights, cycling is a popular mode of transport. The roads are relatively flat and traffic free, so decide for yourself whether the heat is easier to bear on foot or on the saddle of a rented boneshaker. Zaki's bicycle shop is on the town square and he charges 3 NIS per hour. There's a second bike hire place round the corner on Jerusalem St. A passport or a similar suitable document may be asked for as security.

AROUND JERICHO

Eight km before Jericho a road leads right to **Nabi Musa**, a small monastic complex revered by Muslims as the tomb of Moses, with an impressive backdrop of the Judean Desert.

Wadi Qelt is a nature reserve with a natural spring where you can swim in a pool under a waterfall and hike along an aqueduct to **St George's Monastery**, built into the cliff face of a canyon. The hike takes about four hours. The starting point is the Wadi Qelt turn-off on the Jerusalem-Jericho road (get the bus driver to drop you off here) and the finishing point is Jericho, from where you can continue sightseeing in the town or easily find transport back to Jerusalem.

BETHLEHEM

Modern-day Bethlehem may be a cynic's delight, with Manger Square, Manger St, Star St, Shepherds' St, two Shepherds' Fields and an unheavenly host of 'Christmases' but for most travellers with even the remotest Christian background, a trip to the Holy Land without visiting the site of the Nativity is unthinkable, even if only to please a pious relative back home. Besides the pilgrimage sites, there are also some excellent excur-

sions to places just outside the town, such as the Mar Saba Monastery and the Herodion.

Orientation & Information

With the Church of the Nativity on its southern side, Manger Square is the centre of town and, ludicrously, also the town's main car park. Squeeze through the tour buses and taxis, and you'll find around the square the tourist office, police station, post office and various shops, hotels and eating places. Milk Grotto St heads off to the south-east, while Paul VI St heads uphill to the north-west, and the museum, outdoor market and more shops and hotels.

Manger St, which comes off the east side of the square, is the main winding route through the new town. It eventually intersects with the Jerusalem-Hebron highway opposite the Jewish shrine of Rachel's Tomb.

Things to See

The **Church of the Nativity**, one of the world's oldest working churches, is built like a citadel over the cave where it is believed that Jesus was born. Happily, it's a suitably august and venerable building, which unlike Jerusalem's Holy Sepulchre or Nazareth's Basilica manages to avoid the 'holy site as sideshow' feel. Down Milk Grotto St is the **Milk Grotto Chapel**, a kitschy little shrine that owes its existence to the Virgin Mary's lactations (at least that's how the legend goes). North of the square, on Paul VI St, the **Bethlehem Museum** has exhibits of traditional Palestinian crafts and costumes; it's open Monday to Saturday from 10 am to noon and 2.30 to 5.30 pm; closed Sunday.

One of Judaism's most sacred shrines, and also revered by Muslims and Christians, **Rachel's Tomb** is housed in a small white domed building on the edge of town at the intersection of Hebron Rd and Manger St.

Places to Stay & Eat

Accommodation in Bethlehem is limited, especially at Christmas and Easter (some things never change) and it makes more sense to stay in nearby Jerusalem.

The best option is the recently renovated

Franciscan *Casa Nova Hospice* (☎ (02) 674 3980/1; fax 674 3540), right next to the Church of the Holy Nativity. It has great facilities and good food, and costs 57 NIS for B&B, 63 NIS for half board, 81 NIS for full board.

Up among the narrow streets to the northwest of Manger Square, off Paul VI St, the *Handal Hotel* (☎ (02) 674 4488; fax 674 0656) has extremely comfortable singles/doubles for 90/150 NIS, breakfast extra.

There are no outstanding restaurants but there are plenty of felafel and mixed grill merchants competing around Manger Square. The *Reem Restaurant*, down the side street past the bakery on Paul VI St, is inexpensive with houmos and other salads for about 8 NIS.

Getting There & Away

Arab bus No 22 runs frequently from East Jerusalem and stops outside Jaffa Gate en route. It's about a 40 minute ride. Service taxis (costing 2 NIS) from outside Damascus Gate are more convenient; they tend to depart more frequently and make the journey in half the time of the bus.

As they are so close, walking from Jerusalem to Bethlehem is a popular option. At Christmas there's an official procession, but the two to 2½ hour, downhill-all-the-way hike is pleasant all year round.

AROUND BETHLEHEM

Past Rachel's Tomb, in the direction of Hebron, a road heads west to the pleasant Christian Arab village of **Beit Jalla** and continues to the summit of **Har Gillo** with great views. A side road leads to the attractive Salesian monastery of **Cremisan**, renowned for its wine and olive oil. Arab bus No 21 runs from Jerusalem to Beit Jalla.

Various biblical events are associated with the **Field of Ruth** and the two **Shepherds' Fields** at the village of Beit Sahur, a km east of Bethlehem. There are the ruins of a Byzantine monastery, destroyed by the Persians in 614, and a 5th century church built over a cave with a mosaic floor. Arab bus No 47

goes to Beit Sahur from Manger St and the fields are a 20 minute walk further east, three or four km from Bethlehem.

Splendid architecture and a superb location combine to make the Greek Orthodox Monastery of **Mar Saba** one of the most impressive buildings in the Holy Land. Unfortunately, it's strictly closed to women but it is worth a visit if only to view the exterior. The monastery is on the steep bank of the Kidron River in the proverbial middle of nowhere and unless you have your own car, you will have to walk the six km from where the bus stops in the village of Abu Diye (reached by Arab bus No 60 from Bethlehem).

There are more superb views and a major archaeological site at the **Herodion**, the palace complex built by Herod between 24 and 15 BC. The Herodion is eight km south of Beit Sahur. Various buses run infrequently from Bethlehem, despite what the tourist office says; otherwise use taxis, walk or hitchhike. **Solomon's Pools**, with a large reservoir and a Turkish fort, are eight km south of Beit Jalla. Take Arab minibus No 1 to Dashit, the nearby Arab village, or Arab bus No 23.

HEBRON

At the time of writing, Hebron continues to be the place of greatest unrest in the West Bank. The dispute focuses on the Ibrahimi Mosque/Cave of Machpelah, a site holy to both Jews and Muslims. In order to be near the shrine, in the early 1970s a group of Jewish extremists established their presence on the fringes of wholly-Arab Hebron. Since then, they have advanced into the town itself, taking possession of a central street and its buildings. Now 400 strong, the Jewish settler community is guarded by 1200 Israeli soldiers from the 12,000 Palestinians among whom they live. It's an extremely volatile situation that as recently as autumn 1995 erupted in a series of particularly unpleasant confrontations, resulting in a number of deaths. Check on the current state of affairs before visiting.

Orientation & Information
The bus or service taxi will drop you off on King David St on the northern edge of the market. Heading down through the market, directly south, brings you to the Ibrahimi Mosque. It is important that when wandering through the old town you look as touristy (ie non-Jewish) as possible.

The Old Town
Supposed burial place of Abraham, to Jews the site of the **Cave of Machpelah**, over which the **Ibrahimi Mosque** was built in the 12th century, is second in sanctity only to Jerusalem's Western Wall, while to Muslims, of all the Holy Land shrines, only the Dome of the Rock is more venerated. As such the site has always inflamed passions and been a cause of bloody tragedy, as happened in February 1994 when a Jewish settler stepped into the mosque and opened fire on a congregation of Muslims at prayer. The mosque is now segregated into separate Muslim and Jewish sections each with their own entrance. Security is tight and visitors will be brusquely frisked and questioned before being allowed entry.

Hebron's **souq** is a compendium of Crusader and Mamluk facades, vaulted ceilings, tiny shops and narrow alleyways. Despite the tensions in the city, it's still fairly lively first thing in a morning.

Getting There & Away
Arab bus No 23 operates regularly between Jerusalem and Hebron (3 NIS) via Rachel's Tomb at Bethlehem but the service taxis (5 NIS), caught outside Jerusalem's Damascus Gate, depart far more frequently and are much faster.

NABLUS
Beautifully situated between the scenic mountains of Gerizim and Ebal, Nablus is the largest of the West Bank towns. It's a typical bustling Arab town, quite attractive with its breeze-block houses tumbling down the mountainsides and an enchanting old quarter. Only an hour from Jerusalem by service it's well worth a day visit.

Orientation & Information
The centre of Nablus is Palestine/Al-Hussein Square, home to a small market and the terminal for many buses and service taxis. Just south of the square is the Old Town, which stretches to the east along Nasir St. Beyond the Old Town rise the slopes of Mt Gerizim, holy to the Samaritans, while Mt Ebal stands to the north.

The Old Town
From Al-Hussein Square head directly south, homing in on the minaret of **An-Nasir Mosque** on Nasir St – one of 30 minarets punctuating the Nablus skyline. Close by this particular mosque is an old Turkish mansion known as **Touqan Castle**. It's now privately owned, but usually visitors are welcome to look at the architecture and garden. From Nasir St walk south through Al-Beik Gate and the entrance is up the slope on your left.

East of the An-Nasir Mosque on An-Nasir St is Al-Shifa (☎ (09) 838 1176), the oldest working **Turkish bath** in the country. Built around 1480 at the start of the Ottoman period, Al-Shifa has been lovingly restored and as well as the hot rooms there's a central hall with cushion strewn platforms to recline on while you sip black coffee or mint tea and puff on a nargileh. The bath is open daily for men only from about 8 am to 10 pm; Wednesday between 8 am and 5 pm is women only. It costs 10 NIS to use the baths and a massage is 10 NIS extra.

Places to Stay & Eat
Since the intifada all of the hotels in Nablus have closed down. Along with soap, the Nablus speciality is sweets. These include all the various pastries, halvah and Turkish delight, but in particular kanafe (cheese topped with orange wheat flakes and soaked in honey). The best bakery at which to try this rich delicacy is *Al-Aqsa*, next to Nasir Mosque and across from the soap factory on Nasir St in the Old City.

Getting There & Away
Arab buses run to Nablus from East Jerusalem

(Nablus Rd station) via Ramallah. The journey takes two to 2½ hours, which makes the service taxis option (1¼ hours; 11 NIS) very appealing.

AROUND NABLUS
Sebastiya

This quiet little Arab village stands about 15 km north-west of Nablus up on the scenic slopes of the Samarian hills. Just above it on the summit of the peak lie the impressive ruins of Samaria, the capital of the ancient Israelite kingdom.

Inside the village is a Crusader church (dating from the 12th century) that was converted into a mosque by Saladin (Salah ad-Din).

No buses run direct to Sebastiya. Instead, take a service taxi from near Palestine/Al-Hussein Square (4 NIS).

Jordan

Despite a turbulent past, Jordan is one of the most interesting and friendly of the Middle East countries, and also the easiest to visit. The people are extremely helpful and friendly – some travellers say the most hospitable on the entire Asia overland route.

While it's not the cheapest country in the region, Jordan can still be afforded by those with even the most modest resources, and there's plenty to see – the highlight being the unbelievably spectacular Petra, the ruined city of the Nabataeans in the south of the country.

As well as being a destination in itself, Jordan (along with neighbouring Syria) forms part of the important land route between the continents of Europe and Africa, and can also be easily slotted into an 'across Asia' sojourn. Don't miss it.

Facts about the Country

HISTORY

Jordan was one of many countries that escaped from a long period of Turkish rule when the Ottoman Empire collapsed after WWI. The ensuing peace conferences gave Britain a mandate over Palestine, and shortly afterwards the new state of Transjordan was made a separate entity under King Abdullah. What remained of Palestine corresponded more or less to the present state of Israel and the Occupied Territories. London's attempts to accommodate Jewish desires for a homeland in Palestine and keep the Arab populace happy were ultimately unsuccessful. Immediately after WWII the British gave up and referred the mess to the United Nations (UN), which voted in favour of the partition of Palestine into Arab and Jewish states. Agreement could not be reached and war broke out in 1948, ending with a comprehensive Israeli victory and occupation of the zones allocated to them under the UN

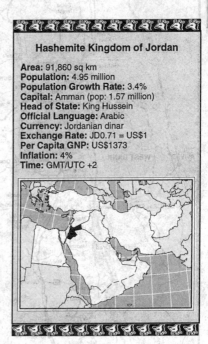

Hashemite Kingdom of Jordan

Area: 91,860 sq km
Population: 4.95 million
Population Growth Rate: 3.4%
Capital: Amman (pop: 1.57 million)
Head of State: King Hussein
Official Language: Arabic
Currency: Jordanian dinar
Exchange Rate: JD0.71 = US$1
Per Capita GNP: US$1373
Inflation: 4%
Time: GMT/UTC +2

plan and virtually all those assigned to the Palestinian Arabs. Transjordan profited from the situation and occupied the West Bank and a part of Jerusalem. This done, King Abdullah changed his fledgling country's name to Jordan.

King Hussein came to power in 1953 and has managed to stay there ever since, despite various insurrection attempts and major disruptions, such as the Arab-Israeli wars, the Palestinian-inspired civil strife of the 1970s and the 1991 Gulf War.

In the 1960s things were pretty rosy in Jordan with aid pouring in from the USA and a boom in tourism, mainly in Jerusalem's Old City. The situation was radically altered by the Six Day War of 1967, in which Jordan

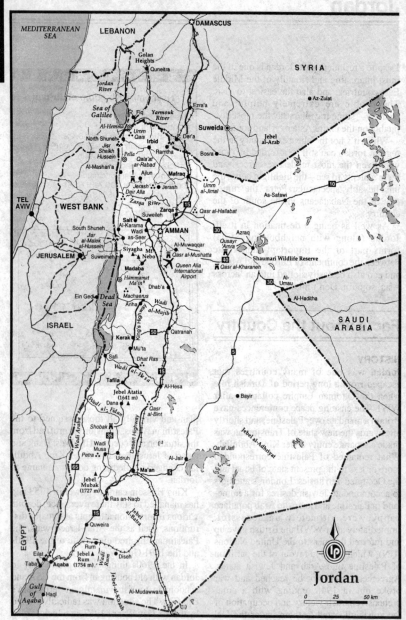

MEDITERRANEAN
SEA

LEBANON

DAMASCUS

SYRIA

Golan
Heights

Quneitra

Az-Zulat

Jordan
River

Ezra'a

Fiq

Sea of
Galilee

Yarmouk
River

Suweida

Al-Hemma

Umm
Qais

Der'a

Jebel
al-Arab

North Shuneh

Irbid

Ramtha

Bosra

Jisr
Sheikh
Hussein

Pella

Qala'at
ar-Rabad

Al-Mashan'a

Ajlun

Mafraq

Jerash
Deir Alla

Jerash

Umm
al-Jimal

TEL
AVIV

WEST BANK

Zarqa River

Zarqa

As-Safawi

10

Salt

Suweileh

Qasr al-Hallabat

Al-Karama

Wadi
as-Seer

AMMAN

15

South Shuneh

Siyagha

Al-Muwaqqar

Azraq

JERUSALEM

Suweimeh

Mt
Nebo

30

Qusayr
Amra

Jisr
al-Malek
al-Hussein

Madaba

Queen Alia
International
Airport

Qasr al-Mushatta

Shaumari Wildlife Reserve

40

Qasr al-Kharaneh

Ein Gedi

Hammamat
Ma'in

Dhab'a

Dead
Sea

Machaerus

Anha

Wadi
al-Mujib

Al-Umau

30

ISRAEL

King's Highway

Al-Haditha

SAUDI
ARABIA

Kerak

Qatranah

50

Mu'ta

Dhat Ras

5

Safi

Wadi al-Hesa

Tafila

Al-Hesa

Bayir

Jebel Atatia
(1641 m)

15

Dana

Qasr
al-Bint

Wadi al-Fidan

Shobak

Jebel al-Adhriyat

35

Wadi
Musa

Petra

Qa'al Jafi

Udruh

Al-Jair

Desert Highway

Ma'an

5

Jebel
Mubak
(1727 m)

Ras an-Naqb

EGYPT

15

Quweira

Jebel
al-Batra

Eilat

Rum

Taba

Jebel
Rum
(1754 m)

Diseh

Haql

Aqaba

Wadi Rum

Jebel al-Khash

Gulf
of
Aqaba

Al-Mudawwara

Jordan

0   25   50 km

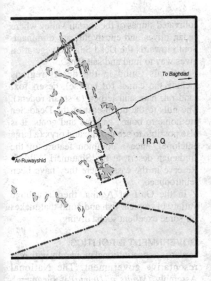

Suggested Itineraries
The main route through Jordan is a fairly straightforward north-south undertaking. As the Desert Highway offers few attractions, the obvious choice for getting from **Amman** to **Aqaba** or vice versa is to follow the **King's Highway**. With a day or two spent on a diversion to **Wadi Rum**, you can pretty much cover all the main, and many secondary, places of interest on or just off this highway. **Petra** lies at its southern end, and on the way you can stop by at the castles of **Kerak** and **Shobak**, cross the great **Wadi al-Mujib** and admire the wonderful Byzantine mosaics of **Madaba**. Further diversions to the **Dead Sea** and the delightful hot springs of **Hammamat Ma'in** suggest themselves along the way, for those who have time.

Apart from this main route, you could take a day or two to do a circuit east of Amman through the **Desert Castles**, and use Amman as a base to visit some of the country's greatest ancient sites, including **Pella**, **Umm Qais** and, of course, **Roman Jerash**. ■

lost the West Bank and its half of Jerusalem to occupying Israeli forces. In a single blow Jordan had lost its two most important income sources – agriculture and tourism. It also experienced another huge influx of refugees.

As the Palestinians, particularly the Palestine Liberation Organization (PLO), became more militant against the Israeli occupation in the early '70s, they also posed a danger to King Hussein, given that most of them operated from Jordanian territory and virtually came to contest power in his Kingdom. After bloody fighting, the bulk of the radicals were forced to move to Lebanon, where they would later become an integral part of that country's woes.

During the Gulf War, King Hussein refused to side against Iraq, largely out of fear of unrest among Jordan's pro-Saddam Palestinian populace. The country avoided total isolation by playing a peace-broker role and complying, officially at least, with the UN embargo on trade with Iraq.

Jordan has recovered remarkably well from that conflict, and despite fears of the threat of Islamic extremism, appears set to capitalise on the peace dividend after signing a full treaty with Israel in 1994.

GEOGRAPHY & CLIMATE
Jordan's 91,860 sq km can easily be divided into three major regions. The fertile Jordan Valley is the country's dominant physical feature. The East Bank plateau is broken only by the gorges cut by streams flowing into the Jordan River. This is the site for the main towns and for most places of interest. All the rest of the East Bank (about 80% of it in all) is a desert stretching to Syria, Iraq and Saudi Arabia, with climatic extremes and minimal rainfall.

Distances are short – it's only about 430 km from Ramtha in the north to Aqaba in the south. From Amman to the furthest point of interest in the east, Azraq, is just 103 km.

The weather in the Jordan Valley is oppressive in summer – daily temperatures are well in excess of 36°C and have been recorded as high as 49°C. To the other extreme, snow in Amman is not unheard of and even Petra gets the occasional fall. Average daytime maximum temperatures in Amman range from 12.6°C in January to 32.5°C in August. The desert areas, with less

JORDAN

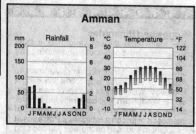

Amman

Rainfall / Temperature charts

than 50 mm of rain annually, have extremely hot summer temperatures that can reach into the high 40s.

ECOLOGY & ENVIRONMENT

The single biggest environmental problem faced by Jordan is the lack of water. A rapidly growing population, rising living standards in the cities and heavy exploitation for agriculture are all contributing factors. Demand far exceeds supply, and wastage on the land and in the cities exacerbates the situation. This has put a huge strain on the country's subterranean aquifers – the most visible result being the virtual disappearance of the Azraq Oasis in the east of the country, and all the wildlife that went with it. Attempts are being made to reverse some of that damage, but the main problem will not simply go away.

Industry also causes problems. The Yamanieh coral reef off the coast at Aqaba is a treasure trove of marine life, but every year thousands of tonnes of phosphates are accidentally dumped at sea by loaders at the Aqaba sea terminal. How much damage this is doing can only be guessed at.

These and other pollution problems have not gone totally unnoticed. A handful of 'Greens' try to make their voices heard, but as yet environmental awareness is far from widespread. In fact, the issue of water in particular is often seen less as an environmental issue than as a bone of regional political contention.

FLORA & FAUNA

The pine forests of the north give way to the cultivated slopes of the Jordan Valley where cedar, olives and eucalyptus are dominant. South towards the Dead Sea the vegetation gives way to mud and salt flats.

Animals found in the desert regions include the camel (of course), desert fox, sand rat, hare and jerboa (a small rodent). The hills to the north-east of the Dead Sea are home to boars, badgers and goats. It is also possible to see gazelle and oryx (a large antelope), once a common feature of the Jordanian desert, at the Shaumari Wildlife Reserve in the east, where they have been reintroduced.

In the Gulf of Aqaba, there's a huge variety of tropical fish and coral that makes for some excellent scuba diving.

GOVERNMENT & POLITICS

Jordan is a constitutional monarchy with representative government. The National Assembly (Majlis al-Umma) is bicameral, the Senate having half the number of members as the House of Representatives. The king is vested with wide-ranging powers, although his power of veto can be overridden by a two-thirds majority of both the houses of the National Assembly.

The 80 member lower house is elected by all citizens over the age of 18 years, but the prime minister is appointed by the king, as are the 40 members and president of the Senate. The prime minister, or the king through him, appoints a Council of Ministers that is subject to the approval of parliament.

Although elections are supposed to take place every four years, the first polls since Jordan lost the West Bank in the 1967 War were held in November 1989.

For administrative purposes the country is divided into eight muhafazat (governorates).

ECONOMY

One of the main economic victims of the Gulf War in 1990-91, Jordan has weathered the storm better than anyone could have expected. One UN assessment put the total cost of the Gulf crisis to Jordan, in the 12 months from August 1990, at more than US$8 billion. A UN blockade of the port of

Aqaba was also costing the country US$300 million a year in lost business until lifted in mid-1994.

Prior to August 1990, Jordan had been selling almost a quarter of its exports to Iraq. All trade came to a halt with the crisis, and Jordan was forced to ration petrol and seek alternative, more expensive sources of oil in Yemen and Syria. At the time of writing, the UN embargo was still in place, but Iraqi oil was reaching Jordan as debt repayment.

Until the war a vital source of income had been remittances from Jordanians and Palestinians working in the Gulf. By early 1992 most had left the Gulf states. The money they brought with them actually unleashed an unprecedented boom – stimulating economic growth by a staggering 11% in 1992.

The success is also partly due to close adherence to an International Monetary Fund reform plan that has greatly boosted confidence in Jordan. Big state monopolies such as Royal Jordanian Airlines and the telephone company are set for privatisation.

Agriculture makes up 8% of the Gross Domestic Product (GDP) and is increasingly concentrated in the Jordan Valley. The various industries account for 26% of the GDP. Jordan produces virtually no oil.

Since the peace deal with Israel in 1994 tourism has again begun to take off.

POPULATION & PEOPLE

The population of Jordan stood at about 4.95 million in December 1995, 900,000 of whom were registered as refugees from the wars of 1948 and 1967 with the United Nations Relief & Works Agency (UNRWA) on the East Bank. The population is growing at a rapid 3.4%.

Some 1.57 million people live in the capital, Amman, and a further 624,000 in neighbouring Zarqa and suburbs.

Ethnic & Religious Groups

The majority of Jordanians are Arabs. In addition, there are 25,000 Circassians (descendants of migrants from the Caucasus in the 19th century) and a much smaller

group of Chechens. Jordan also has a small Armenian population.

About 60% of the population are Palestinians, many still registered as refugees. The desert dwellers, the Bedouin, or Bedu (the name means nomadic), make up the backbone of the original population of Jordan, but not more than 40,000 can now be considered nomadic.

EDUCATION

Jordanians are among the better educated of the Arabs, with 13% illiteracy and 97% of children attending primary school. Of the six state-owned universities, the three big ones are: Jordan University in Amman; Yarmouk University in Irbid; and the military Mu'ta University near Kerak. At the end of 1991 Jordan became the only Arab country to scrap compulsory military service.

SOCIETY & CONDUCT

For the predominantly Muslim population, religious values still greatly inform Jordanian social life. Although Jordan is more westernised than most Arab countries, women here still tend to take a back seat to men in the professions, with the emphasis on family. The old tribal structure of the Bedouin remains more or less intact, but the number of true nomads is shrinking as most settle in towns.

Avoiding Offence

Although fairly used to the odd ways of westerners, immodest dress is still a source of irritation and can be an invitation for trouble for women.

Men can walk around in shorts without getting much of a response. Women are advised to wear at least knee-length dresses or pants and cover the shoulders. Both sexes should dress conservatively when entering mosques.

Although getting your hands on a drink is no problem, moderation is the rule of thumb.

RELIGION

More than 92% of the population are Sunni Muslims, and about 6% are Christians who live mainly in Amman, Madaba, Kerak and Salt. There are tiny Shiite and Druze populations, and a few hundred Baha'is.

The majority of Christians belong to the Greek Orthodox Church, but there are Greek Catholics, a small Roman (Latin) Catholic community, Syrian Orthodox, Coptic Orthodox and, among the non-Arabs, Armenian Orthodox and Catholics.

LANGUAGE

Arabic is the official language of Jordan. For details of the Arabic language, see the Facts about the Region chapter.

Facts for the Visitor

PLANNING
When to Go

Spring is the best time to visit as temperatures are mild and the winter rains have cleared the haze that obscures views for much of the year. Autumn is the next choice.

If you go in summer, don't be caught without a hat and water bottle, especially in Wadi Rum and the south, the Desert Castles and along the Jordan Valley. Winter can be bitterly cold, especially in Amman and the Eastern heights. Aqaba is the only real exception to the general rule – scorching in summer, it can be very pleasant in winter.

Maps

Although it's a bit of a toss-up, Freytag and Berndt's *Jordan* map (scale 1:800,000) is probably about the best available fold-out map.

Lonely Planet's travel atlas, *Jordan, Syria & Lebanon*, is the best of the lot and saves on picking up a lot of unwieldy individual maps.

TOURIST OFFICES
Local Tourist Offices

Tourist information is sparse in Jordan, although the Ministry of Tourism & Antiquities does put out a few glossy brochures, the most useful of which is the *Visitor's Guide*.

There are tourist offices in Amman, Aqaba, Jerash, Kerak and Petra.

Tourist Offices Abroad

Royal Jordanian Airlines' sales offices double as tourist offices all over the world. In London, you could also try the Jordanian Information Bureau (☎ (0171) 630 9277), at the same address as the embassy (see under Embassies later in this section).

VISAS & DOCUMENTS

Visas are required by all foreigners entering Jordan. These are issued at the border or airport on arrival, or can be obtained from Jordanian consulates outside the country. Tourist visas are valid for stays of up to two weeks from the date of entry, but can be easily extended for up to three months (see Visa Extensions below for further details). The cost ranges from nothing for Australian passport holders to some US$60 for US passport holders.

In general, visas can be more cheaply obtained in Damascus or Cairo, where multiple-entry visas are also easily obtained. In some cases you are better off waiting until you arrive at the border (this is true for US and Canadian passport holders), but occasionally it doesn't work like that. UK nationals will get their visas cheaper in Damascus than at the border. Multiple-entry visas are not issued at the border.

Visa Extensions

If you intend to stay beyond the two weeks your initial visa allows, you need to obtain an extension from the police. In Amman, you must go to the Muhajireen police station (see under Information in the Amman section later in this chapter). Extensions of two to three months are issued free of charge and with a minimum of fuss. Failure to do so results in a JD1 fine for each day overstayed – charged on departure.

Other Documents

Keep your passport handy at all times, but especially along Wadi Araba, the Dead Sea and Jordan Valley, where you'll encounter numerous military checkpoints. Keep the card you receive on entry and/or that handed to you with your visa extension. You need to present them on departure. International Driving Permits are not necessary in Jordan.

EMBASSIES
Jordanian Embassies Abroad
Countries with Jordanian embassies and consulates include:

Australia
  20 Roebuck St, Redhill, Canberra, ACT 2603 (☎ (62) 295 9951)
Egypt
  6 Al-Juhaini St, Doqqi, Cairo (☎ (2) 348 7543)
France
  80 Blvd Maurice Barres, 92200 Neuilly-Seine, Paris (☎ 01 46 24 23 78)
Germany
  Beethovenallee 21, 5300 Bonn 2 (☎ (228) 35 70 46)
  Jordanian visas are also available at consulates in Berlin, Düsseldorf, Hanover, Munich and Stuttgart.
Saudi Arabia
  Diplomatic Area, Riyadh 11693 (☎ (1) 454 3192)
Syria
  Al-Jala'a Ave, Damascus (☎ (11) 323 4642)
Turkey
  Mesnevi, Dedekorkut Sokak No 18, Çankaya, Ankara (☎ (4) 439 4230)
UK
  6 Upper Phillimore Gardens, London, W8 7HB (☎ (0171) 937 3685)
USA
  3504 International Drive NW, Washington DC 20008 (☎ (202) 966 2664)
  Consulate: 866 UN Plaza, New York, NY (☎ (212) 752 0135)

Foreign Embassies in Jordan
Most of the foreign embassies and consulates are in Amman. Egypt also has a consulate in Aqaba.

Australia
  Between 4th and 5th Circles, Zahran St, Jebel Amman (☎ 673246)
Egypt
  Between 4th and 5th Circles, Qurtubah St (☎ 605202)
France
  Mutanabi St, Jebel Amman (☎ 641273)
Germany
  4th Circle, 31 Benghazi St, Jebel Amman (☎ 689351)

Iraq
  1st Circle, Jebel Amman (☎ 621375)
Saudi Arabia
  1st Circle, Jebel Amman (☎ 814154)
Syria
  Afghani St, Jebel Amman (☎ 641935)
UK
  Abdoun (☎ 823100)
USA
  Between 2nd and 3rd Circles, Jebel Amman (☎ 820101)

Visas for Neighbouring Countries
Syria Since the beginning of 1996 it has been virtually impossible to obtain a Syrian visa in Amman. Travellers should get one before arriving in Jordan (in Cairo for instance). The situation could, of course, easily revert to normal.

Egypt The embassy is next to the distinctively yellow Dove Hotel, and is open for visa applications Sunday to Thursday from 9 am to noon. Passports can be picked up on the same day at 3 pm. You need a passport photo and the JD17 fee. Visas are valid for presentation for three months and get you one month in Egypt. The consulate in Aqaba is quieter, cheaper and easier to deal with.

Israel Visas of one month duration are issued at the land borders but any evidence of a visit to the Jewish state will bar you from entry into Lebanon, Syria, Iran and any of the Gulf States – see The Israeli Stamp Stigma in the Visas & Documents section of the Israel chapter.

Lebanon Lebanon has followed Syria's example and has virtually stopped issuing visas to non-residents. The Lebanese embassy is open Sunday to Thursday from 8.30 to 11 am. If you wish to try for a visa, take a photocopy of your passport details, a passport photo and JD14 (the fee for all nationalities). The visa, if you get it, is valid for a month.

CUSTOMS
You can import 200 cigarettes and up to one litre of wine or spirits into Jordan duty free.

JORDAN

There are no restrictions on the import and export of Jordanian and foreign currency.

MONEY
Costs
Jordan is not the cheapest country in the Middle East to travel in, but neither is it prohibitively expensive. With careful budgeting about US$15 per day is possible, as long as you don't mind eating felafel and shwarma all day and staying in the cheapest of the cheapies. It wouldn't take too many 'extravagances' to push the daily budget closer to US$20.

Currency
The currency in Jordan is the dinar (JD) – known as the *jaydee* among hip young locals – which is made up of 1000 fils. You will also often hear *piastre* or *qirsh* used, which are both 10 fils, so 10 qirsh equals 100 fils. Often when a price is quoted to you the ending will be omitted, so if you're told that something is 25, it's a matter of working out whether it's 25 fils, 25 qirsh or 25 dinar! To complicate things a little further, 50 fils is commonly referred to as a *shilling*, 100 fils (officially a *dirham*) as a *barisa* and a dinar as a *lira*. In fact, Jordanians rarely use the word fils at all, except for the benefit of foreigners.

Currency Exchange
Australia	A$1	=	JD0.58
Egypt	E£1	=	JD0.21
Germany	DM1	=	JD0.47
Japan	¥100	=	JD0.64
Syria	S£10	=	JD0.17
UK	UK£1	=	JD1.19
USA	US$1	=	JD0.71

Changing Money
It's not difficult to change money in Jordan, with most hard currencies being accepted (you will get nowhere with the New Zealand dollar and the Irish punt, however). American Express (Amex) seem to be the most widely accepted travellers' cheques.

The British Bank of the Middle East, Jordan National Bank and the Bank of Jordan accept MasterCard for cash advances, but only at selected branches.

Visa is more widely accepted for cash advances, but again only at selected branches of the following banks: the Housing Bank; the Bank of Jordan; the Cairo-Amman Bank; the Arab Banking Corporation; the Jordan Arab Investment Bank; and the Jordan Investment & Finance Bank. The first two each have a branch in Aqaba that will give cash advances on Visa, as will a branch of the Bank of Jordan in Irbid.

ATMs have made an appearance, but as yet the only ones that seem to accept foreign cards (including Visa and MasterCard) are those of the British Bank of the Middle East – and there are still precious few about. If an ATM swallows your card, call ☎ (06) 669123 (Amman).

Outside banking hours, there are plenty of exchange houses in Amman, Aqaba and Irbid. Many only deal in cash but some take travellers' cheques. Check their exchange rates with those in the banks before changing – often they are quite OK.

Tipping & Bargaining
Tips of 10% are generally expected in the better restaurants. Bargaining, especially when souvenir hunting, is essential but shop owners are unlikely to shift a long way from their original asking prices.

POST & COMMUNICATIONS
Post
Letters to the USA and Australia cost 400 fils, postcards 300 fils. To Europe, letters are 300 fils and postcards 200 fils.

Parcel post is ridiculously expensive. If you want to send something by air to Australia, for instance, the first kg will cost you JD13.700 and each subsequent kg JD9.400. To the UK the first kg is JD9.500 and each kg after JD3.400.

Telephone
The local telephone system isn't too bad. Calls cost 100 fils and most shop owners and hotels will let you use their phone, which is

better than trying to use the few noisy public telephones.

Overseas calls can be made easily from offices in Amman and Aqaba but cost the earth, with prices up to JD2.750 per minute for a three minute minimum. It may take up to 30 minutes or so to get the connection. In Amman a bunch of private phone/fax offices have sprung up in direct competition. They sometimes provide cheaper rates and do not impose a three minute minimum. It is not possible to make collect (reverse charge) calls from Jordan.

BOOKS

Annie Caulfield's *Kingdom of the Film Stars: Journey into Jordan* unravels some of the tightly-woven western myths about the Arab world, and does so in the intimate framework of a love story. With honest and humour, the author tells of her relationship with a Bedouin man and offers a vividly personal account of Jordanian culture and society. This is one of the many exciting titles in Journeys, Lonely Planet's new travel literature series. For more detailed information on travelling in Jordan, get hold of Lonely Planet's *Jordan & Syria*.

For rock-climbing and walking, *Treks & Climbs in the Mountains of Rum & Petra* by Tony Howard is an excellent handbook full of walks, climbs, and 4WD and camel treks. *Walks & Scrambles in Rum* is a useful pocket guide by Tony Howard.

See also the Books section in the Regional Facts for the Visitor chapter for more general reading matter.

NEWSPAPERS & MAGAZINES

The press in Jordan is given a surprisingly free reign and by the region's standards the controls are loose. The *Jordan Times*, the daily English-language newspaper, has a reasonably impartial outlook and gives good coverage of events in Jordan, elsewhere in the Middle East and worldwide.

RADIO & TV

Radio Jordan transmits in Arabic and English. The English station is on 855 kHz

AM and 96.3 kHz FM in Amman, or 98.7 kHz FM in Aqaba. It's mostly a music station.

Jordan TV broadcasts on two channels; one in Arabic, and the other (Channel 2) in a combination of English, French, Hebrew and Arabic.

PHOTOGRAPHY

Kodak and other brands of film, including slide, are widely available at the tourist sites in Jordan and in Amman itself, but don't expect to pay less than you would at home (anything up to JD8 for a roll of 36 slides). Check the use-by dates before buying.

Always ask permission before photographing anyone, particularly women, and be careful when taking pictures in and around Aqaba as Israel is just 'over there' and the Saudi border is only 20 km away. Photographing military areas is forbidden.

HEALTH

No inoculations are required in order to enter Jordan unless you are coming from a disease-affected area, but it is a good idea to have preventative shots for hepatitis A, polio, tetanus and typhoid before you go.

In the major towns the tap water is safe to drink, but if your stomach is a bit delicate or you find yourself in out-of-the way places bottled water is widely available. Never eat unwashed fruit or vegetables, and take great care with leafy salads. Make sure any meat you eat is thoroughly cooked.

Medical services in Jordan are well developed in the larger towns and cities and many of the doctors have been trained overseas and speak English. Your embassy will usually be able to recommend a reliable doctor or hospital if the need arises.

Many drugs normally sold only on prescription in the west are available over the counter in Jordan, but as the price of antibiotics in Jordan can be outrageous, you may want to bring a supply with you. If you do, make sure you bring a prescription or a letter from your doctor also.

For more general health information see the Health Appendix.

WOMEN TRAVELLERS

Women travelling alone in Jordan will find that Jordanian men are a little less hung-up about western women and sex than a lot of men in other Middle East countries, but it still pays to dress and behave modestly. Walking the streets of Amman in shorts and a singlet would be as embarrassing for the locals as for you.

Women travelling alone should think carefully before hitch hiking to avoid unwelcome proposals.

DANGERS & ANNOYANCES

Jordan is a safe and friendly country to travel in. The military keep a low profile and you are unlikely to experience anything but friendliness, honesty and hospitality. It is generally safe to walk around anywhere day or night in Amman and other towns.

Theft is usually no problem for people who take reasonable care with their gear.

BUSINESS HOURS

Government offices are open from 8 am to 2 pm daily, except Friday. Banks are open from 8.30 am to 1 pm and 4 to 6 pm in summer (3.30 to 5.30 pm in winter) daily, except Friday. Businesses keep similar hours but are more flexible. Museums are generally closed on Tuesday.

Small shops are open for long hours, from about 9 am to 8 or 9 pm. Some close for a couple of hours mid-afternoon. Friday is pretty dead, although a few shops are open, and you can still change money at the airport.

The souqs and street stalls are open daily, and in fact Friday is often their busiest day.

PUBLIC HOLIDAYS & SPECIAL EVENTS

Holidays are either religious (Islamic or Christian) or celebrations of important events in Jordanian or Arab history. For Islamic holidays see the table of holidays near Public Holidays & Special Events in the Regional Facts for the Visitor chapter.

January
    Tree Day (Arbor Day) (15th)

March
    Arab League Day (22nd)
May
    Labour Day (1st) and *Independence Day* (25th)
June
    Army Day and *Anniversary of the Great Arab Revolt* (10th)
August
    King Hussein's Accession (11th)
November
    King Hussein's Birthday (14th)

ACTIVITIES

Diving

The coast south of Aqaba port up to the Saudi border is home to one of the world's better diving spots, with plenty of coral and colourful fish life. There are at least four dive centres in Aqaba and all run PADI and CMAS courses for beginners and beyond, which will cost up to JD290.

Hiking & Climbing

Wadi Rum and Petra are ideal places for long day walks, or in the case of Wadi Rum, treks that could last days on foot or by camel. Rock climbing is also a possibility in Wadi Rum, but only basic gear is available on the site. For more information see the Books section earlier in this chapter.

COURSES

The University of Jordan (☎ 843555) on University St, Amman, offers summer courses in Modern Standard Arabic as well as more leisurely courses through the rest of the year. Enquiries should be addressed to the director of the Language Centre in the Arts Faculty. On occasion it can help find accommodation with Jordanian families. Some of the foreign cultural centres also conduct Arabic courses.

WORK

Work in Jordan is probably not an option for most foreigners passing through. You may be able to get work on archaeological digs but it is usually unpaid. If the Department of Antiquities is no help, try the British Institute for Archaeology & History (☎ 841317) or the American Center of Oriental Research (ACOR; ☎ 846117).

ACCOMMODATION

There are no youth hostels in Jordan. A bed in a shared room in a cheap hotel will not cost under JD1.500 and, generally, will be more like JD3 to JD5 without shower. It's sometimes possible to sleep on the roof, which in summer is a good place to be, but this will still cost at least JD1.

There is a reasonable choice of mid-range hotels in Amman, Aqaba and Petra, where a single may cost from JD8 to JD20.

FOOD & DRINKS

Takeaway outlets from small cafes to street stalls are the cheapest way to eat. You'll find plenty of spiced shwarma, salad and felafel, yoghurt and round, flat bread and syrupy nut-and-pastry cakes. In fact, you'll find the food very similar to the other countries of the region (Lebanon, Syria) but also to that of Greece and Turkey. Meat is relatively expensive but houmos, fuul and yoghurt (especially) are all cheap and good.

Bottled mineral water is widely available, as are locally made soft drinks, beer and wine. Imported liquors are sold in Amman and Aqaba but are prohibitively expensive.

ENTERTAINMENT

Jordan is not exactly thumping with night life. The big hotels offer the usual expensive and often dull discos and nightclubs, and occasionally present Arab musicians and belly dancing. Amman also has a few reasonable cinemas which show comparatively recent movies that haven't been too badly mauled by the censors.

THINGS TO BUY

Jordan doesn't have a lot to offer the souvenir hunter. Most things are overpriced and many come from Syria anyway, such as the inlaid backgammon boards and boxes.

Bedouin rugs and tapestries made by Palestinian women are popular, though you need to check carefully to make sure they are actually handmade.

Brass and copper coffee pots are among the better buys but they're difficult to transport and usually come from Syria, where you can pick them up for less. Small bottles of coloured sand from Petra, skilfully poured into the bottle to form intricate patterns, are sold for anything from 500 fils upwards.

Getting There & Away

AIR

You can fly to Amman from Beirut, Cairo, Damascus or further afield. Royal Jordanian is the national carrier, but from the main European capitals you can generally get cheaper deals with other airlines. One-way fares start at around $US789 from the USA, UK£237 from the UK, US$150 from Athens and İstanbul, E£326 from Cairo, and A$1200 from Australia and New Zealand.

LAND

Bringing Your Own Vehicle

To bring a vehicle into Jordan you should have a *carnet de passage* and your own insurance. Obviously, you will need the vehicle's registration papers, but you do not need an International Driving Permit – your national licence is sufficient.

You will be obliged to take out local insurance, which costs JD17, plus a nominal customs fee of JD7 for most European-registered vehicles.

Syria

Bus The only border crossing between Syria and Jordan is at Ramtha/Der'a.

Air-con Jordan Express Tourism Transport (JETT) and Karnak buses (respectively the Jordanian and Syrian government bus companies) both run once each way between Amman and Damascus. The trip takes about seven hours depending on the border formalities and is the easiest way to make the crossing. It costs JD4.500 from Amman but only JD4 or US$5 from Damascus. You can't pay in Syrian pounds either way and you need to book 48 hours in advance as demand often exceeds supply.

Train The famous Hejaz railway line built early this century to transport pilgrims to Medina from Damascus has been resurrected between Damascus and Amman. A slow diesel train with ancient carriages leaves Amman on Monday at 8 am and returns the following Sunday. Tickets cost JD4 and the journey time is about 8 hours.

Service Taxi The *servees* are slightly faster than the buses and run at all hours, although it gets harder to find one in the evening. They usually get a far more thorough search at the border, so you often save no time at all. They leave from around the Abdali bus station in Amman and from next to the Karnak bus station in Damascus. It costs JD5.500 or S£385.

Hitching It is possible to cross the Jordan-Syria border with a combination of local bus, walking and hitching.

Iraq
Bus There are two daily JETT buses between Amman and Baghdad. They cost JD12, depart at 8.30 am and 2 pm and take about 14 hours.

Service Taxi The service taxis are faster than the buses, but over a long distance the bus is probably more comfortable. You'll find taxis for Baghdad around Abdali bus station and on Shabsough St in Downtown Amman.

Saudi Arabia
There are regular JETT and Saptco buses from Amman to Jeddah (10 am), Dammam (11 am) and Riyadh (11.30 am), all costing JD31 and taking up to 24 hours, depending on your destination. Buses also depart from Aqaba. (Note, however, that it may not be possible to buy a ticket from Riyadh to Amman from companies in Riyadh.) Transport can also be arranged to destinations beyond, such as Abu Dhabi and Kuwait.

Hijazi also has buses to Saudi Arabia for similar prices.

Israel & the Palestinian Territories
Peace with Israel and the setting up of the partially autonomous Palestine National Authority has created a totally new situation. There are now three border crossings. As of April 1996 private cars can be taken across the northern and southern crossings. Israeli vehicles are required to change number plates when they enter Jordan, but no such restriction applies to Jordanian vehicles going the other way. Vehicles with plates from other countries should have no problem. Reportedly, since June 1996, there have also been direct bus services operating between Jordan and Israel.

Wadi Araba This handy crossing (Arava to the Israelis) in the south of the country links Aqaba to Eilat. The border is open Sunday to Thursday from 6.30 am to 10 pm; Friday to Saturday from 8 am to 8 pm. To get there from Aqaba you need to take a taxi (JD3) 10 km to the border. Because the border is only about two km from central Eilat, you can simply walk in from the Israeli side or catch bus No 16 for 4 NIS. Bus No 16 runs between this crossing and the Taba crossing into Egypt, via Eilat's central bus station. If coming to Jordan this way, there are white service taxis to central Aqaba – they cost JD4.

If you're coming down from Jerusalem on the No 392 bus and you want to skip Eilat, ask the driver to let you off at the turn-off for the border, a short walk away.

A bus service between the two towns was due to begin operation in April 1996, but there was still no sign of it at the time of writing.

There are money-changing facilities, phones and cafes on both sides of the border, and if you are coming from Israel the Jordanians will issue visas on the spot. This route makes a viable alternative to the Nuweiba ferry for heading into Egypt. Leaving Israel there is an exit tax of 48.70

NIS. Going the other way the Jordanian tax is JD4.

Jisr Sheikh Hussein The northernmost Jordan River crossing, and perhaps the least convenient for most travellers, the Jisr ('Bridge') Sheikh Hussein links Beit She'an in Galilee with northern Jordan. If coming from Israel, get a Tiberias bus and change at Beit She'an. From here another bus takes you to the Israeli side for 8.40 NIS. The Israeli official name for this crossing point is Jordan Border. After passport formalities, a compulsory bus takes you to the other side for 3 NIS.

From the Jordanian side you can wait for a minibus to Irbid (300 fils) or get a taxi about three km to the main road, where you can try your luck flagging down minibuses.

The Jordanian exit tax is JD4, while the Israelis charge 48.70 NIS. The crossing is open the same hours as the Wadi Araba crossing, and you can obtain a Jordanian visa there.

Jisr al-Malek al-Hussein/Allenby Bridge For many years the only crossing between Jordan and the West Bank (and hence tacitly Israel), this crossing over the Jordan River remains something of an anomaly. The procedure is more straightforward than in the past, and you need no permits as was the case prior to the signing of the Israeli-Jordanian peace treaty.

The border is open Sunday to Thursday from 8 am to 10.30 pm; Friday and Saturday until 1 pm. You can catch the JETT bus from Amman at 6.30 am (JD6). The fee includes the short ride over the bridge. Or you can get a minibus (JD1) or service taxi (JD1.500) to the Jordanian frontier (JD2 going the other way) from Abdali bus station. The odd service taxi also connects from this border crossing to Irbid.

The ride to the Israeli side costs another JD1.500 – although it's extremely short, it can seem to last an eternity with repeated stops for passport checks and the like. The bridge itself is rather disappointing, an unimpressive 30m long structure over what seems little more than a dribble of the Jordan River. It's not possible to walk, hitch or take a private car across.

The historic oddity of this crossing has remained enshrined in the fact that, on departing Jordan, you are not really considered to be leaving it. Prior to 1988 Jordan still laid claim to the West Bank as its own territory, and somehow this idea has remained in the approach to visas. If you wish to return to Jordan from Israel within the validity of your present Jordanian visa, you need only keep the stamped exit slip and present it on returning by the same crossing (it won't work at the other crossings). For this reason there is no Jordanian exit tax either. Going the other way, the Israeli exit tax is a hefty 83.50 NIS (US$31), supposedly because you are paying to leave Israel *and* the Palestine National Authority's territory.

The Israeli passport control process can be a little wearying, with plenty of waiting and bag checking. There is a change booth on your way to the exit. Note that, if you are entering Jordan this way and intend to return to Israel, you must keep the entrance form given to you by the Jordanians – they could well insist on you prolonging your stay in Jordan if you cannot present it.

Once outside you have two choices if you wish to proceed to Jerusalem. First there is the easy way – a direct share taxi (*sherut*) for 26 NIS per person. These taxis arrive at a garage opposite the Damascus Gate in Jerusalem.

Then there is the more complicated route. Since the Palestine National Authority was set up, the cheap Arab bus to Jerusalem of yore is history. You can now catch a bus to Jericho (Areeha) for 5.50 NIS. There you will be told you can change for a bus to Nazareth for 10 NIS and then get another to Jerusalem. This is the long and hard way – four hours. Instead take a service taxi from the south side of Jericho's main square. You should be able to catch one direct to Jerusalem's Damascus Gate (30 minutes; 5 NIS) or at least to Bethany, just outside central Jerusalem, where you can pick up another service taxi to the centre (1.50 NIS).

Although known as the Allenby Bridge to the Israelis, the bridge is the Jisr al-Malek al-Hussein (King Hussein Bridge) to the Jordanians and Palestinians. Asking for the Allenby Bridge is likely to meet with blank stares. Although it can get quiet, the traffic through this crossing is pretty constant, so you shouldn't have too much problem with public transport either way.

Note Middle Eastern politics being what it is, all the above information should be considered highly perishable. Things can alter at short notice, and although the Israeli-Jordanian peace deal appears solid, be prepared for changes – at least in the procedural minutiae.

SEA

Egypt

Ferry & Bus You can book a ferry and bus right through to Cairo at the JETT bus office. The ticket costs US$45, but you can pick up Cairo-bound buses on arrival at Nuweiba anyway.

Ferry & Fast Boat There is at least one daily car ferry and a fast (foot passenger only) boat between Aqaba and Nuweiba in Sinai. This route is far more interesting (and cheaper) than flying to or from Cairo.

Beware of buying ferry tickets in Amman, as you may be charged for nonexistent 1st class places.

The car-ferry trip is meant to take three hours but can often take much longer. Although some travellers have reported the luxury of travelling on a near-empty boat, the more common experience is of ferries packed beyond capacity. Be prepared for a trip that could last as long as eight hours.

The fast turbo-catamaran is a new beast on this route, and on a good day takes just one hour to complete the trip.

The worst time to travel is just after the haj, when Aqaba fills up with *hajis* (pilgrims) returning home from Mecca.

For details on ticket prices see the Aqaba Getting There & Away section later in this chapter.

LEAVING JORDAN

There are three departure taxes from Jordan: JD4 across land borders (except to the West Bank); JD6 from Aqaba by sea; and JD10 by air.

Getting Around

AIR

The modern Queen Alia international airport is about 35 km south of Amman. There is just one domestic route – between Amman and Aqaba. There is also a smaller airfield in the outlying Amman suburb of Marka, from where Royal Wings (a subsidiary of Royal Jordanian) operates daily flights to Aqaba.

BUS

The blue and white buses belonging to the JETT bus company run from Amman to Aqaba, the King Hussein Bridge (Jisr al-Malek al-Hussein), Petra and Hammamat Ma'in. See under Getting Around in the Amman section for details of destinations and fares.

Large private buses, usually air-conditioned, run north from Amman to Irbid (850 fils) and south to Aqaba (JD2).

All smaller towns are connected by 20-seat minibuses. These leave when full and on some routes operate infrequently. The correct fare is nearly always posted in Arabic somewhere inside the front of the bus.

SERVICE TAXI

By far the most popular mode of transport is the service taxi. These are usually Peugeot 504 or 505 station wagons with seven seats or Mercedes sedans with five seats.

They operate on most routes and cost up to twice as much as the minibuses but are faster.

CAR & MOTORCYCLE

If there are four or more of you to split the cost of a rented car, it can be a good way of seeing a bit of the country – especially the desert castles, some of which are not accessible by public transport.

You'll be lucky to find a small car with unlimited km for under JD25 a day with a three day minimum. Limited-km deals work out to be much more expensive if you're going to be doing more than 100 km per day. They cost from about JD20 per day plus 60 to 80 fils for every extra km.

Motorcyclists should be aware that there are precious few mechanics in Jordan able to deal with the average modern bike and its problems.

BICYCLE

Cycling is an option in Jordan but not necessarily a fun one. The desert in summer is not a good place to indulge in strenuous activity. Cycling north or south (most travelling will be done in those directions) can be hard work too. There is a strong prevailing wind from the west that can wear you down. Bring plenty of spare parts.

HITCHING

Hitching is definitely feasible in Jordan. The traffic varies a lot from place to place but you generally don't have to wait long for a lift, although you may be asked to pay.

Make sure you have a hat and some water to fight the heat if you have to wait a while for a lift. Hassles when hitching are rare, but women travelling alone should definitely not hitch. A single male traveller wrote in to warn about the truck drivers who may have 'designs on your body'.

Amman

Amman will certainly never win any prizes for being the most interesting city in the world and, in fact, has only a few attractions. The Downtown area is a busy, chaotic jumble of traffic – human and motorised – and just crossing the street is an achievement. The town council seems bent on making the situation as difficult as possible, erecting barriers along footpaths too narrow

to cope with the squeeze. Nevertheless, Amman is the hub of all roads in Jordan so it's highly unlikely that you will not pass through – and it's really quite pleasant too.

The place has been inhabited since at least 3000 BC. Built originally on seven hills (like Rome), Amman (Philadelphia to the Romans) now spreads across 19. At its heart lies a well restored, 6000 seat theatre, a forum and a street of columns. To the north, across from the theatre on a hill, is the citadel – an old Roman garrison from which you have some of the best views of the city centre.

Amman is also one of the friendliest cities you're likely to visit. Most residents, whether born Jordanians or among the flood of Palestinian refugees from the wars of 1948 and 1967, are well educated, friendly, speak a fair amount of English and are eager to chat with a foreigner. In almost every encounter they will say to you: 'Welcome in Jordan.' And you get the feeling that they really mean it.

Jerash is the most popular day trip from Amman, but you can also visit Madaba, where there are some good mosaics, or Wadi as-Seer, with its restored 2nd century BC castle.

Orientation

The Downtown area of Amman, where you'll find plenty of cheap hotels and restaurants, as well as banks, a post office and the bulk of what little there is to see in the city, is at the bottom of four of the many hills that characterise the city. The main hill is Jebel Amman, where you'll find most of the embassies and some of the flash hotels. On Jebel al-Hussein are the Abdali and JETT bus stations.

Information

Tourist Office There's no tourist office in Amman but the Ministry of Tourism & Antiquities just up from 3rd Circle has a few brochures, the most helpful of which is called simply *Visitor's Guide*.

Police Registration If you plan to stay in Jordan for more than 15 days, you must

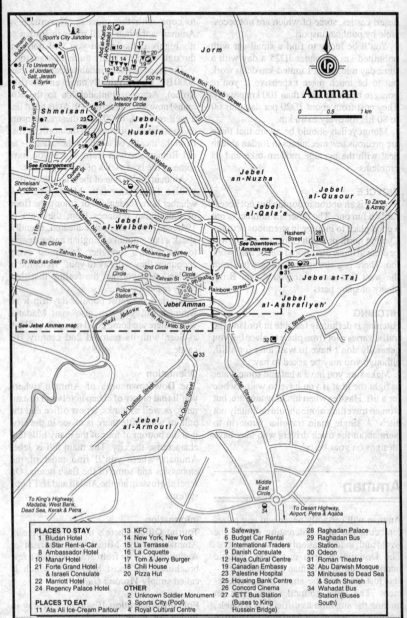

Amman

0   0.5   1 km

PLACES TO STAY
1 Bludan Hotel
   & Star Rent-a-Car
8 Ambassador Hotel
10 Manar Hotel
21 Forte Grand Hotel
   & Israeli Consulate
22 Marriott Hotel
24 Regency Palace Hotel

PLACES TO EAT
11 Ata Ali Ice-Cream Parlour

13 KFC
14 New York, New York
15 La Terrasse
16 La Coquette
17 Tom & Jerry Burger
18 Chili House
20 Pizza Hut

OTHER
2 Unknown Soldier Monument
3 Sports City (Pool)
4 Royal Cultural Centre

5 Safeways
6 Budget Car Rental
7 International Traders
9 Danish Consulate
12 Haya Cultural Centre
19 Canadian Embassy
23 Palestine Hospital
25 Housing Bank Centre
26 Concord Cinema
27 JETT Bus Station
   (Buses to King
   Hussein Bridge)

28 Raghadan Palace
29 Raghadan Bus
   Station
30 Odeon
31 Roman Theatre
32 Abu Darwish Mosque
33 Minibuses to Dead Sea
   & South Shuneh
34 Wahadat Bus
   Station (Buses
   South)

register with the police. In Amman you need to go to the Muhajireen police station (ask for the *Markaz Amn Muhajireen).* You can get service taxi No 35 from near the Church of the Saviour – ask where to be let off. The relevant office at the station opens Saturday to Thursday from 10 am to 1 pm.

Money There are numerous banks all over the Downtown area as well as in Jebel Amman and Shmeisani. The rates don't vary but the commissions and other charges do. For travellers' cheques, the best place is probably the Bank of Jordan branch on 1st Circle. The Downtown branch is also fine, and the British Bank of the Middle East on Al-Malek al-Hussein St has an ATM that accepts several foreign cards, including Visa and MasterCard. The Amex agent is International Traders (☎ 661014) out in Shmeisani, opposite the Ambassador Hotel on Abd al-Karim al-Khattabi St.

Post & Communications The main post office is in the Downtown area on Prince Mohammed St. It is open from 7 am to 7 pm (winter to 5 pm) daily except Friday, when it closes at 1.30 pm. The main office for international telephone calls is on the street up behind the post office, opposite the Al-Khayyam Cinema. It's open from 7.30 am to about 11 pm daily. You'll find private phone offices on the same street.

Bookshops Possibly the best bookshop is the one at the Jordan InterContinental Hotel, which has a range of books on Jordan and the Middle East as well as some fiction and foreign press. The Jordan Distribution Agency is the closest to Downtown Amman, just where 9th Sha'ban and Al-Amir Mohammed Sts meet. It has a reasonable range of books on the Middle East, a small stock of fiction and some foreign press. The Amman Bookshop (☎ 644013) just below 3rd Circle has just been refurbished and offers an excellent range of English-language books. The Mujdalawi Masterpieces Bookshop (☎ 658859) is an excellent bookshop which stocks mainly children's books.

Also good are the Jordan Book Centre (☎ 606882), Al-Jubeiha, and the University Bookshop (☎ 606271), Luweibeh Gardens St.

Cultural Centres & Libraries The British Council (☎ 636147) on Rainbow St (or Abu Bakr as-Sadiq St), Jebel Amman, east of 1st Circle, has a good library, current newspapers and regularly shows films. The American Center (☎ 822471), out by the US embassy in Abdoun, also has a library. The Centre Culturel Français (☎ 637009) is by the roundabout at the top of Jebel al-Weibdeh.

Medical Services Among the better hospitals are the Hussein Medical Centre (☎ 813813/32) in Wadi as-Seer and the Palestine Hospital (☎ 607071) on University St, Shmeisani.

Emergency In case of emergency, you can contact the police by telephone (☎ 192 or ☎ 621111). For an ambulance or first aid call ☎ 193.

Things to See
The restored **Roman theatre**, five minutes walk east of Downtown Amman, is the most obvious and impressive remnant of Philadelphia. It is cut into the northern side of a hill that once served as a necropolis, and has a capacity of 6000 people. It is believed that the theatre was built in the 2nd century AD during the reign of Antoninus Pius, who ruled from 138 to 161. On the eastern end of what was the forum stands the **Odeon**, which is still being restored. Built about the same time as the Roman theatre, it was used mainly for musical performances. Philadelphia's chief fountain, or **nymphaeum**, stands with its back to Quraysh St, west of the theatre and not far from the King Hussein Mosque.

Although much of the **citadel's** buildings have disappeared or been reduced to rubble, you can see evidence of Roman, Byzantine and Islamic construction. Buildings include the **Temple of Hercules**, a trio of whose

JORDAN

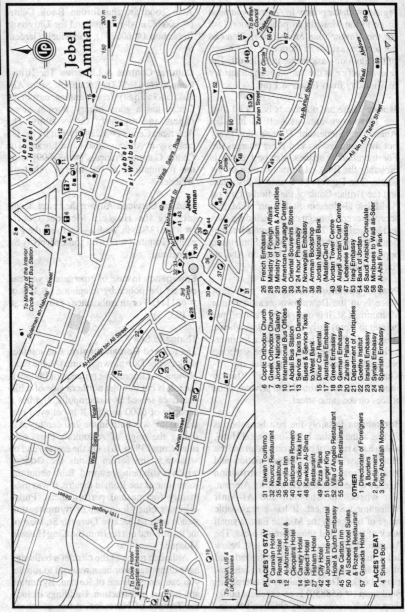

300 m
150
16

Jebel Amman

Jebel al-Hussein

Jebel al-Weibdeh

Jebel Amman

To Ministry of the Interior Circle & JETT Bus Station

Suleiman en-Naouri Street

Al-Hussein bin Ali Street

Wadi Saqra Road

Wadi Saqra Road

Zahran Street

Zahran Street

Queen Alia Street

11th August

4th Circle

Wadi Abdoun

Ali Ibn Abi Taleb Street

Al-Buhturi Street

Amir Mohammed St

Amir Mohammed St

Faleter St

1st Circle

2nd Circle

3rd Circle

To British Council

To Abdoun, US & UK Embassies

To Dove Hotel & Egyptian Embassy

To West Bank

PLACES TO STAY
5 Caravan Hotel
8 Remal Hotel
12 Al-Monzer Hotel & Cleopatra Hotel
14 Canary Hotel
16 Select Hotel
27 Hisham Hotel
42 City Hotel
44 Jordan InterContinental Hotel & Dutch Embassy
45 The Carlton Inn
50 Al Sabeel Hotel Suites & Rozena Restaurant
57 Granada Hotel

PLACES TO EAT
4 Snack Box

31 Taiwan Tourismo
32 Nouroz Restaurant
35 Maatouk
36 Bonita Inn
40 Ristorante Romero
41 Chicken Tikka Inn
48 Kawkab Al-Sharq Restaurant
49 Pizza Place
51 Burger King
52 Villa d'Angelo Restaurant
55 Diplomat Restaurant

OTHER
1 Directorate of Foreigners & Borders
2 Parliament
3 King Abdullah Mosque

6 Coptic Orthodox Church
7 Greek Orthodox Church
9 Jordan National Gallery
10 International Bus Offices
11 Abdali Bus Station
13 Service Taxis to Damascus, Buses & Service Taxis to West Bank
15 Dinar Car Rental
17 Australian Embassy
18 Greek Embassy
19 German Embassy
20 Zahran Palace
21 Department of Antiquities
22 Goethe Institut
23 Iranian Embassy
24 Syrian Embassy
25 Spanish Embassy

26 French Embassy
28 Ministry of Foreign Affairs
29 Ministry of Tourism & Antiquities
30 American Language Center
33 Oriental Souvenirs Stores
34 24 hour Pharmacy
37 Norwegian Embassy
38 Amman Bookshop
39 Jordan National Bank (MasterCard)
43 Alaydi Jordan Craft Centre
46 Lebanese Embassy
47 Iraqi Embassy
53 Bank of Jordan
54 Saudi Arabian Consulate
56 Minibuses to Wadi as-Seer
59 Al-Ahli Fun Park

columns have been re-erected. Artefacts dating to the Bronze Age show that the hill served as a fortress or agora for thousands of years. The **National Archaeological Museum** here is worth a visit. It's open from 9 am to 5 pm Saturday to Thursday (except Tuesday, when it is closed), and from 10 am to 4 pm on Friday and holidays. Entry is JD2.

The **Folklore Museum** is one of two small museums housed in the wings of the Roman theatre. The other is the **Traditional Jewels & Costumes Museum**, which has well-presented displays of traditional costumes, jewellery and utensils. Opening times are the same as for the Archaeological Museum and entry to each costs a rather steep JD1.

The simple and solemn **Monument to the Unknown Soldier** is out by the Sports City complex and houses a small museum on Jordan's military history.

Places to Stay

Downtown Amman is thick with cheap hotels. For the most impecunious, *Zahran Hotel* (☎ 625473) might be the answer. It's about as basic as they come, costs JD1.500 per person (JD3 for a double to yourself if you want) and is virtually welded onto the King Hussein Mosque – just right for early risers.

If that doesn't grab you, there are any number of cheapies charging around JD3 for a bed. The *Yarmouk Hotel* (☎ 624241), on Al-Malek Faisal St, has beds for JD2.500 and doubles for JD5 (whether double or single occupancy). The *Baghdad Grand Hotel* (☎ 625433), on the same street, is much of a muchness and charges JD2.500 for a bed or JD6 for a double (it might knock a JD1 off for single occupancy). You'll find many other hotels in the same sort of category.

That long-time backpacker favourite, the *Cliff Hotel* (☎ 624273), is a slight jump for the better in quality but not the cheapest around. It is up a side alley just off Al-Malek Faisal St. A bed in a double costs JD5, or JD8 for the whole room. You can sleep on the roof for JD2. A hot shower costs 500 fils extra. The owner, Abu Suleiman, is a mine of information.

One lane up towards the post office is the *Vinice* (☎ 638895). Beds in a shared room cost JD3, and doubles JD6 (JD5 for single occupancy). It is quite OK, and becoming increasingly popular as a rival to the Cliff.

By the telephone office is the *Bdeiwi Hotel* (☎ 643394), a spick and span new place on Omar al-Khayyam St. Rooms are clean and comfortable, and you pay JD4 per person (in doubles and triples). Single occupancy of a room costs JD8. Hot showers are free, and the guy here also runs a busy phone and fax business.

Edging a little further up the scale, *Park Hotel* (☎ 648145), Al-Malek al-Hussein St, is not bad at JD10/14 for rooms with phone, TV, balcony and bathroom – staff seem happy to bargain.

A nice deal is the *Select Hotel* (☎ 637101) on Baoniya St in Jebel al-Weibdeh. The rooms, which cost JD11/16, are about the same quality as those of the Park Hotel, but many have shady balconies and the attached Negresco bar is an added attraction.

Tucked away on a side street opposite the police department by Abdali bus station is the *Remal Hotel* (☎ 630670; fax 655751), which has much more comfortable rooms for JD14/18 plus taxes. The *Canary Hotel* (☎ 638353; fax 654353) on Jebel al-Weibdeh, opposite the Terra Sancta college, has good rooms for JD16/24.

Places to Eat

On the alley across Al-Amir Mohammed St from the Vinice hotel is *Hashem*, a cheap restaurant for felafel, houmos and fuul. A filling meal with bread and tea is only about 500 fils, and the place opens 24 hours.

You'll find several shwarma stalls dotted around the Downtown area. The price of a shwarma is around 250 fils, but you'll need a couple to make a halfway decent lunch.

On the same lane as the Baghdad Grand Hotel is a place called the *Abu Khamis & Abu Saleh Restaurant*. It has a good range, including chicken, stuffed green peppers, potato chips, and a variety of meat and vegetable stews. A filling meal will cost between JD1 and JD2.

The best dish at *Al-Quds Restaurant* on

Al-Malek al-Hussein St is the traditional mensaf with a delicious cooked yoghurt sauce. It's not cheap at JD2.200 but it is excellent.

Cheaper, and with a similar range to the Abu Khamis, is the *Cairo Restaurant* one block south-west of the King Hussein Mosque.

Just off Cinema al-Hussein St is the *Beefy Cafe*, a fast-food-type place with good hamburgers, pizzas and chips. Best of all, it must do one of the region's top milkshakes. A basic hamburger is 450 fils.

By far and away superior to all of them is *Snack Box*, on Suleiman an-Nabulsi St

behind the King Abdullah Mosque. The fine stir fries and meat-and-pasta meals (eat in or take away) cost JD2 or under, and are a tasty alternative to the standard fare.

Right on 1st Circle, the *Diplomat Restaurant* has a good range of dishes for JD1 to JD3, including reasonable pizzas. It's open until quite late and has tables on the footpath where you can sip on an Amstel (JD1.800).

Just behind the nearby hospital and down a side street two blocks south of 3rd Circle is the *Taiwan Tourismo*, where a filling and good Chinese meal for two can be had for around JD10.

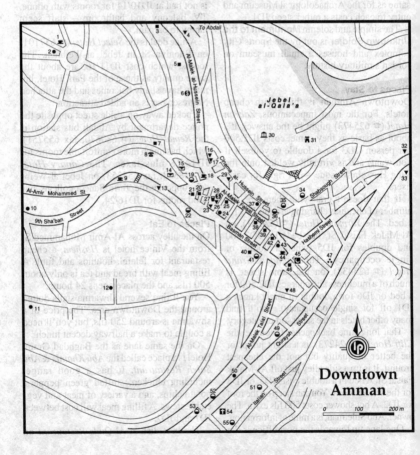

Downtown Amman

0   100   200 m

In Shmeisani is a whole string of places where you won't come away with much change from JD10, except at the western takeaways: *Pizza Hut* and *KFC*.

Popular and somewhat more shishi places include *La Terrasse*, which often has Arab musicians in the evening, *La Coquette*, for French dining, and *New York, New York*. These are all clustered around Queen Noor St, but the easiest thing to do is jump into a cab and ask for the *Jabri* pâtisserie in Shmeisani.

Entertainment

There are numerous tiny little bars tucked away in the rabbit warren of alleys around the Cliff Hotel. They close by 11.30 pm, as do most of the hotel bars. The *Hisham Hotel* has a nice beer garden and the *Dove Hotel*, near 5th Circle, has a thumping Irish pub which stays open until about 1.30 am.

Getting There & Away

Air The only internal air route is between Amman and Aqaba. Royal Wings has a daily flight from Marka airfield at 7.30 am for JD20 each way. Some Royal Jordanian flights also land in Aqaba, as a stop on international routes.

Bus The JETT bus office/station is on King Hussein St, a few minutes walk north past the Abdali bus station. Tickets for JETT buses should be booked at least a day in advance. There are daily departures to the Aqaba (JD4.300), Baghdad (JD12), Damascus (JD4.500), King Hussein Bridge for the West Bank (JD6) and Petra (JD5.500).

The main bus stations in Amman are Abdali for transport north and west, and Wahadat for buses south. From Abdali, minibuses run to Ajlun (450 fils), Deir Alla (400 fils) in the Jordan Valley, Irbid (530 fils), Jerash (370 fils), Salt (175 fils) and Suweileh (85 fils). From the southern end of the station you can get minibuses to the King Hussein Bridge.

From Wahadat there are minibus departures for Aqaba (JD3), Hammamat Ma'in (JD1.500; irregular), Kerak (750 fils), Ma'an (JD1.050), Madaba (220 fils) and Wadi Musa/Petra (JD2). There are also buses

(JD2) for Aqaba. The minibus to Madaba (220 fils) from Raghadan bus station in the centre is more convenient.

Train The Hejaz Railway train to Damascus leaves from a station in Marka (take a service taxi from Raghadan bus station) on Monday at 8 am and costs JD2.500.

Service Taxi The service taxis are faster and more convenient than the buses but are more expensive. They use the same stations as the buses. From Abdali bus station they run to Irbid (850 fils), Jerash (650 fils), Ajlun, Salt, the King Hussein Bridge (JD1.500) and even occasionally to Ramtha, the Jordanian border crossing with Syria (JD1). They also run to Damascus for JD5.500.

Getting Around
The Airports The Queen Alia international airport is about 35 km south of the city. Buses make the 50 minute run irregularly from 6.30 am to 8.30 pm from the Abdali bus station for 750 fils. You can also get special airport taxis for the trip into town. They cost about JD8 (JD10 from about 10 pm to 8 am).

If you need to get to the small airfield at Marka, take a Marka service taxi from the Raghadan bus station.

Service Taxi There's a standard charge of 70 to 80 fils for most service taxis, depending on the route, and you pay the full amount regardless of where you get off. Some of the more useful routes are: No 3 from Basman St for the 3rd and 4th circles; No 6 from Cinema al-Hussein St for the Ministry of the Interior Circle, going past the Abdali and JETT bus stations; and No 27 from near the fruit and vegie souq to the Middle East Circle for Wahadat bus station.

Taxi The flag fall in a standard taxi is 150 fils, and any cross-town journey you want to make should never cost more than 800 fils.

AROUND AMMAN
Wadi as-Seer & 'Araq al-Amir
The narrow, fertile valley of Wadi as-Seer is a real contrast to the bare, treeless plateau of Amman to the east. The ruins of the building of **Qasr al-Abd** (Castle of the Slave) and the caves, known as 'Araq (or 'Iraq) al-Amir (Cave of the Prince), are another 10 km down the valley from the largely Circassian village of Wadi as-Seer.

The caves are up to the right of the road and are in two tiers; the upper one forms a long gallery along the cliff face. The castle is about 500m down the valley and can be seen from the caves. There is still some mystery about when and why it was constructed but it is believed that it was built in the 2nd century BC by Hyrcanus of the powerful Jewish Tobiad family.

Getting There & Away A minibus from Ali bin Abi Taleb St in Amman takes half an hour and costs 100 fils. There are also minibuses from Suweileh and local town buses. From Wadi as-Seer you catch a minibus for 100 fils; it will take you right to the end of the road at 'Araq al-Amir.

North & West of Amman

JERASH
This beautifully preserved Roman city, 51 km north of Amman, is one of Jordan's major attractions, second only to Petra.

The main ruins of Jerash were rediscovered in 1806 but excavations did not begin until the 1920s. They continue today but it is estimated that 90% of the city is still untouched. The site is open daily from 7.30 am until dark, and entry is JD2.

There's a Visitors' Centre with a souvenir shop and post office, and a Government Rest House that sells expensive refreshments and buffet meals.

History
Although discoveries indicate that the site was inhabited in Neolithic times, it was from the time of Alexander the Great (332 BC) that the city really rose to prominence.

In 63 BC the Roman general Pompey

conquered the region and Jerash became part of the Roman province of Syria and, soon after, one of the cities of the Decapolis (the commercial league of 10 cities formed by Pompey after his conquest of Syria and Palestine in 64 BC). Jerash reached its peak at the beginning of the 3rd century, when it was made a colony, but from then on it went into a slow decline.

Things to See

Approaching the ruins from Amman, the **Triumphal Arch** is first to come into view. Behind the arch is the **hippodrome**, the old sports field that used to be surrounded by seating holding up to 15,000 spectators. The **South Gate**, originally one of four in the 3500m long city wall, little of which remains, is the main entrance to the site today.

Once inside the gate, the **Temple of Zeus** is the ruined building on the left. It was built in the latter part of the 2nd century on a holy site from earlier times. The **Forum** is unusual because of its oval shape, and some attribute this to the desire to link gracefully the main north-south axis with the existing Hellenistic sacred site of the Zeus temple or its predecessor.

The **South Theatre**, behind the Temple of Zeus, was built in the 1st century and could once hold 5000 spectators. On the far side of the Forum is the **colonnaded street**, stretches for more than 600m to the North Gate. The street is still paved with the original stones and the ruts worn by thousands of chariots over the years can be clearly seen.

Next along the cardo is the **Nymphaeum**, the main ornamental fountain of the city and a temple to the Nymphs. This is followed by the most imposing building on the site, the **Temple of Artemis**, dedicated to the patron goddess of the city.

In the tiny **museum** just to the east of the Forum, there's a good selection of artefacts from the site. The site is open daily from 7.30 am until dark, and entry is JD2. ■

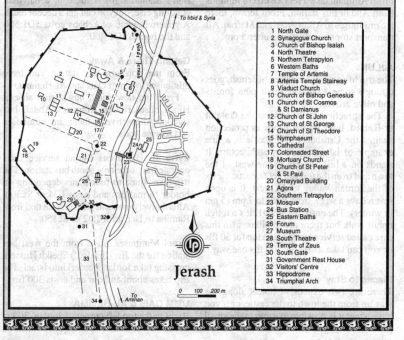

1	North Gate
2	Synagogue Church
3	Church of Bishop Isaiah
4	North Theatre
5	Northern Tetrapylon
6	Western Baths
7	Temple of Artemis
8	Artemis Temple Stairway
9	Viaduct Church
10	Church of Bishop Genesius
11	Church of St Cosmos & St Damianus
12	Church of St John
13	Church of St George
14	Church of St Theodore
15	Nymphaeum
16	Cathedral
17	Colonnaded Street
18	Mortuary Church
19	Church of St Peter & St Paul
20	Omayyad Building
21	Agora
22	Southern Tetrapylon
23	Mosque
24	Bus Station
25	Eastern Baths
26	Forum
27	Museum
28	South Theatre
29	Temple of Zeus
30	South Gate
31	Government Rest House
32	Visitors' Centre
33	Hippodrome
34	Triumphal Arch

To Irbid & Syria

Wadi Jerash

Jerash

0   100   200 m

To Amman

By the middle of the 5th century Christianity had become the major religion of the region and the construction of churches proceeded at a startling rate. With the Persian invasion of 614 and the Muslim conquest of 636, followed by a series of earthquakes in 747, Jerash was really on the skids and its population shrank to about 25% of its former size.

Places to Stay & Eat

Surprisingly, there is no hotel in Jerash, but it's an easy day trip from Amman. The *Government Rest House* by the entrance has an expensive restaurant, and near the bus station there's the usual collection of *cafes* selling the usual felafel and shwarma. About 20m from the site entrance is the pleasant *Al-Khayyam Restaurant*.

Getting There & Away

From Amman, take a service taxi or minibus from Abdali bus station. From Jerash, there are minibuses to Ajlun, Irbid and Mafraq. All transport stops running soon after 5 pm.

AJLUN

The trip to Ajlun, 22 km west of Jerash, goes through some beautiful small pine forests and olive groves.

The attraction of the town is the **Qala'at ar-Rabad**, built by the Arabs as protection against the Crusaders. The castle is a fine example of Islamic military architecture. It stands on a hill two km to the west of the town and from the top you get fantastic views of the Jordan Valley to the west. It is open seven days a week from 8 am to 7 pm (5 pm in winter). The entry fee is JD1. It's a tough uphill walk but there are minibuses (in this case called service taxis) to the top for 50 fils or you can take a taxi for 500 fils one way.

Places to Stay

There are two expensive hotels along the way up from the town to the castle, or if you have a tent it is possible to camp in the small patch of forest just to the west of the castle.

Getting There & Away

There are regular minibuses from Jerash (170 fils) or direct from Amman (450 fils).

IRBID

Irbid has little to offer but is a handy base for the trip to Umm Qais and Al-Hemma, on the Syrian border, as well as to Pella. It can also be a stop-off on the way to or from Syria.

Places to Stay & Eat

There are a few cheapies in the central area. The best is probably the *Hotel al-Wahadat al-Arabiyya* (☎ 242083), with rooms for JD5/8/10.500.

For something a bit more up-market, try the *Al-Umayya Hotel* (☎ 245955) on King Hussein St. It is on the 2nd floor above the Jordan Arab Investment Bank, and has good, clean rooms with ensuite bath, TV and fan at JD14/18.

The *Al-Khayyam Restaurant* (look for the Bell's Scotch sign) is more of a bar than anything else, but you can get a decent meal. A generous plate of kebabs costs JD1.500 and the beer is JD1.400.

Getting There & Away

From the northern bus station you have minibuses to Umm Qais and Al-Hemma.

From the new south bus station air-con Hijazi buses run to Amman's Abdali bus station. Alternatively, there are minibuses and service taxis.

Syria To Damascus Syrian service taxis operate out of the new south bus station. The trip takes three to four hours depending on border formalities and costs JD4 or S£300. Alternatively, you can get a service taxi from Ramtha to Der'a for JD2 or S£150.

Israel Minibuses leave from the west bus station for the Jisr ('bridge') Sheikh Hussein crossing (aka Jordan Border) into Israel. The trip takes about an hour and costs 300 fils.

UMM QAIS & AL-HEMMA

Right in the top left corner of Jordan, 30 km north-west of Irbid, is Umm Qais, with views over the Golan Heights and the Sea of Galilee (Lake Tiberias) to the north and the Jordan Valley to the south. This is the site of the ancient Graeco-Roman town of Gadara, one of the cities of the Decapolis, and where, according to the Bible, the place Jesus cast out the Devil from two men into a herd of pigs (Matthew 8: 28-34) – an alternative site for this episode exists on the eastern shore of Lake Galilee in Israel.

Things to See
The small **museum** (open from 8 am to 5 pm, 4 pm in winter, and closed on Tuesday; entrance free), contains artefacts and mosaics from the area. A most interesting exhibit, found in one of the town's mausoleums, is a 4th century mosaic. It is overshadowed perhaps by the headless, white marble statue of a goddess that was found sitting in the front row of the **Western Theatre**, which is now in a sorry state of repair. Admission to the site, open daily from 8 am to 7 pm (to 5 pm in winter), costs JD1.

The baths of **Al-Hemma** are a further 10 km from Umm Qais, down the hill towards the Yarmouk River and Golan. The baths were famous in Roman times for their health-giving properties and are still used today, but you have to be keen to want to jump into the smelly water.

Places to Stay & Eat
The *Umm Qais Hotel* (☎ (02) 217081; fax 242313) is a very comfortable place that opened in 1995. Room prices vary, but JD6 a person seems the approximate figure. It has a small restaurant too.

In Al-Hemma, there is a hotel by the baths with rooms for JD8, and another in the village at the same rate.

Getting There & Away
There are regular minibuses to Umm Qais from Irbid (220 fils) and on to Al-Hemma. You need your passport for the trip down as there's a military control point on the edge of Umm Qais and at least one other closer to Al-Hemma.

UMM AL-JIMAL
Comparatively little is known about this strange, black-basalt city in the south of the Hauran (also called Jebel Druze), only about 10 km from the Syrian border and about 20 km east of Mafraq.

It is thought to have been founded in about the 2nd century AD and formed part of the defensive line of Rome's Arab possessions. It continued to flourish into Umayyad (or Omayyad) times, but was destroyed by an earthquake in 747 and never recovered.

Things to See
Much of what remains is simple urban architecture – ordinary people's houses and shops – but other buildings which have been identified include a **barracks** and **church** combined, and the building known as the **Western Church**.

Getting There & Away
It is possible to do the trip in a day from Amman, from where you would take a local bus or minibus to Zarqa (up to 150 fils), a minibus from there to Mafraq (350 fils) and from there another for 200 fils.

JORDAN VALLEY
Forming part of the Great Rift Valley of Africa, the fertile valley of the Jordan River was of great significance in Biblical times and is now the food bowl of Jordan. The river rises in the mountains of Lebanon and flows for 360 km, draining into the Dead Sea – the lowest lake on Earth.

The Jordan River marks the boundary between Israel and Jordan from the Sea of Galilee to the Dead Sea.

Ambitious irrigation projects such as the East Ghor (now King Abdullah) Canal have brought substantial areas under irrigation. A new dam is being built at Al-Karama. The hot dry summers and short mild winters make for ideal growing conditions and two or even three crops a year are grown.

Apart from the Dead Sea and Pella, there is little to attract the visitor to the valley today.

Make sure you have your passport with

you when travelling in the area, as military checkpoints are frequent.

The Dead Sea

The Dead Sea is 65 km long, from six to 18 km wide and has no outlet. The name becomes obvious when you realise that the high salt content (30%) makes any plant and animal life impossible. The high water density certainly makes for an unusual swimming experience. Your body becomes so buoyant that drowning or sinking is virtually impossible. While swimming you will probably discover cuts you never knew you had as the water gets into them and stings like crazy.

At the southern end of the sea the Jordanians are exploiting the high potash content of the mineral-rich water.

Places to Stay & Eat

The 'resort' at Suweimeh is where most people go for a float on the east (Jordanian) bank of the Dead Sea. The government-owned *Dead Sea Rest House* here provides day trippers with showers, changing rooms and an air-con restaurant. Well-overpriced rooms are also available, or you can try the expensive *Dead Sea Spa Hotel*, 5.5 km south.

Getting There & Away

There are frequent buses from Al-Quds St in Amman to South Shuneh (400 fils), from where another minibus leaves about every half an hour for Suweimeh. This drops you about one km away – follow the sign to the resthouse. Friday and Sunday are the best days for hitching as families head down to the sea on their day off, although many of the cars are full.

Pella

Near the village of Al-Mashari'a are the ruins of the ancient city of Pella (Tabaqat Fahl), two km east of the road. It is a steep walk up to the site, and the heat can be punishing in summer, so get some water at one of the shops in Al-Mashari'a before heading up.

Pella followed the fate of many other cities in the region, coming successively under the rule of the Ptolemies, the Seleucids and the Jews, who largely destroyed Pella in 83 BC because its inhabitants were not inclined to adopt the customs of their conquerors.

Pella was one of the cities of the Decapolis. It was to Pella that Christians fled persecution from the Roman army in Jerusalem in the 2nd century AD.

Excavations are still in progress by an Australian team.

Things to See The main points of interest include the area known prosaically as the 'main mound', the imposing **Civic Complex Church**, a small 1st century *odeon* or **theatre**, the remains of a Roman **Nymphaeum** or baths and a Byzantine fort.

Getting There & Away From Irbid you can catch an Al-Mashari'a minibus from the west bus station. From Amman, take a minibus for Suwalha and change for Al-Mashari'a. You can also catch a series of minibuses up the valley from South Shuneh or down from North Shuneh.

East of Amman

THE DESERT CASTLE LOOP

A string of what have become known as 'castles' lies in the desert east of Amman. Most of them were built or taken over and adapted by the Damascus-based Umayyad rulers in the late 7th and early 8th centuries. Two of the castles, Azraq and Qasr al-Hallabat, date back to Roman times and there is even evidence of Nabataean occupation.

The castles can be visited in a loop from Amman via Azraq and are never more than a couple of km off the road. With the exception of Qasr al-Mushatta, it is quite feasible to see all the main castles in one day using a combination of public transport and hitching. There are several so far off the beaten track that only 4WDs and experienced guides will do. A private car would simplify matters, or you could arrange a taxi for the day from Amman. The Cliff Hotel can help with this (see Places to Stay in the Amman section earlier in this chapter), or you could negotiate directly with a taxi driver.

Qasr al-Hallabat & Hammam as-Sarakh

Qasr al-Hallabat was originally a Roman fort built as a defence against raiding desert tribes. During the 7th century it became a monastery and then the Umayyads further fortified it and converted it into a pleasure palace. Today it is a jumble of crumbling walls and fallen stone.

A few km down the road heading east is the Hammam as-Sarakh bathhouse and hunting lodge built by the Umayyads. It has been almost completely reconstructed and you can see the channels that were used for the hot water and steam.

Getting There & Away From Amman take a minibus to Zarqa, from where you can get another to Hallabat (230 fils). The same bus drives right by the two sites. From the Hammam as-Sarakh it's probably easiest to hitch to the Azraq highway and on to Azraq.

Azraq

The oasis town of Azraq, 103 km east of Amman, is the junction of the roads heading north-east to As-Safawi and on to Iraq and south-east into Saudi Arabia.

Azraq has the only water in the whole of the eastern desert, and used to be one of the most important oases in the Middle East for birds migrating between Africa and Europe. It was also home to water buffalo and other wildlife. Until a few years ago, the oases had almost run dry because of the large-scale pumping from wells to supply Amman with drinking water. This process has been reversed, but most of the wildlife has been lost – few birds stop here now.

Things to See The large castle here is built out of black basalt and in its present form dates to the beginning of the 13th century. It was originally three storeys high, but much of it crumbled in an earthquake in 1927. Greek and Latin inscriptions date earlier constructions on the site to around 300 AD –

about the time of the reign of Diocletian. The Umayyads followed and maintained it as a military base, as did the 14th century Ayyubids. In the 16th century the Ottoman Turks stationed a garrison there.

After the 16th century the only other recorded use of the castle was during WWI when TE Lawrence made it his desert headquarters in the winter of 1917, during the Arab Revolt against the Turks.

The **Shaumari Wildlife Reserve** is an attempt to reintroduce long-absent wildlife into the region. There are 222 wild oryx, several hundred gazelle, 14 ostriches and other less visible birdlife. Unfortunately, you may not see much apart from the ostriches as the gazelle and oryx largely roam free. The only way to get to this small reserve, about 10 km south of the old junction in Azraq, is by car or hitching.

Places to Stay & Eat The *Al-Zoubi Hotel*, about one km south of the intersection and just back from the road to Saudi Arabia, is the best deal of the four hotels in Azraq. As everywhere else here, prices are negotiable, but you may be able to get a room with up to four beds for JD12. There are no singles. The penniless may choose the *Funduq Al-Waha* (no sign in English), a few hundred metres north of the Al-Zoubi along the same highway. A bed costs JD3 in a shared double. The two hotels north of the intersection are well overpriced.

A bunch of small *restaurants* lines the one km stretch south of the main road junction. These places are all keen for your money, so it is advisable to find out what you'll be paying before eating.

Getting There & Away There is a minibus from near the post office (north of the Qasr) to Zarqa (450 fils).

Qusayr 'Amra

Heading back towards Amman on Highway 40, the Qusayr (Little Castle) 'Amra is the best preserved of the desert castles and the walls of the three halls are covered with frescoes – including several rather risqué

JORDAN

nudes. The castle's plain exterior belies the beauty within.

Qasr al-Kharaneh

This well-preserved castle is a further 16 km along the road to Amman, stuck in the middle of a treeless plain to the left of the highway. It seems it was the only one of the castles built solely for defensive purposes, although no one really knows what its purpose was. Another popular explanation was that it was one of the first Islamic *khans*, or caravanserais, for travelling traders.

Qasr al-Mushatta

Qasr al-Mushatta is 35 km south of Amman near the airport. It was the biggest and most lavish of all the Umayyad castles but for some unknown reason was never finished.

Getting There & Away The Qasr al-Mushatta is only about two km from the airport but cannot be reached on foot. The only option is to drive the 10 km around the airport perimeter (you will need to leave your passport at a military checkpoint).

South of Amman

There are three possible routes south of Amman to Aqaba: the Desert Highway, the Wadi Araba road via the Dead Sea and the King's Highway. The latter is by far the more interesting of the three, as it twists and winds its way south, connecting the historic centres of Madaba, Kerak, Tafila, Shobak and Petra.

Public transport along the route is reliable but infrequent. Hitching is possible and, from Tafila at least, is the quickest way to go.

MADABA

This easygoing little town 30 km south of Amman is best known for its remarkable, mostly Byzantine-era mosaics, including the famous 6th century map of Palestine. There are also excellent mosaics at Mt Nebo, 10 km south-west of Madaba. Madaba makes an

easy day trip from Amman or a good first stop en route between Amman and Petra.

The most interesting **mosaic** is in the Greek Orthodox St George's Church. It is a clear map of Palestine and lower Egypt, and although it is now far from complete, many features can still be made out, including the Nile River, the Dead Sea and the map of Jerusalem showing the Church of the Holy Sepulchre. It was made around 560 AD, originally measuring a staggering 25 by five metres and consisting of more than two million pieces. Admission is JD1.

Careful excavation and restoration from 1991 to 1995 has led to the creation of an **Archaeological Park**. Its core takes in the sites of the 7th century churches of the Virgin and the Prophet Elias, along with parts of an earlier structure now known as the Hippolytus Hall. Between the two churches run the well-preserved remains of a Roman road, which ran east to west between the then Roman city's gates. Several mosaics have been uncovered and ramps built to allow visitors to examine them.

By far the most impressive mosaic is in the Hippolytus Hall, depicting scenes from the classical Oedipal tragedy of Phaedre and Hippolytus. The main mosaic in the Church of the Virgin, a masterpiece of geometrical design, appears to have been executed in Umayyad times, but by Christians, not Muslims.

Yet another extraordinary mosaic, dedicated to the 12 Apostles, is on view in a tastefully designed building to replace what little was left of the Church of the Apostles, down by the King's Highway about one km from St George's Church.

Places to Stay & Eat

Lulu's Pension (☎ (08) 543678) is about a 10 minute walk from St George's Church. Head out along the road for Mt Nebo, but at the second roundabout go straight. The price is JD10 per person in very clean, comfortable rooms, and includes breakfast.

Opposite St George's is the *Coffee Shop Ayola*, a swish new place that offers good but expensive felafel (500 fils), filter coffee for JD1 and great ice cream.

Getting There & Away

Minibuses regularly run between Madaba and Amman's Raghadan (220 fils) and Wahadat bus stations.

AROUND MADABA
Mt Nebo

From this area, west of Madaba on the edge of the plateau, it is possible to see the Dead Sea and the spires of the churches in Jerusalem on a clear day.

The Franciscan Fathers bought the site at Mt Nebo in the 1930s and have excavated the ruins of a 6th century church and monastery. Although little remains of the buildings that housed them, the mosaics from this period can be seen today, protected by a modern structure erected by the Franciscans.

Getting There & Away From Madaba take a minibus from the traffic roundabout (near the tourist office) or by the Jordan Bank heading for Mt Nebo (100 fils). From there it's about a four km walk, and you may be able to hitch.

Hammamat Ma'in

The hot springs and resort of Hammamat Ma'in lie 35 km south-west of Madaba. The serpentine road crosses some of the most spectacular territory around the Dead Sea and drops fairly steeply to the springs after the first 30 km. The therapeutic value of the spring waters was made famous by such figures as Herod the Great.

Before you even get into this place, you are hit for money. It's a minimum JD2 just to get into the area. Or you can pay JD3.850 to use the pool as well (alternatively you can pay for the pool separately once you're inside - and at no extra cost).

As you walk down to the Ashtar Hotel, you'll see a 25m waterfall fed by warm spring water – great for a splash around.

For a free sauna and spa, walk along the road passing under part of the hotel and after a few hundred metres you'll reach a mosque.

Continue past this another 50m and you'll come to a natural sulphur spa bath. The cave to the right is as good a sauna as you'll ever have. This is, unfortunately, generally a male-dominated activity – the usual warnings to women apply.

Places to Stay & Eat The cheapest accommodation is the *Safari Caravans* park just behind the Drop & Shop 'supermarket' on your left shortly after entering the site. These claustrophobic little sweat boxes are JD15/20 a night for singles/doubles – plus 10% tax!

In the *Ashtar Hotel* (☎ (08) 545500), the heart of the resort, singles/doubles are US$70/90. There is a drink stand by the mosque, and like everyone else, it feels entitled to charge over the odds.

Getting There & Away From Amman you can catch the JETT bus from Abdali for JD4 one way, or pay JD10 for the round trip, which includes entry and lunch. From Wahadat there are up to four minibuses in the morning for JD1. Be early and be patient.

From Madaba catch a minibus to Ma'in (150 fils) and hitch. If you're lucky the minibus will go the whole way (500 fils).

MACHAERUS

Perched on a 700m high hill about 50 km south-west of Madaba are the ruins of Herod the Great's fortress Machaerus. His successor, Herod Antipas, had John the Baptist beheaded here. Herod Antipas feared John the Baptist's popularity and did not take kindly to criticism of his second marriage to Herodias.

Things to See

The fort, known to the locals as **Qala'at al-Meshneq**, is approached up a set of stairs. There's not an awful lot to see, but vestiges of Herod Antipas' palace, baths and parts of the fortress wall and defensive towers can be made out.

Getting There & Away

From Madaba take a Muqawir minibus (250

fils) and tell the driver your destination and he'll let you out at an appropriate place. You can see the hill and fort to the west. The minibuses back to Madaba are infrequent and finish at about 5 pm, so keep a look out.

KERAK

The fort town of Kerak lies about 50 km south of the spectacular Wadi al-Mujib, which cuts a massive swathe across the King's Highway. Kerak lies on the route of the ancient caravans that used to travel from Egypt to Syria in the time of the Biblical kings, and were also used by the Greeks and Romans.

The greater part of Kerak lies within the walls of the old Crusader town and is dominated by its fort – one in a long line built by the Crusaders, which stretched from Aqaba in the south right up into Turkey in the north.

The **fort** itself has been partially restored, and is a jumble of rooms and vaulted passages. It is still possible to see the cisterns where water was once stored, but not much else. There is also a small **museum**. The castle is open daily during daylight hours and admission is JD1.

Places to Stay & Eat

The *Castle Hotel* (☎ 352489), near the old fortress is an acceptable cheapy. Singles/doubles/triples go for about JD5/7/10. Showers are communal and the toilets are a little on the nose.

Just around the corner, the same people operate the *Towers Hotel* (☎ 354293), which has clean rooms, some with private shower and toilet. Room prices are flexible but it appears JD10/15 are the basic rates.

Just as good and in the centre of town is the *Cottage Hotel* (☎ 354359). It is clean and has some large rooms. Doubles without private bathroom go for JD7; those with cost JD10.

Next to the castle is the *Karak Rest House* (☎ 351148), which charges JD27.500/40 for comfortable rooms, including taxes and breakfast. The views are excellent.

There are a few cheap eateries around. The *Peace Restaurant*, near the Castle Hotel,

serves up a filling mixed grill of meat with several dips and salad for about JD3.500, including a soft drink. A block on is *Al-Fida* restaurant, where you can get a beer.

Getting There & Away

From the bus station there are minibuses and service taxis for Amman along the Desert Highway. They also run north along the King's Highway as far as Ariha and south to Tafila.

DHAT RAS

The crumbling ruins of a Nabataean and Roman settlement can be seen in this small village about 25 km south of Kerak. The remains of a wall and column belonging to a 2nd century temple lean at a crazy angle and look set to tumble down.

The village is five km east of the King's Highway and minibuses run from Kerak (30 minutes; 250 fils).

TAFILA

Wadi al-Hesa, the second great river gorge to cut the King's Highway, lies 45 km south of Kerak, and 32 km north of Tafila. Tafila was once a Crusader base, but there's little to see from that era. You may well stop here to change minibus on the trip between Petra and Kerak.

DANA NATURE RESERVE

Stretching west from the King's Highway town of Al-Qaddisiyyeh, the newly developed Dana Nature Reserve is something of a novel experiment in Jordan – an attempt to promote ecotourism, protect wildlife and improve the lives of local villagers all at once.

Several walking trails have been marked out and you can camp at an expensive official ground. Alternatively, you can stay in the equally pricey *Dana Guest House* (☎ (03) 368497; fax 368499) in the village of Dana at the east end of the reserve.

SHOBAK

This is yet another Crusader castle/fort in the chain and, like Kerak, it has a commanding position over some incredibly desolate land. Today the place looks more impressive from the outside, as it is built on a small knoll right on the edge of the plateau. The inside is in a decrepit state, although restoration work is underway.

PETRA
If you are only going to see one place in Jordan – or the entire Middle East for that matter – make it Petra. It's worth going a long way to see and certainly is the No 1 attraction in Jordan. Petra is the ruined capital of the Nabataeans – Arabs who dominated the Transjordan area in pre-Roman times – and they carved elaborate buildings and tombs out of the solid rock.

Like Jerash, this lost city was forgotten by the outside world for 1000 years. It was rediscovered in 1812, excavations commenced in 1929 and the central city was not uncovered until after 1958.

The spectacular city was built in the 3rd century BC by the Nabataeans who carved palaces, temples, tombs, storerooms and stables from the rocky cliffs. From here they commanded the trade route from Damascus to Arabia, and through here the great spice, silk and slave caravans passed.

Things to See
The most famous ruin is the **Khazneh** (Treasury), the first main monument you come to after the trek through the incredibly narrow two km long defile known as the *siq*. The carved facade of the treasury is the finest of all the Petra monuments, and should be familiar to viewers of the film *Indiana Jones & the Last Crusade*.

The other monument that shouldn't be missed is the **monastery**, reached by a long, rock-cut staircase on the far side of the site. It has a similar facade to the Khazneh, but is far bigger and the views from there are stunning.

Other sites of interest include the 8000 seat **amphitheatre**, the **Qasr al-Bint** (one of the very few free-standing buildings on the site), the **colonnaded street**, the **Temple of the Winged Lions** and the facade known as the **Royal Tombs**.

There are a number of things well worth seeing that require a bit of hard sweat to reach but the effort is repaid by the spectacular views. The **Crusader Fort** is the easiest and takes just a few minutes, while the **High Place of Sacrifice** near the Siq is a half hour climb best done in the early morning so you have the sun behind you.

The hike up to the top of **Umm al-Biyara**, once thought to be the Biblical Sela, is tough going and takes two to three hours. It is certainly not for the faint-hearted or vertigo sufferers, but the views over Petra and the surrounding area are the best you'll get from anywhere.

Places to Stay
Petra and the neighbouring village of Wadi Musa are crawling with hotels – and there seems no end to the construction under way.

The *Mussa Spring Hotel* (☎ 336310; fax 336910) is the first hotel you come across, right after 'Ain Musa. A bed on the enclosed roof costs JD2, one in a room of three people or more JD4, doubles JD10 (without own bath) and JD16 (with). The hotel can organise a lift to and from the site.

The *Araba Hotel* (☎ 336107; fax 336107), further down the hill, is a good place. The owner charges JD10/15 for good little rooms with bath, but will bargain.

The *Peace Way Hotel* (☎ 336963) is a comfortable place with a good reputation – so good it can often be booked out for months in advance. Singles/doubles with heating, private bathroom and telephone cost JD21/25.

The *Sunset Hotel* (☎ 336579; fax 336950) is the cheapest deal in the area close to Petra. Doubles/singles without private bath cost JD10/15; JD15/20 with.

Petra Hotel & Rest House (☎ 336014), about as close to the entrance as you can get, has good rooms that are not unreasonably priced at JD30.800/60 in the older part and JD40.800/72 in the new wing.

Places to Eat
The *Petra Rest House* and *Forum Hotel* both

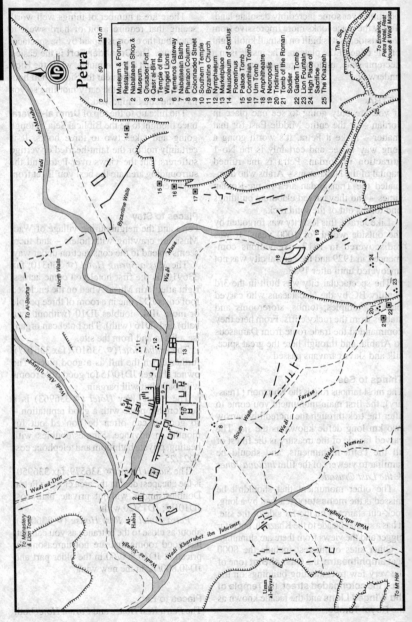

Petra

| 0 | 50 | 100 m |

1 Museum & Forum
2 Restaurant
3 Nabataean Shop & Theatre
4 Museum
5 Crusader Fort
6 Qasr al-Bint
7 Temple of the Winged Lions
8 Temenos Gateway
9 Nabataean Baths
10 Pharaoh's Column
11 Colonnaded Street
12 Southern Temple
13 Byzantine Church
14 Nymphaeum
15 Marketplace
16 Mausoleum of Sextius Florentius
17 Palace Tomb
18 Corinthian Tomb
19 Um Tomb
20 Amphitheatre
21 Necropolis
22 Triclinium
23 Tomb of the Roman Soldier
24 Garden Tomb
25 Lion Fountain
26 High Place of Sacrifice
27 The Khazneh

To Al-Beidha
To Al-Matiha
Wadi al-Matiha
North Walls
Byzantine Walls
Wadi Musa
To Monastery & Lion Tomb
Wadi ad-Deir
Al-Habis
Umm al-Biyara
Wadi Kharrubet ibn Jubeimer
Wadi as-Siyagh
South Walls
Wadi Farasa
Wadi Numeir
To Mt Hor
The Siq
To Entrance, Petra Forum Rest House & Wadi Musa

have expensive restaurants, and all the other hotels have restaurants attached.

For the cheapest eats, investigate the little restaurants clustered in the centre of town – which incidentally is where you can buy your own foodstuffs in shops frequented mainly by locals. The place marked *Fresh Food* is a good little eatery. With luck you can get yourself some decent kebabs or some such meal for JD2 to JD3.

The *Wadi Petra Restaurant*, right on the roundabout in town, is a curious little place where you can eat a few dishes beyond the usual stuff. The chicken and mixed vegetable stew is good value at JD1.800. A big bottle of Amstel costs JD2.750.

Getting There & Away

There is one JETT bus daily from Amman, which you can catch one way for a hefty JD5.500, or take the day tour for JD32, which includes lunch and entry to the site – definitely only for those with strictly limited time. It leaves for Amman at about 3 pm.

There are supposed to be three morning minibus departures for Amman (JD2) and a couple for Aqaba (JD2.500).

The most frequent connection is the minibus to Ma'an (750 fils), which is supposed to leave about once an hour. From Ma'an you can get another minibus or service taxi to Amman or Aqaba, or just get off on the highway and hitch.

At about 6.30 am a minibus leaves for Wadi Rum (JD2.500).

WADI RUM

Wadi Rum has some of the most spectacular desert scenery anywhere in the world, and is well worth the detour. Lawrence of Arabia spent quite a bit of time here during the Arab Revolt and many scenes from the movie were shot here.

The huge jebels rise sheer from the sandy valley floor overshadowing the small but growing settlement of Rum, which features the Desert Patrol Corps fort. All up, villagers and desert nomads throughout the Wadi Rum area number some 4000.

The JD1 you pay to enter Wadi Rum enti-

tles you to a cup of coffee or tea. If you bring in a 4WD you pay an extra JD4 or JD5, depending on whether you've hired it or it's a private vehicle.

To hire a 4WD will cost you anything from JD15 just to get down to Lawrence's Well and back, to JD39 for a full day. You can also hire camels by the hour or day – one great trip is from Wadi Rum to Aqaba.

Apart from trekking around the desert, Wadi Rum also provides some great rock-climbing possibilities. There is little or no gear available, but you should ask around for Sabah Atiq, a local guide and rock climber. Also, try to get a hold of Tony Howard's *Treks & Climbs in the Mountains of Wadi Rum & Petra*.

Places to Stay & Eat

The *Government Rest House* has quite reasonable two-person tents out the back for JD3 a head. Or you can sleep on the roof (it provides mattress and blankets) for JD2. Take note that even in summer it gets pretty cool in the evenings. The resthouse has showers, kitchen and luggage storage.

If this doesn't appeal, head out into the desert and sleep under the stars. You may be asked by Bedouin to sleep under their tents instead – but don't turn up uninvited.

Getting There & Away

There is at least one daily minibus between Wadi Rum and Petra and another to Aqaba. The Petra bus leaves at 8.30 am and costs JD2.500 (it leaves Petra for Wadi Rum about 6.30 am). The bus for Aqaba leaves Wadi Rum at 6.30 am and costs JD1.500. All these times are subject to the usual vagaries of this kind of transport – if they fill up earlier, they leave earlier.

Otherwise, you'll have to stick out your thumb. The turn-off for Wadi Rum is five km south of Quweira and the 26 km road from there is surfaced. From Aqaba take a Quweira minibus (500 fils) or a Ma'an minibus (JD1) to the turn-off.

AQABA

Aqaba was just a small fishing village until

JORDAN

it became a major trading port – Jordan's only outlet to the sea. Since pre-Roman times it has on occasion been a maritime trading centre, and today is also important as a tourist centre. While the rest of the country shivers in winter, the mercury hovers steadily around 25°C in Aqaba. In summer, however, temperatures are uncomfortably high, as is the humidity.

Information

There's a tourist office in the Visitors' Centre in the old fort by the waterfront. The Egyptian consulate in the new part of town issues tourist visas on the spot for JD12 with a minimum of fuss – a great contrast to the shambles at the embassy in Amman. It is open from 9 am to noon daily, except Friday.

If you are stuck without cash on a Friday or holiday, try the branch of the Cairo-Amman Bank at the Arab Bridge Maritime Company, which is open seven days a week. If you have a Visa card, you can process cash advances quickly at the Cairo-Amman Bank in the centre of town. MasterCard holders should head for the Jordan National Bank. There are also quite a few exchange booths operating outside banking hours for cash and travellers' cheques. The agent for Amex, International Traders (☎ 313757), is near the municipality building.

The post and telephone offices are next to one another right in the centre of town. The post office is open daily from 7.30 am to 7 pm, except Friday when it closes at 1.30 pm. The telephone office is open daily from 8 am to 10.30 pm.

Things to See

US-funded excavations have revealed the medieval city of **Ayla**, the heart of old Aqaba. Some portions of the walls have been partly restored. Discoveries here have been used to augment the **museum** at the Visitors' Centre, next to which you can also visit the 14th century **fort**. Finally, there is quite a decent little **aquarium** just south of the passenger terminal on the coast road to Saudi Arabia.

Beaches

There are beaches right in town, and these are OK, but women will feel very uncomfortable – to avoid harassment you are best off trying the beaches at the big hotels or heading south to either the National Touristic Camp or the Royal Diving Centre.

Diving

Many people come to Aqaba just for the diving, and there are four centres here. Most of the best diving is just off the beach on the Yamanieh Reef north of the Saudi Arabian border, and although the general consensus is that Ras Mohammed in Sinai is more spectacular, the diving here is still some of the best in the world.

The Royal Diving Centre (☎ 317035; fax 317097), which has been going since 1987, is right down on the beach, about 12 km out of town. It charges JD15 a dive or JD27 for two on the same day, including all equipment. A one-off trial dive costs JD25. A day's snorkelling costs JD3.500, or you can just hang around the pool for JD2. There is a cafeteria but no accommodation. A private bus does a round of the big hotels in town at about 9 am and returns at 4.30 pm.

The longest established dive centre is at the Aquamarina I Hotel (☎ 316250; fax 314089). It is the most expensive, too. It seems to do boat dives only, although the other places will tell you this is entirely unnecessary. Such a dive costs a whopping JD48, which includes equipment for the entire day – a strong incentive to pay for the second dive too (JD16.800). A half-day trial dive from the boat with basic instruction costs JD45.

The dive centre at the Al-Cazar Hotel (☎ 314131; fax 314133) charges from JD18 to JD28 per dive, depending on the amount of equipment you need.

The Red Sea Diving Centre (☎ 322323; fax 318969) charges JD24 for one dive with full equipment and JD40 for two dives on the same day.

Courses

Professional Association of Diving Instructors (PADI – sometimes known as

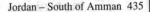

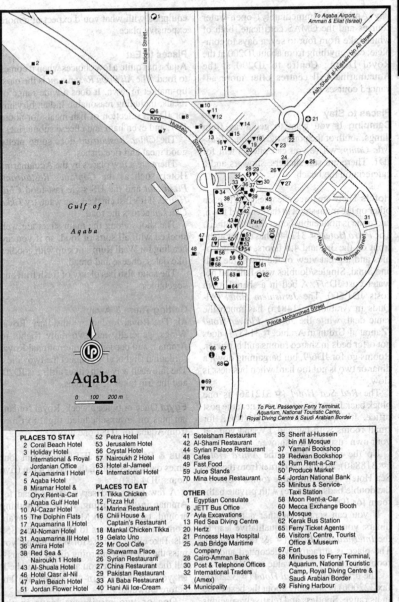

Aqaba

Gulf of Aqaba

To Aqaba Airport,
Amman & Eilat (Israel)

0   100   200 m

To Port, Passenger Ferry Terminal,
Aquarium, National Touristic Camp,
Royal Diving Centre & Saudi Arabian Border

PLACES TO STAY	
2	Coral Beach Hotel
3	Holiday Hotel International & Royal Jordanian Office
4	Aquamarina I Hotel
5	Aqaba Hotel
6	Miramar Hotel & Oryx Rent-a-Car
9	Aqaba Gulf Hotel
10	Al-Cazar Hotel
15	The Dolphin Flats
17	Aquamarina II Hotel
24	Al-Noman Hotel
31	Aquamarina III Hotel
36	Amira Hotel
38	Red Sea & Nairoukh 1 Hotels
43	Al-Shuala Hotel
46	Hotel Qasr al-Nil
47	Palm Beach Hotel
51	Jordan Flower Hotel
52	Petra Hotel
53	Jerusalem Hotel
56	Crystal Hotel
57	Nairoukh 2 Hotel
63	Hotel al-Jameel
64	International Hotel

PLACES TO EAT	
11	Tikka Chicken
12	Pizza Hut
14	Marina Restaurant
16	Chili House & Captain's Restaurant
18	Mankal Chicken Tikka
19	Gelato Uno
22	Mr Cool Cafe
23	Shawarma Place
26	Syrian Restaurant
27	China Restaurant
29	Pakistan Restaurant
33	Ali Baba Restaurant
40	Hani Ali Ice-Cream
41	Setelsham Restaurant
42	Al-Shami Restaurant
44	Syrian Palace Restaurant
48	Cafes
49	Fast Food
59	Juice Stands
70	Mina House Restaurant

OTHER	
1	Egyptian Consulate
6	JETT Bus Office
7	Ayla Excavations
13	Red Sea Diving Centre
20	Hertz
21	Princess Haya Hospital
25	Arab Bridge Maritime Company
28	Cairo-Amman Bank
30	Post & Telephone Offices
32	International Traders (Amex)
34	Municipality
35	Sherif al-Hussein bin Ali Mosque
37	Yamani Bookshop
39	Redwan Bookshop
45	Rum Rent-a-Car
50	Produce Market
54	Jordan National Bank
55	Minibus & Service-Taxi Station
58	Moon Rent-a-Car
60	Mecca Exchange Booth
61	Mosque
62	Kerak Bus Station
65	Ferry Ticket Agents
66	Visitors' Centre, Tourist Office & Museum
67	Fort
68	Minibuses to Ferry Terminal, Aquarium, National Touristic Camp, Royal Diving Centre & Saudi Arabian Border
69	Fishing Harbour

Pay And Dive Immediately) open-water courses and the CMAS certificate, both of which take from four to seven days to complete, cost anything from about JD200 at the Royal Diving Centre to JD290 at the Aquamarina. All centres offer more advanced courses too.

Places to Stay

Camping If you want to get away from things, south of the port is the *National Touristic Camp*, where you can pitch a tent for JD1. There are sun shelters, showers and a cafeteria on the beach.

Hotels There are three cheapies next to each other on the main street in the centre of town, and none is noticeably better than the others. The *Petra Hotel* (☎ 313746) has rooms at the front on the 3rd and 4th floors, with balconies and a great view of the town, the gulf and Sinai. Singles/doubles with fans and hot water cost JD5/7. A bed in a shared room costs JD1.500. The *Jerusalem Hotel* (Al-Quds in Arabic; ☎ 314815) has much the same deal, while the *Jordan Flower Hotel* (Zahrat al-Urdun in Arabic; ☎ 314377) does not offer beds in shared rooms and is pricier. Rooms go for JD6/9, but bargaining down a dinar or two is not too hard when business is slow.

The *Red Sea Hotel* (☎ 312156) is one block back from the main street, near the post office. It's quite decent at JD6/10/18 for small rooms with fan and TV, and you get your own (usually) hot shower.

Up the scale a little, the *Amira Hotel* (☎ 318840), around the corner from the Red Sea Hotel, has comfortable rooms (some of the double beds are huge) with private bathroom for JD12/18.

If you can scrape together a few more dinars, you make quite a qualitative leap to the *International Hotel* (☎ & fax 313403). The place is attractively decorated and the rooms extremely good value at JD18/28.

The brand new *Crystal Hotel* (☎ 322001; fax 322006) is probably about the best value in its range. Spotless and relatively spacious singles/doubles cost JD24/36, and are equipped with what you'd expect of a more expensive place.

Places to Eat

Aqaba has quite a few choices when it comes to food. The *Ali Baba Restaurant* is the most up-market in town. It does a wide range of meals, including reasonable Indian biryanis for JD5, a selection of fish meals for about JD7, and even ham and cheese submarines.

The *China Restaurant* does some pretty good meat and rice dishes.

There are a few places by the Aquamarina Hotel, such as the *Captain's Restaurant*, *Pizza Hut* and the US-style fast-food *Chili House*. If it's fast chicken you want, try *Tikka Chicken* across the road.

The shops along the main street are well stocked with all sorts of food, so if you are heading for Wadi Rum stock up on goodies like dates, cheese and bread.

The souq also has plenty of fresh fruit and vegetables.

Getting There & Away

Air The Royal Jordanian subsidiary, Royal Wings, generally has two daily flights to Amman, and occasional international Royal Jordanian flights also connect the two cities. The fare each way with either airline is JD20, and the trip takes 45 minutes.

Egypt Once or twice a week, Royal Jordanian puts on an unscheduled flight to Cairo from Aqaba for JD84 one way.

Bus & Service Taxi JETT buses run four times daily to Amman, the last at 4 pm (five hours; JD4.300).

A few buses and service taxis head for Amman in the morning. If there's nothing around, take a bus to Ma'an and try again from there. Minibuses to Quweira cost 350 fils. Take either of these for Wadi Rum if you miss the one early morning direct minibus – tell the driver where you are going and he'll let you off at the turn-off, about five km before Quweira.

One or two minibuses leave in the morning for Wadi Musa (Petra) for JD2.500

per person. They are less likely to run on Friday and holidays.

Saudi Arabia Minibuses for the Saudi border (Ad-Durra) leave from the main road near the fort for 250 fils. Saudi Saptco buses depart daily from the JETT terminal for most destinations in Saudi Arabia. The trip to Riyadh costs JD31.

Israel You may get lucky and find a service taxi running to the Israeli border crossing for JD4 (JD1 per person if you can fill it), otherwise the price for a standard taxi is JD3. For more details of the crossing, see the Getting There & Away section earlier in this chapter.

Car There are several car-rental agencies dotted around town but, as in Amman, they are far from cheap. If you're hiring a car for any length of time and want to cover the whole country that way, it would be cheaper to do so in Amman.

Sea The ferry terminal is south of the port, seven km from the city centre – a local minibus runs between the fort and the Saudi border for 250 fils, or a taxi between the terminal and the city centre costs JD1.500. You can buy tickets at the Arab Bridge Maritime Co in central Aqaba.

There is at least a daily car ferry between Aqaba and Nuweiba. On Sunday they leave at noon and 6.30 pm; the rest of the week at 4 pm. There is also a fast turbo-catamaran for foot passengers only. It leaves daily at noon. From Nuweiba the ferry adopts a more or less identical timetable (Sunday at 11 am and 6 pm; the rest of the week 4 pm), while the fast boat leaves at 3 pm. The ferry trip under ideal conditions takes about three hours, while the fast boat can whisk you to the other side in an hour.

The one-way trip from Jordan on the car ferry costs US$19 (plus a 200 fils charge). Return tickets are valid for a year and cost US$32. The one-way fare on the fast boat is US$27 (plus the 200 fils charge), or US$42 for a return (also valid for one year). Departure tax is JD6.

For more details see the Getting There & Away section earlier in this chapter.

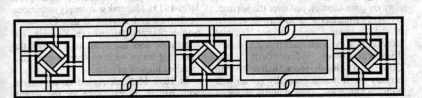

Kuwait

When the Iraqis were driven out in early 1991 and reconstruction work began in the ruins of Kuwait City, the government quickly became obsessed with meticulously re-creating the appearance the country had had prior to the invasion – right down to the pink marble steps at the entrance to Kuwait City's leading five-star hotel.

With the war a fading memory, Kuwait is once again the prototypical oil state. Though it may look the same, it has certainly changed and it may be a few more years before anyone, Kuwaitis included, is really able to say how.

Facts about the Country

HISTORY
The headland now occupied by Kuwait City was settled only 300 years ago. In the early 18th century Kuwait was nothing more than a few tents clustered around a storehouse-cum-fort.

Eventually the families living around the fort divided among themselves the responsibilities attached to the new settlement. The Al-Sabah family, whose descendants now rule Kuwait, were appointed to handle local law and order. The small settlement grew quickly. By 1760, when the town's first wall was built, Kuwait's dhow fleet was said to number 800 and camel caravans based there travelled regularly to Baghdad and Damascus.

By the early 19th century Kuwait was a thriving trading port. But trouble was always, quite literally, just over the horizon. It was often unclear whether Kuwait was part of the Ottoman Empire or not. Official Kuwaiti history is adamant that the shaikhdom was always independent of the Ottomans. During the second half of the 19th century the Kuwaitis generally got on well with the Ottomans. They skilfully managed

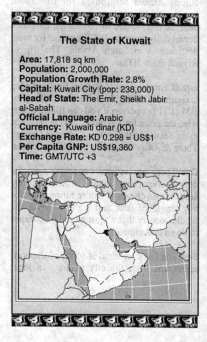

The State of Kuwait

Area: 17,818 sq km
Population: 2,000,000
Population Growth Rate: 2.8%
Capital: Kuwait City (pop: 238,000)
Head of State: The Emir, Sheikh Jabir al-Sabah
Official Language: Arabic
Currency: Kuwaiti dinar (KD)
Exchange Rate: KD 0.298 = US$1
Per Capita GNP: US$19,360
Time: GMT/UTC +3

to avoid being absorbed into their empire as the Turks sought to solidify their control of eastern Arabia (then known as Al-Hasa). They did, however, agree to take the role of provincial governors of Al-Hasa.

That decision led to the rise of the pivotal figure in the history of modern Kuwait: Shaikh Mubarak al-Sabah al-Sabah, commonly known as Mubarak the Great (reigned 1896-1915). Mubarak was deeply suspicious of Turkey and convinced that Constantinople planned to annexe Kuwait. He overthrew and murdered his brother the emir, did away with another brother and installed himself as ruler.

In 1899 Mubarak signed an agreement with Britain. In exchange for the British navy's protection he promised not to give away territory to, take support from or negotiate with any other foreign power without British consent. The Ottomans continued to claim sovereignty over Kuwait but they were now in no position to enforce it. Britain's motive for signing the treaty was a desire to keep Germany, then the main ally and financial backer of Turkey, out of the Gulf.

Kuwait spent the early 1920s fighting off the army commanded by Abdul Aziz bin Abdul Rahman Al-Saud (Ibn Saud), the founder of modern Saudi Arabia. In 1923 the fighting ended with a British-brokered treaty

KUWAIT

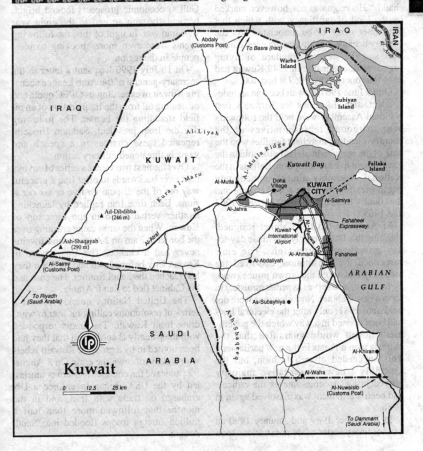

under which Abdul Aziz recognised Kuwait's independence, but at the price of most of the emirate's territory.

An oil concession was granted in 1934 to a US-British joint-venture known as the Kuwait Oil Company (KOC). The first wells were sunk in 1936 and by 1938 it was obvious that Kuwait was virtually floating on oil. The outbreak of WWII forced the KOC to suspend its operations, but when oil exports took off after the war so did Kuwait's economy.

Shaikh Abdullah al-Salem al-Sabah (reigned 1950-65) became the first 'oil shaikh'. His reign was not, however, marked by the kind of profligacy with which that term later came to be associated. As the country became wealthy, health care, education and the general standard of living improved dramatically. In 1949 Kuwait had only four doctors; by 1967 it had 400.

On 19 June 1961 Kuwait became an independent state. Elections for Kuwait's first National Assembly were held the following year. Although representatives of the country's leading merchant families won the bulk of the seats, radicals had a toehold in the government from its inception. Leftists in the National Assembly almost immediately began pressing for faster social change and the country had three cabinets between 1963 and 1965.

In August 1976 the Cabinet resigned, claiming that the assembly had made day-to-day governance impossible. The emir suspended the constitution, dissolved the assembly and asked the crown prince (who, by tradition, also serves as prime minister) to form a new Cabinet. New elections were not held until 1981, only after the electoral laws had been revised in a way which the government hoped would guarantee that the radicals won no seats in the new parliament. This succeeded after a fashion, but the assembly's new conservative majority proved just as troublesome as the radicals had been. Parliament was dissolved again in 1986.

In December 1989 and January 1990 an extraordinary series of demonstrations took place calling for the restoration of the 1962 constitution and the reconvening of parliament. The demonstrators were met by riot police, tear gas and water cannons. In June of that year elections were held for a consultative council which was supposed to spend four years advising the government on possible constitutional changes prior to the election of a new assembly. Pro-democracy activists demanded the restoration of the old assembly and denounced the new council as unconstitutional.

Despite these political and economic tensions, by mid-1990 the country's (and the Gulf's) economic prospects looked bright, particularly with an end to the eight year Iran-Iraq war. In light of this, the following events were even more shocking to most people in the region.

On 16 July 1990 Iraq sent a letter to the secretary-general of the Arab League accusing Kuwait of exceeding its OPEC quota and of stealing oil from the Iraqi portion of an oil field straddling the border. The following day the Iraqi president, Saddam Hussein, repeated these charges in a speech and vaguely threatened military action.

Over the next two weeks a series of envoys bent over backwards to offer Iraq a graceful way out of the dispute on five or six occasions. Each time Iraq replied by launching another verbal salvo in the direction of Kuwait. When the tanks came crashing over the border at 2 am on 2 August, the Kuwaitis never had a chance. The Iraqis were in Kuwait City before dawn and by noon they had reached the Saudi frontier. The emir and his Cabinet fled to Saudi Arabia.

The United Nations quickly passed a series of resolutions calling on Iraq to withdraw from Kuwait. The Iraqis responded with the patently absurd claim that they had been invited in by a group of Kuwaiti rebels who had overthrown the emir. On 8 August Iraq annexed the emirate. Western countries, led by the USA, began to enforce a UN embargo on trade with Iraq, and in the months that followed more than half a million foreign troops flooded into Saudi Arabia.

At the end of November the USA and the UK secured a UN resolution authorising the use of force to drive Iraq out of Kuwait if Baghdad did not pull out voluntarily before 15 January 1991. The deadline passed, the Iraqis did not budge and within hours waves of Allied (mostly US) aircraft began a five week bombing campaign over Iraq and Kuwait.

The ground offensive, when it finally came, lasted only 100 hours and was something of an anticlimax. Iraq's army, which had been touted in the west as one of the most fearsome military machines on earth, simply disintegrated. Allied forces arrived in Kuwait City on 26 February 1991 to be greeted by jubilant crowds and clouds of acrid black smoke from the hundreds of oil wells the Iraqis had torched as they retreated.

The government set about not simply rebuilding Kuwait but rebuilding it exactly as it had been before the invasion. Meanwhile, a heated debate began over the country's political future.

In keeping with a promise the opposition had extracted from the emir during the occupation, elections for a new National Assembly took place in October 1992. The opposition shocked the government by winning over 30 of the new parliament's 50 seats and opposition MPs secured six of the 16 seats in the Cabinet, though the Al-Sabah family retained control of the key defence, foreign affairs and interior ministries.

By the second anniversary of the invasion Kuwait's government had largely succeeded in erasing the physical scars of war and occupation, although tensions with Iraq remained high. Several times in the years since liberation Iraqi troop movements have prompted the Kuwaitis, the US or both to mobilise troops. In 1994 Kuwait convicted several Iraqis on charges of attempting to assassinate former US president George Bush when he visited the emirate in 1993. The plot, according to the Kuwaitis, was uncovered and foiled at the last minute.

GEOGRAPHY

Kuwait's 17,818 sq km of land are mostly flat and arid with little or no ground water.

The desert is generally gravelly. The country is about 185 km from north to south and 208 km from east to west. The only significant geographic feature is the now infamous Al-Mutla ridge, where Allied aircraft massacred a column of retreating Iraqi forces in the closing hours of the war.

CLIMATE

In the summer (April to September) Kuwait is hellishly hot. Its saving grace is that it is nowhere near as humid as Dhahran, Bahrain or Abu Dhabi. The winter months are often pleasant but can get fairly cold, with daytime temperatures hovering around 18°C and nights being genuinely chilly. Sandstorms occur throughout the year but are particularly common in spring.

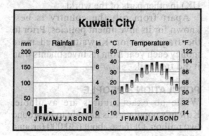

GOVERNMENT & POLITICS

Under Kuwait's 1962 constitution the emir is the head of state. By tradition the crown prince serves as prime minister. The prime minister appoints the Cabinet, usually reserving key portfolios (such as interior and defence) for other members of the ruling family.

The powers of the emir, crown prince and Cabinet are tempered by the 50 member National Assembly, which must approve the national budget and also has the power to question Cabinet members. The emir has the power to dissolve the assembly whenever he pleases, but is required by the constitution to hold new elections within 90 days of any such dissolution (a requirement that, historically, has not always been honoured).

Voting is restricted to adult, male, '1st class' Kuwaiti citizens (essentially those who can trace their family's residence in Kuwait back beyond WWI), and the male children of naturalised Kuwaitis. Naturalised citizens themselves are not permitted to vote. Whether to extend the franchise to all Kuwaitis, and especially to women, is a subject of heated debate in the country.

ECONOMY

Among the Arab Gulf States, Kuwait's oil reserves are second only to those of Saudi Arabia. The government has sought to diversify the country's role in the oil industry to make it a player on all levels, rather than simply being a producer/refiner of crude oil. It has purchased distribution networks and petrol stations (such as the Q8 chain in the UK) in other parts of the world.

Apart from oil, the country is best known for its investment policies. Prior to the Iraqi invasion Kuwait earned more money each year from its investments than it did from oil.

POPULATION & PEOPLE

While no exact figures are available, Kuwait's population is thought to be around two million. Of these about 630,000 (around 32%) are Kuwaitis.

ARTS

The arts scene in Kuwait is fairly limited. Sadu House (see the Kuwait City section later in this chapter) is a cultural foundation dedicated to preserving Bedouin art traditions, especially weaving.

SOCIETY & CONDUCT
Dos & Don'ts

Kuwait is a lot more relaxed about matters of public conduct than other Gulf countries. Aside from things obviously immodest by Muslim standards (skirts above the knee, halter tops etc), women can dress as they want and there is never any need for a woman to wear an *abayya* (a long, cloak-like black garment), veil or headscarf.

Non-Muslims may enter mosques, even

during prayer time, as long as proper dress is observed.

RELIGION

Kuwait's brand of Islam is not as strict as that practised in Saudi Arabia, but the country is not as liberal as Bahrain. Most Kuwaitis are Sunni Muslims, though there is a substantial Shiite minority.

LANGUAGE

Arabic is the official language but English is very widely understood.

Facts for the Visitor

PLANNING
When to Go

If you come in summer it may be a relief to know that Kuwait is somewhat less humid than the Gulf's other cities (but no less hot).

Maps

The *Oxford Map of Kuwait* is the best of the locally available maps. A better map, easy to recognise because of its yellow cover, is published by the Ministry of Information and distributed free at Kuwaiti embassies abroad. We've never seen it on sale in Kuwait.

What to Bring

Aside from the usual Gulf necessities, people visiting in the winter months might want to bring a medium-weight jacket and a jumper.

VISAS & DOCUMENTS
Visas

Everyone except nationals of the other Gulf States needs a visa to enter Kuwait. Kuwait does not issue tourist visas. Large hotels can sponsor visas. To arrange this send the hotel a fax, including your passport data, arrival and departure dates, flight numbers and the reason for your visit (for example, 'business'). The hotels usually prefer a fax copy of the actual passport. Most people will receive a single-entry visa valid for one month and for a one month stay.

The hotel may also charge you a fee for carrying out this service which could be as little as a dinar or two or as much as 10 dinars. Hotels also usually require that you stay with them for three nights. It usually takes three to four working days for a hotel to process a visa.

Once you are informed that your visa has been approved you will have to go to a Kuwaiti embassy to get it. Visas can be picked up at any Kuwaiti diplomatic mission, but the pick-up point has to be specified at the time the papers are filed. The embassies themselves are of little use to the casual traveller as they only issue visas against instructions from Kuwait.

If your passport contains an Israeli stamp you will be refused entry to Kuwait.

Visa Extensions It is difficult to stay in Kuwait for more than one month on a business visa. If you need to hang around for more than a month you will probably have to fly out, get a new visa and return.

EMBASSIES
Kuwaiti Embassies Abroad

There are Kuwaiti embassies in the following countries:

Bahrain
King Faisal Highway, Manama, opposite the Holiday Inn (☎ (973) 534 040)
Oman
Jameat A'Duwal al-Arabiyya St, Medinat Qaboos Diplomatic Area, Muscat (☎ 699626 or 699627). The embassy is on the sea side of Sultan Qaboos St, west of the Al-Khuwair roundabout.
Qatar
Diplomatic Area, beyond the Doha Sheraton Hotel, Doha (☎ 832 111)
Saudi Arabia
Diplomatic Quarter, Riyadh (☎ (01) 488 3500)
UAE
Diplomatic Area, Airport Rd, Abu Dhabi, behind the Pepsi Cola plant, about 10 km south of the city centre (☎ (02) 446 888)
Beniyas Rd, Deira, Dubai, opposite the Sheraton Hotel (☎ (04) 284 111)

UK
45/46 Queen's Gate SW7 (☎ (0171) 589 4533, 581 2698)
USA
2940 Tilden St NW, Washington DC 20008 (☎ (202) 966 0702)

Foreign Embassies in Kuwait

The following countries have diplomatic representation in Kuwait:

Bahrain
Surra District, St 1, Block 1, Building 24 (☎ 531 8530)
Canada
Da'iya District, El-Mutawakil St, Area 4, House 24, adjacent to the Third Ring Rd (☎ 256 3025)
Oman
Udailia District, St 3, Block 3, House 25, by the Fourth Ring Rd (☎ 256 1962)
Qatar
Diplomatic Area, Istiglal St, south of the city centre off Arabian Gulf St (☎ 251 3599)
UAE
Diplomatic Area, Istiglal St, south of the city centre off Arabian Gulf St (☎ 252 7639)
UK
Arabian Gulf St, near the Kuwait Towers and Dasman Palace (☎ 243 2046)
USA
Arabian Gulf St, entrance from opposite the Safir International Hotel (☎ 242 4151)

CUSTOMS

Alcohol is illegal in Kuwait. The duty-free allowance for tobacco is 500 cigarettes or 50 cigars or half a kg of loose tobacco.

MONEY
Costs

Kuwait is expensive. A rock-bottom budget would be KD17.50 (US$62) per day but you are likely to find yourself spending more than that.

Currency

Kuwait's currency is the Kuwaiti dinar (KD). The KD is divided into 1000 fils. Coins are worth 5, 10, 20, 50 or 100 fils. Notes come in denominations of KD¼, ½, 1, 5, 10 and 20. The Kuwaiti dinar is a hard currency and there are no restrictions on taking it into or out of the country.

Currency Exchange

Australia	A$1	=	KD0.240
France	FF1	=	KD0.059
Germany	DM1	=	KD0.199
UK	UK£1	=	KD0.502
USA	US$1	=	KD0.298

Changing Money

For a country with a highly sophisticated financial system, Kuwait can be a remarkably frustrating place to change money. Banks charge excessive commissions and moneychangers often refuse to change travellers' cheques. The only bright spot in this picture is that even Kuwait's cheap (if you can call them that) hotels take credit cards.

Tipping & Bargaining

A tip is only expected in fancier restaurants. Note, however, that the service charge added to your bill in such places goes into the till, not to waiting staff.

Bargaining is not as common as you might think. If you ask for a discount at a hotel or a shop selling, say, electronics, it is likely to be offered. It is equally likely that this new price represents the bottom line. Do not expect to find yourself in lengthy haggling sessions.

POST & COMMUNICATIONS
Post

Post boxes are a rare sight around Kuwait City, so you will probably have to brave the lines at post offices if you need to send anything and do not already have stamps.

The postal rate for aerogrammes and for letters or postcards weighing up to 20g is 150 fils to any destination outside the Arab world. Postage for cards or letters weighing 20 to 50g is 280 fils. Ask at the post office for parcel rates as these vary significantly from country to country.

There is no poste-restante service in Kuwait. Large hotels will often hold mail for their guests but otherwise you are out of luck.

Telephone

Kuwait has an excellent telephone system and calling pretty much anywhere in the world is quick and easy. Payphones take 50 and 100 fil coins. Two different types of card phone are in use, though neither is seen much apart from in telephone centres and post offices.

When calling Kuwait from the outside world, the country code is 965, followed by the local seven digit number. There are no area or city codes.

The USA Direct access code from Kuwait is 800-288. For MCI CallAmerica, dial 800-624.

Fax, Telex & Telegraph

These services are available from the government communications centres, though there are usually long queues.

BOOKS

There are not a lot of good books on Kuwait. Geoffrey Bibby's *Looking for Dilmun* includes several chapters on the archaeological excavations on Failaka Island and also paints an interesting picture of life in Kuwait in the 1950s and '60s.

The New Arabians by Peter Mansfield has a good summary chapter on Kuwait's history. *The Modern History of Kuwait 1750-1965* by Ahmad Mustafa Abu-Hakima is a detailed account written by a Kuwaiti scholar based in Canada. It is widely available in Kuwait and is worth a look, especially for the old photographs documenting life in Kuwait in the early years of the 20th century.

The Ministry of Information publishes a number of books on the Iraqi invasion and the Gulf War. These include a rather gruesome collection of photographs of Iraqi atrocities in occupied Kuwait called *The Mother of Crimes against Kuwait in Pictures*. Michael McKinnon and Peter Vine's book *Tides of War: Eco-Disaster in the Gulf* looks at the ecological consequences of the oil slicks and oil fires left intentionally by the retreating Iraqis. See also the Books section in the Regional Facts for the Visitor chapter for more book information.

NEWSPAPERS & MAGAZINES

Arab Times and *Kuwait Times* are Kuwait's two English-language newspapers. Both provide adequate foreign coverage, largely reprinted from British newspapers and international wire services.

RADIO & TV

Radio Kuwait – aka the Super Station – broadcasts on 99.7 FM; it plays mostly rock and roll with a bit of local news and features mixed in. The US military's Armed Forces Radio & Television Service (AFRTS) can be heard on 104.3 FM; it broadcasts a mixture of music, news and chat shows. Neither station can be heard outside Kuwait City.

Kuwait TV's Channel 2 broadcasts programmes in English each evening from around 5 pm until midnight. Many hotels, even the smaller ones, have satellite TV.

PHOTOGRAPHY & VIDEO

In theory, a photography permit is necessary to take pictures of anything in Kuwait. In practice, this is not something you need to worry about provided you exercise a modicum of common sense. Photographing obvious 'tourist' sites, such as the Kuwait Towers or the Red Fort in Al-Jahra, is never a problem. If you are discreet and do not photograph anything sensitive you should be OK.

HEALTH

Health care in Kuwait is equivalent to what is available in most western countries.

The drinking water in much of the country is not good and you would be well advised to stick to bottled water. See the Health Appendix for more detailed health information.

WOMEN TRAVELLERS

Harassment of women has been an increasingly serious problem in Kuwait since liberation. The best advice is to dress conservatively, not to respond to approaches on the street and avoid eye contact with men. If you are followed go to a public place, such as the lobby of a hotel.

DANGERS & ANNOYANCES

Muggings and having your pocket picked are not among the things you need to worry about in Kuwait. The things that will scare you are much nastier.

You must be aware, above all, of the lingering danger of mines throughout the country. While Kuwait City and the residential sections of other urban centres like Al-Jahra and Al-Ahmadi are clear of mines, much of the desert and, outside of the capital, much of the coastline are unsafe. Seaborne mines remain a problem as well, but this problem is much reduced in scope since 1992-93. Since this situation changes from month to month as mine clearance proceeds, the best course before venturing outside the city is to contact your embassy, which will certainly know which parts of the country are safe and which aren't.

If you are going north toward Iraq, bear in mind that the border is not very well marked. Foreigners travelling in the border zone have regularly been arrested by Iraqi troops and charged with straying into Iraqi territory. Some of these arrests have taken place several km inside Kuwait. If you get into this sort of trouble the UN troops who patrol the border zone have no authority to help you. You'll probably be taken to Baghdad and may be put on trial. The bottom line is that you should not go any further north than the checkpoint on the Al-Mutla Ridge without a very good reason.

BUSINESS HOURS

Shops are open Saturday to Wednesday from 8 or 9 am until about 1 pm and about 4 until 6 or 7 pm. Large shopping centres usually stay open until 9 pm. On Thursday most businesses will only be open in the morning. Friday is the weekly holiday and almost nothing is open during the day, though some shops may open in the late afternoon and early evening.

PUBLIC HOLIDAYS & SPECIAL EVENTS

Secular holidays are New Year's Day (1 January) and National Day (25 February). Liberation Day (26 February) is not an official holiday but everyone seems to treat it as one. In deference to the families of those still missing after the war and occupation there are no official ceremonies or celebrations marking either National Day or Liberation Day.

Religious holidays are tied to the Islamic Hijra calendar. Eid al-Fitr (the end of Ramadan), Eid al-Adha (the end of pilgrimage season), Lailat al-Mi'raj (the Ascension of the Prophet), the Prophet's Birthday and the Islamic New Year are all observed – for dates see the table of holidays near Public Holidays & Special Events in the Regional Facts for the Visitor chapter.

WORK

A business visa cannot be changed to a residence permit while you are in the country. Coming to Kuwait to look for a job is illegal and almost certainly a waste of time.

ACCOMMODATION

Getting a bed for the night in Kuwait was never cheap but prices went up after the war by 100 to 150% at most of the country's hotels and they have not returned to earth since. The bottom end of the market has disappeared and, since the first edition of this book, the mid-range has thinned out. Expect to pay at least KD15 to KD20 for a single and KD23 to KD25 for a double.

FOOD & DRINK

Most of Kuwait's cheapest restaurants are Indian places which rarely have anything other than biryanis on the menu. Aside from these Indian places the only cheap eats are western fast foods such as burgers and pizza.

Cafes, mostly located in either hotels or shopping centres, offer western-style snacks and sandwiches at reasonable prices, and the city is well stocked with good, up-market eateries.

All drinks are nonalcoholic. The usual selection includes soft drinks, mineral water, fruit juice, coffee and tea.

ENTERTAINMENT

There are several cinemas in Kuwait City. They mostly show Indian, Pakistani and Arabic films, though the occasional English-language movie turns up as well, almost invariably starring Arnold Schwarzenegger or Sylvester Stallone.

THINGS TO BUY

Kuwait is not exactly a shopper's paradise. You can buy traditional Bedouin weavings at Sadu House, a cultural foundation dedicated to preserving Bedouin art, but there is little else in the way of locally produced souvenirs on the market. As is the case elsewhere in the Gulf, most of the Arabian-looking things you will see for sale around the country are produced elsewhere.

Getting There & Away

AIR

Kuwait is not a particularly cheap place to fly or from. The airlines and travel agents tightly control prices and few discounted fares are available. Airlines from what used to be the Eastern Bloc offer your best hope for cheap tickets.

Fares to or from the USA start at around US$1200. By comparison Australia is actually a pretty good deal. Return fares to Melbourne come as low as KD276 (US$966) in the low season (early September through mid-December and mid-January through May) even though there is no direct air service. Ten day minimum/three month maximum stay return tickets to London start at KD324 (US$1134) and one-way tickets start from KD278 (US$973).

Fares to the Indian subcontinent are among the better deals available from Kuwait. The cheapest regular fare to New Delhi is KD192 (US$672) for a return ticket allowing a four month stay (seven day minimum).

The cheapest return fares to some other Gulf destinations include Abu Dhabi or Bahrain KD41 (US$144), Dubai KD72 (US$252), Muscat KD102 (US$357) and Riyadh KD56 (US$196).

LAND

Buses operate between Kuwait and Cairo via Aqaba in Jordan and Nuweiba in Egypt. Agents specialising in these tickets (the trip takes about two days) are in the area around the municipal bus station. In Cairo there are a number of agents on Talaat Harb St and Tahrir Square advertising bus transport to Kuwait.

LEAVING KUWAIT

There is an airport departure tax of KD2. Tickets sold outside Kuwait often don't include tax, meaning that you'll have to pay it in cash at the airport. Look for 'KWD 2.000' or something similar in the 'tax' box just below the part of the ticket that shows the cities between which you are travelling.

Getting Around

Kuwait has a very cheap and extensive system of both local and intercity buses. You can also use local taxis to get around, though these have no meters. See the Kuwait City Getting There & Away and Getting Around sections for details.

Renting a car in Kuwait will cost you at least KD8 per day. See the Kuwait City section for information on car-rental agencies and costs.

Kuwait City

In the years since liberation Kuwait City has developed into a remarkably easy-going place, at least compared to what things were like in the late '80s.

Orientation

Kuwait City's commercial centre is the area from the bay inland to Al-Soor St between the Al-Jahra Gate and Mubarak al-Kabeer St. The main shopping and commercial street is Fahad al-Salem St, which becomes Ahmed al-Jaber St north of Al-Safat Square. The souq is the area between the municipal park and Mubarak al-Kabeer St. Up-market shopping places are clustered along the lower end of Fahad al-Salem St (near the Sheraton Hotel) and just east of it.

From the centre the city spreads inland becoming ever broader as it goes. The main arteries are a series of numbered ring roads and Arabian Gulf St, which continues along the coast to Al-Salmiya and beyond.

Information

Money You will find banks evenly distributed throughout the city. Moneychangers can offer slightly better rates than banks (and usually lower commissions) but finding one in the city centre that will change travellers' cheques can be a problem. Try the Al-Jawhara Exchange Centre in the Souq al-Watya shopping centre, next to the Sheraton Hotel. It changes travellers' cheques at decent rates with no commission.

American Express (Amex; ☎ 241 3000) is represented in Kuwait by Al-Ghanim Travel from its office on the 2nd mezzannine level of the Salhiya Commercial Centre. It is open Saturday to Thursday from 8 am to 1 pm and 4 to 7 pm, and closed on Friday. Amex cardholders can cash personal cheques but the office will not hold mail for Amex clients.

Post The GPO is on Fahad al-Salem St near the intersection with Al-Wattiya St. It is open Saturday to Wednesday from 7 am to 7 pm, Thursday until 3 pm and Friday from 9 to 11 am. The Safat post office, at the intersection of Abdullah al-Mubarak and Al-Hilali Sts, is open the same hours as the GPO.

Communications The main telephone office is at the intersection of Abdullah al-Salem and Al-Hilali Sts at the base of the telecommunications tower. It is open 24 hours a day. Bring identification for the checkpoint at the door. Card phones (for which cards are on sale) are available for international calls. You can also book international calls and pre-pay the cost, but this is more expensive than using the card phones. Telex and fax services are available.

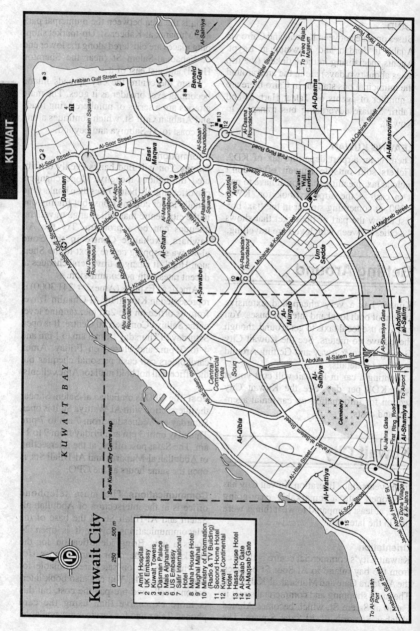

Kuwait City

See Kuwait City Centre Map

KUWAIT BAY

0   250   500 m

1 Amiri Hospital
2 UK Embassy
3 Kuwait Towers
4 Dasman Palace
5 Mais Alghanim
6 US Embassy
7 Safir International
   Hotel
8 Maha House Hotel
9 Mughal Mahal
10 Ministry of Information
   (Radio & TV Building)
11 Second Home Hotel
12 Kuwait Continental
   Hotel
13 Hassan House Hotel
14 Al-Shaab Gate
15 Al-Maqsab Gate

KUWAIT

Travel Agencies Fahad al-Salem and Al-Soor Sts between the Al-Jahra Gate and the Radio & TV building both have lots of small travel agencies. It is pointless to recommend one over another. Despite a theoretical ban on the discounting of published air fares, shopping around might save you some money.

Bookshops The best place to look for English-language books is the bookshop on the basement level of the Al-Muthanna Centre on Fahad al-Salem St. Also good is the Family Bookshop on Salem Al-Mubarak St in Al-Salmiya.

Cultural Centres The Alliance Française (☎ 531 9850) is at the French embassy, Mansouria District, St 13, Block 1, Villa 24.

The British Council (☎ 253 3204) is on Al-Arabi St in the Mansouria district, next to the Nadi al-Arabi stadium. The library is open Saturday to Wednesday from 4 to 8 pm and Thursday from 9 am to 1 pm.

Laundry Al-Shurouq Laundry, on the corner of Abu Bakr al-Siddiq and Al-Wattiya Sts in the city centre, offers 24 hour turn-around. Another option in the city centre is Fajr Kuwait Laundry on Al-Soor St. Washing and ironing a medium-sized load at either place will probably cost KD2 to KD4.

National Museum

The museum was once the pride of Kuwait and its centrepiece, the Al-Sabah collection, was one of the most important collections of Islamic art in the world. During the occupation, however, the Iraqis systematically looted the exhibit halls. Having cleaned out the building, they smashed everything they could and then set what was left on fire.

The remaining ruins of the National Museum are open Saturday to Wednesday from 8 am to 1 pm and 4 to 7 pm, and Thursday and Friday from 8 am to 11 am and 4 to 7 pm. Admission is free.

A hall at the back of the museum complex's courtyard has been restored and is sometimes used for temporary exhibitions.

Sadu House

A small building near the National Museum on Arabian Gulf St, Sadu House is a museum and cultural foundation dedicated to preserving Bedouin arts and crafts. The house itself is built of gypsum and coral. Note the carved decorative work around the courtyard. The building is open daily, except Friday, from 8 am to 12.30 pm and 4 to 7.30 pm. Admission is free.

Sadu House is the best place in Kuwait to buy Bedouin goods. Pillows cost around KD12 and small bags KD7 to KD15.

National Assembly Building

This is the distinctive white building with the sloping roofs on Arabian Gulf St near the National Museum. The building was designed by Jorn Utzon, the Danish architect who also designed the Sydney Opera House. The two sweeping roofs are supposed to evoke Bedouin tents.

Parliamentary sessions are open to the public, though you will have to have your passport or (for foreign residents) iqama to get through the security check at the gate. Check the *Arab Times* to find out when the legislature is in session. Simultaneous translation of parliamentary debates into English is available. Ask for a set of earphones as you enter the chamber.

Sief Palace

At the intersection of Mubarak al-Kabeer and Arabian Gulf Sts north-east of the National Museum, Sief Palace is the official seat of the emir's court. The oldest parts of the building date to the turn of the century. The palace is not open to the public. Do not attempt to photograph it unless you have a photo permit.

Grand Mosque

This huge, modern mosque opposite the Sief Palace was opened in 1986. It cost KD13 million to build and the government says that it can accommodate over 5500 worshippers. The central dome is 26m in diameter and 43m high.

Former Political Agency

About 750m north-east of Sief Palace you will find a modest white house with blue trim. From 1904 until the late 1930s this was the Political Agency, the British headquarters in Kuwait. Freya Stark spent most of March 1937 here. The widow of the last British political agent continued to live in the house for many years, spending her winters here well into the 1980s.

Kuwait Towers

Designed by a Swedish architectural firm and opened in 1979, the towers have become Kuwait's main landmark. The largest of the three towers rises to a height of 187m.

The upper globe houses a two level observation deck. The largest tower's lower globe (at 82m) has a restaurant, a coffee shop and a private banquet room. The lower globe on the largest tower and the single globe on the middle tower are used to store water. The small tower with no globes is used to light up the other two.

The observation deck is open daily from 9 am to 11 pm. Admission to the observation deck costs 500 fils but entry to the restaurants is free. Because the towers overlook the emir's palace, cameras with zoom lenses are not permitted and you will have to leave these at the ticket booth.

Tareq Rajab Museum

This museum, which is housed in the basement of a large villa, is a private collection of Islamic art assembled by Kuwait's first minister of antiquities. The collection is all the more important granted the fate that befell the National Museum's treasures.

The museum is at House 16, St 5, Block 12, in the Jabriya district, on a corner two blocks north and one block west of the New English School, near the intersection of the Fifth Ring Motorway and the Fahaheel Expressway. It is open Saturday to Thursday from 9 am to noon and 4 to 7 pm; closed Friday. Admission is free. There is no sign on the building but it is easily identified by its entrance – a carved wooden doorway flanked by two smaller doors on each side.

All four of the door panels are worked in gilt metal.

Science & Natural History Museum

Though the collection seems to consist largely of stuffed animals, there is some variety. The ground floor also contains animal skeletons, including a few dinosaurs. The 1st floor has a display on space exploration. On Abdullah al-Mubarak St, the museum is open Saturday to Thursday from 8.30 am to noon; closed Friday and holidays. Admission is free.

Old City Gates

Four of Kuwait City's five gates lie along Al-Soor St, the street which follows the line of the old city wall (soor is the Arabic word for 'wall'): Al-Shaab, Al-Shamiya, Al-Jahra and Al-Maqsab. The fifth gate (Dasman Gate) was near the Dasman Palace by the Kuwait Towers. Despite their ancient appearance the wall and gates were only constructed around 1920. The wall was torn down in 1957.

Exhibition of Kuwaiti Sailing Ships

This small, largely unknown, tourist sight consists of about half a dozen different dhows and other traditional sailing vessels ranging in size from small fishing boats to a large ocean-going dhow. All of the boats have been carefully restored and ramps provide access for curious visitors. It's a long drive out from the city but absolutely worth the trip.

The exhibition is open every day from 8 am to 8 pm. Admission is free. To reach the site take the Al-Jahra Rd west out of Kuwait City. Follow the signs for Entertainment City and turn onto the Doha spur road.

Beach & Health Clubs

Most of the health clubs at the big hotels are open to the public. Your best bet is probably the Safir Hotel. If you are not staying at the hotel, use of the pool is KD4 per day. To use the health club also (sauna, squash and tennis courts, weight room etc) costs KD6.

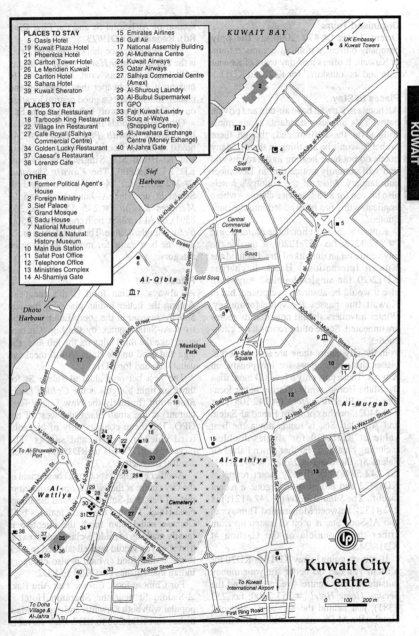

PLACES TO STAY
5 Oasis Hotel
19 Kuwait Plaza Hotel
21 Phoenicia Hotel
23 Carlton Tower Hotel
25 Le Meridien Kuwait
28 Carlton Hotel
32 Sahara Hotel
39 Kuwait Sheraton

PLACES TO EAT
8 Top Star Restaurant
18 Tarboosh King Restaurant
22 Village Inn Restaurant
27 Cafe Royal (Salhiya Commercial Centre)
34 Golden Lucky Restaurant
37 Caesar's Restaurant
38 Lorenzo Cafe

OTHER
1 Former Political Agent's House
2 Foreign Ministry
3 Sief Palace
4 Grand Mosque
6 Sadu House
7 National Museum
9 Science & Natural History Museum
10 Main Bus Station
11 Safat Post Office
12 Telephone Office
13 Ministries Complex
14 Al-Shamiya Gate

15 Emirates Airlines
16 Gulf Air
17 National Assembly Building
20 Al-Muthanna Centre
24 Kuwait Airways
26 Qatar Airways
27 Salhiya Commercial Centre (Amex)
29 Al-Shurouq Laundry
30 Al-Bulbul Supermarket
31 GPO
33 Fajr Kuwait Laundry
35 Souq al-Watya (Shopping Centre)
36 Al-Jawahara Exchange Centre (Money Exhange)
40 Al-Jahra Gate

KUWAIT BAY

UK Embassy & Kuwait Towers

Sief Harbour

Dhow Harbour

Sief Square

Central Commercial Area

Souq

Gold Souq

Al-Qibla

Municipal Park

Al-Safat Square

Al-Murgab

Al-Salhiya

Al-Wattiya

Cemetery

To Al-Shuwaikh Port

To Doha Village & Al-Jahra

To Kuwait International Airport

First Ring Road

Kuwait City Centre

0   100   200 m

Street names visible on map: Abdulla al-Ahmad Street, Al-Kabeer Street, Mubarak, (Al-Khalij al-Arab Street), Al-Maarri Street, Al-Salem Street, Ahmed al-Jaber Street, Abdullah al-Mubarak Street, Abu Bakr Al-Siddiq Street, Arabian Gulf Street, Al-Watiya Street, Al-Hilali Street, Al-Saddiq Street, Al-Salhiya Street, Al-Hilali Street, Abdullah al-Salem St, Al-Wazzan Street, Fahad al-Salem Street, Mohammed Thunayyan Street, Al-Soor Street, Usama ben Monqiz St, Abu Bakr

Organised Tours

Orient Tours (☎ 474 2000) is the only company currently running organised tours in Kuwait. It offers half-day tours of Kuwait City and its 'outskirts' for KD10 to KD11.

Places to Stay

All hotels in Kuwait have air-con and private baths. TVs are also standard, as are mini-fridges (at the bottom end, though there probably won't be anything in them). Many hotels do not have heating in the rooms and you will certainly notice this in December and January. Most of the country's hotels also hit you for a 15% service charge – where applicable this has been added into the rates quoted.

Kuwait's cheapest hotel, the *Maha House* (☎ 252 1218; fax 257 1220), is outside the city centre on an unmarked street behind the Kuwait International Hotel. It charges KD12/20 for singles/doubles. Anywhere else it would be absurdly overpriced, but in Kuwait this passes for value-for-money. Winter travellers should note that its rooms are unheated. Some of the rooms have kitchenettes.

In the city centre there are several decent places that, again, pass for inexpensive in Kuwait. These cost only a few KD more than the Maha House, while offering better locations. The *Phoenicia Hotel* (☎ 242 1051; fax 242 4402), on the corner of Fahad al-Salem and Al-Hilali Sts, is hands down the best value at KD16/20 for singles/doubles, including breakfast. Further down Fahad al-Salem St, the *Carlton Hotel* (☎ 242 3171; fax 242 5848) has slightly larger rooms at KD17/22 and has also undergone a recent facelift. The *Sahara Hotel* (☎ 242 4121; fax 242 4132), between Mohammed Thunayyan and Al-Soor Sts, is a bit of a step up from either the Phoenicia or the Carlton at KD18/24.

If you are going to pay KD18 or KD20 for a room you can do better for your money outside the city centre. We recommend the *Second Home Hotel* (☎ 253 2100; fax 253 2381), just behind the Kuwait Continental Hotel at the Al-Dasma roundabout (the inter-

section of Al-Istiqlal St and the First Ring Rd). Rooms are KD19/23.

The cheapest place that can arrange a visa is the *Carlton Tower Hotel* (☎ 245 2740; fax 240 1624). Rooms cost KD44.500/46, making it a bit cheaper than other top-end places. It also boasts a good central location on Al-Hilali St, just off Fahad al-Salem St.

Other large hotels that can arrange visas include the *Kuwait Plaza Hotel* (☎ 245 8890) at the intersection of Fahad al-Salem and Al-Hilali Sts. Singles/doubles cost KD51.750/59.800. The *Kuwait Sheraton* (☎ 242 2055; fax 244 8032), on Fahad al-Salem St near the Al-Jahra Gate, and *Le Meridien Kuwait* (☎ 245 5550; fax 243 8391), on Al-Hilali St, both charge KD57.500/ 69 for a single/double. The Meridien is probably the best value for money in this price category.

Places to Eat

As always, Indian food is the cheapest. Among the better Indian places is the *Top Star Restaurant* in the souq. Enter the souq from Al-Safat Square by the big 'Citizen' sign, take the third alley on the left after the sign and head up the stairs. A full meal can usually be had for KD1.

The best bet on Fahad al-Salem St for those on tight budgets is the *Golden Lucky Restaurant* (formerly the New Lucky Restaurant) at the small plaza just west of the GPO. The menu consists only of biryanis, fried chicken or fish, and snacks. The biryanis cost 750 fils to KD1 and samosas are 100 fils each.

Another excellent spot for a cheap meal in the city centre is the *Village Inn Restaurant*, just off Fahad al-Salem St behind the Phoenicia Hotel. Though the menu features both Chinese and Indian food, the clientele is mostly made up of middle-class Indian expatriates so you would be well advised to stick to the Indian food (which is also cheaper). Indian main dishes cost KD1 to KD2.

For Chinese food, *Caesar's* on Abu Bakr al-Saddiq St near the Sheraton Hotel is popular with both Kuwaitis and expats. Main dishes cost KD1.200 to KD2. *Cafe Royal* in the Salhiya Commercial Centre is another place where Kuwaitis and foreigners mix easily. It has quite good hot and cold sandwiches for KD1.500 to KD1.800 and salads for KD1.250 to KD2.

If you are looking for a more traditional open-air coffee house try *Beit Lothan* on Arabian Gulf St just north of the intersection with Qatar St (several km south of the centre). It offers coffee, tea and shisha pipes in a quiet garden. The main building also houses an art gallery.

One top-end restaurant must be mentioned in any rundown of Kuwait's eateries. If your budget will bear it, you must visit *Mais Alghanim*. This Lebanese restaurant on Arabian Gulf St, between the Kuwait Towers and the intersection with Al-Soor St, was founded in 1953 and has long been something of a local institution. Meals cost about KD3 to KD4. It is worth going out of your way for; expect queues for the garden tables in the winter and the indoor (air-con) ones in the summer.

Entertainment

The main cinemas in Kuwait City are the Al-Firdaus and Al-Hamrah, both at the Al-Maqwa roundabout (the intersection of Jaber al-Mubarak and Al-Hilali Sts). They show mostly Indian and Pakistani films. Check the *Arab Times* or *Kuwait Times* to see what's on.

Getting There & Away

Air Kuwait international airport is 16 km south of the city centre. Check-in time is officially two hours before your flight is due to depart, but some carriers insist on you being there three hours in advance; call the airline to double check. Security is tight so you should not let this slip too much. Note that Kuwait is pretty serious about enforcing the 'only one carry-on bag' rule. For general information, including flight arrivals and departures, call ☎ 433 5599 or 433 4499.

Bus Kuwait has only a handful of intercity bus routes. All long-haul trips cost 300 or 350 fils. Route 101 runs from the main bus

station in the city centre to Al-Ahmadi and Fahaheel. Route 103 goes to Al-Jahra.

International bus services to Cairo and Dammam (Saudi Arabia) can be booked through any of the small travel agencies around the intersection of Abdullah al-Mubarak and Al-Hilali Sts.

There is no formal service-taxi system operating in Kuwait.

Car Kuwait is the most expensive place in the Gulf to rent a car. Al-Mulla is the cheapest of the larger local agencies, with cars from KD7.500 per day. This rate usually includes unlimited km, but full insurance will cost an extra KD2 per day. Al-Mulla has offices in the Kuwait Plaza (☎ 245 8600) and Safir International (☎ 250 3869) hotels.

If you hold a driving licence and residence permit from another Gulf country you can drive in Kuwait without any further paperwork. Otherwise you can drive on an International Driving Permit or a local licence from any western country, but you'll also be required to purchase 'insurance' for your licence at KD10.

Getting Around

The Airport Taxis charge a flat KD4 between the airport and the city. Bus 501 runs between the main bus station and the airport every 30 minutes from 5.30 am to 9 pm. The fare is 250 fils.

Bus The central bus station is near the intersection of Al-Hilali and Abdullah al-Mubarak Sts. On printed timetables the central station is referred to as 'Mircab bus station'.

Buses start running at around 5 am and continue until around 10 pm. Fares are 100, 150 or 200 fils depending on how far you travel. Some of Kuwait City's main bus routes include:

Route 11 – Sharq bus station (on Dasman Square at the eastern end of the city centre), Ahmed al-Jaber St, Fahad Al-Salem St, Jamal Abdul Nasser St, Al-Sabah Hospital, Orthopaedic Hospital

Route 13 – main bus station, Fahad al-Salem St, Jamal Abdul Nasser St, Airport Rd, Kheitan

Route 24 – main bus station, Abdullah al-Mubarak St, Al-Maghreb St, Qadisiya, Hawalli, Amman St, Rumaithiya, Al-Salmiya bus station

Route 38 – Al-Jahra Gate, Fahad al-Salem St, Al-Istiqlal St, Hawalli, Bayan, Mishrif, Sabah al-Salem district, Messila bus station

Taxi Kuwait's taxis have no meters. Bargaining the fare in advance may save you some grief at the end of the trip but it will also cost you money. Around town, taxis are orange coloured. In general, any trip within the city centre is about KD1. Longer trips just outside the city centre (eg from the Sheraton to the Safir Hotel) cost about KD1.500.

Around Kuwait

FAILAKA ISLAND
The home of Kuwait's main archaeological site, Failaka is definitely worth a visit, though it requires a bit of extra caution. The Iraqis turned Failaka into a heavily fortified base, and after liberation it was found to be filled with mines. While the site is now open, Failaka is one of those parts of Kuwait where you should restrict yourself to well-trodden paths.

Failaka's history goes back to the Bronze Age Dilmun civilisation which was centred in Bahrain. The Greeks arrived in the 4th century BC in the form of a garrison sent by Nearchus, one of Alexander the Great's admirals. A small settlement existed on the island prior to this, but it was as the Greek town of Ikaros that the settlement became a real city or at least a large town.

As you enter the site, the road swings around to the left and ends in front of a group of prefabricated buildings. These are the archaeological museum and the on-site administrative offices. From here it is a short walk to the **temple**, Failaka's centrepiece.

Ferries to Failaka depart from Ras Salmiya (also known as Ras al-Ard) on Arabian Gulf St south of the city centre. At the time of writing there was still only one ferry per day, departing sometime between 8 and 10 am (the schedule varies from day to day and is published a couple of weeks in advance). The trip to the island takes 90 minutes. The ferry then stays at the island for two hours before making the return trip. This is enough time for a quick look at the archaeological site but not much else. If you miss the ferry back you will be stuck on the island until the following day. Since there are no hotels and camping is inadvisable because of the danger of land mines, don't miss the ferry! The fare is KD1 one way and KD2 return. Call the ferry company on ☎ 574 2664 for information on sailing times.

To reach the site from the ferry terminal on Failaka, turn right as you exit the terminal building. Almost immediately you will see the mud house, the one which contains the ethnographic display, on a low hill to the right beyond a wall. The entrance is a gate in this wall with seals on either side marked Kuwait National Museum.

AL-AHMADI
Built to house Kuwait's oil industry in the 1940s and '50s, Al-Ahmadi was named for the then emir, Shaikh Ahmed. It remains, to a great extent, the private preserve of the Kuwait Oil Company (KOC).

The **oil display centre** (☎ 398 2747), on Mid 5th St, is a small, well-organised and rather self-congratulatory introduction to KOC and the oil business. The centre is open Saturday to Wednesday from 7 am to 3 pm. Admission is free. Al-Ahmadi also has a small, pleasant **public garden** that is worth a visit.

To reach the town take the Al-Safr Motorway south out of Kuwait City until you reach the Al-Ahmadi exit. First follow the blue signs for North Al-Ahmadi, and then the smaller white signs for the display centre and the public garden.

AL-JAHRA
Al-Jahra, 32 km west of Kuwait City, is the site where invading troops from Saudi Arabia were defeated (with British help) in 1920. It was also the site of the Gulf War's

infamous 'turkey shoot' – the Allied destruction of a stalled Iraqi convoy as it attempted to retreat from Kuwait. The convoy's remains were pushed off to the side of the road to rust, where, at last report, a few bits and pieces of it are still visible.

The town's only site of the more conventional variety is the **Red Fort** (also known as the Red Palace), a low rectangular mud structure near the highway. The fort played a key role in the 1920 battle. Coming from Kuwait City, take the second Al-Jahra exit from the expressway. The Red Fort is on the right, about 200m south of (inland from) the highway, though you can't see it until you are right in front of it. In winter it is open daily, except Saturday afternoon, from 7.30 am to 1.30 pm and 3.30 to 6.30 pm. During summer the hours are from 7 am to 1 pm and 4 to 7 pm. Admission is free but identification is required. Still photography is permitted but videos are not. Call ☎ 477 2559 for more information.

DOHA VILLAGE

On an arm of land jutting out into Kuwait Bay, Doha Village is the site of several small dhow-building yards and a fishing village of squalid shacks. The dhow yard is not particularly interesting. If you are planning a trip to Bahrain or to Sur, in Oman, the dhow yards there are far more interesting and easier to reach. The fishers' shacks lie along the road, beyond the concrete walls of the dhow yards. The bus from Kuwait City stops at the end of the concrete wall.

Lebanon

Prior to the civil war Lebanon was the international playground of the eastern Mediterranean attracting visitors from the west and from the Arab world. It was a unique blend of tradition and sophistication; Christian and Muslim; European and Middle Eastern. The civil war changed all that. The country was divided and damaged physically, culturally and economically.

The situation is still not ideal; not all of the political problems have been resolved and it will be many years before the infrastructure, which was badly damaged during the war, is rebuilt. The country's economy is starting to recover but with the Lebanese currency having lost a lot of its value, inflation is running high.

However, with Syrian help, the Lebanese army and police have retaken control of most of the country and the security situation has improved substantially. The Lebanese now await tourists eagerly, and travelling independently is once more possible all around the country except in southern Lebanon, which is still periodically under attack from Israel.

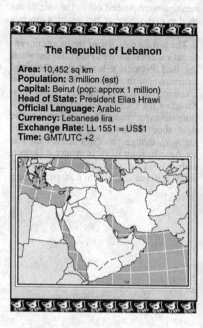

The Republic of Lebanon

Area: 10,452 sq km
Population: 3 million (est)
Capital: Beirut (pop: approx 1 million)
Head of State: President Elias Hrawi
Official Language: Arabic
Currency: Lebanese lira
Exchange Rate: LL 1551 = US$1
Time: GMT/UTC +2

Facts about the Country

HISTORY

Lebanon was another country which emerged from the break-up of the Ottoman Empire after WWI. Between the wars it was under a French mandate and it became fully independent during WWII. Its strategic Middle Eastern location and relatively stable, west-leaning government made it a major trade and banking centre. Many western multinationals had their Middle Eastern head offices in Beirut.

But Lebanon had a fatal flaw in its national make-up – power and control rested with the right-wing Christian part of the population while the Muslims (almost half the popula-

tion) felt they were excluded from real government. Add large numbers of displaced and restive Palestinians and you had a recipe for conflict. The USA helped to put down a Muslim rebellion in 1958, but in 1975 civil war broke out between a predominantly Muslim leftist coalition (allied with Palestinian groups) and Christian right-wing militias. In April 1976, Syrian forces intervened at the request of the Lebanese president, Suleiman Franjieh, to halt the defeat of the Christian forces.

Subsequently, an uneasy peace was forced upon the two sides by the Syrians. Then in 1978 the Israelis marched into southern Lebanon and set up a surrogate militia, the South Lebanon Army (SLA), led by a renegade Christian Lebanese army general, to protect northern Israel from cross-border attacks by the Palestine Liberation Organization (PLO). Following United Nations (UN) pressure, the Israelis withdrew three months later and were replaced by UN peacekeeping forces (UNIFIL). Meanwhile in Beirut, both the Christian and Muslim militias continued building up their arsenals. In the absence of a political solution acceptable to all parties, fighting erupted frequently, only to be stopped by Syrian intervention. At the same time, the Christians started demanding that Syria withdraw its troops from Lebanon.

In June 1982, Israeli troops marched again into Lebanon, this time with the stated aim of eradicating the PLO. They laid siege to Beirut and for seven weeks relentlessly bombarded the Muslim half of the capital by air, sea and land. In August the USA arranged for the evacuation of PLO fighters to other Arab countries, and a Multinational Force (MNF) of US and Western European troops was deployed in Beirut to protect Palestinian and Muslim civilians. After the assassination of Lebanese president-elect Bashir Gemayel, who was also a Christian militia leader, Israeli troops entered west Beirut. Two days later the Israeli-backed Christian militias massacred Palestinian civilians in the Chatila and Sabra camps in west Beirut. Gemayel's brother, Amin, was elected president.

More than a year later Israeli troops withdrew to southern Lebanon. No sooner had they left than fighting broke out between Druze Muslim militias and Christian forces who had been deployed in the Chouf Mountains east of Beirut under Israeli protection. At the same time fighting erupted between Lebanese army units and Muslim militiamen in the capital. The MNF came under repeated attack and suffered heavy casualties; following suicide bombings of the US and French contingents in October 1983, the MNF withdrew in early 1984.

In mid-1985 the Israelis withdrew from the rest of Lebanon, except for a 60 km long border strip which remained under Israeli control. Over the next couple of years the country descended into more chaos as rival factions within both the Christian and the Muslim camps fought each other, and Iranian-backed Muslim fundamentalists (the Islamic Jihad) resorted to taking foreigners hostage. At the request of the then prime minister, Selim al-Hoss, Syrian troops returned to west Beirut in February 1987 to end fighting between rival Muslim militias. The Syrians slowly brought the Muslim areas of Lebanon under their control.

In September 1988, on the expiry of his term, President Gemayel appointed a transitional military government led by General Michel Aoun to succeed him. General Aoun disbanded the Christian militias and then launched a 'war of liberation' against the Syrians in Lebanon. Following fierce fighting Aoun was defeated and sought refuge in France in August 1991. In the meantime a majority of Lebanese MPs met in Taif, Saudi Arabia, to sign an Arab-brokered 'accord for national reconciliation'. The MPs elected a new president, René Moawwad, who was assassinated 17 days after his election. He was replaced by Elias Hrawi, a moderate Maronite Christian with good relations with Syria.

With the help of the Syrians the Lebanese army took control of Beirut and by late 1991 had spread its presence to most Lebanese areas. By early 1992 all surviving foreign hostages had been released, and Syrian troops began withdrawing from the Beirut area.

In August 1992 parliamentary elections were held in Lebanon for the first time in 20 years, and Muslim fundamentalists of the Iranian-backed Hezbollah party won the largest number of seats. A few months later the Cabinet resigned and Rafik Hariri was appointed as the new prime minister.

As the new Cabinet, made up mostly of technocrats, began rebuilding Beirut's infrastructure and rehabilitating the country, the security situation remained tense in southern Lebanon. Israeli forces continued to attack southern Lebanon in 1991 and 1992 as skirmishes between Israeli soldiers in the border strip and Hezbollah fighters increased in frequency. After Hezbollah fighters killed

LEBANON

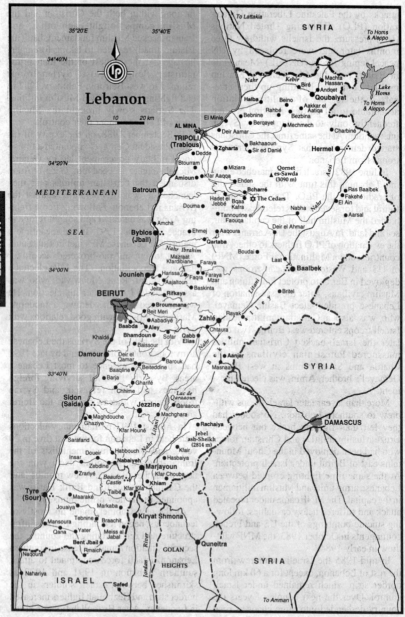

LEBANON

Suggested Itineraries

The capital, **Beirut**, is a convenient base for touring in Lebanon and, even taking into account the war damage, still offers the traveller a taste of the Middle East's most cosmopolitan city.

South of Beirut are the coastal towns of **Sidon (Saida)** and **Tyre (Sour)** which both have ancient ruins which should not be missed. Also to the south is the **Palace of Beiteddine**, a lavish Ottoman style building set in a beautiful landscape.

To the north the ancient port of **Byblos (Jbail)** is a must see for its ruins and picturesque port. **Tripoli (Trablous)** in the far north has a dramatic Crusader castle dominating the city and a number of outstanding Islamic monuments in the old city.

Bcharré and the **Kadisha Gorge** are among the most beautiful sights in Lebanon. Also worth a visit are the famous **Cedars** nearby. Across to the east in the Bekaa valley is **Baalbek**, Lebanon's number one archaeological attraction. If you only have time to visit one place in Lebanon this should be it.

Nowhere in Lebanon is more than a couple of hours by road from Beirut, so each of these places can easily be visited as a day trip. ■

seven Israeli soldiers in July 1993, Israeli forces launched week-long air, sea and land bombardments on some 80 villages in southern Lebanon, killing 113 people and causing more than 300,000 civilians to leave for safer areas. The shelling stopped after US intervention with Tel Aviv.

Trouble flared up again in April 1996 when Israel mounted a wave of air strikes on Hezbollah positions in southern Lebanon and the southern suburbs of Beirut. At the time of writing there was still tension in the air and the Middle East peace process had stalled.

GEOGRAPHY

On the eastern coast of the Mediterranean, Lebanon has an area of 10,452 sq km. It is bounded by Syria to the north and east and by Israel to the south. The Lebanese coastline stretches for 225 km from the rivers Nahr al-Kabir in the north to Ras en-Naqoura

in the south. From west to east the distance ranges from 25 to 90 km.

There are four main geographical areas, running more or less parallel to each other from north to south. They are (from west to east): the coastal plain, the Mt Lebanon range, the Bekaa Valley and the Anti-Lebanon range.

The coastal plain is quite narrow except in the north and is broken at several points by cliffs and buttresses of the Mt Lebanon range which run into the sea. Lebanon's main cities and towns, including Beirut and Tripoli (Trablous), are along this plain.

The Mt Lebanon range rises from the coastal plain in limestone terraces. It is cut by deep gorges and numerous rivers and streams and includes Lebanon's highest summit of Qornet es-Sawda (3090m) and the famous Cedars of Lebanon.

The eastern slopes of the Mt Lebanon range are rocky and arid and fall steeply into the Bekaa Valley, Lebanon's main agricultural region. At 800m above sea level, the fertile Bekaa, with two rivers flowing from it, is cultivated year-round.

The Anti-Lebanon range is an arid massif rising from the eastern side of the Bekaa Valley and marks the border between Lebanon and Syria. Its highest summit is Jebel ash-Sheikh (Mt Hermon) at 2814m.

CLIMATE

Lebanon has a Mediterranean climate – hot and dry in the summer, cool and rainy in the winter. About 300 days of the year are sunny. Humidity is very high along the coast in summer, and daytime temperatures average

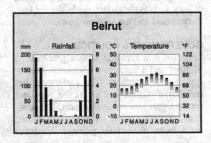

Beirut

30°C, with night temperatures not much lower. Winter is mild with daytime temperatures averaging 15°C.

In the mountains, however, summer days are moderately hot (26°C on average) and the nights pleasantly cool. Winters are cold and it snows above 1300m.

ECOLOGY & ENVIRONMENT

The environment suffered considerable damage during the war; pollutants and rubbish were dumped in the sea and rivers, and unplanned buildings sprang up everywhere. There are still problems but the government and various conservation organisations are attempting to rectify the damage and protect the natural environment with legislation.

FLORA & FAUNA

Lebanon's wildlife has been depleted to almost zero due to over hunting, modern development and the knock-on effects of the war. Travellers are only likely to see domestic animals such as sheep and goats roaming the hills. Even the camel, which was until recently a common sight in the Bekaa Valley, is now a rarity.

A few remote protected sites in the mountains are endeavouring to conserve some of the indigenous species of flora and fauna under threat of extinction. The Horsh Ehden Forest Nature Reserve is the last archetype of the ancient natural forests of Lebanon and is home to several species of rare orchids and other flowering plants. It is also the protected home to mammals such as the badger, the jackal, the porcupine, the Levant vole and many species of shrews and bats and to birds of prey such as the golden eagle, the red kite, the buzzard and the sparrow hawk.

GOVERNMENT & POLITICS

Lebanon is a republic with a president, a Cabinet and a unicameral National Assembly of 128 members. The parliament has legislative powers and elects the president for a six year non-renewable term. The president appoints a prime minister and Cabinet; both have executive powers. Under a National Covenant agreed to in 1943, the president is a Maronite Christian, the prime minister a Sunni Muslim, the speaker of parliament a Shiite Muslim and the armed forces chief of staff a Druze.

ECONOMY

Lebanon's once thriving economy was thrown into turmoil by 17 years of fighting. From a healthy LL 2.50 to the US dollar in 1975, the value of the Lebanese pound declined to LL 1720 to the US dollar in 1993. The public sector has suffered most, as the government lost most of its revenues during the war years.

Agriculture accounts for 10% of GDP and employs about 19% of the workforce. Although Lebanon is not self-sufficient in food, crops such as fruit, cereals, olives and vegetables are major exports.

Industry accounts for some 17% of GDP, and includes food processing, textiles, cement and glass, oil refining, chemicals, tobacco and publishing.

The government has begun the huge task of rebuilding the country's infrastructure, from telephones and electricity to health and education, and rehabilitating its airport and ports. All efforts are geared towards restoring Lebanon's importance as a free trade and banking centre and reviving its tourist and services industries – once Lebanon's main foreign currency earners.

POPULATION & PEOPLE

Lebanon has a population of more than three million people, 60% of whom live in urban areas – about a million of them in Beirut. It is one of the most densely populated countries in the Middle East, with an average density of 307 people per sq km. In addition, there are about 400,000 Palestinian refugees and more than 300,000 other Arabs, Kurds and Armenians.

Although the Lebanese are of mixed ancestry, the majority are of Arab descent.

ARTS

Lebanon's national dance is the *dabke*, an energetic folk dance practised all over the country. Dabke performers wear traditional Lebanese mountain dress and the theme of the dance usually relates to village life.

The main crafts include glass-making, weaving, pottery, embroidery and brass and copper work.

Poetry

One very popular form of poetry in Lebanon is the *zajal*, in which a group of poets enter into a witty dialogue by improvising verses. The verses are sung rather than recited. This is usually done over a meal and drinks of arak, the local spirit, and the poets are generally egged on by the enthusiastic audience. ■

SOCIETY & CONDUCT
Traditional Culture

The traditional lifestyle revolves strongly around the family, socialising and hospitality. This is true for all Lebanese, despite the diversity of customs and traditions associated with the different religious groups and the geographic influences. Outside the big cities and towns people have retained many of the old Lebanese customs and traditions, especially in the mountains.

The Lebanese are extremely friendly and hospitable. They are very helpful to strangers and have no qualms about inviting them into their homes.

Weddings and funerals are big events that often involve whole villages. Religion also plays an important part and most celebrations are related to religious festivals and events.

Dos & Don'ts

In general the Lebanese are quite accepting of foreigners' ways and dress, but outside the big cities and towns people are more traditional. In such places it is better for women to dress modestly. This is especially true when visiting mosques or other religious places. It is also a bad idea to get involved in any political discussions unless you know the person you are talking to really well.

RELIGION

About half the population is Christian and half is Muslim.

The largest Christian group is the Maronite sect, followed by the Greek Orthodox, the Greek Catholic, the Armenian Orthodox, the Armenian Catholic, the Syrian Catholic, the Chaldean, the Protestant and the Syrian Orthodox churches.

The largest Muslim group is the Shiite (Shia) sect, followed by the Sunni and the Druze.

There's also a handful of Roman Catholics, Baha'is and Jews.

LANGUAGE

Arabic is the official language of Lebanon, but French and, to a lesser degree, English are widely spoken around the country. For a list of useful Arabic words and phrases see the Language section in the Facts about the Region chapter.

LEBANON

Facts for the Visitor

PLANNING
When to Go

Spring and autumn are the best times to travel; the climate then is very warm but not uncomfortable. If you want to ski then November to March is the time to go.

Maps

The most comprehensive map is the *Lonely Planet Travel Atlas: Jordan, Syria & Lebanon*. There is quite a good map of Beirut on the back of the GEOprojects map of Lebanon, which you can buy in Beirut. Regional city maps are confined to the ones on the Ministry of Tourism brochures.

What to Bring

A hat and sunglasses are essential in summer, while some warm clothes and a waterproof jacket are needed in winter. A torch is useful for walking around Beirut at night. Most items can be bought cheaply in Lebanon.

TOURIST OFFICES

Local Tourist Offices

The main tourist body is the National Council of Tourism in Lebanon (☎ (01) 340 9404; telex 20898; PO Box 11-5344) on the 1st floor of the Ministry of Tourism building on Rue Banque du Liban in Beirut. Tourist offices elsewhere in Lebanon had not reopened at the time of writing.

Tourist Offices Abroad

You can obtain information before arriving in Lebanon from any of the Lebanese diplomatic missions or the offices of Lebanon's carrier, Middle East Airlines (MEA). They have free, though outdated, hand-out brochures on the major tourist sites and maps of Lebanon and Beirut. You can also contact the Lebanon Tourist & Information Office in the following countries:

Egypt
    1, Talaat Harb St (Midan at-Tahrir), Cairo
    (☎ (02) 393 7529; telex 92227)
France
    124 Rue Faubourg St-Honoré, Paris 75008
    (☎ 01 45 62 34 73; telex 644016;
    fax 45 62 66 13)
Saudi Arabia
    c/o Lebanese General Consulate, Hamra,
    Andalos St, Jeddah (☎ (02) 661 0000;
    telex 401455)
UK
    Piccadilly 90, London W1 (☎ (0171) 409 2031;
    telex 261894)

VISAS & DOCUMENTS

Visas

All foreigners, except Gulf Cooperation Council (GCC) nationals, require a passport and visa to enter Lebanon. GCC nationals are issued three month tourist visas upon arrival at Beirut international airport.

Visas can be obtained at any Lebanese embassy or consulate and require two passport-size photographs and possibly a letter of recommendation from your own mission. They are valid for six months for a stay of two months duration and cost about the equivalent of US$20 for a single-entry visa and US$40 for a multiple-entry visa (useful if you're planning to visit Syria from

Lebanon and return to Beirut). They are usually issued the same day but can sometimes take longer.

If you have an Israeli stamp in your passport, you will be refused entry into the country.

Visa Extensions Visas can be extended for a further three months at no charge at the *amn el-aam*, or General Security office, located on the corner of a block to the west of Cola bridge. The office is on the 2nd floor and the staff speak English. A second extension of three months is possible. It is open every day from 8 am to 2 pm except Sunday.

Other Documents

Keep your passport with you at all times when travelling around Lebanon. There are Lebanese and Syrian army checkpoints all around the country, and even though identification checks have become less frequent, being caught without one will cause you unnecessary delays and hassles.

If you intend to drive in Lebanon an International Driving Permit (IDP) is required. Third-party insurance is not mandatory but recommended. See Car & Motorcycle in the Getting Around the Region chapter for more information about IDPs.

EMBASSIES

Lebanese Embassies Abroad

Some of the Lebanese embassies and consulates abroad include:

Australia
    27 Endeavour St, Red Hill, ACT 2603
    (☎ (02) 295 7378)
    Consulate: 117 Wellington St, Windsor, VIC
    3181 (☎ (03) 9529 4588). Issues visas to
    Victorian residents only.
    Consulate: 70 William St, Kings Cross, Sydney,
    NSW (☎ (02) 9361 5449). Issues visas to NSW
    residents only.
Canada
    640 Lyon St, K1S 3Z5 Ottawa, Ontario
    (☎ (613) 236 5825)
    Consulate: 40 Chemin Côte Ste Catherine, H2V-
    2A2-PQ, Montreal 153 (☎ (514) 276 2638)
Cyprus
    1 Queen Olga St, Nicosia (☎ (41) 442 866/216;
    fax 467 662)

France
  42 Rue Copernic, Paris 75016 (☎ 01 40 67 75 75)
Germany
  Rheinallee 27, Bad Godesberg, 5300 Bonn 2
  (☎ (0228) 35 20 75)
Greece
  Building No 26, Kifissias Ave, Athens 11526
  (☎ (01) 778 5158)
Spain
  178 Paseo de la Castellana, Madrid 16
  (☎ (91) 457 1368)
UK
  21 Kensington Palace Gardens, London W8
  4QM (☎ (0171) 229 7265/6)
USA
  2560, 28th St, Washington DC 20008
  (☎ (202) 939 6300)
  Consulate: Suite 510, 7060 Hollywood Blvd,
  Hollywood Ca 90028 (☎ (213) 467 1253)
  Consulate: 9, East 76th St, NY 10021
  (☎ (212) 744 7905)

Foreign Embassies in Lebanon

Many foreign embassies closed during the war or relocated to temporary offices in different parts of Beirut or to Damascus. At the time of writing many were returning to their former premises, so their telephone numbers and addresses may change without notice.

Australia
  The embassy is in Damascus, but it has an office on the 4th floor of the Farra building, Rue Bliss, Ras Beirut (☎ 868 349/068).
Egypt
  Ramlet el-Bayda (☎ 802 734)
France
  Rue Clémenceau, Ain Mreisseh (☎ 364 600/1)
  Mar Takla, Hazmieh (☎ 429 590)
Germany
  Rue Jurdak, Daouk building, Manara
  (☎ 802 025)
Greece
  Rue Sadat, Sadat Tower, Hamra (☎ 801 590)
Iran
  Sakina Matar building, Jnah (☎ 309 859)
Italy
  Rue Makdissi, Hamra (☎ 340 225)
Russia
  Rue Mar Elias Btina (☎ 867 560)
Spain
  Rue Baalbek, Assaf building, Hamra (☎ 352 448)
Turkey
  Rabieh (☎ 412 118)
UK
  Shamma building, Raouché (☎ 812 849)
  Villa Tohmeh, Rabieh (☎ 417 007)

USA
  Awkar (☎ 417 774, 403 300)
Yemen
  Shaiboub building, Ramlet el-Bayda
  (☎ 832 291)

CUSTOMS

Visitors are allowed to bring in 400 cigarettes and one bottle of spirits or 200 cigarettes and two bottles of spirits. There are no restrictions on the import and export of local or foreign currencies.

MONEY
Costs

Lebanon is far from cheap and the main expense is accommodation. The cheapest realistic budget would be US$30 per day. It is cheaper to stay outside of Beirut where you can get away with spending US$10 a night in a modest hotel. In Beirut the cheapest would cost double that amount. Food is cheap though, and you can live on felafel and shwarma for a few dollars a day. If you shop around you can get a simple restaurant meal for US$5 to US$10. Service taxis and buses are also cheap – even a long trip will only cost about US$5. In Beirut service taxis charge a flat LL 1000 and buses LL 250.

Currency

The currency in Lebanon is the Lebanese lira (LL), also known locally as the *pound*. There are only notes in circulation as the lira lost much of its value during the war and coins (piastres) became obsolete a few years ago.

There are notes of LL 50, 100, 250, 500, 1000, 10,000 and 50,000. Because of the lira's devaluation, most shops, restaurants and hotels accept payment in US dollars.

Currency Exchange

At the time of writing, the exchange rates were:

Australia	A$1	=	LL 1231
Canada	C$1	=	LL 1155
France	FF1	=	LL 305
Germany	DM1	=	LL 1032
Japan	¥100	=	LL 1391

LEBANON

Jordan	JD1	=	LL 2200
Syria	S£10	=	LL 375
Turkey	TL1000	=	LL 156
UK	UK£1	=	LL 2595
USA	US$1	=	LL 1551

Changing Money

Most banks will only change US dollars and UK pounds in cash and travellers' cheques, while moneychangers, found throughout Lebanon, will deal in almost any convertible currency. They also offer better rates than the banks.

Before using moneychangers try to find out what the current exchange rates are. Either ask at a bank or check the previous day's closing exchange rates in the local newspapers. There are no local English-language papers but the exchange-rate list in the French-language *L'Orient-Le Jour* should not be too difficult to decipher.

The rate you'll be offered will never be the same as the published rate, as it includes the moneychanger's commission, but you can always bargain with them to bring the rate closer to it. If you're not happy with the rate offered by one moneychanger try another one.

For travellers' cheques, there's a commission of US$1 per US$50, US$2 per US$100 and US$3 per US$1000 at most places. It pays to shop around.

Travellers' cheques and most international credit cards (American Express, Visa, Diner's Club, Eurocard) are accepted in the larger establishments, and increasingly in restaurants and shops.

Tipping & Bargaining

Tipping is usually expected as a reward for services. Because of the devaluation of the Lebanese currency, salaries and wages are much lower than they used to be. With basic monthly salaries at LL 200,000 (about US$115), tips are an essential means of supplementing incomes.

Most restaurants and nightspots include a 16% service charge in the bill, but it is customary to leave an extra tip of 5% to 10% of the total.

With the exception of a few set prices, everything can be bargained down in Lebanon, from taxi fares to hotel charges. If you feel you're being overcharged while shopping (which is probably the case), offer a price below what you're really willing to pay to leave room for negotiation. If you're still not happy with the price, shop around and you're likely to find the same item cheaper somewhere else.

Many hotels will give you a discount if there are a few of you or if you're staying for more than three days. Or they may offer to throw in a free breakfast.

Service taxis have set prices for their routes, but regular taxis may try to overcharge you. A good way to know how much to pay regular taxis is to multiply the service-taxi fare to your destination by five (the number of passengers in a full car).

POST & COMMUNICATIONS
Post

The GPO is on Rue Riad Solh in Downtown Beirut, but it's a bit out of the way. There are smaller post offices in Hamra, Ashrafieh and Mazraa, and the American University of Beirut (AUB) has its own, very efficient, postal service.

Post offices are open Monday to Saturday from 8 am to 1.30 pm. Lebanon has recently introduced a 'one size fits all' postal charge, which is quite expensive. A postcard to any destination costs LL 1500 and a letter LL 3000.

The Lebanese postal service, affected badly by the war, is slow but quite reliable. Letters can take from 10 to 21 days to reach Europe, the USA or Australia. You can only send letters from a post office. (The government has yet to issue new stamps to reflect the decrease in the currency value.)

Receiving mail takes even longer and there are no poste restante facilities.

Telephone

There's a government-run telephone on Rue de Rome in Beirut, to the south of the intersection with Rue Hamra (near the Ministry of Tourism office) where you can make local calls (LL 500 within Beirut) and international calls (US$2 to US$3 per minute depending on the destination).

Otherwise, all over the country there are private telephone offices which charge LL 1000 to LL 1500 for local calls and US$2 to US$4 per minute for international calls.

At the time of writing it was not possible to make collect calls from Lebanon.

Fax & Telegraph

Faxes and telexes can be sent from large hotels and from the many private bureaus in Beirut. There are many in the area around the AUB campus.

BOOKS

Many books have been written on Lebanon's recent history and the war. Kamal Salibi's *A House of Many Mansions – the history of Lebanon reconsidered* looks at the reasons for Lebanon's civil war. Meir Zamir's *The Formation of Modern Lebanon* is a detailed study of how modern Lebanon was formed in the wake of the disintegration of the Ottoman Empire after WWI. It shows how the creation of Greater Lebanon was bound to lead the country to a civil war.

Pity the Nation – Lebanon at War, by Robert Fisk, is a comprehensive account of the Lebanese war. It chronicles the events of the war since it began in 1975 and explains the different factions and parties involved. Sandra Mackey's *Lebanon – Death of a Nation* is another account of the war and its causes. It also elaborates on the misunderstanding between the Middle East and the western nations.

There are many coffee-table books about Lebanon. One of the better ones is Fluvio Roiter's *Lebanon* (National Council of Tourism, Beirut, 1980). It is full of exquisite colour plates of prewar Lebanon, its heritage and people, but it's rather expensive at US$75.

Prewar travel accounts make good reading. Try Colin Thubron's *The Hills of Adonis* or Philip Ward's *Touring Lebanon*. For ancient history *The Phoenicians*, by Donald Harden, is comprehensive and authoritative. For more general book information see the Books section in the Regional Facts for the Visitor chapter.

NEWSPAPERS & MAGAZINES

There is a new English-language daily called the *Daily Star* and a weekly news magazine, *Monday Morning*, which reviews the week's currant affairs and social events. The local French-language *L'Orient-Le Jour* newspaper is reasonable, as are the weekly magazines *La Revue du Liban* and *Magazine*.

Bookshops and newsagents stock many foreign publications, including the *International Herald Tribune*, *The Independent*, *The Guardian*, *The Times*, *Le Monde*, *Le Figaro*, as well as German, Italian and Spanish newspapers (they're usually one day late). They also have *Time* and *Newsweek* magazines, *The Economist*, *L'Express*, *Le Point* and many more foreign publications.

RADIO & TV

The Lebanese Broadcasting Station has programmes in French and English, as do most of the private radio stations. You can pick up the BBC's 24 hour service on 1323 kHz or 720 kHz medium wave.

There are more than 10 TV stations broadcasting in Arabic, English and French at different times of the day.

PHOTOGRAPHY & VIDEO

Kodak, Agfa, Fuji and other brands are sold everywhere in Lebanon, but good slide film is generally only available in Beirut (the larger towns and some tourist shops (but watch the expiry date!). A regular 36 exposure print film costs LL 6500 to LL 8500, a slide film LL 15,000 (often including developing). Many photo shops have a one hour or same-day developing service (LL 10,000 for a 36 exposure film), and the quality is reasonable. Videotapes are available in all the popular formats.

There's a good range of camera and video equipment and spare parts in Beirut. Check out Kamera (Olympus and Canon) and Lord Camera Shop in Rue Hamra, next door to

LEBANON

each other near the Horseshoe fast-food restaurant.

Generally there is no problem taking photographs anywhere in Lebanon, but there are a few notable exceptions. Never take photos of military checkpoints without first asking permission otherwise you risk having your film confiscated and possibly being detained and questioned. Beware of taking pictures of buildings being used as army barracks; this applies to some of the bombed out buildings in Beirut. Be aware that the security situation is tighter since the Israeli attack in spring '96 and until things relax again it is better to err on the side of caution when taking pictures.

People generally don't mind being photographed but as a matter of courtesy ask for their permission first.

ELECTRICITY

At the time of writing Lebanon was still suffering from electricity shortages as a result of the war. However, this should not affect travellers as most hotels and restaurants have back-up generators.

LAUNDRY

There are dry-cleaning services in all the major cities and towns but no laundrettes – your hotel can direct you to the nearest one. Dry-cleaners usually take at least two days, and their prices start at about LL 2000 for a simple garment.

HEALTH

There are no mandatory vaccinations required for entry into Lebanon, unless you're coming from a disease-affected area. However, it's recommended that visitors have preventative shots for polio, tetanus and typhoid.

The medical services in Lebanon are well developed and most doctors have graduated overseas and speak English or French. The best equipped hospitals are usually the private ones, and a medical insurance policy is essential as they are expensive. Pharmacists can prescribe you medicines for minor ailments, and most drugs are available over the counter.

The main precaution to take is with food and water. Tap water is *not* drinkable in Lebanon, so either drink bottled spring water, which is widely available (LL 750 for 1.5L in grocery stores) or sterilise your water. Always wash fruit and vegetables and avoid eating salads in cheap snack bars. See the Health Appendix for more detailed health information.

TOILETS

Public toilets are nonexistent outside of hotels and restaurants. The standard is usually quite good although you would be advised to take your own toilet paper.

WOMEN TRAVELLERS

Women should have few hassles travelling around Lebanon. The worst they'll be subjected to is leers or attempts at conversation, and sometimes rude remarks. The best thing to do is to ignore your harassers. If some persist ask them loudly to leave you alone and chances are they'll be told off by other passers-by.

Sleeveless tops, shorts and miniskirts are quite common in Beirut, the big towns and along the coast, but it's essential for women to wear bras. Outside the main centres women will feel more comfortable wearing more modest clothing. When visiting mosques make sure that your head, arms and legs are covered.

DANGERS & ANNOYANCES

The main danger spot in Lebanon is the south, which can often be subject to Israeli retaliatory shelling or air raids for cross-border guerrilla operations. The most dangerous zones are in any case off limit to visitors. But outside this area Lebanon is surprisingly safe to travel in. Since the disarming and disbanding of militias in the early '90s, it has become possible to go anywhere at night or day without worries about security. However, the presence of army checkpoints, the bombed-out buildings and the electricity shortages do lend the place an eerie feeling, and some may prefer not to venture out at night.

It is always a good idea to be alert to the current situation; being well informed can save you a lot of trouble later on. Attacks from Israel can happen without warning and at times such as these you would be well advised to stay away from Hezbollah areas (mainly in the south and the Bekaa Valley).

Theft can be a bit of a worry but no more so here than in other places around the world. As a general rule, never leave your belongings unattended or leave money and valuables in your hotel room. Use money belts and avoid showing too much cash.

BUSINESS HOURS

Sunday is the end-of-week holiday in Lebanon. Government offices, including post offices, are open Monday to Saturday from 8 am to 2 pm, and on Friday from 8 to 11 am. However, you'll rarely find anyone before 9.30 am. Banks are open Monday to Saturday from 8.30 am to 12.30 pm.

Shops and private businesses open from 9 am to 6 pm Monday to Saturday. Many grocery stores keep later hours and open on Sunday as well. In summer many places close around 3 pm.

PUBLIC HOLIDAYS & SPECIAL EVENTS

Most holidays are religious, and with so many different sects in Lebanon there are quite a few events to celebrate:

New Year
1 January
Mar Maroun – the patron saint of the Maronites
9 February
Good Friday & Easter Monday
(western and eastern churches)
March-April
Labour Day
1 May
Assumption
15 August
Independence
22 November
Christmas Day
25 December

Also observed are the Muslim holidays of Eid al-Fitr, Eid al-Adha, the Prophet's Birthday, the Muslim New Year and Ashura. For the dates of Muslim holidays see the table of holidays near Public Holidays & Special Events in the Regional Facts for the Visitor chapter.

ACTIVITIES

Water Sports

There are a few public beaches along the Lebanese coast but these lack facilities and are highly polluted. The alternative is to swim in the pools of the many private resorts along the coast. Most offer water sports such as windsurfing, water-skiing, scuba diving and sailing, but they can be very expensive. Admission to these resorts costs from US$6 to US$20 depending on the level of luxury you want.

Skiing

There are several ski resorts of varying degrees of difficulty. The most popular are at Faraya and The Cedars. The ski resorts offer a variety of hotels to suit most budgets (except the very small). A room in a modest hotel should cost around US$25. Ski passes cost on average US$10 per day and ski hire about US$6 per day plus a deposit. The Tourist Board has published a very useful booklet called *Ski Lebanon* which details all the ski resorts and facilities.

ACCOMMODATION

Cheap hotels are very hard to come by as the only hotels which managed to survive the war were the more expensive ones. All of Lebanon's youth hostels have closed down, but there's still one good camping ground remaining and a few bottom-end and mid-range hotels.

Camping

Of Lebanon's five camping grounds only one has survived, the Camping Amchit Les Colombes, just outside Byblos (Jbail) on the northern coast. It's an excellent camping ground on a promontory overlooking the sea, with a capacity for 1500 people and equipped with all the necessary amenities. It's very cheap and safe and is a good base from which to visit the rest of Lebanon (see

Places to Stay in the Byblos section of this chapter). The owner is planning a second camping ground in the mountains which should be open by the time you read this.

Hotels

The cheapest hotels in Beirut were traditionally in the Downtown area but these have gone under the bulldozer to make way for reconstruction. The few cheapies left in the city are listed in the Beirut section. Around the country there are cheap places to stay, but they're few and far between. Tripoli (Trablous) and Zahlé have a few, and there is one (very cheap) hotel in Sidon (Saida).

FOOD

What a treat – Lebanese cuisine is a real delight, with a variety of foods to suit all tastes. What's more, it's not expensive; even the street food is delicious. Beans, fruits and vegetables are plentiful and mutton is the favourite meat. A typical Lebanese meal consists of a few *mezze* dishes (hors d'oeuvres), a main dish of meat, chicken or fish (usually with rice), a salad and dessert. There are two kinds of bread: the flat, pocket variety found everywhere in the Middle East and the *marqouk*, or mountain bread – a very thin bread baked on a domed dish on a wood fire.

There are sandwich and snack bars all over Beirut and in every town around the country. Restaurants also abound, and cover a variety of cuisines from Middle Eastern to European, Chinese and Japanese. They tend to be expensive, though. For more information, *Beyrouth à Table* (1993) has a list of all eateries and restaurants around Lebanon. It gives the addresses (with maps showing locations), notes the average price per person and whether advance bookings are necessary. It also provides other details, plus a summary of the cuisine and atmosphere. Although the guide is in French, it has helpful English summaries for each entry.

Mezze & Snacks

These include *fatayer bi sbanikh* (spinach pies), houmos, *baba ghanouj* (eggplant dips), *labneh* (dried yoghurt cheese), *fatayer bi zaatar* or *man'oushi* (thyme pizza), *lahm bi ajin* (meat pizza), stuffed vine leaves, eggplants and peppers cooked in oil and served cold, *loubieh bi zeit* (string beans cooked with tomatoes, onions and garlic), and many more.

Main Dishes

The national dish is *kebbe*, lamb meat mixed with *burghul*, or crushed wheat, which comes in the form of a baked pie or fried balls stuffed with pine nuts. Other main meals include *kharouf mihshi* (lamb stuffed with rice, meat and nuts), *sayadieh* (fish cooked with rice in an onion and tahina sauce), and *ruz wi djaj* (chicken with rice and nuts). There's also all the variety of kebabs found in the Middle East.

The two favourite salads are *tabouleh* and *fattoush*. The first consists of parsley, mint, onions and tomatoes mixed with burghul and the second has parsley, lettuce, tomatoes, radishes, onions, cucumbers and toasted bread pieces, and is seasoned with *sumak*, a tangy herb.

Desserts & Sweets

In addition to the syrupy *baklava* varieties, sweets include *mahallabiye* (a milk custard with pine nuts and almonds), *maamoul bi joz* or *tamr* (semolina cakes stuffed with walnuts or dates), and *katayef*, pastries stuffed with cream *(bil qashta)* or walnut *(bi joz)*.

DRINKS

Nonalcoholic Drinks

Like other Middle Eastern countries, Arabic coffee is very popular in Lebanon. It's quite strong and served in small coffee cups. You can have it *sadah* (without sugar), *wassat* (medium sugar) or *hilweh* (sweet). Tea is also available but not as popular. Western-style coffee is usually called *Nescafé* and comes in small sachets with a pot of hot water and a jug of milk and is usually expensive.

Other popular nonalcoholic drinks include freshly squeezed vegetable and fruit juices, *limonada* (fresh lemon squash), *jellab* (a delicious drink made from raisins and served with pine nuts) and 'ayran (a yoghurt drink). All kinds of foreign-brand soft drinks are also widely available.

Alcohol

Alcohol is cheap and widely available in Lebanon and you'll find everything from local beers and wines to imported whisky and vodka.

The most popular alcoholic drink is arak, which is mixed with water and ice and usually accompanies meals. Good local brands include Ksarak and Le Brun. There are a few wineries in Lebanon, such as Ksara and Kefraya, producing a reasonable variety of red, rosé and white wines. Local beer brands include Laziza and Almaza, which are quite good. There is also Amstel, a Dutch beer brewed locally under licence. For more information on Middle Eastern food and drinks see the Regional Facts for the Visitor chapter.

ENTERTAINMENT
Cinemas

Many cinemas in and around Beirut show foreign films, sometimes quite recent releases, in their original version with Arabic subtitles.

Classical Music

Occasionally classical concerts are held at the AUB chapel. During March there is an annual festival at the Al-Bustan Hotel in Beit Meri. There are also plans to revive the Baalbek Festival.

Discos & Nightclubs

There are many discos and nightclubs in Beirut and in the major towns, and there's usually no entry fee, although watch out for the price of drinks.

Horse Racing

A good way to spend Sunday in Beirut is at the racecourse. For details see the Beirut section of this chapter.

THINGS TO BUY

Beirut is full of shops, stalls and markets where you can buy everything from locally woven rugs to electronic calculators and the latest fashion wear, often at good prices.

Local handicrafts include pottery, blown glass, embroidered materials, caftans, copperware, brass bowls and trays, mother-of-pearl inlaid boxes and backgammon sets, and rugs. To buy handicrafts, go to La Maison de l'Artisan in Ain el-Mreisseh or Artisans du Liban (Rue Clémenceau, Tajer building, opposite the French embassy). They both collect the work of artisans from around the country and sell them at reasonable prices to promote the local crafts.

Getting There & Away

You can travel to Lebanon by air, overland or by sea. Lebanon's carrier, Middle East Airlines (MEA), connects Beirut with most European capitals, other parts of the Middle East and some African capitals, and with Singapore and Australia. In addition, an increasing number of European, Middle Eastern and Asian airlines have resumed their services to Beirut.

You can also travel overland from Syria and by boat from Cyprus.

AIR
The USA & Canada

At the time of writing it was not possible to fly directly from North America to Lebanon because of some political issue between the Lebanese and US governments. Tickets issued in the USA are not allowed to have Beirut listed on them. However, many European airlines linking Beirut with the USA via a stopover in their capital city will issue you two tickets to get around this problem (check with the airlines).

There are two month Apex return fares from New York to Beirut for US$1050 in the low season and US$1150 in the high season; from Los Angeles they're US$1410 and US$1510, respectively. They have to be

LEBANON

booked at least 14 days in advance. To/from Toronto, there's a three month excursion fare of US$1210.

The UK & Europe

There are daily flights between Beirut and most European capitals and the best fares on offer are youth fares (under 26) and student fares (under 31), as they're usually half the normal economy fare. A London-Beirut student/youth return fare costs UK£310; from Paris it's FF 5860. If you don't qualify for a discount the cheapest fares from London are UK£350 return in the low season up to about UK£450 in the high season.

There's a 35 day Apex fare from Athens on Olympic Airways for US$368/405 in the low/high season. One of the cheapest routes from the UK is on Turkish Airlines via İstanbul for UK£230 return except from 15 June to 15 August.

Australia

MEA has a weekly direct flight between Sydney and Beirut, and Gulf Air flies three times a week to Beirut with a stopover in Bahrain. Both airlines charge the same fare. A full economy return ticket between Melbourne or Sydney and Beirut costs A$2318/2678 in the low/high season, although specials and discounts may be available on application.

The Middle East

Return excursion fares to İstanbul cost US$273, to Cairo US$511, to Damascus US$100, to Amman US$160 and to Abu Dhabi US$680.

LAND

The only way into Lebanon by land is through Syria; the border with Israel is closed and will be for the foreseeable future. If you're bringing your car into Lebanon, you must have an International Driving Permit.

There are daily buses and service taxis between Beirut and Damascus, and between Tripoli in northern Lebanon and Homs. Service taxis from Beirut to Damascus

charge LL 15,000; buses are cheaper at LL 7500. From Tripoli to Homs a service taxi costs LL 7000, buses LL 4000. There is also a frequent bus service to Aleppo and the fare is LL 10,000. The journey takes seven hours.

SEA

It is possible to arrive in Lebanon by sea from Larnaca, Cyprus. The journey by catamaran takes 3½ hours and costs US$90/180 for a single/return fare. The ferry docks at Jounieh, just north of Beirut.

Note: the ferry service has suffered total disruption since the Israeli attack in spring '96. It is due to resume, but is vulnerable to blockades by the Israeli navy.

LEAVING LEBANON

There's a US$15 departure tax if you're leaving by boat. Economy class airline passengers departing from Beirut international airport must pay US$15, while 1st class airline passengers must pay US$30. There is no tax at land borders.

Getting Around

There are no air services or trains operating within Lebanon. Buses cover some parts of Beirut, the airport and a few destinations around Lebanon. There are more new routes starting up all the time. The best way to get around is by service taxi. They are cheap, abundant and cover most city neighbourhoods and major destinations around the country.

BUS

Buses travel between Beirut and the major towns around the country, but they often have only one or two departures a day and there are no timetables. There are two make-shift bus stations in Beirut, one outside the National Museum for buses travelling to destinations north of Beirut and another at the Cola bridge for destinations south of Beirut. They usually have the destination displayed on the front window or above it in Arabic only.

The buses are all run by private companies as the government has not yet restored a nationwide bus service.

TAXI & SERVICE TAXI

Taxis and service taxis are recognisable by their red number plates and, on some cars, a white sign with 'TAXI' written on it in red letters. Most of the cars are old Mercedes models. Before getting in, always check that the number plate is red as there are many unlicenced drivers operating taxis.

Service taxis usually follow an established route and you can stop them anywhere. To signal the driver to stop just say '*indak*' (here). Payment can be made at any point during the trip, though people tend to pay as soon as they get in. To take you anywhere in central Beirut, a service taxi charges LL 1000 (LL 2000 to outlying districts). You may sometimes have to take more than one service taxi if your destination is not straightforward – for example if it includes more than one of the service taxi's routes. Outside Beirut, the fares range from LL 2000 to LL 8000 depending on the destination. Although the fares are not listed anywhere the driver will usually ask for the correct fare. However, always enquire 'Service?' before getting into the car, especially if there are no other passengers, to avoid being charged a full taxi fare.

The same service taxi can become a taxi if you pay for the fare of the four other seats in the car. This avoids the delay of stopping to let other passengers in or out. In addition, the driver will deposit you right outside your destination.

Ordinary taxis are not confined to a set route and take only one fare. You can also order taxis by telephone. They'll take you anywhere in Lebanon and some also have services to Syria and Jordan.

CAR

Road Rules

Driving is on the right-hand side of the road in Lebanon, and this is where road rules end.

Despite the cheap petrol (LL 420 per litre), driving is not exactly recommended in Lebanon. Accidents and traffic jams are frequent hazards.

Despite the attempts of traffic police to organise the flow of cars, very few drivers follow road regulations. Trying to cross at intersections is a real nightmare and depends on who manages to edge their bumper in first.

Driving in cities is frustrating because of the traffic jams, the double parking and service taxis who stop without warning in the middle of the road to let passengers in or out. On the highways it's a pretty scary experience as drivers will zigzag among the cars at crazy speeds. In the mountains, it's rather dangerous as most roads are narrow with hairpin bends and it's not unusual for drivers to overtake on hidden road bends.

In addition, you have to keep an eye out for pedestrians who often walk in the middle of the streets or haphazardly cross highways and roads.

That said, local drivers are quite used to driving in these chaotic circumstances.

Rental

There are several car hire companies in Beirut offering competitive rates. We strongly recommend that you take out the best insurance policy that you can afford. Many of the firms also offer drivers to go with the cars. This will cost you about US$50 per day, but if you are nervous about the driving conditions it is probably a good idea.

Following is a list of rental companies and a sample of their prices.

Avis (☎ (01) 398 850, 861 614). Its cheapest car is a Fiat Uno, which costs US$37 per day, including 100 km free (16c for each km above that), and US$222 per week with unlimited mileage.
Budget (☎ (01) 833 027, 410 791). Its cheapest car is a Nissan which costs US$35 per day or US$220 per week, both with unlimited mileage.
Europcar (☎ (01) 480 480, 363 636). It's a bit more expensive at US$40/260 per day/week for a Datsun March but with unlimited mileage.
Prestige (☎ (01) 866 328). It charges US$35/210 per day/week for a Renault 5, a Nissan or a Subaru 4WD with unlimited mileage.

LEBANON

All companies require a refundable deposit except from credit card holders and offer free delivery and collection during working hours. The minimum age for drivers is 21. At the time of writing you could not take hire cars over the border into Syria.

LOCAL TRANSPORT
Taxi
Service taxis are the best way to get around Beirut and between towns (see Taxi & Service Taxi in the earlier Getting There & Away section earlier in this chapter).

ORGANISED TOURS
There are a few operators organising tours within Lebanon and to Syria and Jordan. They're a good option as the tours cover most of Lebanon's places of interest and are reasonably priced (most include lunch in the deal). All transport is by air-con coaches. The itineraries vary from company to company but they all cover the main places of interest such as Baalbek, Aanjar, Byblos, Tripoli, The Cedars, Sidon and Tyre (Sour). The main tour operators include:

Nakhal & Cie
    Ave Sami Solh, Ghorayeb building (☎ (01) 425 753, 389 507/8; fax 422 302)
Tania Travel
    Rue Sidani, opposite Cinema Jeanne d'Arc (☎ (01) 860 238, 340459; fax 340 473)
Tour Vacances
    A consortium of four tour operators that can be reached on any of these numbers (☎ (01) 352 194, 321 934, 340 375, 423 672; fax 424 509, 580 957). As well as the usual tours this company specialises in ski packages to Faraya and Faqra during the winter season.

Beirut

Beirut is the capital of Lebanon and its largest city, with a population of just over a million. Once dubbed the Paris of the Middle East, Beirut suffered severely from Lebanon's 17 year war. Whole neighbourhoods were destroyed by bombardments, including the old city centre, and the influx of refugees to

the capital was more than the city's infrastructure could deal with.

At first sight the full extent of the destruction, coupled with uncontrolled building construction, overcrowding and a feeling of total chaos, comes as a shock to the visitor. It's a city of contrasts where beautiful architecture exists alongside concrete eyesores; traditional houses set in jasmine-scented gardens are dwarfed by tall, modern buildings; winding old alleys turn off from wide avenues; beggars and wealthy people share the pavement; and expensive new cars vie for the right of way with vendor carts.

But amid this chaos, and partly because of it, Beirut has lost none of its vibrancy and retains a certain charm, due mainly to the warmth and hospitality of its citizens. Though there's not much left to see in Beirut itself, it's a good base for travellers, as it's the country's transport hub, and the most distant part of Lebanon is no more than three hours' drive away.

History
Beryte, as Beirut was originally known, was a modest port during Phoenician times (2nd millennium BC). It became famous in Roman times for its School of Law, one of the first three in the world, which made it a cultural centre until the 6th century AD. Then it went into a long period of decline, and even during Arab times (13th century), when mosques, hammams and souqs were built, it was still relatively obscure. In the 19th century it started gaining importance as a trading centre and gateway to the Middle East and Beirut's port became the largest on the eastern Mediterranean coast. The city soon became a major business, banking and publishing centre and remained so until the civil war, which started in 1975, undermined its position.

Since the war ended, in 1991, the rehabilitation of the city's infrastructure has begun in earnest and the reconstruction of the city centre, or Downtown area, has already started – a major task which will probably take the next 10 years to complete. One positive thing which has come out of all the

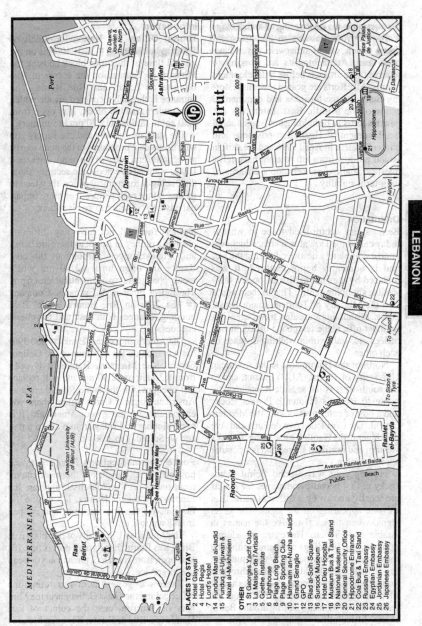

PLACES TO STAY
2 Hotel Glayeul
4 Hotel Regis
7 Ford's Hotel
14 Funduq Manal al-Jadid
15 Funduq al-Urjuwan &
    Nazel al-Mukhliseen

OTHER
1 St Georges Yacht Club
3 La Maison de l'Artisan
5 Goethe Institute
6 Lighthouse
8 Plage Long Beach
9 Plage Sporting Club
10 Hammam an-Nuzha al-Jadid
11 Grand Seraglio
12 GPO
13 Riad al-Solh Square
16 Sursock Museum
17 Hotel Dieu Hospital
18 Museum Bus & Taxi Stand
19 National Museum
20 General Security Office
21 Hippodrome Entrance
22 Cola Bus & Taxi Stand
23 Russian Embassy
24 Egyptian Embassy
25 Jordanian Embassy
26 Japanese Embassy

Beirut

LEBANON

destruction is the uncovering of archaeological sites from Phoenician and Classical times which would otherwise never have been seen. Archaeologists are working to remove these artifacts before redevelopment begins. All efforts are geared towards restoring Beirut as the business and commercial centre of the Middle East. Internally the peace seems to be holding but Israel's aerial bombardment of Hezbollah positions and parts of Beirut in April 1996 and the shift in Israeli politics from left to right have left a question mark over Lebanon's chances of long-term stability.

Orientation

Beirut's city centre used to be in what is today called the Downtown area, which was almost completely destroyed during the war and is currently being restored. It was replaced by the Hamra district, once a fashionable shopping centre. That's where you'll find the Ministry of Tourism, major banks, hotels, restaurants and cafes, travel agencies, the post office, the telephone office, airline offices etc – all within walking distance of each other.

North of the Hamra area is the American University of Beirut (AUB) district, and to the south-west is the seaside Raouché area, home to Beirut's landmark Pigeon Rocks and a host of cafes overlooking the Mediterranean. The Corniche (Ave de Paris and Ave du Général de Gaulle) runs along Beirut's western and northern shores and is a popular spot for walks.

Finding your way around Beirut seems tricky at first because sometimes the streets are locally known by a different name than the one appearing on the signs. The street signs, when they exist, give the names in Arabic and French. There are no address numbers and buildings are known either by the name of their owner or by their function (eg British Bank building). When directing you, people refer to landmarks and the names of commercial institutions. You soon get used to this system and getting around Beirut is less difficult than it may at first seem.

Information

Tourist Office The National Council of Tourism in Lebanon (☎ 340 940/4) is on the ground floor of the office block housing the Ministry of Tourism on the corner of Rue Banque du Liban and Rue Rome. The entrance is through a covered arcade which runs underneath the block. It is open from 9.30 am to midday (12.30 pm in summer).

The staff are friendly and can supply you with up-to-date brochures of the main tourist attractions (and some of the minor ones too). If you want advice about the security situation, being a government office, they tend to paint a rather rosy picture. For more impartial advice it is better to go elsewhere.

Money You will not have any difficulty changing money in Beirut as there are banks and moneychangers throughout the city. Banks are open until 12.30 pm while moneychangers stay open until at least 6 pm. The Beirut Finance & Exchange Company (☎ 864 280) on Rue Hamra, Abdel Baki building, changes both cash and travellers' cheques.

The American Express Bank (☎ 360 390) has a branch on the 1st floor of the Gefinor Centre, Rue Maamari, Hamra. It is open from 8.30 am to 12.30 pm and will replace lost cheques. On the same floor there's an American Express Cards office where you can obtain cash using your Amex card. It is open Monday to Friday from 8 am to 6 pm, and on Saturday to 1.30 pm.

Post & Communications There are several post offices in Beirut, but the most convenient one is on Rue Makdissi, opposite the Embassy Hotel, in Hamra. It's on the 1st floor, above the Star stationer, and is open from 8 am to 2 pm.

The American University of Beirut on Rue Bliss, Ras Beirut, has its own post office. It's also open from 8 am to 2 pm and anyone can use its service.

There's a government-run telephone office behind the Glass Gallery near the Ministry of Tourism, near the corner of Rue Hamra and Rue de Rome. It is open Monday to Saturday from 8 am to 2 pm (to 11 am on Friday). You give your number to an operator who will direct you to a booth.

All over Beirut are private telephone offices where you can make local and international calls (for rates see Post & Communications in the Facts for the Visitor section of this chapter).

The telephone code for Beirut is 1.

Travel Agencies There are travel agencies all over Beirut, including many along Rue Hamra and quite a few in the Gefinor Centre. Among the better ones is Levon Travel (☎ 347 141/2, 351 424) on Rue Banque du Liban, Jallad building (a few metres east of the Central Bank building).

Bookshops & Libraries Beirut has a good selection of foreign-language bookshops stocked with academic books, dictionaries, novels and general-interest books. They also sell European newspapers such as *The International Herald Tribune*, *The Guardian*, *The Financial Review*, *Le Monde* (usually one day late) and magazines including *Time, Newsweek, L'Express, Le Point* and others. There are a few along Rue Hamra, including Librairie Antoine, which has quite an array of English and French-language books. Four Steps Down and Way In, also on Rue Hamra, have mainly English-language books, as do the Lebanon Bookshop and Khayat's Bookshop on Rue Bliss, opposite AUB. Another good bookshop is the Librairie Internationale on the ground floor of the Gefinor Centre.

The British Council and the other cultural centres also have small libraries open to the public where you can catch up with newspapers and magazines from back home and read up about Lebanon.

Cultural Centres There are a few foreign cultural centres in Beirut, including:

British Council
    Azar building, Rue Yamout (off Rue Sidani), Ras Beirut (☎ 730 459, 739 460)

Centro Cultural Hispanico
    Rue Baalbek, Assaf building (☎ 352 448)
Goethe Institut
    Rue Bliss, Gideon building, Manara (☎ 805 880)
Institut Culturel Français
    Cité Bounnour, Rue de Damas (☎ 387 511/2/3)
Italian Cultural Centre
    Rue de Rome, Najjar building (☎ 862 395)
Russian Cultural Centre
    Rue Verdun (☎ 309 889)

Emergency The following numbers can be useful in case of emergency:

Emergency Police: 16
Police: 386 440, 425 250
Fire Brigade: 310 105
Ambulance: 386 675
Red Cross: 865 561
Civil Defence: 394 100

Dangers & Annoyances On the whole Beirut is a safe place to travel around. For pedestrians the traffic poses the biggest hazard. Also beware of masonry falling from damaged buildings, and watch for potholes in the road when walking around, especially at night where there is little or no street lighting.

Museums
Beirut's **National Museum**, which housed an impressive collection of archaeological artefacts, statuettes and sarcophagi covering Lebanon's history from prehistoric times to the present, is due to re-open following restorations in 1996. Other museums include the **American University Museum**, inside the AUB campus, with a fine collection of Phoenician glass and Arab coins, and the **Sursock Museum**, set in a beautiful old house in Ashrafieh, which has regular exhibitions of modern paintings, sculptures and old manuscripts.

Downtown
A walk around the Downtown area (*albalad*) gives you an idea of the extent of destruction. Many churches, mosques and old buildings are currently under restoration, including the *saraya* (Grand Seraglio), a

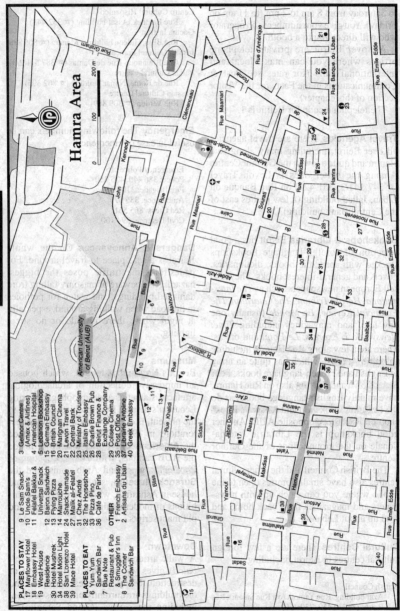

Hamra Area

0   100   200 m

American University
of Beirut (AUB)

PLACES TO STAY
17 Mayflower Hotel
18 Embassy Hotel
19 West House
    Residence
30 Hotel Mushrek
34 Hotel Moon Light
38 San Lorenzo Hotel
39 Mace Hotel

PLACES TO EAT
6   Yum Yum
7   Blue Note
    Restaurant & Pub
8   Smuggler's Inn
    The Corner
    Sandwich Bar

9   Le Sam Snack
10 Uncle Sam's
11 Felafel Bakkar &
    Universal Snack
12 Baron Sandwich
13 Flying Pizza
14 Marrouche
24 Snack Hamade
27 Malik al-Felafel
31 The Zodre
32 The Lordshoe
33 Pizza Pino
36 Café de Paris

OTHER
1   French Embassy
2   Artisans du Liban

3   Gefinor Centre
    (Amex & Airlines)
4   American Hospital
5   Lebanon Bookshop
15 German Embassy
16 British Council
20 Marignan Cinema
21 Lewon Travel
22 Central Bank
23 Ministry of Tourism
25 Italian Embassy
26 Charlie Brown Pub
28 Beirut Finance &
    Exchange Company
29 Coliseé Cinema
35 Post Office
37 Librairie Antoine
40 Greek Embassy

former Ottoman barracks and once the seat of the government.

Corniche

The Corniche is a favourite promenade spot, especially late in the afternoon. You can stop to drink a coffee served from the back of a van or sample the push-cart pedlars' specialities, such as hot chestnuts, iced cactus fruit, *kaak* (crisp bread with sesame seeds and thyme), fresh coconut, corn on the cob and green almonds. Or you can stop at one of the open-air cafes for a beer and nargileh (water pipe). There is a small funfair on the Corniche which is popular with Lebanese families.

Beaches

Unfortunately, the beaches around Beirut are heavily polluted but there are a few seaside resorts in and around the capital where you can sunbathe or swim in a pool. They're rather on the expensive side, with entry fees ranging between US$8 and US$20. Alternatively you can walk down the cliffs near Pigeon Rocks and sunbathe for free.

Hammam

You can indulge yourself with a full massage, sauna and bath at the Hammam an-Nuzha al-Jadid (☎ 641 298) on Rue Kasti, off Ave du General Fouad Chehab. It's open all week 24 hours a day, but women can only go on Monday from 9 am to 2 pm. The hammam provides soap and towels.

Places to Stay – bottom end

Cheap accommodation in Beirut is very hard to find; all the real cheapies used to be in the Downtown district and are now under the bulldozer. The cheapest options are mainly around Hamra. The new *Hotel Moonlight* (☎ 352 308) is off Rue Hamra, tucked down a side street between Rue Ibrahim Abdel Ali and Rue Omar ben Abdel-Aziz. Rooms here cost US$20/22/28 for a single/double/triple.

The *Hotel Mushrek* (☎ 345 773) on Rue Makdissi seems reasonable enough at US$20/26/38 for singles/doubles/triples and like many hotels will probably come down

in price if pressed. The *San Lorenzo Hotel* (☎ 348 604/5) is right on Rue Hamra, above the Taverne Suisse restaurant. You can get a very basic single/double for US$16/22 with shared (funky) bathrooms. If you want a private bath the price is US$20 for a single.

One of the cheapest hotels in Beirut is the *Hotel Glayeul* (☎ 869 690) on Rue Minet al-Hosn, near the St Georges Yacht Club. It only has 11 rooms and is often full. The cost of a double room here is US$20 and the hotel has a terrace restaurant overlooking the sea. Nearby is the *Hotel Regis* (☎ 361 845) which is down a small side street almost opposite the Glayeul. It has 20 rooms and singles/doubles cost US$20/40, although apparently the proprietors will come down in price.

Places to Stay – middle

If you are prepared to pay a bit more the *Mace Hotel* (☎ & fax 344 626/7, 340 720) is recommended. It is off Rue Hamra on the southern side towards the western end of the street. All the rooms have baths, TV and air-con. Singles/doubles are US$35/45 and that includes breakfast. Ask for the 'special price' and you should be offered a discount.

Another popular mid-range hotel is the *Embassy* (☎ 340 814/5), on Rue Makdissi opposite the post office. Singles/doubles with bath go for US$35/55. The well-known *Mayflower Hotel* (☎ 340 680; fax 342 038) is a popular watering hole for expats. It is now offering economy rooms at US$35/45 for singles/doubles, which is a lot less than its regular rate.

A good deal offering more services is the *West House Residence* (☎ 351 051/2/3) on Rue Sourati, near its intersection with Rue Omar ben Abdel-Aziz, Hamra. It has 24 self-contained studio apartments, each with a double bed or twin beds, a small sitting room, coffee and tea-making facilities, TV, air-con and a bathroom with hot water available in the shower 24 hours a day. It charges US$35 per room per night, US$200 per week and US$350 per fortnight, and it gives discounts to groups. The same company owns a similar apartment hotel building on Rue

Artois called *West House Residence* II (☎ 350 450).

At the same price is another apartment hotel, *Residence Haddad* (☎ 342 313), which has just opened up on Rue Sidani off Rue Hamra and has similar facilities.

Places to Eat

Beirut is full of eateries catering to all tastes and budgets, and it would be impossible to list them all in this space. Here is a selection in the Hamra and Ras Beirut areas that should give you an idea of what's on offer and the prices.

Restaurants *Uncle Sam's* (☎ 353 500), on the corner of Rue Jeanne d'Arc and Rue Bliss, has long been a favourite with AUB students. Its main meals cost between US$6 and US$9 and you can have a beer at the bar for US$2. There's a US$1 cover charge and a 16% service charge. It's open Monday to Friday from 7 am to midnight, Saturday to 3 pm; and it's closed on Sunday.

The *Flying Pizza* (☎ 353 975) is a reasonably priced takeaway/sit-down pizzeria on Rue Khalidi. It charges LL 5100 for a small pizza, LL 10,200 for a medium-size pizza, LL 1500 for a soft drink and LL 3000 for a beer. There are no additional charges and it's open from 11 am till midnight.

The *Blue Note* restaurant and pub (☎ 350 426) is on Rue Makhoul (the continuation of Khalidi). It's a pleasant restaurant offering mezze dishes that start at LL 3000 for a houmos or eggplant dip and main courses that start at LL 8500. Or you can have a drink at the bar for LL 3900 for a local beer, LL 5200 for imported brands or spirits. It has live jazz music on Friday and Saturday nights but there's a cover charge of LL 6000. It's open all week except Sunday from noon till late.

Next door is the *Smuggler's Inn* (☎ 354 941), offering Lebanese and international food. It's on the expensive side but they have a plat du jour with salad, coffee and dessert for US$8 plus a US$1 cover charge and 16% service charge. It's open all week except Sunday from noon to 4 pm and 7 pm till late.

Another good option is to eat in the cafeteria of the university. It has meals from LL 3000 from noon to 3 pm and cheap sandwiches and coffee all day. It usually has a good vegetarian selection. The cafeteria is near the Rue Bliss entrance to the campus.

Cafes There are many cafes dotted around the city selling excellent Arabic coffee and sweet pastries. In some of the older establishments you can smoke a nargileh pipe. European-style cafes are also popular; the *Café de Paris* is on Rue Hamra, near Librairie Antoine, and has a 'watch the world go by' feel to it. In most cafes Arabic coffee costs between LL 1000 and LL 1500. Pastries and sweets vary in price between LL 1000 and LL 2000. If you are on a budget avoid ordering Nescafé as it is invariably expensive.

Fast Food Beirut has many fast-food joints of every conceivable variety. It is possible to live very cheaply on fast food alone, although it may get a bit repetitive after a while. The usual system in these places is to order your food and pay at the till and then take your receipt to the food counter. *Snack Hamade* on Rue de Rome, just off Rue Hamra, has Lebanese pizzas on thin bread priced from LL 750 (zaatar, or thyme) to LL 1250 for a cheese or meat pizza.

One block further, on Rue de Rome, is *Maatouk* takeaway, which has chicken and meat shwarma for LL 2000 and a wide variety of Lebanese rice dishes. For felafel sandwiches (LL 1250 to LL 1500) head for *Malik al-Felafel* (King of Felafel) on Rue Roosevelt, just off Rue Hamra, one of the best felafel places in town.

The *Horseshoe* on the corner of Rue Hamra and Rue du Caire is a fast-food joint selling chicken, fish and meat burgers for LL 2000. A few metres down the opposite side of Rue Hamra, inside an arcade, is *Chez André* (☎ 345 662), one of the nicer sandwich bars that survived the war in Lebanon. It has excellent lahm bi ajin and sandwiches for LL 1500 to LL 2000, plus draught beer

(LL 2500) and wine and spirits (LL 3500 per glass). Don't be put off by the dingy arcade. Chez André is the third shop on your left-hand side. It's open all week except Sunday from 8 am to 11 pm.

Quite a few places sell whole roast chickens which are cheap (around LL 7000) and very good. They often come wrapped in bread and with garlic sauce on the side. The *Paulco* chicken takeaway is in Raouché on the Corniche just north of the public beach, and is recommended.

There are a few sandwich and snack bars around the AUB campus catering mainly to students. *The Corner* at the intersection of Rue Makhoul and Rue Jeanne d'Arc makes chicken, meat, cheese and labneh sandwiches for LL 1750. It also has a wide variety of fresh juices for LL 1000 to LL 2500, depending on the mix of fruit.

Yum Yum on Rue Bliss is a grocery/sandwich bar with a variety of sandwiches ranging in price from LL 1750 (cheese, eggplant, potato, labneh) to LL 2000 (meat or chicken). It also sells mineral water (LL 750 for a bottle, LL 500 for a half bottle), soft drinks (LL 750) and canned juice (LL 500 to LL 1750). A few metres further down the street is *Bliss House*, which specialises in fresh juices (LL 1750 for a small glass to LL 3000 for a large one).

Opposite the AUB main gate is *Le Sam Snack*, where you can get a hamburger for LL 2250 and french fries for LL 750.

Further down Rue Bliss *Baron Sandwich* specialises in spicy Armenian sausages (soujouk and pasterma) for LL 2000, which go down very well with a cold yoghurt drink (LL 500).

For good felafel or shwarma head for *Felafel Bakkar*, just around the corner on Rue Jeanne d'Arc. The sign is in Arabic only but it's the second shop on the right as you walk up Jeanne d'Arc from Rue Bliss. A simple felafel sandwich costs LL 1250, an extra one LL 1500. Shwarma sandwiches cost LL 2000. It's open every day except Sunday from 10 am to 10 pm (8 pm Saturday).

Next door is the good-value *Universal Snack* (☎ 342 209), specialising in hamburg-

ers. Here you get your hamburger served on a plate with a generous helping of salad and french fries for LL 3500. It also has a variety of grills and serves English breakfast (bacon & eggs) for LL 7500 and Lebanese breakfast (fuul, labneh etc) for LL 5000. It's open all week from 7.30 am to 11 pm.

Entertainment

Some of the cinemas showing a good selection of foreign films include the *Colisée, Monte Carlo* and *Marignan* in Hamra and the *Vendome* and *Empire* in Ashrafieh. There are more cinemas just outside Beirut in Kaslik and Zouk Mikael.

There are many pubs, discos, bars and nightclubs in and around Beirut. Among others in the Hamra area are the *Charlie Brown* pub at the Cavalier Hotel in Hamra, the *Blue Note Pub/Restaurant* in Rue Makhoul and *Back Street* in Rue Khalidi, near the Flying Pizza.

Spectator Sport

Horse Racing The *Hippodrome* (☎ 632 520) holds regular Sunday race meetings, one of the few events which survived throughout the war. The meetings are very popular and are a great way to soak up the local atmosphere. Admission is US$10 to the grandstand and US$3 to the 2nd class stand. The entrance is on Ave Abdallah Yafi, not far from the museum.

Getting There & Away

Air Beirut international airport is served by the local carrier, Middle East Airlines (MEA), and several Arab, Asian and European airlines.

Several airlines have their offices in the Gefinor Centre in Hamra, including Aeroflot (☎ 364 030), Air Canada (☎ 811 690), British Airways (☎ 364 690), Cathay Pacific (361 230), Gulf Air (☎ 367 270), KLM (☎ 372 100) and MEA (☎ 368 891). Elsewhere are the following:

Air France
    Rue Bliss (☎ 804 250)

Air India
      Sanayeh (☎ 336 282)
Alitalia
      Rue Hamra (☎ 340 280)
Lufthansa
      Rue Hamra (☎ 349 001)

Bus & Service Taxi Buses and service taxis to destinations north and north-east of Beirut gather in front of the National Museum and in Dawra. For destinations south and south-east of Beirut the buses and service taxis leave from the Cola bridge station. (For more information see the main Getting There & Away and Getting Around sections of this chapter.)

Getting Around
The Airport Beirut international airport is approximately five km south of Beirut. There is a bus service (No 5) from the new Lebanese Commuting Company into the port area of the city. The fare is LL 500. From there you can catch bus No 1 to Hamra for another LL 500.

Taxis from the airport are notoriously expensive, charging up to US$25 for the trip into town. A cheaper option is to walk 200m to the highway and hail a service taxi into town for LL 2000.

Bus There are now several new regular bus services from the new Lebanese Commuting Company. It operates on a 'hail and ride' system. Short hops cost LL 250 and longer journeys LL 500. The No 2 runs from Hamra to Dawra via the port and Achrafieh, the No 3 goes from Cola to Hamra and the No 4 goes from Dawra to Jounieh. There are also several buses which run along the Corniche starting at the junction of Ave de Paris and Rue Minet al-Hosn and running round to Blvd Saeb Salem.

Taxi Taxis are not equipped with meters and you have to agree on the fare before getting into the car. Within Beirut they charge from LL 5000 to LL 8000, depending on your destination. They are usually Mercedes with red number plates and can be hailed on the

street. It's also possible to ring for a taxi from taxi offices. They are a bit more expensive but are safer to use, especially at night (make sure you ask for the fare over the phone). They include:

      Caracas Taxi (☎ 808 316)
      Lebanon Taxi (☎ 353 152/3)
      Radio Taxi (☎ 804 026)
      Sadat Taxi (☎ 808 720/741)
      TV Taxi (☎ 862 489)

Service Taxi Service taxis cover the major routes in Beirut. They can be hailed anywhere around town and will drop you off at any point along their established route. The fare is LL 1000 on established routes within the city, LL 2000 to outlying suburbs.

Around Beirut

MOUNTAIN RESORTS
There are a few mountain resorts around Beirut which are easy to get to and are a welcome change from the heat and traffic of the city. You will go through some of them while travelling around Lebanon but some make a nice day trip from Beirut.

Beit Meri & Broummana
Located 16 km east of Beirut, Beit Meri is set in pine forests some 800m above Beirut with panoramic views over the capital. It dates back to Phoenician times and has Roman and Byzantine ruins, including some fine floor mosaics in a Byzantine church dating from the 5th century AD. At the time of writing, however, it was not possible to visit the ruins because of army presence there.

Four km further on from Beit Meri is Broummana, a bustling little town full of hotels, eateries, cafes, shops and nightclubs. Broummana has a lot of charm and it's a nice place to wander around.

Service taxis from the Museum or Dawra stand charge LL 1500 to Beit Meri or Broummana. You can get off to have a look at Beit Meri and from there either walk the four km to Broummana or take another service taxi (LL 500) there.

Faraya

If you're into skiing, Faraya is a ski resort 51 km from Beirut (about an hour's drive). It is equipped with ski lifts and chairs and there are several hotels to stay at, though they are usually fully booked during the ski season. Tour Vacances organises reasonably priced package tours to Faraya (for details see the Getting Around section at the beginning of this chapter).

Six km down the road, **Faqra** is worth visiting for the extraordinary natural bridge of Kferdibian and the remains of Roman and Phoenician temples and tombs in a very picturesque setting.

JOUNIEH

Once a sleepy little village on a magnificent bay, Jounieh, 21 km north of Beirut, is today a modern resort and playground full of high-rise buildings, restaurants, shops and nightclubs. Only the old part of town is of interest, as it has retained some of its previous charm. It is centred around Rue Mina, a narrow street along the bay. You get glimpses of the water between the beach resorts (entry fees LL 8000 to LL 10,000) that line Rue Mina. The telephone code for Jounieh is 09.

Casino de Liban

This famous casino at the north end of the bay has reopened with enormous fanfare. It is a huge complex full of glitter, dancing girls, restaurants and, of course, gambling.

Activities

There's a cable car (*téléphérique*) from Jounieh up to the mountain-top Basilica of Our Lady of Lebanon. The views are quite breathtaking and the return ride costs LL 6000/4500/3500 for adults/students/children. It operates every day except Monday from 9.30 am till sunset; and till 12.30 am between July and October. The *Téléphérique Restaurant* at the top offers nightly entertain-

ment, mezzes and grills for US$15 per person.

Places to Stay & Eat

Hotel St-Joseph (☎ 931 189), on Rue Mina about 50m north of the municipality building, is really a pension charging US$10 per person in single/double rooms with shower and toilet. It's a lovely old house with high vaulted ceilings and 12 spacious rooms and there's a common lounge, kitchen and terrace overlooking the bay on one side and Rue Mina on the other.

The hotel is above *Le Relais* (☎ 830 144), a good-value restaurant/pizzeria with takeaway service. Medium/large pizzas cost from US$3 to US$6; plats du jour of meat, chicken or fish cooked with rice are between US$2 and US$5.25; it has a wide selection of dips, burgers and sandwiches at about US$2. Le Relais is open all week from 11 am to midnight and has a good collection of red wines. We recommend this place.

Another good eatery in Jounieh is *La Crêperie* (☎ 912 491), where you can have a selection of savoury and sweet crepes at reasonable prices (US$6 on average). It's in an old Lebanese house set on a cliff with a magnificent view of Jounieh's bay. It's just before Jounieh's centre on the old Jounieh road.

Otherwise there are several sandwich bars with the standard variety of shwarma, felafel, cheese, meat, chicken etc.

Getting There & Away

Service taxis to Jounieh leave from the Dawra or Museum stands in Beirut. The fare is LL 2500.

North of Beirut

BYBLOS

History

The ancient city of Byblos (biblical Gebal, modern Jbail), with its picturesque port and impressive ruins, is one of the oldest continuously inhabited cities in the world.

Excavations have shown that Byblos was inhabited during the Neolithic period 7000 years ago. In the 3rd millennium BC it became the most important trading port in the area and sent cedar wood and oil to Egypt in exchange for gold, alabaster, papyrus rolls and linen. It continued to be the major Phoenician centre until the 10th century BC, and developed an alphabetic phonetic script which was the precursor of modern alphabets.

The Greeks called Gebal Byblos after the Greek word for papyrus, *bublos*, because papyrus was shipped from Egypt to Greece via the Phoenician port. A collection of sheets were called *biblion*, or book, and from the Greek *ta b blia*, or 'the books', the English word 'Bible' was derived.

As of the 1st millennium BC, Byblos suffered successive invasions, from the Persians to Alexander the Great, the Romans, the Byzantines, the Arabs and, finally, the Crusaders, who built a castle and moat using the large stones and granite columns of the Roman temples. Following the Crusaders' departure Byblos fell into obscurity.

Orientation & Information

The town itself stretches from just outside the perimeter of the ruins to the old port which is sheltered by a craggy headland. A hotel and restaurants are clustered around the port. Opposite the entrance to the ruins are more restaurants and sandwich bars and a few souqs full of souvenir shops.

The telephone code for Byblos is 09.

Ruins

The site is entered through the remains of the Crusader castle which dominates the city's medieval ramparts. Around the site are remains of huts from the 5th millennium BC, the temple of Baalat Gebal (the Lady of Byblos) from 2800 BC, an L-shaped temple from 2700 BC, two royal tombs and the Obelisk temple from the early 2nd millennium BC, and a colonnade, a nymph's shrine and an amphitheatre from the Roman period.

The site is open all year round from 8 am to sunset and entrance is LL 2000 to LL 4000. If you want a guide the gatekeeper can arrange one who speaks English, French, German, Italian or Japanese.

Wax Museum & St John Church

The Wax Museum (☎ 940 463) is on the road to the port, opposite the Maison Paroissal Monastery. It portrays the history and culture of Lebanon through the ages in a series of rather bizarre and sometimes creepy tableaus. The traditional costumes worn by the figures are quite impressive and it is worth a short visit. It's open all year round from 9 am to 6 pm and costs LL 5000 for adults, with a reduction for students.

Near the monastery is the St John Church, a cathedral with three apses built by the Crusaders.

Boat Rides

Down by the old port the fishers take visitors on 15 minute rides in their small boats for LL 4000 per person from spring till autumn.

Places to Stay

Camping About three km north of Byblos is *Camping Amchit Les Colombes* (☎ 940 322, 943 782), a lush camping ground on a promontory overlooking the sea with a capacity for 1500 people. It's fully self-contained and has all necessary amenities, including hot-water showers, toilets (with facilities for handicapped people), kitchen with gas burners, electrical points for caravans (220V), telephone, mail and poste restante service. The owner/manager, François, is extremely friendly and helpful and will provide you with tourist information, change money and arrange cheap transport and tours.

A camp site costs US$3 per person (half price for children); a tent costs US$1 plus 50c for a sleeping bag. In addition to tent and caravan sites, it also rents out fully furnished chalets for US$20 and 'tungalows' (François' invention – a bungalow in the shape of a tent with two beds and toilet) also for US$20. Each tungalow comes with a hammock.

The camping ground is set on a wooded cliff-top with steps down to its own rocky beach. There is a cheap restaurant (see Places to Eat) as well as sports facilities. It's highly recommended and has a great atmosphere as well as weekly beach parties. You can get there by service taxi from Byblos (LL 1000) or Beirut (LL 4000).

Hotels In Byblos the *Ahiram Hotel* (☎ 941 540, 944 726), on the beach just north of town, is reasonable at US$40/55/65 a single/double/triple with breakfast. The price can be negotiated if there are a few of you. It has 30 rooms and there's a beach where hotel residents can swim.

Places to Eat
If you stay at the Amchit camping ground you can get good, cheap meals there (breakfast from US$1.50, lunch or dinner from US$2 to US$4). In Byblos, there are a few cheap takeaways around the town square. Most of the restaurants and cafes around the old port and near the ruins tend to be rather smart and on the expensive side. *El Molino*, down by the port, has meals ranging from US$5 to US$10, including hamburgers for US$5. It's closed on Monday. Near the entrance to the ruins *Abi-Chemou* (☎ 940 484) has a cafe downstairs and a restaurant upstairs where a lunch of mezze, a grill, fruit and coffee will set you back US$10. The owner is quite friendly and may be able to arrange cheap accommodation.

Getting There & Away
The service-taxi stand is at the town's main square. A service taxi to Beirut or Tripoli costs LL 4000.

THE COAST ROAD
Between Byblos and Tripoli are a number of places of interest. At **Amchit** there is an unspoiled collection of 19th century silk merchants' houses, mostly still privately occupied, plus the tomb of Henriette Renan, sister of the famous French writer.

Further north is the town of **Batroûn** with its natural sea wall and atmospheric fishing harbour. A few km past the town, on the new highway, is the fairytale castle of **Moussalya** perched on a pinnacle of rock and visible from the road. The small town of **Enfe** has a couple of notable Byzantine churches and **El Qalamoun** is the place to go if you are interested in copper. The town is full of workshops and souqs selling all kinds of copperware. You can ask to be dropped off at any of these places if you get a service taxi doing the Beirut-Tripoli run. Often you will have to walk the short distance from the highway into the towns.

TRIPOLI (TRABLOUS)
Tripoli (Trablous), 86 km north of Beirut, is Lebanon's second-largest city and the main port and trading centre for northern Lebanon. It gets its name from the Greek word *tripolis* because the city had three parts in ancient times, though there are no remains of Tripoli's Phoenician past.

The Crusaders left their mark in the St-Gilles Citadel which towers over the city, but it's the city's medieval history and (sometimes intact) Mamluk architecture which make it a fascinating place to visit.

Although Tripoli had its share of fighting during the Lebanese war, it was not as badly damaged as Beirut. It has retained the charm of a Middle Eastern city, with its narrow alleys, souqs, slow pace, and especially its friendly and hospitable people.

Tripoli is also famous as the sweets capital of Lebanon, and any trip to the city is not complete without a visit to one of its Arabic sweet shops. The main speciality is *halawet el-jibn*, a delicious sweet made from cheese and served with syrup.

History
Like other Phoenician cities along the eastern Mediterranean coast, Tripoli (ancient Arados) had a succession of invaders from the Romans to the Persians and Byzantines. After its occupation by the Arabs in the 7th century AD, it again became an important trading centre. Then in the 12th century it fell

to the Crusaders, led by Raymond de St-Gilles who built the citadel overlooking the city. The Crusaders remained there for 180 years, until the city was captured by the Mamluks in 1289. The old city, built around the base of the citadel, dates back to this era.

Orientation & Information

The layout of Tripoli is a bit confusing but you can get a free, if somewhat ancient, copy of a tourist map from the Tourist Information Office (☎ 433 590). (The map marks the main monuments by number, and these numbers can be found on plaques on the buildings.) The Tourist Information Office is on the first main roundabout as you enter Tripoli from Beirut – there's an 'Allah' sign in the middle.

There are two main parts to Tripoli: Al-Mina (the port area), which juts out into the sea; and the city proper, which includes modern Tripoli and the old medina. The centre is at Sahet et-Tall (pronounced et-tahl), a large square by the clock tower and municipality building where you'll find the service-taxi and bus stands, cheap eateries and hotels. (This is where you'll be dropped off when arriving by public transport in Tripoli.)

The old city sprawls east of the Sahet et-Tall, while the modern centre is west of the square, along Rue Fouad Chehab. On this street there are banks, moneychangers, travel agencies, bookshops, pharmacies etc.

Between Rue Fouad Chehab and Al-Mina are broad avenues with residential buildings. In Al-Mina, which is also an older part of the city, you'll find more hotels, restaurants and cafes, banks, moneychangers etc.

There are two post offices, the main one on Rue Fouad Chehab near the Bank of Lebanon building, and a branch in Al-Mina on Rue Ibn Sina.

Tripoli's telephone code is 06.

The Old City

The old city, which dates from the Mamluk era (14th and 15th centuries), is a maze of narrow alleys, colourful souqs, hammams, khans (courtyard inns), mosques, and theo-logical schools (madrassas). Although parts of it were damaged during the Lebanese war (at the time of writing, some sites were being renovated while others were closed), it's a very lively place where craftspeople, including tailors and coppersmiths, continue their work in this city as they have done since the 14th century. Among the highlights of Islamic architecture are the **Taynal Mosque** (built in 1336), with its magnificent inner portal; the **Al-Qartawiya Madrassa** (1316-1326) with its facade of alternate black and white facings and honeycomb pattern above the portal; and the **Al-Burtasiya Mosque & Madrassa** (1310) with its intricate mihrab.

St-Gilles Citadel

Towering above Tripoli the citadel was originally built in 1103-4 by the Frankish Crusader Raymond de St-Gilles. It was badly burned in the 13th century, and partly rebuilt in the 14th century by a Mamluk emir. Since then it has been altered many times. However, it's an imposing monument of basalt and limestone, with vaulted rooms, iron gates, courtyards and a baptismal font.

Lion Tower

The Lion Tower is the only surviving example of several towers that were built by the Mamluks along the coast to protect the city. It dates back to the 15th century and is an imposing, impregnable square structure but with numerous decorative elements adorning its entrance. It's near the port in the Al-Mina district, not far from the old railway terminus.

Boat Trips

There are several offshore islands which can be reached from Al-Mina port. The return trip takes two hours, with time for a swim, and costs LL 5000 per person, or you can hire a whole boat (10-12 persons) for LL 50,000. The three far islands are a nature reserve and you need a permit from the Tripoli Tourism Office to visit.

Places to Stay

The cheapest place in town is the rather

basic, family-run *Les Cedres*, which is on Rue Tall near the taxi stand. Rooms with shared bath cost US$6 to US$7.

The *Tall Hotel* (☎ 628 407), on Rue Tall, is a clean hotel charging US$10 per person in single/double/triple rooms with hot-water shower and toilet. It's at the other end of the Rue Tall from the square, opposite the Al-Masri exchange booth and Bijouterie Tahan (jewellery shop).

Also on Rue Tall and overlooking the square is the *Palace* (☎ 432 257), which charges US$10 per person in doubles with shared bath and US$15/25/30 in singles/doubles/triples with private bathroom and air-con. It's in a beautiful old building with high ceilings and stained-glass windows.

In Al-Mina, the *Hotel Hayek* (☎ 601 311, 602 198) has 12 rooms with sea views at US$20/30 for doubles/triples with shared bath and complimentary tea or coffee. It's a pink building on Rue ibn Sina (opposite the post office), and there's Supermarket Hayek on the ground floor. The entrance is from the back; ask at the supermarket.

Also in Al-Mina, the *Qasr el-Sultan* (Sultan's Palace; ☎ 601 627, 611 640) is more expensive at US$36/46 for singles/doubles with bath and breakfast. All rooms have a TV, minibar and air-con. There's a restaurant on the 1st floor. It's right on the Corniche, on the corner of Rue ibn Sina and Rue el-Meshti.

Places to Eat

There are lots of cheap places to eat around Sahet et-Tall, where you can get a plate of fuul or houmos for LL 1500, felafel sandwiches for LL 500 and other sandwiches for LL 1000 to LL 1300. Al-Mina is also a good area to find cheap eats.

Getting There & Away

The service-taxi stand is at Sahet et-Tall. Service taxis to Beirut charge LL 5000. Tripoli is a good place from which to visit Bcharré, Khalil Gibran's birthplace and the site of his museum, and The Cedars. Service taxis to Bcharré charge LL 6000, to The Cedars LL 10,000.

Syria Service taxis to Homs in northern Syria charge LL 8000. They leave when full from Sahet et-Tall.

Getting Around

Service taxis in Tripoli cost LL 500.

BCHARRÉ & THE CEDARS

The trip to Bcharré and The Cedars takes you through some of the most beautiful scenery in Lebanon. The road winds along the mountainous slopes, continuously gaining in altitude and offering spectacular views of gorges. Villages of red-tile roofed houses perch atop hills or cling precariously to the mountainsides. Olive groves and vineyards, lush valleys and mountain peaks rise higher and higher behind every road turn.

Gibran Museum

One of the highlights along this route is the Gibran Museum in the village of Bcharré, the birthplace of the author/artist Gibran Khalil Gibran (1883-1931; better known as Kahlil Gibran) whose most famous work is *The Prophet*. According to his wishes Gibran, who had emigrated to the USA in the 19th century, was buried in an old monastery built into the rocky slopes of a hill overlooking Bcharré. The Gibran Museum, set up in this monastery, houses a large collection of Gibran's oil paintings, drawings and gouaches, and manuscripts. His coffin is in the monastery's former chapel, which is cut straight into the rock. In the same room is his bed, a table and chair and other personal objects, and a 12th century tapestry of Christ on the cross, which Gibran was particularly fond of because it depicted a smiling Christ.

The museum is open Tuesday to Sunday from 9 am to 4 pm and admission is LL 1000.

Cedars of Bcharré

From Bcharré the road climbs up some 400m along a tortuous road until it reaches the last remaining forest of biblical cedars in Lebanon. Known locally as *arz ar-rab* (God's cedars), they are on the slopes of Mt Makmal at an altitude of more than 2000m. It's a small forest as the cedar tree, which once covered most of Lebanon's high summits, has been overexploited throughout the centuries. The site is classified as a national monument as some of these cedars go back more than 1500 years. The Phoenicians exported cedar wood to the Egyptians, who considered it as the sacred wood of the gods, and to Solomon to build his temple.

Skiing

The Cedars region is a prime ski resort in winter for both downhill and cross-country skiing. There are ski-hire shops and accommodation in the village below the forest.

The Kadisha Gorge

Below the town of Bcharré is the spectacular gorge which has the tombs of the early Maronite patriarchs. There are also rock-cut monasteries and retreats. The gorge is a hiker's paradise. You can either walk down the side of the gorge along cut paths or drive to the bottom and then walk along the bottom. Allow a few hours for the walk and take a water bottle.

Places to Stay & Eat

The *Palace Hotel* (☎ (06) 671 460) is just below the main road to Bcharré, about 200m before the village square. It charges US$20/25 for singles/doubles with bathroom, hot water and heating. The hotel has a restaurant where meals range from US$3 to US$8.

A bit more expensive is the *Hotel Chbat* (☎ (06) 671 237/671 230) at US$65/78 for singles/doubles (but ask for a 15% discount). The hotel has a great, homely atmosphere and terrific views over the gorge.

Getting There & Away

From Tripoli service taxis charge LL 5000 to Bcharré or LL 10,000 to The Cedars. Out of the ski season you will probably only get a service taxi as far as Bcharré and then have to take a taxi for about US$5.

South of Beirut

Travelling south of Beirut is OK all the way to Tyre (Sour), 80 km south of the capital, and all over the Chouf Mountains, south-east of Beirut. East and south of Sour the area is under UNIFIL control and is often subject to Israeli shelling, and past UNIFIL's area the border strip is under Israeli control and is out of bounds for visitors – Lebanese and foreigners alike.

Cheap accommodation is hard to come by in areas south of Beirut; fortunately most of the places of interest can be visited on day trips from Beirut.

SIDON

Sidon (Saida) is a small port city, set amid citrus orchards and banana groves, 41 km south of Beirut. It's a very old settlement, going back 4000 years, and once was a prominent and wealthy Phoenician city. Like other Phoenician capitals, Saida was built on a promontory facing an island to shelter its fleet. It had a succession of invaders, from the Persians to the Assyrians, Alexander the Great, the Romans, the Byzantines, the Arabs, the Crusaders and then the Mamluk Muslims. It was destroyed twice by wars between the 7th and 4th centuries BC, and by an earthquake in the 6th century AD, and few remains of the ancient city survived. But it has a particularly good Crusader castle and fine examples of Muslim architecture in its mosques, khans and a maze of vaulted souqs.

Saida is famous for orange-blossom water and a sort of crumbly biscuit called *sanioura* which is delicious.

Orientation & Information

The centre of town is around Sahet en-Nejmeh (En-Nejmeh Square), where you'll find cheap eateries, the bus and service taxi-stations, the municipality building and the police station. Rue Riad Solh, which runs south off Sahet en-Nejmeh (in reality a huge roundabout), has restaurants, banks, money-changers, shops, travel agencies etc. The old city, the harbour and the Sea Castle are west of Sahet en-Nejmeh and Rue Riad Solh, while the modern shopping centres and residential buildings are on the eastern side.

The telephone code for Sidon is 07.

The Old City

Old Sidon is behind the buildings fronting the harbour, just across the wharf. It's a fascinating maze of **vaulted souqs**, tiny alleyways and old buildings dating back to the Middle Ages when most inhabitants lived in the area between the city walls and the harbour. It's a bit difficult to find your way around it, especially if there is no electricity to light up the dark alleys, as was the case when we visited. However, you'll be surrounded by young people who will tag along and they're quite helpful in showing you around (they'll expect a small tip, though).

In the souqs you'll find shops selling everything from spices to fish and vegetables and you'll see the craftspeople at work. There's also the **Khan el-Franj** (Inn of the Foreigners), which consists of vaulted galleries surrounding a large rectangular courtyard with a central fountain. It was built with limestone during the reign of Fakhreddine II in the 17th century to accommodate foreign merchants and promote contact with Europe and has now undergone extensive restoration.

Further inside the old city is the **Great Mosque**, a beautiful mosque with vaulted prayer areas surrounding a central courtyard. It replaced a church built by the Crusaders and its outer walls date back to the 13th century. Visitors wishing to enter the mosque must be modestly dressed and women should cover their hair.

Sea Castle

Built by the Crusaders in the early 13th century, the Sea Castle (Qasr el-Bahr) sits on a small island which was formerly the site of a temple to Melkart, the Phoenician Hercules. It is connected to the mainland by an Arab fortified stone bridge (of a later date). It was one of many coastal castles built by the Crusaders for protection and, like

many others, was destroyed by the Mamluks to prevent the Crusaders from returning to the region.

However, it is still in a fair state of preservation and it consists chiefly of two towers connected by a wall – the west tower is better preserved than the east tower which has lost its top floor. Roman shaft columns used as transverse trusses support the outside walls, and there are two cisterns in the castle's basement.

It's open all year round from 9 am to 6 pm and entrance costs LL 2000.

Echmoun

About two km north of Sidon is the site of Echmoun, a Phoenician temple site which is well worth a visit. The cult of Echmoun is similar to the Adonis story and the temples clearly catered for plenty of worshippers, as the row of ancient shops testifies. The highlight of the site is the throne of Astarte guarded by winged lions. It is possible to walk to the site from town through lanes lined with fruit farms. The walk back to the highway follows the river, and when you hit the highway you can catch a service taxi.

Places to Stay & Eat

The *Nazel ash-Sharq* (Oriental Hotel; ☎ 720 364) is the only cheap place to stay in Sidon. It's really basic with six rooms and one bathroom with cold water only, and the price is US$10 per room for either one or two people. Hot water is extra. It's above a baggage shop on Rue Shakrieh, not far from the Muslim cemetery in the old city. (It's a bit hard to find so look out for a sign on the balcony with the words 'Hotel de L'Orient'.)

There are lots of sandwich stalls and cheap cafes around Sahet en-Nejmeh and the harbour. For a bit of a splurge at a reasonable price (US$5 to US$10) go to the restaurant of the government-run *resthouse* on the seafront opposite the Sea Castle. The food is good and it has a variety of dips, grills, fish and alcoholic beverages. It's built in the traditional Arab style and is worth visiting even if you don't plan to eat there.

Getting There & Away

The bus and service-taxi stands are on Sahet en-Nejmeh. Service taxis charge LL 2000 to Beirut and LL 2000 to Tyre (Sour). Buses are cheaper (LL 1000) but they also wait until they are full to depart so it's quicker to go by service taxi.

TYRE

Ancient Tyre (Sour) was founded by the Phoenicians in the 3rd millennium BC. It originally consisted of a mainland settlement and an island city just off the shore, but these were joined in the 4th century BC by a causeway which converted the island permanently into a peninsula. Its most famous king was Hiram; it was to him that Solomon appealed for cedars to build the temple of Jerusalem and his palace.

History

For a long time, Tyre had a flourishing maritime trade and, with colonies in Sicily and North Africa, was responsible for Phoenician expansion in the west. It was also famous for its purple dye and glass industries.

Tyre suffered successive invasions that left their mark, and excavations have revealed remains of Crusader, Arab, Byzantine and Graeco-Roman cities. It withstood a 13 year siege by Nebuchadnezzar II, King of Babylon, in the early 6th century BC and in the 4th century BC was besieged for seven months by Alexander the Great, who finally stormed the city. In 68 BC it came under Roman rule and by the 2nd century AD had a large Christian population. The Muslims then ruled it from the 7th to the 12th century, when it became part of the Kingdom of Jerusalem under the Crusaders, to be destroyed by the Muslim Mamluks in 1291.

Tyre's most famous site is the remains of the Roman city, but recently a Phoenician children's cemetery, the first ever found in Lebanon, was discovered by accident.

Orientation & Information

The old part of Tyre is on the peninsula jutting out into the sea and covers a relatively small area. The modern town is on the left-hand side as you arrive from Beirut. The coastal route goes all the way to Tyre's picturesque old port, around which are a few cafes and restaurants. Behind the port is the Christian quarter, with tiny alleys and old houses behind shaded courtyards, and a fine church inside the Maronite Patriarchate.

To the left of the port the road forks southward and goes around the excavation site of the Roman ruins. There are three streets running parallel between the northern and southern coastal roads, and that's where you'll find banks, moneychangers, sandwich stalls, travel agencies and the souq.

Tyre's telephone code is 07.

Roman Ruins

Inside the excavation site there's a well-preserved Roman road leading to the ancient settlement, made of big blocks of paving stones. The road stretches in a straight line for about 1.6 km, passing through a monumental archway. It is lined on one side by an aqueduct, and on both sides there are hundreds of ornate stone and marble sarcophagi of the Roman and Byzantine periods. The sarcophagi are intricately carved with the names of the occupants or reliefs drawn from the *Iliad*. There are also the remains of a large civic building, baths and a theatre.

Outside the excavation site, about one km back towards the modern town, there's a Roman hippodrome. The U-shaped hippodrome, built in the 2nd century AD for chariot racing, was one of the largest of the Roman period with a capacity for more than 20,000 spectators.

Places to Stay & Eat

The only place to stay in Tyre is the *Hotel Alisar* (☎ 741 267/8), on the southern side of the peninsula. It has single/doubles with bath for US$35/50 including breakfast. The hotel is nondescript but it's clean and there's a restaurant on the 1st floor where you can get a filling meal for US$5 and a beer for about US$1.70. Otherwise there are the restaurants on the port where you can eat grilled meat or chicken for about US$5, fish at a much higher price or the standard sandwich fare.

Getting There & Away

The service taxi-stand is about 50m before the port on the northern coastal road. Service taxis to Beirut cost LL 4000, to Sidon (Saida) LL 2000.

THE CHOUF MOUNTAINS

The Chouf Mountains, just south-east of Beirut, are the southern part of the Mt Lebanon range. Like their northern counterparts, they're spectacularly beautiful with narrow gorges, lush green valleys, fountains and springs, rivers and waterfalls, and cultivated, terraced mountainsides.

Unlike their northern counterparts, however, they're sparsely populated as many of the inhabitants fled following the Israeli invasion of 1982 and the fighting that broke out in the Chouf in the wake of the Israelis' departure.

At the time of writing, budget accommodation was practically nonexistent in the area. However, all the sites of interest can be visited in day trips from Beirut.

Palace of Beiteddine

The main attraction of the Chouf Mountains is the Palace of Beiteddine, 45 km south-east of Beirut. Sitting majestically atop a terraced hill and surrounded by gardens, the palace was built by Emir Beshir al-Chehabi II in the first half of the 19th century. After WWI the palace was used by the French Mandatory Authorities for local administration. When Lebanon became independent in 1943, the palace became the summer residence of the president. Following the Mountain War in 1983, the palace came under the control of the Druze militias who have transformed it into a museum and cultural centre, renaming it the Palace of the People.

Although conceived by Italian architects, the palace incorporates all the traditional forms of Lebanese architecture. The gate opens onto a vast, 60m courtyard walled on three sides only; the fourth side looks out over valleys and hills. A double staircase on the western side leads into the inner court, which consists of a smaller courtyard with a central fountain bordered by buildings on three sides only. Beyond this court is the Dar el-Harim, or women's quarters, with a beautiful hammam. All the buildings have arcades along their facades.

The main court houses a couple of museums and a craft shop. In July and August there is an arts festival. The inner court and Dar el-Harim contain vast, vaulted rooms decorated and paved with multi-coloured marble or mosaics and richly decorated doorways with exquisite calligraphic inscriptions. The former stables display a collection of Byzantine mosaic floors dating back to the 5th and 6th centuries from Jiyyeh, 30 km south of Beirut.

The palace is open every day except Monday from 8.30 am to 6 pm. Admission is LL 1000 and there are multilingual brochures for LL 2000.

Other Attractions

Further up the hill and overlooking the village of Beiteddine is the **Mir Amin Palace** (a smaller version of the Beiteddine Palace), which belonged to the son of Emir Beshir. It is now a 1st class luxury hotel with 24 rooms, a swimming pool and spectacular views over the hills and valleys. It's worth stopping there for a drink.

The picturesque town of **Deir el-Qamar**, five km from Beiteddine on the way to Beirut, was the seat of Lebanon's emirate during the 17th and 18th centuries. The town square has some fine examples of Arab architecture including a mosque built in 1493. There are a few sandwich stalls around the square.

Another five km on the way to Beirut is the village of Kfar Him which has a small natural **grotto** with stalactites and stalagmites. It is open all week from 7 am to 7 pm and admission is LL 2500. There's a souvenir shop there where you can buy slide film.

Places to Stay & Eat

Staying overnight is not really an option as the few hotels around the area are in the top-end bracket. The cheapest option is the nondescript **Rif Hotel** (☎ (05) 501680), where double rooms with bath cost US$40. It's in the village of Samqaniye, about three km south-east of Beiteddine on the road to Moukhtara.

You'll find sandwich stalls (shwarma, chicken, cheese, etc) in most of the villages and restaurants (mezzes and grills) in the bigger towns. Among the nicer ones is the *Nabeh Mershed* restaurant (☎ (05) 500221), located by a spring *(nabeh)*. It's reasonably priced with mezzes for US$1.25 to US$3 and grills starting from US$3. It's just past the village of Moukhtara, some eight km from Beiteddine.

Getting There & Away

The best way to visit the Chouf Mountains is by car. If there's a few of you travelling, you could hire a taxi from Beirut for the day (US$80); otherwise there are service taxis from the Cola stand to different towns in the Chouf. The fare is from LL 2000 to LL 4000, depending on where you want to be dropped off. You can get off at the places you want to see along the way and then catch service taxis to your next destination, though on certain stretches you may have to wait a while.

The Bekaa Valley

There are two fascinating sites to visit in the Bekaa Valley, the fertile plain that separates the Mt Lebanon and Anti-Lebanon ranges. One is Baalbek, or ancient Heliopolis, with its monumental Roman ruins of gigantic proportions, and the other is Aanjar, where a whole Muslim Umayyad (Omayyad) town was uncovered in the early 1950s.

The Bekaa Valley is reached via the Damascus Highway, which goes through several towns and villages in the Mt Lebanon range. This area was the scene of heavy fighting during the war and you'll see a lot of destruction along the way, especially in Aley, Bhamdoun and Sofar. There are also lots of Lebanese and Syrian army check-points along this route.

Chtaura

The first town in the Bekaa Valley is Chtaura, a main stopover halfway between Beirut and Damascus and the transport hub of the different sites around the valley. It's full of cheap eateries along the main road going through town, and if you want to stay there, the *Hotel Khater* (☎ (08) 840 133), opposite the police station, has singles/doubles/triples (some with private bath) for US$10 per person. It's above a restaurant of the same name. Service taxis from Beirut to Chtaura charge LL 5000.

Zahlé

The other major town in the Bekaa is Zahlé, about seven km north-east of Chtaura. It's a picturesque town nestled along the slopes of a narrow valley and is famous for its river-bank cafes and restaurants specialising in mezzes and grills. A typical meal at one of those place would set you back about US$12, but it's well worth the experience. To get there, take a service taxi from Chtaura (LL 1500) which will drop you in the town centre; from there it's a 15 minute walk to Nahr Birdawni. The telephone code for Zahlé is 08.

Places to Stay There are a few cheapish hotels in Zahlé. On Rue Brazil there is the modest *Hotel de L'Amerique* (☎ 820 635) with rooms for US$10/20. The pick of the cheaper hotels is the *Hotel Akl* (☎ 820 701) which is clean, family run and very much recommended. It costs US$15 per person but is worth it.

BAALBEK

Baalbek, 86 km north-east of Beirut, was originally named after the Phoenician god Baal. The Greeks later called it Heliopolis, or City of the Sun, and the Romans made it a major worship site for their god Jupiter. The modern town is small and centres around a tiny square east of the Roman temples; it's very easy to get around.

Roman Ruins

Baalbek's acropolis is one of the largest in the world. The complex is about 300m long and has two temples with porticoes, two courtyards and an enclosure built during the Arab period. The Temple of Jupiter, completed around 60 AD, is on a high platform at the top of a monumental staircase; only six of its colossal columns (22m high) remain, giving an idea of the vast scale of the original building. The nearby Temple of Bacchus, built around 150 AD, is relatively well preserved except for its roof. Outside the acropolis stands the Temple of Venus. The site is open daily from 8 am to 6 pm and entry is LL 2500.

Outside the site you can go for a short camel ride for LL 2000.

Places to Stay & Eat

The *Ash-Shams Hotel* (no telephone) is a clean little place run by a tailor on Rue Abdel Halim Hajjar. It has four rooms (with washbasins) that sleep up to four people for LL 5000 per person. There's a shared toilet and hot-water shower. It's on the 1st floor.

Otherwise, *the* place to stay in Baalbek is at the *Palmyra Hotel* (☎ (08) 870 230), opposite the ruins on the right-hand side of the road just before Baalbek. It's a beautiful 117 year old building set in shady gardens with singles/doubles with bath for US$28/35. The hotel has a bar and reasonably priced restaurant, but when we were there we were not impressed with the quality of the food.

There are lots of cheap eateries on Rue Abdel Halim Hajjar where you can get a plate of fuul or houmos and sandwiches for

LL 1250. Baalbek's speciality is lahm bi ajin (meat pizza; LL 1200).

Getting There & Away

The service taxis stop just around the corner from Rue Abdel Halim Hajjar. They charge LL 7000 to Beirut, LL 3000 to Chtaura, LL 2000 to Zahlé and LL 8000 to Damascus.

AANJAR

This town, uncovered in the early '50s, is the only Umayyad site in Lebanon and remains a mystery as nothing is known about its history or why it was built in the Bekaa Valley. Parts of it have been reconstructed by the Department of Antiquities but the work was interrupted during the war. However, there's enough here to give an idea of this unusual place that was built in a symmetrical style reminiscent of Roman tradition.

The town is enclosed within four protective walls that form an almost perfect square, with an imposing gate set halfway within each wall and circular towers at intervals reinforcing the walls. There are two 20m wide avenues connecting the gates and a tetrastyle where these avenues meet at right angles, dividing the town into four blocks. Along both sides of the avenues are arcades with numerous shops. The blocks contained two palaces (one has been partially reconstructed), mosques, baths, an enclosure for livestock and residences.

Getting There & Away

You can catch a service taxi from Chtaura which will drop you at the turn-off, leaving you with a two km walk. Alternatively hire a taxi to take you to the site, wait and return for about US$10.

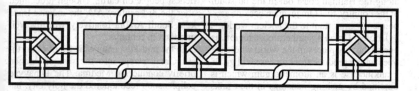

Oman

In contrast to the vast desert wasteland of Saudi Arabia or the tiny city-states of the Gulf, Oman is a land of dramatic mountains and long, unspoiled beaches. Its capital, Muscat, does not have the nouveau-riche feel that typifies much of the Gulf.

Tourism is still a new concept for the Omanis and the country has taken a cautious approach to its development. Oman remains one of the most traditional countries in the Middle East though, at least on the coast, its traditions are often more outward looking than it's given credit for.

Facts about the Country

HISTORY

As in much of the rest of Arabia, the earliest known settlements in Oman date from the 3rd millennium BC. In that era an empire known as Magan developed along the Batinah, Oman's northern coast, exploiting the rich veins of copper found in the hills around Sohar. Magan dominated the ancient world's copper trade, supplying the precious metal to the powerful kingdoms of Elam (in modern-day southern Iran) and Sumer, both of which used it to make weapons and neither of which possessed any copper deposits of their own.

The region's economy declined over the centuries and sometime around 563 BC northern Oman was incorporated into the Persian Achaemenian Empire. It was not until long after Magan's glory days, and not along the Batinah coast but in the far south of the country, that Oman again became economically important to the ancient world.

Dhofar, Oman's southernmost region, is one of the few places in the world where the trees which produce frankincense will grow. Frankincense is an aromatic gum which is obtained by making incisions in the trunks

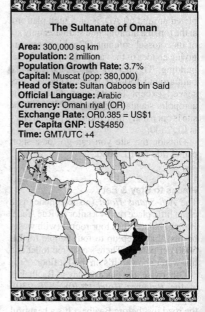

⛧⛧⛧⛧⛧⛧⛧⛧⛧⛧⛧

The Sultanate of Oman

Area: 300,000 sq km
Population: 2 million
Population Growth Rate: 3.7%
Capital: Muscat (pop: 380,000)
Head of State: Sultan Qaboos bin Said
Official Language: Arabic
Currency: Omani riyal (OR)
Exchange Rate: OR0.385 = US$1
Per Capita GNP: US$4850
Time: GMT/UTC +4

of trees of certain species of the *Boswellia* genus.

The incense has a natural oil content, which means that it burns well. It also has medicinal qualities. This combination, and its relative scarcity, made it one of the most sought-after substances in the ancient world. Pliny, writing in the 1st century AD, claimed that control of the frankincense trade had made the South Arabians the richest people on earth. Though it declined after the 3rd century AD, the incense trade kept South Arabia relatively wealthy well into the 6th century.

In the mid-8th century the tribes of northern Oman swept into the rest of Arabia, briefly conquering Medina. The Umayyad caliphs soon reconquered the holy city, but the revolt undermined their rule, contributing to their subsequent overthrow by the Abbasids. Though defeated, Oman managed to remain relatively free of Abbasid control. Until 1506, when the Portuguese arrived in the Indian Ocean, Omani naval power had few rivals in the area.

The Portuguese occupied Oman for more than a century. In 1622 they made Muscat their main garrison in the region, bringing it to prominence for the first time.

In 1650 Imam Sultan bin Saif expelled the Portuguese. Omani independence is usually dated from this victory, making Oman the oldest independent state in the Arab world.

This victory also marked the beginning of a great expansion. By the end of the 18th century the Omanis ruled a far-flung empire. At its peak in the 19th century, under Sultan Said bin Sultan (reigned 1804-56), Oman controlled both Mombasa and Zanzibar and operated trading posts even further down the African coast. It also controlled portions of what are now India and Pakistan. It was not until 1947 that Oman surrendered its last colonial outpost at Gwadar, in what is now Pakistan.

When Said died the empire was divided between two of his sons. One became the Sultan of Zanzibar, and ruled Said's African colonies, while the other became known as the Sultan of Muscat and Oman – the coast and interior of today's sultanate which were then regarded as two separate realms.

The division of the empire cut Muscat off from some of its most lucrative domains, causing the country to stagnate economically during the late 19th century. The British exacerbated this situation by pressing the sultan to end the trade in slaves and arms for which Oman had long been known. This left the sultan a great deal poorer, and lack of money made the interior difficult to control.

When Sultan Faisal bin Turki died in 1913, the interior's tribes refused to recognise his son and successor as imam. This led to a split between the coastal areas ruled by the sultan and the interior, which came to be controlled by a separate line of imams.

In 1938 a new sultan, Said bin Taimur, came to power. When he sought to extend his writ into the interior in the early '50s the British backed him, largely because they believed that there might be oil there. The imam responded by taking his case to the Arab League in Cairo, where he sought recognition of the interior as a separate state. Said did not gain full control of the country until 1959.

Though he ended the long-running revolt in the interior Said, in many other respects, took Oman backwards. He was opposed to any sort of change and sought to isolate Oman from the modern world. Under his rule, a country which only a century earlier had rivalled the empire-builders of Europe became a medieval anachronism.

In 1958 Said boarded himself up in his palace at Salalah, which he rarely left thereafter. The formation of a nationalist rebel group, the Dhofar Liberation Front (DLF), in 1962 did little to change this. The DLF's battle against the state began in 1965 and was far more serious than Said's earlier clashes with the imamate.

The combination of the ever-escalating rebellion and Said's refusal to spend any of the money which he received from oil exports after 1967 soon began to try even London's patience. In July 1970 Said was overthrown by his only son, Qaboos, in a bloodless palace coup. The British denied any involvement in or advance knowledge of the coup, but this is hard to believe as British officers effectively commanded the army at the time. Said spent the rest of his life living in exile in a London hotel.

Sultan Qaboos bin Said was only 30 years old when he came to power. He promptly repealed his father's oppressive social restrictions and began to modernise Oman's semi-feudal economy.

There was a certain urgency in Qaboos' programme to bring the country into the 20th century. In 1970, when development in much of the rest of the Gulf was already well under way, Oman still had only 10 km of surfaced road (between Muscat and Mutrah). There were only three primary schools in the

OMAN

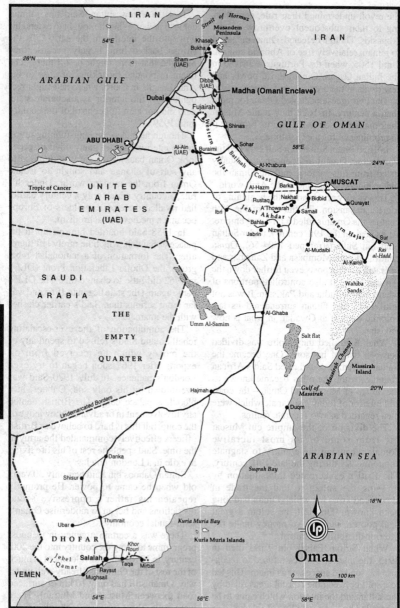

Oman

0   50   100 km

Suggested Itineraries
In Muscat be sure to make time for a trip to the **Mutrah souq** – one of the best traditional markets in the region. The **Sultan's Armed Forces Museum** in the capital's Bait Al-Falaj district and the **Natural History Museum** in Medinat Qaboos are both 'must-see' sites, as are the capital area's three **forts**.

If you have the time and money the best place to visit is the **Musandem peninsula**, home of some of the most dramatic scenery in the Gulf. Other spots worth visiting outside Muscat include the old fortress and the market in **Nizwa** and the fort at **Jabrin** in the north of the country, and **Job's Tomb** just outside of Salalah in the far south. ■

country and no secondary schools. There was one hospital, which was run by US missionaries.

Oman's oil revenues were, and still are, small and its resources limited. Qaboos saw the need to move quickly if the oil wealth was to have any significant effect on his people's lives. He pushed localisation of the workforce much harder than the rulers of the other Gulf countries. Oman, he knew, needed foreign aid and expertise, but it could hardly afford the luxury of the armies of foreign labourers who had built the infrastructure of places like Kuwait.

Despite Qaboos' apparent desire to make a clean break with the past, the Dhofar rebellion continued unabated. It ended only when Oman and South Yemen established diplomatic relations in 1982, and the Aden government cut off its assistance to the rebels.

In foreign affairs Qaboos has carved out a reputation for himself as a maverick. In spite of Oman's past military ties with the Shah, he has managed to maintain friendly relations with post-revolutionary Iran. Oman was also one of only two Arab countries (the other was Sudan) that refused to break diplomatic ties with Egypt after it signed a peace treaty with Israel in 1979. In late 1993 the sultan became the first Gulf leader to welcome a representative of Israel to his country when Prime Minister Yitzhak Rabin paid a brief visit.

GEOGRAPHY

Oman is approximately 300,000 sq km in area. Its territory includes the Musandem peninsula, which is separated from the rest of the country by the east coast of the UAE.

The northern coastal strip, known as the Batinah coast, is a sand and gravel plain separated from the rest of Arabia by the Hajar Mountains. The highest peak in the country is Jebel Akhdar (the 'green mountain') at 2980m. The term Jebel Akhdar, however, generally refers to the entire Hajar range in north-central Oman, rather than to a single peak.

There are also two large areas of salt flats and a sandy desert area, the Wahiba Sands, popular with tourists and expatriates for 4WD trips.

CLIMATE

Oman's varied geography makes for a wide range of climatic conditions. Coconuts are grown in the southern coastal areas while the highlands around Jebel Akhdar produce roses and grapes.

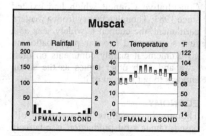

Muscat is hot and very humid from mid-March until October and pleasantly warm from October to March. In the Salalah area, humid weather with temperatures approaching 30°C is common even in December. The Salalah area gets drenched by the monsoon rains every year from June to September.

FLORA & FAUNA

Oman has a fascinating array of animals ranging from various sorts of molluscs to the rare Arabian oryx and the Arabian tahr (a kind of wild goat). An area has been set aside around Ras al-Hadd, the easternmost tip of the Arabian peninsula, as a protected breeding ground for the giant sea turtles which live in the Indian Ocean and come ashore in Oman each year to lay their eggs. The government also runs a breeding centre for endangered species at Bait al-Barakah, west of Muscat.

The same sort of attention has been accorded the country's plant life. The government runs a scheme for protecting coastal areas and there are a number of nature preserves, known as national protected areas, scattered around the country. The most accessible area is the Qurm Public Park & Nature Reserve in Greater Muscat.

GOVERNMENT & POLITICS

The sultan is the ultimate authority. Period. Even relatively minor policy decisions go all the way to his desk before being implemented.

In January 1992 an elected Consultative Council, or *majlis ash-shura*, convened for the first time, replacing an appointed State Consultative Council which had existed since 1981. Though a far cry from a western parliament, the council is widely seen as a first step toward broader participation in government. It mainly comments on draft laws and such other topics as the sultan chooses to put in front of it.

ECONOMY

Though the economy is essentially oil-based, Oman's oil production is relatively modest by Gulf standards. Agriculture in the inland areas and fishing on the coast continue to be important sources of income for much of the population.

The Omani government has been more successful than any other in the region at 'localising' its workforce (ie, replacing foreigners with Omanis wherever possible). It is far more common to see Omanis in service positions or doing manual jobs than it is to see other Gulf Arabs doing similar jobs.

POPULATION & PEOPLE

Oman's population is estimated to be about 2 million. While Omanis are Arabs, the country's long trading history has led to a great deal of mingling and intermarriage of Omani Arabs with other ethnic groups. There has been an Indian merchant community in Muscat for at least 200 years and, in the north, it is common to find people who are at least partly of Persian or Baluchi ancestry.

SOCIETY & CONDUCT
Traditional Lifestyle

Despite the modern appearance of Muscat's Qurm, Al-Khuwair, Ruwi and Medinat Qaboos districts, much of the country, including parts of the capital area, remains intensely traditional.

Dos & Don'ts

Omanis are generous and welcoming to foreigners. However, as Oman has only been open to the outside world for just over 25 years, a degree of caution is required. Taking photographs anywhere in Oman is a sensitive matter and taking pictures of women is almost always unacceptable. In rural areas it is particularly important to dress modestly. Do not drink alcohol in public places. It is offensive to Omani sensibilities and may cause trouble with the police.

Ibadism

Most Omanis follow the Ibadi sect of Islam. The Ibadis are one of the Muslim world's few remaining Kharijite sects, and are a product of Islam's earliest fundamentalist movement. The sect takes its name from a theologian who did most of his important teaching while living in Basra (in today's southern Iraq) during the late 7th century.

Though its origins lie in a very strict interpretation of Islam, modern Ibadism has developed into one of the Muslim world's most tolerant strains. ■

Non-Muslims are not permitted to enter mosques in Oman.

LANGUAGE

Arabic is the official language, though English is widely spoken in business circles. In the northern coastal areas you can find a large number of expatriates from the Indian subcontinent, traders and sailors who speak Fārsī and/or Urdu. Many Omanis who returned from Africa in the early 1970s speak Swahili and in some cases French, languages more common than Arabic in some interior towns.

Facts for the Visitor

PLANNING

When to Go

See the Regional Facts for the Visitor section for general information about when to visit this part of the world. Unusually for the Gulf, southern Oman has a monsoon season, which lasts from June to September, and while you probably do not want to be in Salalah during the rains, it is definitely worth a visit in October when everything in Dhofar is still lush and green.

Maps

The best map is the Bartholomew *Map of the Sultanate of Oman*. It has a light-blue cover with a picture of the Seeb clock tower on one side and palm trees on the other. Unfortunately it is pretty hard to find, and it's even harder to get hold of a copy in English. Also excellent is the National Survey Authority (NSA) 1:1,300,000 scale map printed in May 1994, which includes large scale maps of Muscat and Salalah and can be bought in most of the larger hotel bookshops. The Oxford *Map of Oman*, available in most hotel bookshops in Muscat, is not quite as good but you can navigate well enough with it. When using any of these maps remember that many of the roads shown as 'projected' have now been built.

What to Bring

See the Regional Facts for the Visitor section.

VISAS & DOCUMENTS

Visas

Unless you are a citizen of another Gulf country you need a visa to enter Oman. It is generally possible for citizens of western countries (North America, Western and Central Europe, Japan, Australia, New Zealand, etc) to obtain business and tourist visas at most Omani embassies overseas. Getting a visa is easiest if you apply in your home country.

You will need to produce several (probably four) photographs and fill out two or three copies of the application. Showing an onward or return ticket does not appear to be a requirement, though travellers are sometimes asked to produce these. Costs will vary according to your nationality, but the standard two year multiple-entry tourist visa generally will set you back around US$35 to US$40. These visas usually allow you to remain in the country for up to six months at a time. Processing a visa usually takes between three and six working days.

When filling out the visa application pay careful attention to the section asking where you plan to enter Oman. You are not bound to the entry point or points you declare here, but if you check only Seeb airport there is the possibility that you will receive a visa allowing entry and exit by air only. Tourist visas are valid for entry through any border post unless they specify otherwise.

If you don't carry a western passport or are not conveniently close to an Omani embassy it is possible to obtain a visa through most of the country's four and five-star hotels. Fax the hotel, make a reservation and send it a copy of the part of your passport with your photo and personal data. Be sure to give the hotel your exact arrival details and a contact number so that it can let you know when your visa is ready. This usually takes about a week. The hotel will usually require a three night minimum stay and will add a visa processing fee to your bill.

OMAN

If your passport shows any evidence of travel to Israel you will be denied entry to Oman.

Visa Extensions In theory these are available to tourists and businesspeople through their hotel/sponsor but you are going to have to come up with a good reason why you need it, particularly since most tourist visas issued through Omani embassies allow stays of up to six months.

Other Documents

Site Permits A permit from the Ministry of Culture & National Heritage in Muscat is needed to visit most archaeological sites, old forts, etc. They are issued without fuss at the ministry, which is adjacent to the Natural History Museum in the Ministries Area of Medinat Qaboos. Head for the 2nd floor of the main building and ask for the forts and castles division. The permits are free.

In theory the people in the permit office can also tell you which forts are closed for restoration at any given moment, though in our experience their information on this score is not necessarily up to date.

Road Permits Foreign residents of Oman need a Road Permit to enter or leave the country by land. This regulation does not apply to tourists.

EMBASSIES

Omani Embassies Abroad

Following is a list of some of the Omani embassies abroad.

Bahrain
Diplomatic Area, Al-Fatih Highway (near the National Museum), Manama (☎ 293 663)
Kuwait
Udailia, St 3, Block 3, House 25, by the Fourth Ring Rd (☎ 256 1962)
Qatar
41 Ibn al-Qassem St, Villa 7, Hilal District (fronting on the C Ring Rd), Doha (☎ 670 744)
Saudi Arabia
Al-Ra'id District, Riyadh, behind the petrol station opposite the main gate of King Saud University (☎ (01) 482 3120)

UK
167 Queens Gate, London SW7 5HE (☎ (0171) 589 2840)
USA
2342 Massachusetts Ave, NW, Washington DC, 20000 (☎ (202) 387 1980/1)
866 United Nations Plaza, Suite 540, New York NY (☎ (212) 355 3505)

Foreign Embassies in Oman

Embassies are usually open from Saturday to Wednesday.

Australia
Australian interests are handled by the UK embassy.
Bahrain
Al-Kharjiyah St, just off Way 3015, Medinat Qaboos (☎ 605074, 605133)
Canada
Canadian interests are handled by the UK embassy.
Iran
Jameat A'Duwal al-Arabiya St, Medinat Qaboos Diplomatic Area to the sea side of Sultan Qaboos St, west of the Al-Khuwair roundabout (☎ 696944)
Kuwait
Jameat A'Duwal al-Arabiya St, Medinat Qaboos Diplomatic Area to the sea side of Sultan Qaboos St, west of the Al-Khuwair roundabout (☎ 699626, 699627)
Qatar
Al-Maamoura St, Bait al-Falaj, behind the Al-Falaj Hotel (☎ 701802)
Saudi Arabia
Jameat A'Duwal al-Arabiya St, Medinat Qaboos Diplomatic Area to the sea side of Sultan Qaboos St, west of the Al-Khuwair roundabout (☎ 601744)
UAE
Jameat A'Duwal al-Arabiya St, Medinat Qaboos Diplomatic Area to the sea side of Sultan Qaboos St, west of the Al-Khuwair roundabout (☎ 600302)
UK
Jameat A'Duwal al-Arabiya St, Medinat Qaboos Diplomatic Area to the sea side of Sultan Qaboos St, west of the Al-Khuwair roundabout (☎ 693077)
USA
Jameat A'Duwal al-Arabiya St, Medinat Qaboos Diplomatic Area to the sea side of Sultan Qaboos St, west of the Al-Khuwair roundabout (☎ 698989)

CUSTOMS

Non-Muslims *arriving at Seeb airport* can bring in one bottle of booze. Those arriving by road are not permitted to import alcohol. The customs regulations allow travellers to import a 'reasonable quantity' of cigars, cigarettes and tobacco.

The customs officers are extremely concerned about videotapes and you can expect to have any that you try to import held at customs and scrutinised for several days.

MONEY

Costs

Accommodation is the main barrier to seeing Oman on a budget. Once you get around that problem many other aspects of daily life are quite cheap. Unless you can find a free bed, plan on spending OR15 per day in Muscat and OR20 to OR25 outside the capital. Beds aside, domestic travel and food are very cheap and admission to museums, forts and other places of interest is generally free.

Currency

The Omani riyal (OR) is divided into 1000 baisa (also spelled baizas). Notes come in denominations of 100 and 200 baisa, and OR¼, ½, 1, 5, 10, 20 and 50. Coins are 5, 10, 25, 50 and 100 baisa, though the 25 and 50 baisa coins are the only ones you are likely to see on a regular basis. The riyal is a convertible currency and there are no restrictions on its import or export.

Currency Exchange

Australia	A$1	=	OR0.305
France	FF1	=	OR0.075
Germany	DM1	=	OR0.253
UK	UK£1	=	OR0.620
USA	US$1	=	OR0.385

Changing Money

Banking hours are Saturday to Wednesday from 8 am to noon and Thursday from 8 to 11 am. Moneychangers keep the same hours and usually also open from around 4 to 7 pm. Some of the moneychangers, particularly the ones in and around Muscat's Mutrah souq,

open for an hour or two on Friday afternoon from 4.30 or 5 pm.

ATMs are widespread though few of them appear to be tied into the big international systems. The exception is the British Bank of the Middle East, some of whose machines accept cards on the Plus system.

Tipping & Bargaining

Tipping is not expected in cheaper places while more expensive restaurants tend to include a service charge (though this often goes to the restaurant, not the waiting staff).

As for bargaining, most prices are fixed in Oman. This applies to restaurants, hotels and taxis (ie, the first price you hear is likely to be the only price on offer). The only things you can expect to dicker over will be souvenirs in the souq. Even in the souq, however, bargaining can be a frustrating experience. Shopkeepers may offer a small discount on the marked price but not much more.

POST & COMMUNICATIONS

Post

Post offices are open weekdays from 7.30 am until 2 pm. They close at 11 am on Thursday and are closed all day Friday.

Sending a postcard costs 150 baisa to any destination outside the Arab world. Postage for letters is 200 baisa for the first 10g and 350 baisa for up to 20g.

Poste restante service is available at the GPO in Muscat's Ruwi district. Have your mail addressed to: Your Name, Poste Restante, Ruwi Central Post Office, Ruwi, Sultanate of Oman.

Telephone

There are central public telephone offices in both Muscat and Salalah and in a few smaller cities and towns as well. With the exception of the call booking office in Muscat, however, these mainly offer card phones, and card phones are pretty easy to find almost anywhere.

When calling Oman from the outside world the country code is 968, followed by the local six digit number. There are no area or city codes.

OMAN

BOOKS

Travels in Oman – On the Track of the Early Explorers by Philip Ward combines a modern travel narrative with the best of the 18th, 19th and early 20th century travellers' accounts of the country. *Sultan in Oman* by James Morris is a travelling journalist's account of a visit to Oman in the 1950s, though you should be aware that it is banned in the country.

Some of the action in Wilfred Thesiger's 1959 classic *Arabian Sands* takes place in and around Salalah, which Thesiger visited at the end of one of his journeys into the Empty Quarter. The final section of the book is an account of a trip around Oman's northern interior. For more general book information see the Books section in the Regional Facts for the Visitor chapter.

NEWSPAPERS & MAGAZINES

The *Times of Oman* and the *Oman Daily Observer* are the local English-language newspapers. Foreign newspapers and magazines, available only in the bookshops in Muscat's five-star hotels and in the suburban shopping centres frequented by the western community, are usually about three days old. Outside of Muscat you can forget about finding foreign papers except, maybe, at the Salalah Holiday Inn and the Salalah Family Bookshop.

Oman Today is a magazine-cum-handbook published every two months and widely available throughout the sultanate for 500 baisa. A less thorough listing of activities in Oman can be found in *What's On*, a monthly publication based in the UAE and available in the sultanate.

RADIO & TV

Omani TV broadcasts a daily newscast in English at 8 pm and shows English-language movies two or three nights a week (usually around 11 pm). Satellite TV is also widely available in the sultanate, even in relatively small hotels.

The Sultanate of Oman FM Service is the local English-language radio station. It broadcasts on 90.4 FM (94.3 FM from Salalah) every day from 7 am to 9 pm, with news bulletins at 7.30 am and 2.30 and 6.30 pm. There is also a retransmission of the BBC news. The fare is mostly classical music interspersed with light entertainment.

PHOTOGRAPHY & VIDEO

Oman is a very security-conscious place. An Omani police officer's idea of what is security-related may differ significantly from yours. Don't photograph anything even vaguely military (though forts still in use by the police are generally OK if, like the three forts in the Muscat area, they are also recognised tourist attractions). Do not photograph people, especially women, without asking their permission first. Video cameras are a particularly sensitive subject.

HEALTH

Since his ascension to power Sultan Qaboos has made improving health care and hygiene standards in Oman one of his main priorities. The result today is one of the most squeaky-clean countries you could ever hope to visit. Even the smallest restaurants in the souq are usually held to quite high standards of cleanliness. The tap water is drinkable throughout the country and no special vaccinations are necessary, though a gamma globulin (or Havrix) injection as a Hepatitis A preventative is always a good idea. Malaria, virtually endemic only 30 years ago, is no longer a huge problem, but you may want to consider antimalarial medications, particularly if you plan to travel extensively in the south. See the Health Appendix for more detailed health information.

WOMEN TRAVELLERS

Oman is one of the easiest countries in the Gulf for women to travel in. Still, the usual advice for the region applies: avoid wearing clothing which is overly tight or revealing. Trousers are OK as long as they are loosely cut, though some expatriate women prefer long dresses. There is no need for a foreign woman to wear a headscarf, though in rural areas you will certainly gain respect by doing so. Shorts are always a bad idea outside the big hotels and especially in any traditional area such as the Mutrah souq.

Women should have no problem using the microbuses or taxis – Omani women and expatriate women from the Indian subcontinent use them all the time. Be aware, however, that foreign women travelling alone are an unusual sight throughout Oman. The more conservatively you dress, the less trouble you are likely to experience.

DANGERS & ANNOYANCES

Oman is a very orderly society and harassment, of either women or men, is far less of a problem here than in some of the other Gulf states. In general you should find it a reasonably open and easy place to travel in so long as you dress properly and avoid doing anything which the police might construe as spying.

BUSINESS HOURS

Businesses are open daily except Friday from 8 am to 1 pm and 4 to 7 or 7.30 pm. Most businesses are closed on Thursday afternoons. Many of the shops in Muscat's Mutrah souq are open during the early evening hours on Friday. Shops in the Mutrah souq and in some of Muscat's more up-market shopping malls stay open until 8 or 9 pm most nights.

PUBLIC HOLIDAYS & SPECIAL EVENTS

Secular holidays observed in Oman are New Year's Day (January 1), National Day (November 18) and the Sultan's Birthday (November 19).

The Islamic holidays of Eid al-Fitr, Eid al-Adha, the Islamic New Year and the Prophet's Birthday are all observed – for the dates see the table of holidays near Public Holidays & Special Events in the Regional Facts for the Visitor chapter. Observance of the two Muslim Eids is more traditional than the celebration of National Day. The Eids are often marked with spontaneous dancing in the streets, even in Muscat.

ACTIVITIES

The variety of terrain in Oman makes

weekend mountain and desert motoring particularly worthwhile. The *APEX Explorer's Guide to Oman* is essential reading for anyone planning to see the country by 4WD.

The main five-star hotels in Muscat all either have a beach of their own or have arranged to use somebody else's. Several sport small fleets of sailing boats, windsurfers, pedal boats, etc and have diving gear available for guests to rent.

WORK

One of the quickest ways to make yourself unpopular with the authorities is to start looking for work while visiting the country on a tourist visa. The rules on imported labour are still pretty strict. If you want to work in Oman you should go back home and apply for a job from there.

ACCOMMODATION

There are no formal camping grounds in Oman. Camping is mostly a matter of finding a good spot and setting up shop. Be careful, however, not to intrude on land that may belong to someone.

Muscat has a range of hotels to suit most budgets, all of which are quite clean. Most of Oman's provincial towns, however, have only one or two hotels, and they tend to be pretty expensive.

FOOD & DRINKS

There is little in the way of traditional Omani cuisine. Muscat and Salalah are full of small Indian restaurants where the food is good, if not too varied. Often the menu is little more than whatever curry the cook decided to make on the day but it is usually pretty good.

Beverage-wise, small restaurants are likely to offer you a choice of little more than Coke, Pepsi or water. Larger restaurants will have a wider variety of soft drinks as well as fruit juice, sometimes freshly squeezed. Alcohol is available only in larger hotels and expensive restaurants.

THINGS TO BUY

Oman is unquestionably the best place in the Gulf to go souvenir shopping.

OMAN

OMAN

Khanjars

The country's most distinctive product is the *khanjar*, also spelled *khanja*, the curved dagger worn by Omani men on important occasions, and in rural areas still sometimes worn every day. Traditionally the dagger handles were made from rhino horn, though today they are almost always made from either plastic or wood. Khanjars cost anything from OR30 to OR500, depending on the extent and quality of the decoration on the dagger, scabbard and belt. As a rule, however, anything under OR50 tends to be pretty nasty – either very shoddy or very battered or both. ∎

Traditional jewellery ranges from small silver boxes designed to hold kohl (traditionally used as make-up by both men and women) to huge belts or chest-pieces. It is often very intricately designed. Thin layers of gold or bronze, coloured glass and old coins are all used to decorate the basic silverwork.

Shopkeepers looking for a sale are apt to make great claims for the age of their wares. Bear in mind, however, that most of this stuff will have been made as wedding jewellery. As it was (and still is) considered an insult for a bride to be given used jewellery to wear on her wedding day, the tradition has long been that a woman's jewellery is melted down and sold for its weight after her death. For this reason very little of the jewellery you will see on sale in the souqs of Muscat and Nizwa will be more than 50 to 60 years old. Kohl boxes, starting at around OR8, are usually the cheapest type of jewellery available.

Maria Theresia dollars, commonly known as thallers, are also on sale in many jewellery shops. Along with the Indian rupee these were the common currency of the Gulf for much of the 19th and early 20th centuries. Regardless of when they were minted all Maria Theresia dollars bear the date 1780. As with the jewellery, you can safely assume that the ones you'll see on sale will be nowhere near that old. They contain about 20g of solid silver and sell for about OR3 apiece.

Other things to buy include caftans and the turbans worn by virtually every Omani man. Locally made pottery, usually in the form of incense burners, can be purchased in Dhofar.

Getting There & Away

AIR

Return fares to the eastern USA from Muscat generally cost OR600 to OR650 (US$1560 to US$1690) depending on the season and how badly the agent wants to sell the ticket. The high season is mid-June to mid-October and about 10 days either side of Christmas.

Although you might think that it would be fairly cheap to fly to London because of the sheer number of British expats in Oman, this is not the case. At OR512 (US$1330), a return ticket to London is almost the same price as a return ticket to New York and more expensive than a low-season return ticket to Melbourne (which is OR505, or US$1315).

New Delhi, at OR191 (US$496) for a return ticket allowing a four month stay, is one of the better deals available out of Muscat. By comparison the cheapest regular return ticket to Cairo or Damascus costs OR288, or US$748 (five day minimum stay, two month maximum).

Sample return fares to some other Gulf cities include: Abu Dhabi OR49 (US$127), Dubai OR46 (US$120), Bahrain OR85 (US$221), and Kuwait or Riyadh OR130 (US$338). Note that to the other Gulf states, and particularly to Dubai and Abu Dhabi, cheap 'weekend fares' are often available. Restrictions vary, but these usually allow outbound travellers to leave on a Wednesday or Thursday and return on a Friday or Saturday.

LAND

Entering or leaving by land means travelling between Oman and the UAE. The border with Yemen is not open to travellers. There is a daily bus service between Muscat and Dubai.

LEAVING OMAN

There is a tax of OR3 for all departing international passengers at Seeb airport in Muscat.

Getting Around

AIR

Oman Aviation (also known as Oman Air) has daily flights to Salalah and regular services to Sur, Khasab, Dibba and Massirah Island.

BUS

Intercity buses are operated by the Oman National Transport Company (ONTC) which has daily services to most of the main provincial towns. With the exception of Salalah none of the main intercity routes costs more than OR4 each way.

TAXI & MICROBUS

Oman has an extraordinarily comprehensive system of service taxis and microbuses. The taxis are invariably orange and white, while the microbuses are white. Unlike service taxis in other Middle Eastern cities, Oman's service taxis and microbuses do not wait until they are full to leave. Drivers will depart when they have a few passengers, expecting to pick up and drop off other passengers along the way. This is a very cheap way to get around, provided you are in no particular hurry. You can also, of course, take a taxi or microbus 'engaged' (ie, privately) by paying for all of the seats in it.

CAR

Traffic laws are enforced fairly strictly in Oman, especially in Muscat. Seat-belt use is mandatory for passengers in the front seat of cars. The fine for not wearing one is OR10. Right turns are not allowed at red lights.

Renting a car in the sultanate is fairly easy but not cheap. Most foreign driver's licences are accepted for people on tourist visas as are international driving permits. Rates for compact cars start at about OR12 per day plus OR2 to OR3 per day for insurance. Rentals usually include 100 or 150 free km per day.

LOCAL TRANSPORT

Only Muscat has a local bus system. Local taxis tend to be pretty thick on the ground throughout the country as are 14-passenger microbuses. In smaller areas in particular it is difficult, if not impossible, to distinguish between local and intercity taxis and microbuses.

ORGANISED TOURS

Organised full-day and half-day tours are available in both Muscat and Salalah. See the respective city entries for details.

Muscat

Muscat is a port the like of which cannot be found in the whole world where there is business and good things that cannot be found elsewhere.

So wrote the great Arab navigator Ahmed bin Majid al-Najdi in 1490. Five centuries later Muscat still enchants visitors in a way that no other city in the Gulf can even begin to match. Maybe this is because Muscat does not have that slightly artificial feel which typifies so much of the rest of the region.

Orientation

Muscat, Mutrah and Ruwi are the capital's core districts. Muscat is the old port area. It is the site of the sultan's main palace and a fascinating place to wander around but it has few shops and, except for the old city walls, there is not much to see. Mutrah, three km north-west of Muscat, is the main trading and residential port area. A few km inland from Muscat and Mutrah lies Ruwi, the capital's modern commercial district. Two roads connect the Ruwi valley to Mutrah. There is no direct link between Ruwi and Muscat.

Immediately south of Muscat lie the small

OMAN

villages of Sidab and Al-Bustan and, further south, the huge Al-Bustan Palace Hotel.

Along the coast to the west of Mutrah and Ruwi are a number of new, mostly residential, districts. The main ones are Qurm, which includes the Gulf Hotel, five or six big shopping malls and the Qurm Nature Reserve; Al-Khuwair, an up-market residential area; and Medinat Qaboos, the site of most of the ministries, a couple of museums and many foreign embassies.

Information

Money Most of the big banks are in Ruwi along Markaz Mutrah al-Tijari St. You'll find a plethora of moneychangers (plus a few banks) along Souq Ruwi St. In Mutrah you will find a number of moneychangers on the Corniche around the entrance to the souq and even more inside the souq.

American Express (Amex; ☎ 708035) is represented by Zubair Travel & Services Bureau in Ruwi. It is open daily except Friday from 8 am to 1 pm and 4 to 6 pm. The office will hold mail and cash personal checks for Amex clients. Clients' mail should be addressed to: American Express – clients' mail, PO Box 833, Ruwi, Oman.

Post The GPO is right on the dividing line between Ruwi and Bait al-Falaj at the northern end of Markaz Mutrah al-Tijari St. It is open Saturday to Wednesday from 8 am to 2 pm and 3.30 to 5.30 pm. On Thursday, Friday and holidays it keeps a shorter 8 to 11 am schedule.

There are branch post offices in Mutrah near the Mina Qaboos port services building and in Old Muscat a few metres from the Al-Kabir Gate.

Telephone & Fax The telephone office is on Souq Ruwi St near the intersection with Street 37. Two international call cabins are on the upper floor. You can also send faxes from a desk in the main lobby. The office is open daily from 7.30 am to 9.30 pm.

Travel Agencies The capital's greatest concentration of travel agencies is in and around Markaz Mutrah al-Tijari St in Ruwi. Because of the high turnover rate at many of these agencies your best bet for finding a good agent is to ask for advice from locals or expat friends, or at the reception desk of a big hotel.

Bookshops There really aren't any decent

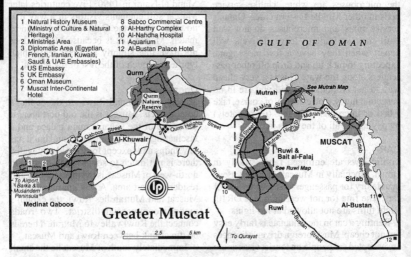

1	Natural History Museum (Ministry of Culture & Natural Heritage)
2	Ministries Area
3	Diplomatic Area (Egyptian, French, Iranian, Kuwaiti, Saudi & UAE Embassies)
4	US Embassy
5	UK Embassy
6	Oman Museum
7	Muscat Inter-Continental Hotel
8	Sabco Commercial Centre
9	Al-Harthy Complex
10	Al-Nahdha Hospital
11	Aquarium
12	Al-Bustan Palace Hotel

Greater Muscat

GULF OF OMAN

0   2.5   5 km

To Qurayat

English-language bookshops in the Muscat-Mutrah-Ruwi area. The best is the Family Bookshop (☎ 786461) which has branches in Medinat Qaboos, the Muscat Inter-Continental Hotel, Qurm and Ruwi.

Cultural Centres The British Council (☎ 600548) is on Al-Inshirah St, parallel to Sultan Qaboos St, in Muscat's Al-Khuwair district. Its library is open to the public on Saturday, Sunday, Monday and Wednesday from 11 am to 8.45 pm and Tuesday from 2 to 8.45 pm. They are closed Thursday and Friday.

Medical Services Should you need hospitalisation this will probably be free, though if things get really serious you are likely to find yourself on the first plane home. The Al-Nahdha Hospital on the outskirts of Ruwi (on the left as you head from Ruwi toward Al-Khuwair) is the main medical centre in the Muscat-Mutrah-Ruwi area.

Emergency Dial 999 for the police, an ambulance or to report a fire.

Greater Muscat

Jalali, Mirani & Mutrah Forts Mutrah Fort sits on a hill overlooking the Mutrah Corniche while Jalali and Mirani forts guard the entrance to Muscat. All three forts took on more or less their present form in the 1580s during the Portuguese occupation of Muscat. Of the three, the Portuguese built only Mutrah Fort from scratch, though their alterations to the other two were so extensive that the forts can be said to be of Portuguese rather than Arab construction.

All of the forts are still used by the police and/or military and are closed to the public. It's OK to photograph them.

Omani-French Museum This museum, in a restored turn-of-the-century building inside Muscat's walls near the Al-Kabir Gate, is largely an extended celebration of the Sultan's state visit to France in 1989 and French President François Mitterrand's state visit to Muscat in 1992. There are several galleries detailing relations between the two countries in the 19th and early 20th centuries. The museum is open Saturday to Wednesday from 8.30 am to 1.30 pm. Admission is free.

National Aquarium Muscat has by far the best aquarium in the Gulf. It is south of old Muscat between Sidab and Al-Bustan. All of the specimens on display are native to Omani waters and most are accompanied by thorough descriptions in English.

Medinat Qaboos

Oman Museum The Oman Museum is in the Ministries Area; look for a small, white building next to the much larger, brown Ministry of Information building on a hill overlooking the rest of Medinat Qaboos. See below for detailed driving directions – it's a bit tricky.

Displays on the ground floor cover Oman history, geography and geology of Oman from the 3rd millennium BC onwards. There is also a display on shipbuilding. The 1st floor has a small display on Islam, consisting mostly of manuscripts, a fair to middling display of Omani arts and crafts and an excellent room on architecture in the sultanate with an emphasis on forts.

The museum is open daily except Thursday and Friday from 7.30 am to 2.30 pm. Admission is free. To get there take the exit off Sultan Qaboos St marked for the Muscat Inter-Continental Hotel (the same exit that has signs for the Children's Museum). If you are coming from the direction of Ruwi or Mutrah go around the roundabout at the exit and take Al-Ilam St across the bridge over Sultan Qaboos St then turn right on Al-Inshirah St. If you are approaching from the other direction (say, from the Natural History Museum or the embassies area in Medinat Qaboos) take the exit marked for the Inter-Continental Hotel, turn right on Al-Ilam St and then left on Al-Inshirah St before you cross the bridge.

Once you are on Al-Inshirah St go 850m and take the fifth left, onto Way 1595, then go 400m and turn left onto Way 1526. After another 250m turn right onto Way 1530. From there, go 550m and turn right at a sign for the Oman Museum (which is actually nearly a 180° turn). Another 150m brings you, at last, to the door.

Natural History Museum The museum is on Al-Wazarat St, which runs parallel to Sultan Qaboos St on the side toward the sea, in the Ministries Area. Look for a small green sign with a drawing of a lynx (the museum's symbol) indicating the exit. The museum is open Saturday to Wednesday from 8 am to 2 pm and Thursday from 9 am to 1 pm. It is also open Sunday and Friday afternoons from 4 to 7 pm.

Adjacent to the museum is the Ministry of Culture & Natural Heritage, which is where you must go to obtain permits for visits to forts and archaeological sites throughout the country. These are usually issued on the spot but you will have to show identification. See Visas & Documents in the Facts for the Visitor section earlier in this chapter for more information about site permits.

Mutrah

Mutrah Fish Market The fish market is at the northern end of the Mutrah Corniche near the Mina and Corniche hotels. The market usually opens around 6.30 am.

Mutrah Souq The Mutrah souq is without a doubt the most interesting souq in the Arab Gulf states. Be sure to stop for a drink at the teahouse on the left-hand side of the main entrance. Sweet tea is 75 baisa a cup, served as you sit on stone benches on either side of the entry archway. No visit to Muscat would be complete without a pit stop here.

As with any good Arab souq the best thing to do is simply to wander at will. The Mutrah souq is not really very big and you are in no danger of getting lost, though there may be moments when it does not look that way.

Watchtower At the eastern end of the Corniche, above and behind the Al-Inshirah restaurant, a restored watchtower looks out over Mutrah. The climb is steep and involves more than 100 steps, but the view from the top is worth it.

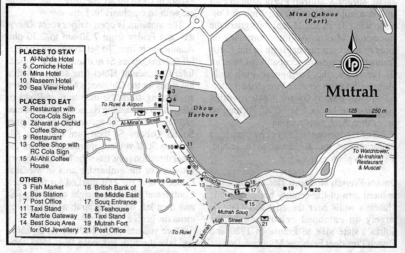

PLACES TO STAY
1 Al-Nahda Hotel
5 Corniche Hotel
6 Mina Hotel
10 Naseem Hotel
20 Sea View Hotel

PLACES TO EAT
2 Restaurant with Coca-Cola Sign
8 Zaharat al-Orchid Coffee Shop
9 Restaurant
13 Coffee Shop with RC Cola Sign
15 Al-Ahli Coffee House

OTHER
3 Fish Market
4 Bus Station
7 Post Office
11 Taxi Stand
12 Marble Gateway
14 Best Souq Area for Old Jewellery
16 British Bank of the Middle East
17 Souq Entrance & Teahouse
18 Taxi Stand
19 Mutrah Fort
21 Post Office

Mina Qaboos (Port)

Mutrah

0   125   250 m

To Watchtower, Al-Inshirah Restaurant & Muscat

Dhow Harbour

To Ruwi & Airport

Al-Mina'a Street

Mutrah Corniche

Liwatiya Quarter

Mutrah Souq

Mutrah High Street

To Ruwi

Ruwi

National Museum The National Museum (☎ 701289), on A'Noor St near the intersection with Al-Burj St, is definitely worth a look. The main exhibit area is on the upper floor, a single large hall with a number of small rooms off to its sides. Much of the central area of this main hall is given over to cases displaying various Omani silverwork. At the back of the room a mural showing trade routes throughout Oman's history covers the entire rear wall.

The museum is open daily except Thursday and Friday from 7.30 am to 2.30 pm. Admission is free. Photography is prohibited.

Sultan's Armed Forces Museum This museum, run by the Omani army, is in the Bait al-Falaj Fort, which gives its name to the Bait al-Falaj district. The fort is one of the oldest buildings in Muscat. It was built in 1845 as a royal summer home, was restored extensively in the early 1900s and served as the headquarters for the Omani army from WWI until 1978. The museum is quite well presented and the lower floor – which provides an excellent outline of Omani history – is definitely worth a visit.

This museum is open Sunday, Monday, Wednesday and Thursday from 8.30 am to 1 pm. On Thursday the museum is also open from 4 to 6 pm. Admission is 500 baisa for adults, and free for anyone under 18. You are usually required to go through the museum with a guide (even if the two of you do not share a common language) and photography is strictly prohibited.

Ruwi Souq The Ruwi souq is a good place for shopping, but it is not exactly a tourist attraction. Like the rest of Ruwi it is a modern creation. Those in search of gold jewellery should try Souq Ruwi St.

Beaches & Beach Clubs

One of the more popular public beaches is at Jussa, south of Al-Bustan off the Qantab Rd. It is a popular picnic spot for Omani families, especially on public holidays, but is a bit difficult to reach unless you have your own transport.

Many of the large hotels will let outsiders use their beach facilities for a fee. While a bit expensive, these beaches should definitely be considered by unaccompanied women, who are far less likely to suffer from harassment at one of the hotels than they would be on a public beach. The Al-Bustan Palace has by far the best facilities, though the entrance fee is pretty steep at OR6 (OR10 on Thursday and Friday). Getting onto the beach at the Muscat Inter-Continental is a bit cheaper at OR4 on weekdays and OR5 on Thursday and Friday.

Organised Tours

Most of Oman's tour operators set their prices by the vehicle – which means that up to four people can take the tour for the quoted price. Bahwan Travel Agencies (☎ 600500 for its office at the Inter-Continental Hotel) offers a day tour of Greater Muscat for OR23. It also offers a full-day tour to Nizwa, Bahla and Jabrin for OR70, and one to Nakhal, Rustaq and Al-Hazm for OR50. For those on a tighter budget there is a bus tour to Nizwa available only on Friday for OR23 per person. Orient Tours (☎ 605066) is another well-established operator with similar offerings and prices.

Places to Stay – bottom end & middle

Muscat's cheapest beds are at the *Al-Hedow Hotel* (☎ & fax 799329) where singles/doubles cost OR7.350/10.500 including tax. Even if you are on a tight budget we can't recommend this place, which looks as though it is falling apart. The cheap hotels along the Mutrah Corniche offer both better rooms and the best views and atmosphere in the city for only a bit more money.

If price remains your main concern but you want to stay on the Corniche try the *Al-Nahda Hotel* (☎ 714196; fax 714994) at the northern end of the Corniche, near the entrance to Mina Qaboos. Singles/doubles are OR8.700/12.800. The cheapest place on the Corniche is all the way down at the opposite end from the Al-Nahda. This is the

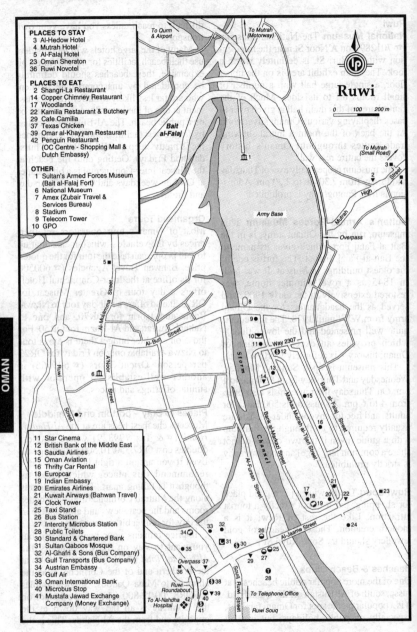

Ruwi

0   100   200 m

PLACES TO STAY
3 Al-Hedow Hotel
4 Mutrah Hotel
5 Al-Falaj Hotel
23 Oman Sheraton
36 Ruwi Novotel

PLACES TO EAT
2 Shangri-La Restaurant
14 Copper Chimney Restaurant
17 Woodlands
22 Kamilia Restaurant & Butchery
29 Cafe Camilia
37 Texas Chicken
39 Omar al-Khayyam Restaurant
42 Penguin Restaurant
    (OC Centre – Shopping Mall &
    Dutch Embassy)

OTHER
1 Sultan's Armed Forces Museum
    (Bait al-Falaj Fort)
6 National Museum
7 Amex (Zubair Travel &
    Services Bureau)
8 Stadium
9 Telecom Tower
10 GPO

11 Star Cinema
12 British Bank of the Middle East
13 Saudia Airlines
15 Oman Aviation
16 Thrifty Car Rental
19 Europcar
19 Indian Embassy
20 Emirates Airlines
21 Kuwait Airways (Bahwan Travel)
24 Clock Tower
25 Taxi Stand
26 Bus Station
27 Intercity Microbus Station
28 Public Toilets
30 Standard & Chartered Bank
31 Sultan Qaboos Mosque
32 Al-Ghafri & Sons (Bus Company)
33 Gulf Transports (Bus Company)
34 Austrian Embassy
35 Gulf Air
38 Oman International Bank
40 Microbus Stop
41 Mustafa Jawad Exchange
    Company (Money Exchange)

To Qurm
& Airport

To Mutrah
(Motorway)

Bait
al-Falaj

To Mutrah
(Small Road)

Street

Mutrah
High

Army Base

Overpass

Al-Mujamma Street

Al-Bur Street

A'Noor Street

Ruwi Street

Street

Way 2307

Storm

Channel

Markaz Mutrah ar-Tijari Street

Bank al-Markazi Street

Bait al-Falaj Street

Al-Fursan Street

Al-Jaame Street

Souq Ruwi Street

Overpass 37

Ruwi
Roundabout

To Al-Nahdha
Hospital

To Telephone Office

Ruwi Souq

OMAN

Sea View Hotel (☎ 714555) at OR8.600/ 12.400.

An extra riyal or two elsewhere on the Corniche gets you a much better room at, for example, the *Corniche Hotel* (☎ 714636; fax 714770). Rooms there start at OR9.500/ 14.700. An equally good bet, offering larger rooms and baths but less atmosphere, is the nearby *Naseem Hotel* (☎ 712418; fax 711728). Rooms there cost OR10.500/ 14.700.

The *Mina Hotel* (☎ 711828; fax 714981) is a bit more up-market than the other Mutrah hotels at OR12/15. It's the only hotel in Mutrah with a restaurant that serves alcohol.

The *Mutrah Hotel* (☎ 798401; fax 790953) is at the Ruwi end of Mutrah High St. Rooms are OR13.650/19.950.

Places to Stay – top end

The cheapest place that can arrange a visa is the *Al-Falaj Hotel* (☎ 702311; fax 795853) on Al-Mujamma St in Bait al-Falaj. Rooms cost OR31.500/37.800. A bit more expensive, but very central, is the *Ruwi Novotel* (☎ 704244; fax 704248) on Ruwi St. It charges OR33.600/38.850. Also in Ruwi is the *Oman Sheraton* (☎ 799899; fax 795791) with rooms at OR66.700/75.900.

Places to Eat

Mutrah Of the several small restaurants at the northern end of the Mutrah Corniche, the best is the place with the green-and-red-on-white *Restaurant* sign near the roundabout near the Mina Hotel. It is fairly spartan, and sometimes water is the only drink available, but the biryanis are quite good and cost only 500 baisa per helping. A short distance inland from the roundabout, the *Zaharat al-Orchid* coffee shop and restaurant has excellent shwarma and also offers cheap sandwiches, burgers and fresh juice. Oddly there are two restaurants with this name a few metres apart. The better of the two is the one further inland.

The semicircular building near the entrance to the souq sporting an RC Cola sign with the words *Coffee Shop* emblazoned on it is a particularly good place for cheap,

quick meals. Try the chickpeas masala for 200 baisa.

Inside the Mutrah souq you should definitely make your way to the *Al-Ahli Coffee House*. The house speciality is fresh juice at 300 to 400 baisa per glass. It also offers an excellent mixed juice 'cocktail' for 600 baisa. Burgers and sandwiches are available for OR300 to 500 baisa apiece. To reach the coffee house from the Mutrah Corniche entrance to the souq, go directly into the souq and keep right at the first fork (the one with the fountain). Follow this street until you reach a T-junction by the Muscat pharmacy. Turn left at this junction and the coffee house will be on your right after 25m.

The only cheapish restaurant in Mutrah that serves alcohol is *Albahr* (which is Arabic for 'the sea', not a misspelling of the English word bar), the restaurant at the Mina Hotel. If you are not staying in the hotel, however, you won't be served booze unless you order a meal. Main dishes cost about OR3, plus drinks. The hotel's street level *coffee shop* is also a popular local gathering spot, particularly on cool evenings when both Omanis and foreigners can be found munching shwarma or felafel and sipping tea in front of the hotel.

Muscat The pickings here are pretty slim. Try the *Al-Badiyeh Restaurant* near the post office. The menu is mostly medium-priced Indian. Most main dishes cost OR1 to OR2.

Ruwi There are several good bets in Ruwi, such as the *Kamilia Restaurant & Butchery* just off Al-Jaame St. The fare here includes biryanis at OR1.500 and grilled dishes, such as kebabs, for OR1.800 including soup and salad. Chinese main dishes cost OR1.200 to OR1.500.

Across Al-Jaame St from the Ruwi bus station *Cafe Camilia* is a good spot for a quick snack with sandwiches and shwarma for 200 baisa.

Texas Chicken on the corner of A'Noor and Al-Jaame Sts has good chicken and burgers but you should really try its excellent, and cheap, Chinese and Filipino noodle dishes, which cost OR1.200 each. A bit more up-market, but still fairly cheap, is the *Omar al-Khayyam Restaurant*, across Al-Jaame St from Texas Chicken, near the Oman International Bank. It has Chinese and Indian food, including a wide selection of Indian vegetarian dishes, most of which are OR2 or less.

If you want to have a drink with dinner and do not want to pay handsomely for the privilege try *Woodlands*, an Indian restaurant off Bank al-Markazi St. The food is pretty good and moderately priced with most main dishes at OR1.500 to OR2.200 and a few under one riyal. Most of the food is fairly spicy.

If you are looking for something up-market, try the *Copper Chimney Restaurant*, just off Markaz Mutrah al-Tijari St near the GPO in Ruwi. It has some of the best Indian food in Muscat and the surroundings are quite dignified. The best place for Chinese food is *Shangri-La* at the Ruwi end of Mutrah High St, near the Oman Hotel. Main dishes mostly cost OR3.500 or more, but the portions are very large.

Entertainment

Muscat is rather thin on entertainment. There are discos at the Muscat Inter-Continental Hotel and at the Oman Sheraton Hotel and many of the big hotels have lounge acts of some sort in their bars.

The *Star Cinema* (☎ 791641) shows both western and Indian films (though rather more of the latter). Tickets are OR1 and 800 baisa. It is the unmistakable round building in Ruwi near the GPO.

Things to Buy

One result of the growth of tourism in Oman has been that the Mutrah souq, while still a great place to wander around and soak in the atmosphere, has become a pretty pricey place to shop for Omani handicrafts. The best place to look for both khanjars and silver jewellery is, oddly enough, a shopping mall out in Qurm. Inside the Sabco Commercial Centre is an area of dagger and jewellery shops called, appropriately, 'the souq',

which includes a government-run handicrafts centre with fixed prices.

Getting There & Away

Air Seeb international airport is 37 km from Muscat or Mutrah. For airport flight information call ☎ 619 223 or 519 456.

Muscat is the hub for Oman Aviation's domestic services. There are two daily flights to Salalah (OR27/50 one way/return in economy class), and four flights per week to Khasab (OR20/40 one way/return) and to Massirah Island (OR17/34). Two of the Khasab flights each week stop in Dibba en route (the fare is the same as to Khasab). There are also three fights each week to Sur (OR14/28).

Bus The Ruwi bus station (☎ 708522) is the main depot for buses in the sultanate operated by the Oman National Transport Company (ONTC). Luggage can be stored in the cargo area (around the side of the ticket office). Timetables in English are posted in the waiting room.

There are daily buses, both express and regular, to Buraimi (OR3.600) via Barka (900 baisa) and Sohar (OR2.200); and to Ibri (OR3.200) via Samail (900 baisa), Nizwa (OR1.600), Bahla (OR2) and Jabrin (OR2.200). There are also extra regular buses to Nizwa via Samail at 6 and 10 am and at 6 pm. Other intercity routes include: Rustaq (OR1.800) via Nakhal (OR1.500); and Sur (OR3.400) via Al-Kamil (OR2.500).

Salalah is the only route on which ONTC has competition. ONTC buses leave daily at 7 am and 7 pm with an extra bus at 6 pm from mid-June to mid-September. All its Salalah buses leave one hour later during Ramadan. The trip takes 12 hours. The fare is OR8 one way and OR16 return. Booking a day or two early is not necessary but would be a good idea if you really wanted to travel on a particular bus.

The competition comes from three companies, all of which have offices in the area behind the Sultan Qaboos Mosque in Ruwi. Gulf Transports, Al-Ghafri & Sons (☎ 707896) and Bin Qasim Transport

(☎ 785059). For what it's worth, ONTC's coaches, though more expensive, are a much better deal. Whichever company you travel with you must have your passport available for inspection at a checkpoint about midway through the trip.

Dubai The only international bus service is to Dubai. Buses leave twice a day, at 7.30 am and 4.30 pm, from the Ruwi bus station. During Ramadan the late bus leaves at 5.30 pm. The trip takes six hours. The fare is OR9 one way, OR16 return.

Taxi & Microbus Greater Muscat has two main service-taxi stands for both taxis and microbuses. One is in Ruwi across Al-Jaame St from the main bus station while the other is out at the Seeb clock tower (formally the Sahwa Tower) roundabout, beyond the airport. A shared taxi from Ruwi to the clock tower costs 500 baisa. Microbuses charge 300 baisa for the same trip. From Mutrah the taxi/microbus fare is 700/300 baisa.

Some sample taxi/microbus fares are:

Barka	OR1/300 baisa
Sohar	OR2.500/1.700
Rustaq	OR2/800 baisa
Nakhal	OR2/OR1
Samail	OR1/500 baisa
Nizwa	OR1.500/OR1
Sur	OR3.500/OR3

Only taxis make the trip to Buraimi, at OR5 per person.

Car There are several rental agencies in the area around the Ruwi roundabout as well as the usual desks in big hotels and at the airport. Europcar (☎ 700190) is a good bet for longer term rentals. Other agencies worth checking out include Thrifty Car Rental (☎ 784275) and Mark Rent-a-Car (☎ 562444).

Getting Around
The Airport Bus Nos 23 and 24 run between the Mutrah bus terminal and the airport twice an hour from approximately 6.30 am until 9.30 pm daily. On Friday there are three

buses per hour, but they do not start running until 7.20 am. The route also passes the Ruwi bus station and the Qurm roundabout. The trip takes about 50 minutes and the fare is 200 baisa.

Taxis between the airport and the centre cost OR6 (Ruwi and Mutrah) and OR5 (Qurm, Medinat Qaboos and Al-Khuwair). If you share a service taxi you should pay 500 to 700 baisa.

Bus ONTC's system of local buses covers greater Muscat fairly thoroughly. Fares are either 100 or 200 baisa (300 baisa to Sultan Qaboos University), depending on the distance travelled. Destinations are displayed on the front of the buses in Arabic and English. Timetables in English are available at the main bus station on Al-Jaame St in Ruwi (the same place that the intercity buses leave from). Bus Nos 2, 4, 23, 24, 28, 31 and 32 all run between the Mutrah and Ruwi stations for 200 baisa. Other main routes include: No 23 and 24 to Qurm and the Ministries Area in Medinat Qaboos, and No 26 to Qurm and Al-Khuwair.

Microbus In Mutrah, local microbuses cruise the Corniche, particularly the end near the Mina Hotel and the Mutrah bus station, while in Ruwi they park en masse in a lot across Al-Jaame St from the main bus station. Mutrah to Ruwi costs 100 baisa, Mutrah to Muscat 150 baisa; no microbus journey within greater Muscat should cost more than 300 baisa, including trips to the airport. The only significant exception to this rule is trips to the main microbus station at the Seeb clock tower (beyond the airport). This trip costs 500 baisa.

Microbus drivers within the city generally go wherever the spirit moves them. Before you get into the bus simply ask the driver 'Ruwi?', 'Medinat Qaboos?', 'Al-Khuwair?', or whatever.

Taxi Muscat's taxis, like all others in Oman, are orange and white and do not have meters. If you bargain you will inevitably pay two or three times what you ought to – the only way to pay the proper fare is to know it before you get into the cab and not to raise the subject of money at all but just hand the driver the proper sum at your destination.

A taxi between Mutrah and Ruwi costs OR1 in either direction if you take it all to yourself ('engaged'), or 200 baisa if shared. Muscat to Mutrah is OR1 engaged and Muscat to Ruwi OR1.500 engaged. There are no shared taxis between Muscat and Ruwi. Mutrah to Qurm is OR3 engaged and 300 baisa shared, and Ruwi to Qurm is OR2 engaged or 300 baisa shared.

Northern Oman

BARKA

Barka, 80 km west of Mutrah and Ruwi, makes an excellent day trip outside the capital, or an easy stopover on the way from Muscat to Sohar. The turn-off from the main Muscat-Sohar highway is well signposted, and this is where you will probably be dropped if you take a microbus. From the junction you can pick up another (local) microbus to cover the extra few km to the centre.

Barka's main site is its **fort**. This will be on your right as you enter town, just before reaching a major intersection at which a number of banks and a few small restaurants can be found. The fort is open every day from 7.30 am to 6 pm. Admission is free.

Barka's other point of interest is **Bait Nua'man**, a restored house that gives you an idea of how wealthier residents of Oman's coast lived several generations ago. Permits from Muscat are required for entry but be warned that the site does not keep the same regular hours as the fort. To reach Bait Nua'man from Barka Fort continue along the road that brought you into Barka from the main highway and go 4.8 km beyond the fort. This will bring you to a left turn onto a paved road. Take this turn (if you reach a roundabout you've gone too far) and follow the road 1.9 km. Bait Nua'man will be on your right.

If you are in need of a meal in Barka try the *Sawahil al-Bathna Restaurant*, on the main intersection across the street from the Commercial Bank of Oman. Look for a small restaurant with a lot of Lipton tea ads pasted on the door. Biryanis cost 500 baisa each.

Getting There & Away

There are four buses per day between Barka and Muscat's Ruwi bus station (one hour express, 1½ hours regular; 900 baisa). The buses all come and go from the roundabout where the road into Barka meets the Muscat-Sohar highway. Taxis and microbuses can be found both around Barka's main intersection and at the roundabout at the junction of the Barka road with the Muscat-Sohar road. A shared taxi from the Seeb clock tower taxi stand to Barka costs OR1 per person and around OR8 engaged. Microbuses charge 300 baisa per person for the trip from the Seeb clock tower roundabout to Barka.

SOHAR

Sohar, home port of the fictional Sinbad the sailor, is one of those places where history casts a shadow over modern reality. A thousand years ago it occupied three times its present area and was the largest town in the country. The fort and its small museum are quite good but only arguably worth the trip by themselves. If time is not a factor, however, or if you can combine Sohar with the Batinah coast's other sites (Barka, Rustaq, Nakhal, etc) it makes a good turnaround point for a two or three day trip out of Muscat and back. If you are passing by anyway (en route from Muscat to Dubai or the Musandem peninsula, for example) it definitely should not be missed.

Orientation & Information

Sohar has two centres – the old centre on the waterfront just north of the fort, and a more modern business district a couple of km inland. The post office and taxi stand are both in the latter area, which is centred on Sohar's main hospital. To reach both areas take the 'city centre' exit off the highway from Muscat and Dubai. For the modern area, turn right at the sign for the hospital. You should spot the taxis and microbuses in a parking lot to your left a few hundred metres before the hospital. The post office is 250m past the hospital along the same road. The modern business district around the hospital is about one km off the highway. Continuing straight ahead on the road from the highway instead of taking the hospital turn brings you to the fort and the coast road.

Sohar Fort

Sohar Fort is a large, whitewashed, slightly irregular rectangle with a single tower rising from its courtyard. It is a dramatic sight after the earth-coloured forts that dominate the rest of Oman. The fort is open Saturday to Wednesday from 7.30 am to 2.30 pm. On Thursday and Friday it is open from 8 am to noon and from 4 to 6 pm. Admission is free and no permit from Muscat is required.

The first fort on the site is thought to have been built in the late 13th or early 14th century. At the far end of the courtyard from the main entrance you can see the excavated remains of the 13th century houses on whose ruins the original fort was built. Much of what you see today dates from the first half of the 17th century. The fort was extensively restored by the Omani government in 1992.

There is a small **museum** in the fort's tower. The tower also houses the **tomb** of Sayyid Thuwaini bin Said bin Sultan al-Busaid, the ruler of Oman from 1856 to 1866 and the son of Sultan Said bin Sultan, the 19th century ruler under whom Omani power reached its height.

The tower's roof offers a sweeping view across Sohar and the sea and is well worth the climb.

Places to Stay & Eat

There are only two places to stay in Sohar. The *Al-Wadi Hotel* (☎ 840058; fax 841997), just off the main highway coming from Muscat, is the cheaper of the two at OR23.100/31.500 for singles/doubles. The other alternative is the *Sohar Beach Hotel* (☎ 843701; fax 843776) where rooms cost OR28.750/34.500 including tax and service

charge. If you can afford the extra money this is one case where the more expensive hotel is definitely better value for money.

To reach the Al-Wadi Hotel coming from Muscat, get off at the second Sohar roundabout, the one whose centrepiece looks like a mosque's dome on stilts. (It's a left turn out of the roundabout if you are coming from Muscat.) The hotel is about 10 km from the centre. The Beach Hotel is about six km north of the centre on the coastal road.

There are a number of good cheap restaurants within easy walking distance of the fort. Two worth trying are *Ahmed bin Mohammed bin Ali & Partners Restaurant* and *Murad bin Abdulrahman bin Musa al-Balushi Restaurant*. Both have biryanis, curries and similar fare for around 500 baisa per serving. If you're in town when the weather is nice the Ahmed bin Mohammed restaurant has a few tables outside overlooking the coastal road and the sea.

Getting There & Away

There are three buses per day between the Sohar hospital and Muscat's Ruwi bus station. The fare is OR2.200.

The daily express buses from Dubai to Muscat and vice versa stop in Sohar at the Penguin Restaurant on the main highway, just south-east of the turn-off for the centre. From there you can get a nonstop lift into Muscat for OR5 or to Dubai for OR4. Tickets can be purchased from the driver but you should phone ahead the Ruwi bus station in Muscat (☎ 708522) to make a booking. The Muscat-bound buses come through daily at approximately 10.30 am and 8.30 pm. The Dubai-bound buses arrive at around 9.30 or 10 am and 6.30 or 7 pm.

Microbuses and taxis come and go from a parking lot across the street from the hospital and 150m to the north of it. A few can also be found at the roundabout where the highway from Muscat meets the road coming up from the centre. Microbuses charge OR1.700 for the trip to the Seeb clock tower roundabout and OR2 to Ruwi. Taxis charge OR2.500 to the clock tower and OR3 to Ruwi. Expect to pay around OR15 if you

OMAN

insist on taking a taxi engaged. There is no direct taxi or microbus service to Rustaq and Nakhal. Expect to pay about OR15 one way to take a taxi to either city engaged.

NAKHAL

Nakhal is a nondescript town dominated by one of Oman's more dramatic forts. The **fort** in question rises from a hill in Nakhal's small town centre. It is open daily from 7 am to 5 pm. Admission is free.

There is only one bus per day between Muscat and Nakhal (OR1.500). The bus leaves the Ruwi bus station in Muscat at 6 pm arriving at 7.55 pm. The return trip leaves Nakhal every morning at 8 am, arriving in Ruwi at 10 am. Since there is no place to stay in Nakhal, this could be a bit awkward. The bus stop is at the junction of the main road from Barka and the small road that leads onward to Nakhal's centre.

You'll find microbuses and taxis both at the junction with the main road and in the area below the fort. Microbuses charge OR1 for the trip to the Seeb clock tower on the outskirts of Muscat and 300 baisa to/from the Barka roundabout on the Muscat-Sohar highway. Taxis charge about OR2 for the same trip, though most of the cabs in the area appear to specialise in short local runs for a couple of hundred baisa (such as between the main road and the town).

A'THOWARAH

A few km beyond Nakhal lies the lush spring known as A'Thowarah. The spring emerges into a wadi here to form a stream and a small oasis. It is a perfect place for a stroll or a picnic. Put your hand into the stream close to the point where it rises from the rocks – the water is surprisingly warm even in winter.

At the spring you will find a couple of small shops selling water, soft drinks and snacks.

To reach A'Thowarah from Nakhal turn right onto Nakhal's main paved street as you leave the fort. After about 500m you will start to see directional signs for A'Thowarah.

RUSTAQ

Some 175 km west of Muscat is Rustaq (Rostaq), a town best known today for its imposing **fort**, though for a time in the Middle Ages it was Oman's capital. A permit from Muscat is necessary to enter the fort, which was under restoration at the time of writing.

There is a small **souq** near the entrance to the fort. It is good for shopping, though in size and variety it is only a pale shadow of the souqs in Nizwa and Muscat. The best time to visit is early morning, especially on Friday.

Rustaq's only other sight is a small, very new-looking, **white mosque** on the edge of town next to a natural spring. There are no hotels in Rustaq, though the town has a few small restaurants.

There is one bus a day to Muscat from Rustaq. The bus originates in the town, departing at 7.05 am and arriving at Muscat's Ruwi station three hours later. The daily bus from Muscat to Rustaq leaves Ruwi at 6 pm. The fare in either direction is OR1.800.

Microbuses can be found a few hundred metres from the fort on the main road to Nakhal and the coast. Microbus fares from Rustaq include: Nakhal, 500 baisa; the junction with the coastal highway, 400 baisa; Sohar OR1; and Muscat-Ruwi, OR1 (800 baisa to the Seeb clock tower). The fare to Muscat in a shared taxi is OR2.

AL-HAZM

The town of Al-Hazm is little more than a **fort** surrounded by a few houses off the road from Muscat to Rustaq, but it is well worth the stop. Al-Hazm is 20 km north of Rustaq and 24.5 km south of the Muscat-Sohar coastal highway. Coming from the coast, make a right turn at the Al-Hazm roundabout at a sign for Hazm. Follow this road for 1.5 km and then turn at a sign for Qal'at al-Hazm. It is impossible to miss.

SUR

Sur (Sour) is a fairly quiet place but has great beaches and several interesting things to see. It is only 150 km down the coast from

Muscat as the crow flies, though by road it is a bit over twice that distance. That makes it a bit too far for a day trip but it is still worth a visit.

Orientation & Information

Sur's commercial centre is several km from the government buildings that make up its administrative and historical centre. The commercial centre includes the taxi stand and bus stop, the cheaper of the town's two hotels, and a few restaurants. The post office is on the roundabout between the Sinesla Fortress and the main mosque. The Sur Beach Hotel can be reached by following the signs on the Muscat road.

Sinesla Fortress

Sur's main fort, which is on a hill overlooking the town, is relatively simple in construction: a defensive wall that is roughly square in shape, with towers at the four corners. Look carefully and you will notice that the two watchtowers facing the sea are slightly taller than the two that face inland. The fort is open daily from 7.30 am to 6 pm. Admission is free.

Bilad Fort

The more impressive of Sur's two forts is just over six km inland from the centre on the road heading back toward Muscat. It is open daily from 7.30 am to 6 pm. The fort is approximately 200 years old. Its basic design – lots of open space, little in the way of accommodation – implies that it was a defensive rather than an administrative centre.

To reach Bilad Fort take the Muscat road from the centre. After six km turn right just past a green sign with a white drawing of a fort and an arrow pointing to the right. From the turn-off go 300m and you will see the fort directly in front of you.

Marine Museum

The highlight of this small exhibit is a collection of photographs of Sur in 1905. These were taken by the French consul in Muscat during a visit to the town and they are a striking contrast to the Sur of today. The

museum is inside the Al-Arouba Sports Club and is open daily from approximately 8 am to noon and from 4 to 7 pm. Admission is free. The club is across the road from the side of Sinesla through which the fort's compound is entered and about 100m closer to the centre. Look for a stone wall with sports figures painted on it.

Dhow Building Yard

At any given time a dozen or more dhows may be under construction in Sur's dhow yard. Since this is a working yard rather than a tourist sight per se there is no ticket booth, and certainly no requirement that you have a permit. The dhow yard is just over three km from the centre.

Ayega

Just beyond the dhow yard is a small ferry that will carry you across the narrow sound to Ayega, a village where many of the dhow builders live. The two storey sand-coloured building near the Ayega ferry landing is the house reserved for the sultan whenever he comes to visit. The ferry crossing is free and takes about two minutes.

Places to Stay & Eat

Cheapish beds can be found in the town centre at the *Sur Hotel* (☎ 440090; fax 443798). Singles/doubles are OR13.800/ 26.200, all with bath. Sur's up-market hotel is the somewhat overpriced *Sur Beach Hotel* (☎ 442031; fax 442228), with rooms at OR25.300/32.200. It is 5.3 km north of the centre and is the only place in town that serves alcohol.

The *Arabian Sea Restaurant* on the ground floor of the same building as the Sur Hotel (though the entrance faces the other side of the block) is a good enough place to eat. Most of its main dishes cost OR1 to OR1.500, though you can also get sandwiches for 200 to 500 baisa. Several similar small restaurants are in the area near the hotel.

Getting There & Away

The airport is south of the centre on the

OMAN

Sur-Muscat road. Oman Aviation has three flights a week between Muscat and Sur. The fare is OR14 a single, OR28 return. Tickets can be purchased, and return flights reconfirmed, through Oman Orient for Travel & Tours (☎ 440279), in the centre.

There are three buses per day between Muscat and Sur (4¼ hours express, 5½ hours regular; OR3.400). Service taxis for Muscat (OR3.500 to the Seeb clock tower roundabout) tout for passengers in the parking lot around the corner from the Sur Hotel. Microbuses make the same trip for OR3, but these are not really major modes of transport along the Sur route.

SAMAIL

From the main Muscat-Nizwa road Samail appears to be little more than a bus stop that people usually head straight past. But 10 km from the junction with the main road is **Samail Fort**, nestled between a wadi and an oasis of palm trees to one side and a hill of dark, loose stone to the other. Even though you cannot get into the fort, it is worth stopping for a look, and making the climb up to the watchtowers for a view out over the oasis.

To reach the fort turn off the Muscat-Nizwa road (a left turn if you are coming from Muscat) at the big green sign welcoming you to the Samail Wilayat. If you are coming from Nizwa look for a sign saying 'Samail 4 km' and pointing right. Follow the road for 10 km until you reach a junction with a road going off to the right and a sign saying 'Luzugh 10 km', pointing in the direction you are travelling. At this point you should be able to see one of the watchtowers on the hill above you and to the left. About 250m beyond the sign turn left onto a dirt track between two whitewashed walls. The fort will be on your left.

The Samail road junction is a stop on the bus route from Muscat to Nizwa. The fare from either city is 900 baisa. Microbuses charge 500 baisa for the trip from the Seeb clock tower (800 baisa from Ruwi). The shared taxi fare from the clock tower is OR1. From Nizwa to Samail the microbus fare is

700 baisa while taxis charge OR1.500. From the junction to the fort the microbus fare is 200 to 300 baisa each way.

NIZWA

Only 45 years ago Wilfred Thesiger was forced to keep well clear of Nizwa. As the seat of the imams who then ruled much of the country's interior it had a reputation for ferocious conservatism. Today, visitors need have no such worries; Nizwa has rapidly emerged as one of Oman's major tourist centres. It is probably the country's most popular destination after Muscat.

Orientation & Information

Nizwa's main landmark is the large, blue-domed mosque which is on your left if you enter the town from the direction of Muscat. The souq is the area immediately around the mosque. Past the mosque the main street swings around to the right into the town's business area. The taxi stand and bus stop are both by the parking lot in front of the mosque. The post office is located in the souq. You can change money at any of the several banks in the centre.

Nizwa Fort

The fort was built in the mid-17th century by Sultan bin Saif, the first imam of the Al-Ya'ribi dynasty. For the next 300 years it was the primary seat of the imamate, serving as a combination palace, seat of government and prison. It is open daily from 7.30 am to 4 pm (until 5 pm from June to September). Admission is free.

Nizwa Souq

The town's other great attraction is its souq. Despite having been moved into more 'modern' quarters a few years ago the souq retains much of its colour and vitality. The bad news is that the souq's popularity with package tours has made it one of the worst places in the sultanate to shop for souvenirs. The best thing to do is to avoid the silver souq altogether and spend your time wandering among the merchants buying and selling fish, meat, fruits and vegetables, household goods, dates and goats.

Places to Stay & Eat

Nizwa's two hotels will both put a dent in your budget. By far the better deal is the *Falaj Daris Hotel* (☎ 410500; fax 410430) where singles/doubles cost OR21/28.350, including tax and service. The hotel is on the Muscat road, 4.5 km from the centre. It's on the left if you are coming from the capital. About 20 km from the centre is the *Nizwa Hotel* (☎ 431616; fax 431619) where the rooms cost OR34.500/40.250. The restau-

rants and bars at the two hotels are the only places in Nizwa that serve alcohol.

For a quick snack in town there's a shwarma stand at the *Fakhry Restaurant & Coffeeshop* on the main street, next to the Habib Bank office. Shwarma cost 150 baisa apiece. For full meals try the *Arab World Restaurant & Cafeteria*, which is across the street and under a large Pepsi sign. A meal usually costs OR1 to OR2 with good chicken and kebab dishes leading the menu. Note, for navigational purposes, that there is another restaurant with the same name a couple of km outside the centre on the road to Muscat. Near Nizwa's taxi stand *Al-Hazfa* has excellent chicken and mutton biryanis and curries for 600 baisa, and the portions are fairly large to boot. The restaurant is on the 1st floor of the small complex of shops facing the mosque and the souq.

Getting There & Away

ONTC operates six buses per day between Nizwa and Muscat (2½ hours express, three hours regular; OR1.600). There are also regular buses from Nizwa to Ibri.

You can catch the south-bound bus from Muscat to Salalah at the roundabout on the edge of Nizwa where the highway from Muscat to Ibri meets the road coming up from Salalah. The buses come through Nizwa at approximately 9 am and 9 pm every day. The fare from Nizwa to Salalah is OR7.200 one way and tickets can be purchased from the driver. You might want to telephone the Ruwi bus station in Muscat (☎ 708522) to reserve a seat in advance.

Taxi/microbus fares from Nizwa to the Seeb clock tower roundabout outside Muscat are OR1.500/1 (to Ruwi add 500 baisa). Microbuses go to Samail for 700 baisa while service taxis charge OR1.500 for the same trip. Ibri is OR2, by taxi or microbus. Other microbus destinations include Bahla (500 baisa) and Jabrin (700 baisa). A taxi to Bahla or Jabrin costs OR8 engaged.

BAHLA

At the time of writing the huge **fort** that dominates the small town of Bahla, 40 km west of

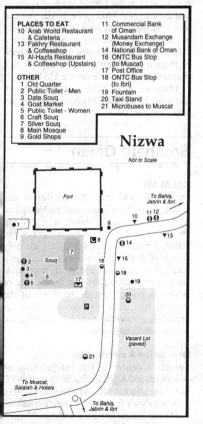

PLACES TO EAT
10 Arab World Restaurant & Cafeteria
13 Fakhry Restaurant & Coffeeshop
15 Al-Hazfa Restaurant & Coffeeshop (Upstairs)

OTHER
1 Old Quarter
2 Public Toilet - Men
3 Date Souq
4 Goat Market
5 Public Toilet - Women
6 Craft Souq
7 Silver Souq
8 Main Mosque
9 Gold Shops
11 Commercial Bank of Oman
12 Musandam Exchange (Money Exchange)
14 National Bank of Oman
16 ONTC Bus Stop (to Muscat)
17 Post Office
18 ONTC Bus Stop (to Ibri)
19 Fountain
20 Taxi Stand
21 Microbuses to Muscat

Nizwa

Not to Scale

Fort

To Bahla, Jabrin & Ibri

Souq

P

Vacant Lot (paved)

To Muscat, Salalah & Hotels

To Bahla, Jabrin & Ibri

OMAN

Nizwa, was undergoing restoration. Parts of Bahla Fort are thought to be pre-Islamic in origin and when work on it is complete the site, which lies smack on the main road from Nizwa to Jabrin and Ibri, should be a major tourist attraction.

Between the bus stop and the fort you can see a **well**, which is still in use, and behind the fort you will find a portion of Bahla's **city wall**. West of the centre, there are more **fortifications** guarding the approach to the town across the adjacent wadi.

The only hotel in the area is the *Bahla Motel* (π 420211; fax 420212), 5.4 km east of the centre on the road coming from Nizwa. It has large, if somewhat pricey, rooms at OR17.250/23 for singles/doubles. Near the fort you can get a bite to eat at the *Nasser al-Wardi Restaurant and Coffeeshop* which offers the usual chicken or mutton curries for 600 baisa each. Half a broasted chicken with rice costs 900 baisa.

Buses for Bahla leave Muscat (three hours express, 3½ hours regular; OR2) three times daily. From Nizwa the trip takes about 45 minutes and costs 300 baisa. Microbuses charge 500 baisa for the trip from Nizwa.

JABRIN

Jabrin (Jibreen) is one of Oman's most dramatic forts. It is large and imposing and its location commands the entire plain and surrounding hilltops. Jabrin is worth visiting if only for the restoration job, which is one of the best in Oman. It is a much more impressive place than Nizwa and its restored state gives one some sense of what it looked like in its prime. Many of the rooms inside the fort are labelled, most of them in English.

To reach the fort from Nizwa follow the Ibri road for 45.5 km then turn at a sign for Jabrin. After another four km the pavement ends at a small roundabout. Turn right, go 500m, and you will reach the fort. The fort is open daily from 8 am to 5 pm. Admission is free.

Buses from Muscat to Ibri and vice versa stop at the road junction for Jabrin. The trip from Muscat takes four hours by express bus

or five hours on a regular bus, and costs OR2.200.

BURAIMI

The long-disputed Buraimi oasis straddles the border between Oman and Abu Dhabi in the UAE. Both the Omani and the Emirati sides of the oasis are covered in this book's UAE chapter. This is because the Omani portion of the oasis is effectively in a customs union with Abu Dhabi.

Approaching the oasis from the Omani side requires that you pass through outgoing Omani customs. Once through this checkpoint (53 km from the border) you can pass freely between the Omani town of Buraimi and the city of Al-Ain in the UAE. You can also continue up the road to anywhere else in the UAE. Approaching the oasis from the UAE side does not involve a customs check or require any documentation beyond that ordinarily required to enter the UAE.

There are three buses per day between Buraimi and Muscat (3¾ hours express, six hours regular; OR3.600).

Southern Oman

SALALAH

Oman's second city, the capital of the country's southern region and the birthplace of Sultan Qaboos, Salalah is a striking change from Muscat. Salalah catches the Indian summer monsoon (virtually the only corner of Arabia which does so) and, as a result, it is cool, wet and green from mid-June to mid-September just as the rest of Arabia is going through the worst of the summer heat. It is also the best base for exploring the villages and archaeological sites of southern Oman.

Orientation & Information

Salalah's centre is the intersection of A'Nahdah and A'Salam Sts. Both the ONTC bus station and the Redan Hotel are a 10 to 15 minute walk from this intersection and the gold souq is right around the corner. Most of the city's businesses are either along, or just off, one of these streets.

Money There are several banks and a few exchange houses around the intersection of A'Nahdah and A'Salam Sts. The Oman United Exchange Company usually offers good rates. For those who arrive by bus and need cash immediately there is a branch of the Commercial Bank of Oman just south of the new souq.

Amex is represented in Salalah by Zubair Travel (☎ 291145) on A'Nahdah St. It cannot cash cheques for Amex clients but it will hold

mail. Mail should be addressed to: American Express – Clients' Mail, c/o Zubair Travels & Service Bureau – Salalah Branch Office, PO Box 809, Postal Code 211, Oman. The office is open Saturday to Thursday from 8 am to 1 pm and from 4 to 7 pm, and Friday from 9 to 11 am.

Post & Communications The GPO is on A'Nahdah St, next to the telephone company's administrative centre (the place with the big antenna), though you have to exit A'Nahdah St and enter the building from the back. It is open Saturday to Wednesday from

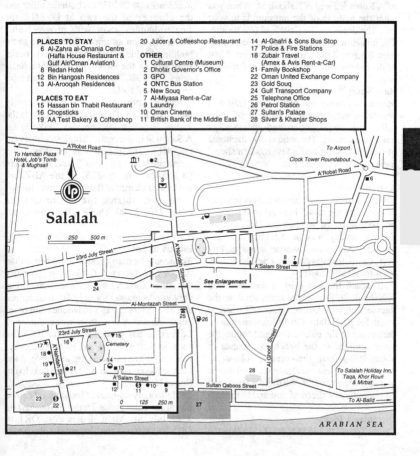

PLACES TO STAY
6 Al-Zahra al-Omania Centre
   (Haffa House Restaurant &
   Gulf Air/Oman Aviation)
8 Redan Hotel
12 Bin Hangosh Residences
13 Al-Arooqah Residences

PLACES TO EAT
15 Hassan bin Thabit Restaurant
16 Chopsticks
19 AA Test Bakery & Coffeeshop

20 Juicer & Coffeeshop Restaurant

OTHER
1 Cultural Centre (Museum)
2 Dhofar Governor's Office
3 GPO
4 ONTC Bus Station
5 New Souq
7 Al-Miyasa Rent-a-Car
9 Laundry
10 Oman Cinema
11 British Bank of the Middle East

14 Al-Ghafri & Sons Bus Stop
17 Police & Fire Stations
18 Zubair Travel
   (Amex & Avis Rent-a-Car)
21 Family Bookshop
22 Oman United Exchange Company
23 Gold Souq
24 Gulf Transport Company
25 Telephone Office
26 Petrol Station
27 Sultan's Palace
28 Silver & Khanjar Shops

To Hamdan Plaza Hotel, Job's Tomb & Mughsail

A'Robat Road

To Airport

Clock Tower Roundabout

A'Robat Road

Salalah

0   250   500 m

23rd July Street

A'Salam Street

See Enlargement

Al-Montazah Street

23rd July Street

Cemetery

A'Salam Street

Sultan Qaboos Street

0   125   250 m

To Salalah Holiday Inn, Taqa, Khor Rouri & Mirbat

To Al-Balid

ARABIAN SEA

7.30 am to 1.30 pm and Thursday from 9 to 11 am but is closed on Friday.

The telephone office is at the intersection of A'Nahdah and Al-Montazah Sts. It's open every day from 7.30 am to 12.30 am. Fax and telex facilities are also available but these close down around 9 pm.

Museum

Salalah's museum is in the Cultural Centre on A'Robat Rd (access is from the back, via A'Nahdah St). There is no English lettering on the building, but it is the huge white place, the second building west of the intersection of A'Robat Rd and A'Nahdah St. When you enter the main door the museum is to your left. The doors on the right lead to a theatre. The museum is open Saturday to Wednesday from 8 am to 2 pm. Admission is free. Most of the exhibits are labelled only in Arabic.

New Souq

Mixed in among the meat, fish, fruit and vegetable vendors are a handful of stalls selling kohl boxes, pottery and other locally–made handicrafts. The souq is also the home of the bus station and a few modern shops, most of which sell textiles.

Al-Balid

The ruins of Al-Balid, site of the ancient city of Zafar, lie about 4.5 km east of the centre on the coast, just west of the Holiday Inn. Zafar's heyday was in the 11th and 12th centuries AD when it was an active trading port. Coins from as far away as China have been found at the site.

To reach the site start in the centre on A'Nahdah St. Follow the street south to the intersection with Sultan Qaboos St (there is a sign for Al-Hafah). Go 400m, turn right on the corner of the palace wall and follow the street straight to the beach (a distance of about 300m from the corner). Follow the beach road for just over three km until it ends at a small roundabout. Al-Balid's fence will be immediately ahead of you and to the left.

Organised Tours

Orient Tours (☎ 235333; fax 235137) in the lobby of the Holiday Inn Hotel, and Al-Miyasa Rent-a-Car (☎ & fax 296521), on A'Salam St next door to the Redan Hotel, offer half-day and full-day tours of Salalah and the rest of Dhofar. Unfortunately these are out of reach of the budget traveller unless you have a group of four people: all tours are priced by the vehicle, and they start at around OR60.

Places to Stay

Salalah's cheapest beds are to be found at two small hotels in the centre, both near the Al-Ghafri & Sons bus stop. The *Al-Arooqah Residences* (☎ 292935) is both the nicer and the cheaper of the two at OR8/12 for singles/doubles, most with private baths. The hotel is on an upper floor of the same building beside which the Al-Ghafri buses stop. Across the street *Bin Hangosh Residences* (☎ 298079) is not as good, and a bit pricier, at OR10/15.

Salalah's other hotels are all significantly more expensive. The cheapest of these is the *Redan Hotel* (☎ 292266; fax 290491) on A'Salam St in the centre. Singles/doubles are OR14/17. The location is good and the rooms are large and clean. The *Haffa House* (☎ 295444; fax 294873) in the Al-Zahra al-Omania Centre at the clock tower round-about just outside the centre charges OR28.750/32.200. This is a large but rather dull place.

Places to Eat

You would be hard-pressed to do better than the *AA Test Bakery & Coffeeshop* (formerly the Antco Bakery) on A'Nahdah St. It has very good samosas for only 50 baisa apiece and also offers cheap sandwiches and other quick snacks. A few doors away, *Juicer & Coffeeshop* has good shwarma for 200 baisa each, as well as sodas and juice. Cheap but substantial Indian meals are available at the *Gareez Restaurant* on A'Salam St next to the Redan Hotel.

Moderately up-market Indian food can be had at the *Hassan bin Thabit Restaurant* on 23rd July St. Main dishes cost OR1 to OR1.500, but you can also get simple curries for 500 to 700 baisa. For anything much fancier – or for alcohol – you'll probably have to head for the *Holiday Inn*.

Activities & Entertainment

What social life there is in Salalah centres on the *Holiday Inn*. Outsiders can use the hotel's pool for the day for OR3. The hotel also has a nightclub with live entertainment, usually a lounge band and a belly dancer, and a disco on weekends.

Things to Buy

Among Dhofar's most distinctive souvenirs are the small, bead-covered plastic bottles used by women to carry kohl for decorating their eyes. These are a far cry from the silver kohl boxes used by both men and women in the northern part of the country, and also a lot more affordable. They can be purchased in the new souq for OR3 to OR5, depending on size.

Other locally made crafts available in the new souq include pottery incense burners. These cost OR1.500 to OR10, depending on size.

Getting There & Away

Air Salalah's small airport is served only by Oman Aviation (☎ 295747). Their office is on the 1st floor of the Al-Zahra al-Omania Centre by the clock tower roundabout. There are two flights per day to Muscat. The fare is OR27 one way and OR50 return.

Bus Buses leave the ONTC bus station in the new souq for Muscat every day at 7 am and 7 pm, with an extra bus at 6 pm from mid-June to mid-September (12 hours; OR8 one way, OR16 return). Departures are one hour later during Ramadan. You can store luggage in the ONTC ticket office at the new souq.

Al-Ghafri & Sons (☎ 293574) also runs buses to Muscat every day at 7 am and 4.45 pm. Departures are from its office on A'Salam St. In Muscat the buses arrive at the company's office near the Ruwi bus station. At OR8 one way and OR14 return, the fare is a bit cheaper than ONTC's, but the buses are older and clunkier.

Taxi & Microbus Salalah's taxis and microbuses hang out in front of the British Bank of the Middle East on A'Salam St in the centre. Taxis will generally only make inter-city trips on an engaged basis, which is invariably expensive (OR10 to Taqa, for example). Microbus fares from Salalah include: Taqa, 300 Baisa; Mirbat, 500 Baisa; Mughsail, OR1; Thumrait, OR1; and Muscat, OR8.

Getting Around

Local taxis and microbuses gather in front of the British Bank of the Middle East on A'Salam St in the centre. Generally a micro-bus ride inside the city costs around 200 baisa and a taxi ride about 500 baisa. To further flung destinations like the Holiday Inn OR1 should be sufficient.

If you want to rent a car in Salalah try Al-Miyasa Rent-a-Car (☎ 296521) on A'Salam St next door to the Redan hotel (look for the large 'Car Rent' sign). It offers small cars for OR14, including insurance and 200 free km per day. Budget (☎ 235160) has a desk at the Holiday Inn. There is an Avis office at Zubair Travel (☎ 291145) on A'Nahdah St and Thrifty has an office in the Al-Zahra al-Omania Centre.

AROUND SALALAH

There are very good **beaches** all along the road to Mughsail once you're about five km out of Salalah. Overnight camping on the beach is not allowed.

MUGHSAIL

Mughsail (Mugsail) is 45 km west of Salalah. It offers beautiful unspoiled beaches as well as some spectacular scenery on the drive out. This includes several groves of **frankincense trees** 15 to 25 km out of Salalah. Most of the trees are along the right-hand side of the road if you are coming from Salalah. When young or not flowering they are mostly small, gnarled and less than impressive.

If you continue beyond Mughsail on the road toward the Yemeni border the landscape gets even more spectacular.

OMAN

Microbuses charge OR1 in either direction for the trip between Salalah and Mughsail.

JOB'S TOMB

In religious terms the mortuary known as Job's Tomb (and referred to in Arabic simply as 'Nabi Ayoub' – Prophet Job) is probably the most important site in Dhofar. Regardless of your religious convictions the tomb – situated on an isolated hilltop overlooking Salalah – is a must-see both for the beautiful drive up to its mountain site and for the excellent view over Salalah that the parking lot affords on a clear day.

The tomb is just over 30 km from Salalah's centre. To reach it take the main west-bound road from the centre toward Mughsail and turn right at the sign for Ittin when you are on the outskirts of Salalah, just after passing the Hamdan Plaza Hotel. From the turn-off follow this road for 22 km and then turn left off the main road at a sign that says 'Al-Nabi Ayoub 1½ km'. After 1.4 km you will come to a fork in the road. Keeping right takes you to the restaurant, while going left takes you to the parking lot outside the tomb enclosure. There is no public transport to or from the tomb.

TAQA

The village of Taqa, 36 km east of Salalah, is definitely worth a stop both for its **castle** and for the **cemetery** where Sultan Qaboos' mother, Maizoun bint Ahmed al-M'ashti, is buried.

The castle is easy to find – just follow the brown and white signs once you enter Taqa. It is open Saturday to Wednesday from 7.30 am to 2.30 pm. Admission is free. To reach the cemetery from the castle turn left out of the castle's door and walk straight toward the main road. Between the castle and the road is the **Mosque of Shaikh al-Affif**. The cemetery is in front of the mosque. Stand facing the mosque and the graveyard and look all the way to your left. At the left-hand corner of the graveyard, near the road, you will see several ornate graves, each marked by two stones. Among these is a single grave with

three stones: this is the grave of Sultan Qaboos' mother.

Microbuses stop on the town's main road a few hundred metres west of the turn for the castle. The fare from Salalah to Taqa is 300 baisa. Taxis will only make the trip from Salalah 'engaged'. This will probably cost around OR10.

KHOR ROURI

Centuries ago Khor Rouri was an important port controlling the southern end of the frankincense route. It was then known as Sumhuram. Today, little remains of the city except the ruins of a palace-cum-fort sitting atop a mound of rather nondescript rubble. The setting, however, is dramatic enough to make the site worth going out of your way to visit.

To reach the site take the road from Salalah toward Mirbat and turn at the Khor Rouri sign, about seven km beyond Taqa's centre. There is another turn-off further down the road, but the first turn, coming from Salalah, is the easier of the two to navigate. The site is 2.5 km off the main road along a bumpy dirt track. Follow the track for 2.1 km to a fork. Keep right at the fork and you will see the mound and the fence on your right after another 400m.

The microbus fare from Salalah should be 300 to 400 baisa, but you will have to walk to the gate from the main road.

MIRBAT

The town of Mirbat (Mirbaat), just over 70 km east of Salalah, is about as far east of Salalah as you can go without a 4WD. The town's small **fort** has a lonely, end-of-the-road feel about it as it overlooks both the town and the coastline trailing off back toward Salalah.

Mirbat's other noteworthy site is the **Bin Ali Tomb**, a small and quite photogenic mosque built in a style typical of Yemen's Hadhramawt region. The tomb is one km off the main road. It is the larger of the two white tombs in the cemetery – the one closer to the parking area.

Musandem Peninsula

Separated from the rest of Oman by the east coast of the UAE, and guarding the southern side of the strategically important Strait of Hormuz, the Musandem peninsula is a land of stark beauty. It is the least developed part of the Gulf's least developed country; an area of fjords, small villages and dramatic, mountain-hugging roads.

It is not a particularly easy place to travel. There are no paved roads in the Musandem outside of the town centres in Khasab, Bukha and the Omani portion of Dibba. Public transport exists more in theory than in practice and some of the region's settlements are accessible only by boat. It is also very expensive, even by Omani standards.

The good news is that the widely held belief that you cannot move about outside of Khasab without a 4WD is not true. This section lists most of the places in the Musandem you can visit using a regular car.

KHASAB

The Musandem peninsula's capital is small but far from sleepy. Its port bursts with activity, much of it involving the smuggling of US cigarettes to Iran, and its souq is filled with both visitors from other parts of the Musandem and an ever-increasing number of tourists.

Orientation & Information

For such a small place Khasab is surprisingly spread out. The town's commercial centre is the port and the small souq a km or so south-east of it. Another 1.5 km to the east is the town's new souq. This consists of a few restaurants and grocery stores, the post office, a couple of banks, Khasab's lone car rental agency and the Oman Aviation office. The Khasab Hotel and the airport lie a short distance to the south.

Khasab Fort

There is nothing especially remarkable about Khasab Fort. What sets this fort apart is the setting. The fort dominates the bit of coast that provides access to Khasab's older sections and the mountains rise dramatically on three sides. Its opening hours are a bit erratic. Government office hours (Saturday to Wednesday from 7.30 am to 2.30 pm) are your best bet. Admission is free.

Kumzan Fort

Kumzan Fort is a ruin, but it is worth the diversion if only for the contrast with Khasab fort. To reach it go east out of the roundabout by the Oman Aviation office (a right turn if you are coming from the Khasab Hotel, straight if you are coming from Khasab Fort and the port) in the new souq area and turn left onto a paved street after 300m. Follow this street for another 1.3 km as it winds through a residential area. The fort will be on your left.

Beach

There is a small beach just outside Khasab.

Musandem Peninsula

0   10   20 km

Road passable with 4WD vehicle only

Strait of Hormuz

Musandem Island

ARABIAN
GULF

Khor Ash Shamm

Kumzar

Al-Harf   Hanah

Quida

Bukha   Tawi   Khasab

Tibat (Oman)

Sham

Khor Najd

Khor Habalayn

OMAN

Sayh

1488 m

Lima

GULF OF OMAN

Ras al-Khaimah

Rawdah Checkpoint

To Dubai (90 km)

1527 m

UNITED ARAB EMIRATES

Dibba Bayah (Oman)
Dibba Hisn (UAE)

Dibba Muhallab (UAE)

To Masafi

To Fujairah

OMAN

Follow the road from the port toward Bukha. The beach is at a lay-by on the right exactly one km after the point where the pavement ends.

Organised Tours

Khasab Travel & Tours (☎ 830464) offers full-day and half-day boat trips around Musandem's fjords. These trips are for groups really and can be very expensive. The company is a bit fuzzy on numbers but the critical mass appears to be four to six people.

Places to Stay & Eat

The only hotel in the entire Musandem is the *Khasab Hotel* (☎ 830267; fax 830989). At OR18.975/32.200 for singles/doubles, including the tax and service charge, it is rather overpriced. There's a pool, and the hotel also has the Musandem's only bar.

In the new souq the *Bukha Restaurant* has biryanis that are more subtly spiced than those one usually finds down in Muscat. These cost 600 baisa per serving. Kebabs are available in the evening and the place is popular with the Iranian cigarette smugglers – always a good sign. For broasted chicken try the *Musandem Restaurant* in the new souq area. Half a chicken costs 600 baisa. Rice is 300 baisa a portion.

Smugglers

What is interesting about Khasab port is the little bay next to the dhow jetty and customs building where, on any given day, 100 or so speedboats from Iran are anchored or pulled up on the shore. The Iranians are smugglers who make the short trip over from Bandar-é Abbas to purchase goods that are expensive or hard to find at home. A quick walk through the souq will show you what the Iranians are in the market for. Maybe half of all the shops in the souq are bulk cigarette merchants. The Iranians buy enormous quantities of cigarettes, wrap the boxes up in plastic and, after dark, head back across the strait. ∎

Getting There & Away

Air Oman Aviation's office (☎ 830543) is on the new souq's main roundabout, between the Khasab Hotel and the port area. It has flights to Muscat four days a week. Fares are OR20 one way and OR40 return, a price you will find hard to beat by going overland unless you have your own car.

Service Taxi The 10-passenger 4WD pick-up trucks that serve as the Musandem's service taxis gather in Khasab's old souq, near the port. The drivers say they travel to Bukha and Tibat for OR1 per passenger but there does not appear to be a lot of action. It's most likely you will have to take a vehicle 'engaged'. The standard engaged rates are: Bukha, OR5; Tibat or Khor Najd, OR10; Dibba, OR25; and Muscat, OR70.

Though it is only about 70 km from Ras al-Khaimah to Khasab there are no service taxis making the run on a regular basis. The Khasab pick-up drivers charge OR15 for the trip to Ras al-Khaimah (about two hours if there are no problems at the border). From Ras al-Khaimah service-taxi drivers demand Dh 200 for the trip to Khasab, though for Dh 40 they will take you to the Sham border post, from where you can try to hitch a ride into Khasab. To leave the UAE by road you will also have to pay a Dh 20 road tax.

Car Khasab's only car rental operation is Bana Rent-a-Car (☎ 830678) on the new souq's main roundabout. Its rates are pretty outrageous – OR10 to rent an ageing compact for use in Khasab only. If you want to take the car to Bukha the rate goes up to OR15, while Khor Najd sends it to OR20. You could, of course, lie to the staff about where you plan to take the car, but if you tell them you are staying in Khasab this fact will be written into your rental agreement – meaning that any accident or damage outside the town will not be covered by the insurance. The company also demands an OR50 cash deposit for all rentals and will only accept cash – no plastic.

Hitching You can also try asking around the

bar at the Khasab Hotel. The problem you are likely to run into is that most of the people propping up the bar at the hotel are expats, many of whom may not be aware that tourists do not need road permits. This may make them reluctant to take you when they discover that you have no road permit.

Getting Around

The Airport Khasab may have the only airport in the world that is completely devoid of taxis. The Khasab Hotel will meet your flight if you have a reservation there and can also give you a lift to the airport when it is time to leave. Either of these services costs OR3. If someone offers you a lift into town but expects to be paid for the service do not agree to pay more than OR2, as the distance is only a few km.

Taxi The Musandem's only form of public transport is open 4WD pick-up trucks with benches in the back. These are the local service taxis, though it is rare to see one actually going anywhere with passengers in it. Should one of these vehicles actually be moving, the driver will charge a couple of hundred baisa for a lift within the town.

TAWI

About 10 km from the spot near Khasab port where the pavement ends lies the village of Tawi, site of a handful of prehistoric **rock carvings**. To reach the carvings turn inland off the Khasab-Bukha road and onto a dirt track at Quida. Coming from Khasab the track is just beyond the sign with the village's name on it but before you pass any of Quida's houses. Follow this track up the Wadi Quida for 2.3 km. The carvings will be to your left on two rocks at a point where the track bends sharply to the right just before a large white house. Across the track from the carvings is an ancient **well** that is still used by Tawi's residents.

BUKHA

Bukha has the distinction of being the only place in the Musandem outside Khasab and Dibba with paved streets or, more accurately,

a paved street. It also has two forts. The more interesting of the two is **Bukha Fort**, on the coast. If you are coming from Khasab the fort is the first thing you will arrive at. The other fort, which is in ruins, is on a hill a short distance inland and north of Bukha Fort.

KHOR NAJD

Khor Najd (Khor A'Najd) is the only one of the Musandem's fjords that can be reached from Khasab in an ordinary car, though it needs to be a car in fairly decent repair considering how steep (both climbing and descending) the last portion of the drive is. It is 24.5 km by road from Khasab's centre, about a 45 minute drive.

To reach Khor Najd go west from the new souq roundabout and turn off the pavement after 350m, on the corner where you see a coffee-pot-shaped sculpture (the 24.5 km mentioned above is measured from this point). After 200m the road forks. Keep left and follow the road for another 3.4 km (the airport perimeter fence will be on your left) until you reach an intersection with a sign reading 'Dabba 110 km'. Continue straight through this intersection. Just over 8.5 km beyond the Dabba intersection you will see a green sign pointing to, among other places, 'Khor A'Najd 10 km'. Turn left, follow this road for another 5.6 km and then turn left again. After another 1.5 km you will come to a three way fork in the road. Take the centre road and you will soon begin a steep ascent. After 2.3 km you will reach the outlook, and your first view of Khor Najd. Another (even steeper) 2.8 km descent brings you to the water's edge.

KUMZAR

Set on an isolated cove at the northern edge of the Musandem peninsula, Kumzar is accessible only by boat. The village's residents do not speak Arabic. Their language, known as Kumzari, is a mish-mash of Fārsī, Hindi, English and Arabic.

The village's only 'sight' is a **well** half a km or so up the wadi that serves as Kumzar's main 'street'. The well, which is now brackish, was Kumzar's sole source of water until

OMAN

the government built a small desalination plant next to the harbour in the '70s. The main attraction of a visit to Kumzar is really the spectacular scenery on the boat trip out and back.

Water taxis travel between Khasab and Kumzar most days, charging OR3 per head. This can be a pretty harrowing trip. Most of the speedboats used as water taxis have no seats and maybe 15 cm clearance between deck and gunwale. Alternatively, you could hire an entire boat. With a little tenacity you should be able to get someone to take you over to Kumzar, wait around there for two or three hours and then bring you back for OR40. If you can split this cost among several people you will have a faster and, probably, safer trip, not to mention a more comfortable ride and a guaranteed lift back. It's not cheap, but it does have its advantages.

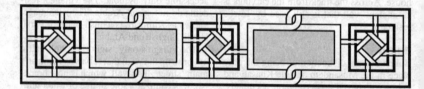

Qatar

Qatar has always had a way of falling off the outside world's radar screens: most foreign maps of Arabia drawn prior to the 19th century do not show the Qatar peninsula. The late British writer Peter Mansfield once remarked that even quiz show champions were likely to have trouble finding the place.

Though the country opened its doors to tourists in 1989, its remoteness kept it off the agendas of even the most intrepid travellers.

Facts about the Country

HISTORY

For most of its recent history, Qatar has been dominated by the Al-Thani family who arrived in the mid-18th century, when Qatar was already well established as a pearling centre, and became the peninsula's rulers about 100 years later. Activity was then centred on Zubara in the north-west. Historically, Doha (now the capital) was never a particularly important trading port, and throughout the 19th and early 20th centuries Qatar remained shockingly poor, even by pre-oil Gulf standards.

In 1915 the Emir of Qatar expelled the Turkish garrison then based in Doha. With Britain and Turkey on opposite sides in WWI, and the British controlling the rest of the Gulf, a switch in alliances seemed like a wise move. After expelling the Turks, Qatar's emir signed an exclusive agreement with the British, under which Britain guaranteed Qatar's protection in exchange for a promise that the ruler would not have any dealings with other foreign powers without British permission.

Even before the collapse of the pearl market around 1930, life in Qatar was rough. With poverty, hunger, malnutrition and disease all widespread, the emir welcomed the oil prospectors who first arrived in the early 1930s. A concession was granted in

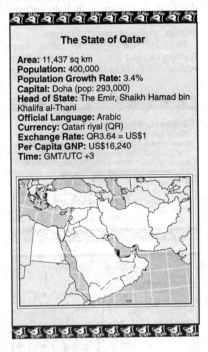

The State of Qatar

Area: 11,437 sq km
Population: 400,000
Population Growth Rate: 3.4%
Capital: Doha (pop: 293,000)
Head of State: The Emir, Shaikh Hamad bin Khalifa al-Thani
Official Language: Arabic
Currency: Qatari riyal (QR)
Exchange Rate: QR3.64 = US$1
Per Capita GNP: US$16,240
Time: GMT/UTC +3

1935 and the prospectors struck oil in 1939. Because of WWII, however, production did not begin for another 10 years.

When the British announced that they would leave the region by the end of 1971, Qatar entered talks with Bahrain and the Trucial States (now the UAE) with the intention of forming a confederation. When Bahrain pulled out of the talks, Qatar followed suit almost immediately, declaring independence on 1 September 1971. Six months later Khalifa bin Hamad al-Thani, a cousin of the emir and for many years Qatar's ruler in all but title, took power in a palace coup.

Like the other small states of the Gulf,

Qatar viewed Iran's 1979 revolution with great alarm. In 1983 the government announced that it had discovered a cache of hidden weapons and foiled a plot to overthrow it. A dispute with Bahrain over ownership of the Hawar Islands has been another consistent source of tension.

In recent years Doha has ruffled some feathers around the Gulf. In 1993 Qatar became the first Gulf country to have open diplomatic contact with Israel when the two countries' foreign ministers met in New York. The country now has contracts to supply natural gas to both Tehrān and Tel Aviv (the latter through a third party).

In June 1995 Shaikh Khalifa was unexpectedly replaced as emir by his son Hamad, until then the crown prince and defence minister. The new emir quickly announced an end to press censorship and has continued to establish Qatar as a maverick voice within the Gulf. Shaikh Hamad walked out of the 1995 Gulf summit when he objected to the choice of a Saudi rather than a Qatari as the new Gulf Cooperation Council (GCC) secretary general, and he was the only Gulf leader to attend the 1996 antiterrorism summit in Egypt in person.

GEOGRAPHY

The Qatar peninsula, which is shaped a bit like a thumb, juts northward into the Gulf from the east coast of the Arabian peninsula. It is about 160 km long and 55 to 80 km wide. The country's total area (including a number of small islands) is 11,437 sq km. The desert tends to be flat (the highest elevation in the country is only about 40m above sea level) and gravelly. There is virtually no natural vegetation.

CLIMATE

Summer (May to September) temperatures in Qatar generally average 35°C, but it not unheard of for them to reach as high as 50°C. The summer weather also tends to be terribly humid. The winter months are much milder with pleasant, cool evenings. Sandstorms are

---

Suggested Itineraries

There is not a lot to see in Qatar, but you can keep yourself occupied for a couple of days. Doha's **National Museum** is well worth a few hours of your time as is its (much smaller) **Ethnographic Museum**. Outside the capital **Al-Khor**, and the fort/museum at **Zubara** make interesting side trips. You can visit both in a single day, provided you get an early start. ■

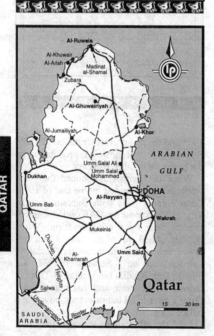

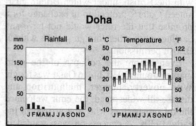

common throughout the year, especially in the spring.

FLORA & FAUNA

Qatar's lack of natural vegetation has meant that it never acquired a large population of Bedouin and, thus, no large herds of camels, at least by Arabian standards. Qatari fauna is limited to birds, such as the houbara, and to animals that are pretty hard to spot, such as bats and sand cats. You will, of course, see camels but not a lot of them.

GOVERNMENT & POLITICS

Qatar is ruled by an emir, Shaikh Hamad bin Khalifa al-Thani, who supplanted his father, Shaikh Khalifa bin Hamad al-Thani, in June 1995. Though he is, in theory, an absolute monarch, the emir must always retain the support and confidence of the other members of the ruling family. Retaining this support requires not only good government but ongoing and wide-ranging consultation with the Cabinet, other members of the ruling family and representatives of the country's larger merchant families.

The emir is also advised by a council whose 30 members he appoints. The council can comment on proposed laws, though it can neither change the proposals nor propose new laws on its own.

ECONOMY

Qatar has an oil-based economy, though in recent years natural gas has been moving to the fore. Its North Field is one of the largest natural-gas fields in the world and can probably produce for a century or more. The government has tried to diversify the economy but, as elsewhere in the Gulf, this has met with only limited success.

POPULATION & PEOPLE

About 400,000 people live in Qatar, of whom about 25% are Qataris. This makes it the smallest country in the Arab world by population. Most Qataris are of Najdi (central Arabian) ancestry, though there are also a number of families of Persian descent.

ARTS

Qatar's National Theatre (☎ 831 333) is in the Ministry of Information's building on the Corniche. Depending on the event, tickets cost from QR25 to QR50 and can be obtained from the box office. To find out what's on, enquire at a big hotel or at the theatre.

The Al-Sadd Art Gallery (☎ 427 333) features exhibitions by both Qatari and foreign artists. It is open Saturday to Thursday from 9 am to noon and 4 to 8 pm. The gallery is outside the city centre on the ground floor of the Ministry of Information's building on Al-Sadd St, near the Shebastan Restaurant.

On Friday afternoons during summer (May to September) various troops performing traditional dances can be seen around Doha and Al-Khor. Montazah Park, just beyond the C Ring Rd in Doha, is a good place to see traditional dancing. Shows usually start around 5 pm.

SOCIETY & CONDUCT
Dos & Don'ts

Qatar is more liberal than Saudi Arabia but a far cry from Bahrain or Dubai. Dress conservatively and do not wear shorts in public, except at the beach or at a hotel's swimming pool where it's more acceptable. Women should always cover their shoulders and avoid clothing that is overly tight or revealing.

RELIGION

Most Qataris adhere to the austere Wahhabi sect of Islam which also dominates in Saudi Arabia. Qatari Wahhabism, however, is less strict than the Saudi variety. For example, alcohol, which is strictly prohibited in Saudi Arabia, is available in Qatar and there is no prohibition on women driving cars.

LANGUAGE

Arabic is the official language, though in Doha it may seem that Urdu, the Pakistani language, would be more useful. In Doha, as is the case in every other capital city in the Gulf, you should have no trouble being understood in English.

QATAR

Facts for the Visitor

PLANNING

When to Go

Because the heat is so fierce in the summer and sandstorms are so common in the spring and winter, the best time to visit Doha is in November or late February and early March. This is the period during which you are most likely to get bearable temperatures with a minimum of wind.

Maps

Most of the available maps of Doha leave much to be desired. The *Tourist Map of Doha*, published by Gulf Air and available free at most big hotels, is probably your best choice.

What to Bring

Visitors during the winter months should bring a light sweater for the evenings.

VISAS & DOCUMENTS

Visas

Nationals of GCC countries and British passport holders with right of abode in the UK do not need a visa to enter Qatar. The following information applies to everyone else.

Tourist visas are available to people of any nationality (except Israelis) and can be obtained either through Doha's larger hotels for pick-up at the airport or in advance through Qatari embassies overseas.

Getting a visa through an embassy involves nothing more than filling out a couple of forms and producing a few passport-size photographs. Processing time is usually five to five working days.

If you go the hotel route the process is also fairly straightforward, but you will be required to stay in the hotel sponsoring you for as long as you are in the country. Contact the reservations department of one of the big hotels with your passport details, reason for visit (business, tourism etc), your arrival and departure dates and flight information. It will get back to you in about a week with your visa number. The visa can then be picked up at Doha airport. Be sure to keep the hotel's acknowledgement that your visa is ready – you may not be able to board your flight without it.

Tourist visas are valid for 14 days and cost QR105.

It is theoretically possible to obtain a 72 hour transit visa on arrival at Doha airport. You are likely to find, however, that the airlines are extremely reluctant to board passengers whose tickets show an overnight transit in Qatar but who do not have a tourist visa.

Visa Extensions Tourist visas can easily be extended for an additional 14 days for QR200. Visa renewal is handled by the hotel or company acting as your sponsor. If you obtained your visa through an embassy you may have to go to the Passports & Immigration Directorate in Doha and handle the process yourself, but if you are staying in a large hotel you may be able to convince the hotel to take care of it for you.

EMBASSIES

Qatari Embassies Abroad

There are Qatari embassies in the following countries:

Iran
    Bozorgrah-é Afrigha, 4 Kheyabun-é Gol Azin, Tehrān (☎ (2) 222 1255)
Kuwait
    Diplomatic Area, Al-Istiqlal St, Kuwait City (☎ 251 3599)
Oman
    Al-Maamoura St, Ruwi, Muscat (☎ 701802)
Saudi Arabia
    Takhassosi Rd, near the Euromarche supermarket, Riyadh (☎ (01) 482 5544)
    Mohammed bin Abdul Aziz St, Area N-23, Al-Andalus District, Jeddah (☎ (02) 665 2538)
UAE
    Al-Muntasser St, 26th District, Abu Dhabi (☎ (02) 435 900)
    Trade Centre Rd, Al-Mankhool District, Bur Dubai, near the Bur Juman Centre, Dubai (☎ (04) 452 888)
UK
    1 South Audley St, London, W1Y 5DQ (☎ (0171) 493 2200)

USA
> Suite 1180, 600 New Hampshire Ave NW, Washington DC 20037 (☎ (202) 338 0111)
> 22nd Floor, 747 3rd Ave, New York, NY 10017 (☎ (212) 486 9355)

Foreign Embassies in Qatar

The following countries have diplomatic representation in Qatar:

Australia
> Australian interests are looked after by the British embassy

Iran
> Diplomatic Area, beyond the Doha Sheraton Hotel (☎ 835 300)

Kuwait
> Diplomatic Area, beyond the Doha Sheraton Hotel (☎ 832 111)

New Zealand
> New Zealand interests are looked after by the British embassy

Oman
> Villa 7, 41 Ibn al-Qassem St, Hilal District, facing the C Ring Rd (☎ 670 744)

Saudi Arabia
> Diplomatic Area, beyond the Doha Sheraton Hotel (☎ 832 030)

UAE
> Khalifa Town District, off Al-Khor St (☎ 885 111)

UK
> Al-Istiqlal St in the Rumailiah District, near Murmar Palace (☎ 421 991)

USA
> At the intersection of Ahmed bin Ali and Al-Jazira al-Arabiya Sts, opposite the TV station on the northern outskirts of Doha (☎ 864 701)

CUSTOMS

You are not allowed to import alcohol or pork products. Videos may also come in for careful scrutiny. There is no limit on the number of cigarettes and cigars or the amount of loose tobacco you can bring in.

MONEY
Costs

On an absolutely rock-bottom budget, you might be able to live in Doha on QR100 (US$28) a day. This assumes you can get a tourist visa through a Qatari embassy. Otherwise, the cheapest hotel that sponsors visas (the Oasis) charges about QR300 (US$82) per night.

Currency

The Qatari riyal (QR) is divided into 100 dirhams, which are also commonly referred to as *halalas*. Coins come in 25 and 50 dirhams. Notes come in denominations of QR1, 5, 10, 50, 100 and 500. The Qatari riyal is fully convertible so there is no black market and there are no exchange controls. Many shops will also accept Saudi riyals at par for small transactions.

Currency Exchange

Australia	A$1	=	QR2.76
France	FF1	=	QR0.72
Germany	DM1	=	QR2.46
UK	UK£1	=	QR5.64
USA	US$1	=	QR3.64

Changing Money

Moneychangers will generally provide you with slightly better rates than banks, though changing travellers' cheques at a moneychanger can often be a trying experience. It is also possible to get money from ATMs throughout the country. All British Bank of the Middle East ATMs are tied into the Cirrus, Plus, ETC and Global Access systems. The ATMs at Commercial Bank of Qatar branches are also tied into Cirrus and Plus, as well as the Diner's Club system.

Tipping & Bargaining

A service charge is usually added to restaurant bills in Qatar but this rarely goes to the waiting staff. Local custom does not require that you leave a tip after a meal, though it would certainly be appreciated.

The traditional shops where serious bargaining usually takes place in the Gulf are becoming quite rare in Qatar. You can almost always negotiate a little bit off the price of electronic goods, rental cars and hotel rooms, but the price of everything else is usually fixed.

POST & COMMUNICATIONS
Post

Most hotels sell stamps and there are several post offices around Doha, including one in The Centre, the capital's main shopping

QATAR

mall. Sending a postcard or a letter weighing up to 10g costs QR1 to any destination in Europe, Australia, Africa or the Americas. The comparable rates for 20/30g letters are QR2/3.

Poste restante is not available in Qatar and American Express (Amex) does not hold client's mail.

Telephone

The telephone system in Qatar is excellent and direct-dialling overseas calls rarely takes more than one attempt. Phonecards worth QR20, QR50 and QR100 can be purchased at the main telecommunications centre in Doha, though as yet there are few card phones outside the city centre itself.

The USA direct access code from Qatar is 0800-011-77.

When calling Qatar from abroad the country code is 974. There are no area or city codes.

Fax, Telex & Telegraph

These services are available through the main telecommunications centre in Doha or through the business centre of any big hotel, and are very reliable.

BOOKS

One of the few books on the market which focuses entirely on Qatar is Helga Graham's *Arabian Time Machine*. Subtitled 'Self-Portrait of an Oil State', the book is a collection of interviews with Qataris about their lives and traditions both before and after the oil boom, and about how Qatari society has coped with its sudden wealth.

Peter Mansfield's *The New Arabians* has a fairly short chapter on Qatari history. 'The Day Before Tomorrow', the Qatar chapter in Jonathan Raban's *Arabia through the Looking Glass*, is probably the best section of this wonderful book. During a short visit in 1979 Raban managed to speak to a particularly interesting cross-section of people – Qatar's leading playwright, a local TV producer and a Jordanian officer working for the Qatari army – in addition to the usual collection of somewhat jaded western

expats. For more book information see the Books section in the Regional Facts for the Visitor chapter.

NEWSPAPERS & MAGAZINES

The *Gulf Daily News* is the local English-language newspaper. The best place to find foreign newspapers and magazines (which usually arrive a day or two after publication) is at The Centre, the shopping complex on Salwa Rd.

RADIO & TV

Qatar FM broadcasts programmes in English from early morning until late evening, with an eclectic selection of music. Its signal goes out on 97.5 FM and 102.6 FM.

Qatar TV's second channel (Channel 37, UHF) broadcasts programmes in English from late afternoon until about midnight seven days a week. With a good antenna you can usually also pick up the English-language stations broadcasting from Abu Dhabi, Bahrain, Dubai and Saudi Arabia. Most hotels, except for the smallest ones, also offer satellite TV.

PHOTOGRAPHY & VIDEO

Film is easy to find in hotels and shopping centres all over town, though getting anything other than colour prints developed can be a hassle. There are no restrictions on taking pictures aside from the usual ban on military sites (including the airport) and the courtesy and caution always required when taking pictures of people in the Gulf.

HEALTH

Unless you are arriving from an area where yellow fever is endemic, vaccination certificates are not required for entry into Qatar.

Like other Gulf countries, the standard of health and medical care in Qatar is very high. There is no need to take malaria prophylactics nor do you need any shots beyond the usual regimen that any traveller should have (mainly DPT or a tetanus booster and gamma globulin). If you do get sick, hospital care is free in Qatar. See the Health Appendix for more detailed health information.

WOMEN TRAVELLERS

Women wearing very tight or revealing clothing will attract leers and comments in public places. A woman should always travel in the back seat when taking a taxi. Women should also avoid making eye contact with men whom they do not know as this is often misinterpreted as a come-on. Single women may also find that they are unwelcome in the cheapest tier of hotels and restaurants.

DANGERS & ANNOYANCES

The main thing to watch out for in Doha is the driving. Much of the city's traffic system is defined by a series of roundabouts. There are often no lights to control entry to these, with the result that when traffic is heavy people have to force their way into a moving stream of vehicles. When traffic is light the situation is worse; many drivers simply sail straight into the roundabout without slowing down at all.

BUSINESS HOURS

Shops and offices are open from around 8 am until noon and may reopen from 4 or 5 until 7 pm. Some of the modern western-style shopping centres stay open until 9 pm. Friday is the weekly holiday and many businesses also close early on Thursday. Embassies and government offices are closed all day Thursday.

PUBLIC HOLIDAYS & SPECIAL EVENTS

The Islamic holidays of Eid al-Fitr (the end of Ramadan), Eid al-Adha (Pilgrimage) and the Islamic New Year are all observed – see the table of holidays near Public Holidays & Special Events in the Regional Facts for the Visitor section.

Qatar's National Day is on 3 September. Embassies and government offices are closed but most private businesses stay open.

WORK

Qatar is not the sort of place where you can expect to pick up a few months of casual work waiting tables or teaching English. To obtain a work visa one usually has to have a job and a signed contract in hand before

arriving in Qatar. It is possible, however, to arrive in the country on a tourist visa, look for a job and then have the employer pick up the sponsorship and convert the tourist visa into a residence visa. This is usually an option only for people with specialised professional skills.

ACCOMMODATION

It is fairly easy to find rooms in good hotels for around QR100, and QR200 will buy you splendid accommodation, but the visa and sponsorship rules are such that you probably won't be staying in any of these places unless you obtained a visa through an embassy in advance.

FOOD & DRINK

Qatar does not have an indigenous cuisine worth mentioning. Outside of the restaurants at the big hotels (which offer fairly predictable fare), Doha itself is filled with the usual collection of western fast-food places and small Indian and Pakistani restaurants offering little more than curries and biryani dishes. At the Pakistani restaurants you can usually eat for about QR10, while western fast food is a bit more expensive.

Fruit juice and soft drinks are the only beverages you will find in the average Qatari restaurant. The cheaper the restaurant, the slimmer your selection is likely to be.

All the larger hotels have one bar and one restaurant that serves liquor. These are open only to hotel guests and those who have purchased memberships. You will have to show either a room key or a membership card at the door. Sometimes this is enforced strictly and sometimes it is not. Memberships are usually pretty nominal (around QR100 per year), which make them cost effective for those who are in the country for a month or more.

THINGS TO BUY

You are not likely to find much in the way of Arabian souvenirs in Doha. If you are flush with money, there are a couple of shops specialising in Persian carpets in the city centre and in the large hotels. Much of the

Arabian stuff you will see (eg incense burners) is actually made in Pakistan or Syria.

Getting There & Away

AIR
Qatar is one of the four part-owners of Gulf Air (along with Abu Dhabi, Bahrain and Oman) and recently launched its own national carrier – Qatar Airways – as well. Competition has not dented prices. Flying between Doha and the USA remains absurdly expensive. From New York, tickets start at around US$1200. From Doha the cheapest regular tickets to New York cost QR6180 (about US$1700). There is daily service between Doha and the UK. The cheapest regular tickets to London cost QR4030 (US$1100).

A low-season (roughly February through August) return fare to Melbourne, Australia, costs QR5830 (US$1600). The high season fare is QR6700 (US$1840).

If you want to get a flight to another Arab country, Syria is your best bet. A one-way ticket to Damascus costs QR1210 (US$332), with return tickets available from QR1610 (US$442).

Flying around the Gulf itself is never cheap and Qatar is no exception to this rule. Return fares to some other Gulf cities include Abu Dhabi QR350 (US$96), Bahrain QR250 (US$68), Dubai QR450 (US$123), Kuwait QR670 (US$184), Muscat QR760 (US$208) and Riyadh QR540 (US$148).

LAND
There are no buses or taxis to Saudi Arabia or the UAE. In theory, one can drive one's car, but this is really only a viable option for those holding residence visas or tourist visas issued overseas.

LEAVING QATAR
You must arrive at Doha airport at least 45 minutes prior to the scheduled departure time of your flight, though it's worth getting

there about an hour in advance. There is no departure tax.

Getting Around

Qatar does not have a bus or service-taxi system, so regular taxis and car rentals are your only options. With a little shopping around you can rent a car for about QR120 per day, less if you are taking it for a week or so. Taxis in Qatar have meters.

Doha

Around the Gulf, Doha has earned the unenviable reputation of being the dullest place on earth. You will be hard-pressed to find anyone who'll claim the place is exciting. That said, there's nothing *wrong* with Doha; the bay is pleasant and there are enough interesting sites around town to keep a traveller occupied for a day or two.

Orientation
The city centre is the string of large buildings along the Corniche between the Qatar National Bank and the Emir's Office. The older section of Doha and much of the main business area lies between the A Ring Rd and the coast. The roundabout where Jasim bin Mohammed St, Al-Asmakh St, Al-Musheireb St and Ali bin Abdulla St come together is the best focal point for the budget traveller. This places you near the souq and what pass in Doha for cheap hotels. Several points of interest are within easy walking distance, as are both the post office and the telecommunications centre.

Information
Money Moneychangers' offices in the souq will provide you with slightly better rates than banks. If you are in search of an ATM there is a British Bank of the Middle East office on Abdulla bin Jasim St and a Commercial Bank of Qatar branch on Grand

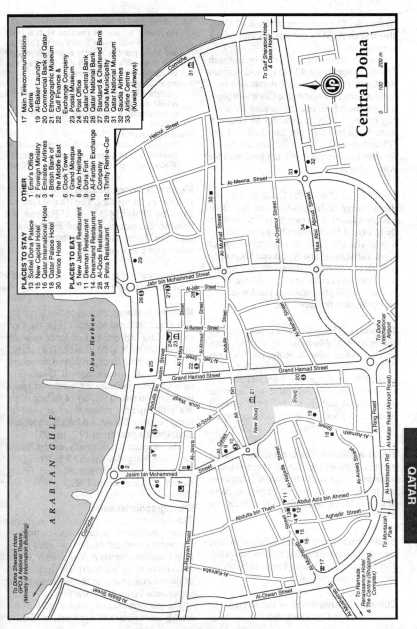

Central Doha

0   100   200 m

PLACES TO STAY
13 Sofitel Doha Palace
15 New Capital Hotel
16 Qatar International Hotel
18 Qatar Palace Hotel
30 Venice Hotel

PLACES TO EAT
5 New Jameel Restaurant
11 Desman Restaurant
14 Dreamland Restaurant
28 Al-Qods Restaurant
34 Petra Restaurant

OTHER
1 Emir's Office
2 Foreign Ministry
3 Emirates Airlines
4 British Bank of the Middle East
6 Clock Tower
7 Grand Mosque
8 Arab Heritage
9 Doha Fort
10 Al-Fardan Exchange Company
12 Thrifty Rent-a-Car
17 Main Telecommunications Centre
19 Al-Baker Laundry
20 Commercial Bank of Qatar
21 Ethnographic Museum
22 Gulf Finance & Exchange Company
23 Postal Museum
24 Post Office
25 Qatar Central Bank
26 Qatar National Bank
27 Standard & Chartered Bank
29 Doha Municipality
31 Qatar National Museum
32 Saudia Airlines
33 Airline Centre (Kuwait Airways)

QATAR

Hamad St. The Commercial Bank of Qatar also has an ATM in the arrivals area of the airport.

Amex is represented in Doha by Darwish Travel & Tourism (☎ 422 411) on Al-Rayyan Rd. Look for the complex dominated by a building with a large Apple Computer logo. It is on the left if you are coming from the city centre. It is open Saturday to Thursday from 8 am to 12.30 pm and 3.30 to 7 pm (Thursday until 6 pm). Cheques are cashed for card holders but it will not hold mail for Amex clients.

Post The GPO is on the Corniche between the Ministry of Information and the Doha Sheraton Hotel. It is open from 7 am to 8 pm daily, except Friday when it's open from 4 to 6 pm. The old GPO, at the intersection of Abdulla bin Jasim and Al-Bareed Sts, is open Saturday to Thursday from 7 am to 1 pm and 4 to 7 pm, and Friday from 8 to 10 am. There is also a small post office in The Centre, the shopping mall on Salwa Rd.

Telephone The main telecommunications centre is on Al-Musheireb St near the intersection where the A Ring Rd becomes Al-Diwan St. It is open 24 hours a day and also offers telephone, fax, telex and telegram services. The least expensive way to make international calls is to dial them yourself from a card phone. Collect (reverse charges) calls are not available.

Travel Agencies There are an astonishing number of travel agencies all over town and, because of high staff turnover, it is impossible to recommend any in particular. Your best bet is to ask the locals if they can recommend one.

Bookshops There is a bookshop in The Centre, the huge shopping mall on Salwa Rd. The selection of English books is heavy on spy novels and romances.

Cultural Centres Some of the foreign cultural centres in Doha include:

Alliance Française (☎ 417 548)
  Ibn Naeem St, just off Ibn Sina St. It is open Saturday to Wednesday from 9 am to 12.30 pm and 5 to 7 pm. On Monday night it stays open until 8 pm. It's closed all day Thursday and Friday and on Sunday morning.
American Cultural Center (☎ 351 279)
  Muaither St, just off Suhaim bin Hamad St, behind the Sherazad Restaurant. The library is open Saturday to Wednesday from 7.30 am to 3.30 pm.
British Council (☎ 426 193)
  Ras Abu Ayoub St opposite the Hardees fast-food restaurant. The library is open Saturday to Wednesday from 10 am to noon and 4 to 7.30 pm.

Medical Services Medical care is free in Qatar even for visitors. The Hamad General Hospital (☎ 446 446) on Al-Rayyan Rd between Suhaim bin Hamad and Mohammed bin Thani Sts offers treatment for tourists on a walk-in basis.

Emergency For fire, police or ambulance services dial ☎ 999.

National Museum
The Qatar National Museum is on the Corniche at the eastern end of town near the intersection with Al-Muthaf St. The exhibits cover everything from geology to astronomy to traditional life in pre-oil Qatar. The museum also includes an aquarium and a small lagoon with a display of sailing ships. It's built around a palace that was used for many years by Shaikh Abdulla bin Mohammed, Qatar's ruler from 1913 to 1951.

The museum is open daily, except Saturday, from 9 am to noon and 3 to 6 pm (4 to 7 pm in summer). It is closed on Friday mornings. Admission is QR2.

Ethnographic Museum
The museum is in a restored traditional Qatari house from the early 20th century, in the centre courtyard of the new souq shopping complex, between Al-Asmakh St and Grand Hamad St. Signs explain the function of the various rooms in the house and their importance in the life of the family.

The museum is open Sunday to Thursday from 9 am to noon and 3 to 6 pm, and Friday from 3 to 6 pm. It is closed on Saturday. Admission is free.

Doha Fort
The Doha Fort is on the corner of Jasim bin Mohammed and Al-Qalaa Sts. The interior consists of a large, paved courtyard with a fountain. The displays run the gamut from model dhows to paintings of Qatari life. Officially, the fort is open Sunday to Friday from 8.30 am to noon and 3 to 7 pm, and Friday from 3 to 6 pm, but the hours seem pretty erratic. It is closed on Saturday. Admission is free.

Postal Museum
If you are a stamp collector this place should figure near the top of your list of things to do in Doha. The museum is adjacent to the old GPO on Al-Bareed St. It is open Saturday to Thursday from 4 to 6 pm, though these hours appear to be loosely interpreted.

Old Police Station
This tiny fort-like building on the corner of Al-Matar Rd and Al-Waab St, between the B and C ring roads, was once a police post on the outskirts of Doha but is now little more than a curiosity within the city's urban sprawl. The interior (closed to the public) is empty.

Zoo
Doha's zoo, on the Dukhan road west of the city, is far from the central area. It is open Sunday to Friday from 3 to 9 pm. The general public is admitted only on Thursday, Friday and Sunday. Monday and Wednesday are for families, and Tuesday for women and children under nine. Admission is QR5 for adults and QR2 for children under nine.

Organised Tours
Qatar Holidays (☎ 495 585 or 495 567) offers half-day city tours for QR60. It also has excursions to camel races (half-day, QR60); dhow trips (half-day, QR175, including lunch); a tour to Al-Khor and other sites in the north of the country (full day, QR175, including lunch); and an all-day

desert safari (QR300, including lunch). Its office in the shopping area of the Gulf Sheraton's lobby is open Saturday to Wednesday from 8 am to 5 pm and Thursday until 1 pm. Doha Tours (☎ 495 585; fax 495 912) has similar offerings and prices.

Places to Stay – bottom end & middle
Bad news: Doha's youth hostel and half of its cheap and medium-priced hotels have disappeared since the 1st edition of this book. On the up side, none of the remaining hotels have increased their prices much since the 1st edition. All of the rooms at these hotels have air-con, TV and private bath. None of these hotels can sponsor visas, and all of them are 'dry'.

If you are looking for the cheapest beds in town head for the *Venice Hotel* (☎ 412 473; fax 412 476) at the intersection of Al-Muthaf and Al-Meena Sts. At QR80/100 for singles/doubles it is OK, but bear in mind that an extra QR30 will get you a significantly better room (in a better location) elsewhere in town.

New Capital Hotel (☎ 445 445; fax 442 233), on Al-Musheireb St between Aghadir St and the telecommunications centre, quotes a rate of QR264.50/299 for singles/doubles, including the service charge, but 19 times out of 20 will discount this to QR125/150 if you just ask. At the lower rate it is a very good deal. This is the cheapest place in town for those who crave a swimming pool.

Next door, the *Qatar International Hotel* (☎ 321 761; fax 442 413) is very clean and modern but not quite as good, with rooms for QR120/150. The Qatar International is a favoured haunt of Russian tourists.

On the other side of the city centre, the *Qatar Palace Hotel* (☎ 421 515; fax 321 515) falls somewhere between the New Capital and the Qatar International in terms of quality. Rooms are QR160/200 plus a 15% tax and service charge, but it will readily discount to QR120/160 net. The hotel is on Al-Asmakh St near the intersection with Al-Areeq St.

QATAR

Places to Stay – top end

These are the places that can arrange your visa. They are also the hotels large enough to have bars. All of these hotels add 17% in taxes and service to the bill (this has been included in the quoted prices). Most will readily offer discounts on the rates listed here.

The *Oasis Hotel* (☎ 423 453; fax 431 171), on Ras Abu Aboud St at the eastern end of the city, is the cheapest hotel in Qatar that sponsors visas for tourists. Rooms are QR287/345 for singles/doubles but with a little bargaining you ought to be able to get that down to around QR220/280.

In the city centre, the *Sofitel Doha Palace* (☎ 435 222; fax 439 186) on Abdul Aziz bin Ahmed St asks QR345/460 for rooms. Further out at the intersection of Salwa Rd and the C Ring Rd, the *Ramada Renaissance Hotel* (☎ 417 417; fax 410 941) has rooms from QR363/410.

Places to Eat

One of the best cheapies in the city centre is the *Desman Restaurant* at the intersection of Abdul Aziz bin Ahmed and Al-Musheireb Sts, across from the entrance to the Sofitel Doha Palace. It has very good Chinese and Indian food. Soups cost QR5 and most main dishes are QR5 to QR10. The portions are large and the service is good. Note that there is another place with the same name nearby. Just look for the one across from the hotel entrance and you are sure to get the right restaurant.

Another good choice in the same neighbourhood is *Dreamland Restaurant* on the corner of Masafi and Aghadir Sts, behind the Sofitel Doha Palace. It has a selection of biryanis, mutton and chicken for QR6, and other Indian dishes at similar prices.

New Jameel Restaurant at the western end of Abdulla bin Jasim St has fresh juice, fairly simple food (a plate of curry with bread for QR4.50) and ice cream. A similar menu of shwarma and other quick meals can be found at the *Al-Qods Restaurant* on the corner of Al-Ahmed and Al-Jabr Sts in the centre. The restaurant's sign is in Arabic only, but it is across from the entrance to the Souq Al-Jabor shopping centre.

On the edge of the city centre, but definitely worth the trip, is the *Petra Restaurant* on Ras Abu Aboud St between Jabr bin Mohammed and Al-Meena Sts. It is mainly a take-away restaurant offering felafel, shwarma, fuul and other such dishes. It's very good and very cheap.

Doha also has two up-market places you should make a point of visiting. The first is *Ya Mal-i-Sham*, a Lebanese restaurant on Al-Matar Rd, directly opposite the main entrance to the airport. Mezzas and soups cost QR5 to QR15, and main courses are QR15 to QR25. The other is the *Caravan Restaurant*, opposite the Ramada Hotel at the intersection of Salwa Rd and the C Ring Rd. It offers a huge all-you-can-eat buffet for QR33 at lunch and QR39 at dinner.

Entertainment

There are a couple of cinemas in town that show Pakistani and Indian films, and once in a blue moon the British Council may bring a travelling theatre company to town. Doha, however, is the kind of place where a night on the town means having dinner out and that's about it. Some of the big hotels offer light entertainment (usually live background music) with their theme-night dinners. Arabic plays and the occasional foreign troop can be seen at the National Theatre on the Corniche.

Getting There & Away

Air Doha has a small, serviceable airport. Gulf Air (☎ 455 444) and Qatar Airways (☎ 430 707) both have their main booking offices on Al-Matar Rd, near the airport entrance.

Bus There are no international or domestic bus services.

Car Rental rates at all of the big agencies start at around QR130 to QR150 per day for a small car, including insurance and unlimited mileage. You might be able to bargain this down to about QR100. Thrifty Rent-a-

Car (☎ 433 800) has an office in the shopping complex attached to the Sofitel Doha Palace. EuroDollar Rent-a-Car (☎ 321 313) is on Al-Rayyan Rd in the same complex as Amex. Avis (☎ 495 578) has an office in the Gulf Sheraton Hotel. Europcar (☎ 438 404) has an office on Al-Rayyan Rd, as well as desks in the Sheraton and Sofitel hotels. All of these agencies also have desks at the airport.

Getting Around
The Airport A taxi between the airport and the city centre will cost QR10 to QR15.

Taxis There are lots of taxis in the city so you should not have too much trouble finding one. A flag fall is QR2 and the meter adds QR1 per km in 10 dirham increments.

Around Qatar

If you are heading south out of Doha, toward Wakrah or Umm Said, take the airport road (Al-Matar Rd) and just keep going. The main road to all points north is 22 February Rd which, as you leave the city, becomes Shimal Rd.

WAKRAH
Sixteen km south of Doha on the Umm Said road, Wakrah has a small **museum** and some good **beaches** just south of town.

UMM SAID
Umm Said is Qatar's answer to Dhahran in Saudi Arabia or Al-Ahmadi in Kuwait – it is the oil-company town. You cannot get into either the industrial or residential areas without an appointment at one of the industrial facilities or an invitation to someone's home.

UMM SALAL MOHAMMED
The attraction of Umm Salal Mohammed (Umm Silal Mohammed), the first town north of Doha, is its **fort**. Once you have made it from the main road into the town you

will come to a roundabout. To reach the fort, take the first right from the roundabout and drive straight through the town for 1.4 km. It's on the left.

UMM SALAL ALI
This town is 37.5 km north of Doha and has a field of **grave mounds**. It is hardly on the scale one finds in Bahrain but if you haven't seen a mound field yet it's worth a quick diversion. The small mound field lies just north of the town and more mounds are scattered in among Umm Salal Ali's buildings.

AL-KHOR
Al-Khor, 67 km north of Doha, is the home of a small **museum** which always seems to be closed. The only other things of note are a number of old **watchtowers** scattered around the town centre, and the ruins of a **mosque** dating from the early 1950s. The view of the ocean is splendid and the setting is quite peaceful. If you have the time, Al-Khor is a pleasant day trip out of Doha.

There are no places to stay in Al-Khor, but the *Ain Helaitan Restaurant & Coffeeshop*, on the Corniche between the ruined mosque and the museum, is a good place for a snack. The Turkish coffee (QR2) is excellent as are the kebabs, though the latter are a bit pricey at QR15.

ZUBARA
Near Qatar's north-western coast, 105 km north of Doha, Zubara (Zubarah) occupies an important place in Qatari history. Its **fort** was built in 1938 as a border post. It is a small four bastion structure built around a courtyard. It was used by the military until well into the 1980s. Today, well-to-do Qataris occasionally travel up here on falconing expeditions, but that's about it.

Until about 100 years ago, Zubara was the main settlement in Qatar. For almost 200 years it was controlled by the Al-Khalifa, Bahrain's ruling family, but hotly contested by Qatar's Al-Thani family. The fort you see today was built shortly after the Al-Thanis wrested the settlement from Bahraini control once and for all. Two km beyond the fort are the ruins of some much older **coastal fortifications**.

AL-RUWEIS

The Qatar peninsula's northernmost point offers little to the traveller. There are a few small grocery stores and restaurants, and

there is a causeway out to the fishing village on **Ras Abu Amran** island.

If you've got a car, a couple of hours to kill and it's not too hot, try the drive between Al-Ruweis and the Zubara Fort. The road passes several abandoned coastal villages, most notably **Al-Khuwair** and **Al-Arish**. The towns were abandoned in the 1970s.

Saudi Arabia

Arabia has intrigued travellers for centuries. Vast and mostly arid, it is the cradle of the Islamic religion, the Arab race and the Arabic language – a language considered holy by Muslims.

Today's Saudi Arabia retains that mystique, in part because it is so incredibly difficult to visit. Yet, contrary to popular belief, the kingdom has an abundance of attractions. Even more intriguingly, Saudi Arabia offers the traveller the rare opportunity of exploring a country where tradition and modernity are still working out their accommodation with one another.

Facts about the Country

HISTORY
Until the 18th century the history of what is now Saudi Arabia is largely the history of the coastal regions. In the Gulf this history goes as far back as any yet recorded. Parts of what is now eastern Saudi Arabia were first settled in the 4th or 5th millennium BC by migrants from what is now southern Iraq. The best known of the western Arabian kingdoms was that of the Nabataeans. At one point their empire, which thrived in the 1st century BC, stretched as far north as Damascus.

In the early 18th century the Al-Saud, the royal family of modern Saudi Arabia, were the ruling shaikhs of the oasis village of Dir'aiyah, near modern Riyadh. What is now called the First Saudi Empire grew from an alliance, cemented circa 1744, between Mohammed bin Saud, the ruler of Dir'aiyah, and Mohammed bin Abdul Wahhab (born 1703), a preacher who espoused a simple, unadorned and strict form of Islam. The result of this alliance was Wahhabism, the back-to-basics religious movement which remains the official form of Islam in Saudi Arabia today.

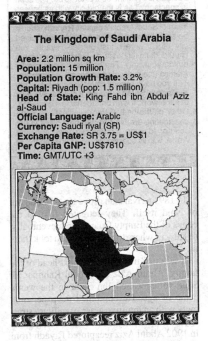

The Kingdom of Saudi Arabia

Area: 2.2 million sq km
Population: 15 million
Population Growth Rate: 3.2%
Capital: Riyadh (pop: 1.5 million)
Head of State: King Fahd ibn Abdul Aziz al-Saud
Official Language: Arabic
Currency: Saudi riyal (SR)
Exchange Rate: SR 3.75 = US$1
Per Capita GNP: US$7810
Time: GMT/UTC +3

Mohammed bin Abdul Wahhab's religious fervour and Mohammed bin Saud's military skill proved to be a potent combination which outlived its two founders. After conquering and converting to Wahhabi doctrine most of the tribes of Najd, the Saudi-led forces swept out across the peninsula. By 1806 they controlled most of the territory of today's kingdom of Saudi Arabia as well as a large section of what is now southern Iraq.

None of this went down well in Constantinople as western Arabia was, at least in theory, part of the Ottoman Empire. An expedition to retake Arabia was launched in 1812. The Saudis were driven out of the Hejaz (western Arabia) and back to Dir'aiyah, which fell in 1818.

Suggested Itineraries

If you can only visit one city in this huge country **Jeddah** is by far the best place to be. The souq is spectacular as is the old city with its houses built from coral. The **Masmak Fortress** at the heart of Saudi Arabia's capital, **Riyadh**, should be seen by every visitor, as should the ruined city of **Dir'aiyah**, just outside Riyadh. You should definitely visit at least one museum during your stay. The best is the one run by Aramco (the national oil company) in **Dhahran**.

If you have several days to spare, a side trip to **Madain Salah** – though it can involve a lot of paperwork, it is an unforgettable experience. Other off-the-beaten track destinations worth considering are **Najran** (the best place in the country to shop for Bedouin jewellery) and **Abha**, with its spectacular mountain scenery. ■

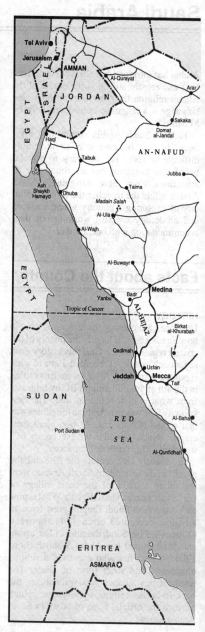

In 1891 a rival clan drove the Al-Saud out of Najd itself. They retreated first to the edges of the Empty Quarter and, eventually, to Kuwait where the ruling shaikh took them in.

It was in Kuwait that the next head of the family, Abdul Aziz bin Abdul Rahman al-Saud (often called Ibn Saud in the west), came of age. He combined deep personal piety with an intuitive grasp of military strategy and diplomacy that bordered on genius. In 1902 Abdul Aziz recaptured Riyadh from the Al-Saud family's traditional rivals, the Al-Rashids, beginning a string of conquests that ended in 1925 when Jeddah surrendered to his troops.

In May 1933, a year after the discovery of oil in commercial quantities in Bahrain, Abdul Aziz granted an oil concession to Standard Oil of California (Socal, the precursor of today's Chevron). Drilling began in 1935 but oil was not found in commercial quantities until 1938. In 1944 Socal and Texaco formed the Arabian American Oil Company, or Aramco, to run their operations in the kingdom. Aramco later sold some of its shares to Standard Oil of New Jersey (now Exxon) and Socony Vacuum (Mobil).

Oil production only really took off after

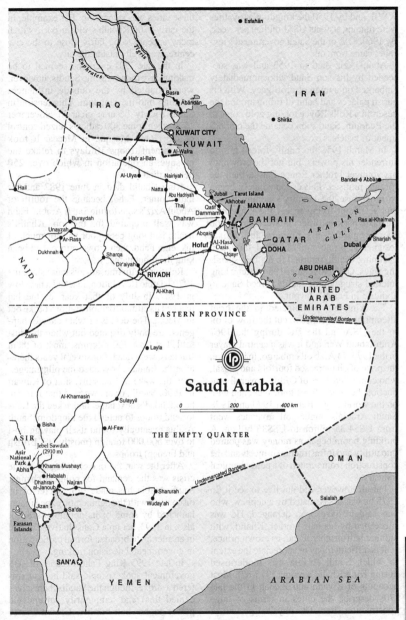

Saudi Arabia

WWII, and by 1950 the kingdom's royalties were running at about US$1 million per week. By 1960, 81% of the Saudi government's revenues came from oil.

Abdul Aziz died in 1953 and was succeeded by his son Saud who immediately embarked on a reign of profligacy. With his garish palaces and habit of riding around the desert in a Rolls Royce tossing gold coins to the Bedouin, Saud soon became the embodiment of tasteless excess.

In March 1958 the family forced him to surrender his powers, but not the crown, to his younger brother Prince Faisal, then the foreign minister. Faisal immediately began to modernise the country's administration and set about trying to get the kingdom's finances back in order. In December 1960 Saud regained his powers and Faisal resigned as prime minister. Saud, though in declining health, returned to his free-spending ways. On 3 November 1964, after a long internal struggle, the family forced Saud to abdicate in Faisal's favour.

The kingdom participated in the brief attempt by Arab states to cut the flow of oil to the USA and the UK during the 1967 Arab-Israeli War, and it was a central player in the 1973-74 Arab oil embargo. In its wake, the price of oil increased fourfold and Faisal, who controlled 30% of OPEC's overall production, became a force to be reckoned with on the world stage. Between 1973 and 1978 Saudi Arabia's annual oil revenues went from US$4.35 billion to US$36 billion. A building boom began as money was poured into utility and infrastructure projects and the construction from scratch of a petrochemical industry.

Faisal, however, did not live to see it. In 1975 he was assassinated by a nephew, who was said to have been deranged. He was succeeded by his half-brother, Khalid, with another half-brother, Fahd, as crown prince.

It is difficult today to appreciate the extent to which Saudi Arabia was modernised during King Khalid's reign (1975-82). Most accounts of Riyadh and Jeddah in the late '70s describe the cities in terms of huge construction sites. The physical growth of these cities was staggering. For example, in the early '70s Riyadh's old airport, which today appears to be fairly close to the city centre, was well outside the city.

In the late '70s everyone seemed to be making easy money. Some Saudis, however, were troubled by the outside influences flooding into the kingdom. This tension in Saudi society became clear in November 1979 when some 300 radicals seized control of the Grand Mosque in Mecca. It took government troops 10 days to retake the mosque, an operation in which over 250 people died.

King Khalid died in June 1982 and his half-brother, Fahd, became the fourth of Abdul Aziz's sons to rule Saudi Arabia. Fahd was well prepared for the job. Khalid's health had long been poor and for much of his reign Fahd, then crown prince, had been king in all but name.

Relations with Iran, always tense since the 1979 Islamic Revolution, reached a new low in 1987. In July of that year, as the haj reached its climax, demonstrations broke out in Mecca. The details of what exactly happened are hotly disputed but when the dust settled at least 400 pilgrims, most of them Iranians, were dead. For several years thereafter the Iranians boycotted the pilgrimage.

In the wake of Iraq's invasion of Kuwait in 1990, Saudi Arabia worried that it might be Baghdad's next target and asked the USA to send troops to defend the kingdom. Saudi Arabia eventually found itself playing host to over 500,000 foreign (mostly US, British and French) troops.

After the war, the one clear legacy of the crisis was the demand for political change. Saudi Arabia has made little secret of its discomfort with the democratic experiments launched by some of its neighbours but it also, in 1993, set up a Consultative Council in an attempt to broaden formal participation in governmental decision making.

In late 1995 King Fahd became ill (US government spokespeople said he had suffered a stroke, though the Saudis themselves denied this) and temporarily surrendered power to his half-brother, Crown Prince

Abdullah. The King resumed his duties in February 1996, but at the time of writing doubts about his health persisted.

GEOGRAPHY

Saudi Arabia is about 2.2 million sq km in area, most of it desert. Western Saudi Arabia is dominated by a mountain chain running the entire length of the country and generally becoming higher and broader as one moves south towards Yemen. About half of the country is taken up by the Rub' al-Khali, or Empty Quarter. This is the largest sand desert in the world, an area about the size of France. Much of the country's central and northern region is a gravelly desert plain. The extreme north-west of the kingdom contains Arabia's second great sand desert, the Nafud.

The Eastern Province is a low-lying area containing a number of *sabkhas* (salt flats). Its main geographical feature is the gigantic Al-Hasa oasis, centred on the town of Hofuf.

CLIMATE

Daytime temperatures rise to 45°C or more from mid-April until October throughout the kingdom, with high humidity in the coastal regions. In places like Jizan this weather continues well into November.

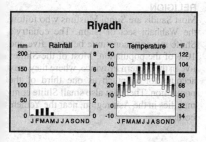

In the dead of winter (December-January) temperatures in the main cities will drop into the teens during the day and even hit single digits in some places, particularly in the central deserts, overnight. In the coastal areas it rains regularly, less often in Riyadh.

FLORA & FAUNA

A drive across Saudi Arabia's deserts will provide you with wonderful opportunities for viewing desert scrub growth and tamarind trees. In the forested areas of Asir there are various sorts of evergreens.

Aside from camels you are not likely to see much wildlife. The desert is full of animals but most of them (hedgehogs and sand cats, for example) are nocturnal. Wild monkeys (Hamadryas baboons, to be precise) can often be seen along the roads in the Asir region.

GOVERNMENT & POLITICS

In theory Saudi Arabia's king is an absolute monarch, but in practice important decisions are rarely taken by the king alone. Before acting he usually consults the Cabinet, senior members of the royal family and the country's religious and business establishments.

King Fahd's creation, in 1993, of a Consultative Council was, in part, a move to formalise and modernise the traditional system of give-and-take. The council's members are appointed by the king. The council can comment on proposed laws and recommend changes but does not have any legislative authority.

After King Fahd, the next person in line for the throne is his half-brother, Prince Abdullah, who heads the National Guard and temporarily assumed the king's powers during Fahd's illness in the early part of 1996.

ECONOMY

Prior to the discovery of oil, the peninsula's economy revolved around the haj in the west, date farming and pearling in the east and tribal raiding in the centre.

After WWII oil quickly replaced these traditional pursuits as the main source of income. In the early '70s Saudi Arabia embarked on a long-term diversification programme. Economic development schemes focused on heavy industry, petrochemicals and agriculture. Today the kingdom churns out huge amounts of steel and cement, boasts one of the world's largest petrochemical industries and is a net exporter of wheat.

All of this costs money (wheat does not grow in the desert without very expensive human assistance), and money in Saudi Arabia usually means oil, of which the country produces between seven and 10 million barrels per day, depending on market conditions.

POPULATION & PEOPLE

Because of its size and history, Saudi Arabia has a very diverse population. Najd is a very homogeneous region but the Hejaz, after 14 centuries of receiving Muslim pilgrims from all over the world, has an extraordinarily mixed population. Hejazis may be as dark skinned as sub-Saharan Africans or as pale as someone from northern Europe. One even encounters a handful of Saudis with distinctly Chinese features. Natives of the Gulf fall somewhere between these extremes. Saudis of the south-western Asir region are distinctly Yemeni in appearance and dress.

The government says there are 15 million Saudi citizens, but most private estimates put the overall population closer to 12 million, of whom about seven million are thought to be Saudis.

SOCIETY & CONDUCT
Dos & Don'ts

Saudi Arabia is one of the most insular societies on earth and an unusual degree of tact and discretion are called for. Dress conservatively. Shorts in public are absolutely out of the question. Women should always cover their shoulders and should not wear clothing that is at all tight or revealing. Take things offered to you with the right, not the left, hand and avoid showing the soles of your feet to people.

Alcohol and pork are illegal, and so are theatres and cinemas. At prayer time all shops must close. The only exceptions are the restaurants in some five-star hotels.

The public profession of all faiths other than Islam is banned. Non-Muslims may not enter mosques in Saudi Arabia, are barred from the area surrounding Mecca (about 25 km from the city in all directions) and may visit only the outskirts of Medina. Public observance of the Ramadan fast is *mandatory* for Muslims and non-Muslims alike. If you are caught smoking, drinking or eating in public – which includes offices, hotel lobbies and even moving vehicles on a highway – you can be sent to prison, usually until Ramadan is over.

The Religious Police Formally known as the Committee for the Propagation of Virtue and the Prevention of Vice, the *matawwa*, or religious police, have a fearsome reputation as a squad of moral vigilantes out to enforce Islamic orthodoxy as they understand it. This overstates matters somewhat, but the bottom line is that the best way to deal with the matawwa is to steer clear of them. If you do find yourself facing an angry-looking religious policeman do not turn the situation into a confrontation. If the matawwa are asking something reasonable of you – not using a payphone during prayer time, for example – obey them.

RELIGION

Most Saudis are Sunni Muslims who follow the Wahhabi sect of Islam. The country's Shiite minority constitute between five and 10% of the population. Most of the Shiites live in the Eastern Province, where they may account for as much as one third of the population. There are also small Shiite communities in the Asir region, near the Yemeni border.

LANGUAGE

Arabic is the official language of Saudi Arabia. English is the universal language of commerce in the kingdom and you should have no trouble getting by with it in all of the main cities and towns.

Facts for the Visitor

PLANNING
When to Go
The best time to visit is between November and February when the climate is mild. The Asir mountains are at their best a bit earlier and a bit later than the rest of the country – during the winter they are often locked in fog. For more information see also the Regional Facts for the Visitor chapter.

Maps
The best maps of Saudi Arabia are the Farsi Maps, available at most bookshops and hotels in the kingdom for about SR 20 each. All are, to varying extents, out of date but still usable. Just remember that roads shown as 'projected' have often been finished.

What to Bring
For the winter months, particularly in desert areas such as Riyadh, Hail and Tabuk, you will need a jumper and a light to medium-weight jacket. Asir's winter climate can be genuinely foul, and warm clothing will definitely be in order. For more details see also the Regional Facts for the Visitor chapter.

VISAS & DOCUMENTS
Visas
Saudi Arabia has a well-deserved reputation as one of the hardest places in the world to visit. As tourist visas are not issued your options consist of visitor's or transit visas and, for Muslims, haj and umrah visas.

To obtain a visitor's visa (ie a business visa) you will need a formal invitation telex from the company or Saudi individual sponsoring you. An 'invitation' is essentially an acknowledgement that your sponsor has obtained a visa on your behalf and that authorisation to issue this visa has been sent to the Saudi embassy in a particular city. At that point all you have to do is appear at the embassy bearing your visa number. If you do not have a visa number do not bother going to the embassy as visas are filed by number, not name. No number, no visa. If you show up with your number in the morning, you can usually pick up your visa the same afternoon. Visitors' visas can be picked up at any Saudi diplomatic mission, though the pick-up site has to be specified when the visa application is filed by the sponsor in the kingdom.

The 24 and 48 hour transit visas are for people passing through Saudi airports. These are issued by Saudi embassies after you have shown them your airline tickets and convinced them that when purchasing the tickets you had absolutely no choice other than an overnight transit in Saudi Arabia.

People driving between Jordan and either Kuwait or Yemen are usually issued three-day transit visas. People driving between Jordan and Bahrain or the United Arab Emirates (UAE) often get seven day transit visas. As a general rule these are only issued in the countries that actually border Saudi Arabia. You have to go to the embassy with your carnet and proof that you already have a visa for the country at the other end of the road. In theory, it is possible to hitch a ride on any of these routes, though in practice you probably will not get a transit visa unless you are already attached to a vehicle. Check your visa carefully as it may contain restrictions concerning the route you are allowed to take through the kingdom.

From the first of Ramadan each year Saudi embassies in Muslim countries issue only haj visas until the haj is over about three months later. There's no longer a ban on issuing visas to people whose passport contains an Israeli stamp but this could cause you problems with some border guards who may not be aware of the new regulations.

A final note: all official business in Saudi Arabia is conducted according to the Muslim Hijra calendar. Any Gregorian date you see on a document is there solely for the foreign community's convenience. A visa valid for a one month stay is valid for a Hijra month, not a Gregorian month. If you stay for a month according to the western calendar you will have overstayed your visa by a day or two – and you will be in trouble.

Other Documents

Travel Letters Foreigners living in the kingdom need permission from their sponsor to travel outside of the city in which they reside. In practice this is only enforced for travel between provinces. Foreigners on a visitor's visa can travel anywhere in the kingdom using only their passport.

Site Permits To visit virtually any fort, ruin or archaeological site in the kingdom you must first obtain a permit. Permits for all sites are issued by the Department of Antiquities office at the Riyadh Museum. Permits for the Eastern Province outside the Al-Hasa oasis can also be obtained from the Regional Museum of Archaeology & Ethnography in Dammam.

In Riyadh you have to file the application one morning and return a day or two later to collect the permit; in Dammam permits can often be issued the same day provided you arrive before 10 am. Resident foreigners will have to bring their *iqama*, or residence permit, and, if the site involves a trip to a province other than the one where they live, a travel letter. People in the kingdom on a visitor's visa require only a passport.

Once you get to the place you plan to visit you may have to take the permit to the local branch of the Antiquities office.

EMBASSIES

Saudi Embassies Abroad

Australia
    12 Culgoa Circuit, O'Malley, Canberra, ACT, 2606 (☎ (06) 286 2099)

Bahrain
    King Faisal Highway, Manama; opposite the Holiday Inn and near the Kuwaiti embassy (☎ 537 722)

Iran
    59 Kheyabun-é Bokharest, Tehrān (☎ (2) 624 294)

Oman
    Jameat A'Duwal al-Arabiya St, Medinat Qaboos Diplomatic Area, Muscat; the embassy is to the sea side of Sultan Qaboos St, west of the Al-Khuwair roundabout (☎ 601744)

Qatar
    Diplomatic Area, beyond the Doha Sheraton Hotel, Doha (☎ 832 030)

UAE
    Karamah St, near the intersection with Dalma St, Abu Dhabi (☎ (2) 465 700)

UK
    30 Belgrave Square, London SW1 (☎ (0171) 235 0303)

USA
    601 New Hampshire Ave NW, Washington DC, 20037 (☎ (202) 342 3800)

Foreign Embassies in Saudi Arabia

All of the following embassies are in Riyadh's Diplomatic Quarter. If you need to visit one of these places call the embassy and ask for directions – it helps to be good with national flags.

Australia	(☎ 488 7788)
Bahrain	(☎ 488 0044)
Canada	(☎ 488 2288)
Ireland	(☎ 488 2300)
Kuwait	(☎ 488 3500)
New Zealand	(☎ 488 7988)
UAE	(☎ 482 6803)
UK	(☎ 488 0077)
USA	(☎ 488 3800)

Embassies outside of the Diplomatic Quarter include:

Oman
    Al-Ra'id District, behind the petrol station opposite the main gate of King Saud University (☎ 482 3120)

Qatar
    Al-Takhassosi Rd, near the Euromarche supermarket (☎ 482 5544)

There are also a few consulates in Jeddah. The UK consulate (☎ 654 1811) is off Al-Andalus St, one block east of the Sheraton al-Bilad Hotel, in the Al-Shate'e district, far to the north of the centre. This consulate also handles diplomatic matters for citizens of Canada, Australia and New Zealand in Jeddah. The US consulate (☎ 667 0080) is on Falasteen St, near the intersection with Al-Andalus St, Ruwais district.

CUSTOMS

The import of anything containing alcohol or pork is strictly forbidden. Customs officers also pay close attention to any books, magazines or photographs you are carrying. Videotapes are often held at the airport for a day or two for screening by censors. Anything deemed pornographic (which, in Saudi Arabia, could include vacation photos of your family and friends at the beach) or politically sensitive may be confiscated.

MONEY
Costs
Saudi Arabia is not a cheap place but it is possible to travel relatively inexpensively if you put your mind to it. Filling your stomach for SR 15 (US$4) or less is never a problem. Beds generally bottom out at SR 8 (US$2) in youth hostels and SR 55 to SR 90 (US$15 to US$24) in hotels. It is possible to cross the peninsula for less than SR 200 (US$53). Travelling around the kingdom can be done on about SR 50 (US$13) a day, though SR 100 (US$26) is a more realistic low-budget estimate (SR 200 if you don't stay in the youth hostels).

Currency
The Saudi riyal (SR) is divided into 100 halalas. It is a hard currency and there are no restrictions on its import or export. Coins come in 5, 10, 25 and 50 halala and SR 1 denominations. Notes come in SR 1, 5, 10, 50, 100 and 500 denominations.

Currency Exchange
The riyal is pegged to the US dollar, so while the US$/SR rate rarely moves by more than a halala or so either side of SR 3.75, the rates against other western currencies change constantly.

Australia	A$1	=	SR 3.04
France	FF1	=	SR 0.74
Germany	DM1	=	SR 2.50
UK	UK£1	=	SR 6.31
USA	US$1	=	SR 3.75

Changing Money
Moneychangers are among some of the kingdom's larger banking operations and usually offer slightly better rates than banks. Changing travellers' cheques can be a pain.

Many banks and moneychangers either will not take them, will only change brands they sell or will only cash them for account holders. You should always carry your original purchase receipt with you as the few places that will change travellers' cheques won't touch them without it.

If you want to withdraw money from an ATM your best bet is the Saudi Cairo Bank. Every branch (and there's one in every Saudi city of any size) has an ATM linked to the Cirrus and Plus networks.

Tipping & Bargaining
Tips are not generally expected in Saudi restaurants. The service charge added to your bill is not an automatic tip but goes straight into the till. Most waiters in the kingdom are paid very little and a few extra riyals would certainly be appreciated.

In Saudi Arabia the price of almost anything is negotiable up to a point. Outside of a Bedouin market, however, bargaining frequently means asking for a discount and being offered it. After that initial offer the price may not go much lower.

POST & COMMUNICATIONS
Post
The queues in Saudi post offices tend to be rather long, especially at the end of the month when many foreign workers send their salaries home to their families. Airmail postage for letters sent to addresses outside the Arab world is SR 1.50 for the first 10g and SR 1 for each additional 10g. Postcards cost SR 1.

There are no poste-restante facilities and American Express (Amex) does not hold mail. The best approach is to find a sympathetic friend who will let you receive mail through his or her company.

Telephone
Saudi Arabia has an excellent telecommunications system. Almost every town has a telephone centre through which international calls can be made. At the time of writing, Saudi Telecom was upgrading its payphones. Card phones are an increasingly

common sight, though the phonecards themselves are hard to find.

USA Direct service is available from pretty much everywhere in the kingdom. The access code is 1-800-10.

The country code for calls to Saudi Arabia is 966 plus the area code for the individual city.

Fax, Telex & Telegraph

In addition to the telephone centres, you can send faxes or telexes from the business centres in most large hotels and from some of the larger copy shops. The latter offer a much better deal.

BOOKS

CM Doughty's *Travels in Arabia Deserta*, originally published in 1888, is the granddaddy of modern Arabian travel literature. If you don't feel like ploughing through its 1400 pages, Penguin publishes an abridged version.

Doughty's writing inspired, among others, TE Lawrence, whose *Seven Pillars of Wisdom* is a classic of modern literature (see the Books section in the Regional Facts for the Visitor chapter). Richard Burton's *Personal Narrative of a Pilgrimage to Al-Madinah & Meccah*, originally published in 1855, is one of the few accounts of the Holy Cities written by a non-Muslim.

The pantheon of Arabian travel classics is completed by Wilfred Thesiger's 1959 memoir *Arabian Sands*, in which he recounts his two journeys across the Empty Quarter in the late 1940s. You might also want to look for *At the Drop of a Veil* by Marianne Alireza, a Californian who married into a Jeddah-based merchant family in the 1940s. The best work on modern Saudi Arabia is Robert Lacey's *The Kingdom*. For more general book information see the Books section in the Regional Facts for the Visitor chapter.

NEWSPAPERS & MAGAZINES

The *Arab News*, *Saudi Gazette* and *Riyadh Daily* are the country's English-language newspapers. Major foreign newspapers and magazines are widely available in the kingdom's main cities. Periodicals usually appear two or three days after publication, by which time they have received a very thorough going-over by Saudi censors.

RADIO & TV

Saudi Arabian TV's Channel 2 broadcasts exclusively in English, except for a French-language newscast every night at 8 pm. The programmes are a mixture of old and heavily edited US shows and locally made documentaries and talk shows. The news in English is broadcast every night at 9 pm. In the Eastern Province you can also receive Channel 3 – the Aramco television station. It tends to be a more up-to-date version of Channel 2 (ie US programmes from two years ago instead of 10 years ago).

In the Eastern Province, Radio Bahrain (98.5 FM) comes in fairly clearly. Aramco also has a radio station that broadcasts mostly country & western music. In Jeddah, Riyadh and the Dhahran area you can also receive the USA's Armed Forces Radio and Television Service (AFRTS) broadcasts on FM.

PHOTOGRAPHY & VIDEO

The old rule of thumb for Eastern bloc travel is still a good guide in Saudi Arabia: never point your camera at anything you might feel inclined to bomb, blow up or shoot at during a war. This always extends to mosques and includes archaeological sites, though in the latter case it is not enforced with any degree of uniformity. Videos are a particularly sensitive subject and are prohibited at some archaeological sites.

Film is easy to find in the kingdom's main cities, but check that it has not passed its expiry date. There are numerous shops specialising in one or two hour photo processing, but most handle only colour prints. Slides or B&W film tend to take a lot longer and the results are often less than satisfactory.

HEALTH

The standard of health care in Saudi Arabia is very high and almost any ailment can be treated inside the country. Many diseases which were once endemic, such as malaria (currently only a problem in the western and south-western provinces), are now virtually unknown in the kingdom. Though a gamma globulin booster (or Havrix injection) as a Hepatitis A preventative might not be a bad idea if you are planning to spend a lot of time far off the beaten track, there are no special precautions that need to be taken before visiting Saudi Arabia.

The quality of drinking water varies greatly in the kingdom. On the whole you should probably stick to bottled water. See the Health Appendix for more detailed health information.

WOMEN TRAVELLERS

Men and women are strictly segregated in Saudi society and the trend over the last few years has been toward increasingly rigorous enforcement of this rule. Restaurants which do not have a family section often will not serve women, and there has been a trend in recent years to bar women entirely from some smaller shops and fast-food outlets. Municipal buses have separate sections for women, and unaccompanied women may not travel by intercity bus or train. Women are also not allowed to drive.

An unaccompanied woman cannot check into a hotel without a letter from her sponsor, and it would probably also be a good idea for the sponsor to contact the hotel in advance. Saudi Arabia's youth hostels are entirely off-limits to women.

Obviously skirts above the knee and tight pants are out. Strictly speaking, it is not necessary for a foreign woman to wear the *abayya* (a long, black cloak-like garment) and a floor-length skirt but, in practice, it's usually a good idea. In the main cities and in smaller places which either have or see a lot of foreigners (Jubail, Yanbu, Taif, Abha, Hofuf), there is no need for foreign women to cover their heads. In more remote or conservative areas (Jizan, Hail, Najran, Sakaka, Tabuk), it is advisable for foreign women to cover their heads. Women who are, or appear to be, of Arab descent are likely to be held to far tighter standards of dress than western or

Asian women, especially outside of the main cities.

Reports of sexual harassment vary widely but leers and obscene comments seem to be fairly common, particularly in closed public spaces, such as aeroplanes. Though men will stare they are less likely to touch. In general, it is best to remain stoic in the face of comments and to shout at, not punch, anyone who gropes you. The social opprobrium that comes from having touched a woman in public is one of your most effective weapons in these situations.

DANGERS & ANNOYANCES

Saudi Arabia is a very safe country and street crime is almost unknown. Petty theft, particularly things being stolen out of cars, is sometimes a problem in the cities.

The main thing that you will have to worry about is the rather frightening way that people drive. As a rule the driving gets crazier as one moves further west in the country.

BUSINESS HOURS

Banks and shops are open Saturday to Wednesday from 8 or 8.30 am until 1 or 1.30 pm. Many shops, and some banks, reopen in the afternoon from about 4 to 7 pm. Big shopping centres, particularly in Riyadh, Jeddah and Alkhobar, may stay open until 10 pm. Few businesses are open on Thursday afternoons and almost everything is shut up tightly on Friday.

At prayer time *everything* closes; even Saudia airlines stops answering its telephones for reservations. The length of the prayer break can be anything from 20 minutes to an hour. If you are already inside a restaurant and eating, the staff may let you hang around and finish your meal, or they may throw you out.

PUBLIC HOLIDAYS & SPECIAL EVENTS

Wahhabism is so strict that the kingdom has no holidays other than Eid al-Fitr and Eid al-Adha (for dates see the table of holidays near Public Holidays & Special Events in the Regional Facts for the Visitor chapter). Saudi

National Day is 23 September, though it is not widely observed.

The kingdom's only cultural and folkloric festival, the Jinadriyah National Festival, takes place every February at a special site about 45 km north-east of central Riyadh.

ACCOMMODATION

Places to stay range from youth hostels to five-star hotels. No matter how cheap the hotel you can count on it having air-conditioning, although a few of the cheaper places in the mountains have ceiling fans. The country's only formal camping grounds are in the Asir National Park.

Saudi Arabia's youth hostels (*beit ash-shabab* in Arabic) are a treat. They are almost always spotless, rarely crowded and are among the best in the world. Beds cost SR 8 per night, for which you often get a single or double room with a private bath. Stays are limited to three nights at any particular hostel, though the management tends to be flexible about this. Saudi hostels are open only to men. Saudi Arabia is an Hostelling International (HI) member and hostel cards are always required.

Saudi law requires the presentation of proper documents to check in at any hotel or hostel. For visitors this means a passport. Expatriates will require their iqama and a travel letter from their sponsor. Small hotels and youth hostels often will ask you to supply a photocopy of these documents if you did not arrive with xeroxes in hand. Women travelling alone need a letter from their sponsor to check into any hotel.

FOOD

Grilled chicken and fuul are the most common cheap dishes. For a quick, and very cheap, meal try shwarma, beef or chicken carved from a large spit and rolled in pitta bread with some or all of the following: lettuce, tomatoes, houmos and hot sauce. They usually cost SR 3 each – two of them and a drink can keep you going for most of the afternoon.

For more up-market dining, every big city has a selection of moderately priced Oriental restaurants. Filipino and Thai food are the cheapest, whereas Chinese food tends to be the most expensive. This is because there are many more low-paid Filipino and Thai workers than Chinese in the kingdom.

DRINKS

The drink selection consists of soft drinks, mineral water and fruit juice. 'Saudi Champagne', which you will sometimes see on menus and can generally be ordered by name, is a mixture of apple juice and Perrier.

Traditional coffee houses, in which everyone drinks tea, not coffee, are becoming rarer. There are a few in Jeddah and in some of the provincial cities but most have yielded to western-style cafes in shopping malls.

ENTERTAINMENT

Almost every form of public entertainment is banned in Saudi Arabia. This includes cinemas, theatres and even lounge singers in hotel restaurants. The exceptions are sporting events and a big folklore festival near Riyadh each year. Soccer and camel racing are the most popular spectator sports. Unless you read Arabic, however, it is very difficult to keep up with the soccer scene in the kingdom. Camel races take place throughout the winter months. The best place to see them is in Riyadh, where there is a large camel track just outside the city centre.

THINGS TO BUY

Among the best buys in the kingdom is silver Bedouin jewellery. Although this is a Yemeni speciality, you can find a really good selection in the souqs of Khamis Mushayt and Najran, and at a few shops in Riyadh and Jeddah. Expect to pay anywhere from SR 100 to SR 700, depending on size and the intricacy of the work, for good quality pieces.

If you have a lot of space in your luggage, woven Bedouin bags make great souvenirs. Prices, after bargaining, range from SR 50 to SR 1000, again depending on the size and the quality of the work. The best place to look for weavings is the Hofuf souq or the weekly Bedouin market in Nairiyah. See the Hofuf and Nairiyah sections later in this chapter for details.

Gold jewellery is also a good buy as the work can be quite striking and the pieces are relatively inexpensive.

Most of the other Arabian souvenirs you will see in shops around the kingdom – incense burners, for example – come from somewhere else, usually Pakistan. The exception is the small pottery incense burners for sale in Jizan.

Getting There & Away

AIR

A return plane ticket from the USA to Saudi Arabia is likely to cost over US$1000, even if purchased from a bucket shop. From Europe it is not a lot cheaper. Flying out of Saudi Arabia to North America, Europe and the Far East is usually much cheaper. Fares fluctuate wildly, and cheap fares are usually available only through travel agents, not the airlines. Youth/student fares are often available for international travel out of the kingdom but they are rarely, if ever, the cheapest way to fly.

LAND

There are five buses per day between Bahrain and Dammam/Alkhobar, and regular daily services between the Eastern Province and Abu Dhabi and Dubai in the UAE.

It is also easy to get a bus from any of the kingdom's major cities to Egypt, Jordan, Syria or even Turkey. On all routes (except Turkey) SAPTCO, the Saudi Arabian bus company, competes with a number of foreign companies. Generally SAPTCO has both the best fares and the best-maintained buses. See the Riyadh, Jeddah and Dammam sections later in this chapter for more information.

SEA

The car ferry connecting Jeddah with Suez is the main seaborne route in and out of the country. There are also regular passenger services from Jeddah to Port Sudan and Musawwa (Eritrea). See the Jeddah section later in this chapter for details and fares.

LEAVING SAUDI ARABIA

Departing from the kingdom through Riyadh, Jeddah, Dhahran or Medina airports is fairly straightforward. You should be at the airport two hours before the scheduled departure time. There is no departure tax.

Getting Around

AIR

All domestic air services in the kingdom are operated by Saudia (Saudi Arabian Airlines), which is quite reliable. The most frequent and efficient service is on the Jeddah-Riyadh-Dhahran corridor. Considering the distances involved, Saudia's domestic services, though no great bargain, are reasonably priced. See the individual city listings later in this chapter for information on direct air connections to and from each city. You can also stop by any Saudia office for an up-to-date timetable.

BUS

Getting around by bus is probably your best bet if you are not pressed for time and do not have a car. Bus fares are one-half to two-thirds of the equivalent airfare. Buses are operated by SAPTCO, which has comfortable, air-conditioned buses that usually run on time. You can buy bus tickets only on the day of departure or one day in advance. When purchasing tickets you will also have to show identification and, for foreign residents, a travel letter.

SERVICE TAXI

Service taxis usually cluster around the bus station in each city and cover most of the destinations the buses go to for the same prices. They leave when full, which could mean anything from five to 11 passengers, depending on the size of the vehicle.

TRAIN

Saudi Arabia has the only stretch of railway track in the entire Arabian peninsula – one line from Riyadh to Dammam, via Hofuf and Abqaiq. Trains leave three times daily in each direction except Thursday, when there is only one train. See the relevant city entries for fares.

CAR

If you are in the country on a visitor's visa and plan to rent a car, a driving licence from most western countries is acceptable. Rental rates are government controlled, with insurance and the collision-damage waiver mandatory. Rates start at SR 110 for a Toyota Corolla or similar size car, which includes insurance and 100 free km per day. Additional km are 40 halalas each. Discounts of 20, 25 or 30% are almost always available for the asking.

HITCHING

Hitching is common in the kingdom among less well-off Saudis and Indians, Pakistanis, Filipinos etc. However, it is so rare for westerners to hitch that anyone trying would be likely to attract police attention. In the Hejaz and Asir regions, hitchers are usually expected to pay the equivalent of the bus fare along the same route.

LOCAL TRANSPORT
Bus

Full-scale municipal bus systems operate in Riyadh, Jeddah and the Dammam-Alkhobar area of the Eastern Province. Smaller scale local services operate in cities like Taif and Abha. Local fares are always SR 2. Riyadh and Jeddah also have confusing minivan systems which operate more or less along the main SAPTCO bus routes. These also charge SR 2 per trip.

Taxi

Taxis in the kingdom's main cities have meters. See the individual city entries for details on the prices of flag falls and per km charges.

Riyadh

While Riyadh, and the nearby oasis town of Dir'aiyah, are the ancestral home of the Al-Saud family, it is only in the last generation that Riyadh has become the centre of government in the kingdom. Though technically Saudi Arabia's capital since the nation's establishment in 1932, it was eclipsed by Jeddah until quite recently. The ministries, embassies and just about everything else were headquartered in Jeddah well into the 1970s.

Orientation

The first thing you should do is learn the names of the main districts. Al-Bathaa is the central, older portion of town around the Masmak Fortress. Al-Murabba and Al-Wazarat are the districts immediately adjacent to it. North of these areas lie Olaya and Sulaymaniyah, the main residential and business areas for the capital's business community.

To the extent that Riyadh has any centre at all it is Al-Bathaa, more or less the area around Al-Bathaa St and Al-Malek Faisal St, which is also called Al-Wazir St, between Al-Washem and Tariq ibn Ziyad Sts. The bus station, GPO and everything else that a traveller needs are in this area, and it is the cheapest part of town.

Informal names are commonly used for some of Riyadh's main streets. These include (formal name first):

Al-Malek Abdul Aziz Rd: Old Airport Rd
Al-Malek Faisal St: Al-Wazir St
Al-Amir Soltan ibn Abdul Aziz St: Tallateen St
Salah ad-Din al-Ayoubi Rd: Sitteen St
Al-Imam Faisal ibn Torki ibn Abdulla St: Al-Khazan St
Al-Ihsa St: Pepsi Cola St

Information

Money Riyadh has no shortage of banks. A good place to look is along Olaya St between the Al-Khozama Hotel and Makkah Rd. They all change money, as do the various moneychangers in Olaya and Al-Bathaa.

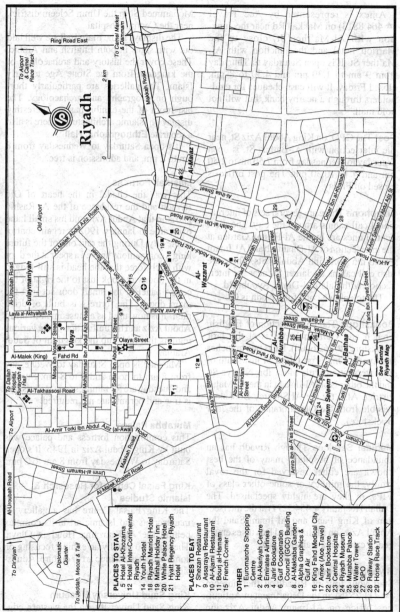

Riyadh

Ring Road East

To Airport & Camel Race Track

To Camel Market & Dammam

To Airport & Camel Race Track

Makkah Road

2 km

1

0

Al-Malaz

Al-Malek Abdul Aziz Road

Old Airport

Al-Insa Street

Omar Ibn al-Khattab Street

Salah al-Din al-Ayubi Road

Al-Dhabzan Street

22

Al-Urubah Road

Sulaymaniyah

29

Al-Amir Salman Ibn Abd Aziz S

Al-Khari Road

20

Al-Malek Abdul-Aziz Road

Al-Wazarat

Al-Amir Abdul Aziz Road

19

18

21

Al-Washem al-Jamian Street

Al-Mazahad al-Edaran Street

Olaya

Mosa Ibn Nosay Street

Layla al-Akhyaliyah St

3

2

Ibn Abdul Aziz Road

Al-Amir Sultan Ibn Abdul Aziz Road

Al-Amir Mohammad

Al-Malek (King) Fahd Rd

Olaya Street

10

9

15

16

Al-Amir Abdul

Kharj Ibn Mosa Ibn Obn Matew Street

17

Omar Ibn Khattab Street

Al-Bathaa Street

Al-Wesham Street

Tariq Ibn Ziyad Street

To Dallah Hospital, Buraydah & Hail

1

13

Al-Matew Street

7

12

Al-Amir (King) Fahd Road

14

Al-Amir Faisal Ibn Fahd Road

Murabba

25

26

27

See Central Riyadh Map

Al-Takhassosi Road

To Airport

Al-Amir Mohammad

11

Abu Feras Al-Hamdani Street

Faisal Street

Al-Malek (King) Faisal Ibn torki Ibn Abdulla Street

Al-Bathaa

24

Umm Saleem

Al-Amir Torki Ibn Abdul Aziz (al-Awal)

6

Makkah Road

Al-Malek Saud Street

Al-Amir Faisal Ibn torki Ibn Abdulla Street

Al-Imam Torki Ibn Abdulla Street

Umm al-Hamam Street

Amro Ibn al-Aas Street

Al-Imam Abdul Aziz Ibn Mohammed St

Al-Malek Khaled Road

Al-Urubah Road

To Dirayah

To Jeddah, Mecca & Taif

Diplomatic Quarter

PLACES TO STAY
5 Hotel Al-Khozama
12 Hotel Inter-Continental Riyadh
14 Youth Hostel
18 Riyadh Marriott Hotel
19 Minhal Holiday Inn
20 White Palace Hotel
21 Hyatt Regency Riyadh Hotel

PLACES TO EAT
7 Shezan Restaurant
9 Assaraya Restaurant
10 Al-Ajami Restaurant
11 Bourj al-Hamam
15 French Corner

OTHER
1 Euromarche Shopping Centre
2 Al-Akariyah Centre
3 Emirates Airlines
6 Jarir Bookstore
8 Gulf Cooperation Council (GCC) Building
13 Alpha Graphics & Gulf Air
16 King Fahd Medical City
17 Amex (Ace Travel)
22 Jarir Bookstore
23 Central Hospital
24 Riyadh Museum
25 Murabba Palace
26 Water Tower
27 GPO
28 Railway Station
29 Horse Race Track

Amex is represented by Ace Travel (☎ 464 8813) on Makkah Rd near the junction with Al-Ma'ther St, close to the Marriott hotel and the junction with Al-Ma'ther St. It is open Saturday to Thursday from 9 am to 1.30 pm and 4.30 to 8 pm, closed Friday. It will cash cheques for cardholders through a nearby bank, but will not hold mail.

Post The GPO, on King Abdul Aziz St, near the intersection with Al-Bathaa St, is open Saturday to Wednesday from 7.50 am to 2.50 pm and 4 to 10.30 pm. The post office is closed on Friday.

Telephone There are several sets of international call cabins around the city. The most central ones are by the Al-Foutah Garden at the intersection of Al-Dhahirah and Al-Imam Faisal ibn Torki ibn Abdulla Sts. There are also call cabins on Jareer St, near the intersection with Salah ad-Din al-Ayoubi Rd.

The telephone code for Riyadh is 01.

Bookshops The best selection of English, French and German books is at the Jarir Bookstore (☎ 462 6000). It has two branches in Riyadh. One is on Olaya St just south of the intersection with Mosa ibn Nosayr St, and the other is on Al-Ihsa St in the Al-Malaz district. Also try the Al Shegrey Bookstore (visible from the Olaya branch of the Jarir Bookstore).

Medical Services Though Riyadh has an abundance of hospitals, many of the best known are either reserved for the royal family, the military or some other class of VIPs, or they are highly specialised. The Dallah Hospital (☎ 454 5277) at the intersection of King Fahd and Al-Imam Saud ibn Abdul Aziz ibn Mohammad Rds takes emergency cases on a walk-in basis.

Riyadh Museum
Start your tour of Riyadh at the museum (☎ 411 2576), in the Department of Antiquities office on Al-Imam Abdul Aziz ibn Mohammed St in the Umm Seleem district, near the Central Hospital.

The displays in the **main hall** are well laid out with signs in both English and Arabic. These cover the history and archaeology of the kingdom from the Stone Age to early Islam. The galleries are particularly thorough on geography and archaeology. The last room of the exhibit has an interesting display on Islamic architecture. There is also a separate **Ethnographic Hall**.

It's open Saturday to Wednesday from 8 am to 2 pm, and admission is free.

Masmak Fortress
This was the citadel in the heart of Old Riyadh and the residence of the Al-Rashid garrison that Abdul Aziz and his small band overcame in January 1902 to regain control of the city. During the raid one of the future king's companions heaved a spear at the door with such force that the head is still lodged in the doorway (look just to the right of the centre panel of the small door set into the main door). The fortress is built of dried mud. It is now used as a museum honouring Abdul Aziz and his unification of the various regions that make up the kingdom of Saudi Arabia.

Masmak is open Saturday to Wednesday from 8 am to noon and 4 to 8 pm. Sunday and Tuesday are for families only. Admission is free and permits are not required.

Murabba Palace
This combination fortress and palace was built by King Abdul Aziz in 1946. It's open Saturday to Wednesday from 8 am to 2 pm.

King Faisal Centre for Research & Islamic Studies
The King Faisal Centre has a gallery of manuscripts and Islamic art in its complex behind the Al-Khozama Hotel in Olaya. There is also usually an exhibit focusing on some aspect of Islamic art or culture. Admission is free.

King Saud University Museum
King Saud University, on the western edge

of Riyadh near the Diplomatic Quarter, has a small museum displaying finds from the university's archaeological digs at Al-Faw and Rabdhah. The museum is open from Saturday to Wednesday, mornings only, but to visit it you must first make an appointment through the university's public relations office (☎ 467 8135).

Camel Market

Around 30 km from the city centre on the outermost outskirts of the city is one of the largest camel markets in the Middle East.

Trading is heaviest in the late afternoon. To reach the market take the Dammam Rd to the Thumamah exit – the last one before the road heads off east across the desert.

Al-Thumairi Gate

On Al-Malek Faisal St, near the Middle East Hotel, this is an impressive restoration of one of the nine gates which used to lead into the city before the wall was torn down in 1950. Across the street, opposite the hotel, is the new Al-Thumairi Gate, a more modern structure vaguely resembling a triumphal arch.

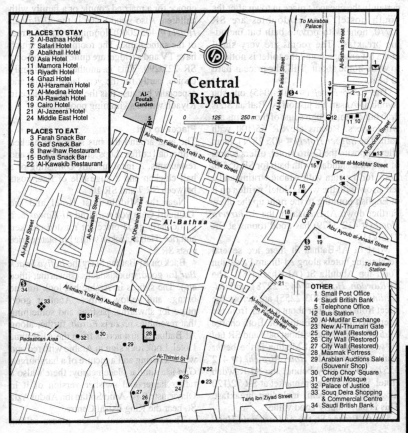

PLACES TO STAY
2 Al-Bathaa Hotel
7 Safari Hotel
9 Abalkhail Hotel
10 Asia Hotel
11 Mamora Hotel
13 Riyadh Hotel
14 Ghazi Hotel
16 Al-Haramain Hotel
17 Al-Medina Hotel
18 Al-Rawdah Hotel
21 Al-Jazeera Hotel
24 Middle East Hotel

PLACES TO EAT
3 Farah Snack Bar
6 Gad Snack Bar
8 Ihaw-Ihaw Restaurant
15 Bofiya Snack Bar
22 Al-Kawakib Restaurant

Central Riyadh

To Murabba Palace

Al-Foutah Garden

0   125   250 m

Omar al-Mokhtar Street

Al-Bathaa

Abu Ayoub al-Ansari Street

To Railway Station

Pedestrian Area

OTHER
1 Small Post Office
4 Saudi British Bank
5 Telephone Office
12 Bus Station
20 Al-Mudifar Exchange
23 New Al-Thumairi Gate
25 City Wall (Restored)
26 City Wall (Restored)
27 City Wall (Restored)
28 Masmak Fortress
29 Arabian Auctions Sale (Souvenir Shop)
30 'Chop Chop' Square
31 Central Mosque
32 Palace of Justice
33 Souq Deira Shopping & Commercial Centre
34 Saudi British Bank

Al-Imam Faisal ibn Torki ibn Abdulla Street
Al-Sowailim Street
Al-Dhahirah Street
Al-Atayef Street
Al-Imam Torki ibn Abdulla Street
Al-Thimiri St
Al-Imam Abdul Rahman ibn Faisal Street
Tariq ibn Ziyad Street
Al-Malek Faisal Street
Al-Bathaa Street
Al-Dhorabi Street
Overpass

Places to Stay

The *Youth Hostel* (☎ 405 5552) is on Shabab al-Ghansani St, a side street off King Fahd Rd in the Al-Namodhajiyah district. Beds are SR 8. The hostel is not on any bus route nor within walking distance of the bus station.

The cheap hotels are all clustered in the vicinity of the bus station. The prices quoted here include the service charges, where applicable. In most cases it should be possible to bargain SR 10 to SR 15 off the quoted price, particularly if you are staying for more than a few days.

The *Middle East Hotel* (☎ 411 1994) on Al-Malek Faisal St is a bit out of the way but certainly the cheapest place in town after the youth hostel. Singles/doubles are SR 45/70, none with private bath but including breakfast. The rooms are very small and a bit cramped, and the toilet is nothing to write home about. Still, the price is hard to beat.

The *Cairo Hotel* (☎ 401 4045) on Abu Ayoub al-Ansari St, just off Al-Bathaa St, is drab but clean, though some of the rooms are windowless. Rooms are SR 65/100 with bath. The *Sageer Hotel* (☎ 405 2871), in an alley opposite the Cairo Hotel, offers rooms of a similar standard with bath for SR 65/90. Look for the sign with Arabic writing and a red arrow with the word 'Hotel' written on it in English pointing to the right up the alley. Further down Al-Bathaa St, the *Al-Jazeera Hotel* (☎ 412 3479) has good rooms at SR 71.50/110.

West of Al-Bathaa St there are several good-value hotels along Al-Imam Faisal ibn Torki ibn Abdulla St (Al-Khazan St). The *Al-Rawdah Hotel* (☎ 412 2278) and *Al-Medina Hotel* (☎ 403 2255) are across the street from each other about a block from the intersection with Al-Bathaa St. Both charge SR 55/83 for rooms without bath and SR 66/99 with bath. The Al-Medina is the better deal of the two. The *Hotel Alrajehi* (☎ 412 3557), up an alley behind the Al-Rawdah Hotel, is a bit more up-market at SR 72/120 for rooms with bath, including breakfast. This is particularly good value.

On Al-Bathaa St, the *Al-Haramain Hotel* (☎ 404 3085) has clean rooms with TV for SR 77/116 with bath, SR 66/99 without.

If you're looking for something a bit more up-market in the Al-Bathaa area, try the *Mamora Hotel* (☎ 401 2111), excellent value at SR 80/120 for singles/doubles. Another good bet is the *Riyadh Hotel* (☎ 402 8777) on Omar al-Mokhtar St, where the staff are friendly but the rooms are a bit dark. Singles/doubles cost SR 80/120. For more good mid-range value try the *Safari Hotel* (☎ 405 5533), on a side street off Al-Bathaa St. Singles/doubles are SR 120/170, though you might be able to talk the price down to SR 80/120. This place would be a good choice for a married couple or a family with children. Also good value is the *Al-Bathaa Hotel* (☎ 405 2000), looming over the street of the same name. The rooms, all of which have TV and a fridge, are quite large and cost SR 225/290. This is another good family choice, partly for the very large rooms and especially because it is the cheapest place in Riyadh with a swimming pool.

Places to Eat

The area around the bus station is packed with small coffee shops, shwarma stands and restaurants. A meal, usually consisting of a half chicken and a huge pile of rice, costs between SR 7 and SR 10.

Near the Middle East Hotel and the Thumairi Gate you will find *Al-Kawakib*, a particularly good place for roasted chicken and rice. Half a chicken with a big plate of rice costs SR 8.

Back on Al-Bathaa St try the *Bofiya Snack Bar* for good, quick snacks (shwarma, juice etc). The sign is in Arabic but look for the orange and yellow stripes. Another good place for shwarma, pastries and something that resembles pizza is *Farah*, further along Al-Bathaa St just across from the Al-Bathaa Hotel. Look for a sign in Arabic with red and white lettering and a picture of a hamburger. *Gad* is a similar place nearby; there's also a rather larger and swisher version of it in Olaya just off Al-Amir Soltan ibn Abdul Aziz St, near the King Faisal Centre.

There are several dozen places selling

cheap Filipino food on the streets behind the Al-Bathaa Hotel. Try *Ihaw-Ihaw*, a couple of short blocks in along the street separating the Al-Bathaa and Safari hotels. Its 'budget lunch', consisting of rice, one selection from its cafeteria line and a drink, is a bargain at SR 7.

Al-Amir Soltan ibn Abdul Aziz St (Tallateen St) in Olaya is a good place to look for affordable food of all types. Good, cheap Lebanese food can be had at *Al-Ajami*, a cafeteria-style restaurant just over one km east of the intersection with Olaya St. Mezze cost SR 5 to SR 10 each and kibbih can be ordered by the piece for SR 2 each. A notch or two up the scale is *Assaraya*, a popular Turkish restaurant, also on Al-Amir Soltan ibn Abdul Aziz St. Excellent kebabs cost SR 12 to SR 15. This place is highly recommended.

French Corner on Al-Amir Abdul Aziz ibn Mosa'ad ibn Jalawi St is the Riyadh branch of a popular kingdom-wide chain. It has good coffee, a wide selection of pastries for SR 5 to SR 7 and full, but generally unimpressive, meals for SR 20 to SR 40.

Things to Buy

Spices and occasional weaving items can be found if you wander deep into the Souq al-Bathaa. The best place in Riyadh to buy Yemeni silver and other Arabian souvenirs is Arabian Auctions Sale, near the Masmak Fortress. A number of smaller shops dealing in (mostly imported) souvenirs are located on and around Al-Thimiri St, near the fortress.

Getting There & Away

Air King Khalid international airport is a long way from the city – nearly 40 km north from Al-Bathaa. Saudia's main reservations office is at the intersection of Al-Amir Torki ibn Abdel Aziz (Al-Thani) and Olaya Sts, north of the city centre.

Riyadh is Saudia's base of operations and there are frequent flights to just about everywhere in the kingdom. Sample one-way economy-class fares include: Abha and Najran SR 270 (US$72); Dhahran and Hofuf SR 140 (US$37); Gassim (Buraydah) SR

130 (US$34); Hail SR 190 (US$50); Jeddah SR 270 (US$72); Jizan SR 310 (US$82); Tabuk SR 380 (US$100); and Taif and Medina SR 240 (US$64).

The cheapest return fares to some other Gulf cities include: Abu Dhabi SR 889 (US$237); Bahrain SR 414 (US$110); Dubai SR 980 (US$261); Kuwait SR 830 (US$221); and Muscat SR 1510 (US$400).

Bus The bus station just off Al-Bathaa St is SAPTCO's intercity depot. You'll need identification to buy a ticket and the queues tend to be long. Unaccompanied women are not allowed to travel by bus.

There are 11 buses every day to Jeddah (13 hours; SR 130) via Taif (10 hours; SR 100). These buses go around Mecca and are OK for non-Muslims. If you are a non-Muslim bound for Jeddah it would be prudent to double-check that the routing has not changed.

Other routes include: ten daily to Abha (13 hours; SR 125); nine daily to Buraydah (4½ hours; SR 60); 11 daily to Dammam (4½ hours; SR 60); three daily to Hail (eight hours; SR 100); three daily to Hofuf (four hours; SR 45), with an extra bus on Thursday; two daily to Jizan (18 hours; SR 160); three daily to Najran (12 hours; SR 115); two daily to Sakaka (14 hours; SR 175); and two daily to Tabuk (17 hours; SR 200).

For Muslims only, buses leave for Mecca (10 hours; SR 115) five times per day, and for Medina (12 hours; SR 140) three times daily.

International service is available to Egypt, Syria, Jordan and Turkey. SAPTCO and a number of foreign companies serve all of these routes. The foreign companies all have offices around the bus station. The foreign companies can often undercut SAPTCO's price, and might throw in a few meals as well. The Amman and Cairo routes are particularly competitive. On the other hand, SAPTCO's buses are often newer and may be more comfortable. Expect to pay around SR 350 to SR 400 to Cairo, SR 200 to Damascus or Amman and SR 260 to İstanbul. SAPTCO will also sell you a through ticket to Bahrain (SR 100) or Abu Dhabi (SR 195), but these routes require a change of bus in Dammam if you're going to Bahrain and in Hofuf if you are headed to Qatar or the UAE.

Service Taxi These also leave from the SAPTCO bus station. In general, the buses are a better bet than the service taxis. If you prefer to catch a service taxi, however, the fare to Buraydah is SR 60. Expect to pay SR 70 to Dammam, SR 120 to Hail, SR 55 to Hofuf and SR 150 to Jeddah. All service taxis leave when they are full. Most carry either five or seven passengers.

Train The railway station (☎ 473 1855) is on Al-Amir Abdul Aziz ibn Abdullah ibn Torki St, a small street off Omar ibn al-Khattab St 2.5 km east of the bus station. Trains leave for Dammam via Hofuf and Abqaiq three times daily, except Thursday, when there is only one train. First class/2nd class fares are SR 52/34 to Abqaiq, SR 60/40 to Dammam and SR 45/30 to Hofuf.

Car Prices are fixed by the government. Expect to pay SR 110 per day, including insurance, for the smallest cars available (usually Toyota Corollas) from all the companies. The net price should drop to SR 90 to SR 100 after you include the discounts available. Most large hotels have a car-rental desk and you can find a number of car-rental offices along Olaya St near the Al-Khozama Hotel.

Getting Around
The Airport There is no bus service to King Khaled international airport. The buses and minibuses marked 'Airport' go to the old airport via Al-Malek Abdul Aziz Rd. Your only option is a taxi. A taxi to the airport could cost anything from SR 30 to SR 70, depending on where in the city you start. From the airport, the white limos have a set tariff of SR 50 or SR 60 to most districts in the city, though a few areas closer to the airport cost only SR 45.

Bus SAPTCO buses and private minibuses cover most of the city. Fares on either are SR 2. Both the buses and the minibuses have their routes posted in the front window, though on the latter this may be only in Arabic. The small (and packed) minibuses follow more or less the same routes as the buses, and the route numbers are applicable in either direction.

Some of the main bus routes include:

No 1 – Mosa ibn Nosayr St, Al-Malek Abdul Aziz Rd, Al-Bathaa St as far as the Ring Rd South

No 7A – Al-Bathaa St, Al-Malek Faisal St, Al-Malek Saud St, Al-Nasiriyah St, Al-Ma'ther St, Al-Jawhrah bint ibn Maamar St, Al-Malek Khaled Rd, Umm al-Hamam St, Al-Uroubah Rd, King Saud University

No 8A – Al-Bathaa St, Al-Washem St, Al-Malek Saud St, Al-Nasiriyah St, Al-Takhassosi Rd

No 9 – Al-Bathaa St, Al-Amir Abdul Aziz ibn Moad'ad ibn Jalawi St, Al-Ma'ther St, Olaya St, Al-Imam Saud ibn Abdul Aziz ibn Mohammad St, Al-Takhassosi Rd

No 10 – Khaled ibn al-Waleed Rd, Obadah ibn al-Samit St, Makkah Rd, Al-Ihsa St, Omar ibn Abdul Aziz St, Salah ad-Din Al-Ayoubi Rd, Al-Jami'ah St, Al-Bathaa St

Taxi There are two kinds of taxis: white-and-orange and yellow taxis. In both cases, a flag-drop is SR 3 after which the meter ticks over in 50 halala increments at SR 1 per km. The drivers in the white-and-orange taxis are more likely to speak English.

AROUND RIYADH
Dir'aiyah
Riyadh's most interesting site is outside the city. On the capital's northern outskirts, about 30 km from Al-Bathaa, lie the ruins of Dir'aiyah, the first capital of the Al-Saud clan and the kingdom's most popular and easily accessible archaeological site (no permits required). The site is open Saturday to Thursday from 7 am to 6 pm and Friday from 1 to 6 pm. Admission is free.

To reach Dir'aiyah from Riyadh, leave the city centre and follow the signs for the airport. Once you're on the expressway to the airport look for signs for Dir'aiyah. Once you exit the expressway you should see the ruins in the distance to your left. Follow the road until you reach a T-junction. Turn left, and left again when you reach a roundabout. Go straight, and look for the small white signs indicating a right turn to reach the ruins.

Najd (Central Region)

BURAYDAH

Buraydah has an unenviable reputation as the least hospitable city in Saudi Arabia. The main city of the Qassim region, it lies 330 km north-west of Riyadh on the road to Hail. It is a place most people pass through as there's not much to see and do. If you do stop here, take a walk through the residential areas two or three blocks on either side of Khobib St, where a few examples of interesting traditional Najdi mud-brick houses are still around to be seen.

HAIL

Hail (pronounced Hay-El), 640 km north-west of Riyadh, was formerly the seat of the Al-Rashid family, the Al-Saud clan's most formidable rivals. It is now the centre of the kingdom's vast agricultural programme, and most of Saudi Arabia's wheat crop comes from the surrounding area.

Hail's main street runs north-south and centres on Commercial District Square by the Saudi Hollandi Bank building. Old Hail is roughly east of this street and the newer areas are west of it, except for the Al-Qashalah Fortress. The bus station is at the Al-Qashalah Fortress, three blocks south of Commercial District Square. The telephone code for Hail is 06.

Things to See

Before doing any sightseeing your permit has to be validated at the Antiquities Section of the Ministry of Education office on the main road (ask for *maktab al-athaar*). The office is on the 1st floor, and is open Saturday to Wednesday from about 8 am until 1 pm.

These are also more or less the hours during which you can visit the sites.

The **Al-Qashalah Fortress**, next to the bus station, was built in the 1930s and was used mostly as a barracks for Abdul Aziz's troops in Hail. The small square building in the courtyard contains a display of artefacts from Hail and the surrounding desert region.

'Airif Fort, on a hill just outside the centre, is much older. It was built about 200 years ago as a combination observation post and stronghold. Also in the city centre, on Barazan Square, you can see two restored **towers**, all that remain of another of Hail's palaces.

Places to Stay & Eat

The *youth hostel* (☎ 533 1485) is at the stadium, a 20 to 30 minute walk south of the bus station. Beds are SR 8. Alternately, walk into town from the bus station and catch a minibus from the parking lot in front of the

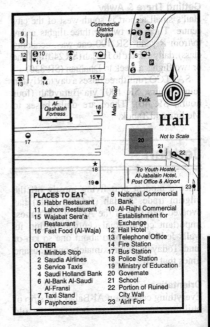

PLACES TO EAT
5 Habbr Restaurant
11 Lahore Restaurant
15 Wajabat Sera'a Restaurant
16 Fast Food (Al-Waja)

OTHER
1 Minibus Stop
2 Saudia Airlines
3 Service Taxis
4 Saudi Hollandi Bank
6 Al-Bank Al-Saudi Al-Fransi
7 Taxi Stand
8 Payphones
9 National Commercial Bank
10 Al-Rajhi Commercial Establishment for Exchange
12 Hail Hotel
13 Telephone Office
14 Fire Station
17 Bus Station
18 Police Station
19 Ministry of Education
20 Governate
21 School
22 Portion of Ruined City Wall
23 'Airif Fort

Saudi Hollandi Bank building. The fare is SR 2.

The *Hail Hotel* (☎ 532 0180; fax 532 7104) is on King Khalid St. Singles/doubles with bath cost SR 132/171, though this price can be readily discounted to SR 120/155. Rooms without private bath cost SR 121/159.50. To reach the hotel walk west from Commercial District Square and turn left at the first set of traffic lights. The hotel will be on your right.

The *Lahore Restaurant*, across from the Hail Hotel, is a decent and cleanish place with the usual selection of chicken dishes and curries. The shakshoka (mildly spiced scrambled eggs) makes a good, cheap breakfast at SR 5. Another good bet is *Wajabat Sera'a*, a small Indian place across from the Al-Bank Al-Saudi Al-Fransi office offering cheap samosas (50 halalas each) and other quick eats. For shwarma and fresh juice try *Fast Food* on the main road across from the southern edge of the park.

Getting There & Away

Hail's small airport is south-west of the city centre. There are two or three flights a day to/from Riyadh (SR 190 one way, economy class), daily service to Jeddah (SR 240) and one or two flights a week to Dhahran (SR 330).

SAPTCO runs three buses a day to Riyadh (eight hours; SR 100) via Buraydah (four hours; SR 40). There are daily buses to Medina and Tabuk.

Jeddah

Once a modest port living mostly off the pilgrim trade, Jeddah (Jiddah, Jidda) has evolved into one of the Arab world's most important commercial centres. Within its walls Jeddah occupied about one sq km of land. Today it is approximately one thousand times that size.

Orientation

Everything centres on Al-Balad: the strip of buildings on the coast between the old

foreign ministry building and the bus station, and on the old city which lies directly inland from them. Al-Madinah al-Munawwarah Rd (Medina Rd, for short) is the principal street running north from the city centre, flanked to the east by Al-Amir Fahd St and to the west by Al-Andalus St.

As in Riyadh, there are a number of streets with commonly used, but unofficial, names. The most important one to know is Al-Amir Fahd St, which is commonly called Sitteen St or King Fahd St. Al-Dahab St is sometimes referred to as King Faisal St. The names of several main streets are commonly anglicised. These include Falasteen St (Palestine St) and Al-Malek Abdel Aziz St (King Abdul Aziz St).

Information

Money There is an Al-Rajhi Banking & Investment Company branch on Al-Malek Abdel Aziz St opposite the Shaheen Hotel and a Saudi British Bank branch in the shopping arcade at the Red Sea Palace Hotel. There are a large number of moneychangers along Al-Qabel St in Al-Balad between Al-Malek Abdul Aziz St and the tunnel that goes underneath Al-Dahab St.

Amex is represented by Ace Travel (☎ 665 1254) on Falasteen St near the intersection with Al-Hamra St. It can replace lost and stolen cards and cash personal cheques for Amex clients but will not hold mail. The office is open Saturday to Wednesday from 9 am to 1.30 pm and 4.30 to 8 pm, and during the morning on Thursday but is closed Friday.

Post The GPO is the large red-and-white building opposite the bus station, between Ba'ashan and Al-Bareed Sts. The entrance is on the Al-Bareed St side of the building. It is open Saturday to Wednesday from 7.30 am to 9.30 pm. On Thursday only the Mumtaz Post (Express Mail) windows are open, from 7.30 am to 2 pm. The post office is closed Friday.

Telephone The telephone office is on Abu Bakr al-Seddeeq St in the Al-Sharafeyyah district, just south of the intersection with Falasteen St. The telephone code for Jeddah is 02.

Bookshops The Al-Mamoun Bookshop, on the 1st floor of the Corniche Commercial Centre, has a reasonable selection of English books. You will find a better selection at the Jarir Bookstore on the south side of Falasteen St between Makarounah and Al-Amir Majed Sts.

Walking Tour & Old City Walls
Many of Jeddah's main sites lie along the

course of the old city walls, which were torn down in the late 1940s. The walls ran along Al-Malek Abdel Aziz St, Makkah al-Mukarramah Rd and Ba'najah St. A circuit of these streets should take a little under an hour on foot.

Along the route are the three reconstructed city gates – all that remains of the wall. Near the North City Gate are several good examples of traditional Jeddah architecture in various states of preservation. Many of the older houses within the old city walls are constructed not of stone but of coral quarried from reefs in the Red Sea.

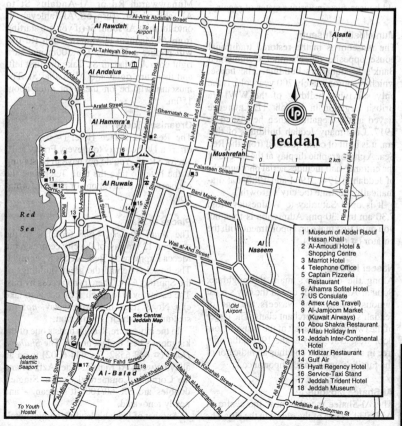

1 Museum of Abdel Raouf Hasan Khalil
2 Al-Amoudi Hotel & Shopping Centre
3 Marriot Hotel
4 Telephone Office
5 Captain Pizzeria Restaurant
6 Alhamra Sofitel Hotel
7 US Consulate
8 Amex (Ace Travel)
9 Al-Jamjoom Market (Kuwait Airways)
10 Abou Shakra Restaurant
11 Alfau Holiday Inn
12 Jeddah Inter-Continental Hotel
13 Yildizar Restaurant
14 Gulf Air
15 Hyatt Regency Hotel
16 Service-Taxi Stand
17 Jeddah Trident Hotel
18 Jeddah Museum

Jeddah Museum

Jeddah's Regional Museum of Archaeology and Ethnography is in an awkward location near the Al-Khozam Palace and the Islamic Development Bank, but if you have not already been to the Riyadh Museum (the displays are quite similar) it is worth the trip. The museum is open Saturday to Wednesday from 8 am to noon. Admission is free.

The Shorbatly House

Just east of the North City Gate, this house is one of the best known examples of the city's traditional architecture. In the immediate area around it you will see several other old houses, also in various states of repair.

Municipality Museum

The museum is in the restored traditional house opposite the National Commercial Bank's headquarters building. The house, which is approximately 200 years old, is the only surviving building of the WWI-era British Legation in Jeddah. TE Lawrence stayed at the Legation when he visited in 1917. Like many Jeddah buildings of that era, it is built of coral quarried from the Red Sea. A photographic display at the far end of the entrance hall includes aerial photographs of Jeddah in 1948, 1964 and 1988 that dramatically illustrate the city's growth.

It is open Saturday to Wednesday from 7.30 am to 1.30 pm. Admission is free, but you must first make an appointment with the curator (☎ 642 4922).

Naseef House

Along the old city's main thoroughfare, Souq al-Alawi, stands one of the city's most famous houses. The Naseefs are one of Jeddah's old-line merchant clans. The larger of the two trees to the left of the house's front door was, as recently as the 1920s, the only tree in all of Jeddah, and thus an indicator of the family's wealth and importance.

Al-Shafee Mosque

The Al-Shafee mosque, near the centre of Al-Balad, is one of the oldest in the city. The easiest way to reach it is to enter the souq near Bab Makkah.

Museum of Abdel Raouf Hasan Khalil

This private museum really has to be seen to be believed. It contains over 10,000 items crammed into four 'houses' that look like the sort of mock-Arab buildings you might expect to see at Disney World. The museum is open Saturday to Thursday from 9 am to noon and 5 to 9 pm, and closed Friday. Admission is SR 20.

Though signs in various parts of Jeddah point to the museum, actually finding it can be a bit tricky. Take either Al-Madinah al-Munawwarah Rd or Al-Andalus St to Al-Tahleyah St. Turn off Al-Tahleyah St onto Ibrahim Al-Jufali St (if you are starting from Al-Madinah al-Munawwarah Rd this will require a U-turn). Go 500m and turn right onto Al-Madani St. Take the first left, and then turn right onto Al-Mathaf St. The museum will be on the right after about 150m.

Organised Tours

The Red Sea Palace Hotel (☎ 642 8555) offers a 1½ hour city tour every Friday at 10 am for SR 25. You do not have to be staying at the hotel to take the tour. Telephone the concierge for reservations or more information.

Places to Stay

The *Youth Hostel* (☎ 688 6692) is at the stadium, 12 km east of the city centre on the Mecca Expressway. Beds are SR 8 per night. The hostel is behind the green buildings of the Sporting City. There is no access by bus. The easiest way to reach it by car is to take exit No 8 from the expressway, *not* the stadium exit which is further on.

In the city centre, Jeddah boasts one of the kingdom's best budget hotels. The *Shaheen Hotel* (☎ 642 6582; fax 644 6302) is on an alley between Al-Malek Abdel Aziz St and the Corniche Commercial Centre. Singles/doubles are SR 60/100. It's clean – and newly renovated.

Another of Jeddah's leading budget hotels

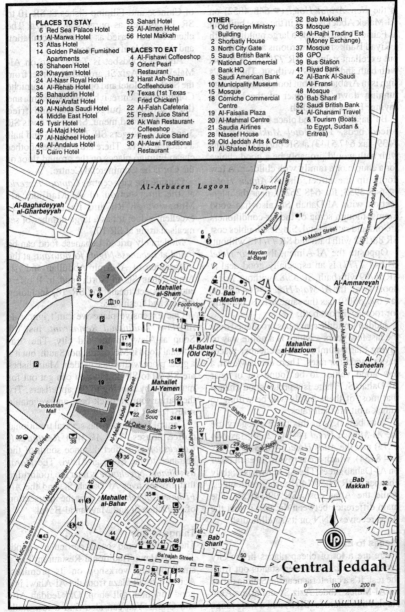

PLACES TO STAY
6 Red Sea Palace Hotel
11 Al-Marwa Hotel
13 Atlas Hotel
14 Golden Palace Furnished Apartments
16 Shaheen Hotel
23 Khayyam Hotel
24 Al-Nasr Royal Hotel
34 Al-Rehab Hotel
35 Bahauddin Hotel
40 New Arafat Hotel
43 Al-Nahda Saudi Hotel
44 Middle East Hotel
45 Tysir Hotel
46 Al-Majd Hotel
47 Al-Nakheel Hotel
49 Al-Andalus Hotel
51 Cairo Hotel
53 Sahari Hotel
55 Al-Almen Hotel
56 Hotel Makkah

PLACES TO EAT
4 Al-Fishawi Coffeeshop
9 Orient Pearl Restaurant
12 Harat Ash-Sham Coffeehouse
17 Texas (1st Texas Fried Chicken)
22 Al-Falah Cafeteria
25 Fresh Juice Stand
26 Ak Wan Restaurant-Coffeeshop
27 Fresh Juice Stand
30 Al-Alawi Traditional Restaurant

OTHER
1 Old Foreign Ministry Building
2 Shorbatly House
3 North City Gate
5 Saudi British Bank
7 National Commercial Bank HQ
8 Saudi American Bank
10 Municipality Museum
15 Mosque
18 Corniche Commercial Centre
19 Al-Faisalia Plaza
20 Al-Mahmal Centre
21 Saudia Airlines
28 Naseef House
29 Old Jeddah Arts & Crafts
31 Al-Shafee Mosque
32 Bab Makkah
33 Mosque
36 Al-Rajhi Trading Est (Money Exchange)
37 Mosque
38 GPO
39 Bus Station
41 Riyad Bank
42 Al-Bank Al-Saudi Al-Fransi
48 Mosque
50 Bab Sharif
52 Saudi British Bank
54 Al-Ghanami Travel & Tourism (Boats to Egypt, Sudan & Eritrea)

Central Jeddah

SAUDI ARABIA

is the *New Arafat Hotel* (☎ 648 4852) on Al-Malek Abdel Aziz St in the same building as Fahad Travel, beside a large building with a Riyad Bank sign. The rooms are a bit bare, but excellent value at SR 77/116 for rooms with bath and SR 66/99 without. The hotel's sign is in Arabic only but look for a large sign running down the corner of the building saying 'Hotel' in English.

Ba'najah St is a good place for moderately priced beds. The *Hotel Makkah* (☎ 647 7439; fax 647 5143) at SR 66/100 for rooms with bath would probably be a good choice for a couple or a family with children. A few doors up the street, the *Al-Almen Hotel* (☎ 648 3953; fax 648 2621), near the intersection with Al-Dahab St, also has good rooms, though some of the air-conditioners are old and rather loud. Singles/doubles cost SR 88/132 with bath and SR 77/115 without.

Opposite the Al-Almen, the *Tysir Hotel* (☎ 647 7777) is an especially good deal at SR 66/99 with bath, SR 55/83 without. A few doors away, the *Al-Majd Hotel* (☎ 647 5354; fax 647 5509) has the same prices, but only for rooms without bath.

Jeddah's middle range has broadened over the last few years – which is a polite way of saying that a number of the cheaper places have raised their rates. There are, however, a few good values to be found on or near Al-Dahab St. There is a pretty good chance that most of these hotels will be willing to knock a bit off their rates.

Your best bets in this price category are the *Al-Marwa Hotel* (☎ 643 2650; fax 644 4273) and the *Atlas Hotel* (☎ 643 8520; fax 644 8454), which are across from each other on Al-Dahab street. The Al-Marwa is slightly cheaper at SR 93.50/140 for singles/doubles, while the Atlas costs SR 99/148.50. The main difference between the two is that the Atlas receives CNN on its satellite dish.

Places to Eat

There are a lot of cheap places in the city centre, *Al-Falah*, however, stands out from the rest. It's a cafeteria near the Saudia office on Al-Malek Abdel Aziz St and offers Arab staples like houmos (SR 5) and a wide range of Chinese and Filipino dishes at SR 10 to SR 15, as well as burgers and pizza. The clientele is as varied as Jeddah's population and the food is always good.

Another good bet is *Texas*, also on Al-Malek Abdel Aziz St, around the corner from the Shaheen Hotel and opposite the Corniche Commercial Centre. It has both shwarma and the traditional burgers, fries and fried chicken fast-food menu. Shwarma costs SR 3 and SR 4, burgers SR 7 to SR 13 and half a chicken SR 12. There are a couple of other cheap Filipino places on the ground floor of the Corniche Commercial Centre.

Outside the city centre, *Captain Pizzeria* at the intersection of Al-Madinah al-Munawwarah Rd and Falasteen St is excellent value. It has a large number of set meals starting at SR 10.

Moderately priced Lebanese food can be found at *Lebanese Nights Restaurant*, at the intersection of Al-Amir Abdullah and Al-Amir Sultan Sts in North Jeddah. It offers enormous set meals for SR 18, including dessert and fresh juice.

One expensive place we can't ignore is *Al-Alawi Traditional Restaurant*, just off Souq al-Alawi in the old city. The 'traditional' food is Moroccan, not Saudi, but it's a great place with a nice garden. Main dishes are SR 30 to SR 45 but you can get out for much less by sticking to the appetisers. Try the harira soup (a thick beef and vegetable soup) for SR 8.

Central Jeddah also has several traditional coffee houses. The *Ak Wan Restaurant-Coffeeshop* is a short distance south of the entrance to the Souq al-Alawi. The *Harat ash-Sham Coffeehouse* is near the footbridge that crosses over Al-Dahab St, and the *Al-Fishawi Coffeehouse* is near the intersection of Al-Dahab St and Maydan al-Bayal.

Things to Buy

The old city's gold souq is particularly good. The Al-Alawi Traditional Restaurant has a small pottery workshop on its premises. Across a small plaza from the Al-Alawi is a good 'oriental' gift shop: Old Jeddah Arts and Crafts. You can also find a few stalls selling silver jewellery and other souvenirs along Al-Qabel St.

Getting There & Away

Air The King Abdul Aziz international airport is about 25 km north of the city on Al-Madinah al-Munawwarah Rd. Saudia flights, both domestic and international, leave from the south terminal. Foreign airlines use the north terminal.

Jeddah is Saudia's second hub, after Riyadh, and you can fly directly from here to pretty much anywhere in the kingdom. There are usually 10 to 15 flights per day to Riyadh (SR 270 one way, economy class) and five or six to Dhahran (SR 410).

Bus The SAPTCO bus station (☎ 648 1131) is on Ba'ashan St. Thanks to a change in routings none of the eastbound intercity buses go through Mecca anymore and, therefore, they are all open to non-Muslims. Non-Muslim passengers, though, would be well advised to double-check this – it changed once so, presumably, it could change back. There are ten buses every day to Riyadh (12 hours; SR 130) via Taif (2¾ hours; SR 30). To Dammam (17 hours; SR 190) there are two direct buses per day at 4.30 and 9 pm. There are also daily buses to Abha (nine hours; SR 90), Al-Baha (seven hours; SR 60), Bisha (8½ hours; SR 100), Jizan (12 hours; SR 100), Khamis Mushayt (9½ hours; SR 90), Najran (8½ hours; SR 120), Tabuk (13 hours; SR 130) and Yanbu (4½ hours; SR 60).

For Muslims only, buses go to Mecca (1¼ hours; SR 15) 16 times a day, and to Medina (five hours; SR 50) 21 times per day.

SAPTCO's international services depart from the same terminal as their domestic ones. There are daily buses to Amman, Cairo and Damascus. Buses to İstanbul leave several times per week. International services are also offered by several Turkish bus companies operating from a small station next door to SAPTCO.

Boat You can travel by sea from Jeddah Islamic Port to Musawwa (Eritrea), Suez and Safaga (Egypt) and Port Sudan. The fares are no great bargain, but they're not unreasonable either. The fares to Egypt start at SR 225 in deck class and run to SR 500 in 1st class. To Port Sudan and Mussawa, tickets cost SR 300 to SR 400. Try Al-Aquel Travel (☎ 647 5337), off Ba'najah and Al-Dahab Sts, behind the Sahari Hotel for tickets and more information.

Car You will find many car-rental offices, including outlets of most of the larger companies, along Al-Madinah al-Munawwarah Rd in the three km or so north of the intersection with Falasteen St.

Getting Around

The Airport Bus No 20 runs to the south terminal (all Saudia flights, both domestic and international) from Maydan al-Bayal. The fare is SR 3. To get to the north (foreign carriers) terminal you will have to take a taxi from the south terminal (SR 35). A taxi to either terminal from the city centre costs SR 30 to SR 50 on the meter.

Set tariffs are charged for taxi trips from the airport to the city centre. From the south terminal to Al-Balad costs SR 40. The same trip from the north terminal costs SR 50.

Bus It's best to stick to the orange-and-white SAPTCO buses for getting around town. Minibuses also prowl the streets of Jeddah but the markings indicating where they are going are written in Arabic only on the side of the vehicle. Bus trips anywhere in the city are SR 2, the sole exception being the airport which costs SR 3. Thrifty Tickets (three trips for SR 5) can be purchased at the SAPTCO intercity depot.

The main bus routes around the city are:

Route 7 – Maydan al-Bayal, Al-Malek Abdel Aziz St, Ba'najah St, Makkah al-Mukarramah Rd, Al-Madinah al-Munawwarah Rd, Abu Bakr al-Seddeeq St, Al-Madinah al-Munawwarah Rd, Hera'a St to Al-Kournaish Rd; returns via same route

Route 8 – SAPTCO garage (Al-Amir Met'ab St), Sawt al-Hegaz St, Al-Amir Majed St, Al-Amir Abdallah St, Al-Makarounah St, Falasteen St,

Al-Amir Fahd St, Makkah al-Mukarramah Rd, Al-Madinah al-Munawwarah Rd, Maydan al-Bayal and vice versa (returns to Makkah al-Mukarramah Rd via Al-Malek Abdel Aziz St and Ba'najah St)

Route 11 – Maydan al-Bayal, Al-Malek Abdel Aziz St, Ba'najah St, Makkah al-Mukarramah Rd, Al-Matar St, Al-Malek Khaled St, Al-Amir Fahd St, Falasteen St as far as the Marriott Hotel, Al-Souq St, Al-Amir Majed St, Bani Malek St, Al-Amir Met'ab St, Falasteen St to the Ring Road Expressway (returns to Maydan al-Bayal by the same route, except that the bus bypasses Al-Amir Majed St and Al-Souq St, remaining on Bani Malek St from Al-Amir Met'ab St to Al-Amir Fahd St

Route 12 – Maydan al-Bayal, Al-Malek Abdel Aziz St, Ba'najah St, Makkah al-Mukarramah Rd, Al-Iskan St, Industrial City; returns via same route

Route 20 – to and from the airport (south terminal) from Maydan al-Bayal via Al-Madinah al-Munawwarah Rd

Taxi The cabs, which are white with an orange stripe down the side, have meters, though you might have to remind drivers to turn them on. They charge SR 3 for a flag fall. The fare then increases in 50 halala increments at a rate of about SR 1 per km.

The Hejaz (Western Region)

USFAN

Usfan (Osfan) was the next to last stop on the pilgrim route from Egypt and Syria to Mecca. Today it is a small town, noteworthy mainly for its **Turkish Fort**, the ruins of which now somewhat incongruously guard the junction of two expressways.

Usfan is about 65 km north-east of central Jeddah. Head north out of the city on Al-Madinah al-Munawwarah Rd past the airport. About nine km beyond the exit for the airport's north (foreign airlines) terminal you will see an exit for Usfan. Take this, and then take another Usfan exit after two km. From there the road will take you straight to the town (it's about 30 km beyond the second exit).

TAIF

Taif (Tai'if, Al-Taif), nestled in the mountains above Mecca, is the summer capital of Saudi Arabia. During the summer months it is noticeably cooler than Jeddah and a great deal less humid. The town's main attractions are its weather, scenery and relaxed atmosphere.

Orientation & Information

Taif centres on a nameless square formed by the intersection of King Faisal and Shubra Sts. It looks like a square because of the large parking lot across from the telephone office. Most of the budget hotels are a bit east of this intersection and cheap restaurants are all over the central area. The bus station and airport are some distance north of the city centre.

To change money there are a number of banks around the main intersection. There is a post office just south of the intersection, opposite the telephone office, though the GPO is north of town, near the bus station. The telephone code for Taif is 02.

Abdallah bin Abbas Mosque

Taif's central mosque on Al-Salamah St is a good example of simple, refined Islamic architecture. The mosque is named for a cousin of the Prophet, who was also the grandfather of the founder of the Abbasid dynasty. Abdullah bin Abbas died in Taif, circa 687 AD, at the age of 70.

Tailors' Souq

One of the few surviving areas of traditional Taif can be found just off the main square at the intersection of Shubra and King Faisal Sts, around the corner from the post office. Next to a Turkish restaurant and several small grocery shops is an archway of sand-coloured stone. The short alleyway behind this arch, part of the tailors' souq, is a quick trip into old Taif. At one time much of the city (and many other Middle Eastern cities) consisted of small, alley-like streets of this kind making up the various souqs.

Shubra Palace

This beautifully restored house on the edge of the city centre doubles as the city's museum. The palace itself was built around the turn of the century. The materials used included marble imported from Italy and timber from Turkey. King Abdul Aziz used to stay here when he visited Taif in his later years and it was also used as a residence by King Faisal. It is open Saturday to Wednesday from 7.30 am to 2.30 pm. Admission is free.

Beit Kaki & Beit al-Khatib

These old houses on Al-Salamah St have also

been maintained (sort of) and were once the summer residences of two of Mecca's leading merchant families.

Places to Stay

Taif is a very crowded city on summer weekends (ie from Wednesday afternoon until Friday afternoon). From May to September reservations are strongly recommended.

The *youth hostel* (☎ 725 3400) is at the King Fahd Sporting City in the Hawiyah district, 22.5 km north of the city centre. The No 10 bus runs from the city centre to the hostel via the bus station and stops about

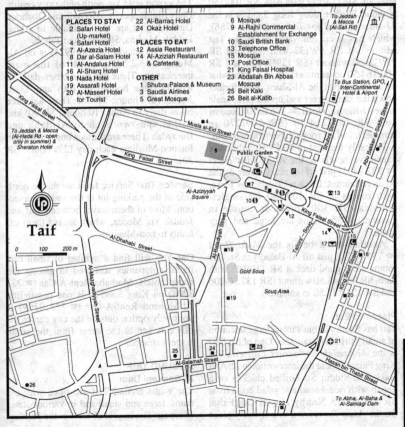

PLACES TO STAY
2 Safari Hotel (Up-market)
4 Safari Hotel
7 Al-Azezia Hotel
8 Dar al-Salam Hotel
11 Al-Andalus Hotel
16 Al-Sharq Hotel
18 Nada Hotel
19 Assarafi Hotel
20 Al-Maseef Hotel for Tourist
22 Al-Barraq Hotel
24 Okaz Hotel

PLACES TO EAT
12 Assia Restaurant
14 Al-Aziziah Restaurant & Cafeteria

OTHER
1 Shubra Palace & Museum
3 Saudia Airlines
5 Great Mosque
6 Mosque
9 Al-Rajhi Commercial Establishment for Exchange
13 Telephone Office
15 Mosque
17 Post Office
21 King Faisal Hospital
23 Abdallah Bin Abbas Mosque
25 Beit Kaki
26 Beit al-Katib

Taif

0   100   200 m

SAUDI ARABIA

100m from the gate. Beds are SR 8. The hostel is infinitely superior to any of the cheap hotels listed under this heading and is far more likely to have space at weekends.

The *Dar al-Salam Hotel* (☎ 736 0124) on King Faisal St, just west of the main intersection, is the only real cheapie in town. Singles/doubles are SR 40/60 (SR 50/70 in summer). The hotel does not have air-conditioning, though all the rooms have ceiling fans.

On King Saud St, the *Al-Sharq Hotel* (☎ 732 3651; fax 732 5093) has good, but not spectacular, rooms for SR 88/132 with bath and SR 77/115.50 without. Summer rates are SR 114/172 with bath, SR 100/150 without. Further along King Saud St is the *Al-Maseef Hotel for Tourist* (☎ 732 4786), which has been renovated since the last edition. At SR 99/132 with bath and SR 77/126.50 without (SR 129/171.50 and SR 100/164.50 in summer), it is a somewhat better value than the Al-Sharq. A bit further down the same street and up the price scale is the *Al-Barraq Hotel* (☎ 736 0610). Rooms cost SR 165/214.50 (SR 209/270 in summer), and all rooms have attached bath.

Probably the best of Taif's slightly more expensive hotels is the *Al-Andalus Hotel* (☎ 732 8491) just off the main square by the Assia restaurant. It is a relatively new place, with rooms at SR 100/150 for singles/ doubles (SR 300 single or double in summer). The rooms are large and very clean.

Another good bet is the *Nada Hotel* (☎ 732 4177), just off Al-Baladiyah St. The rooms are a good deal at SR 110/165 with bath, SR 99/148.50 without (SR 137.50/206 and SR 124/185.50 in summer).

Places to Eat

Taif has Saudi Arabia's usual large selection of small Turkish restaurants. One of the best is the *Al-Aziziah Restaurant Cafeteria*, on King Faisal St near the intersection with Abu Bakker al-Siddiq St. Grilled chicken or a kebab with rice, bread and salad costs from SR 10 to SR 15. Nearby, also on King Faisal St, the *Assia Restaurant* is a friendly place

with similar, though not quite as outstanding, fare. The prices are about the same as those at the Al-Aziziah.

If you are looking for a traditional coffee house try the *Port Said Coffeehouse*, above the Al-Rajhi Commercial Establishment office on the main square. It's entered through a small door on the north side of the building, next to a stationary shop.

Near the youth hostel you will find several small restaurants virtually across the street from the hostel entrance. Try the *Dema Kaffetarea* for shwarma.

Getting There & Away

The airport is 25 km north of the city centre. Daily flights operate to Riyadh and Dhahran. Direct flights are also available to Abha, Jeddah, Medina, Shararah and Tabuk.

The bus station (☎ 736 9924) is on Al-Matar Rd, 2.5 km north of the main intersection. There are nine buses daily to Riyadh (nine hours; SR 100) and 13 to Jeddah (2¾ hours; SR 90). There are three buses daily to Abha (10 hours; SR 90) and Bisha, and two each to Al-Baha and Buraydah. There are thirteen buses to Jeddah for non-Muslims each day (2¾ hours; SR 30).

Service Taxi Service taxis are on the north side of the parking lot at the main intersection. Most of them travel between Taif and Jeddah via Mecca, which makes them off limits to non-Muslims.

Car You will find a number of small car-rental companies scattered in among the cheap hotels. Marhaba Rent-A-Car (☎ 732 3204) on King Saud St is one possibility. Al-Mohand Rent-A-Car (☎ 725 0769) is your only option outside the city centre. Its office is across the street from the youth hostel entrance.

AROUND TAIF
Al-Samlagi Dam

The wadis around Taif are filled with old dams, large and small and in various states of repair. The largest of these is the Samlagi

Dam, approximately 30 km south of the city centre. It was originally built in the early years of the Islamic era, making it at least 1300 years old. Some sources say the dam is actually pre-Islamic.

To reach the dam, head south of Taif on the road to Abha. After 17.5 km turn right at the sign for Tamalah. Follow this road for just over one km and then turn left, again at a sign for Tamalah. Stay on this road for 12 km, then turn left onto a dirt track that goes uphill. When you pass signs for Wadi al-Umar you will know that you are close to this last turn-off.

Follow the dirt track for 300 m. This will take you to a fork. Keep to the right. About 100m past the fork the track splits three ways; keep to the left. About 500m after the fork you will come round a bend to find the dam in front of you. You can reach the dam in an ordinary car, but it requires some careful driving. No permit is needed since the dam is not fenced off.

MADAIN SALAH

The spectacular rock tombs at Madain Salah, some 330 km north of Medina, are Saudi Arabia's most famous archaeological site. The tombs were mostly carved between 100 BC and 100 AD when Madain Salah was ruled by the Nabataeans, in whose empire it was second in importance only to Petra in present-day Jordan. In later centuries the pilgrim road from Damascus to Medina passed near the site and it was by following this that Charles Doughty, in the 1880s, became the first westerner to see the tombs.

The Saudi Arabian Department of Antiquities publishes a useful guide to Madain Salah. It costs SR 15 and can be purchased at the Riyadh Museum or from any number of Saudi men cruising the site in pickup trucks, though they charge SR 20 to SR 30 per copy.

There are no hotels or restaurants at Madain Salah, though accommodation and food can both be found 22 km away at Al-Ula.

Madain Salah's tombs are less spectacular than those at Petra but they're better pre-served. You do not need a 4WD to get around the site, though it might make life easier. You should, however, have a vehicle of some sort as the distances are large.

Be sure to see **Qasr Farid**, the largest tomb at Madain Salah. It is carved from a single large outcrop of rock standing alone in the desert. **Qasr al-Bint**, which translates as 'The Girl's Palace', is another important site. If you step back and look up near the northern end of its west face you'll see a tomb that was abandoned in the early stages of construction and would, if completed, have been the largest at Madain Salah.

The Diwan, or Meeting Room, is carved into a hillside a few hundred metres northeast of Qasr al-Bint. The name owes more to modern Arab culture than to the Nabataeans, who probably used the area as a cult site. Nearby, by the cleft in the rock face, note the small altars carved into the cliff face and the channels which brought water down into several small basins. After passing through the cleft, go straight for 150 to 200m and then climb up to the right for a good view over the site.

On the northern edge of the site is an abandoned station from the **Hejaz Railway**, of *Lawrence of Arabia* fame (though Lawrence never operated this far south). The complex of 16 buildings includes a large workshop building where a restored WWI-era engine is on display.

Organised Tours

Tours to Madain Salah are offered by the Medina Sheraton (☎ (04) 846 0777; fax 846 0385) and Golden Eagle Services of Riyadh (☎ and fax (01) 491 9567). Both charge around SR 900 per person. The Medina Sheraton tour is a day trip, Golden Eagle offers camping trips. Both tours are geared toward groups but allow single people to tack themselves onto groups that are already going. In either case you should book three to four weeks in advance so that the necessary permits can be arranged. Note that Medina airport and the Medina Sheraton are both open to non-Muslims, as is Medina's youth hostel (☎ (04) 847 4092; fax 847 4344).

SAUDI ARABIA

Getting There & Away

Madain Salah is 330 km north of Medina, off the main road from Medina to Al-Ula. To reach the site from Medina, take the north-bound Tabuk/Hail exit when you are about 20 km south of Al-Ula. Follow this road 25 km to another junction, exit, turn right and after a short distance you will see a sign saying 'Madain Salah 18 km'. Eleven km from this sign you will see a paved road running off into the desert to your left – turn here. Note that in the direction you are travelling this road is unposted. After another six km turn right at a sign marked 'Antiquities'. Another 1.7 km brings you to the site gate.

AL-ULA

Al-Ula, the closest town to Madain Salah is nondescript, but it does offer a small museum and a couple of hotels, in case camping out at Madain Salah is not an option for you.

The **Museum**, which contains the usual displays on Saudi Arabia's history, geology and traditions, is open Saturday to Wednesday from 8 am to 2 pm. It is in the town centre

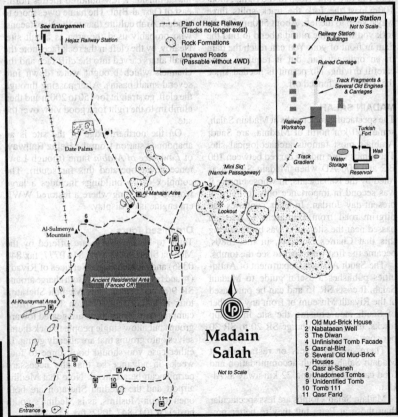

Hejaz Railway Station
Not to Scale

Railway Station Buildings

Ruined Carriage

Track Fragments & Several Old Engines & Carriages

Railway Workshop

Turkish Fort

Track Gradient

Well

Water Storage

Reservoir

See Enlargement

Hejaz Railway Station

Path of Hejaz Railway (Tracks no longer exist)

Rock Formations

Unpaved Roads (Passable without 4WD)

Date Palms

Al-Mahajar Area

Al-Sulmenya Mountain

'Mini Siq' (Narrow Passageway)

Lookout

Ancient Residential Area (Fenced Off)

Al-Khuraymat Area

Area C-D

Site Entrance

Madain Salah
Not to Scale

1 Old Mud-Brick House
2 Nabataean Well
3 The Diwan
4 Unfinished Tomb Facade
5 Qasr al-Bint
6 Several Old Mud-Brick Houses
7 Qasr al-Saneh
8 Unadorned Tombs
9 Unidentied Tomb
10 Tomb 111
11 Qasr Farid

on the main road. The **Al-Khuraibat Tombs**, a site from the Thamudite era, are on the edge of town. The turn-off for the tombs is beside the checkpoint at the entrance to town. Between the checkpoint and the town centre you will pass **Old Al-Ula**, a quarter of abandoned mud buildings that sits on the site of the biblical city of Dedan.

In the town centre, *Madain Salah Rest House* (☎ (04) 884 0249) has singles and doubles for SR 150 per room. The rooms are plain but reasonably good. There is a small restaurant attached to the hotel. To reach it, head straight into town from the checkpoint. When you reach the intersection with a brown mosque on the right make a U-turn, backtrack 150m and turn right at the 'Mada' shop. The resthouse is 100m down this street on the left, on the corner. There is no sign in English.

Asir (The South-West)

The dramatic mountains of the Asir range are on the edge of the same geological fault line that emerges further to the south-west as Africa's Great Rift Valley. The mountain chain includes Jebel Sawdah, the 2910m peak near Abha which is the highest point in Saudi Arabia. Asir was an independent kingdom until it was conquered by Abdul Aziz in 1922. It has long had close ties with Yemen, and the region's architecture has a distinctly Yemeni look about it. The most distinctive features of the houses are the shingles sticking out from their sides. These are designed to deflect rain away from the mud walls of the house.

Another common sight are Hamadryas baboons which can often be seen along the main roads throughout Asir. Allow yourself time to stop and explore this fascinating place.

AL-BAHA
Al-Baha, 220 km south of Taif and 340 km north of Abha, is the secondary tourist hub of the Asir region – it's major attraction is its

lack of development compared to Abha. The **Raghdan and Shaba Forests** are nice spots with some good views, but the scenery is better further south.

Al-Baha has a youth hostel (☎ (07) 725 0368) at its Sporting City, 12 km north of the town centre. The only cheap hotel in town is the *Al-Baha Hotel* (☎ (07) 725 1007; fax 725 2625), on the airport road north of the junction with the Taif-Abha Rd (ie moving toward the airport). Singles/doubles with bath are SR 66/99 (from June to September SR 85/128), including service charge.

For meals try the *Istanbul Servet Restaurant*, on the Taif-Abha Rd, roughly across the street from the Al-Zulfan Hotel. The *Al-Bukhara Restaurant*, a short distance up the street toward the main road junction, is also worth a try.

Al-Baha's small airport is about 30 km north-east of the main road junction. There are daily flights to Riyadh, and several flights each week to Jeddah and Dhahran. There are three buses a day to Abha and Khamis Mushayt, and seven per day to Taif with onward service to Jeddah. The bus station is on the Taif-Abha road, a short distance west of the intersection with the airport road. If you are coming from Taif, it is on the left.

BISHA
Bisha is a large, rambling oasis town in the high desert east of Al-Baha and the main Asir mountain range. It is not really on the way to anywhere and has little to recommend it. If fate leaves you stuck here for any length of time all we can say is that we hope you brought a good book. There is nothing to do in Bisha, and, as far as we can tell, only one traditional house of any size is still standing anywhere in the town centre (it's over on the western edge of town near the agricultural development).

ABHA
If Saudi Arabia ever opens up to tourism, Abha, the capital of the south-western province of Asir, is likely to be one of the main attractions. The relatively cool weather,

forested hills and striking mountain scenery have made it a very popular weekend resort. Like Taif, it is very crowded on summer weekends and reservations are strongly recommended.

You'll need to have a car in Abha as taxis are hard to find and local buses do not serve the main areas of the Asir National Park.

Orientation & Information

The main streets are King Khalid and King Abdul Aziz Sts, and around their intersection is Abha's nominal city centre. (King Khalid St is called Al-Bahar St between King Abdul Aziz and King Faisal Sts.) These names come from the Fārsī maps. On the ground you will find few, if any, street signs. The streets are quite crowded, so if you are driving your best bet is to head out to the Ring Rd and drive around.

You'll find several banks in the area around the main intersection. The post office and telephone office are side by side on King Abdul Aziz St, near the intersection with Prince Abdullah St.

The telephone code for Abha is 07.

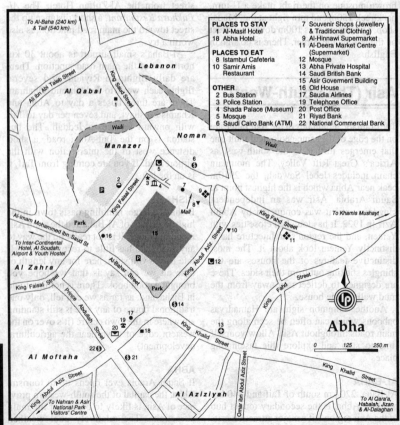

PLACES TO STAY		7 Souvenir Shops (Jewellery
1 Al-Masif Hotel		& Traditional Clothing)
18 Abha Hotel		9 Al-Hinnawi Supermarket
		11 Al-Deera Market Centre
PLACES TO EAT		(Supermarket)
8 Istambul Cafeteria		12 Mosque
10 Samir Amis		13 Abha Private Hospital
Restaurant		14 Saudi British Bank
		15 Asir Goverment Building
OTHER		16 Old House
2 Bus Station		17 Saudia Airlines
3 Police Station		19 Telephone Office
4 Shada Palace (Museum)		20 Post Office
5 Mosque		21 Riyad Bank
6 Saudi Cairo Bank (ATM)		22 National Commercial Bank

To Al-Baha (240 km) & Taif (540 km)

Lebanon

Al Qabal

Manazer

Noman

To Khamis Mushayt

To Inter-Continental Hotel, Al Soudah, Airport & Youth Hostel

Al Zahra

Mall

Park

Al Moftaha

To Nahran & Asir National Park Visitors' Centre

Al Aziziyah

To Al Qara'a, Habalah, Jizan & Al-Dalaghan

Abha

0   125   250 m

Shada Palace

Abha's only city-centre attraction is the Shada Palace. It was built in 1927 as an office/residence for King Abdul Aziz's governors in the region. The palace is the large, traditional tower immediately behind the large police station on King Faisal St, across from the bus station. It is open Saturday to Thursday from 9 am to 1 pm and 4.30 to 7.30 pm. Admission is free; children under 12 are not allowed inside.

Asir National Park Visitors' Centre

The Asir National Park Visitors' Centre sits imposingly on the southern edge of the Ring Rd. It is not a tourist office but rather an introduction to the Asir National Park. It is open only to families and only in summer, when its hours are daily from 4 to 8 pm. If you want to visit in winter, or you are male and are not accompanied by women and/or children, you must first obtain a permit from the park headquarters on the Qara'a road, 1.8 km from the junction with the Ring Rd.

Asir National Park

The park covers some 450,000 hectares of land from the Red Sea coast to the desert areas east of the mountains. The parts easily accessible to visitors amount to a number of non-contiguous mini-parks. The two main mountain areas are **Al-Soudah**, a few km beyond the Inter-Continental Hotel, and the remote **Al-Sahab** area several kilometres beyond Al-Soudah. Al-Soudah, which is near the summit of Saudi Arabia's highest mountain (Jebel Sawdah, 2910m), is the most spectacular part of the park. At the time of writing, a cable car was under construction at Al-Soudah, just beyond the turn-off for the Inter-Continental Hotel.

The main park areas to the south-east of Abha are **Al-Dalaghan** (Dalgan), 26 km from Abha, and, further down the same road, **Al-Qara'a** (Qara), after which the road is named. Both areas consist of a large area of rounded boulders and small evergreen trees, which look rather like a giant's rock garden. Wild baboons can often be seen in both areas.

Organised Tours

The Inter-Continental Hotel (☎ 224 7777; fax 224 4113) in Abha and the Trident Hotel (☎ 223 3466; fax 222 0828) in Khamis have a virtual monopoly on organised tourism in Abha. They both offer several two and three night packages, some of which include excursions to Najran and/or the Red Sea. In addition to staying at these hotels, the tours usually require a group of at least 10 adults.

Places to Stay

For a resort, there are remarkably few places to stay in Abha. The *youth hostel* (☎ 227 0503) is at the Sporting City, 20 km west of Abha and eight km off the Abha-Khamis road. Beds are SR 8. Unfortunately, there is no bus service.

Every place except the youth hostel has higher rates in summer (May to September), so make sure you make reservations if you plan to arrive on a Wednesday or Thursday.

The cheapest hotel in Abha is the *Assir Hotel* (☎ 224 4374; fax 224 3073), on the Taif Rd one km north of the city centre. It charges SR 50/72 (SR 65/99 in summer) for singles/doubles. Only its triples (SR 88 in winter, SR 115 in summer) have private bath. The common baths are rather grim.

Probably the best value for money in Abha, after the hostel, is the *Shamasan Hotel* (☎ 225 1808; fax 226 0074), just outside the city centre. You can see it from the intersection of King Faisal and King Saud Sts. It charges SR 90/135 (SR 117/167 in summer) for rooms without bath and SR 100/150 (SR 130/195 in summer) for rooms with bath.

Right on the edge of the city centre you'll find the *Al-Masif Hotel* (☎ 224 2651; fax 224 2162) on King Saud St. Singles/doubles are SR 100/140 (SR 150/240 in summer). The only hotel right in the city centre is the *Abha Hotel* (☎ 224 8775; fax 224 2592) on King Abdul Aziz St, where rooms cost SR 110/165 (SR 143/240 in summer).

In the mountains, the *Inter-Continental Hotel* (☎ 224 7777; fax 224 4113) has a fairly standard five-star rate of SR 517.50/ 673 (SR 621/805 in summer). The hotel is said to have been designed originally as a palace for a Saudi prince. Whatever your budget, it is worth dropping by for a cup of coffee and an opportunity to marvel at its sheer scale.

Places to Eat

There are a few restaurants scattered around the city centre but, on the whole, the pickings are rather thin. Try the *Samir Amis Restaurant* on King Abdul Aziz St for good kebabs and grilled chicken. The *Istambul Cafeteria* (a sign over the doorway says 'Turkey Cafeteria') near the Al-Hinnawi supermarket is a good place for a quick snack. Grilled chicken, egg, beef or liver sandwiches cost SR 2 each. Several other small places are in the area immediately around the Samir Amis Restaurant.

Getting There & Away

The airport is 25 km from town. To get there, take the Abha-Khamis Rd to the turn-off just beyond the turn for the Sporting City. Saudia's Abha ticket office is near the post office on King Abdul Aziz St. There are several flights each day to Jeddah and Riyadh, and one per day to Dhahran.

The SAPTCO bus station is in the big parking lot on King Faisal St, a couple of blocks north of the intersection of King Khalid and King Abdul Aziz Sts. Buses to Jeddah (8½ hours; SR 90) leave 12 times a day. There are also three buses per day to Taif and two to Jizan. For buses to Riyadh you must go to Khamis Mushayt. See the following section for details.

Local buses run between the Abha and Khamis Mushayt bus stations every half hour from 6.30 am to 10.30 pm. The trip takes about 35 minutes and the fare is SR 2.

Getting Around

Here you are a bit stuck as there do not seem to be a lot of taxis, and none of the bus routes serve the main areas of the park. The usual car-rental rates for Saudi Arabia apply and you can rent a car at the airport or go to one of the small agents in the centre.

KHAMIS MUSHAYT

Khamis Mushayt (Khamis, for short) is 26 km east of Abha. Khamis is usually spoken of as Abha's twin city, though it is a bit difficult to see what the two places have in common. It is as flat and dull as Abha is hilly and interesting.

Khamis' small, modern souq, bus station and two of its three hotels are all clustered around the city's main square and the large parking lot just to the north.

The **Khamis souq** is a good place to shop for silver jewellery. To reach the silver souq start in the main square with your back to the Mushayt Palace Hotel. Standing in front of the hotel turn left, and then left again around the side of the building. Turn right across a small intersection, in front of the Ihaw-Ihaw Restaurant, and continue straight for about 100m. On your left you should see a small shop with a sign saying 'Silver J Courner'. This marks the beginning of the silver souq, a collection of about a dozen shops, all along that alley.

Places to Stay & Eat

On the main square you will find the *Al-Azizia Hotel* (☎ (07) 222 0900; fax 222 1128). Singles/doubles start at SR 132/170.50 (SR 165/214.50 in summer), including service charge. Across the main square, the *Mushayt Palace Hotel* (☎ (07) 223 6220; fax 223 5272) asks SR 264.50/344, including service charge, but discounts are readily available most of the time.

The city's lone top-end hotel is the *Trident Hotel* (☎ (07) 223 3466; fax 222 0828), at the junction of Abha-Khamis and King Faisal Rds. It charges SR 287.50/374 (SR 345/448.50 in summer).

There are a number of small Indian, Turkish and Filipino restaurants in the area around the main square, particularly in the small streets behind the Mushayt Palace Hotel.

Getting There & Away

The bus station on the main square is SAPTCO's hub for the Asir region. Twelve buses leave daily for Jeddah via Abha (nine hours; SR 90), four leave daily to Jizan (five hours; SR 35); three daily to Najran (five hours, SR 30), ten daily to Riyadh (13 hours; SR 125) and three daily to Taif (10 hours; SR 90).

Local buses to Abha leave every half hour from 6.30 am to 10.30 pm. The trip takes about 35 minutes and the fare is SR 2.

HABALAH

The deserted village of Habalah (Habella), about 60 km from the centre of Abha, is one of the most dramatic sites in the Asir National Park. A traditional farming village, Habalah appears to hang from a 300m high cliff face above terraced fields and a broad valley. If you look carefully along the rim of the cliff above the village you can still see the iron posts to which ropes were tied to lower people and goods to the village.

A cable car takes you down to the remains of the village (where you will find a restaurant) for SR 30, but it only runs when eight people are around to make the trip. Assuming sufficient numbers of people are present, the cable car operates daily from 8.30 am to 7.30 pm. The trip down offers some of the most dramatic views in the kingdom and is well worth the long drive from Abha.

To reach Habalah take the Qara'a road from Abha past Al-Dalaghan. Three km beyond the Al-Dalaghan turn-off, the road ends in a T-junction. Turn left and follow the road to the village of Wadiain where you will see a sign pointing toward 'Al-Habla Park'. Follow the sign and keep left at the white sign with a picture of a cable car.

NAJRAN

Najran (Nejran) is one of the most fascinating and least visited places in Saudi Arabia. Yemen's cultural influence is stronger here than anywhere else in the kingdom. This is obvious in both the local architecture and the attitude of the people toward outsiders. Najranis are extremely outgoing and deeply conservative at the same time.

Orientation & Information

Najran is an easy place to find your way around. Driving from Abha, you'll hit a T-junction; this is the only road leading to Najran and everyone calls it the Main Road. Turning left at the junction takes you to the Holiday Inn, Najran airport and the Empty Quarter (in that order). Turning right leads you into Faisaliah, a modern business district just before Najran.

Most of the shops and businesses, the youth hostel, the other two hotels, Saudia, the telephone office, two post offices (the main one in Faisaliah and a smaller one near the turn for the Najran Fort) and the bus station are all along, or a short distance off, the Main Rd in Faisaliah. Except for the bus station all are on the right-hand side of road if you are coming from Abha or the airport. Continue along the Main Rd and you'll reach Najran's centre, where the fort and the souq are located.

The telephone code for Najran is 07.

Najran Fort (Qasr al-Imara)

Though the well in the fort's inner courtyard is said to date from pre-Islamic times, the present fort was begun in 1942 as a royal residence. It was built to be a self-sustaining complex, with its own livestock pens, food storage rooms, guards' quarters and even a radio station. It hasn't been used for this purpose since 1967.

The fort is virtually in the centre of town. From Abha and Faisaliah, follow the Main Rd until you see the fort beyond the houses to your right, then turn right at the first set of traffic lights (the fruit and vegetable market will be across the intersection and to the left). It is open daily from 8 am to 5 or 6 pm (depending on the time of the sunset prayer). Admission is free and you don't need a permit to get in.

Al-Aan Palace

Al-Aan Palace, also known as Saadan Palace, is one of the most remarkable pieces of architecture in the Wadi Najran. The main tower is five storeys high and dominates the entire oasis from above an outcropping of rock. You cannot enter the palace as it is still used as a private residence. It is about five km west of Najran's centre. The best way to reach it is to backtrack toward Faisaliah along the Main Rd and turn (left if coming from Najran, right if coming from Faisaliah) at the sign for Maratah. Follow the road for seven km from this point and turn off in front of the large house surrounded by a white and yellow wall directly beneath the palace.

Museum

Najran boasts one of the kingdom's newest and best museums. It is open Saturday to Wednesday from 8.30 am to 2 pm. Admission is free; photography is prohibited. The museum is several km off the Main Rd and sits in front of the archaeological site of Al-Ukhdood, which was inhabited from about 500 BC through the 10th century AD.

To reach the museum, turn off the Main Rd at the sign for 'Okhdood'. After three km you will reach a T-junction. Turn right. The museum will be on your left after two km.

Najran Valley Dam

The largest dam in the kingdom is in the hills above Najran, controlling the water flow through much of the oasis. The last few km of the drive up to the dam are very pretty. To get there, turn off the Main Rd at the sign for Al-Jurbah. Go 3.3 km and turn right at the traffic lights when you reach a T-junction. Follow this road for just over 22 km. Note that if you are coming directly from the museum you can reach the dam by turning left out of the museum's parking lot. Following this road for 1.8 km will bring you to the T-junction mentioned above; just keep going straight and you will reach the dam.

Places to Stay

Najran's *youth hostel* (☎ 522 5019) is one of the smaller ones in the kingdom but is a clean and friendly place, about nine km from the Najran Fort. As you pass through Faisaliah watch out for the Najran Municipality on your right. Some distance past this, the Main Rd swings around to the left while a smaller street continues on straight. Keep going straight on the smaller road. Take the first right (immediately beyond the first petrol

station) and then take the second right from the street onto which you turned. The hostel will be on your right after less than 200m. It's across the street from a school.

Aside from the youth hostel there are two cheap/mid-range hotels, both just off the Main Rd, approximately 10 km from the fort and three km from the junction with the Abha road. Coming from Abha, the *Okhdood Hotel* (☎ 522 2614; fax 522 2434) is the first you'll pass. It has rooms for SR 132/170.50, including service charge, but will discount these by about 15% when things are slow. The *Najran Hotel* (☎ 522 1750; fax 522 2993), about one km closer to the town centre, is slightly better value at SR 88/132.

Places to Eat

An odd thing about Najran's town centre is how few restaurants one finds there. It's easy to eat cheaply in Faisaliah but hard to eat at all in Najran. The *Samerames Restaurant*, around the corner from the Najran Fort and across the street from the fruit and vegetable market, is so-so. Grilled chicken or mutton and rice costs SR 10.

In Faisaliah there are a number of good places in the general vicinity of the youth hostel. The *Cafeteria al-Beek* has good shwarma served, unusually, in submarine sandwich rolls. The sign is in Arabic only. It is on the south side of the road about 500m back toward Abha from the turn-off for the youth hostel.

One of Najran's best bets is *Al-Ramal ash-Shaabi*, around the corner from the youth hostel (right from the hostel and right again). The kebabs and grilled chicken dishes are excellent, as is the rice. At breakfast, great *hadas* (a spicy bean dish eaten with pitta bread) is served sizzling in front of you for SR 4. The restaurant's sign is in Arabic only. Look for the models of two Yemeni-style houses framing the entrance.

Things to Buy

Najran is famous for its silver jewellery. A lot of (mostly elderly) women have small shops in the souq area behind the fort with silver jewellery for sale, though it may not always be out on display. A lot of new stuff is mixed in with the old and the quality of the workmanship varies hugely. Najran is also famous for its basket weaving, though not all of the numerous baskets you will see in the souq are locally made (most come from Yemen). These cost anywhere from a few riyals to SR 200, depending on size.

Getting There & Away
The Saudia office is on the Main Rd about one km toward the town centre from the turn-off for the youth hostel. There are daily flights to Riyadh and Jeddah. Direct flights also operate to Dhahran, Jizan and Sharurah.

The bus station is on the Main Rd, 1.7 km from the turn-off for Abha. Buses for Riyadh (12 hours; SR 120) leave three times daily and buses to Jeddah (14½ hours; SR 120) via Abha and Khamis Mushayt leave twice daily. There is one bus each day to Sharurah (3½ hours; SR 40).

SHARURAH
The town of Sharurah lies deep in the Empty Quarter, about 340 km east of Najran. The desert scenery on the road to Sharurah is spectacular and includes a drive of about 60 km through what can only be described as a canyon of sand dunes rising to heights of 100m or more on each side of the road.

There is nothing to see in Sharurah itself. The town has two hotels, the *Hotel al-Mahmal* (☎ (07) 532 1137), where singles/doubles cost SR 77/115, and the *Al-Hammami Hotel* (☎ (07) 532 1578), where rooms go for SR 80/120. Of the two, the Al-Mahmal is more modern and comfortable. A good place to eat is *Naseef al-Qamar*, an Egyptian-run restaurant on the street that runs between the two hotels.

There is one bus per day from Najran. The bus leaves at 2 pm (3½ hours, SR 40). The return trip leaves Sharurah every day at 7.30 am, so you will have to spend the night if you do the trip by bus.

JIZAN
Even in November the heat and humidity of Jizan (Gizan) can make the place almost unlivable. There is little of interest in Jizan except for its old souq.

Orientation & Information
The heart of the town is one long street which does not appear to have a name. It begins at a huge roundabout on the town's outskirts, where the road from Abha, the airport road, the road to the Sporting City and several other streets all converge. From there it runs straight down to the Corniche and the port. The bus station is just off the Corniche. The post office and telephone office are two doors apart on a side street that branches off the Corniche opposite the main entrance to the port. The airport is about five km northeast of the town centre.

The telephone code for Jizan is 07.

Things to See
The **Ottoman Fort** overlooking the town is Jizan's most interesting site, but happens to be sitting smack in the middle of an interior ministry police compound. The **old souq**, however, is a treat. To reach it, face the sea and turn left onto the Corniche from the main street. There's also an **animal market** at the base of the artificial hill behind the fort.

Places to Stay & Eat
The *youth hostel* (☎ 322 1875, ext 242) is at the Sporting City, just over eight km from the Corniche. Beds are SR 8. If you are coming from Abha or Jeddah, enter the main roundabout and take the last road you come to before having gone all the way around the traffic circle.

The closest thing to a cheap hotel in Jizan is the *Gizan Sahari Hotel* (☎ 322 0440; fax 317 1386), with rooms with bath for SR 120/170, without bath for SR 88/132. The hotel sign is in Arabic only.

As for food, the *Lulua al-Sahel Broast & Restaurant*, on the main road near the junction with the Corniche, serves rice with chicken, meat or vegetables for less than SR 10. Back by the main roundabout, the *Turky Resturent* is another good place to get a quick, cheap meal. Across the street from the

Lulua, and above a small grocery shop, you'll find a good traditional coffee house.

The North-West

TABUK

Tabuk (Tabouk), the largest city in north-western Saudi Arabia is largely a military town, so be careful where you point your camera. It also has a very conservative reputation, so tread cautiously.

Orientation & Information

Most of Tabuk's essential services are on or near Prince Fahd bin Sultan St. This includes the post office, several banks (including a branch of the Saudi Cairo Bank, whose ATM is tied into both the Plus and Cirrus systems) and the local taxi stand. The local Antiquities office is in the education ministry building 400m west of the Al-Balawi Hotel. Moving from the hotel toward the city centre, you will see two white buildings opposite each other on either side of the street. Coming from the hotel the education ministry build-

ing is the one on the right. The Antiquities office is on the second floor (US third floor).

The telephone code for Tabuk is 04.

Things to See

At the western end of Prince Fahd bin Sultan St, **Tabuk Fort** is not much to look at but has a long history. The first fort on this site was built circa 985 AD. The present fort, the third to occupy the site, was built by the Ottoman Turks circa 1655 and was restored by the Saudi government in the early '90s. Tabuk, and the fort, were a stop on the pilgrim's road from Damascus to Mecca.

Tabuk was one of the major stops along the short-lived **Hejaz Railway**. The extensively restored station stretches along nearly half a km of one of Tabuk's main streets. The view from outside the fence is excellent, though if you want a closer look a permit from the main Antiquities office in Riyadh is required.

Tabuk's most important mosque, the **Mosque of the Prophet**, is just off Prince Fahd bin Sultan St. It takes its name from a mosque built on this site during the Prophet Mohammed's lifetime. The building you see

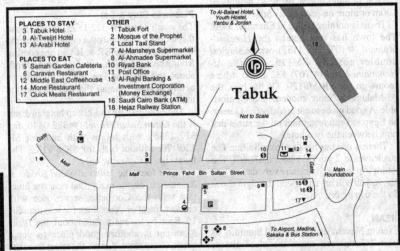

PLACES TO STAY
3 Tabuk Hotel
9 Al-Tweijri Hotel
13 Al-Arabi Hotel

PLACES TO EAT
5 Samah Garden Cafeteria
6 Caravan Restaurant
12 Middle East Coffeehouse
14 Mone Restaurant
17 Quick Meals Restaurant

OTHER
1 Tabuk Fort
2 Mosque of the Prophet
4 Local Taxi Stand
7 Al-Mansheya Supermarket
8 Al-Ahmadee Supermarket
10 Riyad Bank
11 Post Office
15 Al-Rajhi Banking & Investment Corporation (Money Exchange)
16 Saudi Cairo Bank (ATM)
18 Hejaz Railway Station

To Al-Balawi Hotel, Youth Hostel, Yanbu & Jordan

Tabuk

Not to Scale

Gate

Mall

Mall   Prince Fahd Bin Sultan Street

Gate

Main Roundabout

To Airport, Medina, Sakaka & Bus Station

SAUDI ARABIA

today is much more recent, dating from the late 1960s or early '70s.

Places to Stay & Eat

The *youth hostel* (☎ 422 6308; fax 422 1668) is at the Sporting City 14 km north of the centre. From the main roundabout head north, turn right at the first set of traffic lights then left at the Al-Balawi Hotel. Beds cost SR 8 per night.

The one really cheap hotel in town is the *Al-Tweijri Hotel* (☎ 424 0028), just off Prince Fahd bin Sultan St. Singles/doubles cost SR 70/100, though you can probably talk five or 10 riyals off this price. The rooms are plain but clean, and most do not have private bath.

A few doors down Prince Fahd bin Sultan St, the *Tabuk Hotel* (☎ 422 1911) is not particularly good value at SR 90 for doubles. A much better bet is the *Al-Arabi Hotel* (☎ 423 6492; fax 422 4787) near the eastern end of Prince Fahd bin Sultan St, where rooms cost SR 88/132.

One eatery definitely worth visiting is the *Mone Restaurant*, a Turkish place at the eastern end of Prince Fahd bin Sultan St. The menu is extensive, the food is cheap (you can get a full lunch for SR 7) and the atmosphere is relaxed. For a slightly more up-market meal, try the *Caravan Restaurant* on the commercial street parallel to Prince Fahd bin Sultan St and one short block south of it. Its Filipino noodle dishes are a great deal at SR 12.

SAKAKA

Sakaka is the capital of the Jof (Jouf) region and the main town along the northern edge of the Nafud. Though remote, rural and rarely visited by sightseers today, it was an important centre of civilisation in ancient times.

Things to See

The citadel of **Qasr Za'abel**, at the northern edge of town, was built in the early 19th century and restored by the Saudi government in 1993-94 with what, aesthetically, can only be described as mixed results. The

fort has four towers and is irregular in its shape, clinging to the awkward contours of the hilltop. Immediately adjacent to Qasr Za'abel are **Jebel Burnus**, a large outcrop of rock decorated with ancient carvings of dancing figures, and **Bir Sisar**, a large rectangular well, cut some 15m straight down into the solid rock.

Near Sakaka's main intersection you will see **Beit Ibrahim al-'Aishan**, a remarkably large and well-preserved mud house thought to be about 50 years old.

Places to Stay & Eat

The *youth hostel* (☎ 624 1883; fax 624 8341) is 1.5 km west of the main intersection on the street that leads out of the intersection immediately to the west of the mosque. Beds are SR 8 per night. Look for a green sign with white lettering in Arabic and a small blue-and-white HI logo in the upper left-hand corner.

After the hostel, Sakaka's cheapest accommodation is at the *Al-Jof Hotel* (☎ 624 5200), on the road running north and east out of the main intersection. The sign is in Arabic only but it is next door to the larger Al-Yarmook Hotel. Singles/doubles cost SR 65/100 with private bath, SR 55/90 without. At the *Al-Yarmook Hotel* (☎ 624 9333; fax 624 8084) rooms cost SR 88/132, all with bath.

The *Al-Deera Restaurant*, 600m north of the main intersection and on the left as you come from that direction, serves good shwarma. It charges about SR 9 for half a roasted chicken. Near the youth hostel, the *Al-Buraq Restaurant-3* is an excellent cheap eatery. The surroundings are good and the kebabs are especially well seasoned. Lunches and dinners cost SR 7 to SR 15, depending on the size of your appetite.

Getting There & Away

The airport is 28 km down the road toward Domat al-Jandal. It appears in Saudia's time-tables as 'Jouf'. Saudia's office is on the main commercial street near its northern end. There are one or two flights every day to

Riyadh, and service several times a week to Jeddah and Hail.

The SAPTCO bus station is on one of the streets running out of the main intersection, a few hundred metres beyond the Al-Yarmook Hotel if you are coming from the direction of the intersection. There are two buses every day to Tabuk (six to seven hours; SR 80) and two to Riyadh (14 hours; SR 175).

DOMAT AL-JANDAL

Domat al-Jandal is one of the kingdom's little-known gems. This modest town boasts two of the country's most interesting antiquities – the ruined **Qasr Marid** and the still-in-use **Mosque of Omar**, both of which are a short walk from the **Jof Regional Museum**. The museum is open Saturday to Wednesday from 8 am to 1 pm. Admission is free.

The museum is 1.25 km off the main road from Tabuk to Sakaka. Coming from Sakaka and the airport, turn right off the main road just past the second Domat al-Jandal petrol station and 350m beyond the police station. Follow this road for 1.25 km. The museum will be on the right.

Qasr Marid is immediately adjacent to the museum. Its foundations date to Nabataean times, and Roman-era records mention Marid by name. The fortress was repaired in the 19th century and again served as the regional seat of government in the early years of the 20th century. The Mosque of Omar, on the far side of Marid from the museum, is one of the oldest in the kingdom.

Outside the town centre, a small portion of Domat al-Jandal's once-formidable **city wall** has been restored and can be viewed without a permit. The wall is 3.6 km from the museum. Ask at the museum for directions.

The Eastern Province

The growth of the Dhahran area over the past two generations has been as spectacular as that of Riyadh and Jeddah, though if you arrive from either of those cities this may not be immediately evident. The Dhahran-Dammam-Alkhobar area, usually appearing on larger maps as a single dot marked 'Dhahran', is neither huge and new, like Riyadh, nor is it a modern city grown from the core of an ancient port, like Jeddah. Prior to the discovery of oil, Dammam and Alkhobar were tiny fishing and pearling villages and Dhahran did not exist.

DAMMAM

The provincial capital, Dammam, is the longest settled and largest town of the

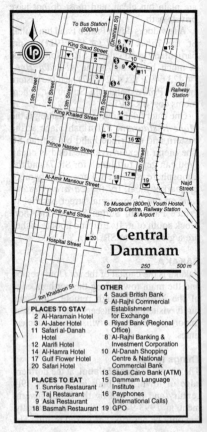

To Bus Station
(500m)

King Saud Street

Old
Railway
Station

King Khaled Street

Prince Nasser Street

Al-Amir Mansour Street

Najd
Street

To Museum (800m), Youth Hostel,
Sports Centre, Railway Station
& Airport

Al-Amir Fahd Street

Hospital Street

Central Dammam

0   250   500 m

Ibn Khaldoon St

PLACES TO STAY
2   Al-Haramain Hotel
3   Al-Jaber Hotel
11 Safari al-Danah Hotel
12 Alarifi Hotel
14 Al-Hamra Hotel
17 Gulf Flower Hotel
20 Safari Hotel

PLACES TO EAT
1   Sunrise Restaurant
7   Taj Restaurant
9   Asia Restaurant
18 Basmah Restaurant

OTHER
4   Saudi British Bank
5   Al-Rajhi Commercial Establishment for Exchange
6   Riyad Bank (Regional Office)
8   Al-Rajhi Banking & Investment Corporation
10 Al-Danah Shopping Centre & National Commercial Bank
13 Saudi Cairo Bank (ATM)
15 Dammam Language Institute
16 Payphones (International Calls)
19 GPO

Dhahran-Dammam-Alkhobar group. It is a bit run-down compared to Alkhobar but a lot cheaper.

Orientation & Information

Central Dammam is roughly the area bounded by King Abdul Aziz St to the north, King Khaled St to the south, 9th St to the east and 18th St to the west. The centre is the area around the intersection of 11th St, which appears on some maps and street signs as Dhahran St, and King Saud St.

There are banks and moneychangers at the intersection of 11th and King Saud Sts. The GPO is on the corner of 9th and Al-Amir Mansour Sts. There are no call cabins in Dammam but there is a payphone complex on 9th St which provides change and sells phonecards.

The telephone code for Dammam is 03.

Regional Museum of Archaeology & Ethnography

The museum (☎ 826 6056) is at the railroad crossing on 1st St near the Dammam Tower and across the street from the Al-Waha mall. Many of the explanatory texts are in Arabic only, though most of the items in the display cases are labelled in English too. It's on the 4th floor, and is open Saturday to Wednesday from 7.30 am to 2.30 pm.

The museum is also the place to pick up permits for visiting the Eastern Province's main archaeological sites. The only exceptions are the sites in the Hofuf area, for which permits must be obtained in Riyadh.

Places to Stay

The *youth hostel* (☎ 857 5358) is at the Sports Centre on the Dammam-Alkhobar expressway. Beds are SR 8 per night. Take bus No 1 from either city and get off midway between the two cities at the buildings in front of the stadium (not the green buildings nearby, and not at the big stadium on the edge of Dammam).

The *Al-Jaber Hotel* (☎ 832 2283), on 11th St between King Saud and King Khaled Sts, is reasonable value, with simple, clean rooms with TV for SR 66/99 with bath, SR 55/83 without. The *Al-Haramain Hotel* (☎ 832 5426; fax 8325785) is just off King Saud St, west of the intersection with 11th St. Rooms are SR 77/115. Most of the rooms have private bath, though some of the doubles do not (the price is the same). The *Gulf Flower Hotel* (☎ 826 2170; fax 827 0709), on 9th St across from the GPO, has rooms at SR 99/132, all with bath, TV and telephone. It's OK, but old and a bit creaky.

A good medium-priced option, though it is a bit out of the city centre, is the *Dammam Hotel* (☎ 832 9000; fax 833 7475), a set of prefabricated buildings behind the five-star Dammam Oberoi. Rooms are SR 165/224, including the 10% service charge. It's much nicer inside than it looks from the street.

Places to Eat

A good bet for a cheap, quick meal is the *Asia Restaurant*, a Filipino place on King Saud St which offers two main dishes, rice, soup, dessert and a soda or mineral water for only SR 10. Roast chicken meals start at SR 12. Even by the standards of the Eastern Province's many cheap Filipino eateries this deal is hard to beat.

Al-Amir Mansour St, a couple of blocks from the GPO, is a good place to look for affordable food. Try the *Basmah Restaurant*, which has good shwarma and fatar (seasoned bread). The service is pretty bad but the food and prices make up for it.

On King Saud St, between 9th and 11th Sts, the Al-Danah shopping centre has a selection of fast-food places. *Pattis France*, on the ground floor, is a good place to stop for a coffee or a light snack, but both the service counter and the adjacent seating area are open to men only.

Getting There & Away

Air Dhahran international airport (DHA) is between Alkhobar and Dhahran, near the University of Petroleum & Minerals and the US Consulate General. A new airport (King Fahd international) is under construction in the desert, 60 km north of the present airport. This project has been underway for years so it is difficult to say when it may open.

There are about eight or 10 flights per day to Riyadh (SR 140, one way, economy class) and four or five to Jeddah (SR 410). There are also daily flights to Abha (SR 410) and Taif (SR 310), and regular service (between one and four flights per week) to Al-Baha (SR 420), Bisha (SR 350), Buraydah (Gassim) (SR 270), Hail (SR 330), Jizan (SR 420), Medina (SR 380) and Najran (SR 410). Saudia's main booking office is at the intersection of Dhahran St and the Corniche in Alkhobar.

Bus The SAPTCO bus station is a few blocks north of the city centre on 11th St between King Abdul Aziz St and the Corniche.

The services to Qatif, Safwa and Tarut Island are classified as local and leave from the same part of the bus station as the routes to Alkhobar and the airport. Bus No 11 goes to Tarut. The fare for any of these trips is SR 2.

There are eight buses to Hofuf (two hours; SR 20) and 11 to Riyadh (4½ hours; SR 60) daily. There are also two buses per day to Jeddah (19 hours; SR 190) via Taif (16 hours; SR 160).

The Saudi-Bahraini Transport Company's buses to Bahrain (three hours; SR 40 one way, SR 70 return) leave five times a day. All the Bahrain buses go via Alkhobar. There is also a daily bus to Kuwait (five hours; SR 80) and one to Abu Dhabi (10 hours; SR 170) and Dubai (13 hours; SR 170). SAPTCO's other international services from the Eastern Province include daily buses to: Amman (24 hours; SR 200); Cairo (SR 455 via Aqaba, SR 410 via Dhuba); and Damascus (36 hours; SR 200). There's also a thrice-weekly service to İstanbul (60 to 72 hours; SR 300).

Train The railway station is south-east of the city centre, near the Dammam-Alkhobar Expressway and a housing development. Trains leave three times daily, except Thursday, for Riyadh (approximately four hours; SR 60/40 in 1st/2nd class) via Abqaiq (45 minutes; SR 10/6) and Hofuf (1½ hours; SR 20/15). On Thursday there is only one train.

Car There are a number of car-rental agencies in the area around the intersection of 11th and King Saud Sts. Two of the bigger agencies, Budget and Abu Diyab, have offices on King Saud St near the intersection with 1st St. There is also the usual collection of car-rental desks at the airport.

Getting Around

The Airport Bus No 3 runs from the bus station to the airport approximately every 30 minutes for SR 2. A taxi between the airport and Dammam costs about SR 40.

Bus Local buses are based at the SAPTCO bus station. All fares are SR 2. Routes and route numbers are posted in the front window of each bus. Virtually all local services are to Alkhobar.

Taxi There is the usual choice of yellow cabs and slightly more expensive white limos. Flag fall is SR 2 and the meter then ticks over in 50 halala increments at SR 1 per km.

ALKHOBAR

Alkhobar (Al-Khubar, Khobar) is the newest – and most up-market – of the three cities that make up the Dhahran area. The central business area is bounded by Pepsi Cola St (officially 28th St, but universally referred to by its nickname) to the north, Dhahran St to the south, the Gulf to the east and King Abdul Aziz St to the west. The Corniche is officially Prince Turky St but you'll be hard-pressed to find anyone who calls it that.

Amex (☎ 895 3862) is represented in the Eastern Province by Kanoo Travel. Its office for Amex business is on the corner of King Khaled and 1st Sts, and is open Saturday to Thursday from 8.30 am to 12.30 pm and 3.30 to 7.30 pm.

The post office is just off Dhahran St near the intersection with the Corniche. The telephone office is on Prince Talal St between 4th and 5th Sts. The telephone code for Alkhobar is 03.

Khobar's main attraction is the **King Fahd Causeway**, a 25 km long engineering marvel linking Saudi Arabia to Bahrain. Restaurants (awful on the Saudi side, tolerable on the Bahraini side) and spectacular views can be found in the twin towers on the island.

Places to Stay & Eat

Khobar doesn't really have any budget hotels. The *Al-Iqbal Hotel* (☎ 894 3538; fax 864 6792), near the corner of Prince Sultan and 1st Sts, is as cheap as they come. The rooms cost only SR 130/170. Nearby, at the intersection of Prince Mansour and 4th Sts, the *Al-Kadisiyah Hotel* (☎ 864 1255; fax 864 3977) has large rooms with rather dowdy decor at SR 125/175, though prices are readily discounted by about 30% when things are slow.

The area bounded by Dhahran St, 4th St, the Gulf and Prince Bandar St is filled with good, cheap restaurants. *Phuket Restaurant*, on King Faisal St one block north of Dhahran St, has good Thai meals for SR 20 to SR 25. Across the street and a few doors down is the *Aristocrat Restaurant*, a newish place with friendly staff and particularly good set meals for SR 10. The *Turkey Cock* on 28th St, across from the Pepsi Cola bottling plant, has excellent set meals for SR 15.

DHAHRAN

Apart from the Aramco visitors' centre, which is the best museum in the kingdom, there is little that is either of interest or accessible in Dhahran. Aside from the Aramco compound, which is a small city in itself, Dhahran consists of the airport, the nearby US Consulate General (☎ 891 3200), and the University of Petroleum & Minerals. Admission to any of these requires identification showing that you live, work, study or have business there.

The **Aramco Exhibit** is open Saturday to Wednesday from 8 am to 6.30 pm, Thursday from 9 am to noon and 3 to 6.30 pm and Friday from 3 to 6.30 pm. Thursday and Friday are for families only; admission is free. The centre is a comprehensive layperson's guide to the oil industry, with a minimum of pro-Big Oil preaching and an emphasis on explaining the technical side of the industry. It's also fun, especially for kids,

with lots of buttons to push, user-participation displays and quizzes.

TARUT ISLAND

For centuries the small island of Tarut has been one of the most important ports and military strongholds on the Arabian side of the Gulf.

Tarut Fort is one of Saudi Arabia's most photographed ruins. The remains you see today were built by the Portuguese in the 16th century on top of a site that has been used since the 3rd millennium BC. Elsewhere on the island is **Qasr Darin**, a site so exposed and so thoroughly ruined that you do not need a permit to see it. It was built in 1875 to guard the seaborne approaches to the island.

Tarut is connected to the mainland by a causeway. Once you're on the island turn right at an intersection-cum-roundabout. Follow a narrow road through Tarut town for about one km and you will see Tarut Fort on the right. To reach Qasr Darin continue on the same road for two km until it swings around to the right. At that point just keep hugging the coastline for another six km and you'll see the ruins on the right, near the pier.

JUBAIL

Jubail was little more than a fishing village until the mid-'70s when the government decided to turn it into one of the kingdom's two showpiece industrial cities – the other is Yanbu, on the Red Sea coast. The industrial city now dwarfs Jubail town.

The only thing to see in the industrial city is the **visitors' centre** at the Royal Commission's headquarters. This is open Saturday to Wednesday from 7 am to noon and 1 to 4 pm. To visit the centre you must make an appointment through the Royal Commission's public relations office (☎ (03) 341 4427). The display covers the history of the Royal Commission and the construction of Jubail.

NAIRIYAH

One of the Eastern Province's most interesting day trips is a visit to the **Bedouin**

market, which takes place every Friday morning in the village of Nairiyah, about 250 km north of Dammam. To reach Nairiyah from Dammam take the Jubail Expressway to the Abu Hadriyah turn-off and follow the signs to Nairiyah. Once in the town, head for the large mosque with a low green dome, and follow the crowd. Get an early start as the market usually disappears by 10 am.

THAJ

The ruined fortress of Thaj is another popular day trip from Dammam and Alkhobar, one often combined with a visit to the Bedouin market in Nairiyah. Today Thaj is a desert village, but two thousand years ago it was a thriving city set beside a substantial lake. The easiest, if slightly roundabout, way to reach Thaj is via Nairiyah, 94 km to the north. From Dammam follow the directions to Nairiyah. Head south out of Nairiyah at the sign that reads 'Riyadh Dammam Exp way 200 km'. After passing through Natta turn left at a sign for Thaj in the village of Al-Sarrar and follow the road until it ends.

HOFUF

The Al-Hasa oasis, centred on the town of Hofuf, is the largest in Saudi Arabia and one of the largest in the world. It seems to go on and on and, if you have time and a car, exploring the small villages scattered through this large, lush area can be a pleasant way to spend an afternoon or two.

Orientation & Information

King Abdul Aziz St is the main commercial street. It intersects Al-Khudod St to form a central square on which you'll find the bus station, a mosque and the Riyad Bank building. Both of the town centre's hotels are an easy walk from this intersection.

There are moneychangers and several banks around the main intersection. The telephone office is north of the city centre at the intersection of the Dammam road (officially Prince Abdullah Ben Jalawi St) and Hajer Palace Rd. It is open daily from 7.30 am until midnight.

The telephone code for Hofuf is 03.

Things to See

The **Hofuf Museum** is especially good on Eastern Province archaeology and, with everything labelled in English, is a much better introduction to the region than the

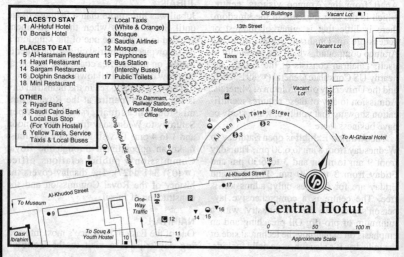

Central Hofuf

PLACES TO STAY
1 Al-Hofuf Hotel
10 Bonais Hotel

PLACES TO EAT
5 Al-Haramain Restaurant
11 Hayat Restaurant
14 Sargam Restaurant
16 Dolphin Snacks
18 Mini Restaurant

OTHER
2 Riyad Bank
3 Saudi Cairo Bank
4 Local Bus Stop (For Youth Hostel)
6 Yellow Taxis, Service Taxis & Local Buses
7 Local Taxis (White & Orange)
8 Mosque
9 Saudia Airlines
12 Mosque
13 Payphones
15 Bus Station (Intercity Buses)
17 Public Toilets

Old Buildings
Vacant Lot

13th Street

Trees

Vacant Lot

Vacant Lot

12th Street

To Dammam, Railway Station, Airport & Telephone Office

Ali ben Abi Taleb Street

To Al-Ghazal Hotel

King Abdul Aziz Street

Al-Khudod Street

One-Way Traffic

To Museum

Qasr Ibrahim

To Souq & Youth Hostel

0   50   100 m
Approximate Scale

Dammam museum where many of the explanatory texts appear in Arabic only. The museum is open Saturday to Wednesday from 8 am to 2 pm. Admission is free. It is about five km from the main intersection, but getting there can be a bit tricky. From the main intersection head west on Al-Khudod St and turn left at the first traffic signal past Qasr Ibrahim. Follow this road for 1.25 km and turn left at the third set of traffic lights (the Al-Safir supermarket will be across the intersection from you). Go about 100m and turn right at the next traffic signal. Follow this road for 1.8 km and turn left at the second traffic signal. Go left again after 700m (at the first traffic signal). The museum will be on your left after a further 600m.

In the town centre is Hofuf's best known site, the Ottoman fortress of **Qasr Ibrahim**, though viewing it involves more than the usual number of hassles. Not only do you need a site permit which has to be issued in Riyadh, but once you arrive in Hofuf you may have to take your permit to the museum.

Inside the fort take a look at the jail next to the mosque, and the underground cells inside it. The Turkish bath near the north-west corner of the compound was used during Abdul Aziz's time to store dates, the smell of which still lingers inside. The stairs along the eastern wall lead to what were the commanding officer's quarters.

Hofuf's real treat is the **souq**. It's just off King Abdul Aziz St, about 300m south of the main intersection. This is one of the few places in the country where handmade Arabian coffee pots can still be found. Several shops also have good collections of Bedouin weavings and a few have old silver jewellery. You will also find a few shops selling weavings near Qasr Ibrahim.

Places to Stay

The *youth hostel* (☎ 580 0028) is at the stadium. It's a long way out and is not served by public transport. Beds are SR 8. To reach the hostel take bus No 2 to the large T-junction by the prison (the white building on the left with a guard tower). There is a stadium behind it but that's not the one. Turn right at

the T-junction and follow the road for half a km until it forks. Keep left at the fork and follow the road for another 2.5 km. A taxi from the bus station costs SR 12 to SR 15.

In town, the *Bonais Hotel* (☎ 582 7700; fax 582 1168) is on King Abdul Aziz St near the bus station. Singles/doubles are SR 110/165, most with bath but some without for the same price. The *Al-Hofuf Hotel* (☎ 587 7082; fax 586 1349) is on 13th St, a five minute walk from the bus station. It's a friendly, mid-range place with rooms at SR 132/198, all with bath and better value for your money than the Bonais. It also offers several organised tours of the Hofuf area, though these usually require a group of at least ten people.

Outside the town centre, the *Al-Ghazal Hotel* (☎ 582 6555; fax 586 9966) is a quite decent place but has a rather inconvenient location several km north-east of the main intersection. Rooms cost SR 138/184 in the hotel's rather dowdy old wing and SR 230/299 in the newer part of the building.

Places to Eat

Hofuf is a bit short on restaurants but there is a very good small place across the main intersection from the bus station. A meal of chicken, rice and salad costs SR 12. It's called *Al-Haramain Restaurant*, but the sign is written in Arabic only. Look for a small black sign with yellow and white lettering.

Near the bus station, the *Sargam Restaurant* has good, cheap Indian food. A meal of chicken or mutton curry with rice costs only SR 7. *Dolphin Snacks*, right next to the bus station, is a good spot for shwarma and other quick fare.

Getting There & Away

The bus station (☎ 587 3687) is at the intersection of King Abdul Aziz and Al-Khudod Sts. Buses run to Dammam (two hours; SR 20) via Abqaiq (one hour; SR 13) eight times a day. To Riyadh (four hours; SR 45), there are four buses daily. SAPTCO's daily bus to Abu Dhabi (8½ hours) and Dubai (12 hours) also stops in Hofuf. Tickets are SR 150 to either city.

Service taxis congregate in the parking lot across the street from the bus station. Seats are SR 55 to Riyadh (SR 300 engaged) and SR 25 to Dammam (SR 125 engaged). All of Hofuf's service taxis are of the five passenger variety. Arrive early if you plan to go anywhere.

The railway station (☎ 582 0571 for information) is a long way from the town centre. To reach it, head north on the Dammam road and turn west onto Hajer Palace Rd at the telephone office. Trains leave three times daily, except Thursday, for Riyadh (2½ hours; SR 45 1st class, SR 30 2nd class) and Dammam (1½ hours; SR 20 1st class, SR 15 2nd class) via Abqaiq. On Thursday there is only one train in each direction.

Syria

As Syria slowly comes in from the cold, its profile as a travel destination is also beginning to rise. Not that travelling there was ever a problem – many visitors find the Syrian people among the most hospitable in the Middle East, or anywhere else for that matter. Long run by a hardline and not entirely benevolent regime, participation on the Allied side in the Gulf War and tentative moves toward peace with Israel, along with a relaxation in internal political and economic strictures, have softened the country's image.

While the image of Syria in the west is still one of a place full of terrorists and other nasties, this is far from the truth; most travellers leave Syria with nothing but good feelings – it's that sort of place.

Places of interest in Syria range from romantic Crusader castles perched on mountain ranges overlooking the coast to Roman ruins in the desert. Damascus, the capital, is claimed by many to be the oldest continuously inhabited city in the world.

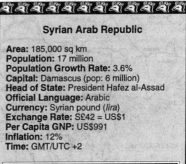

Syrian Arab Republic

Area: 185,000 sq km
Population: 17 million
Population Growth Rate: 3.6%
Capital: Damascus (pop: 6 million)
Head of State: President Hafez al-Assad
Official Language: Arabic
Currency: Syrian pound (*lira*)
Exchange Rate: S£42 = US$1
Per Capita GNP: US$991
Inflation: 12%
Time: GMT/UTC +2

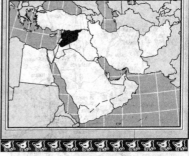

Facts about the Country

HISTORY

Historically Syria included Jordan, Israel, Lebanon and modern Syria. Due to its strategic position, its coastal towns were important Phoenician trading posts and later the area became an equally pivotal part of the Roman, Persian, Egyptian and Babylonian empires – and for that matter many others in the empire-building business. These early civilisations helped shape the region's history.

It finally ended up as part of Ottoman Turkey and (along with Lebanon) was dished out to France when the Turkish Empire broke up after WWI. This caused considerable local resentment, as the region had been briefly independent from the end of WWI until Paris took over in 1920.

The French never had much luck with their Syria-Lebanon mandate and during WWII agreed to Syrian and Lebanese independence. The French proved reluctant to make good on the proposal and it was only in 1946 that they finally withdrew.

A period of political instability followed and by 1954, after several military coups, the Ba'athists in the army rose virtually unopposed to power. A brief flirtation with the Pan-Arabist idea of a United Arab Republic (with Egypt) in 1958 proved unpopular and coups in 1960, 1961 and 1963 saw the leadership change hands yet again. By 1966 the Ba'ath party was back in power, but it was

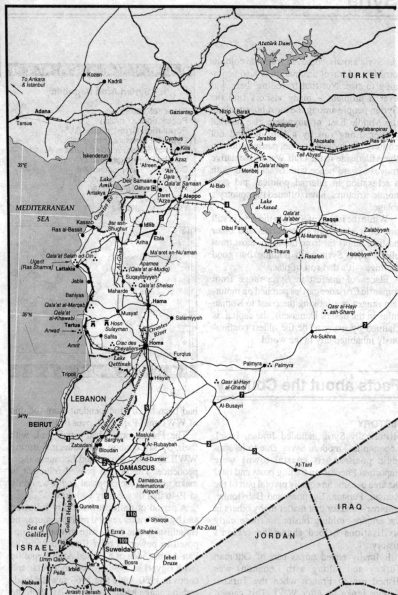

Syria

0   25   50 km

Area under Israeli
or UN control

Suggested Itineraries

Geography and traveller flow have seemingly cut a pretty much set path up and down the country. Increasingly, travellers are using Syria and Jordan as an overland link between Turkey and Egypt, often not spending more than a week in Syria. You could easily dally longer, but the busy mover can take in the main sights in this time. Coming from the north, you could start in **Aleppo** for a day or two and then move down to **Hama**. This makes a good base for several day and half-day trips – including to the Crusader castle known as the **Crac des Chevaliers**. From there you could proceed to Homs, change buses and head east to **Palmyra** for a day or two, and finally slew south-west to **Damascus** and on to Jordan. The same route works just as well in reverse.

If you have more time, another less well-beaten trail takes in the coast. The main towns, **Lattakia** and **Tartus** are nothing too remarkable, but several ancient sites and Crusader-era castles in the mountains just inland are best visited from the coast. You could do this as part of a loop via Aleppo and Hama. The Euphrates River offers a series of mostly little visited ancient sites including the better known ones of **Dura Europos** and **Mari**. An alternative departure route to Turkey (via the border town of Qamishle) would take you up into the rich farming country of the **Jezira**, in Syria's north-east. ■

severely weakened by loss in two conflicts – the Six Day War with Israel in 1967 and the Black September hostilities in Jordan in 1970. At this point, Defence Minister Hafez al-Assad seized power.

Since 1971, Assad has maintained control longer than any other post-independence Syrian government with a mixture of ruthless suppression and guile. In 1992, he was elected to a fourth seven year term with a predictable 99.9% of the vote. Assad rules through the so-called National Progressive Front, a Ba'ath-dominated body of allied parties.

The lack of an obvious successor to Assad remains a glaring problem, but fears of growing instability were lulled in the early '90s by Assad's astute exploitation of the Gulf War and improvements in the economy.

The main dissenting voice comes from the extremist militant group, the Muslim Brotherhood, whose opposition has sometimes taken a violent course. In the first half of the '90s many were freed from jail or allowed to return from exile, a sign that Assad no longer expects serious trouble from their quarter. Their few attempts at stirring the pot have been promptly curtailed by the security forces.

During the Gulf War, Syria joined the Allied anti-Iraq coalition, spurred on by the collapse of the Soviet Union, its main superpower backer. Although no friend of Baghdad, having supported its enemy Iran throughout the first Gulf War, above all Assad saw in 1990 a chance to get into the good books with the west, and the USA in particular. In return for its modest contribution, Syria hoped to be dropped from Washington's list of states supporting international terrorism, for which Syria has a well-entrenched reputation, having long been accused over the 1988 Pan-Am air explosion over Lockerbie.

Assad is dragging behind in the peace process with Israel, with neither side apparently willing to make sufficient concessions to the other on the subjects of security, Israeli withdrawal from the Golan Heights and curtailing terrorist attacks on Israel emanating from Lebanon. Most consider a peace deal inevitable, but at the time of writing none was in sight.

GEOGRAPHY & CLIMATE
Syria has an area of 185,000 sq km, a bit over half the size of Italy. It is bordered in the south-west by Lebanon, in the south by Jordan, in the east by Iraq and in the north by Turkey.

The country has four geographical regions – a fertile, 180 km long coastal strip between Lebanon and Turkey; the Jebel an-Nusariyah mountain range, with an average height of 1000m, an impenetrable ridge running north-south inland from the coast with the Jebel Lubnan ash-Sharqiyyeh (Anti-Lebanon Mountains) forming a 2000m high border between Lebanon and Syria; the cul-

tivated steppes that form an arc on the inland side of the mountain range and include the main centres of Damascus, Homs, Hama, Aleppo and Qamishle; and the stony Syrian desert of the south-east.

Syria has a Mediterranean climate with hot, dry summers and mild, wet winters close to the coast. Inland it gets progressively drier and more inhospitable. On the coast average daily temperatures range from 29°C in summer to 10°C in winter and the annual rainfall is about 760 mm. Temperatures on the cultivated steppe area average around 35°C in summer and 12°C in winter. Rainfall varies from about 250 to 500 mm. In the desert the temperatures are high and rainfall is low. In summer the days average 40°C and highs of 46°C are not uncommon.

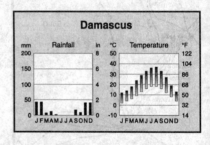

FLORA & FAUNA
Heavy clearing has all but destroyed the once abundant forests of the mountain belt along the coast of Syria, although some small areas are still protected. Yew, lime and fir trees predominate in areas where vegetation has not been reduced to scrub. Elsewhere, agriculture dominates, with little or no plant life in the unforgiving stretches of the Syrian Desert.

Your chances of coming across anything more interesting than donkeys, goats or the odd camel are next to nil. Officially, wolves, hyenas, foxes, badgers, wild boar, jackals, deer, bears, squirrels, and even polecats supposedly still roam around in some corners of the country, but don't hold your breath.

GOVERNMENT & POLITICS

Actual power resides in the president as leader of the Arab Ba'ath Socialist Party. The president has the power to appoint ministers, declare war, issue laws and appoint civil servants and military personnel. At the time of the promulgation of the constitution, which guarantees freedom of religious thought and expression, there was outrage that Islam was not declared the state religion. Bowing (but not all the way) to the pressure, President Assad and his government amended it to say that the head of state must be Muslim.

The country is divided into 14 governorates, or *muhafazat,* which in turn are subdivided into smaller units of local government.

ECONOMY

The outlook for Syria's still greatly-shackled economy has improved in the course of the '90s. This is partly due to oil finds and the gradual relaxation of laws on foreign investment, but reforms have been painfully slow and much remains to be done.

Agriculture accounts for 25% of GDP and employs a quarter of the workforce. Cereals, cotton, tobacco, various fruits, especially citrus, and olives are all intensively grown.

Industry accounts for 23% of GDP, and includes the production of phosphates, fertilisers, iron and steel, and cement. Other products include rubber, glass, paper, food processing, along with the assembly of TVs, fridges, tractors and some other vehicles.

Power generation, while much improved, remains a source of worry as consumption increases. However, the power cuts that once were a regular feature of daily life seem to have been eliminated.

Severe strain is placed on the economy by defence spending, which accounts for over 50% of total expenditure, more than five times what is spent on education. The internal security apparatus also soaks up a sizeable chunk.

Although the black market continues to operate, unusually vigorous action, especially in Lebanon (the main source of illicit goods) has put a severe brake on its activities.

POPULATION & PEOPLE

Syria has a population of 17 million, and its annual growth rate of 3.6% (one of the highest in the world) is way out of proportion with its economic growth.

About 90% of the population are Arabs, which includes some minorities such as the Bedouin (about 100,000). The remainder is made up of smaller groupings of Kurds (about one million), Armenians, Circassians and Turks.

EDUCATION

Officially at least, primary education from the age of six is free and compulsory. Secondary education is only free at the state schools, in which there is fierce competition for places.

About 170,000 students attend higher education institutions and jostling for places in the universities is highly competitive. Damascus and Aleppo have Syria's two main universities.

Most young Syrians have to contend with 2½ years' military service.

SOCIETY & CONDUCT

Syrians are conservative when it comes to clothes and are not accustomed to the bizarre ways some tourists dress. Women should always wear at least knee-length dresses or pants and tops that keep the shoulders covered.

Men will have no problem walking around in shorts but will be considered a bit eccentric and should expect to get stared at a lot. To avoid unpleasant scenes, dress conservatively if you want to enter a mosque. Some mosques, such as the Omayyad Mosque in Damascus, will provide you with a cloak if they feel you're 'indecent'.

RELIGION

Islam is practised by about 86% of the population – one-fifth of this is made up of minorities such as the Shiite, Druze and Alawite, while the remainder are Sunni Muslims.

Christians account for most of the rest and belong to various churches including the

Greek Orthodox, Greek Catholic, Syrian Orthodox, Armenian Orthodox, Maronite, Roman Catholic and Protestant.

Since the government started issuing them passports in 1992, all but a handful of the several thousand Jews who lived in Damascus have emigrated, mostly to the USA.

LANGUAGE

Arabic is the mother tongue of the majority. Kurdish is spoken in the north, especially towards the east, Armenian in Aleppo and other major cities, and Turkish in some villages east of the Euphrates.

Aramaic, the language of the Bible, is still spoken in two or three villages.

English is widely understood and increasingly popular as a second language, while French, although waning, is still quite common among older people.

Facts for the Visitor

PLANNING

When to Go

Spring is the best time to visit as temperatures are mild and the winter rains have cleared the haze that obscures views for much of the year. Autumn is the next choice.

If you go in summer, don't be caught without a hat, sunscreen and water bottle, especially if visiting Palmyra or the northeast. Winter can be downright unpleasant on the coast and in the mountains, when temperatures drop and the rains begin.

Maps

Apart from the free hand-out maps available at Syrian tourist offices, GEOprojects, based in Beirut, publishes a slightly better map of Syria. It's not great, but there's not a lot around. You are better off picking up a copy of Lonely Planet's *Jordan, Syria & Lebanon travel atlas.*

TOURIST OFFICES

Local Tourist Offices

There is a tourist office in every major town,

but don't expect too much in the way of information. All they generally have is a free map of often indifferent quality, although the Damascus one isn't bad.

Tourist Offices Abroad

For information before arriving in Syria, contact any of the Syrian diplomatic missions and Syrianair offices overseas. They often have a complete set of the free maps available for each town in Syria.

VISAS & DOCUMENTS

Passport

Keep your passport handy at all times when travelling in Syria. There are occasional ID checks on buses. Keep the yellow entry card you filled out at the border. You'll be issued with a new one for each visa extension and it has to be handed in when departing.

Visas

All foreigners entering Syria must obtain a visa. These are available at Syrian consulates outside the country, or in some cases on arrival at the border, port or airport. To be on the safe side, however, it is wise to get a visa before showing up at the border. If there's any evidence of a visit to Israel in your passport, you won't be allowed in. Don't be fooled by any trick questions about going to or having been in Occupied Palestine.

A tourist visa is valid for 15 days and expires three months after the date of issue. On entry, you will fill out a yellow entry card, which you'll need to get visa extensions and on leaving Syria.

The cost of visas varies according to nationality and where you get them from. There seems to be little rhyme or reason in deciding which nationalities pay what, except in the case of UK passport-holders, who *always* pay a lot. If you plan to go to Lebanon, try to get a multiple-entry visa.

In the UK, the cost of a single-entry visa varies from UK£3.50 (Canadians) to UK£34 (Australians, British citizens). In Turkey they cost from nothing (Australians) to a whopping US$60 (Britons).

Since the beginning of 1996, a constant

stream of travellers have been stymied in Jordan, once the easiest place to get a Syrian visa and now virtually impossible. This situation may change, but the best advice is to get your Syrian visa *before* you reach Jordan.

Visa Extensions For stays of more than 15 days, a visa extension is required. There are Immigration offices in all main cities. You can get more than one extension but their length appears to depend on a combination of what you ask for and the mood of the official you deal with.

The cost (never more than US$1), number of passport photos and the time taken to issue the extension all vary from place to place. You'll need anything from three (Damascus) to five (Aleppo) photos, and they may be issued on the spot (most places) or at 1 pm the following day (Damascus). There are also several forms to fill in, in French and/or English, usually containing repetitive questions – it is a challenge to think of sensible things to put down.

Other Documents
An International Driving Permit is officially required if you intend to drive in Syria (although national licences often seem to be accepted).

EMBASSIES
Syrian Embassies Abroad
Countries with Syrian embassies and consulates include:

Egypt
　　Sharia Abd ar-Rahim Sabri 18, Doqqi, Cairo (☎ (02) 718320)
France
　　20 Rue Vaneau, 75007 Paris (☎ 01 45 51 82 35)
Germany
　　Otto Grotewohl Str 3, Berlin (☎ (030) 220 20 46)
　　Andreas Hermes Str 5, 5300 Bonn 2 (☎ (0228) 81 99 20)
Jordan
　　Afghani St, Jebel Amman (☎ (06) 641392)
Saudi Arabia
　　Sharia al-Andalus and Sharia Mahmoud Rasif, Jeddah (☎ (02) 660 5801)
　　Intersection of Sharia ath-Thamaneen and Sharia ar-Riyadh, Riyadh (☎ (01) 463 3198)

Turkey
　　Abdullah Cevdet Sokak No 7, Çankaya, Ankara (☎ (312) 440 9657)
　　Consulate: 3 Silahhane Caddesi (aka Maçka Caddesi), Ralli Apt 59, Teşvikiye, İstanbul (☎ (212) 248 2735)
UK
　　8 Belgrave Square, London, SW1 (☎ (0171) 245 9012)
USA
　　2215 Wyoming Ave NW, Washington DC 20008 (☎ (202) 232 6313)
　　Consulate: 820 Second Ave, New York, NY 10017 (☎ (212) 661 1313)

Foreign Embassies in Syria
Australia
　　128/A Farabi St, Al-Mezzeh (☎ 666 4317)
Canada
　　Block 12, Al-Mezzeh (☎ 223 6851)
Denmark
　　Chakib Arslan St, Abu Roumaneh (☎ 333 1008, 333 7853)
Egypt
　　Al-Jala'a Ave (☎ 661 3490)
France
　　Ata Ayoubi St (☎ 224 7992)
Germany
　　53 Ibrahim Hanano St (☎ 332 3800/1)
Japan
　　18 Al-Mahdi bin Baraka Ave (☎ 333 8273)
Jordan
　　Al-Jala'a Ave (☎ 223 4642)
Saudi Arabia
　　Al-Jala'a Ave, Abu Roumaneh (☎ 333 4914)
Sweden
　　Catholic Patriarchate building, Chakib Arslan St, Abu Roumaneh (☎ 332 7261)
Switzerland
　　26 Al-Mahdi bin Baraka Ave, Chora building (☎ 331 1870)
UK
　　11 Mohammed Kurd Ali St, Kotob building, Malki (☎ 371 2561/2/3)
USA
　　2 Al-Mansour St, Abu Roumaneh (☎ 333 2814)

Visas for Neighbouring Countries
Jordan Jordanian visas are available at the border or at the Jordanian embassy in Damascus. Two-week tourist visas, issued the same day, require two passport photos, and cost from nothing (Americans, Australians) to S£1300 (Canadians). Britons should get a visa in Damascus (S£900 single entry), as the charge on the border

is higher. Multiple-entry visas are also available. Visa extensions are easily available in Jordan.

Iraq & Lebanon The Iraqi embassy is closed, and there is no Lebanese diplomatic representation in Damascus.

CUSTOMS
You are allowed to bring in up to US$5000 without declaring it. You can only export US$2000 without declaring (S£5000 to Jordan or Lebanon).

MONEY
Costs
It is quite possible to stay within the US$10 to US$15 a day mark, but only if you are prepared to stay in the cheaper hotels and stick to a diet of felafels, shwarma and juice.

With some exceptions, the cheapest beds in Syrian hotels cost around S£150. An average meal in a mid-range restaurant will cost around S£200 and up. If money is tight, be selective about museums and sights, as some are not worth the S£100 and S£200 admission prices.

Currency
The currency is the Syrian pound (S£), known locally as the *lira*. There are 100 piastres *(qirsh)* to a pound, but the smallest coin you'll find now is one pound. Notes are S£5, 10, 25, 50, 100 and 500.

Currency Exchange

Australia	A$1	=	S£33
France	FF10	=	S£82
Germany	DM1	=	S£28
Jordan	JD1	=	S£59
Turkey	TL10,000	=	S£4 *
UK	UK£1	=	S£69
USA	US$1	=	S£42

*You may find it difficult to change Turkish lira in the banks.

Changing Money
The tourist exchange rates in the banks are set close to the black-market rate; bank transactions are slow but the rates are reasonable.

Some shop owners will accept not only foreign hard currency, but travellers' cheques and even some personal cheques for purchases – they will ask you to be discreet about it.

Although still no good for cash advances (except occasionally on the black market at a poor rate), credit cards are increasingly accepted in bigger hotels, for buying air tickets and making purchases.

The Commercial Bank of Syria's official rate on most currencies has barely moved in the past four years. The 'official rate' of S£11.20 to the US dollar for payment in 'dollar hotels' (hotels where foreigners pay in dollars, rather than the local currency, at an artificially inflated rate) appears to be headed for the bin, creating a single standard rate for all tourist transactions of S£42 to the US dollar – this is still to be implemented, and the hotels concerned are expected to raise their rates considerably to make up for the shortfall in their revenue.

If you leave by land, you can trade your leftover pounds for dinars in Jordan or lira in Turkey with little trouble.

Black Market
The black market is alive and well, and the difference between its rates and what you get in the banks hovers around 15%. Exercise maximum discretion, as heavy prison sentences apply equally to Syrians and foreigners in the unlikely event you are caught.

Tipping & Bargaining
Tipping is expected in the better restaurants and occasionally waiters deduct it themselves when giving you your change.

Whatever you buy, remember that bargaining is an integral part of the process and listed prices are always inflated to allow for it. When shopping in the souqs, bargain – even a minimum effort will see outrageous asking prices halved.

POST & COMMUNICATIONS

Post

The cost of sending a letter or postcard seems to be different every time. Letters to any destination seem to be up to S£18, postcards to Australia and the USA S£11, to Europe S£10. In addition to post offices, you can also buy stamps *(tawaabi')* from most tobacconists.

The Syrian postal service is slow but effective enough. Letters mailed from major cities take about a week to reach Europe and anything up to a month to reach Australia or the USA.

The poste-restante counter at the central post office in Damascus will allow you to look for your mail through piles alphabetically organised under your first name and surname. Take your passport. There is an S£8 pick-up fee.

Telephone

International calls can be made from the telephone offices in major cities or through any of the five-star hotels. There is a three minute minimum charge and you can wait up to two hours for a connection to be made. Bring your passport along, as they'll want to see it. Calls to Australia cost S£115 per minute, calls to Europe S£100. The hotels ask much more. There are also cheap rates at odd hours of the day and night.

Telephone cards have been introduced, but there are few card phones at the telephone offices. Cards cost S£900 and are much more convenient for international calls (there is no three minute minimum). You can use cards for national calls, but local calls still need to be made from coin-operated phone boxes – you're better off calling from your hotel in this case. Reverse charge (collect) calls are impossible in Syria.

BOOKS

Lonely Planet has a travel survival kit to *Jordan & Syria*. In English there are two fine guides to the monuments in Syria. The better of them is *Monuments of Syria*, by Ross Burns, but it's a bit big for your backpack.

The other is Warwick Ball's *Syria – A Historical and Architectural Guide*.

For unique insights into everyday life, read *The Gates of Damascus* by Lieve Joris. Through her friendship with a local woman and her family, the author paints a compellingly intimate portrait of contemporary Syria. This is one of the many exciting titles in Journeys, Lonely Planet's new travel literature series.

The Struggle for Syria by Patrick Seale, an *Observer* correspondent, is a highly readable account of the political intrigues in Syria from independence in 1945 until the ultimately aborted attempts at Pan-Arab union in 1958. For a more general summary, look for Derek Hopwood's *Syria – 1945-1986*.

If it's coffee-table tomes you're after, you could do worse than Michael Jenner's *Syria in View*, which contains some stunning photography and is available in Damascus.

NEWSPAPERS & MAGAZINES

The English-language daily newspaper, the *Syria Times*, is published under direct government control and is predictably big on anti-Zionist, pro-Arab rhetoric and short on news. Foreign newspapers and magazines are irregularly available in Damascus, Aleppo and Homs. Any articles on Syria or Lebanon are so lovingly torn out you'd hardly notice there was something missing.

RADIO & TV

The Syrian Broadcasting Service seems to have dropped much of its foreign language broadcasting. For news of the world, you can tune into retransmitted BBC and VOA broadcasts. Try 9.41 mHz, 9.51 mHz, 21.7 mHz and 15.31 mHz for the BBC and 11.84 mHz for VOA. If you have a shortwave set you'll have no trouble.

The Syrian TV reaches a large audience and programmes range from news and sport to American soaps. There is news in English on Syria 2 at around 10 pm. A few hotels, even at the budget end, have satellite TV.

PHOTOGRAPHY

Print film is readily available but slide film

is much harder to find outside Damascus and Aleppo. There are a number of film-processing places around but the quality is often poor.

Photography is not a problem as long as you avoid taking snaps of military sites and 'strategic areas' like bridges, public buildings (notably the ones with guards outside them) and the like. Be discreet if photographing women – show them the camera and make it clear you want to take a picture of them – some may object, and if they don't, their male companions may instead.

LAUNDRY

Syrian laundries are hard to find and can take forever. Do it yourself or ask your hotel for help.

HEALTH

No inoculations are required in order to enter Syria unless you are coming from a disease-affected area, but it is a good idea to have preventative shots for hepatitis A, polio, tetanus and typhoid before you go. If you plan on spending a great amount of time along the Euphrates River in the north of Syria, your doctor may also recommend that you take anti-malarial tablets such as chloroquine.

The occasional outbreak of cholera still does occur in Syria, but as the vaccine is not very effective, your best bet is to keep your eyes open. A good sign is a notable absence of salad, especially parsley, being served in restaurants. (Cholera can be transmitted via the water that salad greens are washed in.)

In the major towns the tap water is safe to drink, but if your stomach is a bit delicate or you find yourself in out-of-the-way places bottled water is widely available. Never eat unwashed fruit or vegetables, and take great care with leafy salads. Make sure any meat you eat is thoroughly cooked. Milk and cream should be avoided, but yoghurt is always OK. As ice cream in Syria rarely contains dairy products, it's also OK unless you are having problems coping with the water.

Medical services in Syria are well developed in the larger towns and cities and many of the doctors have been trained overseas and speak English. Your embassy will usually be able to recommend a reliable doctor or hospital if the need arises.

For more general health information see the Health Appendix.

WOMEN TRAVELLERS

Women travelling alone or in pairs should experience few problems if they follow a few tips: avoid eye contact with a man you don't know; ignore any rude remarks and act as if you didn't hear them; dress modestly at all times, but particularly in smaller towns, which are likely to be more conservative than the cities.

A wedding ring will add to your respectability in Syrian eyes, but a photo of your children and even husband can clinch it – if you don't have any, borrow a picture of your nephew or niece. If you have to say anything to ward off an advance, *imshi* (clear off) should do the trick.

DANGERS & ANNOYANCES

Syria is a safe country to travel in. You can walk around at any time of the day or night without any problem, although the area around the bars in central Aleppo and the red-light zone in Damascus should be treated with a little caution.

Most Syrians are very friendly and hospitable. Don't hesitate to take up an offer if someone invites you to their village or home.

Theft is generally no problem.

LEGAL MATTERS

The modern Syrian legal system has inherited elements from the Ottoman system and its French successor. The hierarchy of courts culminates in the Court of Cassation – the ultimate appeal court for cases not connected with the constitution.

The law is not necessarily a paragon of equal treatment. The country is full of political prisoners and the law can be an arbitrary arm in the hands of the government. That said, tourists should have few opportunities to get to know the system personally. Drug-smuggling, long a problem through Lebanon, has been heavily clamped down and carrying any kind of narcotics or even marijuana/hash is a foolish undertaking. If you are caught in possession, you could well wind up doing a heavy jail sentence. If you do cross the law in any way, remember that your embassy can do little to help but contact your relatives and recommend local lawyers.

BUSINESS HOURS

Government offices, such as Immigration and Tourism, are generally open daily except Friday and holidays from 8 am to 2 pm. Other offices and shops keep similar hours in the morning and often open again from 4 to 6 or 7 pm. Most restaurants and a few small traders stay open on Friday.

Banks generally follow the government office hours, but there are quite a few exceptions to the rule. Some branches keep their doors open for only three hours from 9 am, while some exchange booths are open as late as 7 pm.

The more important museums and sights generally open daily from 9 am to 6 pm (4 pm from October to end of March), and are in most cases closed on Tuesday. More minor places open from 8 am to 2 pm. Not all strictly adhere to these times.

PUBLIC HOLIDAYS & SPECIAL EVENTS

Most holidays are religious (Islamic and Christian) or celebrations of important dates in the formation of the modern Syrian state. Most Christian holidays fall according to the Julian calendar, which can be as much as a month behind the western (Gregorian) calendar.

For Islamic holidays see the table of holidays near Public Holidays & Special Events in the Regional Facts for the Visitor chapter. Other holidays, not all of which imply any disturbance in day-to-day affairs, are:

January
New Year's Day (15th)
February
Union Day (22nd)

March
Revolution Day/Women's Day (8th)
Arab League Day (22nd)
April
Evacuation Day (17th)
May
Martyrs' Day (6th)
Security Force Day (29th)
August
Army Day (1st)
Marine's Day (29th)
October
Veteran's Day (6th)
Flight Day (16th)
November
Correction Movement Day (16th)
December
Peasant's Day (14th)
Christmas (25th)

ACTIVITIES
Hiking

There are no organised facilities for hikers in Syria, but one or two possibilities suggest themselves. The desert is not really wonderful hiking territory, but the mountainous strip between Lebanon and Turkey (around the Kassab border crossing) might well appeal to some. You could for instance set out to walk between some of the Crusader castles and similar sites. The Crac des Chevaliers, Safita and Hosn Sulayman are all linked by road. The problem with all this is that you are virtually obliged to follow roads as there are simply no maps available to guide you off the asphalt track. Also worth bearing in mind is that in many small villages there are no hotels or banks. Weather is another important consideration. In summer it is really too hot for this sort of caper, and winter can be miserably wet and bitterly cold.

Turkish Baths

If you've never had a full Turkish bath, Syria is not a bad place to start. There are several good public baths in Aleppo and Damascus, and the full wash, steam bath and massage package does wonders for the body. As a rule, the baths are open for men only or women only.

COURSES

If you develop a more than passing interest

in the Arabic language, there are several options in Damascus. The Arabic Teaching Institute for Foreigners (☎ (011) 222 1538), PO Box 9340, Jadet ash-Shafei No 3, Mezzeh-Villat Sharqiyyah, runs two courses, a short one in summer (June to September) and another in winter (October to May). Both cost US$450, so the winter one is obviously better value.

The Goethe Institut and the Centre Culturel Français run courses in colloquial Arabic, and there is an expensive school, MATC (☎ (011) 224 3997), used mostly by embassies and foreign companies.

WORK

Teachers have limited possibilities of finding work. The American Language Center (☎ (011) 332 7236) is the best place to try. It is the biggest English-training school in Damascus, followed by the British Council (☎ (011) 333 8436). The ALC can get you residence papers. The Council should be able to as well.

ACCOMMODATION

Rooms in most of the cheap hotels are let on a shared basis and will have two to four beds. If you want the room to yourself you'll often have to pay for all the beds. For solo male travellers these shared rooms are quite OK and your gear is generally safe. Solo females will usually have to take a room.

Most hotels will want to keep your passport in the 'safe' overnight. This is generally to ensure payment – tell them you need it to change money at the bank. If you want to hang on to it, the hotel may insist on advance payment for the room.

Hotels officially rated two-star and up generally require payment in US dollars or hard currency and often want *cash*. If you feel you may not want to stay in the cheapest places and pay in local currency, it would be advisable to keep a fair amount of cash in US dollars with you. The more expensive hotels sometimes accept credit cards and with some it is possible to change travellers' cheques for the appropriate amounts.

FOOD

Although the bulk of the dishes you'll find in Syria can be found elsewhere in the Middle East, especially in neighbouring Lebanon and Jordan, there are a few items to watch for.

A solid and tasty starter is *maqlubbeh*, steamed rice topped with grilled slices of eggplant or meat, grilled tomato and pinenuts. A good dish that, ordered in sufficient quantity, could easily make a very satisfying main course is *mar-ya*, not unlike Turkish *lahmacun*. It is a thin pastry base with a minced meat and spice topping, folded over and cut into sandwich-like squares.

A dessert native to the town of Hama, and well worth seeking out, is *halawat al-jibna* – a soft doughy pastry filled with cream cheese and topped with syrup & ice cream.

ENTERTAINMENT

There is not a huge range of night-time entertainment to choose from. Most of the cinemas run heavily censored macho-violence drivel or Turkish titillation. A few cinemas and the cultural centres in Damascus occasionally show more serious films.

Other than the belly-dancing and musical performances the big hotels often stage, the only other real possibility is the sleazy night clubs, of which there is no shortage in Aleppo and Damascus.

THINGS TO BUY

In the souqs of Damascus and Aleppo, you can pick up anything from silk and cotton to 100 year old handmade carpets from Iran (the latter are increasingly rare and the local products, while solid, are not outstanding) and antique silver jewellery. Compared with prices in Europe these are incredibly cheap. Gold is also reasonable.

Inlaid backgammon boards and jewellery boxes are popular buys and look great. Other good souvenirs include brassware; nargilehs (water pipes); embroidered tablecloths; and traditional clothing, particularly the *kaffiyeh* (head scarf) and *'iqal* (black cord) so characteristic of the region.

Getting There & Away

AIR

Syria's two international airports are at Damascus and Aleppo. Both, but especially Damascus, have regular connections to Europe, other cities in the Middle East, Africa and Asia.

As it's not a popular destination you won't find much discounting on fares to Syria. Nevertheless, prices and conditions vary wildly from one agency to the other, so take the time to call around. Some of the cheaper deals, such as with Czech Airlines, involve stopovers – which in the case of Prague is not necessarily a bad thing!

From Athens and İstanbul, some agents offer one-way flights with Syrianair for around US$160 (US$320 return). Students fly for less. Shop around!

Syrianair has flights from Delhi and Bombay in India, and to Cairo and Tunis in North Africa.

LAND
Bringing Your Own Vehicle

You will need a *carnet de passage* if you bring your own car or bike (you can get around this by paying temporary customs waivers on arrival).

Third-party insurance has to be bought at the border at the rate of US$36 a month. This supposedly also covers you for Lebanon, but double check. Its value is questionable, and it is worth making sure your own insurance company will cover you in Syria.

An International Driving Permit is supposedly mandatory in Syria, although in fact a national licence is often accepted. You will need your vehicle's registration papers.

Turkey

Bus You can buy tickets direct from İstanbul to Aleppo (approximately 22 hours), Damascus (30 hours) and even beyond to Amman and Medina if you wish. The ticket costs in the vicinity of US$24 to US$30, depending on which company you travel with, regard-

less of whether you are going to Aleppo (ask for Halep) or Damascus (ask for Şam). As a rule you change buses in Antakya and probably again in Aleppo.

Another option is to catch a *dolmuş* (Turkish minibus) from the last Turkish town to the border, cross the border yourself and continue by microbus (called *meecro* – similar to a minibus) on the Syrian side. This is not always easy. At the main Bab al-Hawa crossing, for instance, there never seem to be a microbus or dolmuş on either side. This means hitching.

For buses to İstanbul, book through the Karnak bus offices in Damascus or Aleppo, or at the Turkish bus stations in those cities. You can also find Turkish buses running from Lattakia and Homs. It's cheaper to get local transport to Aleppo and catch a bus from there.

Train Every Thursday a train leaves Haydarpaşa railway station on the Asian side of İstanbul at 8.55 am for the 40 hour trip to Aleppo. No advance booking is necessary. There are no sleepers, and in İstanbul you will only be sold 1st class tickets at TL2,205,000 (about US$45). For details of the journey from Aleppo to İstanbul see the Aleppo Getting There & Away section.

Jordan

There's only one border crossing between Syria and Jordan, at Der'a/Ramtha. For details, see the Der'a section.

Bus A Syrian Karnak bus and Jordanian JETT bus run daily in each direction between Amman and Damascus. For details of departure times and fares see the Damascus Getting There & Away section.

From Amman, the tickets cost JD4.500. Book two days in advance as demand for seats is high. The trip takes about seven hours, depending on the wait at the border.

Train The up to 11 hour narrow-gauge Hejaz railway trip to Amman starts in Damascus on Sunday at 7.30 am and returns the following day at 8 am. Tickets in 1st/2nd class cost S£160/120. From Amman you pay JD2.500.

Service Taxi The service taxis *(servees)* are faster than the buses but tend to get more thoroughly searched. They cost JD5.500 or S£385 either way between Damascus and Amman. Service taxis run between Damascus and Irbid (Jordan) for JD4 or S£300.

Hitching It is possible to cross the Jordan-Syria border with a combination of local bus, walking and hitching.

Lebanon
Bus There are daily buses from Damascus to Beirut and Tripoli. For details see the Damascus Getting There & Away section.

From Aleppo you can get private buses for S£255 to Beirut. Daily Karnak buses from Lattakia cost S£125 to Tripoli and S£175 to Beirut.

Service Taxi Service taxis operating out of Damascus run to Tripoli for S£416 or to Beirut for anything from S£191 to S£291, depending on which part of the city you want to reach.

Saudi Arabia & Kuwait
Bus It is possible to go direct from Syria to Saudi Arabia, simply passing through Jordan. For details see the Damascus Getting There & Away section. There are also irregular services all the way to Kuwait.

Service Taxi For S£3000 per head you can take a service taxi from near the Karnak bus station in Damascus to Riyadh.

SEA
Every Wednesday a ferry leaves Lattakia for Alexandria (Egypt) via Beirut (Lebanon). The trip can last up to three days. In summer the same vessel may call in at Cyprus too. The cheapest fare is US$140 for an airline-type seat, with no meals included.

LEAVING SYRIA
On leaving Syria, you need to hand over the yellow entry card or the equivalent you received on getting a visa extension.

Departure Tax
People flying out of Syria must pay S£200 airport departure tax, but there is no tax for those leaving by land.

Getting Around

AIR
There are internal connections from Damascus to Aleppo, Qamishle, Lattakia and Deir ez-Zur.

BUS
Syria has a well-developed road network and public transport is frequent and cheap. Private cars are relatively rare. Distances are short and so journeys rarely take more than four hours.

Carry your passport with you at all times, as you may need it for ID checks.

Holiday Travel
Note that on most buses, minibuses and the like you are charged up to 25% extra on official holidays (this does not apply to normal Fridays).

Bus/Minibus
The bottom category of buses connect all major towns, and minibuses serve the smaller places. They have no schedule, are often luridly decorated (especially on the inside) and leave when full, so on the less popular routes you may have to wait for an hour or so until one fills up. Note that locals generally call the old minibuses *meecros*. For the sake of clarity, we have distinguished them from the modern vans that are now taking over the roads (see Microbus).

These buses are far less comfortable than the more modern alternatives but as the distances are short it's no real hardship, and it is one of the best ways to meet local people. Conversations on buses can lead to an invitation to someone's house or village. Try to keep your schedule flexible enough to make the most of Syrian hospitality.

Journey times are generally longer than with the other buses, as these ones set people down and pick them up at any point along the route. This has earned them the nickname of 'stop-stops' among some of the locals.

Microbus

The term microbus is blurred, but in general refers to the increasingly popular modern (mostly Japanese) vans on Syrian roads. These are used principally on short hops between cities (such as Homs to Hama) and on many routes to small towns and villages. They are replacing the clattering old minibuses with which they compete, and are more expensive. They too leave when full but because they are smaller and there is no standing room, departures are considerably more frequent. In most (but not all) cases you pay for the trip once on board the microbus.

Karnak & Pullman Buses

The orange-and-white buses of the state-run Karnak company were once the deluxe carriers of the Syrian highways. The company and its buses have barely changed and with so many rival companies employing newer vehicles, Karnak looks a pretty poor cousin. Its buses are perfectly acceptable and connect most major centres, but its network is shrinking. Tickets cost roughly double those on the old buses.

At the end of the '80s, private companies emerged with buses of the same vintage as Karnak, and in some cases superior. As a rule, they were (and remain) cheaper than Karnak by a few pounds and went by the general name of Pullman. The denomination seems to have fallen into disuse, but for the purposes of this guide is as good as any to distinguish them from the most recent crop of modern buses now roaming Syria's roads. Quality of these buses can vary greatly, and the real distinction is between these and the antique buses in circulation mentioned above. As with Karnak, you must always buy a ticket, with seat assigned, prior to boarding.

Luxury Buses

For want of a better word, we are calling the latest crop of buses 'luxury'. These new companies arrived on the scene in the early '90s, and in general fares are at least 50% higher than with Karnak. A rigid no-smoking rule is imposed on most, and in the course of the journey a steward will distribute sweets and the occasional cup of water.

Tickets must be bought in advance and buses leave strictly according to a timetable. In some towns all these companies share a bus station, but in others it is a matter of tracking down each company's office. Among the better companies are Qadmous, Al-Ahliah and Al-Ryan.

> **Warning**
> It is generally considered grossly impolite for men to sit next to women on the buses. If, when boarding, a male traveller only finds free seats next to local women, it would be prudent to remain standing. ■

TRAIN

Syria has a fleet of fairly modern trains made in Russia. They are cheap and punctual, but the main disadvantage is that the stations are usually a few km from the town centres.

First class is air-conditioned with aircraft-type seats; 2nd class is the same without air-con.

The main line connects Damascus, Aleppo, Deir ez-Zur, Hassake and Qamishle. A secondary line runs from Aleppo to Lattakia, along the coast to Tartus and again inland to Homs and Damascus. For further details see the relevant Getting There & Away sections.

SERVICE TAXI

The service taxis (share taxis) only operate on the major routes and can cost three times the microbus fare – sometimes more. Unless you're in a tearing hurry, there's really no need to use them.

CAR

Road Rules

Traffic runs on the right-hand side of the road in Syria and a good dose of common sense is the best advice. Remember that vehicles and people in some places often compete for space. Develop the habit of using the horn liberally. The speed limit in built-up areas is 60 km/h, 70 km/h on the open road and 110 km/h on major highways. The roads are generally quite reasonable in Syria, but when heading off into the backblocks you will find that most signposting is in Arabic only. Night driving can be hairy and is best avoided.

Rental

Europcar has been joined by Budget and Avis, as well as a gaggle of sometimes dodgy local companies. With the latter, keep your eye on insurance arrangements, which seem quite lackadaisical. Budget's cheapest standard rate is US$45 a day for a Ford Fiesta or something similar, including all insurance and unlimited mileage. Rental for a week comes out at US$259. The local companies can be cheaper, but look around.

Fuel

If you are driving a car in Syria you'll be better off if it runs on diesel (*mazout*), which is widely available and dirt-cheap at S£2.66 per litre. Regular petrol (*benzin*) costs S£6.85 a litre and super (sometimes referred to as *mumtaz*) S£20.40. The latter is fairly widely available, but you can forget about lead-free petrol.

BICYCLE

There is no real problem with riding a bike through Syria, although the summer heat is not ideal for it, particularly in desert areas. Decent spare parts are hard to come by.

HITCHING

Hitching is easy as few people have private cars and it is an accepted means of getting around. Some payment is often expected, as drivers will take passengers to subsidise their own trip. As always, women should think twice before hitching alone. It's been done without incident, but it is risky.

LOCAL TRANSPORT

From Damascus airport local buses and taxis serve the city centre. Buses run from 5.30 am to 11 pm. From Aleppo airport there are buses to the city centre.

All the major cities have a local bus/microbus system but as the city centres are compact, you can usually get around on foot.

Taxis in most cities are plentiful and cheap. In Damascus they have meters, although not all drivers use them – a cross-town ride should never cost more than S£25. In Aleppo a cross-town ride should not cost more than S£15.

In some cities, notably Aleppo, there are local service taxis that run a set route, like a bus, picking up and dropping passengers along the way for a set price.

Damascus

Damascus (*ash-Sham* or *dimashq* in Arabic) is the capital of Syria and, with a recently estimated population of six million, its largest city. It owes its existence to the Barada River, which rises high in the Jebel Lubnan ash-Sharqiyyeh (Anti-Lebanon Mountains). The waters give life to the Ghouta Oasis, making settlement possible in an otherwise uninhabitable area.

Damascus is claimed to be the oldest continuously inhabited city in the world – there was an urban settlement here as long ago as 5000 BC. Later it was a Persian capital, fell to Alexander the Great, became a Greek centre and then a major Roman city. In 635 AD, with Byzantine power on the decline, Damascus fell to the Muslims and rose to primacy in the rapidly expanding Muslim Arab Empire. In 1200 it was sacked by the Mongols and then had centuries of slow decline under the Mamluks and the Ottomans before eventually passing to the French mandate and finally independence.

It is a fascinating city of contrasts, retaining much of the mystery of the oriental bazaars and the gracious, somewhat decayed charm of some of the Islamic world's greatest monuments. Exuding just a hint of its more remote past too, Damascus is well worth spending a few days exploring. Many travellers find themselves caught up in its spell and stay much longer!

Orientation

The city centre is compact and finding your way around on foot is no problem. The heart of the city is Martyrs' Square (Saahat ash-Shuhada), and many of the cheap hotels and restaurants are close by. Locals know it as 'Al-Merjeh'.

The main street, Said al-Jabri Ave, begins at the Hejaz railway station and runs northeast, changes its name a couple of times and finishes at the Central Bank building. The whole street is about one km long and on it you'll find the central post office, tourist office, various airline offices and many midrange restaurants and hotels.

The Barada River is unfortunately not much more than a smelly drain flowing through the city. On its banks to the northwest of Martyrs' Square is the Takiyyeh as-Sulaymaniyyeh Mosque and the National Museum, with several bus stations and the Immigration office nearby.

Information

Tourist Office This is on 29 Mai Ave, just up from Youssef al-Azmeh Square. It's open daily except Friday from 9 am to 7 pm, and the friendly, English-speaking staff can be very helpful.

Money There are several branches of the Commercial Bank of Syria as well as exchange booths where you can change money fairly easily. The booth on Martyrs' Square is open daily from 9 am to 6 pm and on Friday from 10 am to 2 pm and will change cash and travellers' cheques. There is also a branch of the Commercial Bank of Syria at the airport, supposedly open seven days a week.

The American Express agent (☎ 221

7813; fax 222 3707) is in the Sudan Airways office in an alley off Fardous St. The postal address is PO Box 1373, Damascus. Thomas Cook is represented by Nahas Travel on Fardous St.

Post & Communications The central post office is on Said al-Jabri Ave and is open daily from 8 am to 7 pm, except Friday and holidays, when it closes at 1 pm. The parcel post office is outside and around the corner.

The telephone office is a block east of the Hejaz railway station on An-Nasr Ave, and is open around the clock. Telegrams can only be sent during vaguely set daytime hours.

Bookshops Possibly the best bookshop in Damascus is the Librairie Avicenne (☎ 221 2911), a block south of the Cham Palace Hotel. It has a fair range of books on Syria, some novels in English and French, and a selection of days-old press, including *The Financial Times*, *The Times* and *Le Monde*. Not quite as good is the Librairie Universelle (☎ 231 0744), on a side street off Port Said St.

The Meridien and Sheraton hotels both have fairly decent bookshops, with some foreign press and a selection of books on Syria and, in the case of the Meridien, even the odd book on surrounding countries. These two shops are owned and operated by Librairie Avicenne.

The Cham Palace Hotel Bookshop (☎ 223 2300) has a good selection of paperbacks, art and design books and books on Syria.

Immigration Office The office is on Palestine Ave (Sharia Filastin), one block up from the Karnak bus station. For visa extensions, go to the 2nd floor to begin the process. You will need three photos and will have to fill in four forms, and buy a revenue stamp for S£3 at a stall outside the building. You can get extensions of up to one month. They cost S£25 and take a working day to process – pick them up at 1 pm.

Cultural Centres The American Cultural Center (☎ 333 8443) is off Al-Mansour St

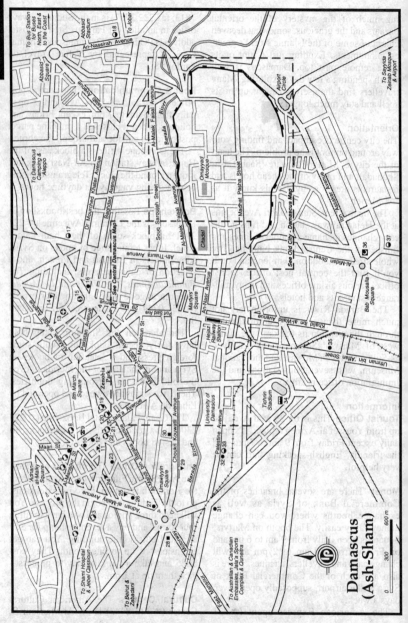

Damascus (Ash-Sham)

0   300   600 m

To Bus Station for Buses North, East & to the Coast
Abbasid Stadium
To Jobar
An-Nassirah Avenue
Abbasid Square
To Damascus Camping & Aleppo
To Sayyida Zainab Mosque & Airport
Airport Circle
Al-Malek Faisal Avenue
Barada River
Souq Saroujah Street
Dr Mourshed Khater Avenue
Baghdad Avenue
Omayyad Mosque
Madhat Pasha Street
Al-Malek Faisal Avenue
Citadel
See Old City – Damascus Map
Al-Midan Street
Bab Mousalla Square
Ath-Thaura Avenue
See Central Damascus Map
An-Nasr Avenue
Martyrs' Square
Khalid Ibn al-Walid Avenue
Port Said Ave
29 Mai Avenue
Maysaloun St
Hejaz Railway Station
Uthman bin Affan Street
Pakistan Avenue
Zenobia Park
8th March Square
Al-Jalaa Avenue
University of Damascus
Tichrin Stadium
Maari St
Adnan al-Malki Avenue
Umaiyyin Square
Choukri Kouwatli Avenue
Palestine Avenue
Barada River
Al-Jazeer Avenue
Al-Mansour St
To Shami Hospital & Jebel Qassioun
To Beirut & Zebdani
To Australian & Canadian Embassies, Jala'a Sports Complex & Quneitra

near the US embassy. Others include the British Council (☎ 333 8436), and French (☎ 224 6181), German (☎ 333 6673), Spanish (☎ 714003) and Russian (☎ 427155) cultural centres.

Things to See & Do

Old City Most of the sights of Damascus are

in the old city, which is surrounded by what was initially a **Roman wall**. The wall itself has been flattened and rebuilt several times over the past 2000 years. The best preserved section is between Bab as-Salama (the Gate of Safety) and Bab Touma (Thomas Gate – named after a son-in-law of Emperor Heraclius) in the north-east corner.

Next to the citadel is the entrance to one of the main covered markets, the **Souq al-Hamadiyyeh**. This cobbled souq with its bustling crowds, hawkers and tenacious merchants is worlds away from the traffic jams and chaos of the streets outside. Most of the shops sell handicrafts.

At the far end of the market the vaulted roof gives way to two enormous Corinthian columns supporting a decorated lintel – the remains of the western gate of the old Roman **Temple of Jupiter** dating from the 3rd century AD.

Opposite the end of the market is the **Omayyad Mosque**. Built on the site of ancient temples and a Christian cathedral, the mosque was built in 705 and designed to be the greatest ever. Despite several disasters, including a huge fire that gutted it last century, it remains a (heavily restored) jewel of Muslim architecture. Of particular note are the mosaics, while the three minarets, although subsequently altered, date to the original construction. The tourist entrance to the mosque is through the northern Bab al-'Amarah. All women, and men in shorts, have to don the black robes supplied. It's quite OK to take photos anywhere inside.

Saladin's Mausoleum was originally built in 1193 and restored with funds made available by Kaiser Wilhelm II of Germany during his visit to Damascus in 1898. It is covered by a red dome and set in a pleasant garden outside the northern wall of the Omayyad Mosque. Saladin is seen as one of the greatest heroes of Arab history, especially for his successful campaigns against the Crusaders. Nearby are two old Qur'anic schools, erected in the 13th century. The **Al-Adiliyya and Az-Zahiriyya madrassas** are especially noteworthy for their facades. In the latter is buried Sultan Baybars, another hero who came after Saladin and pretty much finished off the Crusaders.

Also near the Omayyad Mosque is a modern Iranian-built Shiite mausoleum and mosque, the **Sayyida Ruqqaya Mosque**, dedicated to Ruqqaya, the daughter of the martyr Hussein, son of Ali. It stands out for its decoration – covered in gold and shades of blue – and overall style, a quite alien, if striking, Persian introduction.

The **Azem Palace**, south of the Omayyad Mosque, is another peaceful haven. It was built in 1749 by the Governor of Damascus, As'ad Pasha al-Azem, out of black basalt and limestone, and the alternating layers of white and black give a curious effect. The rooms of the modest palace also house the exhibits of the **Museum of the Arts & Popular Traditions of Syria**. The displays manage to give some idea of Syria as it was. The palace is open daily except Tuesday from 9 am to 6 pm (4 pm in winter). Entry is S£200.

Swinging back to the west, the **Madrassa an-Nuri** is the mausoleum of Saladin's predecessor Nureddin. An outstanding feature is the crimson *muqarnas* cupola.

Just south of the Souq al-Hamadiyyeh, the **Maristan Nur ad-Din** was built by Nureddin in the 12th century as a mental hospital and was for centuries renowned in the Arab world as an enlightened centre of medical treatment. Note again the muqarnas dome and decoration of the entrance. Around the cool, peaceful courtyard inside are displayed the hodge-podge exhibits of the so-called Science & Medical Museum.

About two-thirds of the way along the Street Called Straight (Via Recta) are the remains of a **Roman arch**. This roughly marks the boundary of what might be called the Christian quarter. **St Paul's Chapel** marks the spot where the disciples lowered St Paul out of a window in a basket one night so that he could flee the Jews. The old cellar of the **Chapel of Ananias** (Kaneesat Hananya), is reputedly (but probably not) the house of Ananias, an early Christian disciple.

It is worth taking a stroll down Al-Midan St, from where the annual *haj* (pilgrimage) to Mecca used to begin. It is still lined with mosques and mausolea.

Elsewhere The peaceful **Takiyyeh as-Sulaymaniyyeh Mosque**, just south of the Barada River, was designed by the Turkish architect Sinan in 1554. It is a particularly graceful mosque built in alternating layers of black and white stone with two slender minarets that immediately betray its Ottoman style.

The **National Museum** is well worth at least one visit and is open daily from 9 am to 6 pm (4 pm in winter) except Friday, when it opens from 9 am to 11.15 pm and 1 to 6 pm. The entry fee is S£200. Unfortunately, most of the exhibits are labelled only in French or Arabic and some have no label at all.

The facade of the museum is imposing – it is the entrance to the old Qasr al-Hayr al-Gharbi (a desert palace/military camp near Palmyra dating to the time of the Umayyad caliph Hisham in 688). Inside is a fantastic array of exhibits: written cylinders from Ugarit (Ras Shamra) using the first known alphabet, dating from the 14th century BC; statuary from Mari, dating from the 3rd to 2nd millennium BC; two halls full of marble and terracotta statues from Palmyra; a reconstruction of an underground burial chamber, or hypogeum, from the Valley of the Tombs, Palmyra; frescoes from Dura Europos; sculptures of black basalt from the Hauran around Bosra; Damascene weapons; old surgical instruments from doctors' graves; Islamic glassware from the 13th century; a collection of Qur'ans dating back to the 13th century; a complete room decorated in the style of the 18th century Azem Palace; and an extensive collection of coins and gold jewellery.

The small **army museum** in the grounds next to the Takiyyeh as-Sulaymaniyyeh Mosque is interesting mainly for the leftover hardware from the 1973 Arab-Israeli War.

The **Sayyida Zeinab Mosque**, on the southern outskirts of Damascus, is another Iranian-inspired mosque and mausoleum and a major object of pilgrimage for Shiites.

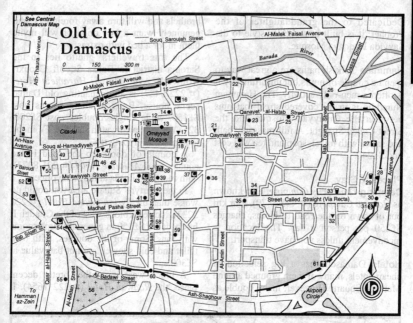

Old City – Damascus

See Central
Damascus Map

Souq Saroujah Street

Al-Malek Faisal Avenue

Barada River

Al-Malek Faisal Avenue

0   150   300 m

Dedicated to the granddaughter of the Prophet, it is built in a similar style to the Sayyida Ruqqaya Mosque.

Hammam Turkish baths are a great way to spend a couple of hours but unfortunately it is often a men-only activity. The Hammam Nureddin is in the covered street that runs between the Omayyad Mosque and the Street Called Straight. A full massage, bath and sauna with towel, soap and tea will cost you S£240.

Places to Stay

Camping *Damascus Camping*, also known as *Harasta Camping* (☎ 445 5870), four km out of town on the road to Homs, charges S£250 per person a day. The location is inconvenient unless you have transport.

Hotels Damascus has a big selection of cheap hotels, many of them grouped around Martyrs' Square. However, many double as

brothels and will turn away foreigners who genuinely want a bed only, or will invite them in for a bed with extras.

The true travellers' ghetto lies in the Sarouja district in Bahsa St, off Choukri Kouwatli Ave. The *Al-Haramein Hotel* (☎ 222 9487) is an enchanting old Damascene house. Beds in share rooms cost S£150, while singles/doubles cost S£200/325. You can even watch satellite TV in the lounge while sipping tea.

A couple of doors up the road is the equally good *Al-Rabie Hotel* (☎ 221 8373), with rooms and beds at the same prices.

In the Martyrs' Square area you could do worse than the *Syrian Grand Hotel* (☎ 221 5233), located a block west of the Citadel. It has beds for S£150 in generally large rooms with fans. Some of the doubles, with own toilet and cold shower, are not bad value at S£300.

A block west is another pretty decent place, the *Radwan Hotel* (☎ 222 1654). It

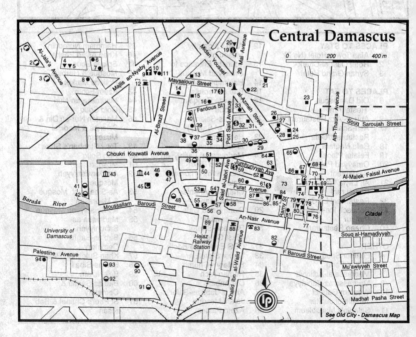

Central Damascus

charges S£200 per person whether you stay in a single, double or bigger shared room. The beds are very comfortable and some rooms also have their own shower and balcony.

A good, clean place is the *Grand Ghazi Hotel* (☎ 221 4581) on Furat Ave. Decent sized rooms with basin and fan cost S£250/350.

One of the best middle level spots is the *Sultan Hotel* (☎ 222 5768), west of the Hejaz railway station on Moussallam Baroudi St. Good, clean rooms with hot water and breakfast are US$22/30.

For a little more you will do even better with the *Alaa Tower Hotel* (☎ 223 1692). This is a chain, but if you try the one tucked away opposite the Centre Culturel Français you'll get quality singles/doubles with satellite TV for S£1300/2200.

Places to Eat

Martyrs' Square is the focus for cheap restaurants. Small stalls and restaurants, where you can get the usual kebabs, chicken, shwarma and felafels, dot the area.

About 30m east of the Omayyad Mosque, just beyond a couple of nice cafes, is about

PLACES TO STAY		79	Al-Arabi Restaurant		Qadmous Bus
13	Cham Palace Hotel	80	Al-Arabi Restaurant		Companies
15	Fardoss Tower Hotel		(No 2)	43	National Museum
	(& The Pub)	85	Shawarma Stands	44	Army Museum
23	Hotel Saadeh	86	Al-Aricha Restaurant	45	Takiyyeh
24	Al-Rabie Hotel	88	Open Air Cafe		as-Sulaymaniyyeh
25	Al-Haramein Hotel				Mosque
27	Alaa Tower Hotel &	**OTHER**		46	Artisanat (Handicraft
	Restaurant	1	Belgian Embassy		Market)
31	Hotel Venezia	2	Egyptian Embassy	47	Ministry of Tourism
52	Hotel Semiramis	3	Jordanian Embassy	48	Bus Station
53	Al-Afamia Hotel	6	Goethe Institut	49	Luxury Bus Station
55	Sultan Hotel	7	Marmou Car Rental	50	DHL (Courier Company)
57	Orient Palace Hotel	8	Lido Music Store	54	Central Post Office
62	Al-Fardous Tower Hotel	9	Church	56	Commercial Bank of
63	Omar al-Khayyam Hotel	11	Dawn Travel		Syria
66	Hotel Altal	14	Librairie Avicenne	58	Syrianair
67	Hotel Al-Imad	16	Syrianair	59	Commercial Bank of
70	Zahraa Hotel	17	Commercial Bank of		Syria
71	Hotel Said		Syria	60	2nd Immigration &
74	Samir Palace Hotel	18	Midan Youssef		Passports Office
76	Radwan Hotel		al-Azmeh (Peasant's	61	Exchange Booth
77	Ghassan Hotel		Monument)	65	Microbuses to
84	Ramsis Hotel	19	Tourist Office		North/East Bus
87	Grand Ghazi Hotel	21	Damascus Workers		Stations & Jobar
89	L'Oasis Hotel		Club	72	Bar Karnak
		22	Haig Camera Repairs	73	Martyrs' Square
PLACES TO EAT		26	Centre Culturel Français		(Al-Merjeh) & Hotel
4	Morocco Restaurant	28	Microbuses to		Siyaha
5	Station One Restaurant		Muhajireen	81	Liquor Store
10	Pizza Roma	29	Zeitouni Bus Company	82	Microbuses to South
12	Shimi Cafe	30	Airport Bus Station		Bus Station &
20	Al-Kamal Restaurant	32	Commercial Bank of		Sayyida Zeinab Stop
34	Cafe Havana		Syria (Cash Only)	83	Telephone Office
35	Cafe	33	Librairie Universelle	90	Microbuses
37	An-Nadwa Restaurant	36	Turkish Bus Station		(Mostly West)
51	Radwan Restaurant	38	Madrassa al-'Aziyya	91	Pullman Buses & Taxis
64	Rooftop Cafe	39	Sudan Airways &		to Saudi Arabia
68	Vegetable Market &		American Express	92	Karnak Bus Station
	Kebab Stalls	40	Nahas Travel &	93	Service Taxis to Amman
69	Al-Awami Restaurant		Thomas Cook		& Beirut
75	Sahloul Restaurant	41	City Microbus Station	94	Central Immigration
78	Ghassan Restaurant	42	Damas Tour &		Office

the best value felafel place in town. A truly fat felafel will cost you S£25.

Along a covered market lane a block west of the Omayyad Mosque is the *Abu al-'Azz Restaurant*. Head upstairs and you'll eat well from a wide menu for under S£200.

Those on a skimpy budget in need of a change from felafel can head for the *Radwan Restaurant*, on Choukri Kouwatli Ave. You can feast on rice, potato and bean stews or even broiled chicken. With a soft drink thrown in you can eat for under S£100.

Pizza Roma, just off Maysaloun St, is run by a guy who used to work for Pizza Hut in Abu Dhabi. He has adapted the idea and this eat-in or take-away joint does a good US-style deep-pan pizza for less than S£100.

You could have a blow-out in the old city at *Old Damascus Restaurant* (☎ 221 88 10), situated behind the citadel. It is sumptuously decked out in the manner of a well-to-do oriental mansion. The food is reasonable but you'll get little change from S£500.

For one of the best ice creams you are likely to taste, head for *Bakdach Ice-Cream Parlour* in the Souq al-Hamadiyyeh.

Getting There & Away

Air Several Syrianair offices are scattered about the city centre. Syrianair fly once or twice daily to Aleppo for S£600. Three times a week (Sunday, Tuesday and Thursday) a flight departs for Qamishle (S£900), and once a week to Deir ez-Zur (Wednesday; S£600) and Lattakia (Friday; S£500).

Bus There are two main bus stations (known as *garages*) in Damascus for regular buses, minibuses and the odd microbus. For buses north, east and to the coast, the station is about three km east of the centre past Abbasid Square. The station for buses south is south of the Bab Moussala Square round-about, about two km from the centre.

The Karnak bus station is about a 15 to 20 minute walk west of Martyrs' Square. JETT and Karnak buses each leave once daily for Amman in Jordan (six or seven hours; US$5/JD4). Buses leave at the same times for Beirut in Lebanon. The trip takes about

three hours and costs S£125. A Saudi bus company, Aman, has a daily service to Riyadh (24 hours; S£2000), although you may have trouble buying a ticket to Damascus from the company in Riyadh. Karnak also has daily departures to many Syrian destinations.

A new station for some of the more expensive bus companies is located about 150m west of the Hejaz railway station. Buses leave from here and other points across the city to all Syrian destinations and Lebanon. Be warned that some of the offices in fact act as agents for buses with different departure points. This is the case with the direct microbuses to Bosra with Damas Tour. These leave seven times a day from beneath the big Jisr ar-Rais (President Bridge) flyover west of the National Museum and cost S£45. Another quality company, Qadmous, is based here.

Sample fares with such buses include: Aleppo (five hours; S£150); Deir ez-Zur (six hours; S£150); Hama (2½ hours; S£100); Lattakia (five hours; S£140); Palmyra (three hours; S£125); Qamishle (10 hours; S£340); Tartus (3½ hours; S£110).

Train Most trains leave from the Khaddam railway station, about five km south-west of the centre (a shuttle bus connects with the Hejaz station in the centre). Trains are infrequent and slower than the buses; they run daily to Homs, Hama, Aleppo, Raqqa, Deir ez-Zur, Hassake, Qamishle, Tartus and Lattakia. The trip to Qamishle can take 16 hours or more.

Service Taxi There is a service-taxi station next to the Karnak bus station. Taxis leave throughout the day and night for Amman (five hours; S£385 or JD5.500) and Beirut (three hours; S£191 or S£291 depending on where in Beirut).

Getting Around

The Airport The airport is 35 km south-east of Damascus. Local buses leave every half-hour from next to the Choukri Kouwatli Ave flyover from 5.30 am to 11 pm. The trip costs S£10 and takes about 45 minutes.

Bus & Taxi Damascus is well served with a local bus and microbus network, but as the centre is so compact you'll rarely have to use them.

All the taxis are yellow, and there are hundreds of them. A ride across town should never cost more than S£25.

South of Damascus

The area from Damascus south to the Jordanian border, about 100 km away, is fertile agricultural land and intensively farmed.

The Golan Heights in the south-west, occupied by Israel since 1967, is the principal bone of contention in the on-again off-again Israeli-Syrian peace talks. The area known as the Hauran is a black basalt plain that straddles the Jordan-Syria border.

SUWEIDA

The only thing of interest in this town 75 km south of Damascus is a fine **museum** that holds an impressive collection covering periods in Hauran history from the Stone Age to Roman times. The main attraction is the mosaics from Shahba, which alone make a visit worthwhile.

Getting There & Away

A minibus from Damascus (from the south bus station) takes 1¾ hours and costs S£22. Or you can take a slightly faster microbus for S£40, which leaves at set times.

BOSRA

The town of Bosra is 40 km east of Der'a across fertile plains littered with black basalt rocks. Once important for its location at the crossroads of major trade and, under the Muslims, pilgrimage routes, it is now little more than a backwater.

Bosra is a weird and wonderful place. Apart from having possibly the best preserved Roman theatre in existence, the rest

of the town is built in, around and over old sections of Roman buildings, and made almost entirely out of black basalt blocks.

Bosra can be seen as a long day trip from Damascus, or you can do things at a more leisurely pace by basing yourself at Der'a.

Things to See

The **citadel** is a curious construction as it is largely a fortified **Roman theatre**. The two structures are in fact one – the fort was built around the theatre to make it an impregnable stronghold. The first walls were built during the Umayyad and Abbasid periods, with further additions being made in the 11th century by the Fatimids.

The big surprise on entering the citadel is the magnificent 15,000 seat theatre – a rarity among Roman theatres in that it is completely free-standing rather than built into the side of a hill.

Other sites in the town include the various **monumental gates**, **Corinthian columns**, **Roman baths**, a **monastery**, and the **Mosque of Omar**, which dates to at least the 12th century.

Places to Stay & Eat

There is only one hotel in Bosra, the expensive *Bosra Cham Palace* (☎ (015) 790488), where singles/doubles cost US$100/120. Otherwise, you can stay in a room inside the citadel for S£200 a night.

Getting There & Away

Damas Tours microbuses leave from the Jisr ar-Rais flyover in Damascus and cost S£45. Book the return trip as soon as you arrive in Bosra. Otherwise, minibuses and microbuses run from Der'a to Bosra fairly regularly for S£9/15. The last one heading back to Der'a leaves at about 4.30 pm.

DER'A

There's not a lot of interest in this southern town, 100 km from Damascus, although it can make a good base for visiting the ruins at Bosra.

Places to Stay & Eat

On the main road is the *Hotel al-Ahram* (☎ 221791), where S£150 will get you a bed in a basic share room. Overpriced but more comfortable doubles with bath cost S£600.

There are a few small felafel, chicken and shwarma places in the main street.

Getting There & Away

Minibuses and bigger buses leave from the south bus station in Damascus (about 1½ hours; S£25). Microbuses do the same run for S£45. Minibuses/microbuses to Bosra take up to an hour and cost S£9/15.

A slow diesel train goes to Damascus twice weekly and Amman on Sunday.

Jordan Service taxis shuttle between the bus stations in Der'a and Ramtha (on the Jordanian side), and cost S£150 or JD2 per head. Alternatively, you can hitch a ride or walk.

Mediterranean Coast

The 183 km long Syrian coastline is dominated by the rugged mountain range that runs along its entire length. The extremely fertile and heavily cultivated coastal strip is narrow in the north and widens towards the south.

The beaches along the coast are certainly nothing to rave about as the water is murky and the sand is littered with garbage, but they are popular with Syrians on holiday.

LATTAKIA

This busy port city on the north coast is probably the most cosmopolitan in the whole country, and the least conservative. It has almost a European feel with its wide tree-lined streets and the occasional cafe with chairs and tables on the footpath.

The city has no real attractions but it makes a good base for visits to the ruins of the ancient city of Ugarit (Ras Shamra).

Information

The Tourist Centre is at the fork in the main road to Aleppo. It is open daily except Friday from 8 am to 7 pm, and the friendly staff are helpful. The post office is south of the centre near the port.

The Immigration office is on the 2nd floor of the police building; it's open daily except Friday from 8 am to 2 pm. Visa extensions are issued on the spot.

Things to See

There's a small **museum** down near the waterfront housed in what was once an old khan, or caravanserai. You'll see some pottery and written tablets from Ugarit, chain-mail suits and a section of contemporary art. It's open daily except Tuesday from 8 am to 2 pm, but at S£200 is a bit of a rip-off.

Places to Stay

The *Hotel Kaoukab al-Chark* (☎ 238452), just by the Assad statue, has basic singles/doubles for S£150/300. Rooms with private bath cost S£200/325.

A marginally better deal is the *Ramsis Hotel* (☎ 238058), where prices are the same. There is a good communal hot shower. Closer to the mosque is the *Afamia Hotel*, where beds cost S£130/250 for singles/doubles. A hot shower costs extra.

Closer to the port is Lattakia's best budget hotel, the *Hotel Al-Atlal* (☎ 236121). This quiet, family-run establishment charges S£250 per person for good beds in homey rooms. The sign on Youssef al-Azmeh St says 'Hotel' only.

Just opposite the Tourist Centre is the *Hotel Riviera* (☎ 421803; fax 418287), where the reception is markedly friendlier and rooms (with hot water, TV and fridge) are more expensive. Singles/doubles cost US$54/59.

Places to Eat

As with hotels, the cheap restaurants and street stalls are centred around the mosque area. A quick hunt around will turn up the old faithfuls – felafel, chicken, kebabs and shwarma.

For a decent pizza try *Mamma*. Their pizzas cost under S£100 and are quite good. They also have spaghetti bolognese, escalope

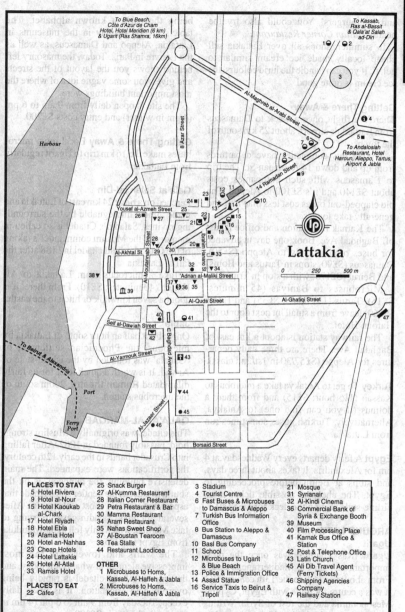

To Blue Beach,
Côte d'Azur de Cham
Hotel, Hotel Meridien (6 km)
& Ugarit (Ras Shamra, 16km)

To Kassab,
Ras al-Bassit
& Qala'at Salah
ad-Din

Al-Maghreb al-Arabi Street

8 Azar Street

Harbour

To Andalosiah
Restaurant, Hotel
Haroun, Aleppo, Tartus,
Airport & Jabla

14 Ramadan Street

Yousef al-Azmeh Street

Al-Akhtal St

Al-Moutanabi Street

Lattakia

0   250   500 m

'Adnan al-Maliki Street

Al-Quds Street

Al-Ghatiqi Street

Seif al-Dawiah Street

c Baghdad Avenue

Al-Yarmouk Street

To Beirut & Alexandria

Port

Al-Jazeer Street

Ferry
Port

Borsaid Street

PLACES TO STAY
5   Hotel Riviera
9   Hotel al-Nour
15 Hotel Kaoukab
    al-Chark
17 Hotel Riyadh
18 Hotel Ebla
19 Afamia Hotel
20 Hotel an-Nahhas
23 Cheap Hotels
24 Hotel Lattakia
26 Hotel Al-Atlal
33 Ramsis Hotel

PLACES TO EAT
22 Cafes

25 Snack Burger
27 Al-Kumma Restaurant
28 Italian Corner Restaurant
29 Petra Restaurant & Bar
30 Mamma Restaurant
34 Aram Restaurant
35 Nahas Sweet Shop
37 Al-Boustan Tearoom
38 Tea Stalls
44 Restaurant Laodicea

OTHER
1   Microbuses to Homs,
    Kassab, Al-Haffeh & Jabla
2   Microbuses to Homs,
    Kassab, Al-Haffeh & Jabla

3   Stadium
4   Tourist Centre
6   Fast Buses & Microbuses
    to Damascus & Aleppo
7   Turkish Bus Information
    Office
8   Bus Station to Aleppo &
    Damascus
10 Basl Bus Company
11 School
12 Microbuses to Ugarit
    & Blue Beach
13 Police & Immigration Office
14 Assad Statue
16 Service Taxis to Beirut &
    Tripoli

21 Mosque
31 Syrianair
32 Al-Kindi Cinema
36 Commercial Bank of
    Syria & Exchange Booth
39 Museum
40 Film Processing Place
41 Karnak Bus Office &
    Station
42 Post & Telephone Office
43 Latin Church
45 Ali Dib Travel Agent
    (Ferry Tickets)
46 Shipping Agencies
    Company
47 Railway Station

and hamburgers! You could also try the nearby *Italian Corner Restaurant*.

In summer, shops all over Lattakia sell cheap locally made ice cream similar to gelati. If you can handle the lurid colours, the ice cream is quite good.

Getting There & Away

There's a flight once a week to Damascus from Lattakia's airport, about 25 km south of the town.

Myriad bus companies have departures from up and down 14 Ramadan St. The trip to Damascus with such companies costs about S£140 and it's S£100 to Aleppo. The old clapped-out buses cost less than half and generally take longer.

The Karnak bus station and office is just off Baghdad Ave. Book one day in advance for buses running daily to Aleppo (S£50), Damascus (S£90, stops in Tartus and Homs) and Beirut (S£175, with a stop in Tripoli).

Microbuses to Baniyas (45 minutes; S£15), Tartus (1½ hours; S£35) and Homs (S£60) leave from a small lot next door to the Haroun Hotel.

The railway station is about a km east of Baghdad Ave. There are three daily departures for Aleppo (S£57/30 in 1st/2nd class).

Turkey To get to Antakya take a microbus to Kassab (1½ hour; S£15) and from there a dolmuş (if you can find one) to Antakya. Alternatively, Turkish buses sometimes run from Lattakia.

Egypt A ferry departs every Wednesday at 4 pm for Alexandria. It takes about three days, and stops at Beirut before proceeding to Egypt. The cheapest possible ticket is an airline-style seat on the deck for US$140.

AROUND LATTAKIA
Ugarit

Ugarit (Ras Shamra) was once the most important city on the Mediterranean coast. From about the 16th to the 13th century BC, it was a centre for trade with Egypt, Cyprus, Mesopotamia and the rest of Syria. Writing on tablets found here is widely accepted as being the earliest known alphabet. The tablets are on display in the museums in Lattakia, Aleppo and Damascus, as well as the Louvre in Paris. Today, the masonry left behind shows you the layout of the streets and gives you some vague idea of where the most important buildings were.

The site is open daily from 9 am to 6 pm (4 pm in winter) and entry costs S£200.

Getting There & Away Local town microbuses make the 16 km trip to Ugarit regularly from Lattakia.

Qala'at Salah ad-Din

Perched on a ridge 24 km east of Lattakia and made almost impregnable by the surrounding ravines, Saladin's Citadel is so called in memory of the Muslim commander's taking of the Crusader-held citadel in 1188 after the fall of Lattakia.

Take a microbus from Lattakia to Al-Haffeh (40 minutes; S£10). From there, it is about a seven km walk or hitch to the castle.

Jabla

Only about half an hour south of Lattakia by microbus, the Phoenician settlement of 'Gabala' was founded by the island-state of Arwad. It is worth a quick look for its fairly dilapidated **Roman theatre**, 200m south of the microbus station.

QALA'AT AL-MARQAB

This citadel was originally a Muslim stronghold, possibly founded in 1062. After falling into Crusader hands in the early 12th century, the fortifications were expanded. The main defensive building, the dungeon, is on the southern side, as the gentler slopes made that aspect the castle's most vulnerable. After several attempts, Saladin gave up trying to take Marqab, which only fell to the Mamluks from Egypt in 1285.

The walls and towers are the most impressive element of what is left today, and the interior of the citadel is rapidly being overrun with vegetation. It is open daily except Tuesday from 9 am to 6 pm (4 pm in winter) and entry is S£200.

Getting There & Away

To get there, take a microbus (S£5) from Baniyas on the coast for Zaoube – it goes right past.

TARTUS

Tartus, Syria's second port, is an easy-going town with what could be a reasonable beach if it weren't so utterly covered in garbage. The compact remnants of the old city (known to the Crusaders as Tortosa) are a fascinating warren of old and new, as is the once fortified island offshore, Arwad. Stench and rubbish seem to be a big theme here – spoiling Arwad as well as the beach.

Things to See

Don't be put off by the rather austere exterior of the 12th century **cathedral**, the interior is all graceful curves and arches and houses a good little museum. From the outside it looks more like a fortress, and that is no coincidence as its construction was conceived with its own defence in mind.

If you head down to the waterfront, pretty well directly in front of the cathedral, you will see remains of the **medieval town walls** and **ramparts**. The area of the **old city** is small and crowded and still buzzing with activity.

The small island of **Arwad**, a few km south-west of Tartus, is a real gem. If only it were not so filthy! There are no cars or wide streets, only a maze of narrow lanes that twist and turn between the tightly packed buildings and, with each turn, reveal something new.

Places to Stay

Among the cheaper alternatives for those on a strict diet of rock-bottom hotels, the *Hotel Tourism & Resort* (☎ 221763) is about the best, especially if you snag one of the rooms with a balcony. You pay S£175/275 and hot water *may* be available. Rooms of a similar quality can be obtained at the *Hotel Republic* (☎ 222580) for the same price. The *Rawda Hotel* is in much the same league.

The *Daniel Hotel* (☎ 220582) charges S£300/600 for rooms of uneven quality and tepid showers – its glory days are fading fast.

The other places start at about US$15 a single. The *Ambassadors Hotel* (☎ 220183) down on the waterfront (the entrance is in the back street) is enormous and has rooms with balconies overlooking the water for US$20/25. Further down the beach and with much better rooms is the *Al-Baher Hotel* (☎ 221687). Singles/doubles cost US$18/25.

Places to Eat

The cheap restaurants and snack places are clustered around the clock tower and Al-Wahda Street. You'll find a juice stand on Khalid ibn al-Walid St.

The small restaurant just behind the boat harbour, *Al-Nabil*, sells baked fish that is heavily spiced and salted. The fish is really quite good, but a meal with extras and a beer or two will set you back almost S£400. They also do more regular dishes (like chicken and kebabs), which cost about half.

Getting There & Away

Bus/Microbus Old buses and minibuses, and the newer microbuses leave from a lot near the railway station when full. The trip to Lattakia by microbus takes about 1½ hours and costs S£35; Baniyas is 30 minutes and S£11 away. There are plenty of buses for Homs (1½ hours; S£23) and Damascus (four hours; S£53).

The Karnak office is across the road from the post office. There is a daily departure at 7 am for Tripoli (S£100) and Beirut (S£150), and another to Damascus (S£75).

The new Qadmous private bus station is next to the Governorate building. The fare to Aleppo is S£115, to Hama S£65 and to Damascus S£110.

Train There is a daily train to Homs and Damascus and another to Lattakia.

AROUND TARTUS
Safita

This peaceful mountain town is dominated by the white tower of the Crusader-era **Castel Blanc**, known to locals simply as the *burj* (tower). To the south-east you can see the Crac des Chevaliers, and directly to the south the snowcapped peaks of northern Lebanon.

Places to Stay & Eat Where the town's two main streets meet in the centre, not far from where the microbuses terminate, there is a small fleapit above a shop, the *Hotel Siyaha*. It charges S£100 for a bed and is only for the desperate.

The only other options are beyond the budget traveller. A few km south-east of the Hotel Siyaha is the hotel *Burj Safita*, which offers decent singles/doubles/triples for US$18/22/25. Even more expensive is the *Safita Cham Palace* (☎ (043) 525980), where rooms cost US$125/160 plus taxes.

There's a good snack place on the intersection with a sign simply saying *Restaurant Bar*. The restaurant by the Castel has great views but is a little expensive.

Getting There & Away The microbus from Tartus to Safita costs S£8 and takes about 45 minutes.

Hosn Sulayman

Some 25 km north of Safita lie the imposing remains of an **ancient temple** at Hosn Sulayman. Its walls were built of huge stone blocks, some of them as great as 10m by three metres! Most of what stands now was built under the Romans.

Minibuses and microbuses (S£7) run at irregular intervals from Safita to the village of Hosn Sulayman.

CRAC DES CHEVALIERS

Qala'at al-Hosn (Castle of the Knights) is one of Syria's prime attractions and should not be missed. It is well preserved and can't have looked much different 800 years ago. The fort is located in the only significant break in the mountain range between

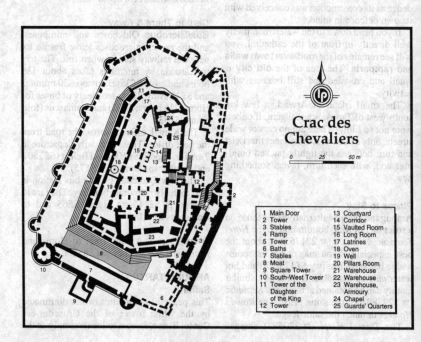

Crac des Chevaliers

0   25   50 m

1	Main Door	13	Courtyard
2	Tower	14	Corridor
3	Stables	15	Vaulted Room
4	Ramp	16	Long Room
5	Tower	17	Latrines
6	Baths	18	Oven
7	Stables	19	Well
8	Moat	20	Pillars Room
9	Square Tower	21	Warehouse
10	South-West Tower	22	Warehouse
11	Tower of the	23	Warehouse,
	Daughter		Armoury
	of the King	24	Chapel
12	Tower	25	Guards' Quarters

Antakya and Beirut, a distance of some 250 km.

The Crusaders built the fort in the 12th century and it could house a garrison of 4000. Local basalt was used in the early stages of construction; later, limestone was also employed. It fell to Mamluk Sultan Baybars in 1271.

The stronghold has two distinct parts: the outside wall with its 13 towers and main entrance; and the inside wall and central construction, which are built on a rocky platform. A moat dug out of the rock separates the two walls.

Places to Stay & Eat

The *Restaurant La Table Ronde* (☎ (031) 734280), about 100m off to the left of the main entrance, has basic rooms with three beds for S£500. They'll also let you camp. It's probably the best choice of place to eat too.

The Crac is an easy day trip from Tartus, Homs or even Hama. The latter especially offers better accommodation possibilities.

Getting There & Away

The Crac lies some 10 km north of the Homs to Tartus motorway.

From Homs there are several microbuses to the village of Hosn (S£20) before noon. They will drop you right at the Crac.

The other alternative, and the only choice from Tartus, is to catch one of the buses shuttling between the two cities and alight at the turn-off. From there you have to hitch or pick up a passing local microbus.

Orontes Valley

The Orontes River (Nahr al-Assi in Arabic – the 'rebel river') has its headwaters in the mountains of Lebanon near Baalbek. The river flows through the industrial city of Homs before reaching Hama, where the only obstruction to the flow is the ancient *norias*, or water wheels. The Orontes once used to flow north-west from Hama and seep away in the swamps of Al-Ghab, but those swamps have long been drained to form one of the most fertile plains in Syria.

HOMS

There's little of interest in Homs, but it is one of those crossroads most travellers have to pass through at some stage. Roads head north to Hama, east to Palmyra and the Euphrates, south to Damascus and west to Tartus and the coast.

There is a small information booth by the footpath on Kouwatli St. For visa renewals, go to the 3rd floor of a multistorey administration building at the end of a tiny side lane north of Kouwatli St.

Things to See

The only building of great note is the **Khalid ibn al-Walid Mosque** on the Hama road about a km north of the town centre. It holds the tomb of the commander of the Muslim armies who brought Islam to Syria in 636 AD.

Places to Stay & Eat

The cheap hotels are on or around Kouwatli St between the tourist office and the souq. The best is the *Al-Nasr al-Jadeed Hotel* (☎ 227423), which has clean singles/ doubles for S£200/300. A hot shower can be cranked up in the corridor.

The *Toledo Restaurant*, set back a little from the gardens around the tourist information booth, serves a reasonable variety of stews, soups and rice dishes and a filling meal can easily be found for under S£200.

Getting There & Away

Bus The Karnak station is about two km north of the city centre. There are several daily buses to Damascus for S£50. Three buses run to Aleppo (calling at Hama) for S£60. There is a daily departure for Safita and another for Tartus – both cost S£30.

The regular bus station is next to Karnak. The old buses will take you to Damascus for S£27, while minibuses will do it for S£35 and modern microbuses for S£60. For Palmyra, a private Pullman-style bus will cost S£90, actually the full fare to Deir ez-Zur. Several microbuses do the trip to Crac des Chevaliers for S£20.

Train The railway station is a half-hour walk from the centre. There are three departures a day south to Damascus (S£47/34 in 1st/2nd class) and north to Aleppo (S£45/32).

Service Taxi Service taxis gather around the corner of the Al-Khayyam Hotel on Kouwatli St and run to Damascus, Aleppo, Beirut and Tripoli (Lebanon).

HAMA

This is one of the most attractive towns in Syria with the Orontes River flowing through the town centre, its banks lined with trees and gardens and the ancient, groaning norias. There's not an awful lot to see, but the town's peaceful atmosphere makes it a pleasant place. The people here are among the most conservative in Syria.

Hama is preferable to Homs as a base for excursions to Crac des Chevaliers and other sights in the area.

Hama became famous, or infamous, in February 1982 when about 8000 troops moved in to quash a rebellion by the Muslim Brotherhood.

For visa extensions go to the Immigration office, which is hidden away up three flights of stairs in a building opposite the footbridge in the centre of town. There is a small sign saying 'passports' in English.

Things to See

For a good view of the city walk up to the park on top of the **citadel**. Apart from a few unrecognisable fragments, nothing remains of the old fortress.

Hama's main attraction is the **norias** – wooden water wheels up to 20m in diameter – built centuries ago to provide water for the town and irrigation. They still turn today, although the water is not used. Because both the wheels and the blocks on which they are mounted are wooden, the friction produces a mournful groaning.

The norias right in the centre of town are

surrounded by a popular park where people gather to relax. The most impressive wheels, however, are about one km east, upstream from the centre. The four norias here, known as the Four Norias of Bichriyat, are in two pairs on a weir straddling the river. About one km west of the centre is the largest of the norias, known as the Al-Mohammediyyeh.

The **Grand Mosque**, about 200m south of the Al-Mohammediyyeh Noria, is gradually being restored after its complete destruction during the 1982 uprising.

The **museum** is housed in the old **Azem Palace**, the residence of the governor, As'ad Pasha al-Azem, who ruled the town from 1700 to 1742. The palace is reminiscent of the more grandiose building of the same name in Damascus. Hardly surprising, as the latter was built by the same man upon his transfer to Damascus.

Places to Stay

Two of the best value-for-money places in Syria are right next to one another in Kouwatli Ave. The *Cairo Hotel* (☎ 237206; fax 511715) is spotlessly clean, has great showers and the friendly owner, Bader, speaks English and German. A bed in a shared room is S£175 (or S£150 if you don't want a shower) and doubles cost S£350. The *Riad Hotel* (☎ 239512) is in direct competition with the Cairo and marginally cheaper.

Bader of the Cairo Hotel has gone up-market with his mid-range *Noria Hotel* (☎ & fax 511715). Singles/doubles cost US$18/28 and are among the highest quality in this price range in Syria.

Places to Eat

In the couple of blocks along Kouwatli Ave west of the Cairo Hotel are the usual cheap kebab and chicken restaurants.

If you want to dine in style, the *Al-Rawda Restaurant* on the banks of the river has a fine setting overlooking the norias. The food is only average, the prices are not. The food is much better in the *Sultan Restaurant*, which you can reach by the low vaulted tunnel under the An-Nouri Mosque.

For a tea or coffee, and maybe a nargileh

and a game of backgammon, you can't beat the shady outdoor *cafe* next to the Al-Rawda.

Although you can find it outside Hama, the halawat al-jibn is a cheese-based dessert speciality of the city.

Getting There & Away
Bus/Minibus The old bus and minibus station is on the southern outskirts of town, about two km from the centre. Regular minibuses go to Homs (30 minutes; S£10), Suqaylibiyyeh (S£10, for Apamea), Aleppo (S£25), Damascus (2¾ hours; S£32) and other surrounding towns.

Microbuses For quicker but more expensive service, you can get microbuses from a separate station virtually across the road.

Karnak & Luxury Buses Several companies, including Qadmous, Al-Nawras and the government-run Karnak have offices in the centre of town. Karnak's is in Cafeteria Afamia and the Qadmous and Al-Nawras offices are next door to it. They run three daily buses to Damascus (S£60) and two a day to Beirut (S£150). The other two companies are more expensive and of a higher standard. Two other companies, Al-Ahliah

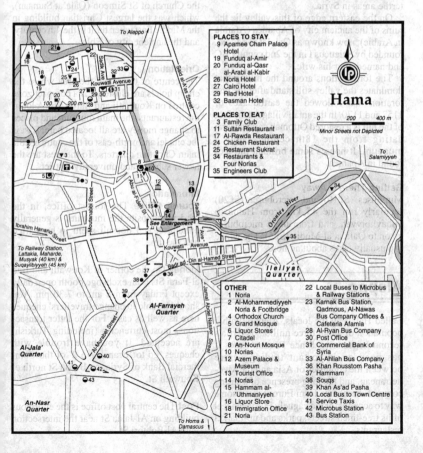

PLACES TO STAY
9 Apamee Cham Palace Hotel
19 Funduq al-Amir
20 Funduq al-Qasr al-Arabi al-Kabir
26 Noria Hotel
27 Cairo Hotel
29 Riad Hotel
32 Basman Hotel

PLACES TO EAT
3 Family Club
11 Sultan Restaurant
17 Al-Rawda Restaurant
24 Chicken Restaurant
25 Restaurant Sukrat
34 Restaurants & Four Norias
35 Engineers Club

Hama

0   200   400 m

Minor Streets not Depicted

To Aleppo

Said al-Aas Street

Sadik Ave

Kouwatti Avenue

0   100   200 m

Abu al-Fida St

Orontes River

To Salamiyyeh

Moutanabbi Street

Ibrahim Hano Street

See Enlargement

Sadik Ave

To Railway Station, Lattakia, Maharde, Musyak (40 km) & Suqaylibiyyeh (45 km)

Kouwatti Avenue

Badr ad-Din al-Hamed Street

Ilellyat Quarter

To Homs & Damascus

Al-Farrayeh Quarter

Jamal Abdel Nasser Street

Al-Murabet Street

Al-Jala' Quarter

An-Nasr Quarter

OTHER
1 Noria
2 Al-Mohammediyyeh Noria & Footbridge
4 Orthodox Church
5 Grand Mosque
6 Liquor Stores
7 Citadel
8 An-Nouri Mosque
10 Norias
12 Azem Palace & Museum
13 Tourist Office
14 Norias
15 Hammam al-'Uthmaniyyeh
16 Liquor Store
18 Immigration Office
21 Noria
22 Local Buses to Microbus & Railway Stations
23 Karnak Bus Station, Qadmous, Al-Nawas Bus Company Offices & Cafeteria Afamia
28 Al-Ryan Bus Company
30 Post Office
31 Commercial Bank of Syria
33 Al-Ahliah Bus Company
36 Khan Rousstom Pasha
37 Hammam
38 Souqs
39 Khan As'ad Pasha
40 Local Bus to Town Centre
41 Service Taxis
42 Microbus Station
43 Bus Station

and Al-Ryan (refer to the Hama map) offer similar services.

Train The railway station is way out of town to the south-west. There are daily trains to Damascus (four hours; S£57/40 in 1st/2nd class) and Aleppo (2½ hours; S£34/23).

APAMEA (QALA'AT AL-MUDIQ)
From Hama, the Orontes River flows north-west and into the vast Al-Ghab depression, some 50 km away. Once a stagnant swamp, this low-lying area of some 40 sq km has been drained and is now one of the most fertile areas in Syria.

On the eastern edge of this valley lie the ruins of the ancient city of Apamea (Afamia in Arabic), now known as Qala'at al-Mudiq, founded by Seleucus I in the 2nd century BC and named after his wife.

The fortifications around the hilltop that dominates the valley still stand after the restoration that followed the earthquakes of 1157 and 1170. In the small village at the foot of the hill is a restored Ottoman caravanserai dating from the 18th century, now a **museum**. It houses some brilliant mosaics found in Apamea.

Getting There & Away
Minibuses (S£10) and microbuses (S£20) regularly run the 45 km from Hama to Suqaylibiyyeh, and from there microbuses go on to Qala'at al-Mudiq (S£5). The whole trip usually takes about an hour.

Aleppo

Called Halab by the locals, Aleppo, with a population of about three million, is Syria's second-largest city. Since Roman times it has been an important trading centre between the countries of Asia and the Mediterranean, and the long presence of a strong corps of merchants from Europe goes some way to account for the vaguely European feel of its tree-lined streets, parks and up-market restaurants.

There is a large Christian population comprised mainly of Armenian refugees from Turkey, and if you walk around certain quarters of the city, you'll see as many signs in the condensed-looking script of Armenian as you'll see in the familiar 'shorthand' with which many people equate Arabic. An influx of traders from the ex-Soviet Union has also left its mark – Russian seems like the third language!

With its fascinating covered souqs, the citadel, museum and caravanserais, it is a great place to spend a few days. There are also interesting sights in the vicinity such as the Church of St Simeon (Qala'at Samaan), which was the largest Christian building in the Middle East when built in the 4th century, and the ancient city of Ebla.

Orientation
The centre of town and the area where the cheap hotels are clustered is a compact zone centred on Kouwatli and Baron Sts. A lot of the restaurants, the main museum and places to change money are all located here. East is the citadel and north-east of the centre are the main Christian quarters. To the west are the newer suburbs and university district.

Information
Tourist Office The tourist office, in the gardens opposite the museum, is generally unhelpful, and doesn't seem to be staffed half the time.

Money On the corner of Kouwatli and Bab al-Faraj Sts is an exchange booth open daily except Friday from 8 am to 7.30 pm. You should be able to change travellers' cheques here as well as cash. For the latter transactions, most currencies (including Turkish) are accepted. If you have trouble with cheques, go to 'Branch No 2' of the Commercial Bank of Syria, on Baron St north of Kouwatli St.

Post The central post office is the enormous building on Al-Jalaa St near the intersection with Al-Bohtori St.

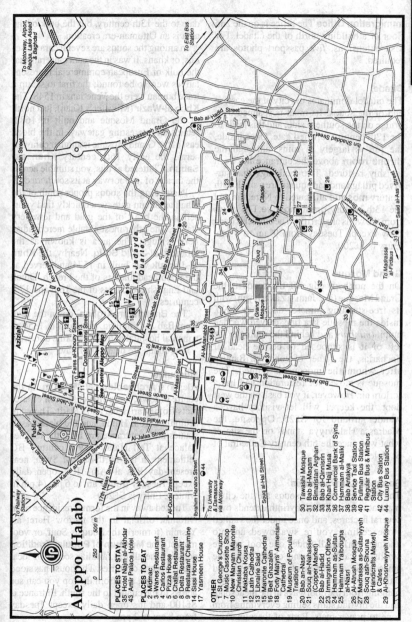

Aleppo (Halab)

0   250   500 m

PLACES TO STAY
35 Hotel Najm al-Akhdar
43 Amir Palace Hotel

PLACES TO EAT
2   Wanes
3   Wanes Restaurant
4   Carlos Restaurant
5   Pizza House
6   Challal Restaurant
8   Delta Restaurant
9   Restaurant Chaumine
14 Sissi House
17 Yasmeen House

OTHER
1   St George's Church
7   Music Cassette Shop
10 New Maryam Maronite
    Christian Church
11 Maktaba Kousa
12 Latin Cathedral
13 Librairie Said
15 Maronite Cathedral
16 Beit Ghazaleh
18 Forty Martyrs Armenian
    Cathedral
19 Museum of Popular
    Tradition
20 Bab an-Nasr
21 Souq an-Nahassen
    (Copper Market)
22 Bimaristan Arghan
23 Immigration Office
24 Khan Hajj Musa
25 Hammam as-Sultan
27 Hammam Yalbougha
    al-Nasri
26 Al-Atroush Mosque
27 Madrassa as-Sultaniyyeh
28 Souq al-Souna
    (Handicrafts Market)
    & Cafes
29 Al-Khosrowiyyeh Mosque
30 Tawashi Mosque
31 Bab al-Maqam
32 Bab al-Hadid
33 Bab al-Qinnisrin
34 Khan Hajj Musa
36 Commercial Bank of Syria
37 Hammam al-Maliki
38 Bab Antakya
39 Service Taxi Station
40 Pullman Bus Station
41 Regular Bus & Minibus
    Station
42 City Bus Station
44 Luxury Bus Station

Immigration Office The office is on the 2nd floor of a building north of the citadel. For visa extensions, *five* passport photos are required.

Citadel

The citadel dominates the city at the eastern end of the souqs. Its moat is spanned by a bridge on the southern side, and this leads to the 12th century fortified gate. Once inside, the fort is largely in ruins, although the **throne room** above the entrance has been lavishly restored. Two buildings that survived pillage and earthquake are a small 12th century **mosque** attributed to Nureddin and the 13th century **great mosque**. The views from the walls are terrific. The citadel is open daily except Tuesday from 9 am to 6 pm. Entry is S£200.

Grand Mosque

On the northern edge of the souqs is the Grand Mosque (aka Jami'a Zakariyyeh) with its free-standing minaret dating to 1090. Inside the mosque is a fine, carved wooden pulpit *(minbar)* and behind the railing to the left of it is supposed to be the head of Zacharias, the father of John the Baptist, after whom the mosque is named. The mosque is closed for restoration and has a forlorn air. However, if you bash on the west door, the keeper will let visitors have a wander around for S£25. Opposite, the Madrassa Halawiyya stands on the site of what was once the 6th century Cathedral of St Helen.

Souqs & Caravanserais

The fabulous covered souqs are the city's main attraction. This labyrinth extends over several hectares, and once under the vaulted stone ceiling, you're swallowed up into another world. All under one roof are the smells of cardamom and cloves from the spice stalls, the cries of the hawkers and barrow pushers, the rows of carcasses hanging from the doorways in the meat souq, and the myriad stalls selling everything from rope to prayer mats. Parts of these markets

date to the 13th century, but the bulk of the area is an Ottoman-era creation.

In among the souqs are several caravanserais, or khans. It was in the caravanserais that the bulk of European commercial representatives were to be found; the first to set up a trade bureau were the Venetians in 1548. The **Khan al-Wazir** (Minister's Khan), just north of the Grand Mosque and built in 1682, retains an interesting gateway. In the block east of the Grand Mosque is another caravanserai, the early 16th century **Khan as-Sabun**. Cluttered as it is, you stumble across the facade of its doorway at its southern end.

Penetrating the souqs proper south of the Khan as-Sabun gate, you quickly find yourself in the heart of the gold and jewellery stands. The other most notable merchandise here is rugs. The area is known as the **İstanbul al-Jadid Souq**. Nearby, the **Khan al-Jumruk** was built in 1574 and served as the main headquarters of the French, Dutch and English merchants of the 16th and 17th centuries.

The **Bimaristan Arghan**, down the road from Bab al-Qinnisrin, was built in 1354 as a mental hospital and boasts a fine doorway.

The souqs are dead on Friday.

Museums

Aleppo's **Archaeological Museum**, in the centre of town, has a fine collection of artefacts from Mari, Ebla and Ugarit. There are sculptures from Hama, and the black basalt statues at the entrance are from the temple-palace at Tell Halaf (a 9th century BC settlement in the north-east of Syria, near present-day Ras al-'Ain). It is open daily except Tuesday from 9 am to 6 pm (4 pm in winter). Entry is S£200.

Tucked away in the former residence of an Ottoman official in the narrow Haret al-Yasmin (formerly the Souq as-Souf, or wool market), the **Museum of Popular Tradition** contains the all too familiar scenes of local life in bygone centuries. The house has stood for 250 years, and from the top you can see across to the citadel to the south. Entrance is S£100 and it's open daily except Tuesday from 8 am to 2 pm.

Christian Quarter

The area immediately surrounding the Museum of Popular Tradition is a Christian, mainly Armenian, quarter called Al-Jadayda, and a number of stately old homes here, dating to the 17th and 18th centuries, can be visited. The whole area is fascinating to wander around on a Sunday, when it's busy with the faithful of five Christian faiths thronging together.

Hammams

Just to the south-east of the bridge to the citadel is the Hammam Yalbougha al-Nasri (☎ 623154). Originally constructed in 1491, it had been destroyed and rebuilt several times before the latest restoration was completed in 1985. Access to the baths, a full massage and sauna costs S£400. Women can only go on Tuesday, Thursday and Saturday from 10 am to 6 pm. It's open to men only on Tuesday, Thursday and Saturday from 5 pm until midnight, and from 10 am to midnight every other day. It's quite touristy now, but you can search out other, less frequented and cheaper hammams around the old city.

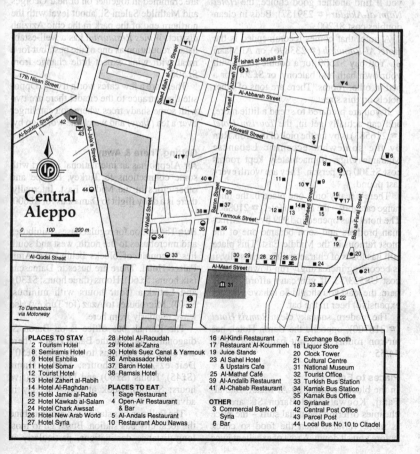

Central Aleppo

0   100   200 m

To Damascus
via Motorway

PLACES TO STAY		
2 Tourism Hotel	28 Hotel Al-Raoudah	16 Al-Kindi Restaurant
8 Semiramis Hotel	29 Hotel al-Zahra	17 Restaurant Al-Koummeh
9 Hotel Eshbilia	30 Hotels Suez Canal & Yarmouk	19 Juice Stands
11 Hotel Somar	36 Ambassador Hotel	23 Al Sahel Hotel
12 Tourist Hotel	37 Baron Hotel	& Upstairs Cafe
13 Hotel Zahert al-Rabih	38 Ramsis Hotel	25 Al-Mathaf Café
14 Hotel Al-Raghdan		39 Al-Andalib Restaurant
15 Hotel Jamie al-Rabie	PLACES TO EAT	41 Al-Chabab Restaurant
22 Hotel Kawkab al-Salam	1 Sage Restaurant	
24 Hotel Chark Awssat	4 Open-Air Restaurant	OTHER
26 Hotel New Arab World	& Bar	3 Commercial Bank of
27 Hotel Syria	5 Al-Andals Restaurant	Syria
	10 Restaurant Abou Nawas	6 Bar

7 Exchange Booth		
18 Liquor Store		
20 Clock Tower		
21 Cultural Centre		
31 National Museum		
32 Tourist Office		
33 Turkish Bus Station		
34 Karnak Bus Station		
35 Karnak Bus Office		
40 Syrianair		
42 Central Post Office		
43 Parcel Post		
44 Local Bus No 10 to Citadel		

Places to Stay

The bulk of the hotels are in the block bounded by Al-Maari, Baron, Kouwatli and Bab al-Faraj Sts. Hot water generally comes only in the evening and/or early morning.

The cheapest place in town is the *Hotel Zahert al-Rabih* (☎ 212790). It's a dingy little number but costs S£125 per person, or S£75 on the roof. A popular choice is the *Hotel Kawkab al-Salam*, where simple but decent rooms have beds for S£150. They have hot water and even satellite TV. If you head east into the winding market streets, you'll find another good choice, the *Hotel Najm al-Akhdar* (☎ 239157). Beds in clean doubles cost S£200.

A hotel that comes recommended is the *Hotel Al-Raoudah* (☎ 233896), on Al-Maari St. You pay S£500 for a double room with your own bath and balcony, or S£200 for a bed in other rooms. There are tons of other hotels on this street.

If you are prepared to spend a little more, and can actually get in, the *Tourism Hotel* (☎ 216583) is by far the pick of the crop. Run by the somewhat eccentric Lebanese Madame Olga, immaculately kept rooms cost S£300 per person. They are worth every last pound.

There's really only one place in the mid-range category – the *Baron Hotel* (☎ 210880). The hotel was opened in 1909 by two Armenian brothers and soon became one of the most famous in the Middle East. This place still has loads of character although, sadly, it is becoming increasingly run-down. Rooms cost US$23/33. If you can't afford to stay here, the least you should do is have a (rather expensive) beer in the bar.

The modern, squeaky clean *Ramsis Hotel* (☎ 216700), opposite the Baron Hotel, has air-con rooms with hot bath for US$30/44/55.

Places to Eat

In the block bounded by Al-Maari, Bab al-Faraj, Kouwatli and Baron Sts are the cheapies offering the usual stuff – the price is more variable than the food so check before you sit down. A row of excellent juice stands lines up at the Bab al-Faraj St end of Yarmouk St.

Al-Chabab is a good alfresco restaurant with a fountain in a side street off Baron St, just up from the Syrianair office. The *Al-Kindi Restaurant* offers quite filling meals of kebabs with the usual side orders for about S£120.

A bright and comparatively recent arrival in central Aleppo is the *Restaurant Abou Nawas*. A full meal will cost about S£200, but they do not serve alcohol.

More than half a dozen classy restaurants are crammed in together on or near Georges and Mathilde Salem St, about level with the northern end of the park in the chic Aziziah district. *Wanes Restaurant* has a well-established reputation as one of the best, but for a meal with wine expect little change from S£500.

There are a few cafes worth trying. Opposite the entrance to the citadel there are two with some shady trees where you can linger over a tea *(shay)* and watch the world go by.

Getting There & Away

Air Aleppo has an international airport with some connections to Turkey, Europe and other cities in the Middle East. Internally, there is a daily flight to Damascus for S£600.

Bus The station for regular buses, minibuses and microbuses to the north, west and south lies a couple of blocks behind the Amir Palace Hotel. There are buses to Damascus (six hours; S£60), Homs (three hours; S£30), and Lattakia (four hours with minibus; S£40). Microbuses to Azaz (for Turkey) also leave regularly from here.

The Karnak bus office is on Baron St diagonally opposite the Baron Hotel. There are daily connections to Lattakia (S£50), Deir ez-Zur (4½ hours; S£90), Hama (S£45), Homs (S£60) and Damascus (five hours; S£100). Book at least one day in advance.

The Pullman bus station is directly behind the local city bus station. Buses go to most long-distance destinations, particularly in the east, and you have to buy the tickets before boarding.

Buses leave from next to the Karnak bus station for Antakya (S£250) and Gaziantep (S£350) in Turkey. The former is the most used service, with departures at 6 am and 2 pm. You can also book a through ticket to other destinations, including İstanbul (24 hours; S£1000).

Most luxury buses operate from a terminal west along Ibrahim Hanano St. On average, you'll pay S£150 for Damascus, S£100 for Homs, S£175 for Qamishle, S£85 for Raqqa, S£100 (microbus) for Lattakia and up to S£350 for Beirut (Lebanon).

Train The railway station, about 15 minutes walk from the central hotel area, is north of the big public park. Local trains run daily to Damascus, Lattakia, Deir ez-Zur and Qamishle in the north-east.

There's a weekly train from Aleppo to İstanbul. It takes forever (anything up to 48 hours) and costs S£530/430 in 1st/2nd class. It leaves Aleppo at 11.07 am on Saturday (winter) and Tuesday and Saturday at 2.14 pm in summer.

Service Taxi Next door to the Pullman bus station is a service-taxi stand.

Car Try the Europcar desk at the Amir Palace Hotel.

AROUND ALEPPO
Qala'at Samaan
This is the Basilica of St Simeon, also known as St Simon of Stylites, who was one of Syria's most unusual early Christians. In 423, he sat on top of a three metre pillar and went on to spend the next 36 years atop this and other taller pillars! After his death in 459, an enormous church was built around the most famous pillar. The church today is remarkably well preserved, with the arches of the octagonal yard still complete, along with much of the four basilicas.

Getting There & Away Microbuses from Aleppo leave every hour or so from the main

microbus station for the one hour trip to the village of Daret 'Azze for S£10. It is about 15 km from Daret 'Azze to Qala'at Samaan and it's a matter of negotiating with a local for transport. Hitching is a reasonable possibility on weekends.

Ebla
About 60 km south of Aleppo on the highway to Hama lay the ancient city of Ebla (Tell Mardikh), dating back as far as the 3rd millennium BC. More than 15,000 clay tablets in a Sumerian dialect have been unearthed, providing a wealth of information on everything from economics to local administration and dictionaries of other tongues. You can still make out the main palace, the former citadel and one of the city gates. Entry costs S£100.

Getting There & Away Take any Hama-bound microbus, or to be sure of not paying the full fare for Hama, one of the less frequent ones to Ma'aret an-Nu'aman, and alight at the turn-off. You should not need to pay more than S£17.50.

The Desert

The Damascus to Aleppo highway marks roughly the division between the cultivable land to the west and the barren desert that stretches east to the Euphrates.

The wide fringe of the desert gets sufficient rain to support enough vegetation to graze sheep and goats. The desert fringe-dwellers build beehive-shaped houses as protection against the extreme heat. You can see them on the road from Homs to Palmyra, in the area south of Lake al-Assad and around Aleppo.

Dotting this desert are the oases – the main one is Palmyra – that once served as way-stations for the caravans on their way between the Mediterranean and Mesopotamia.

PALMYRA
Known to the locals as Tadmor (its ancient

Semitic name), Palmyra is Syria's prime attraction and one of the world's great historical sites. If you're only going to see one thing in Syria, make it Palmyra. Although mass tourism is making itself felt and the place's popularity is growing, there's still a good chance you'll be able to enjoy it with relatively few other people about.

The oasis is really in the middle of nowhere – 150 km from the Orontes River to the west and 200 km from the Euphrates to the east.

The ruins of the 2nd century AD city have been extensively excavated and restored and cover some 50 hectares. The new town is rapidly growing around it, spreading out with particular speed towards the west, and counts 40,000 inhabitants.

History

Palmyra was at one time a Greek outpost of considerable importance. It was an Assyrian caravan town for over 1000 years but only enjoyed its later Greek period of glory for two centuries. It was annexed by Rome in 217 AD and became a centre of unsurpassed wealth.

The city's most famous character was Zenobia, the half-Greek, half-Arab ruler of Palmyra from 267 AD, after the death in suspicious circumstances of her husband Odenathus. Claiming descent from Cleopatra, she was a woman of exceptional ability and ambition. She even set her sights on Rome, although her troops were soundly beaten by the forces of Aurelian in 271, and the city was put to the torch by him two years later.

This was the beginning of the end for Palmyra. It fell to the Muslims in 634 and was finally and completely destroyed by an earthquake in 1089.

Information

The tourist office is about halfway between the town and the site proper. There is no bank or exchange office in Palmyra, although the black market thrives and you can change at the Palmyra Cham Palace Hotel at not terribly favourable rates.

Places to Stay

The cheapest hotel is the *New Tourist Hotel*, where basic singles/doubles cost S£200/325. A bed in a share room is S£150. There is a hot communal shower and some rooms have their own (cold) bath. It's basic but OK. The *Citadel Hotel* (☎ 910537) has a couple of simple rooms that seem popular with backpackers. They charge the same price. Marginally better than all of these is the

Things to See

The **Temple of Bel**, on the eastern edge of the ruins, is in a massive 200m square courtyard. Entrance costs S£200. Across the main road from here is the **Great Colonnade**, an impressive column-lined street that formed the main artery of the town, running from the main entrance to the monumental arch, and then on for 700m or so to end at the **funerary temple**. The **monumental arch** has been restored, although the keystone appears ready to drop out at any moment.

The **theatre** is on the southern side of the street, and in this area are the **marketplace** (Agora) and **banqueting hall**. About a third of the way along the street is the reconstructed **tetrapylon** (four groups of four pillars), which marks a major intersection of the city. Only one pillar is original, the others are rather crude concrete reconstructions.

The **funerary towers** at the foot of the hill are worth visiting, but a pain. A museum attendant with keys is prepared to go out there four times a day (details posted at the museum; tickets S£100), but only if you arrange with a local driver to take a group of people out. The towers are in easy walking distance, and the above procedure is only necessary if you have an undying wish to fossick around *inside* them.

On the hill overlooking Palmyra is the 17th century Arab castle, **Qala'at ibn Maan**. It's a hard, 45 minute scramble up there, but the views from the castle are outstanding, especially in the late afternoon.

The **museum**, between the ruins and the new town, has some excellent pieces from Palmyra, and the labelling is in English. It's on the edge of the new town and is open daily, except Tuesday, from 8 am to 1 pm and 4 to 6 pm (2 to 4 pm in winter). The entrance fee is S£200. ∎

Hotel Odeinat (☎ 911067), which generally charges S£300/500, but it is worth making the effort to bargain.

Of the middle bracket places, the *Hotel Al-Nakheel* (☎ 910744) has comfortable rooms with private bathroom and heating in winter for S£700/1200.

You can camp at the *Hotel Zenobia* out by the ruins but it's expensive at S£200. The hotel itself has rooms for US$55/66/76 in high season.

Places to Eat

Everyone seems to agree that the best place to eat is the *Traditional Palmyra Restaurant*. For S£150 you can have a hearty meal and be plied unfailingly with tea. They do a great soup for S£50.

Next door, the *Sindibad Restaurant* is not nearly as inviting, but they do sell overpriced beer (S£60 a bottle). Both places also do breakfast menus (fried eggs, toast, jam, juice and coffee or tea).

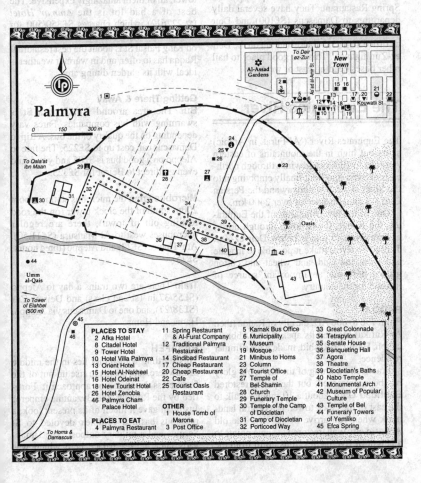

Palmyra

0   150   300 m

To Qala'at ibn Maan

To Tower of Elahbel (500 m)

To Homs & Damascus

Umm al-Qais

To Deir ez-Zur

Al-Assad Gardens

New Town

As'ad al-Amir St

Kouwatli St

Oasis

PLACES TO STAY	11 Spring Restaurant	5 Karnak Bus Office	33 Great Colonnade
2 Afka Hotel	& Al-Furat Company	6 Municipality	34 Tetrapylon
8 Citadel Hotel	12 Traditional Palmyra	7 Museum	35 Senate House
9 Tower Hotel	Restaurant	19 Mosque	36 Banqueting Hall
10 Hotel Villa Palmyra	14 Sindibad Restaurant	21 Minibus to Homs	37 Agora
15 Hotel Al-Nakheel	17 Cheap Restaurant	23 Column	38 Theatre
16 Hotel Odeinat	20 Cheap Restaurant	24 Tourist Office	39 Diocletian's Baths
18 New Tourist Hotel	22 Cafe	27 Temple of	40 Nabo Temple
26 Hotel Zenobia	25 Tourist Oasis	Bel-Shamin	41 Monumental Arch
46 Palmyra Cham	Restaurant	28 Church	42 Museum of Popular
Palace Hotel		29 Funerary Temple	Culture
	OTHER	30 Temple of the Camp	43 Temple of Bel
PLACES TO EAT	1 House Tomb of	of Diocletian	44 Funerary Towers
4 Palmyra Restaurant	Marona	31 Camp of Diocletian	of Yemliko
	3 Post Office	32 Porticoed Way	45 Efca Spring

There are a few cheap restaurants also as far down as the town square. A half chicken and the usual trimmings should not cost more than about S£100.

Getting There & Away
Several minibuses and microbuses leave for Homs (S£50) from the main square when full. The government-run Karnak bus company has all but folded here, with a daily departure for Damascus (S£90) via Homs (S£50). Al-Furat Tours has set up shop in the Spring Restaurant. They have several daily departures to Damascus (S£100) and Deir ez-Zur (S£90). Otherwise, Damas Tour has an office at the Sahara Restaurant on the Deir ez-Zur highway. This is a good place to hail other buses heading east or west.

The Euphrates River

The Euphrates River ('Al-Furat' in Arabic) starts out high in the mountains of eastern Anatolia in Turkey and winds through northeastern Syria into Iraq, finally emptying into the Shatt al-Arab waterway and the Persian Gulf – a total distance of over 2400 km.

One of the few tributaries of the Euphrates, the Kabur, flows down through northeastern Syria to join it below Deir ez-Zur. These two rivers make it possible to irrigate and work the land, and wheat and cotton grown here are an important source of income for the country.

RAQQA
From 796 to 808 AD, the city of Raqqa (then Ar-Rafika) reached its apex as the Abbasid caliph, Harun ar-Rashid, made it his summer residence.

Practically nothing of the city's old glory has been preserved, but the partly restored **Baghdad Gate**, about a 10 minute walk to the east of the clock tower, is a central landmark when you arrive in the city. The old Abbasid city **wall**, restored at some points to a height of five metres, runs north from the gate past the **Qasr al-Binaat** (Daughters'

Palace), which served as a residence under the Ayyubids.

A small **museum**, located roughly halfway between the Baghdad Gate and the clock tower, has some interesting artefacts from excavation sites in the area. It is open daily except Tuesday from 9 am to 6 pm (4 pm in winter), and entry costs S£100.

Places to Stay & Eat
There are a few hotels around the clock tower, all of them amazingly expensive. The best of a bad lot is the *Ammar Hotel* (☎ 222612), which charges S£350/500 for singles/doubles. The *Al-Rasheed Restaurant* on King Faisal St is about the best restaurant Raqqa has to offer, and in warmer weather is ideal with its garden dining area.

Getting There & Away
Bus The area around Ath-Thaura St is swarming with bus companies. Fares vary depending on the quality of the bus. A trip to Damascus can cost up to S£225. The fare to Aleppo on a good bus is S£85 and you could even go direct to Beirut for S£325.

Microbus From the microbus station, about 200m south of the clock tower (on the road leading out of town), there are regular microbuses west to Al-Mansura (S£11.50), Ath-Thaura (S£23) and Aleppo (three hours; S£75).

Train There are two trains a day to Aleppo (S£55/37 in 1st/2nd class) and Deir ez-Zur (S£38/27), and one to Damascus via Aleppo, Hama and Homs.

RASAFEH
This startling walled city lies in the middle of nowhere, and seems to rise up out of the featureless desert as you approach it. Fortified by the Romans, the Byzantine emperor Justinian gave it much of its present look, a religious basilica complex devoted to St Sergius and a military outpost. The Umayyads later built a palace here which was subsequently destroyed by the Abbasids.

Getting There & Away

Catch a microbus from Raqqa to Al-Mansura (20 minutes; S£5) – that's the easy bit. Now it's just a matter of waiting at the signposted turn-off for a pick-up to take you the 35 km to the ruins for about S£20 – or hitching.

HALABIYYEH & ZALABIYYEH

The fortress town of Halabiyyeh was founded by Zenobia and later re-fortified under emperor Justinian. The walls are largely intact, and there are remnants of the citadel, basilicas, baths, a forum and the north and south gates.

Across the river and further south is the much less intact forward stronghold of the main fort, Zalabiyyeh.

Getting There & Away

Neither Halabiyyeh nor Zalabiyyeh are easy to get to. Get a Raqqa bus from Deir ez-Zur and get out at the Halabiyyeh turn-off a few km after the town of Tibni (one hour; S£10). From here you'll have to hitch or, if you feel up to it, do the two hour walk. For Zalabiyyeh, ask at the Deir ez-Zur bus station for the right minibus. You'll be let off on the highway and have to walk a short way.

DEIR EZ-ZUR

This is a pleasant town on the Euphrates and a crossroads for travellers visiting the north-east of Syria. It has prospered recently with oil discoveries in the surrounding areas.

There's not much to see, apart from a poor museum, but a stroll along the riverbank is a popular activity. On the other side of the suspension bridge is a small recreation ground where you can swim with the locals, though this is probably not advisable for women travellers.

For visa extensions, go 500m from the Commercial Bank of Syria, turn left at the roundabout and left again. The big Immigration and passports building is just on the corner. It is open from 8 am to 1.30 pm.

Places to Stay

The very basic *Hotel Damas* (☎ 221481) is probably the best budget bet. It's on the corner of 8 March St. A bed in a shared room costs S£150, including hot shower, and singles/doubles cost S£200/325.

East of the square, along Khalid bin al-Walid St, are several pretty crummy places, including the *Ghassan*, *Semiramis* and the *Hotel al-Arabi al-Kabir*.

For something better try the *Hotel Raghdan* (☎ 222053), which has acceptable if overpriced rooms for US$16/26, or the newer *Hotel Mari* (☎ 224340; fax 221657), which has rooms at US$24/39.

Places to Eat

Around the hotels on the main street you'll find the same roast chickens, kebabs, houmos and salad that you get everywhere.

Restaurant Cairo, across the road from the canal and west of the Hotel Damas, has reasonable food as well as alcohol. Better are the couple of outdoor restaurants right on the riverbank.

Getting There & Away

Air The airport is about seven km east of town and the weekly flight between Deir ez-Zur and Damascus costs S£600.

Bus/Microbus The local bus station is a couple of km south of town. Old buses leave regularly for Damascus (S£125) via Palmyra, Aleppo (S£70), Homs (S£75), Hassake in the north-east (S£75) and on to Qamishle on the Turkish border (S£125). There's an hourly microbus to Raqqa (two hours; S£60) and plenty of microbuses south to Abu Kamal (S£50). The minibus to Abu Kamal costs only S£30, but it is agonisingly slow.

Several private companies operate big comfortable buses to most main destinations from Salah ad-Din al-Ayoubi St. The companies include Qadmous, Raja and Al-Furat, and although timetables vary considerably, prices tend to be similar. Qadmous is about the best, with services to Damascus costing S£175 and to Aleppo S£135.

Train The railway station is across the river to the north of town, about three km from the centre. There are trains to Aleppo (S£87/58 in 1st/2nd class), Damascus (S£153/103), Hassake and Qamishle (S£60/40).

SOUTH OF DEIR EZ-ZUR
The route south-east of Deir ez-Zur follows the Euphrates down to the closed Iraqi border. It is dotted with sites of archaeological and historical interest.

Qala'at ar-Rahba
The 13th century defensive citadel, which was finally abandoned after the battles between Mongols and Mamluks, is a few km south of the town of Al-Mayadin.

Like many castles it is more impressive from the outside than from within, but the views of the desert to the west, and the Euphrates and occasional oil field to the east, are breathtaking.

Tell Ashara
Just 17 km south of Mayadin is the sleepy village of Tell Ashara. Three sites that date back to the early centuries AD are being excavated, but there is little of real interest here. An old mud-brick mosque, with a fragile eight storey minaret, is the main item.

Dura Europos
For the uninitiated, the extensive, largely Hellenistic/Roman fortress city of Dura Europos is by far the most intriguing site to visit on the road from Deir ez-Zur to Abu Kamal. The riverside walls overlook the left bank of the Euphrates, 90m below. It is renowned for its apparent religious tolerance, seemingly confirmed by the presence of a church, synagogue and other Greek, Roman and Mesopotamian temples side by side.

Mari
The ruins of Mari (Tell Hariri), an important Mesopotamian city dating back some 5000 years, are about 10 km north of Abu Kamal. Although fascinating for their age, the mud-brick ruins do not grab the imagination as much as you might hope.

The **Royal Palace of Zimrilim** was enormous, measuring 200 by 120m with over 300 rooms. The palace is the main point of interest; it is now sheltered from the elements by a modern protective roof.

Getting There & Away Local microbuses run alongside the river from Deir ez-Zur to Abu Kamal (three hours; S£50).

The North-East

Bordered by Turkey and Iraq, there are no major monuments or sights in the north-eastern corner of the country, but this does not mean it is empty of attractions. Perhaps the greatest is the chance to meet the Kurds, a people without a country, who have yet to give up their struggle. Only about one million of a total of around 20 million Kurds live in Syria.

The numerous tells (artificial hills) dotted around the place are a sign that the area has been inhabited since the 3rd millennium BC.

HASSAKE
The capital of the governorate of the same name, Hassake doesn't offer the visitor an awful lot to do, but it's not a bad base from which to explore the area, unless you're planning on entering Turkey here, in which case you may as well push on to Qamishle.

Places to Stay & Eat
There are two basic hotels near the clock tower. The *Heliopolis* has simple singles/doubles for S£175/275, and these are better value than those at the *Hotel Ramsis*, for the same price.

There are a few places to eat around the centre, mostly run by Iraqi Christians from the nearby refugee camp at Al-Hol. The *Karnak Restaurant*, in Hafez al-Assad St, offers copious quantities of the usual stuff for around S£200 per person, and they have a garden too.

Getting There & Away
Hassake is serviced by a variety of buses and

microbuses, and there are trains to Qamishle, Damascus, Deir ez-Zur and Aleppo.

QAMISHLE

Situated right at a crossing point on the Turkish border in the north-east, Qamishle is full of Kurds and Turks and the cheaper hotels will sometimes quote prices in Turkish lira rather than Syrian pounds.

There is nothing to see in Qamishle, but the mix of people makes the place interesting. Because of its proximity to the border, you can expect passport checks at the hotels (even during the night), and when getting on or off buses or trains.

Places to Stay & Eat

The cheapest and lousiest is the *Omayad Hotel*, in a side street across from the Hotel Semiramis. A bed here costs S£100. Just around the corner is the *Chahba Hotel*, which is nothing to write home about and asks S£100 a bed (women must take a double). The upstairs terrace is OK.

The *Mamar*, a block south, is better value, although a tad more expensive. Singles/ doubles cost S£300/400. The rooms with balconies are quite good and they have hot water.

Opposite the Chahba is a pleasant restaurant with an outdoor section. A good meal of kebabs and the usual side orders will cost about S£200.

Getting There & Away

The Turkish border is only about one km from the centre of Qamishle – a 15 minute walk.

There are three flights a week to Damascus (S£900).

Several private companies operate buses to Damascus (10 hours; S£340) and Aleppo (five hours; S£175). More rickety buses do the trips for half the price.

There are three daily trains that go as far as Aleppo, and one or two of them go all the way to Damascus (S£740 for a sleeper, S£198/132 in 1st/2nd class).

Turkey

Turkey is the bridge between Europe and the Middle East, both physically and culturally. The Ottoman sultans ruled the entire Middle East for centuries, and traces of Turkish influence remain in all of the countries once controlled from İstanbul.

Turkey was the first formerly Ottoman Muslim land to establish a republic and to achieve real democracy, as well as the first to look westward, to Europe and North America, for cultural models. A tourism boom during the 1980s brought even more European influence, from rock music to topless beaches. It may be the least exotic country you encounter in this region, but it is no imitation Europe. With more ancient cities than any other country in the region, 4000 km of warm-water coastline, varied countryside and excellent food, Turkey has lots to offer. The Turks are mostly quite friendly, especially when you escape the coastal resorts and head into the heartland.

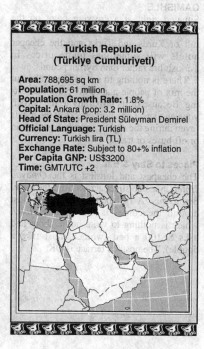

**Turkish Republic
(Türkiye Cumhuriyeti)**

Area: 788,695 sq km
Population: 61 million
Population Growth Rate: 1.8%
Capital: Ankara (pop: 3.2 million)
Head of State: President Süleyman Demirel
Official Language: Turkish
Currency: Turkish lira (TL)
Exchange Rate: Subject to 80+% inflation
Per Capita GNP: US$3200
Time: GMT/UTC +2

Facts about the Country

HISTORY

Traces of early Turkish civilisation date from the 6th millennium BC in Central Asia, but the earliest known in Anatolia (Asian Turkey) is that of the Hittites. Long believed to be a purely mythical people, they were in fact a force to be reckoned with from 2000 to 1200 BC.

After the collapse of the Hittites, Anatolia broke up into small states, and it was not until the Graeco-Roman period that parts of the country were reunited. Later, Christianity spread through Anatolia, carried by the apostle Paul, a native of Tarsus (near Adana).

The Roman emperor Constantine founded a new imperial city at Byzantium (modern İstanbul) in 330 AD. Renamed Constantinople, this strategic city became the capital of the Eastern Roman Empire and was the

centre of the Byzantine Empire for 1000 years. During the European Dark Ages, when the glories of Greece were just a memory and Rome was overrun by barbarians, the Byzantine Empire kept alive the flame of western culture. Through the centuries it was threatened by the powerful empires of both east (Persians, Arabs, Turks) and west (the Christian powers of Europe).

The beginning of the Byzantine Empire's decline came with the arrival of the Seljuk Turks, who had previously conquered Persia, and who were beginning to encroach into Byzantine territory. The threat posed by the Seljuks precipitated the election of a new Byzantine emperor, Romanus IV Diogenes.

Romanus assembled an army to battle the

Seljuks, but in August 1071 he was defeated at Manzikert, near Lake Van (Van Gölü), and taken prisoner. The Seljuks took over most of Anatolia, and established a provincial capital at Nicaea (İznik). Their domains included today's Turkey, Iran and Iraq.

With significantly reduced territory, the Byzantines, under their new emperor, Alexius I Comnenus, endeavoured to protect Constantinople and reclaim Anatolia.

The Crusades

In 1095, Pope Urban II called for crusaders to fight in a Holy War. To reach the Holy Land, it was necessary for the First Crusade to pass through Constantinople. In return for this right of passage, Alexius Comnenus struck a deal with the crusade leaders, demanding that any territories won from the Turks by the Crusaders be returned to the Byzantines. Although the Crusaders failed to cooperate totally with the terms of the pact, in 1097 the Byzantines were able to win back the city of Nicaea from the Seljuks and to reoccupy western Anatolia. The Seljuks maintained their power in the rest of Anatolia.

The Fourth Crusade (1202-04) proved less fruitful for the Byzantines, with a combined Venetian and Crusade force taking and plundering the city of Constantinople. The ravaged city was eventually regained by the Byzantines in 1261.

Ottoman Empire

A Mongol invasion of the late 1200s put an end to Seljuk power, but new small Turkish states were born soon after in western Anatolia. One of these, headed by Osman Gazi (1281-1326), became the Ottoman Empire, and in 1453 (just under 40 years before Columbus left for America), Constantinople fell to the Ottoman sultan Mehmet II (the Conqueror).

A century later, under Süleyman the Magnificent, the Ottoman Empire reached the peak of its cultural brilliance and its power spread deep into Europe, Asia and North Africa. The Janissaries, the first modern standing army, gave the Turks an advantage,

as the European nations had to raise new armies for each war. The Turks also tolerated minority groups, including Christians and Jews.

Ottoman success was based on military expansion, not industry or agriculture. When its march westwards was stalled at Vienna in 1683 the rot started, and by the 19th century Turkey had become the 'sick man of Europe'. A succession of incompetent sultans hardly helped, especially when combined with discontent among the by now totally unreliable Janissaries. The great European powers began to covet the sultan's vast domains.

The nationalist ideal swept through Europe after the French Revolution, and Turkey found itself with unruly subject populations. In 1829 the Greeks won their independence, followed by the Serbs, the Romanians and the Bulgarians in 1878. Mohammed Ali took control of Egypt in 1805, and went to war against the sultan in 1832 and 1839, effectively cutting Egypt off from control by İstanbul. Tunisia was put under a French protectorate in 1881. Italy took Tripolitania (now Libya) from Turkey in 1911, and Albania and Macedonia escaped after the 1912-13 Balkan War. Finally, the unfortunate Turks emerged from WWI stripped of their final non-Turkish provinces – Syria, Palestine, Mesopotamia (Iraq) and Arabia. Anatolia (most of Turkey) was to be parcelled out to the victorious Greeks, Italians, French and Russians, leaving the Turks virtually nothing.

Atatürk

At this low point of Turkish history, Mustafa Kemal, the father of modern Turkey, took over. Atatürk, as he was later called, had made his name by repelling the Anzacs (the Australian and New Zealand forces) in their heroic but futile attempt to capture Gallipoli. Rallying the tattered remnants of the army, he pushed the final weak Ottoman rulers aside and out-manoeuvred the Allied forces in the War of Independence, a desperate affair.

Final victory for the Turks came in 1923

Suggested Itineraries

İstanbul, the Aegean and Mediterranean coasts, and Cappadocia are the areas most people come to see. The Black Sea coast can be travelled in a day or a week, as you wish. Eastern Turkey is for the more adventurous. If your time is limited, consider the following itineraries:

Two days
Explore İstanbul or Selçuk/Ephesus.
One week
See İstanbul and the Aegean coast to Bodrum or Marmaris, with a quick trip to Pamukkale.
Two weeks
Travel from İstanbul south and east along the coasts to Antalya or Alanya, then return via Cappadocia.
Three weeks or more
Consider the following itinerary: İstanbul-İznik-Bursa-Aegean coast-Mediterranean coast to Silifke-Konya-Cappadocia-Ankara-İstanbul.

Eastern Turkey

A route covering north-eastern Turkey, Kars, Erzurum, Doğubeyazıt, Van, Diyarbakır, Şanlıurfa, Nemrut Dağı, ending in Antakya or Cappadocia, can be done in about two weeks, but 2½ or three is better.

Highlights

In **Istanbul**, don't miss Topkapı Palace, Aya Sofya (Hagia Sofia), the Blue Mosque or the Kariye Museum. The battlefields of **Gallipoli**, on the Dardanelles, are particularly moving. Many visitors find **Troy** disappointing, but not so **Ephesus**, the best-preserved classical city on the Mediterranean.

Seljuk Turkish architecture, earlier than Ottoman, is particularly fine. **Alanya**, **Konya**, **Sivas** and **Erzurum** have good Seljuk buildings.

Turkey's beaches are best at **Pamucak** (near Ephesus) on the Aegean, and **Ölüdeniz**, **Bodrum**, **Patara**, **Antalya**, **Side** and **Alanya** on the Mediterranean. The improbable 'lunar' landscapes of **Cappadocia** are perhaps the single most visually impressive feature in all of Turkey. Further east, the great Commagenian stone heads on the mountain peak of **Nemrut Dağı** certainly repay an early start to the day. ∎

at Smyrna – a city with a large Greek population on Turkey's Aegean coast, today known as İzmir – where invading Greek armies were literally pushed into the sea. A Turkish republic was born, based in Anatolia and eastern Thrace. The treaties of WWI, which had left the Turks with almost no country, were renegotiated.

With Turkey reduced to smaller but secure boundaries, Atatürk embarked on a rapid modernisation programme, the essence of which was the establishment of secular democracy, the de-emphasis of religion, the introduction of Latin script and European dress, and equal rights for women. In 1923 the country's capital was moved from 'decadent' İstanbul to Ankara, which was laid out anew to a modern plan. Naturally, such sweeping changes did not come easily, but Turkey has done remarkably well and is now far ahead of most of its neighbours in these areas.

ATATÜRK

It won't take you long to discover the national hero, Kemal Atatürk. Though he died on 10 November 1938, his picture is everywhere in Turkey, a bust or statue (usually equestrian) is in every park, and quotations from his speeches and writings are on every public building. He is almost synonymous with the Turkish Republic.

The best popular account of his life and times is Lord Kinross' *Atatürk: The Rebirth of a Nation*. Kinross portrayed Atatürk as a man of great intelligence and even greater energy and daring, possessed by the idea of giving his fellow Turks a new lease of life. Like all too few leaders, he had the capability of realising his obsession almost single-handedly. His achievement in turning a backward empire into a forward-looking nation-state was taken as a model by President Nasser of Egypt, the shahs of Iran and other Islamic leaders.

Early Years

In 1881, a boy named Mustafa was born into the family of a minor Turkish bureaucrat living in Salonika – now the Greek city of Thessaloniki, but at that time a city in Ottoman Macedonia. Mustafa was smart, and a hard worker at school. His mathematics teacher was so impressed that he gave him the nickname Kemal (excellence). The name Mustafa Kemal stuck with him as he went through a military academy and the war college, and even as he pursued his duties as an officer.

Military Career

He served with distinction, and acquired a reputation as something of a hothead, perhaps because his commanders were not as bold as he was. By the time of the battle at Gallipoli in WWI, he was a promising lieutenant colonel of infantry.

The defence of Gallipoli, which saved Constantinople from British conquest (until the end of the war, at least), was a personal triumph for Mustafa Kemal. His strategic and tactical genius came into full play. His commanders had little to do but approve his suggestions; he led with utter disregard for his own safety. A vastly superior British force (including Anzacs from Australia and New Zealand) was driven away, and Mustafa Kemal became an Ottoman folk hero.

Though he was promoted to the rank of *paşa* ('pasha', meaning general), the powers-that-be wanted to keep him under control. They saw him as a 'dangerous element', and they were right. When the war was lost and the empire was on the verge of being disarmed and dismembered, Mustafa Kemal Pasha began his revolution.

The Revolution

He held meetings and congresses to rally the people, began to establish democratic institutions and held off several invading armies (French, Italian and Greek). He did all of this at the same time with severely limited resources. Several times the whole effort almost collapsed, and many of his friends and advisers were ready to ride for their lives out of Ankara. But Kemal never flinched, and was always ready to dare the worst.

He was skilful – and fortunate – enough to carry through. Many great revolutionary leaders falter or fade when the revolution is won. Atatürk lived 15 years into the republican era, and he had no doubts about what the new country's course should be. He introduced reforms and directed the country's progress with surprising foresight. ■

Modern Turkey

The oil crisis of the 1970s, the Gulf War and continuing problems with separatist Kurds in the east have wreaked havoc on the Turkish economy, forcing the government to introduce unpopular austerity measures.

Still poor by western standards, Turkey is developing rapidly. In 1995 it entered into a customs-union agreement with the European Union (EU), and hopes eventually for full membership in the EU.

Although resurgent Islam has recently gained some influence in the country, and Islamic Welfare Party (Refah) candidates won mayoral elections in İstanbul and Ankara in 1994, Atatürk remains very much the symbol of modern Turkey, and secularism – not Islamic law – is the preference of the great majority of Turks. The collapse of the old Soviet Union has brought Turkey unparalleled opportunities for trade with Eastern Europe and the newly emerging Turkic republics of former Soviet Central Asia, but chronic political crises are delaying the exploitation of those opportunities.

GEOGRAPHY

Turkey is divided into Asian and European parts by the Dardanelles, the Sea of Marmara and the Bosphorus strait. Eastern Thrace (European Turkey) comprises only 3% of the total 788,695 sq km land area. The remaining 97% is Anatolia, a vast plateau rising eastward towards the Caucasus Mountains. Turkey's coastline is over 6000 km long and has grown into a popular resort area.

CLIMATE

The Aegean and Mediterranean coasts have mild, rainy winters and hot, dry summers. In İstanbul, summer temperatures average around 28°C to 30°C; the winters are chilly but usually above freezing, with rain and perhaps a dusting of snow. The Anatolian plateau is cooler in summer and quite cold in winter. The Black Sea coast is mild and rainy in summer, chilly and rainy in winter.

Mountainous eastern Turkey is very cold and snowy in winter, and only pleasantly warm in high summer. The south-east is dry and mild in winter and very hot in summer, with temperatures above 45°C not unusual. In general, spring (April/May) and autumn (September/October) have the most pleasant weather.

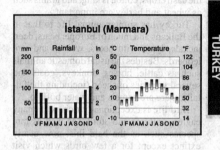

ECOLOGY & ENVIRONMENT

There is an environmental movement in Turkey, and it is making some progress. Some cities attempt to recycle glass and metal, and Bosphorus restaurants now seem to refrain from disposing of food waste right into the water. Sewage treatment plants are being built, but as these projects are expensive and Turkey is hardly a rich country, it will take time. At least vessels – including yachts – in Turkish waters are prohibited by law from emptying waste into the seas, though it still happens because of insufficient enforcement. See also the Ecology & Environment section in the Regional Facts about the Region chapter.

FLORA & FAUNA

Once cloaked in dense forest, after millennia of woodcutting Anatolia is now largely denuded. The government encourages conservation and reforestation, but the great forests will never return. The Mediterranean coast west of Antalya, the Black Sea area and north-eastern Anatolia still have forests of considerable size. Elsewhere, the great swaths of wild flowers which cover the rolling steppes in spring make fine splashes of colour.

Because of Turkey's temperate climate, domesticated plants such as apples, apricots, bananas, cherries, citrus fruit, cotton, date palms, grapes, sugar beet, sunflowers and tobacco thrive. Turkey grows much of the world's supply of hazelnuts (*filberts*), and a large volume of pistachios and walnuts. Of the cash crops, cotton is king, and grains such as wheat and barley are important.

Turkey has similar animal life to that in the Balkans and much of Europe: bears, deer, jackals, lynx, wild boars, wolves and rare leopards. Besides the usual domestic animals such as cattle, horses, donkeys, goats and several varieties of sheep (including the fat-tail), there are camels and water buffalo.

Bird life is exceptionally rich, with many eagles, vultures and storks, as well as rare species such as the bald ibis, now nearly extinct except for a few birds which visit Birecik, between Gaziantep and Şanlıurfa, each year. In several parts of the country reserves have been set aside as *kuş cenneti* (bird paradises).

Turkey's coastal waters have rich varieties of fish, shellfish and other sea creatures, though overfishing and pollution are now serious problems.

GOVERNMENT & POLITICS

Turkey is a multiparty parliamentary democracy. Several times in the last 40 years, the army has stepped in to 'correct' what it saw as an undemocratic drift away from the principles set forth by Atatürk. During the 1970s, in shock from the oil crisis, the country became politically unstable and wracked by terrorism from both the left and the right. To nobody's surprise (and to many people's relief), the army ousted the ineffectual civilian government in 1980, restored order and rewrote the constitution.

By 1983, its popularity gone, the military government held elections and, again to no-one's surprise, lost power to the new centre-right Anavatan (Motherland) party headed by economist Turgut Özal. Motherland held a parliamentary majority through the 1980s, with Özal first as prime minister (1983-89) and then elected as president for a seven year term.

In 1993 Özal died and seven time former prime minister Süleyman Demirel became president, with former economics minister Professor Tansu Çiller as Turkey's first female prime minister under the banner of the centre-right True Path (Doğru Yol) party. Mesut Yılmaz, Çiller's bitter political rival, rose to head the Anavatan party, now out of power.

The elections of 24 December 1995 were a wake-up call against politics as usual: the far-right pro-Islamic Welfare (Refah) party won a plurality of 23%, which was seen as a protest vote against the two big centre-right parties. But no other major party would join Refah in a coalition, so the same two center-right parties – Motherland and True Path – formed a shaky coalition in March 1996 with Mesut Yılmaz as prime minister, to alternate with Çiller according to a predetermined schedule. Recrimination and in-fighting began immediately, however, and the coalition's weakness and unseemly cat-fights only exacerbated the country's political and economic problems and worked to further strengthen the Welfare party.

ECONOMY

Turkey is strong in agriculture, being a net exporter of food. Wheat, cotton, sugar beets, sunflowers, hazelnuts, tobacco, fruits and vegetables are abundant. Sheep are the main livestock, and Turkey is the biggest wool producer in Europe. However, manufacturing and services now dominate the economy. Turkey builds motor vehicles, makes appliances and consumer goods and handles large engineering projects, and exports them throughout the region. There is still a large Turkish workforce in the industries of Europe, particularly in Germany.

POPULATION & PEOPLE

Turkey's nearly 61 million people are predominantly Muslim Turks, with a significant minority (perhaps eight million) of Muslim Kurds and small groups of Jews, Greeks, Armenians, Laz (a Black Sea people) and Arabs. Its five biggest cities are İstanbul (10 million people), Ankara (3.2 million), İzmir

(2.7 million), Adana (1.9 million) and Bursa (1.6 million).

EDUCATION
The Turkish Republic provides five years of compulsory primary (*İlkokul*) and middle-school (*Ortaokul*) education for all children aged from seven to 12 years. Secondary, *lise* (high school, *lycée*), and vocational or technical education is available at no cost to those who decide to continue. Specialised schools are available for the blind, the deaf, the mentally retarded, orphans and the very poor. There are also numerous licensed private schools, *kolej* (colleges, like high schools) and universities which charge tuition fees.

Turkey has 29 government-funded universities to which students are admitted through a central placement system. At Ankara's Middle East Technical University and Bilkent University, and at İstanbul's Boğuaziçi (Bosphorus) University, English is the language of instruction.

ARTS
Ottoman literature and court music were mostly religious, and both sound pompous and lugubrious to western ears. Folk music was (and still is) sprightly; troubadours were highly skilled and very popular, although TV and cassettes have wiped them out.

As with all else, Atatürk changed Turkey's cultural picture overnight, encouraging painting, sculpture, western music (he loved opera), dance and drama. Recently, Ottoman arts such as paper marbling and the Karagöz shadow-puppet plays are enjoying a resurgence, and are seen as valuable traditions worthy of preservation. Carpet-weaving is, was, and always will be a Turkish passion.

SOCIETY & CONDUCT
Ottoman Turkey was ruled by the *shari'a* (Islamic religious law), but republican Turkey – thanks to Atatürk – has largely adapted to a modern westernised lifestyle. Many Turks drink alcohol (though alcoholism is not yet a big problem), don't mind if others drink, and otherwise wink at Islamic law. But they still revere the moral and spir-

itual teachings of their religion, and observe its customs, if sometimes loosely.

Liberal western attitudes born of Atatürk's reforms are strongest in the urban centres of the west and along the coasts, and among the middle and upper classes. You will feel quite comfortable among these Turks, who look to western culture as the ideal, and accept the validity of other religious beliefs.

The working and farming classes, particularly in the east, are more conservative, traditional and religious. There is a small but growing segment of 'born again' Muslims (witness the Refah party's electoral victory), fervent and strict in their religion but otherwise modern. Though always polite, these Turks may give you the feeling that east is east and west is west, and that the last echo of 'Crusaders versus Saracens' has not yet died away.

Dos & Don'ts
When you visit mosques, dress conservatively (no 'revealing' clothing like shorts or sleeveless shirts), remove your shoes, don't take flash photographs and be respectful. Women should cover their head and shoulders.

RELIGION
Turkey is 99% Muslim, predominantly Sunni, with Shiites and Alawites in the east and south-east.

Religious minorities live freely. The small Jewish community is descended from those who fled the Spanish Inquisition in 1492 and found tolerance in the Ottoman Empire. The Ecumenical Orthodox Patriarch is based in İstanbul, but the Orthodox minority dwindled after the Cyprus crisis of the 1970s.

LANGUAGE
Ottoman Turkish was written in Arabic script, but Atatürk decreed a change to Latin script in 1928. In big cities and tourist areas, many locals know at least some English and/or German. In the south-east, Arabic or Kurdish is the first language in some towns.

For a comprehensive list of useful Turkish words and phrases, get a copy of Lonely Planet's *Turkish phrasebook*.

Pronunciation

The new Turkish alphabet is phonetic, and thus reasonably easy to pronounce, once you've learned a few important differences. Each Turkish letter is pronounced; there are no diphthongs, and the only silent letter is 'ğ'.

Vowels Turkish vowels are pronounced as follows:

A, a	as in 'shah'
E,e	as in 'fell'
İ,i	as in 'ee'
I, ı	as in 'uh'
O, o	as in 'hot'
U, u	as the 'oo' in 'moo'
Ö, ö	as the 'ur' in 'fur'
Ü, ü	as the 'ew' in 'few'

Note: ö and ü are pronounced with pursed lips.

Consonants Most consonants are pronounced as in English, but there are a few exceptions:

Ç ç	as the 'ch' in 'church'
C c	just like the English 'j'
Ğ ğ	isn't pronounced but just draws out the preceding vowel a bit; don't pronounce it, ignore it!
G g	hard, as in 'gun'
H h	as the 'h' in 'half'
J j	like 's' in 'measure'
S s	hard, as in 'stress'
Ş ş	as the 'sh' in 'shoe'
V v	as the 'w' in 'weather'

Basics

Hello.	Merhaba.
Goodbye/ Bon Voyage.	Allahaısmarladık/ Güle güle.
Yes.	Evet.
No.	Hayır.
Please.	Lütfen.
Thank you	Teşekkür ederim.
That's fine/ You're welcome.	Bir şey değil.
Excuse me.	Affedersiniz.

Sorry. (Excuse me/ Forgive me.)	Pardon.
How much is it?	Ne kadar?

Language Difficulties

Do you speak English?	İngilizce biliyor musunuz?
Does anyone speak English?	Kimse İngilizce biliyor mu?
I don't understand.	Anlamiyorum.
Just a minute.	Bir dakika.
Please write that down.	Lütfen yazın.

Signs

Camping ground	Kamping
Entrance	Giriş
Exit	Çıkış
Full	Dolu
Guesthouse	Pansiyon
Hotel	Otel(i)
Information	Danışma
Open/closed	Açık/kapalı
Police	Polis/emniyet
Police station	Polis karakolu/ Emniyet Müdürlüğü
Prohibited	Yasak(tır)
Rooms available	Boş oda var
Toilet	Tuvalet
Railway station	Gar/ıstasyon
Student hostel	Öğrenci yurdu

Getting Around

Where is the bus/ tram stop?	Otobüs/tramvay durağı nerede?
I want to go to ...	...'e gitmek istiyorum.
Can you show me on the map?	Haritada gösterebilir misiniz?
far/near	uzak/yakın
Go straight ahead.	Doğru gidin.
Turn left.	Sola dönün.
Turn right.	Sağa dönün.
What time does the ... leave/arrive?	... ne zaman kalkar/gelir?
next	gelecek
first	birinci/ilk
last	son

ferry/boat	*feribot/vapur*
city bus	*şehir otobüsü*
intercity bus	*otobüs*
train	*tren*
tram	*tramvay*

I would like...	*...istiyorum*
a one-way ticket	*gidiş bileti*
a return ticket	*gidiş-dönüş bileti*
1st class	*birinci sınıf*
2nd class	*ikinci sınıf*

Accommodation

Where is a cheap hotel?	*Ucuz bir otel nerede?*
What is the address?	*Adres ne?*
Could you write the address, please?	*Adresi yazar mısınız?*
Do you have any rooms available?	*Boş oda var mı?*

I would like ...	*... istiyorum.*
a single room	*Tek kişilik oda*
a double room	*İki kişilik oda*
a room with a bathroom	*banyolu oda*
to share a dorm	*yatakhanede bir yatak*
a bed	*bir yatak*

How much is it...	*kaçpara?*
for one night	*Bir gecelik...*
per person	*kiğibağına...*
Can I see it?	*Görebilir miyim?*
Where is the bathroom?	*Banyo nerede?*

Around Town

I'm looking for the/a ...	*... arıyorum*
bank	*bir banka*
city centre	*şehir merkezi*
... embassy	*... büyükelçiliğini*
hotel	*otelimi*
market	*çarşıyı*
police	*polis*
post office	*postane*
public toilet	*tuvalet*
telephone centre	*telefon merkezi*

tourist information office	*turizm danışma bürosu*
beach	*plaj*
bridge	*köprü*
castle	*kale/hisar*
church	*kilise*
hospital	*hastane*
island	*ada*
lake	*göl*
mosque	*cami(i)*
old city	*tarihi şehir merkezi*
palace	*saray*
ruins	*harabeler/kalıntılar*
sea	*deniz*
square	*meydan*
tower	*kule*

Food

breakfast	*kahvaltı*
lunch	*öğleyemeği*
dinner	*akşamyemeği*

I'd like the set lunch, please.	*Fiks menü istiyorum, lütfen.*
Is service included in the bill?	*Servis ücreti dahil mi?*
I don't eat any meat.	*Hiç et yemiyorum.*

Health

I'm diabetic/epileptic/ asthmatic.	*Şeker hastasıyım/ sar'alıyım/astımlıyım.*
I'm allergic to anti-biotics/penicillin.	*Antibiyotiklere/peni-siline alerjim var.*

antiseptic	*antiseptik*
aspirin	*aspirin*
condom	*prezervatif*
contraceptive	*gebeliği önleyici*
diarrhoea	*ishal/diyare*
medicine	*ilaç*
nausea	*bulantı*
sunblock cream	*güneş blok kremi*
tampon	*tampon*

Time

What time is it?	*Saat kaç?*
today	*bugün*
tomorrow	*yarın*
in the morning	*sabahleyin*
in the afternoon	*öğleden sonra*

TURKEY

TURKEY

in the evening	akşamda

Days of the Week

Monday	Pazartesi
Tuesday	Salı
Wednesday	Çarşamba
Thursday	Perşembe
Friday	Cuma
Saturday	Cumartesi
Sunday	Pazar

Months

January	Ocak
February	Şubat
March	Mart
April	Nisan
May	Mayıs
June	Haziran
July	Temmuz
August	Ağustos
September	Eylül
October	Ekim
November	Kasım
December	Aralık

Numbers

0	sıfır
1	bir
2	iki
3	üç
4	dört
5	beş
6	altı
7	yedi
8	sekiz
9	dokuz
10	on
11	on bir
12	on iki
13	on üç
14	on dört
15	on beş
16	on altı
17	on yedi
18	on sekiz
19	on dokuz
20	yirmi
21	yirmi bir
22	yirmi iki
30	otuz

40	kırk
50	elli
60	altmış
70	yetmiş
80	seksen
90	doksan
100	yüz
200	iki yüz
1000	bin
2000	iki bin
one million	bir milyon

Emergencies

Help!/Emergency!	İmdat!
Call a doctor!	Doktor çağırın!
Call the police!	Polis çağırın!
Go away!	Git!/Defol!

Facts for the Visitor

PLANNING

When to Go

Spring (late April to May) and autumn (late September to October) are the best times to visit. The weather is fine and usually not too rainy, and the crowds have yet to appear. In high season (July to mid-September) the weather can be quite hot, and major tourist destinations are crowded and high-priced. Though winter weather is rainy and cold, with high air pollution, accommodation prices are low, and there are no crowds. See Climate earlier in this chapter for more information.

Maps

The Bartholomew Euromap of Turkey, in two sheets at 1:800,000, is excellent. The forthcoming Lonely Planet *Turkey travel atlas* will cover the country in an easy-to-carry format. Inspect locally produced maps carefully before you buy to assess their probable usefulness.

What to Bring

You'll find the following items useful in Turkey: mosquito repellent (from April to September); sunblock cream (it's expensive in Turkey); a universal sink plug; a towel; and reading matter. Women should bring their favoured sanitary protection.

TOURIST OFFICES
Local Tourist Offices
Ministry of Tourism (Turizm Bakanlığı) offices are in every tourist-oriented town. There may be provincial or local offices as well. The enthusiasm and helpfulness of the staff vary widely, but most offer regional brochures and local maps of minimal usefulness; the big town maps, however, are excellent. Ask for the *Youth Travel Guide Book* which has lots of advice for budget travellers.

Tourist Offices Abroad
There are Turkish tourist offices in most Western European countries and the USA, including:

UK
> 170-173 Piccadilly, 1st floor, London WV1 9DD (☎ (0171) 734 8681; fax 491 0773)

USA
> 821 UN Plaza, New York, NY 10017 (☎ (212) 687 2194; fax 599 7568)

VISAS & DOCUMENTS
Have a passport valid for at least three months beyond your date of entry. Nationals of many western European countries don't need visas for visits of up to three months. UK subjects pay UK£10, and US citizens US$20, for a visa on arrival.

EMBASSIES
Turkish Embassies Abroad
Australia
> 66 Ocean St, PO Box 222, Wollahra, NSW 2025 (☎ (02) 9328 1155)

Bulgaria
> Blvd Vasil Levski No 80, 1000 Sofia (☎ (359) 872306)

Canada
> 197 Wurtemburg St, Ottawa, Ontario KIN 8LD (☎ (613) 789 4044)

Greece
> Vassileos Gheorghiou B 8, 10674 Athens (☎ (01) 724 5915)

UK
> 43 Belgrave Square, London SW1X 8PA (☎ (0171) 235 5252)

USA
> 1714 Massachusetts Ave, NW Washington, DC 20036 (☎ (202) 659 8200)

Foreign Embassies & Consulates in Turkey
Embassies are in Ankara; many nations have consulates in İstanbul and some also in İzmir, Antalya or other ports or tourist centres.

Australia *(Avustralya)*
> Embassy: Nene Hatun Caddesi 83, Gaziosmanpaşa, Ankara (☎ (312) 436 1240; fax 445 0284)
> Consulate: Tepecik Yolu 58, 80630 Etiler, İstanbul (☎ (212) 257 7050; fax 257 7054) open from 8.30 am to 12.30 pm weekdays

Bulgaria *(Bulgaristan)*
> Embassy: Atatürk Bulvarı 124, Kavaklıdere, Ankara (☎ (312) 426 7456; fax 427 3178)
> Consulate: Zincirlikuyu Caddesi 44, Ulus, Levent, İstanbul (☎ (212) 2269 0478, 269 2216)

Canada *(Kanada)*
> Embassy: Nenehatun Caddesi 75, Gaziosmanpaşa, Ankara (☎ (312) 436 1275/9; fax 446 4437)
> Consulate: Büyükdere Caddesi 107/3, Bengün Han, 3rd floor, Gayrettepe, İstanbul (☎ (212) 272 5174)

France *(Fransa)*
> Embassy: Paris Caddesi 70, Kavaklıdere, Ankara (☎ (312) 468 1154; fax 467 9434)
> Consulate: İstiklal Caddesi 8, Taksim, İstanbul (☎ (212) 243 1852; fax 249 9168)

Germany *(Almanya)*
> Embassy: Atatürk Bulvarı 114, Kavaklıdere, Ankara (☎ (312) 426 5451/65; fax 426 6959)
> Consulates: İnönü Caddesi, Selim Hatun Camii Sokak 46, Ayazpaşa, Taksim, İstanbul (☎ (212) 251 5404; fax 249 9920); Atatürk Caddesi 260, Alsancak, İzmir (☎ (232) 421 6995; fax 463 4023)

Greece *(Yunanistan)*
> Embassy: Ziya-ur-Rahman Sokak (Karagöz Sokak) 9-11, Gaziosmanpaşa, Ankara (☎ (312) 436 8861; fax 446 3191)
> Consulate: Turnacıbaşı Sokak 32, Ağahamam, Beyoğlu, İstanbul (☎ (212) 245 0596; fax 252 1365)

India *(Hindistan)*
> Embassy: Cinnah Caddesi 77/A, Çankaya, Ankara (☎ (312) 438 2195; fax 440 3429)
> Consulates: Cumhuriyet Caddesi 257/3, Harbiye, İstanbul (☎ (212) 296 2128; fax 230 3697); Anadolu Caddesi 37-39,

TURKEY

Koyuncuoğlu Han, Salhane, İzmir
(☎ (232) 486 1064; fax 435 0549)

Iran *(İran)*
Embassy: Tahran Caddesi 10, Kavaklıdere,
Ankara (☎ (312) 429 4320)
Consulate: Ankara Caddesi 1/2, Cağaloğlu,
İstanbul (☎ (212) 513 8230)

Iraq *(Irak)*
Embassy: Turan Emeksiz Sokak 11, Gazios-
manpaşa, Ankara (☎ (312) 426 6118, 426 3907)
Consulate: Halide Edip Adıvar Mahallesi,
İpekböceği Sokak 1, İstanbul
(☎ (212) 230 2930/3; fax 234 5726)

Ireland *(İrlanda)*
Honorary Consulate: Cumhuriyet Caddesi 26/A,
Pegasus Evi, Harbiye, İstanbul
(☎ (212) 246 6025; fax 248 0744)

Israel *(İsrail)*
Embassy: Mahatma Gandhi Caddesi 85, 06700
Gaziosmanpaşa, Ankara (☎ (312) 446 3605;
fax 426 1533)
Consulate: Valikonağı Caddesi 73/4, Nişantaşı,
İstanbul (☎ (212) 225 1040; fax 225 1048)

Japan *(Japon)*
Embassy: Reşit Galip Caddesi 81, Gazios-
manpaşa, Ankara (☎ (312) 446 0500/3;
fax 437 1812)
Consulate: İnönü Caddesi 24, Ayazpaşa, Taksim,
İstanbul (☎ (212) 251 7605; fax 252 5864)

New Zealand *(Yeni Zelanda)*
Embassy: Kızkulesi Sokak 42/1, Gaziosmanpaşa, Ankara (☎ (312) 446 0768, 446 0732;
fax 445 0557)

Russian Federation *(Rusya)*
Embassy: Karyağdı Sokak 5, Çankaya, Ankara
(☎ (312) 439 2122/3; 438 3952)
Consulate: İstiklal Caddesi 443, Tünel, Beyoğlu,
İstanbul (☎ (212) 244 2610, 244 1693;
fax 249 0107)

South Africa *(Güney Afrika)*
Consulate: Esentepe, İstanbul
(☎ (212) 275 4793)

Syria *(Suriye)*
Embassy: Abdullah Cevdet Sokak 7, Çankaya,
Ankara (☎ (312) 438 8704; fax 439 4588)
Consulate: Mecidiyeköy, İstanbul
(☎ (212) 275 4396)

UK *(İngiltere, Birleşik Krallığı)*
Embassy: Şehit Ersan Caddesi 46/A, Çankaya,
Ankara (☎ (312) 427 4310; fax 468 3214)
Consulates: Meşrutiyet Caddesi 34, Tepebaşı,
Beyoğlu, İstanbul (☎ (212) 252 6436, 244 7540;
fax 245 4989); Mahmut Esat Bozkurt Caddesi,
1442 Sokak No 49, İzmir (☎ (232) 463 5151;
fax 421 2914)

USA *(Amerika Birleşik Devletleri, Amerika)*
Embassy: Atatürk Bulvarı 110, Kavaklıdere,
Ankara (☎ (312) 468 6110; fax 467 0019)
Consulates: Atatürk Caddesi, Adana

(☎ (322) 454 3774, 454 2145; fax 457 6591);
Meşrutiyet Caddesi 104-108, Tepebaşı, Beyoğlu,
İstanbul (☎ (212) 251 3602; fax 252 7851);
Turkish-American Association *(Türk-Amerikan
Derneği)* Büyük Efes Oteli Arkası, İzmir

CUSTOMS

You may import, duty-free, two cartons
(that's 400) cigarettes, 50 cigars or 200
grams of smoking tobacco, and five litres of
liquor. Duty-free items are on sale in both
arrival and departure areas of Turkey's international airports.

Turkey is full of antiquities: ancient coins,
figurines, pots, mosaics etc. *It is illegal to
buy, sell or export antiquities!* Penalties are
severe – if caught, *you may go to jail.*
Customs officers spot check the luggage of
departing passengers. For information on
bringing a motor vehicle into Turkey, see Car
& Motorcycle in the Getting Around section
later in this chapter.

MONEY

Costs

Turkey is relatively cheap. You can travel on
as little as US$10 to US$15 per person per
day using buses, staying in pensions and
eating one restaurant meal daily. For US$15
to US$30 per day you can travel more com-
fortably by bus and train, stay in one and
two-star hotels with private baths, and eat
most meals in average restaurants. For
US$30 to US$70 per person per day you can
move up to three and four-star hotels, take
the occasional airline flight and dine in restaurants all the time. Costs are highest in
İstanbul and the big coastal resorts, and
lowest in small eastern towns off the tourist
track.

Currency

The Turkish lira (TL) comes in coins of
1000, 2500, 5000, 10,000 liras, and notes
(bills) of 10,000, 20,000, 50,000, 100,000,
250,000, 500,000 and one million liras, with
higher denominations issued regularly as
inflation (around 80% to 90% per annum)
devalues the currency. Watch for three or
more zeroes to be dropped from the money

in 1997. Prices in this chapter are quoted in more stable US dollars.

Currency Exchange

The Turkish lira is subject to rapid devaluation caused by inflation – so it would be unhelpful to display exchange rates as they were at the time of writing. Check exchange rates shortly before your visit to Turkey and be prepared for currency exchange rates to change during your visit.

Changing Money

Turkey has no black market; you can often spend US dollars or Deutschmarks in place of liras. Exchanging cash of major currencies is fast and easy in most banks, exchange offices, post offices, shops, hotels etc. Cashing major travellers' cheques is less easy (some places resist) and the exchange rate is usually slightly lower. Many places charge a commission *(komisyon)*; ask first.

Tipping

Waiters appreciate 7 to 10% (15% in expensive places); hotel porters 50c to US$1; barbers, hairdressers and Turkish bath attendants 10 to 15%; and cinema ushers a few coins or a small lira note. Porterage at airports and train and bus stations is set and should be posted. Except for special service, don't tip taxi drivers; rather, round up the fare. Minibus *(dolmuş)* drivers are not tipped.

Bargaining

In some shops prices are set, but in others, use *pazarlık* (bargaining). You *must* bargain for souvenirs. Even if the establishment has set prices, bargain if you are buying several items or are shopping in the off season. For hotel rooms, bargain if you visit any time between November and April, or if you plan to stay more than a few days.

Taxes & Refunds

A value-added tax (KDV, *Katma Değer Vergisi*) of 15 to 20% is included in the price of most items and services: it's known as KDV *dahil* (VAT included). A few hotels and shops give discounts if you agree not to request an official receipt; this way, they don't have to pay the tax, and you save. It's illegal but not unusual.

If you buy an expensive item (eg carpet, leather apparel) for export, ask the shopkeeper for a KDV *iade özel fatura* (special VAT refund receipt). Get the receipt stamped as you clear customs, then get your refund at a bank branch in the airport departure lounge (usually not open); or you can mail the receipt and be sent a cheque (be patient...and ever-hopeful).

POST & COMMUNICATIONS

Post

Turkish post offices are called PTT *(posta, telefon, telgraf)*. This has been changed to Posta Telğraf as the telephone system has been separated from it. Look for the black-on-yellow signs. If you have mail addressed to you care of poste restante in a major city, the address should include Merkez Postane (Central Post Office), or the name of the neighbourhood post office at which you wish to retrieve it.

Telephone & Fax

Turkey's public telephones, now separated from the PTT and operated by Türk Telekom, take either *jeton* (tokens) or *telekart* (telephone cards), both sold at telephone centres and some shops. Turkey's country code is 90.

To call from one city to another, dial 0 (zero), then the area (city) code and seven digit number. To call abroad, dial 00, then the country and area (city) codes and number.

It's easiest to send and receive faxes at your hotel for a fee (ask in advance). Türk Telekom centres have faxes, but require more paperwork.

Internet

TURNET, Turkey's national Internet network, was established by Türk Telekom in 1996. IBM also has a Turkish network, but both require that you have a monthly account. A better option is to have an account with CompuServe or America Online, US online services with nodes in most countries.

You can sign up for an account no matter where you live in the world.

Turkish nodes (9600 bps) for these services are:

America Online, Ankara (modem (312) 468 8042)
America Online, İstanbul (modem (212) 234 5168)
America Online, İzmir (modem (232) 446 2034)
CompuServe, Ankara (modem (312) 468 8042)
CompuServe, İstanbul (modem (212) 234 5168)

Both these services levy surcharges on the use of non-US nodes, currently US$6 per hour for America Online's Turkish nodes, US$18 per hour for CompuServe's. Also, you may need to download and install special software (CCLs, etc) to use these nodes. Consult your online service.

Many phones use US-style RJ11 modular plugs (common in expensive hotels). In cheaper hotels you must buy a three-prong Turkish phone plug *(telefon fişi)* and make an adapter.

BOOKS

Lonely Planet publishes the more detailed *Turkey*, now in its 5th edition, as well as the useful *Turkish phrasebook*.

For a short cut to an understanding of Turkey, read *Atatürk: The Rebirth of a Nation* by Lord Kinross. An absolutely gripping account of the decline of the Ottoman Empire from its peak under Süleyman the Magnificent is *Lords of the Golden Horn* by Noel Barber. Freya Stark's *Alexander's Path* retraces Alexander the Great's route across southern Turkey; it's good on the pre-tourist-boom south, if sometimes a little too learned. An easier read is Mary Lee Settle's *Turkish Reflections* which casts a novelist's eye over the whole country. For more general book information see Books in the Regional Facts for the Visitor chapter.

NEWSPAPERS & MAGAZINES

The *Turkish Daily News* is the local English-language paper. In major tourist areas you'll find many day-old European and US newspapers and magazines.

RADIO & TV

Broadcasting is by the government-funded TRT (Turkish Radio & Television) and numerous independent stations. TRT offers short news broadcasts in English each morning and evening on radio, and late each evening on TV.

PHOTOGRAPHY & VIDEO

Film costs about US$6, plus developing, for 24 Kodacolor exposures. Kodachrome is scarce, pricey and can't be developed in Turkey, though the simpler E-6 process films such as Ektachrome and Fujichrome are readily available and speedily processed in city photo shops.

Still cameras are subject to an extra fee in most museums; in some they are not allowed at all. To use a flash or tripod, you must normally obtain written permission from the staff (not easy). Video fees are usually even higher.

Don't photograph anything military. In areas off the tourist track, it's polite to ask *Foto/video çekebilir miyim?* (May I take a photo/video?) before shooting close-ups of people.

LAUNDRY

Attended laundrettes are beginning to appear in the larger cities, but most tourist laundry *(çamaşır)* is done in hotels. Talk to the staff. The cost may be negotiable. Dry cleaners *(kuru temizleme)* are readily found in the cities; ask at your hotel.

HEALTH

Travellers in Turkey may experience 'traveller's diarrhoea', so take precautions. Drink bottled water; make sure fruit is washed in clean water, or peeled with clean hands; avoid raw or undercooked seafood and meat; don't eat food which has been standing unrefrigerated.

Pharmacists can advise you on minor problems and dispense many drugs on the spot for which you would need a prescription at home. Emergency medical and dental treatment is available at simple dispensaries *(sağlık ocağı)*, clinics *(klinik)* and government hospitals *(hastane)*. Look for signs with a red crescent or big 'H'. Payment is required, but is usually low. For more detailed health information see the Health Appendix.

TOILETS
The word is *tuvalet*. All mosques have toilets, though most are at least a bit smelly. Major tourist sites have better ones. Almost all public toilets require payment of a small fee (10c to 30c).

Though most hotels and many public toilets have the familiar raised bowl commode, you'll also see traditional flat toilets, which are simply a hole in the floor with footrests on either side. You'll soon find squatting quite natural. The custom is to wash with water (from a spigot, jug or little pipe attached to the toilet) using the left hand. When not in your hotel, carry toilet paper with you.

STUDENT TRAVELLERS
The International Student Identity Card (ISIC) gets you reductions at museums and archaeological sites (usually 50%), train travel (30%), Turkish Maritime Lines ships (10%) and sometimes on private bus lines and Turkish Airlines.

WOMEN TRAVELLERS
In traditional Turkish society, men and women have lives apart: the husband has his male friends, the wife has her female friends. Younger and richer Turks are shedding these roles, and women now hold some positions of authority, right up to the prime minister's job, recently held by Ms Tansu Çiller.

Still, foreign women are often hassled while travelling in Turkey. Men pinch, grab and make rude noises, which can become very tiresome; more serious assault is uncommon but possible. Travelling with a male improves matters, as does travelling with another female, or preferably two.

Turkish women completely ignore men who speak to them in the street. Wearing a headscarf, a below-the-knee length skirt, a wedding ring and/or sunglasses makes you

less conspicuous. Away from beach resorts you should certainly avoid revealing tops and brief shorts.

GAY & LESBIAN TRAVELLERS
Although homosexuality is not technically illegal in Turkey, there are a number of laws relating to indecency which can be (and have been) used to prosecute homosexuals. So, while there are a few openly gay bars and clubs in major cities and resorts, homosexual activity has a fairly low profile.

There are several gay organisations in Turkey, the most visible being Lambda Istanbul (☎ & fax (212) 256 1150), PK 103, Göztepe, İstanbul, which also has an English gay guide to Turkey on the World Wide Web at http://www.qrd.org/qrd/www/world/europe/turkey.

Club 14 (Abduülhakhamit Caddesi, Belediye Dükkanlari 14, Taksim), Han Cafe (Cumhuriyet Caddesi, Taksim Square) and Private (Tarlabasi Bulvari 28, Taksim) are popular gay hang-outs in İstanbul. See the *Spartacus International Gay Guide* for more information on gay-friendly bars and hotels in Turkey.

DANGERS & ANNOYANCES
Although Turkey is considered one of the safest countries in the region, you must still take precautions. Wear a money belt under your clothing. Be wary of pickpockets and purse-snatchers in buses, markets and other crowded places.

In İstanbul, single men have been victims of a thinly veiled form of extortion: after being lured to a bar or nightclub (often one of those along İstiklal Caddesi) by new Turkish 'friends', the man is then made to pay an outrageous bar bill whether he drank or not.

There have been a few incidents of rape and even murder at resorts, and though very unusual, they had not happened at all before the current tourism boom.

On intercity buses, there have been isolated incidents of theft by drugging: the person in the bus seat next to you buys you a beverage at a rest stop, slips a drug into it and, as you sleep, makes off with your luggage. More commonly, the hard-sell tactics of carpet sellers can drive you to distraction; be warned that 'free' lifts and suspiciously cheap accommodation often come attached with near compulsory visits to carpet showrooms.

BUSINESS HOURS

Banks and offices are open Monday to Friday, generally from 8.30 am to noon and from 1.30 to 5 pm; shops are open Monday to Saturday from 9.30 am to 6 or 7 pm, although some take a lunch break from 1 to 2 pm. Food shops generally open early (6 or 7 am) and close late (7 or 8 pm). One food shop in each neighbourhood opens on Sunday.

PUBLIC HOLIDAYS & SPECIAL EVENTS
Secular Celebrations
1 January
    New Year's Day
Mid-January
    Camel-wrestling in Selçuk
23 April
    National Sovereignty Day (the first republican parliament was convened in Ankara in 1920) and Children's Day
19 May
    Youth & Sports Day (date of Atatürk's landing in Samsun to begin the War of Independence)
Mid-May
    Ephesus Festival of international dance and drama at Efes
June
    Oil-wrestling in Edirne (2nd week); International İstanbul Music Festival (late June-early July)
30 August
    Victory Day (victory over invading Greek armies at Dumlupınar in 1922)
29 October
    Republic Day (proclamation of the republic in 1923)
10 November
    Date of Atatürk's death (1938); although not a legal holiday, special ceremonies are held
December
    Whirling Dervishes in Konya

Religious Celebrations
Muslim holidays follow the lunar calendar. The holy month of Ramadan (Ramazan) is followed by the three day Şeker Bayramı (Sweets Holiday, Eid al-Fitr).

Kurban Bayramı (Sacrifice Holiday, Eid al-Adha), when millions of families slaughter rams to celebrate Abraham's near-sacrifice of Isaac, is a four day national holiday, the biggest of the year. Plan ahead – almost everything closes, including banks; transport and resort hotels may be packed. For more information about the dates of these celebrations see the table of holidays near Public Holidays & Special Events in the Regional Facts for the Visitor chapter.

ACTIVITIES
Archaeology
If you like archaeology, you've come to the right place. Turkey abounds with ancient sites. You may have some of the remote ones all to yourself. The most interesting sites are Ephesus, Hierapolis (Pamukkale), Nemrut Dağı and Pergamum, but there are hundreds of others. Boğazkale and Troy are more impressive for their antiquity than for their extant remains. Many Turkish and foreign universities schedule digs annually in the summer. To volunteer for a dig, you must first find out which team is digging where. There is no centralised registry.

Water Sports
The Aegean and Mediterranean coasts are the places to go; the Black Sea is too chilly, and most lakes are too salty or undeveloped. The larger resort hotels have windsurfing, snorkelling, scuba diving and rowing equipment for hire.

Yacht Cruising
Turkey has lots of possibilities for yacht cruising, from day trips to two week luxury charters. Kuşadası, Bodrum and Marmaris are the main centres, with more resorts developing yachting businesses all the time. You can hire crewless bareboats or flotilla boats, or take a cabin on a boat hired by an agency. Ask anywhere near the docks for information.

Hiking

Hiking and mountain trekking are becoming popular in Turkey, particularly in the north-east. For more information, see Walking in the Getting Around section later in this chapter.

Turkish Baths

The pleasures of the Turkish bath are famous: soaking in the steamy heat, getting kneaded and pummelled by a masseur/masseuse, then being scrubbed squeaky clean and lathered all over by a bath attendant, before emerging swaddled in puffy Turkish towels for a bracing glass of tea.

Traditionally, men and women bathe separately, but in popular tourist areas baths often accept men and women at the same time for higher than usual prices. For safety and comfort's sake, women should know at least some of the men in the bath with them, and females might want to avoid male masseurs (a Turkish woman would only accept a masseuse).

Not all baths accept women. Smaller baths in small towns accommodate men and women on different days or at different times of the day.

WORK

You must have residence and work permits to be legally employed; your employer can help you with these. Some people work illegally (as waiters, English teachers, journalists and such) and cross the border to Greece every three months to keep their visas current. If you're thinking of doing this, remember that after a while the immigration officer checking your passport is going to question all those exit and entry stamps. Job opportunities for English-speakers are listed in the classifieds of the *Turkish Daily News*.

ACCOMMODATION

You'll find camping facilities here and there throughout Turkey. Some hotels and pensions let you camp in their grounds and use their toilets and washrooms for a small fee. Well-equipped European-style camp sites are available in a few resort areas.

Turkey has plenty of cheap hotels, although the very cheapest are probably too basic for many tastes and not always suitable for women travelling alone. The cheaper places (up to US$20 a night) are usually subject to rating by municipalities. Above this level, ratings are by the national Ministry of Tourism.

The very cheap hotels are just dormitories where you're crammed into a room with whoever else fronts up. To avoid this, negotiate a price where you (and yours) have the whole room. Women travellers will get less unwanted attention in hotels by asking for *aile* (family/ladies') accommodation.

There are a few very basic student hostels in the cities, available only in summer when they're not being used by Turkish students, and a couple of accredited Hostelling International (HI) (previously IYHF) youth hostels. In tourist areas look for small 'home pensions' *(ev pansiyonu)*, which sometimes offer kitchen facilities too.

One and two-star hotels offer reasonable comfort and private bathrooms at excellent prices; three-star places can be quite luxurious.

In smaller tourist towns, such as Bodrum, Selçuk (near Ephesus), etc, touts for various hotels and pensions may accost you as you step from your bus. Many are legitimate agents – or even pension owners – looking for customers, but the obnoxious ones are usually freelancers who extort commissions from pension owners for bringing you to them. Most pension owners don't like these guys any more than you do. Don't follow anyone who's pushy or overly eager.

FOOD

Turkish food, which is similar to Greek, only more refined, has often been called the French cuisine of the east, with good reason. Pop into the kitchen and see what's cooking. *Şiş kebap* (shish kebab), lamb grilled on a skewer, is a Turkish invention. You'll find the *kebapçı*, a cheap eatery specialising in roast lamb, everywhere. Try the ubiquitous *döner kebap* – lamb packed onto a vertical revolving spit and sliced off when done.

The best cheap and tasty meal is *pide*,

Turkish pizza. Fish, though excellent, is often expensive – be sure to ask the price before you order. A proper meal consists of a long procession of dishes. First come the *meze* (hors d'oeuvres), such as:

beyaz peynir – white sheep's milk cheese
börek – flaky pastry stuffed with white cheese and parsley
(kuru) fasulye – (dried) beans
kabak dolması – stuffed squash/marrow
patlıcan salatası – puréed aubergine salad
patlıcan tava – fried aubergine
pilaki – beans vinaigrette
taramasalata – Turkish red caviar, fish roe
yaprak dolması – stuffed vine leaves

Dolma are made of all sorts of vegetables (aubergine, marrow, peppers, cabbage or vine leaves) served cold and stuffed with rice, currants and pine nuts, or hot with lamb. The eggplant (aubergine) is the Turks' number one vegetable. It can be stuffed as a dolma *(patlıcan dolması)*, served puréed with lamb *(hünkar beğendi)*, stuffed with minced meat *(karnıyarık)* or appear with exotic names like *imam bayıldı* – 'the priest fainted' – which means stuffed with ground

lamb, tomatoes, onions and garlic. Well might he!

For dessert, try *(fırın) sütlaç* (baked) rice pudding, *kazandibi* (caramelised pudding), *aşure* (fruit and nut pudding), *baklava* (flaky pastry stuffed with walnuts or pistachios, soaked in honey), or *tel kadayıf* or *burma kadayıf* (shredded wheat with nuts in honey).

Finally, Turkish fruit is terrific, particularly the melons.

DRINKS

Good bottled water is sold everywhere. Beers, such as Tuborg or Efes Pilsen, the sturdy Turkish pilsener, supplement the familiar soft drinks. There's also good Turkish wine – red or white – or fierce aniseed *rakı*, which is like Greek *ouzo* or Arab *arak* (the Turks usually cut it by half with water). Turkish coffee *(kahve)* is legendary. Order it *sade* (no sugar), *az şekerli* (slightly sweet), *orta* (medium-sweet) or *çok şekerli* (very sweet). Turkish tea *(çay)*, grown on the eastern Black Sea coast, is served in tiny glasses, with sugar; milk *(süt)* is not always available. A milder alternative is apple tea *(elma çay)*.

Turkish Delight

For a traditional Ottoman treat in İstanbul, walk through the archway to the left of the Yeni Cami in Eminönü, and turn left onto Hamidiye Caddesi. One short block along, on the right-hand (south) side of the street near the corner with Şeyhülislam Hayri Efendi Caddesi, is the original shop of *Ali Muhiddin Hacı Bekir* (☎ 522 0666), inventor of Turkish delight.

History notes that Ali Muhiddin came to İstanbul from the Black Sea mountain town of Kastamonu and established himself as a confectioner in the Ottoman capital in the late 1700s. Dissatisfaction with hard candies and traditional sweets led the impetuous Ali Muhiddin to invent a new confection that would be easy to chew and swallow. He called his soft, gummy creation *rahat lokum*, the 'comfortable morsel'. 'Lokum', as it soon came to be called, was an immediate hit with the denizens of the imperial palace, and anything that goes well with the palace goes well with the populace.

Ali Muhiddin elaborated on his original confection, as did his offspring (the shop is still owned by his descendants), and now you can buy lokum made with various fillings: *cevizli* (JEH-veez-LEE, with walnuts), *şam fıstıklı* (SHAHM fuhss-tuhk-LUH, with pistachios), *portakkallı* (POHR-tah-kahl-LUH, orange-flavoured), or *bademli* (BAH-dehm-LEE, with almonds). You can also get a *çeşitli* (CHEH-sheet-LEE, assortment). Price is according to weight; a kg costs US$3 to US$9, depending upon variety. Ask for a free sample by indicating your choice and saying *Deneyelim!* (DEH-neh-yeh-LEEM, 'Let's try it').

During the winter, a cool-weather speciality is added to the list of treats for sale. *Helvah*, a crumbly sweet block of sesame mash, is flavoured with chocolate or pistachio nuts or sold plain. Ali Muhiddin Hacı Bekir has another, more modern shop on İstiklal Caddesi between Taksim Square and Galatasaray. ■

Carpets

Turkey is famous for its beautiful carpets and kilims and wherever you go you'll be spoilt for choice as to what to buy. Traditionally, village women wove carpets for their own family's use, or for their dowry. Knowing they would be judged on their efforts, the women took great care over their handiwork, hand-spinning and dyeing the wool, and choosing what they judged to be the most interesting and beautiful patterns. These days the picture is more complicated. Many carpets are made not according to local traditions, but to the dictates of the market. Weavers in eastern Turkey might make carpets in popular styles native to western Turkey. Long-settled villagers might duplicate the wilder, hairier and more naive *yörük*, or nomad, carpets.

A good carpet shop will have a range of pieces made by a variety of techniques. Besides the traditional pile carpets, they may offer double-sided flat woven mats such as kilims. Some traditional kilim motifs are similar to patterns found at the prehistoric mound of Çatal Höyük, testifying to the very ancient traditions of flat-woven floor coverings in Anatolia. Older, larger kilims may actually be two narrower pieces of similar but not always identical designs stitched together. As this is now rarely done, any such piece is likely to be fairly old. Other flat-weave techniques include *sumak*, a style originally from Azerbaijan in which coloured threads are wrapped round the warp. In Turkey the sumak technique was only used for saddlebags, so big sumak pieces must be from elsewhere in the Turkic world. Some sumaks are decorated with naive animal patterns and are often (but fantastically) called 'Noah's Ark carpets'. *Cicims* are kilims with small, lively patterns embroidered on top of them. ■

ENTERTAINMENT

İstanbul, Ankara and İzmir have opera, symphony, ballet and theatre. Many smaller towns have folk-dance troupes. Every Turkish town has at least one cinema and one nightclub with live entertainment. The cinemas show a mixture of western films and much-loved Turkish melodrama. In summer the seaside resorts throb to the sounds of innumerable clubs and discos.

THINGS TO BUY

Clothes, jewellery, handicrafts, leather apparel, carpets, brass and copperware, and carved meerschaum are all good buys. Bargaining usually pays off.

Getting There & Away

There are plenty of ways to get into and out of Turkey by air, sea, rail and bus, across the borders of seven countries.

If travelling to or from Turkey by land, you'll need a transit visa for any country except Greece. There are consulates in İstanbul (and a few in İzmir) as well as embassies in Ankara.

AIR

International airports are at İstanbul, Ankara, İzmir, Dalaman, Antalya and Adana. Turkish Airlines has direct flights from İstanbul to two dozen European cities and New York, as well as the Middle East, North Africa, Bangkok, Karachi, Singapore and Tokyo.

Major European airlines such as Aeroflot, Air France, Alitalia, Austrian Airlines, British Airways, Finnair, KLM, Lufthansa, SAS and Swissair fly to İstanbul; British Airways, Lufthansa and the independent airline İstanbul Airlines have flights to Ankara, Antalya, İzmir or Dalaman as well. One-way full-fare tickets from London to İstanbul can cost as much as US$450, so it's usually advisable to buy an excursion ticket (US$250 to US$425) even if you don't plan to use the return portion.

The European airlines also fly one-stop services from many North American cities to İstanbul; Lufthansa has perhaps the most cities and the best connections. Only Turkish Airlines flies nonstop. This service operates from New York (Newark) to İstanbul. Delta flies from various US cities to various European cities including a direct flight from New York to İstanbul via Frankfurt. Round-trip fares range from US$500 to US$1200.

There are no nonstop or direct flights from Australia or New Zealand to Turkey, but you can fly Qantas or British Airways to London, or Olympic to Athens, and get a connecting flight from these cities. You can also fly Qantas or Singapore Airlines from most Australian cities, or Kuala Lumpur, to Singapore to connect with Turkish Airlines' thrice-weekly flights to İstanbul. Excursion fares range from US$2000 to US$2400, which is almost as much as you would pay for a more versatile Round-the-World (RTW) ticket.

Eastern Mediterranean nonstop flights with Turkish Airlines include daily flights from İstanbul to Athens (1½ hours) and Tel Aviv (two hours), two per week to Amman (2⅓ hours), three to Baku (2½ hours), two to Beirut (one hour), four to Cairo (2½ hours), two to Damascus (2½ hours), three to Dubai (6¼ hours), four to Jeddah and Riyadh (5¾ hours), two to Kuwait (4¼ hours), three to Tehrān (4½ hours) and three to Tunis (two hours).

There are daily nonstop flights connecting İstanbul, Ankara and Nicosia (Turkish: Lefkoşa) with Turkish Airlines, Cyprus Turkish Airlines and Istanbul Airlines, and nonstop flights several times weekly between Nicosia and Adana, Antalya and Izmir.

LAND
Europe
The daily *İstanbul Express* train links Munich, Slovenia, Croatia, Yugoslavia and Bulgaria to İstanbul's Sirkeci railway station. Travellers have reported passengers being knocked out with sleeping gas in their compartments and their gear stolen.

Several Turkish bus lines, including Ulusoy, Varan and Bosfor, offer a reliable, comfortable service between İstanbul and major European cities such as Frankfurt, Munich and Vienna. One-way tickets range from US$110 to US$175.

Greece
There are daily train (*Athens Express*) and bus connections between Athens and İstanbul via Thessaloniki. The bus (US$45 to US$75) is much faster than the train.

Syria
Direct daily buses connect Antakya, at the eastern end of Turkey's Mediterranean coast, with the Syrian cities of Aleppo (Halab, 105 km, four hours; US$12) and Damascus (465 km, eight hours; US$20), and Amman in Jordan (675 km, 10 hours; US$28). You may need to obtain a visa from a Syrian consulate before you reach the border.

Armenia
Two trains run daily from Kars to the Armenian border at Doğu Kapı. The slow *Akyaka Postası* departs Kars each Friday afternoon for Ahuryan, just across the border in Armenia, returning to Kars early in the evening each Tuesday. You should obtain an Armenian visa from a consulate before proceeding to the border.

Georgia
The border-crossing post at Sarp, at the Georgian border on the Black Sea coast, is now open to all. Obtain a Georgian visa in advance at the Georgian Consulate in Trabzon, Gazipaşa Caddesi No 20 (☎ (462) 326 2226; fax 326 2296).

Iran
See the Getting There & Away section in the Iran chapter.

SEA
Turkish Maritime Lines (TML) runs car ferries from Antalya, Marmaris and İzmir to Venice weekly from May to mid-October. The charge is US$236 to US$286 one way with reclining seat; mid-price cabins cost US$386 to US$493 per person. Greek and Italian lines also visit İzmir and İstanbul. Taşucu (near Silifke) has a daily service to Turkish Cyprus.

Private ferries run between Turkey's Aegean coast and the Greek islands, which are in turn linked by air or boat to Athens. Service is frequent (usually daily) in summer, several times weekly in spring and autumn, and infrequent (perhaps once a week) in winter. The most reliable winter services are Rhodes-Marmaris, Samos-

Kuşadası and Chios-Çeşme; warm-season services are Lesbos-Ayvalık, Lesbos-Dikili, Kos-Bodrum and Kastellorizo-Kaş.

LEAVING TURKEY
The departure tax is about US$12, and may be included in the cost of your ticket if you bought it in Turkey. Don't have any antiquities in your luggage. If you're caught smuggling them out, you'll probably go to jail.

Getting Around

AIR
Turkish Airlines (Türk Hava Yolları, THY) links all the country's major cities, including the busy İstanbul-Ankara corridor (50 minutes, US$90). Domestic flights fill up; book in advance. İstanbul Airlines competes with Turkish Airlines on a few routes with lower fares, but less frequent flights. Smoking is prohibited on domestic flights.

BUS
Buses go everywhere in Turkey frequently and cheaply (around US$2.25 to US$2.75 per 100 km) and usually comfortably. Kamil Koç, Metro, Ulusoy and Varan are premium lines, more comfortable and with better safety records than most. (Traffic accidents take a huge number of lives on Turkish roads each year.)

The bus terminal (otogar) is often on the outskirts of a city, but the bigger bus companies often have free şehiriçi servis (shuttle minibuses) between the city-centre ticket office and the otogar. Many of the larger otogars have left-luggage rooms called emanet; there is a small charge. Don't leave valuables in unlocked luggage. If there's no emanet, leave luggage at your bus line's ticket office.

Everyone in Turkey – bus drivers included – seems to chain-smoke. Aside from getting a seat near a window-vent, there doesn't seem to be a polite solution. Ask about

sigarasız (no-smoking) buses when you buy a ticket.

TRAIN
Turkish State Railways (Türkiye Cumhuriyeti Devlet Demiryolları, TCDD or DDY) trains have a hard time competing with the best long-distance buses for speed and comfort. Only on the special-express trains such as the Fatih and Başkent can you get somewhere faster than by bus.

Ekspres and mototren services are sometimes one class only. If they have 2nd class it costs 30% less. Student and return fares are discounted too. These trains are a little slower than and comparable in price with buses, and they are sometimes more pleasant (there are no-smoking cars, for one thing). On yolcu and posta trains you could grow old and die before you get to your destination. Trains east of Ankara are not as punctual or comfortable as those to the west.

Sleeping-car trains linking İstanbul, İzmir and Ankara are good value; the cheaper örtülü kuşetli carriages have four simple beds per compartment.

Major stations have emanet (left-luggage rooms).

CAR & MOTORCYCLE
An International Driving Permit may be handy if your driving licence is from a country likely to seem obscure to a Turkish police officer.

Türkiye Turing ve Otomobil Kurumu (TTOK), the Turkish Touring & Automobile Association (☎ (212) 282 8140; fax 282 8042), Oto Sanayi Sitesi Yanı, Seyrantepe, 4 Levent, İstanbul, can help with questions and problems.

Carnets are not required if you're staying for less than three months, but details of your car are stamped in your passport to ensure it leaves the country with you.

Mechanical service is easy to find, reasonably competent and cheap. The most easily serviced models are Fiat, Renault and Mercedes, with Volkswagens and Toyotas starting to show up in large numbers as well.

If you plan to spend time in a major city,

park your car and use public transport – traffic is terrible and parking impossible. Your hotel will advise you on parking. Parking garages are called *katotopark*.

BICYCLE

Although the countryside is varied and beautiful, the road surfaces acceptable (if a bit rough), and Turkish drivers accommodating (though a bit dangerous), cyclists are still an unusual sight here.

HITCHING

Because of the extensive, cheap bus system, hitching is not popular in Turkey. If you ask for rides, drivers will expect you to offer an amount equivalent to the bus fare in exchange. They may politely refuse to accept it, but if you don't offer, you will be considered a freeloader.

Women should not hitchhike alone; if you must hitch, do it with another woman or (preferably) a man, do it only in touristy areas, don't hitch at night, and don't accept a ride in a vehicle which has only men in it.

WALKING

Turkey's varied scenery affords some fine opportunities for treks. The Kaçkar Dağları region is increasingly popular for organised trekking trips of anything from one to 10 days. Provided you bring a tent, sleeping bag and good shoes you could even spend a month exploring the mountains and summer villages (*yaylalar*). If you want to arrange a tour, a good person to talk to would be Adnan Pirikoğlu. Find him by asking at the Pirikoğlu Aile Lokantası in Ayder or by calling ☎ (464) 657 2021 or 655 5084.

BOAT

A comfortable Turkish Maritime Lines car ferry departs from İstanbul each Monday from June to early October, headed for Trabzon and calling at ports along the way. It departs Trabzon on Wednesday for İstanbul, arriving on Friday. Fares from İstanbul to Trabzon (per person, no meals) range from US$15 for a reclining seat to

US$50 for a bed in the best cabin. The fare for a car is US$20.

A similar car-ferry service departs from İstanbul on Friday (year round) and arrives the next morning in İzmir. It departs in the afternoon for the return trip to İstanbul. Fares are US$16 (reclining seat) to US$50 (luxury cabin bed), and US$45 for a car.

A twice-daily ship/train service called the *Marmara Express* links İstanbul and İzmir via Bandırma, costing US$10 one way; there are no ships on Friday or Saturday, though.

LOCAL TRANSPORT

The big towns all have local bus services, and also private *dolmuş* (shared taxis or minibuses). İstanbul has a growing metro system of trains and trams. Ankara's metro is building as well.

In the big cities, taxis have digital meters and are required by law to run them. The greatest risk of taxi rip-offs (drivers refusing to run the meter, taking the long way etc) is in İstanbul. Service is usually fairly honest and efficient in the other big cities. In smaller places, where taxis have no meters, fares are set by the town, but you'll be at a loss to know what they are. Agree on a fare before you get in the car.

ORGANISED TOURS

Most independent travellers find tours in Turkey expensive. Almost all tours park you in a carpet shop for an hour (the guide gets a kickback). In general, it's faster and cheaper to make your own travel arrangements.

İstanbul

İstanbul, formerly Constantinople, is a treasure trove of places and things to see. After a day of wandering around mosques, ruins and tangled streets where empires have risen and fallen, you'll realise what is meant by the word 'Byzantine'. Nor should it be forgotten that it was here, five and a half centuries ago, that the final fragment of the Roman Empire crumbled, and that through Europe's Dark

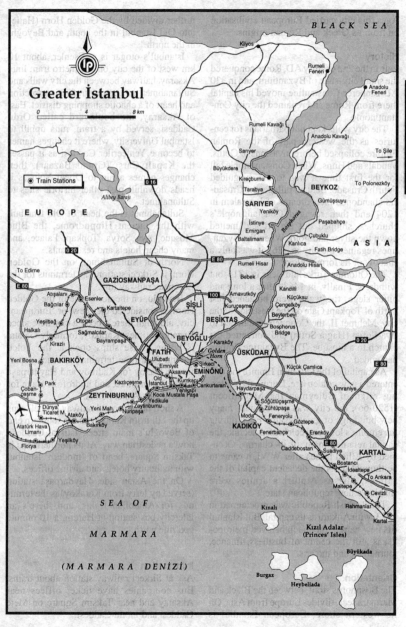

Greater İstanbul

0   4   8 km

● Train Stations

BLACK SEA

Kilyos

Rumeli
Feneri

Anadolu
Feneri

To Şile

Rumeli Kavağı

Anadolu Kavağı

Sarıyer

To Polonezköy

Büyükdere

Kireçburnu

Tarabya

BEYKOZ

Gümüşsuyu

SARIYER

Yeniköy

Paşabahçe

İstinye

Emirgan

Çubuklu

Baltalimanı

Kanlıca

ASIA

Fatih Köprü

Rumeli Hisar

Anadolu Hisarı

EUROPE

Alibey Barajı

Bebek

Kandilli

Küçüksu

O 16

Rumeli Hisar

Çengelköy

Beylerbeyi

GAZİOSMANPAŞA

Arnavutköy

Kuruçeşme

Bosphorus
Bridge

To Edirne

O 20

E 80

ŞİŞLİ

100

E 80

Atışalanı

Bağcılar

Esenler

Kartaltepe

EYÜP

BEŞİKTAŞ

Yeşilbağ

Otogar

Sağmalcılar

BEYOĞLU

Karaköy

O 20

Halkalı

Bayrampaşa

Golden
Horn

ÜSKÜDAR

Kirazlı

FATİH

Ulubatlı

Emniyet

Sirkeci

Küçük Çamlıca

Yeni Bosna

Aksaray

Kumkapı

EMİNÖNÜ

BAKIRKÖY

Kazlıçeşme

Old
İstanbul

Yenikapı

Cankurtaran

Haydarpaşa

Ümraniye

Park

ZEYTİNBURNU

Koca Mustafa Paşa

Söğütlüçeşme

Çoban-
çeşme

Yedikule

Zeytinburnu

Zühtüpaşa

Dünya
Ticaret M.

Ataköy

Yeni Mah.

Nurıpaşa

Moda

Feneryolu

Göztepe

Atatürk Hava
Limanı

Bakırköy

KADIKÖY

Erenköy

Florya

Yeşilköy

Fenerbahçe

E 80

KARTAL

Caddebostan

Suadiye

Bostancı

İdealtepe

To Ankara

SEA OF

Maltepe

Cevizli

MARMARA

Kınalı

Rahmanlar

Kartal

Kızıl Adalar
(Princes' Isles)

MARMARA DENİZİ

Büyükada

Burgaz

Heybeliada

Ages this city carried European civilisation on from its Greek and Roman origins.

History

Late in the 2nd century AD, Rome conquered the small city-state of Byzantium, and in 330 AD Emperor Constantine moved his capital there from Rome and renamed the city Constantinople.

The city walls kept out barbarians for centuries as the western part of the Roman Empire collapsed before invasions of Goths, Vandals and Huns. When Constantinople fell for the first time it was to the misguided Fourth Crusade. Bent on pillage, the Crusaders abandoned their dreams of Jerusalem in 1204 and then ravaged Constantinople's churches, shipped out the art and melted down the silver and gold. When the Byzantines regained the city in 1261 it was only a shadow of its former glory.

The Ottoman Turks laid siege in 1314, but withdrew. Finally, in 1453, after a long and bitter siege, the walls were breached just north of Topkapı Gate on the west side of the city. Mehmet II, the Conqueror, marched to Aya Sofya (Hagia Sofia) and converted the church to a mosque. The Byzantine Empire had ended.

As capital of the Ottoman Empire the city entered a new golden age. During the glittering reign of Süleyman the Magnificent (1520-66), the city was graced with many new buildings of great beauty. Even during the empire's long and celebrated decline, the capital retained many of its charms. Occupied by Allied forces after WWI, it came to be thought of as the decadent capital of the sultans, just as Atatürk's armies were shaping a new republican state.

The Turkish Republic was proclaimed in 1923, with Ankara as its capital. But İstanbul (its new name), the much beloved metropolis, is still the centre of business, finance, journalism and the arts.

Orientation

The Bosphorus strait, between the Black and Marmara seas, divides Europe from Asia. On its western shore, European İstanbul is further divided by the Golden Horn (Haliç) into Old İstanbul in the south and Beyoğlu in the north.

İstanbul's otogar is at Esenler, about 10 km west of the city on the metro tram line. Aksaray, halfway between the city walls and Sultanahmet, is a major traffic intersection and heart of a chaotic shopping district. East of Aksaray, the boulevard called Ordu Caddesi, served by a tram, runs uphill to İstanbul University, where it changes names to become Yeniçeriler Caddesi as it passes the Kapalı Çarşı (Grand Bazaar), then changes names again to Divan Yolu as it heads downhill past other historic sites to Sultanahmet.

Sultanahmet is the heart of Old İstanbul, with the ancient Hippodrome, the Blue Mosque, Aya Sofya, Topkapı Palace, and many cheap hotels and restaurants.

North of Sultanahmet, on the Golden Horn, is Sirkeci station, the terminus for the European railway line.

Beyoğlu, on the north side of the Golden Horn, is considered the 'new' or 'European' city, although there's been a city here since Byzantine times. Karaköy, formerly Galata, is where cruise ships dock at the Yolcu Salonu (maritime terminal). Ferries depart from Karaköy for Kadıköy and Haydarpaşa on the Asian shore, and hydrofoils leave for more distant Asian points.

A short underground railway (Tünel) runs up the hill from Karaköy to the southern end of Beyoğlu's main street, İstiklal Caddesi, now a pedestrian way. At its northern end is Taksim Square, heart of 'modern' İstanbul with its luxury hotels and airline offices.

On the Asian side, Haydarpaşa station (served by ferry from Karaköy) is the terminus for Anatolian trains, and there's an intercity bus station at Harem, a 10 minute taxi ride north.

Information

Ask at Sirkeci railway station about trains. Bus companies have ticket offices near Aksaray and near Taksim Square on Mete Caddesi and İnönü Caddesi.

Tourist Offices The Ministry of Tourism has offices in the international arrivals hall at Atatürk airport (☎ 663 6363); in the Yolcu Salonu (maritime terminal ☎ 249 5776) at Karaköy; in Sirkeci railway station (☎ 511 5888); at the north-east end of the Hippodrome in Sultanahmet (☎ 518 1802); near the UK Consulate in Beyoğlu at Meşrutiyet Caddesi 57, Tepebaşı (☎ 243 2928); in Taksim Square (☎ 245 6876) on İstiklal Caddesi; and in the İstanbul Hilton arcade on Cumhuriyet Caddesi (☎ 233 0592), four long blocks north of Taksim Square.

Money Divan Yolu is lined with foreign exchange offices and travel agencies offering speedy, hassle-free exchange facilities at fairly high rates. Most exchange offices are open daily from 9 am to 9 pm. Other good areas to look are Sirkeci and Taksim/İstiklal.

Post & Communications The main post office *(merkez postane)* is on Şehinşah Pehlevi Sokak, just west of Sirkeci station. Go here for poste restante mail. There are branch PTTs in Aksaray and the Grand Bazaar, and in Beyoğlu at Galatasaray and Taksim, as well as in the domestic and international departure areas at Atatürk airport.

İstanbul has two telephone codes: 212 for the European side and 216 for the Asian. Assume that phone numbers given here are 212 unless stated otherwise.

Travel Agencies Divan Yolu in Sultanahmet is lined with travel agencies, all of them selling cheap air and bus tickets; they can also arrange train tickets. Shop around for the best deals. Most also offer speedy foreign exchange facilities and can arrange minibus transport to the airport.

Ms Filiz Bingöl at the Overseas Travel Agency (☎ 513 4175; fax 513 4177), Alemdar Caddesi 16, Sultanahmet, is a helpful Turkish-Aussie lady.

Backpackers Travel Agency (☎ 638 6343; fax 638 1483), Yeni Akbıyık Caddesi 22, is right among the hotels and pensions of Cankurtaran.

A long-established, reputable travel agency/tour operator with English-speaking staff is Orion-Tour (☎ 248 8437; fax 241 2808), Halaskargazi Caddesi 284/3, Marmara Apartmanı, Şişli, about two km north of Taksim. Orion (pronounced ORyohn) sells tickets to anywhere, and tours to anywhere in Turkey.

Bookshops Aypa (☎ 516 0100), Mimar Mehmet Ağa Caddesi 19, Sultanahmet, just down the hill from Aya Sofya and the Blue Mosque, has guides, maps and magazines in English, French and German.

The best shops are on İstiklal Caddesi around Tünel Square, including Robinson Crusoe (☎ 293 6968), İstiklal Caddesi 389; Dünya Aktüel (☎ 249 1006), İstiklal Caddesi 469; ABC Kitabevi (☎ 279 6610), İstiklal Caddesi 461; and Metro Kitabevi (☎ 249 5827), İstiklal Caddesi 513.

Laundry Try the Hobby Laundry (☎ 513 6150), Caferiye Sokak 6/1, Sultanahmet, by the Yücelt Interyouth Hostel; Active Laundry, Dr Emin Paşa Sokak 14, off Divan Yolu beneath the Arsenal Youth Hostel; and Sultan Laundry, İncili Çavuş Çıkmazı 21, opposite the Hotel Nomade.

Medical Services For hospitals, the Amerikan Bristol (☎ 231 4050), at Güzelbahçe Sokak, Nişantaşı (two km north-west of Taksim Square), and the International (☎ 663 3000), Çınar Oteli Yanı, İstanbul Caddesi 82, in Yeşilköy near the airport, do good work.

Emergency Try the Tourist Police (☎ 527 4503), Yerebatan Caddesi 6, Sultanahmet, across the street from Yerebatan Saray (Sunken Palace Cistern).

The ordinary police (☎ 155 in an emergency) are less experienced in dealing with foreigners.

Things to See – Old İstanbul

Sultanahmet is the first place to go, with all the major sights arranged around the Hippodrome. There is a sound and light show on summer evenings – different nights, different

TURKEY

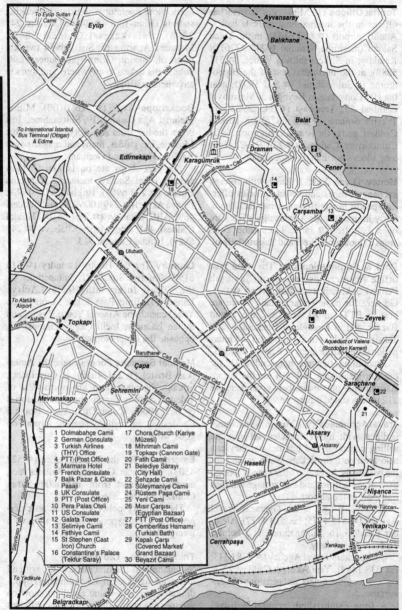

1 Dolmabahçe Camii
2 German Consulate
3 Turkish Airlines (THY) Office
4 PTT (Post Office)
5 Marmara Hotel
6 French Consulate
7 Balik Pazar & Cicek Pasaji
8 UK Consulate
9 PTT (Post Office)
10 Pera Palas Oteli
11 US Consulate
12 Galata Tower
13 Selimiye Camii
14 Fethiye Camii
15 St Stephen (Cast Iron) Church
16 Constantine's Palace (Tekfur Saray)
17 Chora Church (Kariye Müzesi)
18 Mihrimah Camii
19 Topkapı (Cannon Gate)
20 Fatih Camii
21 Belediye Sarayı (City Hall)
22 Şehzade Camii
23 Süleymaniye Camii
24 Rüstem Paşa Camii
25 Yeni Cami
26 Mısır Çarşısı (Egyptian Bazaar)
27 PTT (Post Office)
28 Çemberlitaş Hamamı (Turkish Bath)
29 Kapalı Çarşı (Covered Market/ Grand Bazaar)
30 Beyazıt Camii

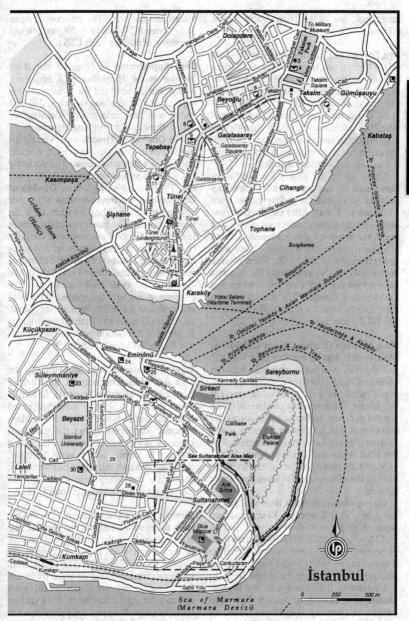

İstanbul

languages. Ask at the Hippodrome tourist office.

Aya Sofya The Church of the Holy Wisdom (also known as Hagia Sofia or Sancta Sophia) was begun under Emperor Justinian in 532 AD and was intended to be the grandest, finest church in the world. For 1000 years it was the largest church in Christendom. The interior reveals the building's true magnificence; stunning even today, it must have been overwhelming centuries ago when it was covered in gilded mosaics.

Climb up to the gallery for a different view, and to see the splendid surviving mosaics (note that the gallery closes from 11.30 am to 1 pm). After the Turkish conquest and the subsequent conversion of Aya Sofya to a mosque, the mosaics were covered over, as Islam prohibits images. They were not revealed until the 1930s, when Atatürk declared Aya Sofya a museum. The minarets were added during the centuries when Aya Sofya was a mosque. The church is open daily except Monday from 9.30 am to 4.30 pm, till 7 pm in summer; entry is US$6.

Blue Mosque (Sultan Ahmet Camii) The Mosque of Sultan Ahmet I, or Blue Mosque, just south of Aya Sofya, was built between 1609 and 1619. It is light and delicate compared with its squat, massive, ancient neighbour. The exterior is notable for its six slender minarets, and a cascade of domes and half-domes, but it is inside where you will find the blue luminous impression created by the tiled walls and painted dome. You're expected to make a small donation when visiting the mosque (and to leave your shoes outside).

On the north side of the Blue Mosque, up the ramp, is a **Carpet & Kilim Museum** (open 9.30 am to 4.30 pm, closed Sunday and Monday; entry US$1). The **Arasta** (row of shops) on the street behind the Blue Mosque to the east provides support for the mosque's upkeep from the shops' rents. In the Arasta is the entrance to the **Mosaic Museum**, a portion of ancient Byzantine pavement showing marvellous scenes of nature and the hunt. The museum is open daily from 9.30 am to 4.30 pm (closed Monday); admission costs US$1.

The Hippodrome In front of the Blue Mosque is the Hippodrome (Atmeydanı), where chariot races and the Byzantine riots took place. Construction started in 203 AD and it was later enlarged by Constantine. Today, three ancient monuments remain.

The **Obelisk of Theodosius** is an Egyptian column from the temple of Karnak, resting on a Byzantine base. The perfectly clear hieroglyphics are nearly 3500 years old. The 10m high rough-stone **Obelisk of Constantine Porphyrogenitus** was once covered in bronze (the Crusaders stole the bronze plates). The base rests at the former level of the Hippodrome, now several metres below the ground. Between these two monuments are the remains of a **spiral column** of intertwined snakes. Erected at Delphi by the Greeks to celebrate their victory over the Persians, it was later transported to the Hippodrome, and the snakes' heads disappeared. At the north-east end of the Hippodrome is a ceremonial **fountain** built to commemorate Kaiser Wilhelm's visit in 1901.

Turkish & Islamic Arts Museum On the west side of the Hippodrome, the Türk ve İslam Eserleri Müzesi is housed in the former palace (built in 1524) of İbrahim Paşa, grand vizier and son-in-law of Süleyman the Magnificent. The exhibits run the gamut of Islamic history, from beautifully illuminated Qur'ans to carpets and mosque furniture, crafts and Turkish miniature paintings. The museum is open daily from 10 am to 5 pm (closed Monday); admission costs US$2.

Sunken Palace Cistern Across Divan Yolu from the north-east end of the Hippodrome is a small park; on the north side of the park is the entrance to Yerebatan Saray, the Sunken Palace Cistern (☎ 522 1259). Built by Constantine and later enlarged by Justinian, this vast, columned cistern held water not only for regular summer use but also for times of siege. It's open daily from 9 am to

5.30 pm, sometimes later on summer evenings; admission costs US$2.

Topkapı Palace Just north-east of Aya Sofya is the fortified, sprawling Topkapı Sarayı, the palace of the sultans from 1462 until the last century (when they moved to Dolmabahçe Palace, across the Golden Horn). Topkapı is not just a palace but a collection of gardens, houses and libraries, and a 400 room harem.

In the vast outer courtyard, where the crack troops known as Janissaries once gathered, is the **Church of Divine Peace** (Aya İrini), dating from around 540 AD. Entrance is through the Ortakapı (Middle Gate).

Within the park-like Second Court are exhibits of priceless porcelain (in the former palace kitchens), silverware and crystal, arms and calligraphy. Also here, right beside the Kubbealtı, or Imperial Council Chamber, is the entrance to the **harem**, a succession of sumptuously decorated rooms that served as the sultan's family quarters.

In the Third Court are the sultan's ceremonial robes, and the fabulous **treasury**, containing an incredible wealth of gold and gems. The **shrine of the Holy Relics** holds a solid-gold casket containing the Prophet Mohammed's cloak, and other Islamic relics. The beautiful little tiled kiosks have fine views of the city. There's also a restaurant here.

Topkapı is open daily from 9.30 am to 5 pm but is closed on Tuesday; admission costs US$6 with an extra US$2.50 payable to visit the harem, open from 10 am to noon and 1 to 4 pm.

Archaeological Museums Down the hill from the outer courtyard, to the west of Topkapı Palace, are the Arkeoloji Müzeleri, a complex of three museums. The **Archaeological Museum** has an outstanding collection of Greek and Roman statuary, and a sarcophagus, said to be that of Alexander the Great. The **Museum of the Ancient Orient** (Eski Şark Eserleri Müzesi) is dedicated to the pre-Islamic and pre-Byzantine civilisations. The **Tiled Pavilion** (Çinili

Köşk), built on order of Sultan Mehmet the Conqueror in 1472, is among the very oldest Turkish buildings in the city. It is now a museum of Turkish tile work. The museums are open from 9.30 am to 5 pm (they're all closed on Monday; the Museum of the Ancient Orient only opens on Wednesday, Friday and Sunday, and the Tiled Pavilion opens on Tuesday, Thursday and Saturday); admission to all three costs US$3.

Down the slope from the museums to the west is **Gülhane Park**, the former palace park, now with a small zoo, restaurants and amusements. It's open daily from 9 am to 6 pm; admission costs 30c.

Divan Yolu Walk or take the tram (30c) westward along Divan Yolu from Sultanahmet. Near the top of the slope, where the street becomes a pedestrian way, on the right, is a complex of **tombs** of several 19th century sultans, including Mahmut II (1808-39), Abdülaziz (1861-76) and Abdülhamid II (1876-1909).

A bit farther along, on the right, is the **Çemberlitaş** (Banded Stone), a monumental column erected by Constantine the Great sometime during the 4th century. Within a century it had to be strengthened with iron bands. During a storm in 1105 Constantine's statue toppled off the top, killing several people sheltering below. In 1779 the column was badly damaged by a fire, and was further strengthened with the iron hoops you see today.

Grand Bazaar The Kapalı Çarşı (Covered Market) is a labyrinthine medieval shopping mall. Most of the old stalls have been converted into modern, glassed-in shops. Still, it's fun to wander among the 65 streets and 4400 shops, and a great place to get lost – which you certainly will.

The bazaar is divided into areas – carpets, jewellery, clothing, silverware and so on. West of the bazaar proper, across Çadırcı╵ Caddesi, beside the Beyazıt Mosque. **old book market** (sahaflar çar╵ many stalls selling second-hand b of them in Turkish. The bazaar is open from Monday to Saturday, 8 am to 7 pm.

Beyazıt & Süleymaniye Beyazıt takes its name from the graceful mosque **Beyazıt Camii**, built in 1506 on the orders of Sultan Beyazıt II, son of Mehmet the Conqueror. In Byzantine times this plaza was the **Forum of Theodosius**, laid out in 393 AD. The great portal on the north side of the square is that of **İstanbul University**. The portal, enclosure and buildings behind it date mostly from Ottoman times, when this was the Ministry of War.

Behind the university to the north-west rises İstanbul's grandest mosque complex, the **Süleymaniye**. Construction was completed in 1557 on orders of Süleyman the Magnificent; he and his foreign-born wife Roxelana (Hürrem Sultan) are buried in a **mausoleum** behind the mosque to the south-east. Süleyman's great architect, Sinan, is entombed near the sultan. The buildings surrounding the mosque were originally a hospital, seminaries (*medrese*), soup kitchen, baths and hospice.

Theodosian Walls Stretching for seven km from the Golden Horn to the Sea of Marmara, the walls date back to about 420 AD, but many parts have been restored during the past decade.

At **Yedikule**, close to the Sea of Marmara, you can visit a Byzantine-Turkish fortress where obstreperous diplomats and inconvenient princes were held in squalor and despair. The fortress is open daily from 9.30 am to 5 pm (closed on Monday); admission costs 75c.

Near the **Edirnekapı** (Adrianople Gate) is the marvellous **Chora Church** (Kariye Müzesi), a Byzantine building with the best 14th century mosaics east of Ravenna. Built in the 11th century, it was later restored, and converted to a mosque, and is now a museum. It's open from 9.30 am to 4.30 pm (closed Tuesday), and admission costs US$3. To get there, take an Edirnekapı bus along Fevzi Paşa Caddesi.

Turkish Baths İstanbul's most interesting historical baths are now quite touristy, and often are not good value for money. The **Cağaloğlu Hamamı**, at Yerebatan Caddesi 34, just a short stroll north-west of Sultanahmet, has separate entrances for men (on the main street) and women (around the corner to the right). The baths are open daily from 7 am to 10 pm (men) and 8 am to 9 pm (women). Prices here would be outrageous anywhere else in Turkey: about US$10 for an assisted bath with massage, supposedly inclusive of tips.

Things to See – Eminönü
At the southern end of Galata Bridge (Galata Köprüsü) looms the large **Yeni Cami** (New Mosque), built between 1597 and 1663. Beside it is the **Mısır Çarşısı** (Egyptian Bazaar), full of spice and food vendors. To the west, in the fragrant market streets, is the **Rüstem Paşa Camii**, a small, richly tiled mosque designed by the great Ottoman architect, Sinan.

Things to See – Beyoğlu
Cross the new Galata Bridge (1992), and head uphill towards the Galata Tower.

Galata Tower In its present form the tower dates from 1216, when Galata was a Genoese trading colony. Later it served as a prison, an observatory, then a fire lookout before it caught fire itself in 1835. In 1967 it was completely restored as a supper club. The observation deck, an excellent place for views and photos, is open every day from 9 am to 6 pm (7 pm in summer) for US$1. Find the sign announcing that during the 17th century an intrepid local 'birdman' launched himself from the top and made the first intercontinental flight clear across to Asian İstanbul.

İstiklal Caddesi & Taksim At the top of the hill is İstiklal Caddesi, once called the Grand Rue de Péra, now a pedestrian way served by a restored tram (50c, always overcrowded). The famed Pera Palas Oteli (rooms for US$180 a double) is off to the west; huge consulates – embassies in Ottoman times – line the avenue. At Galatasaray is the colourful **Balık Pazar** (Fish Market) and **Çiçek**

Pasajı (Flower Passage), an assortment of fish-and-beer restaurants.

Taksim Square, with its huge hotels, park

TURKEY

The Hamam Experience

The history of steam baths goes back millennia and many of Turkey's natural spas were enjoyed by the ancient Greeks and Romans. Turks built beautiful, elaborate baths (hamams) to serve their communities, partly because Islam demands high standards of personal hygiene, and partly because bathing is such a pleasure.

Public baths used to be required because private homes didn't have bathing facilities. Everybody, rich and poor alike, went to the baths. For a worker, a visit to the baths was simply to get clean. For a high-born woman, it was a ritual of attendants and polite courtesies, and many museums display the gorgeous gold-embroidered towels, mother-of-pearl pattens and lovely accessories she would have taken with her.

Most Turkish towns still have hamams of varying degrees of fanciness although they are becoming scarcer in the west as homes acquire modern plumbing. Still, the custom of going to the hamam continues because the public facilities are so much grander than what is available at home, and because, for Turks, it is a social occasion. To steam clean, have a massage, relax, watch TV, sip tea and chat with friends is looked upon as a wonderful, affordable luxury.

What happens in a hamam? Well, you will be shown to a cubicle (camekan) where you can undress, store your clothes, lock up your valuables and wrap the cloth that's provided (the peştemal) round you. An attendant (tellak) will lead you through to the hot room where you sit and sweat for a while.

Then you have to make a choice. It's cheapest to wash yourself with the soap (sabun) and shampoo (şampuan), and use the towel (havlu) you brought with you. The hot room will be ringed with individual basins which you fill from the taps above before sluicing the water over yourself with a plastic scoop. You should try not to get soap into the water in the basin, and avoid splashing your neighbours, especially on a Friday when a Muslim who has completed their ritual wash would have to start all over again if soaked by an infidel.

But it's far more enjoyable to let an attendant wash you. In the hot room you'll be doused with warm water and then scrubbed with a coarse cloth mitten (kese), loosening dirt you never suspected you had. Afterwards you'll be lathered with a sudsy swab, rinsed off and shampooed.

When all this is done you'll be offered the chance of a massage, an experience worth having at least once during your trip. Some massages are carried out on the floor or a table but often you'll be spread out on the great marble bench (or göbektaşı) beneath the dome. In touristy areas (other than İstanbul) the massage is likely to be pretty cursory and unless you're prepared to pay the extra for an 'oil massage' you may be disappointed. Elsewhere, however, a Turkish massage can be an unforgettable, if occasionally rough, experience.

The massage over, you'll be led back to the cold room, where you'll be swathed in towels and taken to your cubicle for a rest. Tea, coffee, soft drinks and beer are usually available.

Traditional hamams have separate sections for men or women or admit men and women at separate times. As the number of baths declines, it's usually the ones for women that go first since there is some ambivalence about how desirable it is for women to be out of the home. Opening hours for women are almost invariably more restricted than for men.

Bath etiquette dictates that men should keep the peştemal on at all times, washing their own private parts without ever removing this modesty wrap. In the women's section, the amount of modesty expected varies considerably: in some baths total nudity is fine, in others it would be a blunder to remove your knickers. Play safe by keeping your underwear on under your peştemal until inside the hot room when you can remove what looks appropriate. Women also wash their own private parts. If you want to shave your legs or armpits, you should do this in the outer warm room rather than in the bath.

In touristy areas, most hamams are happy for foreign men and women to bathe together, usually for a premium price. In traditional hamams women are washed and massaged by other women. No Turkish woman would let a male masseur near her but while Turkish men continue to frequent baths used by tourists, the Turkish women vanish and with them go the masseuses.

Sexual activity has no place in the traditional bath ritual. Women who accept a masseur should have their massage within view of their male companions or friends. At the first sign of impropriety, they should protest loudly. ∎

and Atatürk Cultural Centre, is the hub of 'modern' İstanbul.

Things to See – The Bosphorus

North from İstanbul towards the Black Sea are some beautiful old Ottoman buildings, including the imposing **Dolmabahçe Palace** and several big mosques; **Rumeli Hisar**, the huge castle built by Mehmet the Conqueror on the European side to complete his stranglehold on Constantinople; and many small and surprisingly peaceful villages that are now the city's 'dormitory suburbs'. Towns on the Asian side in particular have charm, open space and good food.

Any bus heading out of Karaköy along the Bosphorus shore road will take you to Dolmabahçe. Get off at the Kabataş stop. Just north is the Dolmabahçe mosque, and beyond it, the palace. To get to Rumeli Hisar, take any bus or dolmuş, going north along the European shore of the Bosphorus to Bebek, Emirgan, Yeniköy or Sarıyer. A ferry ride up the Bosphorus is *de rigueur* for all İstanbul tourists. See also Organised Tours later in this section.

Things to See – The Princes' Isles
Once the site of monasteries and a haven for pirates, this string of nine spotless little islands (*adalar*) is a popular weekend and summer getaway for İstanbul's middle class. With good beaches, lots of open woodland and transport by horse-drawn carriages, the isles make a pleasant escape from the noise and hustle of İstanbul. Ferries (US$3.50) and hydrofoils (*deniz otobüsü*, US$5) depart the dock at Kabataş, just south of Dolmabahçe.

Organised Tours
The standard 1¾ hour tourist cruise from Eminönü (Boğaz dock) to Sarıyer on a normal ferry costs US$4 one way (half-price on Sunday). Or, you can take the shorter 'poor-person's sunset cruise' across the Bosphorus and back by boarding any boat for Üsküdar.

Special Events
Celebration of the conquest of Constantinople from the Byzantines (1453) is held on the anniversary, 29 May, out by the city walls. The İstanbul International Music Festival is held each year from early June to early July, with top name artists from around the world.

Places to Stay
Camping In this big city, camping is not particularly convenient and costs about as much as staying in a cheap hotel (US$8 to US$10 for a tent site). *Londra Camping* (☎ 560 4200) is a truck stop with a large camping area behind it; you'll find it on the south side of the Londra Asfaltı between Topkapı Otogar and the airport (coming east from the airport, follow the *servis yolu* signs). *Ataköy Tatil Köyü* (☎ 559 6000), on the shore south-east of the airport, and *Florya Turistik Tesisleri* (☎ 663 1000) are holiday beach-hotel-bungalow complexes with camping facilities. To get to the Ataköy, take bus No 81 from Eminönü; to get to the Florya, take the *banliyö* (suburban) train from Sirkeci railway station.

Hostels & Hotels The hostels aside, İstanbul's accommodation is quite pricey nowadays. South-east of Sultanahmet is Cankurtaran, an area of quiet streets and good cheap and moderate hotels. For four and five-star hotels, go to Taksim.

Sultanahmet *Yücelt Interyouth Hostel* (☎ 513 6150), Caferiye Sokak 6/1, has dorm beds for US$6, beds in three or four-bed rooms for US$8 and doubles with toilet for US$18.

Arsenal Youth Hostel (☎ 513 6407), Dr Emin Paşa Sokak 12, off Divan Yolu by the

PLACES TO STAY		
4	Hotel Anadolu	
5	Hotel Elit	
6	Hotel Ema	
7	Yücelt Interyouth Hostel & Hobby Laundry	
15	Arsenal Youth Hostel & Active Laundry	
20	Four Seasons Hotel	
21	Yeşil Ev Hotel	
32	Hotel Side Pansiyon	
33	Hotel Park	
34	Star Hostel & Laundry	
35	Guesthouse Berk	
36	Orient Youth Hostel	
37	Yusuf Guesthouse	
38	Hotel Empress Zoe	
39	Alp Guesthouse	

PLACES TO EAT	
12	Pudding Shop
13	Can Restaurant & Sultanahmet Köftecisi
14	Vitamin Restaurant
17	Dedem Börekçisi
25	Yeni Birlik Lokantası

OTHER	
1	Cağaloğlu Hamamı (Turkish Bath)
2	Gülhane Park
3	Aya İrini (Hagia Eirene Church)
8	Imperial Gate (Entrance to Topkapı Palace)
9	Aya Sofya (Hagia Sofia)
10	Tourist Police
11	Yerebatan Saray (Sunken Palace Cistern)
16	Imperial Tombs
18	Tourist Office
19	Kaiser Wilhelm's Fountain
22	Obelisk of Theodosius
23	Turkish & Islamic Arts Museum
24	Law Courts
26	Spiral Column
27	Blue Mosque (Sultan Ahmet Camii)
28	Mosaic Museum
29	Carpet & Kilim Textile Museum
30	Arasta
31	Aypa Bookshop
40	Cankurtaran (Sultanahmet) Banliyö Railway Station

Tarihi Park Hamamı, has dorm rooms with four beds each at US$6 per bed, and showers down the hall.

Yerebatan Caddesi runs west from Aya Sofya. A block past the Sunken Palace Cistern, turn right on Salkım Söğüt Sokak to find *Hotel Ema* and *Hotel Elit* (☎ 512 7566), both on the left, and *Hotel Anadolu* (☎ 512 1035), down the street on the right. The Anadolu and Elit are the cheapest and quietest at US$12 and US$15 per person for rooms with sink; hot showers are free.

Cankurtaran Find the house-like Yeşil Ev hotel on the south-east side of the fountain park between Aya Sofya and the Blue Mosque, and walk down Tevkifhane Sokak on the hotel's left side. Downhill on the corner of Utangaç Sokak is the friendly *Hotel Park* (☎ 517 6596), Utangaç Sokak 26. Basic double rooms cost US$22, those with shower cost US$30, with breakfast included. The neighbouring *Hotel Side Pansiyon* (☎ 517 6590) costs a bit more. Slightly farther downhill, at Kutlugün Sokak 27, is the friendly *Guesthouse Berk* (☎ 516 9671), where clean rooms with bath cost US$35/45 a single/double; it's a good place for single women.

Yusuf Guesthouse (☎ 516 5878), at Kutlugün Sokak 3, is friendly and quiet. Doubles without bathroom cost US$14, with free, hot showers off the hall. Beds in four-bed dorms cost US$5; those on the roof cost US$3. *Star Hostel* (☎ 638 2302), Akbıyık Caddesi 18, has doubles with shower for US$20, and a public laundry as well. Walk down Adliye Sokak for the *Alp Guesthouse* (☎ 517 9570) at No 4; it's family run, for US$35 a double with shower and breakfast.

Around the corner at Akbıyık Caddesi 13 is the cheerful, friendly *Orient Youth Hostel* (☎ 517 9493); doubles cost US$12 with sink, US$3.50 for a dorm bed, and the top-floor cafe has marvellous Marmara views.

Best splurge in this area is the tidy *Hotel Empress Zoe* (☎ (212) 518 2504; fax 518 5699), Akbıyık Caddesi, Adliye Sokak 10, in a Byzantine cistern next to an old Ottoman hamam. The rooms are small but nice, with marble baths, at US$45/60 a single/double. The rooftop bar-lounge-terrace affords fine views of the sea and the Blue Mosque. Run by American expatriot Ann Nevens, it's a fine choice for single women.

Places to Eat

Nowadays, the *Pudding Shop*, officially known as the *Lale Restaurant* and once a legend amongst travellers, is just one of a string of medium-priced *lokanta* (restaurants) along Divan Yolu opposite the Hippodrome – typical meals cost US$4 to US$6. Try the *Can Restaurant*, or the *Vitamin Restaurant*, a brightly lit, hyperactive and shifty place (the food's good, but check your bill). The *Sultanahmet Köftecisi* serves delicious grilled meatballs called köfte with salad, bread and a drink for US$4 or less. *Dedem Börekçisi*, Divan Yolu 21, is a streetside booth selling flaky pastry (börek) filled with sheep's milk cheese for US$2, drink included.

At the far (south-western) end of the Hippodrome, walk up Peykhane Sokak one short block to the *Yeni Birlik Lokantası* (☎ 517 6465), at No 46, a large, light ready-food restaurant favoured by lawyers from the nearby law courts. Meals cost US$2.50 to US$4; no alcohol.

The neighbourhood called Kumkapı, following the shoreline 800m south of Beyazıt along Tiyatro Caddesi, boasts dozens of good seafood restaurants. In fair weather the whole place is one big party. You can eat meat for US$8 or US$10, but are more likely to spend from US$12 to US$20 on fish and rakı. For a cheaper fish lunch, buy a filling fish sandwich from one of the boats near the Galata Bridge for just US$1.

Getting There & Away

Air İstanbul is Turkey's airline hub. Most foreign airlines have their offices near Taksim, or north of it, along Cumhuriyet Caddesi. You can buy Turkish Airlines tickets in Taksim (Cumhuriyet Caddesi 10), or at any travel agency. Most domestic flights with Turkish Airlines cost under US$100. For reservations, call ☎ 663 6363.

İstanbul Airlines (☎ 509 2121; fax 593 6035) flies to Adana, Ankara, Antalya, Dalaman, İzmir and Trabzon, as well as many European cities. Most domestic flights cost US$55 to US$70.

Bus The International İstanbul Bus Terminal (Uluslararası İstanbul Otogarı, ☎ 658 0505) has 168 ticket offices and buses leaving for all parts of Turkey and beyond. Get to it via metro train from Aksaray; get out at Otogar.

Buses depart for Ankara (seven hours; US$9 to US$20; or express buses, six hours; US$15 to $US24) roughly every 15 minutes, day and night, and to most other cities at least every hour. Heading east to Anatolia, you might want to board at the smaller otogar at Harem, north of Haydarpaşa on the Asian shore.

Train Sirkeci is the station for trains to Edirne, Greece and Europe. Haydarpaşa, on the Asian shore, is the terminus for trains to Anatolia. Ask at Sirkeci station (☎ 527 0050) or Haydarpaşa station (☎ (216) 336 0475) for rail information. From Sirkeci there are four daily express trains to Edirne (6½ hours; US$4), but the bus is faster (three hours; US$5.75). The nightly *İstanbul Express* goes to Munich via Bulgaria, Yugoslavia, Croatia and Slovenia.

From the Sarayburnu dock, just north of Topkapı Palace, ships depart each morning and evening (except Friday and Saturday) for Bandırma, from where you continue to İzmir on the *Marmara Express* (10½ to 12 hours; US$10).

From Haydarpaşa there are seven daily express trains to Ankara (7½ to 11 hours; US$11 to US$30); one of them has all sleeping cars.

Boat For information on car ferries to İzmir and along the Black Sea coast to Trabzon, see the introductory Getting Around section in this chapter. Buy tickets at the Turkish Maritime Lines (Denizyolları) office (☎ 249 9222 for reservations, ☎ 244 0207 for information), Rıhtım Caddesi, Karaköy, just east of the Karaköy ferry dock.

Ferries and hydrofoils depart from İstanbul's Kabataş dock, east of Taksim and south of Dolmabahçe, for the Princes' Isles and Yalova on the south shore of the Sea of Marmara, half a dozen times daily in summer. From Yalova buses run to İznik (ancient Nicaea) and Bursa.

Getting Around
The Airport Havaş airport buses depart from the international terminal about every 30 minutes, stopping at the domestic terminal, Bakırköy and Aksaray (get out here for Sultanahmet) before terminating in Taksim Square. The trip takes 30 to 45 minutes and costs US$2.75. The metro is cheaper but less convenient; Dünya Ticaret Merkezi stop is closest to the airport and you will need to take a taxi from there. City buses from the airport to Sultanahmet are infrequent and slow.

An airport taxi costs about US$10 to US$12 for the 23 km trip to Old İstanbul, and US$12 to US$15 to Beyoğlu; it costs 50% more at night. Many of the Divan Yolu travel agencies and Sultanahmet hostels book minibus transport from your hotel to the airport for about US$3.50.

Bus City buses are crowded but useful. Destinations and intermediate stops are indicated at the front and side of the bus. You must have a ticket (50c) before boarding; some long routes require that you stuff two tickets into the box. You can buy tickets from the white booths near major stops or from nearby shops. Stock up in advance.

Train To get to Sirkeci railway station, take the *tramvay* (tram) from Aksaray or Sultanahmet, or any bus signed for Eminönü. Haydarpaşa railway station is connected by ferry to Karaköy (at least every 30 minutes, 50c). *Banliyö tren* (suburban trains, 40c) run every 20 minutes along the southern walls of Old İstanbul and westward along the Marmara shore.

Tram The tramvay between Sirkeci and Aksaray via Divan Yolu and Sultanahmet is useful, and costs just 30c; buy a ticket before boarding from the booths near the stops. A different tramvay, the Hızlı Tramvay (50c), runs west from Aksaray via Adnan Menderes Bulvarı through the city walls to the otogar. A third, restored tramvay trundles along İstiklal Caddesi to Taksim (30c).

Underground The Tünel (İstanbul's underground train) mounts the hill from Karaköy to Tünel Square and İstiklal Caddesi (every 10 or 15 minutes, 35c). An underground line from Taksim north to 4 Levent may be operational in 1997.

Taxi İstanbul has 60,000 yellow taxis, all with digital meters; some are driven by lunatics who will really take you for a ride. From Sultanahmet to Taksim costs US$2.50 to US$3.50; to the otogar costs around US$10.

Around İstanbul

EDİRNE
European Turkey is known as Thrace (Turkish: Trakya). If you pass through, stop in Edirne, a pleasant, untouristed town with decent cheap hotels and several fine old mosques. Have a look at the **Üçşerefeli Cami**, the **Eski Cami**, and especially the **Selimiye Camii**, the finest work of Süleyman the Magnificent's master architect Sinan. The impressive **Beyazıt II Camii** complex is on the outskirts. There are several good, cheap hotels only a few blocks from the tourist office (☎ & fax (284) 225 1518), at Hürriyet Meydanı 17, in the town centre. Buses run every 15 minutes to İstanbul (250 km, three hours; US$5.75), and five times daily south to Çanakkale.

BURSA
Sprawled at the base of Uludağ, Turkey's biggest winter sports centre, Bursa was the Ottoman capital prior to İstanbul's conquest. It retains several fine mosques and pretty neighbourhoods from early Ottoman times, but Bursa's big attraction, now and histori-

cally, is its thermal springs. Besides healthy hot water, Bursa produces lots of succulent fruit and most of the cars made in Turkey. It's also famous for its savoury kebabs.

Orientation & Information
The city centre, with its banks and shops, is along Atatürk Caddesi between the Ulu Cami (Grand Mosque) to the west and the main square, Cumhuriyet Alanı, commonly called Heykel (*heykel* means 'statue'), to the east. The PTT is on the south side of Atatürk Caddesi across from the Ulu Cami. Bursa's Şehir Garajı (otogar) and some cheap hotels are 1500m down the mountain slope from the city centre. Çekirge, with its hot springs, is about six km west of Heykel.

You can get maps and brochures at the Ministry of Tourism office (☎ 251 1834) in the Orhangazi Altgeçidi subway, Ulu Cami Parkı, opposite the Koza Han (silk market).

Bursa's telephone area code is 224.

Things to See & Do
The largest of Bursa's beautiful mosques is the 20 domed **Grand Mosque**, or Ulu Cami (built in 1399), on Atatürk Caddesi in the city centre. About one km east of Heykel in a pedestrian zone is the early Ottoman **Green Mosque** (Yeşil Cami, built in 1424), its beautifully tiled **Green Tomb** (Yeşil Türbe, open daily from 8 am to noon and from 1 to 5 pm; entry free) and the **Turkish & Islamic Arts Museum**, or Türk ve İslam Eserleri Müzesi (open from 8 am to noon, and from 1 to 5 pm). Entry costs 70c and the museum is closed Monday.

A few hundred metres farther east is the **Emir Sultan Mosque** (1805). To get there, take a dolmuş or bus No 18 ('Emir Sultan') from Heykel.

Uphill and west of the Grand Mosque, on the way to Çekirge, are the **Tombs of Osman & Orhan** (dating from the 14th century), the first Ottoman sultans. A km beyond is the **Muradiye Mosque Complex**, with its decorated tombs, dating from the 15th and 16th centuries. Nearby is a restored 17th century house, the **17 Y Y Osmanlı Evi Müzesi**.

On a clear day it's worth going up **Uludağ**. From Heykel you can take bus No 3 or a dolmuş east to the *teleferik* or cable car up the mountain (US$5), or take a dolmuş (US$6) from the otogar for the entire 22 km to the top. Uludağ is Turkey's biggest winter sports centre.

Bursa's **covered market** is behind the Koza Park (fountain plaza), by the Ulu Cami. You can also take a stroll in the vast **Kültür Park** west of the centre on the way to Çekirge. **Mineral baths** can be found in the suburb of Çekirge.

Places to Stay

Camping is along the Yalova Highway at the *Kervansaray Kumluk Mocamp*, six km north, or the *Nur Mocamp*, eight km north.

Bursa's cheapest hotels are pretty seedy. *Hotel Mavi Ege* (☎ 254 8420), Fırın Sokak 17, down a side street opposite the otogar, has singles/doubles with sink for US$6/9; showers cost extra. Nearby, at Menderes Caddesi 168, the *Hotel Belkis* (☎ 254 8322) costs the same. *Öz Uludağ Hotel*, a few doors to the left (west) of the Belkis is not as comfortable. The *Otel Geçit* (☎ 254 1032), Menderes Caddesi 175, charges US$15 a double with shower.

In Tahtakale, south of the Ulu Cami, the *Otel Çamlıbel* (☎ 221 2565), İnebey Caddesi 71, is past its prime; rooms with a shower cost US$13/17 for singles/doubles. Better value at US$18/22 are the excellent, quiet *Hotel Çeşmeli* (☎ 224 1511), Gümüşçeken Caddesi 6, just north of Heykel, and the lower quality *Hotel Bilgiç* (☎ 220 3190), Başak Caddesi 30, south of Heykel.

Staying in Çekirge, you pay more but get free mineral baths. The *Yeşil Yayla Oteli* (☎ 236 8026), behind the Yıldız Hotel at the upper end of the village, charges US$14 a double for rooms with sink, and free use of the mineral baths. The *Hotel Eren* (☎ 236 8099), Birinci Murat Arkası 2, has a pleasant terrace, but charges US$22 for a double with shower.

For real luxury, try the *Termal Hotel Gönlü Ferah* (☎ 233 9210), Murat Caddesi 24, with its panoramic views and marble baths. It costs US$50/70 for a single/double, including breakfast.

Places to Eat

Bursa is renowned for İskender kebap (döner kebap topped with savoury tomato sauce and browned butter). Competition for patrons is fierce among kebapçıs. *Kebapçı İskender*, Ünlü Caddesi 7 just east of Heykel, dates back to 1867 and has a posh atmospheric dining room but low prices – about US$6 with a soft drink. *Adanur Hacıbey*, opposite, costs the same but is less fancy.

Çiçek Izgara, Belediye Caddesi 15, just north of the half-timbered Belediye (city hall) in the flower market, is bright and modern, good for women unaccompanied by men, and open every day from 11 am to 3.30 pm and from 5.30 to 9 pm.

For cheaper eats, head for the small eateries in the Tahtakale Çarşısı (the market across Atatürk Caddesi from the Ulu Cami). For a jolly evening of seafood and drinks, explore Sakarya Caddesi, off Altıparmak Caddesi.

Getting There & Away

The best way to İstanbul is by bus to Yalova (every half-hour, 70 minutes; US$3), then the fast (one hour) Yalova-İstanbul (Kabataş) deniz otobüsü (hydrofoil; five a day) for US$6.

Buses to İstanbul designated *feribot ile* use the Topçular-Eskihisar ferry, which is quicker (2½ hours) than the land route (*karayolu ile*) round the Marmara (four hours; US$9).

Getting Around

Dolmuş and buses to places all over Bursa leave from behind the otogar. Buy BOI city bus tickets (30c) at kiosks and shops. Bursa dolmuş with little 'D' plates on top charge 45c or more for a seat. Those marked 'SSK Hastanesi' go to Çekirge, those marked 'Dev(let) Hast(anesi)' go to the Orhan & Osman tombs, those marked 'Yeşil' go to the Yeşil Cami (Green Mosque) area, and those marked 'S Garaj' go to the bus station.

The Aegean Coast

Olive groves and history distinguish this gorgeous coast. Gallipoli, Troy and Pergamum are only a few of the famous places to be visited.

ÇANAKKALE

Çanakkale is a hub for transport to Troy and across the Dardanelles to Gallipoli. It was here that Leander swam what was then called the Hellespont to his lover Hero, and here too Lord Byron did his Romantic bit and duplicated the feat. The defence of the straits during WWI led to a Turkish victory over Anzac (Australian and New Zealand) forces on 18 March 1916, now a big local holiday.

Orientation & Information

The helpful tourist office (☎ (286) 217 1187), all the cheap hotels and a range of good cafes are all within a block or two of the ferry pier, near the town's landmark clock tower.

Çanakkale's telephone area code is 286.

Aegean Turkey

0   50   100 km

Things to See

The Ottoman **castle** built by Sultan Mehmet the Conqueror in 1452 is now the **Army & Navy Museum**. Just over two km south of the ferry pier, the **Archaeological Museum** holds artefacts found at Troy and Assos.

Places to Stay

Most small hotels and pensions have identical city-regulated prices (singles/doubles for US$6/9, or US$7/10 with shower). All are heavily booked in summer. In spring, rooms are in high demand around Victory Day, 18 March, when Turks celebrate the Ottoman Dardanelles victory in WWI; and Anzac Day, 25 April, when Australians and New Zealanders come to pay their respects to the tens of thousands of their soldiers who died in the battle for Gallipoli.

Hotel Efes (☎ 217 4687), behind the clock tower at Aralık Sokak 5, is modern; rooms have no running water. *Hotel Akgün* (☎ 217 3049), across the street, is similar, as are the *Hotel Erdem* (☎ 217 4986) and *Hotel Umut* (☎ 217 6473) nearer to the clock tower. The *Yellow Rose Pension* (☎ 217 3343) is quiet, tucked out of sight at Yeni Sokak 5. By the clock tower, the *Kervansaray* (☎ 217 8192), an attractive old house with garden, is a good choice, as is the more up-to-date *Konak* (☎ 217 1150).

Hotel Bakır (☎ 217 2908) is old, but has fine sea views and rooms with shower for US$24/30. *Otel Aşkın* (☎ & fax 217 4956), Hasan Mevsuf Sokak 53, less than a block north of the bus station, charges US$14 a double with shower and breakfast. The nearby *Aşkın Pansiyon* (same phone), has waterless doubles for US$8.

For two-star comfort, the *Otel Anzac* (☎ 217 7777), facing the clock tower, charges US$24/30, or there's the *Otel Anafartalar* (☎ 217 4454), right by the docks, for slightly more. Camping is at Güzelyalı Beach, 15 km south, off the road to Troy.

Places to Eat

The *Gaziantep Aile Kebap ve Pide Salonu*, behind the clock tower, serves good cheap pide and more substantial kebabs, while *Trakya Restaurant*, on the main square, always has lots of food ready and waiting 24 hours a day. If you eat at the waterfront fish restaurants, ask for *all* prices in advance.

GALLIPOLI

Always the first line of defence of İstanbul, in WWI the Dardanelles defences proved their worth. Atop the narrow, hilly peninsula, Mustafa Kemal (Atatürk) and his troops fought off a far superior but badly commanded force of Anzac and British troops. After nine months, having suffered horrendous casualties, the Allied forces were withdrawn. A visit to the battlegrounds and war graves of Gallipoli (Turkish: Gelibolu), now a national park, is a moving experience.

The easiest way to get there is on a minibus tour from Çanakkale with Troy-Anzac Tours (☎ (286) 217 5849) for about US$20 per person. However, it's cheaper to take a ferry from Çanakkale to Eceabat and a dolmuş to Kabatepe, and follow the trail around the sites described in a booklet sold at the visitors' centre there.

Turkish Maritime Lines' car ferries cross the straits hourly from Lapseki to Gallipoli and from Çanakkale to Eceabat (50c per person). Small private 'dolmuş' ferries cross more frequently, more cheaply, and faster (15 to 20 minutes) from Çanakkale (in front of the Hotel Bakır) to Kilitbahir. Buses also make the five hour trip to Gallipoli from İstanbul's Esenler otogar.

TROY

According to Homer, Paris abducted the beautiful Helen from her father, Menelaus, king of Sparta, and whisked her off to Troy, thus precipitating the Trojan War. But Troy (Truva) was a thriving city long before the Spartans beat the Trojans by means of a wooden horse secretly filled with soldiers. Troy 1 goes back to the Bronze Age. Legendary Troy is thought to be Troy 6 by some, Troy 7 by others. Most of the ruins you see are Roman ones from Troy 9. Still, it's nice to say you've been there.

Dolmuş run the 32 km from Çanakkale

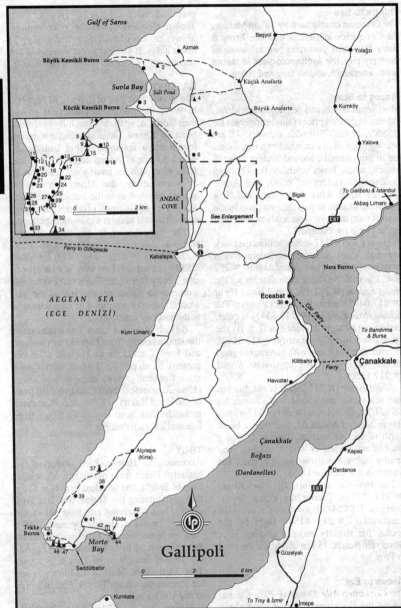

Gulf of Saros

Beşyol

Azmak

Yolağzı

Büyük Kemikli Burnu

Suvla Bay

Salt Pond

Küçük Anafarta

Kumköy

Küçük Kemikli Burnu

Büyük Anafarta

Yalova

To Gelibolu & İstanbul

Bigalı

Akbaş Limanı

E87

ANZAC
COVE

See Enlargement

0   1   2 km

Ferry to Gökçeada

Kabatepe

35

Nara Burnu

Eceabat

36

Car Ferry

AEGEAN SEA
(EGE DENİZİ)

To Bandırma
& Bursa

Kum Limanı

Kilitbahir

Ferry

Çanakkale

Havuzlar

Çanakkale
Boğazı
(Dardanelles)

Kepez

Alçitepe
(Kirte)

37

Dardanos

E87

38

39

40

Abide

41   42

44

Tekke
Burnu

43
45
46 47

Morto Bay

Seddülbahir

Güzelyalı

Gallipoli

0   3   6 km

Kumkale

To Troy & İzmir

İntepe

frequently for US$2. Walk straight inland from the ferry pier to Atatürk Caddesi, and turn right towards Troy; the dolmuş station is at the bridge.

Tevfikiye, the farming village one km before the site, has a few small pensions charging US$8 to US$12 a double. The restaurants by the ruins entrance are inevitably pricey. Troy is open daily from 8 am to 5 pm (7 pm in summer); entry is US$2.50.

BEHRAMKALE (ASSOS)

Once known as Assos, Behramkale, 19 km south-west of Ayvalık, has a hilltop **Temple of Athena** looking across the water to Lesbos in Greece, and was considered one of the most beautiful cities of its time, attracting even Aristotle. It is still beautiful – particularly the little port *(iskele)* two km beyond the village.

On the heights, *Halıcı Han* and other pensions can put you up for US$12 a double and the *Kale Restaurant* will feed you. Port hotels *(Behram, Kervansaray, Şen, Yıldız)*

are more expensive (US$25 to US$60 a double), but also more comfy and atmospheric. *Dost* provides camping at the port for US$5.50. Visit in the low season if you can.

AYVALIK

Once inhabited by Ottoman Greeks, this small, pleasant fishing port and beach resort is the departure point for ferries to Lesbos.

The otogar is 1.5 km north of the town centre, the tourist office (☎ & fax (266) 312 2122) one km south, opposite the marina. Offshore is **Alibey Island**, with open-air restaurants, linked by ferries and a causeway to the mainland (take the red 'Ayvalık Belediyesi' bus north). Six km south is the 12 km Sarımsaklı *plaj* (beach), also called Plajlar. To get there take a blue 'Sarımsaklı Belediyesi' bus.

Places to Stay & Eat

Best value is the *Çiçek Pansiyon* (☎ (266) 312 1201), 200m south of the town centre and one street in from the water (follow the

#		#		#	
1	Büyük Kemikli Picnic Area & Beach	18	Kemalyeri (Scrubby Knoll, Turkish HQ)	35	Kabatepe Information Centre & Museum
2	Hill 10	19	New Zealand No 2	36	Gelibolu Tarihi Milli Park
3	Lala Baba		Outpost Cemetery		(Gallipoli National
4	Green Hill	20	No 2 Outpost Cemetery		Historic Park),
5	Hill 60 New Zealand Memorial	21	Canterbury Cemetery		Ziyaretçi Merkezi (Park Visitors'
6	7th Field Ambulance	22	57th Regiment (57 Alay) Cemetery		Centre) & Picnic Area
7	Cemetery Kocaçimentepe	23	Arıburnu Cemetery	37	Twelve Tree Copse
8	Chunuk Bair New Zealand Memorial	24	Quinn' Post (Bomba Sırt) & Yüzbaşı Mehmet Şehitliği		Cemetery & NZ Memorial
9	Conkbayırı Mehmetçik Memorials	25	Courtney Steele's Post	38	Redoubt Cemetery
10	Place where Atatürk	26	Anzac Memorial	39	Pink Farm Cemetery
	Spent the Night of	27	Johnston's Jolly	40	Kerevizdere
	9-10 August 1915	28	Anzac Cove		Picnic Area
11	Lala Baba Cemetery	29	Kırmızı Sırt (125 Alay	41	Skew Bridge Cemetery
12	Embarkation Pier Cemetery	30	Cephesi) Lone Pine (Kanlı Sırt)	42	French Memorial & Museum
13	Mehmet Çavuş Cemetery	31	Cemetery Shrapnel Valley	43	Lancashire Landing Cemetery
14	Düztepe (10 Alay Cephesi)		(Korkudere) & Plugge's Plateau	44	Çanakkale Şehitleri Abidesi Memorial
15	Talat Göktepe Monument	32	Cemeteries Kanlı Sırt Kitabesi	45	Cape Helles British Memorial
16	The Nek	33	Beach (Hell Spit)	46	İlk Şehitler & Yahya
17	Baby 700 Cemetery & Mesudiye Topu	34	Cemetery Mehmetçiğe Saygı Anıtı	47	Çavuş Memorials 'V' Beach Cemetery

signs), where clean, quiet rooms with shower cost US$11/14 a single/double; the *Biret* and *Melisa* round the corner take the overflow. *Taksiyarhis Pansiyon* (☎ (266) 312 1494), İsmetpaşa Mahallesi, Mareşal Çakmak Caddesi 71, is a renovated Ottoman house charging US$25 a double with shower.

Off İnönü Caddesi are several good, cheap restaurants such as the *Ayvalık* and the *Anadolu Döner ve Pide Salonu*. The ones in the market, east of the main road, are more atmospheric. The *Öz Canlı Balık Restaurant* on the waterfront is pricier but good for seafood.

Getting There & Away
Lesbos Turkish boats make the two hour trip in the morning, Greek boats in the evening, for an outrageous US$50 one way and US$65 same-day return. Boats operate daily from late May to September.

BERGAMA
From the 3rd century BC to the 1st century AD, Bergama (Pergamum) was a powerful and cultured kingdom. A line of rulers beginning with a general under Alexander the Great ruled over this small but wealthy kingdom, whose **asclepion** (medical school, 3.5 km from the city centre, entry US$2.50) grew famous and whose library rivalled that of Alexandria in Egypt. The star attractions here are the city's ruins, especially the **acropolis** (a hill-top site six km from the city centre, entry US$2.50), and an excellent **Archaeology & Ethnography Museum** (in the city centre, entry US$2.50).

The tourist office (☎ (232) 633 1862) is at Cumhuriyet Meydanı in the town centre. Taxis wait here, and charge US$5 to the acropolis, US$10 total if they wait and bring you back down. If you're a walker, follow the path down through the ruins instead. A tour of the acropolis, the asclepion and the museum costs US$21.

Places to Stay & Eat
There are *mocamps* (motorists' camping grounds) including *Bergama Camping* (US$3 per person) between the town and the coast highway.

The spotless, family-run *Böblingen Pension* (☎ (232) 633 2153), Asklepion Caddesi 2, is at the start of the road to the asclepion, with doubles for US$15. Near the *çarşı hamamı* (Turkish bath, for men only) on the main street, *Pergamon Pension* (☎ (232) 633 2395), Bankalar Caddesi 3, has rooms of all sizes for US$8 to US$12. Across the street, *Acroteria Pension* (☎ (232) 633 2469), set back from the road and thus quiet, charges just a bit more.

For luxury, there's the *Hotel Berksoy* (☎ (232) 633 2595) east of the town, charging US$55 a double amid well-kept gardens with a pool.

About 150m south-west of the old Red Basilica on the main street is a square, where you'll find the *Meydan Restaurant* charging about US$5 or US$6 for a three course meal on vine-shaded terraces. The simpler *Sarmaşık Lokantası* has no outdoor seating, but is cheaper. Heading south-west towards the museum and pensions, the *Şen Kardeşler* and *Çiçek Sever Kebap Salonu* are good, cheap eating alternatives.

Gözde Yemek ve Kebap Salonu, next to the Çarşı Hamamı, is also good.

Getting There & Away
Buses shuttle between Bergama and İzmir every half-hour in summer (1½ hours; US$4). Four buses connect Bergama's otogar and Ayvalık daily; or you can hitch out to the highway and catch a bus.

İZMİR
İzmir (once named Smyrna), Turkey's third-largest city, was the birthplace of Homer, about 700 BC. Today it's a transport hub, but otherwise a good place to skip if you can manage it. It's spread out and baffling to find your way around, and its hotels are over-priced.

Orientation
Central İzmir is a web of plazas or *meydan* linked by streets that aren't at right angles to

each other. Instead of names the back streets have numbers. You'll go mad without a map.

Budget hotel areas are near the Basmane railway station. To the south-west, Anafartalar Caddesi twists and turns through the labyrinthine venerable bazaar to the waterfront at Konak, the commercial and government centre. Atatürk Caddesi, also called Birinci Kordon, runs north-east from Konak along the waterfront 1400m to Cumhuriyet Meydanı and its equestrian statue of Atatürk, the main post office, luxury hotels, tourist and airline offices.

At Atatürk Caddesi's northern end is the harbour (Alsancak Yeni Limanı) and the smaller, mostly suburban Alsancak railway station. İzmir's otogar is two km east of Alsancak railway station.

Information

The tourist office (☎ 484 2147; fax 489 9278) is next to the Turkish Airlines office in the Büyük Efes Oteli at Gaziosmanpaşa Bulvarı 1/C, Cumhuriyet Meydanı, with another at Adnan Menderes airport. There's a good city information desk at the otogar.

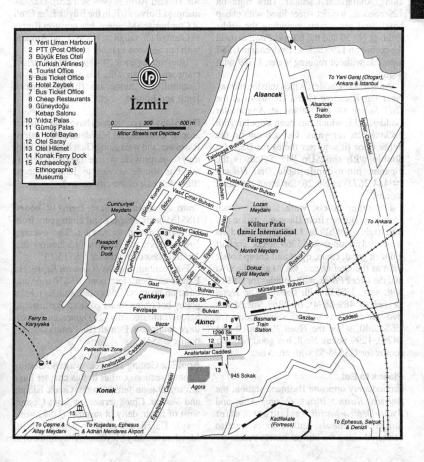

1 Yeni Liman Harbour
2 PTT (Post Office)
3 Büyük Efes Oteli
   (Turkish Airlines)
4 Tourist Office
5 Bus Ticket Office
6 Hotel Zeybek
7 Bus Ticket Office
8 Cheap Restaurants
9 Güneydoğu
   Kebap Salonu
10 Yıldız Palas
11 Gümüş Palas
   & Hotel Baylan
12 Otel Saray
13 Otel Hikmet
14 Konak Ferry Dock
15 Archaeology &
   Ethnographic
   Museums

İzmir

0   300   600 m
Minor Streets not Depicted

Yeni Liman Harbour
To Yeni Garaj (Otogar),
Ankara & İstanbul

Alsancak
Alsancak
Train
Station

İşçiler Caddesi

Cumhuriyet
Meydanı

Pasaport
Ferry
Dock

Atatürk Caddesi
Cumhuriyet Bulvarı
(Birinci Kordon)
(İkinci Kordon)

Gaziosmanpaşa Bulvarı

Talatpaşa Bulvarı

Vasıf Çınar Bulvarı

Dr Mustafa Enver Bulvarı

Plevne Bulvarı

Lozan
Meydanı

Kültür Parkı
(İzmir International
Fairgrounds)

Montrö Meydanı

To Ankara

Bozkurt Cad

Ferry to
Karşıyaka

Gazi Bulvarı

Çankaya

Fevzipaşa Bulvarı

Bazar

Pedestrian Zone

Şehitler Caddesi

Necati Bey Cad

Şehit Nevresbey Bulvarı

Hürriyet Bulvarı

Şair Eşref Bulvarı

Dokuz
Eylül Meydanı

1368 Sk

Akıncı

1296 Sk

12 11 10
Anafartalar Caddesi

13
945 Sokak

Anafartalar Caddesi

Eşrefpaşa Caddesi

Konak

15

To Çeşme &
Altay Meydanı

To Kuşadası, Ephesus
& Adnan Menderes Airport

Agora

Mürselpaşa Bulvarı

7

Gaziler Caddesi

Basmane
Train
Station

Kadifekale
(Fortress)

To Ephesus, Selçuk
& Denizli

TURKEY

Germany, India, the UK and the USA maintain consulates in İzmir. See the Facts for the Visitor section earlier in this chapter.

İzmir's telephone area code is 232.

Things to See

If you stay in İzmir, enjoy the good **bazaar**, the 2nd century Roman **agora**, the hilltop **Kadifekale** fortress, and the **Archaeology and Ethnographic museums**.

Places to Stay

From Basmane railway station, walk south along Anafartalar Caddesi. Turn right on 1296 Sokak, a quiet street lined with cheap hotels and restaurants including the *Yıldız Palas* at No 50 and the *Gümüş Palas* around the corner on 1299 Sokak. Both charge US$7 a double without running water, US$9 with a sink.

Anafartalar Caddesi winds into the bazaar. Near the Hatuniye Camii (mosque) is the *Otel Saray* (☎ 483 6946) at Anafartalar Caddesi 635, which has been popular with backpackers for years. Get a room on the upper floor (it's quieter there) for US$14 a double with sink. Up 945 Sokak is the cleaner, more comfortable *Otel Hikmet* (☎ 484 2672) at No 26, for about the same money.

For other hotels, walk straight down Fevzipaşa Bulvarı from Basmane station and turn right (north). In 1368 Sokak and its westward continuation, 1369 Sokak, are half a dozen good, clean, quiet and cheap hotels such as the *Otel Özcan*, the *Akgün*, the *Ova* and the *Çiçek Palas*, with doubles for US$12 with sink, US$18 with shower. The *Hotel Zeybek* (☎ 489 6694), on 1368 Sokak, has two-star comforts in very small rooms for US$32/40, while the *Hotel Baylan* (☎ 483 1426), 1299 Sokak No 8, has good two-star rooms for US$35/53 with breakfast.

Places to Eat

Immediately opposite Basmane station, the *Ankara, Karaca Birtat, Ödemiş Azim* and *Aydın-Denizli-Nazilli* restaurants offer quick, cheap meals. Little eateries are also scattered along the budget-hotel streets.

On 1296 Sokak is the cheap *Güneydoğu Kebap Salonu*, where a kebab plate and drink cost US$4 or less. But the restaurants on 1368 and 1369 sokaks, just across Fevzipaşa Bulvarı, are much more pleasant and some serve alcohol. The *Dört Mevsim Et Lokantası*, 1369 Sokak No 51/A, specialises in meats, serves drinks, and will fill you up for about US$5 or US$6.

The up-market restaurants are along Atatürk Caddesi, by the sea.

Getting There & Away

Air Turkish Airlines (☎ 484 1220), Gaziosmanpaşa Bulvarı 1/F, in the Büyük Efes Oteli at Cumhuriyet Meydanı, has nonstop flights to İstanbul (50 minutes, US$85) and Ankara, with connections to other points.

İstanbul Airlines (☎ 489 0541), Gaziosmanpaşa Bulvarı 2/E, has some flights to İstanbul, and numerous flights between İzmir and Europe.

Bus Many bus companies have ticket offices around Dokuz Eylül Meydanı, just north of Basmane, and west along Gazi Bulvarı. They may also provide a free (*şehiriçi servis*) minibus shuttle service to İzmir's otogar (three km east of the city centre).

Train An evening Mavi Tren (14 hours; US$13) hauls sleeping and dining cars from Basmane station to Ankara. The evening *İzmir Express* to Ankara (15 hours) has 1st/2nd class carriages for US$15/13.

For İstanbul, take the *Marmara Express* to Bandırma, then a ferryboat (US$10 train and boat; no boats on Friday or Saturday). Four pokey but cheap trains go from Basmane to Selçuk/Ephesus daily (2½ hours; US$1.50); three continue to Denizli (for Pamukkale, six hours; US$4).

Boat The Getting There & Away and Getting Around sections earlier in this chapter have information on ferries to the Greek Islands and Venice. Chios ferries go from Çeşme, west of İzmir, daily in summer (US$25 one way). Catch a bus from Dokuz Eylül Meydanı to Altay Meydanı (Altay Square) in

TURKEY

western İzmir. From there, buses go to Çeşme every 20 minutes.

Getting Around
The Airport A Havaş bus (45 minutes, US$2) departs from the Turkish Airlines office at the Büyük Efes Oteli several times daily for the 25 km trip to Adnan Menderes airport. Trains (50c) run hourly from Alsancak railway station to the airport, and *some* south-bound trains from Basmane also stop at the airport. From Montrö Meydanı, 700m north of Basmane, south-bound 'Adnan Menderes Belediyesi' buses go to the airport during the day for US$1. A taxi costs about US$12.

Local Transport City buses and dolmuş connect the bus and railway stations for 70c; signs say 'Basmane' or 'Yeni Garaj'. The No 50 city bus (40c, buy your ticket before boarding) links the Yeni Garaj and Konak;

Çankaya Meydanı is the closest stop to Basmane. A taxi costs about US$3.

SELÇUK & EPHESUS
Selçuk is an easy 1¼ hour (80 km) bus trip south of İzmir. Almost everybody comes here to visit the splendid Roman ruins of Ephesus (Efes). In its Ionian heyday only Athens was more magnificent, and in Roman times this was Asia's capital.

Orientation & Information
Selçuk, although touristy and Europeanised, is modest compared with coastal playpens like Kuşadası. On the east side of the highway (Atatürk Caddesi) are the bus station (otogar), restaurants, some hotels and the railway station; on the west side behind the museum are the pensions. There's a tourist office (☎ & fax 892 6328) and town map in the park on the west side of the main street, across from the bus station.

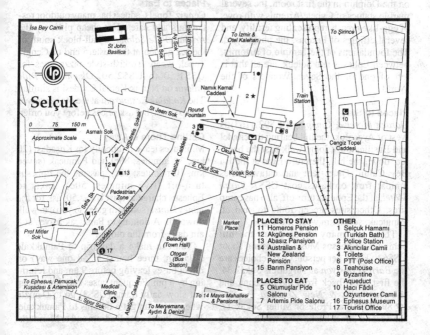

Selçuk

0   75   150 m
Approximate Scale

İsa Bey Camii

St John Basilica

To İzmir & Otel Kalehan

To Şirince

Namık Kemal Caddesi

Train Station

Round Fountain

Cengiz Topel Caddesi

Pedestrian Zone

Prof Mıller Sok

Market Place

Belediye (Town Hall)

Otogar (Bus Station)

Medical Clinic

To Ephesus, Pamucak, Kuşadası & Artemision

To Meryemana, Aydın & Denizli

To 14 Mayıs Mahallesi & Pensions

PLACES TO STAY	OTHER
11 Homeros Pension	1 Selçuk Hamamı (Turkish Bath)
12 Akgüneş Pension	2 Police Station
13 Abasız Pansiyon	3 Akıncılar Camii
14 Australian & New Zealand Pension	4 Toilets
15 Barım Pansiyon	6 PTT (Post Office)
	8 Teahouse
PLACES TO EAT	9 Byzantine Aqueduct
5 Okumuşlar Pide Salonu	10 Hacı Fâdıl Özyurtsever Camii
7 Artemis Pide Salonu	16 Ephesus Museum
	17 Tourist Office

The telephone area code for Selçuk is 232.

Ephesus is a three km, 35 minute walk west from Selçuk's bus station along a shady road (turn left (south) at the Tusan Motel). Alternatively, there are frequent minibuses from the bus station to the motel, leaving you just a one km walk.

Things to See

The immense **Great Theatre** at Ephesus holds 24,000 people. The **Temple of Hadrian**, the **Library of Celsus**, the **Sacred Way** (where the rich lived) and the **Fountain of Trajan** are still in amazingly good shape, or under painstaking restoration. The site, permanently swamped with coach groups, is open daily from 8 am to 5 pm. Entry fees are US$6, plus US$1 to park a car.

The excellent **Ephesus Museum** in Selçuk (open from 8.30 am to noon and 1 to 5.30 pm; closed Monday; entry US$3.50) has a striking collection of artefacts. Don't miss the small, exquisite figure of the Boy on the Dolphin in the first room, the several marble statues of Cybele/Artemis with rows of egg-like breasts representing fertility, and several effigies of Priapus, the phallic god. The foundations of the **Temple of Artemis**, between Ephesus and Selçuk, are all that is left of one of the Seven Wonders of the World.

Places to Stay

Garden Motel & Camping (☎ 892 1163) is west of Ayasoluk, the hill bearing the citadel and Basilica of St John; walk past the basilica, down the hill, then turn right at the İsa Bey Camii. Quiet tent and caravan sites amidst fruit orchards cost US$7. *Tusan Motel*, at the Ephesus turn-off, also has camp sites. Other sites are en route to, and at, Pamucak, seven km west of town.

There are many pensions up the hill behind the Ephesus Museum, costing about US$6 to US$8 per person. Good choices are the *Barım Pansiyon* at Turgutreis Sokak 34, the first street back from the museum, and the *Australia & New Zealand Pension* (☎ 892 6050) at Profesör Mitler Sokak 17, the second street back. Also worth seeking

out are the *Homeros Pension* (☎ 892 3995), Asmalı Sokak 17; *Abasız Pansiyon* (☎ 892 1367), Turgutreis Sokak 13, with nine rooms (some with views); and the eight room *Akgüneş Pension* (☎ 892 3869), Turgutreis Sokak 14, with private showers.

For even cheaper rooms but without private showers, walk east from the otogar uphill to the section called 14 Mayıs Mahallesi and follow the signs to the *Yayla, Zümrüt* and *Panorama* pensions.

For luxury, the best place is the atmospheric 50 room *Otel Kalehan* (☎ 892 6154), on the main road just north of the Shell station. Rooms with showers, mini-fridges and air-con cost US$30/50/70 a single/double/triple. There's a pool as well.

Cengiz Topel Caddesi, a pedestrian street between the Cybele fountain at the highway and the town square by the railway station, has several decent hotels with private bath for US$25 a double.

Places to Eat

Cengiz Topel Caddesi has many outdoor restaurants and cafes. For cheap pide, try the *Artemis Pide Salonu*, a half-block south of the tea garden at the eastern end of Cengiz Topel, where Turkish-style pizza goes for US$1.50 to US$2.50. *Okumuşlar Pide Salonu* on Namık Kemal Caddesi is similar. The *Kodalak Restaurant* at the otogar serves cheap stews, but ask prices before you order.

Getting There & Away

Minibuses leave frequently for Kuşadası (20 km, 30 minutes, 80c) and Pamucak (seven km, 10 minutes, 70c), passing the Ephesus turn-off (five minutes; 50c). Taxis to Ephesus charge at least US$2.50; ask for the *güney kapısı* (southern gate) so you can walk downhill. A dolmuş to Pamucak leaves at 8 am daily from the otogar.

You can make a day trip to Pamukkale (195 km, three hours; US$8 one way) on direct buses leaving before 9 am and returning by 5 pm. Frequent buses and three cheap but slow daily trains (US$3) go to Denizli, where you can get a dolmuş to Pamukkale. Hourly buses go to Bodrum and to Marmaris.

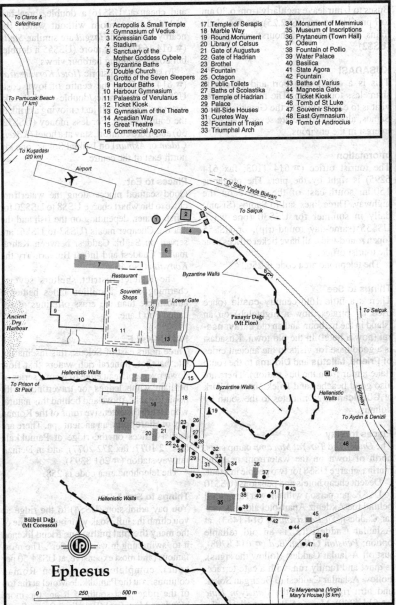

1 Acropolis & Small Temple	17 Temple of Serapis	34 Monument of Memmius
2 Gymnasium of Vedius	18 Marble Way	35 Museum of Inscriptions
3 Koressian Gate	19 Round Monument	36 Prytaneum (Town Hall)
4 Stadium	20 Library of Celsus	37 Odeum
5 Sanctuary of the	21 Gate of Augustus	38 Fountain of Pollio
Mother Goddess Cybele	22 Gate of Hadrian	39 Water Palace
6 Byzantine Baths	23 Brothel	40 Basilica
7 Double Church	24 Fountain	41 State Agora
8 Grotto of the Seven Sleepers	25 Octagon	42 Fountain
9 Harbour Baths	26 Public Toilets	43 Baths of Varius
10 Harbour Gymnasium	27 Baths of Scolastika	44 Magnesia Gate
11 Palaestra of Verulanus	28 Temple of Hadrian	45 Ticket Kiosk
12 Ticket Kiosk	29 Palace	46 Tomb of St Luke
13 Gymnasium of the Theatre	30 Hill-Side Houses	47 Souvenir Shops
14 Arcadian Way	31 Curetes Way	48 East Gymnasium
15 Great Theatre	32 Fountain of Trajan	49 Tomb of Androcius
16 Commercial Agora	33 Triumphal Arch	

To Claros & Seferihisar

To Pamucak Beach (7 km)

To Kuşadası (20 km)

Airport

Dr Sabri Yayla Bulvarı

To Selçuk

Byzantine Walls

Restaurant

Souvenir Shops

Lower Gate

Panayır Dağı (Mt Pion)

To Selçuk

Ancient Dry Harbour

Hellenistic Walls

To Prison of St Paul

Byzantine Walls

Hellenistic Walls

To Aydın & Denizli

Hellenistic Walls

Bülbül Dağı (Mt Coressos)

lp

Ephesus

0   250   500 m

To Meryemana (Virgin Mary's House) (5 km)

Buses to İzmir leave regularly from 6.30 am to 7 pm (1¼ hours; US$2.25); the four daily trains are slower (2½ hours) but cheaper (US$2).

KUŞADASI

This is a cruise-ship port and cheerfully shameless tourist trap. The main reason to visit is to catch a boat to the Greek island of Samos, although there are several places of interest in the environs.

Information

The tourist office (☎ 614 1103; fax 614 6295) is right by the pier. The otogar is 1500m south-east of the centre on the highway. Three lines sail to Samos (Sisam) daily in summer for US$30 (one way), US$35 (same-day round-trip), or US$55 (open round-trip); all have ticket offices near the tourist office.

The telephone area code is 256.

Things to See

There's a little 16th century **castle** (once used by pirates, now a nightclub) on an island in the harbour, and an old **caravanserai** (now a hotel) in the old town. Kuşadası is a good base for visits to the ancient cities of **Priene**, **Miletus** and **Didyma** to the south (take a tour from the bus station). There are also good beaches and Dilek National Park at **Güzelçamlı**, 25 minutes to the south by dolmuş.

Places to Stay

The *Önder* and *Tur-Yat Mocamp* camp sites, north of town on the waterfront near the marina, charge US$8 for two people in a tent.

Decent cheap hotels and pensions (US$10 to US$12 per person with shower) are uphill behind the Akdeniz Apart-otel along Aslanlar Caddesi. *Su Pansiyon* (☎ 614 1453), at Aslanlar Caddesi 13, is an old reliable option; *Pension Golden Bed* (☎ 614 8708), just off Aslanlar Caddesi (follow the signs), is quiet and family run, with a cafe terrace. Follow Aslanlar Caddesi to Bezirgan Sokak and turn right to find the *Pansiyon Dinç* (☎ 614 4249), Mercan Sokak, small, simple,

and cheap at US$16 a double, breakfast included, in a room without water; the nearby *Enişte* and *Hasgül* are similar. *Stella* (☎ 614 1632) costs more (US$55 a double) but boasts stunning harbour views.

To stay in the historic *Hotel Kervansaray* (☎ 614 4115) in the centre of town costs US$50/65 for singles/doubles with breakfast; you're better off just enjoying a drink in the courtyard bar. For less money (US$22/36) and more comfort, stay at a hotel *(Köken, Çidem* or *Akman)* on İstiklal Sokak, one km north-east of the centre.

Places to Eat

Good seafood places along the waterfront close to the wharf charge US$8 to US$20 for a fish dinner, depending on the fish and the season. Cheaper meals (US$3 to US$6) are served on Sağlık Caddesi between Kahramanlar Caddesi and İnönü Bulvarı. Try the *Konyalı* at No 40.

The Kaleiçi district shelters several charming cafes, a million miles better in atmosphere than the crass offerings of so-called Pub Lane.

PAMUKKALE

Three hours east of Selçuk, this fascinating site has hot, mineral-rich waters that flow down over a plateau edge to form a series of brilliant white ledges, or travertines, with pools in each. Above and behind this natural wonder are the extensive ruins of the Roman city of **Hierapolis**, an ancient spa. There are tourist offices on the ridge at Pamukkale (☎ 272 1077; fax 272 2077), and in Denizli railway station (☎ 261 3393).

The telephone area code is 258.

Things to See & Do

You pay admission (US$4) to the ridge as you climb the hill. Soak your bones in one of the many **thermal baths**; one friend likened it to 'swimming in warm Perrier'. The most famous (and most expensive, at US$4.50 per hour), complete with sunken Roman columns, is at the Pamukkale Motel at the top of the ridge. Just south of it are the more mundane Municipal (Belediye) Baths. Some pensions in the town, at the bottom of the ridge, have pools too.

If time allows, on your way back to Selçuk or Kuşadası take a detour to **Aphrodisias**, south of Nazilli near Karacasu, a beautiful ruined city thought by many to rival Ephesus.

Places to Stay

The government has said that the ridge-top hotels must soon close. In the meantime the *Tusan Moteli* (☎ 272 2010) and the *Motel Koru* (☎ 272 2429) charge US$65/80 a single/double, breakfast and dinner included.

The bargain pensions and hotels (over 60 of them) are below in the village – the further from the highway, the cheaper they are. For cheerful service and decent rooms, good bargains are the *Kervansaray Pension* (☎ 272 2209), where rooms cost US$12/18, and the nearby *Aspawa* (☎ 272 2094). The friendly, tidy *Koray Otel* (☎ 272 2300), a few streets south, has a restaurant, bar and pool; doubles cost US$18, including breakfast.

Places to Eat

Taking meals in your pension or hotel is usually best here – but ask prices in advance! Of the restaurants in the town, the *Gürsoy*, opposite the Yörük Motel in the village centre, has the nicest terrace, but the *Han*, around the corner facing the square, offers best value for money. Meals at either cost US$4 to US$6.

BODRUM

Bodrum, formerly Halicarnassus, is the site of the Mausoleum, the monumental tomb of King Mausolus, which is another of the Seven Wonders of the World.

Orientation & Information

The otogar is 500m inland along Cevat Şakir Caddesi from the Adliye Camii, a small mosque at the centre of the town. The PTT and several banks are on Cevat Şakir. The tourist office (☎ 316 1091; fax 316 7694) is beside the Castle of St Peter.

Bodrum's telephone area code is 252.

Things to See

There is now little left of the **Mausoleum**. Placed between Bodrum's perfect twin bays is the Gothic **Castle of St Peter**, built in 1402 and rebuilt in 1522 by the Crusaders, using stones from the tomb. It's now the **Museum of Underwater Archaeology**, and contains finds from the oldest Mediterranean shipwreck ever discovered. The museum is open from 8 am to noon and from 1 to 5 pm; entry costs US$3, with another US$1.75 each to visit the ancient wreck and a model of a Carian princess' tomb.

Walk west past the marina and over the hill to **Gümbet**, which has a nicer beach than Bodrum proper, though a bit polluted. **Gümüşlük**, to the far west of the Bodrum peninsula, is the best of the many smaller villages nearby. Dolmuş run there every hour.

Places to Stay

Some of the smaller villages on the peninsula such as Bitez Yalısı and Ortakent Yalısı have camp sites. There are more on the peninsula's north shore.

Bodrum is full of pensions and hotels costing US$6 to US$10 per person; prices rise steeply as you approach the waterfront, but they drop in the off season.

Behind the Belediye (town hall) on Türkkuyusu Sokak, try the *Sevin Pansiyon* (☎ 316 8361) which has doubles with shower for US$24, or the cheaper *Titiz* (☎ 316 1534) at No 18, or *Melis* (☎ 316 1487), at No 50.

Two nearly identical quiet, modern places renting double rooms with showers for US$20 are on Menekşe Çıkmazı, a narrow alley which begins between Neyzen Tevfik 84 and 86: the *Yenilmez* (☎ 316 2520) at No 30, and the *Menekşe* (☎ 316 0537) at No 34. Off season, breakfast is included.

The *Şenlik Pansiyon* (☎ 316 6382), at No 115 is right on the street and a bit pricey at US$28 a double, but behind it is the family-run *Sedan* (☎ 316 0355), Türkkuyusu Sokak 121. Newer double rooms with shower go for US$20; older doubles without water are US$15.

Best of all is the wonderful *Su Otel* (☎ 316 6906), Turgutreis Caddesi, 1201 Sokak (follow the signs), with a charming flower-filled courtyard, a swimming pool and rooms decorated in local crafts; doubles with bath cost US$40 to US$55 in summer.

Places to Eat

For very cheap eats, buy a dönerli sandviç (dur-nehr-LEE sahn-DVEECH, sandwich with roast lamb) for less than US$2 at a streetside *büfe* (buffet). Look for the words in the window.

In July and August, the cheapest food is at simple local eateries well inland, without menus in English and German. Most serve no alcohol.

In the grid of small market streets just east of the Adliye Camii are several restaurants. *Babadan*, *Ziya'nin Yeri* and *Üsküdarlı* are patronised by locals as well as foreigners, and serve plates of döner for about US$2.75, beer for US$1.30. For cheaper fare, continue eastward to a little plaza filled with open-air restaurants serving pide and kebab. The *Nazilli* is the favourite here, but the *Şahin*

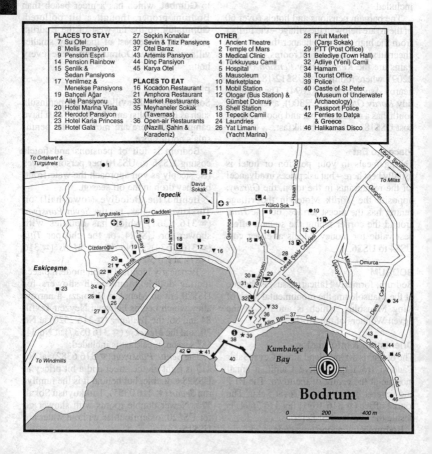

PLACES TO STAY	
7	Su Otel
8	Melis Pansiyon
9	Pension Espri
14	Pension Rainbow
15	Şenlik & Sedan Pansiyons
17	Yenilmez & Menekşe Pansiyons
19	Bahçeli Ağar Aile Pansiyonu
20	Hotel Marina Vista
22	Herodot Pansiyon
23	Hotel Karia Princess
25	Hotel Gala
27	Seçkin Konaklar
30	Sevin & Titiz Pansiyons
37	Otel Baraz
43	Artemis Pansiyon
44	Dinç Pansiyon
45	Karya Otel

PLACES TO EAT	
16	Kocadon Restaurant
21	Amphora Restaurant
33	Market Restaurants
35	Meyhaneler Sokak (Tavernas)
36	Open-air Restaurants (Nazili, Şahin & Karadeniz)

OTHER	
1	Ancient Theatre
2	Temple of Mars
3	Medical Clinic
4	Türkkuyusu Camii
5	Hospital
6	Mausoleum
10	Marketplace
11	Mobil Station
12	Otogar (Bus Station) & Gümbet Dolmuş
13	Shell Station
18	Tepecik Camii
24	Laundries
26	Yat Limanı (Yacht Marina)
28	Fruit Market (Çarşı Sokak)
29	PTT (Post Office)
31	Belediye (Town Hall)
32	Adliye (Yeni) Camii
34	Hamam
38	Tourist Office
39	Police
40	Castle of St Peter (Museum of Underwater Archaeology)
41	Passport Police
42	Ferries to Datça & Greece
46	Halikarnas Disco

and the *Karadeniz* are almost as good. A pide topped with meat or cheese costs only US$3 or so.

In warm weather, check out Meyhaneler Sokak (Taverna St), off İskele Caddesi. Wall-to-wall tavernas serve food and drink to happy crowds nightly for US$12 to US$18.

Of the up-marketplaces, *Amphora* (☎ 316 2368) on the western bay is the best, with meals for around US$15 a head. More expensive, but quite pleasant, is *Kocadon* (☎ 316 3705), back toward the centre a bit.

Getting There & Away
Bodrum has a fast and frequent bus service to all points in the region and to some beyond, including Antalya (11 hours; US$22), Fethiye (4½ hours; US$14), İzmir (four hours; US$9), Kuşadası and Selçuk (three hours; US$9), Marmaris (three hours; US$8) and Pamukkale (five hours; US$13).

Hydrofoils and boats go to Kos (İstanköy) frequently in summer for US$22.50 one way, US$29 return (plus a US$13 Greek port tax at Kos). In summer there are also boats to Datça, Didyma, Knidos, Marmaris and Rhodes; check with the tourist office.

The Mediterranean Coast

Turkey's Mediterranean coastline winds eastward for more than 1200 km from Marmaris to Antakya on the Syrian border. East of Marmaris the 'Turquoise Coast' is perfect for boat excursions, with many secluded coves and quiet bays all the way to Fethiye. The rugged peninsula east of Fethiye to Antalya – immortalised by Homer as 'Lycia' – and the Taurus Mountains east of Antalya are wild and beautiful. Farther east you pass through fewer seaside resorts and more workaday cities. The entire coast is liberally sprinkled with impressive ruins, studded with beautiful beaches and washed by pellucid water ideal for sports.

MARMARİS
Marmaris, like Bodrum, is sited on a beautiful bay at the edge of a hilly peninsula. The sculptured coastline and crystalline waters are probably the reason Marmaris has become Turkey's premier yachting port. The Greek island of Rhodes is a short voyage south.

Orientation & Information
Marmaris has a small castle overlooking the town centre. İskele Meydanı (the main square) and the tourist office (☎ 412 1035) are by the ferry pier just north-east of the castle. The centre is mostly a pedestrian precinct, and new development stretches many km to the south-east around the bay.

The otogar is north of the yacht harbour. Hacı Mustafa Sokak, otherwise known as Bar St, runs down from near the otogar to the bazaar; action here keeps going until the early hours of the morning.

The post office (PTT) is on Fevzipaşa Caddesi. Marmaris' telephone area code is 252.

Things to See & Do
The **castle** has a few unexciting exhibition rooms but offers fine views of Marmaris. It's open daily except Monday from 8 am to noon and 1 to 5 pm; entry is US$1.

There are daily **boat trips** in summer to nearby Paradise Island (about US$15 a head) and further afield to **Dalyan** and **Caunos** (about US$30 a head). The beach at **İçmeler**, 10 km away by minibus, is marginally better than that at Marmaris.

Datça, a village two hours out on the peninsula, has now been 'discovered' but is still a great place to visit; less spoilt is **Bozburun**, not as far west. At the tip of the peninsula are the ruins of the ancient port of **Knidos**, accessible by road or excursion boat.

Places to Stay
Marmaris has hundreds of lodgings, but few are cheap. Ask at the tourist office about *ev pansiyonları* (home pensions), renting double rooms for US$8 to US$12. Some are

inland from Abdi İpekçi Park on 97 Sokak, including the *Altun*, the *Taşkın*, the *Erdel*, the *Cihan* (☎ (252) 412 4312), and the *Etem*.

For lodgings and camping on the beach, take a 'Siteler-Turban' minibus along the waterfront road to the last stop at the *Turban Marmaris Tatil Köyü* holiday village, four km south-west of the main square. Besides *Berk Camping*, with tent sites for US$6 and cabins for US$18, there are several small pension-like hotels renting double rooms for around US$20: the *Birol*, *Yüzbaşı*, *Sembol*, *Panorama* and *Tümer*.

The original *Interyouth Hostel* (☎ 412 6432) at Kemeraltı Mahallesi, İyiliktaş Mevkii 14, has been joined by a second hostel deep in the bazaar at Tepe Mahallesi, 42 Sokak 45 which has cheekily co-opted the same *Interyouth Hostel* (☎ 412 3687) name. Neither is ideal – the original stranded in Marmaris' rear wastelands, its newer rival in the noisy bazaar. Both charge US$6 for a dorm bed, US$8 in a double.

A few small old hotels remain just off the main square near the tourist office, including the *Otel İmbat* (☎ 412 1413) and the unsigned *Otel Karaaslan* (☎ 412 1867);

both charge US$14 a double with private bath, but this area is now *very* noisy with disco-bars.

Pricier but charming is the *Hotel Begonya* (☎ 412 4095), Hacı Mustafa Sokak 101, north-west of the yacht harbour, one street inland. A stone house around a courtyard filled with flowers, it has singles/doubles with shower for US$35/45, including one of Turkey's best breakfasts. Noise from nearby bars goes on until the early hours, though.

Places to Eat

The 'resort rule' applies: the farther you go inland from the water, the higher the quality and the lower the price. Have some Marmaris honey while you're here – it's famous.

The *Ayyıldız Restaurant*, near the mosque in the bazaar, is fairly dependable, with three course meals for US$7.50 or so. Of the open-air restaurants along Fevzipaşa Caddesi (the street with the PTT), the *Marmaris Lokantası* is one of the best, offering İskender kebap for US$4. The *Yeni Liman* is also good and cheap, with full meals for US$8 to US$10, as is the *Öz 49*.

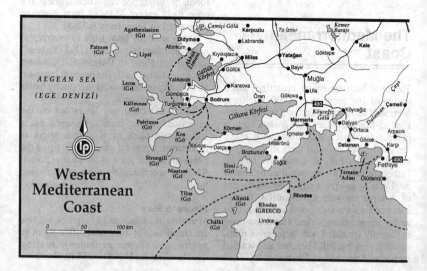

Hacı Mustafa Sokak (Bar St) harbours all sorts of possibilities for cheap eating from filled baked potatoes through to pizzas. *Beyoğlu Café-bar* has cheap fish meals for US$7.50. *Pizza Napoli* offers tasty, filling pizzas for around US$6.

Surprisingly, the pizza and steak meals at the posh *Pineapple International Restaurant* (☎ 412 4999) in the Netsel Marina (new yacht harbour) cost only US$15 to US$20.

The best place for a sundowner is *Panorama Bar*; follow the signs from the castle end of the bazaar.

Getting There & Away

Marmaris otogar, north of the new yacht marina, has frequent direct buses and minibuses to all places in the region, including Antalya (eight hours; US$14), Bodrum (three hours; US$8), Dalyan (via Ortaca, two hours; US$4), Datça (1¾ hours; US$4), and Fethiye (three hours; US$6.50). Bozburun minibuses run once daily (1½ hours; US$2), more frequently in summer. Small car ferries run to Rhodes daily except Sunday in summer (less frequently in the off season) for US$41 one way or US$56 return (plus US$13 port tax at Rhodes and US$10 to re-enter Turkey).

KÖYCEĞİZ & DALYAN

Köyceğiz, 75 km east of Marmaris, stands at the edge of a great placid lake. Although a pleasant, peaceful farming town with a few pensions and hotels, it's overshadowed by its smaller but more touristy neighbour, the town of Dalyan.

Set in lush river-delta farming country, Dalyan has it all: fertile soil, a placid river meandering by, excellent fishing and, to the south at İztuzu, beautiful **beaches** which are the natural nesting ground of the *carretta carretta*, or ancient sea turtle.

As if that were not enough, Dalyan has ruins: dramatic rock-cut **Lycian tombs** in the cliff facing the town, and the ruined city of **Caunos** within easy boat excursion reach downriver. Upriver on the shores of Köyceğiz Lake are **hot springs** at Sultaniye Kaplıcaları.

You will need little help finding your way around Dalyan. Dozens of pensions and small but comfortable hotels are ranged north and south of the town centre. The local boaters' cooperative sets rates for river excursions to points of interest.

DALAMAN & GÖCEK

Dalaman, 23 km south-east of Dalyan, is another farming community, but with an international airport *(hava limanı)*. A few scheduled flights supplement the holiday charters. The town has hotels and pensions covering all price ranges, and you can camp in the Belediye Koru Parkı pine forest 300m north of the otogar. Buses run to all points along the coast and beyond.

Göcek, 23 km east of Dalaman through fragrant pine forests, is a small fishing town getting used to tourism. With an odd mix of cheap pensions and camping grounds for backpackers, and white-tablecloth restaurants for sailing enthusiasts, Göcek is pleasant and laid-back, even though it lacks good beaches.

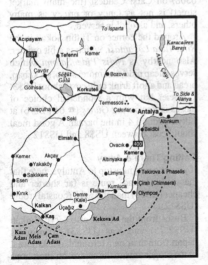

FETHİYE & ÖLÜDENİZ

Fethiye has superb beaches and cheap lodgings, crowded in summer but worth the diversion off the road. This is the site of ancient Telmessos, with giant Lycian stone sarcophagi from about 400 BC littered about, and the rock-cut Tomb of Amyntas looming from a cliff above the town.

Orientation & Information

The otogar is two km east of the centre. As you come into town you pass near the government buildings, the PTT and the museum, skirt the market district on the left, then curve round the bay past the tourist office (☎ & fax 614 1527) next to the Dedeoğlu Otel, and then by the yacht marina on the western side of the town.

The telephone area code is 252.

Things to See & Do

The **Tomb of Amyntas** is open from 8 am to 7 pm; entry costs US$1. There's a marked hiking trail over the hills to the Ottoman Greek 'ghost town' of **Kayaköy**. The beach at **Çalış** to the north of the tomb is many km long, and backed by hotels and pensions.

To the south, 17 km over the mountains, is the gorgeous lagoon of **Ölüdeniz** ('Dead Sea'), too beautiful for its own good and now one of the most famous beach spots on the Mediterranean. Inland from the beach are moderately priced bungalow and camping areas, as well as some hotels.

If you stay in Fethiye longer than overnight, be sure to take the '12 Island Tour' **boat excursion**. With its swimming, cruising and sightseeing, it may be your most pleasant day in Fethiye. Prices range around US$8 per person. Don't miss the **Turkish bath** in the bazaar either. It's open from 7 am to midnight and the full treatment costs about US$10.

Places to Stay

There's a cluster of pensions near the stadium just west of the otogar. To find them walk straight down the road heading north from the minibus station.

Next to the stadium, *Göreme Pansiyon*

(☎ 614 6944), Dolgu Sahası, Stadyum Yanı 25, has spotless rooms for US$10/16 a single/double, and a proprietor who lived in London. Across the road is the similar but cheaper *Moonlight Pension* (☎ 614 2178). Turn right and follow the signs for the *Olimpiyat Pansiyon* (☎ 614 3444), Yergüz Caddesi 48, with big, clean rooms for US$14 a double, breakfast included.

Other pensions are uphill from the yacht marina along Fevzi Çakmak Caddesi. The *Yıldırım* (☎ 614 3913), the *Pınara* (☎ 614 2151), the *Derelioğlu* (☎ 614 5983), the *Polat* (☎ 614 2347) and the *İrem* (☎ 614 3985) all charge US$7 to US$9 per person; breakfast costs US$1.

The *İdeal Pension* (☎ 614 1981), Zafer Caddesi 1, has superb views from its terrace, but is a bit more expensive. Even farther uphill, the *İnci Pansiyon* (☎ 614 3325) has marvellous views and is blissfully quiet, with similar prices. *Cesur Pansiyon* (☎ 614 3398) across the street is similar.

Places to Eat

The market district is packed with open-air restaurants, where you should watch out for bill fiddling. The *Tahirağa Lokantası* (☎ 614 6308) on Çarşı Caddesi (the main market street) is not as fancy or pricey as many others, and alcohol is served.

Around the corner on Tütün Sokak is the *Rifat Tuna Lokantası*, which is a bit quieter. Also nearby is *Nefis Pide Salonu* which serves cheap pide, and more: soup, şiş kebap, bread and a soft drink only costs about US$3.

Pricier but with a wonderful choice of mezes is *Restaurant Güneş* (☎ 614 2776) at Likya Caddesi 4 in the bazaar. A good meal should cost between US$8 and US$12.

Getting There & Away

If you're going nonstop to Antalya, note that the *yayla* (inland) route is far shorter and cheaper (US$8) than the *sahil* (coastal) route (US$12).

Buses from the otogar also serve Kalkan (US$2.75) and Kaş (US$3). Minibuses depart from their own terminal, one km west of the otogar toward the centre, on short hops to other points along the coast, like Patara (US$2.75), Kınık (for Xanthos, US$2) and Ölüdeniz (US$1).

RUINS NEAR FETHİYE

Lycia was heavily populated in ancient times, as shown by the large number of wonderful old cities, reachable by minibus from Fethiye. **Tlos** is far up into the mountains near Kemer on the *yayla* (inland) route to Antalya. **Pınara**, 46 km east of Fethiye then six km south, right off the road, is also a mountainous site.

Letoön, 63 km east of Fethiye, a few km off the highway in a fertile valley filled with tomato greenhouses, has excellent mosaics, a good theatre and a pool sacred as the place of worship of the goddess Leto.

Xanthos, a few km east of Letoön above the village of Kınık, is among the most impressive sites along this part of the coast, with its Roman theatre and Lycian pillar tombs. At **Patara**, seven km farther east (turn at Ovaköy), the attraction is not so much the ruins as the incredible 20 km beach. Lodgings in Patara village, 2.5 km inland from the beach, range from camping to cheap pensions and hotels to the three-star *Otel Beyhan Patara* (☎ (242) 844 5098).

KALKAN

Kalkan, everybody's idea of what a small Turkish fishing village should be, is 11 km east of the Patara turn-off. It tumbles down a steep hillside to a yacht marina (in ancient times, the port).

Kalkan's old stone and wood houses have been restored as lodgings – some expensive, some moderate, some still fairly cheap. The streets above the marina are chock-a-block with atmospheric open-air restaurants. There are no good beaches to speak of, but the inevitable excursion boat tours (or minibuses) can take you to Patara Beach and secluded coves along the coast. More information on things to do is available from the tourist office (☎ 844 1339).

Kalkan's telephone area code is 242.

Places to Stay

If you decide to stay, look for cheap pensions (US$10/15 a single/double) at the top of the town.

On the main shopping street, *Özalp Pansiyon* (☎ 844 3486) charges US$9/13 for modern rooms with shower. *Çelik Pansiyon* (☎ 844 2126), Yalıboyu 9, is simple, charging US$9/16, breakfast included. *Holiday Pension* and, up the hill across from it, the *Gül Pansiyon* (☎ 844 3099), are both more primitive and slightly cheaper.

Towards the harbour, the *Akın Pansiyon* (☎ 844 3025) has some waterless rooms for US$17 a double; rooms lower down with private showers cost US$22, breakfast included. The *Akgül* (☎ 844 3270) around the corner is similar.

Çetin Pansiyon (☎ 844 3094) is quieter, at US$16 a double, as is the nearby *Altan Pension* (☎ 844 1044).

Kalkan Han (☎ 844 3151) is charming at US$38/55, including breakfast.

KAŞ

Kaş, called Antiphellus in ancient times, has a picturesque quayside square, friendly people and a big **market** on Sunday. It's a fine, laid-back place to spend some time. The tourist office (☎ 836 1238; fax 836 1368) is on the square.

The telephone area code is 322.

Things to See & Do

Lycian stone **sarcophagi** are dotted about the streets, and tombs are cut into the cliffs above the town. The Greek island of **Kastellorizo** is visible just a short distance across the water and can be reached by daily boat.

Apart from enjoying the town's ambiance and a few small pebble beaches, you can walk west a few hundred metres to the well-preserved **theatre**, then take a boat excursion to Kalkan, Patara, the Blue Cave, Üçağız or Demre. The tourist office has brochures.

Places to Stay

Kaş has everything from camp sites to cheap pensions and four-star hotels. *Kaş Camping*, in an olive grove a km west of town past the theatre, also has simple bungalows.

At the otogar you'll be accosted by pension-pushers. Yenicami Caddesi (or Recep Bilgin Caddesi), just south of the otogar, has lots of places including the *Orion Hotel* (☎ 836 1938), with tidy rooms and sea views for US$13/22 a single/double, breakfast included. Farther along the street, or just off it, are the *Akkın Pansion* (☎ 836 1232), the *Anıl Motel* (☎ 836 1791), *Hilal* (☎ 836 1207), and the *Melisa* (☎ 836 1068). At the southern end of the street by the mosque is the *Ay Pansiyon* (☎ 836 1562), where the front rooms have sea views.

Turn right at the Ay Pansiyon and follow the signs to the quieter *Çetin Pension* and the *Pansiyon Kale* (☎ 836 1094), right by the theatre ruins. Opposite the Çetin is the slightly pricier *Korsan Karakedi Motel* (☎ 836 1887) with a lovely roof terrace with bar. Rooms here cost US$13/17 a single/double.

On the other (eastern) side of town many more pensions offer similar accommodation. Try the *Koştur* (☎ 836 1264).

For more comforts and services, try the two-star *Hotel Kayahan* (☎ 836 1313) above Küçük Çakıl Plaj, where rooms with wonderful sea views cost US$28/30; or the three-star *Hotel Club Phellos* (☎ 836 1953), the fanciest place in town, with a swimming pool and comfortable rooms for US$40/65, including breakfast.

Places to Eat

Five popular restaurants fill a shady alley between the marketplace and the main square: the *Aslı Ocakbaşı, Derya, Orkinos, Evakent* and *Baba'nın Yeri*. All serve three course meals for US$4 to US$8.

On the main square, the *Noel Baba* is a favourite cafe-restaurant for breakfast and light meals from US$1.50 to US$4. The *Corner Café*, at the PTT end of İbrahim Serin Caddesi, serves juices or a vegetable omelet for US$1, yoghurt with fruit and honey for US$1.50. The *Café Merhaba* across the street is good for cakes.

The *Eriş*, behind the tourist office, is a

favourite, as much for its setting as its food. Also popular is *Smiley's Restaurant* nearby, where pizza or seafood meals cost around US$3 to US$6.

Round off the evening in the wonderfully decorated *Sun Café*, at the western end of the quay behind the mosque, which sometimes has live music.

KEKOVA & ÜÇAĞIZ

Up in the hills 14 km east of Kaş a road leads south to Kekova and Üçağız, two villages amid partly sunken ancient ruins. Üçağız, 20 km from the highway, is a farming and fishing hamlet with a handful of very basic pensions and a few simple waterfront restaurants built right atop the ruins of ancient Teimiussa. Boat owners will take you on a tour (US$10 to US$16 per person) of the bay.

KAŞ TO ANTALYA

Hugging the coast backed by pine-clad mountains, the main road goes east from Kaş, then north to Antalya, passing the ruins of a dozen ancient cities.

Demre (Kale)

Demre (ancient Myra, also known as Kale), set in a rich alluvial plain covered in greenhouses, is interesting because of its generous 4th century bishop who, according to legend, gave anonymous gifts to dowryless girls, thus enabling them to marry. He was later canonised as St Nicholas, the original Father Christmas or Santa Claus (Noel Baba in Turkish). For US$3 you can visit the restored 12th century **Church of St Nicholas** built to hold his tomb. Two km inland from the church at Demre is a rock face honeycombed with ancient **tombs**, right next to a large **Roman theatre**. Both are open daily from 8 am to 5.30 pm; entry costs US$1.

Most people don't stay overnight here, but if you do, head straight for the *Kekova Pansiyon* (☎ (242) 871 2804), İlkokul Caddesi 38, 800m south of the main square past the bus station towards the beach. The rooms are US$6/9 a single/double. If it's full, try the neighbouring *Otel Topçu* (☎ 871 2200). The pricier *Hotel Simge*

(☎ 871 3674), a block east of the main square near the PTT, charges US$20 for doubles with balconies, bathrooms and breakfast, but it needs updating.

As for meals, the *Şehir* and *Çınar* near the main square provide basic sustenance. In high season, better fare is offered five km west at **Çayağzı**, the ancient Andriake, Demre's harbour, where the beach, the views and the food are fine.

Olympos

After climbing into the mountains, you reach a turn-off marked for Olympos. From here it's just over eight km down a winding unpaved road to the village, and a farther 3.5 km along an ever-worsening road to the site of **ancient Olympos**. A wild, abandoned place, the Olympos ruins peek out from forest copses, rock outcrops and riverbanks. It's perfect for the rough camper. A few small restaurants provide sustenance. The beach is magnificent, although pebbly.

Çavuşköy/Adrasan, on the next cove to the east, has half a dozen hotels and pensions, ranging from the very simple to the quite comfortable.

Chimaera

According to legend, the Chimaera (Yanartaş), a natural eternal flame, was the hot breath of a subterranean monster. Easily sighted by mariners in ancient times, it is today a mere glimmer of its former flamy self.

Turn off the highway less than a km east of the eastern Olympos turn-off; the road is marked for Çıralı, seven km towards the sea. Çıralı has lots of good cheap pensions and camping grounds, including the *Barış, Sahil and Bizim Cennet*, all charging US$4 or US$5 per person. Keep walking westwards for the small but friendly *Rüya Pansiyon* (☎ (242) 825 7055), tucked away behind a school, and for the *Blue Blue Pansiyon* (☎ (242) 825 7013). The *Florya Pension* trumpets its health-minded food as a selling point.

To see the Chimaera, go three km east down a neighbouring valley. If you're

driving, park at the end of the valley, then follow the signs for the half-hour climb.

Phaselis

Two km from the highway, Phaselis is a collection of ruins framing three small, perfect bays. It's a good place for a swim; bring a picnic. The ruins are open daily from 7.30 am to 7 pm; entry costs US$1.

Kemer

Built to the specifications of resort planners and architects, Kemer was custom-made for the package holiday traveller. Its white buildings and straight streets seem sterile, but there's a nice little beach by the marina and, above it, a **Yörük Park** (Nomad Park), with exhibits showing aspects of traditional life from the region. The place to stay here is the *King's Garden Pension* (☎ (242) 814 1039), on the north side of town, 400m north-east of the minibus station. There is camping, simple rooms (US$40 for two with all meals) and good meals.

ANTALYA

The main town of the coast, Antalya has one of the most attractive harbour settings in the Mediterranean. It's fun to kick around in **Kaleiçi**, the old restored Ottoman town by the Roman harbour – now the yacht marina. The **bazaar** is interesting and the archaeological museum outstanding. The **beaches** are out of town, to the west (Konyaaltı Plaj, a pebble beach) and the east (Lara Plaj, a sand beach).

Orientation & Information

The main otogar is four km north of the centre on the D 650 highway to Burdur. The city centre is at Kalekapısı, a major intersection right next to Cumhuriyet Meydanı, with its dramatic equestrian statue of Atatürk. Kaleiçi, the old town, is south of Kalekapısı down the hill.

The Doğu Garaj (eastern otogar) is 600m east (left) of Kalekapısı along Ali Çetinkaya Caddesi. Atatürk Caddesi, 100m east of Kalekapısı, goes south past Hadriaynüs

Kapısı (Hadrian's Gate). A bit farther along is the pleasant Karaali Park.

There are two tourist offices. One (☎ 247 6298) is in Kaleiçi on Mermerli Sokak across from the Hotel Aspen. The other (☎ 241 1747), at Cumhuriyet Caddesi 2, is 250m west of Kalekapısı (look for the sign 'Antalya Devlet Tiyatrosu' on the right-hand side; it's in this building). The Turkish Airlines office (☎ 241 0558) is in the same building. The PTT is around the corner on Güllük (Burdur) Caddesi.

The telephone area code is 242.

Things to See

Behind the clock tower is Antalya's symbol, the **Yivli Minare** (Grooved Minaret), which rises above an old building which was once a mosque, and is now an art gallery.

From Kalekapısı, go east 100m along Ali Çetinkaya Caddesi to Atatürk Caddesi, then south to the **Hadriaynüs Kapısı** (Hadrian's Gate), a monumental gate built for the Roman emperor's visit in 130 AD. A bit farther along is **Karaali Park**, perched on cliffs above the sea.

In Kaleiçi, the **Kesik Minare** (truncated minaret) marks a ruined Roman temple.

Cumhuriyet Caddesi leads west to the **Antalya Museum**, two km from Kalekapısı. It is open from Tuesday to Sunday, 9 am to 5 pm for US$2. Past the Sheraton and Falez hotels along Cumhuriyet Caddesi is **Konyaaltı Beach**.

Places to Stay

The *Parlar Mocamp*, 14 km north on the Burdur highway (D 650), has unshaded tent and campervan sites. *Camping Bambus* (☎ 321 5263), on the road to Lara Plajı, has modern facilities on the beach.

Kaleiçi is full of pensions; find them by following the little signs. *Garden Pansiyon* (☎ 247 1930), Zafer Sokak 16 (or Hesapçı 44), has a few US$9 rooms, but most have showers and cost US$18, including breakfast. The *Bahar Aile Pansiyon* (☎ 248 2089), Akarçeşme Sokak 5, is unrestored and frankly unattractive, but its simple, basic clean waterless rooms are low in price:

US$12 a double; the showers are clean. Other cheap places include *Adler* (☎ 241 7818) at Civelek Sokak 16, and the *Saltur Pansion* (☎ 247 6238), on the corner of Hesapçı and Hıdırlık sokaks, charging US$15 for a double with shower and breakfast. The *Bermuda* and *Senem* across the street are other good bets.

For a bit more money Kaleiçi has many other beautiful pensions and hotels, including the prettily decorated *Atelya Pension* (☎ 241 6416) at Civelek Sokak 21 where doubles cost US$26 including breakfast.

Pricier but worth it is the *Frankfurt Pension* (☎ 247 6224), Hıdırlık Sokak 25, a spotless place for US$28/38 a single/double.

Places to Eat

Many pensions serve good meals at decent prices; ask at yours.

Eski Sebzeciler İçi Sokak, a short street just south-west of the junction of Cumhuriyet and Atatürk caddesis, is filled with open-air restaurants where a kebab, salad and drink can cost as little as US$4. The speciality is Antalya's own tandır kebap (mutton cooked in an earthenware pot), but döner kebap is also served.

Cheaper meals are to be had on a back street running from near Eski Sebzeciler İçi Sokak to Kalekapısı. Try the *Surkent Restaurant* for cheap lahmacun (Arabic soft pizza) and pide, or the nearby *Sultanyar* for more substantial meals.

For grills, you can't beat the *Parlak Restaurant* (☎ 241 6553), a block up Kazım Özalp/Şarampol Caddesi on the left. Skewered chicken and lamb kebabs sizzle as patrons drink rakı and beer. A full meal of meze, grills and drinks costs from US$8 to US$12 a person. The neighbouring *Plaza Fast Food* is the sanitised version of the Parlak.

Getting There & Away

Turkish Airlines has daily nonstop flights from Antalya to Ankara and İstanbul, and weekly nonstop flights to Amman, Lefkoşa (Nicosia), London, Tel Aviv and Zürich. İstanbul Airlines also has frequent flights to

İstanbul. The airport bus costs US$1, a taxi about US$10, or take any eastbound minibus and walk the final two km.

Beach buses leave from the Doğu Garaj on Ali Çetinkaya Caddesi – the Konyaaltı minibus goes west, the Lara minibus east. You can get to the local ruins from here too: take an 'Aksu' dolmuş for Perge, and 'Manavgat' for Side.

From the otogar hourly buses go to Alanya (two hours; US$44), Konya (six hours; US$12), Nevşehir (for Cappadocia, nine hours; US$18), Side (1½ hours; US$3), and other towns.

AROUND ANTALYA

This stretch of coast has plenty more Greek and Roman ruins if you can take them. **Perge**, east of Antalya just north of Aksu, includes a 12,000 seat stadium and a theatre for 15,000. **Aspendos**, 47 km east of Antalya, has Turkey's best preserved ancient theatre, dating from the 2nd century AD; it is still used for performances during the Antalya Festival in September. **Termessos**, high in the mountains off the Korkuteli road, to the west of Antalya, has a spectacular setting and demands some vigorous walking and climbing to see it all.

SİDE

Once an idyllic seaside village, Side ('SEE-deh') has been overrun by tourists, and by carpet and leather shops. It is now a raucous, tawdry, overcrowded caricature of its former self. It was once the main slave market at this end of the Mediterranean, and a base for pirates. Its impressive ancient structures include a **Roman bath** (now an excellent small museum, open daily from 8 am to 5.15; entry is US$2), the old **city walls**, a huge **amphitheatre** (open daily from 8 am to 5.15 pm; entry is US$2) and seaside marble **temples** to Apollo and Athena. Its excellent beaches are packed in summer.

The village is three km south of the highway at Manavgat; minibuses (70c) will take you between the two. To and from Antalya and Alanya you'll have more (and probably cheaper) connections at Manavgat.

The tourist office (☎ (242) 753 1265; fax 753 1830) is on the road into town, 1.5 km from the centre.

The village itself is packed willy-nilly with pensions and hotels, all of which fill up daily in summer. The little pensions on the road into town from Manavgat are cheaper but less convenient. The larger hotels and motels are west of the town along the beach.

ALANYA

Dominated by the ruins of a magnificent Seljuk fortress perched high on a promontory, Alanya is second only to Antalya as a Turkish Mediterranean resort. Indeed, it was a resort in the 13th century, when the Seljuk sultans came down from Konya for sun and fun. Once a pretty, easy-going place, it has grown in recent years into a big, bustling, noisy city. The good beaches to the east and west are now lined with hotels.

The bus station is three km west of the centre; you can get to town in a dolmuş or a municipal bus (marked 'ALSO') and get off at the roundabout by the little mosque. Downhill towards the big mosque is the old waterfront area with trendy shops and good food; uphill (south) above the harbour are some good cheap hotels. The tourist office (☎ & fax 513 1240) is on the western side of the promontory.

The telephone area code is 242.

Things to See & Do

If you stop here, visit the Seljuk **Kızıl Kule** (Red Tower, built in 1226), down by the harbour. It's open daily except Monday from 8 am to noon and from 1.30 to 5.30 pm for US$2. Also worth checking out is the **kale** (fortress, also built in 1226) atop the promontory. It's open daily from 8 am to 7pm for US$2. Hire a boat (US$17 to US$27) for an excursion to caves beneath the promontory.

Places to Stay

Camping is available at the Forestry Department site of İncekum, 19 km west of town. Sadly, cheap accommodation has virtually disappeared as pensions give way to self-catering flats for package holiday-makers.

There are a couple of places left on noise-ridden İskele Caddesi, above the harbour. *Baba Hotel* (☎ 513 1032), at No 6, has cheap doubles without/with bath for US$13/16. The adjacent *Alanya Palas* (☎ 513 1016) is similar. The *Hotel Emek* (☎ 512 1223), at İskele Caddesi 12, has rooms with bath and balcony for US$18. The *Çınar Otel* (☎ 512 0063), Hürriyet Meydanı 6, on the plaza just north of the Hotel Baba, rents basic rooms for US$9/12 a double without/with shower.

Places to Eat

The best cheap-and-friendly food area is between the first two waterfront streets, near the big mosque, where the alleys are filled with tables and chairs. Most places here will give you a big döner kebap, salad and beer for US$4.50. The *Yönet* and *Mahperi* along the waterfront promenade are worth visiting for evening meals (around US$8 to US$12).

THE EASTERN COAST

East of Alanya the coast sheds some of its touristic freight. Seven km east of **Anamur** there is a wonderful castle, built by the emirs of Karaman in 1230, right on the beach, with pensions and camping grounds nearby. The ghostly ruins of Byzantine **Anamurium** are 8.5 km west of the town.

Silifke has a Crusader castle and a ruined Roman temple, but is mostly a transport point. At **Taşucu**, 11 km south-west of Silifke, boats and hydrofoils depart daily for Girne (Kyrenia) in Turkish Cyprus. **Kızkalesi** (Maiden's Castle) is a small holiday town with a striking Crusader castle offshore. **Mersin** is a modern city of no great interest apart from being a port for car ferries to **Famagusta** (Gazimagosa) in Turkish Cyprus. **Tarsus**, just east of Mersin, was the birthplace of St Paul and the place where Antony first ran into Cleopatra. Little is left to testify to these events, however. Smoky industry prevails.

Adana is the country's fourth largest city, an important agricultural centre and a major bus interchange for eastern Turkey.

HATAY

South-east of Adana, a tongue of Turkish territory licks at the mountains of north-western Syria – the land is called Hatay. You'll pass several impressive castles on the way to İskenderun (formerly Alexandretta), where Alexander the Great defeated the Persians and Jonah is thought to have been coughed up by the whale. It's still an important port city, with several Crusader buildings in evidence.

ANTAKYA

The biblical Antioch, where St Peter did a spell of converting, was said to be the most depraved city in the Roman Empire. You can see his church, the **Senpiyer Kilisesi**, three km outside the town. There are magnificent Roman mosaics in the **Antakya Museum** (open from Tuesday to Sunday, 8 am to noon and 1.30 to 5 pm; entry is US$2.50). Buses run from here to Aleppo and Damascus in Syria.

The provincial tourist office (☎ (326) 216 0610) is one km north of the museum. Cheap hotels are south of the otogar. The *Jasmin Hotel* (☎ (326) 212 7171), İstiklal Caddesi 14, has decent double rooms with shared baths for US$12. *Hotel Güney* (☎ (326) 214 9713), İstiklal Sokak 28, one narrow street east of İstiklal Caddesi, serves Turkish families who spend US$10 for a double without shower, US$14 with. The *Divan Oteli* (☎ (326) 215 1518), İstiklal Caddesi 62, costs about the same, and the cross-ventilation is fairly good.

Hotel Orontes (☎ (326) 214 5931), İstiklal Caddesi 58, is the best mid-range choice at US$24/34 a single/double for its 35 air-con rooms, some with river views.

Central Anatolia

The Anatolian plateau is Turkey's heartland. Atatürk realised this, and moved the capital to Ankara. Don't think of this area as a great central nothingness; cruise across the undulating steppe to Cappadocia and you'll be amazed by a region that looks as if it belongs in another world.

ANKARA

The capital of Turkey since 1923, Ankara's site was a Hittite settlement nearly 4000 years ago. Apart from a few interesting things to see it's not of special interest, but because of its central location there is a good chance you'll at least pass through here.

Orientation

Ankara's *hisar* (fortress) crowns a hill one km east of Ulus Meydanı (Ulus Square), centre of 'old Ankara', and near most of the cheap hotels. 'New Ankara' (Yenişehir) is 3.5 km to the south, centred on Kızılay Meydanı (KızılaySquare).

Atatürk Bulvarı is the city's main north-south axis. Ankara's mammoth otogar is 6.5 km south-west of Ulus Meydanı, the historic centre, and six km west of Kızılay Meydanı, the modern centre. The Turkish Airlines city bus terminal is next to the railway station (*gar*), 1400m south-west of Ulus Meydanı.

Opera Meydanı (Opera Square, also called İtfaiye Meydanı), just south of Ulus Meydanı, has lots of cheap hotels.

Information

The tourist office (☎ 229 2631) is at the square called Tandoğan Meydanı. The main post office is on Atatürk Bulvarı just south of Ulus Meydanı, although there's a handy branch beside the railway station where you can also change cash and travellers' cheques. In an emergency, you could try the tourist police at Boncuk Sokak 10/2, but the tourist office is probably a better bet.

The telephone area code is 312.

Embassies The diplomatic area is Çankaya, five km south of Kızılay, and the adjoining districts of Gaziosmanpaşa and Kavaklıdere. See Facts for the Visitor, earlier in this chapter, for a list of foreign embassies in Ankara.

Things to See

The **Anadolu Medeniyetleri Müzesi** (Anatolian Civilisations Museum; ☎ 324 3160),

Hisarparkı Caddesi, is Ankara's most worthwhile attraction. With the richest collection of Hittite artefacts in the world, it's an essential supplement to visiting central Turkey's Hittite sites. It's uphill from Ulus Meydanı, next to the citadel, and is open from 8.45 am to 5.15 pm; entry is US$2.50. The museum is closed on Monday in winter. When you're done at the museum, go to the top of the hill and wander among the old streets of the castle.

The **Ethnographic Museum** (☎ 311 9556) is at the junction of Atatürk Bulvarı and Talatpaşa Caddesi, just south of Opera Meydanı.

North of Ulus Meydanı, on the east side of Çankırı Caddesi (the continuation of Atatürk Bulvarı north of Ulus Meydanı), are some **Roman ruins**, including the **Jülyanüs Sütunu** (Column of Julian, erected in 363 AD) and the **Temple of Augustus & Rome**. Right next to the temple is the **Hacı Bayram Camii**, a sacred mosque commemorating the founder of a dervish order established in 1400. On the west side of Çankırı Caddesi are the **Roma Hamamları** (Roman Baths).

The **Anıtkabir** (Mausoleum of Atatürk), two km west of Kızılay Meydanı, is a monumental tomb and memorial to the founder of modern Turkey. It's open daily from 9 am to 4 pm; entry is free.

Places to Stay

Along the east side of Opera (or İtfaiye) Meydanı, on the corner of Sanayi Caddesi and Tavus Sokak near the Gazi Lisesi high school, try the *Otel Devran* (☎ 311 0485), Tavus Sokak 8, with doubles for US$16 with shower, US$18 with bath. The *Sipahi* (☎ 324 0235), Kosova Sokak 1, is old and dingy but serviceable in a pinch, and cheap at US$10 for a double with sink, US$13 with shower. Perhaps the best value on the street is at the *Otel Fuar* (☎ 312 3288), Kosova Sokak 11, where the same US$10 gets you a decent double room with sink, and showers down the hall.

For more comfort, the *Otel Mithat* (☎ 311 5410), Tavus Sokak 2, has shower-equipped doubles for US$18, and is a better choice

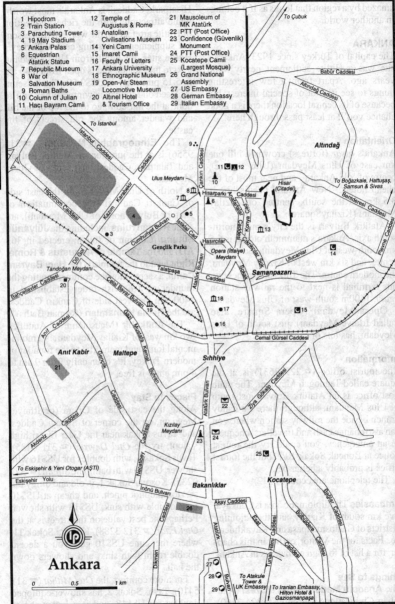

1 Hipodrom
2 Train Station
3 Parachuting Tower
4 19 May Stadium
5 Ankara Palas
6 Equestrian
  Atatürk Statue
7 Republic Museum
8 War of
  Salvation Museum
9 Roman Baths
10 Column of Julian
11 Hacı Bayram Camii

12 Temple of
   Augustus & Rome
13 Anatolian
   Civilisations Museum
14 Yeni Cami
15 İmaret Camii
16 Faculty of Letters
17 Ankara University
18 Ethnographic Museum
19 Open-Air Steam
   Locomotive Museum
20 Altinel Hotel
   & Tourism Office

21 Mausoleum of
   MK Atatürk
22 PTT (Post Office)
23 Confidence (Güvenlik)
   Monument
24 PTT (Post Office)
25 Kocatepe Camii
   (Largest Mosque)
26 Grand National
   Assembly
27 US Embassy
28 German Embassy
29 Italian Embassy

To Çubuk

Altındağ Caddesi

Babür Caddesi

Altındağ Caddesi

To İstanbul

İstanbul Caddesi

Altındağ

Hipodrom Caddesi

Kazım Karabekir Caddesi

Çankırı Caddesi

Ulus Meydanı

Hisar
(Citadel)

To Boğazkale, Hattuşaş,
Samsun & Sivas

Hisarparkı Caddesi

Bentderesi Caddesi

Cumhuriyet Bulvarı

İstiklal Cad

Gençlik Parkı

Konya Caddesi

Çiçekdağı Sok

Payitre Caddesi

Hasırcılar

Opera (İtfaiye)
Meydanı

Ulucanlar

Samanpazarı

Talatpaşa   Caddesi

Atatürk Bulvarı

Tandoğan Meydanı

Bahçelievler Caddesi

Celal Bayar Bulvarı

Gazi Mustafa Kemal Bulvarı

Anıt Caddesi

Anıt Kabir   Maltepe

Cemal Gürsel Caddesi

Sıhhiye

Ziya Gökalp Caddesi

Kızılay
Meydanı

Akdeniz   Caddesi   Gençlik   Caddesi

To Eskişehir & Yeni Otogar (AŞTİ)
Eskişehir   Yolu

Necatibey Caddesi

Bakanlıklar

İnönü Bulvarı

Kocatepe

Akay Caddesi

Büyükdere Caddesi   Caddesi

Atatürk   Bulvarı

Dikmen

Tunalı Hilmi Caddesi

Tunus   Caddesi

To Atakule
Tower &
UK Embassy

To Iranian Embassy,
Hilton Hotel &
Gaziosmanpaşa

Ankara

0   0.5   1 km

than the adjoining *Otel Akman* (☎ 324 4140), Tavus Sokak 6, which charges more.

North of Ulus and one street west of Çankırı Caddesi, the three-star *Hotel Oğultürk* (☎ 309 2900), Rüzgarlı Eşdost Sokak 6, has rooms with TV and minibar for US$26/40 a single/double, breakfast included. The nearby *Yıldız* (☎ 312 7581) is similar.

In 'new' Ankara south of Kızılay Meydanı, the one-star *Hotel Ergen* (☎ 417 5906), Karanfil Sokak 48, near Olgunlar Sokak, charges US$30/42 a single/double for rooms with bath.

Places to Eat

There are some good, cheap spots around Opera Meydanı. *Uğur Lokantası*, Tavus Sokak 2, is a clean aile (family-oriented) that serves full meals for US$5 or less. At the south-eastern corner of Ulus at Atatürk Bulvarı 3 is the *Akman Boza ve Pasta Salonu*, in the courtyard of a huge block of offices and shops. Order a pastry, omelet, sandwich or snack, and consume it at terrace tables around a tinkling fountain. Overlooking this place, on the upper storey, is *Kebabistan*, a family kebab place with good food and low prices – about US$3 to US$5 for a full meal of roast lamb, or less for just pide.

Çankırı Caddesi north of Ulus Meydanı also has numerous restaurants. *Çiçek Lokantası* is quite attractive, and serves drinks with meals (US$6 to US$9).

For a memorable meal at a very reasonable cost (US$9 to US$16 per person), try the *Zenger Paşa Konağı* (☎ 311 7070), Doyran Sokak 13, in Ankara's hisar. It's an old house with wonderful crafts and ethnographic displays, as well as good Ottoman-style food. *Kınacılar Evi* (☎ 312 5601), Kalekapısı Sokak 28, straight uphill from the hisar entrance, is an imposing place with airy rooms and some traditional dishes such as mantı (Turkish ravioli).

Getting There & Away

Air Turkish Airlines (☎ 309 0400), at Atatürk Bulvarı 167/A, Bakanlıklar, has daily nonstop flights to most Turkish cities.

Most international routes require a connection in İstanbul. İstanbul Airlines (☎ 432 2234), Atatürk Bulvarı 83, Kızılay, serves several Turkish cities, but more foreign ones.

Bus Ankara's huge otogar (AŞTİ) is the vehicular heart of the nation, with coaches to all places day and night. For İstanbul (seven hours; US$9 to US$20. Express buses, six hours; US$15 to US$24) they go at least every 15 minutes. Other sample fares are Antalya (10 hours; US$17), Bodrum (13 hours; US$20), Erzurum (15 hours; US$23), İzmir (8½ hours; US$14.50 to US$20) and Ürgüp/Cappadocia (five hours; US$9).

Train Seven daily express trains (7½ to 11 hours; US$11 to US$30), two of them with sleeping cars, connect Ankara and İstanbul. The *Fatih* and *Başkent* express are the fastest and most expensive.

The *İzmir Mavi Tren* (14 hours; US$13) hauls sleeping and dining cars. The evening *İzmir Express* (15 hours) has 1st and 2nd class carriages (US$15 and US$13).

Trains heading east of Ankara are not as comfortable or punctual as those travelling westward. The *Doğu Express*, hauling carriages and sleeping cars, departs each evening for Erzincan, Erzurum (25 hours; US$15, or US$32 for a bed) and Kars. On alternate mornings the *Güney Express* departs for Diyarbakır (26½ hours; US$15), and the *Vangölü Express* departs for Tatvan (31 hours; US$16; both haul sleeping cars (US$35).

Getting Around

The Airport Ankara's Esenboğa airport is 33 km north of the city centre. Havaş buses (40 minutes in light traffic; US$3.50) depart the Turkish Airlines city terminal at the railway station 1½ hours before domestic and two hours before international Turkish Airlines flights. A taxi costs US$20 or more. Cheaper shared taxis run from the railway station to the airport as well.

Local Transport Ankara's metro (underground transit system) is under construction.

Many city buses run the length of Atatürk Bulvarı. Buy a *bilet* (ticket, 50c) from kiosks by bus stops, or from a shop with the sign 'EGO Bilet(i)'.

City bus 198 departs the otogar headed for the railway station and Ulus; bus 623 goes via Kızılay to Gaziler.

Taxis are multitudinous, metered, and often suicidal, charging about US$3 for an average ride, or US$4 to US$6 from one end of the city to the other.

BOĞAZKALE

The Hittites ruled central Anatolia from about 2000 to 1180 BC. Boğazkale (called Hattuşaş in Hittite), 29 km off the Ankara-Samsun road (to the south), was the ancient capital of the Hittites until it was destroyed by the Phrygians. There is little left today apart from the walls and foundations of the buildings. But what walls! Crumbling though they are, they stretch for over 10 km and have five entrances, including the **Royal Gate**, the **Lion Gate** (flanked by stone lions) and the underground tunnel, **Yer Kapı**. The foundations are also inspiring – massive and imposing – although visited only by the occasional curious sheep. Largest is the site of the **Great Temple of the Storm God**, which has no fewer than 70 storerooms. The natural rock temple of **Yazılıkaya**, two km from the main site, has bas-reliefs of Hittite deities carved into the rock face.

In the village of Boğazkale is a small **museum**. Several small hotels are open in the warm months, with camping facilities. Take a bus to Sungurlu, then a minibus to Boğazkale.

Alacahöyük, 36 km north-east of Boğaz-kale near the main Ankara-Samsun road, is a pre-Hittite site, probably 6000 years old. The remains, however, including the Sphinx Gate, are Hittite. There is another small museum here.

KONYA

Known as Iconium in Roman times, Konya, due south of Ankara, is a conservative place, but it's one of the oldest continually occu-pied cities in the world, and is a showplace

for some striking Seljuk architecture. It was the capital of the Seljuk Turks, and it was here, in the 13th century, that the poet Mevlana Rumi inspired the founding of the whirling dervishes, one of Islam's important mystical orders. You can see them whirling here during the **Mevlana Festival** every December.

Orientation & Information

The centre of the city stretches from Alaettin Tepesi, the hill topped by the Alaettin Mosque (1221), along Alaettin Caddesi and Mevlana Caddesi to the tomb of Mevlana, now called the Mevlana Müzesi.

Outstanding Seljuk buildings around the Alaettin Tepesi are the **Büyük Karatay Müzesi**, once a Muslim theological semi-nary, now a ceramics museum; and the **Seminary of the Slender Minaret** (İnce Minare Medresesi), now the Museum of Wood & Stone Carving. Mevlana's **tomb** is topped by the brilliant green-tiled tower near the tourist office (☎ (332) 351 1074; fax 350 6461) and hotel area. The otogar is 3.5 km north of the centre. Minibuses will ferry you to the town centre for 25c.

Places to Stay & Eat

If you're staying, good budget places near the Mevlana Müzesi are the *Mavi Köşk* (☎ (332) 350 1904) and *Derviş* (☎ (332) 351 1688) hotels, side by side in Bostan Çelebi Sokak and both charging US$9/11 a sin-gle/double. Just doors away from them is *Öztemel Konya Fırın Kebap Salonu* where you can sample Konya's own *fırın kebap*, oven-roasted mutton, with a drink for US$4.

CAPPADOCIA

Cappadocia (Turkish: Kapadokya), the region between Ankara and Malatya, between the Black Sea and the Taurus Moun-tains, is famous for the fantastic natural **rock formations** of its valleys. Over the centuries people have carved rooms, houses, churches, fortresses, even complete underground cities into the soft, eerily eroded volcanic stone. Attractions include the Göreme and nearby Zelve valleys; rugged Ihlara Valley (south of

Aksaray) dotted with ancient churches, and Soğanlı with its scores of stone-cut chapels (early Christian monastics sought refuge throughout the region); and the huge underground cities at Kaymaklı and Derinkuyu (open from 8 am to 5 pm, 6.30 pm in summer; entry is US$2.50).

Information

Nevşehir is the biggest town. Touristy Ürgüp has a good selection of hotels and pensions, but Göreme village is most attractive to low-budget travellers. You can camp almost everywhere, most conveniently in the gardens of pensions.

Transport is easy between Nevşehir and everywhere else, and buses run on the hour between Avanos and Ürgüp, stopping in Göreme. Good, reasonably priced tours of the region are offered by Turtle Tours (☎ (384) 271 2388) across the road from Göreme otogar; and Hiro Tour (☎ (384) 271 2542), in the otogar. Nevşehir tourist office

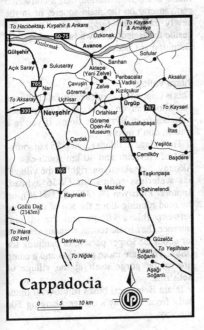

Cappadocia

0   5   10 km

(☎ (384) 213 3659) is sympathetic to budget travellers. Smaller, less useful offices are in Ürgüp and Avanos.

Nevşehir

This is a loud, unattractive town but it's good for information and for transport all over Cappadocia. Catch minibuses here for the astonishing underground cities at **Derinkuyu** and **Kaymaklı**. Much farther south at **Niğde** are rock-carved monasteries and churches, Hittite traces and interesting mosques.

Göreme & Zelve Valleys

The Göreme Valley is one of the most amazing sights in Turkey. Over the centuries a thick layer of volcanic tufa has been eroded into fantastic, eerie shapes. Early Christians carved chambers, vaults and labyrinths into them for use as churches, stables and homes.

Painted **church murals** can be seen in the rock-hewn monastery, nunnery and several dozen cave churches of the **Göreme Open-Air Museum** (Göreme Açık Hava Müzesi). Some murals date from as early as the 8th century, though the best are from the 10th to 13th centuries. Unlit for many centuries, they've hardly faded at all, though vandals have left their indelible mark. The museum is open daily from 8 am to 5.30 pm (4.30 pm in winter); entry is US$5.

Less touristed is the nearby **Zelve Valley** on the road to Avanos (same price and opening times).

Three km away is **Uçhisar**, a picturesque town built around, and into, a prominent peak. A room-to-room scramble through its rock citadel leads to fine views from the summit.

Places to Stay At the lower end of the Göreme Valley, Göreme village (Göreme Köyü) has basic but convenient pensions, some carved into the rocks. You can camp in the gardens of many pensions, or at the *Dilek* or *Berlin* camp sites, side by side amid wonderful rock formations on the road leading from Göreme village to the open-air museum.

The many pensions in Göreme village charge identical rates of US$3.50 per bed in a dorm, US$4.50 in a waterless private room, or US$7 per bed with private facilities. One of the most popular is *Köse* (☎ (384) 271 2294), on the right side of the flood channel, with a good cafe and a book-exchange scheme. Other favourites are the *Tan* (☎ (384) 271 2445), *Rock Valley* (☎ (384) 271 2153), *Paradise* (☎ (384) 271 2248), *Ufuk (Horizon)* (☎ (384) 271 2157), and the *Peri* (☎ (384) 271 2136). The pretty *Cave Hotel Melek* (☎ (384) 271 2463), high on the valley wall, has rock-cut waterless double rooms for US$10, or US$16 with private bath, breakfast included. The aptly-named *Ottoman House* (☎ (384) 271 2616) offers luxury at affordable prices: US$9 a head.

Restaurants offering standard fare at slightly above average prices are clustered around the otogar. For a splurge, head uphill to the *Konak Türk Evi* where a 19th century paşa's house is now a fine restaurant. Expect to pay around US$8 to US$15 to dine in such opulence.

Avanos

Set on the north bank of the Kızılırmak (Red River), Avanos is known for its pottery. Pensions here tend to be cheaper than in Göreme. Good value is *Kirkit Pansiyon* (☎ (384) 511 3148), where beds cost US$6 in waterless doubles, US$8 with shower, breakfast included; from the tourist office (☎ (384) 511 4360) at the northern end of the bridge, walk east and bear left at the first alley.

Other cheapies in the old town up behind the main square include the basic *Nomade* and the slightly cheerier *Panorama* and *Kervan*, all with doubles for US$6 to US$8. Moving up the price and comfort scale, the *Sofa Motel* (☎ (384) 511 4489), across the bridge from the tourist office, has tastefully decorated rooms in a group of old houses for US$15/20 a single/double with private bath.

Ürgüp

Despite busloads of tourists, this low-rise town still has appeal, with its old sandstone buildings, cobbled streets and a stone hill carved full of rooms and passages. Cappadocia's best wineries are on the outskirts. The tourist office (☎ & fax 341 4059) is in the park, downhill on Kayseri Caddesi.

The telephone area code is 384.

Places to Stay The *Belde* and *Yeni Hitit* hotels, with rooms for US$10/16 a single/double, are along Dumlupınar Caddesi, east of the otogar. The *Elvan*, west of the otogar past the Dutlu Cami, has doubles with shower for US$21. Follow Ahmet Refik Caddesi up the hill towards Nevşehir and you'll find *Born Hotel* (☎ 341 4756), an old paşa's house with singles/doubles costing US$5/10.

Prettiest of all is the pristine *Esbelli Evi* (☎ 341 3395; fax 341 8848) behind the Turban Hotel, at US$45/55, excellent breakfast included; reserve in advance.

Good food at reasonable prices can be found at the *Sofa Restaurant*, a converted caravanserai on the main square, or in the newly expanded *Cappadocia Restaurant* beside the Belediye (town hall) and just off Dumlupınar Caddesi.

Ihlara Valley

This is Cappadocia with a physical challenge – a remote canyon full of carved and painted churches from Byzantine times. If you're a walker, don't miss it.

The village of Ihlara Köyü is 85 km south-west of Nevşehir and 40 km south-east of Aksaray. *Star Pansiyon*, right in the village, has waterless rooms for US$6 a head. *Anatolia Pansiyon* (☎ (382) 453 7128), on the road running along the top of the gorge between Ihlara village and the official entrance, has basic rooms without showers for about US$6 per person, or camping for US$2. There are more pensions and a camp site in the gorge itself at the village of Belisırma.

Ihlara Belediyesi buses run several times daily from Aksaray's otogar, charging 50c one way.

Kayseri

Sitting in the shadow of snowy Mt Erciyes, Kayseri (known as Caesarea in Roman times) was the provincial capital of Cappadocia. Thankfully its once notoriously persistent carpet merchants are learning the art of soft sell.

The telephone area code is 352.

Things to See A religiously conservative town, Kayseri is full of mosques, tombs and old seminaries. Near the tourist office (☎ 222 3903; fax 222 0879) is the beautiful **Hunat Hatun mosque, tomb** and **seminary** (now the Ethnographic Museum). Opposite, behind the massive 6th century city walls, is the **bazaar** and the **Ulu Cami** (Great Mosque), begun by the Seljuks in 1136. Pride of place goes to the **Twin Seminaries** (Gıyasiye ve Şifaiye Medreseleri) in Mimar Sinan Park, a Seljuk hospital now set up as a medical museum. The **Güpgüpoğlu Konağı** is a stone mansion from the 18th century, now a museum of domestic decoration.

Places to Stay Cheapest is the *Hunat Oteli* (☎ 432 4319), Zengin Sokak 5, behind the Hunat Mosque, with waterless rooms priced at US$5/8 a single/double. Much better is the *Hotel Sur* (☎ 222 4367), Talas Caddesi 12, not far from the tourist office, with good double rooms for US$20 with private shower. *Hotel Çamlıca* (☎ 231 4344), Bankalar Caddesi, Gürcü Sokak 14, is in the bazaar, and has serviceable rooms for US$16 a double with sink, US$18 with shower. One block from the Vezirhanı (historic caravanserai, now a market), try the *Hotel Berlin* (☎ 222 4368) at Maarif Caddesi, Yeni Han Çıkmazı 12.

For comfort, there are three good hotels near Düvenönü Square charging US$30 to US$35 for a double with breakfast: *Hotel Çapari* (☎ 222 5278; fax 222 5282), *Hotel Konfor* (☎ 320 0184; fax 331 7911), and *Hotel Almer* (☎ 320 7970; fax 320 7974).

Safranbolu & Amasra

A charming antique town of half-timbered houses, Safranbolu, near the steel-making city of Karabük, is off the beaten track 250 km north of Ankara. Come for a look at the wonderful old houses, especially the *Havuzlu Konağı* (☎ (372) 712 2883; fax 712 3824), now a hotel (US$22/31 a single/double with bath), and the Kaymakamlar Evi mansion, now a museum. *Çarşı Pansiyon* (☎ (372) 725 1079), not far from the Cinci Hanı (historic caravanserai, now a market), is Ottoman style and costs only US$7 per person, breakfast included. The *Arasta* and *Asya* are similar. Ask at the tourist office (☎ & fax (372) 712 3863) next to the Köprülü Mehmet Paşa Camii mosque in the Çarşı district.

After Safranbolu, take a quick side trip 90 km north to the small, untouristy seaside town of Amasra (different from Amasya, below), where there's a Byzantine fortress and numerous small, cheap hotels.

Amasya

A mountain town set dramatically on river banks hemmed in by sheer cliffs, Amasya has rock-cut tombs of the Pontic kings dating from before Christ, a lofty citadel, nice old houses, and several fine Seljuk buildings. The tourism office (☎ 218 7428), Mustafa Kemal Bulvarı 27, is on the riverbank in the centre.

Amasya's telephone area code is 358.

Things to See Look for the **Gök Medrese Camii** (1276), the **Burmalı Minare Camii** (Spiral Minaret) (1242), the Mongol-built **Bimarhane Medresesi** (1308), the octagonal **Büyük Ağa Medresesi** (1488) and the Ottoman **Sultan Beyazıt II Camii** (1486). The **museum** is good, with the bonus of some gruesome mummies.

Places to Stay The best place to stay is in the beautifully restored old mansion called *İlk Pansiyon* (☎ 218 1689; fax 218 6277), Hitit Sokak 1, for US$8 to US$21 a single, US$13 to US$29 a double. A similar place is *Yuvam Pension* (☎ 218 1324), Atatürk Caddesi 24/5. For modern comforts there's the *Büyük Amasya Hotel* (☎ 218 4054; fax

218 4056), Elmasiye Caddesi 20, for US$14/20 a single/double with bath.

The Black Sea Coast

This region is dramatically different from the rest of Turkey – steep and craggy, damp and lush, isolated by the Pontic Mountains along most of its length. It's the country's dairy-land, and its hazelnuts make Turkey the world's biggest exporter. The tea you drink in İstanbul probably comes from east of Trabzon; the cigarette smoke you endure probably comes from tobacco grown west of Samsun.

Legend has it that the coast was first settled by a tribe of Amazons. Its kingdoms have tended to be independent-minded; Trabzon was the last Byzantine bastion against the Ottomans. Even tourism hasn't penetrated very far, though you'll find plenty of cheap hotels and camping. With the exception of Samsun and Trabzon, less English is spoken here than in other areas of Turkey.

Partly because of heavy industry around Zonguldak, the coast west from Sinop to the Bosphorus is almost unknown to tourists, though the fishing port of Amasra, with its Roman and Byzantine ruins, and Safranbolu with its traditional timber houses, are worth a look (see Cappadocia in the Central Anatolia section, earlier).

SİNOP

This fishing and boat-building town three hours north-west of Samsun was the birth-place of Diogenes, the Cynic philosopher. Thanks to the development of Samsun's harbour, Sinop is a fine little backwater now. There are beaches on both sides of the pen-insula, as well as a few historic buildings, and numerous good, cheap hotels.

SAMSUN

Under the Seljuks, Samsun was a major trading port and had its own Genoese colony. When the Ottomans looked set to capture it in the 15th century, the Genoese fled after burning the city to the ground. Consequently, there's little of interest here now, but it's a good starting point for coastal travel and a port of call for the ferry from İstanbul. Atatürk landed here on 19 May 1919 to begin the Turkish War of Independence.

The bus station is three km east of town; take the dolmuş. The town centre is the traffic roundabout near the Atatürk statue. Inland to the north-east, next to the Archaeo-logical Museum, is the tourist office (☎ (362) 431 1228).

SAMSUN TO TRABZON

There are excellent cold-water beaches around the cheerful resort town of **Ünye**, on a wide bay 85 km east of Samsun. Beaches are the only reason to stop in the glum town of **Ordu**, 80 km east of Ünye. A tourist office (☎ & fax (462) 223 4178) is half a block east of the central Atatürk statue and mosque.

Europe's first cherry trees came from **Giresun** courtesy of Lucullus, the Roman general and famous epicure, and the town is still surrounded by cherry orchards.

One of the more dramatic remains of a large Byzantine fortress, free for the explo-ration, is on a headland beside the friendly village of **Akçakale**, about 22 km west of Trabzon.

TRABZON

Trabzon is certainly the most interesting place on the Turkish Black Sea coast, with good-natured people, mild weather, lots of Byzantine architecture, a bazaar full of honest merchants, beaches, mountain trek-king, even white-water boating – and the amazing Sumela Monastery. Known as Trebizond in Byzantine times, this was the last town to fall to the Ottoman Turks, and an earlier holdout against the Seljuks and Mongols as well.

Orientation & Information

Modern Trabzon is centred on Atatürk Alanı (Atatürk Square), on a steep hill above the harbour. The helpful government tourist office (☎ & fax 321 4659) is on the south side of the square (the Atatürk statue faces east). Up behind it is an Ulusoy bus ticket office. Turkish Airlines is on the west side of the square and Turkish Maritime Lines (TML or Denizyolları) is to the east, in front of the Hotel Usta.

On the coast highway at the foot of the hill are two regional minibus yards: north of the bazaar for points west, and on the east side near the ferry pier for points east. A third yard, north of Atatürk Alanı, has buses to Rize. To reach Atatürk Alanı from any of them, just take the steepest climb up. Three km to the east is the otogar for long-distance buses.

The telephone area code is 462.

Things to See

A 20 minute walk west of Atatürk Alanı are the dark walls of the Byzantine city. The **old town**, with its timber houses and stone bridges, still looks medieval.

Trabzon has many **Byzantine churches**, the oldest being the 7th century St Anne's, and the best preserved the 13th century Aya Sofya, now a museum (take a minibus from Atatürk Alanı). Among its more beautiful **Ottoman mosques** are the Gülbahar Hatun Camii (1514) west of the city walls and the Çarşı (or Osmanpaşa) Camii in the bazaar. For a look at a beautiful 19th century villa, visit the **Atatürk Köşkü** high above the town.

Some travellers come to Trabzon just to visit the 14th century **Sumela Monastery**, built into a cliff face like a swallow's nest. It was inhabited right up to this century and has many fine murals (much damaged by vandals) and amazing views. Special Ulusoy buses (US$4) depart for Sumela from a small terminal on Taksim Caddesi, across the street and uphill a few steps from the tourist office. Entry to the Sumela National Park costs US$2.50 (half-price with a student card) per person, US$1 per car.

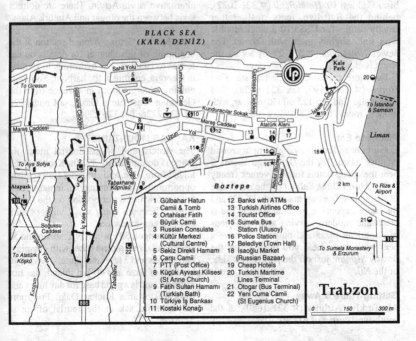

TURKEY

BLACK SEA
(KARA DENİZ)

Trabzon

1 Gülbahar Hatun Camii & Tomb
2 Ortahisar Fatih Büyük Camii
3 Russian Consulate
4 Kültür Merkezi (Cultural Centre)
5 Sekiz Direkli Hamam
6 Çarşı Camii
7 PTT (Post Office)
8 Küçük Ayvasıl Kilisesi (St Anne Church)
9 Fatih Sultan Hamamı (Turkish Bath)
10 Türkiye İş Bankası
11 Kostaki Konağı
12 Banks with ATMs
13 Turkish Airlines Office
14 Tourist Office
15 Sumela Bus Station (Ulusoy)
16 Police Station
17 Belediye (Town Hall)
18 İsaoğlu Market (Russian Bazaar)
19 Cheap Hotels
20 Turkish Maritime Lines Terminal
21 Otogar (Bus Terminal)
22 Yeni Cuma Camii (St Eugenius Church)

To Giresun
To Aya Sofya
To Atatürk Köşkü
To İstanbul & Samsun
To Rize & Airport
To Sumela Monastery & Erzurum

Sahil Yolu
Cumhuriyet Cad
Gazipaşa Caddesi
İskele Cad
Kale Park
Kunduracılar Sokak
Maraş Caddesi
Atatürk Alanı
Liman
Uzun Yol
Kazım Sokak
Sakarya
Tabakhane Köprüsü
İç Kale Caddesi
Boztepe
Değirmen
Soğuksu Caddesi
Tanjant Yolu
Kuzgun
Tabakhane Deresi
Maraş Caddesi
Atapark

0   150   300 m

2 km

Places to Stay

Çınaraltı Camping is five km west of Trabzon and *Dalyan Camping* is nine km to the west. Just before Dalyan, take the turn-off to Derecik; it's 1.5 km to the camping area at Sera Gölü lake. On the road to Sumela there's a camping ground two km beyond Maçka, and on the road to the monastery.

Petty traders and prostitutes from the former Soviet states often fill the cheapest hotels, so you may have trouble finding space late in the day. Look for rooms east of Atatürk Alanı on Güzelhisar Caddesi and surrounding streets. *Hotel Toros* (☎ 321 1212), north of Atatürk Alanı at Gençoğlu Sokak 3/A, has clean doubles without bath for US$12, or with showers for US$14. *Gözde Aile Oteli* (☎ 321 9579), just off Güzelhisar, offers reasonable rooms with private sinks and showers but no toilet for US$4 a head.

Doubles with bath cost just a bit more (US$18) at the *Anıl* (☎ 321 9566), Güzelhisar Caddesi 10. *Hotel Benli* (☎ 321 1022), behind the Belediye, rents small, rather smelly rooms for US$5/10 a single/double with sink, slightly more with shower. The newer *Hotel Nur* (☎ 321 2798) across the street is cleaner.

For more comfort, try the two-star *Otel Horon* (☎ 321 1199; fax 321 6628), Sıra Mağazalar Caddesi 125 off Güzelhisar, with modern rooms for US$30/40 a room.

Places to Eat

Lots of cheap food is available right around Atatürk Alanı. Try the *Derya* and *Volkan 2* near the cheap hotels for sulu yemek (ready food). *Murat Balık Salonu* on the north side of the square fries up mackerel (US$3) and the more expensive trout (alabalık). *Tad* is clean and modern, serving approximations of American pizza and burgers. To have a beer with your meal you must suffer the dowdy *Şişman*, just off the park's west side, or the *Nil*.

Getting There & Away

Air Turkish Airlines (☎ 321 1680), at the south-west corner of Atatürk Alanı, has daily nonstop flights to Ankara and İstanbul. An airport bus (US$1) leaves from the Turkish Airlines ticket office at the west end of Atatürk Alanı; minibuses run from the square as well.

Istanbul Airlines (☎ 322 3806), at Kazazoğlu Sokak 9, Sanat İşhanı, on the north-west corner of Atatürk Alanı, flies to İstanbul on Monday, Tuesday, Wednesday and Sunday.

Bus West-bound dolmuş go as far as Ordu, from the minibus yard on the highway below the bazaar. Dolmuş going east as far as Rize, and minibuses to Maçka and Sumela, go from the yard east of Atatürk Alanı near the ferry terminal. Rize city buses leave from the foot of Gazipaşa Caddesi, north below Atatürk Alanı. From the otogar, minibuses go every 30 minutes to Rize, Hopa and Artvin. A dozen buses a day go to Erzurum, a beautiful ride via Gümüşhane made slow by construction work; an equally beautiful alternative is via Artvin. There are dolmuş taxis between the otogar and Atatürk Alanı.

Boat See the Getting Around section at the beginning of this chapter for details on car ferries to İstanbul. For hydrofoils to Batumi in Georgia, enquire at the harbour. You must obtain a Georgian visa in advance from the Georgian consulate at Gazipaşa Caddesi 20 (☎ 326 2226; fax 326 2296).

KAÇKAR MOUNTAINS

The eastern end of the coastal mountain range is dominated by 3937m Kaçkar Dağı, inland from Rize, and around it are excellent opportunities for camping, wilderness treks, and even white-water boating on the Çoruh River. There are many small villages with cheap accommodation.

At Uzungöl, 50 km east of Trabzon and 50 km inland, is an **alpine lake**, with camping, bungalows and a few small hotels. Ayder, 40 km east of Rize and 40 km inland, has **hot springs**, and is a good base for day hikes and trekking towards Kaçkar Dağı. For more information, ask at the tourist office in Trabzon.

Eastern Turkey

Turkey's eastern region is the harshest, hardest part of the country, but it rewards visitors with dramatic landscapes – like majestic views of 5165m Mt Ararat (the legendary resting place of Noah's Ark) – and some unusual historical relics. In the winter, bitterly cold weather is imported direct from the Russian steppes, so unless you are well equipped and something of a masochist, avoid travelling in this region from October through to April.

For full coverage of this region see Lonely Planet's *Turkey*.

Warning
In recent years, the Kurdistan Workers' Party (PKK) has carried out terrorist raids throughout Turkey, but particularly in the east, in pursuit of its goal of an independent Kurdistan. On isolated occasions the PKK have even kidnapped tourists to attract publicity.

At the time of writing, the region was still unstable, with incidents between the Turkish army units deployed in force there and guerrilla fighters. Check with your embassy or consulate before travelling east, especially to Diyarbakır, Mardin or any points east of them. If you do travel here, stick to the main roads and large towns, and travel only in daylight on recognised bus lines, trains and airlines. ■

SİVAS

Sivas, on the central route through Turkey, was an important crossroads on the caravan route to Persia and Baghdad, and has many marvellous Seljuk buildings to prove it. In 1919, Atatürk convened the second congress of the War of Independence here.

The tourist office (☎ (346) 221 3535) is in the Vilayet building on the main square. The buildings to see are in the adjoining park: the **Twin Minaret Seminary** (Çifte Minare Medrese), **Şifaiye** and **Bürüciye** seminaries, the **Ulu Cami** and the **Blue Seminary** (Gök Medrese).

The better cheap hotels are 700m southeast of Konak Meydanı, at the junction of Atatürk Caddesi and Kurşunlu Sokak.

Best is the *Otel Çakır* (☎ (346) 222 4526) which charges US$7/9 for a clean single/double with bath, including breakfast. The nearby *Otel Fatih* (☎ (346) 233 4313), Kurşunlu Caddesi 15, charges a bit more.

Across the road is the cheaper *Otel Yuvam* (☎ (346) 221 3349). Round the corner at Atatürk Caddesi 176, the friendly *Otel Ergin* (☎ (346) 221 2301) offers beds from US$4. Single women would probably be better off at the *Çakır* or *Fatih*. Top places are the *Otel Sultan* (☎ (346) 221 2986; fax 221 9346), Eski Belediye Sokak 18, at US$23/42, and the cheaper, older *Otel Köşk* (☎ (346) 221 1150; fax 223 9350), Atatürk Caddesi 11.

For cheap meals look behind the PTT on 1 Sokak, just off the main square.

ERZURUM

Eastern Turkey's main transport hub and military centre, as it has been for thousands of years, Erzurum is a fairly drab town famous for its harsh climate, although it has some striking Seljuk buildings that justify a stay of a day or so.

Orientation & Information

The tourist office (☎ 218 5697; fax 218 5443) is on Cemal Gürsel Caddesi, the main street, just west of the Atatürk statue. The bus station (otogar) is inconveniently located three km from the centre on the airport road, but the centre itself is compact and all the main sites are within walking distance.

The telephone area code is 442.

Things to See

The well-preserved walls of a 5th century **Byzantine fortress** loom over a maze of narrow streets. From here you get a good view of the town's layout and the bleak plains that surround it.

The **Çifte Minareli Medrese** (1253), is a seminary famous as an example of Seljuk architecture. It is beautifully symmetrical, with a classic carved portal flanked by twin

TURKEY

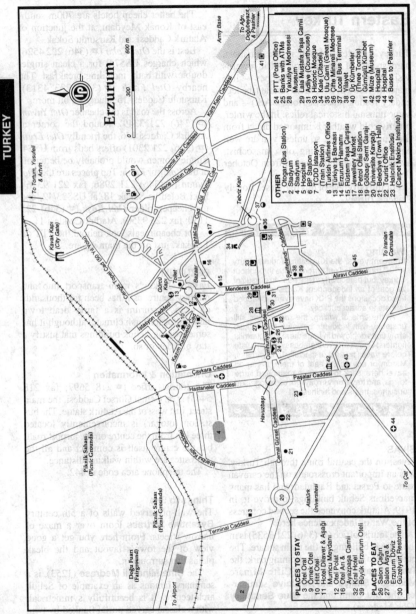

Erzurum

To Ağrı,
Doğubeyazıt
& Pasinler

Army Base

0   300   600 m

To Tortum, Yusufeli
& Artvin

Kars Kapı Caddesi

Nene Hatun Cad

Demir Ayak Caddesi

Tahtacılar Cad Gül Ahmet Cad

Kavak Kapı
(City Gate)

Gürcü Kapı

Toilet

Bazaar

Menderes Caddesi

Tebriz Kapı

Şeftelendri Caddesi

Alirav Caddesi

To Iranian
Consulate

İstasyon Caddesi

Kasım Karabekir Cad

Cumhuriyet Caddesi

Çaykara Caddesi

Hastaneler Caddesi

Paşalar Caddesi

Havuzbaşı

İstanbul Kapı Caddesi

Cemal Gürsel Caddesi

To Çat

Piknik Sahası
(Picnic Grounds)

Piknik Sahası
(Picnic Grounds)

Doğu Fuarı
(Fairground)

Atatürk
Universitesi

Terminal Caddesi

To Airport

OTHER

24 PTT (Post Office)
25 Banks with ATMs
28 Museum
29 Lala Mustafa Paşa Camii
31 Adliye (Courthouse)
33 Historic Mosque
34 Ulu Cami (Great Mosque)
35 Kale (Citadel)
36 Çifte Minareli Medrese
37 Üçe Minarele Minare
38 Vilayet
40 Üç Kümbetler
   (Three Tombs)
41 Gümüşlü Kümbet
42 Müze (Museum)
43 Belediye (Town Hall)
44 Hospital
45 Buses to Pasinler

1 Shogaar (Bus Station)
2 Stadyum
4 Stadyum
5 Hospital
6 BP Station
7 TCDD İstasyon
   (Train Station)
8 Turkish Airlines Office
13 Türkiye İş Bankası
14 Erzurum Hamamı
15 Rüstem Paşa Çarşısı
17 Rüstem Paşa Çarşısı
18 Pevel Ofisi Station
19 Gölbaşı Semt Garajı
20 Universite Kavşağı
21 Belediye (Town Hall)
22 Tourist Office
23 Halıcılık Enstitüsü
   (Carpet Making Institute)

PLACES TO STAY

3 Otel Oral
9 Örnek Otel
10 Hitit Otel
11 Hotel Dilaver & Aşağı
   Mumcu Meydanı
12 Otel Polat
16 Otel Arı &
   Ayazpaşa Camii
32 Kral Hotel
39 Büyük Erzurum Oteli

PLACES TO EAT

26 Salon Çağın
27 Salon Asya &
   Erzurum Döviz
30 Güzelyurt Restorant

minarets, which also frame a conical dome behind.

The oldest mosque is the **Ulu Cami** (1179), next door to the Çifte Minareli. Farther west along Cumhuriyet Caddesi is an open square in the centre of town with an Ottoman mosque and, at the western corner, another seminary, the **Yakutiye Medresesi**, built by the local Mongol emir in 1310, and now a museum of Turkish arts.

Places to Stay

Erzurum has lots of cheapies, although showers and winter heating may cost extra, and some of the places are pretty dismal. *Otel Arı* (☎ 218 3141), at Ayazpaşa Caddesi 8, next to the Ayazpaşa mosque, charges only US$8 for a double with sink. *Otel Polat* (☎ 218 1623), Kazım Karabekir Caddesi 4, costing around US$7/10 for singles/doubles, is well situated between the railway station and the town centre. There are plenty of other, mostly ordinary, choices in the same street, such as the *Hitit Otel* (☎ 218 1204), at No 26, charging US$8/11 with sink, US$10/13 with shower. Next door is the similarly priced *Örnek Otel* (☎ 218 1203), with 35 rooms, all with private showers.

The *Büyük Erzurum Oteli* (☎ 218 6528; fax 212 2898), Aliravi Caddesi 5, has better rooms and more services for US$20/32 a single/double, but the best rooms in town are at the three-star *Hotel Dilaver* at Aşağı Mumcu Caddesi Petit Meydanı (☎ 235 0068; fax 218 1148), with TV, air-con and minibar for US$40/60.

Places to Eat

There are several reasonable choices along Cumhuriyet Caddesi near the Yakutiye Medresesi. *Güzelyurt Restorant*, though Erzurum's fanciest, is cheap and good: have the mantarlı güveç (lamb-and-mushroom casserole), with drinks, for less than US$7. *Salon Çağın* and *Salon Asya*, a block away, are even cheaper, and still quite good.

Getting There & Away

Air Turkish Airlines (☎ 218 1904), at 100. Yıl Caddesi at the north-western end of Kazım Karabekir Caddesi, has at least one and sometimes two daily nonstop flights (US$85) to Ankara, with connections to İstanbul and İzmir. The airport bus (US$1) departs 1½ hours before flight time.

Bus Catch a No 2 bus into town from the bus station. There are plenty of bus company offices uphill from the railway station at Gürcü Kapı.

The Gölbaşı Semt Garajı, about one km north-east of Gürcü Kapı through the back streets, handles minibuses to towns to the north and east of Erzurum.

Train The *Doğu Express* (US$9.50/14 in 2nd/1st class, US$30 for a sleeping berth) takes you to İstanbul (via Ankara) in 25 hours. The bus is much faster.

TORTUM VALLEY

Don't miss the chance to hike in the fruit-filled Tortum Valley, north of Erzurum. To get there, take a minibus to Yusufeli from Erzurum's Gölbaşı Semt Garajı, stay in one of the many cheap hotels, and trek to the old Georgian churches in Haho (Bağbaşı), Öşk Vank, İşhan, Barhal (Altıparmak) and Dörtkilise (near Tekkale).

ARTVİN

Capital of a poor but beautiful mountain province, Artvin is set on a small mountain and has a frontier feel. The scenery is breathtaking, the hotels are grotty but cheap, and during the third week in June the Caucasus Culture and Arts Festival (Kafkasör Kültür ve Sanat Festivali) is held.

KARS

About 260 km north-east of Erzurum, in the shadow of Mt Ararat, this frontier town was much fought over and has a suitably massive fortress. Nearby are the ruins of ancient Ani on the border with Armenia.

There is quite an interesting **museum** (closed on Monday) north-east of the railway station on Cumhuriyet Caddesi, with exhibits dating from the Bronze Age. The tourist office (☎ & fax (474) 223 2724) is on

Ali Bey (Ordu) Caddesi; come here to get your permit for Ani. Look also at the Kümbet Camii (Church of the Apostles) by the river.

Among hotels, *Hotel Temel* (☎ (474) 223 1376), at Kazım Paşa Caddesi 4/A, offers the best value for US$7/12 a single/double. *Otel Kervansaray* (☎ (474) 223 1990), at Faik Bey Caddesi 124, charges only US$5 for a double with sink, US$7 with shower; the neighbouring *Otel Nur Saray* (☎ (474) 223 1364) is similar. *Hotel Güngören* (☎ (474) 212 0298; fax 223 1636), at Halit Paşa Caddesi, Millet Sokak 4, has pretensions and a bit more comfort for US$15/25 with bath.

For real comfort, go to the three-star *Hotel Karabağ* (☎ (474) 212 2585; fax 223 3089) at Faik Bey Caddesi No 84, with good rooms for US$35/45 a single/double.

For breakfast, have tea, bread, butter and the excellent Kars honey at the *Lale Pastanesi* on Halit Paşa Caddesi. *Kristal* on Atatürk Caddesi is the town's brightest and most cheerful place to eat.

ANİ

Ani, 45 km east of Kars, was completely deserted in 1239 after a Mongol invasion, but before that it had been an important city and a capital of both Urartian and Armenian kingdoms. Surrounded by walls, the ruins lie in fields overlooking the Arpaçay River, which forms the border with Armenia. The ghost city is extremely dramatic and there are several notable churches, including a cathedral built between the years 989 and 1010.

You must apply at the museum in Kars for permission to visit Ani, buy a ticket (US$2), then have your application approved (usually no problem) at the Emniyet Müdürlüğü (Security Headquarters). A taxi to Ani costs between US$29 and US$35, fair enough for a group but a hefty sum if you're on your own.

MT ARARAT

When the 40 days and 40 nights finally ended, Mt Ararat (Turkish: Ağrı Dağı) is where Noah and his flock are said to have landed. A nice theory, but difficult to test, since climbing is only allowed with permis-

sion from Ankara. You must go with an organised group.

Rising sheer from a level plain, the snow-capped dormant volcano makes an impressive view from the main road between Erzurum and the border with Iran.

DOĞUBEYAZIT

Known jocularly as 'dog biscuit', this drab town is the last Turkish town on the road to Iran. The town is dramatically sited at the far side of a sweeping grass plain that runs to the foot of Mt Ararat. It doesn't take long to get your bearings and find the cheap hotels, as everything is within five minutes walk.

Apart from spectacular views of Mt Ararat, there is an interesting **palace-fort**, the İshak Paşa Sarayı (open daily from 8 am to 5 pm; entry US$2), five km east of town. Perched romantically among rocky crags, it overlooks the town and the plains. The occasional dolmuş passes nearby, but, unless you want to walk, you'll probably have to negotiate for a taxi (US$5).

Take excursions to the **meteor crater, Diyadin hot springs**, another supposed resting-place of **Noah's Ark**.

If you decide to stay, *Murat Camping*, on the road to the İshak Paşa Sarayı, has tent spaces for US$1. *Hotel Erzurum* (☎ (472) 312 5080), on Belediye Caddesi, with spartan waterless rooms for US$7 a double, is typical of the hotels. *Hotel Tahran* (☎ (472) 311 2223), Büyük Ağrı Caddesi 86, is much better and only a bit more expensive; it's strictly Muslim, as is the similar, nearby *Gül. Hotel İsfahan* (☎ (472) 215 5139; fax 215 2044), Emniyet Caddesi 26, has comfy rooms (some with real bathtubs) for US$25/38/46 a single/double/triple.

SOUTH-EASTERN TURKEY

In the south-east corner of Turkey, along the border with Syria and Iraq, is the region once known as Upper Mesopotamia, drained by the historic Tigris (Dicle) and Euphrates (Fırat) rivers. The cities of Şanlıurfa, Mardin and Diyarbakır were all centres for the Hurri-Mitanni civilisation of 4000 years ago.

Nemrut Dağı

North of Şanlıurfa, south of Malatya, pretty much in the middle of nowhere, is Nemrut Dağı (Mt Nimrod), on whose summit is a 2000 year old **memorial sanctuary** for an obscure Commagene king, with enormous statues of gods and kings, their heads toppled off by earthquakes and scattered on the ground.

You can trek to Nemrut Dağı from the north via Malatya, a farming city that specialises in apricots, or from the south via the oil- prospecting towns of **Adıyaman** and **Kahta**. Daily minibus tours (under US$30) go from the tourist office (☎ (422) 323 3025; fax 324 2514) in Malatya, and include a sunset visit, a night at a hotel near the summit, and a dawn visit. From Kahta the bonus is stops at other ancient sites along the way: Karakuş, a Roman bridge, Yeni Kale, and Arsameia.

In Malatya, try the *Park Otel* (☎ (422) 321 1691), Atatürk Caddesi across from the Belediye, for US$9 a double, or the cheaper *Otel Kantar* (☎ (422) 321 1510), at Atatürk Caddesi 81, or *Otel Pehlivan* (☎ (422) 321 2609), Cumhuriyet Caddesi 26, which are alright in the centre. Best in town is the

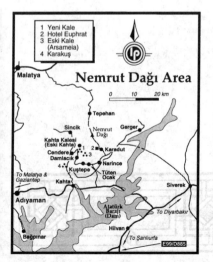

Malatya Büyük Otel (☎ (422) 321 1400; fax 321 5367), with fine doubles for US$25.

In Adıyaman the hotels are expensive and usually full of oil prospectors. *Beyaz Yılancı Pansiyon* (☎ (416) 216 2100), Atatürk Bulvarı 136, on the highway in the eastern part of town, has rooms with shower for US$7/12/15 a single/double/triple. The nearby three-star *Hotel Antiochos* (☎ (416) 216 3377; fax 213 8456), Atatürk Bulvarı 141, is the best, with good rooms for US$14/18 a single/double, breakfast and swimming pool included.

Cheaper rooms are in Kahta, 35 km to the east, in the *Anatolia Pension* (☎ (416) 725 2479), at US$5 per person; in the *Hotel Mezopotamya* (☎ (416) 725 5112) and neighbouring *Zeus Camping*; and the *Hotel Kommagene* (☎ (416) 725 1092; fax 725 5548), at the start of the Nemrut road. Kahta's tourist office (☎ (416) 725 5007) is on the main road near the Hotel Kommagene.

Şanlıurfa

Once known as Edessa and commonly called Urfa, this hot, dusty city boasts that it harbours the **cave** where the patriarch Abraham was born. Pilgrims come, pay their respects, then feed fat carp in a shady pool nearby. You can visit the fine old bazaar, some mosques, a good museum, the citadel, and the sacred pool. The highlight, however, is a day trip south 50 km to **Harran** (Altınbaşak), one of the oldest continuously occupied settlements on earth, with distinctive beehive mud-brick houses.

Diyarbakır

The great basalt walls of Diyarbakır surround a city of medieval mosques, narrow streets, and Kurdish separatist feelings. At the centre of the Kurdish insurgency, Diyarbakır now feels somewhat like an armed camp.

Ask at the tourist office (☎ (412) 221 2173; fax 224 1189), in the Kültür Sarayı, 5th floor, office 28, for a map showing the many mosques. If you walk along the tops of the walls, do it in a group, as robbery and mischief are now problems.

Take a dolmuş from the otogar to Dağ Kapısı (3.5 km) to find cheap hotels such as the *Hotel Kenan* (☎ (412) 221 6614), İzzetpaşa Caddesi 24, with shower-equipped double rooms for US$7.50, and the nearby, quieter *Hotel Malkoç* (☎ (412) 221 2975), İnönü Caddesi, Sütçü Sokak 6, charging US$8/11 a single/double with shower and TV.

Van

Van, on the south-east shore of the vast salt lake of the same name, has a 3000 year old **citadel** at the Rock of Van, and an interesting **museum**. There is a 10th century church on **Akdamar Island** in the lake, a fascinating piece of Armenian architecture in a beautiful setting, with frescoes inside and reliefs outside depicting biblical scenes. Ferries make the trip from near Gevaş for US$3 return; you can get a dolmuş to the harbour from Beş Yol in Van. You can also make an excursion to Çavuştepe, an Urartian city from about 760 BC, and the dramatic

Kurdish castle at Hoşap (1643). The helpful tourist office (☎ (432) 216 3675) is at the southern end of Cumhuriyet Caddesi (No 127).

Places to Stay Adequate cheapies are the *İpek Otel* (☎ (432) 216 3033), Cumhuriyet Caddesi, Eski Hal Civarı, and the Lüks Aslan Oteli (☎ (432) 216 2469) nearby, with beds for US$3.50 per person. *Hotel Çaldıran* (☎ (432) 216 2718), Sıhke Caddesi, Büyük Cami Karşısı, two short blocks from Beş Yol, has 48 well-used, noisy rooms for US$8/12 a single/double with private shower.

The best value for money is the three-star, 50 room *Otel Sirhan* (☎ (432) 214 3463; fax 216 2867), Cumhuriyet Caddesi, Hükümet Konağı Yanı, on the south side of the Van Valiliği provincial government headquarters, which charges US$28 a double, breakfast included. The *Büyük Urartu* (☎ (432) 212 0660; fax 212 1610) is the high-status place, but quite overpriced at US$42/60, including breakfast.

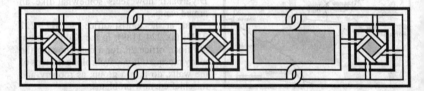

The United Arab Emirates

The United Arab Emirates (UAE) is a union of seven sovereign shaikhdoms which was formed in 1971 when the British withdrew from the Gulf. Despite the small size of the emirates, each has its own, distinct features. The capital, Abu Dhabi, is one of the most modern cities on earth, while Dubai is unquestionably the most vibrant city in the Gulf, sporting the region's best night life. In the other emirates – Sharjah, Ajman, Umm al-Qaiwain, Ras al-Khaimah and Fujairah – life moves at a slower pace.

Travel agencies in Europe are pushing the UAE as a land of contrasts: mountains, beaches, deserts and oases, camel racing, Bedouin markets and the legendary duty-free shopping of Dubai. Brochures trumpet the 'Arabian Experience' and are clearly aimed at up-market tourists in search of an exotic but comfortable destination. But the UAE is also one of the best places in the Gulf for the independent traveller, and with over 100,000 tourists already making the trip each year, you should see it soon before mass tourism really hits its stride.

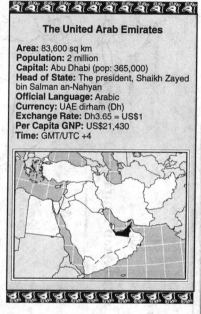

The United Arab Emirates

Area: 83,600 sq km
Population: 2 million
Capital: Abu Dhabi (pop: 365,000)
Head of State: The president, Shaikh Zayed bin Salman an-Nahyan
Official Language: Arabic
Currency: UAE dirham (Dh)
Exchange Rate: Dh3.65 = US$1
Per Capita GNP: US$21,430
Time: GMT/UTC +4

Facts about the Country

HISTORY

Like much of the rest of the Gulf, what is now the UAE has been settled for many centuries. The earliest significant settlements are from the Bronze Age. In the 3rd millennium BC a culture known as Umm an-Nar (after the island where it was discovered) arose near modern Abu Dhabi. Umm an-Nar's influence extended well into the interior and down the coast of what is now Oman. There were also settlements at Badiyah (near Fujairah) and at Rams (near Ras al-Khaimah) during the second half of the 3rd millennium BC.

The Greeks were the next major cultural influence in the area. Ruins showing strong Hellenistic features have been found at Meleiha, about 50 km from Sharjah, and at Al-Dour in the emirate of Umm al-Qaiwain.

During the Middle Ages much of the area was part of the Kingdom of Hormuz, which controlled the entrance to, and most of the trade in, the Gulf. The Portuguese first arrived in 1498 and by 1515 they had occupied Julfar (near Ras al-Khaimah) and built a customs house through which they taxed the Gulf's flourishing trade with India and the Far East. The Portuguese stayed on in the town until 1633.

The rise of British naval power in the Gulf in the mid-18th century coincided with the rise of two important tribal confederations along the coast of the lower Gulf. These were the Qawasim and the Bani Yas, the ancestors

711

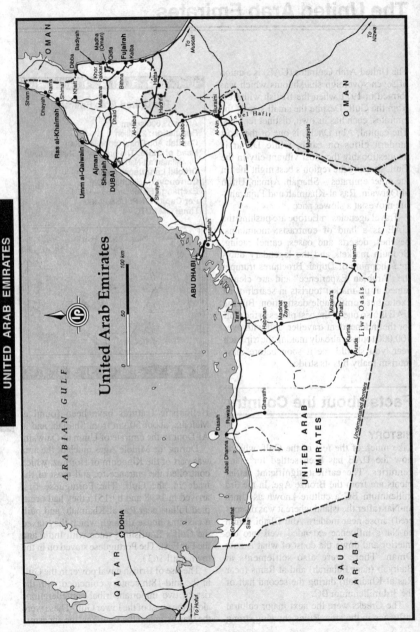

UNITED ARAB EMIRATES

Suggested Itineraries

Dubai is the most vibrant city in the Gulf, and should be a stop on any traveller's itinerary. The museum and gold souq are worth a look, but the city's real attraction is its atmosphere.

The **Buraimi oasis**, where you can cross freely between the UAE and Oman should be your second stop. There are a number of historical and archaeological sites in the area, and the contrast between the Emirati and Omani sides of the oasis is greater than you might think. If you have more time, consider a trip to **Fujairah** on the east coast or to the mountain areas around **Ras al-Khaimah**. ■

of the rulers of four of the seven emirates which today make up the UAE.

The Qawasim, whose descendants now rule Sharjah and Ras al-Khaimah, were a seafaring clan based in Ras al-Khaimah. Their influence extended, at times, to the Persian side of the Gulf. This eventually brought them into conflict with the British, who dubbed the area the Pirate Coast and launched raids against the Qawasim in 1805, 1809 and 1811. In 1820 a British fleet systematically destroyed or captured every Qawasim ship it could find, imposed a General Treaty of Peace on nine Arab shaikhdoms in the area and installed a garrison in the region. As life there quieted down Europeans took to calling the area the Trucial Coast, a name it retained until 1971.

Throughout this period the main power among the Bedouin tribes of the interior was the Bani Yas tribal confederation, made up of the ancestors of the ruling families of modern Abu Dhabi and Dubai. The Bani Yas were originally based in Liwa, an oasis on the edge of the Empty Quarter desert, but moved to Abu Dhabi in 1793. They engaged in the traditional Bedouin activities of camel herding, small-scale agriculture, tribal raiding and extracting protection money from caravans passing through their territory. The Bani Yas divided into two main branches in the early 19th century when Dubai split from Abu Dhabi.

So long as their rivals were kept out of the region and the lines of communication to India remained secure the British, who formally established a protectorate over the Trucial Coast in 1892, did not really care what happened in the Gulf. The area became a backwater. Throughout the late 19th and early 20th centuries the shaikhdoms were all tiny enclaves of fishers, pearl divers and Bedouin.

It was the prospect of oil that changed the way the British ran their affairs on the Trucial Coast. After the collapse of the world pearl market in the early part this century, the entire coast was plunged into abject poverty. In 1939, Shaikh Shakhbut, the ruler of Abu Dhabi, granted the first of several oil concessions on his territory. It was not until 1958, however, that oil was found in the emirate. Exports began in 1962 and, with a population at the time of only 15,000, Abu Dhabi was obviously on its way to becoming very rich.

Throughout this period Dubai was cementing its reputation as the region's busiest trading centre. In 1939 Shaikh Rashid bin Saeed al-Maktoum became the regent for his ailing father, Shaikh Saeed. (Rashid formally succeeded to the leadership in 1958.) He quickly moved to bolster the emirate's position as the lower Gulf's main entrepôt. Dubai was already becoming a relatively wealthy trading centre when, in 1966, it was found to have oil of its own.

Britain's 1968 announcement that it would leave the Gulf in 1971 came as a shock to most of the ruling shaikhs. Britain's original plan was to form a single state consisting of Bahrain, Qatar and the Trucial Coast. Plans for such a grouping were announced in February 1968 but collapsed almost immediately. Negotiations over the next three years eventually resulted in independence for Bahrain and Qatar and the formation, in July 1971, of a new federation: the United Arab Emirates. The new country came into existence on 2 December 1971.

At the time many outsiders dismissed the UAE as a loosely assembled, artificial and largely British creation. While there was some truth in this charge, it was also true that the emirs of the smaller and poorer shaikhdoms knew that their territories had no hope of surviving as independent states. Despite the doomsayers, since independence the UAE has been one of the most stable and untroubled countries in the Arab world.

Though it is rapidly becoming an important, world-class business centre, the UAE today rarely produces much news of interest to the outside world – aside from an ever-growing list of major sporting events hosted by Dubai and Sharjah. In 1990-91, the UAE contributed troops to the anti-Iraq coalition and foreign soldiers and sailors were based here during the months prior to the liberation of Kuwait. The result was a strengthening of the country's already strong ties with the west.

GEOGRAPHY

The UAE is about 83,600 sq km in area. The Emirate of Abu Dhabi represents over 85% of this total. The smallest of the emirates by area is Ajman, with only about 250 sq km of land.

The coastal areas, particularly along the Gulf, are marked by salt flats. Much of the inland area of the UAE is a nearly featureless desert running to the edges of the Empty Quarter. The northern end of the Hajar Mountains runs through the UAE and the country's northern and eastern sections are green and inviting, with striking mountain scenery.

CLIMATE

From May to September, daytime temperatures are around 40°C in Abu Dhabi and

Dubai. In the east coast cities of Fujairah and Khor Fakkan, the climate is not quite so bad – it is just as hot and humid but you're more likely to have a breeze. The mountains above Ras al-Khaimah also provide some relief. In the winter months all of the emirates enjoy very good weather, though it can get very windy in Abu Dhabi, Dubai and Sharjah.

FLORA & FAUNA

The varied terrain of the UAE makes for an equally wide variety of plants and animals, though few of these will be visible to the casual observer. Outside of the mountain areas around Fujairah and Ras al-Khaimah, much of the vegetation you are likely to see is, in fact, not indigenous but rather part of the local government's 'greenery' programme. Even in the Buraimi oasis natural groves of date palms have been supplemented by acres of grass and trees planted in municipal parks.

The UAE's fauna includes the Arabian leopard and the ibex but you are unlikely to see them. You could get lucky, of course, but your glimpses of wildlife is not likely to extend beyond camels and wild goats. In the spring and the autumn, flocks of birds migrating between Central Asia and East Africa can sometimes be seen in the northern emirates.

GOVERNMENT & POLITICS

The UAE consists of seven emirates: Abu Dhabi, Dubai, Sharjah, Ajman, Umm al-Qaiwain, Ras al-Khaimah and Fujairah. Though there is a federal government over which one of the emirs presides (in practice this is always Shaikh Zayed of Abu Dhabi), each of the rulers is completely sovereign within his own emirate. Each emirate is named after its principal town.

The degree of power which the seven emirs should cede to the federal government has been one of the country's hottest topics of debate since independence in 1971. Over the years, Abu Dhabi has been the strongest advocate of closer integration while Dubai has fought hardest to preserve as much of its independence as possible.

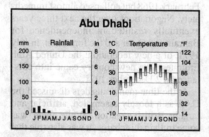

	Abu Dhabi			
mm	Rainfall	in	°C	Temperature	°F
200		8	50		122
			40		104
150		6	30		86
100		4	20		68
			10		50
50		2	0		32
			-10		14
0	J F M A M J J A S O N D	0		J F M A M J J A S O N D	

The forum where these issues are discussed is the Supreme Council. Its members are the seven emirs and tends to meet informally. There is also a Cabinet in which the posts are distributed among the emirates.

The Cabinet and Supreme Council are advised, but cannot be overruled, by the Federation National Council. This is a 40 member consultative body whose members are appointed by the respective emirs. All the council's members come from leading merchant families.

ECONOMY

The seven emirates are quite diverse economically. Only Abu Dhabi, with 9% of the world's oil and 5% of its natural gas, is an oil state in the same sense as Qatar or Kuwait. Like the other big Gulf producers, Abu Dhabi has diversified into petrochemicals and other oil-related industries. Dubai is the second-richest emirate. It too has a lot of oil, but the real foundation of the city's wealth is trade. Dubai is the home of a huge dry-dock complex, one of the Middle East's busiest airports and a large free-trade zone at Jebel Ali.

Sharjah, once the most prosperous of all the emirates, has spent most of this century living in the shadow of Dubai. It has received a modest income from oil since the early '70s but found itself deeply in debt after the oil price collapse of the mid-1980s. Sharjah's airport and seaport facilities derive much of their income from cargo.

Ras al-Khaimah, too, derives much of its income from oil but it has also invested heavily in tourism in recent years. Fujairah has also entered the tourist market though it still remains primarily a cargo port. Fujairah, Ajman and Umm al-Qaiwain all receive rather substantial subsidies from the federal government.

POPULATION & PEOPLE

There are estimated to be just over two million people living in the UAE, of whom about 25% (500,000) are UAE citizens (or 'nationals' as they are usually referred to in the local media).

SOCIETY & CONDUCT

The UAE is probably the most liberal country in the Gulf but it is still a very conservative place by western standards. In Dubai in particular you can wear clothing that would get you arrested in, say, Saudi Arabia, but that does not mean you should do so. You are, after all, a guest, and what might be appropriate in a disco is not necessarily appropriate on the street.

Women should not wear overly tight or revealing clothing (eg miniskirts, short shorts, bikini tops etc) and men should not walk around bare-chested in public. Women may want to stick to one-piece bathing suits at the beach, though bikinis are probably OK around the pool at big hotels. Conservative dress is particularly in order in rural areas.

RELIGION

Most Emiratis are Sunni Muslims subscribing to the Maliki or Hanbali schools of Islamic law. Many of the latter are Wahhabis, though UAE Wahhabis are not nearly as strict and puritanical as the Saudi Wahhabis. There are also smaller communities of Ibadi and Shiite Muslims.

LANGUAGE

Arabic is the official language of the UAE but English is very widely understood. In Dubai, you could also get by using the Persian language, Farsi. Urdu can be reasonably useful in Abu Dhabi and Dubai because a large number of Pakistani expatriates live there.

Facts for the Visitor

PLANNING

When to Go

For information about when to visit this part of the world see the Regional Facts for the Visitor chapter and the Climate section earlier in this chapter.

UNITED ARAB EMIRATES

Maps

The best all-round map of the country is the yellow-covered *Dubai Town Map and Street Guide*, which is available at most hotels for about Dh20. It has a very good map of Dubai and, on the back, one of the most up-to-date maps of the country. There are no really good city maps of either Abu Dhabi or Sharjah. The tourist map distributed free by all the hotels in Al-Ain and Buraimi is not very good but it is the only one available.

What to Bring

See the Regional Facts for the Visitor chapter for information about what you should bring from home when travelling in the Middle East.

VISAS & DOCUMENTS

Visas

Citizens of other Gulf Cooperation Council (GCC) countries and British nationals with the right of abode in the UK do not need visas to enter the UAE. Britons can stay for a month and can renew their entrance stamp for another two months.

US and German citizens can obtain visas for business or tourist visits through UAE embassies. These visas are also available to most western passport holders who have a residence/work visa in another GCC country. In all cases you may be issued anything from a single-entry visa valid for use within three months to a 10 year multiple-entry visa, and the period of stay may be anything from two weeks to three months. It depends mainly on what you ask for and what the people at the embassy choose to give you. On paper these visas eliminate the need for sponsorship but in practice UAE embassies often still ask for some form of written documentation such as a hotel reservation, a letter from your company saying that it wants you to travel to the UAE, or an invitation to visit a friend.

In general, if you are not American, British, German or a Gulf Arab you will probably have to arrange a transit or visit visa through a hotel. The most common way to enter the UAE is on a 15 day transit visa. This

cannot be extended or renewed. Your other option is a 30 day visit visa. This not only allows you to stay in the country longer but it can also be renewed. Both types can be arranged through most medium-sized, and all large, hotels. These visas are almost always deposited at the airport for you to pick up on arrival. Transit visas cost Dh120 and visit visas Dh60, though most hotels will charge you at least Dh170, and in some cases Dh300 or more, for arranging either one.

To arrange a visa through the hotel make a reservation and fax through the first page of your passport (the one with your photograph) along with the purpose of your visit (tourism is OK) and your flight arrival data. Be sure to get the hotel to fax you back a copy of the visa when it is ready or the airline may not let you travel. The hotel will usually require you to stay one to three nights. Once you have the visa, however, you are free to go anywhere in the country or to move to a cheaper hotel, though if you are moving down-market, it would be wise not to advertise it. Processing the visa can take anywhere from two days to three weeks. Generally, the biggest and most expensive hotels in Dubai are the fastest while smaller hotels anywhere, and big hotels in out-of-the-way places like Fujairah, take the longest.

While there are a lot of cheap hotels which claim to sponsor visas, many of them provide rather questionable service. It makes far more sense to splash out and stay at a good hotel and get the visa organised right the first time.

If you enter the UAE by road from Oman through the crossing points at Dibba, Buraimi or Hatta – where there are no customs posts on the Emirati side of the border – you are considered to be in transit and have 48 hours to leave whether by air, sea or road. After that you will incur a fine of Dh100 per day when you do try to leave. Having a valid UAE visa in your passport makes no difference.

If your passport shows any evidence of travel to Israel you will be denied entry to the UAE.

EMBASSIES
UAE Embassies Abroad
As outlined earlier, UAE embassies still do not issue many visas (residence visas excepted).

Iran
  Kheyabun-é Vali-yé Asr, Kheyabun-é, Shahid Sartip Vahid Dastgerdi, Tehrān (☎ (2) 222 1333, 229 5029)
Kuwait
  Istiglal St, Diplomatic Area, Kuwait City, south of the centre off Arabian Gulf St (☎ 252 7639)
Oman
  Jameat A'Duwal al-Arabiya St, Medinat Qaboos Diplomatic Area, Muscat, to the sea side of Sultan Qaboos St, west of the Al-Khuwair roundabout (☎ 600302)
Qatar
  Khalifa Town District, off Al-Khor St, Doha (☎ 885 111)
Saudi Arabia
  Diplomatic Quarter, Riyadh (☎ (1) 482 6803)
UK
  30 Princes Gate, London SW1 (☎ (0171) 581 1281/4113)
USA
  600 New Hampshire Ave NW, Washington DC 20037 (☎ (202) 338 6500)

Foreign Embassies in the UAE
Following is a list of some of the embassies in Abu Dhabi:

Australia
  The Australian government covers the UAE from its embassy in Riyadh although the UK embassy also handles some Australian affairs.
Canada
  The Canadian ambassador accredited to the UAE is resident in Kuwait, although the UK embassy also handles some Canadian affairs.
Kuwait
  Diplomatic Area, Airport Rd, behind the Pepsi Cola plant, about 10 km south of the centre (☎ 446 888)
Qatar
  Al-Muntasser St, 26th District (☎ 435 900)
Saudi Arabia
  Al-Karamah St, near the intersection with Dalma St (☎ 465 700)
UK
  Khalid bin al-Waleed St, just south of the Corniche (☎ 326 600)
USA
  Sudan St, between Al-Karamah St and the intersection where King Khalid bin Abdul Aziz St becomes Al-Nahayan St (☎ 436 691)

A number of countries also have consulates in Dubai.

Australia
  World Trade Centre, 6th floor, on the Dubai side of the Creek (☎ 313 444)
Kuwait
  Beniyas Rd, Deira, opposite the Sheraton Hotel (☎ 284 111)
Qatar
  Trade Centre Rd, Al-Mankhool District, Bur Dubai, near the Bur Juman Centre (☎ 452 888)
UK
  Al-Seef Rd, on the Dubai side of the Creek, near the Dhow Restaurant (☎ 521 070)
USA
  World Trade Centre, 21st floor, on the Dubai side of the Creek (☎ 313 115)

CUSTOMS
The duty-free allowances for tobacco are huge: 2000 cigarettes, 400 cigars or two kg of loose tobacco (this is *not* a country cracking down on smoking). Non-Muslims are allowed to import two litres of wine or spirits, unless they are arriving in Sharjah, where alcohol is prohibited. You are generally not allowed to bring in alcohol if you cross into the country by land.

MONEY
Costs
The UAE is not a low-budget country but it is possible to keep costs under reasonable control. Decent hotels can be found for Dh100 to Dh150 (US$27 to US$41) – less in Dubai. Eating for Dh10 to Dh15 (US$2.70 to US$4) is rarely a problem though if your taste runs to alcohol the bill is going to be a lot higher. Getting around by service taxi is very cheap. Plan on spending approximately Dh150/200 (US$41/54) per day for budget/mid-range travel. In Dubai and Fujairah, which have good youth hostels, you might be able to keep your budget down to close to half that.

Currency
The UAE dirham (Dh) is divided into 100 fils. Notes come in denominations of Dh5, 10, 50, 100, 200 and 500. Coins are Dh1, 50 fils, 25 fils, 10 fils and 5 fils. The dirham is

fully convertible and is pegged to the US dollar.

Currency Exchange

Australia	A$1	=	Dh2.93
France	FF1	=	Dh0.72
Germany	DM1	=	Dh2.45
UK	UK£1	=	Dh6.16
USA	US$1	=	Dh3.67

Changing Money

Moneychangers sometimes have better rates than banks but some of them either will not take travellers' cheques or will take only one type. Many places will only exchange travellers' cheques if you can produce your original purchase receipt.

Automatic teller machines (ATMs) have become very widespread in the UAE in recent years and cash machines at all of the larger banks are tied into one or more of the global ATM systems.

Tipping & Bargaining

Tips are not generally expected in the UAE but they would certainly be appreciated as most waiters receive extremely low salaries. The service charge added to your bill usually goes to the restaurant, not the waiter.

Most hotels will offer a discount if you ask for it, but the prices of meals, service taxis, consumer goods etc are almost always fixed.

POST & COMMUNICATIONS
Post

The UAE's postal system is very modern and the post offices are among the most efficient in the Gulf. They also have the shortest queues. Mail generally takes about a week to Europe or the USA and eight to 10 days to Australia.

Letters are charged per 10g. To Europe, the rate is Dh2 per 10g; to the USA and Australia it's Dh2.50. Postcard rates are Dh1.50 to Europe, Dh2 to the USA and Australia.

Poste restante facilities are not available in the UAE, but the American Express offices in Abu Dhabi and Dubai will hold mail for Amex clients (ie, card holders and people with Amex travellers' cheques).

Telephone

The UAE has a splendid telecommunications system and you can connect up with just about anywhere in the world from even the remotest areas. Coin-operated phones take Dh1 and 50 and 25 fils coins but card phones are increasingly common throughout the country. The state telecom monopoly, ETISALAT, has offices in even the smallest towns. To call the UAE from abroad, the country code is 971, followed by the city code and the local number.

Home Country Direct services are available to the USA and France. To reach an ATT operator in the USA dial ☎ 800-121. For MCI the access code is ☎ 800-1-0001. The access number for France Direct is ☎ 800-1-9971.

Fax, Telex & Telegraph

Most ETISALAT offices are also equipped to send and receive fax, telex and telegraph messages.

BOOKS

Books about the UAE's history are hard to find. *The New Arabians* by Peter Mansfield has a short chapter on the UAE's history. *The Merchants* by Michael Field gives a brief sketch of the rise of Dubai as a trading centre.

Looking for Dilmun by Geoffrey Bibby includes an interesting account of the early archaeological work at Umm an-Nar and in Buraimi and gives some idea of life in Abu Dhabi just before and after the beginning of the oil boom. For a more intimate view of life on the Trucial Coast before oil was discovered, read Wilfred Thesiger's classic *Arabian Sands*, originally published in 1959. Jonathan Raban's *Arabia Through the Looking Glass* has lengthy sections on Abu Dhabi, Dubai and Al-Ain and is well worth reading.

For more general book information, see the Book section in the Regional Facts for the Visitor chapter.

NEWSPAPERS & MAGAZINES

Gulf News and *Khaleej Times*, both based in Dubai, are the UAE's two English-language newspapers. Both cost Dh2 and carry pretty much the same international news, though *Gulf News* is widely regarded as the better of the two.

What's On is a monthly magazine catering mostly to the expatriate community. It's a pretty good source of information about what's new at the UAE's hotels, bars, clubs and discos.

RADIO & TV

Abu Dhabi and Dubai each have an English-language TV channel, though outside the two main cities reception is decidedly mixed. In various parts of the country you can also pick up English-language signals from Qatar and Oman. Most hotels, even small ones, offer satellite TV.

Abu Dhabi and Dubai also have English-language FM radio stations. Dubai FM is at FM 92. Abu Dhabi's Capital Radio is at FM 100.5.

PHOTOGRAPHY & VIDEO

Aside from the usual provisos about photographing women or anything military-related, there is no problem with taking photographs in the UAE.

Getting colour prints developed is never a problem – one hour services are advertised by photo developers on nearly every street in the country. Developing slides or B&W film is much more difficult and you might want to wait and do this somewhere else.

HEALTH

The standard of health care is quite high throughout the UAE. Should you get sick consult either the hotel doctor, if you are in a big hotel, or your embassy or consulate. The city listings include phone numbers for hospitals in some of the larger cities.

No particular shots are necessary for travel in the UAE. An International Health Certificate is required only from travellers arriving from an infected area.

The tap water in Abu Dhabi and Dubai is

safe to drink, but it often tastes horrible and is heavily chlorinated. Most residents stick to bottled water. See the Health Appendix for more detailed health information.

WOMEN TRAVELLERS

In general, the UAE is probably the easiest country in the Gulf for women to travel in. Checking into hotels is not usually a problem, though unaccompanied women might want to think twice about taking a room in some of the cheaper places in Dubai.

This is not to say that all of the usual problems that accompany travel in the Middle East will not arise in the UAE as well: unwanted male visitors knocking on your hotel room door at night, lewd looks and comments in the street etc. Apply common sense and retain your self-confidence whatever happens.

DANGERS & ANNOYANCES

The UAE, like much of the rest of the Gulf, has a road system built around traffic circles, or roundabouts. People have a tendency to zoom into these at frightening speeds and to try to turn out of them from inside lanes, paying little attention to other cars. Eternal vigilance is the price of avoiding fender-benders. This problem exists throughout the country but is particularly acute in Dubai and Sharjah.

BUSINESS HOURS

Banks, private companies and shops open Saturday to Wednesday from 8 or 9 am until 1 or 1.30 pm and reopen in the afternoon from 4 to 7 or 8 pm. Shops may or may not be open on Thursday afternoon. The larger shopping centres and supermarkets in Abu Dhabi and Dubai will stay open until 9 or 10 pm every night. Everything is closed during the day on Friday though some shops may open on Friday evenings.

In Ras al-Khaimah all shops are required to close for about half an hour at prayer time.

PUBLIC HOLIDAYS

Religious holidays are tied to the Islamic Hijra calendar. Eid al-Fitr (the end of

Ramadan), Eid al-Adha (Pilgrimage), Lailat al-Mi'raj (the Ascension of the Prophet), the Prophet's Birthday and the Islamic New Year are all observed.

Secular holidays observed in the UAE are New Year's Day (1 January) and National Day (1 December, though the celebrations often last to 2 December). Each emirate may also observe its own holidays. In Abu Dhabi, for example, 6 August is a holiday marking the accession of Shaikh Zayed.

ACTIVITIES

Water sports are popular throughout the UAE, and the tourist industry is increasingly pushing the country as a winter 'sea & sun' destination. Most water-sports facilities are tied either to a big hotel or a private club and are not generally accessible to budget travellers. The UAE has several dive centres, most of which are also attached to large hotels.

The UAE has most of the Gulf's golf courses with real grass. There are three courses in Dubai and a pitch-and-putt course in Al-Ain, all of which are expensive.

WORK

The UAE is not the place to look for work. Since 1984 the government has applied what is known as the Six Months Rule. This states that if you enter the country on a visit or transit visa you must leave for six months before you can return on a residence visa. Exceptions to this are rare.

ACCOMMODATION

There are no camping grounds adjacent to the UAE's cities but camping in the desert is quite common.

There are youth hostels in Dubai, Sharjah and Fujairah. At all three hostels HI cards are required and a working knowledge of Arabic would be useful.

Most of the country's cheap hotels are in and around the Dubai souq. These bottom out at around Dh60/100 for a single/double. The cheapest places that provide reliable visa service cost from Dh250/350.

FOOD & DRINKS

Eating cheap in the UAE means eating either in small Indian/Pakistani restaurants which often seem to have only biryani dishes on the menu, or having street food, such as shwarma. In Dubai and, to a lesser extent, Abu Dhabi, cheap oriental food is also fairly easy to come by.

Nonalcoholic drinks such as soft drinks, fruit juices and mineral water are available throughout the country. Alcohol can only be sold in restaurants and bars attached to hotels (in practice, three-star hotels or better). The selection is what you would expect to find in any well-stocked bar. The prices are pretty outrageous – expect to pay around Dh20 for a pint of beer. Alcohol is not available in Sharjah.

ENTERTAINMENT

Western theatre companies regularly visit the UAE and perform in the five-star hotels. Watch the local English-language press and look for flyers in the lobbies of the big hotels for details.

Most cinemas in the UAE show Indian and Pakistani films, though there is a cinema in Dubai specialising in recent English-language films.

If you want to dance the night away Dubai is the place to be. While there are discos and bars with dance floors in most of the larger hotels elsewhere in the country, Dubai is clearly the centre of the UAE's night life.

The main spectator sport in the UAE is camel racing. This takes place in various spots around the country during the winter (see the Dubai, Al-Ain and Ras al-Khaimah sections later in this chapter).

THINGS TO BUY

If you are looking for old Arabian souvenirs the UAE may be a bit disappointing. There are a few shops in Al-Ain, Abu Dhabi and Dubai which deal in Bedouin jewellery, most of which comes from Oman. If you have a lot of money to spend try the gold souq in Dubai or the carpet merchants in Sharjah's new souq. Dubai is also the cheapest place outside of Iran to buy Iranian caviar.

Getting There & Away

AIR

Dubai and Abu Dhabi are the country's main international airports, though an increasing number of carriers serve Sharjah as well. There are also small international airports at Ras al-Khaimah, Fujairah and Al-Ain.

Flying to Europe or the USA tends to be a bit less expensive out of Dubai than from Abu Dhabi, though it is not cheap from either city and Abu Dhabi offers the only direct service to the USA and Australia. There is daily or near-daily service from both Abu Dhabi and Dubai to major European cities such as London, Paris and Frankfurt and to major Middle Eastern cities such as Cairo, Damascus and Beirut, as well as to the other Gulf capitals.

LAND

There is a daily bus service between Dubai and Muscat, though the lack of a UAE border post on the road used by the bus can present some visa problems for travellers.

SEA

There are passenger services between Sharjah and Bandar-é Abbās in Iran. For more details contact Oasis Freight Company (☎ 596 325) in Sharjah.

LEAVING THE UAE

There is no airport departure tax. If you leave by boat or road, there's a Dh20 tax, though at some crossing points there are no border posts to collect it.

Getting Around

There are no air or bus services between the emirates (though there are a few intercity routes within the Abu Dhabi and Dubai emirates). If you do not have your own car, the only way to travel between the emirates is by service taxi.

SERVICE TAXI

Service taxis can be a bit cramped but they are cheap and a great way to meet people. The main problem is often that, aside from the busy Abu Dhabi-Dubai route, they do not fill up very quickly. Between Abu Dhabi and Dubai there are also minibuses which carry 14 people and charge a few dirhams less than the service taxis.

CAR

Most foreign driving licences are accepted in the UAE so long as you are either a citizen or a resident of the country that issued the licence. Rental for small cars starts at about Dh140 per day with another Dh20 to Dh30 for insurance, though you may be able to negotiate this down to a net rate of around Dh130 per day, including insurance. The first 100 or 150 km per day are usually free, with additional km costing 40 or 50 fils each. If you rent a car for more than three days you will usually be given unlimited mileage.

HITCHING

Hitching is not illegal but it is not very common either. A foreigner with his (we do not recommend that women try this) thumb out might get lifts because the drivers are curious, or he might be passed by on the theory that something so strange has to be a bit suspicious.

LOCAL TRANSPORT

Bus

Only Abu Dhabi, Al-Ain and Dubai have municipal bus systems and these are of varying usefulness. Abu Dhabi's offers little help for the traveller. The bus systems in Dubai and Al-Ain are much more comprehensive and can get you to most points of interest fairly easily.

Taxi

Taxis in Abu Dhabi and Al-Ain have meters but those in Dubai and the other emirates do not. In these cities you should negotiate the fare in advance. See the individual city entries for more information.

ORGANISED TOURS

There are several companies in Dubai, Sharjah and Ras al-Khaimah offering half-day and full-day tours of the various emirates. They also run desert safaris. See the relevant city entries for more details.

Abu Dhabi

Everything in the UAE's capital is modern, sleek and shiny. Abu Dhabi is often accused of being a rather soulless place, but that is probably going a bit too far: it may not be the most exciting place around but it does have its attractions.

Orientation

The city of Abu Dhabi sits at the head of a T-shaped island. It is not a compact place, and distances here tend to be bigger than they look (especially once you start trying to get around on foot!). The airport is on the mainland about 30 km from the centre.

The main business district is the area bounded by Shaikh Khalifa bin Zayed and Istiglal Sts to the north, Zayed the Second St to the south, Khalid bin al-Waleed St to the west, and As-Salam St to the east. The GPO and the telephone office are just outside this area. The main terminal for buses and service taxis is further to the south.

Some of the streets also have names which are in more common use than their official ones. These include (formal name first):

Shaikh Rashid bin Saeed al-Maktoum St – Airport Rd or Old Airport Rd
Zayed the Second St – Electra St
Hazaa bin Zayed St – Defence St
Al-Falah St – Passport Street

Information

Money In the centre, and especially along Shaikh Hamdan Bin Mohammed and Khalifa bin Zayed Sts, it often seems like every third building is a bank. If you're looking for a moneychanger instead of a bank, try the souq or Shaikh Hamdan Bin Mohammed St near the Gulf Air office.

American Express (☎ 213 045) is represented by Al-Masaood Travel & Services on Al-Nasr St near the intersection with Khalid Bin al-Waleed St. All the usual Amex services are provided, including cheque cashing and holding mail. Mail should be addressed c/o American Express, PO Box 806, Abu Dhabi, UAE, and should be clearly marked 'Client's Mail'. The office is open Sunday to Thursday from 8.30 am to 1 pm, and from 4 to 6.30 pm.

Post The GPO is on East Rd between Al-Falah and Zayed the Second Sts. It is open Saturday to Wednesday from 8 am to 8 pm, Thursday from 8 am to 6 pm and Friday from 8 to 11 am.

Telephone & Fax The ETISALAT office on Shaikh Rashid bin Saeed al-Maktoum St is open 24 hours a day. You can book international calls through the operator or dial them direct on card phones. Fax, telex and telegram services are also available. This is the old ETISALAT building and, regardless of what you may hear, the office providing these services has not moved into the new headquarters building down the street. The telephone code for Abu Dhabi is 02.

Bookshops It is hard to find bookshops with a good selection of English-language books in Abu Dhabi. All Prints Bookstore (☎ 338572) has a good selection. It is two blocks behind the British embassy off the Corniche, near Avis Rentacar. You will also find English-language books in Spinney's Supermarkets and major hotels.

Medical Services Most hospitals will take walk-in patients for consultations and/or treatment. Abu Dhabi's central hospital (☎ 214 666 for the general switchboard or 344 663 for the emergency unit) is on Al-Manhal St. The emergency entrance is on the corner of Al-Manhal and Karamah Sts.

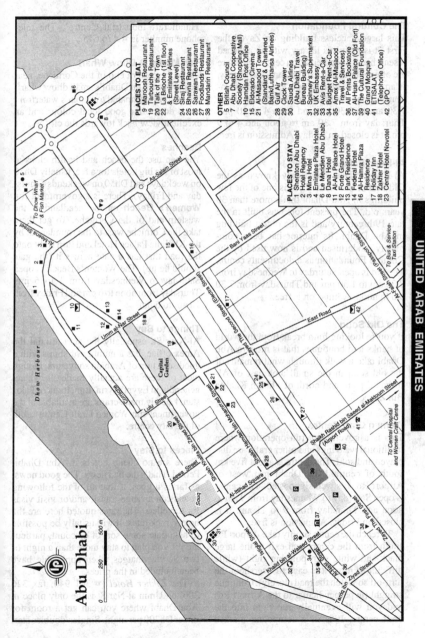

Abu Dhabi

0   250   500 m

PLACES TO EAT
9   Maroosh Restaurant
19   Tarbouche Restaurant
20   Talk of the Town
22   La Brioche (1st floor)
     & Emirates Airlines
     (Street Level)
24   Siraj Restaurant
25   Bhavna Restaurant
26   Sarawan Restaurant
27   Foodlands Restaurant
38   Mandarin Restaurant

OTHER
5   British Council
7   Abu Dhabi Cooperative
     Society (Shopping Mall)
10   Hamdan Post Office
15   Al-Masood Tower
21   Eldorado Cinema
     Standard & Chartered
     Bank/Lufthansa Airlines
28   Gulf Air
29   Clock Tower
30   Saudia Airlines
     Abu Dhabi Travel
     Bureau Building
31   Spinner's Supermarket
32   UK Embassy
33   Avis Rent-a-Car
34   Budget Rent-a-Car
35   Al-Masood
     Travel & Services
36   All Prints Bookstore
37   Al-Husn Palace (Old Fort)
39   The Cultural Foundation
40   Grand Mosque
41   ETISALAT
     (Telephone Office)
42   GPO

PLACES TO STAY
1   Sheraton Abu Dhabi
2   Hotel Regency
3   Mina Hotel
6   Emirates Plaza Hotel
8   Le Meridien Abu Dhabi
11   Dana
12   Al-Ain Palace Hotel
13   Forte Grand Hotel
14   Federal Hotel
16   Al-Hamra Plaza
     Residence
17   Park Residence
18   Zakher Hotel
     Holiday Inn
23   Centre Hotel Novotel

The Cultural Foundation

This large, faceless building on Zayed the First St is mainly a library with an attached research and documentation centre, but there are often interesting exhibits on local history, Islamic art, old manuscripts etc. The foundation is open Saturday to Wednesday from 7.30 am to 1.30 pm and from 4 to 10 pm, Thursday from 7.30 am to noon and 4 to 9 pm. It is closed on Friday. Admission is free.

Al-Husn Palace

Al-Husn Palace, commonly known as the Old Fort or the White Fort, is one of the few buildings in Abu Dhabi that's more than 30 years old. The present fort was built in the late 19th century and is the oldest building in Abu Dhabi. Its interior has been completely modernised and is now used by the Cultural Foundation as a documents centre. The fort is open Saturday to Wednesday from 7.30 am to 1.30 pm and Thursday from 7.30 am to noon. Admission is free.

The Old Souq

If you're looking for a break from the world of banks and boutiques that is modern Abu Dhabi take a walk through what remains of the old souq in the small area east of Al-Ittihad Square and north of Shaikh Khalifa Bin Zayed St.

Women Craft Centre

This is a government-run operation where traditional weavings and other crafts are displayed and sold. The centre is about five km south of central Abu Dhabi just west of Airport Rd. It's well signposted. The centre is open Saturday to Wednesday from 9 am to noon and Thursday from 9 to 11 am. It is closed on Friday. Admission is free.

To reach the centre simply take Airport Rd south from the centre and exit at the large black-and-white sign pointing right (while difficult to miss, it is easy to overshoot the turn-off so watch the road closely). Continue straight (ie perpendicular to the Airport Rd) and you will eventually run right into the craft centre. It is in a compound marked

'Handicraft Industrial Centre'. The telephone number is ☎ 476 645.

Fish Market & Dhow Wharf

Out at the eastern end of the Corniche, near the port, lies Abu Dhabi's small dhow wharf. It is nothing compared to Dubai's waterfront but it does offer good local colour and an excellent view back towards the city.

Beaches

You can use the beach and health clubs at most of the big hotels for a fee, usually Dh30 on weekdays and Dh50 on weekends (Thursday and Friday). There is a government-run **Women's Beach** on the headland at the western end of the Corniche. To get there take the Corniche west to the roundabout by the Khalidia Palace Hotel and turn right onto the road that has a gate across it (the gate should be up). The Women's Beach is open Saturday to Wednesday from 1 to 6 pm, Thursday from noon to 6 pm and Friday from 10 am to 6 pm.

Things to Buy

Al-Nasr St, especially the area around the Amex office, has a number of shops with a good selection of Arabian souvenirs, though most of these are actually made elsewhere, generally in Egypt, Syria, Iran, India or Pakistan. Locally made crafts are available at the government-run Women Craft Centre south of the city centre.

Places to Stay

There are no cheap hotels in Abu Dhabi. Period. That's the bad news. The good news, as far as it goes, is that all of the following hotels can arrange transit and/or visit visas for travellers. The rates quoted here are the hotels' rack rates. It will usually be possible to negotiate some sort of discount, particularly if you plan to stay more than a night or two. Service charges, where applicable, have been included in the prices.

The *Zakher Hotel* (☎ 341 940; fax 326 306) on Umm al-Nar St is the only place in Abu Dhabi where you can get a room for under Dh200 per night. Singles/doubles start at Dh195.50/264.50. Abu Dhabi's cheapest doubles are just down the street from the Zakher at the *Federal Hotel* (☎ 789 000; fax 794 728). Rooms are Dh200/225.

The *Mina Hotel* (☎ 781 000; fax 791 000), at the intersection of the Corniche and Al-Meena St, is under the same management as the Federal but has higher rates. Singles/doubles cost Dh250/350. The *Emirates Plaza Hotel* (☎ 722 000; fax 723 204) off Al-Meena St is slightly more expensive still at Dh262.50/367.50.

The *Khalidia Palace Hotel* (☎ 662 470; fax 660 411) at the western end of the Corniche is one of the better value hotels in this price category. Singles/doubles cost Dh287.50/ 402.50. If you do not mind being somewhat removed from the centre, it offers a number of restaurants and a beachfront location.

Places to Eat

One good place for cheap food is the *Siraj Restaurant* on Zayed the Second St. It has hot tea for 75 fils a glass as well as a selection of sodas, cakes and sandwiches. There are a number of other small restaurants and tea shops on Zayed the Second St between Shaikh Rashid bin Saeed al-Maktoum St and East Rd.

One of Abu Dhabi's best value places to eat is *Talk of the Town* on Shaikh Khalifa bin Zayed St, west of the intersection with Lulu St. For Dh7 you'll get an omelette or two pieces of fried chicken, as well as soup, bread and fries. Burgers cost Dh5 to Dh7. The food and service are both great.

One of the best biryanis we have ever had was at the *Sarawan Restaurant* on Zayed the Second St. The portions are large and, at Dh8, excellent value. Cheap vegetarian Indian food can be found at the *Bhavna Restaurant* on Zayed the Second St. Samosas are Dh2.50 each and there's quite a good masala dosa (curried vegetables in a pastry shell) for Dh3.

A place you should definitely try is *Tarbouche* on Shaikh Hamdan bin Mohammed St. The fare on offer is almost entirely Lebanese. Appetisers and main dishes cost Dh6

to Dh22 (most of the mezzes are Dh6 to Dh8) and the freshly baked Arabic bread is served hot at your table. Cheaper, but arguably better, Lebanese fare in less fun surroundings can be found at *Maroosh* near the intersection of Shaikh Hamdan bin Mohammed and As-Salam Sts.

A good bet at any time of day is *La Brioche* on Shaikh Hamdan Bin Mohammed St. It is on the 2nd floor of the same building that has the Emirates Airlines office at street level. It offers coffee and cappuccino which, at Dh7 to Dh10, is worth the extra dirham or two. For breakfast, croissants and various other pastries are available for Dh3 to Dh6. It also makes excellent sandwiches.

For cheap Chinese food, try the *Mandarin Restaurant* on Zayed the First St. It has generous combination plates starting at Dh24 for a full meal, including drink.

Entertainment

Abu Dhabi is probably not as boring as its reputation but it has neither Dubai's energy nor its nightclub scene. *The Tavern*, a British-style pub at the Sheraton Hotel, is a good place for a drink. The closest approximation of a real sports bar is *The Island Exchange*, the bar on the 1st floor of the Forte Grand Hotel.

The *Eldorado Cinema* on Zayed the Second St shows western films.

Getting There & Away

Air Abu Dhabi international airport (AUH) is on the mainland, about 30 km from the centre. You should be at the airport about 90 minutes before departure for short-haul flights (ie, within the Gulf) and two hours before departure for flights to Europe and Asia. Call ☎ 757 611 for airport information.

Abu Dhabi is one of the co-owners of Gulf Air (☎ 332 600). The airline's booking office is on the corner of Shaikh Rashid bin Saeed al-Maktoum and Shaikh Hamdan bin Mohammed Sts. Return fares to some other Gulf cities include: Bahrain Dh500, Doha Dh360, Kuwait Dh1040, Muscat Dh520 and Riyadh Dh880.

Bus The main bus terminal is on East Rd, south of the centre. Intercity service is only available within the Abu Dhabi emirate. Buses run to both Al-Ain and Madinat Zayed (2½ hours; Dh10 to either city) 15 times daily from early morning until about 9 pm. Change at Madinat Zayed for Liwa.

Service Taxi Service taxis and minibuses leave from a station adjacent to the main bus terminal on East Rd. Minibuses carrying 14 passengers charge Dh20 per person to Dubai. Taxis, carrying five to seven people, charge Dh30. Taxis also regularly go to Al-Ain (Dh20) and Sharjah (Dh30).

Car Car rental rates start at about Dh140 to Dh150 per day plus insurance, though you will probably get some sort of discount on these rates if you ask for one. There are a number of rental places in the city centre.

Getting Around

The Airport Bus No 901 runs from the main bus terminal to the airport around the clock, departing every 20 minutes (every 30 minutes between midnight and 6 am). The fare is Dh3. Airport limos charge Dh70 from the airport to the city, while airport taxis charge Dh40 to Dh60. The taxis are orange and white. A taxi from the city centre costs around Dh40.

Bus You will notice municipal buses running throughout Abu Dhabi. These are cheap – fares are only Dh1 to Dh4 depending on the distance travelled – but they are nearly useless for the traveller because they follow no fixed routes. Really. All of the buses originate at the main bus and service-taxi station on East Rd. From there they go down one of the three main roads that lead back onto the mainland. The buses end up in various industrial zones and labourers' camps on the mainland, where they turn around and head back into the souq. Outbound they take whatever road the driver feels like taking. On the way back they do the same thing, driving around the souq and Corniche area until there are no passengers left on the bus. The only, limited, exception to this system is the Airport bus, No 901. Even this bus, however, does not follow a set route on its way back into town.

Taxi Taxis are equipped with meters. A flag fall is Dh2 and the meters turn over at 50 fils a click.

AL-AIN & BURAIMI

The Buraimi oasis straddles the border between Abu Dhabi and Oman. There are a number of settlements in both parts of the oasis but in the UAE the entire area is referred to by the name of the main town in Abu Dhabi's section: Al-Ain (pronounced so that it rhymes with 'main'). Buraimi technically refers to the entire oasis but is also used when referring to the Omani section.

Once in the oasis, you can cross freely between the UAE and Oman – people driving up from Muscat pass through customs before reaching the Omani town of Buraimi – and it is this fact (plus the dry climate) that makes the oasis so appealing. Note, however, that if you have rented a car in the UAE, your insurance will not cover accidents occurring on Omani territory. Use of seat belts in mandatory in Oman and this, like the speed limits, is strictly enforced.

Orientation

The Al-Ain/Buraimi area can be very confusing. All of the streets in Al-Ain look pretty much the same. Basically, Al-Ain wraps around an arm of Omani territory with most of Al-Ain's business district lying just south of the border. The main streets in Al-Ain are Khalifa ibn Zayed St and Zayed ibn Sultan St, both of which run roughly east-west. Khalifa ibn Zayed St is also the road to both Abu Dhabi and the airport. The main north-south cross streets are Abu Bakr al-Siddiq St, which extends into Buraimi, and Al-Ain St. The two landmarks you need to know for navigational purposes are the clock tower and coffeepot roundabouts.

The streets in Buraimi don't appear to have names, but there are fewer of them, so getting around is not very difficult.

PLACES TO STAY
2 Al-Buraimi Hotel
11 Al-Dhahrah Hotel
31 Al-Ain Hilton
32 Al-Ain Inter-
Continental

PLACES TO EAT
3 Coffeehouse
7 Yameen Restaurant
8 Muscat Restaurant
10 Al-Karawan Restaurant
13 Safsuf Cafeteria
14 Cafeteria Beirut
15 Pizza Hut

16 Golden Fish
19 Muslim Restaurant
25 Golden Gate Restaurant

OTHER
1 Muraijib Fort & Park
4 Buraimi Souq &
Al-Hilla Fort
5 Royal Oman Police
6 Buraimi Post Office
9 Al-Khandaq Fort
12 Buraimi Bus Station
17 Grand Mosque
18 Al-Ain Service-
Taxi Stand

20 UAE Exchange Centre
(Money Exchange)
21 Camel Market
22 Old Prison
23 Al-Ain Souq
24 Al-Ain Bus Station
26 Al-Ain GPO
27 ETISALAT
(Telephone Office)
28 Al-Ain Club (Stadium)
29 Eastern Fort &
Al-Ain Museum
30 Livestock Souq

Al-Ain & Buraimi

UNITED ARAB EMIRATES

Distances in both Al-Ain and Buraimi are large. You could, in theory, walk from the bus or taxi station to the oasis' one semi-cheap hotel, which is just over the Omani border, but with any luggage at all it would be a hell of a hike, especially when it is hot, which is most of the time. You also require your own transport to visit some of the sights, like Jebel Hafit.

Information

There is no tourist office in either city but it's fairly easy to find most of the things worth seeing in Al-Ain by following the big purple road signs. Buraimi has no tourist signs but the market and both of the old forts are adjacent to the main road which runs across Omani territory.

Money There are lots of banks in Al-Ain near the Clock Tower roundabout and the GPO. The area around the Grand Mosque has several moneychangers. In Oman you'll see several banks on the main road. UAE dirhams and Omani riyals are accepted on both sides of the border.

Post & Communications Al-Ain's GPO and telephone office are side by side at the Clock Tower roundabout. The GPO is open Saturday to Wednesday from 8 am to 8 pm, Thursday from 8 am to 6 pm and Friday from 8 to 11 am. The ETISALAT office is open every day from 7 am to midnight. Buraimi's post office is across the street from the Yameen restaurant. It is open Saturday to Wednesday from 8 am to 2 pm, and Thursday from 8 to 11 am. It is closed on Friday.

The phone systems of the two cities are separate. Thus, if you're in the Hotel Al-Buraimi and want to ring someone 200m away in Al-Ain, it's an international call and will be billed as such. The UAE telephone code for Al-Ain is 03. There are no telephone area codes in Oman.

Eastern Fort & the Al-Ain Museum

The museum and fort are in the same compound, south-east of the overpass near the Coffeepot roundabout. As you enter the museum, take a look at the Bedouin *diwan* (divan) set up to the left of the manager's office. Also be sure to see the display of photographs of Al-Ain in the 1960s.

There's not a lot to see in the fort beyond the old cannon in the courtyard. The fort was the birthplace of Abu Dhabi's current ruler, Shaikh Zayed. It was built in 1910 by Zayed's father.

The museum is open Sunday to Wednesday from 8 am to 1 pm, Thursday from 8 am to noon and Friday from 9 to 11.30 am. It reopens every afternoon from 3.30 to 5.30 pm (4.30 to 6.30 pm from May to October) and is closed all day Saturday. Museum admission is 50 fils (if somebody is at the door to collect it).

Livestock Souq

You can see the entrance to the livestock market from the museum/fort parking lot. The souq attracts Bedouin and townspeople from all over the southern UAE and northern Oman. The best time to be there is early in the morning (before 9 am) when the trading is at its heaviest.

The Old Prison

The prison is the fort-like building on Zayed ibn Sultan St near the Coffeepot roundabout. It is open rather erratic hours but if you get into the courtyard, it is usually possible to climb to the roof of the prison tower for a view out over the oasis and the camel market.

The Camel Market

Al-Ain's camel market is immediately behind the prison. It's quite small but worth visiting for local colour. It is open from early morning until about noon every day, and the best time to visit is as early in the day as possible, before the heat intensifies both the dust and the smell.

Buraimi Souq & Al-Hilla Fort

Buraimi's souq is bigger than it looks from the road. It's a very practical place selling fruit, vegetables, meat and household goods. The Al-Hilla Fort, immediately behind the souq, was being restored at the time of writing. Technically it is not open to the public but if you ask the workers nicely they may let you wander around.

Al-Khandaq Fort

This fort, which is much larger than Al-Hilla, is said to be about 400 years old. If you're entering Buraimi from the centre of Al-Ain you'll see it about 200m off the road to your left, about 750m past the border. It was recently restored and is now open Saturday to Wednesday from 8 am to 6 pm and Thursday and Friday from 8 am to 1 pm and 4 to 6 pm. Admission is free.

Muraijib Fort & Park

This small fort is on Al-Jimi St, several km north-west of Al-Ain's centre. The restored remains of the fortifications are scattered within a beautifully landscaped garden. The garden is open daily from 4 to 11 pm (10 am to 11 pm on Friday and holidays). Admission is Dh1 but this is not always strictly enforced. In theory the park is only open to women and small children but this, too, is not always enforced.

Muraijib can be reached by bus No 80 to Hili Jimi. The fare is Dh1.

Jebel Hafit

The views from the top of this mountain are well worth making the effort to see. The summit is about 30 km by road from the centre of Al-Ain (a taxi should make the round trip for about Dh40 after a bit of bargaining).

Ayn al-Fayda

Ayn al-Fayda is a resort south of the oasis, 1.5 km beyond the Jebel Hafit turn-off. The area is a resort favoured mostly by expatriate Arab families. The spring itself is a sulphur pool which is not suitable for swimming.

Hili Gardens

This combination public park and archaeological site is about eight km north of the centre of Al-Ain, off the Dubai Rd. The site is open daily from 4 to 11 pm (holidays from 10 am to 10 pm). Admission is Dh1.

The main attraction is the **Round Structure**, a 3rd-millennium BC tomb, possibly connected with the Umm an-Nar culture. The park can be reached by bus Nos 80, 100 and 203. The fare is Dh1.

Zoo

Al-Ain's zoo, one of the better ones in the Gulf, is south of town. It is open daily from 7 am to 5.30 pm. Admission is Dh2. It has indigenous species including Arabian oryx and gazelle, saluki dogs and bustards. It also has kangaroos, pigmy hippos, vultures etc. The zoo can be reached via bus No 110 to Ayn al-Fayda or bus No 60 to Zakhe.

Activities

Visitors can use the sports facilities at both the Hilton and the Inter-Continental hotels for Dh30 per day (for free if you're staying in the hotel). The Hilton also has a par-3 golf course. Greens fees are Dh50 for the first nine holes and Dh25 to play a second nine. You can rent clubs for Dh20.

Al-Ain's camel racecourse is about 20 km from the centre on the road to Abu Dhabi. Races usually take place early on Friday mornings during the winter months.

Organised Tours

Al-Ain Camel Safaris (☎ (050) 470 700, 477 268) offers a variety of desert trips, ranging from short one hour rides into the desert to overnight trips including dinner and breakfast. It has an office in the lobby of the Hilton.

Most of the tour companies operating out of Dubai, Abu Dhabi and Sharjah also run trips to Al-Ain.

Places to Stay

There are only four hotels in the two towns and only one of them remotely qualifies as cheap. This is the *Al-Dhahrah Hotel* (☎ 650 492; fax 650 881). It's a good place, sitting almost smack on the border, and will be on your right if you enter Oman from the centre of Al-Ain. Singles/doubles are Dh130/160 or OR13.700/16.900. The Al-Dhahrah has a small restaurant but it does not serve alcohol. The other hotel on the Omani side of the oasis is the *Al-Buraimi Hotel* (☎ 652 010; fax 652 011; in the UAE call ☎ (050) 474 954), which you can find easily enough by following the blue-and-white signs strategically positioned throughout the Omani part of the oasis. Singles/doubles are Dh351/427 (OR37/45) plus 15% tax and service charge, though discounts are often available.

Back in the UAE, your choices are the *Al-Ain Hilton* (☎ 686 666; fax 686 888) and the *Al-Ain Inter-Continental* (☎ 686 686; fax 686 766). Both charge Dh420/500 plus 16% for singles/doubles, but discounts, again, are usually available.

Places to Eat

Al-Ain The best area for cheap eateries is near the Grand Mosque and the Clock Tower roundabout. The *Muslim Restaurant*, just north of the overpass on Abu Bakr al-Siddiq St, offers the usual fare of rice with mutton, chicken or fish for Dh7. It also makes very good hadas (a spicy lentil paste) for Dh3. *Cafeteria Beirut* on Khalifa ibn Zayed St has excellent shwarma and also offers felafel, sodas and fresh juice.

For more up-market eating, there is the *Golden Gate Restaurant* at the intersection of Khalifa ibn Zayed and Al-Ain Sts for good Chinese and Filipino food. Main dishes are Dh15 to Dh30. Another good bet is *The Hut*, a coffee shop on Khalifa ibn Zayed St near the large *Pizza Hut*. It offers good cappuccino as well as a wide selection of cakes.

For alcohol and more expensive fare, you have to head for the hotels. *Paco's*, at the Hilton, has surprisingly good Mexican food with main dishes at about Dh30 apiece. The *Horse & Jockey Club Pub* at the Inter-Continental is the best bar in town and usually has good pub meals on offer.

Buraimi Buraimi has fewer eating places than Al-Ain. You will probably find your options limited to the standard cheap fare of a helping of biryani rice with fish, chicken or mutton for about Dh10/OR1. Try the *Al-Karawan Restaurant* and the *Muscat Restaurant*, both opposite the turn for the Al-Khandaq Fort. On Buraimi's main com-

mercial street, the *Yameen Restaurant* has more of the same.

Things to Buy

There are (expensive) shops in the lobbies of the Hilton and the Inter-Continental hotels selling Omani jewellery and other souvenirs. You can also buy these things in the Buraimi souq where they will definitely cost less but are also likely to be in much worse condition.

Getting There & Away

Air Al-Ain's airport is approximately 20 km from the centre. Gulf Air offers direct service from Al-Ain to Bahrain, Doha, Muscat, Karachi and a number of major Arab cities. EgyptAir, Royal Jordanian and PIA also serve the airport a couple of times per week. For airport information call ☎ 855 555, ext 2211.

Bus Buses run from Al-Ain to Abu Dhabi (2½ hours; Dh10) 15 times per day starting around 6 am, with the last trip at about 9.30 pm. The bus station is behind the Al-Ain Cooperative Society's supermarket.

Oman's bus company, ONTC, has three buses a day to and from the Ruwi station in Muscat (six hours regular, 4½ hours express; OR3.600) via Sohar.

Service Taxi Al-Ain's taxi station is in the big parking lot behind the Grand Mosque. The fare to both Dubai and Abu Dhabi is Dh20.

Getting Around

The Airport Bus No 500 is an express service that runs every 30 minutes between the Al-Ain's bus station and the airport. The fare is Dh3 and the trip takes about 40 minutes. A taxi to or from Al-Ain running on the meter should cost about Dh25.

Bus All of Al-Ain's buses run roughly on the half-hour from 6 am to midnight. All fares are Dh1 except for Ayn al-Fayda and the airport, both of which are Dh3.

You cannot get to the Inter-Continental Hotel by bus, but bus No 120 will take you to the Hilton. Bus No 110 goes to Ayn al-Fayda and the zoo. Bus No 60 also goes to the zoo. Several buses serve Hili.

There are no local buses in Buraimi.

Taxi It is better to use Al-Ain taxis than Omani taxis because only the Al-Ain taxis have meters.

MADINAT ZAYED
Madinat Zayed, also called Badr Zayed, is the administrative centre for the huge desert region that includes the Liwa oasis. It lies some 50 km south of the coast road along a stretch of tarmac that takes you through one of Abu Dhabi's main onshore oil production areas. There is nothing to see in Madinat Zayed itself but it makes a useful base for exploring the Liwa area.

The only place to stay is the *Rest House* (☎ (088) 46281) run by Abu Dhabi National Hotels Co. All the rooms cost Dh165, single or double. There are 15 buses per day from Abu Dhabi to Madinat Zayed (2½ hours; Dh10) and a similar number running back to Abu Dhabi. There are also nine buses daily, and 12 on Friday, from Madinat Zayed to Liwa (one hour; Dh4).

LIWA
The Liwa oasis has long been a popular weekend getaway spot for Emiratis and expatriates alike. The extension of the paved roads deep into the desert has made it possible to see some of Liwa's scenery without a 4WD. Liwa is not a single stand of greenery, like the huge Al-Hasa oasis in eastern Saudi Arabia; rather it is a collection of small villages spread out over a 150 km arc of land.

Mizaira'a is where the road from Madinat Zayed ends in a roundabout. Approaching from the north, the bus station is to the right of this roundabout opposite some shops and restaurants. There are nine buses per day (12 on Friday) to Madinat Zayed (one hour; Dh4). Two local routes serve the oasis communities. The more interesting route goes east to the village of **Hamim** (Dh3), where the paved road ends and the bus turns around. The other route, 40 km west to **Karima**

(Dh2), is flatter, more open and much less interesting.

Liwa's *Rest House* (☎ (088) 22 075; fax 29 311) is about seven km west of the bus station along the Arada road. Book ahead if you plan a weekend visit.

Dubai

In all the Middle East, there is no place quite like Dubai. It is a bastion of anything-goes capitalism – sort of an Arab version of Hong Kong. There isn't actually a lot to see in Dubai, but you will not find a more easy-going place anywhere in the Gulf – or a place with better night life. There's almost nothing 'old' in Dubai but it is the one place in the Gulf where that hardly seems to matter.

Orientation
Dubai is really two towns: Deira to the east, and Dubai to the west. They are separated by the Creek (*al-khor* in Arabic), an inlet of the Gulf. The Dubai side is sometimes referred to as Bur Dubai when someone wants to make it clear that he or she means the Dubai side as opposed to the entire city. Deira, however, is the city centre.

Activity in Deira focuses on Beniyas Rd (which runs along the Creek), Beniyas Square (which used to be called Nasr Square and is still generally known by that name) and the area along Al-Maktoum Rd, Al-Maktoum Hospital Rd, and Naif Rd. The Deira souq, where most of the cheap hotels are located, is most of the area west of Beniyas Square and south of Naif Rd.

Information
There is no tourist office in Dubai, though you might be able to get some information from the tour operators listed under Organised Tours both in this section and in the Sharjah section.

Money In central Deira, especially along Beniyas Rd and on Beniyas Square, every other building seems to contain a bank or a

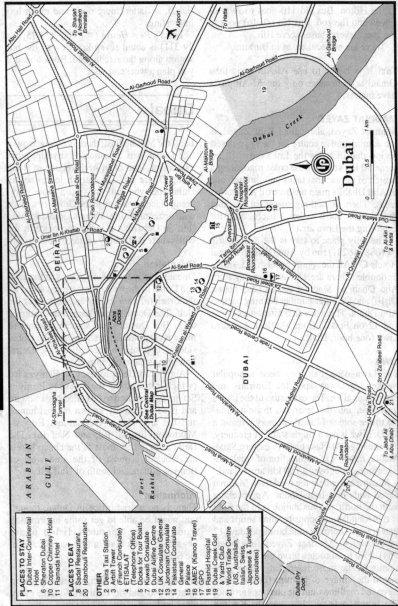

Dubai

1 km

0.5

0

Dubai Creek

PLACES TO STAY
1 Dubai Inter-Continental Hotel
6 Sheraton Dubai
10 Copper Chimney Hotel
11 Ramada Hotel

PLACES TO EAT
8 Sadaf Restaurant
20 Istanbouli Restaurant

OTHER
2 Deira Taxi Station
3 Arbift Tower (French Consulate)
4 ETISALAT (Telephone Office)
5 Docks for Tour Boats
7 Kuwaiti Consulate
9 Dubai Airline Centre
12 UK Consulate General
13 Jordanian Consulate
14 Pakistani Consulate
15 Palace
16 AMEX (Kanoo Travel)
17 GPO
18 Rashid Hospital
19 Dubai Creek Golf & Yacht Club
21 World Trade Centre (US, Australian, Italian, Swiss, Japanese & Turkish Consulates)

moneychanger. In Bur Dubai there are a lot of moneychangers (though most of them only take cash) around the *abra* (water taxi) dock. In either case it is worth shopping around if you are changing more than a few hundred US dollars.

Amex (☎ 524 400) is represented in Dubai by Kanoo Travel. Its office is on the Dubai side of the Creek, on Za'abeel Rd in the National Bank of Umm al-Qaiwain building next to the GPO. It is open daily except Friday from 8.30 am to 1 pm and 4 to 6.30 pm. Cheques are cashed for card holders and mail is held for Amex clients. Address mail c/o American Express, Client's Mail, PO Box 290, Dubai, UAE.

Post The GPO is on the Dubai side, on Za'abeel Rd. It is open Saturday to Wednesday from 8 am to 11.30 pm, Thursday from 8 am to 10 pm and Friday from 8 am to noon. There is also a small post office on the Deira side of the creek, on Al-Sabkha Rd near the intersection with Beniyas Rd.

Telephone & Fax The ETISALAT office on the corner of Beniyas and Umar ibn al-Khattab Rds is open 24 hours a day. In addition to telephones, the office has fax, telex and telegram facilities. Note that the building you want is the new one – the glass and steel tower with a thing that looks like a golf ball on top – not the older, white building across the street. Dubai's telephone code is 04.

Bookshops Dubai's best bookshop, Magrudy Books (☎ 444192) is on Beach Rd, Jumeira, near the Jumeira Mosque. In the centre, try Aalam al-Kotob (World of Books) in the Al Ghurair Centre on the corner of Umer Ibn Al-Khattab and Al-Rigga Rds, or the bookshops in the big hotels.

The Creek

The obvious place to start your tour of Dubai is at the waterfront. The best idea is to hire an abra for an hour or so. For around Dh30 (for the whole boat, not per person) the captain should take you up to the Al-

Maktoum Bridge and back. For Dh40 he ought to extend that route to include a trip down to the mouth of the Creek and back.

Dubai Museum

Dubai's museum occupies the Al-Fahaidi Fort on the Dubai side of the Creek, next to the Ruler's Office. Al-Fahaidi Fort was built in the early 19th century and is thought to be the oldest building in Dubai. The museum has recently been remodelled and expanded and is definitely worth visiting. Expect to spend at least two hours here, as it is much bigger than it looks.

It is open Saturday to Thursday from 7.30 am to 2 pm and 3 to 9 pm and Friday from 3 to 9 pm. Admission is Dh3.

The Ruler's Office

This is the white building, decorated with mock wind towers, fronting onto the Creek. Near it are a few old buildings with (real) wind towers.

Shaikh Saeed's House

The house of Shaikh Saeed, the grandfather of Dubai's present ruler, has been restored as a museum of pre-oil times. The 30 room house sits beside the Creek on the Dubai side. At the time of writing the museum was closed for renovations. When it reopens (possibly by the time you read this), it will probably keep hours similar to those of the museum.

World Trade Centre

The World Trade Centre Tower is Dubai's tallest building. There is a viewing gallery on the 37th floor. You can only visit the gallery as part of a tour. These leave from the information desk in the tower lobby at 9.30 am and 4.30 pm. Admission is Dh5.

Activities

Many activities, such as sailing and water sports, are organised through clubs. *What's On* is a good source of information for these clubs and other leisure activities. Dubai has three golf courses: Emirates Golf Club (☎ 480 222), Dubai Creek Golf & Yacht

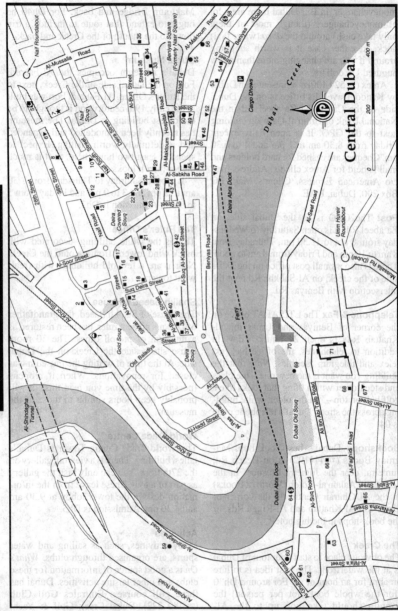

Central Dubai

400 m

200

0

Dubai Creek

Cargo Dhows

Ferry

Deira Abra Dock

Dubai Abra Dock

Dubai Old Souq

Al-Seef Road

Umm Hurair Roundabout

Mussala Rd (Dubai)

Al-Ittin Abi Talib Road

Al-Hisn Street

Al-Faghidi Road

Al-Esbij Street

Al-Nahda Street

Al-Rifa'a Street

Al-Suq Road

Al-Mussala Road

Naif Roundabout

28th Street

38th Street

Deira Street

Naif Road

Al-Soor Street

Al-Khaleej Road

Al-Shindagha Road

Al-Shindagha Tunnel

Al-Burj Street

Street 38

Al-Maktoum Hospital Road

Beniyas Square
(Formerly Nasr Square)

Road 14

Al-Maktoum Road

Beniyas Road

Street 1

Al-Sabkha Road

Al-Suq Deira Street

Suq Deira Street

Al-Khail Street

Deira Covered Souq

Deira Souq

Gold Souq

Old Baladiya Street

Al-Sabkha Street

Al-Buteen Street

Sikkat

Al-Suq Al-Kabeer Street

Beniyas Road

Al-Ras Street

Al-Abba

Al-Hadd Street

Al-Khor Street

UNITED ARAB EMIRATES

Club (☎ 821 000), and the Dubai Golf & Racing Club (☎ 363 666). Playing at any of them is expensive (around Dh250) and requires an advance booking. You may be asked to produce a handicap certificate, but they tend to be flexible about this.

Camel racing takes place early on Friday mornings during winter and spring, at the track south of the centre off the 2nd Za'abeel Rd on the Dubai side. Admission is free but try to get there by 8 am.

Organised Tours

Arabian Adventures (☎ 317 373; fax 314 696) is a Dubai-based company run in tandem with Emirates Airlines. It offers full-day and half-day tours of Dubai and the other emirates for Dh100 to Dh300 per person, depending on the itinerary. Net Tours (☎ 666 655; fax 668 662) has a similar selection of tours at similar prices.

Coastline Leisure (☎ 450 867; fax 452 497) offers boat tours of the Creek by dhow starting at Dh35 per person. The boats depart from the Deira docks, across from Chamber of Commerce building.

Places to Stay – bottom end & middle

Dubai's *youth hostel* (☎ 625 578) is on Qusais Rd, on the eastern outskirts of the city, between the Al-Ahli Club and the Jamiat al-Islah relief agency. Beds are Dh35 per night in two and three-bed dorm rooms. Women as well as men can be accommodated, though the manager reserves the right to turn away unaccompanied women if the hostel is full of rowdy young males. Bus Nos 13 and 19 go to the hostel.

Dubai's hotels are scattered over a wide area but the cheapies are concentrated in the Deira souq, particularly along Al-Sabkha Rd and in the side streets off Suq Deira St. You can probably negotiate some kind of discount, especially for longer stays, at almost any hotel listed here. Few of Dubai's cheapest hotels still arrange visas, which is probably just as well considering the chequered record some of these places had in

PLACES TO STAY		
2	Green Line Hotel	
3	Metro Hotel	
4	Al-Ikhlas Hotel	
8	Hotel Delhi Darbar	
9	Hariri Palace Hotel	
11	Imperial Palace Hotel	
13	Ramsis Hotel	
14	Gold Tower Hotel	
15	Al-Khayam Hotel	
17	Arabian Island Hotel (Branch)	
18	Al-Najah Hotel	
19	Stars Hotel	
20	Al-Buteen Plaza Hotel	
21	Al-Amal Hotel	
22	Shatt al-Arab Hotel	
23	Sina Hotel	
25	Vienna Hotel	
26	Miriana Hotel	
27	Avon Hotel	
28	Dubai Orient Hotel	
29	Royal Prince Hotel	
31	Phoenicia Hotel	
33	Rex Hotel	
35	Swiss Hotel	
36	Anahita Hotel	
37	Shams al-Sahraa	

38	Al-Sheraa Hotel	
39	Al-Aman Hotel	
40	Bin Sadoon Hotel	
41	Red Sea Hotel	
43	Mirage Hotel	
44	Victoria Hotel	
45	Al-Khaleej Hotel	
53	Riviera Hotel	
54	Carlton Tower Hotel	
62	Peninsula Hotel	
63	Ambassador Hotel	
65	Astoria Hotel	
66	Time Palace Hotel	
68	Regent Palace Hotel	

PLACES TO EAT		
6	Najaf Restaurant	
10	Bab-U-Sabkha	
16	Al-Burj Cafeteria	
24	Gulf Restaurant & Cafeteria	
30	Entezary Restaurant	
32	Golden Fork	
47	Cafeteria al-Abra	
48	Pizza Corner	
49	Hatam Restaurant	
52	Popeye Restaurant	
57	Cafe Mozart	

67	Bhavna Restaurant	

OTHER		
1	Deira Bus Station	
5	Mosque	
7	Police Station (Old Fort)	
12	Wind Tower	
34	Tide Drycleaners & Laundry	
42	Small Exchange Kiosks	
46	Deira Post Office	
50	Saudia Airlines	
51	British Bank of the Middle East	
55	Emirates Airlines	
56	Al-Maidan Laundry	
58	Emirates Bank International (ATM)	
59	Shaikh Saeed's House	
60	Plaza Cinema	
61	Dubai Bus & Service-Taxi Station	
64	Moneychangers Souq	
69	Wind Towers	
70	Ruler's Office	
71	Dubai Museum	

UNITED ARAB EMIRATES

terms of getting the paperwork done properly and on time.

An exception to this rule is the *Mirage Hotel* (☎ 260 004; fax 260 293), in an alley just off Al-Sabkha Rd across from the much larger Al-Khaleej Hotel. The rooms are tiny but at Dh60/100 for singles/doubles (plus a Dh10 'registration fee' applied on your first night only) you won't beat the combination of price and cleanliness.

Only two other bottom-end hotels credibly claim to be able to arrange visas. One is the *Al-Sheraa Hotel* (☎ 265 213; fax 254 866) on Al-Buteen St. At Dh80/100 for singles/doubles without bath it is a definite step down from the Mirage. The other is the *Red Sea Hotel* (☎ 264 281; fax 265 249), also on Al-Buteen St. Rooms are Dh60/80; none have private baths.

Moving on to cheap hotels which require you to arrive visa-in-hand, and staying on Al-Buteen St, the *Bin Sadoon Hotel* (☎ 264 236; fax 259 825) is a somewhat spartan affair but the place has character. Singles/doubles without bath cost Dh60/80. Next door the *Al-Aman Hotel* has doubles only at Dh70 apiece, none have attached bath. Nearby, the *Shams al-Sahraa* (☎ 253 666; fax 253 647) is a bit more expensive at Dh80/120. Further up Al-Buteen St, and across the street from the Red Sea, the *Al-Najah Hotel* (☎ 263 931; fax 266 092) has OK rooms for Dh80/120.

In an alley between Sikkat al-Khail St and Al-Soor St is the *Metro Hotel* (☎ 260 040; fax 262 098). It has doubles at Dh100 per room but accepts only families (ie, no single males).

If you really want to be in the thick of things, head back to Al-Sabkha Rd and take a look at the *Shatt al-Arab Hotel* (☎ 258 587) overlooking the bus stop at the intersection of Al-Sabkha Rd and Deira St. Rooms are Dh30 per person; none have private baths. Many of the guests look like permanent residents and the place is often full. It's the grimiest place in Dubai and the air-conditioning is deafening, but it has character.

If you are looking for something a bit more up-market try the *Royal Prince Hotel*

(☎ 239 991; fax 219 757) on Al-Sabkha Rd where the rooms are very good value at Dh140/180.

Since the first edition of this book there has been quite a lot of hotel-building along Naif South St. Places here tend to be bottom-end hotels with lower mid-range prices. One of the more established is the *Imperial Palace Hotel* (☎ 211 344; fax 223 770) with rooms at Dh150/180, which makes them reasonable value but nothing special. Among the newer places the *Tehran Hotel* (☎ 222 392; fax 222 823) is worth a look. It only has doubles, all at Dh140. The *Swiss Hotel* (☎ 212 181; fax 211 779), on Al-Mussalla Rd, is a very friendly place. Rates are Dh207/264.50 but discounts are readily given.

The *Hotel Delhi Darbar* (☎ 267 474; fax 266 464) on Naif Rd is, as its name implies, an Indian-oriented establishment. At Dh201/287.50 for large, spotless rooms, it is one of the better deals in this price range. It does not, however, sponsor visas.

Places to Stay – top end

All of the hotels in this category will arrange visas. Rates are negotiable, and the service charge is already included in the prices listed here.

Deira One of the better-value top-end places in the city is the *Al-Khaleej Hotel* (☎ 211 144; fax 237 140) between Beniyas Square and Al-Sabkha Rd. Singles/doubles are Dh288/408. The *Phoenicia Hotel* (☎ 227 191; fax 221 629) has a prime location on Beniyas Square. At Dh230/360 its rates are OK by local standards for its rather ostentatious rooms.

The *Victoria Hotel* (☎ 269 626; fax 269 575), in an alley off Al-Sabkha Rd, is a decent if dull place at Dh220/260.

Along Beniyas Rd the *Carlton Tower Hotel* (☎ 227 111; fax 228 249) is a good 'budget' top-end place with rooms starting at Dh367.50/472.50. Next door, the *Riviera Hotel* (☎ 222 131; fax 211 820) has similar prices but is less plush and does not serve alcohol.

Dubai Unless it's for business reasons, it is a bit hard to see why one would want to stay on the Dubai side. Deira is a lot more fun, and there are no cheap hotels on the Dubai side.

The *Time Palace Hotel* (☎ 532 111; fax 539 948) does not arrange visas, but it has a good location on the edge of the Bur Dubai souq. Rooms cost Dh172.50/230. Just off Khalid ibn Al-Waleed Rd, the *Harbour Hotel* (☎ 511 223; fax 511 248) is the only other cheapish place in Bur Dubai, at Dh175/250.

Places to Eat

On Beniyas Square between the Phoenicia and the Rex hotels, the *Golden Fork* has an odd combination of oriental dishes and western fast food. Two pieces of chicken, french fries, bread and a soda cost Dh7 – a hard price to beat. A few doors down the *Entezary Restaurant* offers equally good value for money. A dinner of kebab, rice, soup, salad, houmos, bread and tea costs only Dh15.

The *Hatam Restaurant*, just off Beniyas Square behind the Saudia Airlines office, serves excellent Persian food at very reasonable prices. A traditional chelo kebab (which appears on the menu as sultan kebab) costs Dh17, including soup and salad.

Across Beniyas Rd from the abra dock, *Pizza Corner* is a good medium-priced place with pizzas and burgers. Its sandwiches go for Dh9 to Dh16. For a quick and cheap meal out on Beniyas Rd, *Cafeteria al-Abra* has good shwarma and samosas along with fruit juice and soda. A bit further up the road, *Popeye* has shwarma, burgers and other snacks. A full meal can easily be had for Dh10 or less.

For coffee you must try *Cafe Mozart*, which re-creates the atmosphere, food, coffee and service of a Viennese coffee house. The pastries and croissants cost about Dh3 each and are good. The coffee and cappuccinos are excellent.

In Deira's budget hotel district there are many cheap restaurants, most of them serving Indian and Pakistani food (though many have menus consisting only of biryanis). Naif South St has particularly good pickings. Try *Bab-U-Sabkha* for good, cheap Pakistani food. On the Dubai side of the Creek try *Bhavna*, an Indian vegetarian restaurant on Al-Faghidi Rd, opposite the Dubai Museum, which has similar fare and prices.

Entertainment

After-hours social life centres around expensive restaurants, bars and discos in the big hotels (only hotels are allowed to serve alcohol). A night out on the town is not going to be cheap. If you're drinking, plan on spending well over Dh150, and even non-drinkers could easily go through half that in cover charges and overpriced glasses of Pepsi.

Pancho Villa's, at the Astoria hotel, is a Dubai institution and often has decent live music. Other popular spots include *The Pub* at the Inter-Continental Hotel and *The Old Vic* at the Ramada Hotel. If you're looking for a disco try the *Jumeira Beach Club*.

You can catch relatively recent western flicks at the *Galleria*., the shopping complex attached to the Hyatt Regency Hotel.

Things to Buy

If you are looking for cheap electronics try the area at the Al-Sabkha Rd end of Beniyas Square. The gold souq is further west, along Sikkat al-Khail St. This area has to be seen to be believed: even veterans of Middle-Eastern gold markets are likely to be blown away be the sheer scale of Dubai's gold souq.

If you are looking for Middle Eastern-looking souvenirs, including Bedouin jewellery, there are a couple of small shops along Beniyas Rd between the abra dock and the Inter-Continental Hotel that are worth browsing around.

Getting There & Away

Air In late 1995 Dubai's government announced plans for a massive expansion of airport facilities over the next four years, so be prepared to run into a lot of construction work around the airport. For general airport information call ☎ 245 777 or 245 555.

Dubai is the base for Emirates Airlines. Its main booking office (☎ 215 544) is on Beniyas Square. Dubai airport is one of the Middle East's main transport hubs, and service is available to just about anywhere in Europe, the Middle East or Asia.

Sample return fares from Dubai to some other Gulf cities include: Bahrain Dh580, Doha Dh450, Jeddah Dh1560, Kuwait Dh1050, Muscat Dh480 and Riyadh Dh960.

Bus Intercity buses only operate within the Dubai emirate. There are six buses daily to Hatta (80 minutes; Dh7). The Hatta buses leave from the Deira bus station, near the gold souq, and also stop at the Dubai bus and service-taxi station.

There are also two buses per day to Muscat, Oman. These depart from the parking lot of Dubai Airline Centre on Al-Maktoum Rd, Deira. The trip takes five to six hours and costs Dh85 one way, Dh150 return. For information, call ☎ 203 3799. Tickets are sold at a desk in Dubai Airline Centre.

Service Taxi There are two service-taxi stations in Dubai, one on either side of the Creek. The Deira taxi station is near the intersection of Umar ibn al-Khattab and Al-Rigga Rds. Fares (per person) are: Sharjah Dh4, Ajman Dh5, Umm al-Qaiwain Dh7, Ras al-Khaimah Dh15, Fujairah Dh25.

Service taxis for Abu Dhabi and Al-Ain leave from the Dubai bus and service-taxi station on Al-Ghubaiba Rd, on the Dubai side of the Creek. It's Dh30 per person to Abu Dhabi or Al-Ain in a service taxi. Minibuses to Abu Dhabi cost only Dh20 per person and carry 14 passengers. There are also service taxis from the Dubai station to Jebel Ali for Dh7.

Car For rentals of more than a few days, Cars Rent-a-Car (☎ 692 694) can usually undercut the bigger agencies. It has an office in Bur Dubai at the Bur Juman Centre. It also has offices in a number of other cities around the UAE. Small cars start at Dh120 per day plus Dh20 per day for insurance, though it,

and the other agencies, are usually willing to discount that rate. We've also had good experience with Hanco Emirates Rent-a-Car (☎ 699 544) on Al-Ittihad Rd just outside the centre.

Getting Around
The Airport From the Deira bus station, bus Nos 4 and 11 go to the airport about every half-hour for Dh1. Only special airport taxis are allowed to pick up passengers at the airport. These charge Dh30 to any point in the city centre. A ride from the Deira souq area to the airport in a metered cab costs Dh10 to Dh12.

Bus Local buses operate out of stations in both Deira and Bur Dubai. The Deira bus station is off Al-Khor St, between that street and the back of the gold souq. The Bur Dubai bus and service-taxi station is on Al-Ghubaiba Rd (the station on the Dubai side is the main terminal). Note that in the official timetables the two stations appear as 'Gold Souq Bus Stn' and 'Ghubaiba Bus Stn' respectively. Fares are Dh1 to Dh3.50 depending on the distance travelled, and you will find that most trips work out at Dh1.50.

Some of the main municipal bus routes are:

Route 4 – Deira bus station, Naif roundabout, Umar ibn al-Khattab Rd, Fish roundabout, Deira taxi station, Al-Maktoum Rd, Clock Tower, Dubai Islamic Bank, Dubai Airline Centre, Flame roundabout, Al-Garhoud Intersection, Airport roundabout, Dubai airport, Dubai municipality garage, Emirates Airlines office, Al-Ramool Industrial Area, Rashidiya Clinic, Rashidiya library and vice versa

No 5 – Deira bus station, Naif roundabout, Umar ibn al-Khattab Rd, Fish roundabout, Deira taxi station, Al-Maktoum Rd to the Clock Tower roundabout, Tariq ibn Ziyad Rd, Al-Maktoum Bridge, Rashid Hospital, Broadcast roundabout (Dubai TV), Consulate Area, Za'abeel Rd, GPO, Karama District, Trade Centre Rd, Ministry of Health, Al-Saeediya Interchange, Khalid bin al-Waleed Rd, Dubai Marine Hotel, Falcon roundabout, Dubai bus and service-taxi station and return

Route 6 – Deira Bus Terminal, Naif roundabout, Umar ibn al-Khattab Rd, Fish roundabout, Salah ad-Din Rd, Ministry of Interior, Muraqqabat police station, Hamarain Centre, Abu Baker al-Siddique Rd, Clock Tower, Dubai Airline Centre, Dubai Islamic Bank, Tariq ibn Ziyad Rd, Al-Maktoum Bridge, British Council, Rashid Hospital, Broadcast roundabout (Dubai TV), Karama district, Trade Centre Rd, Bur Juman Centre, Immigration Department, Bur Dubai police station, Al-Dhiyafa Rd, Satwa Rd, Al-Safa St, Al-Wasl Rd, Jumeira fire station, Al-Amal Hospital, Al-Safa housing and return

No 8 – Al-Khabesi Industrial Area, Muraqqabat Rd, Abu Baker al-Siddique Rd, Al-Rigga Rd, Deira taxi station, Beniyas Rd, Dubai municipality, abra dock, Dubai public library, Deira bus station, Al-Shindagha Tunnel, Falcon roundabout, Dubai bus and service-taxi station, Al-Mina Rd, Dubai dry dock, Jumeira Mosque, Dubai Zoo, Umm Suqaim Municipality, Jumeira Beach Park, Chicago Beach Hotel, Mina Siyahi, Jebel Ali power station and return

Route 13 – Deira bus station, Naif roundabout, Umar ibn al-Khattab Rd, Fish roundabout, Salah al-Din Rd, Ministry of Interior, Muraqqabat police station, Tolaitala school, Al-Qiyada roundabout, Dubai police headquarters, Al-Ahli Club, Ministry of Information, Jamiat al-Islah, Al-Qusais Commercial Centre, Qusais Police Station, Qusais Clinic, Qusais Residential Area, Labour Camps and vice versa

Route 17 – Deira bus terminal, Hayatt Regency Hotel, Al-Khaleej Rd, Al-Khamsaa School, Kuwaiti Hospital, Al-Hamriya Port, Al-Wuhaida Rd, Al-Mamzar Library, Al-Ahli Club, Jamiat al-Islah, Ministry of Information, Al-Qusais commercial centre, Dubai abattoir, Moh family quarters and return

No 90 – Dubai bus and service-taxi station, Trade Centre Rd, Immigration Department, World Trade Centre, Shaikh Zayed Rd, Emirates Golf Club, Jebel Ali village, Ducab, Jebel Ali Free Zone

Taxi Most of Dubai's taxis have no meters. You can negotiate the fare in advance (and pay too much) or get in, tell the driver your destination, pay him what you think is appropriate once you get there and hope that there is no argument.

Should you go the latter route, pay Dh4 or Dh5 for trips around the centre that do not involve crossing the Creek. For trips across the Creek pay Dh7. Drivers will expect a 50% premium after midnight.

Or, you can call Dubai Transport (☎ 313 131), whose cabs have meters. Its taxis are

all cream coloured and charge Dh2 for flag fall and Dh1 per km thereafter.

Boat Abras leave constantly from early morning until about midnight. On the Deira side of the Creek the dock is at the intersection of Al-Sabkha and Beniyas Rds. On the Dubai side the dock is in front of a shop called Captain's Stores. The fare is 25 fils, which is collected once you are out on the water.

The Northern Emirates

SHARJAH

The third-largest of the seven emirates, Sharjah (*Ash-Sharqa* in Arabic) is a place that too many visitors to the UAE either miss entirely or pass through too quickly. Sharjah has some of the most interesting architecture in the country. Its new souq offers shopping to rival that of Dubai and its recently restored old souq offers a window on an older way of life that has now all but disappeared.

Orientation

Sharjah's business district is the area between the Corniche and Al-Zahra Rd, from the Central Market to Shaikh Mohammed bin Saqr al-Qasimi Rd (or Mohammed Saqr St). This is not a huge area and it's pretty easy to get around. During the day, however, it is a dreadful place for driving because the streets are both narrow and crowded. Central Sharjah's main street is Al-Arouba Rd.

Information

On Boorj Ave, just about every building houses a bank. Moneychangers can be found on the small streets immediately to the east and west of it. The GPO is on Government House Square. It is open Saturday to Wednesday from 8 am to 8 pm and Thursday from 8 am to 6 pm. ETISALAT's office is on Al-Safat Square (formerly Kuwait Square). It is open 24 hours a day. In addition to telephones, telex and fax services are also available.

The telephone code for Sharjah is 06.

UNITED ARAB EMIRATES

Sharjah Archaeological Museum

This museum is on Cultural Square on the corner of Shaikh Mohammed bin Saqr al-Qasimi Rd (which is an extension of Al-Wahda Rd, coming from Dubai). It is open daily from 8.30 am to 12.30 pm and from 5 to 8 pm. On Friday it is open only in the afternoon. Admission is free. All exhibits are labelled in English, French and Arabic.

The exhibits, as you might guess, focus on archaeological work in the emirate, though there are also displays on Sharjah's geography and traditional *falaj*-based irrigation

systems and on the emirate's history during the Iron Age (1200 to 400 BC).

Rolla Square

Sharjah's main square lies just inland from the intersection of Boorj Ave and Al-Arouba Rd. On holidays and other ceremonial occasions it is used for big, formal parades. The rest of the time it is a public park.

Old Souq

The Sharjah government has been restoring the old souq, large sections of which fell to

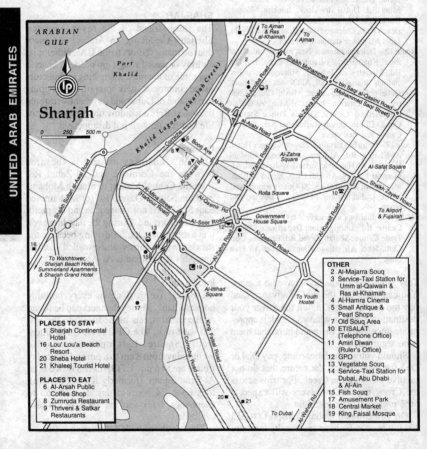

PLACES TO STAY
1   Sharjah Continental Hotel
16 Lou' Lou'a Beach Resort
20 Sheba Hotel
21 Khaleej Tourist Hotel

PLACES TO EAT
6   Al-Arsah Public Coffee Shop
8   Zumruda Restaurant
9   Thriveni & Satkar Restaurants

OTHER
2   Al-Majarra Souq
3   Service-Taxi Station for Umm al-Qaiwain & Ras al-Khaimah
4   Al-Hamra Cinema
5   Small Antique & Pearl Shops
7   Old Souq Area
10 ETISALAT (Telephone Office)
11 Amiri Diwan (Ruler's Office)
12 GPO
13 Vegetable Souq
14 Service-Taxi Station for Dubai, Abu Dhabi & Al-Ain
15 Fish Souq
17 Amusement Park
18 Central Market
19 King Faisal Mosque

pieces during the 1970s and 1980s. At the time of writing one large-ish section of the covered market had opened for business. The shops are a mixture of craft and souvenir outlets along with a few run-of-the-mill houseware places.

Central Market

From certain angles, the Central Market (also called the new souq or the Sharjah souq) looks like a set of monster-size oil barrels which have tipped over and had wind towers glued to their sides. Inside, hundreds of shops and stalls sell just about everything imaginable. The Central Market is reputed to be the best place in the UAE to shop for Persian carpets.

King Faisal Mosque

Sharjah's central mosque is the largest mosque in the UAE. It is said to be able to accommodate 3000 worshippers. The mosque dominates Al-Ittihad Square next to the Central Market.

Old Watchtower

Old, and much restored, watchtowers dot the landscape of Sharjah. One worth noting for its location is the lone watchtower that stands guard over a small patch of the coastline on the corner of Khan Rd and Shaikh Sultan al-Awal Rd.

Organised Tours

The main tour operators based in Sharjah are SNTTA Emirates Tours (☎ 351 411) and Orient Tours (☎ 549 333). Both offer half-day and full-day tours of Sharjah and the other emirates starting from Dh100 per person.

Places to Stay

Sharjah's *youth hostel* (☎ 321 897) is at the Sharjah Sports Club on Al-Qasmia Rd, about 3.7 km from the GPO. Beds cost Dh15 per night and HI cards are required. The hostel is only open for men.

There are only two fairly cheap hotels in town, both on King Faisal Rd. The *Khaleej Tourist Hotel* (☎ 597 888; fax 598 999)

charges Dh105/160 for singles/doubles. It is clean but has unbelievably small bathrooms (some with Turkish toilets). Across the street the *Sheba Hotel* (☎ 522 522; fax 354 357) is much better value at Dh95/130, with better rooms and larger baths. Neither hotel can arrange visas.

If you are looking for a visa as well as a room try the *Federal Hotel* (☎ 354 106; fax 541 394) on King Faisal Rd. Singles/doubles are Dh176/220. Nearby, at Municipality roundabout, the *Sharjah Plaza Hotel* (☎ 377 555; fax 373 311) is particularly good value at Dh126/157.50.

Outside the centre, along Shaikh Sultan al-Awal Rd, the *Sharjah Carlton Hotel* (☎ 283 711; fax 284 962) asks Dh345/460, more if you want a seaview from your room. It will only sponsor visas for Americans and Western Europeans. Further down the road, the *Lou' Lou'a Beach Resort* (formerly the Golden Beach Motel, ☎ 285 000; fax 285 222) is a bit nicer. It charges Dh345/460 for rooms, again without a sea view.

Places to Eat

There is one place that you really must try while in Sharjah. The *Al-Arsah Public Coffee Shop* in the restored section of Sharjah's old souq. For Dh10 you not only get a fairly large biryani but also salad and a bowl of fresh dates for dessert. The restaurant is a traditional-style coffee shop, with seating on high benches. Shisha pipes and backgammon sets are available and sweet tea is served out of a huge urn.

Rolla Square and Al-Ghazali Rd (parallel to Al-Arouba Rd but one block closer to the sea) have a plethora of cheap Indian eateries. Try the *Zumruda Restaurant* on Al-Ghazali Rd with biryanis at Dh6 to Dh7.

The *Al-Anqood Restaurant* on the edge of Rolla Square is a vegetarian Indian restaurant. Further up Rolla Square try the *Thriveni Restaurant* or the slightly fancier *Satkar Restaurant* immediately above it. The Satkar offers good Thali set meals (a selection of vegetables with bread and rice) from as little as Dh6. The surroundings are nicer and the view out over the square is worth the extra dirham or two. You can, however, get out of Thriveni with a pretty good meal for under Dh5.

Getting There & Away

Sharjah international airport is 15 km from the centre. The phone number for airport information is ☎ 581 111.

There is no bus service to, from or through Sharjah but the city does have two service-taxi stations. Taxis for Umm al-Qaiwain (Dh7) and Ras al-Khaimah (Dh15) leave from the lot on Al-Arouba Rd across from the Al-Hamra cinema. Taxis for Dubai (Dh4), Abu Dhabi and Al-Ain (Dh30 to either city) depart from a stand next to the vegetable souq.

Getting Around

Since Sharjah has no bus system, getting around without your own car means either taking taxis or walking. The taxis have no meters and trips around the centre should cost Dh5 to Dh10 (agree on the fare before you get in). When the heat is not too debilitating Sharjah's centre can be covered on foot quite easily.

AROUND SHARJAH

Sharjah Natural History Museum

Opened with much fanfare in November 1995 the Sharjah Natural History Museum is quite extraordinary – possibly the slickest, most modern museum in the entire Gulf. Unfortunately for the casual visitor, it also happens to be out in the desert 35 km east of Sharjah's centre on the road to Fujairah. At least the exit is well marked.

Many of the museum's exhibits are aimed at children – most can be touched and there are a large number of interactive displays – but grown-ups will probably find it fascinating as well. Everything in the museum is labelled in both English and Arabic. Particularly impressive is the 35m long diorama (allegedly the longest diorama in the world) that portrays the emirate's different geographical features.

At the time of writing the museum had just opened and it was uncertain what its regular

hours would eventually be. The expectation, according to the museum's manager, was that it would be open Sunday to Thursday from approximately 9 am to 1 pm, Friday from 10 am to 9 pm and closed Saturday.

AJMAN

The smallest of the seven emirates, Ajman is hardly the mere extension of Sharjah that some people imagine. The emirate occupies a small stretch of coast between Sharjah and Umm al-Qaiwain and also has two inland enclaves.

Ajman's central square is within walking distance of pretty much everything, including the museum, Ajman's lone hotel, a couple of small restaurants and the coastline. Leewara St follows the section of the coast containing most of the city's few sites other than the museum.

The telephone code for Ajman is 06.

Things to See

The **Ajman Museum** occupies the old police fort on the emirate's central square. It is open from 9 am to 1 pm except Thursday, when it closes at noon. The museum reopens in the afternoon from 4 to 7 pm (5 to 8 pm from May to August). It is closed on Saturday. Admission is Dh4. Photography is not permitted.

The fort was built in the late 18th century and served as the ruler's palace and office until 1970. From 1970 to 1978, it was Ajman's main police station. It was opened as a museum in 1981. It is one of the best museums in the UAE and is well worth the drive from Dubai.

Fruit and vegetables and meat and fish are sold in two purpose-built **souqs** along the coast, off Leewara St. The best time to come shopping is early in the morning, around 7 or 8 am, when the fishers are back in port with the day's catch and the fish souq is at its busiest.

Around the parking lot in front of these markets an area known as the **Iranian souq** has grown up in the last few years. The Iranian souq is a fascinating place to prowl around. You are unlikely to find much in the way of souvenirs (unless your idea of a souvenir is a plastic washing bucket), though you can sometimes find interesting pottery.

Places to Stay & Eat
The only place to stay in Ajman is the *Ajman Beach Hotel* (☎ 423 333; fax 423 363). It has decent singles/doubles for Dh175/250. The hotel will arrange visas for travellers arriving through Dubai airport.

The *Kuwait Restaurant,* at the junction of Humaid Bin Abdul Aziz St and Abu Baker al-Siddiq St, has good biryanis for Dh7. You'll find a number of similar places along Leewara St. The *Dhow Restaurant* is actually a coffee house in a traditional *barasti* shelter (made of woven palm leaves) along the waterfront. It's a nice place for a cup of coffee or tea late in the afternoon. Look for the blue-and-white sign with two coffee pots and a rose-water urn on it.

Getting There & Away
Ajman has no bus service and there's no taxi stand. But taxi drivers on the Sharjah route generally don't mind travelling here as it's only a few extra km.

AROUND AJMAN
Manama
No, not the capital of Bahrain. This Manama is an enclave of Ajman lying near the junction of the southbound road from Ras al-Khaimah and the east-west road linking Dubai and Sharjah with the east coast. The only thing to see is the **fort** near the main roundabout. It is quite well preserved, probably because the police still use it. It is not open to the public.

UMM AL-QAIWAIN
With a population of around 40,000, Umm al-Qaiwain (Umm al-Quwain, Umm al-Qawain) is the least populous of the seven emirates. It lies on a narrow peninsula of sand jutting north from the main road linking Dubai and Sharjah with Ras al-Khaimah. The old town and the emirate's small business district are at the northern tip of the peninsula, particularly along King Faisal Rd. The telephone code for Umm al-Qaiwain is 06.

The small **fort** at the intersection of Al-Hason Rd and Al-Lubna Rd and the **mosque** next to it are the town's only sights. The

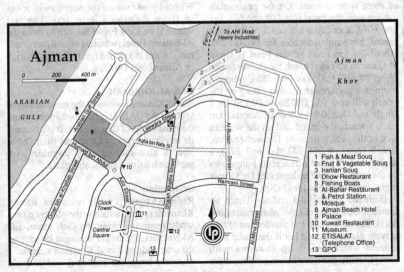

Ajman

0   200   400 m

ARABIAN GULF

To AHI (Arab Heavy Industries)

Ferry

Ajman Khor

1 Fish & Meat Souq
2 Fruit & Vegetable Souq
3 Iranian Souq
4 Dhow Restaurant
5 Fishing Boats
6 Al-Bahar Restaurant & Petrol Station
7 Mosque
8 Ajman Beach Hotel
9 Palace
10 Kuwait Restaurant
11 Museum
12 ETISALAT (Telephone Office)
13 GPO

Arabian Gulf Street
Leewara Street
Aqba bin Nafa St
Humaid bin Abdul Aziz Street
Omer bin al-Khattab Street
Shaikh Khalifa Street
Ramrani Street
Al-Butain Street
Al-Mina Street

Clock Tower
Central Square

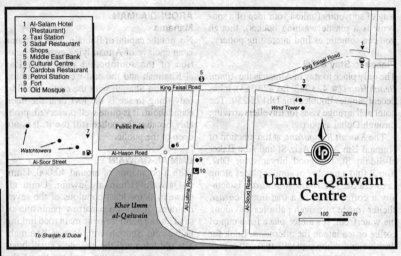

1 Al-Salam Hotel
   (Restaurant)
2 Taxi Station
3 Sadaf Restaurant
4 Shops
5 Middle East Bank
6 Cultural Centre
7 Cardoba Restaurant
8 Petrol Station
9 Fort
10 Old Mosque

King Faisal Road

King Faisal Road

Wind Tower

Public Park

Watchtowers

Al-Hason Road

Al-Soor Street

Al-Lubna Road

Al-Soug Road

Khor Umm
al-Qaiwain

To Sharjah & Dubai

**Umm al-Qaiwain
Centre**

0   100   200 m

mosque was built in 1962. A few old **watch-towers** are scattered around town.

Places to Stay & Eat

All three of Umm al-Qaiwain's hotels are south of the centre. None are cheap and none of them sponsor visas. On the peninsula's eastern side, the *Pearl Hotel* (☎ 666 678; fax 666 679), about five km south of the town centre, has singles/doubles for Dh200/220. About 2.5 km north of the Pearl is Umm al-Qaiwain's newest hotel, the *Palma Beach Hotel* (☎ 667 090; fax 667 388), where a room in a prefabricated cabin sitting on the beach will cost you Dh220 or Dh250 for a single and Dh330 for a double. Another km back towards the centre and on the western side of the peninsula is the *Umm al-Quwain Beach Hotel* (☎ 666 647; fax 667 273), a slightly musty place which rents bungalows by the bedroom: one bedroom for Dh350 per night, two bedrooms for Dh500.

Both the Pearl Hotel and the Umm al-Quwain Beach Hotel have restaurants (and bars). The centre also has a collection of tiny biryani places. A good bet is the *Sadaf Restaurant* which serves up shwarma with exceptionally generous helpings of meat for

Dh2. Half a fresh-roasted chicken will set you back Dh7. Similar fare can be found at the *Cardoba Restaurant* near the intersection of King Faisal and Al-Hason Rds.

Getting There & Away

Without your own car the only way in or out of Umm al-Qaiwain is by taxi. The taxi station is on King Faisal Rd, across from the Al-Salaam Hotel (which is actually a restaurant). A seat in a shared taxi to Dubai, Sharjah or Ajman costs Dh7.

RAS AL-KHAIMAH

Ras al-Khaimah is one of the most beautiful spots in the UAE. It is the northernmost and the most fertile of the emirates. It is a favourite weekend getaway for people from Dubai and is also increasingly popular with package tourists from Scandinavia.

Orientation

Ras al-Khaimah is really two cities. Ras al-Khaimah proper, which is the old town on a sandy peninsula along the Gulf coast, and Al-Nakheel, the newer business district on the other side of Ras al-Khaimah's creek.

Aside from the museum and the old

town's souq, there isn't very much to Ras al-Khaimah proper.

Most of Al-Nakheel's shops and offices are on Oman St, between the Hospital roundabout and the Cinema roundabout (both of which, despite the names, are intersections, not roundabouts). This area includes the city's one cheap hotel and a number of small restaurants.

Information

You can change money at any of the many banks along Al-Sabah St in Ras al-Khaimah or Oman St in Al-Nakheel. The GPO is a red brick building on King Faisal St, about four km north of the Bin Majid Beach Hotel. The ETISALAT office is one km east of the Cinema roundabout in Al-Nakheel.

The telephone code for Ras al-Khaimah is 07.

Things to See

Ras al-Khaimah's **museum** is in the old fort on Al-Hosen Rd, next to the police headquarters. All the signs are in both Arabic and English. The fort was built in the mid-18th century. Until the early 1960s it was the residence of the ruling Al-Qasimi shaikhs. It

is open daily except Tuesday from 8 am to noon and from 4 to 7 pm. Admission is Dh 2.

Ras al-Khaimah's **old town** is a wonderful place to stroll around. The **souq area**, south of the museum, has a number of small tailors' shops but the main attraction is the unspoiled atmosphere.

Camel Racing

Ras al-Khaimah's camel racecourse is in Digdagga, about 10 km south of town. Races usually take place on Friday during the winter and sometimes also on Tuesday or Wednesday. Admission is free but come early. The races usually start around 6 am and continue until 9 or 9.30 am.

To reach the racecourse, take the airport road south from Al-Nakheel and turn right at the Ras al-Khaimah Poultry & Feeding Company (there's a yellow sign on the building). Look for a large, free-standing minaret at the turn-off. Keep following the road from there until you reach the track.

Places to Stay & Eat

There are four hotels in Ras al-Khaimah. The one cheapie is the *Al-Sana Resthouse* (☎ 229 004; fax 223 722) on Oman St immediately

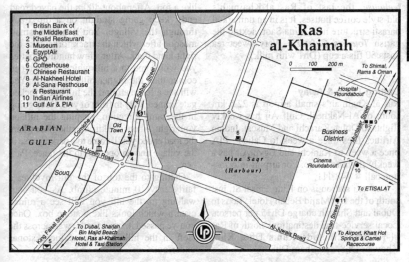

```
1  British Bank of
   the Middle East
2  Khalid Restaurant
3  Museum
4  EgyptAir
5  GPO
6  Coffeehouse
7  Chinese Restaurant
8  Al-Nakheel Hotel
9  Al-Sana Resthouse
   & Restaurant
10 Indian Airlines
11 Gulf Air & PIA
```

Ras al-Khaimah

0   100   200 m

To Shimal,
Rams & Oman

Al-Sabah Street

Corniche

Old Town

ARABIAN GULF

Al-Hosen Road

Souq

King Faisal Street

Mina Saqr
(Harbour)

Hospital
'Roundabout'

Business District

Muntasser Street

Cinema 'Roundabout'

To ETISALAT

Oman Street

To Dubai, Sharjah
Bin Majid Beach
Hotel, Ras al-Khaimah
Hotel & Taxi Station

Al-Juwais Road

To Airport, Khatt Hot
Springs & Camel
Racecourse

behind the Al-Nakheel Hotel. Singles/doubles cost Dh100/120. The *Al-Nakhel Hotel* (☎ 222 822; fax 222 922), on Muntaser St in Al-Nakheel, has the cheapest bar in town but not much else to recommend it. Rooms are Dh120/180.

The *Bin Majid Beach Hotel* (☎ 352 233; fax 353 225) is the favoured haunt of Russian tour groups. Rooms are Dh192.50/275, including the service charge. The *Ras al-Khaimah Hotel* (☎ 352 999; fax 352 990) has rooms for Dh264/374, including service charge.

The *Al-Sana Restaurant*, immediately behind the Al-Sana Resthouse, is still one of the best deals in Ras Al-Khaimah. It has western, Chinese and Filipino food. Meals should not run to more than Dh20. Another very good place to eat in Al-Nakheel is the *Libanese House Restaurant*, next door to the Al-Nakheel Hotel on Muntaser St. It serves great Lebanese mezzes for Dh5 to Dh12 apiece. Main dishes cost Dh10 to Dh12. In the old town, the *Khalid Restaurant* on Al-Sabah St remains dependably clean. However, at Dh12 or Dh13 for a biryani, it is rather expensive for this sort of place.

You should definitely drop in at the *Coffeehouse*, the last of Ras al-Khaimah's old-style coffee houses. It is in an unmarked barasti structure near Mina Saqr, next to the garish *Tourists Cafeteria*. Very sweet tea costs 50 fils a cup (Dh1 with milk).

Getting There & Away

Ras al-Khaimah's small airport is 22.5 km south of Al-Nakheel. Gulf Air has weekly flights to Doha, Karachi and Muscat. Indian Airlines flies once a week to Calicut, PIA once a week to Karachi and EgyptAir has a weekly flight to Cairo. For airport information call ☎ 448 111.

The taxi station is on King Faisal St, just south of the Bin Majid Beach Hotel. Taxis to Dubai and Sharjah charge Dh15 per person. Local service-taxi destinations north of Ras al-Khaimah include Rams Dh6, Khor Khowair Dh8, and Sham Dh8.

Getting Around

Taxis into Ras al-Khaimah's centre are Dh2 shared and Dh10 engaged.

AROUND RAS AL-KHAIMAH
Shimal

The village of Shimal, five km north of Ras al-Khaimah, is the site of some of the most important archaeological finds in the UAE. The main attraction is the **Queen of Sheba's Palace**, a set of ruined buildings and fortifications spread over two small plateaus overlooking the village. Despite its name, the palace was not built by the Queen of Sheba. It may, however, have been visited by Queen Zenobia, who ruled a sizeable chunk of the Near East in the 4th century.

To reach the site go north for 4.5 km from the Hospital roundabout in Al-Nakheel and turn right onto a paved road. Look for a white sign with the UAE crest and a big red arrow (for those who read Arabic, the sign points to the Shimal Health Centre). Follow this road for approximately 1.5 km until you reach a roundabout and take the first right turn out of the roundabout. Follow the road for another 2.3 km and take the first paved turn to the left at a new building built to look like a fort. After about 400m the paved road ends; keep going straight on a dirt track through the village. You'll pass a small mosque after which the track forks; take the right-hand track. After a few hundred metres you will come to a hill which is lighter in colour than the higher hills behind it. You will see a fence around the hill and a locked gate immediately in front of you. Keep going in the same direction, keeping the hill on your right. About one km after the place where the road ended you'll come to a parking area in the village and an opening in the fence. Park here.

Getting to the top of the hill involves a fairly easy 10 minute climb. As you start walking up the hill you will see a ruined cistern which looks like a stone box. Once you've passed it, head for the wall across the cleft in the hill. Beware of loose stones underfoot.

Rams

A quiet village 12 km north of Ras al-Khaimah, Rams has a nice coastline and a few old **watchtowers**. Service taxis between Rams and Ras al-Khaimah cost Dh6 per person regular and Dh30 engaged.

Dhayah

Another 3.5 km beyond Rams is Dhayah. It was here that the people of Rams retreated in the face of the advancing British in 1819 and surrendered after a four day siege. The **fort** sits atop a sharp, cone-shaped hill behind the modern village.

To reach the hill, turn right off the road from Ras al-Khaimah immediately after you pass Dhayah's new white mosque and the Lehamoodi Grocery, both of which are also on the right (the turn is 14.5 km north of the Hospital roundabout). If you pass a sign saying 'Sha'm 15 km', you have gone too far. Leaving the main road you follow a dirt track which swings around to the right behind the village. After about 500m you'll see the Al-Adal Grocery; keep to the left of this and continue for another 300m. When the main track swings to the left continue straight on a smaller track towards an old watchtower which you pass on your left. From there the track twists around for another 400m; take a right turn and then proceed for another 300m straight towards the hill and park on its northern side.

Khatt Hot Springs

The popular Khatt Hot Springs are open daily from 5 am to 11 pm. Admission is Dh3. There are separate areas for men and women. You might want to wear sneakers if you are going in – the rocks inside the pool look quite sharp!

To reach Khatt head south out of Al-Nakheel following the signs for the airport; you'll see signs for Khatt further along the road. The spring is about 25 km from the centre. When you reach the roundabout in the village of Khatt, turn left. The spring is another 800m down the road.

HATTA

An enclave of Dubai nestled in the Hajar Mountains, Hatta is a popular weekend getaway spot. It is 105 km from Dubai by road, about 20 km of which runs through Omani territory. There is no customs check as you cross this portion of the road but remember that if you are driving a rental car your insurance will not cover accidents in Oman.

There is not much to see in Hatta itself. Its main attractions are its relatively cool, dry climate (compared to that of the coast) and the mountain scenery. It is also a good jumping-off point for off-road trips through the mountains. At the time of writing the government was building a **Heritage Village** in Hatta, a re-creation of a traditional mountain village from the pre-oil era.

The only place to stay in Hatta is the *Hatta Fort Hotel* (☎ (085) 232 11; fax 235 61) where singles/doubles cost Dh350/450, plus 20% for tax and the service charge.

There are six buses per day from Dubai to Hatta (80 minutes; Dh7) and vice versa. In Hatta, the buses depart from the red bus shelter near the Hatta Palace Grocery. Purchase tickets from the driver.

The East Coast

FUJAIRAH

Fujairah is not cheap but it is attractive and a good base for exploring the east coast.

Orientation & Information

Fujairah is quite spread out but most of the services travellers will need are in a fairly compact area. The main business area is Hamad bin Abdulla Rd, between the Fujairah Trade Centre and the coast. Along this stretch of road you will find the main post office, several banks and, at the intersection with the coast road, the central market. There is a concentration of good, cheap restaurants near the Hilton hotel. The ETISALAT office is on Al-Nakheel Rd, between Fahim and Shaikh Zayed bin Sultan Rds. The telephone code for Fujairah is 09.

The coastal road changes its name three times, which can be confusing. Passing through the city from south to north it is called Regalath Rd, Gurfah Rd and Al-Faseel Rd, in that order.

Museum

Fujairah's museum is at the intersection of Al-Nakheel and Madab Rds. It has an archaeology gallery and an ethnographic display. The former is much the more inter-

esting of the two. It's open daily from 8 am to 1.15 pm and 4 to 6 pm. On Friday the museum is open only in the afternoon. Admission is Dh2.

The Old Town

Spooky might be the best word to describe the old town, which consists of a fort at least 300 years old overlooking the ruins of old Fujairah. The fort has been partially restored.

Ain Al-Madab Garden

On the edge of town, this park-cum-hotel is

```
PLACES TO STAY
1   Fujairah Beach Hotel
3   Youth Hostel
8   Fujairah Hilton
19  Fujairah Plaza Hotel

PLACES TO EAT
9   Diner's Inn
10  Arous al-Bahr
    Restaurant
12  National Restaurant
13  Al-Zahra Restaurant

OTHER
2   Sports Club
4   Shaikh's Palace
5   Fujairah Fort &
    the Old Town
6   Fujairah Museum
7   ETISALAT
    (Telephone Office)
11  Ghorfah Post Office
14  Central Market
15  National Bank of
    Abu Dhabi
16  British Bank of
    the Middle East
17  Indian Airlines
18  GPO
20  Fujairah Trade
    Centre (Gulf Air)
```

Fujairah

0   0.5   1 km

To Khor Fakkan

GULF OF OMAN

Al-Faseel Road
Shamkam Road
Kuweit Road
King Faisal Road
Al-Kalaa Road
Madab Road
Date Gardens
Al-Nakheel Road
Shaikh Zayed bin
Date Gardens
Al-Muntazar Rd.
Fahim Road
Sultan Road
Date Gardens
Gurfah Road
New Coast Road

To Ain al-Madab Garden & Hotel
Al-Njaimat Road
Mohammed bin Mathar Road
Ittihad Road
Hamad bin Abdulla Road
Al-Maktoum Rd.
20   19   18
17   16   15

To Taxi Station, Sharjah & Dubai
Road No 17
Road No 18
Al-Sharq Road
Tunis Road
Jerusalem Road
Jamal Abdul Nasser Street
Meraishid Road
Regalath Road

Airport
Airport Terminus

To Kaiba & Oman

a pretty sorry sight. None of the kiddie rides dotted around the park look as if they have been used in a very long time. The garden is open during daylight hours and admission is Dh2.

Places to Stay

Fujairah's *youth hostel* (☎ 222 347) is just off Al-Faseel Rd near the sports club. Beds are Dh15 apiece. The hostel will only accommodate women if it is empty enough to segregate them from the men. Considering how small the hostel is, that means a single woman stands a fairly high chance of being turned away.

There are only three hotels in Fujairah and none are cheap. The *Fujairah Beach Hotel* (☎ 228 051; fax 228 054) is several km north of the centre. It is good, if slightly musty. Single/double rooms are Dh194/241.50 including tax and service charge. In the centre the *Fujairah Plaza* (☎ 232 000; fax 232 111) is an all-suites hotel. Rooms start at Dh275/330. It does not sponsor visas.

The *Fujairah Hilton* (☎ 222 411; fax 226 541) represents the local top end. Singles/ doubles go for Dh425/485.

Both the Hilton and the Beach Hotel will sponsor visas for tourists with 15 days notice.

Places to Eat

The *Diner's Inn* on Al-Faseel Rd, across from the Hilton, has good, cheap Indian and Chinese food served in reasonably large helpings for Dh8 to Dh10. Nearby, also on Al-Faseel Rd but on the other side of the intersection with Al-Nakheel Rd, the *National Restaurant* has cheap chicken, rice and biryani dishes. A meal costs about Dh10. The same sort of fare can be found down the street at the *Al-Zahra Restaurant*.

A bit more up-market is *Arous al-Bahr*, a medium-priced Lebanese restaurant. It is at the intersection of Al-Nakheel and Al-Faseel Rds.

Getting There & Away

Fujairah international airport is served by Gulf Air (one flight a week to Bahrain and Doha and two to Muscat) and Indian Airlines (one flight a week to Calicut). It is on the southern edge of town.

The taxi station is on the edge of town on the road to Sharjah and Dubai. The fare to Dubai or Sharjah is Dh25 per person. Seats to Dibba are Dh20, Dhaid Dh10, Masafi and Khor Fakkan Dh5.

AROUND FUJAIRAH

The largely residential town of **Kalba**, just south of Fujairah, is part of the Sharjah emirate and has nice beaches.

The *Marine Hotel* (☎ 778 877; fax 776 769) in Kalba, 13 km south of Fujairah on the coast road, charges Dh250/300 but those rates can drop by up to Dh100 if things are slow.

BITHNA

The village of Bithna, in the mountains some 12 km from Fujairah, has several interesting archaeological sites. It is an easy trip from Fujairah (even by taxi it should not be too expensive) and well worth the effort.

The **T-Shaped Site**, or the Long Chambered Tomb, is fenced in, though part of the excavations are visible. Its main period of use appears to have been between 1350 and 300 BC but the tomb itself may date from an earlier period. Bithna's other sight of note is its **fort**, which is more impressive than its counterpart in Fujairah.

To reach the T-Shaped Site take the main road from Fujairah inland towards Sharjah and Dubai. About 12 km out of Fujairah, turn right at the exit marked 'Bithnah'; the town will be to the right of the road. Immediately after exiting the highway you will come to a T-junction; turn right and follow the paved road to the radio tower (a distance of 500m). At that point there will be a dirt road to your left. Turn onto this road. After 100m it will fork; keep right and look for the metal sun-shade that covers the site. It will be on your right.

To reach the fort, exit the main road as above and turn right at the T-junction. Go 250m and turn left, off the paved road, at the Rabia tailor's shop. Follow this dirt track straight through the village and over the first of two inclines that take you down into the wadi. When you are 350m beyond the paved road keep left as you go down a second incline and into a rocky area. You should see a clump of trees up the wadi and to your right, about 500m away. The fort is behind those trees. The wadi is passable in a regular car but only barely. Be careful.

QIDFA
Near this village, 18 km north of Fujairah on the road to Khor Fakkan, you will notice a turn on the inland side of the road (on the left if you are coming from Fujairah) with a sign welcoming you to the Omani Governorate of Madha (in English; in Arabic it welcomes you to the Musandem Governorate). This marks the boundary of the small Omani enclave of **Madha**, which is completely surrounded by the UAE. Qidfa itself has nothing of interest.

KHOR FAKKAN
One of Sharjah's enclaves and the largest town on the east coast after Fujairah, Khor Fakkan is a large port with a long, scenic Corniche. It's also a trendy weekend resort, but while the port has proved to be a roaring success, the development of tourism has been somewhat held back by Sharjah's ban on alcohol.

The four km long Corniche is bounded by the port at the southern end and the luxury Oceanic Hotel to the north, with lots of nice beaches in between. There is very little to see except for a few lonely looking watchtowers perched on the hills above the city. The fort which once dominated the coast is long gone.

Singles/doubles at the *Oceanic Hotel* (☎ (09) 385 111; fax 387 716) cost Dh391/506, including the service charge. Special cheap deals are sometimes available on weekends. The only other place to stay is the *Al-Khaleej Hotel* (☎ (09) 387 336), about 3.5 km inland on the road to Fujairah. It only has doubles, which cost Dh100 without a private bath and Dh150 with bath. The rooms are very clean, if somewhat sparsely furnished.

On the Corniche there are two seaside restaurants north of the roundabout that marks the Corniche's junction with the road from Fujairah. The *Lebanon Restaurant* is the better of the two, with both Lebanese mezze and the usual cheap Indian fare of biryanis and tikka dishes. Main dishes cost around Dh20 apiece. Further north along the Corniche the *Green Beach Cafeteria & Restaurant* has similar fare. The restaurant on the top floor of the *Oceanic Hotel* is expensive but try to drop in for a cup of coffee and a chance to admire the view over the bay.

BADIYAH
Badiyah, eight km north of Khor Fakkan but in the Fujairah emirate, is one of the oldest towns in the Gulf. Archaeological digs have shown that the site of the town has been settled more or less continuously since the 3rd millennium BC. Today, it is known mainly for its **mosque**, a small whitewashed structure of stone, mud-brick and gypsum which is the oldest mosque in the UAE. Its exact date of construction is uncertain but was probably not much more than a few hundred years ago. The mosque is still in use. It is built into a low hillside along the main road just north of the village. On the hillside above and behind it are several ruined **watchtowers**.

There is no place to stay in Badiyah but six km to the north, near the village of Al-Aqqa, there's the *Sandy Beach Motel* (☎ (09) 445 354; fax 445 207). Singles/doubles are Dh315/475 in bungalows near the sea.

DIBBA
Dibba's name lives in Islamic history as the site of one of the great battles of the Ridda Wars, the reconquest of Arabia by Muslim armies in the generation after the death of the Prophet. The Muslims were fighting against a number of tribes and towns which had sworn allegiance to Mohammed during his lifetime but did not feel themselves bound to the new religion following his death. The victory at Dibba in 633, a year after the

Prophet's death, traditionally marks the end of the Muslim reconquest of Arabia.

Today, Dibba is a quiet set of seaside villages. In fact, there are three Dibbas, each belonging to a different ruler: Dibba Muhallab (Fujairah), Dibba Hisn (Sharjah) and Dibba Bayah (Oman). As at Al-Ain, you can walk or drive freely across the Omani

border and explore some of the Omani villages at the southern edge of the spectacular Musandem peninsula.

There is nothing to see except the **fort** in Dibba Hisn, which is still used by the police, and there are no hotels. Nevertheless, the quiet pace of life in Dibba makes it worth the trip.

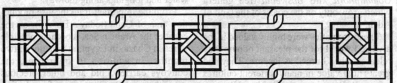

Yemen

Over 3000 years of recorded history has left Yemen with a unique cultural heritage, evident in the architecture of the towns and villages of the country. Today Yemen is furiously modernising a society that only opened up to the rest of the world a generation ago. It is the privilege of today's traveller to witness the endurance of the world of *The Thousand and One Nights* in the grip of an abrupt change.

Yemen is more accessible today than it has ever been. After an era of isolation, which for some parts of the country had lasted decades, for other parts 1000 years, tourists have been cautiously welcomed since the late 1970s. Yet lack of resources and recurrent political crises have hampered the development of tourism: there are no holiday resorts in Yemen, western-style hotels are rare and many of the country's attractions are inaccessible. However, many visitors have found their trip far too short, dictating a return.

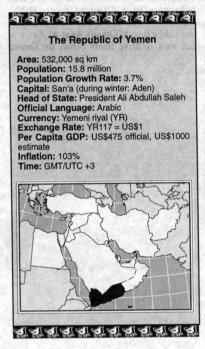

The Republic of Yemen

Area: 532,000 sq km
Population: 15.8 million
Population Growth Rate: 3.7%
Capital: San'a (during winter: Aden)
Head of State: President Ali Abdullah Saleh
Official Language: Arabic
Currency: Yemeni riyal (YR)
Exchange Rate: YR117 = US$1
Per Capita GDP: US$475 official, US$1000 estimate
Inflation: 103%
Time: GMT/UTC +3

Facts about the Country

HISTORY
Pre-Islamic Kingdoms
The earliest known civilisations in southern Arabia existed more than 1000 years before Christ.

The Frankincense Trade The ancient kingdoms based their existence primarily on agriculture and, secondly, on trade. The most important products of southern Arabia were myrrh and frankincense, the resins of the *Commiphora* and *Boswellia* tree genera which grow only on the coasts of the Gulf of Aden.

These aromatics were highly valued in the civilised world for the pleasant odours they released when burned as incense. They had great ritual value in many different cultures – from the Egyptian to the Greek and Roman.

These commodities were carried by sea or land. Around the 11th century BC, overland travel through Arabia vastly improved with the introduction of camels as they could walk much longer distances without requiring as much rest or water as donkeys. This meant that routes could be plotted through dry lands, with only a few stops needed for food, water and lodgings along the way.

From the important frankincense production area of Qana (today's Bir Ali), on the coast of the Arabian Sea, it became possible to reach Ghaza, in Egypt, in a matter of two months. In addition to fragrances, the convoys carried gold and other precious items that came to Qana by sea from India.

Saba & its Rivals In southern Arabia, several mighty kingdoms along the trade route rose and fell within a period of 1500 years. The most important of these was Saba, which existed for at least 14 centuries from about 1000 BC. Saba is first mentioned in the Old Testament when the Sabaean Queen Bilqis visits King Solomon.

The capital of Saba was located in Ma'rib, in a strategically important area crossed by the natural land route from Qana running north through the Hadhramawt valley. The agricultural wealth of Saba was based on the famous dam in Ma'rib, which was built in the 8th century BC and stood for over 1000 years.

However, Saba had powerful rivals along the trade route: Najran (in present-day southern Saudi Arabia), Ma'in, Awsan, Qa'taban and Hadhramawt (all in present-day Yemen). Between the 6th century BC and 2nd century AD, these states alternately fell under Sabaean rule and freed themselves from it.

In the 1st century AD, Greeks and Romans discovered how to utilise monsoon winds on their voyages to India, transferring their cargo from camels to ships. This created a boom for the ports of Al-Muza north of Bab al-Mandab strait, and Aden, at the expense of those using the land-based routes.

Among the people who gained from this development were the Himyarites, with their capital Dhafar (now a small village in the Ibb governorate) close to the Bab al-Mandab strait, and the Ethiopians on the opposite shores of the strait. From the 2nd to 6th centuries AD, Ethiopians and new Sabaean rulers from the Yemeni highlands alternated with the Himyarites in control of the region.

With the rise of Christianity on the shores of the Mediterranean, the use of 'pagan' ritual fragrances was abandoned. In 395 AD the emperor, Theodosius, ruled that Christianity was to be the state religion of the Roman Empire, putting an end to the demand for frankincense.

Consequently, the Sabaean kingdom faced a decline. Maintenance of the great Ma'rib dam was neglected and in 570 AD the dam broke. The inhabitants abandoned Ma'rib, wandering the Arabian peninsula to settle in new locations.

In the same year, the Ethiopians were finally defeated by the Himyarites who had allied themselves with the Persians. By 575 AD the Persians managed to subdue this region, as they had already done to the rest of the peninsula.

Medieval Islamic Yemen In 628 Badhan, the Persian governor of Yemen, converted to Islam and the general population soon followed. Prominent Yemenis visited the Prophet Mohammed, and by the early 630s the first Yemeni mosques were built in San'a, Al-Janad and near Wadi Zabid. The first two still stand today.

After the Prophet's death in 632, the capital of the newly founded Islamic empire was quickly moved away from the Arabian peninsula: first to Damascus in 661 by the Umayyad (Omayyad) caliphs and then to Baghdad in 750 by the Abbasid caliphs. With its status diminishing to that of a distant province of the empire, Yemen saw numerous small, short-lived, semi-independent states and dynastic kingdoms.

The most important rulers in the northern part of Yemen were the Zaydis of Sa'da, a dynasty founded in 897 by a descendant of the Prophet Mohammed, Yahya bin Hussein bin Qasim ar-Rassi. Based on strict Islamic values, they established an exceptionally strong and stable state, which was only occasionally conquered by foreigners. The Zaydi dynasty lasted well into the 20th century, ending in 1962 with the revolution.

The Hadhramawt area was stabilised in the 15th century by the Kathirids, who remained in power until the 1967 revolution of the south. The Zaydis and the Kathirids were the last Yemeni houses to rule the country.

Arrival of Europeans The emerging European colonial powers first made themselves felt in Southern Arabia when the Portuguese annexed the island of Suqutra in the Arabian Sea in 1507 and attacked Aden in 1513.

The Portuguese operations prompted the

YEMEN

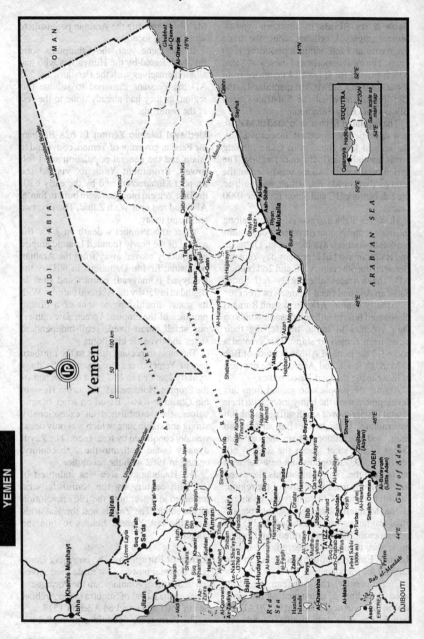

Suggested Itineraries
If you only have one week in Yemen, the North Yemeni triangle San'a/Al-Hudayda/Ta'izz/San'a with overnight stays at Manakha, Al-Hudayda, Ta'izz and Ibb plus a side trip to Ma'rib will leave you with an itch to return to Yemen. Two weeks will allow you to travel at a more leisurely pace and visit Hajja, Al-Mahwit and Sa'da also.

The eastern round trip San'a/Ma'rib/Wadi Hadhramawt/Al-Mukalla/Aden/San'a requires one week of sitting in a car if you don't fly, add the time to see sights at the destinations also. Four weeks will allow you to see most of the places covered in this chapter, although some ready-made tours try to make it in two weeks. ■

Mamluk rulers of Egypt and the Ottoman Turks to compete for Yemen in the following years. The duel was won in 1517 by the Ottomans, who managed to conquer most of Yemen, from Aden to San'a, by 1548.

This first Ottoman occupation ended in 1636 when the Zaydi imams finally freed all of Yemen from Turkish oppression. The Zaydis' realm extended from Hadhramawt in the east to 'Asir in the north, and their rule lasted for more than 200 years. In the south, the Shafai Sultan of Lahej put an end to Zaydi domination in 1728 by blocking their access to the Arabian Sea, but in the central highlands, Zaydi rule continued.

British Occupation of Southern Yemen In 1839 the British conquered Aden, and it became known as the Aden protectorate. This important port along the sea route to India was highly valuable because of the artesian wells in Sheikh Othman, which provided plentiful supplies of drinkable water. Moves towards full colonisation of southern Yemen continued into the next century, with a series of 'protection' treaties between the British and local sheikhs. By the 1950s they had extended their reach to Hadhramawt.

The Second Ottoman Occupation The Turks returned to Yemen in 1849, first occu-

pying the Tihama but extending their control to the highlands after the opening of the Suez Canal in 1869. By 1882 they even occupied Sa'da, the Zaydi capital.

However, the local sheikhs kept rebelling against the foreign authorities and several mountain fortresses were never conquered by the Turks. In the first decade of the 20th century, Zaydi Imam Yahya ibn Mohammed and a leader of North Tihama tribes, Sayyid Mohammed al-Idrisi, instigated effective insurrections against the Turks.

In 1911 the Treaty of Da"an gave Imam Yahya and the Zaydis certain autonomy in the Yemeni highlands, but hostilities between the Turks and the Idrisi forces continued in the Tihama. By the time the Turks finally retreated from Yemen in 1919, WWI had stripped the Ottoman state of its imperial status. The country was left to Imam Yahya, who became the king of Yemen.

The Imamate of Yemen Imam Yahya quickly established his rule in the Tihama, forcing the Idrisi forces to retreat to the 'Asir region by the late 1920s. Al-Idrisi, however, allied with the head of the evolving Saudi state, Ibn Saud. In the Saudi-Yemeni war of 1934 the imam was forced to sign a treaty on Saudi terms, leaving 'Asir under Saudi rule for 40 years. In 1974 the treaty was extended for another 20 years, and Yemen recognised Saudi sovereignty of the area in 1995.

During the reigns of Imam Yahya and his son, Imam Ahmad, Yemen remained isolated and underdeveloped. By the end of Imam Ahmad's rule in the early 1960s, there were still no paved roads, almost no doctors, the Qur'an schools were attended by one child in 20 and the legislation was based on Qur'anic *shari'a* law.

The 1950s saw frequent border disputes between Yemen and the Aden Protectorate state. In 1958 Imam Ahmad sought protection from Cairo. These negotiations led to the foundation of the United Arab States, a union of Yemen, Egypt and Syria. The short-lived pact served only to promote Egyptian interests when the revolution broke out in Yemen one year later.

YEMEN

Birth of the Yemen Arab Republic (YAR)

A week after Imam Ahmad's death in September 1962 a group of army officers led by Colonel Abdullah Sallal started a revolution. The new regime founded the Yemen Arab Republic (YAR).

Imam Ahmad's son Mohammed al-Badr fled to the northern mountains and his forces (the Royalists) began a bitter, eight year civil war supported by Britain and Saudi Arabia. The YAR forces (Republicans) were supported by Egypt and the Soviet Union. Casualties were heavy on both sides.

After a power struggle in the Republican party, the frustrated Egyptians finally left Yemen in late 1967, having lost almost 20,000 troops in the war. The winning faction decided to establish friendly relations with Saudi Arabia. President Sallal was exiled to Iraq and was replaced by Qadi Abdul Rahman al-Iryani.

The Royalists were not able to defeat the Republicans after the Egyptians' departure, although they attacked and captured San'a from December 1967 to February 1968. The war was finally ended in 1970: Imam al-Badr was exiled to Britain and the Yemen Arab Republic was recognised by Saudi Arabia.

Birth of the People's Democratic Republic of Yemen (PDRY)

Britain certainly did little to develop its protectorate states in southern Arabia during its 100 year presence. The 31 small sultanates forming the South Arabian Protectorate served as a mere buffer against possible threats from the north, with Britain maintaining only a minimal presence outside Aden.

In the 1960s nationalistic spirit was revived, fed by the 1962 Republican revolution in the north, coupled with the British support for the Royalists. The National Liberation Front (NLF) of South Yemen was formed by Marxist and nationalistic militants, starting a guerrilla war in 1963 in the Radfan Mountains. The struggle gradually spread, and in late 1967 intense fighting forced the British to leave Aden. The People's Republic of South Yemen was born.

The economy was on the verge of collapse following the departure of the British and the closure of the Suez Canal in 1967, and the country only managed to survive with economic support from Communist countries. The government moved further to the left with the so-called Corrective Movement in 1969, with the new constitution nationalising much of the economy. The name of the first and only Marxist Arab state was changed to the People's Democratic Republic of Yemen (PDRY) in 1970.

The Two Yemens

The 1970s marked an era of mutual suspicion between the two Yemens (YAR and PDRY) exacerbated by internal security problems in both countries. The short border wars of 1972, 1978 and 1979 were futile for both parties. The YAR experienced one bloodless coup and two presidential assassinations during the decade, and a South Yemeni president was ousted and executed.

In 1978 Lieutenant Colonel Ali Abdullah Saleh of the Hashid tribe became president of the YAR. The country enjoyed a period of increasing stability under his rule in the 1980s. Conflicts between competing interest groups were contained within the army and the stability of the 20 minister Cabinet was guaranteed by carefully balancing the representation of different tribes. Political parties were banned in this Islamic Arab state, with the constitution paying attention to western-like values such as personal freedom and private property.

Meanwhile, in the PDRY, the ruling Yemen Socialist Party was seeking to steer a path between Chinese and Soviet influences. The country was plagued by internal power struggles, which culminated in the fierce two week civil war of Aden in January 1986, followed by stagnation.

One Yemen

In the last years of the 1980s, with the Gorbachev era and the collapse of the Soviet economy, the flow of both ideological and financial aid to the already bankrupt PDRY dried up. The government had few friends to turn to; they chose their brothers next door, the YAR.

In fact, the quest for unification of Yemen had continued since the birth of the two states, and the mid-1980s discovery of oil fields in the desert area on both sides of the undemarcated border accelerated the progress towards unity. The unified Republic of Yemen was declared on 22 May 1990, and the unification was sealed in a referendum held in May 1991.

Unfortunately, however, the leaders of the new country could not agree on how to share the power. Vice President Ali Salim al-Baydh, a southerner, soon found his party politically isolated and retreated back to Aden, excluding himself from the work of the San'a-based government.

The rift led, in May 1994, to a full-scale civil war, and the governorates of the former PDRY seceded to form the Democratic Republic of Yemen. However, no country ever recognised the division, and the southern troops were crushed in two months, reinforcing the unity on President Saleh's terms.

GEOGRAPHY

Yemen is 532,000 sq km in area, with two thirds of it uninhabited. Saudi Arabia and Oman are its neighbours. In the Red Sea, the Hanish Islands are claimed by both Eritrea and Yemen.

The topography of the country is the most varied of any country in the Arabian peninsula. From the 20 to 50 km wide coastal strip, the Tihama, the western mountains rise to well over 3000m, with the highest peak, Jebel an-Nabi Shu'ayb, rising 3760m above sea level. Between the western and the lesser eastern mountains, fertile high plateaux lie at over 2000m. The capital San'a sits at the centre of the San'a basin at an altitude of 2250m.

Several parts of the highlands are still volcanically active with hot springs and occasional earthquakes. The eastern mountains slowly descend to about 1000m at the Omani border. From the north, the great sands of the vast Arabian desert, Ar-Ruba'

al-Khali (the Empty Quarter), extend to the southernmost tip in the middle of Yemen.

CLIMATE

Yemen is the most arable spot on the Arabian peninsula. Twice-yearly monsoon winds often bring ample rains from the south and south-west. The rains are irregular, however; in different years, they may come in different months and, some years, a monsoon may pass delivering no rain.

Temperatures vary considerably according to location and calendar. The Tihama and the southern coast are hot and arid but the air is very humid, with maximum daytime temperatures ranging from 32°C in winter to over 40°C in summer. Night-time temperatures fall to about 20°C from December to February and to about 27°C to 35°C in June and July. Rainfall is scant, with most of the rain falling between late July and September.

The highlands are mild and San'a's maximum daily temperatures range from 25°C to 30°C throughout the year. Minimum nightly temperatures are around 0°C in January (the dry season) and 10°C in July, between the two rainy seasons. The western mountains receive most of the rainfall; in the governorate of Ibb, daily rains bring a monthly rainfall of almost 500 mm in July and August, while San'a may get a fourth of that. During the winter and mid-summer no rainfall at all occurs except infrequently in Ibb. Towards the east, the rainfall gradually diminishes. In Ruba' al-Khali no rain ever falls.

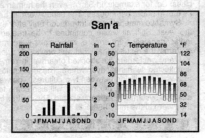

ECOLOGY & ENVIRONMENT

Yemen faces most of the ecological problems shared by the region's other arid, ancient countries. Intense cultivation and hunting have impoverished the natural flora and fauna. Deforestation in turn has caused erosion and lead to recurrent, violent floods. Centuries of irrigation has salified the soil, resulting in desertification. Although exacerbated by today's explosive population growth, these processes are nothing new: the surroundings of the ancient capital of Shabwa are extremely saline, suggesting that the city might have been abandoned partly due to the worsened conditions for agriculture in the area.

In the 1970s and 1980s many Yemeni terrace fields suffered much damage because of the en-masse emigration of farmers to oil-rich Arab countries, for work. A couple of years' negligence was often enough for the rains to wash the fertile soil away from the untended fields, leaving only the rocky structures behind. Another recent development is the sinking levels of ground water due to widespread pumping for irrigation and household use. Developing water resource management is the country's top environmental priority.

Due to its recent start and limited area of operations, oil mining has not yet caused major environmental problems in Yemen.

Tourism has also been limited enough not to have caused a visible impact on even the most visited sites in the country, unlike other Middle-Eastern destinations such as Egypt and the Gulf States.

FLORA & FAUNA

All over Yemen's arable regions, intense cultivation has all but destroyed the natural vegetation.

The Tihama's vegetation varies from the mangroves and salt-resistant plants of the seashore to the sparse grasses and shrubs of inner Tihama's dune valleys. Further inland, the wadi shores and mountain foothills are moist enough to sustain evergreen plants such as palms and acacias.

The natural vegetation of the western and southern mountain slopes is tropical, with evergreen forests of acacia, ficus and tamarisk. Cultivation of tropical fruit is common on the lower slopes. At higher altitudes (up to 1500m) cereals are typical. From 1500m to 2500m cash crops of coffee and qat (a mild narcotic) are grown.

On the central highland plateaux, sorghum is widely cultivated at about 2300m above sea level. All kinds of vegetables abound, as well as various spice plants. The wadis and springs of the highlands also provide a suitable environment for various fruit trees.

Western Waste in a Developing Country

As recently as the early 1960s, the Yemeni economy was completely based on recyclable materials. No 'waste' existed – everything was useable and anything that was thrown away was immediately absorbed in a process of natural circulation. This applied both to rural agricultural communities and to cities. So, for example, in San'a, even the human excrement was dried, carefully collected and used as fuel in public bathhouses. The ashes were, in turn, sold to gardeners to be used as fertiliser.

Synthetic materials were introduced only after the revolutions when the country started to open to the west. Still, all waste continues to be treated as though it were organic and is disposed of indiscriminately. Furthermore, water pipes were introduced to the towns and villages before sewage systems; the result is that what was previously dried up into neat cakes now flows along the streets.

Many westerners get shocked on arrival in Yemen because of the huge quantities of rubbish lying uncollected seemingly everywhere. These ubiquitous 'wrecking yards in the streets' are the outcome of a violent collision between two cultures. The west has taken several hundred years to solve this problem; eventually, the Yemenis will also come to terms with it. In fact, the development of waste disposal systems has already started. The centres of the big cities today are much cleaner places than they were in the mid-1980s. ■

As for fauna, intense hunting has long since driven all sizeable wild animals to the brink of extinction. For ornithologists, Yemen is a great place to watch migratory birds on their way to and from East Africa.

GOVERNMENT

After the civil war of 1994, President Ali Abdullah Saleh stands out as the undisputed leader of Yemen.

Yemen held the first free elections in the whole Arabian peninsula on 27 April 1993, and almost 40 parties competed for the 301 seats of the parliament. The People's General Congress of the North won 122 seats and the biggest religious party, Islah, won 62 seats. These two parties form the present government with Abdulaziz Abdulghani from the former party as Prime Minister. The Yemen Socialist Party of the South lost its influence in the civil war and its 57 seats today weigh nothing. The rest of the seats are held by independents and small parties.

ECONOMY

Yemen is a developing country, with very low industrialisation. The estimated per capita GDP was less than US$1000 in 1994. Despite the high potential, agriculture is mostly small-scale and intended for the sustenance of the family. Oil was not discovered in Yemen until the mid-1980s. Production levels are still very low at 350,000 barrels per day and the estimated reserves are modest when compared to the Gulf States.

A significant factor in the early 1970s to late 1980s was labour export. Both Yemens practically lived on the remittances from Yemeni oil workers working in the oil-rich Gulf States, which peaked at 70% of the PDRY's GNP in 1975. The system was brought to an abrupt end in October 1990 when Saudi Arabia expelled more than one million Yemenis because of San'a's lack of support for UN resolutions against Iraq during the Gulf crisis.

Yearly inflation broke the 100% barrier in 1994 and unemployment stays around 35%. While the relations with Saudis have recently been formally re-established, any recovery is bound to be slow.

POPULATION & PEOPLE

According to the census of December 1994, the population of the united Yemen was 15.8 million, with more than 80% from the former YAR.

Yemen is still very much a tribal society. The tribes form even bigger units that could be called tribal federations. Two powerful federations remain in the northern part of Yemen today: the Hashids and Bakils of the mountains. These tribal units still have a strong influence in Yemen to the extent that no Cabinet can be formed without balancing tribal representation.

The Zaraniqs of Tihama no longer have a strong role and neither do the fragmented tribes of the south and the east.

EDUCATION

The government allocates one quarter of the total public expenditure to education. Schooling is free but not compulsory, and only six out of 10 children attend the nine year primary school. Severe shortage of teachers hampers the efforts in education, and teachers have been recruited from Egypt, Sudan and Iran. There are universities in San'a and Aden.

ARTS

Architecture Yemeni architecture is unique. Houses are built from local materials: mud, brick and reed are used for structures on the plains and along the wadis, and stone is used in mountain areas. The building styles and facade decorations vary from region to region. Human settlements always display a fantastic harmony with the natural surroundings.

In the Tihama, houses are low; the only structures of considerable height are the minarets of mosques. The most common type of house in the countryside is the African-style reed hut – a round or rectangular house with one room and a sharply pointed roof. In the larger villages and towns, one or two storey houses are built of brick. Decorations on the

YEMEN

outer walls include patterns of protruding unfinished bricks or elaborate plastered ornaments.

In the highlands, the most commonly seen dwellings are multistorey tower houses. These buildings are made of stone, brick or mud, depending on locally available material, and embody the architectural style so reminiscent of Yemen. Each house is home to one extended family.

The biggest tower houses have five or six floors, each serving a different function. The ground floor is typically for house animals and bulk storage. The rooms on the 1st floor often serve as storage spaces for agricultural products and household items. The 2nd floor may include the *diwan*, or reception room for guests.

The next two or three floors are generally used as bedrooms for the several generations of families occupying the house. The kitchen is on one of these storeys, often equipped with a well which goes straight through the lower storeys into the ground.

On the top floor is the large *mafraj*, or the 'room with a good view', where the owner's guests gather to chew qat in the afternoons. The *manzar*, a separate attic on the roof, serves the same purpose.

In the wadis of the southern governorates,

mud-plastered mud brick architecture dominates. In Al-Mukalla and the Hadhramawt valley, the decoration of many houses shows Indian and Indonesian (especially Javanese) influences. Sa'da, in the north, has some fine examples of *zabur* architecture. Walls are built by laying clay courses on top of each other, letting one layer dry before the next one is laid.

Music The most celebrated Yemeni instruments are *al-oud*, from which the name of the western lute is said to derive, and the lyre-like *simsimiya*. Traditional music styles vary greatly from region to region; the feverish rhythms of the Tihama hardly appeal to the dignified *oud* player from San'a.

SOCIETY & CONDUCT

Yemenis are set apart from other Arabs by their passionate love of weapons – there are an estimated 45 million guns in the country – and qat, the national narcotic, the value of which is said to equal twice that of all other agricultural production.

Visiting Mosques

Non-Muslims are not allowed to enter most Yemeni mosques. A few mosques allow visitors but only outside prayer times. Some

Chewing Qat

Yemenis love to chew the fresh leaves of *Catha edulis*, a small, evergreen tree or bush which prospers only at relatively high altitudes (1500 to 2500m). The leaves are not swallowed, instead the chewed paste is pushed against one's cheek, which bulges as the slimy lump grows – no wonder old Yemenis' cheeks appear so wrinkled when empty!

Qat is a mild stimulant, above all a social drug, chewed at qat parties which take place in the afternoons in the mafraj of Yemeni houses. Every male Yemeni has to attend the chews at least once a week lest he be regarded as a loner, a voluntary social outcast. Each one offers his house in turn, and qat parties serve to enforce the social fabric of the local community. When asked if you, the foreigner, have chewed qat, a negative answer reveals you are either new or want to retain your foreigner's status, while a positive answer shows you have some Yemeni friends, which will win you respect.

Although most talk in the qat chews is just everyday chattering, decision-making also requires qat: nobody has a say in Yemeni politics if he's not invited to President Saleh's qat parties.

Qat is not cheap. A *rubta*, or small bundle of six or 10 qat branches containing enough leaves for a typical three to four-hour chewing session, may cost anything from YR200 to YR1500 (a quarter to double of an unskilled labourer's daily wage) depending on supply and demand, the season and the quality of the qat. The ability to pay for one's qat is an important means to show affluence. ■

historical mosques that are not in active ritual use can be entered. Never enter a mosque without asking permission. If you are granted entry, take off your shoes. Women should not expose hair or any skin other than face, hands and ankles. Visitors may not be allowed into certain parts of the mosque.

RELIGION

The state religion of Yemen is Islam. Most people in the Tihama and the southern and eastern parts of the country belong to a Sunni sect called the Shafai, while the northernmost governorates are inhabited mainly by Zaydis, a Shiia minority sect. The Zaydis make up a third to a half of the Yemeni population. Members of another Shiia sect, the Ismailis, constitute a very small percentage of the population. A small but important Jewish minority existed throughout the first 14 Islamic centuries. After the creation of the state of Israel, about 50,000 Jews left Yemen; a few hundred remain in the country.

LANGUAGE

Arabic is the official language of Yemen and the only language of most of the inhabitants. Having some Arabic at your command makes all the difference. In the northern governorates, English has been taught in the schools since the end of the 1960s civil war, with pretty poor results. It is easy to get by with English (or Russian) in Aden due to the city's recent history. For more details about the Arabic language, see the Facts about the Region chapter.

Facts for the Visitor

PLANNING

When to Go

Climatic conditions vary greatly between regions. If you plan to visit the Tihama region or Aden and Hadhramawt, avoid the unbearably hot summer. In contrast, nights in the highlands can get quite cold in winter. From late November to early January, San'a may have nightly frosts and, in the moun-

tains, it is chilly indeed. The dry season of late October to early February causes most of the country to become parched and dusty.

The rainy seasons – the lighter one in March-April and the heavier one in August-September – offer pleasant temperatures but heavy downpours and fogs make the mountains less pleasant. The moderate periods just after the rainy seasons, April-May and September-October, might be your best bet.

Maps

There are few maps available in the major cities. The General Tourist Corporation has low-quality maps of San'a, Al-Hudayda and Ta'izz. The *Tourist Map of the Republic of Yemen* is a good road map in a 1:1,500,000 scale, published by the Survey Authority in 1993.

What to Bring

When packing for your trip to Yemen, be selective. In the bigger cities of Yemen, you can buy all the little things for your daily activities, from personal hygiene requirements to stock medicines. Don't expect to find these items in smaller villages, though. It's a good idea to have a flashlight with you; when night falls, Yemeni towns and villages are dimly lit, if at all. A medical kit is advisable; see the Health Appendix for a list of what to include.

VISAS & DOCUMENTS

Everybody needs a visa to enter Yemen. Any Yemeni consulate will issue you an entry visa as long as there are no stamps of Israel in your passport – even after the September 1993 signing of the PLO-Israel peace agreement Yemen has not relaxed this ban.

The entry fees are generally about US$35 for citizens of the country where the embassy is located, more for others. The period covered by an entry visa varies from one to three months. The maximum duration of stay is usually one month for tourist visas.

Depending on the embassy, you will need one or two photographs for your visa application. For the question about religion, it is perfectly safe to write 'Christian'. Given the still disputed Palestinian question, it might not be prudent to proclaim yourself to be a Jew, and stating 'none' might create a stir among the highly religious Yemenis.

If you're travelling on business, you will need a reference in Yemen – a letter from the Yemeni company or organisation with which you are dealing.

Visa Extensions
You can get two week extensions of your visa from the Immigration office of the Ministry of Interior at no cost. There are Immigration offices in San'a, Ta'izz, Al-Hudayda and Aden.

EMBASSIES
Yemeni Embassies
Yemen has embassies all over the world but not in all countries – apply for the visa at the embassy most convenient for you.

Australia
    Australian travellers in Yemen are asked to register their presence with the Australian embassy in Riyadh, Saudi Arabia (☎ (1) 488 7788; fax 488 7973).
Canada
    Suite 1100, 350 Sparks St, Ottawa, Ontario K1R 7S8 (☎ (613) 232 8525; fax 232 8276)
Egypt
    28 Sharia Amin ar-Rafi'i, Doqqi, Cairo (☎ (02) 360 4806)
France
    21 Ave Charles Floquet, 75007 Paris (☎ 01 43 06 66 22)
Germany
    Adenauerallee 77, 5300 Bonn (☎ (228) 22 02 73, 22 05 54)
Iran
    Bucharest Ave, No 26, Tehrān (☎ (021) 628 011)
Jordan
    PO Box 3085, Jebel Amman, 3rd Floor, Zabram St, Amman (☎ 642 381/2)
Kuwait
    PO Box 4626, 13047 Safat, Rawadah, Block 3, Yousef as-Sabih St, Villa 15, Kuwait City (☎ 251 8827)
Lebanon
    Shaiboub building, Ramlet al-Bayda, Beirut (☎ (1) 832 291)
Netherlands
    Noordeinde 41, 2414 GC Den Haag (☎ (703) 653 937)

Oman
    PO Box 105, 115 MQ, Muscat (☎ 696966)
Qatar
    Villa Mohammad' Maayouf, al-Naimy, Doha (☎ 671 050/1)
Saudi Arabia
    PO Box 94356, Riyadh 11693 (☎ (1) 488 1757)
Syria
    Abu Roumaneh, Charkassieh, Damascus (☎ (11) 335 643, 339 807)
UAE
    PO Box 2095, Abu Dhabi (☎ (02) 829 825, 822 800)
UK
    57 Cromwell Rd, London SW7 2ED (☎ (0171) 584 6607; fax 589 3350)
USA
    Suite 705, 2600 Virginia Avenue, NW, Washington, DC 20037 (☎ (202) 965 4760/1; fax 337 2017)
    United Nations, 8th floor, 747 3rd Ave, New York, NY 10017 (☎ (212) 355 1730/1)

Foreign Embassies in Yemen
All of the following are in San'a (the telephone area code for San'a is 1):

Canada
    Building 4, Street 11, off Haddah St (☎ 208 814; fax 209 523)
France
    Al-Bawniya Area (☎ 268 888)
Germany
    Rd No 22, Hs No 9-49 (☎ 413 184/77/80)
Netherlands
    Hadda St (after Ring Rd) (☎ 215 626/7/8)
UK
    129 Haddah Rd (☎ 215 630; fax 263 059)
USA
    Dhahr Himyar Zone, Sheraton Hotel District (☎ 238 843/54; fax 251 563)

MONEY
Yemeni currency is called the riyal (YR). The riyal is divided into 100 fils.

Costs
By eating and sleeping cheaply and travelling at a leisurely pace, you should be able to travel in Yemen for as low as YR1000 a day (US$8.50). If you're looking for western-style luxury and hurrying around in private taxis, you'll spend 10 times more.

YEMEN

Currency Exchange

In the beginning of 1996 the Yemeni riyal was set floating with no official exchange rate. During the first half of the 1990s, the fixed official rate had been lagging far below parallel market rates, which kept fluctuating significantly.

US$1 = YR117
YR1 = US$0.009

Changing Money

To avoid unpleasant surprises, keep watch where you change money and make comparative enquiries on your arrival. The worst rates are offered at the airports and at top-notch hotels. Change money in commercial banks or with moneychangers in the souqs of larger cities. The moneychangers sometimes offer considerably better rates than the banks but their operations are periodically outlawed. San'a is your best bet for reasonable rates. In smaller towns you won't be able to exchange money at all.

It is best to bring US dollars in cash; major European currencies are also accepted. US$100 bills will get you better rates than smaller denominations. Travellers' cheques are a nuisance, and credit cards are practically useless outside a few of the biggest hotels.

Tipping & Bargaining

The practice of tipping is unknown in Yemen as service is included in restaurant and hotel prices. Fares for taxis and the like are best negotiated in advance. Time-consuming bargaining never was the rule in Yemen, but tourists have recently introduced the habit in the more populated silver souqs and even hotels. Compare the prices and use your judgement.

POST & COMMUNICATIONS
Post

Postal services in Yemen are relatively developed, and you can send your postcards from San'a and Aden in fair confidence that they will reach, say, Europe in a week or two. Post offices can also be found in towns everywhere in the country but not in smaller villages. Print the country of destination in Arabic after the address to make sure the local handlers route your mail first to San'a or Aden, the hubs of international traffic. Receiving mail is only possible at San'a poste restante or big hotels belonging to international chains.

Telephone

Phone services are quite good in the towns of the former northern republic but are still developing in rural areas and the south-eastern provinces, where most connections have to be placed through an operator. In the bigger towns you can find International Telephone Centre offices with phone booths for domestic and international calls. Domestic rates are very reasonable, while international rates comply with the international price level anywhere.

The international dialling code for Yemen is 967.

BOOKS

Highly recommended are Jacques Hébert's *Yemen – Invitation to a Voyage in Arabia Felix* (1989) and *Arabian Moons – Passages in Time Through Yemen* by Pascal & Maria Maréchaux (1987). Check the bookshop of the Taj Sheba hotel in San'a for its random selection. See also the Books section in the Regional Facts for the Visitor chapter.

NEWSPAPERS & MAGAZINES

The most interesting newspaper for the English-reading visitor is the political weekly *Yemen Times*, proof of the freedom of Yemeni press. *Time* and *Newsweek* are also available in some centrally located newsstands in the bigger cities and at a couple of luxury hotels in San'a.

RADIO & TV

The two radio stations in Yemen, San'a and Aden, broadcast mainly in Arabic. All TV programmes are in Arabic, except for the 7.30 and 10 pm news which are broadcast in English. Dish antennas for receiving satellite broadcasts became legal in 1991 and are rapidly gaining popularity.

PHOTOGRAPHY & VIDEO

Photographers will find that film is readily available in bigger cities, though not in the remote villages.

Have respect for the Islamic traditions which prohibit the making of pictures of people. Before snapping a photo of anybody first show them your camera and ask permission using the phrase 'mumkin sura?' ('May I take a picture?'). It is not customary to photograph women, with or without veils. On the other hand, many younger Yemenis insist on being photographed.

Military installations and buildings are strictly prohibited subjects. It is OK to take photographs of mosques (but not of the worshippers inside).

HEALTH

Although you may see a lot of waste lying around on the roadsides, it is not threatening to your health. Soap and tap water are available in restaurants for washing your hands before eating. It is still best to exercise caution when choosing your food. For more detailed health information, see the Health Appendix.

WOMEN TRAVELLERS

Yemen is a strict Muslim society, which means that you don't come here for a suntan. Western women are not required to wear veils but it is wise to dress appropriately; wear full-length, loose-fitting clothes, and shirts preferably with long sleeves. Covering your hair might make you feel more comfortable.

For both sexes, loose clothing and protective headgear also make sense as protection against the climate.

DANGERS & ANNOYANCES

In some northern mountain regions like Sa'da, children throwing small rocks at tourists have become a nuisance. You can try to slow down and talk to the children although this may not be the perfect precaution.

In certain Bedouin governorates (especially Ma'rib, Al-Jawf and northern Shabwa), tourists may inadvertently become involved in skirmishes between local tribes or tribes and government forces. Some travellers and expats have found themselves kidnapped by local groups trying to blackmail the government for various ends. Fortunately, even the worst incidents have only lasted a few days and no traveller has been physically harmed to date.

Enquire about the current situation at the Tourist Corporation or local tour operators.

BUSINESS HOURS

Government offices and banks are open from 8 or 9 am to about noon or 1 pm and are closed in the afternoon. On Friday and other holidays, the offices stay closed. Most shops and restaurants are open mornings and evenings, closing for a few hours in the early afternoon for qat time.

PUBLIC HOLIDAYS

In addition to those in the Muslim calendar (for dates see the table of holidays near Public Holidays & Special Events in the Regional Facts for the Visitor chapter), the following secular holidays are observed:

May
  Labour Day (1st)
  Day of National Unity (22nd)
September
  Revolution Day (26th)
October
  National Day (14th)
November
  Independence Day (30th)

ACCOMMODATION

In classifying Yemeni hotels, the conventional no-star to five star system is not very descriptive. A better method is to look at what you will find on the beds. The lowest standard of hotels offers no sheets (but with blankets) on the filthy beds, of which there may be four or six in a room or 10 to 20 in a dormitory; cold water in buckets or from a tap may be available in the toilets for washing. A bed costs YR100 to YR300 a night.

Not much better is the one-sheet hotel (one sheet on the bed, usually changed according to a weekly schedule). It may offer doubles but usually quadruples or more, common bathrooms with mostly cold tap water, and the price per bed typically ranges from YR200 to YR400.

A cleaner variation of the no-sheet theme is the palace hotel found in heavily tourist-populated towns and villages: an old-style Yemeni house converted into a hotel serving western tourists only, charging negotiable prices from YR500 to YR1000 per mattress on the floor.

In the western-style two sheet hotels, pricing is set by the room, and doubles cost YR500 to YR3000. Bathrooms are common or private (not good value) with hot showers. In the Tihama and the southern governorates, air-conditioning is worth paying for.

The deluxe category consists of a few members of western and Indian hotel chains, charging in dollars only from US$100 to US$250 a night for fabulous service in the four biggest cities.

FOOD & DRINK

Yemeni restaurants are eateries instead of places of social interaction. Lunch is the main meal of the day. A knife and fork are not used; fingers of the right hand and a piece of bread usually do the job. Bottled mineral water and soft drinks are readily available around the country, even in the tiniest villages. *Never* drink water from the standard plastic jars in restaurants.

Bread is baked once or twice daily and comes in several varieties: *khubz tawwa* (ordinary bread fried at home), *ruti* (bought from stores) and *lahuh* (a festive pancake-type bread made of sorghum).

The ubiquitous *kebabs* are cheap but the national dish is a thick, fiery stew called *salta*. It contains lamb or chicken with lentils, beans, chickpeas, coriander, spices and any other kitchen leftovers and is served on a bed of rice. Yemenis also like their *shurba* – a cross between a soup and a stew. Varieties include *shurba bilsan* (a lentil soup) and *shurba wasabi* (lamb soup). Fenu-greek (the celebrated *hilba* soup) is something you can't help encountering.

A typical Yemeni dessert is *bint al-sahn*, an egg-rich, sweet bread which you dip into a mixture of clarified butter and honey.

The everyday drink in Yemen is *shay*, or tea, drunk from small glasses with or without milk; it's sometimes flavoured with a leaf of mint. *Qahwa*, or coffee, often flavoured with ginger and other spices, is not so common. It is made from either the beans themselves or from their shells. Tea and coffee are always very sweet.

As for alcohol, the Qur'anic ban was enforced in the former YAR and extended to the whole of the country after the civil war of 1994. Of course, you can find expensive illegal liquor smuggled into the country.

THINGS TO BUY

Yemen is not exactly a popular shopping stop, lacking many traditional 'Arab' items, but some typical Yemeni products can be nice souvenirs.

In the silver markets of the souqs of San'a and Ta'izz, old and old-looking jewellery is sold. Traditionally, all Yemeni silverware was crafted by the Jews of Yemen.

A special form of silverware is the Maria Theresa thaler of Austrian origin. The Ottoman Turks brought the coin to Yemen, where it served as the currency until the end of the imamate; it remained in limited use up to the 1980s.

An object that is indisputably typical of countries in southern Arabia is the sharply curved tribesman's ceremonial dagger, known as a *jambiya*. It is worn by men on a special belt at the waist. The elite, such as a *qadi* or a *sayyid*, wear more slenderly curved *dhumas*. The prices range from a few hundred riyals for a simple jambiya to tens of thousands for more ornate dhumas with silver and gold decorations.

The most highly valued daggers have handles made from African rhinoceros horn. In fact, Yemen is the chief consumer of this rare material, jeopardising the survival of the entire species.

YEMEN

Getting There & Away

AIR
Europe

The national carrier of Yemen, Yemenia, offers direct flights from San'a to Frankfurt, Moscow, London, Milan, Paris and Rome; there are one to three flights a week. Air France flies weekly from Paris to San'a and Lufthansa has twice weekly flights from Frankfurt. Economy-class return fares to San'a are typically US$1250 to US$1500 or more. Many of the Arab countries' national carriers such as Royal Jordanian also offer flights from Europe to San'a via their respective capitals.

Aeroflot (Russian Airlines) offers 10 to 35 day excursion tickets from Europe to San'a via Moscow at US$750 to US$800.

Africa

From Aden, Yemenia has flights to Djibouti, Nairobi (Kenya), Zanzibar and Daressalam (Tanzania). Yemenia also flies directly to Addis Ababa (Ethiopia), Asmara (Eritrea), Djibouti and Khartoum (Sudan) from San'a. Prices for a one-way economy-class flight range between US$150 to US$450.

Egyptian, Ethiopian, Sudanese, Tanzanian and Djibouti airlines also serve the country. Ethiopian Airlines offers the best connections to many parts of Africa.

Middle East & Asia

For the Middle East, Yemenia or the national carrier of each Middle Eastern or Asian country will offer a connection. In Asia, Yemenia flies directly to Karachi and Bombay.

Australia & The USA

There are no direct connections between Yemen and Australia nor the USA. It is probably best to fly to Yemen via the Middle East or Europe.

LAND

There are no bus lines crossing Yemeni borders so you'll have to arrange to hire a car.

The border between Oman and Yemen was opened late 1992. The only route, the coastal road through Salalah, is very long and tiring, but a new road is being planned.

From Saudi Arabia, only the Tihama road from Jizan to Bajil is open. Yemeni customs and immigration formalities are handled in Haradh. The paperwork is horribly time-consuming – expect to spend a full day at the border.

You must get a *carnet de passage* for your vehicle and hefty insurance is essential. Should you be involved in an accident in which a Saudi or Yemeni citizen dies, you will be held liable for considerable compensation of up to tens of thousands of dollars to the victim's family. Make sure to check the procedures with your insurance company beforehand.

LEAVING YEMEN

An airport tax of US$10 is also payable in Yemeni currency. Don't count on exchanging money at the airport.

Getting Around

AIR

Flight services inside Yemen are frequent, and useful if you are in a hurry. Domestic economy-class tickets cost about three times as much as ground transport fares.

BUS

Buses go along all major asphalt roads. Usually they leave terminal towns between 6 and 9 am, with afternoon buses leaving between 1 and 3 pm on shorter and more frequented lines. On some long-haul lines such as Aden to Al-Mukalla (nine hours) there may only be a 6 am bus. Buy tickets beforehand from offices at every bus terminal and at major stops along the way. Ticket offices are only open an hour or so before departures.

City Bus

The bigger cities have plenty of minibuses, *dhabar*, that drive along defined routes and pick up passengers from the streets. Prices are around YR10 to YR20 per person. There are no route maps nor schedules.

TAXI

Service Taxi

Service taxis run on predetermined routes. They have no timetables – they wait until full and then leave. Main taxi routes are also served by buses but the taxis travel on non-asphalt roads as well. Often, a service-taxi station is a little way from the centre of town, along the road to the final destination.

Fares are structured on a fixed per person basis but must be agreed on before you get in. A rule of thumb is that the fares are some 15% to 50% higher than the corresponding bus fare.

Taxis are painted white with broad horizontal stripes and a big circle on the front door, with the route often painted in Arabic inside the circle. Ordinary city taxis and short-haul service taxis have black stripes, while the stripes on long-haul service taxis are coloured according to their routes.

Private Taxi

Private taxis abound in bigger cities. You should be able to get almost anywhere within the city boundaries for well below YR200 in San'a or Aden, less than YR100 in Ta'izz or Al-Hudayda, though some patience may be required in finding the right taxi with the right price.

CAR RENTAL

Cars are usually hired complete with driver from local travel agencies. A 4WD vehicle with a driver will cost you at least the equivalent of US$60 (YR7000) a day.

Universal Travel Company (☎ (1) 272 861), PO Box 10473, San'a, and Yemen Arab Tourism Agency (☎ (1) 224 236), PO Box 1153, San'a, are two of the many travel and tourist agencies in San'a. There are plenty of others around Ali Abdul Mogni and Az-Zubeiry Sts in San'a.

Renting cars without drivers is rare. It is cheaper but don't think about renting a 4WD vehicle unless you know how to handle it across the very rough terrain. Moreover, while driving along Yemeni roads you are subject to Islamic and tribal law.

HITCHING

It is relatively easy to get a ride in Yemen, except on the asphalt roads served by buses and taxis. However, in remote areas where tourists are rare, people may wish to avoid contact with strangers. After the ride, always offer some money, equivalent to what you would pay for a seat in a service taxi.

San'a

History

According to Yemeni folklore, San'a is one of the first sites of human settlement, founded by Noah's son, Shem. The first written history testifies the city wall was built in the late 2nd century AD. The name San'a literally means a fortified city.

Later, San'a served as the capital of the Himyarites during the reigns of several kings. Following the arrival of Islam in Yemen in 628 AD, all non-Muslim palaces were destroyed and mosques were built in their place.

During subsequent centuries, San'a often served as a capital but new sultans on various occasions seized power and moved the throne elsewhere. The city was destroyed by Abbasid troops in 803 AD, by the Zaydis in 901 AD and internal dynastic battles in 1187 AD. During the two Turkish Ottoman occupations, San'a was again conquered, first in 1636, then again in 1872. In 1918 the city became the capital of the independent Kingdom of Yemen. However, in 1948, Imam Ahmad moved the capital to Ta'izz.

After the 1962 revolution, San'a regained its capital status. In 1990, when the two Yemens united, San'a became the capital of the new Republic of Yemen.

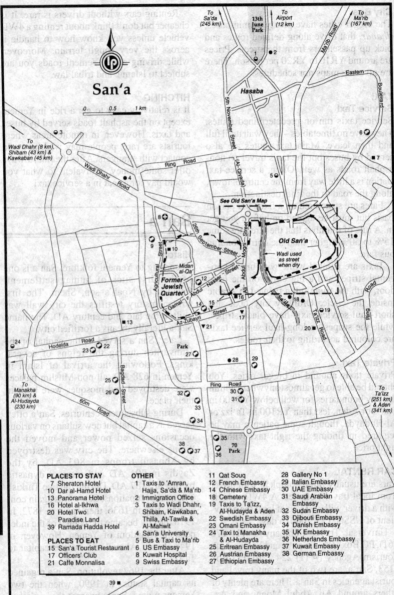

San'a

0   0.5   1 km

Hasaba

Old San'a

Wadi used as street when dry

Former Jewish Quarter

Midan al-Qa'

See Old San'a Map

To Sa'da (245 km)

13th June Park

To Airport (12 km)

To Ma'rib (167 km)

To Wadi Dhahr (8 km), Shibam (43 km) & Kawkaban (45 km)

To Manakha (90 km) & Al-Hudayda (230 km)

To Ta'izz (251 km) & Aden (341 km)

To Hadda (3 km)

PLACES TO STAY	OTHER		
7 Sheraton Hotel	1 Taxis to 'Amran,	11 Qat Souq	28 Gallery No 1
10 Dar al-Hamd Hotel	Hajja, Sa'da & Ma'rib	12 French Embassy	29 Italian Embassy
13 Panorama Hotel	2 Immigration Office	14 Chinese Embassy	30 UAE Embassy
16 Hotel al-Ikhwa	3 Taxis to Wadi Dhahr,	18 Cemetery	31 Saudi Arabian
20 Hotel Two	Shibam, Kawkaban,	19 Taxis to Ta'izz,	Embassy
Paradise Land	Thilla, At-Tawila &	Al-Hudayda & Aden	32 Sudan Embassy
39 Ramada Hadda Hotel	Al-Mahwit	22 Swedish Embassy	33 Djibouti Embassy
	4 San'a University	23 Omani Embassy	34 Danish Embassy
PLACES TO EAT	5 Bus & Taxi to Ma'rib	24 Taxi to Manakha	35 UK Embassy
15 San'a Tourist Restaurant	6 US Embassy	& Al-Hudayda	36 Netherlands Embassy
17 Officers' Club	8 Kuwait Hospital	25 Eritrean Embassy	37 Kuwait Embassy
21 Caffe Monnalisa	9 Swiss Embassy	26 Austrian Embassy	38 German Embassy
		27 Ethiopian Embassy	

In 1962 the city wall was completely intact, embracing the city of 34,000 inhabitants in the midst of green fields. After the revolution San'a experienced a period of unprecedented growth, doubling in size every four years. By the mid-1980s the city had spread in all directions, swallowing the nearby villages. Today the population is about one million.

Orientation

San'a is best defined in terms of its main squares by the old gates. Midan at-Tahrir (Liberation Square), or simply Tahrir, at the point joining the separate parts of the old city, is the post-revolutionary centre of the city. It is connected to the other squares by intracity buses.

Bab al-Yaman, the Gate of Yemen, south of the old city's eastern part, gathers the greatest crowds of people. Less important squares include Bab ash-Sha'ub, by the north gate, and Midan al-Qa', by the west gate.

Information

Tourist Office The office of the General Tourist Corporation is at the western end of Midan at-Tahrir. It is open from 9 am to 1 pm. Its Handicraft Exhibition (souvenir shop) is worth checking for maps, postcards, posters and other items.

Money Several banks in the vicinity of Midan at-Tahrir deal with both cash and travellers' cheques. In Souq al-Milh by Bab al-Yaman you can find private enterprisers exchanging cash only, as well as at Gamal Abdel Nasser St behind Tahrir.

Post & Communications The main post office is at the south-eastern corner of Midan at-Tahrir. The coin-operated phones there are for calls within Yemen only.

For overseas calls, there are several International Telecommunication Centres in the city. A central one is at Qasr al-Jumhuri St, three blocks from Ali Abdul Mogni St. You can place domestic calls there, too.

The telephone code for San'a is 1.

Immigration Should you need a visa extension, the Immigration office is in Hasaba, halfway between Midan at-Tahrir and San'a International Airport. A taxi will take you there from Tahrir for YR10 per person.

The Old City

The most imposing sight in San'a is the old city, especially the eastern part. Many houses are more than 400 years old and all are built in the same unique style of 1000 years ago. The old walled city is one of the largest completely preserved medinas in the Arab world.

Old San'a is highly regarded for its cultural heritage, and in 1984, UNESCO launched an international campaign hoping to raise US$223.5 million to safeguard the city. The success of this campaign has since spawned several bilateral daughter campaigns on a national level.

San'a houses represent a mix of Yemeni styles and materials. The lower floors are built of dark basalt stone and the upper storeys of brick. Facades are ornamented with elaborate friezes, and plastering with white gypsum is used imaginatively. The *takhrim* windows, with their complex fretwork of superimposed round and angular shapes, are made of alabaster panes or coloured glass.

Plenty of mosque minarets rise high above the roofs of the beautiful tower houses. *Hammams*, or bathhouses, abound in the city, many dating from the Turkish era. Private gardens hide behind mud walls.

On the south-eastern tip of the walled city, the old citadel stands on an elevation. It is used by the military forces and cannot be entered.

Souq al-Milh

The central market area begins at Bab al-Yaman and extends past the Great Mosque, half a km north of the Bab. Bab al-Yaman was built in the 1870s by the Turkish occupiers.

The souq is open daily but is best visited in the morning, when activity peaks, or between 6 and 7 pm in the evening. The area

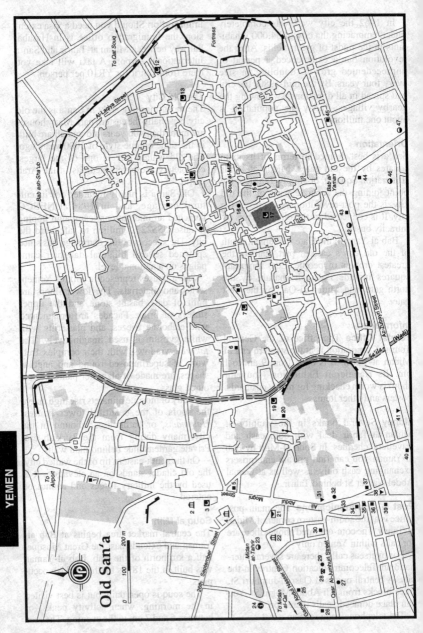

Old San'a

is called Souq al-Milh (Salt Market) but it consists of about 40 smaller souqs, each specialising in things like vegetables, spices, qat, corn, raisins, pottery, clothes, woodworks or copper.

Near Bab al-Yaman, modern consumer items are sold. Moving further into the souq, better defined sub-souqs emerge, many of them selling traditional products. In the Jambiya Souq you can watch the complicated manufacture of ceremonial weapons. The prosperity of the silver market is largely based on tourists paying high prices.

Traditionally, within each souq there was a *samsara*, a building that served as both storehouse for the wares and an inn for those bringing the wares for sale. Fifteen of them can still be found next to the corresponding souqs; many have been restored in the 1990s. **Samsarat an-Nahas** and **Samsarat al-Mansura** today house handicraft and modern art centres.

Mosques
For Muslim visitors, the place to visit in San'a is, of course, **Al-Jami' al-Kabir**, or the Great Mosque, on the westernmost side of Souq al-Milh. Entrance is not granted to non-Muslims. The mosque was built around 630 AD, when the Prophet Mohammed was still alive. Most of the present structures, including the minarets, date from the 12th century.

Salah ad-Din Mosque, in the eastern part of the city, is built in authentic Yemeni style, while the **Qubbat Talha**, in the western part of the medina, shows Turkish influence in its cupolas.

The beautiful, brightly lit minaret of the small **Al-'Aqil Mosque** can be seen at night, overlooking Souq al-Milh. The relatively recent Turkish-style **Al-Mutwakil Mosque** is on Ali Abdul Mogni St, near the northernmost corner of Midan at-Tahrir next to the Museum of Arts & Crafts. It was built by Imam Yahya in the early 20th century.

The **Qubbat al-Bakiriya**, in the eastern part of the old city by Al-Laqiya St, was built in the early 17th century and restored in the latter part of the 19th century, both times by the Turks.

YEMEN

Museums

The **National Museum** is by Ali Abdul Mogni St, about 100m north of Midan at-Tahrir, after Al-Mutwakil Mosque. It is housed in Dar as-Sa'd (House of Good Luck), a former royal palace built in the 1930s. The museum occupies five floors, with rooms dedicated to ancient kingdoms such as Saba, Ma'rib, Ma'in and Himyar, Yemen's Islamic past and an ethnographic section of 20th century Yemeni folk culture. It's open daily from 9 am to noon and from 3 to 5 pm, except on Friday (mornings only).

The **Museum for Arts & Crafts**, in Dar ash-Shukr (House of Thanks), another imamic palace near Tahrir, specialises in traditional everyday artefacts of Yemen.

The **Military Museum**, by the southwestern corner of Tahrir, is easy to spot; the building is exuberantly decorated with military hardware. This surprisingly good museum tells the story of Yemen from the very relevant military point of view.

The museum is open daily (except Friday and the last Thursday of each month) from 9 am to noon and from 4 to 8 pm.

Places to Stay

For rock-bottom prices forget the no-sheet and one-sheet holes in San'a and instead try the old and neglected *Alexander Hotel* on Qasr al-Jumhuri St or the better-kept *Funduq Arwa* and *Manakha Hotel* on Gamal Abdul Nasser St. These hotels have fairly good two-sheet doubles at YR400 to YR600, with shared bathrooms.

Ali Abdul Mogni St has several newly renovated and clean two-sheet hotels, with private bathrooms. These places offer doubles from YR800 to YR1500. *Shabwa Hotel Tourism* (☎ 273 183), *Say'un Hotel* (☎ 272 318) and *Gulf of Oman Tourist Hotel* (☎ 278 817) are all on Ali Abdul Mogni St, near the Shazarwan Restaurant.

In old San'a, several traditional tower houses have been turned into hotels with doubles for YR1000 to YR2000, depending on the season. Among the best are the central *Taj Talha Hotel* (☎ 237 674) north of Souq al-Milh, and *Sultan Palace Hotel* (☎ 273 766) to the west of Sa'ila.

Moving towards the top, the new *Plaza Hotel* (☎ 274 346) on Ali Abdul Mogni St has singles/doubles at YR2500/3000. Opposite the street the gorgeous *Taj Sheba* (☎ 272 372) accepts US dollars only, with doubles at US$210. Further away from the centre are the *San'a Sheraton Hotel* (☎ 237 500), on Ring Rd in the eastern suburbs, and *Ramada Hadda Hotel* (☎ 215 214), on Hadda St.

Places to Eat

Small restaurants abound all around San'a, but the best selection can be found near Bab al-Yaman and Midan at-Tahrir.

The *Shazarwan Restaurant* is by the Gulf of Oman Tourist Hotel, opposite the cinema on Ali Abdul Mogni St. It is clean and busy; the grilled chicken is some of the best you will find in Yemen. Another good one is the *Al-Afrah Restaurant* on Az-Zubeiry St between Ali Abdul Mogni St and the Sa'ila.

In the small street near Ali Abdul Mogni St, between the post office and Qasr al-Jumhuri St, there are a couple of inexpensive restaurants serving excellent fish.

On St No 35, north of Az-Zubeiry St, a few blocks east from the Hadda St junction, the *San'a Tourist Restaurant* offers Ethiopian food and excellent cappuccinos.

Getting There & Away

There are a few bus and taxi stations in San'a, each serving a different destination.

Buses to Ta'izz, Aden and Al-Hudayda leave from Az-Zubeiry St, south-west of Bab al-Yaman. Taxis leave from the huge taxi station on Ta'izz Rd, just south of Az-Zubeiry St behind the house blocks.

If you are going in the direction of Wadi Dhahr, Thilla and Shibam, the taxi station is in Matbah, inconveniently far in the north-west of the town. No buses run in this direction.

Brown-striped taxis going to Hajja and Sa'da leave from Hasaba, at the junction of the Sa'da road and the road to the airport.

Buses to Hajja, Sa'da and Ma'rib leave from the station in Al-Jomhuriyya St, half a km north of Bab ash-Sha'ub, where the city bus leaves you. Buses actually start from Bab al-Yaman and stop at this station on the way. Yellow-striped taxis to Ma'rib operate from the square next to the bus station.

Getting Around

The Airport Only private taxis serve the airport, with all drivers charging the 'standard' (official) fare of YR500! A hundred meters from the airport building you can find shared taxis for YR50 per seat, sometimes reluctant to serve foreign tourists.

Bus San'a's most important sub centres, Bab al-Yaman, Bab ash-Sha'ub and Midan al-Qa', are linked to Midan at-Tahrir by city buses. They leave when all seats are full and cost YR10 per person. The route between Tahrir and Bab al-Yaman is served most frequently.

Black-striped minibuses shuttle along main streets such as Az-Zubeiry St, Ali Abdul Mogni St (the airport road), Hadda St and parts of Ring Rd. The fare is YR10 per person.

Taxi Black-striped shared taxis often operate on the same principle as minibuses, driving back and forth along a certain street. The charge may vary from YR10 to YR20 per person, according to the length of the ride. Check the price before entering.

Within the urban area you'll need private taxis if you are uncertain about how to get to your destination. Even then, be prepared to encounter a driver no wiser than yourself.

Around San'a

To the north-west of San'a there are several places of interest, suitable for half or full-day excursions. Wadi Dhahr, Shibam and Thilla are served by black-striped taxis stationed in Matbah, north-west of San'a. The fares are YR50 to YR100 per person for the one hour ride.

WADI DHAHR

Only about 15 km north-west of San'a lies Wadi Dhahr, a fertile valley of small villages and clay-walled orchards. The taxi will probably take you to the front of **Dar al-Hajar**, (the Rock Palace). The five storey palace was built in the 1930s by Imam Yahya as a summer residence. It was built over the ruins of a prehistoric building on top of the most extraordinary rock formation. The well, penetrating the rocks by the house, is said to be original.

The palace is government property and has remained empty from the time of the revolution. The renovation and furnishing project started in 1990 is about ready now. The building may occasionally be visited.

To the north of Dar al-Hajar you'll find the beautiful village of **Qaryat al-Qabil** with its small Friday market. It is shadowed by an impressive precipice formed over millions of years by fast-flowing waters. The region was already inhabited in Himyarite times; you should be able to spot several caves in the cliff. Ancient rock paintings of animals and hunters can be found a couple of km from the village. Ask the children for directions.

SHIBAM & KAWKABAN

Not to be confused with the Shibam of Hadhramawt, Shibam is a smaller town with quite a past. It stands on the edge of the San'a basin, by a mountain rising steeply from 2500 to 2850m and is the easternmost town of the Al-Mahwit governorate.

During the 1st century AD, it was the capital of one of the small and short-lived independent states then common in the highlands. Both Sabaean and Himyarite inscriptions can be found on stones in the city gate of Shibam, in the mosque and in other older constructions.

From 845 to 1004 AD, Shibam again became the capital, when the Bani Ya'fur dynasty ruled here. They built the Shibam mosque on the site of a Himyarite temple.

Kawkaban, on top of the 350m cliff shadowing Shibam, originally served as the town's fortification. During crises, the inhabitants were evacuated to the fortress.

Water cisterns carved out of the rock collected water during the rainy seasons and grain silos were filled during the years of peace, enabling the population to survive a crisis of almost any length.

The steep path winding its way from Shibam was easily defended; many an attacker found their sophisticated guns useless against Yemenis throwing rocks down the cliffs. A walk from Shibam to Kawkaban takes one hour. The paved footpath starts from behind the big mosque.

From Kawkaban, another ancient town with a mountain fortress can be seen in the distance: Thilla, only nine km from Shibam, is also well worth a visit.

The Historic Fart

Shibam has the honour of being the only locality in all of Yemen to host a tale from *The Thousand and One Nights*.

In the tale a man fouls up his wedding ceremony by letting out a tumultuous fart at the peak of the festivity. In utmost shame, the man flees the scene, riding his horse all the way to India and finally settling there. Years later he decides to put an end to his exile and returns home to Yemen. On the outskirts of his adored village, he dismounts by a house and happens to overhear a conversation through a window. A young girl asks her mother about her age and is told that she was born 'on the day of Hussein's historic fart'. Facing the horror of the fact that his fart will never be forgotten or forgiven, the man mounts his horse and rides away, this time for ever. ■

Places to Stay

If you plan to extend your visit to Thilla or Al-Mahwit, you can stay overnight in the basic no-sheet *Funduq Hanida* in traditional Yemeni style. Prices start from YR200 for a mattress, and fluctuate considerably by the season. To find the place, walk down the At-Tawila Rd from the central market square until you see a small arch, about 30m on the right. Go through the arch and you will find the modern-looking house directly in front of you.

In Kawkaban *Hotel Jabal Kawkaban* and *Kawkaban Hotel* in old-style tower houses are no-sheet places geared for tourists. The latter is cleaner and offers better value with hot showers and a reasonable restaurant. An outrageous scenery tax brings the cost of staying overnight to around YR1000 per double, but you may try to bargain.

AL-MAHWIT GOVERNORATE

This small governorate is to the west of the San'a governorate. It is a most impressive mountain district, full of small villages and hamlets and very suitable for trekking. From Shibam you can catch a service taxi to At-Tawila (75 minutes; YR100) or to the governorate's capital, Al-Mahwit (55 km; YR160), where a new two-sheet hotel near the market offers doubles at YR1500.

MANAKHA

The western Haraz Mountains benefit from ample monsoon rains and are intensely cultivated. In the centre of the region stands the proud mountain village of Manakha (altitude 2200m). Its location was of strategic importance during the Ottoman occupation of Yemen; from here the Turks were able to protect the supply lines between San'a and Al-Hudayda, in the Tihama.

Manakha is an excellent base for trekking, although no maps are available. In the Haraz region, old fortified villages and hamlets are scattered on hilltops and between the terraces that extend across the steepest slopes. The place of pilgrimage for members of the Ismaili sect, **Al-Khutayb**, lies only about five km downhill, south-east from Manakha. Another fine village, the tightly built **Al-Hajjara** is five km south-west of Manakha.

Places to Stay

Just after the entrance of the village, on the right-hand side, the *Manakha Tourist Hotel* is a no-sheet hotel in a traditional Manakhan house. This place is frequented by western tour groups and its prices are accordingly high but negotiable, varying from YR500 to

YR750 per person. Another hotel further in the town is run by the same family.

Getting There & Away

Buses and taxis to Al-Hudayda leave from Bab al-Yaman in San'a; buy a ticket to the village of Al-Maghraba (82 km from San'a by the old Al-Hudayda road), a small roadside market. The fare to Al-Maghraba is YR180 by bus, taxis charge YR200 per seat.

From Al-Maghraba, a six km road takes you up to Manakha. Local taxis charge YR20 for the ride but walking the distance could be a substitute for more extensive trekking.

Hajja

The town of Hajja (also spelt Haddzhah or Haggah) is a modern provincial capital standing on top of a mountain. There is little to see in the town but the Hajja road, winding through the heart of the Yemeni highlands, makes a trip to Hajja worthwhile, even if you take the next taxi or bus back.

The 65 km stretch between 'Amran and Hajja offers spectacular views of terraced mountain slopes. The Chinese-built road first climbs to an altitude of 2800m then, after crossing the highest pass, descends steeply and serpentines all the way down to Wadi Sharas, a mere 1000m above sea level. Hajja itself stands at 1700m.

Despite its modern look, Hajja is an old town and once served briefly as the capital of the Zaydi state. The citadel on top of Hajja's highest peak was built by the Turks and served the Zaydi imams when the country was no longer occupied.

Places to Stay

There are some very modest hotels on San'a St, near the central taxi station. The expensive *Funduq Ghamdan Hajja* (or Ghamdan Hotel Hajah) is your only decent alternative. It stands on top of the hill to the west of central Hajja, a 10 minute walk from the central cross-roads (take the road left from

San'a St). It offers singles/doubles for YR900/1200.

Getting There & Away

Buses from San'a to Hajja cost YR80 and leave at 8 am and 2 pm from Bab ash-Sha'ub. Taxis leave from Hasaba, and cost YR300. The 115 km ride takes 2½ to three hours.

SHIHARA

Shihara (also spelt Shaharah) in the northern Hajja governorate is one of the most famous mountain fortress villages in Yemen. Situated on top of the 2600m high Shihara mountain, the almost inaccessible village of Shihara was never conquered during the Ottoman occupations. Only during the 1960s civil war, when Shihara served as the headquarters of the Royalists, was it defeated for the first time, a victim of the Republican air force.

Shihara has 23 water cisterns. The two parts of the village, located on neighbouring mountain peaks, are connected over a 300m deep gorge by a stone bridge built in the early 17th century.

Places to Stay

The price of an overnight stay in one of the no-sheet dormitories at *Funduq Shihara* varies greatly, from YR500 to YR1000 per person.

Getting There & Away

Unfortunately, it is very expensive to get to Shihara as you can only visit using a tour operator from San'a, who will provide you with a car and driver for YR8000 a day. Due to bad road conditions near Shihara, you'll need two days for the visit.

At Al-Qabai, a village at the foot of Jebel Shihara, the locals won't allow the San'a tour operators to drive you to the top of the mountain. Instead, you have to hire a local car and pay another YR5000!

You may choose to walk up for the extraordinary views. However, the 1400m ascent will take at least five to seven hours.

Sa'da

The northernmost provincial capital of
Yemen, Sa'da (also spelt Saadah) was inhabited long ago in the days of frankincense
trade but the history of Sa'da begins in 901
AD. An outsider from Basra, in Iraq, Yahya
bin Hussein bin Qasim ar-Rassi had been
called to Sa'da in 892 to mediate between
warring Hashid and Bakil tribes. He was a
follower of Zaydism, a Shiia sect. He proclaimed himself the imam and made Sa'da
his capital.

The Zaydi state is led by the imam, chosen
from the *sada*, or those descended directly
from Ali and Fatima, the son-in-law and
daughter of the Prophet. The Zaydi dynasty
lasted for more than 1000 years, with Sa'da
remaining the spiritual if not always the governmental capital of the country. It was the
holy city of the imamate up to the 1962
revolution, and it still has an influence in
Yemeni politics.

Orientation & Information

You will be dropped off in front of Bab
al-Yaman, Sa'da's southern gate. The hotels,
restaurants, bus office, taxi station, police
and hospital are on San'a St, within a few km
of the city wall.

The telephone code for Sa'da is 51.

Things to See

The holiest place of the Zaydis is the **Great
Mosque of Sa'da**, built in the 12th century.
Imam Yahya, who introduced Zaydism to
Yemen, is buried here with 11 later imams,
under 12 cupolas. Entry into this mosque is
not allowed to non-Muslims. The fortification on the central hill is used by the
government and cannot be entered either.

The town's wall is largely intact and has
been partly renovated. Of special interest is
Bab Najran, the northern gate, surrounded
by imaginatively twisted walls. The houses
of Sa'da are an excellent example of zabur
architecture with the walls built of layers of
clay.

In town, the Sunday market is best. If you
buy a Maria Theresa thaller in Yemen, do it
here since the silver coin, the sole monetary
currency before the revolution, served in
actual use the longest in Sa'da.

Just outside the town, to the west, is a huge
Zaydi graveyard. Among the many elabo-
rately carved stone plates and tombstones
there are a few small domes, marking the
graves of distinguished Zaydis.

Places to Stay

There are a few hotels on San'a St close to
Bab al-Yaman. Rock-bottom one-sheet
hotels just outside the old town are *Sa'da
National Hotel* with shared cold showers and
Funduq an-Nil (Nile Hotel) with warm
showers; prices per bed range from YR200
to YR400.

A classier choice is the two-sheet *Rahban
Hotel* nearby, in a modern house curved like
a dhuma. Similarly priced is the even better
Al-Mamoon Hotel (☎ 2203) a couple of km
from the old town towards San'a. It has
friendly staff, singles/doubles for YR800/
1200 and a bathroom to every three rooms.

Places to Eat

Several eateries along San'a St and around
the market area inside the city walls offer
modest but tasty food. The *Yemen Unity Restaurant* continues to gather favourable
mentions from travellers.

Getting There & Away

From San'a, Sa'da is best reached by bus or
taxi. Buses leave from near Bab ash-Sha'ub
at 7 am and 2 pm; the fare is YR360. Brown-
striped taxis will take you to Sa'da for
YR400 a seat from Hasaba. The 244 km trip
takes about four hours.

Tihama

The coastal plain of the Red Sea, the Tihama,
is economically the most important part of
Yemen with approximately a third of the
country's population and almost half the

country's agricultural output produced here. For the visitor, it's of limited interest due to monotonous landscape, lack of spectacular architecture, and extremely hot and humid climate, exacerbated by sandy winds.

AL-HUDAYDA

Al-Hudayda (also spelt Hodeida) is the largest city of the Tihama. It is a young city, plagued by recurrent wars in the 19th and 20th centuries. Only after the Saudi-Yemeni war, in 1934, has Al-Hudayda been allowed to develop without disturbance. The real boom for the port city began after the revolution and especially after the 1960s civil war, in the explosive years of foreign (import) trade. Today, Al-Hudayda is Yemen's fourth largest city.

Orientation & Information

Al-Hudayda is a fairly large city but it is quite easy to find your way around it. The main street, San'a St, enters the city from the east as a continuation of the San'a and Ta'izz roads. San'a St ends at the modern park of Hadiqat ash-Sha'b (People's Garden), which has a huge fountain.

Everything of interest in Al-Hudayda lies within one or two km of the People's Garden, between San'a St and the coastline – bus stations, taxis, accommodation, the 'old' city, shops, markets, pharmacies, banks and the fishing port.

The telephone code for Al-Hudayda is 3.

Things to See & Do

The oldest part of Al-Hudayda is formed by the Turkish quarters near the old market area, which is as lively as any Yemeni market but with the extra flavour of sailors from various countries.

The typical old Red Sea house found in Al-Hudayda is three or four storeys high with wooden balconies or window covers

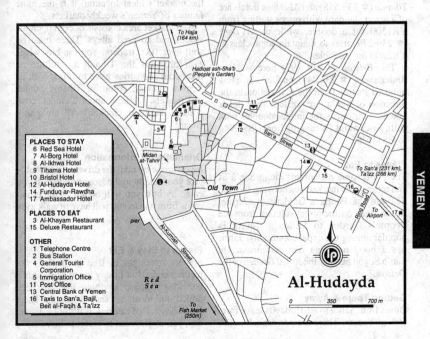

PLACES TO STAY
6 Red Sea Hotel
7 Al-Borg Hotel
8 Al-Ikhwa Hotel
9 Tihama Hotel
10 Bristol Hotel
12 Al-Hudayda Hotel
14 Funduq ar-Rawdha
17 Ambassador Hotel

PLACES TO EAT
3 Al-Khayam Restaurant
15 Deluxe Restaurant

OTHER
1 Telephone Centre
2 Bus Station
4 General Tourist Corporation
5 Immigration Office
11 Post Office
13 Central Bank of Yemen
16 Taxis to San'a, Bajil, Beit al-Faqih & Ta'izz

To Hajja (164 km)

Hadiqat ash-Sha'b (People's Garden)

San'a Street

To San'a (231 km), Ta'izz (266 km)

Midan at-Tahrir

Old Town

To Airport

Ring Road

Al-Kurnish Street

pier

Red Sea

To Fish Market (250m)

Al-Hudayda

0   350   700 m

YEMEN

and plaster-decorated walls. One of the best examples, with a rare dome on its roof, faces the Red Sea by Al-Kurnish St.

In the mornings the fishing port in the south abounds with fishers coming back from the sea carrying numerous different species of fish and shellfish. Many fishers still use traditional wooden vessels.

Places to Stay

If you arrive by taxi from San'a or Ta'izz and walk a few blocks along San'a St, after passing a couple of no-sheet, no-sign *dormitories* you'll find the *Funduq ar-Rawdha*, a gorgeous-looking but not very clean two-sheet hotel where an air-con double with private bathroom costs YR1000 a night. The *Al-Hudayda Hotel* (☎ 226 100) half a km further along, on the same side of the street, is good value at YR1100 for a double.

On the southern side of the People's Garden, no less than five two-sheet hotels stand in a row. The *Red Sea* (☎ 239 430), *Tihama* (☎ 239 558) and *Al-Ikhwa* hotels are of a lower standard with prices starting from YR1500 for a double, while the *Al-Borg* (☎ 239 279) tries to maintain some class at YR2500 for a double.

The *Bristol* (☎ 239 197) here and the *Ambassador* (☎ 231 247), on San'a St, a few hundred metres from the taxi station in the direction of San'a, are western-style dollar hotels, with prices for singles/doubles with bath, air-con and TV ranging from US$38/44 to US$55/65.

Places to Eat

There are some restaurants along San'a St and more in the market area between the Red Sea and the People's Garden. *Al-Khayam Restaurant*, on the street running from the People's Garden to Midan at-Tahrir, is popular among the expat community. Tahrir has a good no-name fish *restaurant*. On San'a St you may try the *Royal Golden* or the *Deluxe*.

Getting There & Away

Buses from San'a to Al-Hudayda leave from Bab al-Yaman. There are two asphalt roads;

the northern one passes through the western mountains near Manakha. Most buses and taxis nowadays choose the less scenic southern route via Ma'bar and the monotonous Wadi Siham.

The bus station of Al-Hudayda is on San'a St, some 500m from the People's Garden. The fares to San'a and Ta'izz are YR360 to YR400. You can also buy a ticket to an intermediate stop.

The station for taxis serving San'a and Ta'izz is further along San'a St. Taxi fares are about YR450.

BEIT AL-FAQIH

The age-old system of weekly markets is well-established in the northern part of Yemen, where almost every village has its market day.

The Friday market of Beit al-Faqih (southeast of Al-Hudayda) began in the early 18th century as a trading point for coffee. Due to the market's ideal location, it is the most famous of Yemen's weekly markets.

The market area consists of both open-air spaces and covered alleys. There must be well over 1000 traders. You can buy whatever products the Tihami agriculture or handicraft industries have to offer, such as Yemeni pottery, colourful Tihami clothes and baskets. Or how about a camel, cow, donkey, lamb or chicken? All are going cheap!

Orientation & Information

If you arrive by taxi, the driver will probably take you straight to the 'supermarket'. If you come by bus, you will be left at the crossroads from where you will have to walk a km or so.

Places to Stay & Eat

Staying overnight in Beit al-Faqih is not recommended but Friday lunch here is not a bad idea. Choose anything that has been boiled; full meals are served indoors. There is an alley full of eateries. If it's not a market day, you might want to resort to biscuits.

Getting There & Away

Buses (YR80) depart from Al-Hudayda at 7 am and taxis (YR100) leave at any time. The 55 km trip along an asphalt road takes only an hour. Coming from Ta'izz is less practical because the trading activities peak between 7 and 10 am, and you may be late for the market. By Friday afternoon the town is almost as quiet as it is during the rest of the week.

From Beit al-Faqih, YR80 should take you to Zabid, and YR300 to Ta'izz by taxi.

ZABID

About 37 km south of Beit al-Faqih lies Zabid, a town with a remarkable past. Zabid was founded in 820 AD by Mohammed ibn 'Abdullah ibn Ziyad who also laid the foundations for the 200 year Ziyadid dynasty. He brought a prominent Mufti (Islamic religious expert), At-Taghlabi, from Baghdad, who founded an Islamic university, an ever-growing compound of Qur'an schools and mosques. Zabid became a famed centre of learning, attracting scholars from abroad.

Besides Islamic law, other disciplines were studied in the university: grammar, poetry, history and mathematics. The word 'algebra' has been attributed to a Zabidi scholar, Ahmad Abu Musa al-Jaladi, who created a mathematical system called al-jabr.

The Zabid university outlived the Ziyadid dynasty, reaching its peak during the Rasulid era (1229-1454), when approximately 5000 students occupied the 200 or more schools and mosques of Zabid. During the Tahirid rule (1454-1526) the Zabid university started its gradual decline, which continued for centuries.

In 1994 UNESCO included Zabid on its World Heritage list.

Orientation

From the junction on the Al-Hudayda to Ta'izz road, an alley leads through the eastern gate to the souq area of Zabid. To your left there is a large square just before the town itself, with a citadel and other imposing buildings behind it.

Once in the town, closely built winding alleys and blocks provide no visual axes or hills. The city appears reserved, because the modest street facades of the houses conceal the splendour of their interiors. If you manage to get a glimpse of the inner courtyards of these houses, the dazzling white, richly ornamented walls will reveal the aesthetic preferences of the Zabid elite.

Things to See

During the golden days of the Zabid university there were 236 mosques. Over the centuries two out of three mosques have vanished but Zabid, with its 86 mosques, is still extraordinary.

The cupolas of many of these remarkable mosques, including the vast **Al-Asha'ir Mosque** (Great Mosque), don't reach great heights but extend over a wide area. The **Iskandar Mosque** with its 60m high minaret stands just outside the old city, inside the citadel walls. The **Mustafa Pasha Mosque** is another mosque of Turkish origin, standing with a dozen cupolas on the eastern side of the Ta'izz to Al-Hudayda highway.

The **Nasr Palace** by the citadel was built in the late 19th century and today serves as a government building. Signs on the walls of the 1st floor bear an account of Zabid's history.

Places to Stay

Don't plan to stay overnight in Zabid as the nights are unbearably hot and no decent inns exist.

AL-MAKHA

This coffee-trading and manufacturing port in the southernmost part of Tihama gave mocha coffee its name but is today a small village with few (if any) attractions. As one disappointed visitor put it, Al-Makha is 'for name-addicted romantics only'.

By the time Europeans appeared in the 16th century, Al-Makha was already a prospering city. Coffee, grown in the Yemeni mountains and the latest craze in Europe, was Yemen's most important product. Trade had started in the late 15th century, greatly expanded under the first Ottoman rule, and flourished during the first half of the Zaydi rule, and Al-Makha was the main export port.

In 1618 the English and Dutch built Al-Makha's first coffee factories. They were soon followed by other Europeans, even Americans. By the 1630s coffee houses were being opened in Venice, Amsterdam and elsewhere, and the demand for coffee rose to such heights that Yemen was no longer able to meet it on its own. Prices soared and the prosperous coffee merchants of Al-Makha built gorgeous villas in the city.

Yemen's monopoly on the coffee beans was broken by the early 18th century, when coffee plants were smuggled out of the country, and new plantations were established in Ceylon. The decline of Al-Makha had begun. The final blow came in 1839, when the British captured Aden and started to develop it as the main port of southern Arabia, robbing Al-Makha of the remaining trade.

Things to See
The Ash-Shadhli Mosque, with its beautiful Zabidi-influenced architecture, is about 500 years old. Some of the ruins of the coffee merchants' villas still stand, but most have already become sand-covered rubble.

Places to Stay
Until recently, no facilities for an overnight stay existed in Al-Makha, but when this edition leaves the printers the new *Mokha Tourist Hotel* should be opened.

Getting There & Away
A seat in a taxi from Ta'izz should not cost more than YR150 for the 105 km ride.

Ta'izz

Ta'izz is dramatically located at an altitude of 1400m in the northern foothills of the majestic Jebel Sabir. In 1175 AD the Ayyubid ruler Turan Shah decided to live in Ta'izz because of its pleasant climate.

During the Rasulid era (1229-1454), Ta'izz prospered as Yemen's capital. The period of Rasulid rule was followed by the 'dark centuries' when the city was controlled by various foreign conquerors and local rulers.

In 1948 Imam Ahmad made Ta'izz his residence and the new capital of Yemen. Much of the current prosperity of Ta'izz derives from the period between 1948 to 1962.

Orientation & Information
Two main streets wind their way through the city in an east-west direction. Gamal Abdel Nasser St serves as the main thoroughfare and buses leave at either end of the street. The southern 26th September St passes by the walls of the old town. At one point, near the Haud al-Ashraf part of town, the streets run very close to each other. There are plenty of hotels and restaurants in this area.

There is an office of the General Tourist Corporation on Gamal Abdel Nasser St, about 200m from the junction with San'a St. The staff are very helpful and you can get a map of Ta'izz.

Besides banks, some jewellery shops in the souqs may occasionally exchange money.

The telephone code for Ta'izz is 4.

Things to See
The liveliest part of the old town is definitely the market area by the northern wall of the old town. The market is small: just a couple of parallel alleys joining the wall's two main gates, Bab Musa (the Gate of Sheikh Musa) and Bab al-Kabir (the Great Gate).

The twin minarets of the **Al-Ashrafiya Mosque** overlook the old town. The mosque was built in the 13th and 14th centuries. Children from the Qur'an school may be willing to guide you around in the afternoon, and even take you to the minaret.

West of Al-Ashrafiya Mosque is another remarkable mosque, **Al-Mu'tabiya**, built in the 16th century by the Turks. Also notable is the 13th century **Al-Mudhaffar Mosque**, to the north of Al-Ashrafiya, with one minaret and more than 20 cupolas.

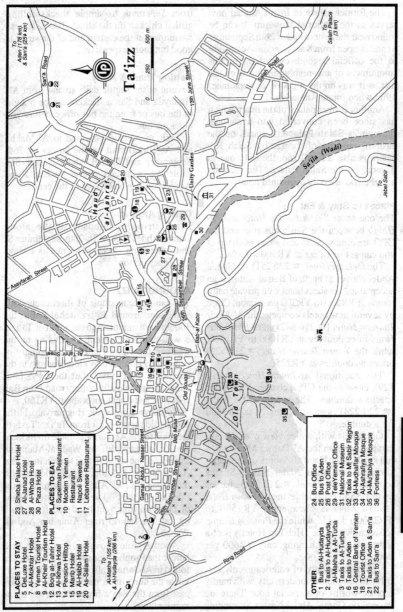

Ta'izz

To Aden (178 km)
& San'a (254 km)

San'a Road

To Salah Palace
(3 km)

San'a Road

13th June Street

Unity Garden

Sa'ila (Wadi)

To Jebel Sabir

San'a Street

Haud al-Ashrat

500 m

250

0

Asayfarah Street

Al-Tahrir Street

26th September Street

Bab-al Kabir

Old Town

Gamal Abdul Nasser Street

26th September Street

Bab Mūsā

Ring Road

To Al-Makha (105 km)
& Al-Hudayda (266 km)

To Al-Makha, Al-Hudayda,
Al-Makha & At-Turba

PLACES TO STAY
5   DeLuxe Hotel
7   Al-Mokhtar Hotel
8   Yemen Tourist Hotel
9   Al-Kheir Tourism Hotel
12 Borg at-Tahrir Hotel
13 Al-Ikhwa Hotel
14 Pension Hilltop
15 Marib Hotel
19 Al-Habib Hotel
20 As-Salam Hotel
23 Sheba Palace Hotel
27 Al-Janad Hotel
28 Al-Whda Hotel
30 Plaza Hotel

PLACES TO EAT
4   Superman Restaurant
10 Modern Yemen
    Restaurant
11 Napoli Sweets
17 Lebanese Restaurant

OTHER
1   Bus to Al-Hudayda
2   Taxis to Al-Hudayda,
    Al-Makha & At-Turba
3   Taxis to At-Turba
6   Taxis to Aden
16 Central Bank of Yemen
18 Tourist Office
21 Taxis to Aden & San'a
22 Bus to San'a
24 Bus Office
25 Bus to Aden
26 Post Office
29 TeleYemen Office
31 National Museum
32 Taxis to Mt Sabir Region
33 Al-Mudhaffar Mosque
34 Al-Ashrafiya Mosque
35 Al-Mu'tabiya Mosque
36 Fortress

YEMEN

The former palace of Imam Ahmad now serves as the **National Museum**. It can be found near the eastern end of 26th September St and is open from 8 am to noon. According to the official legend, everything in this 'monument of anti-revolution' has been left just as it was on the night of 26 September 1962 when Imam Ahmad died.

Another former palace of the imam which has since been converted into a national museum is **Salah Palace**. It stands on the eastern outskirts of Ta'izz, by Salah Rd. There is also a small zoo, the only one in Yemen, by the Salah Palace. The museum and the zoo are only open until noon.

Places to Stay & Eat
The one-sheet *Sheba Palace Hotel* and *Al-Habib* between the San'a bus stop and the GPO are almost clean and about as cheap as you can get in Ta'izz at YR300 a double.

The *DeLuxe Hotel* (☎ 226 251), on Gamal Abdel Nasser St north of Bab al-Kabir, is an acceptable two-sheet hotel with private bathrooms at YR250 to YR300 per person. Close by several new hotels compete: the *Al-Kheir Tourism Hotel* (☎ 216 647) and *Al-Mokhtar Hotel* offer doubles at YR1000 to YR1500, while the *Yemen Tourist Hotel* (☎ 219 522) prices its doubles at YR2250.

The traditional *Al-Janad Hotel* (☎ 210 529), close to the GPO, charges YR800 for spacious doubles. The nearby *Plaza Hotel* (☎ 220 224) is more expensive at YR2150 for a double.

Old hotels with a nice view over the city can be found on the Al-Dabwa Mountain, a hill north of the Haud al-Ashraf, on the opposite side of Gamal Abdel Nasser St: the top-class *Marib Hotel* (☎ 210 350) charges up to US$50 per double, the *Al-Ikhwa Hotel* (☎ 210 364) is cheaper at YR1500 to YR2500 a double, while the *Pension Hilltop* (also known as the 'Hel Top Hotel') is of a lower standard, charging only YR600 per double.

Ta'izz has plenty of eateries evenly distributed around the modern city, with hardly a place worthy of a special note. There are several on Gamal Abdel Nasser St, ranging from *Superman* to simple shacks selling grilled chicken on the street. The *Lebanese Restaurant* at the eastern end of the street is good but more expensive.

Getting There & Away
Several buses shuttle daily to and from Al-Hudayda and San'a. Tickets can be bought in the bus or from the bus office before you enter the bus.

Taxis to Al-Hudayda (and to Al-Makha and At-Turba) wait on the corner of 26th September and Gamal Abdel Nasser Sts, while the main taxi station for San'a and Aden is on San'a Rd, east of the centre.

Getting Around
Black-striped minibuses shuttle along Gamal Abdel Nasser St, 26th September St and other long streets. The fare is always YR10 per person.

AROUND TA'IZZ
You can make a couple of short excursions in the area around Ta'izz. **Jebel Sabir**, the 3006m high mountain to the south of Ta'izz, is well worth the ascent. Depending on the weather, the views can be extraordinary or completely obscured by clouds or rain in the afternoon. 4WD taxis start their 1½ hour climb along the really bumpy road from Bab al-Kabir, and a seat costs about YR160.

Hujjariya (also spelt Huggariyah) is the countryside south-west from Ta'izz. Taxis to the main town, At-Turba, notable for its location on a steep cliff by Wadi al-Maqatira, leave from the western taxi station in Ta'izz. A seat for the 1½ hour trip should not cost more than YR160. After about a third of the ride there is the 500 year old white mosque of Yifrus on your right-hand side. It was built by the last Tahirid ruler Amir bin Abd al-Wahab.

Another fine mosque, originally built before the Prophet's death in 632 AD, can be found in **Al-Janad** (also spelt Al-Ganad), six km to the north of Ta'izz and another five km east from the San'a highway, served by no regular taxis.

IBB

Ibb was originally built on a hilltop (1850m). The old town of stone tower houses is definitely well worth visiting. Ibb is also a good stopping place between San'a and Ta'izz for a side trip to Jibla (see the Jibla section, following).

Orientation & Information

The San'a to Ta'izz highway no longer passes through the centre of Ibb. If you arrive by bus, you will be dropped off at the junction of the Al-Udayn Rd; look for a black-striped taxi to take you east to the town centre, just below the old town.

Places to Stay & Eat

There are many one and two-sheet hotels within 100m of the street junction which is a station for taxis to Jibla and San'a. Prices vary from YR250 to YR400 per bed.

The two-sheet *Arhab Hotel Garden* (or Alrehab) is at the junction of the old San'a Rd and the new Al-Udayn Rd. A double costs YR450 and warm showers are available. *Ibb Tower Tourism Hotel* by the Jibla taxi station, 100m towards Ta'izz, has not-so-clean doubles for YR450. The *Bilqis Palace Hotel*, a 10 minute walk along the old Ta'izz road, has clean doubles for YR550.

The *Mat'am az-Zahban* close to Ibb Tower Tourism Hotel, towards Ta'izz, is a good place to eat, with a family room upstairs. Or try *Kentaky Alekil* on your way up to the old town.

Getting There & Away

The bus fare from San'a (193 km) is YR280, from Ta'izz (65 km), YR120. For a seat in a shared taxi, add YR40 from San'a and YR20 from Ta'izz.

JIBLA

A small town with a big history, Jibla is only eight km south from Ibb, three km from the Ta'izz road. It is another former capital of Yemen from the time of the Sulayhids, a dynasty founded by Ali as-Sulayhi in 1064. He was a follower of an Ismaili branch of the Shiia Islamic sect, from the Haraz region

near present-day Manakha. After the death of his son, his daughter-in-law, Arwa bint Ahmad, became the queen. She moved the capital to Jibla and ruled for almost 70 years until her death in 1138. Jibla still bears signs of prosperity from her time.

Things to See

Jibla is attractively located on a basalt hill between two wadis that join immediately under the town. Once in town after crossing the bridge, take the first street to the left, just after the *funduq* (hotel) and before the Qubbat Beit az-Zum Mosque. You will see the souqs and, eventually, the **Mosque of Queen Arwa**. It is big with two minarets and can occasionally be visited. Queen Arwa is buried in the mosque.

As you enter the town you can choose to continue straight through, past the beautiful small mosque, **Qubbat Beit az-Zum**, to your left. This road leads to the upper slopes of the hill. From here an aqueduct, built in the days of Queen Arwa, still brings water from the mountains past the graveyard to the town.

Places to Stay

There is a small one-sheet hotel as you enter the town. It has doubles for prices subject to bargaining and common cold-water bathrooms only. A new alternative, higher up in the village, opened in early 1993, charging YR350 for a double.

Aden

The natural deep port of Aden is built on a site of past volcanic activity. It served as the port for the ancient kingdom of Awsan between the 5th and 7th centuries BC. A long sequence of changes in the sovereignty included Saba and other ancient kingdoms, continuing with local sheikhs and sultans of the early Islamic era, and finally distant colonists from Egypt and Europe. All were attracted by the port's convenient location on the major sea route between India and Europe.

YEMEN

The British ruled their South Arabian Protectorate from Aden, and the city served as the capital of the PDRY after their exit in 1967. However, the development of the city was stalled under the Communist rule. When the two Yemens united, Aden became a free trade zone. The city suffered badly in the 1994 civil war, but was declared the winter capital of Yemen and is finally showing signs of recovery.

Orientation & Information

The hot and steamy Aden actually consists of several towns: the classical port city of Aden, the industrial Little Aden with its huge oil refinery and the new government centre, Madinat ash-Sha'b. North of the old city are the suburbs of Khormaksar and Sheikh Othman. Between these two is Aden's international airport.

The old city is scattered around the almost 600m high volcano that forms Cape Aden.

The oldest part is the Crater (or Critir). To the west of Crater is the modern centre of Ma'alla. Around the western tip (the colonial Steamer Point) of the cape is At-Tawahi, and further to the south you'll find the beaches of Gold Mohur.

Banks in Aden are open from 7.30 am to 12.30 pm. Moneychangers operate on Main Bazaar Rd in central Crater. The Yemenia offices for international flights is on Queen Arwa Rd in Crater.

The telephone code for Aden is 2.

Things to See

The so-called **Tanks of Aden** high above Crater on the slopes of Jebel Shamsan are among the oldest sights in Aden. The 18 cisterns, probably built by the Himyarites in the 1st century AD, can store a total of 45 million litres of water. The present appearance of the tanks is the result of renovations carried out by the British in the mid-19th century.

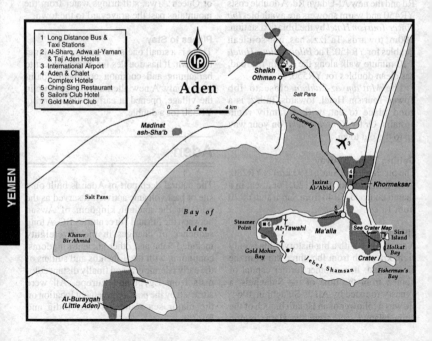

1 Long Distance Bus & Taxi Stations
2 Al-Sharq, Adwa al-Yaman & Taj Aden Hotels
3 International Airport
4 Aden & Chalet Complex Hotels
5 Ching Sing Restaurant
6 Sailors Club Hotel
7 Gold Mohur Club

The **Aden Museum**, in a garden just by the tanks, is only open on request. The **Military Museum**, the pride of the former PDRY, on Sayla (Sa'ila) Rd in central Crater, has been closed since the civil war of 1994 but is bound to reopen.

The **National Museum of Antiquities**, with numerous treasures from excavations at Awsan kingdom towns, such as Qa'taban, Shabwa and Hadhramawt, and the **Museum Popular of Legacy**, with a fine ethnographic exhibition, are both housed in the old sultan's palace in northern Crater. The museums are open daily from 8 am to 1 pm.

The **Al-'Aydarus Mosque** (also spelt Al-Aidrus), on Aidrus St, is one of the oldest mosques in Aden as it was first built in the 14th century AD, then rebuilt in 1859. The blazingly white **Aden Minaret** in central Crater, not far from the central post office, belonged to an 8th century mosque.

The **Rimbaud House** near the GPO serves as the French Cultural Centre, renovated in 1991 as homage to the French poet Arthur Rimbaud. He frequented Aden from 1880 to 1891 while occupied as an arms trader in Harare, Ethiopia.

Places to Stay

The cheapest hotels in Aden can be found in Crater. The one-sheet *Al-Iqbal*, *Red Sea* and *Al-Nasser* (pronounced An-Nasr) are all modest establishments, costing YR200 to YR300 per bed. The just-renovated two-sheet *Al-Hurriya* (☎ 352 217), also known as the *Liberty Hotel*, and the central *Al-Wafa* are good value at YR750 for a double with air-con and shared bathrooms. Top-end in Crater is the brand-new *Al-Amer Hotel*, with prices for doubles starting at US$20.

In At-Tawahi, the *Sailor's Club* (☎ 203 209) is recently renovated and offers spotlessly clean singles/doubles at YR950/1840.

Aden Hotel Moevenpick (☎ 232 911) in

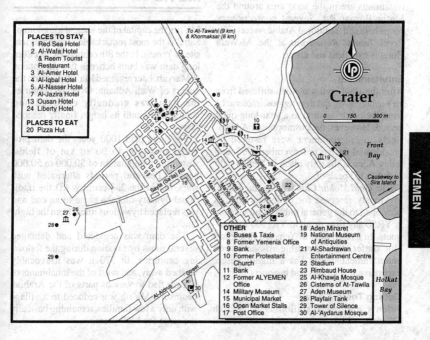

Khormaksar, near the airport, is the most luxurious hotel in Aden, at US$210 per double. The *Chalet Complex Hotel* (☎ 341 301) nearby is somewhat cheaper.

In Sheikh Othman, next to the long-distance taxi station, three hotels stand in a row: the *Al-Sharq Hotel* is a filthy no-sheet place charging YR350 per bed, the brand-new two-sheet *Adwa al-Yaman* (☎ 386 498) charges YR4000 for a double, while the *Taj Aden* tries to get US$70 for a similar room; all prices are bargainable.

Places to Eat

In At-Tawahi, you can't miss the *Cafeteria Broast Roasting*, in the Aden Gardens. The popular *open-air cafe* next to it is a pleasant place. The *Osan Broast Restaurant Tourist* nearby is modern and clean, and the restaurant at the Sailor's Club is good also. The *Ching Sing Restaurant* in eastern Ma'alla is an expensive Chinese restaurant.

In Crater, the best teahouses and small restaurants are in the souq area around the Ma'in Bazaar Rd. Several confectionery shops here sell traditional Arabic sweets. The *Reem Tourist Restaurant* at the Al-Wafa Hotel is excellent and cheap.

Entertainment

After the 1994 civil war Aden suffered from an onslaught of Zaydi religious intolerance from the north, leading to a year-long quiet period. However, the cosmopolitan Adenis' rights to entertainment were restored by presidential decree in November 1995, and today Aden is the only place in Yemen with nightlife to speak of.

The *Gold Mohur Club* with its fine beach, previously reserved for diplomats only, is now open to the general public. Entrance fee is YR50 any time or up to YR1500 for banquets. In Crater, next to Yemen's first Pizza Hut outlet, the incredible *Al-Shadrawan* entertainment centre has a nightly disco, expensive restaurants and banquets.

Getting There & Away

Aden's main bus station is in Sheikh Othman, which is connected with central Aden by both city buses and taxis (YR15). Buses leave at 6 am for Al-Mukalla (YR500 per person), at 6.30 am for Ataq (YR300), and at 7 am to Ta'izz (YR230).

Buses are often full but you can always use taxis. The station is a couple of blocks from the bus station in Sheikh Othman. Shared taxi fares are some 20% higher than bus fares. Taxis to Al-Mukalla also leave from the city bus station in Crater. It is advisable to show up no later than 7 am to be sure of getting a seat for longer hauls.

Getting Around

Small buses and shared taxis shuttle straight between the stations in the city's sub centres. Seats cost YR15 regardless of distance. The private cabs should take you between any two points on the cape of Aden for YR100 and to Sheikh Othman for YR200.

Ma'rib

Ma'rib, the capital of the ancient kingdom of Saba, is the most remarkable archaeological site in Yemen. In the 8th century BC, a 680m long dam was built between two mountains in Maryab, later renamed Ma'rib, to catch the waters of Wadi Adhana. Over the centuries the dam was gradually enlarged and strengthened until its height finally reached 16m.

For more than 1000 years the dam provided irrigation to 96 sq km of fields, sustaining a population of 30,000 to 50,000 people. Peaceful periods alternated with wars, but in the 2nd century AD the traditional dynasty of Saba came to an end and was replaced by various rulers from the highlands.

The dam was neglected and damaged several times by flooding during the following centuries. In 570 it was irrevocably washed away, and most of the inhabitants of Ma'rib fled to various parts of the Arabian peninsula. Ma'rib was reduced to a village with only a few families, remaining basically the same for 1400 years.

In the 1970s, pump irrigation revived agriculture in the region, and in the early 1980s, Hunt Oil Corporation found oil east of Ma'rib. Yemen's first oil well went into production in 1986, and the new town of Ma'rib and even a new dam have been built. Today, Ma'rib is a bustling place.

Orientation & Information

The 'New Ma'rib' is a collection of shops and petrol stations just past the rancid Ma'rib airport. You can have something to eat and buy bottles of fresh water to endure the heat of the Ma'rib afternoon.

The old village of Ma'rib is visible in the distance. Just before the village a new road branches to the right, leading to the sites of the dams a little way upstream. To see all the archaeological sites, widely scattered around the wadi, involves a 30 km round trip along the asphalt roads winding through the sands.

If you are travelling on your own, you should be able to get lifts with passing Toyotas. Another possibility is to hire a car; YR300 is the general price but YR100 might do.

The telephone code for Ma'rib is 6.

Things to See

On a tiny hill by the wadi bank stands **Old Ma'rib**. Of the almost demolished village, some impressive small-windowed mud buildings remain, their stone basements often sporting stones with ancient Sabaean inscriptions.

On the other side of the wadi, just a couple of km south-west of Old Ma'rib, you will find the remnants of remarkable Sabaean temples. They are marked by a sign reading 'Balqis Palace'. A few hundred metres to the west stand the five and a half remaining pillars of the Temple of the Moon (called **'Arsh Bilqis**, or the Throne of Bilqis by the locals, after the Yemeni name for the legendary queen of Saba).

Continuing further in the direction of Safir and turning right at the sign reading 'Sun Temple' you find the **Mahram Bilqis**, or 'Temple of Bilqis'. Archaeological studies from 1950 to 1952 indicate that the temple

was built around 400 BC. Today the desert has reclaimed much of the temple, leaving only pillars rising from the sands.

Back on the road that leads to the dams, you come to the ancient **Great Dam of Ma'rib**, some eight km from Old Ma'rib. Only ruins of the sluice gates on each bank remain. Continuing just a couple of km upstream, you will come to the 40m high and 760m long **New Dam of Ma'rib**, built in the 1980s as a US$75 million gift from Sheikh Zayed bin Sultan al-Nahyan, the ruler of Abu Dhabi. His ancestors lived in Wadi Nahayan, near Ma'rib, and migrated to the shores of the Persian Gulf after the great disaster of 570 AD.

Places to Stay & Eat

The one-sheet *Brothers* hotel, by the gasoline station in new Ma'rib, offers filthy quadruples (YR300 per bed) with shared bathrooms.

For something better, head towards old Ma'rib until you reach the '1st-class' *Funduq al-Jannattyn* (☎ 2306) on your right. A double costs YR700 or YR1400 with air-con. A holiday resort hotel, the gorgeous *Bilqish Mareb Hotel* (☎ 2666), offers doubles for YR2000.

For simple eating, there are a few Yemeni-style restaurants near the bus station, all about the same.

Getting There & Away

Buses to Ma'rib leave from Bab ash-Sha'ub in San'a at 8 am and 2 pm; the 158 km trip takes 2¾ hours and costs YR300. Yellow-striped taxis offer an alternative to the buses; they charge YR360 a seat.

BARAQISH

In the Bedouin governorate of Al-Jawf, only 35 km off the San'a to Ma'rib road, stand the impressive ruins of Baraqish. This was the original capital of the Ma'in kingdom from around the year 400 BC. The 14m high town walls still stand.

Hadhramawt

The sparsely populated governorates of Shabwa and Hadhramawt form the bigger part of eastern Yemen.

SHABWA

The ancient Shabwa, capital of the Hadhramawt kingdom for maybe 1000 years before its fall in the 220s AD, is today a less-visited archaeological site. It's about 165 km to the north of Habban which is a wadi settlement of striking appearance, about 340 km east of Aden on the Al-Mukalla road. The road to Shabwa goes through Ataq, 45 km from Habban, or you can more conveniently visit it on your desert trip from Ma'rib to Wadi Hadhramawt.

About 180 km to the west of Ataq or 150 km south-east of Ma'rib is Bayhan, the site of ancient Timna', in the midst of the desert. Timna' was the capital of the state of Qa'-taban and is thought to have been originally founded by the Sabaeans around 400 BC.

To visit Shabwa or Bayhan you might want to hire a car and driver since public transport is scarce. Sometimes unrest in these Bedouin regions prevents visits.

The southern end of the frankincense route was in ancient Qana on the coast of the Arabian Sea. The place is marked by today's fishing village of Bir Ali on the Aden to Al-Mukalla road.

AL-MUKALLA

Al-Mukalla in southern Hadhramawt is a prosperous sea port and fishing centre. Founded as a fishing village in 1035 AD, today it has more than 100,000 inhabitants.

The beautiful but shrinking old town with white buildings represents a fascinating mix of Yemeni, Arabic and Indian elements. The notable **Ar-Rawdha Mosque** and the **Mosque of Omar** on Main al-Mukalla St are worth a look. The **Al-Mukalla Museum** by the bay has been closed for renovation since 1990. Just out of the town **Husn al-Ghuwayzi**, a photogenic tiny fortress, is poised on an imposing cliff.

Places to Stay & Eat

Funduq ash-Sa'b in the northern part of Al-Mukalla has two-sheet doubles with common baths for YR900. The *Al-Atemad Hotel* in the western town and the *Awsan Hotel* in the northern suburbs offer clean doubles starting from YR1500.

Instead of the hotel restaurants, try the numerous small fish or chicken *restaurants* in the old town. Tuna, pilchard and lobster are common here but the real winner in Al-Mukalla is dried shark.

Next to the Mosque of Omar is a traditional teahouse with a fine atmosphere.

Getting There & Away

Buses and taxis to Aden leave from the eastern bank of the wadi dividing Al-Mukalla in two. Buses leave daily at 6.30 am – arrive at the station 30 minutes before the bus leaves. A ticket to Aden costs YR800.

The taxi station serving the direction of Say'un is in the northern suburb of Hai Uktubr. The trip to Say'un costs YR700 and takes six hours, with traffic starting only in the morning.

The desert airport of Riyan is some 20 km north-east of Al-Mukalla. Taxi fare for the 30 minute ride is YR400. The Yemenia office is in the western part of the town facing the wadi.

WADI HADHRAMAWT

Wadi Hadhramawt, the biggest wadi in the Arabian peninsula, runs for 160 km, west to east, amidst the most arid stone desert, about 160 km from the coast. The main valley is about 300m deep, with the wadi bottom at an altitude of 700m.

Wadi Hadhramawt with its numerous tributaries is very fertile, making it possible for a population of 200,000 to live on agriculture and goat-herding. Archaeological sites show that the region has been settled throughout human history. Before the 3rd century AD the area was ruled from Shabwa, at the far western end of the wadi.

In 951 Sayyid Ahmad ibn Isa al-Muhajir, a descendant of the Prophet Mohammed, settled in Hajrayn, in the eastern part of the wadi, establishing Shafaism in the region. The tomb of Al-Muhajir is still an important place of pilgrimage.

In 1488 the Kathirids of Hamdanis, a San'a tribe, conquered Hadhramawt and eventually settled in the eastern part of the wadi, with Tarim then Say'un as its capital.

In the 16th century the western part of the wadi fell under the rule of the Qu'aitis, a Yafi'i tribe originally brought to the region by the Kathirids as paid soldiers. The Qu'aiti sultanate made the town of Al-Qatn the capital. The disputes and wars between Qu'aitis and Kathirids continued throughout the centuries, resulting in division of the wadi between Shibam and Say'un in the mid-19th century.

The colonial power of Britain slowly extended its rule to the hinterlands, mediating between the sultanates of Al-Qatn and Say'un by the 1940s. The 1967 revolution brought about a final resolution to the dispute; sultans fled to Saudi Arabia and old ruling institutions were replaced by Communist ones.

Orientation & Information

Say'un, in the middle of the wadi, has an airport, other central traffic facilities and several hotels.

The asphalt road from Al-Mukalla descends to the wadi at the town of Haura, passing the towns of Al-Qatn and Shibam before reaching Say'un. The road then continues to Tarim and beyond. Numerous tributaries are also worth exploring, most notably Wadi Daw'an.

Getting There & Away

Direct flights arrive four days a week from San'a, once a week from Aden at US$120.

The traditional land route through Aden and Al-Mukalla takes three full days in a taxi or bus. You can also skip Aden and ride from San'a to Al-Mukalla via Al-Baydha. Another alternative is to hire an expensive Bedu taxi from Ma'rib to Say'un. The Bedus used to request US$300 per car for the eight hour ride, but the San'ani tour operators entered the market in 1995 and forced the prices down to US$100.

Getting Around

Taxis shuttle along the asphalt road that links

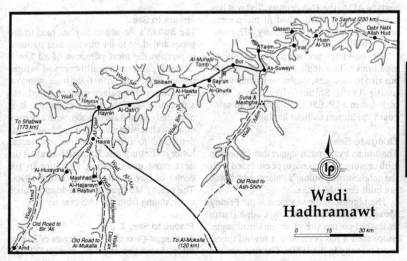

YEMEN

Hadhrami Emigration

Yemen has always been a great source of emigrants, but Wadi Hadhramawt exceeds all other regions in this respect. Throughout its history, Wadi Hadhramawt has sent waves of emigrants to other parts of the world. Hadhramis were numerous among the Arabs who spread Islam in its early centuries, but this was just an episode in an exodus that has lasted for thousands of years.

The explanation is in geography: a fertile valley surrounded by inhospitable deserts breeds more people than it can feed. The proximity of the sea has meant that emigrants have flocked to shores all over the Indian Ocean. While the nearby Arabic countries along the Red Sea and the Persian Gulf have certainly received their share of emigrants, Hadhramis have settled in East Africa, India, Malaysia and Indonesia in great numbers.

Because the number of returnees has also been high, Wadi Hadhramawt has been more susceptible to outside influences than most other regions in the mountains of western Yemen. One of the very first cars in Yemen outside Aden was imported by Sultan al-Kaf in Tarim in 1933.

Wadi Hadhramawt has also prospered economically from emigrants who have sent part of their earnings home, and returnees who have brought their successes back with them. South-East Asian influence is evident in the architecture of towns from Al-Mukalla to Tarim. ∎

the towns of the wadi. Seats cost YR50 from Say'un to Shibam and YR70 from Say'un to Tarim.

SHIBAM

Shibam is the 'Manhattan of the desert', a tight collection of about 500 tower houses, five to seven storeys high, crammed into an area of perhaps only half a sq km. It is a very old city, having served as the capital of the Hadhramawt area several times since the 3rd century AD to the 16th century. Today it has a population of 7000. Most of the present houses date from the 16th century AD; many were rebuilt about 100 years ago.

The buildings are made exclusively of mud bricks. This applies not only to houses but also to mosques, tombs, wells and walls. In the 1980s Shibam, like San'a, was included in a UNESCO programme to safeguard the human cultural heritage.

Things to See

The citadel by the main square dates from the 13th century AD. It is not to be confused with the neighbouring Sultan's Palace, which was not built until the 1920s.

The biggest of the mosques is the **Friday Mosque**, built in 904 AD by Caliph Harun ar-Rashid on the site of an earlier mosque. Since then it has been rebuilt several times, most recently in the 1960s. The first mosque

you see as you enter the city through the main gate is the **Ma'ruf Mosque**, also over 1000 years old, but rebuilt in the 1940s.

In the western palm grove stands the splendid white **Mosque of Sheikh Ma'ruf**, over 400 years old.

SAY'UN

Say'un, 'the town of a million palm trees', with its 30,000 people, is the largest town in the Hadhramawt valley.

Things to See

The **Sultan's Palace** in Say'un, next to the souqs and close to the bus and taxi stations, is perhaps the most pompous of all South Yemeni palaces: a multistoreyed white-plaster colossus with light-blue window decorations. The palace was converted into a museum after the 1967 revolution. It is open daily from 8 am to noon, with a permanent archaeological show and sections dedicated to folklore themes and recent history. The turquoise **Tomb of Habshi** is the next most eye-catching structure in the centre of Say'un. It dates from the 1910s. The nearby **Mosque of al-Haddad** is much older, dating from the 16th century AD.

Places to Stay & Eat

Funduq al-Qasr in the very centre of Say'un offers basic two-sheet doubles at YR600.

YEMEN

The two-sheet *Trade & Housing Tower Hotel* (☎ 3575), half a km from the centre on the northern road to Tarim, offers modern doubles at YR1200. The *As-Salam Hotel* (☎ 2341), a couple of km from the town centre in the direction of Tarim, has doubles with air-con for YR2000, including breakfast. New up-market hotels in the outskirts of the town, requiring transport of your own, include *Seiyun Hotel* (☎ 3124), *Chalets Sam City Hotel* and *Samah Seiyun Hotel* (☎ 3623).

In the centre of Say'un, next to the new souq and the taxi station, a pleasant cafe serves tea and cold drinks. For food, try the *Ash-Shaab* restaurant, on the 1st floor of the building opposite, or the *Park Cafe & Restaurant* by the park.

TARIM

Tarim, with its 15,000 inhabitants, is about 35 km to the east of Say'un. It is overshadowed by vast rock cliffs on one side and surrounded by palm groves on the other.

From the 17th to the 19th centuries the numerous mosques of Tarim were as important in spreading the Shafai teachings in and from Hadhramawt as those of Zabid were in the Tihama.

Things to See

Tarim is a beautiful town marked by the high minarets of its many mosques. The most famous, the **Al-Muhdar Mosque**, with its 50m high square minaret, is the symbol of the town.

The **Al-Afqah Library** was founded in 1972 to preserve the spiritual heritage of the region's Islamic teachers. About 14,000 volumes, including 3000 antique manuscripts, were gathered from all over Wadi Hadhramawt. The books are locked behind glass doors.

The finest palace in Tarim with its 19th century Javanese Baroque style is **Sayyid Omar bin Sheikh al-Qaf**, near the Al-Muhdar Mosque.

The graveyards of Tarim, to the south of the town centre, are worth a glimpse through the gates. The uniformly designed sandstone monuments with their deft calligraphy represent a style unique in Yemen.

YEMEN

Health Appendix

Travel health depends on your predeparture preparations, your day-to-day health care while travelling and how you handle any medical problem or emergency that does develop. While the list of potential dangers can seem quite frightening, with a little luck, some basic precautions and adequate information few travellers experience more than upset stomachs. For more information, see also the individual country chapters.

Travel Health Guides
There are a number of books on travel health, including:

Staying Healthy in Asia, Africa & Latin America, Dirk Schroeder, Moon Publications, 1994. Probably the best all-round guide to carry, as it's compact but very detailed and well organised.

Travellers' Health, Dr Richard Dawood, Oxford University Press, 1995. Comprehensive, easy to read, authoritative and also highly recommended, although it's rather large to lug around.

Where There is No Doctor, David Werner, Macmillan, 1994. A very detailed guide intended for someone, such as a Peace Corps worker, going to work in an underdeveloped country, rather than for the average traveller.

Travel with Children, Maureen Wheeler, Lonely Planet Publications, 1995. Includes basic advice on travel health for younger children.

There are also a number of excellent travel health sites on the Internet. From the Lonely Planet homepage, *http://www.lonelyplanet.com*, there are links, at *http://www.lonelyplanet.com/health/health.htm/h-links.htm*, to the World Health Organization, Centers for Diseases Control & Prevention in Atlanta, Georgia, and Stanford University Travel Medicine Service.

Predeparture Preparations
Health Insurance A travel insurance policy to cover theft, loss and medical problems is a wise idea. There is a wide variety of policies and your travel agent will have recommendations. The international student travel policies handled by STA or other student travel organisations are usually good value. Some policies offer lower and higher medical expenses options but the higher one is chiefly for countries like the USA which have extremely high medical costs. Check the small print:

- Some policies specifically exclude 'dangerous activities' which can include scuba diving, motorcycling, even trekking. If such activities are on your agenda you don't want that sort of policy.

- You may prefer a policy which pays doctors or hospitals direct rather than you having to pay on the spot and claim later. If you have to claim later make sure you keep all documentation. Some policies ask you to call back (reverse charges) to a centre in your home country where an immediate assessment of your problem is made.

- Check if the policy covers ambulances or an emergency flight home. If you have to stretch out you will need two seats and somebody has to pay for them!

- Many policies exclude cover for travel in war zones, which may include several countries in the Middle East. (Some insurers, particularly in the USA, still consider the Gulf a war zone, for example.)

Medical Kit It's wise to carry a small, straightforward medical kit. The kit should include:

- Aspirin or paracetamol (acetaminophen in the USA) – for pain or fever.

- Antihistamine (such as Benadryl) – useful as a decongestant for colds and allergies, to ease the itch from insect bites or stings or to help prevent motion sickness. Antihistamines may cause sedation and interact with alcohol so care should be taken when using them.

- Antibiotics – useful if you're travelling well off the beaten track, but they must be prescribed and you should carry the prescription with you.

- Loperamide (eg Imodium) or Lomotil for diarrhoea; prochlorperazine (eg Stemetil) or metaclopramide (eg Maxalon) for nausea and vomiting. Antidiarrhoea medication should not be given to children under the age of 12.

- Rehydration mixture – for treatment of severe diarrhoea, this is particularly important if travelling with children, but is recommended for everyone.

- Antiseptic such as povidone-iodine (eg Betadine), which comes as a solution, ointment, powder and impregnated swabs – for cuts and grazes.

- Calamine lotion or Stingose spray – to ease irritation from bites or stings.

- Bandages and Band-aids – for minor injuries.

- Multivitamins are a worthwhile consideration, especially for long trips when dietary vitamin intake may be inadequate. Men, women and children each have different vitamin requirements so obtain multivitamin tablets which are specific to age and gender.

- Scissors, tweezers and a thermometer (note that mercury thermometers are prohibited by airlines).
- Insect repellent, sunscreen, suntan lotion, chap stick and water purification tablets.
- A couple of syringes, in case you need injections in a country with medical hygiene problems. Ask your doctor for a note explaining why they have been prescribed.

Ideally, antibiotics should be administered only under medical supervision and should never be taken indiscriminately. Take only the recommended dose at the prescribed intervals and continue using the antibiotic for the prescribed period, even if the illness seems to be cured earlier. Antibiotics are quite specific to the infections they can treat. Stop immediately if there are any serious reactions and don't use them at all if you are unsure if you have the correct one. Some individuals are allergic to commonly prescribed antibiotics such as penicillin or sulpha drugs. It would be sensible to always carry this information when travelling.

In many countries if a medicine is available at all it will generally be available over the counter and the price will be much cheaper than in the west. However, be careful of buying drugs in developing countries, particularly where the expiry date may have passed or correct storage conditions may not have been followed. Bogus drugs are common and it's possible that drugs which are no longer recommended, or have even been banned, in the west are still being dispensed in many Middle Eastern countries.

Health Preparations Make sure you're healthy before you start travelling. If you are embarking on a long trip make sure your teeth are OK; there are lots of places where a visit to the dentist would be the last thing you'd want to make.

If you wear glasses take a spare pair and your prescription. Losing your glasses can be a real problem, although in many places you can get new spectacles made up quickly, cheaply and competently.

If you require a particular medication take an adequate supply, as it may not be available locally. Take the prescription, with the generic rather than the brand name (which may not be locally available), as it will make getting replacements easier. It's wise to have a legible prescription or a letter from your doctor with you to show you legally use the medication – it's surprising how often over-the-counter drugs from one place are illegal without a prescription or even banned in another.

Immunisations Vaccinations provide protection against diseases you might meet along the way. For some countries no immunisations are necessary, but the further off the beaten track you go the more necessary it is to take precautions.

It is important to understand the distinction between vaccines recommended for travel in certain areas and those required by law. Essentially the number of vaccines subject to international health regulations has been dramatically reduced over the last 10 years. Currently yellow fever is the only vaccine subject to international health regulations. Vaccination as an entry requirement is usually only enforced when coming from an infected area.

Smallpox has now been wiped out worldwide, so immunisation is no longer necessary.

All vaccinations should be recorded on an International Health Certificate, which is available from your physician or government health department.

Plan ahead for getting your vaccinations: some of them require an initial shot followed by a booster, while some vaccinations should not be given together. It is recommended you seek medical advice at least six weeks prior to travel.

Most travellers from western countries will have been immunised against various diseases during childhood but your doctor may still recommend booster shots against measles or polio, diseases still prevalent in many developing countries. The period of protection offered by vaccinations differs widely and some are contraindicated if you are pregnant.

In some countries immunisations are available from airport or government health centres. Travel agents or airline offices will tell you where. Vaccinations include:

Tetanus & Diptheria Boosters are necessary every 10 years and protection is highly recommended.

Polio A booster of either the oral or injected vaccine is required every 10 years to maintain our immunity from childhood vaccination. The risk of contracting polio is low in most Middle Eastern countries, with the exception of Turkey and Yemen.

Typhoid Available either as an injection or oral capsules. Protection lasts from one to five years depending on the vaccine and is useful if you are travelling for long in rural, tropical areas. You may get some side effects such as pain at the injection site, fever, headache and a general unwell feeling. A single-dose injectable vaccine, Typhim Vi, has few side effects, but is more expensive. Side effects are unusual with the oral form but occasionally an individual will have stomach cramps.

Hepatitis A & B Hepatitis A, the most common travel-acquired illness, exists in all Middle Eastern countries, but can easily be prevented by vaccination. Protection can be provided in two ways – either with the antibody gamma globulin or with the vaccine Havrix 1440.

Havrix 1440 provides long-term immunity (possibly more than 10 years) after an initial injection and a booster at six to 12 months. It may be more expensive than gamma globulin but certainly has many advantages, including length of protection and ease of administration. It is important to know that, being a vaccine, it will take about three weeks to provide satisfactory protection – hence the need for careful planning prior to travel.

Gamma globulin is a ready-made antibody which has proven very successful in reducing the chances of hepatitis infection. It should be given as close as possible to departure because it is at its most effective in the first few weeks after administration and the effectiveness tapers off gradually between three and six months.

Hepatitis B is endemic in all Middle Eastern countries. Travellers at risk of contact, such as anyone who anticipates contact with blood and other bodily secretions, are strongly advised to be vaccinated. The vaccination course comprises three injections given over a six-month period then boosters every three to five years. The initial course of injections can be given over as short a period as 28 days then boosted after 12 months if more rapid protection is required.

Meninogococcal Meningitis Vaccination is recommended for travellers to Egypt. It is also required of all haj pilgrims entering Saudi Arabia. A single injection will give good protection against the A, C, W and Y groups of the bacteria for at least a year. The vaccine is not, however, recommended for children under two years because they do not develop satisfactory immunity from it.

Rabies Pretravel rabies vaccination involves having three injections over 21 to 28 days and should be considered by those who will spend a month or longer in a country where rabies is common, especially if they are cycling, handling animals, caving, travelling to remote areas, or children (who may not report a bite). If someone who has been vaccinated is bitten or scratched by an animal they will require two booster injections of vaccine.

Tuberculosis TB risk should be considered for people travelling more than three months to high-risk areas such as Asia, Africa and some parts of the Americas and Pacific. As most healthy adults do not develop symptoms, a skin test before and after travel to determine whether exposure has occurred is usually all that is required. Vaccination for children who will be travelling for more than three months is recommended.

Basic Rules

Care in what you eat and drink is the most important health rule; stomach upsets are the most likely travel health problem but the majority of these upsets will be relatively minor. Don't become paranoid; trying the local food is part of the experience of travel, after all.

Water The number one rule is *don't drink the water* and that includes ice. If you don't know for certain that the water is safe always assume the worst. Reputable brands of bottled water or soft drinks are generally fine, although in some places bottles refilled with tap water are not unknown. Take care with fruit juice, particularly if water may have been added. Milk should be treated with suspicion, as it is often unpasteurised. Boiled milk is fine if it is kept hygienically and yoghurt is always good. Tea or coffee should also be OK, since the water should have been boiled.

Water Purification The simplest way of purifying water is to boil it thoroughly. Vigorously boiling for five minutes should be satisfactory; however, at high altitude water boils at a lower temperature, so germs are less likely to be killed.

Simple filtering will not remove all dangerous organisms, so if you cannot boil water it should be treated chemically. Chlorine tablets (Puritabs, Steritabs or other brand names) will kill many pathogens, but not those causing giardia and amoebic cysts. Iodine is very effective in purifying water and is available in tablet form (such as Potable Aqua), but follow the directions carefully and remember that too much iodine can be harmful.

If you can't find tablets, tincture of iodine (2%) can be used. Four drops of tincture of iodine per litre or quart of clear water is the recommended dosage; the treated water should be left to stand for 30 minutes before drinking. Iodine crystals can also be used to purify water but this is a more complicated process, as you have to first prepare a saturated iodine solution. Iodine loses its effectiveness if exposed to air or damp so keep it in a tightly sealed container. Flavoured powder will disguise the taste of treated water and is a good idea if you are travelling with children.

Food Salads and fruit should be washed with purified water or peeled where possible. Ice cream is usually OK if it is a reputable brand name, but beware of ice cream that has melted and been refrozen. Thoroughly cooked food is safest but not if it has been left to cool or if it has been reheated. Take great care with shellfish or fish and avoid undercooked meat. If a place looks clean and well run and if the vendor also looks clean and healthy, then the food is probably safe. In general, places that are packed with travellers or locals will be fine, while empty restaurants are questionable.

Nutrition If your food is poor or limited in availability, if you're travelling hard and fast and therefore missing meals, or if you simply lose your appetite, you can soon start to lose weight and place your health at risk.

Make sure your diet is well balanced. Eggs, tofu, beans, lentils and nuts are all safe ways to get protein.

Fruit you can peel (eg, bananas, oranges or mandarins) is usually safe and a good source of vitamins. Try to eat plenty of grains (including rice) and bread. Remember that although food is generally safer if it is cooked well, overcooked food loses much of its nutritional value. If your diet isn't well balanced or if your food intake is insufficient, it's a good idea to take vitamin and iron pills.

In hot climates make sure you drink enough – don't rely on feeling thirsty to indicate when you should drink. Not needing to urinate or very dark yellow urine is a danger sign. Always carry a water bottle with you on long trips. Excessive sweating can lead to loss of salt and therefore muscle cramping. Salt tablets are not a good idea as a preventative, but in places where salt is not used much adding salt to food can help.

Everyday Health A normal body temperature is 98.6°F or 37°C; more than 2°C (4°F) higher is a 'high' fever. A normal adult pulse rate is 60 to 100 per minute (children 80 to 100, babies 100 to 140). You should know how to take a temperature and a pulse rate. As a general rule the pulse increases about 20 beats per minute for each °C (2°F) rise in fever.

Respiration (breathing) rate is also an indicator of illness. Count the number of breaths per minute: between 12 and 20 is normal for adults and older children (up to 30 for younger children, 40 for babies). People with a high fever or serious respiratory illness (such as pneumonia) breathe more quickly than normal. More than 40 shallow breaths a minute usually means pneumonia.

Many health problems can be avoided by taking care of yourself. Wash your hands frequently – it's quite easy to contaminate your own food. Clean your teeth with purified water rather than straight from the tap. Avoid climatic extremes: keep out of the sun when it's hot, dress warmly when it's cold. Avoid potential diseases by dressing sensibly. You can get worm infections through walking barefoot or dangerous coral cuts by walking over coral without shoes. You can avoid insect bites by covering bare skin when insects are around, by screening windows or beds or by using insect repellents. Seek local advice: if you're told the water is unsafe due to jellyfish, crocodiles or bilharzia, don't go in. In situations where there is no information, discretion is the better part of valour.

Medical Problems & Treatment
Self-diagnosis and treatment can be risky, so wherever possible seek qualified help. Although we do give treatment dosages in this section, they are for emergency use only. Medical advice should be sought before administering any drugs.

An embassy or consulate can usually recommend a good place to go for such advice. So can five-star hotels, although they often recommend doctors with five-star prices. (This is when that medical insurance

really comes in useful!) In some places standards of medical attention are so low that for some ailments the best advice is to get on a plane and go somewhere else.

Environmental Hazards
Sunburn In the desert or at high altitudes you can get sunburnt surprisingly quickly, even through cloud. Use a sunscreen and take extra care to cover areas which don't normally see sun – eg, your feet. A hat provides added protection, and you should also use zinc cream or some other barrier cream for your nose and lips. Calamine lotion is good for mild sunburn.

Remember that too much sunlight, whether it's direct or reflected (glare) can damage your eyes. If your plans include being near water, sand or snow, then good sunglasses are doubly important. Good quality sunglasses are treated to filter out ultraviolet radiation, but poor quality sunglasses provide limited filtering, allowing more ultraviolet light to be adsorbed than if no sunglasses were worn at all. Excessive ultraviolet light will damage the surface structures and lens of the eye.

Prickly Heat Prickly heat is an itchy rash caused by excessive perspiration trapped under the skin. It usually strikes people who have just arrived in a hot climate and whose pores have not yet opened sufficiently to cope with greater sweating. Keeping cool but bathing often, using a mild talcum powder or even resorting to air-conditioning may help until you acclimatise.

Heat Exhaustion Dehydration or salt deficiency can cause heat exhaustion. Take time to acclimatise to high temperatures and make sure you drink sufficient liquids. Salt deficiency is characterised by fatigue, lethargy, headaches, giddiness and muscle cramps and in this case salt tablets may help. Vomiting or diarrhoea can deplete your liquid and salt levels. Anhydrotic heat exhaustion, caused by an inability to sweat, is quite rare. Unlike the other forms of heat exhaustion it is likely to strike people who have been in a hot climate for some time, rather than newcomers.

Heat Stroke This serious, sometimes fatal, condition can occur if the body's heat-regulating mechanism breaks down and the body temperature rises to dangerous levels. Long, continuous periods of exposure to high temperatures can leave you vulnerable to heat stroke. You should avoid excessive alcohol or strenuous activity when you first arrive in a hot climate.

The symptoms are feeling unwell, not sweating very much or at all and a high body temperature (39°C to 41°C or 102°F to 106°F). Where sweating has ceased the skin becomes flushed and red. Severe, throbbing headaches and lack of coordination will also occur, and the sufferer may be confused or aggressive. Eventually the victim will become delirious or convulse. Hospitalisation is essential, but in the interim get patients out of the sun, remove their clothing, cover them with a wet sheet or towel and then fan continually.

Fungal Infections Hot-weather fungal infections are most likely to occur on the scalp, between the toes or fingers (athlete's foot), in the groin (jock itch or crotch rot) and on the body (ringworm). You get ringworm (which is a fungal infection, not a worm) from infected animals or by walking on damp areas, like shower floors.

To prevent fungal infections wear loose, comfortable clothes, avoid artificial fibres, wash frequently and dry carefully. If you do get an infection, wash the infected area daily with a disinfectant or medicated soap and water, and rinse and dry well. Apply an antifungal powder like the widely available Tinaderm. Try to expose the infected area to air or sunlight as much as possible and wash all towels and underwear in hot water as well as changing them often.

Motion Sickness Eating lightly before and during a trip will reduce the chances of motion sickness. If you are prone to motion sickness try to find a place that minimises disturbance – near the wing on aircraft, close to midships on boats, near the centre on buses. Fresh air usually helps, reading or cigarette smoke doesn't. Commercial antimotion-sickness preparations, which can cause drowsiness, have to be taken before the trip commences; when you're feeling sick it's too late. Ginger (available in capsule form) and peppermint (including mint-flavoured sweets) are natural preventatives.

Infectious Diseases

Diarrhoea A change of water, food or climate can all cause the runs; diarrhoea caused by contaminated food or water is more serious. Despite all your precautions you may still have a bout of mild travellers' diarrhoea but a few rushed toilet trips with no other symptoms is not indicative of a serious problem. Moderate diarrhoea, involving half-a-dozen loose movements in a day, is more of a nuisance. Dehydration is the main danger with any diarrhoea, particularly for children, so fluid replenishment is the number one treatment. Weak black tea with a little sugar, soda water, or soft drinks allowed to go flat and diluted 50% with water are all good. With severe diarrhoea a rehydrating solution is necessary to replace minerals and salts. Commercially available oral rehydration salts (ORS) are very useful; add the contents of one sachet to a litre of boiled or bottled water. In an emergency you can make up a solution of eight teaspoons of sugar to a litre of boiled water

and provide salted cracker biscuits at the same time. You should stick to a bland diet as you recover.

Lomotil or Imodium can be used to bring relief from the symptoms, although they do not actually cure the problem. Only use these drugs if absolutely necessary – eg, if you *must* travel. For children under 12 years Lomotil and Imodium are not recommended. Under all circumstances fluid replacement is the most important thing to remember. Do not use these drugs if the patient has a high fever or is severely dehydrated.

In certain situations antibiotics may be indicated:

- Diarrhoea with blood and mucous. (Gut-paralysing drugs like Imodium or Lomotil should be avoided in this situation.)
- Watery diarrhoea with fever and lethargy.
- Persistent diarrhoea not improving after 48 hours.
- Severe diarrhoea, if it is logistically difficult to stay in one place.

The recommended drugs (adults only) would be either norfloxacin 400 mg twice daily for three days or (for very serious problems only) ciprofloxacin 500 mg twice daily for three days.

The drug bismuth subsalicylate has also been used successfully. It is not available in some countries. The dosage for adults is two tablets or 30 ml and for children it is one tablet or 10 ml. This dose can be repeated every 30 minutes to one hour, with no more than eight doses in a 24 hour period.

The drug of choice for children would be co-trimoxazole (Bactrim, Septrin, Resprim) with dosage dependent on weight. A five day course is given.

Giardiasis The parasite causing this intestinal disorder is present in contaminated water. The symptoms are stomach cramps, nausea, a bloated stomach, watery, foul-smelling diarrhoea and frequent gas. Giardiasis can appear several weeks after you have been exposed to the parasite. The symptoms may disappear for a few days and then return; this can go on for several weeks. Tinidazole, known as Fasigyn, or metronidazole (Flagyl) are the recommended drugs for treatment.

Dysentery This serious illness is caused by contaminated food or water and is characterised by severe diarrhoea, often with blood or mucous in the stool. There are two kinds of dysentery. Bacillary dysentery is characterised by a high fever and rapid development; headache, vomiting and stomach pains are also symptoms. It generally does not last longer than a week, but it is highly contagious.

Amoebic dysentery is more gradual in developing, has no fever or vomiting but is a more serious illness. It is not a self-limiting disease: it will persist until treated and can recur and cause long-term damage.

A stool test is necessary to diagnose which kind of dysentery you have, so you should seek medical help urgently. In case of an emergency, the drugs norfloxacin or ciprofloxacin can be used as presumptive treatment for bacillary dysentery, and metronidazole (Flagyl) for amoebic dysentery.

For bacillary dysentery, norfloxacin 400 mg twice daily for seven days or ciprofloxacin 500 mg twice daily for seven days are the recommended dosages.

If you're unable to find either of these drugs then a useful alternative is co-trimoxazole 160/800 mg (Bactrim, Septrin, Resprim) twice daily for seven days. This is a sulpha drug and must not be used by people with a known sulpha allergy.

In the case of children the drug co-trimoxazole is a reasonable first-line treatment. For amoebic dysentery, the recommended adult dosage of metronidazole (Flagyl) is one 750 mg to 800 mg capsule three times daily for five days. Children aged between eight and 12 years should have half the adult dose; the dosage for younger children is one-third the adult dose.

An alternative to Flagyl is Fasigyn, taken as a two gram daily dose for three days. Alcohol must be avoided during treatment and for 48 hours afterwards.

Viral Gastroenteritis This is caused not by bacteria but, as the name suggests, by a virus. It is characterised by stomach cramps, diarrhoea, and sometimes by vomiting and/or a slight fever. All you can do is rest and drink lots of fluids.

Cholera Cholera vaccination is not very effective. The bacteria responsible for this disease are waterborne, so attention to the rules of eating and drinking should protect the traveller. Outbreaks of cholera are generally widely reported, so you can avoid such problem areas. The disease is characterised by a sudden onset of acute diarrhoea with 'rice water' stools, vomiting, muscular cramps, and extreme weakness. You need medical help – but treat for dehydration, which can be extreme, and if there is an appreciable delay in getting to hospital then begin taking tetracycline. The adult dose is 250 mg four times daily. It is not recommended for children aged eight years or under nor for pregnant women. An alternative drug is Ampicillin, though people with allergies to penicillin should not take it.

Typhoid Typhoid fever is another gut infection that travels the fecal-oral route – ie, contaminated water and food are responsible. Vaccination against typhoid is not totally effective and it is one of the most dangerous infections, so medical help must be sought.

In its early stages typhoid resembles many other illnesses: sufferers may feel like they have a bad cold or flu on the way, as early symptoms are a headache, a sore throat, and a fever which rises a little each day until it is around 40°C or more. The victim's pulse is often slow relative to the degree of fever present and

gets slower as the fever rises – unlike a normal fever where the pulse increases. There may also be vomiting, diarrhoea or constipation.

In the second week the high fever and slow pulse continue and a few pink spots may appear on the body; trembling, delirium, weakness, weight loss and dehydration are other symptoms. If there are no further complications, the fever and other symptoms will slowly go during the third week. However, you must get medical help before this because pneumonia (acute infection of the lungs) or peritonitis (burst appendix) are common complications, and because typhoid is very infectious.

The fever should be treated by keeping the victim cool and dehydration should also be watched for. The drug of choice is ciprofloxacin at a dose of one gram daily for 14 days. It is quite expensive and may not be available. The alternative, chloramphenicol, has been the mainstay of treatment for many years, but there are fewer side affects with Ampicillin. The adult dosage is two 250 mg capsules, four times a day. Children aged between eight and 12 years should have half the adult dose; younger children should have one-third the adult dose.

Patients who are allergic to penicillin should not be given Ampicillin.

Hepatitis Hepatitis is a general term for inflammation of the liver.

Hepatitis A is the more common form of this disease and is spread by contaminated food or water. The first symptoms are fever, chills, headache, fatigue, feelings of weakness and aches and pains. This is followed by loss of appetite, nausea, vomiting, abdominal pain, dark urine, light-coloured faeces and jaundiced skin; the whites of the eyes may also turn yellow. In some cases there may just be a feeling of being unwell or tired, accompanied by loss of appetite, aches and pains and the jaundiced effect. You should seek medical advice, but in general there is not much you can do apart from resting, drinking lots of fluids, eating lightly and avoiding fatty foods. People who have had hepatitis must forego alcohol for six months after the illness, as hepatitis attacks the liver and it needs that amount of time to recover.

Hepatitis B, which used to be called serum hepatitis, is spread through sexual contact or through skin penetration – it could be transmitted via dirty needles or blood transfusions, for instance. Avoid having your ears pierced, tattoos done or injections where you have doubts about the sanitary conditions. The symptoms and treatment of type B are much the same as for type A.

Tetanus This potentially fatal disease is found worldwide. It is difficult to treat but is preventable with immunisation. Tetanus occurs when a wound becomes infected by a germ which lives in the soil and faeces of horses and other animals, so clean all cuts, punctures or animal bites. Tetanus is known as lockjaw, and the first symptom may be discomfort in swallowing, or stiffening of the jaw and neck; this is followed by painful convulsions of the jaw and whole body.

Rabies Rabies is a fatal viral infection found in all Middle Eastern countries and is caused by a bite or scratch by an infected animal. Dogs and cats are noted carriers. Any bite, scratch or even lick from a mammal should be cleaned immediately and thoroughly. Scrub with soap and running water, and then clean with an alcohol or iodine solution. If there is any possibility that the animal is infected, medical help should be sought immediately to prevent the onset of symptoms and death. Even if the animal is not rabid, all bites should be treated seriously as they can become infected or can result in tetanus. A rabies vaccination is now available and should be considered if you are in a high-risk category – eg, if you intend to explore caves (bat bites could be dangerous) or work with animals or travel so far off the beaten track that medical help is more than two days away.

Meningococcal Meningitis Sub-Saharan Africa is considered the 'meningitis belt' but there are recurring epidemics in other regions including Saudi Arabia and the Nile Valley.

The disease is spread by close contact with people who carry it in their throats and noses, spread it through coughs and sneezes and may not be aware that they are carriers.

This very serious disease attacks the brain and can be fatal. A scattered, blotchy rash, fever, severe headache, sensitivity to light and neck stiffness which prevents forward bending of the head are the first symptoms. Death can occur within a few hours, so immediate treatment is important.

Treatment is large doses of penicillin given intravenously, or, if that is not possible, intramuscularly (ie, in the buttocks). Vaccination offers good protection for over a year, but you should also check for reports of current epidemics.

Tuberculosis Although this disease is widespread in many developing countries, it is not a serious risk to travellers. Young children are more susceptible than adults and vaccination is a sensible precaution for children under 12 travelling in endemic areas. TB is commonly spread by coughing or by unpasteurised dairy products from infected cows. Milk that has been boiled is safe to drink; the souring of milk to make yoghurt or cheese also kills the bacilli.

Schistosomiasis Known as bilharzia, this disease is carried in water by minute worms. The larvae infect certain varieties of freshwater snails, found in rivers, streams, lakes and particularly behind dams. The worms multiply and are eventually discharged into the water surrounding the snails. The Nile and the Nile Delta are infested with the bilharzia parasite. The disease is common in Yemen and is also found in Iraq, Saudi Arabia, Syria and the south-west of Iran.

The worm enters through the skin, and the first symptom may be a tingling and sometimes a light rash around the area where it entered. They attach themselves to your intestines or bladder, where they produce large numbers of eggs. Weeks later, a high fever may develop. A general feeling of being unwell may be the first symptom; once the disease is established, abdominal pain and blood in the urine are other signs. The infection often causes no symptoms until the disease is well established (several months to years after exposure) and damage to internal organs irreversible.

Avoiding swimming or bathing in fresh water where bilharzia is present is the main method of preventing the disease. Even deep water can be infected. If you do get wet dry off quickly and dry your clothes as well. Seek medical attention if you have been exposed to the disease and tell the doctor your suspicions, as bilharzia in the early stages can be confused with malaria or typhoid. If you cannot get medical help immediately, praziquantel (Biltricide) is the recommended treatment. The recommended dosage is 40 mg/kg in divided doses over one day. Niridazole is an alternative drug.

Diptheria Diptheria can be a skin infection or a more dangerous throat infection. It is spread by contaminated dust contacting the skin or by the inhalation of infected cough or sneeze droplets. Frequent washing and keeping the skin dry will help prevent skin infection. Treatment requires close medical supervision.

Sexually Transmitted Diseases (STDs) Sexual contact with an infected sexual partner spreads these diseases. While abstinence is the only 100% preventative, using condoms is also effective. Gonorrhoea, herpes and syphilis are the most common of these diseases; sores, blisters or rashes around the genitals, discharges or pain when urinating are common symptoms. In some STDs, such as wart virus or chlamydia, symptoms may be less marked or not observed at all in women. Syphilis symptoms eventually disappear completely but the disease continues and can cause severe problems in later years. The treatment of gonorrhoea and syphilis is with antibiotics.

There are numerous other sexually transmitted diseases, for most of which effective treatment is available. However, there is no cure for herpes and there is also currently no cure for HIV/AIDS.

HIV/AIDS HIV, the Human Immunodeficiency Virus, may develop into AIDS, Acquired Immune Deficiency Syndrome. HIV is not a major problem in the Middle East, but this does not mean you should not take the usual precautions. Any exposure to blood,

blood products or bodily fluids may put an individual at risk. In many developing countries transmission is predominantly through heterosexual sexual activity. This is quite different from industrialised countries where transmission is mostly through contact between homosexual or bisexual males, or via contaminated needles shared by IV drug users. Apart from abstinence, the most effective preventative is always to practise safe sex using condoms. It is impossible to detect the HIV-positive status of an otherwise healthy-looking person without a blood test.

HIV/AIDS can also be spread through infected blood transfusions; some developing countries cannot afford to screen blood for transfusions. It can also be spread by dirty needles – vaccinations, acupuncture, tattooing and ear or nose piercing can be potentially as dangerous as intravenous drug use if the equipment is not clean. If you do need an injection, ask to see the syringe unwrapped in front of you, or better still, take a needle and syringe pack with you overseas – it is a cheap insurance package against infection with HIV.

Fear of HIV infection should never preclude treatment for serious medical conditions. Although there may be a risk of infection, it is very small indeed.

Insect-Borne Diseases
Malaria This serious disease is spread by mosquito bites. It does not occur in Bahrain, Kuwait, Israel, Jordan, Lebanon or Qatar, but is endemic in certain rural areas of other Middle Eastern countries (see Health in each individual country chapter). If you are travelling in endemic areas it is extremely important to take malarial prophylactics. Symptoms include headaches, fever, chills and sweating which may subside and recur. Without treatment malaria can develop more serious, potentially fatal effects.

Antimalarial drugs do not prevent you from being infected but kill the parasites during a stage in their development. Expert advice should be sought, as there are many factors to consider when deciding on the type of antimalarial medication, including the area to be visited, the risk of exposure to malaria-carrying mosquitoes, your medical history, and your age and pregnancy status. It is also important to discuss the side-effect profile of the medication, so you can work out some level of risk-versus-benefit ratio. It is also very important to be sure of the correct dosage of the medication prescribed to you. Some people have inadvertently taken weekly medication (chloroquine) on a daily basis, with disastrous effects. While discussing dosages for prevention of malaria, it is often advisable to include the dosages required for treatment, especially if your trip is through a high-risk area that would isolate you from medical care.

The main messages are:

1) Primary prevention must always be in the form of mosquito-avoidance measures. The mosquitoes that

transmit malaria bite from dusk to dawn and during this period travellers are advised to:

- wear light-coloured clothing
- wear long pants and long-sleeved shirts
- use mosquito repellents containing the compound DEET on exposed areas (overuse of DEET may be harmful, especially to children, but its use is considered preferable to being bitten by disease-transmitting mosquitoes)
- avoid highly scented perfumes or aftershave
- use a mosquito net – it may be worth taking your own

2) While no antimalarial is 100% effective, taking the most appropriate drug significantly reduces the risk of contracting the disease.
3) No one should ever die from malaria. It can be diagnosed by a simple blood test. Symptoms range from fever, chills and sweating, headache and abdominal pains to a vague feeling of ill-health, so seek examination immediately if there is any suggestion of malaria.
4) Contrary to popular belief, once a traveller contracts malaria he/she does not have it for life. Two species of the parasite may lie dormant in the liver but they can also be eradicated using a specific medication. Malaria is curable, as long as the traveller seeks medical help when symptoms occur.

Leishmaniasis This is a group of parasitic diseases transmitted by sandfly bites, found in many parts of the Middle East. Cutaneous leishmaniasis affects the skin tissue causing ulceration and disfigurement and visceral leishmaniasis affects the cells of internal organs. The disease rarely causes serious illness, but it is often misdiagnosed and therefore treated incorrectly. Treatment of the disease is with drugs containing antimony.

Avoiding sandfly bites is the best precaution. The bites generally occur at night, are usually painless, only slightly itchy and are yet another reason to cover up and apply repellent, especially between late afternoon and dawn.

Cuts, Bites & Stings
Cuts & Scratches Skin punctures can easily become infected in hot climates and may be difficult to heal. Treat any cut with an antiseptic solution such as povidone-iodine. Where possible avoid bandages and Band-aids, which can keep wounds wet. Coral cuts are notoriously slow to heal, as the coral injects a weak venom into the wound. Avoid coral cuts by wearing shoes when walking on reefs, and clean any cut thoroughly with hydrogen peroxide if available.

Bites & Stings Bee and wasp stings are usually

painful rather than dangerous. Calamine lotion will give relief or ice packs will reduce the pain and swelling. There are some spiders with dangerous bites but antivenenes are usually available. There are also various fish and other sea creatures which can sting or bite dangerously or which are dangerous to eat.

Scorpions Scorpion stings are a serious cause of illness and occasional deaths in the Middle East, although effective antivenenes are available. Shake shoes, clothing and towels before use. Inspect bedding and don't put hands or feet in crevices in dwellings where they may be lurking. A sting usually produces redness and swelling of the skin, but there may be no visible reaction. Pain is common, and tingling or numbness may occur. At this stage, cold compresses on the bite and pain relief (eg, paracetamol) are called for. If the skin sensations start to spread from the sting site (eg along the limb), then immediate medical attention is required.

Snakes To minimise your chances of being bitten always wear boots, socks and long trousers when walking through undergrowth where snakes may be present. Don't put your hands into holes and crevices, and be careful when collecting firewood.

Snake bites do not cause instantaneous death and antivenenes are usually available. Keep the victim calm and still, wrap the bitten limb tightly, as you would for a sprained ankle, and then attach a splint to immobilise it. Then seek medical help, if possible with the dead snake for identification. Don't attempt to catch the snake if there is even a remote possibility of being bitten again. Tourniquets and sucking out the poison are now comprehensively discredited.

Jellyfish In the Gulf and Red Sea, jellyfish are the most common problem. Local advice is the best way of avoiding contact with these sea creatures and their stinging tentacles. Stings from most jellyfish are simply rather painful. Dousing in vinegar will deactivate any stingers which have not 'fired'. Calamine lotion, antihistamines and analgesics may reduce the reaction and relieve the pain.

Bedbugs & Lice Bedbugs live in various places, but particularly in dirty mattresses and bedding. Spots of blood on bedclothes or on the wall around the bed can be read as a suggestion to find another hotel. Bedbugs leave itchy bites in neat rows. Calamine lotion or Stingose spray may help.

All lice cause itching and discomfort. They make themselves at home in your hair (head lice), your clothing (body lice) or in your pubic hair (crabs). You catch lice through direct contact with infected people or by sharing combs, clothing and the like. Powder or shampoo treatment will kill the lice and infected clothing should then be washed in very hot water.

Women's Health

Gynaecological Problems Poor diet, lowered resistance due to the use of antibiotics for stomach upsets and even contraceptive pills can lead to vaginal infections when travelling in hot climates. Keeping the genital area clean, and wearing skirts or loose-fitting trousers and cotton underwear will help to prevent infections.

Yeast infections, characterised by a rash, itch and discharge, can be treated with a vinegar or even lemon-juice douche or with yoghurt. Nystatin, miconazole or clotrimazole suppositories are the usual medical prescription. Trichomonas and gardnerella are more serious infections; symptoms are a smelly discharge and sometimes a burning sensation when urinating. Male sexual partners must also be treated, and if a vinegar and water douche is not effective medical attention should be sought. Metronidazole (Flagyl) is the prescribed drug.

Pregnancy Most miscarriages occur during the first three months of pregnancy, so this is the most risky time to travel. The last three months should also be spent within reasonable distance of good medical care, as quite serious problems can develop at this time. Pregnant women should avoid all unnecessary medication, but vaccinations and malarial prophylactics should still be taken where possible. Additional care should be taken to prevent illness and particular attention should be paid to diet and nutrition.

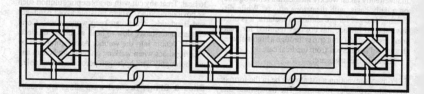

Glossary

Here, with definitions, are some unfamiliar words and abbreviations you might meet in the text or on the road in the Middle East:

abayya – woman's full-length black robe
Abbasids – Baghdad-based successor dynasty to the *Umayyads*. Ruled from 750 until the sack of Baghdad by the Monguls in 1258.
abd – servant, slave
abra – small motorboat
abu – father; saint
acropolis – high city, hilltop citadel and temples of a classic Hellenic city
agal – (also *'iqal*) headropes used to hold a *kaffiyeh* or *gutra* in place
agora – open space for commerce and politics in a classic Hellenic city
ahwa – see *qahwa*
aile salonu – family room for use of couples, families and single women in a Turkish restaurant
'ain – (also *ein*, *ayn*) spring, well
al-Ahram – the pyramids
arg (Persian) – citadel
Ayyubids – Egyptian-based dynasty founded by *Saladin* (1169-1250)

bab – gate
bait – see *beit*
barasti – traditional method of building palm-leaf houses and the name of the house itself
barjeel – wind towers
bazbort – (also *basbut*, *pispot*) passport
beit – house
biblion (Greek) – book
bijous (Egyptian) – service taxi
Book of the Dead – ancient Egyptian theological compositions, or hymns, that were the subject of most of the colourful paintings and reliefs on tomb walls. Extracts from these so-called books were believed to assist the deceased person safely into the afterlife via the Kingdom of the Dead. The texts were sometimes also painted on a roll of papyrus and buried with the dead.
bublos (Greek) – papyrus
burj – tower (*burg* in Egypt)
buzkashi – Afghan bloodsport involving a sheep's carcass

caliph – Islamic ruler
cami(i) (Turkish) – mosque
Canopic jars – pottery jars which held the embalmed internal organs and viscera (liver, stomach, lungs, intestines) of the mummified Pharaoh. They were placed in the burial chamber near the sarcophagus.
caravanserai – see *khan*
çarşı (Turkish) – market, bazaar
cartouche – oblong figure enclosing the hieroglyphs of royal or divine names
chador – one-piece head-to-toe black covering garment, as worn by many Iranian women

deir – monastery, convent
dervish – Muslim mystic; see also *Sufi*
dhabar (Yemeni) – minibus
dhuma (Yemeni) – nobleman's curved dagger
Diaspora – Jewish dispersion or exile from the Land of Israel; the exiled Jewish community worldwide
dishdasha – name of man's shirt-dress worn in Kuwait and the UAE
diwan – reception room
doner kebab – see *shwarma*

Eid al-Adha – Feast of Sacrifice marking the pilgrimage to Mecca
Eid al-Fitr – Festival of Breaking the Fast; celebrated at the end of *Ramadan*
emām (Persian) – see *imam*
emir – Islamic ruler, military commander or governor; literally, prince
Eretz Y'Israel – the Land of Israel, commonly used today by Israel's right wing to refer to their preferred borders for the

modern Jewish State, which includes the Gaza Strip, the West Bank and sometimes Jordan and/or the Sinai, too

falaj – irrigation channel
Fatimids – a Shiite dynasty (908-1171) from North Africa, later based in Cairo, claiming descent from Mohammad's daughter Fatima; founders of Al-Azhar, the oldest university in the world
felafel – deep-fried balls of chickpea paste with spices served in a piece of flat bread with tomatoes or pickled vegetables
fellahin – the peasant farmers or agricultural workers who make up the majority of Egypt's population; fellahin means 'ploughman' or 'tiller of the soil'
funduq – hotel
fuul – paste made from fava beans

galabiyya – full-length robe worn by men
GCC – Gulf Cooperation Council; members are Saudi Arabia, Kuwait, Bahrain, Qatar, Oman and the UAE
gebel (Egyptian) – see *jebel*
gutra – white headcloth worn by men in Saudi Arabia and the Gulf States

haj – annual Muslim pilgrimage to Mecca
Hamas – militant Islamic organisation which aims to create an Islamic state in the pre-1948 territory of Palestine; acronym (in Arabic) for Islamic Resistance Movement
hammam – (also *hamam(ı)*) Turkish steam bath
hared or hasid – (pl *haredim* or *hasidim*) member of an ultraorthodox Jewish sect
hejab – woman's headscarf, worn for modesty (*hegab* in Egyptian)
hijra – migration; also name of Islamic calendar
hisar – fortress, citadel; same as *kale*
hypostyle hall – hall in which the roof is supported by columns

imam – prayer leader, Muslim cleric
Intifada – the Palestinian uprising against Israeli authorities in the Occupied Territories and Jerusalem (literally 'shaking off')
iskele(si) (Turkish) – landing-place, wharf, quay
iwan – vaulted hall, opening into a central court in the madrassa of a mosque

jambiya – tribesman's ceremonial dagger
jebel – hill, mountain
jihad – literally: striving in the way of the faith; holy war

ka – spirit, or 'double', of a living person which gained its own identity with the death of that person. The survival of the ka, however, required the continued existence of the body, hence mummification. The ka was also the vital force emanating from a god and transferred through the Pharaoh to his people.
Kaaba – (also *Qabaa*) the rectangular structure at the centre of the Grand Mosque in Mecca (containing the Black Stone) around which haj pilgrims circumnambulate
kaffiyeh – headscarf
kale(si) (Turkish) – fortress, citadel; same as *hisar*
karez – Afghan form of irrigation
khan – (also *caravanserai* or *wikala*) a travellers' inn usually constructed on main trade routes, with accommodation on the first floor and stables and storage on the ground floor around a central courtyard
khanjar – (also *khanja*) Omani curved dagger
khedive – Egyptian viceroy under Ottoman suzerainty (1867-1914)
kibbutz – (pl *kibbutzim*) communal settlement; originally farms, but now involved in additional industries
kibbutznik – member of a *kibbutz*
kiosk – open-sided pavilion
knanqah – *Sufi* monastery
Knesset – Israeli parliament
kosher – food prepared according to Jewish dietary law
köy(ü) (Turkish) – village
kufic – a type of highly stylised old Arabic script

Likud – major Israeli right-wing political party, headed by Prime Minister Binyamin Netanyahu

liman(ı) (Turkish) – harbour

madrassa – Muslim theological seminary; also modern Arabic word for school

mafraj – room with a view; top room of a tower house

mahalle(si) (Turkish) – neighbourhood, district of a city

majlis – formal meeting room; also parliament

Mamluk – slave-soldier dynasty that ruled out of Egypt from 1250-1517

manzar – attic; room on top of a tower house

mashrabiyyah – ornate carved wooden panel or screen; a feature of Islamic architecture

mastaba – Arabic word for 'bench'; a mud-brick structure above tombs from which the pyramids were developed

medina – old walled centre of any Islamic city

medrese(si) (Turkish) – see *madrassa*

menorah – seven pronged candelabra; an ancient Jewish symbol associated with the Hanukkah Festival

meydan(ı) (Turkish) – see *midan*

midan – town or city square

mihrab – niche in a mosque indicating the direction of Mecca

minbar – pulpit used for sermons in a mosque

Misr – another name for Egypt and Cairo; also written as Masr

moshav – cooperative settlement, with a mix of private and collective housing and industry

moulid – festival celebrating the birthday of a local saint or holy person

muezzin – cantor who sings the *ezan*, or call to prayer

nargileh – water pipe used to smoke tobacco

Nilometer – pit descending into the Nile and containing a central column marked with graduations. The marks were used to measure and record the level of the river, especially during the inundation.

obelisk – monolithic stone pillar, with square sides tapering to a pyramidal, often guilded, top; used as a monument in ancient Egypt. Obelisks were usually carved from pink granite and set up in pairs at the entrance to a tomb or temple. A single obelisk was sometimes the object of cult worship.

OPEC – Organisation of Petroleum Exporting Countries

otogar – bus station

pansiyon – pension, B&B, guesthouse

PLO – Palestine Liberation Organization

PTT – Posta, Telefon, Telğraf: post, telephone and telegraph office

pylon – monumental gateway at the entrance to a temple

qahwa – (also *ahwa*) coffee

qasr – castle

qat – mildly narcotic leaves commonly chewed in Yemen

Qur'an – the holy book of Islam; also spelt Koran

rakats – cycles of prayer during which the Qur'an is read and bows ad prostrations are performed in different series

Ramadan – the Muslim month of fasting

ras – cape or headland; also head

sabil – public drinking fountain

Saladin – (in Arabic *Salah ad-Din*) Kurdish warlord who retook Jerusalem from the Crusaders; founder of the *Ayyubid* dynasty

Şehir (Turkish) – city; municipal

serdab – hidden cellar in a tomb, or a stone room in front of some pyramids, containing a coffin with a life-size, lifelike, painted statue of the dead king. Serdabs were designed so that the Pharaoh's *ka* could communicate with the outside world.

settler – a term used to describe those Israelis who have created new communities on territory captured from the Arabs during the 1967 War

Shabbat – the Jewish sabbath and shutdown, observed from sundown Friday to sundown Saturday

shaikh – see *sheikh*

shari'a – Islamic law

shay – tea

sheikh – (also *shaikh*) a venerated religious scholar

sherut – shared taxi (fixed route)

shisha – see *nargileh*

shwarma – grilled meat sliced from a spit and served in a pitta bread with salad; also known as doner kebab

souq – market

stele – (pl *stelae*) stone or wooden commemorative slab or column decorated with inscriptions or figures

Sufi – follower of any of the Islamic mystical orders which emphasise dancing, chanting and trances in order to attain unity with God

sultan – the absolute ruler of a Muslim state

ta'amiyah – see *felafel*

takiyya – Ottoman name for a *khanqah*

TC – Türkiye Cumhuriyeti (Turkish Republic) which designates an official office or organisation

tell – an ancient mound created by centuries of urban rebuilding

thobe – term used in Saudi Arabia, Bahrain and Qatar for man's shirt-dress; similar to a *dishdasha*, but more tightly cut

THY – Türk Hava Yolları: Turkish Airlines

Torah – the five books of Moses (the first five Old Testament books); also called the Pentatuch

Umayyads – (also *Omayyad*) first great dynasty of Arab Muslim rulers, based in Damascus (661-750)

wadi – dried up river bed; seasonal river

wikala – see *khan*

zawiya – a small school dedicated to the teaching of a particular *sheikh*

Index

TEXT

Map references are in **bold** type.

A'ali Burial Mounds (B) 131
A'Thowarah (O) 514
Aanjar (L) 491
Ābādān (Irn) 284
Abbasids 16-17, 112
Abdul Aziz (SA) 542-4
Abha (SA) 573-6, **574**
Abu Dhabi (UAE) 722-26, **723**
  entertainment 725
  getting around 726
  getting there & away 725-6
  places to eat 725
  places to stay 724-5
  things to see & do 724
Abu Kamal (Syr) 632
Abu Simbel (E) 193-4
Abydos (E) 176
accommodation 70, see also
  individual country entires
Achaemenian Empire 227
Ad-Diraz Temple (B) 131
Adana (T) 694
Aden (Y) 783-6, **784**, **785**
Adıyaman (T) 709
Adrasan (T) 691
Afghanistan 99-111, **100**
  accommodation 106
  books 105-6
  cultural considerations 104
  drinks 106
  embassies 105
  food 106
  history 99-102
  money 105
  shopping 106-7
  visas 105
Agiba (E) 205
Ahvāz (Irn) 282-3
'Ain as-Siliin (E) 172
'Ain Furtaga (E) 222
'Ain Mahmed (E) 222

air travel 74-82, 91, see also
  individual country entries
  air travel glossary 76-7
Ajlun (J) 424
Ajman (UAE) 742, **743**
Akçakale (T) 702
Akdamar Island (T) 710
Akko (Isr) 365-8, **366**
Al-'Areen Wildlife Sanctuary
  (B) 132
Al-Ahmadi (K) 454
Al-Ain (UAE) 726-31, **727**
Al-Arish (E) 225-6, (Q) 540
Al-Assad, Hafez 25, (Syr) 590-1
Al-Baha (SA) 573
Al-Balid (O) 520
Al-Bathaa (SA) 560
Al-Dalaghan (SA) 575
Al-Faiyum (E) 172-3
Al-Ghab (Syr) 619, 622
Al-Ghardaka, see Hurghada
Al-Hajjara (Y) 774
Al-Hasa Oasis (SA) 586
Al-Hazm (O) 514
Al-Hemma (J) 425
Al-Hudayda (Y) 777-8, **777**
Al-Jahra (K) 454-5
Al-Janad (Y) 782
Al-Jasra House (B) 131-2
Al-Karama (J) 425
Al-Khalifa family 112
Al-Khor (Q) 539
Al-Khuraibat Tombs (SA) 573
Al-Khutayb (Y) 774
Al-Khuwair (Q) 540
Al-Mahwit (Y) 773
Al-Mahwit Governorate (Y) 774
Al-Makha (Y) 779-80
Al-Mashari'a (J) 426
Al-Mayadin (Syr) 632
Al-Milga (E) 224
Al-Minya (E) 173-5
Al-Mukalla (Y) 788
Al-Mutla Ridge (K) 445

Al-Qabai (Y) 775
Al-Qaddisiyyeh (J) 430
Al-Qara'a (Qara) (SA) 575
Al-Qasr (E) 195
Al-Quseir (E) 216
Al-Ruweis (Q) 540
Al-Sabah family 438
Al-Sahab (SA) 575
Al-Samlagi Dam (SA) 570-1
Al-Saud family 541
Al-Soudah (SA) 575
Al-Ula (SA) 572-3
Alacahöyük (T) 698
Alanya (T) 693-4
alcohol 73
Aleppo (Halab) (Syr) 622-7,
  623, **625**
Alexander the Great 14, 227
Alexandria (E) 198-204, **199**,
  201
Aley (L) 490
Alibey Island (T) 675
Alkhobar (SA) 584-5
Allenby Bridge, see Jisr al
  Malek al-Hussein
Altınbaşak, see Harran
Amadiya (Irq) 313
Amasra (T) 701
Amasya (T) 701-702
Amchit (L) 483
Amman (J) 415-22, **416**, **418**,
  420
  entertainment 421
  getting around 422
  getting there & away 421-2
  places to eat 419-21
  places to stay 419
  things to see 417-19
  tourist office 415
'Amran (Y) 775
Anamur (T) 694
Anamurium (T) 694
Ani (T) 708
Ankara (T) 695-8, **696**

THANKS

Thanks to the many travellers who took the time and trouble to write to us about their experiences in the Middle East. They include:

Haico Aaldering, JM Allfrey, Douglas Andersen, Philip Anthony, Phoenix Arrien, Susanne Bader, Emre Balta, Chris Beckley, Joseph Bellestri, Maria Grazia Benedetti, Dane Birdseye, S Bishop, David Black, Christoph Blocher, Pia Blonden, Cian Boland, Barbara Boorman, Kevin Brackley, Oliver Bradley, Mark Brizland, David Browning, Lynne Brunton, Brooke Bullinger, Heather Burles, David Caloia, Heath Cameron, Jonathan Carroll, Sarah Clacha, Bruce & Julie Cook, Paul Cook, Christopher Corbett, SD Corr, Alison Couch, Nick Dallas, Pat Daniel, Jenni Davies, Kevin Davies, Michael Donovan, Leo Falk, Andrea Fechter, Hanne Finholt, SE & PR Fletcher, Lars Frid, Jan Frith, Fergus Gallagher, Ian Galloway, Sarah Gault, William Gets, Stephanie Gibson, Claude Patrick Giraud, David Gould, Tim Gourlay, Robert Gutterman, Paul Hamidavi, Jonathan Harris, Jacqueline Harrison, John Harrison, Steve Harrison, Jodi Hayes, Steven Heymann, Stuart Hickox, T Hickson, Richard Hill, David Hirsch, Simone Hoppler, Mark Horobin, Mary Horvers, Philip Housraux, SM Jagger, Anne James, J Japper, Kristin Jensen, Lisa Jessup, Kristin Johannsen, Graham Jones, Tony Joyce, Patrick Joynt, Joakim Kardell, Christoph Kessel, Dr Mojgan Khademi, Magnus Killander, Rob Kimmel, Andre Klarenberg, Wolfgang Kniese, Christoph Kock, Michael Kolodner, Mark Korenhof, AH & J Koutsaplis, Mike Kramer, D Kramer, Thomas Kramer, Jeremy Kull, Stephane La Branche, Patrick Lambourne, Terry Last, F Leenders, Cas Leiber, Paul Lewtas, John Lumley-Holms, Trish Manning, Rose-Anne Manns, Alex Marcovitch, Katherine Martys, Oliver Maruna, Neil McAllister, Barrie McCormick, Brian McGinty, Kym McKenzie, Colin Michell, Dennis Moors, Richard Moss, Stuart Nargrove, Scott Newman, Catherine Noventa, Orlinda & Tim Ornelas, Stephen O'Neil, Leen Ouweneel, Wim Pannecoucke, Ward Petherbridge, Vanessa Pollett, Tamara Prischnegg, Renee Pyburn, Ehab Raad, Annette Reeves, Paul Regan, David Retzleff, Miss L Rex, Marco Riccomini, Dr A Robertson, Don Rose, J Rosmalen, Esam Y Sabr, Kelly Salloum, Michael Schmidt, John Sellich, Luke Shannon, Tamsin Sharp, Cate Shaw, Geri Sheppard, Steve Silk, Emily-Maria Silva, Andrew Smith, Colin Smith, Matthew Smith, Sally Smith, Andrew Sneddon, Claire Stewart, Terry Sustig, Yusuke Suzuki, Oscar Szanto, Richard Tanner, Mary Tappenden, Marisa Texter, Neil Thody, Sarah Thompson, Oscar Valle, Peter van Pelt, Bram van der Waals, Jim & Beryl Walter, Lawrence Webb, Bill Weir, Cyprian Wilkowski, Kathryn Williams, Sonya Williams, Tim Williams, Mike Williamson, Matt Willis, Garry Wilson, Jean Philippe Wispelaere and Michael Zemble.